Women and Politics Worldwide

Women
and Politics
Worldwide

EDITED BY

BARBARA J. NELSON &

NAJMA CHOWDHURY

YALE UNIVERSITY PRESS

NEW HAVEN & LONDON

For Mainur Reza Chowdhury

and

Betty-Jane James   *Bernard J. Nelson*

and   *and*

George Knox   *Rachel Wayne Nelson*

Published with assistance from the foundation established in memory of Philip Hamilton McMillan of the Class of 1894, Yale College.

Designed by Nancy Ovedovitz. Set in Galliard type by The Composing Room of Michigan, Inc. Printed in the United States of America by Edwards Brothers, Ann Arbor, Michigan.

Library of Congress Cataloging-in-Publication Data

Women and politics worldwide / edited by Barbara J. Nelson and Najma Chowdhury.

    p. cm.

  Includes bibliographical references (p.   ) and   index.

  ISBN 0-300-05407-6 (cloth : alk. paper). —

  ISBN 0-300-05408-4 (paper : alk. paper)

    1. Women in politics—Cross-cultural studies. 2. Women's rights—Cross-cultural studies. I. Nelson, Barbara J., 1949– .

II. Caudhurī, Nājamā, 1942– .

HQ1236.W6363 1994

320'.082—dc20   93-28668

                 CIP

A catalogue record for this book is available from the British Library.

The paper in this book meets the guidelines for permanence and durability of the Committee on Production Guidelines for Book Longevity of the Council on Library Resources.

10   9   8   7   6   5   4   3   2   1

Contents

Contents   vii

Acknowledgments

Few books have enjoyed the support of as many individuals and institutions as *Women and Politics Worldwide*. Our first thanks go to each other for nearly a decade of friendship, affection, and scholarly collaboration that crossed the globe. We both thank Nancy Johnson, associate director of the Center on Women and Public Policy, who managed this project with consummate skill and intelligence. The center, located in the Hubert H. Humphrey Institute of Public Affairs at the University of Minnesota, served as the secretariat of the project, and its administrative assistants, Ellen Carlson, Stacey Grimes, Karen Schuster, and Linda Colbeth, have our profound thanks.

To the authors in the volume we extend our heartfelt thanks. They are smart and wise, talented and adventurous, patient and generous, and we enjoyed their companionship on this long journey of international research and feminist development. The women of the world, whose political conditions and aspirations are partially analyzed here, were always in our thoughts.

A large group of dedicated graduate students worked on this project. Their intelligence, enthusiasm, and willingness to tackle questions of politics and feminism in many countries contributed importantly to its success. In Bangladesh and the United States we thank Sarita Ahuja, Lavon Anderson, Abul Kalam Azad, Melissa Bass, Tom Gilles, Clare Gravon, Stephanie Hawkinson, Alissa Hummer, Sarah McGrath Johnson, Gary Keese, Karen Kingsley, Janet Larsen, Julie Luner, Renée Monson, Barbara Naramore, Stefanie Novacek, Paula O'Loughlin, Gülhan Ovalioglu, Paula Prahl, Polly Prunuske, Katie Shea, Kris Thalhammer, Whitney Thompson, Rita Ulrich, Nancy Vivian, Kristin Watkins, Margaret Woods, and Gayle Zoffer. In addition, we thank the many individuals who undertook translations for the book, read chapters as regional specialists, or consulted on a host of topics ranging from international debt to the changing configuration of nationalism. We are grateful to them for their talent and commitment.

We owe a special debt of gratitude to Kathryn A. ("Mandy") Carver for her sustaining role in the project. In 1985 she represented the United States at our session "Educating Women for Political Participation Worldwide" at the Nairobi Non-Governmental Forum that closed the U.N. Decade for Women. She traveled extensively to confer with authors, and, as a research fellow, she contributed to the research and editing of many chapters.

We thank Carlos Ruiz of the Cartography Laboratory at the University of Minnesota for his excellent cartography and for his colleagueship in designing a map that reflects the great changes in political geography that occurred during the research.

To our many funders we give thanks for their moral and material support. Each supported a vision, a process, and a product. Foremost, we would like to thank the Ford Foundation and the University of Minnesota for their commitment to and continuous support of the Women and Politics Worldwide project. We also thank the Rockefeller Foundation for making available to us the hospitality of the Villa Serbelloni in Bellagio, Italy, where, joined by Nancy Johnson, we spent a month together drafting the four overview chapters; the Kellogg National Fellowship Program for support for Barbara Nelson to establish the network of scholars who participated in this project; and the Ford Foundation, Dhaka, and the Norwegian Agency for Development Cooperation (NORAD), Dhaka, for travel grants to Najma Chowdhury to attend conferences in Nairobi, New York, and Buenos Aires.

We are grateful to the government of the People's Republic of Bangladesh for the support extended to Najma Chowdhury to participate at the U.N. Non-Governmental Forum at Nairobi and for her nomination as member of the Bangladesh delegation to the U.N. General Assembly in 1986, and to the University of Dhaka, Bangladesh, for granting the leave over the past years that enabled her to participate in this collaborative work as coeditor and author. We are also grateful to the International Visitor Program and the Fulbright Program of the U.S. government, under which Najma Chowdhury visited Minneapolis in 1984 and resided as visiting scholar at

the University of Minnesota in 1988, and to the Humphrey Institute for the friendship extended to Najma during her visits.

We thank those remarkable individuals whose unflagging belief in the project made it possible for scholars and activists across the world to work together: June Zeitlin of the Ford Foundation for early and continued support; G. Edward Schuh, Dean, and Paul Light, former Associate Dean, of the Humphrey Institute for institutional, monetary, and intellectual support; Anne Peterson, Dean, and Robert Holt, former Dean, of the Graduate School of the University of Minnesota for continued support of Barbara Nelson through the faculty grants program; Shamsul Huda Harum and Emajuddin Ahmed, who chaired the Department of Political Science, University of Dhaka, during 1987–92, and M. Nazrul Islam, Kamaluddin Ahmed, Dalem Ch. Barman, and Dil Roushan Zinnat Ara Nazeen of the department for their cooperation and assistance; Carol Pateman, President, and Guillermo O'Donnell, former President, of the International Political Science Association for designating this project an official research endeavor of IPSA; Catherine Rudder, Executive Director, and Robert Hauck, Assistant Director, of the American Political Science Association for assistance with the mid-project meeting; Fazle Hasan Abed, Executive Director of the Bangladesh Rural Advancement Committee (BRAC), for extending access to fax facilities to Najma Chowdhury; Adrienne Germain and Susan Davis, formerly of the Ford Foundation office in Dhaka; Zakia Hassan of NORAD, Dhaka; Susan Garfield of the Rockefeller Foundation; and Francis and Jackie Sutton and Gianna Celli of the Villa Serbelloni in Bellagio.

In addition, we would like to acknowledge the contributions of universities, nongovernmental organizations, and government agencies for research and travel grants for authors of the chapters on Argentina, Australia, Brazil, Canada, China, Egypt, France, Germany, Great Britain, Greece, Hong Kong, Hungary, India, Israel, Japan, Korea, Mexico, Morocco, Nepal, the Netherlands, Norway, Palestine, Papua New Guinea, the Philippines, Puerto Rico, the former Soviet Union, Spain, Sudan, Switzerland, Turkey, and Uruguay.

Yale University Press has been a faithful partner in this effort. We thank John S. Covell, the political science editor, for believing in the special place of *Women and Politics Worldwide* in the social sciences and in women's studies. We thank Mary Pasti and Heidi Myers, who edited the book, joining us in our interest in preserving the unique analysis and voice of each chapter. Theirs was a monumental task—editing in one volume the writings of 61 authors who speak 23 native tongues.

We would especially like to thank our families, who lived with the book for many years. Barbara thanks Mandy Carver, Bernard and Rachel Nelson, Betty-Jane James, and George Knox for their constant love and support. They were excited about the many international trips the book required, patient during absences, and joyous at homecomings. Najma thanks her husband, Mainur Reza Chowdhury; her daughters, Lamiya and Bushra; and her parents, C.I. Zaman and Atiya Zaman, for their love, inspiration, and support and for their understanding—born out of a sense of commitment to the book itself—of the demands made on her time and presence.

Barbara J. Nelson   Najma Chowdhury
Minneapolis   Dhaka

POLITICAL DIVISIONS

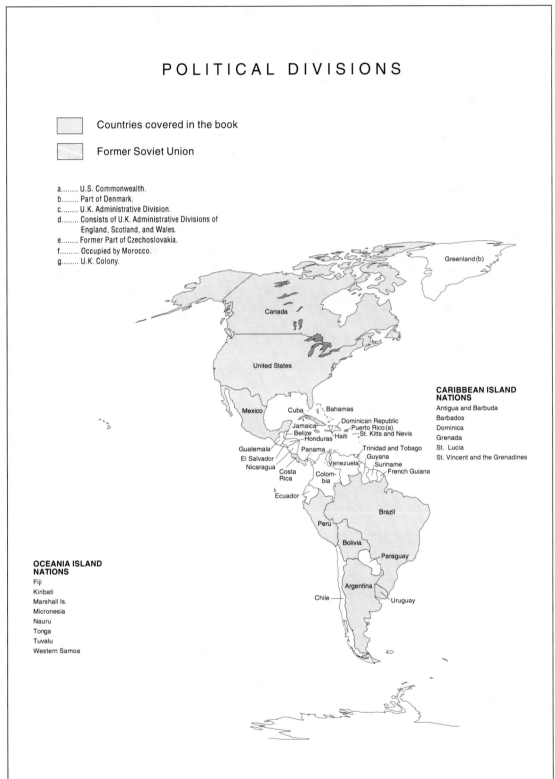

Countries covered in the book

Former Soviet Union

a........ U.S. Commonwealth.
b........ Part of Denmark.
c........ U.K. Administrative Division.
d........ Consists of U.K. Administrative Divisions of
           England, Scotland, and Wales.
e........ Former Part of Czechoslovakia.
f......... Occupied by Morocco.
g........ U.K. Colony.

Greenland (b)

Canada

United States

CARIBBEAN ISLAND NATIONS
Antigua and Barbuda
Barbados
Dominica
Grenada
St. Lucia
St. Vincent and the Grenadines

Mexico   Cuba   Bahamas
                     Dominican Republic
Jamaica   Puerto Rico (a)
Belize   St. Kitts and Nevis
Honduras   Haiti
Guatemala   Trinidad and Tobago
El Salvador   Panama   Guyana
Nicaragua   Venezuela   Suriname
Costa   French Guiana
Rica   Colom-
Ecuador   bia

Brazil

Peru

Bolivia

Paraguay

OCEANIA ISLAND NATIONS
Fiji
Kiribati
Marshall Is.
Micronesia
Nauru
Tonga
Tuvalu
Western Samoa

Argentina

Chile   Uruguay

OF THE WORLD

EUROPE

1	Andorra	11	Liechtenstein	21	Yugoslavia (Serbia and Montenegro)
2	Monaco	12	Austria	22	Bosnia and Herzegovina
3	Malta	13	Czech Republic(e)	23	Croatia
4	San Marino	14	Slovak Republic(e)	24	Slovenia
5	Belgium	15	Hungary	25	Macedonia
6	Luxembourg	16	Romania		
7	Switzerland	17	Moldova		
8	Netherlands	18	Bulgaria		
9	Denmark	19	Greece		
10	Germany	20	Albania		

AFRICA

26 Tunisia
27 Burkina Faso
28 Benin
29 Togo
30 Cameroon
31 Central African Republic
32 São Tomé and Príncipe
33 Uganda
34 Rwanda
35 Burundi
36 Malawi
37 Zimbabwe
38 Djibouti

MIDDLE EAST

39 Lebanon
40 Israel
41 Bahrain
42 United Arab Emirates

CARTOGRAPHY BY CARLOS J. RUIZ

1 ▲ Redefining Politics: Patterns of Women's Political Engagement from a Global Perspective

NAJMA CHOWDHURY AND
BARBARA J. NELSON
WITH KATHRYN A. CARVER,
NANCY J. JOHNSON,
AND PAULA L. O'LOUGHLIN

In its most general formulation, the major finding of this book comes as no surprise: *in no country do women have political status, access, or influence equal to men's*. The sweep of women's political subordination encompasses the great variety of cultures, economic arrangements, and regimes in which they live.

Our point is not that women are never powerful or that they never enjoy political equality with men. Women frequently exercise political power in a particular arena, and in many situations their political activism is distinctive or unopposed. Rather, our point is that these situations are always exceptional in some manner. Neither do we mean that all women experience their subordinate political status in the same way or that all groups of women are equally subordinate to all groups of men. In most cultures there is a complex matrix of political power composed of many social hierarchies, of which gender is only one component. Nonetheless, men of any group are more able to be active in politics than can the women of their group.

The ubiquity of women's secondary political status demonstrates how politics is intertwined with other aspects of life. We see politics, economics, culture, religion, and law as mutually constitutive, each creating itself and the others at the same time. The secondary status of women in each realm is reinforced by the total pattern of men's privileges. But each sphere of society also creates unique elements of gender inequality and its own opportunities for resistance, innovation, and transformation.

These findings and the many others in this book derive from a study of women's political engagement in 43 countries. The countries were chosen systematically to represent a variety of political systems, levels of economic development, and regions, and together they cover a quarter of the world's political units and three-quarters of its population. The editors and a group of country chapter authors designed the research protocol. Each country chapter investigates how women in all their variety express their political demands and what solutions they devise in their communities or extract from their governments. Most of the country chapters trace the history of three political or policy issues important to women in that country today. In Chapter 2 we detail the research design and methodology that guided the project.

The study took nine years to complete: four to design the research, raise the funds, and find the locally based contributing scholars; three to research, write, and edit the chapters; and two to publish this book. The project brought together 61 scholars from 43 countries who spoke 23 native languages written in 12 alphabets or symbol systems. The idea for the study arose in 1985 from a session entitled "Educating Women for Political Participation Worldwide," organized by Najma Chowdhury and Barbara Nelson at the Nongovernmental Forum of the U.N. Conference on Women in Nairobi. The history of the project and its connection to international feminist scholarship and activism are recounted in Chapter 3.

Although the research focused on political activism, an overall picture of women's political, economic, and demographic characteristics was also important. Each country chapter contains a chart of these indicators, and in Chapter 4 we describe how the information was gathered and also discuss the problems in collecting international data on the status of women.

Each country chapter begins with a political introduction to the history and institutions of the country in question, and then summarizes the organization of women's movements or activism there. The chapters continue with an analysis of how diverse groups of women articulate their interests in specific issues and conclude with a discussion of the patterns of response. Authors found their own balance among these parts and chose the issues they would cover.

We had a strong vision of what the book would be: we wanted each country chapter to provide an integrative and interpretive analysis of the patterns of women's political activism. We expected that chapters would approach the analysis of women, gender, politics, and policy making from a variety of points of view. Although we wanted comparability among chapters, our aim was not to produce a handbook or an encyclopedia.

This chapter extends and adds nuance to the general finding of women's secondary political status. There are many causes of women's secondary status and many modes of response. Through recounting and theorizing this variety, it may be possible to develop strategies for improving specific conditions and changing the general pattern. We begin by examining the historical moment in which the country studies were done, looking particularly at international economic, political, and religious trends that mold national events. This overview provides a context for the next section of the chapter, which summarizes issues discussed in the country chapters and offers a global view of the concerns that bring women to political activism. We then ex-

amine the position of women in formal politics, emphasizing the role of parties within civil and political life. Finally, we discuss activism outside formal politics and propose a model of women's mobilization into women-defined activism based on the relation of gender ideologies to action potentials.

INTERNATIONAL FORCES AND THE HISTORICAL MOMENT

Although the country chapters offer a picture of women's political engagement at the national and subnational levels, it is important to view the chapters in the wider frame of international systems and changes within them. The forces that affect women's political engagement do not reside wholly within nation-states, regardless of how established or strong they are. An examination of the international processes and historical moment in which these country analyses were done widens the context and deepens the historical roots of our understanding of women's political activism and accomplishments.

Most of the chapters cover the period from the early 1960s to the early 1990s. The specific time frames depend on when the current wave of the women's movement emerged in each country. During these years women's political engagement was influenced by fundamental changes in international economic relations, reduced national capacities to solve problems, remarkable transformations in political regimes, and a rise in religious fundamentalism, as well as growth in the international component of the women's movement. The international changes often set the stage for distinctly national dramas.

International Economic Forces

Perhaps the most notable international changes have been the policies promoting macroeconomic stabilization and internal structural transformation introduced by the World Bank and the International Monetary Fund to respond to economic instability, first in Third World countries and then in the emerging democracies of Central Europe.[1] The problems faced by African, Asian, and Latin American countries are rooted in the extractive capitalism practiced first by colonial powers and later by indigenous elites and multinational corporations. These practices have extended to slavery and forced migration as well as to plantation economies, artificially low commodity prices, controlled distribution policies, and payment arrangements that were extraordinarily favorable to colonial powers.[2] Political independence has sometimes improved productivity and standards of living, but improvement has been uneven within and among less industrialized countries.[3]

Where improvement did occur, it was not shared equally by women and men. Indeed, there is good evidence that men's share of resources and their control over women's lives often increased dramatically with economic development. The evidence comes from many sources, ranging from statistical data showing that boys have had much greater access to education than girls in most Third World countries to sociological analyses showing that cash-export agriculture can lead to increased male income in households and thereby to an increased number of wives in polygynous societies.[4] Conventional development economics asserts that men and women in a family have a fundamental unity of interest and that men are benevolent distributors of family wealth. This assumption has been contradicted repeatedly by empirical household analyses.[5] Likewise, assumptions that treat women's paid employment as marginal or like men's are wrong. Women's work is rarely marginal to household or national economies, but neither is it very much like men's, because national and international productive systems are deeply stratified by sex.[6] Women often benefit from increasing real family or personal income, but the processes by which they extract these benefits are more complex and conflictual than the theories or practices of development investment have taken into account.

Over the past 20 years new economic and political conditions have exacerbated the economic problems of less industrialized countries and the place of women within these economies. The two shocks in oil prices in the 1970s had a doubly negative effect on oil-importing nations. First, they raised the prices of the inputs to production with noticeable negative effects on standards of living and productive capacities. Second, the profits from the increase in oil prices put an enormous amount of extra money into the world monetary system, encouraging private and in some cases international lending agencies to lend more money to developing countries. Third World leaders, the banking community, and international policy analysts debate whether banks used due prudence in making the loans, indeed whether the banks thought that the loans would ever be repaid in full. Externally generated price shocks—including rising interest rates, falling world commodity prices, balance-of-payment problems, and the effects of internal financial and political decisions—led to other serious economic problems, including mounting debts, inability to extend credit, runaway inflation, and declining standards of living.[7] Although these problems have changed over time, they have always had serious political consequences for less industrialized countries. In many cases, the problems have strained the political and economic capacities of Third World democracies, sometimes to the breaking point.[8]

The World Bank introduced adjustment lending in 1979 to provide temporary balance-of-payment loans while governments pursued changes in internal economic policies. By the end of the 1980s adjustment lending accounted for about 25 percent of World Bank lending and more than 50 percent of lending to some severely indebted countries.[9] With adjustment lending came requirements for internal economic reordering, called "conditionality." Although the conditions imposed on each country differ, the general strategy developed during the 1980s and early 1990s was to undertake macroeconomic stability procedures first (especially disinflation) and then economic restructuring in favor of more exports and more accurate internal and external pricing of goods. Considered as a whole, these conditions have meant a reconfiguration of the political winners and losers in each country, usually reducing the power of the public sector, organized labor, and urban white-collar interests and increasing the power of the commercial agriculture, private industry, and export sectors.[10]

During the years of structural adjustments, overall levels of central government expenditures in the social sector, as well as per capita social expenditures, have fallen somewhat in most countries receiving adjustment loans.[11] According to aggregate figures, some effects of disinvestment in human capital appear to hit women and men or girls and boys equally. For example, UNESCO figures reporting whether a child who starts primary school persists for four years show that many of the declines in persistence were countrywide, rather gender specific. Panama, for example, reported a persistence rate of 97 per 100 students for both girls and boys in 1973, declining to 90 per 100 for girls and 89 per 100 for boys in 1984.[12] Other measures suggest that the full effects of structural adjustment policies on women have yet to be reflected in social indicators. One indicator to watch is maternal mortality: rates have been declining for 20 years, but the rate of decline slowed in the first decade of structural adjustment.[13]

These figures do not tell the human stories or calculate the invisible adjustment costs, however. The country chapters show that structural adjustment policies have often had severe consequences for women, although the nature of the hardships has varied from country to country. Decreased public spending on education, health, and food subsidies means that increased costs must be borne by women, who work longer hours, look for less expensive food, spend more resources on basic health care, make difficult choices about which children will get an education and which will work to sustain the family economy, and face lower wages or fewer job opportunities as the wages in female-dominated industries decline or as the returns to agricultural labor are not sustained.[14] Women's labor and women's bodies often absorb the impact of reduced public spending. The result is more need for activism in the face of dwindling resources for it.

The experience of Malawi shows the dramatic effects that structural adjustment policies can have on women. Women-headed households have borne the brunt of the decline in real income brought on by structural adjustment policies. Child nutrition is deteriorating because women, who must increasingly seek wage work, do not have enough time to prepare the four or five maize meals that children need each day for adequate calories and protein. The macroeconomic changes in men's labor affect the status of women and children in Malawi as well. Children receive better nutrition when the father in the household migrates for work and sends money back home than they do when he lives at home and earns his income growing cash crops like tobacco or groundnuts. It appears that cash crops reduce women's ability to create food security by storing food, which cannot be "spent" as easily as cash.[15]

The Changing Nature of Nationalism

Two other international forces—changes in the nature of nationalism and the rise of many forms of religious fundamentalism—have also affected women's status in the past three decades. Modern nationalism, born of the modern nation-state at the end of the eighteenth century, is a complex and variable set of ideas and practices. How it is experienced at a particular moment depends not only on the identities of individuals, their communal connections, and the way they define those not in their group but also on the level and type of political sovereignty over a particular territory that a people or its leaders can establish.[16] Achieving and strengthening the political power of the nation-state were the dominant foci of nationalism in the immediate post–World War II era of rebuilding and decolonizing.

For most of the world's women, this state-focused political nationalism was accompanied by formal (though not actual) legal equality. For many women, formal legal equality was accompanied by secularism in government, which officially (though not always in practice) disentangled the power of the state from the power of religious denominations, most of which had a tradition of treating men and women unequally.

Universalism and secularism expanded women's political opportunities in civil society as well as with the state.[17] In recent decades, however, state-focused political nationalism has been increasingly challenged by the rise of ethnic, communal, and regional forces that seek to alter the nature of national control of politics. In some instances, these forces also seek to change national boundaries in fact or in meaning.

In North America and Western Europe the strains on state-focused political nationalism are felt both in the growth of regional and ethnic identities (the French and Native Americans in Canada, the Basques in Spain) and in the expansion of international regional organizations (the reconfiguration of the European Economic Community, the proposed North American Free Trade Zone). European feminists on both sides of the former iron curtain fear that the new regionalism, combined with economic restructuring, will mean a decrease in nationally supported social programs designed to help women manage child rearing and paid employment.[18] This fear coexists with the recent positive experiences of regionalism for Western European feminists, mostly arising from applying progressive European Economic Community (EEC) policies to reluctant member countries. For example, equal-rights advocates in Great Britain used the European Court of Justice to challenge national pay laws that did not conform with the EEC policy of equal pay for work of equal value.[19]

Two types of reasoning explain why activists worry about the future friendliness of pan-European institutions toward women. The European Court has assisted women most strongly in programs that required equal hiring and pay. These programs are indirectly redistributional, in contrast with the more obviously redistributional aspects of child allowances and subsidized child care. Moreover, these decisions were made when the EEC was a somewhat weaker institution. A more powerful and reconfigured European Community might in fact reinforce nationally sanctioned gender inequalities. The codicil to the proposed Treaty of Maastricht that allows the Republic of Ireland to have a national policy on abortion that is significantly more restrictive than that of the European Community demonstrates a willingness on the part of this regional body to retreat from universalism and secularism as these values apply to women. This retreat parallels quite strikingly the growing responsiveness to gendered ethnic and religious communalism within nation-states.

The nations established in the wake of decolonization, revolution, and outside intervention, with shorter national histories and different processes of state formation, experience the strains on state-focused political nationalism somewhat differently from Western European and North American countries. These new nations were not the product of national self-determination based on common identity. National boundaries based on colonial history ignored common identity as often as they acknowledged it.[20] The result has been nation-states with serious internal ethnic and communal conflicts and often only a veneer of representative government to find solutions. There has been a tendency, especially in sub-Saharan Africa, toward one-party or military rule, in part to manage the ethnic conflicts that are elements of the colonial legacy.[21] Indeed, one-party rule in the less developed world and in state socialist nations has been a favored strategy for managing ethnic diversity, attempting rapid economic growth, and concentrating political power. The excesses of this system lead to demands for more active and competitive democracy on the one hand and for more meaningful, immediate, and communally defined problem-solving institutions on the other. The tensions between the universalism of democracy and the particularism of communalism are poignantly evident in the recent history of minority relations in the nations formed by the breakup of the Soviet Union and in the bitter ethnic fighting in an unraveled Yugoslavia.

These tensions can have a gender component as well. The experience of a Kenyan woman, Wambui Otieno, exemplifies the equivocal place of women when accommodations to ethnic power politics conflict with formal universalism. Otieno, a Christian Kikuyu, wanted to bury her late husband, the well-known lawyer S. M. Otieno, a Christian Luo, in Nairobi, where they had lived. Her husband's male relatives objected and ultimately the High Court awarded the body to them. Mr. Otieno's Luo kinsmen rallied support among the Luo for their interpretation of "ethnic essentialism"—the view that ethnic identity cannot be overridden by national citizenship. In accepting their argument, the High Court reinforced the growing collaborative hegemony between male ethnic power structures and male state power.[22]

The Rise of Religious Fundamentalism

Religious fundamentalism, like increased ethnic identity, responds to the failures of meaning, community, and political effectiveness in the modern nation-state. There has been a remarkable growth in religious fundamentalism in the major religions of the world over the past three decades. The political repercussions of Jewish, Catholic, evangelical Protestant, and Hindu fundamentalism have been felt regionally, but none of these has been as important a political force or had such wide-ranging effects on women as has the worldwide growth in the various types of Muslim fundamentalism.[23] In its several modes, Muslim fundamentalism appeals to both men and women because it offers plans for right living supported by institutions that address immediate problems. The extent to which Muslim fundamentalism enhances the well-being of ordinary people can be seen in the more than 20,000 medical facilities established by the Muslim Brotherhood in nongovernmental mosques in Egypt.[24]

Deniz Kandiyoti has analyzed the rise of Islamic fundamentalism and its problematic relation to women's status in the context of nation building and state development.[25] She argues that women come to represent an "inner sanctum" of national, ethnic, or religious identities, a cultural resource and marker against Western imperialism or other religious and ethnic traditions. But Kandiyoti argues that the power of Muslim fundamentalism to define women's position in society also needs to be understood in terms of the relation of religious organizations to state institutions. A nation-state must establish a national identity, which often supplants or coexists with kin-based or ethnic identities. Powerful elements in the state have differing beliefs about whether family structures should control women's bodies and their social status—a view supported by fundamentalist Islamic tradition—or whether women's bodies and status should be controlled by national or universalistic systems that contribute to nation building. Whether leaders favor secular or religious control of personal laws depends in part on their national goals and their independence in promoting them. For example, differences in the balance of power among the national, state, and local communities in Tunisia, Morocco, and Algeria during the drive for independence account for significant differences in women's status in family legislation in these three countries.[26]

The economic dependence of non-oil-producing Muslim nations on richer oil-producing Islamic countries also helps account for the rise of Islamic fundamentalism. The wealthy oil-producing states of the Persian Gulf have strong traditions of religious fundamentalism. Their economies use male migrant workers in part because of cultural and political resistance to mobilizing women into the paid labor force. Male migrants from countries like Egypt, Yemen, Bangladesh, Turkey, and Pakistan participate in a more fundamentalist culture when working abroad. The Persian Gulf states also contribute grants and capital investment to poorer Islamic countries. The aid packages from gulf nations seek to strengthen religious education, whereas aid packages from international nongovernmental agencies or the World Bank can have secularizing goals for women.[27]

The Growth of International Feminism

The increasing power of nationalism and fundamentalism coincided with similar localizing and internationalizing trends in women's political organizing. Over the past several decades, women's movements—or, where movements did not exist, women's activism—have grown stronger, more varied, and more accepted as indigenous expressions of women's interests. Early in this wave of organizing, nationalists in developing countries and Marxists worldwide often discredited women's movements as imperialist or bourgeois. They voiced concerns about the applicability of feminist ideas originating in Western Europe and North America. The effect of these arguments was to reduce the appeal and legitimacy of women's organizing and thus to contain the range of their political activism. Women in these societies came to develop their own awareness of male domination and its relevant cultural forms. As a result, nationalist and Marxist objections now more rarely close down debate or stop women's organizing. In most countries stalwart groups of women are vigorously inventing ways to respond to women's subordination.

Growing recognition of the many national and community-based forms of women's activism and of the fundamentally plural nature of women's understandings of their problems has occurred simultaneously with increased international communication, disagreement, and cooperation among women.[28] The major forms of these interactions were networks, committees, and caucuses, rather than organizations (though important permanent organizations were created as well). These groups, born of common interests and limited resources, sustained international efforts to improve women's place in economic development, to mobilize opposition to violence against women, to encourage collaboration among scholars, and to facilitate hundreds of other causes defined by women as important to women and to the world.[29]

The U.N. International Women's Year (1975) and Decade for Women (1976–85) nourished the international connections among women in innumerable large and small ways. Whether it planned to or not—even whether it wanted to or not—the United Nations was perhaps the most important resource a resource-poor social movement could have. In much the way new national social movements are often sheltered by established organizations, the United Nations promoted the development of international feminisms and women's movements by creating national and international forums for action.[30] The international spotlight on women, the impetus to gather and compare data, the ability of women's groups to hold their governments to account, and the occasions for international coalition building represented by the three U.N. women's conferences (in Mexico City, Copenhagen, and Nairobi) all catapulted the international connections among women to a qualitatively different level.[31]

The networks and other groups that were encouraged by the U.N. Decade for Women allowed women to experiment with new ways of managing the complexities of simultaneous similarities and differences among themselves. In many ways the feminist theorizing about differences among women and the international experiences of participating in networks have yet to come together. Feminist theories of difference have until recently emphasized the separate identities and histories of groups of women based on religion, race, ethnic heritage, nationality, sexual orientation, and economic position.[32] These differences are important not only in themselves but also because they are often constructed hierarchically and enforced by violence. Theories of difference are central to feminist thinking because they explore the many ways that social cleavages are connected and how they affect women's lives. Theories of difference also act as a corrective to early Western feminist writings that gave primacy to gender over other social cleavages and that often took as normative the experiences of white middle-class women. An exclusive interest in difference can, however, yield a dangerous fatalism about unbridgeable differences among women. A narrow approach to difference saps agency from women and denigrates their efforts to change their lives in anything other than homogenous groups.[33]

Networks, committees, and caucuses were like reefs that protected the experiments on which women of different backgrounds worked together. And, like reefs, these groups could be damaged by the sea raging around them or by their own inattention to their fragile internal environments. The groups were very valuable inventions for three related reasons. First, they were task oriented, so discussions about effective and proper ways of acting occurred in the same setting as the action itself, adding much-needed praxis to efforts to create theories of difference. Second, these groups were often established not only to be an arena for women with differences but also to create a setting where differences became a potential source of valued solutions. Third, women participating in these networks came to understand that they were nurtured by more homogenous groups in ways that they were not as likely to experience in international networks. Home communities were important to participants because it was often difficult, conflictual, and tiring to figure out how to act together and to complete their tasks. The experiences of these international networks, committees, caucuses, and organizations are scattered through the literature on women's movements and deserve much more careful attention.[34] Bernice Johnson Reagon captures the importance and difficulty of the strategic alliance, a short-term type of networking, when she says that "in a coalition you have to give, and it is different from your home. You can't stay there all the time."[35]

WHAT DO WOMEN WANT? A GLOBAL REVIEW OF WOMEN'S ISSUES

In a world defined by this much variety and change, one of the first questions to ask is, What issues mobilize women into political action? The phrase "women's issues" has been used recently in two ways. One definition begins with the distinction between gender and sex. Gender is defined as the social construction of the relations between women and men and among various groups of women or men. Sex is defined as the biological similarities and differences between and among women and men.[36] The first definition of women's issues includes those issues usually associated with women through the traditional sex-gender division of labor: maternal and child health, child care, income generation, support for mothers, and education. Women have

contributed significantly to articulating their own, their children's, and society's needs in these areas, which have often been of secondary concern for men. Indeed, some men have worried that an interest in such topics "feminizes" them and makes them politically less powerful and less acceptable to other men.[37]

The second meaning associated with the discussion of women's issues includes every issue as it is analyzed from a multicultural gender perspective. The assumption is that women's practical and theoretical knowledge about their distinctive positions in deeply gendered social institutions gives them prisms through which they can evaluate not only their own needs but also all the issues facing their society. For example, if women are the only water gatherers in a particular culture, and if they walk many miles a day to fetch water, then building a village well—certainly not a "typical" women's issue according to the first definition—has a specific impact on women.[38]

Analyzing the issues raised in the country chapters requires special attention to the methodology of the research. As we discuss in detail in Chapter 2, the contributing authors were asked to choose three issues of importance to women as vehicles for analyzing the variety and meaning of interest articulation and aggregation in their countries. It is crucial to note that the absence of an issue from the analysis of a country does not mean that the issue is unimportant to women there. The analysis in this book is not, therefore, a ranking of the most urgent problems facing the world's women. Such a ranking would be open to dispute even if social indicator data, survey research on the problems facing women, or independently commissioned panels of experts had generated the topics discussed in each chapter.[39] Instead, our interpretations of what women want are more qualitative and inquiring, directed at piecing together the mosaic of meaning that comes from the variety and spontaneity of women's efforts to act politically.

Three conclusions on the issues that currently command the political attention of women stand out in a global assessment. First, women choose issues of importance to themselves using both definitions. They see the issues typically associated with women in the sex-gender division of labor as especially important, but they consider the full range of political and social problems their concern as well. Second, any issue can appear anywhere. As conveyed in the country chapters, no issues are tied solely to one political context or economic condition, though these contexts and conditions shape the way issues are experienced. Third, the political problems facing women that emerge from these chapters cluster into four topics: ensuring personal safety, security, and autonomy; providing abortion, reproductive rights, and maternal and child health programs; equalizing access to public, communal, and market resources for problem solving and empowerment; and remaking the political and legal rules of the game.

One of the most powerful findings emerging from the country chapters is the extent to which any issue can be important to women anywhere. For instance, violence against women and women's ability to participate fully in economic activities are two issues mentioned as severe problems in rich countries as well as poor ones, democratic nations as well as state socialist or authoritarian regimes. No region or culture is immune. There are of course limits to how women frame these issues and how much they can do about them by themselves, in their communities, and through government action—limits firmly imposed by the specific characteristics of each country.[40] The fact that issues of all types arise everywhere suggests, however, that important political commonalities coexist with marked social differences.[41]

The wide geographical dispersion of all types of problems is an important finding for two reasons. First, it illuminates the profound difficulties that all societies experience in organizing reproductive, domestic, productive, communal, and political activities in a gender-fair manner. Women everywhere define their political interests in terms of coping with or changing the demands that they contribute so much to reproductive and domestic activities that they can-

not make full, valued, and self-directed choices in the other spheres of life. In China, for instance, workers have one day of rest per week. On that day—Sunday—most adults do housework. Women contribute an average of eight to nine hours to domestic tasks, compared with six to eight for men. As Yue Daiyun and Li Jin report, this leads to "uptight Saturdays, fighting Sundays, exhausted Mondays."[42]

Second, the potential for an issue to be taken up by women in any country shows the power of women's experiences as a mobilizing force. Even in the face of powerful ideologies that suggest either that women do not have problems worthy of note or that current solutions will provide remedies, women's experiences act as a catalyst for their political engagement. Marxist ideologies tell women that their problems are secondary to a reordering of productive arrangements. Liberal ideologies tell women that the mechanisms of government are really gender neutral. Authoritarian ideologies tell women that leaders are attending to their needs with fatherly benevolence. When given a chance, women expose the inadequacies of these ideologies to solve problems from women's perspectives, even when they agree with other tenets of these belief systems.

Violence, Safety, and Security

The issues that engage women politically today belie the notion that women and men experience all issues similarly as "human" issues or that only the public versions of women's home roles take up their political time. Women's issues are rooted in the particularity of their experiences in the face of the false universality of men's experiences. Nowhere is this more evident than in issues of safety and security. Women routinely experience the risk of sexual assault in ways that have no immediate parallels for men. Women's concerns for the safety and security of their bodies are discussed in roughly a quarter of the countries examined in this book—in nations as diverse in their social organization as Bangladesh, Great Britain, Mexico, and Australia. The vulnerability and powerlessness of women accruing from their sex and their inability to fully protect themselves make women subject to violence and aggression, physical oppression and exploitation. Women's organizations in these countries have mobilized against brutalization, battery, and sexual abuse through strategies ranging from social services to sexual politics. They seek to engage the state in punishing offenders and helping survivors.

The chapter authors also provide a glimpse of another face of violence—state militarism—and its effect on a defenseless populace. Argentina, Uruguay, South Africa, Ghana, Nigeria, and the Philippines have all recently endured state violence. Women feel the effects of this violence in special ways. The mass arrest and kidnapping of large numbers of people in Argentina during the military regime of Gen. Jorge Rafael Videla and his successors mobilized women to speak as mothers for their missing children, allowing a nonpartisan maternalism to be a wedge against authoritarian rule when much of civic life was repressed.[43] Sexual torture and rape by the police and military, used routinely in the Philippines during the martial law period imposed by Ferdinand Marcos, are also forms of military violence with special meaning to women as individuals and as symbols of family and cultural purity.[44]

The weight of state violence has another more diffuse but still corrosive effect on women. Women who have come through the cold winter of militarism also speak of the need to democratize everyday life, whose practices became more patriarchal as part of the gestalt of military rule. Graciela Sapriza describes the effect of Uruguayan militarism and state terror on family life this way: "The assault on institutions and the banning of political parties and labor unions all combined to limit women's political participation to the home and neighborhood. The public world of men also disappeared; the household became the place in which men could exercise power—as fathers, husbands, and brothers. This testifies to the power of a patriarchal system with no more legitimacy than that of gender hierarchy."[45]

Reproductive Rights, Abortion, and Maternal and Child Health

Reproductive rights and abortion are issues for women in about a quarter of the countries as well. In Europe and North America legal recognition of a woman's option to have an abortion early in pregnancy is articulated not only as a woman's right but also as a human right. At stake is the ability of women to retain some control over the conditions of conception and motherhood in a world where intercourse is not always joyous or freely chosen. Even when intercourse is experienced lovingly, the consequence may still be a pregnancy that will endanger a woman's health or welfare. Pregnancy, often eagerly awaited, is also the nexus through which women's secondary economic and political status is constructed.[46] As such, supporters of legal abortion argue that all of women's human rights depend on retaining a voice in deciding the outcome of unwanted pregnancy.

In response to this approach, anti-abortion groups and conservative forces have mobilized against the gains made so far. For some anti-abortion activists, the issue revolves around religious beliefs that accord personhood to a being from the moment of conception. Other anti-abortion activists see their efforts as an important contribution to resisting a male-defined, acquisitive individualism or a state-supported disregard for human relations, both of which they feel are harmful to society, and especially to women. The newly developing opposition to abortion in Poland encompasses both these objections: "A politically powerful Catholicism has produced a public discourse that accuses feminism of being both too left and too right, both too close to the remnants of Polish communism (which gave nominal equality to women and granted them the rights to abortion) or too much the vanguard of a self-interested capitalism."[47]

In less developed regions of the world, reproductive freedom and abortion rights take on an additional characteristic: the policy of the state toward the size of the population. In China, Turkey, and Brazil, respectively, abortion is widely required, legally available in the first ten weeks, and socially tolerated because the government believes that its economic growth strategies depend on managing population growth. Families and individual women here and around the world often make abortion decisions in ways that balance household resources with the mouths they already have to feed.

The health and survival of pregnant women and young children are also tremendously important to women. In poorer countries, where adequate food and health care are often unavailable, women organize to provide these services themselves and to demand that governments and donor agencies place high priority on maternal and child health. This concern is covered in most of the chapters on less industrialized countries, but it is especially evident in the discussions on Sudan, Nigeria, Ghana, Kenya, and South Africa. War and natural disasters also add to the difficulties that women face in nurturing their children. Drought, famine, and internal warfare have left Sudan awash in refugees. Women in refugee camps in Sudan despair for their children, who are subjected to the grinding poverty of camp life. Hawa, a 20-year-old married woman with one child, describes the precariousness of life in Abu Zeid Refugee Camp: "The government doesn't supply us with any of the necessities such as sugar, tea, milk, flour, and so on. For two years we depended on the relief agencies to support us, but now they stopped. We used to exchange the food of the relief agencies that is not familiar to us for sugar, tea, second-hand clothes, and things like that. Last year many children were poisoned because they ate the powdered soap that mothers thought was a baby food."[48]

Equalizing Strategies

Women also focus their political efforts on what can be called equalizing strategies, which represent attempts to improve women's access to existing education, employment, healthcare, credit, and other resource opportunities and ultimately to make these resources more responsive to women's needs. The country authors understand both the potentially transformative nature of this equality and the often fierce resistance to it. As a result, they embrace a wide variety of strategies to promote women's status: equal and equivalent treatment, equal and equivalent outcomes, and separate or special opportunities. The interest in equalizing strategies goes beyond merely giving women access to institutions and opportunities that are defined by men's needs and life cycles.

The content of equalizing strategies varies by level of economic development. In Japan, women have organized to improve access to education and to reduce stereotyping in curricula. Feminists in the United States want to participate in policy discussions about the provision of universally available health insurance. In contrast, Nepalese women are experimenting with increasing women's autonomy and economic productivity by extending credit to women. In Kenya, women want a say in government and family decisions to move from subsistence to export crops, and they want guarantees that they, not the men in their family, will be paid for their own labor.

In their demands for greater access to and substantive equality in the distribution of resources, women are posing a fundamental question of distributive justice: Can a society have equality, even equality of opportunity, without a social commitment to distributive justice that understands the sex-gender organization of life? When read together, the country chapters extend a collective invitation to John Rawls, the philosopher of justice, to live as a poor man's wife in a village, squatter settlement, or town in one of their countries. Rawls's design for a just society includes equal basic liberty, fair equality of opportunity, and substantive equality built on the principle that differences in the treatment of people are permissible only when the differences help those people least advantaged in society. In this just world, each head of a household must agree to the ordering of society without knowing "his" position in the eventual distribution of individual and social attributes (Rawls's veil of ignorance). Susan Moller Okin notes the inadequacy of this formulation for women. She argues that although Rawls's analysis could be applied to remedy women's subordination, his use of heads of households as the basis of the social contract and his inattention to the gendered construction of society mean that women are ignored in this theory of justice as in others. Rawls's theory does not address the fact that by his criteria the family and the entire gender system are unjust institutions.[49] His failure arises from an inability to see the particularity of men within his theory about individuals and from his lack of knowledge about how the world's women live—especially how women's status in the family is connected to their status in other realms of society.

Politics and the Law

The political and legal rules of the game, defined by access to political institutions and as critiques of systems or processes, are featured in nearly half the country chapters, including those on Argentina, Bangladesh, Egypt, Ghana, Great Britain, India, Nepal, Peru, the former Soviet Union, Sudan, and the United States. Concerns with political representation and electoral participation are directed at the limited involvement of women in formal politics, their minimal presence in parliaments and legislative bodies, and their virtual absence from the top echelons of political parties, cabinets, and bureaucracies. In a notable change from a decade ago, chapter authors report an increased pragmatism on the part of feminists in democratic regimes who, while retaining concerns over the potentially co-opting character of working within parties and governments, are much less willing to turn their backs on the state as an arena of activism. Maria Teresa Gallego Mendez describes the tentative moves of Spanish feminists toward an activism that includes direct engagement with the state:

Only recently has there been some change in the pattern of the feminist debate about politics. Participants at a feminist workshop in 1990 in Madrid stated: "We consider that the feminist movement should be transformed into a political voice, because it is the only way equality of rights and opportunities will reach every woman. . . . Feminism cannot stop at the frontier of the small, self-conscious group, but must expand to more open spheres in which women can walk quietly,

express ourselves, be in contact with each other, and participate without the need of heroic efforts, breaks or extraordinary tensions. To be capable of acquiring this social presence the feminist movement needs to develop structures of consensus and coordination . . . and discern what kind of political rules we should learn to use rationally and what kind we should regret and change."[50]

For women living under corrupt or brutal regimes, or in countries where they have no real representation, the choices are more difficult. Active resistance, noncooperation, and disengagement from official politics are often neccessary strategies. Here too, however, women defer rather than abandon imagining a world where their political participation as women citizens would matter.

The country authors note the changes in women's autonomous organizing as well. Where they existed, older independent women's political organizations, many of which began life in suffrage campaigns earlier in this century, were reinvigorated by increasing interest in women's issues. New types of organizations sprang up, too. The non-hierarchical groups that characterized radical feminism in North America and Western Europe in the 1960s and 1970s did not translate well into larger-scale action.[51] This organizational form, which represented a move away from establishment-oriented, male-dominated organizations, was useful in consciousness-raising and bequeathed a legacy of leadership sharing to feminist organizations in these countries.

Worldwide, women's political organizing has made another central contribution to how politics is done and what it means. Women's activism has demonstrated the inaccuracy of assuming that more players merely cut the political pie into smaller pieces. As often as not, increasing the number and variety of political players changes the nature of politics and generates additional political resources. The Glass of Milk committees in Peru, whose activism strengthens the civic sector, have expanded political access and increased political resources. More than 9,000 committees, with a total membership of 300,000 women, prepare and distribute one glass of milk each day to young children. Virginia Vargas Valente and Victoria Villanueva describe the program as "one of the most organized action groups [in Peru], with a substantial capacity for mobilization. It has exercised political pressure not only to assure the donation of the milk but also to prevent the state and the political parties from manipulating the committees for their own purposes."[52]

WOMEN'S EXCLUSION FROM FORMAL POLITICS

What happens in formal political organizations when women voice their concerns over issues of violence, reproductive and child health, equalizing policies, and the political and legal rules of the game? Too often, very little happens, in large measure because women are barely visible in formal political institutions. Political systems, whatever the ideology, form, and mobilization capacity, rest on the virtual exclusion or marginalization of women from formal politics. The ubiquity and extremity of that exclusion deserves attention. Why is it that half of the world's population routinely holds only 5–10 percent of the formal positions of political leadership? Why, when disparities in ethnic and racial representation engage the attention of politicians worldwide, are calls for efforts to research and remedy the barriers to women's formal political participation greeted with concern about special interests?[53]

The country chapters and the charts that accompany them paint a bleak picture of women's participation as national leaders, cabinet ministers, members of national legislatures, and incumbents in the high civil service. At the end of 1990, only 6 of the 159 countries represented in the United Nations had women as chief executives. In nearly 100 countries men held *all* the senior and deputy ministerial positions in 1987–88. Worldwide, only 10 percent of national legislative seats were held by women in 1987. The percentage is declining because the legislative quotas allotted to women (usually 20–30 percent) in the former Soviet Union and the state socialist regimes of Central Europe are no longer

in effect. The democratic regimes that replaced them have failed to mobilize women for legislative offices in the same proportions. Cross-national figures comparing women's representation in the top echelons of civil service are not readily available. But if the sex of senior managers in the United Nations can be used as a proxy, as U.N. experts on women suggest that it should, then women are very poorly represented in high administrative positions. Less than 5 percent of the senior managers in the U.N. system are women.[54]

The irony of women's exclusion from formal politics is aptly conveyed by the situation of women in India before and after the ouster of the British. In the decades before independence, women constituted 10 percent of those jailed for anti-British activities. In the decades since independence, however, women have never held more than 8 percent of the seats in the Lok Sabha, the lower house of Parliament. It was easier to get arrested for supporting democracy than it is to get elected to the democratic institutions that Indian nationalists were fighting to obtain.[55]

To explain women's exclusion from formal politics, the authors in this book look beyond the two traditional theories of women's exclusion from formal politics: women's socially shaped "choices," especially to concentrate on child rearing and homemaking; and social norms, which comprise the thousands of big and little gender-based rules about proper political activity that make up "political socialization." These explanations are inadequate because they make women's absence from formal political institutions either their own fault or no one's fault; the explanations are either too individualistic or epiphenomenal. The traditional explanations focus only on the supply of women for formal activism, not the demand.[56] In contrast, the country chapters emphasize how political institutions mold the expectations, careers, and activities of those who aspire to participate in them.

Patriarchy and Fraternalism

The contributors write incisively about the male culture and ethos of formal politics, which is fashioned by male lifestyles and characterized by an aggressiveness and a competitiveness that are often viewed as male traits. The maleness of politics has two aspects, both of which are theoretically and practically important. One construction is found in the traditional fatherly connotation of patriarchy, in which politics is seen as having patron-client relationships that reiterate patriarchal father-son family structures. This political form excludes women from the material rewards of politics in much the way they are excluded from the material rewards of other male-controlled economic obligation and reciprocity networks. In Kenya, the patron-client quality of the "man-made political machinery" is one of the primary reasons development policies and programs rarely respond to women's needs.[57]

The other male aspect of politics is rooted in fraternalism, or what in Great Britain is called the "chaps" mentality of politics.[58] To some extent, all formal representative governments are descendants (through colonialism, reinvention, or imitation) of British parliamentary experiments with shared power and of the French Revolution's initial participatory impulse. Both of these political experiences emphasized the brotherhood of men. In the British experience, the king grudgingly shares his exclusive power first with a brotherly band of powerful landholders and later with rich commercial entrepreneurs. In the French experience, the power of the king—and the king himself—were swept away in a tide of what comes to be understood as the fraternity of male citizenship.

Carole Pateman captures the distinctions between the patriarchal and fraternal maleness of contract theory, itself an integral part of the development of formal representative institutions. She also acknowledges that feminists must struggle to promote recognition of the male meanings of so-called universal terms so that their applicability to women can be gauged. "A very nice conjuring trick has been performed so that one kinship term, fraternity, is held to be merely a metaphor for the universal bonds of humankind, for community, solidarity or fellowship, while another kinship term, patriarchy, is held to stand for

the rule of fathers which has passed away long ago. The modern civil order then can be presented as universal ('fraternal') not patriarchal. Almost no one—except some feminists—is willing to admit that fraternity means what it says: the brotherhood of *men*."[59]

The significance of fraternalism as a source of political power is that the exclusiveness of brothers is just as effective as the protection of fathers in limiting women's access to formal politics. In France, fairly typically, the political costs of fraternalism are extracted by the eternal dilemma between equality and difference faced by French women elected to office. They have the choice of a male-defined equality that renders them invisible or a male-defined difference that renders them secondary.[60]

Political Parties and Civil Society

The clear message in the country chapters is that the culture and processes of formal political institutions—especially parties, their affiliated labor or employer groups, their youth wings, and even their women's auxiliaries—are major barriers to women's equal participation in institutional politics. The barriers include the concrete expressions of patriarchal and fraternal privilege found in men's expressive and problem-solving styles, their networks, their workday, their domestic and child-care obligations, and even their traditions of making sexual access to women one of the perquisites of power. Even the Green Party in Germany, whose platform stands for gender equity, was tainted by a scandal arising from the sexual exploitation of women by a Green parliamentarian.[61]

Moments of system change, when the distribution and forms of power are in flux, underscore the importance of parties in structuring women's opportunities to participate in formal politics. There has been growing recognition that even though social disjunctures like war, revolution, or economic distress may temporarily increase the range or intensity of women's political activism, these changes do not endure after political consolidation.[62] The role of parties in returning politics to the gender status quo is demonstrated in the chapters discussing the transitions from authoritarian or state socialist regimes to democracies. Taken as a whole, these examples show the importance of parties and their relation to civil society. During periods of transition to democracy, parties lack the virtual monopoly of interest articulation that comes with political routinization. They have not incorporated the deep social tension of simultaneously being part of the governmental system while also being, in theory at least, the premier example of civic voluntarism. In this more fluid and often less efficient political period, women can have more influence on parties from within, as well as from without. The disorderliness that makes political life in this period tenuous opens up opportunities for women if they are organized, willing to act, and not thoroughly opposed by entrenched interests whose patriarchal gender ideologies and interests must be placated.

Brazil, Greece, and Hungary offer different examples of the relations among political parties, civic life, time available for political organizing, and women's fortunes in the transition to democracy. The element unifying these dissimilar transitions was the adoption of electoral systems with proportional representation, which offer the greatest opportunity to elect more women to legislatures because ticket balancing can occur on party lists.[63] In none of these transitions did proportional representation have any important effect on promoting women's formal participation, however. Such experiences reaffirm that the advantages of proportional representation for women lay dormant without political leadership and social pressure.[64]

The transition from military rule to democracy in Brazil that took place in the early 1980s was influenced by the existence during the military period of certain kinds of activism that promoted civic variety when democracy was finally allowed. The Roman Catholic church had encouraged mothers' clubs; the political left had organized poor urban communities; the military regime had not, in the main, exercised brutal repression against women's organizing; and the process of democratization was lengthy enough to allow in-

stitutions in these areas to develop. Civil society rather than political society dominated in the transition, and parties were not the primary vehicle of democratization. When elections regularized, however, political society began to triumph over civil society, and women's access to decision makers and their ability to be leaders themselves declined.[65]

A similar but much-attenuated situation occurred in Greece in the transition to democracy in 1974 and 1975. Civil society had always been weak in Greece, and "underground" party organizations had survived repeated military governments. This combination meant that the period during which civil and political life were balanced was much briefer in Greece than in Brazil. In this moment Greek women made another foray into cooperative, non-party-dominated political activism, but the routinization of political life made these experiments difficult to sustain.[66]

The transition to democracy in Hungary in 1989 was somewhat different because this regime change was from state socialism, and the place of the Communist Party in the new regime had to be resolved during the transformation. The official women's organization of the Communist Party was discredited, though the group survived. Its Marxist ideology of women's liberation through work left many women deaf to discussions on women's status. Independent organizing by all groups had been forbidden by the former regime. The few new women's organizations directed at women's political engagement declined to be affiliated with any party, and the new democratic parties did not court them, in part because they had no organized constituency. The rapid decline in economic conditions meant that women spent more time managing household economies, which lessened the time they could spend on political activism. Together, these factors reduced the period of openness and therefore the time during which women were likely to be especially effective in redesigning their place in the political system.[67]

Women's increased participation in formal politics will depend, then, not only on the more equitable sharing of reproductive, domestic, productive, and communal activities, but also on the transformation of the norms of parties and their affiliated organizations and on the strength of civil society. To the extent that there are few groups in civil society that encourage women to voice their demands politically, or to the extent that parties are impervious to women's demands, parties will remain a significant structural barrier to women's political participation. These barriers will remain, even when party systems begin to age and when citizen demands and party platforms are out of sync. By itself, party dealignment, a trend in many Western European nations and in the United States, will not increase women's representation in formal political bodies.[68] But changes within the organizational cultures of parties, strong connections among parties and groups active in civil society, and attention to the electoral rules of the game can promote women's formal participation.

THE POLITICS OF EVERYDAY LIFE

The richest, most varied, and most typical arena of women's political engagement is found in the politics of everyday life. The site of this activism is the terrain between the state and family that is usually ignored in conventional investigations of politics.[69] Viewed globally, the diversity of civic activities is staggering, even though countries vary dramatically in the form and extensiveness of civic life and the place of women in it. For instance, during the demise of the Soviet Union and the creation of more than a dozen new countries in its place, Soviet women struggled to hold their first public independent feminist conference. Its motto was, "Democracy without women is not democracy." In Ghana, market women alternately offer and withdraw their support of political parties and leaders in response to their needs as small traders and as they evaluate the potential of effective activism in a one-party (often militarily controlled) state. In Bolivia, rural women fight to make the politically dominant mining union recognize their simultaneous roles as mothers, workers, and citizens.[70]

Gender Interests

What patterns of activism emerge from these examples? Maxine Molyneux has distinguished between strategic and practical gender interests as a basis for understanding how women organize as women:

Strategic gender interests are derived in the first instance deductively, i.e., from the analysis of women's subordination and from the formulation of an alternative, more satisfactory set of arrangements to those that exist. These ethical and theoretical criteria assist in the formulation of strategic objectives to overcome women's subordination, such as the abolition of the sexual division of labor, the alleviation of the burden of domestic labor and child care, the removal of institutionalized forms of discrimination, the establishment of political equality, freedom of choice over childbearing, and the adoption of adequate measures against male violence and control over women. . . . *Practical gender interests* are given inductively and arise from the concrete conditions of women's positioning by virtue of their gender within the division of labor. . . . Practical interests are usually a response to an immediate perceived need and they do not entail a strategic goal such as women's emancipation or gender equality. . . . [Practical gender interests] cannot be innocent of class effects . . . [and they] do not in themselves challenge prevailing forms of gender subordination, even though they arise directly out of them.[71]

Scholars of Latin America and the Caribbean have found this distinction particularly useful in creating typologies of women's groups. In this region, women-created, neighborhood-based groups with practical gender interests are called feminine organizations. As originally portrayed by Molyneux, feminine groups do not question the gender-role divisions of everyday life but use those role obligations as a moral claim for public activism to accomplish women's usual tasks. In contrast, feminist organizations are women's groups that seek to advance strategic gender interests by changing the relations between the sexes.[72] The United Nations implies a similar classification when it divides women's groups into community-based problem-solving organizations and nongovernmental organizations with policy or program objectives.[73] Both of these categorizations resemble the somewhat different distinction in the United States between womanist and feminist organizations or perspectives. A womanist orientation, articulated by African American women, asserts the inseparability of race and gender in the thought and experience of Black women and presents a view of the gender identity of Black women as ineluctably located in racial and community consciousness.[74] As such, gender conflict is seen in terms of its racial meanings as well as its relevance for relations between women and men.

These typologies all react against a notion of unified, undifferentiated "women's interests," especially as they were defined in the universalistic approach to structural social change that characterized much of the early feminist movement in many countries. The value of each of these typologies is that it asks how gender interacts with other social cleavages.

Molyneux's typology, devised to explain women's activism on a global scale, goes the furthest in suggesting how women mobilize for action, but it also raises the most questions. In her definitions of strategic and practical gender interests, Molyneux strongly implies two kinds of causal social linkages. Practical gender interests arise in the popular classes from the immediate problems of women, and the solutions to these problems are not perceived by the women experiencing them to require a change in gender relations. Strategic gender interests arise in the old and new middle classes as women deduce the long-term structural changes necessary to alter the systems of male domination. This formulation aptly summarizes much of women's mobilization into political activism in Latin America and the Caribbean in the 1970s and early 1980s. But it has a number of serious limitations: too many causal factors are too firmly linked. Popular classes, immediate problems, short-term solutions, and unwillingness to question existing sex-gender systems are juxtaposed against middle classes, structural and distant problems, long-term solutions, and the willingness to question sex-gender systems. Political and historical research on Latin America shows that women's activism is not fixed in this mold. For example, as a result of coming together to solve immediate problems like inadequate health care (a practical gender interest), feminine groups often took up the problem of domestic violence (a strategic gender interest).[75] These historical events suggest the importance of rethinking the types of women's concerns and the relation between concerns and activism.

Gender Ideologies and Action Potentials

We suggest a model of women's mobilization into women-defined activism based on the relationship of gender ideologies and action potentials. At their core, gender ideologies describe actual and preferred relations between men and women and among members of the same sex. They include personal theories of power, and they evaluate possibilities for individual or social change. They are complex, amenable to alteration through experience, and redolent of connections to other belief systems. As such, gender ideologies are interconnected with ideologies about actual and preferred relations among other social groups, such as classes and races.

The content of gender ideologies revolves around the evaluation of two organizing principles: domination and difference. Gender ideologies must address men's general domination of women and how women avoid or reverse it. One of the principal ways that male domination is managed is through beliefs about what the differences between women and men mean. In its most reduced form, the relation between domination and difference can be thought of as a matrix defined by two dimensions. On the first, individuals support or resist male domination. On the second, they accept or reject the importance of large or significant differences between women and men.[76]

As the table shows, when male domination is unquestioned and sex-gender differences are thought to be large or significant, gender ideology emphasizes *distinct obligations* for women and men. When male domination is unquestioned but sex-gender differences are believed to be small or insignificant, gender ideology empha-

Importance of Sex-Gender Differences	Response to Male Domination	
	Accept	Reject
Accept	Distinct obligations Ideologies	Separate spheres Ideologies
Reject	Male privilege Ideologies	Gender system change Ideologies

sizes men's *unfettered privileges,* there being little other justification for men's advantages. In contrast, when male domination is rejected, and sex-gender differences are believed to be large or significant, gender ideology emphasizes *separate spheres of activities.* When male domination is rejected, and sex-gender differences are believed to be small or insignificant, gender ideology emphasizes *change* toward equal or equivalent treatment. Because the nature of domination and the meaning of sex-gender differences can vary with the type of activities or relations considered, an individual may have different gender ideologies for different realms of life.

Gender ideologies predispose women individually and in groups to particular types of action. The ideologies of distinct obligations and separate spheres predispose women to preserve their capacities to be successful in their gender-defined responsibilities. At the moment of initial activism, a gender ideology based on distinct obligations would predispose women not to engage politically in ways that question male dominance. This may have been the ideology of the Latin American feminine groups when they began their activism, but experience changed the ideology of many women active in these groups. A distinct obligations gender ideology that preserves male dominance through social activism in the name of sex-gender differences characterizes conservative social activism by women in many other countries as well. It is different from the better-known separate spheres ideology, which predisposes women toward the social housekeeping activism that brings their special characteris-

tics to bear on social and public problems. Here sex-gender differences are accepted but men's political domination is not. A change-based gender ideology predisposes women to work to end male domination by increasing similarity of treatment or outcome for women and men. Women who hold unvarnished male-privilege gender ideologies are not predisposed to be active politically in the name of women.

A woman's decision about how and where to act politically in response to her view of her position as a woman arises not only from the predispositions set by gender ideologies but also from choosing goals, evaluating repertoires of action, and assessing opportunity structures. These choices create action potentials that can change with experience and in response to settings. New skills are developed, individual problems are seen as collective in the wake of conversations with people who have similar experiences, opportunities come and go, regimes become more or less repressive, family members are more or less supportive. In the context of gender ideologies and action potentials, individuals and groups make tactical decisions about whether to take up immediate or long-term problems or to accept or challenge existing systems of sex-gender relations.

Women who live in societies in which group formation is possible establish civic-sector institutions that promote particular goals. The specialization and experience of organizations grant longevity to these goals. Women's political activism must then address the maintenance of organizations and the organizations' capacities to endure and change. Throughout the country chapters we see that women in this wave of international activism were startled by the complexities and costs of sustaining the institutions they created, especially when added to child care, household work, paid work, other community activities, and, sometimes, formal politics. In Norway and Australia, for example, the feminist rape crisis centers faced dilemmas over whether to accept government money. Feminists not only feared losing control of the services, they were saddened to acknowledge the difficulty of maintaining social services as a voluntary political activity.

Overall, the future of women's political engagement—in formal politics and in the politics of everyday life—depends on the gender construction of the family, civil society, the economy, and official political institutions. When formal institutions are impermeable to women's self-defined claims, civil society becomes the major arena for women's activism. When civil society is weak or shaped by polarized gender ideologies, women have fewer opportunities to create the experiments whose successes help to transform the institutions in which they live. And when eking out enough to eat takes the whole day or when the fear of a policeman's knock consumes the night, women's activism is even more limited. The message of these chapters is, then, that women's political engagement occurs against long odds. When it is successful, women find it pleasurable, difficult, surprising, and worthwhile, all at the same time.

NOTES

1. All the phrases used to describe poorer and richer countries are deeply flawed. We use "less developed," "developing," "less industrialized," and "Third World" to denote the poorer countries and "more developed," "more industrialized," and "First World" to denote the richer ones. Each phrase has unfortunate hierarchical connotations, but each is also well known and understood. No ready alternatives are available and we continue this practice, recognizing its many limitations.

2. See GHANA and NIGERIA.

3. D. Michael Shafer, "Sectors, States, and Social Forces: Korea and Zambia Confront Economic Restructuring," *Comparative Politics* 22 (January 1990): 127–50.

4. United Nations, "Literacy: Tool for Empowering Women," U.N. Department for Public Information Document DPI/1075 (July 1990); and KENYA. For a summary of the problems of standard economic development models as they are applied to women see Irene Tinker, ed., *Persistent Inequalities: Women and World Development* (New York: Oxford University Press, 1990).

5. See, e.g., Mohammad Abdullah and Erica F. Wheeler, "Seasonal Variations and the Intra-Household Distribution of Food in a Bangladeshi Village," *American Journal of Clinical Nutrition* 41 (June 1985): 1305–13; Amartya Sen, *Poverty and Famines: An Essay on Entitle-*

ment and Deprivation (Oxford: Clarendon Press, 1981); Amartya Sen, "Well-Being, Agency, and Freedom: The Dewey Lectures," *Journal of Philosophy* 85 (April 1985): 169–221; Gary Becker, *A Treatise on the Family* (Cambridge, Mass.: Harvard University Press, 1981); Susan C. Bourque and Kay B. Warren, *Women of the Andes: Patriarchy and Social Change in Rural Peru* (Ann Arbor: University of Michigan Press, 1981); Hanna Papanek, "The Work and Non-Work of Women," *Signs* 4 (Summer 1979): 775–81; Bina Agarwal, "Women, Poverty and Agricultural Growth in India," *Journal of Peasant Studies* 13 (July 1986): 165–220; and Caroline H. Bledsoe, "Women's Marital Strategies Among the Kpelle of Liberia," *Journal of Anthropological Research* 32 (Winter 1976): 372–89.

6. Vina Mazumdar and Kumud Sharma, "Sexual Division of Labor and the Subordination of Women: A Reappraisal from India," in Tinker, ed., *Persistent Inequalities,* 185–97.

7. Stanley Fisher and Vittorio Corbo, "Structural Adjustment: What Have We Learned From the Eighties?" World Bank, Country Economics Department; Policy, Research, and External Affairs Working Paper no. 5, series 4, Macroeconomic Adjustment and Growth, May 1991.

8. Guillermo O'Donnell, "Tensions in the Bureaucratic-Authoritarian State and the Question of Democracy," in David Collier, ed., *The New Authoritarianism in Latin America* (Princeton: Princeton University Press, 1979), 285–318.

9. Fisher and Corbo, "Structural Adjustment," 1.

10. John Waterbury, "The Political Management of Economic Adjustment and Reform," in Joan Nelson, ed., *Fragile Coalitions: The Politics of Economic Readjustment* (New Brunswick, N.J.: Transaction Books, 1989), 27–28.

11. Fisher and Corbo, "Structural Adjustment," 24–25.

12. World Bank, *World Development Report, 1990* (New York: Oxford University Press, 1990), 240.

13. United Nations, *1989 World Survey on the Role of Women in Development* (New York: United Nations, 1989), 42–43.

14. See EGYPT, PERU, BRAZIL, and ARGENTINA.

15. Uma Lele, "Women, Structural Adjustment, and Transformation: Some Lessons and Questions from the African Experience," in Christina H. Gladwin, ed., *Structural Adjustment and African Women Farmers* (Gainesville: University of Florida Press, 1991), 53–54.

16. On the history and study of modern nationalism see Sylvia Bashevkin, *True Patriot Love: The Politics of Canadian Nationalism* (Toronto: Oxford University Press, 1990); Benedict R. Anderson, *Imagined Communities* (London: Verso, 1991), 37–46; and Partha Chatterjee, "Colonialism, Nationalism, and Colonized Women:

The Contest in India," *American Ethnologist* 16 (November 1989): 622–33.

17. One of the first systematic cross-national observations of the importance of universalism and secularism for women is found in Gabriel A. Almond and Sidney Verba, *The Civic Culture: Political Attitudes and Democracy in Five Nations* (Princeton: Princeton University Press, 1963), 387–400. One of the authors' more remarkable findings was that in the early 1960s, 25 percent of women and 28 percent of men in the United States were current or past officers in volunteer associations.

18. Dorothy J. Rosenberg, "Shock Therapy: GDR Women in Transition from a Socialist Welfare State to a Social Market Economy," *Signs* 17 (Autumn 1991): 129–51.

19. Joyce Gelb, *Feminism and Politics: A Comparative Perspective* (Berkeley: University of California Press, 1989), 107–14. National courts in Western Europe and North America had been much less supportive of equal-value wage policies. On the U.S. case see Sara M. Evans and Barbara J. Nelson, *Wage Justice: Comparable Worth and the Paradox of Technocratic Reform* (Chicago: University of Chicago Press, 1989).

20. Eric Hobsbawm, *Nations and Nationalism Since 1780: Programme, Myth, Reality* (Cambridge, Eng.: Cambridge University Press, 1990), 171.

21. Vicky Randall, "Conclusion," in Randall, ed., *Political Parties in the Third World* (London: Sage, 1988), 188–89.

22. Patricia Stamp, "Burying Otieno: The Politics of Gender and Ethnicity in Kenya," *Signs* 16 (Summer 1991): 808–45. For a discussion of collaborative hegemony see Zakia Pathak and Rajeswari Sunder Rajan, "'Shahbano,'" *Signs* 14 (Spring 1989): 558–82.

23. See the denominational essays in Martin E. Marty and R. Scott Appleby, eds., *Fundamentalisms Observed* (Chicago: University of Chicago Press, 1991), for analyses of North American fundamentalist Protestantism; Roman Catholic traditionalism in the United States; Latin American fundamentalist Protestantism; Jewish fundamentalism in the United States; Jewish fundamentalism in Israel; Sunni fundamentalism in Egypt and Sudan; activist Shiism in Iran, Iraq, and Lebanon; South Asian Islamic fundamentalism; Hindu fundamentalism; Sikh fundamentalism; fundamentalist movements in Theravada Buddhism; Islamic fundamentalism in Malaysia and Indonesia; the Confucian revival in industrial East Asia; and Japanese political and religious fundamentalist links.

24. Saad Eddin Ibrahim, "Egypt's Islamic Activism in the 1980s," *Third World Quarterly* 10, no. 2 (1988): 642–43, in John O. Voll, "Fundamentalism in the Sunni Arab World: Egypt and the Sudan," in Martin E. Marty and R. Scott Appleby, *Fundamentalisms Observed*, 346.

25. Deniz Kandiyoti, "Women, Islam, and the State," *Middle East Report* 173 (November–December 1991): 9–14.

26. Mounira Charrad, "State and Gender in the Mahgrib," *Middle East Reporter* 163 (March-April 1990): 19–24, in Kandiyoti, "Women, Islam, and the State," 11.

27. Ibid.

28. On the multiple origins of feminisms and women's activism see Jane Mansbridge and Susan Moller Okin, "Feminism," in Robert E. Goodin and Philip Petit, eds., *A Companion to Contemporary Political Philosophy* (Oxford: Blackwell, forthcoming 1993).

29. Jessie Bernard, *The Female World from a Global Perspective* (Bloomington: Indiana University Press, 1987), 156–66.

30. See, e.g., David Knoke, "Resource Acquisition and Allocation in U.S. National Associations," in Burt Klandermans et al., eds., *Organizing for Change: International Social Movements Research*, vol. 2 (Greenwich, Conn.: JAI, 1989), 129–54; and Jack Walker, "The Origins and Maintenance of Interest Groups in America," *American Political Science Review* 77 (June 1983): 390–406.

31. Irene Tinker and Jane Jaquette, "U.N. Decade for Women: Its Impact and Legacy," *World Development* 15 (March 1987): 419–27.

32. On the importance of identity and the separations among women see Maria C. Lugones and Elizabeth V. Spelman, "Have We Got a Theory for You! Feminist Theory, Cultural Imperialism, and the Demand for 'The Women's Voice,'" *Women's Studies International Forum* 6, no. 6 (1983): 573–81; and Spelman, *In Essential Woman* (Boston: Beacon, 1988).

33. On the limits of identity feminism and a call for political coalitions and action see Linda Gordon, "On Difference," *Genders* 10 (Spring 1991): 91–111; and Shane Phelan, *Identity Politics: Lesbian Feminism and the Limits of Community* (Philadelphia: Temple University Press, 1989). On the relations between communitarian and political social movements see Claus Offe, "New Social Movements: Challenging the Boundaries of Institutional Politics," *Social Research* 52 (Winter 1985): 823–58.

34. See, e.g., Nancy Saporta Sternbach, Marysa Navarro Aranguren, Patricia Chuchryk, and Sonia F. Alvarez, "Feminisms in Latin America: From Bogotá to San Bernardo," *Signs* 17 (Winter 1992): 397–411. In the chapter on networking in *The Female World from a Global Perspective,* Jessie Bernard demonstrates that many of the sources that would help us know about networks remain unpublished.

35. Bernice Johnson Reagon, "Coalition Politics: Turning the Century," in Barbara Smith, ed., *Home Girls: A Black Feminist Anthology* (New York: Kitchen Table Press, 1983), 356–57.

36. See Barbara J. Nelson, "Women and Knowledge in Political Science: Texts, Histories, and Episte-

mologies," *Women & Politics* 9 (Spring 1989): 1–25. This usage derives from Gayle Rubin's classic article "The Traffic in Women: Notes on the 'Political Economy' of Sex," in Rayna R. Reiter, ed., *Toward an Anthropology of Women* (New York: Monthly Review Press, 1975), 157–210.

37. For a historical example from the United States of how issues get sex-typed in the development of national bureaucracies see Cindy Sondik Aron, *Ladies and Gentlemen of the Civil Service: Middle Class Workers in Victorian America* (New York: Oxford University Press, 1987). For contemporary analyses of how this process works in development agencies see Nüket Kardam, *Bringing Women In: Women's Issues in International Development Programs* (Boulder, Colo.: Lynne Rienner, 1991); Sue Ellen M. Charlton, *Women in Third World Development* (Boulder, Colo.: Westview, 1984); and Kathleen Staudt, *Women, Foreign Assistance and Advocacy Administration* (New York: Praeger, 1983).

38. Alison Jaggar, "Teaching Sedition: Some Dilemmas of Feminist Pedagogy," *Report from the Center on Philosophy and Public Policy* 4 (Fall 1984): 6–9.

39. On the limits of public opinion polling in determining these kinds of rankings see Shanto Iyengar and Donald R. Kinder, *News That Matters: Television and American Public Opinion* (Chicago: University of Chicago Press, 1987).

40. Changing laws covering violence against women without changing the social conditions that promote violence or increasing women's specific skills to respond to violence is not sufficient. For a sobering account of the limits of legal reform in the area of violence against women in India see Flavia Agnes, "Protecting Women Against Violence: Review of a Decade of Legislation, 1980–89," *Economic and Political Weekly*, April 25, 1992, WS-19—WS-33.

41. David Snow et al., "Frame Alignment Processes, Micromobilization, and Movement Politics," *American Sociological Review* 51 (August 1986): 464–81.

42. See CHINA.

43. María del Carmen Feijoó and Monica Gogna, "Women in the Transition to Democracy," in Elizabeth Jelin, ed., *Women and Social Change in Latin America* (London: Zed Books, 1990), 79–114.

44. Dorothy Friesen, "The Women's Movement in the Philippines," *NWSA Journal* 4 (Summer 1989): 677; and personal interviews by Kathryn A. Carver and Barbara J. Nelson with women working with survivors of military rape, Manila, 27–28 June 1989.

45. See URUGUAY.

46. Wendy Brown, "Reproductive Freedom and the Right to Privacy: A Paradox for Feminists," in Irene Diamond, ed., *Families, Politics, and Public Policy: A Feminist Dialogue on Women and the State* (New York: Longman, 1983), 322–38; and Eli Zaretsky, "The Place of the Family in the Origins of the Welfare State," in Barrie Thorne with Marilyn Yalom, eds., *Rethinking the Family: Some Feminist Questions* (New York: Longman, 1982), 188–224.

47. Ewa Hauser, Barbara Heyns, and Jane Mansbridge, "Feminism in the Interstices of Politics and Culture: Poland in Transition," in Nanette Funk and Magda Müller, eds., *Gender Politics and Post-Communism* (New York: Routledge, forthcoming 1993).

48. See SUDAN.

49. Rawls offers an essentially liberal theory of justice, but one that is open to public or private ownership of property; as such it has had tremendous influence on theories of justice located in other political traditions. See John Rawls, *A Theory of Justice* (Cambridge, Mass.: Harvard University Press, 1971); and Susan Moller Okin, *Justice, Gender, and the Family* (New York: Basic Books, 1989).

50. See SPAIN.

51. Jo Freeman, "The Tyranny of Leaderlessness," in Jane Jaquette, ed., *Women in Politics* (New York: Wiley, 1974), 202–14; and Judith Adler Hellman, *Journeys Among Women: Feminism in Five Italian Cities* (New York: Oxford University Press, 1987).

52. See PERU.

53. On the efforts to ensure representation of ethnic or racial minorities in legislatures see Arend Lijphart, "Proportionality by Non-PR Methods: Ethnic Representation in Belgium, Cyprus, Lebanon, New Zealand, West Germany, and Zimbabwe," in Bernard Grofman and Arend Lijphart, eds., *Electoral Laws and Their Political Consequences* (New York: Agathon, 1986), 113–23.

54. United Nations, *The World's Women: Trends and Statistics, 1970–1990* (New York: United Nations, 1991), 31–36.

55. See INDIA.

56. For discussions on the limits of women's choices and on socialization explanations for the absence of women from high offices see Vicky Randall, *Women and Politics: An International Perspective*, 2d ed. (Chicago: University of Chicago Press, 1987), 123–30.

57. See KENYA.

58. See GREAT BRITAIN.

59. Carole Pateman, *The Sexual Contract* (Stanford, Calif.: Stanford University Press, 1988), 78.

60. See FRANCE.

61. Carol Schmid, "Women in the West German Green Party: The Uneasy Alliance of Ecology and Feminism," in Guida West and Rhoda Lois Blumberg, eds., *Women and Social Protest* (New York: Oxford University Press, 1990), 238.

62. Carol Berkin and Clara Lovett, *Women, War and Revolution* (New York: Holmes and Meier, 1980); and Muthoni Likimani (with an introductory essay by Jean

O'Barr), *Passbook Number F.47927* (New York: Praeger, 1985).

63. For a discussion of how to improve women's representation in legislatures see Barbara J. Nelson, "The Role of Sex and Gender in Comparative Political Analysis: Individuals, Institutions, and Regimes," *American Political Science Review* 86 (June 1992): 491–95.

64. Yael Azmon discusses the necessity of leadership and social pressure for women to achieve gains through proportional representation in "Women Politics: The Case of Israel," *Women & Politics* 10 (1990): 43–57.

65. Sonia E. Alvarez, *Engendering Democracy in Brazil: Women's Movements in Transition Politics* (Princeton: Princeton University Press, 1990), 262–63; and BRAZIL.

66. See GREECE.

67. See HUNGARY; and Julia Szalai, "Some Aspects of the Changing Situation of Women in Hungary," *Signs* 17 (Autumn 1991): 152–70.

68. On party dealignment see Russell J. Dalton, Paul Allen Beck, and Scott C. Flanagan, "Electoral Change in Advanced Industrial Democracies," in Russell J. Dalton, Scott C. Flanagan, and Paul Allen Beck, eds., *Electoral Change in Advanced Industrial Democracies: Realignment or Dealignment?* (Princeton: Princeton University Press, 1984), 3–22.

69. *The Civic Culture* is a notable exception. Almond and Verba measured participation in voluntary organizations when they studied how political life is sustained. Their approach to women's participation in voluntary organizations prefigures and has the same limitations as later discussions of republican motherhood, in which women's participation is praised as contributing to the democratic education of children, but the structural biases against women's participation in formal politics are unexamined.

70. See USSR, GHANA, and BOLIVIA.

71. Maxine Molyneux, "Mobilization Without Emancipation? Women's Interests, State, and Revolution," in Richard R. Fagen, Carmen Diana Deere, and Jose Luís Coraggio, eds., *Transition and Development: Problems of Third World Socialism* (Boston: Monthly Review Press, 1986), 283–84.

72. Alvarez, *Engendering Democracy in Brazil*, 24–25; and Sternbach et al., "Feminisms in Latin America," 401–02. In Latin America feminine groups are often described as belonging to the women's movement, as opposed to the feminist movement.

73. United Nations, *World's Women*, 33.

74. Alice Walker, *In Search of Our Mothers' Gardens: Womanist Prose* (New York: Harcourt, Brace, Jovanovich, 1983); Elsa Barkley Brown, "Womanist Consciousness: Maggie Lena Walker and the Independent Order of Saint Luke," *Signs* 14 (Spring 1989): 610–33; and Evelyn Brooks Higginbotham, "African-American Women's History and the Metalanguage of Race," *Signs* 17 (Winter 1992): 251–74.

75. Alvarez, *Engendering Democracy in Brazil*; and Sternbach et al., "Feminisms in Latin America."

76. We acknowledge that there is a range of values on each dimension, specifically that there are many positions between supporting or resisting male domination and accepting or rejecting the importance of large and significant differences between women and men.

2 ▲ Research Design and Practice: Methodological Issues in Feminist Comparative Politics Research

NAJMA CHOWDHURY AND
BARBARA J. NELSON
WITH NANCY J. JOHNSON
AND PAULA L. O'LOUGHLIN

To make the idea of a systematic worldwide study of women's political engagement into reality required a research design and a set of practices appropriate to the size and scope of the project. The research design for this book developed from two questions: How should countries be chosen, and what analytical frameworks and narrative structures should be used within country chapters? The answers could not be found solely in traditional political science, which routinely disregards the substance and meaning of women's activities. Neither could they be found only in feminist analysis, which has been inattentive to formal politics and has not fully placed women's community-based activism into a wider political context. Both in theory and in action, the answers came from integrating the two research traditions when possible and ultimately from experimenting with new research practices.

COUNTRY CHOICE

From the beginning the methodological task was to translate an interest in regional diversity into a structure for choosing countries. We decided at the outset to include a larger than usual number of countries so that we could avoid making the traditional comparative politics choice between most different and most similar nations.[1] The larger number of countries that we wanted to include changed rather than eliminated difficulties of selection, however.

Three problems had to be solved in the course of choosing countries. The first was the problem of using the nation-state as the exclusive unit of analysis. In a world of contested sovereignties, we needed to acknowledge that nation-states are not the only geopolitical units that claim people's allegiance or organize their everyday lives. The second problem was how to assure systematic variations in cultures, political systems, and economic arrangements among the selected countries. Here the goal was that elusive combination of specificity and parsimony that would sharpen comparisons without splintering the categorization scheme. The third problem was finding, to the extent possible, contributing authors native to and living in the countries that we had chosen who would be available throughout the project. Scholars specializing in women and politics are scarce in many countries. The ideal country-choice system needed to be adaptable to a world where discrimination against women as scholars and as the subject of inquiry permeates every aspect of educational institutions.

The Unit of Analysis: Problems of Nationhood and Sovereignty

Much of the work in comparative politics has focused on the nation-state. Indeed, a recent definition called comparative politics "the systematic and comparative study of nations and their political systems."[2] This definition has a number of acknowledged problems, especially its concentration on the nation-state at the expense of other levels and units of analysis.[3] Making the nation-state, with its fixed rather than evolutionary connotations, the sole subject of comparison tends to obscure the contested processes of nation building. Similarly, the statism encouraged by considering the nation-state the primary unit of analysis reinforces the public (male)–private (female) dichotomy that predominates in traditional political inquiry. Feminist theories investigate rather than accept as axiomatic the origins and the consequences of the gendered public and private divisions in political life.[4]

Nevertheless, the nation-state presents an important summation of the political, economic, and cultural attributes of a geographical setting. It offers a middle ground between narrower concepts like government (or its specific institutions) and broader, more amorphous concepts like society. But most important for this analysis, the nation-state brings up the question of sovereignty. Not all the political units of the world are nation-states with complete sovereignty, and a number of ostensibly secure nation-states are beset by internal and external threats to self-rule.

It became important, then, to organize the book around nation-states and the other political entities that encounter problems in establishing sovereignty. At the beginning of the project, four cases illustrated the contested nature of the nation-state as the organizing principle of the book: the situations in Northern Ireland, Hong Kong, and Puerto Rico, and the conflict between the Israelis and the Palestinians. These cases form a rough continuum: in Northern Ireland, incorporation into an existing state is the major political question; in Hong Kong and Puerto Rico, colonial and quasi-colonial relations dominate political arrangements; in the Israeli and Palestinian conflict, two struggles for national identity are waged over much the same territory. We were able to get chapters on Great Britain, Hong Kong, Puerto Rico, Israel, and Palestine. We were not able to get chapters on Northern Ireland and the Republic of Ireland. Later, we considered seeking an author in one of the Baltic republics but concluded that it was too late in the

project, and perhaps too early in the remaking of Baltic independence, to begin that effort. This process demonstrates how continually problematic sovereignty is. If this book had been written 20 years ago, the array of nation-states and other political units would have been different, as they surely will be if the project is repeated 20 years from now.

Dimensions of Country Comparisons

Once we had decided to use both nation-states and other political entities, we faced the questions of what to call this variety of political units and how to categorize them. We use the term *nation-state* to convey our interest in the issues of state formation and sovereignty. Following conventional usage, we employ the terms *nation* and *country* generically as a shorthand for the geographical area that each political unit occupies, even if that occupation does not mean full control.

We chose a categorization that arrayed countries across four dimensions: type of political regime, level of economic development, cultural milieu as approximated by region, and legal tradition concerning women's status. The assumption was that within each dimension the categories imply different sets of institutions and processes. The dimensions were certainly not independent of one another; political, economic, cultural, and legal activities and institutions usually form patterns. But because there was so little research on women's political engagement undertaken on a global scale, we felt that we could achieve greater analytical power by choosing countries on the basis of a four-dimensional matrix than by grouping countries by often problematic national typologies using categories like traditional, emerging, and modern. These typologies were developed without much attention to women and gender analysis, and we were skeptical that they would—to use Giovanni Sartori's term—"travel well" to global research on women's political engagement.[5]

Each of the dimensions posed complex conceptual questions about which definitions or categorization schemes to use. On the political dimension, we categorized countries as democratic, state socialist, or authoritarian. But what constitutes each type of regime is of course debated. There are, for instance, disagreements over whether purely procedural definitions of democracy that emphasize voting in multiparty elections are stringent enough to denote a democracy,[6] questions about the degree to which state socialist regimes require a wholly centrally planned economy or can be tolerant of private enterprise,[7] and debates about whether to apply the term authoritarian to right-wing regimes only or to repressive regimes of both the left and right.[8] In general, we defined democracies as having competitive elections open to everyone, state socialist countries as supporting government direction of the majority of the economy, and authoritarian countries as following repressive policies regardless of their other political orientations. We were keenly aware that these definitions were not always mutually exclusive. The classification of each country was based on the political information provided by the *Political Handbook of the World: 1986.*[9] Using a single source as much as possible minimized differences in definitions that might arise from using several sources. Occasionally we used mixed categories if the formal political system and actual practices were in conflict.

Each type of regime is sustained by ideologies and practices that have different views of women. Each creates a secondary status for women, but through different processes and with different consequences. Gayle Rubin suggests that one of the tasks of feminist analysis is determining "the endless variety and monotonous similarity" of women's oppression, and the gender ideologies embedded in regime type offer an important avenue of research.[10] Broadly speaking, classical democratic theory presupposed the existence of a separate female domestic sphere (and a sphere of material labor populated by noncitizen women and men) that supported limited male citizenship. The ideology of equal participation has been grafted onto this theory and practice, meaning that women's mobilization currently takes place within the language of equality and

the denial of structural inequality. State socialist regimes are guided by Marxist-Leninist views that hold that sexual oppression is a "secondary contradiction" that will take care of itself or be taken care of when the victory of the proletariat occurs. In state socialist systems, officially sanctioned "leading institutions" mobilize women's interests from a vanguardist model of party and state leadership. Authoritarian systems, by and large, support ideologies of maternal purity that conflate womanhood with motherhood. While state-generated popular mobilizations or mass parties are often established by authoritarian regimes, most society-generated efforts at autonomous popular movements, including women's movements, are suppressed.

The chapters were written during a moment in history when tremendous pressures for regime change were unleashed. Bangladesh moved from authoritarian practices within the framework of a formal democratic regime to a more democratic politics. Nepal moved from an authoritarian to a democratic regime. Czechoslovakia, Hungary, Poland, and the Soviet Union shifted from state socialist regimes to democratic ones, and Czechoslovakia and the Soviet Union ultimately ceased to be. The two Germanies were reunited, removing the German Democratic Republic from the roster of nations. These transitions were all moves toward democratic politics, but such changes are neither inevitable nor even typical. In the 1960s and 1970s many of the regime transformations worldwide were changes to state socialist or authoritarian types of government.[11] Transformations undertaken in the 1980s and 1990s are far from complete or secure in a number of countries; the question of sustainable democratic transformation may hold crucial significance for the future in some countries. Regime transformations have also occurred within the past 15 years in other countries covered in the book, including Sudan, Nigeria, Ghana, the Philippines, Bolivia, Argentina, Brazil, Greece, Turkey, and Spain.

On the economic dimension we classified countries by using a modification of the formula devised by the World Bank. That formula, which used 1982 data available in 1985, defined the per capita gross national product of low-income countries as less than U.S. $400, the per capita GNP of low-middle-income countries as $400 to $999, the per capita GNP of upper-middle-income countries as $1,000 to $3,499, and the per capita GNP of high-income countries as $3,500 or more. We chose this categorization because it was the most sensitive to variations in per capita GNP in countries that were not abjectly poor, thus reflecting differences of economic infrastructure as much as is possible in income measures. We also recognized that GNP figures significantly underestimate women's contribution to national production, a topic that we address in Chapter 4 when we discuss the problems of measuring women's activities. As we looked for contributors we kept other economic groupings in mind, especially the newly industrialized countries and the members of the Organization of Petroleum Exporting Countries, but these categories were not as important as representation by income level.[12]

Finding a broad-brush way to represent cultural differences on a global scale was difficult. No scheme could embrace the complexity and variation of cultural forms within and among countries. Ultimately, after considering a variety of categorizations based either on traditionalism-modernity or religion-race-ethnicity, we chose to use the regional divisions of the Overseas Development Council (ODC) as reported in *Economic Development in the Third World*.[13] These divisions combine geographic proximity and historical similarity to create a proxy for cultural characteristics. As with all such systems, there are legitimate questions of categorization. Where should Turkey, a Muslim nation organized as a secular state that is a member of the North Atlantic Treaty Organization and OPEC, be categorized? Is it in Europe, where the ODC places it, or in Asia, where the United Nations places it? This uncertainty about regional categorization reflects disagreement among Turks, as well as among scholars and international bureaucrats, and indicates the imperfections of regional qua cultural classification schemes.

The legal dimension categorized countries by former colonial status, if any, as a basis for examining how received legal systems interacted with locally developed ones to affect women's status. For example, at the moment of independence in the nineteenth century, many former Spanish colonies in South America chose or kept the Napoleonic Code, a legacy shared with former French colonies in Africa. The Napoleonic Code more severely limited women's civil status than did the British legal tradition.[14] The interaction between colonial and local legal systems is useful in research on the historical patterns of changes in women's civil status. It was not very helpful in this study, however. The research presented by the country authors shows that legal systems do matter in other ways. A more useful categorization for future research would distinguish between those countries where personal status laws covering marriage, divorce, inheritance, child custody, and the like are determined by religious codes and those countries where uniform secular civil laws define personal status. In the table, the nation-states and other political units of the world are arrayed across the first three dimensions of categorization (not including legal tradition).

Locating Contributing Authors

The forty-three nations included in this book reflect our efforts to create a representative categorization scheme and the realities of finding authors. Two goals guided our search for contributors. First, we wanted to create a network of scholars and activists interested in women's political engagement—a network that would endure after the project was completed. Toward that end, we strove to find contributors at various points in their careers and of many ages. Second, we wanted, when possible, to have writers who were native to and living in the countries about which they would write. We believed that in addition to scholarly excellence, indigenous writers would add the perspective of understanding women's experience in that nation and knowing the country's politics firsthand. No decision shaped the course of the project as much as this one.

28   Najma Chowdhury and Barbara J. Nelson

Countries by Region, GNP per Capita, and Regime Type
(Countries in this book are listed in boldface)

Low Income (Less than U.S. $400)	Low-Middle Income (U.S. $400–999)	Upper-Middle Income (U.S. $1,000–3,499)	High Income (U.S. $3,500 and up)
Africa			
Benin S/A	Angola S	Algeria A	Gabon A
Burundi A	Botswana D	Congo A/S	Libya A
Cape Verde A	Cameroon A	Ivory Coast A	Réunion
Central African Republic A	Djibouti A	Mauritius D/A	
Chad A	**Egypt** D	Namibia	
Comoros D	**Ghana** A	Seychelles A	
Equatorial Guinea A	**Kenya** A	**South Africa** D/A	
Ethiopia S	Lesotho A	Tunisia A	
Gambia	Liberia A		
Guinea A	Mauritania A		
Guinea-Bissau A	**Morocco** A/D		
Madagascar A	**Nigeria** A		
Malawi A	Senegal A/D		
Mali A	Swaziland A		
Mozambique S	Zambia A		
Niger A	Zimbabwe A		
Rwanda A			
São Tomé and Príncipe A			
Sierra Leone A			
Somalia A			
Sudan A			
Tanzania A			
Togo A			
Uganda A			
Upper Volta			
Zaire A			
Asia			
Afghanistan A	Indonesia A	Iran	Bahrain A
Bangladesh A	Mongolia S	Iraq	Brunei A
Bhutan A	**Philippines** D	Jordan D	**Hong Kong**
Burma A	Thailand D	North Korea S	**Israel** D/A
China S	Yemen Arab Republic A	**South Korea** D/A	**Japan** D
India D	South Yemen S/A	Lebanon	Kuwait A
Kampuchea A		Macao	Oman A
Laos S		Malaysia D	Qatar A
Maldives		Syria A/S	Saudi Arabia A
Nepal A		Taiwan	Singapore D
Pakistan A			United Arab Emirates A
[Palestine]			
Sri Lanka D			
Vietnam S			
North America			
			United States D
			Canada D

(*continued*)

Countries by Region, GNP per Capita, and Regime Type
(continued)

Low Income (Less than U.S. $400)	Low-Middle Income (U.S. $400–999)	Upper-Middle Income (U.S. $1,000–3,499)	High Income (U.S. $3,500 and up)
Latin America			
Haiti A	**Bolivia** D/A	**Argentina** D	Bahamas D
	Cuba S	Belize D	Barbados D
	Dominica D/A	**Brazil** D	Guadeloupe
	El Salvador D/A	Chile A	Martinique
	Grenada D/A	Colombia D	Netherlands Antilles
	Guyana D/A	**Costa Rica** D	Trinidad and Tobago D
	Honduras D/A	Dominican Republic D	Venezuela D
	Nicaragua S	Ecuador D	
	St. Lucia D	Guatemala D	
	St. Vincent A	Jamaica D	
		Mexico D	
		Panama A	
		Paraguay A	
		Peru D	
		Puerto Rico	
		Suriname A	
		Uruguay D	
Oceania			
	Pacific Islands Trust Territory	Fiji D	**Australia** D
	Papua New Guinea D		French Polynesia
	Solomon Islands D		Guam
	Tonga A		New Caledonia
	Western Samoa D		New Zealand D
Europe			
	Albania S	Portugal D	Austria D
	Romania S	**Greece** D	Belgium D
		Turkey D	Bulgaria D
		Yugoslavia S	Channel Islands
			Cyprus
			Czechoslovakia S
			Denmark D
			Finland D
			France D
			Germany D
			Hungary S
			Iceland D
			Ireland D
			Italy D
			Luxembourg D
			Malta D
			Netherlands D

(*continued*)

Countries by Region, GNP per Capita, and Regime Type
(continued)

Low Income (Less than U.S. $400)	Low-Middle Income (U.S. $400–999)	Upper-Middle Income (U.S. $1,000–3,499)	High Income (U.S. $3,500 and up)
			Norway D
			Poland S
			Spain D
			Sweden D
			Switzerland D
			USSR S
			United Kingdom D

Sources: The countries and their political regimes were drawn from Arthur S. Banks, ed., *Political Handbook of the World, 1986* (Binghamton, N.Y.: CSA Publications, 1986). When the *Handbook* did not provide regime information, none was included in the chart. Economic data and regional classifications were drawn from Michael Todaro, *Economic Development in the Third World*, 3rd ed. (New York: Longman, 1985). For details see Chapter 2.

Note: Regimes are coded A (authoritarian), D (democratic), and S (socialist) as of their status in 1986.

We located contributors in a variety of ways. We contacted individuals through lists provided by the International Political Science Association (IPSA) Research Committee 19 on Sex Roles and Politics and IPSA Study Group 30 on Women, Politics, and Developing Nations. We also contacted a number of nonnative experts who generously forwarded to us the names of in-country colleagues. Authors proposed collaborations across countries that were fruitful to them and enriched the book. Most of the contributors are social scientists (political scientists predominate) who are politically active in the women's movement or are personally committed to improving women's status if no organized activism exists or is permitted. It is important to add, however, that the array of countries in this book reflects not only our initial ability to locate authors but the exigencies of authors' schedules and their other responsibilities. In three years of writing and editing, some authors left the project, and we were not always able to find replacements in time to meet the publishing schedule.

There were drawbacks, as well as benefits, to emphasizing the power of locally situated contributors, mainly because it was difficult to locate authors in countries controlled by authoritarian regimes. These individuals were approached with great care after consultation with people knowledgeable about local conditions. (We also made more efforts to reach authors from authoritarian countries living abroad.) The responses were complex, ranging from no reply to implicit and explicit messages about the difficulties of participating. It was the most difficult to find writers in poor authoritarian countries, the vast proportion of which are in Africa. In the less prosperous state socialist countries outside Central Europe, particularly in Africa and Southeast Asia, potential authors also faced the problem of government control of political writing. In its final form this book comprises countries from almost every level of economic development in every region. Not every type of regime is represented within income and regional groups because it was not always possible to locate authors.

STRUCTURING THE CHAPTERS

We wanted each chapter to provide an integrative and interpretive analysis of patterns of women's political engagement shaped by a common chapter outline and an interest in hearing women's voices in every text. The outline, which included a political introduction, a discussion of how women identify their interests and represent them to themselves and others, and an analysis of three issues important to women, provided the general framework for each discussion. This approach to the analysis and narrative structure evolved from our desire, shared by the chapter authors, to find a format that did not over-emphasize formal politics, encompassed discussions of political activity that existed primarily in civil society, and encouraged comparisons of different types of activity within countries as well as among them. Authors chose the issues they analyzed on the basis of the national contexts in which they lived. In countries undergoing dramatic regime change, the change itself became the major issue, in part because of its central importance but also because the established political and policy processes often collapse in times of grave political instability. We asked that the issues chosen be among those that seriously affected women in that country, but there was no assumption that these would be *the most* pressing problems facing women (who would decide that in any case?) or that other scholars from that nation would have chosen exactly the same topics.

The intellectual and narrative design of the chapters was guided by attention to several recurring questions in research on women, gender, and politics: What kinds of activities should be included in the study of women's political engagement when politics is usually defined in part on the basis of the exclusion of women and their perspectives from certain spheres of life? How can women's interests (in the political sense) be defined in ways that encompass both the commonalities and the differences among groups of women and between women and men? How should women's opportunities for individual and group action be understood in relation to the force of large social structures and processes? What constitutes evidence—indeed, what constitutes knowing—when women are made significant actors in political life? Our perspectives on these questions shaped the structure of the country chapters, the communication with authors, and the editing process.

New Definitions of Politics

Because women are rarely prominent political actors in any political system, and because the char-

acter of women's secondary political status differs from country to country, defining political activism for women requires rethinking the definition of politics. For example, in contemporary Japan the near exclusion of women from politics rests in part on Japan's status as a late-comer to capitalism and on the remnants of feudalism. Machiko Matsui states that "since 1868, under the restored Emperor structure, patriarchal values have been reinforced in order to transfer family loyalty to the Emperor by identifying Emperor-loyalty with filial piety. The nation is regarded as a large extended family sanctified by the 'sacred and inviolable' Emperor-patriarch. In such a system women and children are deprived of their rights and subordinated to the patriarch."[15]

The gender implications of the political remnants of Japanese feudalism have resonance not only for other political systems that retain feudal characteristics but also for polities in which state structures are supposed to reproduce kin structures more generally. In contrast, state structures in the Western European and North American experience supposedly ignore kin structures. Sue Ellen M. Charlton writes that the public-private distinction "reinforces the asymmetrical nature of political authority between women and men in the contemporary nation-state. . . . Insofar as the private sphere lies outside the authority of the state (in theory) and historically outside the realm of politics, the female reality of subordination to men and male institutions eludes most theorizing about states."[16]

Until recently, political science as a discipline has reproduced these and other forms of female political subordination in its research paradigms by failing to acknowledge and investigate the gender ideologies implicit in these worldviews. The most prevalent paradigm has been the "stable democracy model" developed out of the post–World War II experiences of Western Europe and North America.[17] The problem with this paradigm is that it magnifies the importance of the state, formal institutions, and social stability at the expense of investigating the political aspects of society, informal organizations, instability, and change.[18] Even when the role of civil society is recognized, the stable democracy paradigm oversimplifies the relationship of state institutions to civil life. In the stable democracy approach, a state is often characterized as "strong" or "weak," and society is described as its reciprocal.[19] Recognizing this limitation, recent research has explored the multidimensionality of the state's capacities.[20] Less attention has been paid, however, to the implications of state strength or weakness for those members of civil society—such as women—not fully captured in the state's embrace.[21]

The state can be the veiled as well as the obvious focus of the stable democracy approach. The emphasis on electoral participation in the stable democracy literature is an example of the shadow presence of the state. Whereas much of the typical electoral research is barely about government, let alone the state, the objective of elections is maintaining the state as well as choosing leaders and, implicitly, the packages of policies they favor. The disproportionate amount of research undertaken on electoral participation has had a generally negative effect on how women are viewed politically, in both less industrialized and more industrialized countries. When seen through the lens of electoral research, women tend to be viewed as "small men," doing what men do, only less often and less well.[22] The conventional electoral research has not been guided by questions about the nature of representation and participation that make evident women's political marginality.[23] The country authors often ask the questions that have been ignored in traditional approaches to women's political participation and relations to the state, thereby reconfiguring the study of formal politics through a gender analysis.

To move away from the overemphasis on democratic electoral activities and state politics usually implied by the term *political participation,* we asked contributors to focus on *political engagement,* which included the development of self-identity, actions in the civil as well as political arenas, and grass-roots as well as elite behaviors. We did not want to foreclose the analysis of for-

mal politics; rather, we wanted to encourage the consideration of many arenas of life as political spheres. Many contributors use the term *political participation* in this expansive way while others reinvigorate it with richer meanings.[24]

Interest Articulation and Aggregation

Covering three issues of concern to women in each chapter encouraged the search for the politics in different spheres of life. The issue approach also provided insights into whether there were variations within countries in the ways that women's interests are articulated and aggregated. Here, too, we needed to employ these political science concepts in ways that transformed, and perhaps transcended, their original meanings. In the early comparative politics literature, interest articulation and aggregation offered a way to analyze the processes that facilitate and inhibit movement from the discovery of political voice to the insertion of organized preferences into the political system. There was an assumption that modernization, economic development, and democratization would reduce the barriers between expressing interests and having them incorporated into the mediating structures, such as parties, in a nation-state.[25] Although the distinction between finding a political voice and finding a listener is crucial to the analysis of women's political position, we do not support the developmentalist assumptions about the way the struggles for voice and attention are waged. Instead, we retain these concepts because each one of the terms—*interest, articulation,* and *aggregation*—offers larger possibilities for understanding women's political activism.

We use *interests* in much the way Anna G. Jónasdóttir uses the term. She writes that the origin of the word is the Latin *inter esse,* meaning "to be among or between." She argues that two aspects of a political understanding of interests exist: the conditions for choosing valued social arrangements and the consequences of choice. The conditions and consequences of coming to identify, claim, and express valued social arrangements— in other words, the processes of interest articulation and aggregation—are rooted historically in the subjectivity of the people who make these choices and in the congruence and conflict of these choices with established social values.[26]

This definition looks for an older understanding of interests than the more typical utilitarian usage, with its links to liberal individualism and self-aggrandizing decision making on the part of autonomous individuals. The emphasis on individual singularity in utilitarian definitions of interests has given feminist scholars pause for two related reasons.[27] Either women's interests are viewed through the same rationalist, individualist lens as men's interests, in which case women—like men—are not seen as relational beings, or their interests are seen as confined by social fabrics so tightly woven that women could not possibly have any self-located preferences or views. The latter approach is often applied to women living in less industrialized countries with traditional patriarchal cultures of father and husband control of women. Amartya K. Sen refutes this approach in his discussion of whether poor rural women in India have a concept of "personal welfare." He writes: "It has often been observed that if a typical Indian rural woman was asked about her personal 'welfare,' she would find the question unintelligible, and if she was able to reply, she might answer the question in terms of her reading of the welfare of her family . . . . It is far from obvious that [this reading is] the right conclusion to draw. . . . The process of politicization—including a political recognition of the gender issue—can itself bring about sharp changes in these perceptions, as can processes of economic change."[28]

Similarly, we use *articulation* and *aggregation* in nontraditional ways. In particular we wanted to avoid treating interest articulation and aggregation like the output produced in the factory of politics. In the systems approach to politics, inchoate needs are transformed into wishes and preferences, which are turned into demands (aggregated interests) on the political system. This view not only denigrates needs by making them irrational, it also assumes that the direction of interest articulation and aggregation is the state or formal politics.[29] Instead, we assert that the

processes that promote or inhibit women's ability to voice their interests and then have those interests considered in conjunction with other interests are not confined to formal politics, which is conventionally established in ways that systematically deflect women and their views from consideration. Individual women or groups of women, like other individuals or groups, may struggle primarily to find a voice for their own needs and demands. Their purposes may be to develop self-identity, to change their place in civil society as viewed distinct from or in contradiction to their place in official political institutions, to resist oppressive state structures, to get around disinterested official organizations, or to create a new, sometimes political discourse in society. Women may also direct their interests to the state and official political machinery, but solely statist understandings of women's processes of interest articulation and aggregation will distort the understanding of women's political engagement.

In essence, examining women's political activism outside formal politics opens a window on the density and variety of interest articulation and aggregation processes existing in any country at a particular time. For example, in Bangladesh the rural women's group Saptagram (Seven Villages) employs an empowerment strategy that builds on the consciousness of women about their own subordination and their strength in solidarity. Saptagram's strategy of activism bypasses the organized and mediating hierarchies of the state and local community. Instead, women may directly confront a local influential man in order, for instance, to make more accessible a well that is the only source of drinking water near their homesteads. Similarly, women may *gherao* (surround and refuse to leave) the local government land registration office as they did in 1989 to assert ownership rights to land they purchased. These actions are not part of regularized political party or state processes. The transfer of strategies effective in local areas and within well-defined social relations to larger and more complex political structures of interest articulation and aggregation or conflict resolution may prove to be problematic, however.[30]

In another example of politics located in civil society, many feminists in Milan in the 1970s created a politics of *autocoscenzia* (self-knowledge, consciousness-raising) that was primarily about the development of autonomous women's voices. In other Italian cities, notably Turin, this approach confronted worker-based notions of activism that encouraged women to cast their needs as women into a class-related framework and to direct their demands through unions to the union hierarchy, management, and government—an approach that quickly moved women's interest articulation into the processes of aggregation (and competition) with the demands of other groups.[31]

Structure and Agency

In addition to encouraging political analysis outside formal politics, the discussion of several issues in most chapters also allowed for consideration of the variety of ways women's interests are voiced and considered in each country. The emphasis on women's diversity and the range of issues that mobilized them contributed to an understanding of the political opportunity structures that shape women's political engagement.[32] The consideration of political opportunity structures was an important component of how we approached the perennial scholarly questions about the relative causal importance of social structures and individual agency. Highly structural arguments, such as orthodox Marxism, tend to overdetermine women's position in society and reduce the scope of women's agency, while highly individualist arguments, such as neoliberalism, underestimate the force of social structures and overestimate the efficacy of individual actions.

The questions we posed to authors during the editing process approached the structure-agency problem through a concept we call contingent political agency. Contingent political agency means that within a social setting, the political activities of individuals of various social identities are shaped but not determined by complex political opportunity structures, themselves shaped by the organization of state and society as well as the

actions of individuals and groups as they constitute these institutions. Each of the components of this definition—social identities, political activities, and opportunity structures—is influenced by the specificity of social arrangements and the historical moment. In our approach to the structure-agency debate we use a definition of theory that expands on the one offered by Lata Mani: here, theory includes a who, when, and where, not merely a what.[33] The concept of contingent political agency is useful because it offers one method of thinking about the similarities and differences in political activities and meanings among groups of women—or any other social group, for that matter. Feminist theorizing has grappled with the importance of social difference as a source of variation in women's life experiences. Feminists have come to respect the importance of the social reality of the adjectives that modify women. But this theorizing has often conflated social identity with political opportunity, foreclosing questions about how social and political systems map onto each other. Political opportunity structures, especially as they refer to state politics, are often much less differentiated than are social identities, thus people with very different social identities face roughly similar political opportunity structures.[34] The political opportunity structures outside state activity may be more or less flexible or varied than those associated with state activities, depending on the regime or the historical moment. By including analytically separable components of social identity and political opportunity structures, the concept of contingent political agency opens up a large set of questions that help us to know more about the patterns of women's political engagement.

Epistemology and Praxis: Knowing Through Practice

Our search for patterns of women's political engagement, using as it did a number of new or changed political definitions, raised interesting questions about feminist ways of knowing—questions that were ever present through the process of country research and creating the anthology.[35] Through reading many versions of the chapters and through extensive correspondence with authors about research and writing, we were able to observe the relationship between feminist research practices and feminist theories of knowledge in action.[36]

Feminist theorists have contributed significantly to the analysis of the three prominent theories of knowledge that inform social research: empiricism, standpoint epistemologies, and postmodernism. In the research for their chapters, contributors often combined several theories of knowledge. In the main, the authors worked within feminist empirical epistemologies. These approaches retain a belief in the "justificatory power" of observation and hypothesis testing arising from the social science versions of the scientific method, while opposing the "point-of-viewlessness" of the observer and the necessary progress toward universal and timeless social laws.[37] There was no doubt expressed to us by the participants in this project that there could be bounded generalizations about the meanings of women's political experiences that also respected particularities.

Standpoint approaches to knowledge made a more complex and contradictory contribution to the research project. In standpoint epistemologies knowledge arises from socially situated and understood experiences (standpoints). The best-known example of standpoint theory is Marx's assertion that the oppressed position of the working class gives its members a more accurate understanding of their personal condition and a more complete worldview than their bourgeois counterparts. A few of the authors, especially but not only those who live under state socialist regimes, used a standpoint approach to understanding women's political participation that privileged the perspectives on women offered by Marxist or revolutionary interpretations of the needs of women in the working, peasant, or popular classes.

But for most authors, standpoint epistemologies had a less direct effect on how they came to know and interpret women's political activism. Standpoint epistemologies emphasize knowing one's own place in society and thinking about that position in terms of the social order. Many chapters suggest that by experiencing male domination women potentially have a greater understanding of the system of sex-gender oppression than is easily available to men. For these authors, their own experiences of male oppression (either firsthand or by observation) were very important because these experiences potentially created the conditions whereby the authors avoided the point-of-viewlessness of traditional empirical social sciences. Sympathetic observation was as important to female as to male authors because it became part of the process by which all authors understood the varieties of women's political activism. Intellectual empathy rather than distance contributed to the insights of the research by keeping the limits of generalizability clearly in focus, thus improving the accuracy and clarity of findings.

In some respects, this research process looks like a version of feminist postmodernism, one that does not deny the possibility of knowing general if not universal aspects of the world, while at the same time avoiding the belief in ideologically determined end states toward which human endeavors evolve or struggle.[38] But postmodernism makes two other assumptions with which writers in this project appear to disagree. Many postmodernists are skeptical about the possibility for "authentic" voice, identity, and speech. In contrast, a central premise undergirding this project was the importance and authenticity of local voices and the authority of the contributors to write accurate syntheses of women's political engagement. The assumption was that chapters could be authentic and authoritative without claiming to be universalistic or complete. The other problem with defining the writings in this book as postmodernist is that it is not clear how authors felt about the place and substance of various philosophical metanarratives, or the encompassing philosophies or schools of social criticism that provide systemwide explanations of social relations. Much of postmodernist analysis views metanarratives—whether democratic, Marxist, or feminist—with skepticism. The chapters show, however, that many contributors were unwilling to give up the power of democratic critiques of nonparticipatory political systems, Marxist critiques of class systems, and feminist critiques of gender systems, even if the writers did not believe these approaches should be cast in terms of the search for universal truths or accepted in their often totalizing original form.

The authors convey concern with each of the theories of knowledge for not being more connected to the actual practices of doing research about women. This concern leads us to suggest that the integration of knowing and doing is necessary for building feminist theories of knowledge and to argue that the problems of research design in the comparative study of women's political engagement need more attention overall.

NOTES

1. See Arend Lijphart, "The Comparable Cases Strategy in Comparative Research," *Comparative Political Studies* 8 (July 1975): 158–77; and Theda Skocpol and Margaret Somers, "The Uses of Comparative History in Macrosocial Inquiry," *Comparative Studies in Society and History* 22 (1980): 174–97.

2. Howard J. Wiarda, "Comparative Politics Past and Present," in Howard J. Wiarda, ed., *New Directions in Comparative Politics* (Boulder, Colo.: Westview, 1985), 3. Wiarda acknowledges the ethnocentrism implicit in this definition of comparative politics, which grows out of a historical American isolationism, though he does not mention that political isolationism often masked the drive for other forms of international domination. Nor does he confront the paradoxical legacy of enforced "otherness" that applies to non-American countries and people, combined with a search for universal theories that will resolve the duality, usually by changing the "other."

3. For a critique from the perspective of feminist studies of the overemphasis on the nation as an established entity see Kumari Jayawardena, *Feminism and Nationalism in the Third World* (London: Zed Books, 1986); and Miranda Davies, *Third World, Second Sex: Women's Struggles and National Liberation* (London: Zed Books, 1983). For a critique of the emphasis on the nation in comparative political science see Sidney Verba, "Comparative Politics: Where Have We Been, Where Are We Going?" in Wiarda, *New Directions in Comparative Politics,* 26–38; and M. Catharine Newbury, "Colonialism, Ethnicity, and Rural Political Protest: Rwanda and Zanzibar in Comparative Perspective," *Comparative Politics* 15 (April 1983): 253–80.

4. On the origins of the gendered public-private split in Western political thought see Jean Bethke Elshtain, *Public Man, Private Woman* (Princeton, N.J.: Princeton University Press, 1981).

5. Giovanni Sartori, "Guidelines for Concept Analysis," in Giovanni Sartori, ed., *Social Science Concepts: A Systematic Analysis* (Beverly Hills, Calif.: Sage, 1984), 15–85. See also Alasdair MacIntyre, "The Essential Contestability of Some Social Concepts," *Ethics* 84 (October 1973): 1–9.

6. We were aware of more richly specified typologies, especially within regime types. Scholars have given considerable attention to distinguishing among types of democratic political systems. Feminist research has usually concentrated on the historic division between liberal and social democracies (which may be more or less corporatist in nature). These categorizations have been applied most frequently to questions of the balance between individual and state responsibility for women's economic security in the face of the gender division of reproductive and paid labor in advanced capitalism. For example, Helga Hernes argues in "The Welfare State Citizenship of Scandinavian Women" that although liberal democracies require women to reconcile their economic dependency through bargains made with individual men in a patriarchal structure of home life, social democracies offer a second solution in form of the social programs of the patriarchal guardian state, bargains that are less personalistic than those available in systems of individual patriarchal dependence but often more intrusive. Helga Hernes, *Welfare State and Power: Essays in State Feminism* (Oslo: Norwegian University Press, 1987), 133–63.

In the context of advanced industrial democracies, political science has offered a variety of typologies. Peter Lange and Hudson Meadwell discern two approaches to these typologies, the first emphasizing democratic stability as it is produced by individual inputs and the second focusing on political and economic outputs as they are mediated by bureaucratic and political structures. Social fissures of the type like gender relations, which are not reproduced in political cleavages, especially in party organizations or corporatist patterns of interest intermediation, are rarely considered in creating or evaluating these typologies. See Peter Lange and Hudson Meadwell, "Typologies of Democratic Systems: From Political Inputs to Political Economy," in Wiarda, *New Directions in Comparative Politics,* 80–112.

7. Scholars have also developed classification schemes for state socialist regimes. Most are based on dependency relations within geographic spheres of influence or on the preferred modes of economic development. See H. Gordon Skilling, *The Governments of Communist Eastern Europe* (New York: Thomas Y. Crowell, 1966); Chalmers Johnson, "Comparing Communist Nations," in Chalmers Johnson, ed., *Change in Communist Systems* (Stanford,

Calif.: Stanford University Press, 1970), 1–32; and Samuel L. Popkin, *The Rational Peasant: The Political Economy of Rural Society in Vietnam* (Berkeley: University of California Press, 1979). For a discussion that includes a gender component see Sharon Wolchik, "Women and the State in Eastern Europe and the Soviet Union," in Sue Ellen M. Charlton, Jana Everett, and Kathleen Staudt, eds., *Women, the State, and Development* (Albany: State University of New York, 1989), 44–65.

8. For a variety of related reasons we chose not to use totalitarian regimes in our classification. In the 1970s and 1980s a number of scholars and politicians, Jeane Kirkpatrick most prominent among them, promoted using a regime typology that compared democratic, authoritarian (right-wing anti-democratic), and totalitarian (left-wing anti-democratic) political systems; see Jeane Kirkpatrick, "Dictatorships and Double Standards," *Commentary* 68 (November 1979): 24–45. The use of *totalitarian* to describe state socialist systems defied the scholarly practice of describing totalitarian regimes as those that engaged in systematic, widespread, and total repression of individual liberties; lacked political representation; and regularly used deadly force against the population. Application of such a description always required a judgment about the severity of repression. Such a description is appropriately applied to Germany under the National Socialists, the Soviet Union under Stalin, and Kampuchea under Pol Pot. It might describe Argentina under the military government of the 1970s, although the political basis of the term totalitarian would limit its application to right-wing dictatorships. We did not agree with the political equation of totalitarianism with left-wing political systems, when totalitarian practices and governments were found in many types of political systems. Similarly, we found flaws in the intellectual argument that saw market economies as a restraint on despotism. The social origins and factual limits of this idea are described in detail in two important works: Albert O. Hirschman, *The Passions and the Interests: Political Arguments for Capitalism Before Its Triumph* (Princeton, N.J.: Princeton University Press, 1977); and Albert O. Hirschman, "The Turn to Authoritarianism in Latin America and the Search for Its Economic Determinants," in David Collier, ed., *The New Authoritarianism in Latin America* (Princeton, N.J.: Princeton University Press, 1979), 61–98.

9. Arthur S. Banks, ed., *Political Handbook of the World, 1986* (Binghamton, N.Y.: CSA Publications, 1986).

10. Gayle Rubin, "The Traffic in Women: Notes on the 'Political Economy' of Sex," in Rayna R. Reiter, ed., *Toward an Anthropology of Women* (New York: Monthly Review Press, 1975), 160.

11. Hirschman, "The Turn to Authoritarianism," 61–98; Richard L. Harris, "Marxism and the Transition to Socialism in Latin America," *Latin American Perspectives*

15 (Winter 1988): 7–54; and William I. Robinson and Kent Norsworthy, "A Critique of the 'Antidemocratic Tendency' Argument: The Case of Mass Organizations and Popular Participation in Nicaragua," *Latin American Perspectives* 15 (Winter 1988): 134–41.

12. Michael P. Todaro, *Economic Development in the Third World*, 3d ed. (New York: Longman, 1985), 22.

13. The regional classification scheme used in *Women and Politics Worldwide* derives from table A2.2, "Economic and Social Indicators of Development, 1981–1984," in Todaro, *Economic Development in the Third World*, 48–58. Todaro's sources are the Overseas Development Council, *U.S. Foreign Policy and the Third World: Agenda, 1983* (New York: Praeger, 1983), 210–21, and the Population Reference Bureau, *1984 World Population Data Sheet* (Washington, D.C.: 1984).

14. Marsha Freeman, "Measuring Equality: A Comparative Perspective on Women's Legal Capacity and Constitutional Rights in Five Commonwealth Countries," *Berkeley Women's Law Journal* 5 (Spring 1990): 110–38.

15. Machiko Matsui, "Evolution of the Feminist Movement in Japan," *NWSA Journal* 2 (Summer 1990): 445.

16. Sue Ellen M. Charlton, "Female Welfare and Political Exclusion in Western European States," in Charlton, Everett, and Staudt, eds., *Women, the State, and Development*, 23–24.

17. See, e.g., Seymour M. Lipset, *Political Man* (Garden City, N.Y.: Doubleday, 1960); and Gabriel Almond and James Coleman, eds., *The Politics of the Developing Areas* (Princeton, N.J.: Princeton University Press, 1960).

18. Russell J. Dalton, Paul Allen Beck, and Scott C. Flanagan, "Electoral Change in Advanced Industrial Democracies," in Russell J. Dalton, Scott C. Flanagan, and Paul Allen Beck, eds., *Electoral Change in Advanced Industrial Democracies: Realignment or Dealignment?* (Princeton, N.J.: Princeton University Press, 1984), 3–22; W. Phillips Shively, "The Development of Party Identification Among Adults: Exploration of a Functional Model," *American Political Science Review* 73 (1979): 1039–54; G. Bingham Powell, "Party Systems and Political System Performance: Voting Participation, Government Stability and Mass Violence in Contemporary Democracies," *American Political Science Review* 75 (December 1981): 861–79.

19. See, e.g., Joel S. Migdal, *Strong Societies and Weak States: State-Society Relations and State Capabilities in the Third World* (Princeton, N.J.: Princeton University Press, 1988); Eric Nordlinger, *On the Autonomy of Democratic States* (Cambridge, Mass.: Harvard University Press, 1981); and Stephen Krasner, "Approaches to the State: Alternative Conceptions and Historical Dynamics," *Comparative Politics* 16 (January 1984): 223–45.

20. Two good recent examples of this work are Alfred

Stepan, "State Power and the Strength of Civil Society in the Southern Cone of Latin America," in Peter Evans, Dietrich Rueschemeyer, and Theda Skocpol, eds., *Bringing the State Back In* (Cambridge, Eng.: Cambridge University Press, 1985), 317–43; and Lawrence R. Jacobs, "The Recoil Effect: Public Opinion and Policymaking in the U.S. and Britain," *Comparative Politics* 24 (January 1992): 199–218.

21. An exception to this is Charlton, Everett, and Staudt, eds., *Women, the State, and Development.*

22. Carolyn K. Ban and Barbara J. Nelson, "Decisions by Line Bureaucrats: Do Sex and Race Affect the Results of Applications for Public Social Benefits or Services" (Paper presented at the annual meeting of the American Political Science Association, Washington D.C., 1977); Karen Beckwith, "The Cross-Cultural Study of Women and Politics: Methodological Problems," *Women and Politics* 1 (Summer 1980): 7–28; and Vicky Randall, *Women and Politics: An International Perspective,* 2d ed. (Chicago: University of Chicago Press, 1987).

23. Scholars of women and politics have begun to ask these questions. See, e.g., Sonia E. Alvarez, *Engendering Democracy in Brazil* (Princeton, N.J.: Princeton University Press, 1990); Neera Desai, ed., *A Decade of Women's Movement in India* (Bombay: Himalaya Publishing House, 1988); Joyce Gelb, *Feminism and Politics: A Comparative Perspective* (Berkeley: University of California Press, 1989); Judith Adler Hellman, *Journeys Among Women: Feminism in Five Italian Cities* (New York: Oxford University Press, 1987); Deniz Kandiyoti, "Women, Islam, and the State," *Middle East Report* 173 (November–December 1991): 9–14; Randall, *Women and Politics;* Earl L. Sullivan, *Women in Egyptian Public Life* (Syracuse, N.Y.: Syracuse University Press, 1986); and Marjory Wolf, *Revolution Postponed: Women in Contemporary China* (Stanford, Calif.: Stanford University Press, 1985).

24. Fanny Tabak, author of the Brazilian chapter, contributed to the development of the political engagement concept, stressing that the development of political consciousness and the decision to engage in other political activities may be separated by a great deal of time, especially in repressive political regimes.

25. See, e.g., Gabriel A. Almond, *Political Development: Essays in Heuristic Theory* (Boston: Little, Brown, 1970).

26. Anna G. Jónasdóttir, "On the Concept of Interest, Women's Interests, and the Limitations of Interest Theory," in Kathleen B. Jones and Anna G. Jónasdóttir, eds., *The Political Interests of Gender* (London: Sage, 1985), 33–65. For a general critique of the limits of rational individualism in political science see Jane J. Mansbridge, "The Rise and Fall of Self-Interest in the Explanation of Political Life," in Jane J. Mansbridge, ed., *Beyond Self-Interest* (Chicago: University of Chicago Press, 1990), 3–22.

27. Virginia Sapiro, "When Are Interests Interesting?

The Problem of Political Representation of Women," *American Political Science Review* 75 (September 1981): 701–16; and Irene Diamond and Nancy Hartsock, "Beyond Interests in Politics: A Comment on Virginia Sapiro's 'When Are Interests Interesting? The Problem of Political Representation of Women,'" *American Political Science Review* 75 (September 1981): 717–21.

28. Amartya K. Sen, "Gender and the Cooperative Conflicts," in Irene Tinker, ed., *Persistent Inequalities: Women and World Development* (New York: Oxford University Press, 1990), 126. For a discussion of how politicization and interest formation go together for women see Vina Mazumdar, *Emergence of Women's Questions in India and the Role of Women's Studies* (New Delhi: Centre for Women's Development Studies, 1985).

29. Jónasdóttir, "On the Concept of Interests," 40–41.

30. See BANGLADESH. The information about Saptagram is based on an interview with the founding member and former project director. Begun in seven villages, the Saptagram Nari Swanirvar Parishad (Saptagram Women's Self-Reliance Movement) now reaches more than 600 villages. See also Naila Kabeer, "Organising Landless Women in Bangladesh," *Community Development Journal* 20 (1985): 203–11. On women's organizing in South Asia see Gita Sen with Caren Grown, *Development, Crisis and Alternative Visions: Third World Women's Perspectives* (New Delhi: Development Alternatives with Women for a New Era [DAWN], 1985), 82–89.

31. Hellman, *Journeys Among Women,* 55–110.

32. For a summary of the political opportunity structure literature in the United States and Western Europe see Sidney Tarrow, "Struggle, Politics, and Reform: Collective Action, Social Movements, and Cycles of Protest," Occasional Paper no. 21 (Ithaca, N.Y.: Cornell University, Center for International Studies, Western Societies Program, 1989), 25–39. Some of the political dependency literature, which focuses on less industrialized regions, employs versions of the political opportunity structure approach. The extent to which aspects of political opportunity structures dealing with a country's position in the international political economy were viewed to be largely fixed or malleable varies within the dependency literature. See J. Samuel Valenzuela and Arturo Valenzuela, "Modernization and Dependency: Alternative Perspectives in the Study of Latin American Underdevelopment," *Comparative Politics* 10 (July 1978): 535–57; David G. Becker and Richard L. Sklar, "Why Postimperialism?" in David Becker, Jeff Frieden, Sayre Schatz, and Richard Sklar, eds., *Postimperialism: International Capitalism and Development in the Late 20th Century* (Boulder, Colo.: Lynne Rienner, 1987), 1–18; and Sylvia Maxfield, "Bankers' Alliances and Economic Policy Patterns: Evidence from Mexico and Brazil," *Comparative Political Studies* 23 (January 1991): 419–58.

33. Lata Mani, "Multiple Mediations: Feminist Scholarship in the Age of Multinational Reception," *Inscription* 5 (1989): 1-24.

34. Seymour M. Lipset and Stein Rokkan, "Cleavage Structures, Party Systems, and Voter Alignments: An Introduction," in Seymour M. Lipset and Stein Rokkan, eds., *Party Systems and Voter Alignments: Cross-National Perspectives* (New York: Free Press, 1967), 1–64; and Philippe C. Schmitter, "Interest Intermediation and Regime Governability in Contemporary Western Europe and North America," in Suzanne Berger, ed., *Organizing Interests in Western Europe: Pluralism, Corporatism and the Transformation of Politics* (Cambridge, Eng.: Cambridge University Press, 1981), 285–327.

35. Sandra Harding, "Introduction: Is There a Feminist Method?" in Harding, ed., *Feminism and Methodology* (Bloomington: Indiana University Press, 1987), 2–3. For a longer treatment of some of these questions see Sandra Harding, *The Science Question in Feminism* (Ithaca, N.Y.: Cornell University Press, 1986); and Sandra Harding and Merrill Hintikka, eds., *Discovering Reality: Feminist Perspectives on Epistemology, Metaphysics, Methodology and Philosophy of Science* (Dordrecht, Neth.: D. Reidel, 1983).

36. For a brief discussion of some of these questions in the discipline of political science as it is practiced in the United States see Barbara J. Nelson, "Women and Knowledge in Political Science: Texts, Histories, and Epistemologies," *Women & Politics* 9 (Spring 1989): 1–25.

37. Sandra Harding, "Conclusion: Epistemological Questions," in Harding, ed., *Feminism and Methodology*, 181–84. See also Marcia Millman and Rosabeth Moss Kanter, "*Another Voice: Feminist Perspectives on Social Life and Social Science,*" in Harding, ed., *Feminism and Methodology*, 29–37.

38. Nancy Fraser and Linda J. Nicholson, "Social Criticism Without Philosophy: An Encounter Between Feminism and Postmodernism," in Linda J. Nicholson, ed., *Feminism/Postmodernism* (New York: Routledge, 1990), 19–38.

3 ▲ Global Research on Women's Political Engagement: The History of the Women and Politics Worldwide Project

NAJMA CHOWDHURY,
NANCY J. JOHNSON,
BARBARA J. NELSON, AND
PAULA L. O'LOUGHLIN

It has taken many years and the energy and imagination of many people to bring *Women and Politics Worldwide* to completion. We always think of it in the first person plural, as a book "we" planned and made, though the individuals composing the we have changed over time. Najma Chowdhury and Barbara Nelson are the we of designing and directing the project. Nancy Johnson and Paula O'Loughlin joined Barbara and Najma to become the we of managing and implementing the project. The we of the book as a whole includes the chapter authors, the editorial team, and the women whose experiences are chronicled here. This is our history, told by several speakers.

DESIGNING A GLOBAL FEMINIST RESEARCH PROJECT

On the warm Kenyan afternoon of 15 July 1985, two of us, Najma Chowdhury and Barbara Nelson, sat on a low wall surrounding the commons of the University of Nairobi. We were preparing for our session "Educating Women for Political Participation Worldwide," a panel in the Non-Governmental Forum organized to coincide with the U.N. conference that ended the U.N. Decade for Women. As we planned our session we worried about whether all the panelists would locate our room on time. In the bustle of an international conference of women of all colors and races located across several campuses

and housed in hotels throughout the city, our final preparation for the panel had been difficult. By the morning of the panel we had been able to reach only a few of the speakers.

Another worry weighed on us as we sat in the sunshine. We had requested a roundtable facility from the forum organizers; instead, we had been allotted an auditorium designed to hold 300. We were concerned that there would be too few people to fill the hall and too much empty space for sustained interaction.

We went to the auditorium in the Education Building about 20 minutes before the panel was to begin. When we pushed open the door we found that the room was nearly full. We stepped back, thinking the previous session had not finished. As we stood nearby, however, we realized that people were going in and not coming out. We looked inside again, and one glance at the empty rostrum at the far end of the auditorium convinced us that the people gathered in the auditorium were waiting for us to begin. We went to the rostrum, greeted the panelists, and began the session. What was intended as a roundtable was quickly modified to fit the format required for a packed auditorium. As more and more people came in, they had to sit on the steps leading down to the rostrum or stand crowded at the back.

The program was an engaging session of presentations by ten panelists from eight countries.[1] The speeches and the discussion with the audience lasted for three hours—an hour longer than the time officially allotted. Finally, at 5:00 P.M., the interpreters put down their microphones, signaling the end of their workday. The session continued for a while nonetheless, with people leaving reluctantly only after university administrators said that the building had to be closed for the night.

We were certain that the overwhelming number of women at the session and the keen participation of the audience were due not just to the overflow of women gathered at the conference, nor even to the general concern about women's issues that engaged the scholars and activists there. At other panels we had seen a desolate look prevail when participants failed to attend or panelists did not arrive. We were convinced that the interest shown at our panel indicated a global concern about the nature of women's political engagement in diverse cultural and national settings.

Over the past eight years the questions about women's political engagement that arose from the Nairobi conference have formed the basis of an international scholarly collaboration and a deep friendship that together have created this book. With a team of assistants, we have worked together through every phase of planning and crafting *Women and Politics Worldwide*. With the help of the contributing authors, we elaborated and refined the initial response to the panel at Nairobi into a framework of analysis that strove for sensitivity to context and diversity, as well as commonality. We have lived through the Nairobi experience time and again, recounting the event in professional meetings and informal gatherings when people ask how and where the project began. We see Nairobi as the beginning of the research.

Four Years of Planning

Nairobi was also the beginning of our friendship. In fall 1984 Najma Chowdhury, a professor of political science at the University of Dhaka, Bangladesh, was in the United States on a tour sponsored by the U.S. International Visitor Program. She was traveling with a multi-national group of women political scientists, politicians, activists, and journalists. The program, which focused on women and politics in the United States, involved travel through seven cities, including Minneapolis, where Barbara Nelson was a professor of public policy at the Hubert H. Humphrey Institute of Public Affairs, at the University of Minnesota. We were brought in touch with each other by a fellow political scientist who had passed along Barbara's request that Najma ring her up. Najma called just before rushing to a bus bound for the airport. Barbara was hoping to organize a panel at the Nairobi conference and inquired if Najma would like to co-sponsor it. Najma agreed, and the conversation ended with the exchange of addresses and the promise of letters.

Barbara and Najma corresponded for eight months in preparation for the Nairobi meeting, introducing our lives and our work to each other prior to our face-to-face meeting, which would occur in Kenya. The correspondence was marked by small but significant changes. Our first letters were highly formal. We came to call each other by our first names only after several months of letter writing and then only after a rather Victorian exchange professing better acquaintance.

The idea of a book emerged in the excitement of organizing the panel and as a logical response to the disappointing search for cross-cultural political science literature that incorporated a gender dimension. The response in Nairobi further impressed on us the need to undertake a project that would ground the analysis of women's political engagement in systematic cross-cultural study. Armed with the list of people who had indicated at our panel a willingness to collaborate on the book, and filled with enthusiasm, we sat down in Barbara's hotel room in Nairobi to plan the project. Over endless cups of tea, we worked out a month-by-month timetable, charting the conceptualization, collaboration, writing, and editing of 15 to 20 chapters. In the plan, we would produce a final manuscript in exactly two years, finishing by June 1987. This schedule proved wildly optimistic. Instead of taking two years, the making of *Women and Politics World-*

wide evolved into a nine-year commitment composed of four years of planning the project, three years of intensive writing and editing, and two years of preparation for publication. In its final form this book has four overview chapters and 43 country chapters written by 61 authors speaking 23 mother tongues written in 12 alphabets or symbol systems.

The process of creating this global project was guided by hope and sometimes fraught with despair. To succeed, it needed funding, time, skills, and infrastructure. As the editors, we needed an initial period of close interaction to set the groundwork for intellectual collaboration and for mapping the direction of the project. Our search for writers had to be guided by our concern that the countries selected for the book be representative. The study also had to be grounded in a common set of research questions formulated through a participatory process and sensitive to multicultural contexts. This meant that we would have to interact with prospective writers either through correspondence—a time-consuming and laborious process—or through face-to-face brainstorming sessions, which were unlikely events, given the realities of organizing international meetings. By June 1987, our original projected completion date, we had made little substantive progress, in large part because we did not have the resources to spend an extended period of time together for planning.

On her return from Nairobi, Barbara began exploring funding possibilities, and we both began to search in earnest for writers. Najma's visit to New York in September 1986 as a member of the Bangladesh delegation to the U.N. General Assembly created the opportunity for her to visit Minneapolis for a speaking engagement, an opportunity that we also utilized for planning. In October we took a preliminary proposal to the Ford Foundation in New York and were encouraged to develop a full proposal.

The turning point came in 1988, when Najma spent the fall quarter at the Humphrey Institute as a visiting Fulbright professor. Those four months together enabled us to lay the intellectual groundwork for the book. Before Najma went to

Minnesota, we met in Washington, D.C., at the 14th World Congress of the International Political Science Association. IPSA's Research Committee 19 on Sex Roles and Politics, for which Barbara organized a panel, and Study Group 30 on Women, Politics and Developing Nations, of which Najma was the convener, provided opportunities for us to launch the project informally and obtain author commitments.[2] Importantly, theoretical discussions were organized among many of the scholars present, some of whom later joined the project as chapter authors. At special sessions on the project, a group of 18 scholars responded to our research design and chapter structure, providing the basis of a jointly fashioned chapter outline. Invigorated by these meetings, we further developed our proposal during the first weeks of Najma's stay in Minnesota, visited the Ford Foundation again in November, and submitted a final project proposal in early 1989. With the commitment of support for the project from the Ford Foundation and the University of Minnesota, *Women and Politics Worldwide* was placed firmly on the launching pad in June 1989.

Three Years of Writing and Editing

The process of international collaboration was shaped by our commitment to creating a network of scholars and activists that would sustain the "building" of the book. During travels in summer 1989 Barbara met with chapter authors and potential authors in ten countries. As part of the collaborative process, we also made sustained efforts to have the participants meet at as many international conferences as possible. In this way the chapter authors could present their preliminary findings, draw on each other's comments and critiques, share a commitment to the book, and establish personal bonds with one another.

The project sponsored official panels and concurrent book-related sessions at several conferences: the IPSA congress in 1988; three back-to-back meetings in June 1990 in New York (the mid-congress meeting of IPSA Study Group 30; the annual meeting of member centers of the [U.S.] National Council for Research on

Women; and the Fourth International Interdisciplinary Congress on Women); the annual meeting of the American Political Science Association (APSA), held in San Francisco in September 1990; and the 15th World Congress of IPSA, held in July 1991 in Buenos Aires. In conjunction with the September 1990 APSA meeting we met with a group of the authors to review the preliminary chapter findings. At all these meetings we tried to organize gatherings of different groups of chapter authors, subject to their availability, access to travel funds, and their other responsibilities at such meetings. During the course of the project, one or both of us met some 70 percent of the chapter contributors.

In 1989 IPSA recognized *Women and Politics Worldwide* as an official association research endeavor and thereby renewed its commitment to the study of women and politics that began in the early 1950s. At that time, the association recognized Maurice Duverger's research for his landmark study *The Political Role of Women,* the first systematic cross-national electoral analysis of women's participation to use survey data and election returns.[3]

The *Women and Politics Worldwide* project moved to its final phase when we chose the publisher in July 1991 during the IPSA conference in Buenos Aires. During November and December 1991, while at the Rockefeller Foundation Study and Conference Center at Bellagio, Italy, the editors and Nancy Johnson, the project manager and literary editor, reviewed all 43 country chapters. During this period we drafted the chapters on findings, methodology, history, and data sources. Working simultaneously in Minnesota were the coauthors Paula O'Loughlin, Kathryn Carver, and Whitney Thompson. The core project team now consisted of Najma, Barbara, Nancy, and Paula; working with us every step were a number of graduate research assistants.

Throughout the crafting of *Women and Politics Worldwide,* the project team was continuously aware that the endeavor was located in the interstices of important historical forces. The International Women's Year and the U.N. Decade for Women contributed to the generation of data on women, particularly in developing countries, which led to increased recognition of women's experiences. Feminist, or, more broadly, women's movements had emerged since the 1960s in many countries with varying degrees of resonance. Activism increasingly addressed issues in both traditional and innovative ways to build power and create solidarity. The development of the field of women's studies—which recorded, analyzed, and theorized about the experiences of women—promoted feminist scholarship. Scholars began raising epistemological questions aimed at situating gender concerns within the central foci of disciplines, challenging the dominant center-periphery and public-private dichotomies. *Women and Politics Worldwide* draws on this history, mobilizes these resources, and brings together activists and academics from political science and allied disciplines to look at issues of gender and politics on a global scale.

MANAGING INTERNATIONAL
FEMINIST RESEARCH

Our key to keeping such a large international collaboration on track was always to think of management and intellectual issues as linked. The design of the process was tied to the goals of the book, and it became clear that both the means and the end would be important research products of this project.

As with many collaborative scholarly projects, the creation of *Women and Politics Worldwide* required a strong vision of both the process and the result; a robust system of frequent communications among the authors and the editors and between the editors themselves; and a deep respect, established at each step of the way, for each other and the work. But there were significant differences from other projects as well. The international nature of this undertaking meant that even though all the chapter drafts were submitted in English, there was still a significant amount of what we all came to think of as translation—in style, in word choice, and in attempts to clarify and protect the authors' original meanings.

In addition, we were made aware of many ways

in which feminist debates on difference applied to this project, as we discussed in Chapter 1.[4] Indeed, given the breadth of *Women and Politics Worldwide,* difference became an assumed condition—not a barrier to overcome but a vehicle through which to interrogate one another's narratives and analyses and to explore the range of women's voices and political actions.

Project Infrastructure

The resources available for this project fell broadly into four categories: funding, staff, technology, and communication. Major funding came from many sources (see the Acknowledgments) and helped to cover the substantial costs of doing international collaborative feminist research. These costs included partial salaries or consulting fees for project staff members; support for graduate research assistants; institutional overhead expenses, such as contributions to wages for secretarial and accounting personnel; postage, fax and telephone costs (which were considerable); travel and conference expenses; and chapter author stipends. While virtually any project could use more funding than it has, the support for this project allowed us to move forward according to plan.

At the University of Minnesota the project was located in the Hubert H. Humphrey Institute of Public Affairs, through its Center on Women and Public Policy. Of Barbara and Najma's two home institutions, Minnesota was the natural place to locate the project secretariat because of its strong organizational infrastructure and the availability of the resources needed to complete the project in a timely way. In all, 27 graduate students in public affairs, political science, feminist studies, public health, and education were employed at the University of Minnesota as project research assistants for one- to three-year periods from 1985 through 1993. Their responsibilities included editing chapters, gathering data, sustaining communication between the editors and the authors, and planning author meetings. Najma also had a research assistant for two years at Dhaka University to assist her with project duties. The students were eager to work on a feminist project that brought together so many of their academic and applied interests.

When planning for the book began in 1985, the Minnesota project secretariat was lodged in a small faculty office outfitted with one typewriter. The project was computerized in 1986, and in 1988 the Humphrey Institute obtained a fax machine. By 1990 the Minnesota end of the project had taken on something of the atmosphere of a small business; it had spread into several offices and had engaged the efforts of five or six people a year. The growing infrastructure facilitated the frequent communication among project participants that kept the project moving forward. Throughout the project, the editors sent 24 mass mailings to chapter authors, and the chapter authors and the editors exchanged an average of 20 personal letters per chapter.

The Process of Chapter Editing

The conferences, letters, and, most important, the chapter editing and author responses allowed the chapters to speak to one another. When the first chapter draft (from the People's Republic of China) arrived in March 1990, the editorial team was both excited and sobered as a new phase of the project began. As the chapter drafts came in, first in a trickle and then in a deluge, we had to develop an editing system that would respond to the volume and variety of the work.

Chapter authors generally submitted their drafts simultaneously to Najma in Dhaka and Barbara in Minneapolis; when a draft was submitted only to the Minnesota office, a copy was sent to Najma. In Minnesota, copies of each draft were distributed to all members of the project team. Each week we read one or more chapters in common, on which we made notes and commented extensively, and held one- to two-hour project meetings. During the early part of the project Najma conveyed her comments by mail, but as deadlines neared we turned to frequent phone conversations and fax messages. We also asked area specialists in women and politics to join the review process.

After the group discussion one member of the

team was assigned responsibility for editing the chapter. This was the most time-consuming part of the editing process, taking anywhere from 8 to 250 hours per chapter. At this point a member of the editorial team put the chapter on disk if it was not already available in electronic form. The chapter editor made grammatical, stylistic, and organizational suggestions and offered queries and comments on the text. During this process we asked authors to define—by exposition, example, or context—terms like feminism and women's movement that were used differently in many chapters. Najma and Barbara reviewed the edited drafts before returning them to the authors. Each chapter went through at least three drafts.

Because of the number of languages spoken by the authors, the task of editing was more complicated and time-consuming than we anticipated. But the authors' responses to our detailed queries and comments were far more enthusiastic and rich than we could have hoped. They were enormously generous with their time and resources in helping to make the chapters accessible to readers knowledgeable about women and politics at home but new to these issues elsewhere.

Challenges of Editing

By the final months of the project, we realized that we had confronted three major editorial challenges, each of which had profound implications for the intellectual content of the book. These challenges involved reading silences, reading differences, and respecting voice.

Reading silences refers to the political difficulties some authors faced in joining the project and to their choices to be silent on some points. In some chapters authors have left important things unsaid. It is particularly clear in the context of women's relationships to the state and to authority that silence frequently does not connote consent. Neither does it equate with lack of comment. Silences speak loudly in this volume, often representing voices yet to be found and discussions yet to begin. Some omissions originate in long historical silences, and others are the

silences of the moment, especially those imposed by repressive political systems.

Reading differences is another theme running through this volume in several ways. Differences in political engagement between men and women in specific country contexts are made explicit by the chapter authors. Additionally, differences exist among women (or men) in any individual country—whether they are thought to be located in the social "cleavages" of political science, the "difference" of feminist theorizing, or the many varieties of political activism and expression in women's experiences. There are also differences among project participants themselves, including the editors. Reading these differences in ways that are instructive, synthesizing, and creative has been one of the major aims of our learning to work together. Some feminist theorizing might conclude that a project such as this one is impossible; we do not agree. This work, rooted in experience and pointed toward analysis, demonstrates the rich possibilities of international feminist collaboration.

Our chapter editing reflects a concern for voice in two senses: the voice of the author as expressed in standard U.S. usage and the voices of the women whose interests and actions the author describes. Thus we found it important to question and clarify early drafts to ground the work in the best possible understanding of each author's style, themes, and intention. Also reflected in the editing is our view of the project as a whole, which required us to consider both how individual chapters complemented and augmented each other and how they contributed distinctively to the book. Transcending the other editorial responsibilities and embedded as a basic principle of this endeavor was another dimension of respect for voice, however: the chapters represent the interpretations of events and the intellectual perspectives of the respective contributors; theirs are the authoritative voices that speak through the chapters.

Clocks and Calendars

We came to understand vividly the extent to which a variety of conceptions of time have shaped this book. One of the most influential schedules was the "publishing clock," whose manuscript and publication deadlines shaped the rhythm of writing, editing, and even the possibility of including specific countries. Another timepiece, so prevalent in the West, was the "write it up fast, get it published soon" social science clock that assumed, incorrectly and androcentrically, that the basic material needed for analysis of women's political engagement must surely be available in official statistics and could be cranked out in a hurry. The assumption created a surreal backdrop against which the time-consuming research process actually took place. Much of the material, data, and theory in each chapter went far beyond anything previously written about that country, and we grew increasingly aware of how dependent the traditional Western social science research clock is on the labor of hundreds of people who collect primary data and undertake initial analyses. In many instances in this project, the labor and analyses were provided by the authors themselves.

Another measure of time that played a major role in our understanding of this project involved the life cycles of the women who participated. In the public, professional realm there have been job changes, promotions, at least one retirement, and the return home of at least one witness to testify to the political atrocities of a previous regime. At some time in their lives, at least two of the authors have been political prisoners; one has gone into hiding for political reasons with her newborn child. During the writing of this book at least two children have been born to chapter authors; at least one child has died. Several authors have faced serious illnesses or surgeries. Many have borne heavy responsibilities for the care of elderly parents, small children, or other family members.

Political events and natural disasters also have intervened. The devastating cyclone and floods in Bangladesh; earthquakes in Costa Rica; regime transformations in Central Europe; the Intifada in the Middle East; the reuniting of the two Germanies; the dramatic unraveling of the Soviet Union; the assassination of India's prime minister; the democracy movements in Nepal and Bangladesh; the events in Tiananmen Square; the breakdown of apartheid in South Africa; and many other events have figured prominently in the project's calendar and timing.

Conclusions Concerning Project Management

Three findings seem especially important to us regarding the management of this project. One is the need for such an undertaking to develop a heuristic, flexible, innovative management system that is open to change at each step. Openness and learning by experience helped the project team to make corrections along the way and still follow the overall plan and vision.

A second finding is the value of respect and conversation in creating project boundaries and methods. As editors, Najma and Barbara saw their responsibilities for intellectual leadership as an equal partnership and their responsibilities for management and production as a proportionate partnership. Although the project could not have established two secretariats, one in Bangladesh and one in the United States, given the differences in national and institutional infrastructure and resources, neither could it have been completed without the rich international collaboration and intense personal friendships that developed from the work. For Najma and Barbara especially, "sisterhood" took on a new meaning rooted in the experience of having invented, tested, and utilized this collaborative process to a successful end.

Finally, through the last nine years we have always imagined this work as a book, not just a collection of country-based essays. The voices of the chapter authors and the women they represent have sounded like a new kind of world chorus of women's polyphonic music, in which many voices sing at once. Some take only brief parts, leaving before the melody ends and contributing to harmonies that quickly change; others are percussion, interrupting what might otherwise be predictable traditional melodies; still others suddenly move into new and unexpected keys, changing the tone and mood of the piece. It is our hope that no voice dominates and that no voice is unheard. Although the music may not yet be comfortable and familiar, its newness may create sounds that can enrich and expand on what has come before.

NOTES

1. For a transcript of the session see Najma Chowdhury and Barbara Nelson, "Educating Women for Political Participation Worldwide: A Report from the United Nations Conference on Women, FORUM '85, Nairobi, Kenya" (Minneapolis: Center on Women and Public Policy, Hubert H. Humphrey Institute, University of Minnesota, 1985). Kathryn A. Carver assisted us as we prepared for our session in Nairobi, and she participated in the original planning session for the book. Nancy J. Johnson edited the taped transcript of the session.

2. Two groups within the International Political Science Association have been invaluable in creating the intellectual community and initial network that sustained this project. They are Research Committee 19: Sex Roles and Politics; and Study Group 30: Women, Politics, and Developing Nations. Both groups address feminist and gender issues within the discipline of political science. Interactions with both groups, of which Najma Chowdhury and Barbara Nelson are members, were fruitful.

3. Maurice Duverger, *The Political Role of Women* (Paris: UNESCO, 1955).

4. See Chapter 1 for a summary of the feminist theorizing on difference.

4 ▲ Measuring Women's Status, Portraying Women's Lives: Problems in Collecting Data on Women's Experiences

BARBARA J. NELSON
WITH KATHRYN A. CARVER,
PAULA L. O'LOUGHLIN,
AND WHITNEY THOMPSON

Each country chapter in this book includes a chart of political, demographic, educational, and economic information, with special attention paid to how women and men fare on measures that can be compared by sex. The numerical data for all the countries in the book are also presented together in the appendix, Selected Information from the Country Charts. These data provide a quick reference to conditions in each country and an easy way to make general comparisons among countries. Through these charts and appendix we describe the *conditions* of life in each country in a way that complements the analysis of the social and political *processes* discussed in the chapters. In this chapter, a guide to the statistics and other material presented in *Women and Politics Worldwide,* we describe the process of gathering the data presented with each chapter and evaluate the strengths and weaknesses of those data (all from secondary sources) and the measures.

Until recently, most efforts at social accounting failed to consider whether women's lives and activities were accurately portrayed by commonly used measures. Indeed, Ruth Leger Sivard, author of *Women: A World Survey,* an important data compendium produced at the end of the U.N. Decade for Women, argues that careful attention to gender considerations in social accounting is largely a result of pressure generated by the U.N. Decade.[1] During this period it became increasingly clear to activists and scholars

that governments and other large data-collection agencies had given scant attention to the reliability and validity of commonly used social and economic indicators when they were applied to women's experiences.[2]

One outcome of this recognition was the addition of a recommendation for better data-gathering efforts to the *Forward-Looking Strategies* document. All the 158 governments represented at the deliberations that closed the Decade for Women conference in Nairobi endorsed the document. The writers of the *Forward-Looking Strategies* recognized the need to collect and present data about women to give "concrete evidence concerning many of the harmful consequences of unequal laws and practices and [to measure] progress in the elimination of inequalities."[3] This recommendation was preceded by the publication—by the U.N. Statistical Office and the International Research and Training Institute for the Advancement of Women (INSTRAW)—of two books, one promoting better use of existing sources of data and the other detailing how data definition and collection could be improved.[4]

THE DATA COLLECTION PROCESS

We developed a system in which information was collected centrally and verified by chapter authors. In choosing specific measures we emphasized variables that gave specific examples of a country's living conditions. For this reason, we chose not to include aggregate quality of life measures even though several good ones, like the Physical Quality of Life Index, exist.[5] We originally collected data on 29 general measures, some of which—like literacy—were further disaggregated by sex or other variables. However, data on three of the measures proved difficult to gather or were unreliable in most countries, and those measures were dropped. These were "the percentages of men and women voting for the highest national office in the last election"; employment status, classified by "own account," "employee," and "unpaid family workers"; and "access to safe drinking water."

We compiled the data from such international sources as the United Nations and the World Bank and from academic handbooks on political systems. The collected information was sent, along with the definitions used in the secondary sources, to chapter authors to verify, expand upon, or correct. This method worked well and had several advantages. First, most international data-collecting organizations have gone to great lengths to standardize definitions and to record the departures from these standards. Thus international organizations provided the best guarantee of comparability of data in a field where variability of measures is more common than uniformity. Second, we were aware that the data we wished to include were not always available to researchers in every country because of political and financial considerations. The collect-and-verify procedure eased the burden on those authors who would have had the most trouble collecting the information, though some authors faced similar difficulties verifying it. This process had a notable disadvantage, however. By using existing measures and sources, the information reported in the country charts would, by and large, reproduce any gender biases in data collection or definitions.

In 1989 we collected the political, demographic, educational, and economic data, and in 1990 we added health data to the demographic measures. Although we used the most recent material available, most of the sources were at least a couple of years old, and some, like national censuses, were occasionally a decade old. (In some countries, estimations from sample surveys were used to update census data.) In 1990 many countries undertook their decennial censuses, but little of that information was available on a systematic basis by late 1991. More important, two international secondary sourcebooks appeared after the data had been collected: the World Bank's *World Development Report,* published in 1990, and *World's Women, 1970–1990: Trends and Statistics,* published by the United Nations in 1991.[6] We compared every measure we used that appeared in either of these sources for seven countries and found that the differences, where they existed, were small and that the chapter authors had in some cases supplied more complete or up-to-date information. Thus, we chose not to alter the data we had collected, with one exception: we replaced our measures of school enrollment with those used by the United Nations in its 1991 publication after determining that the measures were based on a definition far superior to the previously available one.

Double-checking our data with chapter authors often proved surprisingly useful and instructive. For example, we found that particular types of data are regularly reported in incomplete or misleading ways. In some sources the year that women received the right to vote is listed as the year the first large group of women received suffrage; in others it is listed as the year universal womanhood suffrage was achieved. The first date implies that women's suffrage occurred earlier than it did; the second obscures the often long process by which women won suffrage in many countries. In Great Britain, for example, women age 30 and older received voting rights in 1918, but universal womanhood suffrage did not occur until 1928. Because of the iterative process of collecting and verifying this data, our charts now present the highlights of the history of women's suffrage in countries where there were distinct phases in winning the vote.

Similarly, few countries collect electoral statistics by sex. The percentage of women voting for the highest office in a country is therefore available only where governments or private polling agencies undertake sample surveys to determine this figure (e.g., the United States) or where experts have privately estimated the figure from published or unpublished data (e.g., Greece). This measure ultimately was dropped for lack of data.

Authors often reported the limits of the data available in their countries with candor and immediacy. Writing a politically risky letter from a then state socialist country, one author said with humor and conviction that the U.S. government probably had more accurate figures about her country than any she could find in publicly available sources. Conversations with authors in several countries indicated that figures were routinely falsified in national sources and when they were reported to international agencies but that nothing could be done in this instance to correct those errors. In addition to the problems of purposefully inaccurate or unavailable data, other countries experienced difficulties providing accurate data even when they wished to do so. When Nigeria's Office of the Census (which was not computerized) burned in 1991, all records were lost and it became impossible to check our data. This loss of records was a great tragedy for Nigeria, where officials, businesspeople, scholars, and others needed the data to plan for the country's future.

SOURCES OF DATA

The data that countries send to international organizations are gathered by census, sample surveys, or administrative records. In the main, all three types of collection assume that the typical respondent will be a man and that men's place in society and the economy is the norm by which to define social indicators and to evaluate the accuracy and adequacy of information. According to the United Nations, the most problematic data on women are those drawn from current measures of economic activities and those that detail the sex and age distribution of household resources. While problems still exist, data about fertility, education, and mortality are more accurate.[7]

Measures of economic activity demonstrate the problems that arise from taking the experiences of men as normative. In both the more developed and less developed parts of the world, definitions of work assume that the way men relate to the economy is the standard. Questions that use terms like *job, work, occupation,* and even *main activity* often presuppose men's patterns of activity and may not encourage women to reveal their productive activities for consumption and exchange. As a result, women's contributions to their families' well-being are routinely undervalued, and their contributions to the gross domestic product of their countries are not accurately reported. Even though the U.N. System of National Accounts suggests that all food production for consumption or exchange and all small-scale capital formation (such as building a house) be included in national accounts, this definition—which would increase the recognition of women's work in agricultural economies—is not widely used. But even this definition excludes other important activities if the goods or services are not sold or exchanged. The lack of attention to domestic work and child rearing as a necessary precondition of other activities also contributes to the systematic undervaluing of women's economic contributions, lowering estimates of gross domestic products by 25 to 30 percent.[8]

Beyond the limitations imposed by a view of the world located in men's experiences, each type of data collection has general advantages and limitations that can be further specified when analyzing its success in gathering information from and about women. National censuses, which attempt to reach every household, are unparalleled in providing general labor force, demographic, and often educational information about both men and women. (Interestingly, censuses rarely gather information about income or wealth. This information affects taxation, and governments fear that the incentives to report income and wealth conservatively might bias all census data collection.)[9] One advantage of national censuses is their use of a closed-ended question format that increases the generalizability and comparability of results but also forces preclassification of responses. This format, together with scale and cost considerations, limits the number of questions that can be asked on any single topic. Because census data are collected infrequently and because great delays and expenses are often encountered in the dissemination of results, the data are frequently outdated by the time they are published.

Gender bias may arise in census data through definitions, methodology, and the actions of enumerators. In most parts of the world, census data are collected by household, with the "head of household" reporting for everyone. This method of reporting is efficient, but heads of households—usually designated as the oldest man or the oldest "economically active" man—may introduce respondent biases into the data. Cultural concerns about prestige or status, as well as ignorance of women's actual situations, may influence what male heads of households report about female household members. In particular, men may underreport women's economic activity because they do not view certain actions as economic or because they have status concerns over acknowledging to outsiders that women undertake certain economic tasks.[10]

All countries depend to some extent on enumerators who go from door to door to collect census data, but that dependence is greater in countries where literacy rates are low or where governmental infrastructure is weak. Mailed census questionnaires are used extensively in countries with high levels of literacy and strong governmental infrastructure. In less developed countries, the need for a large number of enumerators often means that the training of data collectors is limited, increasing the likelihood that additional gender bias may be introduced by enumerators. In the Third World the majority of enumerators are male. Like male heads of households, enumerators may introduce gender bias into census data by making erroneous assumptions about women's roles. For example, enumerators may presume that women are not heads of households, even when men are not present. Although the stereotype holds that women-headed households are found primarily in more developed countries, such is not the case. The percentage of households headed by women has grown rapidly in Africa, Latin America, and the Caribbean. In these regions, 30 countries report that at least 20 percent of all households are headed by women, and most of these households consist of women and children.[11]

A second important source of data on women is sample household surveys undertaken by governments to augment or update census information. Similar surveys can be undertaken by universities, donor agencies, or, in more wealthy countries, commercial firms. The U.N.'s Statistical Office and INSTRAW suggest that well-designed public sample surveys of households can help to correct flaws in definitions and data collection caused by the scope and methods of censuses, especially but not solely in less developed countries.[12] Sample surveys allow for a greater number of questions on topics of interest and provide an arena for experimentation with new measures. In particular, less rigid notions of who can head a household, a willingness to interview any adult available at the time of the interview, and the possibility of using definitions of *household* that emphasize residence over relationships can improve the quality and quantity of data about women. An emphasis on residence in household definitions (the eating-from-one-pot approach) means that when a wife and children live in the country and the husband lives in town, the presumption is of two households rather than one. This presumption means that economic transfers between the households have to be determined through questioning rather than assumed by virtue of the marriage.[13]

Government records, the third source of data on a country's population, offer a more current picture of births, deaths, marriages, divorces, and the like than is available from census data. But registration of these events may not be mandatory in poorer countries, and records may be poorly kept. Many citizens of developing countries may consider such recordkeeping unnecessary or illegitimate and may, therefore, fail to participate.

Three factors affect gender bias in administrative recordkeeping: decisions made by heads of households about the importance of establishing a relationship with the state for girls or women, the consequences of social practices that favor boys and men over girls and women, and state policies that enforce male dominance. In rural areas of China it is more likely that the birth of boys will be officially registered than the birth of girls.[14] Such practices can substantially reduce girls' chances to participate fully in their societies because access to important public benefits like healthcare or education depends on birth registration. Accurate registration is also an important resource in determining the extent of imbalances in sex ratios, a growing problem in Afghanistan, Bangladesh, Bhutan, China, India, Nepal, Pakistan, Papua New Guinea, and Turkey, where males often outnumber females 100 to 92.[15] When girls and boys receive the same medical care and nutrition, girls have a better survival rate. Sex ratios that favor boys after the earliest months of life suggest that social practices favor boys.[16] Bias against women in administrative recordkeeping can also be a policy choice. Since colonial times, the process of registering land titles in many developing countries gives ownership solely to men, even when women have a customary or religious claim to partial, joint, or full ownership.[17]

DEFINITIONS

In this section we list the specific definitions that we drew from secondary sources and used for the measures in the country charts. The references after the definitions give the sources of the data. If chapter authors provided information based on other definitions, these exceptions are noted in the references to those charts. Most applicable information is available for each nation or non-nation entity, with the exception of Palestine.

Political Measures

Type of Political System: Regime types are designated as democratic, partial democratic, state socialist, or authoritarian—a slight refinement of the types used in the country-choice matrix (see Chapter 2). The problems of defining regime types for entities that are not nations are dealt with in the charts for Great Britain, Hong Kong, Palestine, and Puerto Rico.

Administrative Organization: A country is defined as a federal system if the subnational units have considerable independent powers. Unitary systems are states in which the subnational units are political extensions of the central government.

Number of Parties: Party systems are defined by the number of parties—none, one, two, or multiple. Where several nominally separate parties act as one, they are counted as one.

Names of Political Parties: All active parties are listed for each country, with updates where possible as necessitated by regime changes. Nominally separate parties that act together are referred to by their joint name. See the references for each chart for details.

Year Women Granted the Right to Vote: Listed is the first year that universal womanhood suffrage was established in that jurisdiction. If women's suffrage was granted in stages, the country charts report this information.[18]

Year Women Granted the Right to Stand for Election: Listed is the first year that women were allowed to stand for election.

Percentage of Women in Legislature: The figure is the proportion of women in each house of the national legislature (or in the one house of a unicameral legislature), using the most recent election results. The election year closest to 1990 was used unless otherwise noted.

Percentage of Electorate Voting for Highest Elected Office in Most Recent Election: The percentage is determined from the total population eligible to vote. The year of the election is also reported.[19]

Demographic Measures

Population: Unless otherwise noted, figures refer to the de facto population within current boundaries. The most recent official estimate of the total population is presented.[20]

Percentage of Population in Urban Areas: This

figure reports the percentage of urban dwellers in the total population. While definitions of *urban* vary, the term generally refers to communities of more than 2,000 inhabitants.[21] Figures are reported separately for women and men.

Percentage of Population Below Age 15: The figures are drawn from the most recent census.[22]

Birthrate (per 1,000 population): The figures report the annual number of live births per 1,000 population in a year.[23]

Maternal Mortality Rate: The figures report the annual number of women dying from pregnancy-related causes per 100,000 live births.[24]

Infant Mortality Rate: The figures report the annual number of deaths of children under one year of age per 1,000 live births.[25]

Mortality Rate for Children Under Five: The figures report the annual number of deaths of children under five years of age per 1,000 live births.[26]

Average Household Size: The internationally recommended definition of *household* is based on a housekeeping concept that requires one or more persons to make common provisions for food or other essentials for living. Households may be composed of related or unrelated people or a combination of both. People living in collective living quarters of institutions, as in military institutions, correctional institutions, hospitals, and the like, are not considered to be living in households.[27]

Mean Age at First Marriage: The figures were prepared by the United Nations from a worldwide review of available information on patterns of first marriage. Specific laws or customs within individual countries have been taken into consideration in the original compilation.[28] These figures are reported separately for women and men.

Life Expectancy: The figures are the average number of years of life for males and females if they were to remain subject to the mortality factors experienced during the time the data were gathered.[29] These figures are reported separately for women and men.

Educational Measures

Ratio of Female to Male Enrollment in First-Level Education: The figure is the ratio of female pupils in the primary grades to male pupils in the primary grades, multiplied by 100. Primary education is generally regarded as beginning between the ages of five and seven and lasting about five years. Actual age ranges vary with educational practices in each country.[30]

Ratio of Female to Male Enrollment in Second-Level Education: The figure is the ratio of females in the secondary grades to males in the secondary grades, multiplied by 100. At the first stage, second-level education is generally defined as beginning between the ages of 10 and 12 and lasting about three years. At the second stage, second-level education is defined as beginning between 13 and 15 and lasting about four years. Figures for this measure include secondary enrollment levels at both stages. Actual age ranges vary with educational practices in each country.[31]

Ratio of Female to Male Enrollment in Third-Level Education: The figure is the ratio of the number of women enrolled in third-level educational institutions to the number of men enrolled in third-level educational institutions, multiplied by 100. Third-level education, which includes training at universities and colleges, is generally defined as beginning between the ages of 17 and 19 and lasting at least three years.[32] This figure routinely excludes students studying in foreign institutions of higher learning.

Literacy Rate: The figures generally pertain to people age 15 years and older. People are defined as illiterate when they cannot, with understanding, both read and write a short, simple statement about their everyday life. However, the interpretation and application of this concept may vary among countries, depending on national, social, and cultural circumstances.[33]

Economic Measures

Gross National Product per Capita: GNP gauges total domestic and foreign output claimed by residents and is calculated without making deductions for depreciation. The preparer of these figures, the World Bank, cautions that differences in accounting and indexing systems prevent figures from being uniformly comparable across nations.[34]

Percentage of the Labor Force in Agriculture: The figure is the proportion of the total labor force involved in agricultural production, livestock production, or agricultural services.[35] These figures are reported separately for women and men.

Distribution of Agricultural Workers by Sex: The figures break down the total agricultural work force into the percentage that are women and the percentage that are men.[36]

Economically Active Population by Sex: The International Labour Organization defines people as economically active if they worked for pay or profit, or were seeking such work, during a specified time-reference period. Work need not be full time for a person to be considered economically active. As has been noted above, the economic activity of women is often substantially understated because of the inappropriateness of market-based definitions of work and because of interviewer and respondent bias. In many countries, women account for the major proportion of people engaged in those economic activities that are the most difficult to measure.[37]

NOTES

1. Ruth Leger Sivard, *Women: A World Survey* (Washington, D.C.: World Priorities, 1985), 42.

2. For a review of how the United Nations, World Bank, and Ford Foundation responded to the challenges of collecting better data on women see Nüket Kardam, *Bringing Women In: Women's Issues in International Development Programs* (Boulder, Colo.: Lynne Rienner, 1991). The Ford Foundation sustained a greater interest than the other organizations in the reliability and validity of data collected on and from women.

3. United Nations, *Improving Statistics and Indicators on Women Using Household Surveys* (New York: United Nations, 1988), 4.

4. United Nations, *Improving Concepts and Methods for Statistics and Indicators on the Situation of Women* (New York: United Nations, 1984); and United Nations, *Compiling Social Indicators on the Situation of Women* (New York: United Nations, 1984).

5. John P. Lewis and Valeriana Kallab, eds., *U.S. Foreign Policy and the Third World, Agenda 1983* (New York: Praeger, 1983), 206–22.

6. World Bank, *World Development Report, 1990* (New York: Oxford University Press, 1990); and United Nations, *World's Women, 1970–1990: Trends and Statistics* (New York: United Nations, 1991).

7. United Nations, *Improving Statistics,* 7–10. See also Nancy Baster, "The Measurement of Women's Participation in Development: The Use of Census Data," Discussion Paper 159 (Overseas Development Administration, February 1981); and Ester Boserup, "Economic Change and the Roles of Women," in Irene Tinker, ed., *Persistent Inequalities: Women and World Development* (New York: Oxford University Press, 1990), 14–24.

8. United Nations, *World's Women,* 90. See also Marilyn Waring, *If Women Counted: A New Feminist Economics* (San Francisco: Harper and Row, 1988), 54 et passim; Amartya K. Sen, "Gender and Cooperative Conflicts," in Tinker, ed., *Persistent Inequalities,* 123–49; and Barbara J. Nelson, "Family Politics and Policy in the United States and Western Europe," *Comparative Politics* 17 (April 1985): 351–71.

9. United Nations, *Improving Statistics and Indicators on Women Using Household Surveys,* 7.

10. Baster, *Census Data,* 10.

11. Among Western Europe, the former Warsaw Pact countries, North America, Australia, New Zealand, and Japan (the U.N. group of developed countries), 13 countries report that more than 20 percent of their households are headed by women, and these households are mostly composed of women living alone. See United Nations, *World's Women,* 17–19.

12. United Nations, *Household Surveys,* 1–21.

13. Ibid., 44.

14. See CHINA.

15. Rhona Mahony, "On the Trail of the World's 'Missing Women,'" *Ms. Magazine* 2 (March–April 1992): 12.

16. Ibid. Sex ratios favoring boys early in life may also represent higher levels of female infanticide or fetal sex selection.

17. See KENYA.

18. Country authors provided the data about the year that women won the vote and the year that women won the right to stand for election.

19. The initial information in the section on political measures comes from Alan J. Day, *Political Parties of the World,* 3d ed. (Chicago: St. James Press, 1988); and George E. Delury, *World Encyclopedia of Political Systems and Parties* (New York: Facts on File, 1987).

20. United Nations, *Population and Vital Statistics Report, 1989* (New York: United Nations, 1989).

21. United Nations, *Demographic Yearbook, 1988* (New York: United Nations, 1990).

22. United Nations, *World Statistics in Brief, 1988* (New York: United Nations, 1988).

23. World Bank, *World Development Report, 1987* (Washington, D.C.: World Bank, 1987).

24. UNICEF, *The State of the World's Children, 1988* (New York: Oxford University Press, 1988).

25. Ibid.

26. Ibid.

27. Thomas Kurian, *New Book of World Rankings* (New York: Facts on File, 1984).

28. United Nations, *Compendium of Statistics and Indicators on the Situation of Women, 1986* (New York: United Nations, 1989).

29. United Nations, *Demographic Yearbook, 1988.*

30. United Nations, *World's Women.*

31. Ibid.

32. Ibid.

33. Kurian, *New Book of World Rankings.*

34. World Bank, *World Development Report, 1987.*

35. Kurian, *New Book of World Rankings.*

36. United Nations, *Compendium of Statistics and Indicators on the Situation of Women, 1986.*

37. Ibid.

PART II

▲ *Argentina*

POLITICS

Type of Political System: democracy
  Sovereignty: republic
  Executive-Legislative System: presidential
Type of State: federal
Type of Party System: multiparty
Major Political Parties[a]

Movimiento Nacionalista Justicialista (MNJ, or Justicialist Nationalist Movement): Developed from Gen. Juan Perón's nationalist movement of 1946–55. Reformed in 1973; has experienced numerous splits.

Unión Cívica Radical (UCR, or Radical Civic Union): Has experienced intense factionalism; dates from the late nineteenth century. Represents the moderate center left; is the primary rival of the MNJ but lost the 1989 presidential elections.

Year Women Granted Right to Vote: 1947
*Year Women Granted Right to Stand for
  Election:* 1947
*Percentage of Women in the Legislature
  (1989)*[b]
  Lower House: 5.9%
  Upper House: 8.9%
*Percentage of Electorate Voting for Highest
  Elected Office in Most Recent Election
  (1989):* 85.0%[c]

DEMOGRAPHICS

Population: 31,497,000
Percentage of Population in Urban Areas
  Overall: 84.7%
  Female: 86.0%
  Male: 83.3%
Percentage of Population Below Age 15: 31.0%
Birthrate (per 1,000 population): 23
Maternal Mortality Rate (per 100,000 live
  births): 85

Infant Mortality Rate (per 1,000 live births):
  33
Mortality Rate for Children Under Five (per
  1,000 live births): 39
Average Household Size: 3.8
Mean Age at First Marriage
  Female: 22.9
  Male: 25.3
Life Expectancy
  Female: 72.7
  Male: 65.5

EDUCATION

Ratio of Female to Male Enrollment
  First-Level Education: 97
  Second-Level Education: 112
  Third-Level Education: 113
Literacy Rate
  Female: 92.0%
  Male: 94.0%

ECONOMY

Gross National Product per Capita: U.S.
  $2,130
Percentage of Labor Force in Agriculture:
  14.8%
Distribution of Agricultural Workers by Sex
  Female: 6.4%
  Male: 93.6%
Economically Active Population by Sex
  Female: 26.6%
  Male: 81.4%

a. Arthur S. Banks, ed., *Political Handbook of the World, 1991* (Binghamton, N.Y.: CSA Publications, 1991), 33.
b. Chamber of Deputies, 1989.
c. Ministry of Home Affairs.

From Family Ties to Political Action: Women's Experiences in Argentina

MARÍA DEL CARMEN FEIJOÓ

Argentina is a large federal republic located in the Southern Cone of South America. Its population is highly urban—85 percent of the population of 31.5 million reside in urban areas—and boasts a literacy rate of 93 percent. The majority of the population is white and of European descent and coexists with a *criollos* minority, people of mixed European-native heritage.

Colonized by Spain in the sixteenth century, Argentina has been independent since 1816. According to the constitution, the state's powers are equally divided among the executive, legislative, and judiciary branches of the government and the provincial governors. Historically, however, the state's powers have not been shared equally. Argentina has been ruled in a highly personalist fashion by its presidents and, when the military has taken over the government, by its military dictators.[1]

Although the electoral system is ostensibly multiparty, politics has been dominated by one or two parties—for the first 100 years of independence, by different parties of the landowning agricultural elite. But their monopoly on electoral politics, as well as the stability of the political system as a whole, ended in the early twentieth century with the rise of a party called Unión Cívica Radical (UCR, or the Radical Civic Union), which drew members primarily from the emerging middle class.[2] Since then each of the main social groups—the middle class and the popular class—has been represented by one of two major parties: the Radicalismo and the Peronismo (the Peronist Party), also known as Justicialismo. The Peronist Party, which appeared in the 1940s, draws its members primarily from the trade unions and the working class. Yet neither the Radicals nor the Peronists have been any match for the most powerful player in Argentine

politics for the past 50 years: the military, which has always been closely linked to the dominant classes. Beginning in 1930, when it deposed the third Radical government, the military has stepped into civil politics and appointed a new president or established military rule whenever it has felt its interests or "national security" were threatened. As a result, Argentina has had only 15 years of democratically elected governments between 1955 and 1991.

The cost of this military intervention has been more than just electoral instability. When the military has chosen itself to rule, the population has endured brutal repression and state terror, especially during the rule of Jorge Rafael Videla and Leopoldo F. Galtieri (1976–83). Under their leadership more than 30,000 Argentines were kidnapped, tortured, or murdered. In 1983, after the defeat in the Malvinas/Falklands war, the government was compelled to call elections. Raúl Alfonsín of UCR was elected on a program based on the defense of life, democracy, and human rights. Since then Argentina has been under civilian rule, though the specter of the military continues to haunt politics in the country, significantly affecting the political engagement of men and women.

Slightly less influential forces structuring women's political engagement are the trade unions and the state.[3] The unions, which developed in the early twentieth century, addressed women's issues from the beginning. The Union Gremial Femenina (Feminine Trade Union), founded in 1904, performed an important role in improving working conditions for women. During the 1940s a new trade unionism that incorporated workers from modern industries and services helped give birth to Peronism, a national popular movement that resulted in the Peronist

Party. Even though both unionism and the Peronists had male-dominant views of unions, especially regarding women's problems, both tried to represent working women. Their focus was on women in traditional female industries and occupations, such as food, chemistry, and textile factories, or in service activities like teaching or telephone work.

The primary realm of the state's influence has been the economy, both directly, through its role as employer, and indirectly, through its regulation of other actors in the economy. For example, the state was able to exercise a good deal of influence on labor because unions must often bargain with the Department of Labor before negotiating with individual industries.[4] The state has also played a crucial role in politics by giving and withholding legal recognition of parties and unions and effectively keeping the Peronist Party out of electoral politics from 1955 to 1973.[5]

Women's political engagement has also been shaped by the economy and politics and the contradictions within them. Among Latin American countries Argentina has shown high levels of industrialization, literacy, health, and resource distribution. The military governments of Videla and Galtieri supported a neoliberal economic approach, however. They attempted to open the internal market economy, and they eliminated subsidies to home industries. This process was supported by foreign loans to sustain the import of consumer goods, which led to a large debt. A shrinkage in the productive activity of the economy, a fall in salaries, and a rise in unemployment resulted.[6] At the same time, the military government began to curtail spending on health, education, and welfare programs, further lowering the living standards of the popular sector.[7] Because of its foreign debt, Argentina has been in an economic crisis for the past ten years, with increasing levels of unemployment and high inflation. With the transition to democracy the new civilian government had to confront this difficult situation while trying to consolidate the new democracy. Strong demands were placed on the newly democratic state, which had no resources to answer them. The economic crisis has served as both a

catalyst for Argentine women's political engagement because of its human costs and a constraint on it because survival has at times taken precedence over political action.[8]

By far the most important influence on women's involvement in politics in Argentina has been women's position in the family. In some ways this appears unexceptional. Women's oppression and economic role in the family shape women's experiences, and thus their political engagement, in many countries. But the centrality of the family in shaping Argentine women's political engagement stems more directly from women's identity as wives and mothers.[9] Argentine women are expected to protect the family unit and human life, and both the forms and objectives of Argentine women's political engagement grow out of these commitments.

FROM WORKERS TO CITIZENS

Argentine women's involvement in politics began with the urbanization of the population and the industrialization of the economy in the late nineteenth century. Women as a whole—and particularly those in the urban centers of Buenos Aires, Córdoba, and Rosario—began to work outside the household. In addition to the usual adversity women face in the private sphere, this growing participation in the economy outside the home led to new kinds of oppression for Argentine women: exploitation as workers and discrimination against them as women in the labor market. It also led to women's first engagement in public politics.

Because women were workers, the workers' movement showed some concern for their position in society. As in many other countries, however, this concern on the part of the overwhelmingly male early labor movement did not come from a sincere interest in women's liberation but from traditional male paternalism. The male labor leaders saw women workers' problems as evidence of their need for protection. Despite this paternalism, women did become actively engaged in shaping the political agendas of the anarchist trade union movement and the early Partido Socialista (Socialist Party).[10] Their concerns ranged from an expansion of their rights as workers to an affirmation of their citizenship rights as women to a redefinition of their position within the family. As the range of their demands suggests, both the issues considered most important and the strategies adopted by these first women to engage in public politics varied. The anarchists were primarily concerned with changing the conditions of women workers' lives in the private sphere, which they regarded as the key to women workers' public as well as private oppression. The socialists' agenda and the engagement of some progressive Catholic women's groups was directed to the public sphere: the workplace and working conditions, salaries and wage discrimination, protection of motherhood, the franchise, and women workers' participation in politics.[11]

During the first decade of the twentieth century, middle-class socialist women of European origin were active in groups like the Centro Socialista Femenino (Feminine Socialist Center), Centro Unión y Labor (Union and Work Center), and the Liga Feminista Nacional de la República Argentina (National Feminist League of the Argentine Republic). They wrote in the Socialist Party newspaper, *La Vanguardia* (The Vanguard), and one of them was even able to join the Executive Board of the Socialist Party. Anarchist women, on the other hand, were mainly poorly educated workers. In 1899 they published a newspaper, *La Voz de la Mujer* (Women's Voice), and later they created the Centro Anarquista Feminista (Feminist Anarchist Center). They organized women's strikes in 1904 and 1907. Highly educated women, who were beginning to enroll in even higher education, created the Centro de Universitarias Argentinas (Argentine University Women's Center), the Primer Centro Feminista del Libre Pensamiento (First Feminist Center of the Free Thinking), and the Consejo de Mujeres (Women's Council), which had strong ties to women's organizations in other countries.[12] Meanwhile, organizations inspired by the Catholic church tried to "protect" women, especially young women, and did not question the roots of women's social situation.

In spite of their differing viewpoints, socialist and anarchist women struggled against the subordination of women. Although the anarchists felt that radical changes in the family structure—including free love, communal care of children, and collective families—were the best ways to change the conditions faced by women workers, the socialists concentrated on taking advantage of existing governmental institutions for legal reforms.[13] This engagement on issues related to women's status as workers quickly led to the first wave of the Argentine feminist movement (1895–1914), which originated with socialist women who demanded that their oppression as women be attended to separate from their condition as workers. These women adopted the socialist strategy of pursuing change through legal reforms.

The efforts of the early activists did not radically change women's position in Argentine society, but they did lead to advances in women's legal position. Law 5291, protecting women and children factory workers, was passed in 1907. A law strengthening women's rights in marriage was created in 1926. Women obtained the right to vote in 1947. In present-day Argentina no one dares deny women's equal status, even if it is only given lip service in many cases.[14]

These legal gains made significant changes in women's opportunities. Since the mid-1950s there has been an increase in the number of women in scientific and professional careers, as well as an increase in the number of women educators. The current opportunities and living conditions of Argentine women—especially of middle-class professional women—are better than they are for women in many other Latin American countries. But gender-based discrimination is ingrained in many social practices, and women's position in Argentine society is still far below men's position and privileges.

During the 1970s groups related to the new wave of international feminism appeared. They dealt specifically with women's problems in terms of gender subordination. Among the most important were the Movimiento de Liberación Femenina (Feminine Liberation Movement), the Organización Feminista Argentina (Feminist Argentine Organization), and the Unión Feminista Argentina (Argentine Feminist Union), which began to introduce the new feminist European and American writers locally. Another group tried to develop feminist organizations—like the Movimiento Feminista Popular (Popular Feminist Movement) or the Agrupación de Mujeres Socialistas (Group of Socialist Women)—linked to progressive political parties. All these efforts were limited by the last dictatorship, however.[15] Many of the exiles who have returned since the 1983 transition to democracy have also played a vital role in disseminating feminist thought. Because of their efforts and factors like the growth of Latin American feminism, the Movimiento Feminista Argentino (Argentine Feminist Movement) was created in 1990 as a national-level organization trying to support the networking of small, isolated groups. Gatherings of women from all over the country have been held every year since 1985. The July 1991 Encuentro Nacional de Mujeres (National Meeting of Women) drew about 6,000 women from feminist groups, grass-roots organizations, and political parties. Differences between feminists and other women's groups are not as clear-cut as these groupings may suggest; the ideological trends of both are continuously changing. Even if the boundaries are indistinct, however, feminine or women's groups intend to improve women's condition without questioning male dominance and social organization. Feminist groups sustain critical views of male dominance, patriarchy, machismo, and discrimination. Even though their strategies are different, both help to pose the women's question in the public agenda.

WOMEN AND POLITICAL PARTIES

Legal gains have had little impact on the formal politics of parties and governing institutions or on women's participation in these structures. Argentine political parties still are male dominated,

and for the most part women have been the rank-and-file members, performing menial tasks. The few women who have managed to attain positions of party leadership have usually had a family relationship with a male party leader. Eva and Isabel Perón are unusual because of the heights they reached, but the way they rose to power is typical of how women reach such positions within the parties. Eva Perón, who was Gen. Juan Perón's wife, played an important role in Argentine politics from 1946 until her death in 1952.[16] Although she preferred to deal with social welfare issues, she was able to pose her action not in the traditional terms of help to the poor but in terms of social justice—fighting oligarchy and powerful groups. She never held a formal elected political position, and when she was nominated for the vice-presidency the military objected, citing her radical views on social matters. Isabel Perón, third wife of General Perón, was elected as her husband's vice-president in 1973. After his death the next year she became president, holding the position until she was overthrown by a military coup in 1976.[17]

In general the parties have made little effort to place issues important to women on their agendas. Supporting women's issues has been considered risky for party leaders, who fear losing their less progressive voters. And because the feminist movement is generally considered a middle-class women's movement, adopting a feminist stance has been thought of as politically dangerous for parties and politicians trying to win over the popular classes. On the few occasions when male politicians have made specific attempts to win support from women, they have done so only to achieve their electoral or legislative goals. As a result, a serious long-term commitment to women's issues has yet to be built, both among Radicals and Peronists.

This neglect of women's concerns has not been limited to the major parties. Only one of the minor parties—the Socialist Party—has allowed women into leadership or shown any sensitivity to women's issues. Since the beginning of the twentieth century the Socialist Party has been relatively open to women's concerns, thanks to the role played by Alicia Moreau de Justo in its early leadership. Alicia Moreau was a young English émigré whose parents were exiles from the Paris Commune. She was one of the first physicians in the country and specialized in women's health. She also published several magazines and newspapers and wrote the 1945 book *La Mujer en la democracia* (Women in democracy).[18] In spite of her age during the last dictatorship (she was past 90), she performed a crucial role in defending human rights by linking historical socialist feminism, modern feminism, and human rights defense. But even the Socialist Party does not always see women's issues as relevant. Socialists often approach women's condition as women simply as an outgrowth of women's condition as workers.

The one attempt to create a party more geared to women's interests was short-lived. Following the rise of Eva Perón and the attainment of suffrage, the Partido Peronista Femenino (Feminist Peronist Party) was created. One of the main goals of the party was to incorporate women into politics; women had little experience within the institutional life of parties until then. Social and welfare activities also were among the objectives of the party. These newly organized women educated their children and their communities through Peronist *unidades básicas* (political community centers), which they built in their neighborhoods. This kind of organization became an example of grass-roots development as various generations of women learned to participate in activities outside the household. With Eva Perón's death, however, the Feminist Peronist Party rapidly declined in political power and became one of the most conservative branches of the Peronist movement.[19]

This lack of gender sensitivity among the parties has affected the number of women elected to government positions. For the most part, women have not been nominated on either the national or local level. On the rare occasions when a party has picked women as candidates, it has generally placed them at the bottom of the list. Consequently, few women have been elected on either the national or local level. Since 1951,

when a quota system was briefly instituted, there have never been more than 29 women in Parliament.[20]

Even when elected, women have not had the same opportunities in policy making as men. They have rarely been appointed to the more powerful parliamentary committees that deal with the budget and the armed forces. Rather, the women elected to Parliament are asked to concentrate on education, social services, health, and child care—less influential areas related to women's traditional roles.[21] This situation is a result of men's discrimination and women's self-exclusion: women perceive themselves as being in the right place only when dealing with problems related to their supposedly natural interest in motherhood.

Because women's participation is rising in almost all realms of public life, and because family and private relations are growing more democratic, women's greater involvement in formal politics should have been expected. On the contrary, women's participation in parties and governing institutions has been declining since 1952, dropping dramatically in 1958 when only two of the national deputies were women.[22] Professional women have increasingly stayed away from political party activity, and no other women have taken their place. Some of this decline can be explained by the generally unstable political conditions of the last 50 years and the continuing military involvement in politics, but even this has a gender-specific dimension. It is clear that women's and men's understanding of their civic rights has developed in a climate that does not favor the growth of democratic behavior. Learning the rules of formal democratic politics has perhaps been difficult for everyone under military regimes, but at least men have had the chance to participate in politics and state administration. The patriarchal approach to government that underlies military rule has excluded women from government positions. As a result, women find it more difficult to participate in political parties and state institutions when democracy is reinstated. In addition, women have not yet been strong enough to demand a gender-based distribution of power within formal politics, like the quota system.

Argentine women have maintained a capacity for political engagement in other forms, however, primarily in the grass-roots social movements of "informal politics" or the "new ways of doing politics." Women's active presence in the 1907 tenant strike in Buenos Aires, when poor families living in *conventillos* (tenements) confronted the owners, may be the earliest example of this kind of mobilization.[23] Since then, though using different approaches, women have mainly been involved in struggles related to their homes and living conditions. Whether these kinds of actions indicate political concerns is still under discussion. This kind of spontaneous, circumscribed participation does not easily give birth to the more conventional pattern of political participation.

These movements are again playing a remarkable role as an answer to state terrorism and in regard to the "human and family costs" of adjustment policies. Their size and scope have varied, from large nationwide movements like the one that opposed human rights abuses to the activities of *sociedades de fomento* (neighborhood associations). Although women are not the exclusive members of these movements, they have been the primary participants and catalysts in their creation.[24]

During the 1976–83 dictatorship of Videla and Galtieri, one form of state terrorism was to kidnap, torture, and detain political militants, then murder them and hide their remains. Between 20,000 and 30,000 individuals disappeared during the period. In early 1977, a group of mothers and grandmothers banded together to find their missing children and grandchildren. The group, which became known as the Madres (Mothers) de Plaza de Mayo, raised the first public voice against the military regime and state terrorism. The women drew on their identity as mothers by wearing diapers, traditional symbols of motherhood, as scarves on their heads. By taking advantage of the sacred value of motherhood to gain public support and to decrease their chances of being repressed, the Madres de Plaza

de Mayo were a decisive force in mobilizing national and international public opinion against the military regime.[25]

The group performed (and continues performing today) its weekly Thursday march at Plaza de Mayo square, the historical center of the city since colonial times. It is surrounded by the Government House, the old Cabildo (colonial government house), the town hall of Buenos Aires, and the national cathedral. Who were these women? The women, in general, were middle-class housewives and women engaged in traditional women's jobs, such as teaching. They met each other casually while struggling with civil and military red tape to find out about their missing children. When they realized how many individuals were missing—usually adolescents and young people—they decided to organize. Although the mothers used this type of protest to take advantage of the supposedly sacred role of motherhood, which they thought would protect them from direct attacks or prison, their choice of activity was more than tactical in the long term. Fathers were never able to sustain public activity in the face of the harsh military regime. Their reluctance may also be explained by society's understanding of family and child care as women's responsibilities. Nor was sacred motherhood strong enough to prevent the mothers from being jailed or even from being disappeared themselves. Azucena Villaflor, one of the first organizers of the Madres disappeared in 1977 while attending a mass for missing children.

Until the Malvinas, or Falklands, war in 1982 the group was one of the few to publicly denounce the government's violation of human rights. It was involved in numerous activities against the dictatorship, and it played an extraordinary role in disseminating information about Argentina's internal situation to the international community. At the same time, it developed an agenda that sought trial and imprisonment for those involved in human rights violations.

In spite of the group's tremendous influence and political power, the Madres de Plaza de Mayo has chosen not to become a formal political player since the transition to democracy. The group does not want to negotiate its demands or to be identified with political parties; in this way it has retained its identity as a defender of ethical principles.

The Madres said that the struggle for human rights was of an ethical nature and thus could not be subsumed in any political trend. Later, as democracy consolidated, the movement developed a subgroup, the Línea Fundadora (Founding Line), that became involved in the Comisión Nacional de Desaparición de Personas (National Commission for the Disappeared). Perhaps the most important difference between the subgroup and the original group was related to their expectations about democratic justice and its ability to punish the military for its abuses. Unluckily, Alfonsín's government suffered constant pressure from the military, and many of those deserving punishment, including some found guilty in trials, were released. Carlos Menem, the Peronist president elected in 1989, has continued this trend, finally passing an *indulto* (general amnesty) in December 1990 for those convicted in court. The goal of the indulto was the reconciliation of society.

WOMEN'S RESPONSE TO THE ECONOMIC CRISIS

This commitment to family and the concern with the human costs of adjustment policies reappear in women's political engagement in the movement that formed in response to the economic crisis. Argentina, having experienced several Peronist governments, was one of the oldest welfare states in South America until the mid-1970s.[26] But the shift in social and economic trends supported by the last dictatorship focused on destroying these structures. Additionally, since the return to democracy in 1983, the state has intentionally worsened living conditions to meet strict conditions imposed by the International Monetary Fund for economic aid. The historically high inflation rate increased to exorbitant levels in the latter half of the 1980s, reaching a peak in 1989 with an annual increase of 4,927 percent. Meanwhile, salaries fell and unemployment grew.[27] In 1988 the poverty rate reached 45 percent of the Buenos Aires metropolitan population.[28]

In this context women's consumer organizations, dormant since the military took over, reappeared. Some were the old middle-class groups that dealt with the traditional problem of the cost of living and the difficulties it created in household economies. But most were new and dealt instead with survival issues. This change indicated the degree that living conditions had worsened. With huge groups of the population unable to afford daily subsistence, lower-class women returned to the social scene in dramatic numbers.

These loosely organized groups are scattered throughout the most important urban centers, especially in and around Buenos Aires, an area that holds one-third of the population of the country. Group members perform activities at the household and grass-roots level—responding to survival issues with communal kitchens, for example. Their collective action has not developed enough to constitute leagues or federations, as in Peru and Bolivia, where the population has been confronting the problem of worsening living conditions for at least two decades. In many cases, neighborhood women's groups in Argentina have close relations with churches or nongovernmental organizations rather than with political parties.

Since 1988 the leaders of this movement have come from the popular classes, which are especially affected by structural adjustment policies. In 1989, as the cost of living continued to grow and the problem of hunger became increasingly pervasive, women and men of the popular classes began the first bread riots in Argentine history, expressing their frustration in the form of *saqueos* (pillages). These spontaneous grass-roots protests in the poorest districts of Buenos Aires were an unpleasant surprise for the whole society. Rather than revolutionary answers to poverty, they were hopeless answers to hunger and uncertainty in a hyperinflationary context. Though the state was democratic, it responded to these riots with repression: sixteen civilians were killed, and about 200 were wounded.[29] Since the state's crackdown the rioting has subsided, and many new groups are trying to ease the hunger problem by creating multifamily kitchens and communal gardens. Women consider these activities an extension of their maternal role—taking care of family reproductive conditions under special constraints—rather than collective or political action. Perhaps this is why all these activities are performed by women and why there is no women's leadership appearing as a result. These women are unaware of the magnitude of this process. Each views herself as providing individual solutions, answering a social emergency that might one day disappear and restore the "natural" order to family life and the male to the position of breadwinner.[30]

The nature and form of women's future engagement in these key areas are unclear. As long as Argentina remains under democratic rule, there is little need for women to continue defending human rights, with the exception of Madres de Plaza de Mayo, which will continue demanding justice. Still, as long as democratic governments follow a path of reconciliation with the military and forgive the violations of human rights, the women's human rights organizations will continue to play an important role in maintaining ethics in politics and in preserving the collective memory of the genocide. In regard to popular-sector women's involvement in issues related to living conditions and survival, we can predict that the role of women will be increasingly relevant because recession and poverty are becoming the main threats to society. Even if women's participation is rooted in their identity as wives and mothers (what has been called the vicarious identity), both types of experiences have the potential to bring about radical changes in women's identity.

There is little doubt that women's participation in these causes, and especially in the human rights movement, has affected Argentine politics. In the dictatorship's breakdown after the Malvinas/Falklands war, women were crucial to delegitimating the government.[31] Whether or not the movements have chosen to institutionalize and become forces in the formal political arena, they still are influential and recognized political actors. And by raising issues through movements directly related to the family women have enlarged the arena of politics.

Women's engagement also suggests the need for changes in, or at least further reflection on, the common understanding of women's political engagement and the shape of politics in general. At the least, the forms and goals of women's political engagement suggest the need for a reevaluation of the traditional understanding of their political behavior as wives who merely follow their husbands' political lead. In addition to women's greater participation in the new social movements, there has been a difference in their electoral behavior. In 1983 women voted overwhelmingly for Alfonsín while their husbands and sons voted for the Peronist candidate, Italo Luder.[32]

Their engagement also suggests the need to let go of the assumption that women's political positions can be evaluated in terms of the traditional left/right axis. Their political orientation seems based on ideas and values, democratic norms, and the preservation of life and family, which do not fit the traditional left and right labels. As such, these new movements, and especially the Madres, support an argument made by both Julieta Kirkwood and Rossana Rossanda, who assert that women's engagement in politics, based on "women's" values like preservation of life, and their interest in upholding of principles rather than achieving tangible results, is profoundly different from men's way of doing politics. Their involvement may signify not only an expansion of the political arena but also the beginning of a new kind of political action centered on "female" values.[33]

Democratic stability is a necessary though insufficient condition for building women's movements. If women's participation reflects problems related to the political scenery and to specific gender questions, democratic stability will make it possible to address gender problems. To reinforce what has been built up so far, however, the women's movements must produce new leaders. The challenge lies in moving from past actions to a clear empowerment with a gender orientation and new leadership. To reach these objectives, it will be necessary to have different strategies for different fields, including political parties, survival organizations, and human rights groups.

Although these new movements represent a widening of the political arena, the birth of new issues, and the development of new political actors, it must be remembered that the movements were shaped by the attitudes and practices of Argentine politics. The success of these movements may be due less to a new family-centered way of politics than to the mobilizing effects of authoritarianism. Some authors have posed that, as a rule, dictatorships help to mobilize political movements. After mobilization comes institutionalization of democracy and the search for "the rule of the law." If this is true, the time for the rule of the law has come for Argentine women. Their success may also be the result of new ideas and issues that could not be accommodated within the old political party platforms.[34]

Most of the optimism over the coming of a new kind of politics arose during the height of the transition to democracy. Since then the movements have subsided. Even if there is a crisis of meaning in the party system, the parties still appear to be the main vehicles for participation. Whether or not women's political engagement represents the arrival of a new way of doing politics, it should not be forgotten that there are problems with adopting the tactics they have adopted as a democratic norm. One must consider why that engagement appears only during times of crisis.[35]

Perhaps this form of engagement is related to women's position within the family, which legitimizes their actions in moments of crisis but sends them back home afterward. To strengthen women's presence in the public world, another new rationale must be built to legitimize them outside the household during "normal" periods and to support their rights as autonomous individuals. If this viewpoint cannot be developed, women will continue their activities in matrifocal and feminized neighborhood networks only, performing communal tasks, unable to strengthen the participation of women as such. The worst possible result will be one of high visibility in informal politics coupled with a persistent absence from the formal democratic party-linked structures.

PROSPECTS

The character of women's political engagement for the past 40 years can be summed up in the two major symbols: Eva Perón and the Madres de Plaza de Mayo. In spite of their differences, both represent the high profile women have had in Argentine politics. Both also became involved in politics through their roles as wives and mothers. They entered politics during times of crisis and decisively affected history, yet neither was able to change women's position in politics. The future for Argentine women depends on the forces that made the change impossible and the ways Argentine women can use the structures of power to their own advantage.

There are signs that women's engagement in the political parties may increase. A small group of women recently attained leadership positions in a right-wing party, Unión de Centro Democrático (UCEDE, or Union of the Democratic Center). The new Trotskyist party, Movimiento Al Socialismo (Movement Toward Socialism), also has shown some openness to women's issues and to women's participation in party leadership. There has also been discussion over the use of quotas to increase the number of women in Parliament thanks to women from the Radical Party who complained about the absence of women from party lists and Parliament. Even though quota participation is not new to Argentina, the pros and cons are again being discussed. Today, the issue is posed as an example of positive discrimination. Use of quotas by the Feminist Peronist Party in 1952 resulted in the highest number of women ever elected to Parliament.[36] But adopting a quota system will not ensure that women's interests are represented because not all Argentine women are feminists, nor do they all have an interest in women's issues. In fact, the women who have attained power in UCEDE do not appear to have any interest in women's issues. Neither will it mean that more women—or more diverse types of women—will become involved in politics. Nevertheless, using quotas would ensure that some women will always be present in Parliament. The quota system, which usually sets aside one-third or one-quarter of the party list for women, would help to develop women's leadership because the availability of positions would be previously known to potential candidates, thus stimulating women's nominations. Under current rules, women will only be included if they can mount certain types of pressure or have certain like linkages—family ties—with party structures. In November 1991 a law was passed requiring party lists for national positions to be made up of at least 30 percent women. The law was scheduled to go into effect for the first time with the November 1993 elections.

Because women's current political engagement grows out of their economic role and their position within the family, it is likely that women's future engagement will be affected by changes occurring in both these areas. As a result of the economic crisis, women's role in the family and the economy are in transition. During the past decade, their participation in the economically active population, especially among women heads of household and middle-aged women, has grown markedly. The amount of time women spend on housework and the domestic production of the goods and services they no longer can purchase has also been growing. Women are becoming increasingly involved in communal networks for economic survival because of neoliberal state policies that cut budgets for activities historically performed by the state, transferring them to society.[37] Studies of Argentina and other Latin American countries show that the new social actors who become responsible for these activities are women. Women shape informal communal networks, based on solidarity and mutual support.[38] The impact of this changing economic role on the nature of Argentine women's political engagement is unclear. If women's political engagement has been determined by the role a woman's family plays in her political identity,

then women's changing economic role within the family may mean more commitment to issues related to the survival of the family and the human costs of state policies. But it implies a relevant presence in the public sphere as women confront the state in their struggle for livelihood.

Another factor that will affect women's political engagement is the state's approach to women's concerns. In response to political campaigns that raised women's issues and to the impact of the U.N. Decade for Women, the state has made efforts to address those issues. A law that criminalized sex discrimination, another on divorce, and a third on *patria potestad* (parenthood rights shared by both parents) were passed under Alfonsín. During Alfonsín's term the Undersecretariat of Women, a subcabinet-level department, was created. The goal of the undersecretariat was to support government programs on gender-related issues. Unfortunately, the undersecretariat's power has been limited by its placement in the Ministry of Social Welfare and in the Secretariat of Children and Family, a traditional setting for women's issues.[39] The provincial governments have also developed state programs to deal with women's issues. Generally these state programs have been caught between looking at these issues in terms of traditional social welfare issues or approaching them only in terms of class inequalities, ignoring the issue of gender subordination.

The province of Buenos Aires, the largest provincial state, has adopted a new approach to bringing women into the government by creating a council modeled on the *conselhos da mulher* (women's councils) in Brazil.[40] The proposed council offers a broad structure in which women's problems may be represented. Instead of ministries, secretariats, or undersecretariats, the idea is to organize horizontal structures involving a variable number of people (five or six or more) to represent the multiple ways of being a woman in a society where women confront subordination in terms of gender, class, regional origins, race, and culture.

Argentine women's political engagement will

also depend on whether a broadly based women's movement can be formed. But even though a formal movement does not exist, feminism has made some women's concerns unavoidable social and political issues. During the democratic consolidation, women's activities assured that laws governing divorce and nondiscrimination were passed by Parliament. Despite the absence of a strong feminist movement, the role played by women in mass media must be stressed. Some have made important contributions to the understanding of women's problems within a gender perspective. Male Argentine politicians have been forced to take stands on some women's issues and face the electoral consequences of their stances, but there has also been silence and opposition surrounding many women's issues.

One of those issues is reproductive rights. Argentine governments have historically supported pro-natalist viewpoints, given the low population density of the country as a whole. In 1974, during the third Peronist government, decree number 3938 prohibited the public distribution of contraceptive devices, thus affecting human rights, especially those of women. Small groups of women lobbied against this decree, and it was revoked in 1986. Other groups continue to make demands related to reproductive rights, access to contraception, and the decriminalization of abortion.[41] But many politicians still oppose granting reproductive rights and permission for abortion under such special circumstances as rape. In spite of Argentine women's capacity to break through a similar silence surrounding the repression practiced by the Videla and Galtieri governments, women have had little success in raising reproductive issues under Alfonsín and Menem.

Until recently there has been no attempt to bring together the different movements in which women have been engaged. An initial step toward building networks among these groups and an attempt to remove the perception that the women's movement is a middle-class movement was taken in several cities when women politicians, feminists, women from the human rights movement, women, from the popular sectors, and others were invited to meet and exchange experiences. By coming together with women from different classes and different experiences, Argentine women can begin to realize their commonalities as women. But transcending these differences will require a gender-inspired will and the capacity to build a common gender-based language. If there is to be an Argentine women's movement, the Third World feminism of other Latin American countries must become the goal of the movement as well.

Developing a feminist movement will also require efforts to expand the number and type of women involved in politics. Observations by Caroline Moser and Cecilia Blondet on women's grass-roots involvement in Ecuador and Peru ring true for Argentina as well. Most of the Argentine women who have been politically engaged in the formal political arena or in the informal social movements have been middle-aged women with grown children. They have usually belonged to the wide social stratum called the popular sectors. Broadening the base to younger women, who still have significant familial responsibilities, would have the practical benefit of providing future members and leadership. It would bring into politics women who have been occupied solely with their families, and it would affirm women's growing independence from the family. Broadening the base will likely strengthen the connection between women's political engagement and their role in the family.[42]

The future success of Argentine women's political engagement will require further emphasizing the female face of hunger and poverty.[43] Although women and politicians acknowledge the problem, they have spent little time trying to reform the gender bias within urban and social policy that leads to it. Urban and social policy makers do not even question the gender division of labor within the household and take it for granted that women will work for free in the home. As a result, having or not having food on the table is considered a private issue and women's responsibility. Recently, some middle-class consumers' leagues have become involved in this problem, but it requires more attention. Groups like Asociación de Defensa del Consumidor (Consumer's Defense Association) and Liga de Amas de Casa (Housewives League) defend the interests of householders with average incomes who are worried about the high cost of living. The effort to broaden their scope to act in the way consumer associations do in highly developed countries is hindered by the difficult economic situation. Whether women's engagement in movements based on the family will help or hurt their drive for full equality in citizenship is unclear. By anchoring their political engagement in the private realm, these movements have expanded what is understood as public and political. Yet women, by initially engaging in these movements as mothers and wives and keepers of the family, may not gain the equal citizenship they also seek.[44] In fact, women's political engagement in these movements may end up tying them even more tightly into their traditional roles. But it may be, as Maruja Barrig's research on women in Peru suggests, that this new type of participation merely changes the dimensions of women's imprisonment in the private sphere, from the household to communal boundaries and the physical space of the neighborhood.[45]

What seems most likely is that any type of political engagement on the part of women will produce changes in the dynamic of power in the household, which in turn will produce changes in the male-dominated power structures of public life. Thus, even if women's political engagement stems from their identities as wives and mothers, these identities will, in the end, affect their lives positively. Demanding a water supply in the neighborhood, for example, compels women to go out of the household and confront the state.[46] If this is a regular activity, as these kind of demands increasingly are, housewives will need to change the structure of the household, looking for support from other people—older daughters or even husbands and men. When they go back to their homes, these women will have gone through an experience that, independent of their goals, has empowered them as women and as citizens. Both kinds of change will probably have

an impact on their household relationships and on their private lives.

The most influential determinant of women's political engagement will probably be whether they are able to build a different understanding of women's position in the family, especially as mothers, which retains the importance and symbolism of the identity but at the same time allows for an autonomous person with interests separate from those of her children and family. If Argentine women are able to "take back" motherhood, gain control of the public meanings of their identity within the family, and reclaim their experiences, politics and the understanding of what is political will be fundamentally changed.

NOTES

1. Peter Snow, "Argentina: Politics in a Conflict Society," in Howard J. Wiarda and Harvey F. Kline, eds., *Latin American Politics and Development*, 2nd ed. (Boulder, Colo.: Westview, 1985), 153–55.

2. Ibid., 130.

3. Ibid., 145–57.

4. Ibid., 155.

5. Ibid.

6. Roberto Frenkel and Mario Damill, *Política de estabilización y mercado de trabajo: Argentina 1985–1987* (Stabilization policy and the labor market: Argentina 1985–1987) (Buenos Aires: CEDES, 1988).

7. Adriana Marshall, *Políticas sociales: El modelo neoliberal* (Social policies: The neoliberal mode) (Buenos Aires: Legasa, 1988).

8. María del Carmen Feijoó and Elizabeth Jelin, "Women from Low Income Sectors: Economic Recession and Democratization of Politics in Argentina," in UNICEF, *The Invisible Adjustment* (Santiago: UNICEF, 1988).

9. Beatriz Schmukler, *Las estrategias de negociación de las madres en familias populares* (The negotiation strategies of mothers in popular families) (Buenos Aires: FLACSO, 1986).

10. María del Carmen Feijoó, "Las feministas" (The feminists), in Oscar Troncoso, *La vida de nuestro pueblo* (Buenos Aires: CEAL, 1980).

11. Iacov Oved, *El anarquismo y el movimiento obrero en la Argentina* (Anarchismo and the labor market in Argentina) (Mexico: Siglo XXI, 1978).

12. Ibid., 10.

13. Maxine Molyneux, "No God, No Boss, No Hus-

band: Anarchist Feminism in Nineteenth Century Argentina," in *Latin American Perspectives* (Beverly Hills, Calif.: Sage Publications, Winter 1986).

14. Marysa Navarro, *Evita* (Buenos Aires: Corregidor, 1981).

15. Inés Cano, "El movimiento feminista argentino en la década del 70" (The Argentine feminist movement in the 1970s), in *Todo es historia,* no. 183 (Buenos Aires, August 1982).

16. Navarro, *Evita*, 14.

17. David Rock, *Argentina, 1516–1987: Desde la colonización española hasta Alfonsín* (Argentina, 1516–1987: From Spanish colonization to Alfonsín) (Buenos Aires: Alianza, 1989).

18. Lily Sosa de Newton, *Diccionario biográfico de mujeres argentinas* (Biographical dictionary of Argentine women) (Buenos Aires: Diccionarios Biográficos Argentinos, 1972).

19. Susana Bianchi and Norma Sanchis, *El partido peronista femenino* (The feminist Peronist party), vol. 2 (Buenos Aires: CEAL, 1988).

20. Nelly Casas, "Qué pasó con las mujeres políticas a partir del 51" (What has happened with political women since 1951), in *Formación política para la democracia* (Buenos Aires: Redacción, 1982).

21. *La Nación,* 15 September 1990.

22. Ibid., 20.

23. Juan Suriano, "Las mujeres en la huelga de conventillos en 1907" (Women in the tenement house strike of 1907) (Buenos Aires, 1987, Mimeographed).

24. Ibid., 8.

25. María del Carmen Feijoó and Mónica Gogna, "Las mujeres en la transición a la democracia" (Women in the transition to democracy), in Elizabeth Jelin, ed., *Ciudadanía e identidad: las mujeres en los movimientos sociales en America Latina* (Ginebra: UNRISD, 1987), 79–114.

26. Ernesto Suani et al., *Estado democrático y política social* (The democratic state and social policy) (Buenos Aires: Eudeba, 1989).

27. *El Cronista Comercial,* 24 September 1990.

28. Instituto Nacional de Estadística y Censos, *La pobreza en el conurbano bonaerense* (Poverty in the Buenos Aires suburbs) (Buenos Aires: INDEC, 1989).

29. *Ambito Financiero,* 1 August 1989.

30. Alberto Minujin, "From 'Secondary Workers' to Breadwinners: Poor and Non-Poor Women Facing the Crisis" (Buenos Aires, 1990, Mimeographed).

31. Ibid., 25.

32. María del Carmen Feijoó, "The Challenge of Constructing Civilian Peace: Women and Democracy in Argentina," in Jane Jaquette, ed., *The Women's Movement in Latin America: Feminism and the Transition to Democracy* (Boston: Unwin Hyman, 1989), 72–94.

33. Julieta Kirkwood, *Ser política en Chile: Las feministas y los partidos* (To be political in Chile: Feminists and the parties) (Santiago: FLACSO, 1986); Rossana Rossanda, *Las otras* (The others) (Barcelona: Gediba, 1982).

34. Francisco Weffort, "Dilemas de la legitimidad política" (Dilemmas of political legitimacy), *Revista de la CEPAL,* no. 35 (Santiago, Chile: CEPAL, 1988).

35. Ibid., 32.

36. Ibid., 19.

37. Ibid., 28.

38. Servicios Urbanos y Mujeres de Bajos Ingresos, *Servicios para las mujeres: Programas y políticas* (Services for women: Programs and policies) (Lima: SUMBI, 1986).

39. Fundación Arturo Illía/Fundación Plural, *Políticas públicas dirigidas a la mujer* (Public policies addressed toward women) (Buenos Aires: Fundación Illía and Fundación Plural, 1987).

40. Sonia Alvarez, "Women's Movements and Gender Politics in the Brazilian Transition," in Jaquette, ed., *Women's Movement in Latin America,* 18–71.

41. Jorge Balán and Silvina Ramos, *La medicalización del comportamiento reproductivo: un estudio exploratorio sobre la demanda de anticonceptivos en los sectores populares* (The medicalization of reproductive behavior: An exploratory study of the demand for contraceptives in the popular sectors) (Buenos Aires: CEDES, 1989).

42. Caroline Moser, "Women's Needs in the Urban System: Training Strategies in Gender-Aware Planning," in Marianne Schmink, Judith Bruce, and Marilyn Kohn, eds., *Learning About Women and Urban Services in Latin America and the Caribbean* (New York: Population Council, 1985); and Cecilia Blondet, "Las organizaciones femeninas y la política en época de crisis" (Women's organizations and politics in a time of crisis) (Buenos Aires, 1989, Mimeographed).

43. María del Carmen Feijoó, *Las respuestas de las mujeres frente a la crisis* (Women's responses to the crisis) (Buenos Aires, 1990, Mimeographed).

44. Feijoó and Gogna, "Las mujeres en la transición a la democracia," in Jelin, ed., *Ciudadanía e identidad,* 79–114.

45. Maruja Barrig and Amelia Fort, *La ciudad de las mujeres: Pobladoras y servicios. El caso del Agustino* (The city of women: Squatters and services. The case of Agustino) (Lima: SUMBI, 1987).

46. María del Carmen Feijoó, "Las mujeres en los barrios: de los problemas locales a los problemas de género" (Women in the neighborhoods: From local problems to gender problems), in *Materiales para la comunicación popular,* no. 5 (Lima: CET, 1984).

▲ Australia

POLITICS

Type of Political System: democracy
  Sovereignty: constitutional monarchy
  Executive-Legislative System: parliamentary
Type of State: federal
Type of Party System: multiparty
Major Political Parties

Australian Labor Party: Founded in 1891 as the political wing of the labor movement; in government in 1992 in four of the six states and at the federal level. Affiliated with the Socialist International.

Liberal Party of Australia: Founded in 1944; took the place of a series of parties that had represented conservative interests. Not affiliated with the Liberal International; more akin to the British Conservative Party than to liberal parties elsewhere.

National Party of Australia: Founded in 1920 as the Country Party to represent rural interests. At the federal level, in coalition with the Liberal Party in 1992.

Australian Democrats: Founded in 1977 in a breakaway of progressives from the Liberal Party; in 1992 held the balance of power in the Australian Senate. Strong commitment to environmental and social justice issues.

Green Independents: Have achieved some parliamentary representation in recent elections.

Year Women Granted Right to Vote: 1894/1902[a]
Year Women Granted Right to Stand for Election: 1894/1902[b]
Percentage of Women in the Legislature[c]
  Lower House: 6.7%
  Upper House: 25.0%
Percentage of Electorate Voting for Highest Elected Office in Most Recent Election (1990): 95.8%[d]

DEMOGRAPHICS

Population: 16,532,000
Percentage of Population in Urban Areas
  Overall: 85.7%
  Female: 86.6%
  Male: 84.8%
Percentage of Population Below Age 15: 23.6%
Birthrate (per 1,000 population): 15
Maternal Mortality Rate (per 100,000 live births): 8
Infant Mortality Rate (per 1,000 live births): 9
Mortality Rate for Children Under Five (per 1,000 live births): 10
Average Household Size: 3.1
Mean Age at First Marriage
  Female: 23.5
  Male: 25.7
Life Expectancy
  Female: 78.8
  Male: 72.3

EDUCATION

Ratio of Female to Male Enrollment
  First-Level Education: 95
  Second-Level Education: 99
  Third-Level Education: 111[e]
Literacy Rate
  Male: 100%
  Female: 100%

ECONOMY

Gross National Product per Capita: U.S. $10,830
Percentage of Labor Force in Agriculture: 6.9%
Distribution of Agricultural Workers by Sex
  Female: 27.5%
  Male: 72.5%
Economically Active Population by Sex[f]
  Female: 52.3%
  Male: 75.4%

a. In 1894 women in South Australia gained the right to vote; in 1902 the federal franchise was extended to all women over 21 years of age.

b. In 1894 women in South Australia were allowed to stand for election; in 1902 the right was extended to all women over 21 years of age.

c. Department of the Parliamentary Library Information Service, Parliament House, "Current List of Women Members of Federal and State Parliaments" (Canberra, July 1992).

d. Australian Electoral Commission, *Election Statistics, 1990* (Canberra: Australian Government Publishing Service, 1990).

e. Commonwealth of Australia, *Women in Australia:*

Australia's Second Progress Report on Implementing the United Nations Convention on the Elimination of All Forms of Discrimination Against Women (Canberra: AEPS, 1992).

f. Australian Bureau of Statistics, *The Labour Force, Australia: April 1991,* no. 6203.0.

Locked Out or Locked In? Women and Politics in Australia

MARIAN SAWER

Australia, an island continent of almost 3 million square miles, lies in the Southern Hemisphere between the Pacific and Indian oceans. Because much of the interior is arid, nearly two-thirds of the population of 17 million is concentrated in the two southeastern states of New South Wales and Victoria and more than one-third in the state capitals, Sydney and Melbourne. Since the nineteenth century Australia has been one of the most urbanized countries in the world. The national capital is the small city of Canberra.

The main landmass and its surrounding islands were inhabited by Aboriginal people thought to have come from Southeast Asia some 40,000 years ago. Australia was colonized by the British in 1788; its first European settlers were convicts from English, Irish, and Scottish jails. Because immigration policy favored Northern European groups until the 1950s, three-quarters of Australians are of British or Irish extraction. After World War II policy was liberalized, and through large-scale immigration from the Mediterranean region and more recently from Southeast Asia, people from non-English-speaking countries and their children now constitute about one-fifth of the population.

Significant numbers of foreign-born Australians were recorded during the 1986 census, including those who were German-born (3.8 percent of the total population), Italian-born (3.7 percent), Greek-born (2 percent), Dutch-born

(1.4 percent), and Chinese-born (1.2 percent). The census also recorded an increase—to 1.4 percent—in the proportion of the population identifying themselves as Torres Strait Islanders or Aborigines. Torres Strait Islanders are a Melanesian people who arrived after the mainland Aborigines.

The first industries developed for export were wool, meat, and wheat. Since World War II mineral exports, particularly coal and iron ore, have been of increased importance. Australia, which possesses 30 percent of the world's uranium reserves, does not have a nuclear industry, and the restricted mining of uranium for export ("the three mines policy") has been highly controversial.

Nineteenth-century settlers imported the radical demands of the British Chartists, and Australia became a pioneer of such democratic innovations as manhood suffrage (introduced in the 1850s), the secret ballot, payment of members of Parliament, and electoral systems designed to achieve "one vote, one value." Since the founding of the colonies, government has played an important role in providing economic and social infrastructure. Australians have always had an instrumental approach to government, seeing it first as an engine of economic development and later as a guarantor of material welfare.

Wages and conditions of employment for the majority of the Australian work force have been determined by quasi-judicial industrial tribunals since the early 1900s. Australia became one of the first countries to establish a minimum wage based on a worker's need to support a family. Through a series of national wage case decisions, the family wage was replaced by the equal pay concept, most notably with the 1972 "equal pay for work of equal value" decision. In spite of significant increases in women's wages prompted by this decision, women—who currently constitute 42 percent of the paid work force—still earn only 85 percent of the average weekly wage earned by men. There is a high degree of gender segregation, and undervaluing of female jobs contributes to the pay differential.

The colonies were granted self-government during the nineteenth century. The movement for federation in the 1890s led to the creation of the Commonwealth of Australia in 1901, with the six colonies becoming states of the Commonwealth. National political institutions reflect the British heritage and the influence of North American federalism. The system of responsible government, with the party or coalition with a majority in the House of Representatives forming the government, is complicated by the existence of an upper house, the Senate, with powers almost equal to those of the House. The Senate is elected by proportional representation, so the government is unlikely to have a Senate majority. Equal numbers of senators are elected from each state, reflecting the original intention that the Senate function as the states' house. Federal elections are held at least every three years, and normally all the seats in the House of Representatives and more than half the seats in the Senate are up for election. State senators are elected for six-year terms and territory senators for three-year terms.

According to the constitution, executive power "is vested in the Queen and is exercisable by the Governor-General as the Queen's representative." (The constitution makes no mention of the prime minister or the cabinet.) Normally the role of the governor-general is restricted to representing the queen as ceremonial head of state. Thanks to strong conventions of responsible govern-

ment, the powers vested in the governor-general were not taken seriously until 1975, when a governor-general made controversial use of his constitutional powers to dismiss a prime minister whose supply bills were being blocked by the Senate.

At the federal level, government has alternated between the Australian Labor Party and a coalition of the Liberal Party and the National Party. The Labor Party emerged in the early 1890s as the political arm of the trade unions, which continue to have an important role in the structure of the party. The Liberals have maintained strong ties to the business community and since the 1980s have increasingly emphasized free-market policies. The National Party, previously known as the National Country Party and the Country Party, reflects the concerns and interests of farmers and upholds conservative values. Other minor parties, whose supporters are less geographically concentrated than those of the National Party, have been unable to break through the barriers posed by the single-member constituency system used for the House of Representatives. Minor party representation flourishes in the Senate, however.

The Australian Democrats, founded in 1977, reject traditional party politics as dominated by sectional interests, have a participatory party structure, and emphasize environmental and social justice issues. The party has consistently fielded the largest number of women candidates for federal elections, and in 1991, five of the AD's eight senators were women. Another woman senator represented the Greens (Western Australia).

In 1902 Australian women gained the vote and the right to stand for the new national Parliament. Voting has been compulsory in Australia since 1915 in Queensland, since 1924 at the federal level, and in all states since the end of World War II. Hence women vote in equal numbers to men but have been unable to realize the potential of the "women's vote." Australia has traditionally had a high level of party identification, and party loyalties largely determine women's as well as men's voting patterns. There has been some erosion of traditional party loyalties over the past decade, which has been attributed to a number of factors, including the influence of "economic rationalism" (free-market ideology) on major parties and the increased importance of environmental issues. The Australian Democrats, originally led by a former Liberal cabinet minister, advocate more state regulation of the economy in the interest of equity and more environmental protection measures than does the Labor Party.

Radical movements in Australia have traditionally sought to satisfy their demands through new state structures, such as the system of third-party intervention in industrial disputes created at the turn of the century, the system of statutory marketing boards created to serve the interests of farmers, and the women's policy structures in government and state-funded women's services (run for and by women) resulting from second-wave feminism.

WOMEN'S MOVEMENTS

In the 1880s, Australian women, frustrated in their efforts to attain social reform in areas such as temperance, child welfare, and the age of consent, began their campaign for the vote. A period of intense institution building on the part of women was followed, after World War I, by a relative decline in organized feminism despite mobilizations around employment issues and equal pay in the 1930s and around postwar reconstruction in the 1940s.

The first women's liberation groups appeared in late 1969 in Sydney and Canberra and grew largely among anti–Vietnam War activists inspired by their sisters in the United States. By 1970 consciousness-raising groups had been formed in most federal, state, and territory capital cities. Early influences included Australian Germaine Greer and overseas writers Kate Millet and Juliet Mitchell.

In 1972 a number of those involved in women's liberation groups created the Women's Electoral Lobby (WEL), a nonpartisan and nonhierarchical organization with members from all political parties. Activists for women's liberation also created the first women's refuges and many other services in the early 1970s.[1] By 1974 it was clear that the demand for such services could not be met without federal funding, and, helped by women who had taken up government policy positions, the word *submission* took on new meaning. In 1975, the International Women's Year, women made numerous submissions to the government for funding of women's services and other feminist projects.[2]

There is no peak (umbrella) organization for women in Australia comparable to such bodies as the Australian Council of Social Service (ACOSS), the Federation of Ethnic Community Councils of Australia, or the Australian Council on the Aging. Instead, there are a number of national organizations for women or groups in which women are predominant. Some of them—the National Council of Women, the Women's International League for Peace and Freedom, the Country Women's Association, the Young Women's Christian Association, the Federation of Family Planning Associations of Australia, and the Australian Federation of Business and Professional Women—long predate the second wave of the women's movement, which began in the 1970s. The National Council of Women has some 570 affiliated organizations and, like the Country Women's Association, has been associated with the conservative side of politics, though it is officially nonpartisan. Newer organizations include WEL, the National Council of Single Mothers and their Children, the Australian Women's Education Coalition, and the National Association of Community-Based Children's Services.

More recently, women from non-English-speaking backgrounds formed the Association of Non-English Background Women of Australia, but Aboriginal and Torres Strait Islander women have not created a similar national organization on their own. Most national women's organizations are active in their international counterparts and through them have consultative status at the United Nations. For example, WEL is affiliated with the International Alliance of Women, in which Australia has been involved since Australian suffragist Vida Goldstein attended the planning session in Washington in 1902.

The women's organizations, which are represented on the National Women's Consultative Council, a federal advisory body, receive operational grants under a program administered by the Office of the Status of Women. The absence of a peak body independent of government reduces the political effectiveness of the women's movement, and the process of overcoming traditional rivalries and differing perspectives to create such an entity is an awesome political task. In the meantime, WEL has often taken the lead in creating broad-based coalitions of women's organizations for specific purposes, such as to support federal sex discrimination legislation in 1983–84 and to defeat a proposed consumption tax in 1985. (Organizations claiming to represent 5 million Australian women gathered for the National Women's Tax Summit that year.) WEL put together a coalition to support its intervention in the 1992 National Wage Case to oppose the drift toward enterprise bargaining. The National Foundation of Australian Women, created with a bequest from a former WEL national coordinator, is attempting to improve communications among women's organizations in Australia and funded the WEL intervention in enterprise bargaining.

There are thousands of local women's organizations, including vocational groups (lawyers and builders), environmental groups, ethnic organizations, organizations within political parties, union committees, campus organizations, writing and publishing groups, theater and art associations, church groups, lesbian groups, issues-oriented action groups, and service collectives. In most Australian cities there is a thriving feminist culture and social life that is often not linked to broader political action.

In spite of government contributions, most women's organizations in Australia run on tiny budgets, typically with part-time office staff. Financial worries are constant, given the large number of government inquiries, reviews, and consultations in which women's organizations

are expected to participate. A peak advocacy body for women's organizations would attract more funding and allow groups to hire full-time professional lobbyists and media liaisons, argue supporters of such a body.

Organizations may apply to the government for project grants after tailoring those projects to the "flavor of the month" in government priorities. Project funding may also be a catalyst for organization (e.g., the role of government AIDS funding in the creation of collectives for prostitutes or sex workers). Lack of organizational clout and agenda-setting capacity means that women's organizations need to plug in to established agendas. State governments have provided relatively little funding for women's advocacy groups (apart from those directly associated with women's services), though they may provide office space or facilities. In 1985 the Victoria government became the first state government to establish a Women's Trust to provide annual grants for nonprofit projects that address the social, cultural, political, and economic needs of women. This bequest has been supplemented by donations and fund-raising events.

Australia does not have a tradition of private philanthropic foundations as the belief has been that legitimate social demands should be met by government. Only recently have women's demands been viewed as having the same legitimacy as those of other groups. There was brief debate in the early 1970s over whether women's liberation would be compromised or bought off by government funding. But it was quickly recognized that there was no alternative; as Sara Dowse commented, "The debate that scarcely happened is closed." A vast range of orientations exists among women's organizations, from the radical separatism of some collectives running women's refuges (which are fully funded by the government) to the socialist feminist outlook of people employed in Working Women's Centres (run by some state governments) to the liberal reformism articulated by the Federation of Business and Professional Women (which receives little operation funding).

For policy reasons, recognition is sought of

needs that arise from the characteristic location of women in the division of paid and unpaid work. The recent debate over a proposal to introduce timed local telephone calls drew attention to the disproportionate impact that such a policy would have on women, who characteristically make longer calls as part of their unpaid work in maintaining the invisible welfare state. Attention was also drawn to the impact the policy would have on older women and on women from non-English-speaking backgrounds, who are the major users and providers of the government-funded Telephone Interpreter Service.

The basic demands of the women's movement were for equal pay, equal employment opportunity, equal access to education, free contraceptive services, abortion on demand, and free 24-hour child care. The movement was at first largely made up of university-educated "Anglo" women, many of whom had been convent girls.[3] Only when the movement began providing services—refuges and women's health services—did it start reaching a broader constituency.

In 1972 a reform wing was developed to put women's demands onto the political agenda and get more women into political positions. This wing created WEL, made up of well-educated but underemployed middle-class women interested in going beyond discussion to action. Many were in their 20s and had given up their careers when they had children.

That year the idea of rating candidates running for federal office regarding their attitudes toward women's needs caught fire. A questionnaire was drawn up, and soon women all over Australia were interviewing politicians and coding the responses. Because of the hundreds of candidates and large distances involved, women with no political experience had to be drafted into the work of tracking down and interviewing candidates. Their confidence rapidly increased as they discovered the ineptitude and ignorance of politicians on issues such as child care. The apparent novelty of the WEL activity caught the attention of the media, and the survey received excellent coverage. Women's demands became a prominent feature of the campaign and part of the mood for

change that was sweeping the country after 23 years of conservative government.

WEL, which exposed women to skill sharing and empowerment, provided a training ground for many women who moved into important political or governmental positions. A 1985 survey of state and federal women MPs found that 28 percent had been or still were WEL members.[4] In June 1991 three of five women cabinet ministers in Western Australia were former WEL activists, including the state premier. WEL activists are similarly represented in other states.

The organization is still an active lobby group, though its energies have been depleted with so many of its former members now in demanding senior government jobs, and there is little new blood. In 1991 WEL and the National Foundation for Australian Women led a coalition of women's groups in opposition to the federal government's proposed "new federalism," which would return authority to the states in many areas of concern to women, such as community services. As governments continue to reduce the size of the public sector, WEL and other groups devote much time to defending the forms of social investment needed by women.

The relation of Aboriginal women to the "white women's movement" has been complex and subject to change. Pat O'Shane, the first Aboriginal admitted to the bar and head of the New South Wales Ministry of Aboriginal Affairs since 1981, summed up Aboriginal attitudes in her 1976 article "Is There Any Relevance in the Women's Movement for Aboriginal Women?" O'Shane wrote, "Sexist attitudes did not wipe out whole tribes of our people, sexist attitudes are not slowly killing our people—racism did, and continues to do so."[5]

The main issues of concern were racism or survival for most Aboriginal women, who believed that they had little in common with the women in the movement. A number of Aboriginal women decided not to participate in International Women's Year activities on the grounds that talking about women's rights was irrelevant when they were oppressed by racism and poverty. The demand for abortion rights was seen as particularly irrelevant by Aboriginal women who were more concerned with racial survival and stopping forced sterilization.[6]

O'Shane and other Aboriginal activists argued that the destruction of Aboriginal society had an even greater effect on men than on women. Having been deprived of status and self-respect, Aboriginal men were often caught in the pub-to-jail syndrome. In this context, "We don't want to down our men" became a refrain among Aboriginal women.[7] On the other hand, concern for Aboriginal rights and welfare had been a traditional issue of Australian women's organizations. In 1972, Elizabeth Reid, soon to be named women's adviser to the prime minister, had worked as campaign manager for Pat Eatock, an Aboriginal candidate for the federal seat of the Australian Capital Territory.

The failure of white bureaucracy to come to grips with the sex-segregated nature of traditional Aboriginal society became a major issue in relation to the land claim process. Neither Aboriginal nor white male anthropologists and bureaucrats were able to identify the sites sacred to women and used in women-only ceremonies. Feminist anthropologists such as Diane Bell played a crucial role in helping Aboriginal women contest the view of Aboriginal society imposed by European anthropologists.[8]

From 1979 to 1983 Aboriginal women pressured the federal government to establish a task force on Aboriginal women that would emphasize their role and status in land rights negotiations. European settlement in Australia had largely proceeded on the assumption of *terra nullius* (the land belonged to no one) and ignored the traditional relation of Aboriginal people to the land. The land rights movement sought recognition of prior Aboriginal ownership of the land and, in particular, restoration of crown land to its traditional owners in the form of inalienable land rights. Land rights claims are conducted by government-sponsored land councils dominated by male Aborigines.

The task force got off the ground largely through the patient work of Mary Sexton in the Office of the Status of Women. It was headed by

two Aboriginal women, Phyllis Daylight and Mary Johnstone, with 11 other Aboriginal women acting as regional coordinators. This historic consultation with Aboriginal women, which included the first national conference of Aboriginal and Islander women, was considered a landmark in enabling Aboriginal women to develop a nationwide perspective. The women demanded recognition of their status as landowners and custodians of land and sacred sites and representation on land councils.[9]

Since then, there has been widespread support in the women's movement for the demands of Aboriginal women, and those demands are regularly addressed at women's conferences. The government's *National Agenda to the Year 2000* includes specific commitments to Aboriginal and Torres Strait Islander women as the most disadvantaged Australian women, but it stops short of land rights. The Commonwealth Labor government has backed away from national land rights legislation under pressure from its state counterparts, particularly in Western Australia, where the mining industry has spent large sums to whip up community fears about the supposed threat land rights pose to the "family farm."

The complex and localized kinship politics of Aboriginal communities, vast distances between communities, differences between urban and traditional Aboriginal women, and the perennial lack of financial resources make national organization extremely difficult for Aboriginal women. Nonetheless, they have a growing role in women's conferences and advisory councils and are beginning to speak out strongly about the prevalence of domestic violence, child sexual abuse, and rape in Aboriginal communities, all long-term effects of European colonization.[10]

Although they have yet to follow Aboriginal men into parliamentary politics, women play an important role in community politics and occupy key governmental positions. Lois O'Donoghue, for example, holds the most powerful position in Aboriginal affairs as chairperson of the Aboriginal and Torres Strait Islander Commission. The agency is a unique bureaucratic structure responsible to the federal Parliament and to commissioners and councillors elected by Aboriginal and Torres Strait Islander communities.

Women from non-English-speaking backgrounds (NESB) constitute a far larger group than Aboriginal women but have faced equivalent or greater problems in gaining recognition of their needs. Cultural and linguistic differences and lack of resources have impeded effective organization at the national level. As noted above, the vast distances in Australia and the high cost of air travel have often hindered the national organization of disadvantaged groups.

Immigrant women from Southern Europe, the Middle East, Southeast Asia, and South America have been particularly disadvantaged. Because they came to Australia as wives, mothers, and daughters rather than as principal applicants under the immigration program, they have had relatively little access to English-language courses or to such services such as culturally appropriate (if any) child care. Immigrant women have traditionally been employed in large numbers in such labor-intensive industries as food processing; contract cleaning; and textile, clothing, and footwear manufacturing—all industries that are facing technological change, retrenchments, and restructuring. Many immigrant women have become outworkers in the clothing industry, a form of work that lacked union protection until recently.

At home or in the factory, immigrant women have been particularly vulnerable to exploitation and have had a high rate of occupational injury and disease. Furthermore, immigrant women have often been poorly served by male trade union officials who neglected the nonwage issues of primary concern to them: child care, working conditions, occupational health problems, and on-the-job English classes.[11]

Although individual immigrant women have been active in the women's movement, many have felt excluded from organizations dominated by articulate, middle-class Anglo women. On the other hand, ethnic community organizations have traditionally been dominated by men. Women in the Federation of Ethnic Community Councils of Australia (FECCA), a peak advocacy body, became acutely aware of the need for a separate women's organization when they tried to obtain greater representation in national decision making. With some government assistance, two such organizations were established: the Women's Network of FECCA and the Association of Non-English-Speaking Background Women of Australia (ANESBWA).

Immigrant women in key government positions—such as German-born Ursula Doyle in the minister's office; Dutch-born Frederika Steen, who was the immigrant women's adviser; and Singapore-born Choon Siau Lee on the National Women's Consultative Council—were among those who saw the importance of developing national structures. Matina Mottee, of Greek origin, became the first convenor of ANESBWA. In 1989 the Commonwealth and State Council on NESB Women's Issues was formed; it was made up of government and community representatives, sometimes mutually suspicious, reporting to the prime minister and other ministers.

In the 1980s there was rapid growth in ethnic women's organizations, some of which received funding for delivering services or for providing information and advocacy to women of specific cultural backgrounds. The first immigrant women from non-English-speaking backgrounds were also elected to Australian parliaments, and these women—such as Italian-born Franca Arena in the New South Wales (NSW) Parliament—were active in promoting networks of women involved in ethnic affairs.[12] Helen L'Orange, the daughter and granddaughter of Greek immigrants, became head of the Women's Co-ordination Unit in the NSW government in 1980 and of the federal Office of the Status of Women in 1988. Immigrant women are playing an increasingly assertive role in women's conferences and in ethnic community conferences, often complaining of the relative lack of interest in their issues. Groups becoming more visible and vocal include Islamic women, whose values are often far removed from other groups demanding greater visibility, such as lesbian women. At the Commonwealth level and in most states, government departments and other public agencies are not required to develop access and equity plans to ensure that services are designed to meet the needs of Australians from non-English-speaking backgrounds. However, as reported in one study conducted by ANESBWA, "most policies, programmes and practices deal only with the disadvantages faced by women from non-English-speaking backgrounds and redressing them. This approach makes them a 'special needs group,' implies a deficit approach and immediately marginalizes them. . . . Women from non-English-speaking backgrounds are rarely presented as a substantial proportion of the population with the right to influence the development and delivery of the services they will use."[13]

In the 1990s the women's movement has become more diverse than in the 1970s, with feminism percolating much further into Australia's heterogeneous population. There has been a growth of feminist organizations in ethnic communities and in social, economic, and cultural bodies. Many young women are espousing eco-feminist perspectives. As in comparable countries, feminism has moved from the streets and into the institutions, its increased complexity and diversity replacing the mobilizing power of simple slogans.

REPRESENTATION

In 1902 Australia became the first country where women obtained both the right to vote and the right to stand for election to the Commonwealth Parliament. Despite this early success and the involvement of women in Australia's early welfare reforms, women were notably absent from public life until the 1970s. It took 41 years for women to be elected to the federal Parliament, and during this period only a handful of women were elected to state parliaments.

The passage of women's suffrage had rested on reassurances that the overall division of labor would be maintained and that home and family would not be neglected. Having achieved victory on these terms, the suffragists were placed in a paradoxical position: although they complained about the lack of women in public life who could direct policies toward protecting the family, the strength of the family structure and its role expectations prevented women from obtaining the organizational support required for entering Parliament. Regardless of how women politicians addressed themselves to upholding the family, their very presence in the male sphere of public power and authority was seen as a threat to a family structure premised on women's dependence. Women's sections set up by the parties early in the century to defuse the threat of non-party feminism contributed to the containment of women in political housekeeping roles.[14]

During the 1960s, Australian women became increasingly impatient with the motherhood roles imposed on them in politics. Women's sections within parties were seen as holding back women, and some were dismantled over the next decade only to be replaced by more overtly feminist structures. A number of women politicians attempted to escape identification with "women's issues" and expressed the belief that gender was irrelevant in politics. These women repudiated any collective identification with women and resented any suggestion that their experience and the ways that they were held accountable might differ from those of their male colleagues.[15] This orientation is still found to some degree among women politicians, particularly those identifying with economic rationalism (free-market ideology), now the dominant strand of the Liberal Party. The traditional maternal orientation is still found among representatives of the rural-based National Party and is often expressed in terms of the need to defend the family and the traditional roles of wife and mother from the depredations of radical feminism.

Beginning in the 1970s there was a steady influx of women into Australian parliaments; the percentage of women MPs went from 2 percent in 1972 to more than 13 percent in December 1991. The majority of these women (63 of 113) were Labor MPs encouraged by the party's national affirmative action policy. Following a disastrous defeat in the 1977 federal election, the Labor Party identified this "gender gap" as a major problem. Historically, some 6 to 8 percent fewer women than men voted Labor—enough to keep the party out of power at the federal level. It was suggested that the party's image as a "working man's party" was to blame, so in 1981 the party adopted an affirmative action policy aimed at achieving representation of women at all levels of the party in proportion to their membership (then between 25 and 30 percent).[16] A comprehensive women's policy was also developed as part of the Labor Party's strategy to close the gender gap. The policy was discussed with women's organizations, including groups never before courted by Labor. In 1981, Sen. Susan Ryan introduced a Sex Discrimination Bill that further focused attention on what the Labor Party was offering women.

Through pressure from women's organizations and advisory bodies, momentum had been building for an all-Commonwealth sex discrimination legislation. The failure of the coalition government (held back by the National Party) to enact antidiscrimination legislation, despite the clear demand for it, has been held responsible for the Liberal Party's loss of its electoral advantage among women.[17] In 1983 the Labor Party closed the gender gap and took office. In return, the Labor government under Prime Minister Robert J. L. Hawke delivered substantial increases in funding for child care, the Sex Discrimination Act of 1984, and the Affirmative Action Act (Equal Employment Opportunity for Women) of 1986, which required large private employers and all higher education institutions to develop EEO programs.

In 1987 the opposition government decided to fight the extension of EEO programs to government business enterprises. This decision led to the resignation of the (male) shadow minister responsible for the Status of Women and prompted one-quarter of the Liberal senators (all male) to vote for the Labor government in support of the bill.[18] This large-scale defection was unprecedented in Australia, where party discipline is strong and MPs rarely defy party whips. The front-page stories about the resignation co-incided with a 10 percent drop in female support for the Liberals, according to the *Age* Saulwick polls published 1 April 1987.

Since 1985 the Liberal and National Parties have been fielding more women candidates, often for seats held by Labor women. Currently the National and Liberal Parties have 35 women in Australian Parliaments. The Australian Democrats, who have consistently fielded the largest number of women candidates, have the highest proportion of women MPs, have had a woman national president almost continuously since 1984, and had a woman federal leader from 1986 to 1991 (with Sen. Janet Powell replacing former Sen. Janine Haines in 1990). The Australian Democrats have escaped the institutional drag of the older political parties, and their participatory structures favor women. Some women have entered parliaments as Green Independents—an indication of the important role women have been playing in the environmental movement. The same movement has brought more women into local government, and by June 1991 they constituted 18.4 percent of those elected nationwide.

The increased prominence of women in formal politics (e.g., in 1991 women held the position of premier in two states, as well as the position of chief minister in the ACT) has led to talk of the "feminization of politics" and to suggestions that Australians are disillusioned with traditional adversarial and machine politics. But there is no indication that the major parties are prepared for such a shift. In the Labor Party, policy and positions are determined by negotiations among three formal factions. Overall policy making is a masculine activity conducted by "numbers men" (whose chief attribute is their ability to command and control the votes of party members). The Liberal Party is now dominated by men committed to free-market doctrines who appear to place little value on the community perspectives contributed by women in the party. In the electorate, polls show that women are more concerned than men about economic strategies that increase inequalities and are now more pro-Labor than men.[19]

The Australian Labor Party and Labor governments were most receptive to the demand for specialized machinery (structures and processes) to ensure that government addressed women's needs. Australia's national machinery for the advancement of women began under the reformist government of Prime Minister Gough Whitlam (1972–75).

The question of how to introduce a feminist machinery of government was the subject of much discussion by WEL members and the first femocrats. The term *femocrat* was invented in Australia to describe feminists recruited to fill women's policy positions in government. Feminists faced the problem of how to develop bureaucratic machinery appropriate to the structural philosophy of the feminist movement. The movement had developed non-hierarchical collectives intended to empower women, but the government bureaucracy was characterized by hierarchies of power and status. Another problem was how to combine the need for concentration of resources—which would give the feminists some clout in the bureaucracy—with the need to prevent marginalization in a separate department or agency.

The answer feminists came up with was a center-periphery model of women's policy coordination. The central unit was to be located in the Department of the Prime Minister and Cabinet, where it would have access to all cabinet submissions. Departmental units would monitor policy development for gender equity implications at the point of initiation. The center-peripheral network model was seen as corresponding to the antihierarchical philosophy of the women's movement while using the clout conferred by being located in the prime minister's own department.[20]

In addition to policy structures, the machinery included women's information and referral services, which are run by women in the Australian capitals, and a number of regional centers. These services, which are provided by government, were originally run by women's movement volunteers in the 1970s. They are a bridge to government for women, particularly those isolated at home, and they provide important feedback on how government policy changes affect women locally.

Key components of Australian women's policy machinery include the central women's policy units found in the prime minister's department, the units found in premiers' departments or chief ministers' departments at the state and territory levels, and the network of departmental women's units. Within a federal system, intergovernmental meetings of women's advisers are also critical to maintaining morale when local political contexts become unfavorable.[21]

The major strength of Australian women's policy machinery has been the institutional recognition that no government activity can be assumed to be gender neutral in its effects. Because men and women have different roles in the family and in the labor market, government policy is likely to affect them differently. This recognition of different outcomes has been entrenched in mechanisms for monitoring and auditing government policy for gender impact. Australia was the first country to introduce comprehensive analysis disaggregated by gender, as presented in the annual Women's Budget Statement. This statement was introduced at the federal level in 1984 (as the Women's Budget Program) and has since been introduced by most state and territory governments. In other words, Australian women tried to build bureaucratic means of monitoring and evaluating the outcomes for women of all government activity and not simply programs intended to advance the status of women.

Positioning women's policy machinery within the central agencies of government put great pressure to conform on surrounding hierarchical structures. The term *femocrat* reflects the ambivalence feminists felt about the associated costs. For example, the editorial collective of a Sydney women's liberation paper, *Mejane*, protested the appointment of the first women's adviser to the prime minister, telling the government that "no woman chosen by men to advise upon us will be acceptable to us. We believe that it is not your right to choose for us our spokeswoman, anymore than it is any woman's right to act as the single spokeswoman for the rest of us."[22]

Anne Summers, a founding member of the first women's refuge in Australia and later the head of the Office of the Status of Women and owner and editor of *Ms.* magazine in the United States, has suggested two possible models for how women policy advisers operate in government: the *missionary* and the *mandarin* approaches.[23] Missionaries engage in public advocacy and private proselytizing, and mandarins use the bureaucratic system by adopting its techniques and structures. Most women policy advisers are seen simultaneously as missionaries by career bureaucrats and as mandarins by women outside the women's movement. These problems of perception exacerbated the relationship between femocrats and their supposed constituency in the women's movement and weakened the femocrats' political base. Those inside were aggrieved by the lack of understanding and support from those outside, particularly as they themselves were constantly under suspicion from the rest of the bureaucracy because of their assumed closeness to the women's movement.[24]

Those outside felt that the femocrats had become careerists and had joined the patriarchy rather than challenging its structures. Lesley Lynch wrote, "Given the nature of the bureaucracy, feminist bureaucrats are subjected to strong pressures and temptations which specifically undermine their capacity to function as feminists."[25] There has been little understanding of the battles waged within the bureaucracy or of the pressure under which femocrats have operated. Gillian Calvert, of the Child Protection Council secretariat in New South Wales, has commented that "a femocrat is a public servant who is feminist and is perceived to have control over either policy or funding or both. The fact that femocrats often do not really *have* that power is the source of friction with the women's movement at large, which is disappointed when femocrats fail to effect the sort of changes it would like." Despite the tensions, Calvert said, many femocrats have a clear understanding of the complementary relationship between femocrats

and the movement outside: "The radical demands of the women's movement prepare the ground for the less threatening but nevertheless important changes in policy and legislation that are pushed through by feminists in the public service."[26]

Networking among feminists in government, in both the bureaucracy and in Parliament, has become an increasingly important form of resistance to the new managerialist and economic rationalist agendas. Feminists from diverse backgrounds have a common interest in resisting the thrust toward deregulation and privatization that is threatening the structure of social intervention in the economy as well as introducing market behavior into the public sector. Regular contact with other feminists may be crucial in reaffirming feminist values.

An Australian antifeminist group similar to Phyllis Schlafly's Eagle Forum in the United States emerged in 1979 to oppose the influence of the women's movement on government. The group, called Women Who Want to be Women (wwww, now Endeavour Forum), was headed by the indefatigable Indian-born Babette Francis. Much of the initial energy of the group, which had close links to the Catholic National Civic Council and access to church networks, was devoted to parliamentary petitions seeking to abolish the National Women's Advisory Council and to disruptive activities relating to the U.N. Decade for Women.

The influence of wwww peaked in 1980–82 when its antifeminist message coincided with the philosophy—then popular with some members of the conservative coalition government—that Australia needed to "strengthen the family" as an alternative to expensive welfare provision.[27] But the extremist views of wwww were not palatable to most Australian conservative politicians. Although feminist strands within the Liberal Party have been weakened with the party's move to the right in the 1980s, they still are able, particularly in South Australia, to provide a basis for bipartisan support for women's policy machinery. Women's advisory bodies have been a useful means to garner such bipartisan support.

After the election of a federal Labor government in 1983, groups such as WWWW that opposed the U.N. Convention on the Elimination of All Forms of Discrimination Against Women were excluded from advisory bodies or grants programs designed to promote the status of women. Jackie Butler, Queensland coordinator of WWWW, was the lead signatory of a propaganda sheet circulated through church networks that gave rise to a flood of petitions, letters, and telegrams to Parliament. Those messages contended that ratification of the U.N. Convention would lead to the Bible becoming a banned book, the state taking control of children from infancy, and Australia being placed under the control of foreign powers. As part of its campaign against "unisex" education, WWWW has brought Michael Levin, an American professor of philosophy, to Australia on speaking tours. Levin focused so extensively on the limitations posed by the structure of the female brain that some Australian newspapers referred to him as a professor of physiology.

Even after becoming politically marginalized at the federal level, WWWW continued to receive a sympathetic hearing from the Bjelke-Petersen National Party government of Queensland. With the fall of Bjelke-Petersen, revelations of the corruption in his government, and election of a reformist Labor government in Queensland in 1989, WWWW lost its last bastion of governmental influence.

Despite such opposition, two issues—domestic violence and equal pay—highlight the variety of actors and strategies employed by the feminist movement in the 1970s and 1980s. Each issue had some success raising public awareness and institutionalizing women's needs within government.

DOMESTIC VIOLENCE

Through such self-help services as refuges, health centers, and rape crisis centers, the women's movement in the 1970s revealed a level of unmet need that required government rather than volunteer action.

The first women's refuge, Elsie, was established in March 1974 by the squatting action of Sydney Women's Liberation group members in two houses owned by the Church of England. The government took over the estate and leased the houses to the refuge at a "peppercorn" (token) rent, but Elsie was run purely on donations and fundraising activities such as dances until the federal Health Commissions provided money for staff and equipment in January 1975. The refuge, which catered to a large number of women who had had no previous contact with feminism, helped reveal the prevalence of domestic violence. But revolutionaries described Elsie as dangerously close to a traditional charity; reformists argued that by stepping in and meeting an identified need, the feminists absolved the government of having to take responsibility for this need.[28]

Eleven refuges were operating in capital cities by 1975, but it was clear that they could not continue without secure government funding. There were bureaucratic problems because refuges did not fit into established government programs. For example, the definition of "homelessness" did not extend to the needs of women who had nowhere to go to escape a violent partner. When the Commonwealth minister for Social Security attempted to visit Elsie to assess needs for himself, he was sent away by refuge workers who explained that men were not allowed inside. Elizabeth Reid, the women's adviser to the prime minister, took the principled stand that the Social Security Department should take responsibility for the issue, despite that department's traditional dislike for community-initiated programs. Her stand frustrated other femocrats aware that the Community Health Program, a new agency eager to establish itself, was flush with funds and eager to take on refuge funding as a new program anxious to establish itself. Reid was eventually persuaded to take the Community Health proposal for more secure funding to the prime minister just before her departure for the U.N. conference in Mexico City and the end of the 1974–75 financial year.[29]

During the 1980s all the state governments set up task forces on domestic violence that included women's service representatives and achieved important legislative reforms. As in other countries, the major goals of such reforms have been to make it easier to obtain protection orders; to encourage police to lay charges; to extend protection to other members of the family; to make spouses compellable as witnesses; and to extend police powers of entry and ouster. Protection orders are issued under civil law, with its less onerous burden of proof; the breach of a protection order is a criminal offense. Refuge workers help train police officers and other service providers.

By 1990 the government was funding 265 women's refuges, the majority run in accordance with feminist collectivist principles, as well as a large number of rape crisis centers, incest centers, domestic violence crisis services, women's health centers, and women's information services. These services provide input to government policy and legislation.

Government-funded community education campaigns on domestic violence, rape, or sexual assault of children have been noted for their feminist perspectives. Public endorsement has been given, through such programs as the National Domestic Violence Education Program launched by the prime minister in 1988, to the view that the answer to the abuse of male power lies in the empowerment of women.[30] This philosophy also justifies the non-hierarchical organizational form of the refuge collectives.

Still, there has been tension between women's service workers and feminists within these policy areas of government. For example, the feminists' attempt to promote a national lobby for women's services was misinterpreted in 1975 as an attempt to extend bureaucratic control.[31] Radical feminist collectivism has more scope within women's services than within central policy coordinating departments. But it is the combination of feminist advocacy from within government and the grass-roots work of the refuges that has put the domestic violence crisis on the public policy agenda and directed resources to it. Few members of the women's movement are outside the structures of the state in Australia, though some

are more closely constrained by them than others.

EQUAL PAY

Another major issue of the 1980s was equal pay, a goal now generally referred to as pay equity. Australia has a centralized wage-fixing system, and employers, unions, and governments make submissions to national wage cases conducted by the Industrial Relations Commission (previously the Conciliation and Arbitration Commission) as well as to the state equivalents. Industrial awards—the determinations by industrial tribunals of rates of pay and conditions of employment—are legally enforceable. There has been a drop in award coverage since the mid-1980s, and now only 80 percent of all employees (and 83.5 percent of female employees) are covered. Although the principle of equal pay for work of equal value has been in place since 1972, the maintenance of historical relativities (comparative wage justice) has posed constraints on its implementation.

Nonetheless, the existence of a centralized system that affords some protection to the less strongly organized sections of the labor market has considerable advantages. This can be seen in the area of over-award payments, which are payments above the federal and state awards. Such payments are determined by collective bargaining at the enterprise level, where women are most disadvantaged, earning less than half the over-award payments earned by men.[32]

Equal pay is not a new issue. The Council of Action for Equal Pay was formed in 1937 by the trade unionist Muriel Heagney to fight a wage policy that had been in place since 1919. That policy set women's wages at 54 percent of the male "family" wage, and Heagney was seeking "the rate for the job," a common rate regardless of the sex of the worker. Trade unions and feminist organizations such as the United Associations of Women, led by Jessie Street, joined the council, which won support for equal pay from the Australian Council of Trade Unions (ACTU) and the Labor opposition by the beginning of

World War II. Despite the pressure, the wartime Labor government did not fulfill this commitment because of strong opposition by employers. It did establish, however, a Women's Employment Board that awarded a high percentage (between 70 and 100 percent) of the male wage rate to women entering war industries, but the 54 percent rate was retained for women in traditional female industries and occupations.

In 1949 the female wage rate was raised to 75 percent. Feminist organizations such as the Australian Federation of Women Voters had to intervene in the 1953 national wage case to prevent an attempt by employers to roll back even this advance. In the late 1950s, after the International Labor Organization's Convention on Equal Remuneration went into effect and following long agitation by teacher unions, state governments began to pass equal pay acts for teachers. In 1967 the then Commonwealth Conciliation and Arbitration Commission invited unions, employers, and governments to pursue equal pay, and that pursuit led to the 1969 "equal pay for equal work" decision. Because of the high degree of occupational gender segregation, the decision benefited only 18 percent of the women in the paid work force. In protest, a Melbourne union activist, Zelda D'Aprano, chained herself to the Commonwealth Building.

In 1972 Australian women, supported by a newly elected and reform-minded Labor government, won the right to equal pay for work of equal value in the national wage case. This principle has never been systematically applied, however, because of the lack of union resources to conduct work value studies and because of the ambiguity in the decision itself regarding how much of a departure from traditional wage-fixing principles was intended.[33] Wages in female occupations increased following the decision, but the basis of comparison was generally a related award, and sometimes a female one. The comparisons examined similarities in job content or tasks rather than assessing work value by using more generalized criteria. The belief overseas was that Australian women had achieved equal pay, and American economists were convinced that

widespread unemployment of Australian women would surely follow.

In 1984 the Council of Action for Equal Pay (CAEP) was reestablished by a number of feminist activists in Victoria and NSW. They included women active in the union movement and feminist academics such as Meredith Burgmann (now in the NSW Parliament) and Clare Burton (now a femocrat), as well as women in the relevant women's policy units. The council investigated the possibility of using the concept of comparable worth, as developed in North America, to improve wages in feminized areas. In 1985 the Australian Council of Trade Unions and CAEP supported a test case by nurses to try to gain acceptance of the comparable worth principle. The work of nurses was to be compared, for example, with that of ambulance officers.

The Conciliation and Arbitration Commission rejected the principle of comparable worth as running counter to historical wage-fixing principles in Australia. While reaffirming the principle of equal pay for work of equal value, the commission rejected the concept of assessing work in terms of its value to the employer, rather than in terms of the value to an award determined by the commission itself. It has been pointed out that the concept of comparable worth was developed for law courts rather than for industrial tribunals that try to maintain flexibility to consider a wide range of political, economic, and industrial factors, articulated in the early days as the needs of a human being in a civilized community.[34]

Nonetheless, the nurses won their increase under the anomalies provision of the wage-fixing principles. It was acknowledged that in their case the 1972 principle of equal pay for work of equal value had not been implemented. They were helped by the shortage of nurses, industrial action that included strikes, and the shifting of nurse education out of hospitals into higher education (thus increasing "work value").

Considerable debate ensued among feminists over whether the concept of comparable worth should be pursued, as it seemed to run counter to the principles involved in the centralized wage-fixing system.[35] Critics of the comparable worth approach pointed to the benefits for women of centralized wage fixing through the arbitration system, rather than through decentralized enterprise bargaining.

Unions, employers, and government present their cases to industrial tribunals, and other interested parties may also be given leave to appear. Women's organizations that have presented pay equity arguments in national wage cases include the National Council of Women, the Union of Australian Women, WEL, CAEP, and the Australian Federation of Business and Professional Women. Decisions in national wage cases—whether relating to pay, maternity leave, or parental leave—eventually benefit most workers.

Progress on equal pay issues has been inhibited by women's lack of representation in bodies affiliated with the major players. Progress has been slow among the unions affiliated with ACTU, despite an Action Plan for Women. In 1991 women occupied only 10 of 38 positions on the ACTU Executive; three of the positions were created in 1987 specifically for women. None of the 80 members of the Business Council of Australia, a peak employer body, was a woman.

The marginalizing of women's interests was underscored by ACTU's 1987 agreement with the government to place a greater emphasis on industry-based "productivity" rather than cost-of-living wage increases and comparative wage justice. This approach was largely adopted by the Industrial Relations Commission in its 1987 and 1988 national wage decisions. Since 1988, wage increases have been predicated in part on award restructuring and have intended to promote a more flexible and skilled work force.

Feminists maintain that ACTU's use of "productivity" principles as guides for equal pay may disadvantage women, who are concentrated in service sectors, where productivity is hard to establish, and in feminized industries with little fat to trade away. Well-off unions within male industries have been able to pursue their claims more quickly than unions in feminized sectors. Women's conferences inside and outside govern-

ment have focused on how to obtain some advantage from the process of award restructuring through the revaluing of women's skills and the creation of proper career paths (for example, the successful negotiation of a proper career structure for child-care workers).

In its renegotiation of its accord with the Labor government in 1990, ACTU attempted to mitigate some criticisms, including the demand for an Equal Pay Bureau. The bureau, which had been sought by women's organizations such as CAEP, was established in the Industrial Relations Department after the 1990 federal election. Its aim was to see that the award restructuring process worked to narrow the wage gap rather than entrench women in the secondary labor market. In 1990, Australian women in full-time work still earned only 84.5 percent of the average ordinary-time earnings of Australian men.

Although the opposition coalition was committed to moving toward enterprise wage bargaining—which would have been even more disadvantageous for women than industry-based productivity principles—pay equity did not become an issue in the 1990 federal election. Press releases on the subject from labor ministers and women's organizations were not picked up by industrial relations reporters, who tend to be men with little grasp of gender issues.

Thus, the immediate future of equal pay in Australia depends on the survival of Labor governments and the accord, despite the problems for women involved in the "structural efficiency" or productivity approach to wage fixing adopted in recent years. The opposition coalition is currently very much influenced by the "new right" ideology in the United States. Should it come into government, it will attempt to reduce the power of unions and of the centralized wage-fixing system. Under a system of enterprise bargaining such as the coalition proposes, the gender gap would be likely to widen to the degree associated with such systems in other countries. Because of economic problems, in part the result of financial deregulation and other "level playing field" economic policies, Labor governments are highly unpopular, making a coalition victory likely even though their policies are even more deregulatory.

Thus, on a superficial level, women seem to have made more gains in the area of public policy relating to domestic violence. However, the gains have been made in part because domestic violence policy is not "the main game in town." Women have been able to make more progress in determining public policy in what has been regarded as a soft issue of relatively little interest to male decision makers than in the area of pay equity, which relates to central economic issues.

PROSPECTS

The women's movement in Australia has been less threatened by organized antifeminism than by the increasing influence of economic rationalism and managerialism, doctrines with little room for the feminist concerns of equity and empowerment. The public sector has placed increasing faith in English-speaking economics, the social science least influenced by feminist critique. There is a decreasing commitment on all sides of politics to the forms of public investment needed by women. While most of the new hard-nosed managers and economic rationalists are men, a few would-be Margaret Thatchers have appeared on the conservative side of politics.

The new language of public administration—in which everything must be justified in terms of the national accounts—is difficult for feminists to speak. Nonetheless, feminists have contributed much to government. They have brought expertise in areas of female experience that were beyond the competence of the prefeminist bureaucracy. They have created systems for monitoring the impact on women of all government activity, and they have institutionalized the awareness that most decisions will have a different effect on women than men.

But in the course of being translated into public policy and bureaucratic structures, the revolutionary goals of the early women's liberation movement have inevitably been diluted. Political parties, unions, and governments persuaded to take on feminist initiatives inevitably have their own agendas. Compromise is inseparable from brokerage. Feminists in the bureaucracy, like those in political parties and in the union movement, are confronted by the fact that organizational loyalty is the precondition of effectiveness, let alone of career prospects.

Femocrats have to operate within a system of bureaucratic politics. Sometimes they may be able to manipulate this to women's advantage, but they also may have to seek the least harmful outcomes rather than optimal ones and then defend these decisions against women in the community.[36] They are caught up in a system still fundamentally based on hierarchy, secrecy, and, increasingly, individual competition and managerial control. Whether feminists are able to preserve their values, including their solidarity, in this environment depends greatly on the presence of supportive networks inside and outside government.

Meanwhile—despite the existence of a flourishing cultural and vocational feminism (there are even feminist shipbuilders)—there has been a decline in political feminism that can be traced to the absorption of activists into senior government positions. The older generation worries about how to hand on the torch. Feminists inside the bureaucracy bemoan the lack of organized pressure from outside. Although feminist organizations have increased their public policy expertise, particularly in economic areas, and have succeeded in effective coalition building and mobilizations, they have not on the whole inspired the younger generation of women.

The political environment has become increasingly unfriendly to the feminist enterprise. The entire political spectrum has moved to the right, and there has been an increasing commitment to the market as the ultimate arbiter of value. Economic inequalities among Australians are growing, and families headed by women remain the segment of the community most vulnerable to poverty. There has been a loss of confidence in the state's role in promoting progressive social reform. Those on the far right blame feminists for the growth of "social engineering" and big government and demand that wasteful community services be dismantled and responsibility handed back to the "family."

Australian political science has proved largely uninterested in unquantifiable questions on the meaning and significance of women's political participation.[37] Insights on this participation have largely come from the practitioners themselves, whose own academic training has often been in sociology or history. While the insight that no political activity is gender neutral in its effects has been institutionalized in government, it is far from institutionalized in political science.

NOTES

1. Women's refuges in Australia are similar to the shelters for battered women in the United Kingdom and United States, providing supported accommodation for survivors of domestic violence, defined in Australian government brochures as "violence of a physical, psychological, emotional, sexual or economic nature."

2. Pat Giles, "Pamela Denoon Memorial Lecture," *WEL National Bulletin* 11, no. 9 (1989): 5.

3. The term *Anglo* is used in Australia to refer to Australians of Anglo-Celtic origin and to distinguish them from Australians from non-English-speaking backgrounds.

4. Kate White, "Is the Women's Movement Turning Inward?" *National Times,* 20–26 May 1983.

5. Pat O'Shane, "Is There Any Relevance in the Women's Movement for Aboriginal Women?" *Refractory Girl* (September 1976): 33.

6. Meredith Burgmann, "Black Sisterhood: The Situation of Urban Aboriginal Women and Their Relationship to the White Women's Movement," *Politics* 17, no. 2 (November 1982): 34.

7. Department of Aboriginal Affairs, "Aboriginal Women Today," in Fay Gale, ed., *We Are Bosses Ourselves* (Canberra: Australian Institute of Aboriginal Studies, 1983), 158.

8. Diane Bell, *Daughters of the Dreaming* (Melbourne: McPhee Gribble, 1983).

9. Phyllis Daylight and Mary Johnstone, *Women's Business: Report of the Aboriginal Women's Taskforce* (Canberra: Australian Government Publishing Service, 1986). The only major exception to the male domination of the land-claim process is the Pitjantjatjara Women's Council, established in 1980.

10. Judy Atkinson, "Violence in Aboriginal Australia: Colonization and Its Impact on Gender," *Refractory Girl* 36 (August 1990): 21–24.

11. Des Storer, *But I Wouldn't Want My Wife to Work Here* (Melbourne: Cura, 1976).

12. Franca Arena, "No More Crumbs," in Jocelynne Scutt, ed., *Different Lives* (Ringwood: Penguin, 1987), 33–42.

13. Maria Eliadis et al., *Issues for Non-English Speaking Background Women in Multicultural Australia* (Canberra: Office of Multicultural Affairs, Department of the Prime Minister and Cabinet), 26.

14. Marian Sawer and Marian Simms, *A Woman's Place: Women and Politics in Australia,* 2nd ed. (Sydney: Allen and Unwin, 1992), chap. 7.

15. Marian Sawer, "From Motherhood to Sisterhood: Attitudes of Australian Women M.P.s to their Roles," *Women's Studies International Forum* 9, no. 5 (1986): 534.

16. Australian Labor Party, "National Committee of Inquiry," Discussion Papers (Adelaide: Australasian Political Studies Association, 1979).

17. Louis Asher, "The Liberal Party and Women," in George Brandis et al., eds., *Liberals Face the Future* (Melbourne: Oxford University Press, 1984), 104–16.

18. Under the system of responsible government in Westminster countries, government ministers are faced within Parliament by an opposition front bench, whose members are referred to as shadow ministers.

19. See the Saulwick polls conducted for *Age* and *Sydney Morning Herald* in 1991.

20. Sara Dowse, "Power in Institutions—The Public Service" (Paper presented at the Women and Politics Conference, Australian National Library, 1975, and a transcript of the discussion).

21. On the nature of Australian women's policy structures, including intragovernmental and intergovernmental machinery, see Marian Sawer, *Sisters in Suits: Women and Public Policy in Australia* (Sydney: Allen and Unwin, 1990).

22. Editorial Collective, *Mejane,* 26 March 1973.

23. Anne Summers, "Mandarins or Missionaries: Women in the Federal Bureaucracy," in Norma Grieve and Ailsa Burns, eds., *Australian Women: New Feminist Perspectives* (Melbourne: Oxford University Press, 1986), 62.

24. Sara Dowse, "The Plight of the Femocrat," *National Times* (22–28 April 1983).

25. Lesley Lynch, "Bureaucratic Feminisms: Bossism and Beige Suits," *Refractory Girl* 27 (1984): 38–44.

26. "Feminism in the Public Service," *Hersay* (September 1987).

27. Irene Webley, "The New Right and Women Who Want to Be Women in Australian Politics in the 1980s," *Hecate* 9 (1983): 7–23.

28. Anne Summers, "The Women's Movement," in Henry Mayer and Helen Nelson, eds., *Australian Poli-*

tics: A Fourth Reader (Melbourne: Longman Cheshire, 1977), 172.

29. Sara Dowse, "The Bureaucrat as Usurer," in Dorothy Broom, ed., *Unfinished Justice: Social Justice for Women in Australia* (Sydney: Allen and Unwin, 1984), 149.

30. Sabine Erika, "Break the Silence: The State and Violence Against Women," *Refractory Girl* 36 (August 1990): 13–16. See also Andrew Hopkins and Heather McGregor, *Working for Change: The Movement Against Domestic Violence* (Sydney: Allen and Unwin, 1991).

31. Ludo McFerren, "Interpretation of a Frontline State: Australian Women's Refuges and the State," in Sophie Watson, ed., *Playing the State: Australian Feminist Interventions* (Sydney: Allen and Unwin, 1990), 195.

32. National Women's Consultative Council, *Pay Eq-uity for Women in Australia* (Canberra: Australian Government Publishing Service, 1990), 38–41.

33. Carol O'Donnell and Philippa Hall, *Getting Equal* (Sydney: Allen and Unwin, 1988), chap. 3.

34. Laura Bennett, "Comparable Worth—What Happened?" *Journal of Industrial Relations* 30, no. 4 (1988): 533–46.

35. *Australian Feminist Studies,* 1987.

36. See, e.g., Margaret Levi and Meredith Edwards, "The Dilemmas of Femocratic Reform," in Mary F. Katzenstein and Hege Skjeie, eds., *Going Public: National Histories of Women's Enfranchisement and Women's Participation Within State Institutions* (Oslo: Institute for Social Research, 1990), 141–72.

37. Felicity Grace et al., "Written Out of Politics: Gender and Australian Politics Textbooks," *APSA Newsletter* 53 (May 1991): 2–7.

▲ Bangladesh

POLITICS

Type of Political System: parliamentary
   democracy[a]
   Sovereignty: republic
   Executive-Legislative System: parliamentary
Type of State: unitary
Type of Party System: multiparty
Major Political Parties

There are approximately 90 political parties in Bangladesh registered under the Political Parties Regulation of 1976. This list does not indicate the splits that have taken place in most of the parties from time to time, with splinter groups taking the name of the original party and adding the name of their leader in parentheses. These new parties have occasionally consolidated, disappeared, become weakened through further fragmentation, or gone back to the original party. Most of the parties have an extremely weak organizational base.

Bangladesh Awami League (AL): Centrist party founded in 1948; a major force in the struggle for independence.[b] Headed by Sheikh Hasina Wajed.

Bangladesh Nationalist Party (BNP): Centrist party, in power in 1992. Chaired by Khaleda Zia.

Jatiyo Dal (National Party): Formerly the National Front; formed in 1985 as a coalition of conservative Muslims and Marxists who wished to cooperate with President Hussain Muhammad Ershad. Headed by former president Ershad.

Jamaat-i-Islami (Islamic Assembly): Pro-Pakistani and religious fundamentalist party, re-formed in 1979. Headed by Abbas Ali Khan.

Bangladesh Communist Party (CPB): A socialist party that became legal again in 1978. Chaired by Moni Singh.

Jatiyo Samajtantric Dal (JSD; National Socialist Party): Leftist party formed in 1972 by a group, primarily students, that separated from the Awami League. Repressed under President Zia, the party became legal again in 1978. Chaired by A. S. M. Rab.

Bangladesh Krishak Sramik Awami League: Center-left party; originally a left-wing faction of the Awami League. Works closely with the Communist Party. Chaired by Abdur Razzaq.

Bangladesh Muslim League (BML): Conservative Islamic parties opposing independence from Pakistan formed this center-right league in 1971. Headed by M. A. Kader.

National Awami Party (NAP): Center-left party founded by the late A. H. I. Bashani. Principal opposition party until the 1975 coup. Headed by Muzaffar Ahmed.

Ganatantric League (Democratic League): Founded in 1976; a centrist party. Headed by Khondokar Mushtaque Ahmed.

Year Women Granted Right to Vote: 1947[c]
Year Women Granted Right to Stand for
   Election: 1947
Percentage of Women in the Unicameral
   Legislature: 10.3%[d]
Percentage of Electorate Voting for Highest
   Elected Office in Most Recent Election
   (1991): not available

DEMOGRAPHICS

Population: 109,877,000[e]
Percentage of Population in Urban Areas [f]
   Overall: 15.7%
   Female: 14.0%
   Male: 17.0%
Percentage of Population Below Age 15: 40.9%[g]
Birthrate (per 1,000 population): 32[h]
Maternal Mortality Rate (per 100,000 live
   births): 600
Infant Mortality Rate (per 1,000 live births):
   114[i]
Mortality Rate for Children Under Five (per
   1,000 live births): 180[j]
Average Household Size: 5.3[k]

Mean Age at First Marriage [l]
  Female: 18.1
  Male: 25.2
Life Expectancy [m]
  Female: 55.4
  Male: 56.4

EDUCATION

Ratio of Female to Male Enrollment [n]
  First-Level Education (ages 6 to 10): 79
  Second-Level Education (ages 11 to 15): 44
  Third-Level Education (ages 16 to 25): 24
Literacy Rate (for age 5 and above) [o]
  Female: 21.8%
  Male: 36.1%

ECONOMY

Gross National Product per Capita: U.S. $180 [p]
Percentage of Labor Force in Agriculture: 73.8% [q]
Distribution of Agricultural Workers by Sex [r]
  Female: 50.7%
  Male: 49.3%
Economically Active Population by Sex [s]
  Female: 61.6%
  Male: 80.9%

a. Although the constitution embodies democratic principles, the military intervened in politics twice between 1971 and 1990 and governed the country under martial law. Both times the military regimes initiated a process of civilianization that led to the election and functioning of the legislature.

b. Arthur S. Banks, ed., *Political Handbook of the World 1991* (Binghamton, N.Y.: CSA Publications, 1991), 54–55, is the source for much of the information here under Major Political Parties.

c. An extremely limited franchise [...] women in the 1920s; universal adult f[...] granted after independence from British rule i[...]

d. The figure given reflects the results of the 19[...] election and includes reserved seats. The constitutional provision for 30 reserved seats for women lapsed in December 1987 but was restored in June 1990.

e. Bangladesh Bureau of Statistics, *Statistical Pocket Book of Bangladesh, '92* (Dhaka: Bangladesh Bureau of Statistics, 1992), 74.

f. Calculations are based on Bangladesh Bureau of Statistics, *Statistical Yearbook of Bangladesh, 1991* (Dhaka: Bangladesh Bureau of Statistics, 1991), 47. The preliminary report of the 1991 census does not include data on urbanization.

g. Ibid., 85.

h. Bangladesh Bureau of Statistics, *Bangladesh Demographic Statistics, 1992* (Dhaka: Bangladesh Bureau of Statistics, 1992), 11.

i. *Human Development Report, 1992* (New York: U.N. Development Program, 1992).

j. Ibid.

k. Bangladesh Bureau of Statistics, *Statistical Pocket Book of Bangladesh, '92,* 74.

l. Bangladesh Bureau of Statistics, *Bangladesh Demographic Statistics, 1992,* 8.

m. Ibid.

n. Computed from data in Bangladesh Bureau of Statistics, *Bangladesh Education in Statistics, 1991* (January 1992); and Bangladesh Bureau of Educational Information and Statistics (BANBEIS), Ministry of Education, *Bangladesh Educational Statistics, 1991* (March 1992).

o. Bangladesh Bureau of Statistics, *Bangladesh Demographic Statistics, 1992,* 5.

p. Computed from Bangladesh Bureau of Statistics, *Statistical Yearbook of Bangladesh, 1991,* 523; and the corresponding official exchange rate for 1989–90.

q. Bangladesh Bureau of Statistics, *Report on Labour Force Survey, 1989* (April 1992), 25.

r. Based on data in ibid., 30.

s. Ibid., x, 20.

Ban_ _ _ _ _ Asian country of 55,598 square mil_ _ _ ds at the threshold of the Southeast Asian region. It is bounded on the west, north, and east by India (except for a short stretch on the east where it shares a border with Burma) and on the south by the Bay of Bengal. The land, mainly an alluvial plain, is at the confluence of the mighty Ganges-Brahmaputra river system, which originates in the Himalayas. The Padma, Meghna, and Jamuna rivers, along with their many tributaries, wash down the land toward the bay, bringing both joys and sorrows, with prospects of rich harvests from fertile fields, as well as the specter of severe floods if the rivers swell.

With a population of nearly 110 million, Bangladesh is extraordinarily crowded—an agricultural country with a population density of 1,918 persons per square mile.[1] The physical and material infrastructure for economic development is scanty and weak. Heavily aid-dependent and very poor—one of the poorest of the less developed countries—Bangladesh has a per capita yearly income of approximately U.S. $180. Nearly 60 percent of the population live below the poverty line, where the basic human requirements with regard to food, clothing, and shelter remain unmet. Although class and gender intersect, women nevertheless constitute a majority of the poor and bear the major brunt of poverty.[2] The means of production, both land and industrial facilities, are owned and controlled by men. Men own capital as well as control women's labor.

The traditional society of Bangladesh is permeated with patriarchal values and norms of female subordination, subservience, and segregation. A high premium is placed on female chastity; and purdah, the veiling and segregation of women, shapes the norms of societal and gender relations. Purdah reinforces not only the view that society is dichotomized into public and private spaces but also the stereotyped gender roles that assign women to the seclusion of the domestic sphere. The custom of purdah, molded by culture, tradition, and age-old religious interpretations, legitimizes the exclusion of women from public spaces, enhances their dependence on and subordination to men, and marginalizes their social status. Purdah is a manifestation of the male proprietary approach to gender relations that is inherent in a patriarchy.[3] In reality, the practice of purdah is being eroded, primarily by sheer survival needs as women venture out of their secluded world in search of livelihoods and partly by modernization, which involves education and mobility. The purdah values persist, however. Social norms uphold female subordination and dependence; women's mobility and their interactions with the outside world and with men are bound by socially acceptable constraints; and gender relations are governed by female deference and acquiescence to male authority.

Sons are expected to provide old-age security for their parents in the absence of a state-provided social security system, and they are expected to eventually take responsibility for their natal families, as well as head their own. Sons get preferential treatment in the allocation of the severely limited resources of a family, for they are considered the natural heirs in a patrilineal and patrilocal society.

Poverty and purdah combine to deprive girls of education, thus of employment opportunities and a sense of self-identity. The culturally prescribed and economically sanctioned subordination of women reinforces their inferior and dependent status in family and society. Upon marriage, a woman's dependence and loyalty to the natal family are transferred to the family of her husband, who replaces the father as the authority figure. The pernicious practice of giving dowry accentuates the inequality in marriage, often causing women to be subjected to abuse and violence within the confines of home for their inability or failure to bring adequate or promised dowry.[4]

Social conservatism is buttressed by religious orthodoxy. The religious opinion leaders, the ulemas and maulanas, generally tend to gravitate toward a narrow and rigid interpretation of Islamic tenets, relegating women to a subordinate status, to the private sphere, to seclusion. According to the Quran, for example, a daughter's inheritance is half the share of a son, and a male inherits more or even twice as much as a female at almost every stage of succession.[5] Although the law of inheritance is irrelevant for many people, who have practically nothing to bequeath, it and other such religious precepts guiding marriage, divorce, child custody, and inheritance are taken to imply that by divine will girls are inferior to boys, and women occupy a status unequal to and subordinate to men's.

Women's political engagement in Bangladesh occurs in the context of the country's poverty, the culture of female subordination, and weak political institutions. Regimes change frequently and have been democratic only fleetingly, and the mechanisms that sustain political articulation and mobilization are not well grounded. In this type of political culture and system, both formal and informal politics must be analyzed to understand women's position.

Any discussion of the formal political system must cover the electoral, legislative and party processes. Although these processes exclude or marginalize women and their interests, formal politics nonetheless shapes the contours of the economic and political life experienced by women in all sectors of society. The distinctions between public and private spheres—the male and the female domains—are sharply drawn. Women's access to the material bases of politics is circumscribed. The interlocking of the public

with the political tends to prevent their entry into politics, not to mention survival and advancement. In discussing women's engagement in formal politics, the chapter addresses the issue of women's representation and focuses on the seeming paradox of women's political leadership—both the government and the opposition in Bangladesh are now led by women—in a patriarchal political culture. Admittedly, neither the state nor the civil society in Bangladesh is structured in a gender-neutral way. The institutional capacities of the state are weak; regime changes and periods of authoritarian rule have undermined the efficacy of political structures. Given the political realities, creating a favorable political climate is necessary for improving the status of women.

The discussion of the informal political process includes a review of women's organizations whose aim is to raise women's status, create awareness of women's issues, and build platforms from which women's demands can be made. In seeking to find a public voice with which to demand change, these ostensibly nonpolitical organizations do in fact venture into the realm of politics. Although civil society has weak institutions in Bangladesh, women's voluntary groups—which have yet to occupy a significant space in the political landscape—provide women an important venue for making their demands known and for transforming the so-called social issues into matters of public policy. Because the Mahila Parishad (Women's Council) exemplifies the opportunities and barriers that women face in overcoming disadvantages and discrimination, this chapter focuses on it and on the nascent women's movement, emphasizing the value of social activism.

Violence, legal inequities, family planning, health needs, income generation, skill formation, education, and credit are all crucial questions for women in Bangladesh. These issues and others have engaged the attention of women social activists, grass-roots activists in many nongovernmental development organizations that advocate alternative paths to development, and the government in formulating its policy agenda. All these issues link women's private, domestic lives with their public and political capacities, interconnecting their concerns about, and hopes for, development and equality, autonomy and empowerment for women in Bangladesh. Finally, women's education is discussed here because of its vast transformative potential.

THE EMERGENCE OF THE STATE OF BANGLADESH

Bangladesh, comprising the former eastern province of Pakistan, became an independent nation-state in 1971. The Pakistan state itself was based on Muslim nationalism and was carved out of British India in 1947 when the British raj withdrew the imperial scepter from the Indian subcontinent. The cultural distinctiveness of the Bengalis inhabiting the eastern wing of Pakistan, or East Bengal, combined with economic exploitation and political domination, helped to transform a strident East Bengal push for autonomy into a vibrant nationalist movement. Nationalist sentiments came to a head in 1970–71, when the East Bengalis' electoral victory in the national Parliament was thwarted. When the Pakistani military junta unleashed a policy of state terror and imposed a military crackdown, the Bengalis responded with armed resistance. They emerged victorious after a bloody nine-month-long war of liberation and became independent of the internal colonialism of the Pakistan state structure.

Since independence Bangladesh has experienced continuing political instability. Weak democratic institutions, a legacy of the Pakistan period, have lacked nurturing during the two decades of Bangladesh's existence. First came a parliamentary system of government, next one-party rule, then two military takeovers—each followed by a period of civilianization to lead to civil government and representative institutions. The debate on the form of government continued through the 1980s. Finally, after the fall from power of Lt. Gen. Hussain Muhammad Ershad in December 1990 and the general election of February 1991, the Parliament passed a constitu-

tion amendment bill to establish parliamentary government. The 12th Constitution Amendment Bill, ratified in a September 1991 referendum, thus embodies a national consensus. After a lapse of sixteen years, Bangladesh is again governed by a parliamentary system.

The Awami League (AL, or People's League)—which had, under the leadership of Sheikh Mujibur Rahman, harnessed Bengali aspirations for a strong regional and later national identity and had subsequently formed the provisional government-in-exile during the war of liberation—formed the first government in independent Bangladesh. The country adopted a parliamentary system of government with a unicameral legislature consisting of 315 members. Of these, 300 were elected on the basis of universal adult franchise and single-member territorial constituencies; they in turn acted as an electoral college for the 15 seats reserved for women. Early in 1975 the multiparty parliamentary system was supplanted by a presidential one, and Bangladesh became a one-party state. A military coup intervened in August 1975; the charismatic Bengali nationalist leader Sheikh Mujibur Rahman, who was then the president of the country, was killed along with his entire family—except his two daughters, Sheikh Hasina and Sheikh Rehana, who were abroad at the time.

Lieutenant General Ziaur Rahman—who had made the historic declaration of the independence of Bangladesh over the radio on 27 March 1971 after the Pakistan army crackdown and who had been a valiant freedom fighter in the war of liberation—emerged as the strongman and ultimately became president.[6] He promoted the organization of a political party called the Bangladesh Jatiyotabadi Dal (Bangladesh Nationalist Party, or BNP), of which he became the leader. During the civilianization that culminated with the election of the national Parliament and the formation of a civilian and representative government in 1979, General Zia made a presidential proclamation that enlarged the number of legislative seats reserved for women to 30 and extended the period during which seats would be reserved from the original ten years to fifteen years following the promulgation of the constitution. A presidential form of government with a multiparty system was introduced. General Zia died in an abortive coup in May 1981, leaving behind his wife, Khaleda, and two minor sons.

In March 1982 a military coup toppled the civilian government. In the course of the civilianization initiated by Lt. Gen. Hussain Muhammad Ershad (a process that was, however, beset with crises), he encouraged the formation of a political party, the Jatiyo Party (JP, or National Party), under his leadership. In the beginning of the 1980s first Sheikh Hasina and later Khaleda Zia emerged in leadership roles in the Awami League and the Bangladesh Nationalist Party, respectively. These two women, who headed their respective parties and alliances, played principal and often crucial roles in the mobilization against Ershad. The eventual fall of Ershad in December 1990 ensured their ascension to state power as the heads of their parties. After the February 1991 election, Khaleda Zia was sworn in as the prime minister of the People's Republic of Bangladesh. Sheikh Hasina, heading the second-largest party in Parliament, thus became the leader of the opposition.

Broadly speaking, the AL, the BNP, and the JP are centrist parties, with the BNP occupying a right-to-center position and the JP further to the right. Another political force, however, has also entered the scene. The Jamaat-i-Islami, an Islamic fundamentalist party that had opposed the nationalist aspirations of the liberation war, carved out a political niche chiefly through participation in the democratic movement of the 1980s. By winning 18 seats in the Parliament in the February 1991 election the Jamaat increased its parliamentary strength. The aim of the party is to establish an Islamic way of life in Bangladesh. Its approach to what constitutes an Islamic way of life reflects a fundamentalist interpretation of the religion. The Jamaat philosophy propagates a sharp public-private dichotomy and assigns women to the private world.[7] The party thus holds potential significance for the future.

WOMEN IN FORMAL POLITICS

The early history of women's awakening in British India reflected the differential processes of the social formation of Hindus and Muslims. The social reform movement, the women social reformers, and the freedom movement fashioned the pattern of women's participation in public life in the immediate preindependence era.[8] With regard to women's issues, Muslim reformers turned their attention mainly to education, purdah, and the preservation of what was perceived as a Muslim way of life. Strong social norms upheld purdah as a determinant in societal and gender relations. Like some Hindu women in an earlier period, Muslim women who came to the public forum generally belonged to aristocratic political families and followed their male relatives into politics.[9]

While Bangladesh was East Pakistan (1947–71), it was part of a patriarchal political culture in which men dominated and controlled the spheres of power—political, military, and bureaucratic. Only a few women appeared in the political arena in Pakistan, generally in roles appended to those of husbands or male relatives. In politics, as in society, women played subordinate, supportive, and dependent roles. The handful of women who pursued politics on the basis of individual identity or within opposition and leftist political organizations were exceptions rather than socially accepted role models and were at times labeled deviants. This social legacy is at odds with women's formal political equality.

The constitution of Bangladesh provides for formal political equality of men and women. There is no legal barrier to women contesting or voting for any elective office, including that of the head of state. Women and men must meet the same qualifying tests for representative offices at both the national and local levels. Women are entitled to the same fundamental rights as men, including those of association, assembly, speech, and expression—which form the basis of political activity in a civil society. The social contract, epitomized in modern times by the constitution, implicitly recognizes that half of the citizens, whose interests the social contract upholds, have unequal access to the benefits of the state, and it declares the intent of the body politic to bring about the desired equality. Generally citizens are entitled to their rights without any discrimination on grounds of race, religion, or sex. Article 10 of the constitution says that steps shall be taken to ensure the participation of women in all spheres of national life. Article 28 (2) declares that women shall have rights equal to men's in all spheres of the state and public life. Article 9 promotes the special representation of women in local government while article 65 (3) provides for reserved seats for women in the Parliament, or Jatiyo Sangsad.[10] But the equality of participation by women in all spheres of national life and their equal rights in all spheres of the state and public life is more ideal than real. Sociocultural factors shape and limit the nature of women's political engagements, constitutional safeguards notwithstanding.

The assumption in colonial India that different communities and interests should be represented in the legislative assemblies was adapted in Pakistan to provide for women's representation through the reservation of legislative seats. Although the specific number of seats reserved for women changed over time, all along constituting a small proportion of the total, the electoral process remained basically the same: except in the 1954 election in East Bengal, women were elected indirectly to the reserved seats by the legislature.[11]

The Pakistan constitutional documents left a legacy for the framers of the Bangladesh constitution. Together with the right to vote and to run for the 300 general or open seats of the Parliament, the provision of reserved seats was considered a way to "safeguard" a minimum representation of women in view of their disadvantaged position in society.[12] Women were provided with "protected" representation because they were not in a position to compete successfully with male politicians for territorial constituencies.

The reservation of seats reflects a paternalistic approach to women's representation. The patriarchal political culture of society led to the transformation of such "protections" and "safeguards" into instruments of patriarchal domination and contributed to the marginalization of women in the political sphere. The ruling parties did not nominate women for general seats in the first two elections—held in 1973 and 1979—but treated the reservation provision as a device to exclude women from the general seats, which thus came to be treated as seats for men.[13]

Indirect election to the reserved seats by simple majority vote ensures the control of these seats by the party obtaining a numerical majority (51 or more seats) in the legislature. This has, on the one hand, dissuaded other political parties from putting forward candidates for the reserved seats.[14] Women candidates nominated by the ruling party were elected uncontested in 1973 (AL), 1979 (BNP), and 1986 (JP). After the general election in February 1991, however, the party obtaining the largest number of seats but not a clear majority in the legislature, the Bangladesh Nationalist Party, conceded two seats to the Jamaat-i-Islami in return, it was hinted, for support in forming a cabinet. On the other hand, the system has encouraged excessive political dependence of the aspiring candidates on party leadership, predominantly male, and on the regime. So-called elite contact has been a more crucial factor in the nomination process for some women than has political support based on contacts with local constituencies.[15] The nomination process and the electoral principle of reserved seats for women render women's participation in the legislature dependent on the patronage of the male elite in the party in power and accentuate women's dependence and subordination in the political sphere. Successive governments have also found the reserved seats for women to constitute block votes that they can conveniently control. Reservation also undermines women's representative status. Dividing the country into 300 constituencies for the general seats and into 30 electoral zones for the reserved seats has made the latter constituencies roughly ten times larger than the former. By implication, one woman in a reserved seat represents an area that ten people (usually male) in general seats also represent, resulting in feeble constituency linkages and a weak local power base for women.

Generally, however, indirect election for the reserved seats has found support among a section of women politicians because it eliminates the need for, as well as the risk of, electoral investments, both political and material. They also regard electoral politics as heavily weighted against women's participation. Male politicians have an overwhelming advantage in terms of financial resources, networking capabilities, and organizational strength, which adversely affects women's electoral prospects even at the stage of nominating candidates.

The reservation of seats lapsed in December 1987 after the president dissolved the 1986 assembly to counter opposition moves to destabilize the regime. The government's attitude toward reincorporating the provision into the constitution was ambivalent as the 1988 elections approached.[16] Several ideas were floated during this time—for example, abolishing the indirect election of women representatives and filling the reserved seats by direct election from territorial constituencies, and establishing quotas for women nominated by the party to run for general seats.[17] Ultimately, however, the 10th Amendment of the constitution, enacted in June 1990, provided for 30 reserved seats for women in the Parliament for ten years from the commencement of the next Parliament. The Parliament elected in 1988 was dissolved after the fall of General Ershad from power. The Parliament elected in February 1991 contains the 30 reserved seats.

In this Parliament several women MPs in reserved seats have attained greater political stature and more visibility, with commensurate public and political roles, than ever before, primarily through their association with the BNP and its leadership—personified by Prime Minister Begum (a female title of rank) Khaleda Zia—in the 1980s. The apparent positive trend needs to be consolidated by grounding women's political and electoral strength directly in local constituencies. It is also necessary to ensure the effective representation of women and the prominence of their concerns within the party.[18] These matters touch upon issues of constitutional principle, electoral organization, and party orientation. A degree of consensus among political actors is therefore necessary with regard to the desired intervention strategies, as is an awareness that these could impact favorably on women's political engagement. A policy of protection hardly ever guarantees equality unless it is intended as a temporary device and orchestrated with measures designed to eliminate the factors that warrant the protection.

A quick overview of elections for the general seats in the Parliament underscores the marginality of women and the androcentric bias in the political process. In the parliamentary election of 1973 women were only 0.3 percent of the total candidates; in 1979 they accounted for 0.9 percent. The percentage rose to nearly 1.3 in the 1986 election, and in the election of February 1991, women constituted slightly over 1.5 percent of the contending candidates.

The 1991 election was held under the caretaker government of Acting President Chief Justice Shahabuddin Ahmed. Unlike the elections of 1973, 1979, and 1986, there was no ruling party (or party backed by the ruling power) that expected to obtain a majority at the polls and thereby win the 30 seats reserved for their women party members. This realization was partly responsible for the nomination of women candidates by all the major parties. There were more than 40 women candidates, more than double the figure for the 1986 elections and the most so far.[19]

Over the years women candidates have increased their voter support. In the 1991 election they polled over 30 percent of the votes in sixteen constituencies, and in five of these they were able to secure more than 50 percent of the votes cast. Khaleda Zia and Sheikh Hasina drew a high level of voter support, and a few candidates lost to their male opponents by narrow margins.[20] Since the 1986 election, when women first won general seats (by-elections excluded), they have won between 1.3 and 2.6 percent of the seats in the general elections—though the number of seats actually filled by women has been lower than the number of women elected, because some candidates have run in several constituencies. In 1986 Sheikh Hasina contested in four and won in three constituencies; in 1991 she won in one of three contested constituencies. Khaleda Zia won all five seats that she contested in 1991; her party, the BNP, did not participate in the 1986 election. In 1986 and 1991 Sheikh Hasina contested from multiple constituencies in the general elections, and Zia did so in 1991.[21] The general seats are acknowledged to wield greater power, and claims of political leadership and effective representation in the legislative arena are rooted in these seats, which are linked to grass-roots support at constituency levels.

Women's limited participation in electoral politics is illustrative of, first, male control of party organizations and of men's greater ability to build viable constituency and party support in favor of nominations; second, women's lack of access to the kind of money and patronage that are increasingly crucial factors in candidates' ability to win elections; and third, the aggressive electioneering tactics often employed, which are likely to dissuade women from entering the fray.[22] These forces have to be viewed in the wider social context of women's limited autonomy, mobility, and economic standing and the overall social framework of unequal gender relations.

The emergence of Sheikh Hasina and Khaleda Zia in political leadership roles represents a paradox in a patriarchal culture that is best explained by their kinship linkages to male authority. The political capital of Sheikh Hasina and Khaleda Zia is their kinship to the powerful male political leaders Mujibur Rahman (leader of the Awami League) and Ziaur Rahman (leader of the Bangladesh Nationalist Party), who were assassinated while serving as presidents of the country in 1975 and 1981, respectively. The two women's political value lies in their symbolizing the former leaders in the absence of any direct male heirs capable of taking their places. Their transformation from housewives to party leaders during 1981–83 underscores their potential as uni-

fying forces; in the background of party internal crises the (male) party stalwarts turned to the bereaved daughter and grieving widow and practically co-opted them as leaders.[23] Sheikh Hasina and Khaleda Zia have inherited the haloes of the slain leaders, which sanctified their status, at least initially. Blood or inheritance has legitimated their leadership. As a result, factions seceding from the parties have either dissipated into insignificance or returned to the fold.[24] Those close associates of Mujibur Rahman who have had reason to feel alienated do not, therefore, effectively challenge Sheikh Hasina's leadership. In spite of secessions and some splintering, the parties led by Sheikh Hasina and Khaleda Zia are recognized as the legitimate successors to those led by Mujibur Rahman and Ziaur Rahman.

The political careers of other leading Awami League women illustrate that women without famous political fathers and husbands can still advance to the higher echelons, mostly through decades of extensive political involvement and sacrifice. Similarly, the instances of political consolidation by a few women within the party organization during the movement phase of the BNP in the 1980s also seem to be politically significant. But the authority and appeal of Sheikh Hasina and Khaleda Zia transcend the routine and formal structures of the parties. Both women have proved adept at creating and consolidating support and forging networks based on personal loyalties within their parties.[25]

The emergence of women political leaders raises issues relevant to consolidating the position of women in public life and creating a necessary power base. Having socially acceptable role models for women diminishes the risk of social stigmatization for entering public life—which entails high visibility, mobility, public contact, and networking. One of the liabilities of entry into public life remains the threat of character assassination by whisper and innuendo that is damaging to the honor of the women concerned. Women leaders conform publicly to the traditions of purdah, albeit symbolically and notionally, by covering their heads with their saris. Some degree of accommodation to the customs and values prescribed by religious-cultural tradition is necessary, for the national constituency remains conservative and imbued with patriarchal values. The power balance of interest groups and factions within the party, as well as organized power and pressure groups in society, leaves little flexibility for women leaders on policy issues, such as a feminist agenda.[26] Nor have women leaders pushed women's issues beyond the framework of national development.

The women's wings of political parties have been more active in party mobilization, particularly during elections, than in interest articulation. Political power has tended to flow through the main organizational bodies of parties and through their respective front organizations (where these exist) of students, youth, labor, and peasants, rather than through women's organizations.

In this cultural and political setting, how are women's concerns and issues of equality addressed? In a developing country, the views of the ruling party and indeed of the opposition are important because the government does act as a change agent in society. The approach to the status of women so far has been one of welfare and development, paternalism and protection, and not one of social transformation and equity.

Women's concerns do not figure prominently in the political discourse. They are not often perceived as major issues, hidden as they are behind the country's poverty and underdevelopment. The major parties project women's issues to the electorate not as central but as marginal, and women's issues remain peripheral in the political debate. The Awami League, in its 1991 election manifesto, takes a stand against policies that discriminate on the basis of gender, expresses a commitment to women's social and economic independence, promises facilities and training to transform women into a skilled labor force and make them full partners in national development, and recognizes women's oppression as a social evil. The Bangladesh Nationalist Party likewise pledges to integrate women into national development efforts, guarantees an honorable role for women in every aspect of national development, and promises to implement gradually all U.N. conventions on women. The leftist Five-Party Alliance promises to accept and implement the U.N. Convention on the Elimination of All Forms of Discrimination Against Women (CEDAW), to stop the practice of dowry, and to push for measures that severely punish oppressors of women. Some of the issues propounded by Jamaat-i-Islami, however, touch on the core of gender relations in society. Among other things, the Jamaat program envisages separate educational institutions and workplaces for women, takes a stand against dowry and the oppression of wives, and expresses a determination to eradicate all forms of moral degradation, including prostitution, by eliminating their causes. The Jamaat is also committed to making Bangladesh an Islamic state and declaring the Quran and the Sunnah the sources of law.[27]

Bangladesh was one of the first countries to set up a focal point within the governmental machinery for women's concerns. The office had developed into a full-fledged ministry by the end of 1978. Though innovative and widely acclaimed at the time for reflecting women's needs and goals, the ministry did not become a powerful lobby for and mechanism to monitor women's advancement and equality.[28] It suffers from a low political profile because of its clientele (women) and mandate (advocacy for women) in the absence of a strong political commitment. However, the procedure (as revised in 1990) for preparing, processing, and appraising government development projects calls for, among other things, assessing the impact of the projects on different socioeconomic groups, including women, and envisages a preapproval screening by the Ministry of Women's Affairs for all projects, whether women specific or not. Whether or not the ministry is a good "watchdog of women's interests" remains to be seen.[29]

The government is paying increasing attention to women's education, both as a means of developing human resources and as a strategy for curbing the rate of population growth. The government's policies with regard to the female recruitment quota in public service employment is being assessed in positive terms, although some operational drawbacks still exist. The government has also enacted legislation to protect women against violence and physical abuse and to strengthen their status, although the basic personal laws governing marriage, divorce, inheritance, and custody have not been touched.[30] The five-year plans of the government reflect a growing concern for women's development needs.[31]

This progress has taken place as a result of the government's interventionist role and also in response to the women's lobby, which consists of women's organizations and voluntary groups, research bodies, and activists. The impact of the U.N. Decade for Women, the policies and program activities of U.N. agencies, and donor priorities have been contributory factors.

BUILDING THE WOMEN'S MOVEMENT

The tradition of voluntarism in Bangladesh has been one of dedication to the welfare and amelioration of the condition of distressed women. Gradually the approach has shifted to development and skill formation. And as the demand for equality has arisen, the state has been urged to redress oppression and discrimination and ensure the exercise of equal rights by women. The aims that at first focused on providing succor now encompass literacy and skill formation, income generation, legal aid, an increase in women's awareness, and information accessing. The strategies used to attain these goals involve mobilization, sensitization, group formation, and solidarity as a basis of taking action. Through mobilization and organization, women's organizations articulate a women's agenda in the public forum, create awareness in society, and seek to have an impact on the formal political system. The techniques generally include rallies, demonstrations, processions, petitions, press conferences, protest actions, and memorandums to the government.

The many women's organizations in Bangladesh reflect their organizational and ideological biases in their modes and areas of operation. They are involved in a wide range of social activities according to their mandate, organizational base, and clientele. For example, the Women's Voluntary Association, the Lionesses, the Rotary, and the Zonta Club carry on the tradition of humanitarian services to women. The Business and Professional Women's Club and the Bangladesh Federation of University Women are run by professional and highly educated women, and other women's organizations represent women of certain professions, such as women lawyers. Broadly speaking, the leadership and membership of these welfarist organizations are drawn from the elite classes of society. The target population is needy and distressed women. Other women's organizations, based more in the middle class, pursue a broad range of activities aimed at eradicating discrimination against women and achieving equality while developing a national structure and presence through a continuous recruitment of members. The Mahila Parishad (Women's Council) and the Mahila Samiti (Women's Association) exemplify this category. Yet another kind of organization has also emerged, typified by Naripokkho (For Women), which may also enlist men as supportive partners. Organizations like Naripokkho, which are also largely middle class, take an actively profeminist stand and view women's subordination and the unequal gender relations in society as basically political issues. Innovative in their approach to mobilization and interest articulation, these groups appeal to limited sectors of society. Research has also played a role in focusing attention on the discrimination and oppression experienced by women. Women for Women, a research and study group, uses research, publication, networking, and advocacy to highlight the situation of women and promote the incorporation of gender concerns into public policies.

Like these autonomous groups, state- and party-directed women's organizations mobilize women and claim to represent their interests. The Jatiyo Mahila Sangstha (JMS, or National Women's Organization), which is under the administrative and budgetary control of the government, has provided support and approval to the government's women-related policies, but its contribution to gender awareness and the articulation of women's needs and concerns has been marginal.[32] Women's organizations may also be extensions of political parties or have informal linkages with them, but they generally eschew political connections and work as social organizations. Gender concerns may also figure prominently in the development programs and projects of national and international nongovernmental organizations (NGOs), even those without an exclusive focus on women.

Women's engagement in social action has given rise to an increased awareness of the need for concerted action. Insofar as women's organizations carry women's voices to the public arena and seek women's advancement and equality, a nascent women's movement exists in Bangladesh. The visibility of women—students, activists, and housewives, women from the performing arts and from political, social, cultural, and women's organizations—on the streets of the capital during the final surge of the democracy movement in November and December 1990 that toppled the Ershad regime points to their heightened political awareness and suggests their potential collective strength.

The early 1980s were years of tentative coalition building. The U.N. Decade for Women (1976–85) had increased awareness among members of women's organizations and consequently their level of activity. Women worked together on issues like violence against women, dowries, and ratification of the Convention on the Elimination of All Forms of Discrimination Against Women. Such alliances proved short lived, however; and it was in the context of the proposed World Conference on Women to be held in Moscow at the initiative of the Women's International Democratic Federation in June 1987 that the seeds for a more lasting, broader alliance of women's organizations were sown. In preparation for the world conference, some 20 women's organizations in Bangladesh established a national committee to formulate and adopt a united program. The gains of concerted action began to be consolidated in the latter half of 1987. A coalition of 14 organizations called

the Oikkyo Baddha Nari Samaj (United Women's Forum) issued a 17-Point Program in February 1988 demanding equal rights for women—as enunciated in the constitution—on a broad range of legal, economic, and social concerns, but the program falls short of advocating gender equality and feminism. The number of member organizations has now increased to about 20.[33]

The forum comprises diverse groups, ranging from those that could be described as generally progressive to those that are feminist in the Bangladesh context and from large-scale organizations to research bodies and activist groups. The organizations have differing approaches and ideological orientations to women's questions: some have a nonpolitical mandate, and others are formal or informal extensions of political parties. Likewise, some member organizations mobilize their own or local resources, whereas others rely on external funding. The leadership of these organizations rests mainly with women from the middle and upper classes—elite women. The forum's funding consists of annual subscriptions from member organizations, which are also expected to take turns serving as its secretariat.

Unity, however fragile, remains operative at the national level. There have been few visible coalitions at the district level, primarily because the activities of most of the organizations in the forum are either based in towns and limited rural areas or based in Dhaka by mandate or organizational necessity. Only a few are broad-based national organizations. The forum mainly coordinates member organizations in taking common stands. It protested the Eighth Amendment Bill, passed in 1988, which declared Islam the state religion; and it took part in several programs during the final days of the democracy movement in 1990.[34] In December 1990, during the transition to democracy after the fall of the Ershad regime, the forum submitted a memorandum to the acting president that incorporated many of the demands earlier put forward in its platform. With a few exceptions, the demands put forward by the forum have already been voiced by the Mahila Parishad, one of its strongest and most active members. Although the forum serves to carry women's collective voice to the public arena, it hardly adds any new dimensions or sharpens the focus and direction of the women's movement.

The strategies and objectives of Mahila Parishad, the largest organization in the forum, typify those of women's organizations in Bangladesh that fight against gender discrimination and organize women to assume a public voice. The Parishad was founded in 1970 during the stirring political developments leading to the war of liberation from Pakistan. Its membership, activities, and program initiatives make it a major force.

The Parishad takes well-defined positions in the areas of women's education, employment, and health, and it raises social, economic, and political demands designed to remove discrimination and to attain equality for women in Bangladesh. Politically, the Parishad stands for an exploitation-free society and full realization of women's equal rights as enunciated in the constitution of the country. Its stand on secularism, in opposition to what it terms the Islamization of Bangladesh, rests on its understanding of the implications of Islamization for both politics and gender. In the interplay of political forces in the country, the Parishad sees signs of a resurgence of Islamic fundamentalism that would relegate women to a more inferior and discriminated-against status and to a more circumscribed existence than they already have.

The Parishad argues that questions of women's emancipation are linked with the broader issue of reconstructing an exploitation-free society. Its view that gender exploitation is one manifestation of class exploitation brings the Parishad near to socialist feminism on the ideological spectrum.

The Parishad had 25,000 members in December 1988, nearly double its 13,000-strong membership in 1980. The membership has a strong urban bias and is heavily represented by middle-class women. It does not yet have branches in larger rural areas.[35] Although lower-income women remain its major target clientele, it has not devised ways to recruit them into the organizational structure and positions of leadership.

Like most voluntary organizations, it is plagued by the need for more time and money.[36]

Though eschewing a partisan political role for itself, the Parishad is perceived by some as having linkage with the Communist Party of Bangladesh (CPB), which could undermine its wider acceptability. Such ties are denied by the Parishad leaders, who point out that such views may have been created by the apparently closer collaboration with party activists during the formative years of the Parishad, the likely involvement of a section of the Parishad leadership with the party, and the Parishad's movement-oriented program. The Parishad was partisan in the 1986 parliamentary election, however, in supporting the Awami League–led 15-Party Alliance, whose left block included the Communist Party of Bangladesh. The Parishad has created a cadre of dedicated and committed workers and played a pioneering role in the emergence of a nascent women's movement in Bangladesh. The Parishad nonetheless needs to consider whether to reassess its intellectual underpinning and whether to reexamine the rationale for its latent political leaning, so that it may carry the weight of a neutral political force and build alliances as necessary for the realization of its goals.

In spite of the political implications of these ideological positions, Parishad claims to have gained increased acceptance by the government over the years. The Parishad cites two instances in particular when it was able to exert pressure on the government through the mobilization of public opinion. In 1980, in a drive to build public opinion and act as a pressure group, the Parishad collected 17,000 signatures of women who opposed the practice of dowry and submitted them to the Parliament. With some justification the Parishad asserts that this led to the framing of the antidowry legislation. The Parishad also waged a campaign for government ratification of the Convention on the Elimination of All Forms of Discrimination Against Women through public meetings, rallies, and press conferences and worked with 13 women's organizations in 1984–85 to mobilize public opinion.[37] The Parishad claims partial success, for the government of

Bangladesh ratified the convention before the 1985 World Conference at Nairobi, though with certain reservations.

The social activism of Bangladeshi women can be seen in the breadth of their work on the political issues underlying gender relations and the subordination of women. The protest raised by women's organizations at the passage of the Eighth Amendment Bill in 1988, which established Islam as the state religion of Bangladesh, is a case in point. Alarmed by the increasing reliance of the regime on Islamic symbolism, many women's groups saw in the move a possible symbiosis of state power with religion and the ascendancy of orthodox and fundamentalist forces, which could have adverse repercussions on women's lives and status. The United Women's Forum, reflecting the views of its membership, saw the move as an exploitation of the religious sentiments of the common people for political reasons and as a relegation of women to a more backward status in society. The forum organized protest rallies and demonstrations. The Parishad, both as a member of the forum and on its own initiative, undertook activities aimed at rallying women around the issue. Five activists in Naripokkho, a radical feminist organization, filed a writ petition before the Supreme Court challenging the validity of the Eighth Amendment Act with respect to article 2A, which proclaims Islam the state religion.[38]

Women's groups have also agitated and lobbied to end economic exploitation (e.g., by lending support to women garment workers' demands) and to change public policies (e.g., by promoting the mainstreaming of women in national development plans).[39] It is on issues concerning violence and oppression, however, that women's groups have responded with the most vigor. The brutalization of women's persons and lives seems to epitomize women's subordination, oppression, and vulnerability in society. Women's organizations generally take up instances of rape, acid throwing, and murder—first, to create social awareness and supportive public opinion so that the perpetrators are brought to trial and punished and, second, to raise the demand for

strict enforcement of the law and more stringent legal measures.[40] Women's organizations like the Mahila Parishad that have legal aid cells and good organizational capabilities follow such incidents closely. Other groups issue statements to the press and support coordinated activities of public protest and mobilization. Some highly publicized cases illustrate the strategies and options of the women's organizations in ensuring a voice for women in the public arena on the issues of women's oppression and exploitation.

A sensational murder brought women's groups to the streets in 1989. The victim was a young, newly married woman, the daughter of a journalist martyred during the war of liberation. The accused was the son of a wealthy family having—it was hinted in press reports—access to the corridors of power. There was also a paramour, an older married woman, with whom the accused allegedly had an illicit relationship before his marriage.[41] The forum held protest rallies and processions; the Mahila Parishad, along with several other women's organizations, marched to the courthouse with placards demanding justice and the death sentence for the murderer. Parishad members also attended the trial, at times along with colleagues from other women's groups. Naripokkho protested against the attitudes of society that give rise to such incidents of murder and violence. The accused and the paramour were sentenced to death by the trial court. The High Court Division of the Supreme Court, in the process of reviewing the death sentences and on appeal, upheld the conviction of the husband but acquitted the paramour on grounds of insufficient proof of instigation.[42] The Parishad and other women's groups continue to watch further legal developments.

An attempt in October 1991 to evict prostitutes from the red-light areas in a district adjacent to the capital—organized by a group that calls itself the Un-Islamic Activities Resistance Committee (UARC)—aroused considerable concern and led to some concerted protests by many women's groups. The UARC said its action was directed at cleansing the social environment and eradicating an immoral and un-Islamic activity. It mobilized in the name of Islam and used Islamic symbolism—including a procession toward the eviction site that started after the Friday midday prayer, an important congregational prayer for Muslims—thereby enlisting wide support and putting those who opposed eviction on legal and humanitarian grounds in the predicament of appearing to support an un-Islamic activity.

Women's groups and a section of the press claimed that the eviction move was the outward culmination of an internal feud between two (male) groups for influence, money, and control over business and property. The prostitutes themselves, with a leader of their own, made statements to the press and prepared to resist eviction. Several women's groups established contact with the prostitutes, and some carried out on-the-spot investigations. The district administration averted eviction for the time being and diffused tension by enforcing law-and-order measures and forming a committee of local officials from the magistracy and police, a journalist, and two members of the UARC to find a solution to the problem. The vigilance of the women's groups and their alacrity in raising the voice of protest and expressing solidarity on the issue of women's oppression and exploitation, together with the supportive role of a section of the media, apparently served as a deterrent to any hasty move or use of force.

The incident recalled the tragic death of a child prostitute in 1985, when women's groups had galvanized the public into demanding adequate rehabilitation of prostitutes and legal measures to eradicate prostitution.[43] Six years later they established direct contact with the prostitutes affected to keep them from being unduly harassed by the police or the UARC. The women's organizations also made public statements identifying the underlying issues and calling for adequate measures to provide for the women's social and economic rehabilitation and the eradication of prostitution. They also requested the identification of the male patrons and clients who were involved with the business of prostitution. Several women's groups that took public stands also joined in attempts—initiated by women's groups and NGOs (such as Naripokkho and the Coordinating Council for Human Rights in Bangladesh)—to bring out a common voice of protest by women and lay a basis for immediate and long-term joint action.[44]

WOMEN AND EDUCATION: A POLICY ISSUE

The education system in Bangladesh is elitist; it has a predominantly urban base and serves mostly male beneficiaries.[45] National statistics provide a grim picture of the overall status of women in education. The literacy rate is modest: only 36.1 percent of the males over five and 21.8 percent of the females over five have the ability to write a letter in any language.[46] The low literacy rate shapes the education policy, the major components of which could be identified as follows: the elimination of illiteracy, the introduction of universal, compulsory primary education, and the strengthening of technical, scientific, and technological education and training at the secondary and tertiary levels.

Certain inherent inequities stemming from the education system itself and the socioeconomic base on which it is built further limit women's educational opportunities. There are three major areas of concern. A wide gender disparity in enrollment and in drop-out rates begins at the primary level (grades one through five), and the disparity in enrollment becomes more pronounced through the successive levels of education.[47] For most families, the actual costs, as well as the opportunity costs—in terms of financial investments and missed child labor—outweigh the perceived gains from enrolling and keeping girls in school. At the same time, the curricula content and ideology reinforce and perpetuate gender stereotypes by promoting and transmitting through succeeding generations the dominant patriarchal values. Finally, the material and infrastructural aspects of education affect women's opportunities. These include the location of schools and colleges, the flexibility of school hours, the availability of female teachers, the provision of facilities for special needs (e.g., toilets on school premises or accommodations for female teachers), and the overall gender imbalance in the planning, administration, and delivery of education. In the higher levels of education, the self-selection or segregation of women in certain fields and women's extremely limited participation in the vocational and technical training institutes are also problematic. Nonformal education to promote literacy, numeracy, sanitation and hygiene, and skill formation has a vast potential for reaching the huge female population bypassed by the formal education system.[48]

The redress of the existing gender imbalances in education initially received only peripheral attention in the policy discourse. Discernible, however, is a growing national emphasis on women's education, dictated mainly by considerations of "social expediency," dictated by pro-natalist and development concerns, and not geared toward the personhood of women nor guided by commitment to the principles of distributive social justice.[49] In successive Education Commission reports, the gender disparity is noted, and special provisions to reduce the gap are called for, but the issue of women's education is marginalized in the context of the policy framework and in terms of the specified objectives and strategies of the government.[50] The First Five-Year Plan (1973–78) set forth the importance of women's education for efficient household management, better care of children, and other private and social matters. The Second Five-Year Plan (1980–85) tried to accelerate the development of women's education through incentives. In the Third Five-Year Plan (1985–90) the gender focus was slightly sharpened.[51] The Fourth Five-Year Plan (FFYP, 1990–95), however, emphasizes the gender dimension of development issues and incorporates the concept of mainstreaming women in the macroeconomic development process—a consequence, in part, of well-orchestrated advocacy and networking activities by women's groups and by international organizations and donor agencies, undertaken during the formulation stages of the draft plan.[52]

Women's initiatives at various forums articulating demands to bring women into the main-stream of the development process or at least to consider women an integral factor in the process as both agents and beneficiaries were aimed at encouraging the government to take a proactive approach toward women in its development efforts. There was also enhanced government awareness and an overall positive stance on the issue of women and development. The U.N. Decade for Women and the follow-up activities seem also to have helped situate women in the context of national development priorities and options. During the 1980s the women of Bangladesh gained greater visibility in economic production processes as they moved to nontraditional areas of economic activity, representing a significant shift to the informal labor market, and as their traditional home-based economic activities were being highlighted by newer research and data, thus demanding greater attention from policy planners.

The FFYP emphasizes education—reducing the gender gap in literacy and promoting girls' education in grades one to twelve—and envisages extensive incentives.[53] The provisions for compulsory primary education, satellite schools, and free studentship (fees) for girls up to grade eight in schools outside municipal areas, if effectively implemented, hold out relatively greater prospects for girls than for boys, because girls constitute the bulk of those traditionally bypassed or shut out from the formal education system, as well as the bulk of those who drop out.[54]

Some initiative has also been taken by the government to remove the patriarchal biases from educational materials. A Women in Development Unit was established at the National Curriculum and Textbook Board in mid-1991 to "exclude discriminatory language and situations and to reflect women's concerns in curriculum and textbooks."[55] The review of the curricula and textbooks for schools at the primary level has just begun. The lengthy task is stupendous, requiring that patriarchal values and culture be delinked from formal education, but it is also potentially transformative.

In the FFYP the government envisages a partnership with nongovernmental organizations that have developed successful models of nonformal education and that could enlarge their bases of operation. NGOS work in closer proximity to the target group than the government does, and they have been exponents of alternative models of development. The Grameen (Rural) Bank and the Bangladesh Rural Advancement Committee (BRAC), which have innovative programs in the fields of credit, income generation, health, and nonformal education, have demonstrated remarkable success in reaching out to the most marginalized and disadvantaged groups—including poor rural women, who remain outside the pale of conventional development efforts. The widely acclaimed credit programs of the Grameen Bank help women acting to break out of poverty and identify women as development actors.[56] BRAC has been a leading exponent of nonformal education to combat illiteracy and underdevelopment, and it, too, focuses on women.[57] The success of the BRAC primary schools has led policy makers to consider replicating them and expanding their number.[58] The modality for cooperation between the government and NGOS like BRAC in the field of nonformal education is being worked out. The many NGOS have differing approaches to teaching, different teaching materials, and different curricula, so overlapping, duplication, and lack of uniformity in class content and educational standards are all possible unless there is adequate coordination of projects and mapping of project boundaries.

The present government, in power since March 1991, has pledged its commitment to the advancement of women's education and has stressed the provision of incentives—particularly free education up to grade eight for girls outside municipal areas—and the introduction of compulsory primary education. The trends augur well for women, provided that policy commitments are built into sustained and effective implementation and delivery processes. In Bangladesh, plans and policies have a history of falling behind stated targets and objectives.

For women's organizations in Bangladesh, women's education is basically an issue of literacy and primary education, given the magnitude of female illiteracy. Women's exploitation, powerlessness, and vulnerability are considered to be rooted in their dependent status, which in turn results from women's lack of education, earned income, and awareness of their rights and status. Women's organizations engaged in consciousness-raising, skill-formation, and income-generation activities have also been involved in nonformal and adult education and programs to teach functional and legal literacy and impart knowledge about basic survival needs and the immediate environment, health, nutrition, hygiene, sanitation, and so on, to girls and adult women. Some organizations, like the Mahila Parishad, use the readers and manuals prescribed by the textbook and curriculum board of the government. Others, like the Saptagram Nari Swanirvar Parishad (Saptagram—Seven Villages—Women's Self-Reliance Movement) create their own teaching materials that reflect their approach to social issues and women's concerns. Still others, like Naripokkho, do not embark on education programs as such but try to generate awareness through cultural media and open forums. Women's organizations are engaged in educating women, however informally and indirectly, insofar as they direct their efforts toward equipping women with physical and social survival skills, with strength and solidarity, with the awareness that changes in their lives and status are possible.

NOTES

1. Bangladesh has a predominantly Muslim population (86.6 percent), along with Hindus (12.1), Buddhists (0.6), and Christians (0.3). The population is ethnically homogeneous except for the roughly 1 percent that comprises tribal peoples. According to the 1981 census, 83.4 percent of Bangladeshis live in rural areas. Women constitute about 48 percent of the population.

2. The burden of poverty falls disproportionately on women, as is set forth in Hossain Zillur Rahman et al., *Rethinking Poverty: A Case for Bangladesh* (New Delhi: Sage Publications India, forthcoming 1993). Rahman and his colleagues estimate that 55 percent of the population of Bangladesh live in poverty. The following statistics attest to the gender disparity in poverty as well.

Although the infant mortality rate per 1,000 live births is higher for male children, the pattern reverses in early life (at one to four years) to a higher female mortality rate. A typical Bangladeshi girl consumes 20 percent fewer calories per day than her brother. Girls also suffer from a higher incidence of stunting and wasting. Malnutrition is significantly higher among young girls (14 percent) than boys (5 percent). The enrollment ratio in primary schools is lower for girls, with the male-female gap widening at successively higher stages of learning and in technical and professional education. A quarter of the female population aged 45 to 49 are widowed or divorced, with sharp increases at higher ages—indicating that a large proportion of Bangladeshi women live in or face the threat of economic and social insecurity. For some relevant statistical information and analyses see Bangladesh Bureau of Statistics, *Selected Statistics and Indicators on the Demographic and Socio-Economic Situation of Women in Bangladesh* (Dhaka: Bureau of Statistics, 1989); UNICEF, *An Analysis of the Situation of Children in Bangladesh* (Dhaka: UNICEF, 1987); and Mahmuda Islam, *The Girl Child in Bangladesh: A Situation Analysis Report* (Dhaka: UNICEF, 1990). For an examination of the disadvantaged status of women in various fields and for related government policies and measures see *Bangladesh: Strategies for Enhancing the Role of Women in Economic Development*, World Bank Country Study (Washington, D.C.: World Bank, 1990); Gul Afroze Mahbub et al., "Sectoral Study on Women in Development," vols. 1–3 (Unpublished report sponsored by the Canadian International Development Agency, 1986).

3. For some discussions on patriarchy and purdah in Bangladesh see Rafiqul Huda Chowdhury and Nilufer Raihan Ahmed, *Female Status in Bangladesh* (Dhaka: Bangladesh Institute of Development Studies, 1980), 5–17; Martha A. Chen, *A Quiet Revolution: Women in Transition in Rural Bangladesh* (Cambridge, Mass.: Schenkman, 1983), 59, 75; Naila Kabeer, "Subordination and Struggle: Women in Bangladesh," *New Left Review* 168 (March–April 1988): 101–9; Najmir Nur Begum, *Pay or Purdah: Women and Income Earning in Rural Bangladesh* (Dhaka: Winrock International and BARC, 1987), 1–20; Rokeya Sakhawat Hossain, Sultana's Dream *and Selections from* The Secluded Ones, ed. and trans. Roushan Jahan (New York: Feminist Press, 1988). See also Hanna Papanek, "Caging the Lion: A Fable of Our Time," in Hossain, Sultana's Dream, 58ff.; Shapan Adnan, *"Birds in a Cage": Institutional Factors and Changes in Women's Position in Bangladesh* (Dhaka: Winrock International and Bangladesh Agricultural Research Council, forthcoming). On purdah see also Mazharul Huq Khan, *Purdah and Polygamy* (Delhi: Chanakya, 1982); and Jamila Brijbhushan, *Muslim Women in Purdah and Out of It* (New Delhi: Vikas, 1980).

4. For example, see Latifa Akhanda and Ishrat Shamin, *Women and Violence: A Comparative Study of Rural and Urban Violence on Women in Bangladesh* (Dhaka: Women for Women, a Research and Study Group, 1984); for a legalistic discussion see Rabia Bhuiya, *Aspects of Violence Against Women* (Dhaka: Institute of Democratic Rights, 1991).

5. For an examination of the legal status of women under the sharia, or personal laws, see Salma Sobhan, *Legal Status of Women in Bangladesh* (Dhaka: Bangladesh Institute of Law and International Affairs, 1978), 19–32; for a brief overview of women's legal status see Rabia Bhuiya, "Legal Status of Women in Bangladesh," in Qazi Kholiquzzaman Ahmad et al., eds., *Situation of Women in Bangladesh* (rpt., Dhaka: Ministry of the People's Republic of Bangladesh, 1988), 245–61.

6. For contemporary events see Talukder Maniruzzaman, *The Bangladesh Revolution and Its Aftermath* (Dhaka: Bangladesh Books International, 1980).

7. For the ideology and organization of the Jamaat see *Constitution of the Jamaat-i-Islami, Bangladesh* (1985); *Organizational System, Jamaat-i-Islami, Bangladesh* (1984); Ghulam Azam, *Ikamat-i-Deen* (Daily) (1981). All are published in Dhaka (in Bangla). In 1989 the leader of a conservative rightist party stated that Islam does not allow a woman to be head of state. *New Nation* (Daily), 27 December 1989.

8. For an account of women's role in the Indian freedom movement see Manmohan Kaur, *Role of Women in the Freedom Movement (1847–1947)* (Delhi: Sterling, 1968); Committee on the Status of Women in India, *Towards Equality: Report of the Committee on the Status of Women in India* (New Delhi: Ministry of Education and Social Welfare, 1975).

9. For some idea of the role that Muslim women played in the movement to form the state of Pakistan see Sarfaraz Hussain Mirza, *Muslim Women's Role in the Pakistan Movement* (Lahore: University of the Punjab, 1969); National Committee for Birth Centenary Celebrations of Quaid-i-Azam Mohammad Ali Jinnah, *Quaid-i-Azam and Muslim Women* (Islamabad: Pakistan Ministry of Education, 1976). See also Kaur, *Women in the Freedom Movement.*

10. Constitution of the People's Republic of Bangladesh (modified up to 31 May 1986), articles 9–10, 27–28, 37–39, 65–66, 122. The 10th Amendment of the constitution reinserted the reservation of seats in the Parliament. See *Bangladesh Gazette Extraordinary,* 23 June 1990. The 12th Amendment introduced a parliamentary form of government. Ibid., 18 September 1991.

11. For the history and practice of reserved seating for women in Pakistan see the Constitution of the Islamic Republic of Pakistan (1956), articles 44, 77; and the Constitution of the Republic of Pakistan (1962), articles 20, 71, 162, 169. For later constitutional amendments see the articles in the Constitution of the Islamic Republic of

Pakistan as amended up to 1965; see also Pakistan Election Commission, *Report of the General Elections in Pakistan, 1964–65*, 1:138–39, 197–205. Also see Najma Chowdhury, *The Legislative Process in Bangladesh: Politics and Functioning of the East Bengal Legislature* (Dhaka: University of Dhaka, 1980), 18–20, 170; Herbert Feldman, *The End and the Beginning: Pakistan, 1969–71* (Karachi: Oxford University Press, 1976), 62–75.

12. See *Bangladesh Constituent Assembly Debates* (in Bangla) (Dhaka: Government Printing Press, 1972), 2:277, 360.

13. Najma Chowdhury, "Women in Politics in Bangladesh," in Ahmad et al., eds., *Situation of Women in Bangladesh*, 272–73.

14. After the 1979 elections the election commissioner urged consideration of an electoral system for these seats that would offer equal opportunity to all women candidates irrespective of their political party affiliations. See Bangladesh Election Commission, *Report on Parliamentary Election, 1979* (Dhaka: Government Printing Press, 1979), iii.

15. The nomination and election of women to the reserved seats in the 1986 Parliament evoked criticism and innuendos from certain sections of the press. Prior to the election General Ershad amended the Representation of the People Order (1972), concerning seats for women members, to provide for a "package election" and thereby effectively preclude any possibility of contestation. *New Nation,* 7 July 1986. The amendment was dropped and the previous provision restored for the 1991 election.

16. The president, in his inaugural address to the newly elected legislature, called upon the members to consider "whether or not to extend for another 15 years the constitutional provision to keep seats in Parliament reserved for women." *Inaugural Address of President Hussain Muhammad Ershad at the Bangladesh Parliament* (in Bangla), 25 April 1988. See also "Jatiyo Party Rejects Women Quota," *Holiday* (Weekly), 27 February 1989.

17. See Bangladesh Federation of University Women, *Proceedings of the Seminar on Direct Election in the Reserved Seats for Women in the Jatiyo Sangsad (Parliament)* (Dhaka, 1988); see also *New Nation,* 11 June 1989. Various women's organizations and research and professional bodies (such as the Mahila Parishad, Women for Women, and the Bangladesh National Women Lawyers' Association) were in favor of an increase in the number of reserved seats, direct elections, and quotas in party nominations for general seats.

18. The Task Forces on the Role of Political Parties in the Development Process and on Women recommended direct election of women from territorial constituencies to reserved seats in the legislature and a 10–15 percent quota of party nominations to women in general seats. The caretaker government standing in after the fall of Ershad instituted 29 task forces to make recommendations to the elected representatives and the government on various issues and problems of development in Bangladesh. See *Report of the Task Forces on Bangladesh Development Strategies for the 1990s* (Dhaka: University Press, 1991), vols. 1 and 2.

19. This increased participation is not reflected in the percentage because of the overall increased participation at the polls.

20. A list of candidates (cyclostyled) and election figures for the 1991 elections were obtained from the Election Commission. For a list of successful candidates see *Bangladesh Gazette Extra Ordinary,* 6 March 1991; for a list of women elected to reserved seats see ibid., 31 March 1991. Some 42 percent of the candidates received less than 1 percent of the votes cast in their constituencies, however. The corresponding figures for 1986 and 1979 were about 13 percent and 44 percent, respectively.

21. A candidate may run in more than one constituency, but under article 71 of the constitution she or he may take oath as a member of Parliament representing only one constituency. A politician may undertake to run in more than one constituency for several reasons: to establish a claim of political popularity, to win a seat for the party in case a suitable candidate is not available, to obtain voter support so that during a subsequent by-election the support may be transferred to a protégé in the party or family, or simply to maximize his or her electoral chances of obtaining at least one seat.

22. The Representation of the People (Amendment) Ordinance (1991) introduced stringent measures to curb and regulate election expenses and enforce financial accounting. See *Bangladesh Gazette Extra Ordinary,* 6 January 1991. The Election Commission, on the basis of a consensus among political parties, also laid down certain rules of conduct to curb election violence and aggressive electioneering. See Bangladesh Election Commission, *Rules of Conduct to Be Followed by Political Parties, Parliamentary Election, 1991* (in Bangla). Money and muscle power were identified in the course of the 1991 election as two evils vitiating the election process.

23. On political socialization and the assumption of roles by political women see Rita Mae Kelly and Mary Boutilier, *The Making of Political Women: A Study of Socialization and Role Conflict* (Chicago: Nelson-Hall, 1978). Sheikh Hasina grew up in a politician's home, participated in student politics, and canvassed in her father's constituency, but she was basically a housewife after marriage. While president, Ziaur Rahman kept his family life private and his family away from politics and the trappings of power. Khaleda Zia was mainly seen accompanying the president on public and ceremonial occasions. On the emergence of women political leaders in South Asia, see Rounaq Jahan, "Women in South Asian Politics," *Third World Quarterly* 9 (July 1987): 848–57. Also note the effort of Congress Party politicians in India to induct

Sonia Gandhi into a leadership role following the assassination of her husband, Prime Minister Rajiv Gandhi.

24. Some former party leaders were accommodated in important positions in the Jatiyo Party and in the government during the Ershad regime; they did not return.

25. Although their routes to political power were similar, they are politically antagonistic to each other. Their mutual accusations and allegations are reported in press and political circles alike.

26. The Awami League advocates equality of inheritance in its *12-Point Program* (in Bangla). In an interview with the author in 1986, Sheikh Hasina mentioned that she played a role in its incorporation. The matter, however, was given little publicity.

27. Bangladesh Awami League, *Jatiyo Sangsad Nirbachani Ishtehar* (Manifesto for parliamentary election) (1991); Bangladesh Jatiyotabadi Dal, *Nirbachani Ghoshona* (Election declaration) (1991); Panch Dal (Five-Party Alliance), *Nirbachani Ishtehar* (Election manifesto) (1991); Jamaat-i-Islami Bangladesh, *Nirbachani Ishtehar* (Election manifesto) (1991). All are in Bangla. Interestingly, a survey of 522 candidates in 100 constituencies conducted by Gonotantric Udyog (Democratic Initiative) and Market Research Consultants of Bangladesh during the 1991 election found that 71 percent of the candidates believed in equality for women and men, and 94 percent thought that women in Bangladesh are oppressed (preliminary findings).

28. For the organization and mandate of the ministry and an evaluation see Mahmuda Islam, "National Machinery for Women" (Geneva: International Labor Organization, 1990).

29. Ibid., 32–34 (quotation on p. 33).

30. For details on the government's policies see Salma Khan, *The Fifty Percent: Women in Development and Policy in Bangladesh* (Dhaka: University Press, 1988), 46–61. On the laws see Sobhan, *Legal Status of Women in Bangladesh;* see also Hasna Begum, "Rights of Women in Bangladesh," *Journal of the Asiatic Society of Bangladesh* (June 1990): 21–36. Women's organizations have demanded a change in personal laws directly in their platforms or indirectly by calling for ratification of all provisions of the U.N. Convention on Eliminating Discrimination Against Women. Also, although several legal measures to protect women have been enacted, women's groups have voiced concern at women's lack of legal knowledge and their inability to resort to legal remedy.

31. See, e.g., Planning Commission, *The Fourth Five-Year Plan, 1990–95* (Draft, October 1990).

32. Islam, "National Machinery," 13–14. The JMS was established in 1976 by a resolution of the government. It was given legal status in an ordinance and later in legislation. For the act see *Bangladesh Gazette Extraordinary,* 4 May 1991.

33. See National Committee for World Congress of Women, Bangladesh, *National Seminar '87;* Bangladesh Mahila Parishad, *Central Committee Report* (1984–88), 50–51, 56, 71–72; Oikkya Baddha Nari Samaj, *17-Point Program* (in Bangla) (N.d.). The forum members include the Mahila Parishad, Mahila Samiti, Democratic Women's Movement, Socialist Women's Forum, Bangladesh Women Writers' Association, Saptagram Women's Self-Reliance Movement, Dhaka Business and Professional Women's Club, Bangladesh Child Care and Rehabilitation, Women for Women, YWCA, Bangladesh Federation of University Women, Soroptomist International, Women's Voluntary Association, Women's Rights Movement, and others. (Some Bangla names have been rendered into English approximations.)

34. Ayesha Khanam, "Women and the Struggle for Democracy in Bangladesh," in Sirajul Islam Chowdhury and Abul Hasnat, eds., *The Mass Movement of 1990* (in Bangla) (Dhaka: Muktadhara, 1991), 94–99.

35. The membership in 1991 is estimated to be 35,000. What proportion is fully active is debatable. See *Mahila Samachar* (in Bangla) (April–June 1991): 5. *Samachar* is the mouthpiece of the Parishad. An earlier assessment put 90 percent of its members in the middle class, 5 percent in the upper class, and 2 percent in the lower class, with 95 percent of the members being urban. See Bangladesh Mahila Parishad, *Organizational Report* (in Bangla), Fifth National Conference (1984), 16–20. Since 1985 the Parishad has run a home, called Rokeya Sadan (Home) after the first Bengali Muslim feminist, Rokeya Sakhawat Hossain (1880–1932), where distressed women are sheltered and taught skills with a view to rehabilitation.

36. On the organization, activities, and ideological position of the Parishad see Bangladesh Mahila Parishad: *Declaration and Constitution; Women's Movement for Emancipation and the Bangladesh Mahila Parishad* (1983); *Report of the General Secretary* and *Organisational Report,* both from the Fifth National Conference (1984); *Central Committee Report* (1984–88) and *District Reports* (Draft), both from the Sixth National Conference (1988). See also Maleka Begum, *Women's Movement in Bangladesh: Problems and Future* (Dhaka: Gyan Prakashani, 1988); and selected issues of *Mahila Samachar* (1984–91). All are in Bangla.

37. See Parishad, *Central Committee Report,* 51. For wider dissemination and awareness, the Parishad has translated the convention into Bangla in collaboration with the U.N. Information Centre in Dhaka.

38. *New Nation,* 19 July 1988. The petition is pending and has not yet been moved for issuance of rule.

39. For a study of women in the garment industry see Hamida Hossain et al., *No Better Option? Industrial Women Workers in Bangladesh* (Dhaka: University Press, 1990); on mainstreaming women in national plans see

Women for Women, *Women and National Planning in Bangladesh* (Dhaka, 1990).

40. The victims of acid throwing are usually girls and women; the perpetrators are men. The intention is to disfigure the face or body of the victim as a punitive or terrorizing measure. In 1984 the government amended the penal code so that causing grievous hurt by means of a corrosive substance can be punished with death or transportation (imprisonment). Bhuiya, *Aspects of Violence Against Women,* 11.

41. The murder was allegedly committed because the wife refused to compromise on the issue of the illicit relationship and the reportedly shady business dealings of the accused.

42. See the judgment in the *Daily Star,* 6 July 1992.

43. Also see Zarina Rahman Khan and Helaluddin Khan Arefeen, *Potita Nari: A Study of Prostitution in Bangladesh* (Dhaka: Centre for Social Studies, 1989).

44. This discussion is based on press releases and reports, pamphlets, leaflets, informal discussions, and other such sources.

45. The gender disparity in spending on education in a given year (1987) is indicative of the trends: girls are the beneficiaries of 44 percent of the expenditures for primary education, 32 percent for secondary education, and 13 percent for university education. *Bangladesh,* World Bank Country Study, 50–52. Also, the recurrent cost per child for rural-based primary education is only 76 takas (U.S. $2), as against the cost per university student of 10,333 takas ($313). Khan, *Fifty Percent,* 27.

46. Bangladesh Bureau of Statistics, *Bangladesh Demographic Statistics, 1992* (Dhaka: Bangladesh Bureau of Statistics, 1992), 5.

47. For a breakdown of enrollment figures at the primary and post-primary levels by sex for 1990 see *Fourth Five-Year Plan,* chap. 15, pp. 25–26. Some increase in girls' enrollment compared to boys' is evident, for example, at the primary and secondary levels, reflecting the small numerical base of girls in school, as well as the efforts to widen the base. The pace of change will not bring parity in the near future. An annual growth rate of 20 percent is needed for female enrollment to achieve parity, but the current rate is only 5 percent in the secondary schools. Proposed Female Secondary School Assistance Project Preparation Mission, Aide Memoire, 1991. Also see UNICEF, *Situation of Children,* 65–69.

48. The marginalization of women in education is also evidenced by their exclusion or near exclusion from certain schools, e.g., *madrasah* (schools with a focus on religious education), cadet colleges (secondary and higher secondary levels; only one of ten is reserved for girls), the Islamic University, and the Islamic Center for Vocational Training and Research. On overall trends in women's education see Shamima Islam, *Women's Education in Bangladesh: Needs and Issues,* 2nd ed. (Dhaka: Foundation for

Research on Education Planning and Development, 1982); Ellen Sattar, *Universal Primary Education in Bangladesh* (Dhaka: University Press, 1982); Women for Women, *Women and Education: Bangladesh, 1978* (Dhaka, 1978); Zaheda Ahmad, "Female Education in Bangladesh," in Ahmad et al., *Situation of Women in Bangladesh,* 159–85; and Women for Women, *Education and Gender Equity: Bangladesh* (Dhaka, 1992). A number of research publications and mimeographs, as well as conference, seminar, training, and survey reports are available, covering aspects of female education. Although the quantitative aspects relating to enrollment and retention have received extensive attention, the qualitative aspects of the gender dimension in education have not yet done so.

49. Social expediency is an expression used by Usha Nayar in "Designing Education for Women's Development" (Paper presented at the Sub-Regional Workshop on Women and Development Management in South Asia organized by the Asian Pacific Development Centre, Kuala Lumpur, October 1989).

50. *Bangladesh Education Commission Report* (May 1974), 192–93; *National Education Advisory Committee Recommendations* (in Bangla) (1979), 33; *Bangladesh National Education Commission Report* (in Bangla) (February 1988), 119–20. These reports, while making general note of the gender disparity, also devote brief chapters or subchapters to female education. Both the *Recommendations* and the 1988 *Report* include a subchapter on women's education under a broad chapter entitled Special Education, which also includes subchapters on fine arts, population studies, education for the physically and mentally retarded, and so forth!

51. Planning Commission, *First Five-Year Plan,* 479–80; Planning Commission, *Second Five-Year Plan,* 288–303; Planning Commission, *Third Five-Year Plan* (1985–90), 365–82. For comments and a brief assessment of the First Five-Year Plan (1973–78), the bridging Two-Year Plan (1978–80), and the Second Five-Year Plan (1980–85) with regard to female education see Islam, *Women's Education,* 78, 107–18. Also see Sattar, *Universal Primary Education,* 82–87.

52. The Fourth Five-Year Plan added for the first time a macro chapter on women in development and paid specific or greater (though criticized by some as not adequate) attention to gender concerns in the sectoral policies, program activities, and projects. NGOs, particularly Women for Women, the Sub-Group on WID (Women in Development) of the Local Consultative Group of Donors, and the SKYSWAM (Sports, Culture, Youth Development, Social Welfare, Women's Affairs, and Mass Media) wing of the Planning Commission played important roles. See Women for Women, *Women and National Planning;* see also Jowshan A. Rahman, "Women in Development: National Plan and Related Issues," *In Touch,* VHSS *Health Newsletter,* vol. 10, no. 100 (December 1991).

Several reports and policy and strategy papers were initiated during 1989–90 while the plan was being formulated. See Rounaq Jahan, *Women and Development in Bangladesh: Challenges and Opportunities* (Report commissioned by the Ford Foundation, March 1989); Salma Kahn, *Integration of Women in Development in the Fourth Five-Year Plan: 1990–95* (Report commissioned by UNICEF, November 1989); Marilyn Waring et al., "Initial Notes: WID/UNDP Mission Bangladesh" (December 1989); *Bangladesh,* World Bank Country Study.

53. Possible incentives are free school uniforms and midday meals. Also being considered for implementation is the ambitious Female Secondary School Assistance Programme, or FSSAP—to be financed by the Government of Bangladesh, IDA, and other foreign development partners—which is modeled on the earlier successful Female Education Scholarship Programme, for wider application in selected areas nationwide. The FSSAP (proposed implementation period 1993–2000) is intended to be the first in a series of follow-up projects until gender parity is reached in the secondary system.

54. The government piloted a bill in the Parliament making primary education compulsory on the eve of the World Conference on Education for All sponsored by the UNDP, UNICEF, UNESCO, and the World Bank. For the act see *Bangladesh Gazette Extra Ordinary,* 13 February 1990. The FFYP incorporated compulsory primary education, shifting from the previous plan's position calling for universal primary education.

55. Also see "Women's Programs Included in the General Education Project," in *Bangladesh,* World Bank Country Study, 146–47.

56. The bank provides loans without collateral and makes credit available to landless women who own absolutely nothing to offer as collateral. On December 1989 women constituted 89 percent of the members of the bank, which is now 25 percent owned by the government. Grameen Bank, *Annual Report* (in Bangla) (1989).

57. There are an estimated 4,500 schools for boys and girls aged eight to ten, under the three-year nonformal primary education program of BRAC. Girls accounted for 70 percent of the enrollment, and women for 75 percent of the teachers. The drop-out rate was only 1.5 percent, and daily attendance was high—an average of more than 95 percent. Catherine H. Lovell and Kaniz Fatema, *Assignment Children: The BRAC, Non-Formal Primary Education Programme in Bangladesh* (UNICEF, 1989). Both BRAC and the Grameen Bank have other programs as well.

58. See FFYP; and Bangladesh Ministry of Education, "Country Documents: Bangladesh" (Paper presented at the South and Central Asia Conference on Education for All, Dhaka, December 1989). Also see *Bangladesh,* World Bank Country Study, 147.

▲ Bolivia

POLITICS

Type of Political System: democracy

Sovereignty: republic

Executive-Legislative System: presidential

Type of State: unitary

Type of Party System: multiparty

Major Political Parties [a]

Acción Democrática Nacionalista (ADN, or Nationalist Democratic Action): Right-wing party founded in 1979 under the slogan "Peace, order, and work." Has previously formed legislative alliances with the Historic Nationalist Revolutionary Movement; in August 1989 it formed an alliance with the Movement of the Revolutionary Left. Led by former President Hugo Banzer Suárez.

Conciencia de Patria (CONDEPA, or Conscience of the Nation): Alliance of eight leftist parties that participated in the 1989 election. Coalition disbanded after the election and re-formed with different members.

Izquierda Unida (IU, or United Left): Left-wing party with strength in urban areas.

Movimiento Nacionalista Revolucionario Histórico (MNRH, or Historic Nationalist Revolutionary Movement): Formed in 1941; ruled 1952–64 but was outlawed for a time after the 1964 coup. MNRH leader Victor Paz Estenssoro elected president in 1985 but was unable to retain the presidency.

Movimiento de la Izquierda Revolucionaria (MIR, or Movement of the Revolutionary Left): Center-left, non-communist Marxist party; splinter of the Partido Demócrata Cristiano (Christian Democratic Party). Leader, Jaime Paz Zamora, is president of the republic.

Partido Demócratica Cristiano (PDC, Christian Democratic Party): Left-wing, predominantly Roman Catholic party.

Year Women Granted Right to Vote: 1953

Year Women Granted Right to Stand for Election: 1956

Percentage of Women in the Legislature

Lower House: 3.8%

Upper House: 7.4%

Percentage of Electorate Voting for Highest Elected Office in Most Recent Election (1985): not available

DEMOGRAPHICS

Population: 6,797,000

Percentage of Population in Urban Areas

Overall: 47.7%

Female: 48.3%

Male: 47.2%

Percentage of Population Below Age 15: 43.8%

Birthrate (per 1,000 population): 42

Maternal Mortality Rate (per 100,000 live births): 480

Infant Mortality Rate (per 1,000 live births): 113

Mortality Rate for Children Under Five (per 1,000 live births): 179

Average Household Size: 4.0

Mean Age at First Marriage

Female: 22.1

Male: 24.5

Life Expectancy

Female: 55.4

Male: 50.8

EDUCATION

Ratio of Female to Male Enrollment

First-Level Education: 88

Second-Level Education: 86

Third-Level Education: not available

Literacy Rate

Female: 51.0%

Male: 75.0%

ECONOMY

Gross National Product per Capita: U.S. $470

Percentage of Labor Force in Agriculture: 46.9%

Distribution of Agricultural Workers by Sex
  Female: 13.4%
  Male: 86.6%
Economically Active Population by Sex
  Female: 24.6%
  Male: 84.1%

a. All political party information is from Arthur S. Banks, ed., *Political Handbook of the World, 1991* (Binghamton, N.Y.: CSA Publications, 1991), 76–77.

Women and Politics: Gender Relations in Bolivian Political Organizations and Labor Unions

GLORIA ARDAYA SALINAS
TRANSLATED BY
SAMUEL M. DUBOIS

Bolivia, a landlocked country in west-central South America with nearly 7 million people, has a history of political instability, authoritarian rule, and frequent military governments. From 1964 to 1982 Bolivian political life was dominated by a succession of military governments that repressed and manipulated the population to maintain power. In 1982 the government returned to civilian rule when Hernán Siles Zuazo was permitted to assume the office of president that he had won in the 1980 elections.

Although the political situation has stabilized somewhat with the transition to democracy, Bolivia is plagued by severe economic problems and a staggering foreign debt. The predominantly rural population of Aymara and Quechua Indians work primarily in agriculture and tin mining, usually at subsistence wages. Bolivia is one of the poorest countries in Latin America—second only to Haiti in the Western Hemisphere—with high rates of illiteracy, infant mortality, and poverty. Spanish is the official language, though it is most often spoken in urban areas. Class and race distinctions are intertwined, with the urban middle class primarily of Spanish descent and the

rural and urban working class from Indian or mixed-race backgrounds.

Bolivia is a country of great heterogeneity, owing to the unequal redistribution of revenue, interregional conflicts generated by insufficient services in rural areas, and growing regional demands. The country's indigenous populations have expanded their fight for greater participation in the political system and for recognition of their cultural and national identity.

The mainstay of Bolivia's parallel economy is the coca leaf, most of which is used in the illegal cocaine trade. A growing number of Bolivians have become involved in coca production as economic instability in the tin-mining sector has increased and as the government has imposed stricter austerity measures limiting wages and increasing prices. Efforts to prosecute drug traffickers and eradicate coca production have been met with sometimes hostile resistance. Hunger strikes by miners, teachers, and rural peasants still occur, as well as clashes with government forces, especially given the unpopular austerity measures.

Notwithstanding this history of political and economic instability, Bolivia is also one of the few

Latin American countries to experience a true national revolution. Like the Mexican Revolution in 1911, the 1952 revolution in Bolivia was led by a coalition of workers and middle-class reformers united in the Movimiento Nacionalista Revolucionario (MNR, or National Revolutionary Movement), which altered the entire political system.

The MNR was formed after the Chaco War (1932–35), a conflict with Paraguay that left Bolivia with a social crisis. Ex-fighters from the Chaco War and intellectuals joined to form a new political instrument, and they channeled their protest against the oligarchical state through the MNR, later bringing together the individuals who would enter politics.

The MNR called for national and democratic reaffirmation. Its party discourse, Revolutionary Nationalism, criticized the oligarchy of mining and landholding capitalists and later developed into a critique of the state system from the petit bourgeoisie sector. Nevertheless, now in power in government, Revolutionary Nationalism is set up like a fan that spreads to cover vast social sectors and diverse social and economic policies.

The MNR overcame the oligarchical state between 1952 and 1964, laying the foundation of a modern capitalist state with a high level of social participation. In 1985, the MNR dismantled the state-dominated economy, replacing it with the current neo-liberal policy.

With its victory in 1952 the MNR, led by Siles Zuazo and Victor Paz Estenssoro, carried out redistributive measures. It gave land to the peasants, nationalized the tin mines into Corporación Minera de Bolivia, the state-owned mining corporation known as COMIBOL, expanded educational opportunities, provided universal adult suffrage, limited foreign investment, and stripped the military of its power. The democratic governments that followed the revolution, however, were plagued by economic woes and were unable to control the growing power of the military, which assumed control with a coup in 1964. During the dictatorial period that ended in 1982, the MNR's presence on the political scene ranged from direct collaboration to non-participation with military governments.

With the return to civilian rule, Bolivia reestablished a democratic government. Under this system, executive power is vested in the president, who is directly elected for a four-year term. Voting is compulsory for all adults age 21 and older. If no presidential candidate wins an absolute majority of the vote under direct elections, the president is elected by Parliament. The bicameral legislature consists of a 27-member Senate and a 130-member Chamber of Deputies elected based on proportional representation. The country is divided for administrative purposes into nine regional departments, each of which is governed by a prefect appointed by the president.

All political parties in Bolivia claim ties to the revolutionary period and the MNR. Other important parties in the 1989 presidential elections were Acción Democrática Nacionalista (ADN, or Democratic Nationalist Action), Movimiento de la Izquierda Revolucionaria (MIR, or Movement of the Revolutionary Left), Conciencia de Patria, (CONDEPA, or Conscience of the Nation), and Izquierda Unida (IU, or United Left).

Bolivian women historically have maintained a significant level of social participation. And their political participation in the indigenous rebellions of 1780–81 and in struggles for independence between 1809 and 1825 is well known. But only since the beginning of the twentieth century has the participation of urban women become visible and permanent. Organizations were created to allow women to voice specific demands related to the conditions of subordination forced on them by society.

Earlier in this century, upper- and middle-class urban women, as well as those from the popular sector, called for the right to political citizenship and for equality in the labor market through such autonomous organizations as Ateneo Femenino (Women's Club) and Legion Femenina de Educación Popular America (Women's Legion of American Popular Education), and through such labor organizations as Federación Obrera Femenina (Federation of Women Workers). The economic contribution of women from rural sectors as family laborers and as paid and unpaid agricultural laborers was substantial. In the urban economy of today some women hold paid positions in the formal sector, but more women work in the informal sector—though statistics tend to ignore women's participation in the labor force.

During the past few years, social scientists have witnessed the emergence of a variety of social actors and movements in South America, movements that are grounded in definite, concrete societies and that in turn affect and modify those societies. One such movement is the growing protest by women in the economic, social, and political fields. From "below"—from their daily lives and subordination—women are redefining their identity and rights in a struggle to broaden the possibilities for action and transformation.

There are a number of national organizations for women from the popular sectors (for rural women, working women, and women from the informal sector) that are independent of parties and government. The most important include the National Housewives Committee of the Nationalized and Privatized Mining Industry; the Bartolina Sisa National Federation of Peasant Women; the National Federation of Mothers' Clubs; and the National Federation of Housewives Committees of the Popular Neighborhoods. On the institutional level, a group of nongovernmental organizations has sprung up in support of women, among which are the Gregoria Apaza Women's Center, Centro de Investigación y Desarrollo de la Mujer (CIDEM, or Women's Center for Research and Development), Instituto Femenino de Formación Integral (IFFI, or Feminine Institute for Training), and Centro de Promoción de la Mujer (CEPROMU, or Center for the Promotion of Women). These organizations assist women in the areas of education, organization, and production, but there is no specific state policy that incorporates women into its plans for development and into its social policies.

The academic study of the women's movement in Bolivia has encountered a number of challenges and difficulties, in large part because women are not a social group with an acknowledged identity in political life. In fact, women do not constitute a social group per se but a frag-

mented social category that cuts across classes, ethnic groups, communities, and nations.[1] The Bolivian context shows that women's situation is heterogeneous, as are the discrimination and subordination they undergo. The social reception to women's issues has been varied within politics in general, and in political parties and labor unions in particular.

In this context, carefully researched information on women's status is still lacking. The theory that will make it possible to "see" women in their particular, day-to-day reality is only now being constructed. Nevertheless, women have been active in social struggles at a grass-roots level since the founding of the republic in 1825, though official history mentions only those women whose exemplary work eclipsed the collective work of ordinary women. There has been significant involvement of women in the struggle for a fairer, more egalitarian society, even though their involvement has gone unnoticed and unrecognized by society.

The retrieval of knowledge about women is hindered not only because Bolivian society as a whole does not consider women's participation important enough to include in official history but also because women themselves have not assumed or valued this history as their own. "Please do not remember that black history of my life," said a National Women's Command leader who refused to be interviewed regarding her involvement in the MNR. Moreover, certain women's sectors have constantly diminished or concealed information on the protagonists of women's action in Bolivia. In this sense, it is true that "we women have inherited a general history, and a history of politics in particular, narrated and acted only by men; therefore, it is reasonable to assume that both are somewhat slanted toward the masculine, which has left us in silence, invisible in the face of history."[2]

Adding to the problem is the perpetual political instability of Bolivia during the past 20 years, which has prevented the preservation of important documents and of the history of major political figures. For this reason, it has been necessary to resort to personal testimonies to reconstruct important events in women's political action. This investigation has shown that most women felt that their participation was not important.

Because women's political participation achieved fuller expression and visibility in moments of social and political crisis, women's specifically gender-related demands were ignored or subordinated to the "main contradiction." That is, depending on the group, women in Bolivia have appeared to be fighting for their nation in some cases or for their class in others. This approach has concealed women's protest even from the women themselves, who have not regarded their efforts as part of the history of their gender. In this context MNR women, in their discourse and in practice, have adopted the struggle for the nation as expressed by the party itself and by the women of the housewives committees. Discourse and practice in defense of the working class guide their struggles, but the effort to improve family living conditions is evident.

In contrast, a smaller group of upper-class women has worked for its class. There has been only one women's social movement tied to the dominant class in Bolivia: Las Damas Crucenas (Ladies of the Cross), an organization linked to the Falange Socialista Boliviana, (FSB, or Bolivian Socialist Falange), the opposition party to the MNR. The movement was limited to the party's 12-year reign in government.

The lack of recognition of gender interests is no accident; women daily endure the authoritarianism imposed by the private world, to which they have been relegated and thereby kept out of politics.[3] Thus women's participation in public affairs has most often occurred as an extension of their traditional roles. They are wives, mothers, and housewives who enter politics to assure the well-being of their families. Women's participation is not explicitly geared to transforming private relationships, and any political action they undertake is governed by the customs of politics.

In this context, it is interesting to examine and establish the meaning of political involvement for women, who are often treated as objects because Bolivian society and especially politics have no notion of women in their own right. The identity of women is strongly shaped by the experience of men's political action, and women today enter the political system by pursuing the aims of men's politics. Women's rebelliousness has not become social rebellion or found expression in women's own issues.

In spite of women's growing participation in social struggles, their identity as women has not been incorporated into the Bolivian political system. A new identity of women making politics like men, while representing women's interests as wives and mothers, has not yet been consolidated. Women adopt and carry on the discourse and practice of nation and class without incorporating the claims of each of the women's sectors or seeking space for the organizations that defend their interests. In consequence, women's political action is riddled with conflicts and contradictions. Old and new forms of politics converge, producing an incongruity between tradition and rebellion in women's political action. The process of forming a new identity has not yet enabled women to accumulate force, recover their history, or use the political power they have wielded previously. But women's participation has generated new forms of action and organization in relation to political parties and labor unions and, therefore, in society. In spite of the limitation to testimonies—and even though many protagonists are dead—recollections have emerged of substantial resistance to men's politics. Within this unformed, many-faceted identity, women have carried forward their opposition, perhaps unconsciously.

To illustrate this phenomenon in Bolivian politics, I shall discuss the "incorporation" of women into political citizenship and the emergence of two social movements on the basis of two case studies: the National Women's Commands of the MNR and the Housewives Committees of the Federación Sindical de Trabajadores Mineros de Bolivia (FSTMB, or Trade Union Federation of Bolivian Mine Workers). There is no precise information available as to when the Women's Commands were formed, in part because the militants were not continually active in the commands. Some women speak of having come together between 1946 and 1952, when the MNR was forced underground to continue its operations, which were often carried out by women militants. Nevertheless, the period of greatest political and organizational action was between 1956 and 1964. The presence of the Women's Commands later became limited to the action of small urban groups. In contrast, the housewives committees arose in 1961, and their political and organizational importance continues to grow.

POLITICAL REPRESENTATION: THE NATIONAL WOMEN'S COMMANDS

The commands, established through the MNR, were among the most important political entities for Bolivian women after the 1952 revolution. Both the Women's Commands and the MNR were major political actors in the fight against the oligarchy. Because women were subordinated within the party, however, it has been extremely difficult to reconstruct the different actions and forms of women's participation; many actions were never recorded or deemed important.

In this context, the MNR was the first political party to include women in its rank and file. Women entered politics and made politics through the MNR. The women who joined the party between 1946 to 1952 were relatives of those martyred, imprisoned, or persecuted during the 21 July 1946 coup d'état. During that time, this small group swelled to include other women's sectors and began to carry out clandestine party work to overthrow the oligarchical regime in power. Its main tasks were holding masses and other homages in remembrance of those who died, aiding political prisoners, editing and distributing party news and propaganda, transferring arms, providing an underground postal service, and recruiting militants. Their most prominent political action was a hunger strike carried out in the Palace of Justice in La Paz, the seat of government in Bolivia. The strike's central objective was to liberate party political prisoners to run in the May 1951 elections.

Several times during this period MNR women verbally and physically confronted the police and agents of the oligarchy. During the 1949 civil war and the April insurrection of 1952, MNR women played an important role in ensuring the safety of the principal militants and in maintaining a presence at the main sites where confrontations broke out with the government.

During the national revolution, MNR women became part of the overall social movement. While they assumed the identity and the oppositional stance of the MNR, they delicately raised a number of specific women's issues and created a minimum level of organization that enabled them to speak on behalf of the party's female members.

In spite of the long struggle waged during the revolution, women were unable to create an identity that would express their specific problems and demands regarding the profound discrimination and subordination to which state and society subjected them. After the triumph of the revolution in 1952, the gains won by women ran parallel with those won by society as a whole: universal suffrage and expansion of the educational and social security systems. Nevertheless, women were not asked to participate in the distribution of political power. Many saw their work as active militants come to an end after the revolution. Under the first MNR government (1952–56), women disappeared from the political scene and were called together only to support party action or to work in social assistance for MNR militants. The first sign that the Women's Commands would reorganize came as a result of the first elections held by the party in power, whose candidate was Siles Zuazo. After women succeeded in running a female candidate for Parliament in these elections, the National Women's Command emerged as a more stable organization under the leadership of Lydia Gueiler, who was later also elected as a government representative.

Women's political identity thus hinged on the identity granted by the party—an identity based on the sexual division of labor. Women in the MNR were above all the mothers, sisters, and daughters of the leaders and militants of the revolution. After the revolution they became militant citizens and did not resist the code of values imposed by the patriarchal society and state. In this context, women were not recognized as political actors.

Although women's action had been a key factor at the start of the revolution because of their links to grass-roots women and the national social movement, their action became an instrument to serve the needs posed by the state's new relations with international capital and dominant groups. After 1956, MNR policy followed economic, political, and military guidelines set up by the U.S. Eder Mission, which were designed to stabilize the economy, reorganize the military, and suppress labor unions. The reality of this arrangement was captured in an FSTMB document dated in 1958 in Colquiri that states, "Imperialism has imposed its plans on the government."

The MNR women's movement was co-opted by the state and the party, in which there was no room for self-determination and autonomy. Nor were women free from corruption, featherbedding, and sexual dealings among militants. Given this situation, MNR women were called upon more and more frequently to act as shock troops in confrontations with the opposition. Women took to the street against strikers, were active against coup attempts made by the opposition through the Bolivian Socialist Falange, and worked as spies for the government.

The initial impulse given to actions of the women's movement faded, as did the capacity for social transformation that women had won through contact with workers and the urban masses. As a result, the postrevolutionary women's movement organized by the MNR was national but essentially urban. Rural women channeled their participation to the National Rural Command, where they were mobilized for elections. It is important to point out that in spite of agrarian reform, rural women were not able to own land directly. Even today women's title to land is in most cases held by men.

One of the constants of MNR women's political participation during this period was involvement in activities that were outside the women's movement per se. The adversary was defined by the party, and women's protest actions were directed by party interests. In many cases, MNR women directed their opposition against sectors of the popular movement, actions contrary to their own interests as women of the lower classes.

The party was able to direct women's actions toward issues alien to them because women never proposed to transform their private relationships. MNR women did not propose an alternative to the approach imposed by the party, and they made no attempt to prepare an all-encompassing project that would include the ideal of equality. They acted not as women but as party militants, bound by men's way of being and thinking. Women did not demand policies that would help them overcome the subordination and discrimination found in political, labor-related, and educational plans. The demands they did formulate centered on achieving better economic and social conditions for their husbands and children.

The MNR women as a group battled for years, but not toward a utopia that would guide their fight for liberation. Without intellectual organizers to formulate such a utopia, they waited for the party and the patriarchal state to give them the guidelines, failing to take into account that men had designed the policies and made the rules. The MNR women's lack of independent political identity also impeded the generation of alliances that would have helped them attain their objectives. At the same time, the men in the party had no interest in or capacity to cope with women's emancipation because they would have had to confront fundamental problems in the organization of society and daily life.

In essence, the process of emancipating women meant linking all the complex matters comprising the public and private worlds, creating new options and ways of being and a new horizon that would displace and change women's traditional status. To do this would require constructing an autonomous institutional strategy in which women and men worked equally to solve the problems of the institutions' operations. But because MNR women focused on confrontation with the political opposition, they conceived politics as war rather than as the achievement of consensus and order for all. It was common for them to confront and clash with the party's internal and external enemies. Instead of pursuing a political vision in which women would be stakeholders with their own identity within a heterogeneous Bolivian society, the democracy attained with the MNR tended toward the homogenization of individuals rather than a mediation that could have brought together diverse groups.

Although women won the right to vote when the MNR took power in 1952, they lacked collective power because they were never present in the smoke-filled rooms where political decisions were made. Women had no power even in civil society, yet this does not mean that the issue of political power was not addressed. Gueiler, the only woman to remain a member of the MNR during and after the National Revolution, stated that "since 1955 I had been thinking about the need to have power, to fight for it, despite the criticism that I might receive for doing so. Even when I was appointed President of the Republic [in 1979], I insisted, because I feel that the only way to obtain any results is by having power."[4]

Nevertheless, there was a long period of time between the recognition of the need for power, its achievement in reality, and its generalization in culture. For that reason, MNR women delegated all the political and organizational power for their collective activities to the men of the party.

Although the MNR women did not formulate any collective proposals to transform private relationships or the prevailing order, they did become incorporated into the political system as collective actors, which ultimately proved subversive for the Bolivian political system and for society. Their actions—as women and as members of an overall social movement—allowed them to enter the public sphere by participating in a organized manner in the social conflict of the time.

DEMANDS OF THE HOUSEWIVES COMMITTEES

The activities of the Housewives Committees of the Federación Sindical Trabajadores Mineros de Bolivia (FSTMB, or Trade Union Federation of Bolivian Mine Workers) were grounded in the economic difficulties of rural mining communities. The *housewives* label refers to the social space that women occupy within the family, a role women laid claim to and accepted as their standard. This housewife identity was built around two roles: the traditional housewife who does all the housework and the woman who is wholly dependent on men and mine workers in politics.

The economic organization of mining structured the lives of the mine workers and their wives. After the revolution, the tin mines went from oligarchical to state control. Since then, the mining industry has been the site of confrontation between the state, represented by the government, and the working class, represented by the FSTMB. After the 1958 Congress of Colquiri, the rupture between the FSTMB and the government was in the open, thanks to the mine workers' constant mobilizations and the relentless use of force by the MNR government.

Even though the mining families were in the political and economic vanguard, their everyday lives were reduced to the simple effort of conserving enough strength to work and to reproduce the work force. Mining families could count on only one source of income, which came from COMIBOL, the state-owned mining corporation. COMIBOL often paid part of miners' salaries by subsidizing the cost of such goods or services as housing, electricity, water, and some foodstuffs available through the *pulperías* (company stores).

Mining families were large; generally women were concerned with the rearing and socialization of their children. But low wages and large families drove many women to become involved in different economic survival strategies. The most common of these strategies were linked with the service sector: selling food, taking in washing, or establishing small businesses or cottage industries.

The first housewives committee was formed on 8 June 1961 in Miraflores, Catavi, the principal mining center of the country at that time. It was organized in the context of an open confrontation between mine workers and the government. As Olga De Toro, first president of the housewives committee of Miraflores noted in an interview in 1984: "Since the pulperías had almost nothing for us we decided to get organized. Afterwards we needed to support our husbands and children because we made so little money and so we organized the housewives committee. Later the leaders were arrested and we worked in order to get them out of jail. At that time we women were courageous. We had to fight side by side with the men. We even held the manager of the mine here hostage to get provisions. . . . Now, on the other hand, women have other political aspirations and they answer to their parties. Before, our families were our political party."[5] The committee's actions initially were local, but as the confrontation with the government intensified, activism spread to other areas until it reached the government in La Paz.

For the women of the mining communities, participation in the housewives committees was their first organized political involvement. They waged their battles from their daily lives, their domestic, private experience, and their role as organizers of family consumption. Essentially, the political and economic crisis of the mining sector enabled housewives to abandon their traditional domestic role to defend their family economy. The space for women's public activities was opened precisely on the basis of expanding their traditional and legitimized role. They were responsible mothers and housewives defending their families' well-being in an area where only women operate and which was therefore not seen as dangerous.[6] As one housewife put it, "We have left our children alone in the mine; we cannot leave them with empty hands, we cannot endure to be trampled on."[7]

There was a feeling among housewives that they were organizing not only to achieve political objectives but fundamentally to improve their families' actual living conditions. One housewife said, "I used to give little importance to the housewives committees. I would say that they were political and were working for some political party, but then I saw that they got some results."[8] Another committee member added that "it's more work for us, because first we have to leave our houses nice and clean, with everything washed, ironed, cooked and ready, before we can attend the committee meeting. . . . But we like to go."[9]

Three general themes emerged in the demands made by the committees. First, the women supported the demands and protests of the mine workers regarding the formation of their labor movement, including the utopia of socialism and the more immediate issues of political and labor-union freedoms, wage increases, and the liberation of political prisoners. Second, they issued demands regarding the collective consumption infrastructure, such as food supply, medicines, the health system, and services (electricity, housing, water, gas). Third, the members of the committees made less explicit demands that arose from their status as women and focused mainly on occupational alternatives for the widows of mine workers. In their first organized action, a group of housewives staged a hunger strike in 1961 to pressure the government to liberate union leaders who had been arrested during the 12th Congress in Colquiri. They also demanded the payment of outstanding wages by COMIBOL and a salary increase.

Repression against mine workers and other social sectors grew with the 1964 coup. The new economic policy of the military government decreased salaries for mine workers and began denationalization. Military governments later elevated the repression of mine workers to a permanent policy. The FSTMB went underground, and its principal leaders were assassinated, imprisoned, or exiled. The 1967 Massacre of San Juan is an infamous example of this period of repression.

During the military dictatorship and with the absence of male leaders, the women of the committees carried on the mining protest using the system of mining radio stations and an underground postal service. Their goal was to ensure the leaders' safety and, in general, support the work done by protest leaders. In 1965 the housewives made public their opposition to the military government of Gen. René Barrientos when he decided to decrease workers' wages. Later, during the military government of Gen. Hugo

Banzer (1971–78), the committees organized protests to maintain leadership of the movement and the capacity of the mining communities to resist the government. In the absence of the principal union leaders, the women led actions to defend the miners and their acquired rights. During mining strikes, the housewives were active in enforcement and also organized soup kitchens that became the meeting places where strikers received information.

The housewives received national attention for their actions in 1978 when four women from the mines—Aurora de Lora, Nelly de Paniagua, Angelica de Floras, and Luzmila de Pimentel—and their 14 children began a hunger strike that had historical significance for the country. They demanded that the government grant general unrestricted amnesty and respect for union and political freedoms. Their action was repeated throughout the country by university students and professors, urban and rural workers, and part of the Catholic church. The strike lasted 24 days. In the end, the military government was obliged to hold general elections on the basis of general amnesty. All of this happened because of the actions of "four brave mining women," whose feat was mentioned in every subsequent political speech.

Through their actions, the women on the housewives committees worked in opposition to the government. It was no accident that the demands of the housewives were directed against the state because the mine workers depended on the state and the government to solve their major problems. In effect, the perception of a "providential state" by union and political leaders, workers, and consumers led them to seek solutions to their problems within the government. This behavior meant that the government had ample leeway to reject or negotiate the demands made by workers and their wives because the miners had no instruments of their own to propose self-managed solutions.[10]

Relations between the workers and the government led women to a certain way of making politics: one that emphasized confrontation and warfare. Like the MNR women, the housewives took up politics as a war in which the enemy must be destroyed. Some of the battle cries of the housewives committee members were, "We shall defend our country with our blood," "We shall fight to our dying breath," "We ratify our unfaltering will," "It is better to be shot to death than to starve," "We shall never be forced to our knees." The emergence of the housewives committees was vital to the mine workers because it brought a combative element to their struggle. As collective agents, the committee women contributed by radicalizing the struggles of the union. They assumed "to their dying breath" the union's objectives. The mining movement thereby ratified its role as the vanguard of the country's social and political movements.

CLASS BEFORE GENDER

In their identity as mining women, the housewives assumed the overall objectives of the workers' movement and focused their protests on the state, not on the miners. The housewives, like the miners, visualized the capitalistic state and the dominant classes as their adversary and were committed to the struggle to transform the current social order into socialism. As Domitila de Chungara, a leader of the housewives committees, stated, "My people are not fighting for a minor conquest. My people are fighting to attain socialism."[11] When women entered politics, their actions were grounded in the distinction between the bourgeoisie and the proletariat. Class categories were determined by the mine workers, and the role of housewives was assigned on the basis of the relationship their husbands had with the means of production. In this case, women were not considered autonomous beings. They had no freedom or control over their lives, as did their wage-earning husbands.

The housewives committees concentrated on the question of capitalism, and thus the economic position of their class, societal production relationships, and the public world predominated in their analysis. The hierarchical sexual structure of society (reproductive relationships, the private world, the domestic work performed by housewives) was not taken into account in women's analysis and struggles. While the initiative came from the women themselves, their actions were born as instruments for other purposes. As the National Housewives Committee stated, "Our first task, in view of the serious risks that the country had been exposed to, was to leave aside a series of urgent workers' issues in order to take up the defense of the democratic process and the period of freedom and rights."[12] But this stance meant that it was impossible to find a single public issue to express the situation of discrimination against housewives. On the contrary, the housewives' identity as mining women reinforced the claim that their interests coincided completely with those of the miners. As Domitila de Chungara put it, "We ended up supporting everything that had been decided by the labor unions . . . [because] we felt that our first and foremost work was not to fight against our male comrades, but to work with them to change the system in which we live, so that men and women will have the right to live, to work and to organize. . . . Prostitution, birth control and all those things are real problems, but not the fundamental ones."[13]

The patriarchal discrimination to which women were subjected thus was not denounced or formulated in the committee speeches. The committees' demands did not include the elimination of the domestic violence suffered by housewives or the provision of day-care facilities because this would have provoked direct confrontations with the union. In fact, only one nursery, established by the Housewives Committee of Catavi, is known to have existed in the entire nationalized mining sector. Feminism and its issues as a social movement were associated with the bourgeoisie and imperialism, so its demands were regarded as spurious. In fact, workers in general considered feminism to be alien to the working class, dividing the labor union movement and blurring class contradictions.

Yet it is not that women did not suffer from the existing sexual hierarchy. Rather, "the response must be sought in the working class culture prevailing in the leadership and even among the grass roots, which is a mixture of doctrinal elements still rooted in revolutionary nationalism and Marxism. The utopia of liberation and socialism present in the miners' theses is doubtlessly set in Marxist terms. It is this learning process and the confusion and insufficiency of the classics of Marxism to address women's issues that have inculcated in the male and female miners an aversion to the claims pertaining to women."[14]

According to this concept, the fight against the patriarchal sexual hierarchy is a matter for bourgeois movements because it divides the working class and subordinates the conflict between the classes. The miners' paradigm of the proletarian dictatorship assumes that all social demands and identities will be overridden by the common project of the class. Therefore, women's demands will remain postponed, secondary to the miners' more general strategy.

FOCUS ON GENDER

Notwithstanding this dominant paradigm, the real novelty of women's political participation was that the mode of making politics affected women's daily lives and produced some changes. As one housewife noted, "sometimes I have to fight so I can leave home to go to the committee meetings, and I know that it will be worse when I get back home, who knows what will happen, but I don't care. What concerns me is to fight and win for the children, above all, who are the important ones."[15]

There recently has been a slight but growing awareness of the oppression suffered by women. Housewives committee members began their work of solidarity with the widows of mine workers. When mine workers die, their widows no longer receive the benefits of the indirect salary paid to workers through groceries at the company store, housing, and so on. For this reason, the committee worked intensively to get the widows hired by the company, whether in the service area or through marginal employment. In effect, the housewives committee organized a committee for the placement of unemployed women. These efforts produced a sizable group of women who became *palliris,* women who gathered and sorted the tailings from the tin mines and were employed through informal contracts with the company.

The housewives' identity as women was undoubtedly expressed most clearly through the redemocratization of Bolivia in 1982. In fact, after political democracy was achieved, most labor unions recovered their full freedoms and the housewives committees began to fade or disband. The unions emerged politically invigorated by the dictatorship and no longer needed these allies in their fight against the government.

An economic and social crisis still existed in Bolivia, however. The contraction of the world minerals market, along with domestic factors, contributed to the problem. Within this setting, the housewives committees regained political importance by mobilizing workers. By this time, however, women had already made plans to form the National Federation of Housewives Committees after reorganizing the committees in each mining center. In this regard, the housewives were greatly influenced by the formation in 1980 of Bartolina Sisa (the National Federation of Peasant Women).

The first time the committees explicitly called for a national organization was in the Mining Congress of Matilde in April 1984, attended by 22 women as associate members. They urged the Mining Congress to organize a national summit of housewives committees to establish the national organization, but the congress put off the proposal.

Such encounters led many committee women to begin perceiving and verbalizing the discrimination that they were subjected to within the miners' federation and the unions. As one housewives committee member testified:

They use us to support their own actions, but that is all they want. When we talk about organizing nationally, then they don't like that, and they ask us, "If you are in politics, who will cook, who will take care of the children at home?" The younger leaders understand better, they listen, they support us, but they don't have any judgment. For that reason, we must organize ourselves and set our own goals, because if we leave this to the [miners'] federation, they only want to order us

around and have us do what they want. But we also have our own opinion, because who does the crisis hit the hardest? Us women. Of course our husbands give us their paychecks, but who stretches them so that they will reach to the end of the month? We are the ones who suffer the most.[16]

Committee meetings attended only by women offered a chance to discuss discrimination against women, though it was still difficult to make their condition understood. In fact, oppression was verbalized only in private conversations and did not result in any actions by the committee. Complaints remained in the private realm, as individual problems requiring no collective action.

In this connection, mining women remained zealous guardians of working class unity. It took a long time for them to confront the paradigm of the proletarian dictatorship because addressing and making public the problems of women's emancipation entailed facing profound, fundamental problems regarding the organization of society. In the case of the miners' unions, such change meant dealing with a working-class approach to politics—one rooted in the mining identity, which had been forged through decades of conflict. This confrontation also called for radical changes in the membership structures of the committees and the unions and adopting a new approach to politics that took advantage of the specific characteristics of women.

By making politics from the union base, however, the housewives committees began to redefine relations with the union and the overall social movement. They worked with increasing coherence toward relative autonomy and objectives geared to constituting a differentiated gender identity and an ever greater awareness of gender contradictions. The increasing institution building achieved by the housewives committees and their interaction with other social actors and movements has gained significant legitimacy for their actions and demands within the political system. In practice, the committees have formed a major informal network of mutual assistance and support.

For women in the MNR and the housewives committees, it has been a long, hard battle to construct a new way of participating in the economic, political, and social fields and to connect the public and private spheres. To accomplish this more fully will require the formation of an institutional strategy that will enable women to deal not only with the miners' federation and the MNR but also with other social, union, and political institutions, both male and female. Finally, women will have to realize that their political actions are based on men's methods of action. They must free themselves of these old modes and assume a political mode of operation based on their own womanhood.

NOTES

1. Elizabeth Jelin, *Identidad y ciudadanía: Mujeres en los movimientos sociales* (Identity and citizenship: Women in social movements) (Buenos Aires, 1986, Mimeographed).

2. Sheila Rowbotham, *Femenismo y revolución* (Feminism and revolution) (Madrid: Debate Publishers, 1978).

3. Julieta Kirkwood, *Ser política en Chile* (To be political in Chile) (Santiago, 1985).

4. Interview with Lydia Gueiler, La Paz, 1983. As president of the Chamber of Deputies, Gueiler was appointed as interim president in a deal between the military and the Parliament. She followed the presidency of Walter Guevara, who had been president of the Senate. Her presidency ended after nine months in a military coup.

5. No citation provided.

6. Teresa Caldeira, *Mujeres: cotidianidad y política* (Women: Everyday life and politics) (Spi, 1986, Mimeographed).

7. Noemi, speaking at the National Committee Meeting.

8. Peguy Lara, speaking at the National Committee Meeting.

9. Margarita N., speaking at the National Committee meeting.

10. Godofredo Sandoval, "Las mil caras del movimiento social boliviano" (The thousand faces of the Bolivian social movement), *Revista Estado y Sociedad* 2 (1986).

11. Moema Viezzer and Domitila Barrios de Chungara, *Si me permiten hablar* (If they allowed me to speak) (Mexico City: Siglo XXI, 1978).

12. National Housewives Committee Meeting, 1986.

13. No citation given.

14. Gustavo Rodriguez, *Las compañeras del mineral* (The companions of the mineral) (Caracas: Nueva Sociedad, 1987).

15. Margarita N., speaking at the National Committee Meeting.

16. Ibid.

▲ Brazil

POLITICS

Type of Political System: democracy
 Sovereignty: republic
 Executive-Legislative System: presidential
Type of State: federal
Type of Party System: multiparty
Major Political Parties [a]

Partido do Movimento Democrática Brasileiro (PMDB, or Party of the Brazilian Democratic Movement): Primarily a center-right party, founded in 1979.

Partido da Frente Liberal (PFL, or Liberal Front Party): Arising from opposition to the presidential candidacy of Paulo Maluf. Formed in 1984; second largest party in Congress by 1986.

Partido Democrático Social (PDS, or Social Democratic Party): Founded in 1979. PDS, a conservative party, supported the military regime.

Partido Democrático Trabalhista (PDT, or Democratic Labor Party): Leftist party organized in 1979 by Leonel da Moira Brizola, former leader of the Partido Trabalhista Brasileiro (Brazilian Labor Party) exiled from Brazil for 15 years.

Partido da Social Democracia Brasileira (PSDB, or Party of Brazilian Social Democracy): Center-left party founded in 1988 by deputies from several other parties, mainly a dissident group of MPs from the PMDB.

Partido dos Trabalhadores (PT, or Workers' Party): Founded by trade unions in São Paulo in 1979, gathering qualified workers and leftist intellectuals. Made significant gains throughout the late 1980s, including election of its candidate as the first woman mayor of São Paulo.

Year Women Granted Right to Vote: 1932
Year Women Granted Right to Stand for Election: 1932

Percentage of Women in the Legislature
 Lower House (1990): 6.0%
 Upper House: 0.4%
Percentage of Electorate Voting for Highest Elected Office in Most Recent Election (1989): 86.2%

DEMOGRAPHICS

Population: 150,368,000[b]
Percentage of Population in Urban Areas
 Overall: 70.8%
 Female: 71.9%
 Male: 69.6%
Percentage of Population Below Age 15: 36.4%
Birthrate (per 1,000 population): 29
Maternal Mortality Rate (per 100,000 live births): 154
Infant Mortality Rate (per 1,000 live births): 65
Mortality Rate for Children Under Five (per 1,000 live births): 89
Average Household Size: 4.9
Mean Age at First Marriage
 Female: 22.6
 Male: 25.9
Life Expectancy
 Female: 67.6
 Male: 62.3

EDUCATION

Ratio of Female to Male Enrollment
 First-Level Education (1980/1984): 95
 Second-Level Education: not available
 Third-Level Education (1980/1984): 100
Literacy Rate
 Female: 63.0%
 Male: 69.0%

ECONOMY

Gross National Product per Capita: U.S. $1,640
Percentage of Labor Force in Agriculture: 46.0%

Women in the Struggle for Democracy and Equal Rights in Brazil

FANNY TABAK

Brazil is the largest country in South America, occupying nearly half of the continent. The country and its indigenous Indians were colonized by the Portuguese in the 1500s, and Brazil became an independent monarchy in 1822 and a republic in 1889. For most of the time since independence the country has shifted from democracy to authoritarian state to military regime.

Today's multiracial population of 150 million is governed under a federal system of 23 states, one territory, and a federal district. On the national level is a presidential system with a bicameral legislature made up of the Senate and the Chamber of Deputies. The states have legislative assemblies and governors, and at the local level are mayors and municipal councils.

In the early twentieth century, government regimes were characterized by the repression of workers and of liberal social and political organizations. A number of so-called revolutions headed by young military officers took place at the beginning of the 1920s. The officers wanted to modernize the country, diminish the absolute economic power that lay with the landowners, and reduce the role of foreign capital. In the 1930s important sectors of the new bourgeoisie gained access to political power, and urbanization spread. General elections were held in 1933—the first time that women were allowed to vote—and in 1934 liberal ideas were included in the constitution for the first time.

But in November 1937 Getúlio Vargas, one of the leaders of the officers' rebellion, took over. He closed the National Congress, canceled the presidential elections, and proclaimed the Estado Novo (New State), which lasted until the end of World War II. His model was Mussolini's fascist Italy.

Women's organizations played a crucial role in fighting Vargas's government and in demanding that Brazil support the Allied forces in Europe. Women shared in the effort made by Brazilian democratic forces to send an expeditionary group of soldiers to fight in Italy. With the defeat of nazism and fascism Vargas's reign ended, and it was possible to obtain political amnesty for thousands of prisoners (including many women), to hold general elections for the executive and legislative branches at all levels, to allow political parties to exist legally, and to hold public meetings and demonstrations. In 1946 a new democratic constitution passed in Parliament.

But in April 1964 a military coup ended the longest period of democratic rule in Brazil, and a strict authoritarian regime remained in power until March 1985. The military did not close down the National Congress as it did in Chile but used various "institutional acts" (extremely repressive decrees). The military suspended the mandates of the MPs and heads of state and local governments, and for ten years it suppressed the political rights of hundreds of political leaders.

The military also persecuted intellectuals, religious leaders, and artists and imposed rigid censorship on the media. By the end of the 1970s, the transition to democracy was accelerated with the so-called political openness. General elections in 1978 and 1982 gave women the opportunity to enter their own candidates at the local, state, and federal levels. Some of those female candidates were active in the feminist movement or at least supported its campaigns.

The party system in Brazil has undergone considerable change throughout this history. It went from a pluralistic system in which more than 30 parties were allowed to participate in elections to a de facto two-party system in which only two parties had any real chances of electing their candidates, regardless of how many parties existed. Finally, during the military regime of 1967–79, all parties but two were banished, and only one of those was allowed to win.

Since March 1985, when a civilian government replaced the military one, Brazil again has had a pluralistic system, and in the general elections of November 1990 more than 30 parties participated. Most parties are not really representative, however, for they attend to the legal requirements merely as a formality shortly before the elections take place only to allow their candidates to run for a seat. In the National Congress and the state assemblies, several parties maintained their strength, or representativeness, in elections held in 1982, 1986, and 1990. Two of them were formed in the 1970s: the Partido do Movimento Democrático Brasileiro (PMDB, or Brazilian Democratic Movement Party), which opposed the military, and the Partido da Frente Liberal (PFL, or Liberal Front Party), which supported the military but agreed to help end the authoritarian regime and permit the transition to democracy. The Partido Democrático Social (PDS, or Social Democratic Party) also supported the military; despite its name, it has nothing in common with the European social democratic parties.

There are a few progressive and democratic parties. The Partido dos Trabalhadores (PT, or Workers' Party) was formed in the late 1970s as an outgrowth of the strong labor movement in the state of São Paulo, where one of the most impressive strikes took place among skilled automobile workers in 1978. PT has also attracted a large number of leftist intellectuals and academics. The Partido Democrático Trabalhista (PDT, or Labor Democratic Party) was created in 1982 after a split among members of the Partido Trabalhista Brasileiro (PTB, or Brazilian Labor Party), which was formed in 1945 by Vargas. The PDT claims to resemble the social democratic parties in Europe and is affiliated with the Socialist International. Its most important leader—Leonel Brizola—is a vice-president of the latter organization.

Two communist parties currently exist in Brazil: both participated in the 1986 and 1990 elections and have representatives in the National Congress. There is also Partido Socialista Brasileiro (PSB, or Brazilian Socialist Party), a revival of the party created in 1945 that has representatives at national and state levels. Among the social movements that were growing rapidly during the 1980s was the ecology movement, which resulted in the creation of the Green Party. Some of its leaders have been elected to legislative bodies.

The Roman Catholic church plays an extremely important role in Brazil and has influenced the attitudes of many women in regard to politics and social issues, as well as in regard to the demands put forward by the feminist movement. Through the so-called Base Ecclesiastical Communities, the church has helped to organize millions of women from the poor popular sectors and from the middle and upper classes. During the era of military repression a number of representatives of the high leadership of the church led a continuous struggle to denounce the torture and murder of political prisoners and to help the democratic social forces. Other religions in Brazil, including Baptists and Evangelicals, also have a great amount of prestige and influence among women.

At present Brazil has a modern economy and such high-technology industries as weapons manufacture. Two-thirds of the people live in urban areas. But, in spite of all the attempts at change made during the second half of the 1980s, problems are rife. They include high inflation, recession, unemployment, and discrimination in the workplace on the basis of sex.

Since 1975 U.N. efforts to help women overcome these problems and others—like illiteracy, poverty, and discrimination—together with the rise of many women's organizations have helped improve the status of women in Brazil. Public bodies were created at the national, state, and local levels, including the Comitês de Defesa dos Direitos da Mulher (Committees in Defense of Women's Rights) in many of the most developed areas, which helped governments to define a number of public policies and were instrumental in articulating a common platform and program of action; Associações de Moradores (Neighborhood Associations), whose active members are mostly women; and professional organizations that also brought together large numbers of women demanding equal rights. In other words, the U.N. Plan of Action and International Decade for Women, the transition to democracy, and the larger female representation in Parliament meant that much more visibility was given to women's issues.

Three struggles related to Brazilian women's political participation are the struggle for a democratic regime; the struggle for equal rights; and the struggle for the implementation of public policies. The struggle for democracy is the central issue if one considers that authoritarian and military rule accounts for almost one-third of the 100 years under a republican system. Even before 1930 there were insurrections, military uprisings, and other presidential periods under siege. This situation is not exclusively Brazilian; in Latin America democracy and political stability are more the exception than the rule. I will deal mainly with the most recent transition to democracy—from 1978 to the writing of the new constitution in October 1988—when women's participation in politics became most visible and intense. Through an examination of the forms and nature of women's participation in Brazil, one can gain insight into the diverse roles played

by different groups in Brazilian society during various historical periods.

WOMEN'S ORGANIZATIONS

A powerful suffragist movement existed in Brazil by the 1920s. A small but active group of professional women, some of whom had been involved in politics and supported the republican movement, developed a persistent campaign for the right to vote. By the end of the first decade of the twentieth century a group of women who called themselves feminists were publishing a few newspapers in Rio de Janeiro.[1] Some of these women had participated in international conferences and were well informed about the social advances made by women in other countries. For instance, the leader of the movement for the enfranchisement of women was Bertha Lutz, a scientist who had attended the 1906 suffrage convention in Baltimore. All these factors influenced the creation in 1921 of a Brazilian Women's League, a group that was transformed into the Brazilian Federation for the Progress of Women in 1922 and still exists. Since its heyday in the 1920s it has been reduced to a rather small group of educated middle-class women from Rio.

Part of the Brazilian press supported women's demand for enfranchisement. In 1921 a proposal made by one of the senators was accepted for consideration, but no bill was passed. Women had created their own political parties, as they thought this would help them win the vote. These included the Women's Republican Party, Women's Liberal Party, Women's National Alliance, and Brazilian Women's Legion. Unlike the Brazilian Federation for the Progress of Women, these parties and alliances were oriented toward active political participation. The first of these organizations was founded in 1909 to support one of the candidates in the presidential elections. By writing articles, giving talks, and conducting interviews, women were able to gain the support of some representatives, who then promoted suffrage. The most prestigious newspapers, particularly those in Rio, endorsed the campaign for the vote.

In 1932 Brazilian women finally gained the right to vote, and in 1933 the first woman was elected to Parliament. She was Carlota Pereira de Queiroz, a physician from São Paulo and a member of a traditional and wealthy family. Interestingly, women's suffrage was obtained in Brazil even before some European countries accorded women the right. Suffrage was one of the most significant results of efforts to modernize the country—the so-called bourgeois revolution, which occurred in 1930 after lengthy protest against government incompetence and corruption, the concentration of property ownership in a few hands, and the young officers' uprisings.

In this respect, extending the vote to women was vital to moving Brazil forward. But the democratic process and women's efforts to take advantage of their newly acquired right to vote were abruptly interrupted by the Vargas coup in 1937. With the fall of Vargas in 1945, women's hopes for increased participation in the decision-making process and society's hopes for a stable democracy bloomed anew. Although many women and their organizations had fought fascism and the Estado Novo, they unfortunately were not represented in the National Congress when the new constitution was created, nor were any women elected to the new government. A few women were voted into local councils and state legislatures, but the complicated party system made it difficult for female candidates to get enough support (financial and otherwise) to be elected. At that time the parties did not consider women priority candidates.

It was not until 1950 that a woman—Ivete Vargas, a relative of Getúlio Vargas—became a member of Parliament.[2] She was affiliated with the Brazilian Labor Party, which Getúlio Vargas had founded, and she became president of the party in 1980 when the military regime was coming to an end. Few other women were able to get seats in Parliament before 1964 and the onset of another period of authoritarian rule, however.

In the 1970s only one woman, Lygia Maria Lessa Bastos, won a seat in Parliament. A representative from Rio, she was first elected in 1945 as a local councillor after accepting the nomination of a new party called the União Democrática Nacional (National Democratic Union), which had been opposing Estado Novo. She came from a middle-class family and worked as a volleyball instructor. She was elected to the position every four years until 1960, when she became a state deputy. She was then elected in 1974 and 1978 to the National Congress. In 1982 she retired after one of the longest political careers ever for a woman representative in Brazil. She supported the authoritarian regime to some extent but not the repression.

There are many reasons for women's low profile in formal political institutions from the 1930s through 1978, when the transition to democracy began with the so-called political openness. Women's organizations did exist, but most of them focused on raising the standard of living. They fought the effect of inflation on the price of goods and paid attention to people's basic needs. Day-care centers were always at the top of the list of demands put forward by these organizations.

Thanks to U.N. efforts to expand the political agenda to include women's concerns, as well as the increasing influence of feminist ideas, women's organizations after 1975 tended to address issues that were more political. Many more women became involved in politics, especially during the 1978 elections, and some of the women candidates active in the feminist movement were elected to the legislature.

THE STRUGGLE FOR WOMEN'S REPRESENTATION IN A DEMOCRATIC REGIME

Despite society's overall progress since the first democratic constitution in 1946, the benefits of democratization have been problematic for women's efforts to obtain representation. From the 1950s until the end of the 1980s enormous changes were introduced into the Brazilian economy and social structure as industry and the working class grew, the rate of urbanization increased, and public services (water supply, sewage system, healthcare) expanded. But the extensive damage in the political arena caused by 20 years under a repressive military regime prevented women from reaping the benefits of living in a democracy.

The women who had been active in gathering other women to discuss the issues while the country was under military rule became known as feminists. They focused on the right of "option" (in regard to contraception), abortion, sexual and domestic violence, and the belief that the private is public. The feminists usually belonged to small groups of professional women, many of them already active in political parties or political organizations. Women also had actively opposed the military regime, and their role in denouncing torture and murder, as well as other forms of persecution and repression, was crucial not only to publicizing what was going on, but also to winning political amnesty for the hundreds of exiled women.

Women's groups had a larger presence in the electoral process in 1978, especially the feminist groups that had been created in 1975, stimulated by the U.N.'s International Women's Year. A few feminist candidates were also elected at the state and local level.

Although it was not until 1982 that a real feminist platform became an issue in the electoral campaign, during the 1978 elections there was a months-long discussion in Rio about the best way to use the political openness to serve the women's cause. On one side were the representatives of feminist groups who argued that it was important to participate in the elections by nominating women and men who would help get projects presented and bills passed. On the other side were those who refused to participate in the elections because the military regime was still in power and many political parties were still considered illegal.

The solution was to circulate what was called the Alerta Feminista (Feminist Warning), a document outlining the demands and proposals of the movement as a whole. Each candidate was expected to support it if he or she wanted the backing of the various women's groups. The participation of hundreds of feminist women from all over the country did help elect a few dozen women to local councils and state legislatures, and this allowed for the introduction of a few bills benefiting women.

The 1978 campaign differed from previous ones in part because issues that were raised by feminist groups in 1975 began to be discussed by all the candidates—male and female. In this respect the mass media, especially television, helped to widen public debate around sex-based discrimination, sexual and domestic violence, and other feminist issues. Each candidate had to take a stand on women's issues, which served to identify his or her position and thus helped to define the support or rejection of the female electorate.

In 1982 almost 2,000 women councilors were elected from five different political parties: PMDB, PDS, PT, PDT, and PTB. A total of 134 female candidates were nominated to the state legislatures, but only 28 were elected: sixteen by the PMDB, seven by the PDS, three by the PDT, and one each by the PT and the PTB. The total number of female candidates for the House of Representatives was 58, but only eight were elected: three by the PMDB; two each by the PDS and the PT; and one by the government's party. The eight representatives elected corresponded to no more than 3 percent of the House. There were women candidates for the Senate, but no one was elected.

The PMDB, PDT, and PT opposed the military government, and women who were affiliated with them and were nominated as the party's candidates were usually women who had resisted authoritarianism and struggled for democracy. PT has been supportive of women's demands from the beginning and has been the party with the highest percentage of female candidates elected to legislative bodies. It is also the party that supported Maria Luiza Fontenele, the first woman to become mayor of a capital city (Fortaleza, in the northeast), and that in 1988 elected another woman, Luiza Erundina, mayor of São Paulo, the most developed and industrialized metropolis in Latin America. Erundina is a migrant from the northeast, the least developed part of the country.

WOMEN AT THE NATIONAL CONGRESS AND THE 1988 CONSTITUTION

The 1986 elections for the National Constituent Assembly were particularly important for Brazilian women. Twenty-six women from 16 different states were elected. Even so, the proportion of female representatives at the National Congress increased by only 3.7 percent from the 1982 election. The two parties that elected the largest number of women were those that supported the government: PMDB and PFL. The former elected eleven representatives and the latter, six. Together, the parties had two-thirds of the entire female representation. But the left-oriented parties (the PT, the two communist parties, and the Socialist Party) had 15 percent, the most significant percentage of women among their representatives.

By 1986, as women's issues became much more visible in the mass media, political action regarding them increased. Feminists denounced sexual violence against women and demanded equal rights, an end to wage discrimination and the lack of equal opportunities, and an end to the exclusion of women from the political process. As a consequence, a certain number of positive results were achieved, including the creation of women's rights commissions and the appointment of more women to top public administration positions in areas where women were rarely seen before the 1980s.

At the 1986 National Constituent Assembly women had the opportunity to include in the 1988 constitution some of the demands formulated during the U.N. Decade for Women, as well as those long proposed by women's organizations. The MPs were pressured to sanction proposals that would simplify the approval and enactment of ordinary laws and thus indirectly contribute to the implementation of other demands and claims by women. Women previously had to deal with unenforced or rarely enforced laws because there were no prescribed penalties or because there was an intentional omission in the law. For example, all companies that employ 30 or more women older than 16 have been obligated since 1910 to establish day-care centers for their workers' children, but the law has rarely been enforced.

The exposure of sexual violence against women—including domestic violence that is often concealed by the victim herself—and the proliferation of protests and actions by feminist groups like SOS Mulher (SOS Woman) over such violence demonstrated the need to include in the new constitution penalties for crimes such as rape.[3] These articles were included to produce laws that would regulate and discipline social relations, as well as eliminate discrimination against women.

Also discussed was a new concept of family that would mandate equality between unmarried partners and redefine the rights, duties, and civil capacities of each partner. Statistical data for the 1980s showed an enormous increase in the number of single mothers, many of whom were women who decided to have a child without getting married. Others were young women who became pregnant through ignorance of contraceptive methods, and still others were women of the popular sectors who had migrated from the countryside to urban areas for work and were responsible for raising children on their own. As a result, an updated understanding of the social function of motherhood through a new perception of the family was crucial. A recognition of that function would imply government responsibility for educating and caring for the "child-citizen," as many feminist groups put it. This would mean, first of all, allocating more public funds to public education, healthcare, day-care centers, and parks.

Interest in these issues and the idea of influencing a new constitution prompted many more women to seek office in 1986. The main reason for the interest in getting a seat at the National Congress was the increased importance this institution had assumed, as it was expected to elaborate a new democratic constitution after the military rule ended. In addition, many feminist groups were already aware of the importance of having female representatives in Parliament to advance the recognition of equal rights.

The state of Rio de Janeiro, where a number of feminist groups had been active since 1975, placed 48 women candidates from many different parties on the lists for the 1986 elections. This time it was not just the big parties that were concerned with nominating women. Even small parties created shortly before the election exclusively to field candidates decided to include women in their lists.

The candidates were nominated by 18 parties, only some of which had obtained the candidate's agreement before placing her name on the list. Some of the candidates said they had no knowledge of their party's structure or program, or even of its proposal for the new constitution. The parties realized that women's issues had gained visibility and media support and were trying to capitalize on the fact that women voters constituted the majority in many cities. A few of the women candidates, however, had gained support from the communities or organizations with which they had been working for many years, and the general expectation was that they could be elected. Also, according to existing legislation on elections, a large vote for one of the candidates would benefit other candidates of the same list or party.

Some of the feminist groups resisted participating in the 1978 and 1982 election campaigns, claiming that a complete separation between the women's movement and political parties was the only way to ensure the movement's autonomy. This belief underestimated the role and function of parties and the help they could provide to women's causes. Many feminists insisted that women, including candidates running for office, unite regardless of political and ideological affiliations, but others were unwilling to establish closer ties with political parties. As a result, in 1982 Rio and São Paulo—the two most developed states and ones in which women's groups had been greatly active—were unable to elect women candidates supported by the feminist movement.

An authoritarian regime and military governments had been in power in Brazil for 20 years, and political parties and ideological forces had been outlawed, so when the possibility of a political opening appeared, the parties realized they could participate in the general elections and help to accelerate the transition to democracy. Although many active feminists were affiliated with these parties, others feared that the parties would be willing to manipulate the feminist movement for their own benefit.

In a study made for UNESCO, 34 of the 48 candidates were interviewed.[4] One of the most striking findings was the variety of motives behind each candidate's choice of political party. Some of those choices were made randomly, and some revealed a certain amount of political opportunism, as the chances of winning were supposed to be greater for the incumbent party. In addition, some women were candidates or affiliated with certain parties simply because their husbands had been in that party for many years. Most of the other studies in Brazil have shown that other people—generally men—have influenced women candidates' decisions to enter party politics.

Some women candidates, however, emerged from social and community movements in which they were recognized as leaders. One of the candidates who was successful was Benedita da Silva, a black woman who for many years had been active in the Neighborhood Associations of the slums of Rio de Janeiro, where she lived. She was elected by the Workers' Party to the National Congress in 1986 after she finished her term as a local councilor. In 1990 she was reelected to the House of Representatives after playing an important role in the debates on the new constitution.

In spite of the growth of women's participation in the elections since 1978 and during the widening of the "opening process" that followed these elections, women continued to experience both overt discrimination and passive resistance from their parties whenever national or state positions were at stake. They faced many difficulties even after women were nominated in the electoral campaign for the National Constituent Assembly in 1986. Those who had been "invited" to be candidates were often left to their own devices, receiving no effective support from the party. All parties lacked financial resources (except the one in office in central government, which controlled the money), but other difficulties that women faced—such as lack of access to television and radio time or invitations to be key speakers at important gatherings—resulted from simple prejudice or machismo.

All the candidates, no matter what their parties, complained about the limited amount of free television and radio time granted by the Tribunal Regional Electoral (Regional Electoral Court), the public body responsible for the electoral process. Few women candidates were seen on television during the 60-day campaign, and those who did appear were allowed just a few seconds to discuss their proposals for the new constitution. Although the large number of candidates made it difficult to distribute broadcast time equitably, women's share was small nonetheless.

Women candidates' lack of credibility was evident inside and outside the parties. Inside there was the old tendency to "instrumentalize" women, to use them as convenient flip sides of the traditional double ticket. A double ticket is a joint campaign conducted by two candidates, each running for office on a different level: local and state, or state and federal. A woman's personal effort and presence on the ticket could help a male candidate in the same party win. But her own candidacy might not be taken seriously by the party.

Outside the party, politics was still considered men's business, especially among the popular sectors, where machismo is deeply rooted. Although a few (male) candidates criticized women's self-deprecation or alienation from political life and insisted on the need to "change people's attitudes," even those candidates did very little to help women.

The women candidates in 1986 who had ties to the women's movement subscribed to the proposals sanctioned at a national conference held in Brasília early that year. The conference was attended by 2,000 women from all parts of the country who approved the Carta das Mulheres (Women's Charter) through which they sought

resolution of some basic problems: the allotment of public funds to create day-care centers; a revision of the laws that established motherhood as a "social responsibility"; and an end to discrimination in the labor market. The candidates, if elected, intended to pursue the demands in the new constitution.

SOCIAL MOVEMENTS AND THE STRUGGLE FOR EQUAL RIGHTS

In spite of women's difficulties with the parties and with obtaining representation, the political opening enabled women to engage politically in many other ways. The participation of large groups of Brazilian women in social movements during the 1980s contributed enormously to reinforcing the trend toward democracy. Three of these social movements were crucial to raising women's consciousness about their rights, their basic needs, and the ways in which they could be recognized and attended: the feminist movement, the Base Ecclesiastical Communities movement, and the Neighborhood Associations movement.

The first feminist groups, as well as a feminist press, were created in Brazil in 1975, the International Women's Year. These groups were mainly formed in the metropolitan areas by middle-class women who were lawyers, professors, and artists.

The new groups differed from the organizations that had existed after the end of World War II not only in their goals and activities but also in the social origin and class backgrounds of their members. In the 1950s hundreds of women's organizations were created all over the country: mothers' clubs, housewives' associations, committees against the high cost of living, and professional organizations (e.g., women's departments in trade unions). Many of the members came from the popular sectors, and their main issues included welfare, health services, and public transportation. After 1975, however, the feminist groups addressed issues that have been approached all over the world by similar groups since the end of the 1960s.

In Brazil, the feminist movement began with

the "groups of reflection" that had existed before 1975 for a couple of years in many parts of the country. These groups brought together a number of women—almost all middle-class, educated, and professional—who discussed social status, sex-based discrimination, and such personal psychological problems as anxiety, loneliness, and conflict with husbands or companions. These women began to realize how much they had in common with each other and sought to learn about feminist theory.

Some of the slogans that became famous—such as "The private is public" or "The personal is political"—were heard for the first time. Some of the groups were transformed into centers or associations. The feminist press helped to articulate the movement nationwide and promoted the groups' activities. The celebration of International Women's Day (March 8) was one of the primary joint activities.

In the 15 years that followed, many banners were unfurled and many battles were fought. Feminists claimed they had the right to decide about the use of their bodies and demanded public policies to attend to their specific needs. Oppression and discrimination against women became much more visible to society after the military regime ended in March 1985, and with the end of censorship, "women's issues" won time and space in the mass media. The feminist movement also contributed to a critical revision in academia in 1980 when the first women's studies center was created in the Pontifical Catholic University of Rio.

When the election of state governors resumed in 1982—it was prohibited from 1964 to 1981—a number of new democratic and progressive governors helped advance the feminist movement in some of the states. That was the case in São Paulo, where the new governor—Franco Montoro, a Christian Democratic—created the first Conselho Estadual da Condicao Feminina (State Council on the Status of Women) at the beginning of his term in 1983.

Other such councils were also created in a few other states, and in 1985 a Conselho Nacional dos Direitos da Mulher (National Council for Women's Rights) finally was formed within the administrative structure of the Ministry of Justice. Its main task was to serve as an advisory body to the federal government by proposing public policies, and it reported directly to the president.

The council has profited from the rich experience accumulated by the feminist movement. Its board is composed almost entirely of women who have taken an active part in the movement in different parts of the country. Thus the council has succeeded in bringing together the expertise garnered from the varied activities conducted by the similar councils at state and local levels. With the financial help of the federal government, the council was able to publish educational materials, support research projects and studies, and collect a considerable amount of data on women all over Brazil. The national council also received funding from other sources—such as UNIFEM, UNESCO, and UNICEF—to support special conferences, roundtables, and a data center.

The role of the national council was particularly important while the 1988 constitution was being discussed.[5] Through the lobbying efforts of its members, a number of the proposals to advance the status of women were included in the federal constitution. Such efforts also helped to include the same, and sometimes even more progressive, articles and paragraphs in the 1989 state constitutions.

Another important element of the feminist movement in Brazil was the protest against sexual and domestic violence. For a long time such violence was accepted by the courts, the mass media, and a large part of the public. Husbands or companions could kill their female partners if they were even suspected of having committed adultery—it was seen as a "legitimate defense of their honor." After 1975 feminist groups organized demonstrations at courts where these cases were being tried and demanded that the killers be jailed.

In response to feminist protest over sexual violence, some state and local governments created police stations run by women as a means of protecting battered women and punishing the batterers. By the beginning of the 1990s there were 100 such police stations operating nationwide, trying to put an end to the usual impunity that protected male abusers who committed sexual violence against their female partners. Women victims of violence, including domestic violence, did not usually register a complaint at a regular police station, where all the staff members were male, because they did not believe that their complaint would have consequence. Besides, they were often treated as though they themselves were responsible for the assault. The number of registered complaints increased extraordinarily after the women's police stations were created, as did the number of men who were sentenced and sent to jail.

In the 1970s and 1980s opposition to the military regime and the number of social movements engaged in the struggle for democracy expanded considerably. Large groups of women participated in these movements, not only in the largest and more developed metropolitan areas but also in small communities and in the countryside.

Three such movements involved thousands of women. The first was linked to the Catholic church, which has played a crucial role in Latin America in defining its "priority option for the poor" (effort to help the poor) and in consciousness-raising about social problems and the roots of the misery and famine they experience. In doing so, the church has touched millions of women who are the core of the popular sectors that live at the periphery of the cities or are landless peasants forced to abandon the countryside.

The Comunidades Eclesiais de Base (CEBs, or Base Ecclesiastical Communities), which are oriented toward the theology of liberation, spread rapidly throughout the country. This new approach of the church was designed to help women understand the roots of their oppression and to discuss how to end, or at least reduce, their subordinate condition.

These communitarian movements—social movements that bring together large groups of people who typically live in poor areas with inadequate or nonexistent public services—have developed in cities and in the countryside. The role of the CEBs in mobilizing women was crucial. Mothers' clubs, for example, were formed mainly through the grass-roots work conducted by Catholic and other Christian churches. They were created during the 1970s and are still active. It is usually much easier to bring women together to discuss problems related to child care, health assistance, education, and water supply, because mothers are the ones who are supposed to face (and attend) such basic needs.

These clubs, while based on women's identity in the private sphere, allow women to participate in the public sphere as well. "In the CEBs meetings, women meet together to discuss the Bible but also to discuss women's communities, city quarters and the country's interests. . . . In leaving the domestic sphere for the world of labor— the communitarian experience—women bring their former identity to a critical point and conquer the public space, where they have to face new challenges and come to a wider vision of their social and ecclesiastical responsibility."[6]

A group of female theologians who accept feminist ideas have also had a role in this movement by defending a critical theology that fights for the liberation of women. This new theological approach has helped to raise "the consciousness [of poor women] about the patriarchal structure of society and the church, and its consequences upon women's lives, as it conducts an articulated fight against the ideology of the subordination of women to men. The awareness [exists] that it is not possible to make theology in women's perspective without the mediation of the feminist movements."[7] As a result, women's participation in the CEBs has had a tremendous indirect effect on their lives as "the initiative of all sorts of organizations in the sense of changing society has been taken by women of the CEBs. They create female organizations, mothers' clubs, domestic servants' associations, communitarian ovens, kitchen gardens and laundries, groups to defend the creation of day-care centers and schools, health, mutual help to build houses, groups to work with prostitutes, groups of wives or [groups] simply to discuss women's issues."[8]

This "rereading of the Bible, through the eyes

of women" has helped millions of Brazilian women become conscious of the marginality of their situation and of the discrimination in society. The CEBS played a crucial role in the most recent transition to democracy.

An economic crisis has existed in Brazil for many years, and it has been especially severe since the military coup in 1964. The crisis had left the country with an enormous external debt of more than U.S. $120 billion at the beginning of the 1990s. The inflation rate reached 80 percent *per month* in March 1990. Poor women must face problems of hunger, misery, and urban violence, as well as inadequate sewer systems, public healthcare, hospitals, schools, public transportation, and housing. These problems have prompted significant mobilization among women and the creation of Neighborhood Associations.

A large number of associations were created in urban settlements on the periphery of large metropolitan areas, and most of their activists were poor women, migrants, or landless peasants. These organizations also exist in middle-class urban districts. The motivations behind the associations have been extremely diverse, as have been their articulated goals. In many cases, the association organizers wanted to preserve a high level of environmental quality of life or to prevent the local government from implementing bills considered harmful to the residents of a particular district. Hundreds of such associations have developed around a platform accepted by large groups of people who have united to demand better living conditions and public services and a more responsible government. The issues addressed by these associations were not usually feminist, but many of the women who participated in demonstrations and actions organized by feminist groups were also active members of Neighborhood Associations.

Some improvements were achieved after the associations pressured local governments. For example, the quality of life has been raised for millions of women living in slums or deteriorated housing. Women always made up the majority of the activists in these associations, and equally important, women often have led the actions con-

ducted by these organizations. In this respect women in the Neighborhood Associations were able to train for the practice of democracy even before the military leadership was gone and the country could return to constitutional rule. Thanks to the accumulated experience of the neighborhood associations, women have learned to deal with governmental agencies and have lost the fear or timidity they might have had before joining the associations of facing the public arena and going into politics. Many of the women who have been elected leaders of these associations— and who have learned to deal with government agencies—have been elected as local councilors or state legislators.

THE STRUGGLE FOR THE IMPLEMENTATION OF HEALTHCARE POLICIES

One of the issues that has mobilized large segments of women from popular urban sectors nationwide is public health policy. The feminist movement has propagated the idea of self-help and of the need for women to know about their bodies, to decide freely about reproduction, and to receive more information on contraceptives. But because health conditions for the majority of the population still are extremely unsatisfactory, the Neighborhood Associations demanded better services from public hospitals and clinics.

As it has in many countries, the feminist movement has also brought the controversial issue of abortion to the public agenda. At one end of the debate in Brazil has been the Catholic church, which still exercises a strong influence and is opposed to any attempt to decriminalize abortion. Currently, abortion is punishable by imprisonment for the woman and the doctor. At the other end are the feminists, who have insisted that the country no longer accept that 3 million Brazilian women have abortions each year and that a large but undetermined number of these women die after undergoing unsafe or unsanitary procedures.

Feminists note that laws on abortion and other women's issues—which were enacted before

1920—do not reflect the extraordinary social changes that have taken place in society. A number of legal restrictions and forms of discrimination against women (especially married women) were lifted in 1962, when a bill was passed at the National Congress after receiving strong support from the women's movement. Although the federal constitution of 1988 improved the status of women in Brazil in many fundamental ways, the old civil code still denies men and women equal rights in regard to the ownership of property, control of children, access to credit, and so on.

Large and intensive campaigns were developed in the 1980s to pressure the government to design public health policies that would benefit women. The creation of special bodies at all levels of government—the state and national councils and the Committees in Defense of Women's Rights—have been critical to the formulation of some of those public policies. The councils have organized dozens of meetings and discussions on proposals offered by women's organizations, and held special conferences in Brasília. Popular education materials published by state and local councils were circulated. As a result, the health issue became the main concern for millions of women. "The expansion of the area of influence of the feminist movements in issues related to the use of one's body, sexuality and reproduction was appropriated by the media and so called the attention of the whole of the society to the historical, ideological and political aspects of the problem."[9]

Feminist groups sought more public funds for women's health programs with campaigns and demonstrations. They protested the inadequacy of the existing services, which were limited to assisting with maternity. Because of the pressure exerted on the government by these groups and the Committees in Defense of Women's Rights, a plan to prevent high-risk pregnancy was introduced by the Ministry of Health in 1987, and it was expected that public hospitals provide special help to qualified women.

The CEBs and the Neighborhood Associations also urged the government to provide better local health services to reduce mortality rates. These groups proposed creating Auxiliary Units for First Aid to lower the rates of infant and maternal mortality, as well as offering inexpensive health assistance. A variety of proposals were thus formulated alongside the official public health system. Beginning in the late 1970s many feminist groups and women's organizations created services that taught women how to prevent illness and how to use contraceptive methods. Those services, called SOS Mulher (SOS Woman), still exist. One of the most successful is in Recife, the capital city of the state of Pernambuco in the northeast, the least developed part of the country.

Their success attracted the attention of the Ministry of Health, and some feminists were even hired to teach courses and train health agents. Most important, their work prompted the ministry to approve the Program of Integral Assistance to Women's Health in 1983. That program aimed for global improvement in the standards of women's health, and not just in connection with reproduction. The plan was to assist women through their entire pregnancy, improve the assistance at delivery, and raise the percentage of mothers who breast-feed their babies, as well as improve control of gynecological cancer and sexually transmitted diseases. One of the basic features of the program has been its decentralization; medical care and information are provided locally through health centers, which are considered the base of the pyramid of the medical institution.

Because of these efforts by feminist groups and women's organizations, Brazilian women are at present much better informed about using contraception, dealing with common diseases, reducing the risk of breast cancer, and so forth. The health education campaigns led by these organizations during the 1980s have also helped raise women's self-confidence in their dealings with medical doctors, reducing the power those professionals have exercised over female patients for ages.

PROSPECTS

The 1980s in Brazil were viewed as the period of propagating feminist ideas and conquering important spaces. The 1990s are expected to be a challenge, as many feminists feel there is a pronounced need to critically revise some of the approaches taken so far. This would mean, for example, eliminating such stereotypes as the view that feminists are not interested in politics.

This analysis of women's political participation in Brazil from the 1940s through the 1980s points to an extraordinary increase in the number of women who have demanded that their basic needs be attended to by all levels of the state. It also demonstrates that a variety of segments of the female population can be impelled to action if there is an important cause and able leaders who can convince women that they can reach their goals and defend their interests through political action.

In spite of the strong influence of ideas such as "women vote conservative," "politics is for men," "feminist groups should stay outside politics," large sectors of poor, noneducated women do engage in political activities when they feel that their actions will improve the quality of life for their families. Brazilian women often have had to become politically active to ensure their own survival and that of their children. Yet there continues in some circles a discussion of how "political" are the "strategies of survival" poor women of the Third World have been using for decades. Many authors would not accept such activities as being politics, yet the feminist movement has forced a revision of the social sciences—and particularly of political science—on this point. It is necessary to use the findings of the last four decades to reformulate some of the assumptions underlying political science, mainly those concerned with women and politics.[10] Social analyst Judith Astelarra is correct in her conclusion regarding the consequences of the feminist reflection about women's political participation: "Instead of questioning women, the option was to question politics itself, its functioning and organization. The result was a different perspective for analyzing the relationship between women and politics."[11]

Nonetheless, the problems most Brazilian women faced at the beginning of the 1990s—economic recession, persistent inflation, unemployment, lack of good public services—have led some of the most active feminists to conclude that much of the effort they have put into changing women's status has not yet improved women's standard of living. In spite of the social advances I mention in this chapter, discrimination based on sex continues, and women's access to top positions in the decision-making process is not guaranteed. In the last decade of the twentieth century politically conscious women in Brazil will be required to expend much more effort to reinforce the democratic system and overcome the obstacles to equal rights between men and women—not only in the law but also in daily life.

NOTES

1. A study of the suffragist movement in Brazil was made by Branca Moreira Alves, *Ideologia e feminismo: A luta da mulher pelo voto no Brasil* (Ideology and feminism: Women's struggle for the vote in Brazil) (Rio de Janeiro: Vozes, 1980).

2. See Fanny Tabak, *A Mulher Brasileira no Congresso Nacional* (Brazilian women at the National Congress) (Brasília: Câmara dos Deputados, 1989). The study analyzes 50 years of legislation and the role of female representation at the National Congress. The main changes in law regarding the status of women are discussed.

3. SOS Mulher (SOS Woman) is the common expression adopted by many feminist groups to make explicit the sort of activity they perform: helping battered women and victims of rape and other forms of sexual violence.

4. Fanny Tabak, *A Nova Ordem Legal—Mulheres na Constituinte* (The new legal order: Women in the Constituent National Assembly) (Rio de Janeiro: NEM-PUC/RJ, 1989).

5. Committees in Defense of Women's Rights had interviewed women all over the country about the proposals to be addressed to the MPs and asked for their support. The organization established a lobby at the National Congress while the new constitution was being discussed.

6. Margarida L. R. Brandão, "Uma reflexão ético-teológica sobre o simbolo da maternidade e suas implicações práticas" (An ethical-theological reflection on the symbol of maternity and its practical implications) (Rio de Janeiro: SALALM, 1990).

7. Fanny Tabak, "Movimentos Sociais no Brasil e participação feminina," *Desarrollo*, no. 2 (1985): 79–89.

8. Teresa Cavalcanti, "Sobre a participação das mul-

heres no VI Encontro Intereclesial da CEBs" (On women's participation in the sixth interecclesiastical conference of the CEBs) *Revista Eclesiastica Brasileira* 47, no. 188 (1987): 803–819.

9. Suely Rosenfeld, "A Mulher e os serviços de saúde" (Women and health services), in *Mulher, Saúde e Sociedade no Brasil* (Petrópolis: Vozes, 1989).

10. The need for a reconceptualization of the political participation of women was felt by many female social scientists gathered at various conferences during the early 1980s. See Fanny Tabak, "The Re-Conceptualization of the Political Participation of Women," in Hemlata Swarup, ed., *Women, Power and Religion* (Delhi: Vedam, 1990).

11. Judith Astelarra, ed., *Participation Politica de las Mujeres* (The political participation of women) (Madrid: CIS, 1990).

▲ Canada

POLITICS

Type of Political System: democracy
  Sovereignty: constitutional monarchy
  Executive-Legislative System: parliamentary
Type of State: federal
Type of Party System: multiparty
Major Political Parties

Progressive Conservative Party: Led by Prime Minister Brian Mulroney at the federal level. Won majority governments in 1984 and 1988 federal elections; held minority government 1979–1980.

Liberal Party: In opposition 1984–90 and in government under the leadership of Prime Minister Pierre Trudeau 1968–84 (except briefly during 1979–80).

New Democratic Party: Social democratic party led by Audrey McLaughlin, first female leader of a major federal party in Canada. Has never formed the government at the federal level.

Reform Party: Originated as a protest grouping in Western Canada but seeks to broaden its electoral base in the rest of country. In 1992 held one seat in the House of Commons.

Year Women Granted Right to Vote: 1917
Year Women Granted Right to Stand for Election: 1920
Percentage of Women in the Legislature [a]
  Lower House: 13.2%
  Upper House: 12.5%
Percentage of Electorate Voting for Highest Elected Office in Most Recent Election (1988): 75.3% [b]

DEMOGRAPHICS

Population: 25,652,000
Percentage of Population in Urban Areas
  Overall: 75.7%
  Female: 76.8%
  Male: 74.7%

Percentage of Population Below Age 15: 21.5%
Birthrate (per 1,000 population): 15
Maternal Mortality Rate (per 100,000 live births): 3
Infant Mortality Rate (per 1,000 live births): 7
Mortality Rate for Children Under Five (per 1,000 live births): 8
Average Household Size: 3.0
Mean Age at First Marriage
  Female: 23.1
  Male: 25.2
Life Expectancy
  Female: 76.0
  Male: 72.7

EDUCATION

Ratio of Female to Male Enrollment
  First-Level Education: 93
  Second-Level Education: 95
  Third-Level Education: 113
Literacy Rate
  Female: 98.0%
  Male: 98.0%

ECONOMY

Gross National Product per Capita: U.S. $13,680
Percentage of Labor Force in Agriculture: 5.7%
Distribution of Agricultural Workers by Sex
  Female: 23.0%
  Male: 77.0%
Economically Active Population by Sex
  Female: 49.9%
  Male: 78.2%

a. Both houses had vacancies at the time of publication. These percentages represent 13 of 104 Senate members (eleven vacancies) and 39 of 295 House members (one vacancy).

b. Appendixes to the *Report of the Chief Electoral Officer* (Ottawa: Elections Canada, 1989).

Building a Political Voice:
Women's Participation
and Policy Influence
in Canada

SYLVIA BASHEVKIN

Within the limits imposed by a federal multiparty parliamentary system, Canadian women have sought to build their own political voice. In this discussion, political voice refers both to the basic "women's issues" common to Western liberal democracies—notably, legal rights, employment, and reproductive choice—and to female participation at decision-making levels.[1] Because the absence of women's voices in the political system has itself become a policy issue, in this chapter I consider female marginalization at elite levels, explanations of this phenomenon, and efforts to increase representation.

The conceptual framework used here can best be described as integrative and political. It rejects standard pluralist, statist, and neo-Marxist paradigms as not only deterministic but also heavily weighted toward the analysis of men's experiences.[2] For example, rather than adopting neo-Marxist assumptions that capitalist relations of production fully explain political marginalization, I focus on political, historical, and socioeconomic factors.

The federal system, above all else, has been a crucial constraint on political voice in this setting. With a population of more than 25 million, Canada is organized as a confederation, with ten provinces and two territories spread across a vast geographical space. The federal government is centered in Ottawa. Both levels of government function as parliamentary democracies; each province has its own elected legislature and premier, and each has fairly distinctive patterns of party competition and political involvement.[3]

The federal system developed over time from a highly centralized arrangement envisaged in the British North America Act of 1867—in which the federal government was almost as powerful as a British-style unitary state, and the provinces were dependencies of that central government—toward a situation in which the provinces are, according to some observers, like ten countries, and the federal government is the weak dependency of the provinces.[4] Jurisdictional control in Canada is thus divided between federal and provincial governments, often after extensive wrangling, bartering, and bickering among elite representatives of both levels. Canadian federalism from the end of World War II through the early 1980s has been described as executive federalism; high-ranking politicians and bureaucrats from both levels of government met frequently to "resolve" issues ranging from highways and taxation to the constitution and women's rights.[5]

Most analysts agree that this federal-provincial division of powers was introduced to accommodate French, English, and regional interests. Conflict between French and English cultures has required the federal government to balance the competing interests of the two language groups (about 6 million Francophones, mostly living in Quebec, and 19 million Anglophones) and, in English Canada, the competing regional interests. Both cleavages cut across many political issues; for example, comprehensive Canada-U.S. free trade was generally opposed by English-speakers and supported by Quebeckers in the 1988 federal elections.[6] Voters in Quebec defeated a 1980 referendum that would have given the provincial government a mandate to negotiate sovereignty-association with the rest of Canada, but the issue of provincial independence remains alive in Quebec through the early 1990s.

The Meech Lake Accord of 1987, which required ratification by the federal parliament and all ten provincial legislatures by 23 June 1990, would have expanded the jurisdictional powers of provincial governments and recognized Quebec as a "distinct society" within Canada. The accord reflected an attempt by the federal government to add Quebec's signature to the 1982 Constitution Act, but the failure of Manitoba and Newfoundland to ratify the accord essentially ended that round of constitutional initiatives. Since the death of Meech Lake, Quebec has pursued a bilateral strategy of direct federal-provincial negotiations over many issues addressed in the accord, including jurisdiction over immigration policy.[7]

Federal arrangements have overwhelmingly shaped not just the Canadian state and government narrowly construed but also the operations of virtually all societal interests. Most major groups concerned with policy issues have organized themselves along lines that closely mirror the structure of the federal political system. The principal Canadian women's organization, the National Action Committee on the Status of Women (NAC), has organized along federal lines, and it has faced many of the same internal tensions that confront the federal system generally.

Canada has a multiparty parliamentary system, and two parties have held power at the federal level: the Liberals led by Pierre Elliott Trudeau formed the government for most of the period between 1968 and 1984, and the Progressive Conservatives led by Brian Mulroney have held power since 1984. Other parties that have formed governments at the provincial level include the New Democratic Party (NDP), a social democratic organization with links to the Canadian Labor Congress; and the Parti québécois (PQ), an independentist organization that first won power in Quebec in 1976.

These partisan cleavages have tended to complicate the organization of women as a cohesive political interest. Even before suffrage was formally granted in 1917, substantial numbers of politically active women were organized into auxiliaries of the Liberal and Conservative parties, a pattern that divided females along partisan

lines. Major Canadian women's organizations have attempted to remain formally independent of the parties, believing that independence could guarantee autonomy, control, and a degree of distance from established party organizations.[8] For example, the first-wave National Council of Women of Canada, established in 1893, was a traditional, conservative group composed primarily of middle-class Anglophone women; it focused on issues affecting women and children and used a national structure that duplicated the larger federal system.[9]

The second-wave National Action Committee on the Status of Women began in 1972 with a Toronto-based steering committee. But activists in Atlantic Canada, Quebec, and western Canada questioned how the national organization of women, which had a decidedly Toronto voice, could speak for everyone. In 1980, NAC adopted a regionally based national board system with provincial and territorial representatives. As an umbrella group, NAC attracted older organizations, such as the National Council, along with newer and more radical women's liberation and women's rights groups; it grew from 15 member groups in 1972 to 586 in 1988, meaning that about 5 million Canadian women were members in NAC's constituent groups by the late 1980s.[10]

NAC's ability to draw together diverse interests was in part a result of its original mandate to press for implementation of the recommendations in the 1970 *Report* of the Royal Commission on the Status of Women (RCSW).[11] Women's organizations ranging from the traditional National Council to the Federation des femmes du Québec (FFQ), formed in 1966, united to seek federal government action on women's issues. The creation of the Canadian Advisory Council on the Status of Women in 1973 represented a partial response to one RCSW recommendation, while the formation of groups pressing for greater political representation (Women for Political Action, Committee for '94), reproductive choice (Canadian Abortion Rights Action League, Ontario Coalition for Abortion Clinics), improved child-care provisions (Canadian Day Care Advocacy Association), employment rights (Equal Pay Coalition), and constitutional reform (National Association of Women and the Law, Ad Hoc Committee of Canadian Women on the Constitution) indicated the degree to which Canadian women believed that their demands had *not* been met. Most of these newer groups joined NAC and helped widen its focus beyond the recommendations of the RCSW.

In spite of the emphasis on building a varied constituency, it was clear that NAC could not claim to represent all Canadian women all the time. For example, the growth during the 1980s of anti-abortion organizations (notably R.E.A.L. Women) modeled on groups in the United States constituted a fundamental challenge to NAC's ability to speak for the women of Canada.[12] Even more damaging from the perspective of a national voice were differences between Anglophone and Francophone women's groups inside NAC. Those differences were reflected in the decision of the Federation des femmes du Québec to withdraw from NAC during two specific rounds of constitutional debate.[13]

In 1980, Canadians elected a majority Liberal government that was dedicated to constitutional reform and to preventing the province of Quebec from seceding from the confederation. Under the banner of "national unity," the Trudeau Liberals set out to revise the federal constitution and to entrench within it a charter of rights and freedoms.[14] Constitutional conflict in 1981–82 caused rifts in NAC as well, especially after the federal government proposed that provinces be granted jurisdiction over family law. Women's organizations in Quebec supported the proposal, believing that family law and a host of other matters would be best handled by a provincial government sensitive to the needs of people in Quebec. In contrast, most women's groups in English Canada opposed the proposal, arguing instead for national standards, uniform legislation, and the primacy of the federal government.[15] One of the many casualties in this round of constitutional bargaining was French-English cohesion within NAC; the FFQ withdrew from the committee but reaffiliated in the mid-1980s after constitutional matters had quieted.

A similar scenario developed during the late 1980s in debates over the Meech Lake Accord, which offered substantial additional powers to *all* provincial governments—not just Quebec's. As in the early 1980s, English Canadian women's groups generally opposed this devolution of power, believing that further decentralization would damage the cause of women's rights, that the closed-door procedures involved in reaching the accord were flawed, and that the terms of the accord would jeopardize the progress made on equality rights in 1982.[16] The FFQ, however, strongly supported the five points in the Meech Lake Accord that had essentially been proposed by the Quebec provincial government. In 1989 the FFQ again withdrew from NAC. In short, just as the government of Quebec announced in 1990 that it would conduct direct bilateral negotiations with the federal government and would not participate as "just another province" at any other federal-provincial meetings, organized feminists in Quebec announced that they would not speak about constitutional politics within the umbrella of NAC. This decision was not surprising given the strength of a nationalist or independentist stream among second-wave Quebec women's groups, notably the Front de libération des femmes (FLF).

PARTISANSHIP VERSUS INDEPENDENCE

In addition to the influences of the federal system, women's engagement has been shaped by a long-standing strategic dilemma between political independence and conventional partisanship. Feminist and suffragist organizations, particularly in English Canada, were part of a broader progressive challenge to the two-party federal system during the early decades of this century. These groups faced a difficult dilemma: on the one hand, they were attracted to a position of political independence that could guarantee organizational autonomy and control; on the other, they were drawn toward conventional partisanship, which might better ensure political influence and legislative success. This tension between independence and partisanship within the context of a changing party system has characterized women's political history for much of the twentieth century.

In practical terms, tensions between independence and partisanship have limited the exercise of effective political power. Even though women in some parts of English Canada obtained the right to vote—primarily in local school board elections—as early as the eighteenth century, and though many were organized into such party affiliates as the Toronto Women's Liberal Association before the formal extension of the franchise, few entered the electorate as politically skilled or equal participants. This situation resulted in part from the ideology of leading suffrage groups, which maintained that women could spread a mantle of purity from their private domestic sphere to the public, political domain. New women voters were encouraged to avoid the corrupting, immoral party organizations and to adopt an independent, nonpartisan route to national influence. The limitations of this strategy in a partisan, parliamentary system, combined with the two major parties' efforts to shunt female activists into auxiliaries, meant that women remained rare in the corridors of power.[17] Agnes Macphail, the first woman elected to the House of Commons (1921), was considered a "freak" whose presence symbolized the vast distance between legal rights and political power for Canadian women.[18]

The impact of this history can be discerned in the careers of other individuals who attempted to become politically active. Nellie McClung, for example, was a prominent prairie suffragist who recognized the importance of developing a partisan as well as an independent voice in parliamentary politics. She campaigned successfully as a provincial candidate for the Alberta Liberals in 1917 but found it difficult to operate as an independent legislator within a partisan system. When McClung broke party ranks to vote her conscience in the Alberta legislature, other Liberals questioned her partisan loyalty, leading McClung to wonder how women could obtain parliamentary influence while remaining committed feminists.[19]

Although individuals like McClung have tried to transcend the dilemma between partisanship and independence, a more common pattern has been for women's organizations to become wedged in the political tension. In cases in which groups have organized to achieve well-defined and primarily legalistic objectives—such as the granting of the federal franchise (1918) and the right to be appointed to the federal Senate (Persons Case, 1929), the establishment of the Royal Commission on the Status of Women (1967), and the provision of equality rights in the 1982 Constitution Act (sections 15 and 28)—divisions between partisan and independent approaches to power have been apparent.[20]

Tensions grew during the early 1980s and the push for constitutional reform. The president of the federally appointed Canadian Advisory Council on the Status of Women, Doris Anderson, was unwilling to bow to government pressure by canceling a planned conference on the subject of women and the constitution; her resistance to pressure from the federal minister responsible for the status of women led to polarization inside the advisory council and, ultimately, to Anderson's resignation. Activists in the governing Liberal Party, which had appointed Anderson, felt betrayed by her public challenge to cabinet control, though others who were less identified with the party believed that Anderson (along with Canadian women in general) was the victim of government manipulation.

These deep-seated perceptions of betrayal and manipulation spilled over into other groups involved in the constitutional process—including NAC, which had formally maintained an independent political position since its formation but had vigorously opposed some government policies and attracted many committed partisans to its leadership. During the early 1980s, NAC's efforts to push for constitutionally entrenched legal rights were often frustrated by the internal maneuverings of partisan activists. As retiring NAC President Lynn McDonald observed in 1981, "Women's organizations, with their fragile interparty compositions, have been sorely tried by the Constitution debate."[21] In short, women's political involvement through the 1980s was enmeshed in a complex and uneasy tension between nonpartisanship and independent feminism and the demands of a party-structured parliamentary system.

NATIONALISMS AND FEMINISMS

The strategic tension between independence and partisanship, along with the constraints imposed by the federal system, exist alongside complications in the construction of the identity known as women within the larger identity known as Canada. As the broader environment for women's struggles, Canada is itself an elusive unit. The country feels pressure—from media spillover, trade, and foreign investment—to integrate culturally and economically with the United States, its southern neighbor. Debate over the controversial Canada–U.S. Free Trade Agreement, which went into effect in January 1989, revealed long-standing tensions between nationalists, who advocate a more independent approach to the United States, and integrationists, who encourage closer continental relations.[22]

These debates held enormous implications for women. Important sources of second-wave feminism in English Canada during the late 1960s included new left, peace, and student groups, many of which were committed to the nationalist position. Not surprisingly, this nationalist element was absorbed by the Anglophone women's movement that began in the early 1970s, and it reappeared during debates over free trade. The National Action Committee on the Status of Women was active in efforts to defeat free trade and the Conservative federal government that sponsored it, even though many prominent women's groups (including NAC) were dependent on federal funding, and even though the Conservative partisans who were involved in NAC opposed this position.[23]

The trade agreement was widely criticized in English Canada as an arrangement that would integrate and ultimately submerge Canada within a continent dominated by the United States, but in Quebec it was viewed far more favorably.

Quebec nationalists in particular had long viewed the United States as a political and economic counterweight to English Canada, and they believed that Francophone culture was insulated by virtue of its language from the media spillover so feared in English Canada.[24] Because reaction to the trade agreement was so favorable in Quebec, the opposition from feminists and other groups in the province was less vigorous than in the rest of Canada.[25]

In many respects, modern Quebec feminism traces its beginnings at least as much to nationalist developments inside the province as it does to the roots it shares with the women's movement in the rest of Canada. Although Canadian women obtained the federal franchise in 1918, they did not have the right to vote in Quebec provincial elections until 1940.[26] And, just as suffragism evolved in a distinctive fashion in Quebec, so too did the second wave of feminism.[27] Reacting to their less-than-equal treatment in nationalist ideology and, more specifically, in the Front de libération du Québec (FLQ, founded in 1963), radical Francophone women established their own organizational vehicle in the Front de libération des femmes (FLF). The latter shared the FLQ's basic commitment to an independent socialist Quebec, and it remained separate from women's groups that did not hold the same objectives. For example, the FLF organized its own protests against abortion policy, purposefully excluding Anglophone feminists in Quebec and the rest of Canada.[28]

Relations between the respective feminisms and nationalisms of Quebec and English Canada became even more complicated after 1976. With the election of the independentist Parti québécois (PQ) to power in Quebec, the stage was set for a spring 1980 referendum on the province's future in confederation. Survey data gathered before the referendum vote suggested that Francophone women in general were more supportive of keeping Quebec in the Canadian federation and were less supportive of provincial independence or sovereignty-association than Francophone men. The poll also indicated more limited support for the PQ among women than men, a pattern linked to the strong base of the provincial Liberal Party among older females. The Quebec Liberals had sponsored suffrage legislation in 1940 and had tended to pursue a more federalist position than the PQ in relations with Ottawa and the other provinces.[29]

Gender played an important role in the 1980 Quebec referendum campaign, when provincial voters were asked whether the PQ government should be granted a mandate to negotiate sovereignty-association. Federalist or *non* (no) forces, which rejected sovereignty-association, organized a rally of about 15,000 women in Montreal and a series of smaller gatherings in response to statements by Lise Payette, the PQ minister of state for the status of women. In March 1980 Payette compared women who voted against sovereignty-association to the passive Yvette character in Quebec schoolbooks. Furthermore, she said, the leader of the provincial Liberal Party, who opposed sovereignty-association, was himself married to an Yvette.[30]

The support given to the Yvette movement and to the federalist side more generally by prominent women in English Canada tended to further divide Francophone from Anglophone women. Although some feminists endorsed the federalist position in both Quebec and English Canada, and some women and men on the English Canadian left were sympathetic toward the independentist position, the broad circumstances of the referendum campaign drew a line between the core federalism of the mainstream English Canadian women's movement and the core independentism of Quebec women's liberation.[31]

Moreover, tensions between feminists in Quebec and English Canada also appeared in their choice of governmental targets. Like other groups that had formed in a Quebec nationalist milieu, many Francophone women's organizations tended to focus on achieving change within Quebec. In contrast, the leading Anglophone women's groups have remained focused on the federal capital, Ottawa, and to a lesser extent on provincial governments in English Canada. Co-

ordination between federal and provincial lobbying efforts can prove useful because of frequent overlap in statutory control, yet it has been limited in the case of women by the separate and sometimes irreconcilable agendas of feminist groups in the two cultures.[32]

POLITICAL CLEAVAGES IN ENGLISH CANADA

Just as feminists in Quebec have been split along federalist and independentist lines, the English Canadian women's movement has been divided into factions. One of the most important of these internal cleavages concerns ideology—specifically feminist belief systems. Suffragism and early feminism in English Canada originated among groups of predominantly white middle-class urban women. The National Council of Women of Canada saw itself as a "parliament of women" that could advance the cause of women's rights without undermining prevailing political institutions or social norms.[33] This dominant stream of liberal feminism, with its emphasis on equal rights in the context of reformed structures, was the foundation for efforts during the mid-1960s to create the Royal Commission on the Status of Women.[34] It continues to inform many efforts to increase the numbers of women involved at decision-making levels in the political parties, as well as the defense of women's legal rights under the Canadian Charter of Rights and Freedoms, which forms the first part of the 1982 Constitution Act.

The primacy of liberal feminism within the English Canadian women's movement was increasingly challenged during the 1980s, however.[35] One challenge from the left or socialist feminist community took issue with what it identified as the status quo, middle-class orientation of liberal feminism. Rather than merely tinkering with established institutions like political parties, socialist feminists sought to transform existing structures of Canadian capitalism, government, and society. Although some socialist feminists did work on issues of numerical representation, notably in parties of the left and on legal rights, their primary focus has been the economy, particularly employment conditions.

Second, liberals were challenged in this period by radical feminists who emphasized the sexual origins of women's oppression. Frequently working at the grass-roots level in rape crisis centers, shelters for battered women, and abortion clinics, radical feminists argued for non-hierarchical structures and for a degree of gender exclusivity that was less likely to be advocated by liberal and socialist activists. Again, although some crossover of priorities has occurred between the liberal and socialist streams, it would seem that the major concerns of radical feminism have related to sexuality and, above all, to such issues as reproductive choice and violence against women.

Under pressure from these socialist and radical streams, organized feminism in Canada by the late 1980s set out to elevate the concerns of abused, visible minority, disabled, and homosexual women.[36] This response to criticisms that it had been preoccupied with the professional mobility of a handful of privileged white women imparted to the movement a far different vision and face. However, the identities and sub-identities that had emerged by 1990 ran the risk of competing with each other and fracturing or fragmenting the collectivity known as the women's movement and weakening its position vis-à-vis the governments of English Canada.

As if these internal problems were not enough, organized feminism was also forced to confront a major external challenge during the 1980s. The rise of conservative anti-abortion groups, most notably R.E.A.L. Women, meant that basic notions of gender equality again were subject to vigorous public threat, as were the federal funds that had supported equality efforts.[37] Like similar groups in the United States, R.E.A.L. Women attempted to articulate a pro-family position that rejected feminist views of abortion, equal pay, child care, and women's legal rights, even though its membership was small and its agenda essentially reactive *against* feminist efforts.[38] The election of successive Conservative majority governments at the federal level in 1984 and 1988

meant that a number of legislators sympathetic to R.E.A.L. Women obtained political power; after winning the free trade election of 1988, the Conservatives announced a series of major budget cuts to NAC and to various feminist publications and grass-roots women's services.[39]

BARRIERS TO ELITE ENGAGEMENT

In attempting to build a political voice, women have confronted each of these obstacles specific to the Canadian case. Yet important barriers that transcend international boundaries also exist; they are particularly relevant for liberal feminist efforts to increase representation at the elite level. As in most Western democracies, Canadian women have access to fewer of the resources required for intensive political engagement. One survey of party delegates, for example, found that women had significantly less university education, lower annual family income, and were less likely to be employed outside the home than men.[40] Closely related to the question of resources is the social-psychological barrier of gender roles. Canadian research on candidacy for public office demonstrates that women have been constrained by household and particularly child-rearing responsibilities. According to Janine Brodie, "Mothers and homemakers often delayed their entry into the electoral field and more often confined their political ambitions to the local level of government. In addition, a good proportion of these women indicated that reservations about their children and marriage delayed their political careers. . . . The equal integration of women in politics . . . is unlikely until the prescriptions of traditional gender roles are relaxed and redirected. As long as women are assigned primary responsibility for homemaking and child rearing, their political activism will be constrained."[41]

Although some Canadian research suggests that the political motivations and expectations of female party activists may differ from those of men, little empirical evidence supports the ambition argument.[42] A party delegates study, for example, found that mean levels of participation and ambition did *not* vary significantly by sex in two of the three major Ontario parties. As might be expected, younger, university-educated, and unmarried female delegates, as well as those with limited child-rearing responsibilities, were found to be more politically ambitious than older, less educated delegates and those who were married with young children.[43]

A somewhat different set of ideas follows from structural or opportunity-based arguments that female involvement is constrained by limited opportunities for recruitment and mobility within political parties. Canadian data show the extent to which women candidates and officeholders are disproportionately involved at the municipal level of government. According to Jill Vickers, this pattern is attributable to the lower financial and personal costs incurred by local activists and to "the relatively low level of power and influence which has the effect of reducing competition [and of weakening] structures such as political parties," which tend to limit access to recruitment channels.[44] On the basis of evidence that female legislative candidates are clustered in weak or marginal seats, Brodie and Vickers suggest that party control over elite recruitment constitutes a crucial barrier to women's political engagement.[45] And, according to Brodie, 50 percent of female candidates in competitive districts experienced "at least one negative party incident," compared with 32 percent among an overall sample of women candidates.[46] These incidents frequently involved changing the date or location of the nomination meeting and failing to inform female candidates or closing child-care services early in the evening so that women's supporters were unable to remain for late ballots.

CONVENTIONAL FORMS OF POLITICAL ENGAGEMENT

Given this background, the more limited involvement of Canadian women than men at elite levels begins to make some sense. The percentage of females active in party organizations tends to decline with the more visible and powerful positions.[47] On average, women's participation

in major Canadian party organizations during the 1980s ranged from about 70 percent of local riding secretaries to about 40 percent of convention delegates, 25 percent of party executive members, 20 percent of campaign managers, 15 percent of candidates, 10 percent of legislators, and 5 percent of cabinet members. Neither major federal party was led by a woman in this decade.

This pattern of "the higher the fewer" must be understood in light of an important corollary, namely "the more competitive the fewer." Although some women have obtained important positions outside of pink-collar or clerical constituency positions, they have frequently done so when their party has had little chance of electoral success. The data indicate that in Ontario increasing numbers of women are involved at all levels but that they continue to cluster in less competitive categories.[48] For example, 44 percent of the ninety-five women who ran as major party candidates in the 1987 Ontario provincial elections finished third; fewer than 30 percent of the men who sought provincial office in 1987 finished third. Moreover, 137 of the 301 women (or 45.5 percent) who ran as major party candidates in Ontario between 1971 and 1987 contested under the banner of the New Democratic Party, a social democratic grouping that had never held power until 1990, when it won a majority government.

The relative absence of women in elite political positions, particularly in competitive party organizations, is also reflected in the federal House of Commons, where the number of female MPs has grown from one (Agnes Macphail) in 1921 to twenty-seven (9.6 percent) in 1984 and thirty-nine (13.2 percent) in 1993. As was the case in other jurisdictions, including Ontario, in 1987 and 1990, much of this increase was attributable to landslide elections that replaced many incumbent government (and usually male) legislators with marginal (and often female) opposition candidates. In other words, some women were in the right place at the right time in these elections, but it is not at all clear that barriers to elite-level involvement in competitive party organizations had necessarily diminished.[49]

Campaigns for leadership in competitive party organizations point toward similar conclusions. Most Canadian parties use either delegated conventions or a ballot vote by party members to select their leaders.[50] In the past, women have obtained party leadership in organizations that did not hold the reins of power at the time and were unlikely to become the governing party in the near future. Canadian women have led a host of parties that were not in a competitive political position at the time of their selection, as is typified by the case of Thérèse Casgrain, who headed the Cooperative Commonwealth Federation (precursor to the New Democratic Party) in Quebec during the 1950s. In some instances, notably those of Sharon Carstairs in the Manitoba Liberal and Audrey McLaughlin in the federal New Democratic organizations, parties led by women subsequently gained a more competitive position.[51]

There remain a number of cases in which women have broken out of this mold to contest competitive party leadership. For example, Flora MacDonald ran in 1976 for the leadership of the federal Progressive Conservatives, Muriel Smith in 1979 for the Manitoba NDP, Grace McCarthy and Kim Campbell in 1986 for the British Columbia Social Credit Party, Sheila Copps in 1982 and 1990 for the Ontario and federal Liberal Parties, respectively, and McCarthy and Rita Johnston in 1991 for the British Columbia Social Credit Party. In each instance except the last, these campaigns have been unsuccessful in the sense that the candidates lost. But they have been successful to the extent that women's claims to competitive party leadership were taken increasingly seriously.[52] Johnston won in 1991 and became Canada's first female premier; she led a right-of-center political party, however, that was not sympathetic to feminist issue positions and was defeated in the next provincial election.[53]

CONFRONTING THE BARRIERS

Are committed feminists in Canada prepared to cast their lot with the traditional party system? Is the party system a hospitable or useful environment for feminist activism? Can women cooperate across French-English and regional lines, not to mention across partisan and ideological divisions? Three basic responses to underrepresentation at the elite level have been put forward in Canada. First, beginning with the establishment in 1972 of a Toronto group known as Women for Political Action, organizations have been established across the country to push for more numbers. Led for the most part by liberal feminists both inside and outside the parties, women and politics groups have sponsored seminars, books, press conferences, television programs, legislative internships, skills-training workshops, and other activities to try to elect more women.[54]

Second, proposals have been made to institute structural changes in the political process. The Committee for '94 in Toronto, for example, was established in 1984 with a goal of electing women to half the seats in the House of Commons by 1994. In studying and, in the case of some members, experiencing the difficulties involved in reaching this goal, the committee developed a policy statement that advocated reform of party finance laws, including complete public funding of nomination contests, elections, and party leadership campaigns.

Third, attempts have been made by the political parties, often in response to pressure from these women's groups, to institute formal and informal reforms. At the level of constitutional change, for example, some federal and provincial parties have adopted rules that specify equal proportions of male and female constituency delegates to conventions and encourage similar provisions in local riding association executives.[55] In addition, some parties have worked actively to recruit women as candidates for party and public office, established separate campaign funds to assist these candidates, and offered campaign schools designed to attract and train new candidates.

IN SEARCH OF INFLUENCE:
THE CASE OF LEGAL RIGHTS

Because policy clout is assumed by liberal and in some cases socialist feminists to follow from enhanced legal rights, women's organizations have often focused on judicial and constitutional issues. As Beverley Baines observes, "Throughout this century, Canadian women have asserted their claims to sex equality in a significant number of legal cases," including those that established their rights to practice law and to serve in the Senate.[56]

More recently, attempts by two native women, Jeanette Lavell and Yvonne Bedard, to challenge a provision of the Indian Act and by Stella Bliss to challenge one section of the Unemployment Insurance Act started a powerful movement toward improved legal rights. In the cases of Lavell and Bedard, which were decided in a single 1973 ruling, the Supreme Court of Canada rejected arguments that denying Indian status only to native women who married non-Indian men (and not to native men who married non-Indian women) violated the sex equality provision of the 1960 Bill of Rights. In the 1979 Bliss case, the Supreme Court maintained that denying unemployment benefits to a pregnant applicant was permissible because "any inequality between the sexes in this area is not created by legislation but by nature."[57]

The frustration that greeted these decisions led legal rights activists to doubt the value of the Bill of Rights, which was not constitutionally entrenched and thus did not supersede other federal laws; Canadian women pressed instead for a comprehensive set of equality provisions that would be entrenched in a revised federal constitution. Two sets of circumstances made legal advancement possible by 1982. First, the National Action Committee on the Status of Women was committed to legal rights issues during the late 1970s and early 1980s. NAC could coordinate its efforts with a growing core of legal policy specialists in the National Association of Women and the Law as well as the Ad Hoc Committee of Canadian Women on the Constitution, which was formed in response to Doris Anderson's resignation from the federal Advisory Council on the Status of Women.

Second, constitutional reform, including the entrenchment of a Charter of Rights and Freedoms, was high on the agenda of the federal government after 1980. Although neither that government nor those of the ten provinces initially recognized the importance accorded to equality provisions by women's organizations, they did respond to concerted pressure by including sections 15 and 28 in the charter:

15(1). Every individual is equal before and under the law and has the right to the equal protection and equal benefit of the law without discrimination and, in particular, without discrimination based on race, national or ethnic origin, color, religion, sex, age or mental or physical disability.

15(2), Subsection (1) does not preclude any law, program or activity that has as its object the amelioration of conditions of disadvantaged individuals or groups including those that are disadvantaged because of race, national or ethnic origin, color, religion, sex, age or mental or physical disability. . . .

28. Notwithstanding anything in this charter, the rights and freedoms referred to in it are guaranteed equally to male and female persons.[58]

Although section 15 has been in effect since 1985, the impact of the charter on women's legal rights remains unclear. In one equality case decided by the Supreme Court of Ontario, the judges stated that the right under section 15(1) of a 12-year-old girl to play minor league hockey had been violated by a provincial human rights provision allowing boys-only teams.[59] Many of the same activists and groups that had mobilized to secure charter reforms became involved in debates over the 1987 Meech Lake Accord, arguing that it ceded too much power to provincial governments, which could then run roughshod over the equality provisions of the 1982 Charter. Yet a major study of charter litigation, published in September 1989, offered far more pessimistic conclusions. According to Gwen Brodsky and Shelagh Day, "The news is not good. Women are initiating few cases, and men are using the Charter to strike back at women's hard-won protections and benefits. At the time of writing, the Supreme Court of Canada had not delivered its first judgment concerning the equality guarantees. But the theories of equality and interpretive tests that, to date, have been applied by other courts in Canada will not improve women's condition."[60]

CHALLENGING EMPLOYMENT POLICY

Among Canadian feminists, frustration with the slow pace of legal change is matched by sustained questioning of the basic enterprise of legal reform. Critics of the legal rights stream—many of whom are socialist and radical feminists—say that women, like other disadvantaged groups, are misguided if they expect courts to solve inequalities. This line of argument maintains that "the courts are, by nature, undemocratic and elitist. By and large, judges are white, middle-aged, middle-class men with no direct experience of disadvantage."[61] Instead, these critics continue, organized feminism should pursue social change through public demonstrations and legislative lobbying rather than through the courts.

Activists who question the legal rights focus have devoted their efforts to a number of other areas, including employment policy. Before World War I, minimum wage laws for women working outside the domestic and agricultural sectors were enacted in most provinces, and some groups of employed women organized strikes for higher pay. Yet these demands ran into serious obstacles through the 1960s. At one level, governments, employers, and most trade unions held fast to the belief that married women were required in the home except during wartime. In this environment, they were expected to reproduce the future labor force and to nurture the present (male) one.

As the demand for workers grew following World War II, however, this convention began to give way to a view that employed women could "make a more effective contribution to the development of Canada."[62] To this end, federal and provincial governments during the 1950s introduced statutes to ensure equal pay for men and women who performed the same or similar jobs—a provision that had little substantive effect because of patterns of occupational segregation in the labor force.

With the emergence of second-wave feminism,

especially on the socialist left and in trade union organizations, demands for more fundamental change in employment policy were voiced. Expanding the availability of child care was an initial priority of the National Action Committee in 1972, and in 1975 NAC adopted "equal pay for work of equal value" as an additional core priority. Child care was seen very early as a major difficulty facing working mothers; in its 1970 Report, the Royal Commission on the Status of Women noted that 20 percent of women with children younger than 14 were working for pay. By 1987 this figure had increased to 65 percent.[63] Similarly, a series of federal, provincial, and academic studies documented the far lower average pay of employed women as compared with men.[64]

Pressure from the feminist community to address employment issues like child care and equal pay has been met with mixed results. Policies for both legal and employment rights have reached the formal political agendas of federal and provincial governments; indeed, some feminists express concern that the issue of child care has been "mainstreamed" to the point of institutionalization.[65] Yet the increased political attention has not necessarily translated into effective policy action.

In the case of child care, a patchwork of facilities, funding schemes, and standards has developed in the absence of a coherent national policy. As Susan Phillips demonstrates, federal governments remain reluctant to act assertively in a policy area where ideological conflicts over the "proper" role of women as mothers exist, where jurisdiction is shared with the provinces, where the costs may be high, and where interest groups are themselves divided over precisely what reforms should be introduced.[66]

Pressure from NAC, the Canadian Advisory Council on the Status of Women, and major trade unions, as well as the Canadian Day Care Advocacy Association (CDCAA) did produce some action, notably the introduction in 1987 of what the Conservative government termed its National Strategy on Child-Care.[67] The principal legislative component of this strategy, the Canada Child-Care Act (Bill C-144), died on the order paper at the dissolution of Parliament in

1988. NAC and other groups opposed the Conservatives' reliance on the tax system to provide what child-care advocates saw as a crucial social and employment policy. Operating as an umbrella for child-care organizations, the CDCAA remains committed to "universally accessible, publicly-funded, high quality, non-profit, comprehensive care"—a position that would seem to be incompatible with the laissez-faire, minimalist government approach of the Conservatives.[68]

In the equal pay area, feminists again established the importance of their claim, arguing that older equal pay for equal work laws had no effect on low-wage female job ghettos. In demanding legislation to establish equal pay for work of *equal value,* feminists proposed that positions be evaluated not on the basis of their similarity to men's work, but rather on the basis of such neutral criteria as skill, effort, and level of responsibility. Jobs rated similarly would be assigned equal value and equal remuneration.

Equal value legislation was enacted by the federal government in 1977 and applied to the approximately 10 percent of the Canadian labor force employed by the federal government, federal crown corporations, and federally regulated industries.[69] Since the rest of the workers in Canada are governed by provincial labor legislation, feminists directed many of their efforts during the 1970s and 1980s toward achieving reform at that level, winning equal value concessions in Quebec, Manitoba, and Ontario. The Ontario Pay Equity Act (Bill 154) of 1987 was one of the most comprehensive statutes of its type in North America; it required all firms with ten or more workers to implement the principle of equal pay for work of equal value on a timetable beginning in January 1991. Categories of work in which women dominate are to be compared with male-dominated categories using the criteria of skill, effort, responsibility, and working conditions. If two jobs are found to be comparable but the female-dominated category is paid less, then employers must make adjustments. Pay equity is considered to be achieved when remuneration for the female job is at least equal to that for the male job.[70]

Many feminist groups that pushed for the Ontario law are frustrated with its limitations. The Equal Pay Coalition, which helped to make equal value legislation a condition of NDP support for a minority Liberal government, was unable to secure further action after the Liberals won a parliamentary majority in 1987. The group's efforts to obtain further progress on pay equity under an NDP majority government (elected in September 1990) were hindered by two main factors. First, a burgeoning public deficit in Ontario and elsewhere in Canada focused public attention on the fiscal costs of additional equal value legislation. Second, a political backlash against the concept of equity policy began to emerge in Canada, parallel to that which had already developed in the United States. Hundreds of thousands of women workers are left outside the legislative purview of Bill 154 because it excludes not only firms with fewer than ten employees but also situations in which no male-dominated job categories exist. Redressing inequalities in sectors of the economy that are predominantly female, such as child care, healthcare, and textiles and clothing industries, as well as many part-time and seasonal categories, is unlikely under the terms of Bill 154.

ABORTION POLICY

The third priority of the National Action Committee when it was formed in 1972, following child care and legal rights, was the decriminalization of abortion. Under the terms of section 179 of the Criminal Code, enacted in 1892, it was an indictable offense to advertise or sell materials "intended or represented as a means of preventing conception or causing abortion."[71] This blanket restriction against what feminists later came to term reproductive choice was eased only slightly by the introduction in 1969 of section 251 of the Criminal Code. That law permitted legal abortions under specified conditions: when the woman's "life or health" would likely be endangered by continued pregnancy; when a therapeutic abortion committee of at least three medical doctors would so certify; and when an accredited or approved hospital would perform the abortion.

Two sets of responses to section 251 could be discerned by 1970. First, women's groups were not prepared to accept a law that gave individual (and primarily male) doctors and local hospital boards control over access to abortion. The 1970 Abortion Caravan, beginning in Vancouver and ending in the visitors' gallery of the House of Commons in Ottawa, reflected the ability of new women's liberation groups to attract masses of women as well as national media attention. By organizing a demonstration of 400 protesters who chained themselves to the railing of the visitors' gallery, prochoice activists made clear their demands to decriminalize abortion and to end therapeutic committees.[72]

Second, in June 1970 a medical doctor, Henry Morgentaler, was issued the first of a long series of charges in Montreal, Winnipeg, Toronto, and Halifax for performing abortions outside an accredited hospital and without the certification of a therapeutic committee.[73] The judicial and political challenge represented by Morgentaler's decision to provide abortion services in freestanding clinics across the country reached a crescendo in 1988. Supported by the many prochoice groups that had developed out of the Abortion Caravan—including the Canadian Abortion Rights Action League, the Ontario Coalition for Abortion Clinics, and groups affiliated with NAC—Morgentaler's case finally reached the Supreme Court of Canada.

In a crucial decision delivered on 28 January 1988, a majority of justices declared that section 251 of the Criminal Code violated the constitutional guarantee of "security of the person," as established in section 7 of the Charter of Rights and Freedoms.[74] The judgment was celebrated by prochoice activists, who had worked toward decriminalization for nearly 20 years and who believed that the decision obviated the need for federal legislation in this area. Not surprisingly, the same decision was denounced by groups like R.E.A.L. Women, who viewed it as an attack on the traditional family and the rights of the unborn child.

After the decision, organized feminists maintained that Canada needed no new abortion law to replace section 251, arguing that reproductive decisions should be made by individual women in consultation with their doctors. Moreover, prochoice groups opposed the reintroduction of therapeutic abortion committees and prohibitions against freestanding clinics, maintaining that these older provisions had created limited accessibility and unnecessary delays.[75] The federal government twice attempted to introduce a new abortion law, and in spring 1990 it passed Bill C-43, which would recriminalize the procedure. Both sides of the abortion debate opposed the legislation, which was ultimately defeated after a tie vote in the Senate.[76]

LOOKING TO THE FUTURE

This discussion of political engagement points toward a number of generalizations concerning women in Canada. First, it suggests that the visibility of feminist issues, including the question of numbers at the elite level, has increased during recent decades. Public awareness of problems of legal rights, child care, equal pay, and reproductive choice has clearly grown, including among legislative and judicial elites who are in a position to act on these issues. Similarly, concern over the underrepresentation of women in decision-making positions has grown as demands for reform in the major parties and in the broader electoral process received greater attention.

This growing visibility has generated a second pattern: a vocal countermovement. Although most progressive movements for social change encounter opposition from traditional groups that feel threatened by the implications of reform, the Canadian women's movement faces a particular problem in that antifeminist beliefs have struck a responsive chord among some conservative interests. As organizations like R.E.A.L. Women demand an end to equal pay laws or argue that child care be provided only by children's own mothers in their own homes, they reflect a traditional social vision that appeals directly to some legislators, especially those in right-of-center political parties. Organized feminism in Canada is trying to protect and expand the progress that has been made, despite sustained opposition from antifeminists and their political allies.[77]

Third, I have suggested that the influence of women's groups is limited not so much by issues and policies as it is by the priorities and ideological predilections of the party in power. At the federal level, feminist organizations since 1984 have confronted a Conservative government that contains some supporters, as well as some antifeminist and many nonfeminist elements. The women's movement successfully "educated" key players in previous Liberal governments between 1968 and 1984, yet demands for substantive policy reform in the areas of child care and abortion remained unanswered. Furthermore, changes in the fields of equal pay, legal rights, and women's numerical representation were won only after considerable struggle.

Whether any degree of organized pressure during the 1990s can bring about an acceptable federal child-care policy, for example, remains to be seen. It appears that a fundamental ideological gap divides the economic interventionism and, in the case of English Canadian feminism, demands for strong federal leadership in the social policy field, on the one hand, from the Conservative emphasis on market forces and cooperative relations with the provinces, on the other.[78] Similarly, while feminist efforts in Quebec have been helped by a strong tradition of assertive provincial action, they have had to contend with serious concerns about a low fertility rate among Francophones—concerns that have led to pronatalist policies by both PQ and Liberal provincial governments.[79]

Fourth, Canadian women are themselves divided—by language, culture, region, ideology, and political strategy. Yet it would be naive to expect the cleavages that divide Canadians as a whole to disappear among the collectivity that constitutes 52 percent of the population. Women's groups have attempted to make a virtue out of this diversity, to demonstrate their ability to build consensus and work toward compromise within a larger society that prides itself on seeking the middle ground. The National Action Committee has reflected this larger political tension in a microcosm by attempting to link a large number of diverse groups, including conservative first-wave women's organizations, Francophone groups, and socialist and radical organizations.

For political analysts, the intriguing question for the future is whether women's groups will be squeezed out of that middle position. Pressures from within the feminist movement as well as from external forces can affect both the gains that have been made and the prospects for additional change. Analysts suggest that constraints on political engagement are themselves often highly political, turning on questions of internal cohesion, strategy, and the ability to translate increasing numbers of women in the political elite into concrete policy reforms.

In short, the prospects for women's engagement in Canada bring us full circle to matters of political action. Having more feminist women at elite levels in provincial and federal parties could provide one answer to the political squeeze facing the women's movement. And for feminists who are more comfortable with independent, nonpartisan routes to power, the need for continued action outside the party system remains clear. These efforts can continue to build an effective—if at times discordant—political voice for women in Canada. Having developed their organizations, support bases, and public visibility through the 1970s and 1980s, it is unlikely that Canadian women will disappear as a political force, yet the threats to internal cohesion and external influence are nevertheless significant. In particular, the need to reconcile so many differing interests within NAC, combined with the impact of antifeminist groups on elected politicians, are important brakes on the development of women's political voice in Canada.

NOTES

1. The phrase *women's issues* is misleading because it suggests that these policy questions concern only

women. Given the widespread use of this term, however, including its appearance in the titles of government departments in Canada, it is introduced here.

2. For Canadian critiques of these standard research paradigms see Mary O'Brien, "Hegemony and Superstructure: A Feminist Critique of Neo-Marxism," in Jill McCalla Vickers, ed., *Taking Sex into Account: The Policy Consequences of Sexist Research* (Ottawa: Carleton University Press, 1984), 85–100; Heather Jon Maroney and Meg Luxton, "From Feminism and Political Economy to Feminist Political Economy," in Heather Jon Maroney and Meg Luxton, eds., *Feminism and Political Economy: Women's Work, Women's Struggles* (Toronto: Methuen, 1987), 5–28; and Jill McCalla Vickers, "Feminist Approaches to Women in Politics," in Linda Kealey and Joan Sangster, eds., *Beyond the Vote: Canadian Women and Politics* (Toronto: University of Toronto Press, 1989), 16–36.

3. Canada is a member of the British Commonwealth, with the governor-general representing the British monarch as head of state. The "repatriation" of the Canadian constitution in 1982 ended formal British control over Canadian constitutional matters. See Roger Gibbins, *Conflict and Unity: An Introduction to Canadian Political Life*, 2nd ed. (Toronto: Nelson Canada, 1990); David J. Elkins and Richard Simeon, *Small Worlds: Provinces and Parties in Canadian Political Life* (Toronto: Methuen, 1980); and David Milne, *Tug of War: Ottawa and the Provinces Under Trudeau and Mulroney* (Toronto: Lorimer, 1986).

4. On the evolution of the federal system see Donald V. Smiley, *Canada in Question: Federalism in the Eighties* (Toronto: McGraw-Hill Ryerson, 1980); and Garth Stevenson, *Unfulfilled Union: Canadian Federalism and National Unity*, 3d ed. (Toronto: Gage, 1989).

5. For an introduction to executive federalism see R. D. Olling and M. W. Westmacott, eds., *Perspectives on Canadian Federalism* (Scarborough, Ontario: Prentice-Hall Canada, 1988), sec. 5.

6. See Lawrence LeDuc, "Voting for Free Trade? The Canadian Voter and the 1988 Federal Election," in Paul Fox and Graham White, eds., *Politics: Canada*, 7th ed. (Toronto: McGraw-Hill Ryerson, 1990), 350–66.

7. The voluminous literature on Meech Lake includes Katherine E. Swinton and Carol J. Rogerson, eds., *Competing Constitutional Visions: The Meech Lake Accord* (Toronto: Carswell, 1988); Ad Hoc Committee of Women on the Constitution, "We Can Afford a Better Accord"; and Barbara Roberts, *Smooth Sailing or Storm Warning? Canadian and Quebec Women's Groups and the Meech Lake Accord* (Ottawa: Canadian Research Institute for the Advancement of Women, 1988).

8. The argument regarding partisanship versus independence is developed at greater length in Sylvia B. Bashevkin, *Toeing the Lines: Women and Party Politics in En-*

glish Canada (Toronto: University of Toronto Press, 1985), chap. 1.

9. See Veronica Strong-Boag, *Parliament of Women: The National Council of Women of Canada, 1893–1929* (Ottawa: National Museums of Canada, 1976).

10. See Sylvia Bashevkin, "Free Trade and Canadian Feminism: The Case of the National Action Committee on the Status of Women," *Canadian Public Policy* 15 (December 1989): 363–75; and Jill Vickers, Chris Appelle, and Pauline Rankin, "Politics As If Women Mattered: A Political Analysis of the National Action Committee on the Status of Women" (Manuscript, 1990).

11. Royal Commission on the Status of Women, *Report* (Ottawa: Information Canada, 1970).

12. R.E.A.L. is an acronym for Realistic, Equal, Active, for Life. See Karen Dubinsky, *Lament for a Patriarchy Lost: Anti-Feminism, Anti-Abortion and R.E.A.L. Women in Canada* (Ottawa: Canadian Research Institute for the Advancement of Women, 1985); and Lorna Erwin, "R.E.A.L. Women, Anti-Feminism and the Welfare State," in Sue Findlay and Melanie Randall, eds., *Feminist Perspectives on the Canadian State*, a special issue of *Resources for Feminist Research* 17 (September 1988): 147–49.

13. See Vickers et al., "Politics As If Women Mattered," 101, 131, 134, 279.

14. See David Milne, *The New Canadian Constitution* (Toronto: Lorimer, 1982).

15. French-English differences among feminists in this period are shown clearly in Audrey Doerr and Micheline Carrier, eds., *Women and the Constitution in Canada* (Ottawa: Canadian Advisory Council on the Status of Women, 1981).

16. Women's organizations in English Canada, notably the Ad Hoc Committee of Women on the Constitution, did not oppose the goal of bringing Quebec within the constitutional fold. Although proponents of the Meech Lake Accord suggested that feminist critics were anti-French and insensitive to the concerns of Quebec, the ad hoc committee said that "notwithstanding anything we say, anything we have said, or anything we are reported to have said—the women of Canada support the intent of the Meech Lake Constitutional Accord. We are in favor of bringing in the Government of Quebec as a signatory to the Canadian Constitution." See Ad Hoc Committee of Women on the Constitution, "We Can Afford a Better Accord: The Meech Lake Accord," in Findlay and Randall, eds., *Feminist Perspectives on the Canadian State*, 142.

17. On the streaming of women into auxiliaries of the Liberal and Conservative parties see Bashevkin, *Toeing the Lines*, chap. 5.

18. Agnes Macphail, "Men Want to Hog Everything," *Maclean's*, 15 September 1949, p. 72. See also Terry Crowley, *Agnes Macphail and the Politics of Equality* (Toronto: Lorimer, 1990).

19. See Veronica Strong-Boag, "'Ever a Crusader': Nellie McClung, First-Wave Feminist," in Veronica Strong-Boag and Anita Clair Fellman, eds., *Rethinking Canada: The Promise of Women's History* (Toronto: Copp Clark Pitman, 1986), 178–90.

20. For further details see Bashevkin, *Toeing the Lines,* chap. 1.

21. Lynn McDonald, "The Charter of Rights and the Subjection of Women," *Canadian Forum* (June–July 1981): 18.

22. For an overview of the trade agreement see David Leyton-Brown, "The Canada-U.S. Free Trade Agreement," in Andrew B. Gollner and Daniel Salée, eds., *Canada Under Mulroney: An End-of-Term Report* (Montreal: Véhicule Press, 1988), 103–18.

23. See Bashevkin, "Free Trade and Canadian Feminism."

24. On Quebec's ties with the United States see J. L. Roy, "The French Fact in North America: Quebec-United States Relations," *International Journal* 31 (Summer 1976): 470–87. The varied perceptions of Canada's two nationalisms are discussed in Philip Resnick, *Letters to a Québécois Friend* (with a reply by Daniel Latouche) (Montreal: McGill–Queen's University Press, 1990); and Sylvia Bashevkin, "Solitudes in Collision? Pan-Canadian and Quebec Nationalist Attitudes in the Late 1970s," *Comparative Political Studies* 23 (April 1990): 3–24.

25. On the more limited opposition in Quebec to free trade see Rick Salutin, *Waiting for Democracy: A Citizen's Journal* (Markham, Ontario: Penguin, 1989); and Sylvia Bashevkin, *True Patriot Love: The Politics of Canadian Nationalism* (Toronto: Oxford University Press, 1991), chap. 7.

26. For details on the granting of franchise in Canada see Bashevkin, *Toeing the Lines,* table 1.1.

27. See Susan Mann Trofimenkoff, *The Dream of Nation: A Social and Intellectual History of Quebec* (Toronto: Gage, 1983), chap. 20; and Sylvia B. Bashevkin, "Social Change and Political Partisanship: The Development of Women's Attitudes in Quebec, 1965–1979," *Comparative Political Studies* 16 (July 1983): 152–54.

28. See Diane Lamoureux, "Nationalism and Feminism in Quebec: An Impossible Attraction," in Maroney and Luxton, eds., *Feminism and Political Economy,* 51–68; and Alison Prentice et al., *Canadian Women: A History* (Toronto: Harcourt Brace Jovanovich, 1988), 354–55. For an early FLQ manifesto see Pierre Vallieres, *White Niggers of America,* trans. Joan Pinkham (New York: Monthly Review Press, 1971).

29. See Bashevkin, "Social Change and Political Partisanship," 148.

30. See R. Dandurand and E. Tardy, "Le phénomène des Yvettes à travers quelques quotidiens," in Y. Cohen, ed., *Femmes et politique* (Montreal: Le Jour, 1981); M. Jean and M. Lavigne, "Le phénomène des Yvettes," *Atlantis* 6 (1981): 17–23; J. Lamothe and J. Stoddart, "Les Yvettes ou," *Atlantis* 6 (1981): 10–16; and Lise Payette, *Le pouvoir? Connais pas* (Montreal: Québec/Amérique, 1982), chap. 6.

31. On the prospects for a "post-nationalist" feminism see Lamoureux, "Nationalism and Feminism in Quebec."

32. The implications of federalism for policy change are explored in Audrey Doerr, "Overlapping Jurisdictions and Women's Issues," in Doerr and Carrier, eds., *Women and the Constitution in Canada,* 123–48.

33. See Strong-Boag, *Parliament of Women.*

34. See Cerise Morris, "'Determination and Thoroughness': The Movement for a Royal Commission on the Status of Women in Canada," *Atlantis* 5 (Spring 1980).

35. These developments are treated in detail in Nancy Adamson, Linda Briskin, and Margaret McPhail, *Feminist Organizing for Change: The Contemporary Women's Movement in Canada* (Toronto: Oxford University Press, 1988); and Prentice et al., *Canadian Women,* chaps. 13–16.

36. This emphasis is reflected in Findlay and Randall, eds., *Feminist Perspectives on the Canadian State.*

37. R.E.A.L. Women eventually received about $21,000 in federal funds to support a conference held in Ottawa in April 1989.

38. See Dubinsky, *Lament for a Patriarchy Lost.*

39. See Bashevkin, "Free Trade and Canadian Feminism."

40. Sylvia B. Bashevkin, "Social Background and Political Experience: Gender Differences among Ontario Provincial Party Elites, 1982," *Atlantis* 9 (1983): 3, 7.

41. M. Janine Brodie, "The Constraints of Private Life: Marriage, Motherhood and Political Candidacy in Canada" (Paper presented at Canadian Political Science Association meetings, Dalhousie University, Halifax, Nova Scotia, May 1981), 29.

42. See M. Janine Brodie, "Recruitment of Men and Women Political Party Activists in Ontario" (M.A. thesis, University of Windsor, 1976); Allan Kornberg, Joel Smith, and Harold D. Clarke, *Citizen Politicians—Canada* (Durham, N.C.: Carolina Academic Press, 1970), chap. 8; and M. Janine Brodie, *Women and Politics in Canada* (Toronto: McGraw-Hill Ryerson, 1985).

43. Sylvia B. Bashevkin, "Political Participation, Ambition and Feminism: Women in the Ontario Party Elites," *American Review of Canadian Studies* 15 (Winter 1985): table 1.

44. Jill McCalla Vickers, "Where are the Women in Canadian Politics?" *Atlantis* 3 (Spring 1978): 46.

45. M. Janine Brodie and Jill Vickers, "The More Things Change . . . Women in the 1979 Federal Campaign," in Howard R. Penniman, ed., *Canada at the Polls: 1979 and 1980* (Washington, D.C.: American Enterprise Institute, 1981), 323–28.

46. Brodie, *Women and Politics in Canada*, 112.

47. For more detailed data see Bashevkin, *Toeing the Lines*, fig. 2.

48. See Sylvia Bashevkin, Marianne R. Holder, and Karen Jones, "Women's Political Involvement and Policy Influence," in Graham White, ed., *The Government and Politics of Ontario*, 4th ed. (Toronto: Nelson, 1990), 293–310.

49. A Liberal landslide in 1987 and an NDP landslide in 1990 elected record numbers of female provincial legislators in Ontario. In September 1990, 29 of 130 provincial legislators elected were women, and 20 of those were members of the 74-person NDP government caucus. See Marilyn Domagalski, "The Role of Canadian Women in Federal and Provincial Politics," in Robert J. Fleming, ed., *Canadian Legislatures: The 1986 Comparative Study* (Toronto: Office of the Legislative Assembly, 1986).

50. Organizations that use the one member, one vote scheme include the Parti québécois and the Ontario Progressive Conservative Party.

51. Provincial parties that have been led by women include the British Columbia Liberals, Saskatchewan Liberals, New Brunswick Conservatives, New Brunswick New Democrats, and Nova Scotia New Democrats. In the case of Sharon Carstairs's leadership of the Manitoba Liberals, the party was not in a competitive political position at the time of her selection as leader; Carstairs led the official opposition in Manitoba from 1988 until 1990. In the case of Audrey McLaughlin, the federal NDP improved its standing in public opinion polls after her election.

52. See Bashevkin, *Toeing the Lines*, 89–97.

53. See Hal Quinn, "A Winning Way," *Maclean's* (29 July 1991), pp. 12–14.

54. These groups have adopted different names across the country and developed a communications network that connects the 51 Percent Solution in Newfoundland, Femmes régroupées pour l'accessibilité aux pouvoirs politique et economique in Montreal, the Committee for '94 in Toronto, and Winning Women in Vancouver. Materials include Josephine Payne-O'Connor, *Sharing Power: A Political Skills Handbook* (Victoria: Kachina Press, 1986) and a six-part television series by TVOntario based on a 1986 conference organized by the Committee for '94.

55. See Bashevkin, *Toeing the Lines*, chap. 4.

56. Beverley Baines, "Women and the Law," in Sandra Burt, Lorraine Code, and Lindsay Dorney, eds., *Changing Patterns: Women in Canada* (Toronto: McClelland and Stewart, 1988), 157.

57. Ibid., 173. See also Leslie A. Pal and F. L. Morton, "'Bliss v. Attorney General of Canada': From Legal Defeat to Political Victory," *Osgoode Hall Law Journal* 24 (Spring 1986): 141–60; Beverley Baines, "Women, Human Rights and the Constitution," in Doerr and Carrier, eds., *Women and the Constitution*, 46–59; and Sally M. Weaver, "The Status of Indian Women," in Jean Leonard Elliott, ed., *Two Nations, Many Cultures* (Scarborough: Prentice-Hall Canada, 1983), 56–79.

58. *Canadian Charter of Rights and Freedoms*, part 1 of the *Constitution Act, 1982*, being schedule B of the *Canada Act, 1982* (U.K.), 1982. Because of a three-year waiting period designed to permit governments to bring their laws into conformity, section 15 did not come into effect until 17 April 1985. See Chaviva Hosek, "Women and the Constitutional Process," in Keith Banting and Richard Simeon, eds., *And No One Cheered* (Toronto: Methuen, 1983), 280–300; and Penney Kome, *The Taking of Twenty-Eight* (Toronto: Women's Press, 1983).

59. See Baines, "Women and the Law," 178–81.

60. Gwen Brodsky and Shelagh Day, *Canadian Charter Equality Rights for Women: One Step Forward or Two Steps Back?* (Ottawa: Canadian Advisory Council on the Status of Women, 1989), 3. For an equally pessimistic view see Margaret Buist, "Elusive Equality: Women and the Charter of Rights and Freedoms," in Findlay and Randall, eds., *Feminist Perspectives on the Canadian State*, 103–5.

61. Brodsky and Day, *Canadian Charter Equality Rights for Women*, 3. See also Lise Gotell, *Canadian Women's Movement, Equality Rights and the Charter* (Ottawa: Canadian Research Institute for the Advancement of Women, 1990).

62. Department of Labor, Women's Bureau Draft Material, 1958, as quoted in Sandra Burt, "Legislators, Women and Public Policy," in Burt, Code and Dorney, eds., *Changing Patterns*, 138.

63. The figures are from Susan D. Phillips, "Rock-a-Bye, Brian: The National Strategy on Child Care," in Katherine A. Graham, ed., *How Ottawa Spends, 1989–90* (Ottawa: Carleton University Press, 1989), 166. In addition to the 1970 *Report* of the Royal Commission on the Status of Women, the child-care issue was addressed in Royal Commission on Equality in Employment (Abella Commission), *Report* (Ottawa: Supply and Services Canada, 1984); and Task Force on Child Care (Cooke Task Force), *Report* (Ottawa: Status of Women Canada, 1986).

64. These sources included the reports of the Royal Commission on the Status of Women (1970) and the Abella Commission (1984), as well as Pat Armstrong and Hugh Armstrong, *The Double Ghetto: Canadian Women and their Segregated Work* (Toronto: McClelland and Stewart, 1975).

65. Susan Prentice, "The 'Mainstreaming' of Daycare," in Findlay and Randall, eds., *Feminist Perspectives on the Canadian State*, 59–63.

66. Phillips, "Rock-a-Bye, Brian."

67. Ibid., 166–67.

68. Prentice, "'Mainstreaming' of Daycare," 62.

69. See Lorna R. Marsden, "The Role of the National Action Committee on the Status of Women in Facilitating Equal Pay Policy in Canada," in Ronnie Steinberg Ratner,

ed., *Equal Employment Policy for Women: Strategies for Implementation in the United States, Canada and Western Europe* (Philadelphia: Temple University Press, 1980), 242–60.

70. On the background to this law see Bashevkin, Holder, and Jones, "Women's Political Involvement and Policy Influence."

71. See Angus McLaren and Arlene Tigar McLaren, *The Bedroom and the State: The Changing Practices and Politics of Contraception and Abortion in Canada, 1880–1980* (Toronto: McClelland and Stewart, 1986).

72. It should be noted that the Front de libération des femmes refused to join the Abortion Caravan. See Prentice et al., *Canadian Women*, 355.

73. See Stan Persky, "Introduction," in Shelagh Day and Stan Persky, eds., *The Supreme Court of Canada Decision on Abortion* (Vancouver: New Star Books, 1988), 3–9.

74. Ibid.

75. See Ontario Coalition for Abortion Clinics, "State Power and the Struggle for Reproductive Freedom: The Campaign for Free-standing Abortion Clinics in Ontario," in Findlay and Randall, eds., *Feminist Perspectives on the Canadian State*, 109–14.

76. Bill C-43 made abortion punishable by up to two years in prison unless a doctor determined that continuing the pregnancy would threaten a woman's physical, mental, or psychological health.

77. For similar conclusions see Sandra Burt, "Canadian Women's Groups in the 1980s: Organizational Development and Policy Influence," *Canadian Public Policy* 16 (March 1990): 26.

78. See Phillips, "Rock-a-Bye, Brian"; and Louise Delude, "The Status of Women Under the Mulroney Government," in Gollner and Salée, eds., *Canada Under Mulroney*, 253–64.

79. Quebec provincial governments have introduced a variety of parental leave, housing assistance, and tax credit provisions, including a system of cash bonuses that become increasingly lucrative with each additional child.

▲ China

POLITICS

Type of Political System: state socialist
  Sovereignty: not applicable
  Executive-Legislative System: not
  applicable
Type of State: unitary
Type of Party System: one party (leading the
  cooperation of several historically separate
  parties)[a]
Major Political Parties

  Communist Party of China (CPC): Founded
in 1920; has controlled the government since
1949.
Year Women Granted Right to Vote: 1949
*Year Women Granted Right to Stand for
  Election:* 1949
*Percentage of Women in the Unicameral
  Legislature:* 21.3%[b]
*Percentage of Population Voting for Highest
  Elected Office in Most Recent Election:* not
  applicable

DEMOGRAPHICS

Population: 1,100,000,000[c]
Percentage of Population in Urban Areas
  Overall: 20.6%[d]
  Female: 20.3%
  Male: 20.8%
Percentage of Population Below Age 15:
  28.7%[e]
Birthrate (per 1,000 population): 21[f]
Maternal Mortality Rate (per 100,000 live
  births): 44
Infant Mortality Rate (per 1,000 live births):
  31
Mortality Rate for Children Under Five (per
  1,000 live births): 43
Average Household Size: 4.2[g]
Mean Age at First Marriage
  Female: 22.4
  Male: 25.1
Life Expectancy[h]
  Female: 69.0
  Male: 66.0

EDUCATION

Ratio of Female to Male Enrollment
  First-Level Education: 82
  Second-Level Education: 69
  Third-Level Education: 42
Literacy Rate[i]
  Female: 54.8%
  Male: 80.8%

ECONOMY

Gross National Product per Capita: U.S. $310
Percentage of Labor Force in Agriculture:
  71.0%[j]
Distribution of Agricultural Workers by Sex[k]
  Female: 47.4%
  Male: 52.6%
Economically Active Population by Sex
  Female: 69.5%
  Male: 87.0%

a. China Zhi Gong Dang: composed mainly of returned overseas Chinese. China Democratic League:
founded in 1941; composed mainly of intellectuals from
educational and cultural circles. China Democratic National Construction Association: founded in 1945; composed mainly of national capitalists, business people, and
industrialists. China Association for Promoting Democracy: founded in 1945; composed mainly of literary intellectuals and primary and secondary school teachers.
Chinese Peasants' and Workers' Democratic Party:
founded in 1930; composed mainly of intellectuals in
medical and pharmaceutical circles and educational and
cultural circles. Revolutionary Committee of the Guomindang: founded in 1948; composed mainly of former
Guomindang members who struggled against Guomindang counterrevolutionaries.

b. China National Statistics Bureau, *China Statistics
Yearbook, 1989* (in Chinese) (Beijing: China Statistics
Publishing House, 1989).

c. "Congress Held to Mark the Population Day of
1,100,000,000 in Beijing" (in Chinese), *People's Daily,*
14 April 1989.

d. People's Republic of China Yearbook Editing Office of XinHua News Agency, *People's Republic of China
Yearbook* (in Chinese) (Beijing: Beijing XinHua Publishing House and Hong Kong New China News Company,
1988).

e. China National Statistics Bureau, *China Statistics*

Yearbook, 1988 (in Chinese) (Beijing: China Statistics Publishing House, 1988).

    f. China National Statistics Bureau, *China Statistics Yearbook, 1989.*

    g. Ibid.

    h. Population Statistics Department, China National

Statistics Bureau, *China Population Statistics, 1988* (in Chinese) (Beijing: China Expectations Publishing House, 1988).

    i. Ibid.

    j. Ibid.

    k. Ibid.

Women's Life in New China

YUE DAIYUN AND LI JIN

The People's Republic of China (PRC)—often called the New China—was formally established on 1 October 1949 after Communist revolutionary forces defeated the Nationalists (Guomindang). The constitution of 1982 defines the country as a "socialist state under the people's democratic dictatorship led by the working class and based on the alliance of workers and peasants."[1] At the township, county, provincial, and national levels two parallel governance structures exist: a state structure alongside the politically dominant party structure. At the national level the primary state structure is the National People's Congress (NPC), whose legislative duties are carried out by the Standing Committee of the NPC when the congress is not in session. The primary national party structure is the National Party Congress of the Communist Party of China (CPC). This body elects the Central Committee, which in turn elects a Political Bureau (Politburo). The Standing Committee of the Politburo is responsible for formulating the party's policies and ideological direction.

The movement for the emancipation of Chinese women is a component of the Chinese revolution; it has not become an independent movement. Chinese women have no history of struggle to win the right to vote and to stand for election; rather, the victory of the Chinese revolution granted Chinese women the right to participate politically. The Chinese revolution gave women legal equality. Women walk out of their families, go into society, and obtain their social rights just as men do; they realize the prediction that the emancipation of women must be inte-

grated with the Chinese revolution. The women's rights movement in China thus possesses a special form different from that of women's rights movements in the West, for it does not strive to win women's rights from a government by men. Chinese women have never appeared on the political stage as an independent force but have played their role as part of the Chinese revolution and depended on the revolution to establish their liberation.

The consciousness of Chinese women as women is not well developed, nor do Chinese women manifest a political sensibility rooted in an analysis of their position as women in society. They are accustomed to playing a subordinate and supplementary role in all spheres of social life. In spite of the actual inequality between men and women, the tensions existing between the sexes have not been acknowledged. Women take the traditional road: they do not develop their character and take back a portion of their rights from men; instead, they swallow humiliation, bear heavy loads, and cooperate with men.

Women keep a foothold in the political domain mostly because there are quotas for women cadres (i.e., trained political personnel). Women cadres are found among writers, actors, technicians, teachers, doctors, and office workers. In 1982 there were more than 8 million women cadres; of those, 1 percent were department directors in the party or government.[2] Women make up 14 percent of the Communist Party as a whole.

The political and policy-making activities of women most frequently take place through the official organization that represents women's interests to the party and conveys party policies to women. The All-China Women's Federation, founded in 1949, is a mass organization supported by the party and operating at every level of government. The principal work of the federation is to unite and educate the broad masses of women in carrying out the general party line, and its secondary task is to defend women's and children's legal rights and promote the cause of women's emancipation. Although the All-China Women's Federation has the right to help formulate laws, regulations, and rules concerning women and children and to supervise the implementation of those laws, it has no power to make decisions. Thus it has a contradictory role: it can suggest action, but—in accordance with the democratic centrist practice of the Chinese socialist system—it must follow in the direction set by the party.

Chinese women have many concerns, but we shall concentrate on three important issues: marriage and divorce, family planning in the context of population policy, and women's employment. Even this discussion must be more abbreviated than the issues warrant. China is a country with several thousand years of history. Over 1 billion people live in China, the most populated country in the world. About 80 percent live in the countryside, and there are significant regional differences in language, tradition, and economic development. No one chapter can easily analyze the concerns of women in such a large and varied country.

MARRIAGE AND DIVORCE

A series of laws and regulations were passed just before and after the founding of the People's Republic of China in order to establish its socialist nature: the Common Program of the Chinese People's Consultative Conference (the substitute for a constitution), the Organic Act of the Central People's Government, the marriage law, the agrarian reform law, the Trade Union Act, labor insurance regulations, and so on. The promulgation and enforcement of these laws and regulations provided a legal basis for carrying out socialist reforms politically, economically, and in everyday life.

The marriage law, which represented the policies of the Chinese Communist Party concerning marriage and family, came into effect on 1 May 1950 and played an enormous role in establishing women's independence before the law and in society, transforming the feudal marriage and family system, and establishing a free, democratic, and united marriage based on mutual love. In 1978 the Third Plenary Session of the 11th Central Committee of the CPC began the process of revising the marriage law of 1950. This effort was part of the legislative response to the Cultural Revolution of 1966–76, when laws and regulations were smashed and chaos reigned. A revised marriage law was passed at the Third Meeting of the Fifth National People's Congress on 10 September 1980 and went into effect on 1 January 1981.

The marriage law of 1980 incorporates the principles of the 1950 marriage law and retains many of its useful and effective stipulations. At the same time, a number of important revisions have enriched and developed it. The 1950 marriage law abolished the system of arranged marriages that supported the superiority of men over women and ignored the interests of children, and established a democratic marriage system based on freedom of choice, monogamy, equal rights, and protection of the legal interests of women and children. The law also prohibited many traditional practices: polygamy, concubinage, child daughters-in-law (taking a very young girl into a family as a daughter-in-law-to-be or as a child bride), interference with the remarriage of widows, and requests for wedding money or presents—by parents, for example. The law marked the thorough abolition of the feudal marriage system and the establishment of a new marriage system throughout the country. It won the heartfelt support of women at all levels.

The feudal marriage system that the marriage law overturned was a powerful force in Chinese society. It was characterized by the authority of the husband over his wife or wives, and its supreme purpose was to produce sons to offer sacrifices to the husband's ancestors. In the feudal period patriarchal marriage was the basis of society; it was an organic part of a centralized society stratified by class that combined imperial, clan, and husbandly authority. The political order was constructed of a set of hierarchical relationships: ruler over subject, father over son, and husband over wife. Thus patriarchal marriage possessed an inviolable sacred dignity. All the rites of marriage were formed to guard the integrated political order.

A man who had a legal wife was forbidden to take another wife, but the rites and the law did not forbid him to take concubines. In practice, the marriage system was a type of polygyny that took remarriage or the acquisition of concubines as its main form—bringing bitterness and humiliation to the broad masses of women. The status of wives and concubines was strictly hierarchical. A wife had to regard her husband as her king, and the concubines had to regard the wife as their queen so that the order of clan and family would not be upset.

The chief virtues of a woman were obedience and submission. We can even say that this is the cultural definition of the nature of a woman in China. In the *Book of Rites,* Confucius said: "A woman is a submissive person, submitting to her father and elder brothers when young, submitting to her husband after marriage, submitting to her son after her husband dies."[3] During a woman's whole life, she had no independence; she had to obey whoever had authority over her.

A husband could divorce his wife, but never a wife her husband. In the chapter on natural destiny in the *Book of Rites,* it is clearly stipulated that a wife could be divorced when accused of one of the following: "disobeying her parents, which is virtueless; having no son, which is heirless; being licentious, which is incestuous; being jealous, which is disorderly; having a nasty disease, which disqualifies one to offer sacrifices to the ancestors; being long tongued, which foments discord; stealing, which is against righteousness."[4] With these "seven reasons for divorce" as general grounds and legal bases, a man could easily justify

divorcing his wife. But the *Rites* went further, limiting women's access to divorce and remarriage, even remarriage after widowhood: "The husband has a reason to remarry, but the wife has no cause to do so."[5] "A loyal official will not serve two countries; a virtuous woman will never remarry."[6]

The feudal patriarchal marriage system threw women into the lowest tier of society. Although marriage was their den of suffering, it was also the center of their lives. For thousands of years women scrupulously abided by the moral teaching of submissiveness to parents, husband, and sons, sacrificing themselves for the stability of society, paying with their tears, blood, and bodies. Perhaps the historical dialectics present a paradox: Chinese feudal society deprived women of their rights, but the political order rested on women. Therefore, when women rise against feudal marriage, the patriarchal ruling order is in jeopardy. Not surprisingly, then, the antifeudal revolutionary era in the New China began with efforts to end feudal marriage and emancipate women.

The 1950 marriage law was simultaneously embraced and resisted after its enactment. Both marriage and divorce practices changed. Before 1949 almost 42 percent of all marriages were arranged, 26 percent were initiated through introductions by relatives, 21 percent were initiated through introductions by friends, 10 percent were initiated by the parties themselves becoming acquainted, and 1 percent were initiated in other ways. Between 1950 and 1965 the rate of arranged marriages dropped to 11 percent, and it fell to 1 percent between 1977 and 1982. In this last time period just over half of all marriages came about through introductions by friends.[7]

Since the revolution, the proportion of arranged marriages has been quite small in cities; most urban women choose their own spouse. In the countryside, however, difficult economic conditions and feudal customs prevail, and arranged marriages, made with mercenary considerations, are rife. In the 1980s the amount of money and presents requested by the bride's family and given by the groom upon betrothal and marriage rose sharply. In rural Qingliu County, Fujian Province, for example, the average annual income per person in 1981 was no more than 400 yuan (U.S. $73). That year betrothal gifts cost 2,341 yuan ($429), and the amount rose thereafter, reaching 4,126 yuan ($756) in 1985. Worse, in 1981 almost 8 percent of the marriages in this county involved betrothal gifts costing more than 5,000 yuan ($917). This level of giving was found in 68 percent of the betrothals in 1985.[8] If we count other expenses, such as feasts, furniture, and home construction, it is clear that the cost of getting married far surpasses income for most peasants. Many families have to borrow money to raise marriage funds.

Peasants who can neither borrow nor pay for betrothal gifts resort to exchanging their daughters and sons: Householder A marries his daughter to B's son and takes B's daughter in exchange for his own son's wife. Sometimes the exchange involves more than two families. At present this form of marriage is popular in the countryside. Such a marriage is an arranged and mercenary marriage in disguise; it creates mental and physical hardships for many women.

The 1950 and 1980 marriage laws changed divorce practices, with similarly uneven consequences. After the first marriage law was passed, courts all over the country saw a substantial increase in divorce cases, from about 190,000 cases in 1951 to an estimated 600,000 in 1952. (A similar rise took place after the promulgation of the marriage law of 1980.) Women constituted the great majority of those seeking divorce. They were struggling to abolish the feudal marriage system and to win their own emancipation through this democratic reform.

The old system and the old ideology of marriage had a strong social foundation, however. Most of the resistance to the marriage law came from men who disliked the reduction of their patriarchal power over women. In 1951 more than 10,000 women in the Central South District —generally the provinces of Henan, Hubei, Hunan, Guangdong, and Guangxi—were killed for striving to win the freedom to choose mates and divorce them on an equal basis with men or

committed suicide because their attempts were frustrated.[9]

In 1953, in response to events like these, the State Council of the Central People's Government and the Central Committee of the Communist Party of China issued successive directives about implementing the marriage law. To develop a well-planned movement to carry out the marriage law, all governments above the county level established special councils. Each council worked with the procuratorate, the civil administrative organs, the judicial institutions, the local units of the women's federation, the youth leagues, the trade unions, and other mass organizations to propagate the law through all possible means. This effort systematically uncovered and criticized feudal thinking and feudal marriage customs. Women's federations were the place where women reported what they had suffered; and because cadres in women's federations helped women gain their legal rights within marriage, women often called women's federations the "mothers' home."

Part of the problem with divorce was the grounds on which it was permitted. The court was strict, especially in regard to the 1950 marriage law. When deciding whether to approve a request, the court always emphasized the justification for the divorce, paying no attention to the feelings of the parties. Unless a good reason could be provided to persuade the judge, it was very hard to get a divorce. In response to this problem, the marriage law of 1980 stipulates that "the people's court should mediate in divorce cases. If the relationship between the couple has ruptured and mediation is ineffective, the divorce should be approved."[10] This article further states that issues of divorce should be judged on the basis of feelings, too. It broadens the conditions for divorce and thus legally protects the right to choose and divorce a spouse.

FAMILY PLANNING IN THE CONTEXT OF POPULATION POLICY

The personal freedom in marriage established by law and policy does not extend to family size because of the relentless pressures that the size of the Chinese population puts on economic development. On 14 April 1989 the population of China reached 1.1 billion. An additional 15 million people are added to the population each year. If the population continues to grow at the current rate, it will top 1.3 billion by the year 2000.

The rapid population growth has again and again sounded an alarm bell because only 7 percent of China's land is arable and that land must feed 22 percent of the world's population. Furthermore, the arable land decreases by approximately 8,000 to 10,000 acres per year. If these trends continue, it is feared that basic living standards cannot be sustained. Thus the government has instituted a nonvoluntary policy of one child per family. Although this policy is not quite just or reasonable, at present there is no other option. Generations of women are called upon to sacrifice their desire to have children, to subject their wishes to the needs of the state, and to have only one child.

In old China birthrates and death rates were high for a variety of reasons: small-scale agricultural production, political oppression and economic exploitation, frequent wars, natural and human-made calamities, and the ravages of disease. Under these conditions Chinese women often gave birth to seven or eight or even ten children, very few of whom lived to grow up.

Since the founding of the New China in 1949, the death rate has fallen substantially, but the birthrate initially remained high. In the short 40 years since the revolution—given increased social stability, quicker economic development, better medical care, and more hygienic conditions —China's population doubled, and this itself became a serious social problem. Controlling the birthrate is an attempt to keep the population at a sustainable level and to coordinate population growth with economic development.

The establishment of a population control system in China has taken arduous efforts. The first national census on 1 July 1953 was published in June 1954, and the enormous size of the Chinese population aroused grave concern in the Com-

munist Party, in the government, and among many specialists. In December 1954, President Liu Shaoqi himself presided over a birth-control forum and said, "Now we must be certain on this point: the party approves of birth control." A birth-control study group was set up then; and in 1956, in the Second Five-Year Plan for developing the national economy, Premier Zhou Enlai also remarked that birth control should be promoted properly.[11] Population studies flourished.

A number of farsighted people voiced their views on the contradiction between rapid population growth and economic development. In "A New Theory on Population," published in 1957, Ma Yinchu pointed out the negative results of the population explosion.[12] He struck the first note of warning for the Chinese nation, suggesting that administrative measures ought to be taken to control the size of the population, improve maternal and infant health, and establish a policy of birth control. Unfortunately Ma's theory on population was repudiated during the struggle against the bourgeois rightists in 1957 by those who held that population growth was good in and of itself. Because the struggle occurred at the high tide of economic construction in China, the population problem did not seem as important as it might have been in less prosperous times. Those advocating a larger population got the upper hand for the time being.

The Great Leap Forward in 1958–60 and the following three years of droughts and floods brought the economy to a standstill and also forced the leaders of the Communist Party and the state into a clearer understanding of the population problem. In 1962 the party's Central Committee issued a directive stating, "family planning must be promoted in all cities and in densely populated rural areas to control the natural population growth rate properly and lead gradually from unplanned to planned growth."[13] In 1963 the State Council decided to set up family planning committees at the central and local levels to provide leadership, and it formally put forward the policy "one is enough, two is just right, three is superfluous." But the Cultural Revolution stopped the work of population control, which was just about to make progress. This interruption lasted for a whole ten years, during which time population growth was unprecedented.

When the Cultural Revolution ended in the mid-1970s, the national economy had come to the brink of collapse and the population had reached 940 million. The problem of population control rapidly exacerbated the arduous task of rehabilitating the national economy. In January 1980 the Central Committee of the Communist Party issued Directive 1: "In carrying out the work of family planning, legislative, administrative and financial measures must be adopted to attain the goal of lowering the natural population growth rate to 1 percent."[14] In September 1980 the Central Committee issued "An Open Letter to All Party Members and League Members on the Issue of Controlling Population Growth in Our Country," in which it said, "The State Council has called on the people of the whole country to strive to keep our population under 1.2 billion at the end of this century and has advocated that a married couple give birth to only one child."[15] The publication of the open letter greatly enhanced the implementation of the one-child policy, and the letter itself became a directive on population control for a certain period of time.

To implement this family-planning policy, the State Birth Control Commission was formed in March 1981. Family-planning institutions in cities, urban neighborhoods, counties, and towns were set up with full-time cadres to do the work. The women's federations joined the State Birth Control Commission in advising women to have only one child. Thus a nationwide family-planning network reaching from the central government to the grass roots was established, and contraceptive devices and drugs, as well as sterilization operations and abortions, were made available free of charge. (After 1987 a nominal charge was levied for these goods and services.) The success of these policies can be seen in the decline in the average number of children born to a woman throughout her reproductive life—from 5.8 in 1970 to 2.3 in 1984.[16]

The success of family planning in China is felt beyond its borders, as well as within the country. If we take the birthrate in 1970 as standard, we can estimate that about 200 million fewer births took place from 1970 to 1987 than if family planning had not been instituted. This reduction in births meant that the date when China's population reached 1.1 billion was delayed by five years. This delay meant that the date when the population of Asia reached 3 billion was postponed for four years and the date when the population of the world reached 5 billion was postponed for two years.

Family planning has also had a positive influence on women, who shoulder the special task of reproducing humanity. The All-China Women's Federation heard many of the complaints that women voiced about the effects of giving birth too often or without adequate spacing—effects on child and maternal health, on women's opportunities for work and study, and on family finances. In 1955 the federation distributed a publication titled "Notice on Family Planning" in which the health benefits of birth control for mothers and children were described and birth control was treated as an issue "to be decided by oneself, not by others."[17] The purpose of family planning was to allow women to have fewer but healthier offspring, thus liberating women from excessive domestic responsibilities so that they would have more time and energy to engage in work beneficial to society and so that they could promote their own social position.

Since 1980 family planning in China has been compulsory. For a married couple perhaps having only one child is not ideal. But for China this policy is necessary, and in cities it is largely successful. In 1989, in Beijing, Tianjin, and Shanghai 98 percent of all couples had only one child.[18]

It is, however, still difficult to implement the one-child policy in rural areas. About 80 percent of the population live in the countryside, where agricultural labor still depends on many hands and where health and social services are not widespread. The death rate of children is often high, especially in remote regions. Peasants understandably fear that having only one child may actually mean having no offspring. Even having one child cannot guarantee that a family will have adequate safeguards against penury in old age or in case of disability. Because sons traditionally provide these safeguards, the one-child family seems a special hardship to peasants. The forces working against family planning in the countryside are consequently very strong. Although city dwellers rarely have a second child these days, rural couples frequently have two or even three children. Data from the State Statistics Bureau show that 17 percent of the total number of births in rural areas in 1986 occurred in families with at least two children.[19]

In 1984, in view of the realities of rural life, the central government suggested "opening a small hole but stopping the gap" to improve family planning policy. This policy permits the 10 to 20 percent of the masses for whom the one-child policy will cause real hardship to have two children. Even so, enforcing family planning is difficult in rural areas. Lots of parents do not register subsequent children. On 30 June 1988 the *People's Daily* reported that about 1 million children—called "black children"—were unregistered.[20]

Another factor influencing some couples' willingness to have more than the one allotted child is the strong cultural preference for boys. To have a boy, some couples not only secretly exceed the quota but even get rid of baby girls. The death rate of baby girls in rural areas is conspicuously œigh. Furthermore, the ratio of boys to girls is increasing in the youngest groups in the population. In 1989 the ratio of boys to girls from newborns to four-year-olds was 108–11 to 100. Newborn boys outnumbered newborn girls by a million. If this trend continues, men will outnumber women by 10 million in ten years, and the lack of marriage partners will be critical twenty years from now.[21]

The problem of contraception has become a hidden trouble for married women of childbearing age because of the one-child policy. Contraceptive failures affect their physical and mental health, their work, and their lives. There were about 10 million abortions per year nationwide

from 1971 to 1985. A study of 90 mothers associated with one workplace found that 73 women had had abortions to remedy birth-control failures, and 39 of these had had three or more abortions. What is more, 4 women had had eight operations each, and 12 had had two operations within one year. The women in the study also had serious gynecological diseases: 63 women experienced inflammation of the uterus, blisters, or tumors.[22] In rural areas where medical services and supplies are short, the situation is even worse, and women suffer greatly.

WOMEN AND EMPLOYMENT

The legislative principle of equality of the sexes established by the socialist system in China is embodied in the policy of equal pay for equal work. Under the protection of this policy, the broad masses of Chinese women march out from their families and engage in all kinds of social and economic activities together with men. Women are found in every occupational category but predominate in agricultural, service, and commercial work, as the table shows. The figures indicate women's importance in the economic development of China. But we must also note that almost four-fifths of all women are employed in agricultural production, the basic characteristic of which is manual labor. In technical and professional jobs (and in other skilled occupations) women are a minority. The deployment of women's labor is clearly irrational.

The employment conditions of women in cities and the countryside reflect the huge differences between urban and rural life and between industry and agriculture. Before 1978 collective ownership was practiced in the countryside, and the production team was the basic accounting unit, which meant that all means of production and all products were possessed, allocated, and used by the production team. Throughout China the principle "to each according to her or his labor" was applied in appraising work and allotting work points and therefore in deciding upon payment.[23] Rural workers, however, not only received lower pay than urban workers but also

Kinds of Jobs	Percentage of Women Employed in Each Sector	Percentage of Women's Employment Accounted for by Each Sector
Professionals & technicians	38.2	4.4
Leading cadres	10.4	0.4
Clerks, etc.	24.4	0.7
Commercial workers	46.1	1.9
Service workers	47.1	2.4
Agricultural and related workers	46.8	77.1
Factory and transportation workers	35.4	13.0
Other workers	41.6	0.1
All sectors (weighted average)	43.7	

Source: Population Study Center of the Chinese Academy of Social Sciences, *Almanac of China's Population, 1986* (in Chinese) (Beijing: Beijing Publishing House Social Science Documents, 1987), 170.

Notes: Extra-organizational workers are not included in employment statistics. Percentages are rounded to the nearest tenth of a percent.

received no labor insurance and few of the material benefits stipulated by the state. Production teams in the vast countryside were unable to provide the necessities of life for their laborers when they were old, sick, or disabled. Nor, under the strict control of census registration, could peasants easily leave their native villages to win better employment in the cities. Women in rural areas were entitled to the same social rights as men and urban women, but they never enjoyed such rights: although classified as employed, they were in fact often unemployed. They got no fundamental protection against such life crises as old age and sickness.

Since 1978, China has reformed its economy, putting a system of responsibility production into wide use in rural areas.[24] By the end of 1982, more than 90 percent of all production teams employed the responsibility system, under which a worker is responsible for the output of the con-

tracted work and workers' wages depend on the completion of contracted work. Families with a contract responsibility to a team made up 70 percent of the total agricultural households. Under this reform, land and other important means of production belong to the production team, but management and operations are carried out by households—a change that has greatly stimulated the labor enthusiasm of the peasants.

The move from collective to individual responsibility has made the surplus population issue even more striking. According to some estimates, the surplus labor force in rural areas amounts to 100 million to 250 million persons.[25] About 30 million surplus workers, mostly men, have already been transferred to new realms of production.[26] These men rushed to enterprises operated by towns and villages to seek new ways of life while the women remained on the land and managed agricultural production. The effects of changes in production policies and migration patterns can be seen in an investigation of 4,700 peasants in 1,100 households in three townships in Fuguo County, Henan Province. The researchers found that the division of labor in rural areas has been changing. The agricultural laborers are mainly women; in contrast, 70 percent of the men are engaged in communication, transportation, handicraft production, or production for export.[27]

Managing agricultural production in their own families has brought many of women's talents into full play. Women engage not only in agricultural work but also in sidelines, such as specialty crops or livestock. They even separate some sidelines from general family agriculture and become professional pig or chicken farmers. In 1988 a third of all the households that specialized in raising pigs or chickens had women directing the efforts. These women worked hard to earn money and improve their lives. They craved a stable life and wanted to modernize the countryside with their own hands.

City women have a different place in the labor force. Guaranteed employment, an enormous group of employed urban women has gradually formed in the 40 years since the establishment of the New China. According to figures from the Statistics Bureau, 82 percent of all urban women between 16 and 54 were employed in 1986.[28]

Workers in urban state-owned and collective enterprises enjoy similar labor insurance and material benefits. Until the late 1980s the state recruited workers; and once recruited, each worker had access to the "iron rice bowl," or government guarantees that basic needs would be met. The unit employing a worker had no power to dismiss him or her. Wages were egalitarian, with little difference between wage grades no matter how skilled or unskilled the work was or how well or badly a worker performed. Equal pay for equal work was the law. Over the last 30 years the defects of "eating from one big pot" have become even more obvious, especially in regard to women's employment.

These egalitarian policies came face to face with the differences between women's and men's responsibilities for childbearing, child care, and domestic life. Although the extensive employment of women enables them to go into society, it does not lighten their heavy burden of housework. Wage employment does not emancipate women from their families; rather, it adds to the work to be done. Household appliances are not technologically advanced, and social services are rare, so not only women but men, too, must devote lots of time and energy to housework. On workdays men and women might spend from three to five hours doing household chores. Sunday was originally intended to be a day of rest, but in some Chinese cities Sunday has become housework day, with men spending six to eight hours and women as many as eight to nine hours on domestic tasks. They wash the week's laundry, clean out storage spaces and vegetable cellars, line up at the grain store to stock up for the week, line up elsewhere around town to buy those hard-to-get items, or take care of other chores. The common saying "uptight Saturdays, fighting Sundays, exhausted Mondays" vividly describes this situation.

Nearly 73 percent of the women workers surveyed in seven cities in 1988 said that their primary motive for working was the economic well-being of their families. Low wages and guaranteed employment, along with equal pay for equal work, have shaped the structure of family income, making equal dedication to work from both husband and wife necessary for family well-being. (The sex stratification of the labor force means that women often make at least 15 percent less than their husbands, however.)[29] If a woman resigns from her job, she endangers the family's standard of living. Chinese women therefore have to clench their teeth and take up strenuous household chores after finishing their full eight-hour workday.

The status of women who work in the nonagricultural sector has been in flux since the economic reforms instituted by the Third Plenary Session of the 11th Central Committee of the party in 1978. Enterprises have been encouraged to assume sole responsibility for profits and losses by using the contract system and to pay attention to economic efficiency and productivity.[30]

The result of these changes is that women face serious competition for employment. Part of this crisis derives from the cost of female workers to enterprises. Each unit or enterprise that employs a women has to pay the wages and fees and absorb the cost of lost time associated with pregnancy, childbirth, and breast-feeding. Enterprises that employ more women have heavier costs to bear. According to a 1988 report, a woman averages 320 quota hours per month, whereas a man averages 442 quota hours. Both get the same monthly pay, but the man does 38 percent more productive work than a woman (and much less reproductive work).[31] From the employer's point of view, there is equal pay but not equal work. From the women's point of view, they have received no reasonable recompense from society as a whole for undertaking the task of reproducing the human race.

Today's crisis of employment troubles working women. Young women constitute 70 percent of those waiting for employment.[32] In 1984 the labor bureau in one county in Jiangsu Province posted a notice announcing that 351 workers would be recruited for several enterprises, including the chemical fiber industry and the Postal and Telegraph Bureau. The notice further specified that 269 of the recruits would be male and 82 female, even though almost twice as many women as men had taken the job examination.[33] One of the most extreme cases occurred in Tianjin, where at the end of 1984 it was stipulated that 97 percent of the total number of workers recruited would be men. The All-China Women's Federation protested and, after a prolonged series of arguments with the city labor bureau, succeeded in getting the percentage of women recruited raised to 20.[34]

Employed women also face a crisis. In response to the Third Plenary reforms enterprises tried at first to raise efficiency by reorganizing the workplace and listing the superfluous workers as extra-organizational personnel. Whether on the permanent roster or hired to meet special, temporary production needs, workers cannot be fired; so extra-organizational workers are furloughed at 60–70 percent of their salaries as they wait at home for new work assignments. Those listed as such are mostly women.

In 1988 the magazine *Chinese Women* initiated a discussion of the problem of women's employment that lasted for over a year. Two entirely different views were presented. One view held that China is in its preliminary stage of socialism. Given the restricted level of economic development, it is impossible to achieve sufficient employment for women. Many women workers are exhausted from doing endless housework and strenuous social labor. If women stay at home and receive 60–70 percent of their wages while they wait for a new assignment, they are rid of their tiring double day, and their work units are relieved of their economic burden, thus benefiting both the family and society. The other view held that the basic issue in achieving equality between the sexes is for women to win financial independence. For women to give up their right to employment is equivalent to giving up the right to own the property bestowed on them by the socialist economic system. Relinquishing economic independence and self-sufficiency means traveling back on the old road of dependency

and, more fundamentally, abandoning the right of political equality. According to the discussion, most people still believe that the idea of going home is unacceptable for the great majority of women, as well as for society. As we see it, the task now is to strengthen women's ability to compete, and spur society to improve all kinds of regulations and systems to create better conditions and opportunities for women to become employed. It is wrong to let women take the road back to dependency.

Members at every level of the All-China Women's Federation have worked hard to ensure women's legal rights, including equal pay for equal work and equality of employment opportunities. In 1980 the secretariat of the federation wrote to Wan Li and Peng Chong, chairman and vice-chairman of the Standing Committee of the National People's Congress, expressing disapproval of the view that working women should go home to do housework. In response, the State Council issued "Regulations on Labor Protection for Women" in July 1988, a document that provides a legal basis for preventing and remedying the special work- and home-related difficulties created by women's physiology. The regulations stipulate that "all units that are suitable for women to work in must not refuse to recruit women; must not lower the basic wages of women during pregnancy or confinement or while breastfeeding; and must not cancel their contracts."[35] The regulations also stipulate which jobs women are not permitted to take and what special allowances should be made for women during pregnancy and maternity leave and while breastfeeding.

Besides working on the labor protection regulations, the women's federation convened a large group of people interested in women's employment problems to formulate a more rational way to compensate women's maternity needs. Their preliminary policy suggestion was that all the wages and medical fees of pregnant women now paid solely by the women's work unit should be shared by the unit that employs the husband, paid from a fund collected by the enterprises, or regulated through variable taxes. These options are being tested in several cities. The final law is for the state to draft.

THE FUTURE

To a great extent, Chinese women's problems are social problems. Family planning, for instance, is not only a personal issue for married couples but also a national issue about the speed of economic development and, more important, about the future existence of the Chinese nation. The employment crisis of women reflects the social problem of surplus labor and low economic efficiency. Even the arranged and mercenary marriages in rural areas are a consequence of small-scale labor-intensive agricultural production. The future of Chinese women will be closely linked with political and economic development. For a future with equality between the sexes, Chinese women must rely on themselves to win a democratic and free political system and must use their own hands to change the backward economic features of China. This will take a very long time and will involve no miraculous changes.

NOTES

1. Editorial Department of the Encyclopedia Yearbook of China, *General Conditions in China, 1981–1983* (in Chinese) (Shanghai: Knowledge Publishing House, 1984), 1.

2. Li Xiaojiang, *The Way Out for Women* (in Chinese) (Liaoning People's Press, 1989), 97.

3. Confucius, *Jiaotesheng: Book of Rites,* in Zheng Xuan and Kong Yingda, eds., *The Thirteen Classics with Notes* (in Chinese) (Beijing: Zhonghua Publishing House, 1980), 1456.

4. Confucius, *Benming: Book of Rites,* in Dai De, ed., *Collection of Books: First Series, Book of Rites* (in Chinese) (Beijing: Zhonghua Publishing House, 1985), 220–21.

5. Fan Ye, "Heroines," in *History of Houhan Dynasty* (in Chinese) (Beijing: Zhonghua Publishing House, 1965), 2790.

6. Feng Menglong, *History of the New States* (in Chinese) (Shanghai: Classics Publishing House, 1987), 1184.

7. Shang Xiaoyun, *The Self-Restraining Personality of the Chinese People: An Analysis of the Minds of Townspeo-*

ple in a Commodity Economy (in Chinese) (Yunnan: People's Publishing House of Yunnan, 1989), 122.

8. Zhang Yanhua and Liu Zongyi, "A Large Sum of Betrothal Money Is a Heavy Burden for Peasants in Qing Liu County, Fujian Province" (in Chinese), *Women in China* 12 (December 1986): 16.

9. Women's Service Department of the All-China Women's Federation, *A Summary of How the Women's Federation Helps the Government Carry Out Marriage Law: A Collection of Documents About the Women's Movement in China,* 2 vols. (in Chinese) (Beijing: Beijing Publishing House for Chinese Women, 1987), 2:107.

10. Editorial Group of the Book, *Selected Collections of Laws and Regulations* (in Chinese) (Beijing: Law Publishing House, 1987), 182.

11. "Births Should Be Properly Controlled" (editorial) (in Chinese), *People's Daily,* 5 March 1957, p. 1.

12. Ma Yinchu, "A New Theory on Population" (in Chinese), *People's Daily,* 5 July 1957, p. 11.

13. Qiao Xiaochun and Liu Shuang, *The Overloaded Land* (in Chinese) (Truth-Seeking Publishing House and Shenyang Publishing House, 1989), 123.

14. Ibid., 124.

15. "An Open Letter to All Party Members and League Members on the Issue of Controlling Population Growth in Our Country" (in Chinese), *People's Daily,* 26 September 1980, p. 1.

16. Cai Wenmei, "Where To? China's Population," *Tomorrow* 2 (1989): 21.

17. All-China Women's Federation, "Notice about Family Planning," in *A Collection of Documents About the Women's Movement in China,* 2 vols. (in Chinese) (Beijing: Publishing House for Chinese Women, 1987), 2:224.

18. Tianjee, "History Has Left Us Little Room to Maneuver. The Future Again Sounds the Alarm: Crisis of Population Quality" (in Chinese), *Worker's Daily,* 29 April 1989, p. 4.

19. Cai Wenmei, "Where To?" 24.

20. Zhang Xinyang, "About a Million Children Have No Census Registration" (in Chinese) *People's Daily,* 30 June 1988, p. 3.

21. Ye Ling, "What a China We'll Leave to Posterity" (in Chinese), *Chinese Women's Paper,* 17 April 1989, p. 1.

22. Zheng Fabi, "The Issue of Women's Birth Control Should Not Be Overlooked" (in Chinese), *Chinese Women's Paper,* 17 October 1988, p. 4.

23. The work of a peasant is appraised and work points are allocated according to scheduled time. At the end of the year the work points of all the peasants on the production team are added together, and the production team's income is divided by that sum, giving the

value of a work point. Peasants get paid according to their number of work points.

24. Responsibility production is a system of management in which the production unit and the individual workers have joint responsibilities and rights in the process of production.

25. Zhang Xinyang, "About a Million Children," 59.

26. Editorial Department, *General Conditions in China,* 319.

27. Wang Wei and Gao Li, "Heavy Manual Work Is Done Mostly by Women; Some of Them Want to Engage in Industry and Commerce" (in Chinese), *Chinese Women's Paper,* 24 August 1988, p. 1.

28. Tie Ge and Liu Jixin, "Employment of Urban Women Reaches 82 Percent" (in Chinese), *Chinese Women's Paper,* 14 September 1987, p. 1.

29. Tang Jun, "What Makes Women Go Out of the Home" (in Chinese), *Chinese Women's Paper,* 18 July 1988, p. 3.

30. The contract system, a new way of trying to recruit workers, is a way of establishing work relations through labor contracts between the unit that employs recruits and the workers employed. Workers so recruited within the quota issued by the state are official workers. They enjoy all benefits enjoyed by the permanent employees. Because the labor contract defines the rights, responsibilities, and duties of both sides, and because the period of employment can be long or short, renewed or terminated, the contract system enables an enterprise to be flexible in its employment practices and also enables workers to be flexible in choosing jobs.

31. Zhang Yigong, "Why Enterprises Want No Women" (in Chinese), *Women in China* 2 (February 1988): 6. A quota hour is not a workhour. It is a way to calculate labor production by creating a production standard. The quota hour for each task is fixed separately, making it possible to compare different products to check the fulfillment of a production plan. For example, a turner in a certain machinery plant who finishes processing two 15-millimeter screw bolts and three matching nuts and two 22-millimeter screw bolts and one matching nut in an eight-hour day has completed tasks allotted, respectively, one-half quota hour, one quota hour, one and one-half quota hours, and two quota hours. Hence, the turner does $(2 \times 0.5) + (3 \times 1) + (2 \times 1.5) + (1 \times 2) = 9$ quota hours' work within eight workhours.

32. State Bureau of Labor, Labor Force Department, "Give Full Pay to Women's Superior Labor Power, Lay Stress on Employing Women," in *A Collection of Documents about the Women's Movement in China,* 2 vols. (in Chinese) (Beijing: Beijing Publishing House of the Chinese Women, 1987), 2:566.

33. Hong Liu, "The Tendency of Employers to Choose More Males Shouldn't Be Encouraged" (in Chinese), *People's Daily,* 26 January 1984, p. 7.

34. Emily Honig and Gail Hershatt, *Personal Voices: Chinese Women in the 1980s* (Stanford, Calif.: Stanford University Press, 1988), 245.

35. "Regulation of Labor Protection for Women Workers and Staff" (in Chinese), *Women in China* 9 (September 1988): 10.

▲ Costa Rica

POLITICS

Type of Political System: democracy
  Sovereignty: republic
  Executive-Legislative System: presidential
Type of State: unitary
Type of Party System: multiparty
Major Political Parties

Partido Unidad Social Cristiana (PUSC, or Social Christian United Party): In power since 1990; coalition of several parties. Affiliated with the Christian Democratic International. Members traditionally were opposed to the National Liberation Party, proposing a liberal economic state.

Partido Liberación Nacional (National Liberation Party): Created under the leadership of Pepe Figueres. Proposed "capitalism with responsibility," funding state institutions to influence the economic development. Member of the Socialist International.

In addition, there are many small political parties of differing ideologies and interests. Several regions have local parties, such as Cartago Agricultural Action, which have won seats in the National Assembly. Electoral support for socialist, communist, and leftist parties (such as United People, Popular Avant-Garde, and the Socialist Workers' Organization) has diminished because of internal splits and the ideological crisis in the socialist countries.

Year Women Granted Right to Vote: 1949
Year Women Granted Right to Stand for Election: 1949
Percentage of Women in the Unicameral Legislature: 12.3%[a]
Percentage of Electorate Voting for Highest Elected Office in Most Recent Election (1986): 82.2%[b]

DEMOGRAPHICS

Population: 3,015,000[c]
Percentage of Population in Urban Areas
  Overall: 44.5%
  Female: 46.4%
  Male: 42.6%
Percentage of Population Below Age 15: 36.7%
Birthrate (per 1,000 population): 29
Maternal Mortality Rate (per 100,000 live births): 24[d]
Infant Mortality Rate (per 1,000 live births): 18
Mortality Rate for Children Under Five (per 1,000 live births): 22
Average Household Size: 5.7
Mean Age at First Marriage
  Female: 21.7
  Male: 25.4
Life Expectancy
  Female: 75.7
  Male: 70.5

EDUCATION

Ratio of Female to Male Enrollment
  First-Level Education: 94
  Second-Level Education: 104
  Third-Level Education: not available
Literacy Rate[e]
  Female: 93.0%
  Male: 93.0%

ECONOMY

Gross National Product per Capita: U.S. $1,300
Percentage of Labor Force in Agriculture: 38.3%
Distribution of Agricultural Workers by Sex
  Female: 11.5%
  Male: 88.5%
Economically Active Population by Sex[f]
  Female: 21.2%
  Male: 53.9%

a. The Costa Rican legislature has 57 seats, seven of which are held by women.

b. *Tribunal Supremo de Elecciones* (Supreme Elected Tribunal) (San José, 1990, Mimeographed).

c. United Nations, *The Situation of Women 1990, Selected Indicators* (New York: United Nations, 1990).
d. Ibid.
e. Ibid.

f. Ministerio de Planificación (MIDEPLAN, Ministry of Planning), *MIDEPLAN: Estadísticas de empleo por regiones* (MIDEPLAN: Statistics of employment by region) (San José: MIDEPLAN, 1989).

With Patience and Without Blood: The Political Struggles of Costa Rican Women

MIRTA GONZÁLEZ-SUÁREZ

Costa Rica, known for its political neutrality, has built a reputation as a peaceful democratic welfare state in a politically volatile region. Sandwiched between strife-torn Nicaragua and Panama and bordered by the Pacific Ocean and the Caribbean Sea, scenically beautiful Costa Rica is one of the most stable republics in Latin America, celebrating 100 years of democracy in 1989.

Costa Rica was inhabited by Mesoamerican cultural groups (Chorotegas, Nicaraos, and Malekus) as well as by the southern Indian nations (including Borucas, Guaymíes, Cabécares, Bribrís) when the Spanish colonized the country in the seventeenth and eighteenth centuries, but diseases from abroad ravaged the small native population. Mountain ranges kept Costa Rica fairly isolated from the other distant Spanish colonies and from the colonial capital in Guatemala. Epidemics, the export of native people, and the scattering of native settlements allowed foreign values to become established in the country. The scarcity of precious metals and the small population led to an economy based on subsistence farming, which linked Costa Ricans through their feelings of isolation, solidarity, and tolerance. Constantino Láscaris, Eugenio Rodríguez, and Carlos Monge propose that this "rural democracy," based on generalized poverty, provided the historical support for Costa Rican democracy.[1]

The 3 million people who now inhabit Costa Rica are predominantly of Spanish descent; 5 percent of the population are Blacks of Jamaican ancestry, mostly concentrated in the Caribbean region; and 1 percent are natives distributed among six ethnic groups—the Malekus, Térrabas, Borucas, Guaymíes, Cabécares, and Bribrís—that settled mostly in rural areas. Spanish became the official language. Though the constitution guarantees freedom of religion, Catholicism was imposed as the dominant faith, and about 90 percent of the population define themselves as Catholics. Costa Ricans are considered to be "mild" Catholics, however, with flexible beliefs that are reflected in their moderate, tolerant, and even indifferent way of being.[2] Láscaris traces this indifference toward church doctrine to colonial times, when peasants refused to fund the church and even hid when the priests neared their homes. This contradiction is often misunderstood by foreigners, who tend to believe that being Catholic means fully accepting the papal directives. But here—as in many other Latin American countries—Catholics have developed ways to satisfy their own goals without openly opposing the church. That attitude explains the widespread acceptance of divorce, illicit sexual relations, and the bearing of children out of wedlock. On the other hand, abortion is illegal in Costa Rica and is considered unethical by most.

The economy is largely based on agriculture, with coffee, bananas, and beef constituting the major exports, though the manufacturing and government sectors have grown in recent years. During the 1970s a sharp rise in coffee prices helped fuel government spending on social programs, but economic problems related to the 1982 recession and rising oil prices have exacerbated Costa Rica's foreign debt problems, slowing the growth of the welfare state and increasing economic dependence on the United States. The development toward an economy based mainly on manufacturing for export and of a general cut in state expenses have permitted a refinancing of International Monetary Fund loans, which helped stabilize the economy but lowered the standard of living.

Since its independence from Spain in 1821, Costa Rica has maintained fairly steady development as a democracy. Under the current political system there are a president, two vice-presidents, and a 57-member unicameral Legislative Assembly. Legislators, elected to four-year terms, represent geographical areas based on a proportion of the population and are directly elected by popular vote. Costa Rican elections are huge demonstrations in which flags of the different parties are displayed in each household and schoolchildren help voters find their way through the crowd. To guard against a monopoly of power, elected officials are limited to a single term in office, though legislators may run again after being out of office for eight years. Elections are regulated by the Supreme Electoral Tribunal, an independent body of magistrates appointed by the Supreme Court of Justice to avert fraud and prevent violence during elections.

Such checks on power are the result in part of a 1948 civil war between the Partido Liberación Nacional (PLN, or National Liberation Party) and government forces over charges of fraud in the presidential election. After a three-month war the rebels won control of the government, ousting the president and instituting social and electoral reforms. True to Costa Rica's tradition of democracy, a new president was elected and a new constitution established in 1949. The constitution abolished the armed forces, nationalized the banking industry, and granted the vote to all Costa Ricans. Contrary to most countries' tradition of spending an enormous amount of their income on the military, Costa Rica opted to invest its resources in public health and educa-

tion. State involvement in these programs was defined by the creation of "autonomous institutions" that regulate such programs as social security, child care, housing, distribution of produce, and healthcare. Through these large state-run agencies—which now employ 25 percent of the population—the country has achieved the highest life expectancy, lowest infant mortality, and highest literacy rates in the region.

The president of Costa Rica since 1990 has been Rafael Angel Calderón Fournier, leader of the Partido Unidad Social Cristiana (PUSC, or Social Christian United Party), a coalition of moderately conservative groups formed in 1983. Calderón is the son of Rafael Angel Calderón Guardia, leader of the forces that fought the rebel leader José Figueres in 1948. The other major political party in Costa Rica is the PLN, the social democratic party that took power following the civil war.

The political engagement of Costa Rican women must be viewed within this context of relatively stable democracy. In such a context women have struggled patiently with a system traditionally defined and controlled by patriarchal values. Combating the notion that their activities exist only in the home, women have been active in a number of arenas and political organizations within and outside formal government. The focus of their efforts has been not only on achieving equality with men but on improving the basic living conditions of their families as well.

WOMEN'S ACTIVISM IN HISTORICAL CONTEXT

From precolonial times to the present women have been active in Costa Rican politics on matters ranging from the personal to the macrosocial. Although their participation has been systematically omitted in the historical documentation, a careful reading of the available files reveals women's involvement in public life as warriors, tribal matriarchs, community activists, and revolutionaries.[3]

Women's struggle for access to the government has required constant intervention against the power systems, which have long been considered entirely male. Because the government has a great influence on regulating everyday life, however, it is essential for democracy that all groups participate in it. It is not enough to organize and fight for women's rights; it is also important that the struggle lead to women's access to important government posts. The alternative of "not considering the state as a struggle field . . . [produces] a lack of interest in the political meaning of gender issues, as well as a limited understanding of the varied levels at which masculine power reveals itself."[4]

Costa Rican women fought their struggle to participate in politics "with patience and without blood," meaning that they were more committed to compromise and persuasion than to outright revolution. Negotiation, however, was not a distinct strategy of women but a widespread social value that Láscaris refers to as *a la tica* (the *tica*, or Costa Rican way)—a commitment to compromise without violence.

Two changes in legislation in the late eighteenth and early nineteenth centuries aided popular access to the government. The first of these was the constitution of 1869, which proclaimed primary education obligatory and free for boys and girls and reduced an 80 percent illiteracy rate in 1889 to 25 percent by 1927. A good education was considered necessary for obtaining access to the media and participating in mass discussions. Second, electoral reform in 1913 eliminated the election of representatives designated to choose the president and vice-presidents and opted for the direct vote. Even though women did not have suffrage at the time, they participated in the media by proposing their own views. Women's political participation was also promoted through the Colegio Superior de Señoritas (Girls' High School), established by the state in 1888. Although high school diplomas were not granted until 1934, and those who wanted to get into the university had to earn their degrees from the Liceo de Costa Rica (the Boys' High School), access to secondary public instruction provided an opportunity for women to meet and share points of view. In 1915 the Escuela Normal (Teachers' School) was founded in Heredia, giving women access to the teaching profession. The University of Costa Rica, which began offering classes in March 1941, was the only institution of higher education in the country for the next 35 years. Currently, about 49 percent of the students at the university are women.

It was not until 1953 that women actually voted in a national election. From the first proposal for women's suffrage in 1890 to the final legislative battle in 1949, the discussion of women's right to vote led to a questioning of their social roles, which were restricted mainly to domestic activities.[5] The primary arguments against women's right to vote as presented in the newspapers (usually by men) were that women did not have the capacity to participate in politics and that they would neglect their obligations as wives and mothers. Opponents also argued that suffrage contradicted the civil code, which stated that women must obey their husbands and thus did not possess the freedom and independence required of citizens. Most comments on suffrage were characterized by mockery and jokes, an approach that Costa Ricans often use to criticize political ideas and minimize their importance.

Those who favored women's suffrage affirmed the equal capacities of men and women and denounced the lack of training opportunities for women. One anonymous writer in the 25 January 1913 issue of *Hoja Obrera* (The Worker's Page) demanded, "Let us not wait for permission, which we shall never receive, from our exploiters in order to become associated: our emancipation must be the result of our own work as women." Her statement shows how the interests of women were viewed as distinct from any other struggle in society.

In the following years, numerous proposals for women's suffrage were made by members of the Legislative Assembly, all of whom were men. One proposal followed the restoration of democratic government after the fall of the dictatorship of the Tinoco brothers in 1920. Women had been especially active during the struggle against the dictatorship, organizing demonstrations and protests with the support of political parties and unions. During the 30-month dictatorship, popular dissatisfaction was enormous, and people became passionate. During a demonstration directed by a teacher known by the pseudonym of Carmen Lyra, the offices of the official newspaper, *La Información*, were set on fire on 13 June 1919, leading to the overthrow of the Tinoco government. Nevertheless, women were still not awarded the vote, as some opponents argued that women's struggle during the dictatorship had taken place under extraordinary circumstances and should not be the cause of drastic changes in the country's social life.[6]

In June 1920 a group from the Colegio Superior de Señoritas presented the Legislative Assembly with a new proposal regarding women's right to vote. This time women were not using intermediaries in the legislature but presenting their reforms directly. Their efforts were unsuccessful, and years later one of the members of the group, Angela Acuña, said, "We knew that our activities were still not taken seriously. Our demands were surrounded by silence with the hope of maintaining the situation as it was. Luckily, women fought with patience and without blood."[7] Two years later Acuña, Cristina Castro, and Ana Peralta represented Costa Rica at the Panamerican Women's Conference, held in New York, with the participation of Carrie Chapman Catt as president of the International League for Women's Suffrage.

The fight for women's right to vote was taken up in 1923 by Liga Feminista (Feminist League), which supported women's rights to suffrage, education, and social welfare. The organization was an autonomous group formed by members of the academic staff at the Colegio Superior de Señoritas, and the opening session was chaired by President Julio Acosta and his wife, Elena Gallegos. The league was especially active during the following three decades as popular requests for social reform increased. The influence of the socialist revolutions in Europe led to the formation of the Communist Party in 1931, which questioned the exploitation of workers. Three years later a strike against the United Fruit Company

set the stage for the approval of the *garantías sociales* (social rights) during the government of Rafael Angel Calderón Guardia. This bill provided for the eight-hour workday, the right of workers to organize in unions, and such benefits as vacations and medical assistance.

Women were openly active during this period of social reform. The Feminist League participated in the demonstration held on 15 May 1943, which was the most significant protest regarding women's right to vote, and the women's meeting of 2 August 1947, in which more than 8,000 women took part. The demonstrators met in downtown San José, the capital. They held white flags, symbolically requesting fairness in the coming elections, a demand that led to civil war a year later. After the PLN took power, an Assembly of Representatives—made up entirely of men—was charged with writing the new constitution. In June 1949 an amendment was proposed to article 10 based on a request by the National Teachers Association, an organization composed predominantly of women, to define citizenship as "the political duties and rights that pertain to all Costa Ricans, of either sex." The proposal was approved by a vote of 33 to 8. After fifty years of struggle few could express doubts about the justice of women's vote.

WOMEN'S PARTICIPATION IN ELECTIONS AND POLITICAL PARTIES

The 1953 national elections were the first to take place with the full participation of women. In these elections, three women were voted into the Legislative Assembly; they made up 7 percent of its members. This percentage decreased during the following three elections but has stabilized at 12 percent. Similar percentages are seen among town hall representatives. Voter turnout among women is 80 percent, a scant 2 percent less than men.

The electoral process requires that each party propose a full list of candidates plus substitutes in case of resignation, death, and so forth. Therefore each party must submit a list with 57 candidates, ranked by preference, plus substitutes.

Since it is unlikely that any party will get 100 percent of the votes, a candidate's position on the list indicates the probability of that candidate getting a post. Women are more likely to be substitutes or to be listed in the lower ranks. A similar situation prevails in the election of town hall representatives. Women's efforts to be included on the party lists are apparent in the gradual increase in elected substitutes—18.6 percent in 1989. This tendency might indicate that social pressure—mostly from women's groups within the party—to include women in electoral lists has grown, even though it has not been enough to get women into positions of power.

It is crucial to analyze women's position within the political parties because it is the parties that control access to government posts and thus the distribution of power. Although the lack of public documentation enormously hinders an analysis on this topic, it appears that the traditional female activity of feeding party supporters has given way to more active participation in decision making within the parties.

The PLN has shown a special interest in encouraging studies on female participation, though most of the results have been for internal use.[8] After the civil war the management of the women's organization of the PLN was directed by the wife of the candidate or president. In 1961 a department on women's issues, Secretaría de la Mujer (Secretariat of Women's Affairs), was formed, but it lasted only a year. By the end of the 1970s, Karen Olsen, the former wife of José Figueres and a member of the Legislative Assembly, had started the Acción Femenina de Evolución Social (Women's Action for Social Progress), whose main objective was to organize women and develop communities.

After the PLN lost the presidential election in 1979, a restructuring took place within the party. Since then the party's Movimiento Femenino (Women's Movement) has been governed by a permanent board of directors, though the presidency is assumed by the candidate's wife during the campaign, and the first lady is honorary president. This tradition is being challenged, and it undoubtedly will need to be changed if the next presidential candidate is a woman. The Women's Movement has had a substantial impact on the development of women's rights, especially within the party and during periods when the PLN has controlled the government.

The other major party in Costa Rica is Partido Unidad Social Cristiana (PUSC, or Social Christian United Party) which is to remain in power until 1994. PUSC has no data on its policies regarding women's participation, partly because it is a recent coalition of political groups with a wide range of ideological positions that tend toward a free-market policy and privatization of the state as opposed to state control of the main factors of the economy. In 1989, however, a National Women's Meeting took place within PUSC in preparation for the primaries. The group elected Gloria Bejarano, who later became first lady, president of the women's party organization, Frente Femenino (Women's Front). Among the tasks of the Women's Front is the restructuring of state institutions related to women and the family.

The minority parties on the left have shown a particular interest in supporting women's full participation in society. In 1931 the Communist Party became the first party to include a proposal for women's equality in its platform. Yet the stated intention of the Marxist parties has not resulted in the designation of women to the few electoral posts these parties have won (one to three representatives at the Legislative Assembly during the past 20 years). Even at the union level, where leftist parties have traditionally concentrated their efforts, men almost always occupy the more powerful positions. Internal crises in orthodox Marxism and external controversies regarding the governance of international communist organizations, particularly the Eastern bloc, have caused confusion and a lack of common projects on the left. And given that context, some women have decided to continue their struggle separately from the parties.

The participation of women within political parties so far has not led to a significant number of women appointees in important government positions. Women's goals, especially those related to grass-roots organizations, have been achieved mostly through the efforts of women's groups, which usually are supported by the few women who have gained access to state power.

WOMEN AND THE STATE IN COSTA RICA

The consciousness raised by the national and international discussion of women's issues during the U.N. Decade for Women (1976–85) was significant for Costa Rican society. Early in the decade the number of women appointed to ministry posts increased, independent of the party in power. The increase was not stable, however, and during the presidency of the PLN leader Alberto Monge (1982 to 1986), all cabinet posts were again filled by men. Currently there are two women cabinet members in the PUSC government. One minister, Elizabeth Odio, who heads the Justice Department, has always participated in the feminist movement, but the other, Aida Fishman, the minister of culture, youth and sports, reported to a journalist that she neither favored equality between the sexes nor did she consider herself a feminist.[9]

During the Women's Decade the number of women appointed by the president to the boards of the autonomous institutions also increased, though these positions were usually related to stereotyped female concerns in such organizations as the Caja Costarricense del Seguro Social (Social Security Institute), Instituto Nacional de Seguros (Costa Rican Social Insurance), Instituto Nacional sobre Alcoholismo (National Institute on Alcoholism), and the Patronato Nacional de la Infancia (Children's Supervisory Committee).

Women currently constitute 41 percent of the judges in Costa Rica, but they are concentrated in the family and criminal courts. According to statements by Tirza Bustamante, a former representative to the Legislative Assembly, these assignments reflect the stereotype that women are more knowledgeable about family issues and the reality that judges in the criminal courts earn less than those in the administrative or commercial courts.[10] On the Supreme Court of Justice, which is elected by the Legislative Assembly, there is only one female justice.

Another arena for the struggles among political parties is the state universities, where elections for executive offices often show the acceptance as well as the relevance of potential national candidates. It was not until 1988 that a female candidate ran for the rectorate of a university. Janina del Vecchio lost the election in 1988 by only three votes at the University of Costa Rica. During the campaign a series of sexist remarks were questioned and made public in the university newspaper. Although the newspaper referred to the male candidate as intelligent and popular, the female candidate was described mainly in terms of her beauty and elegance. In 1989 Rose Marie Ruiz won the election at the National University, becoming the first woman rector of a university in Costa Rica. Ruiz strongly supported the women's program at her university and in 1991 promoted it to the higher status of Institute of Women's Issues.

In the 1986 presidential election, which was won by Oscar Arias of the PLN, special attention was given for the first time to choosing a woman as vice-president. Victoria Garrón was selected for the job because of her role as a scholar who would garner wide support from women and because the main issues of the Arias administration —peace and housing—are highly valued by the female electorate. The electoral experts of the PLN linked Arias' victory to the young people and women who supported his consistent policy of pacifism.

Women have gained access to political power mostly through direct vote, not through appointments. The question remains as to whether women's access to political positions has provided real gains for women in general. On the one hand, some women's activists believe that women who do not share a feminist consciousness are usually absorbed by the dominant patriarchal scheme and thus make insignificant contributions to their own group. On the other hand, some feminist leaders believe that women who attain important government positions usually identify with pro-woman actions more easily because of their experience with discrimination.

Women's access to positions of political power in Costa Rica has been especially important to promoting feminist goals. In fact women in government ministries have been influential enough to overcome bureaucratic sluggishness and achieve changes even when those who proposed the changes have already left office. As minister of justice, Odio has helped transform the legal codes and equalize the legal rights of men and women. When initiatives are presented in the Legislative Assembly, the female members are the first to be contacted for support. Even though one representative, Norma Jiménez, was one of the heartiest opponents of the Law for Real Equality, most female members give their open support to proposals related to their gender.

Another example of the importance of women's access to government posts is the formation of the Oficina de la Mujer (Women's Bureau) in 1975 on the initiative of the minister of culture, youth and sports, Carmen Naranjo, a member of the PLN who is known for supporting women's demands. The Women's Bureau, funded by the government, in 1987 moved to larger premises and has changed its name to Centro Nacional para el Desarrollo de la Mujer y la Familia (National Center for the Development of Women and the Family). It is the base for a vast amount of activity, including promoting and consolidating women's communal groups; supporting the revision of the family, criminal, and labor codes; and formulating plans with the Ministry of Education to eliminate sexism in the schools. The center currently directs its efforts to altering attitudes and situations that prevent the full participation of all women and to encouraging national consciousness on this topic. It also funds training for women community leaders in urban and rural areas and endows activities organized by a range of grass-roots women's groups. It has a library on women's issues, which is open to the public, and it publishes research results, books, leaflets, and educational brochures. During the past few years the center has focused on three basic areas: the training and organization of women's groups, research on women's issues, and coordination of the programs that affect women in the ministries and agencies.[11]

The PUSC government attempted in 1990 to establish another state institution known as the Institute for the Family. This project, coordinated by the Women's Front of PUSC, would have restructured and united all the government agencies that deal with women and children. The plan was to incorporate into one large agency the Children's Supervisory Agency, the welfare system, the National Center for the Development of Women and the Family, and programs for peasant women, abused women, and the elderly. Feminist organizations were concerned about this change, fearing that women's issues would not be considered important within this massive institute. This criticism from grass-roots groups, as well as academics, did not go unheeded. In May 1991 First Lady Gloria Bejarano and Mary Albán, head of the National Center for the Development of Women and the Family, presented to the Legislative Assembly a proposal to create the Instituto de la Mujer (Women's Institute). That agency would have larger resources and responsibilities for women's issues than the National Center for the Development of Women and the Family.

WOMEN'S ACTIVISM OUTSIDE GOVERNMENT

The political engagement of Costa Rican women is not limited to formal government agencies. Although the number of autonomous women's organizations varies according to the definition used in data collection, the most recent research indicates that there are 154 women's organizations in Costa Rica. According to their own main goals, 140 are economic groups organized for the purpose of survival, professional associations, or assistance organizations; 12 concentrate on gender issues; 1 is primarily political; and 1 deals with human rights.[12]

The Women's Decade was of special importance in the creation of groups because it was mainly in the early 1980s that new associations of all kinds were formed. These included Colmena (Beehive), which provides information, training, and support for women; Ventana (Window), a feminist group that publishes a journal of the same name; Las Entendidas (The Knowledgeable), a lesbian rights group; Liga Internacional de Mujeres pro Paz y Libertad (Women's International League for Peace and Freedom); Asociación de Desarrollo Laboral Femenino (Women's Association for Labor Development); and Colectivo Pancha Carrasco (Pancha Carrasco Collective), organized for political and communal promotion.

The need to obtain enough resources for their families has prompted the foundation of groups organized around material survival. Even though most of these groups are formed by low-income women, they are often supported by women in better economic situations, including professionals. Access to such organizations is more difficult in rural areas, where the possibilities of communication are scarce and women have an overload of work. In urban areas the opportunity to share experiences and to organize around problems has systematically increased the number of women who struggle for housing, water, electricity, child-care centers, and healthcare. Women participate in solving problems, rebelling against stereotyped attitudes, and demonstrating that the issues of daily survival are not only "men's work." One community activist remarked that "many women work with a pick and shovel, mix cement, stack bricks, carry tiles and do all kinds of work."[13]

Because women's communal activities are so closely connected to their basic survival, some women have turned to violence to achieve their goals. Such was the case in 1983 when women and men together protested an increase in electricity rates. Entire low-income communities on the outskirts of San José refused to pay their light bills and made barricades in the streets to keep the government from cutting off power. During these demonstrations women fought openly with the police, and many were imprisoned.[14]

Women have also been active in forming self-promoted businesses, which allow them to earn an income at the same time they join with other women in making collective decisions. The 1982 economic crisis forced the establishment of self-promoting cooperatives (i.e., factories owned by the workers), mainly in the agricultural and industrial sectors. At the time, special importance was given to making clothing, which was in great demand as an export, thereby improving women's standard of living.

Even though women tried to solve the everyday problems of infrastructure and considered it important to participate in communal organizations, a survey of 156 women conducted by the National Center for the Development of Women and the Family in 1981 revealed that only 18 percent were members of an organization. One reason for this contradiction between desire and real activity was women's double shift of salaried and household work. Other drawbacks included conformism on the part of women, a lack of training in management responsibilities, and the media image of women as engaged primarily in domestic activities.

Another survey conducted in 1982 to determine the reasons for the lack of female participation on the boards of directors of different Associations of Communal Development discovered that marital status, number of children, education level, and age influenced women's ability to participate politically. Statistics showed that married women were less likely to participate than single women because wives had more housework and their husbands disapproved of outside activities; women with more children were less likely to participate; women with less education had less time to participate because of greater household duties—educated women were of a higher social class and could pay someone to do their housework; and women age 30 to 35 participated at the highest rate. In addition, women's ability to participate was limited by the persistence of sexist cultural attitudes and women's own lack of self-esteem.

Women's participation in communal and work organizations demonstrates that the struggle for social justice must address the requirements of survival at both an individual and group level. Access to the distribution of wealth is thus fundamental for state political involvement. Yet the heavy load of obligations placed on women does not allow for such extra activities as political meetings. And their economic dependence on their husbands or parents hinders women's ability to participate fully in the decision making of society.

NONGOVERNMENTAL ACTIVISM:
TWO EXAMPLES

To highlight Costa Rican women's activism in the nongovernmental arena I will examine two associations, Alianza de Mujeres Costarricenses (ACW, or Alliance of Costa Rican Women) and Centro Feminista de Información y Acción (CEFEMINA, or Feminist Center of Information and Action). The former is one of the oldest women's groups in the country, and the latter is a good example of the approach that came with the U.N. Decade for Women. Both nonprofit organizations have had an enormous impact, especially at the popular level, and base their activities primarily on voluntary work. They are funded through membership dues (the amount depends on one's income) and state or international financing of specific programs.

ACW was formed in 1952 out of the remnants of the Carmen Lyra Union of Women, which was related to the then illegal Marxist-Leninist party Vanguardia Popular (Popular Vanguard Party). Even though the ACW was an autonomous organization, many members, including a majority of blue- and white-collar workers, also supported the Popular Vanguard Party. In accordance with the ideological point of view of its members, ACW was linked directly to such popular struggles as national and international worker solidarity and the improvement of labor conditions. It also pursued improvements in such basic areas as health, housing, and child care. ACW's capacity to generate popular struggles was underscored in the 1970s when poor communities organized to defend their rights to services such as water and electricity. At the same time ACW actively supported popular movements in other Central American countries, especially during the uprising against the Somoza dictatorship in Nicaragua. One of the main aspects of the current work of ACW is a nationwide network that promotes organization, education and consciousness-raising.

During the 1980s ACW widened its areas of interest, supporting the creation of self-promoted businesses owned by women and establishing a legal and psychological counseling program. ACW provided counseling and support at the self-promoted factory Cooperativa de Costura (Seamstresses' Cooperative) in San Ramón. The cooperative began in 1987 with a group of women factory workers whose employer had fled the country without paying his employees. To prevent the company from being closed permanently the workers took over the factory and established themselves as a cooperative with 22 associates. Although the company is struggling to meet market demands given the high levels of exploitation in industry, the ability to control their own income has improved the living conditions of the workers. The women's main problem is a lack of permanent contracts for their products.

The ACW joined with university professors to conduct research on political training and analyze women's specific problems. The general tendency to use a methodology of action research or participative research in these projects frequently gave the researchers a heightened awareness of the everyday problems of women. Nevertheless, many ACW members were unwilling to call themselves feminists until 10 years ago because they felt the term overlooked the fact that women's struggle was immersed in an even larger battle for social justice.

The Popular Vanguard Party split over ideological differences in 1984, and a small group left ACW to form the Carmen Lyra Association in 1985. ACW retained most of its members, and in 1987, partly because of the national and international crisis faced by orthodox Marxism, a confrontation over the direction of the party took place. As a result, ACW decided to sever its links to any political party and to concentrate on issues directly related to women. Thus, even if women's issues up to that time had been analyzed within the context of the class struggle, contradictions related to the importance of the class struggle versus the women's struggle led to the formation of a more independent women's organization. In essence, the objectives of the organization were refocused from the perspective of class-gender to gender-class.

CEFEMINA, founded in 1981, was preceded by the Movimiento de Liberación Femenina (Women's Liberation Movement), created in 1974. The initial group, formed mainly by scholars who had studied abroad, tried to activate feminist issues in a manner similar to the experiences of North America and Europe. The issues included the right to abortion and birth control, subjects that still evoke enormous social resistance. Abortion remains one of the most difficult subjects to discuss publicly in Costa Rica. For example, a series of sex education books for secondary school students was disapproved by the Catholic bishop, Monseñor Arrieta, who demanded that he be allowed to analyze the written materials. The church has still not given its final position on this issue, and the Ministry of Public Education is not giving them to the schools as planned.

The CEFEMINA programs concentrate on supporting women from a range of socioeconomic levels. Its members help squatters get land and housing, provide therapy for battered women, and organize international and academic congresses on women's issues. CEFEMINA has participated in the organization of two university congresses on women (in 1984 and 1988) and the Fifth International Meeting on Women and Health in 1987. It has also promoted the program Woman, You Are Not Alone, a center that supports abused women. Resources for the program were raised from international donors and from the Center for the Development of Women and the Family, which provided the facilities and paid the overhead.

A highlight of CEFEMINA's work with low-income women is the Guararí Community Development Project, referred to in an internal document as "a unique experiment in low-cost housing in the crowded central valley."[15] CEFEMINA encouraged women with severe economic problems to organize to achieve their own goals. Many women joined CEFEMINA and broadened their demands, requesting not only the minimal material requirements for living but also a voice in the decision making. In this project "the government facilitates land acquisition and materials, and the beneficiaries provide the labor. To qualify for a house, a head of household needs 900 hours of credits of work done on the site, most of which will be construction work but can also include training in construction, day-care of children, helping in the communal kitchen, road cleaning and maintenance service." According to Marta Trejos, president of CEFEMINA, 69 percent of the families in Guararí are headed by women, and 87 percent of the managers of the project are women.

Guararí is part of CEFEMINA's national program of Salud Vivencial (Living Health), an approach to health services that integrates nutrition, personal and social hygiene, family planning, and prevention of disease. According to a survey conducted in 1988 by the Costa Rican Demographic Association, the areas served by the Living Health programs, including Guararí, produced higher family-planning acceptance rates than the national average.

As independent organizations, CEFEMINA and ACW are improving the living conditions of Costa Rican women while supporting women who are acting on their own behalf. Organizing these women did not lead to a form of dependency but instead helped women set their own goals and design their own ways of solving problems. Both organizations have found a way to interrelate women's rights and the class struggle, always questioning the relevancy of each aspect.

COLLABORATION BETWEEN THE ACADEMY AND THE GRASS ROOTS

The political struggle for women's rights is central to the relation between the academy and the community. Collaboration was prompted in part by the Decade for Women, during which many professional women took part in associations in search of social change and began to view their research as a vehicle for accomplishing their goals. This contact provided the means of spreading the impact of academic activities at the same time it changed the usual research process from one defined by the researchers to a more participatory model that starts with the communities' interests. In such a model, grass-roots groups are involved in choosing the research topic and collecting and analyzing data. Neither theoretical nor topical academic priorities are established aprioristically; they generally are based on the concerns and circumstances of grass-roots groups.

Through such collaboration women from different socioeconomic and education levels have been able to identify their common problems. In turn, the opportunity to share information has led to a continuous exchange between universities and women's organizations.[16] In addition to increasing the popular sector's level of political development, participative, action-oriented research has prompted calls for the inclusion of women's studies in the universities. Gender studies centers were formed in the two major state universities in 1987, as well as in the coordinating agencies for Latin American higher education: Confederación de la Educación Superior Centroamericana (Confederation of Central American Universities) and Facultad Latinoamericana de Ciencias Sociales (FLASCO, or Latin American College of Social Sciences).

The research conducted by women has in general encouraged the consideration of women as active beings, not simply as subjects, and has challenged the accuracy of public documents that systematically deny women's active participation in society. The recovery of women as participants in history does not constitute a mere academic interest, however, but transcends it, valorizing women's group experience accumulated over the years. It is in this sense that the combination of efforts by women with different ideologies allowed a more rapid advance toward real equality.

THE LAW FOR REAL EQUALITY

An important manifestation of the collaboration among women was the battle for passage of the Law for Real Equality. The issue of equality in participation in government was one on which people from different social and cultural backgrounds could unite. From 1988 to 1990 one of the main activities of the National Center for the Development of Women and the Family was coordinating support for the Project for Real Equality, which was being considered by the Legislative Assembly. The proposed law was presented to the assembly by former President Oscar Arias with the support of the center and many women's groups, among them CEFEMINA and ACW.

The Law for Real Equality was designed to secure gender equality not only on paper but in real life. When presented, the law included chapters on political rights, economic and social rights, sexual protection, education, and a public defender for women. Women's activists supported the law, though it was clear from the beginning that some of the articles would be controversial. The law incited a long-running discussion in the assembly and in the media, making the topic of women's rights one of the most important issues of the time.

The discussion of each article received widespread media coverage, as did the many mass demonstrations that were held. One of the largest demonstrations in Costa Rican history took place in front of the Legislative Assembly on 22 June 1988. It was organized by the National Center for the Development of Women and the Family and an organizing committee of representatives of women's organizations. Thousands of women marched through the main avenue carrying banners and calling for their rights. There were rural women with children demanding land tenure, low-income urban women advertising their housing projects, and academics wearing T-shirts that proclaimed, "I support a real equality." At the end of the year thousands of women again gathered in downtown San José, as well as in each provincial capital, for a national public meeting on the proposed law. This mobilization did not come easily. A year before the bill was presented it was sent for discussion to women's groups, which met periodically to keep up with the latest amendments. During this intense process the bill was considered not just any bill but "our bill."

Although the support from grass-roots women's organizations was impressive, getting a bill through the Legislative Assembly is not an easy task. Each law has to be discussed first in a specific committee, in this case the Comisión de Asuntos Sociales (Committee of Social Affairs). During this deliberation changes can be made; then a final version is presented to the plenary. One of the most controversial aspects of the proposed law would have established a quota system for women's political representation. The article required that the list of candidates for national and municipal offices proposed by the parties include a proportion of male and female candidates reflecting the proportion of men and women in that election district. Essentially, this was a request that half the candidates be women. Another provision said that "25 percent of the election funds must be allocated to stimulate female political participation, organization, and affiliation."

A group of lawyers argued that the proposed quota system was unconstitutional, however, restricting individual liberties and threatening the equality of society. Neither provision was approved by the Social Affairs Committee. Although few dared to voice open doubt of the justice inherent in women's participation in government, opponents argued that a quota system would privilege one group over another and that women would be elected to fill a quota, not because of their abilities.

The only female member of the committee, Norma Jiménez of PUSC, opposed the project. She viewed the law as a way of manipulating and weakening the women's struggle and said the quota system prevented women from making the necessary efforts to be elected. Some members of the ruling PLN were also opposed to the law but in a rather paternalistic fashion: they thought the law would label women as needing special assistance to accomplish as much as men.

These arguments came from a conception of a liberal state in which all members have the same opportunities, even if such equality is a utopian way of contemplating the distribution of power. In this context, accepting a quota system for women would be revolutionary, opening the door to other groups suffering discrimination—such as Blacks and natives—and therefore threatening the power structure.

Given the strong opposition, it seemed at one point as though the law would not be endorsed at all. But Margarita Penón, wife of President Arias and a strong supporter of the project, arranged a meeting with members of the Legislative Assembly to negotiate a compromise. Through her efforts and the arduous negotiation with each representative of the Legislative Assembly by Mimi Prado, then vice-minister of culture, and Marta Trejos from CEFEMINA, the law was approved, though in a very different form from the one optimistically proposed two years before.[17] While the strategy of asking for maximum benefits and then accepting lesser ones has proved an intelligent method of social negotiation, there is a certain sadness in not achieving all the goals. In this case the project has been mutilated, annulling the changes at the electoral level and leaving female participation an internal party decision. In fact the chapter on political rights has been practically eliminated, and the law was renamed the Law for the Promotion of Women's Social Equality. The law nevertheless is still referred to by its original name, something all its supporters have shared. As Macarena Barahona has pointed out, "We are far from being able to say that the Costa Rican woman enjoys the social conditions to be able to fully exercise the rights society has given her and that historically she herself has attained."[18]

PROSPECTS FOR COSTA RICAN WOMEN

The experiences of women in the Costa Rican political arena have been comprehensive. But there are some groups—Blacks, natives, and rural women—whose demands are still neglected and who still need to find the space to be heard. The creation of the Women's Institute has raised new expectations of moving closer to this goal. As often occurs in government agencies, however, state actions will depend on the level of consciousness of the directors and staff toward women's issues. Since the heads of state agencies are chosen by the ruling members of the party in power, the influence of the women's association of PUSC or PLN will be important to the success of this institute.

The current headlines on women's issues do not usually refer to the Women's Institute, however, but to the primaries of the PLN, whose candidate Penón is one of the strong hopes for the presidency. Her opponent, José María Figueres Olsen, is the son of José Figueres and Karen Olsen (a member of the Legislative Assembly). The election is the first in which a majority party may nominate a woman for president. This possibility has shaped the campaign, in which discussion on gender roles is predominant. The personalities of the candidates—with Penón portrayed as a peaceful and charming woman and Figueres Olsen as a strong man who will follow in his father's path—have led to a necessary analysis of the impact of gender stereotypes on voters. Among academic feminists, one of the main issues to consider is that the requirements for a woman candidate are more stringent than those for a man seeking the same position. Penón must prove her knowledge of state philosophy and economics at the same time that some supporters demand she become a representative not only of women but also of such minority groups as gay men and lesbians.

For the male candidates mere presence is enough for voters to assume that they are capable of assuming the presidency and representing everyone's interests. This experience shows that there are different approaches to male and female candidates and makes one consider the different symbols of power each gender has been trained to accept as natural.

Estela Quesada, a former minister of education and labor under PUSC who currently does not belong to any major party, has recently questioned the two-party political structure in Costa Rica. She has claimed in the media that minority parties have little chance to enlarge their membership because of the law that allows the parties to receive state funding in accordance with the percentage of votes they received in the last election. This means that the two major parties get an enormous amount of money to use during the election campaign.

Quesada presented an appeal to the constitutional court requesting that such funding be eliminated and began a national discussion on improving democratic conditions by granting media space to each party. This would permit the participation of smaller parties on an equal basis, but because the Legislative Assembly is controlled by the two major political parties it seems unlikely that this change will be approved. Nevertheless, the discussion on how to improve democracy by permitting more comprehensive participation in state power would benefit women who want to present their own perspective outside the mainstream of a bipartisan system.[19]

NOTES

1. Constantino Láscaris, *El Costarricense* (The Costa Rican) (San José: EDUCA, 1985); Eugenio Rodríguez, *Biografía de Costa Rica* (Biography of Costa Rica) (San José: Editorial Costa Rica, 1982); and Carlos Monge, *Historia de Costa Rica* (History of Costa Rica) (San José: Imprenta trejos, 1977).

2. Mavis Biesanz, Richard Biesanz and Karen Zubris de Biesanz, *Los Costarricenses* (The Costa Ricans) (San José: EUNED, 1979).

3. The political participation of upper-class women was mostly performed through *tertulias* (cultural gatherings in the home). In this setting the interchange of artistic and philosophical opinions rapidly led to the formation of a nucleus for subversive activities.

4. Ana Sojo, *Mujer y política: Ensayo sobre el feminismo y el sujeto popular* (Women and politics: Essay on feminism and the popular subject) (San José: DEI, 1985), 85. There is a tendency for government to interfere in private matters. For example, many women encountered difficulties in attending the International Lesbian Meeting in San José in 1990. The interior minister restricted participants' entrance to the country after being pressured by individuals and social groups, specifically the archbishop of Costa Rica, whose criti-

cism of the event was broadcast on radio and television. The restrictions were applied even though the meeting was to take place in a private villa and not in a public place.

5. For peasants, domestic activities include the unpaid agricultural work performed around the home.

6. As a legislator mentioned at the plenary, giving women the vote would "distract women from their worthy household occupations in order to have them involved in the turmoil of our politics." Quoted by Macarena Barahona, "Las luchas sufragistas de la mujer en Costa Rica, 1890–1949" (The suffragist struggles of women in Costa Rica, 1890–1949) (Thesis, Ciudad Universitaria Rodrigo Facio, 1986).

7. Angela Acuña, *La mujer costarricense a través de cuatro siglos* (The Costa Rican woman across four centuries) (San José: Imprenta Nacional, 1969), 356.

8. See, e.g., Ana Cecilia Escalante, Macarena Barahona, and Laura Guzmán, "Balance sobre la situación de la mujer en las política de Costa Rica" (Evaluation of the situation of women in politics in Costa Rica), *Seminario de Estudios de la Mujer* (September 1986): 73–86.

9. *La República,* 8 May 1990, p. 3B.

10. University Radio, 2 April 1990.

11. Nidia Morera and Cecilia Ling, "Planificación y política pública en el campo de la mujer" (Planning and public policy with respect to women), *Primer seminario nacional: Mujer, políticas públicas y desarrollo* (San José: MIDEPLAN, 1990).

12. Other researchers have found different results. In 1985, Sibille identified 175 non-governmental organizations, private groups, state organizations and international entities that have a direct relation to women's issues; a similar study conducted by Centro de Orientación Familiar (Center for Family Guidance) in 1986 found 456 groups of that kind. Mafalda Sibille, Yadira Calvo, Laura Guzmán and Elizabeth Aguilar, *Diagnóstico de la situación actual y propuesta del sistema de información para la mujer en Costa Rica* (A diagnosis of the current situation and a proposal for a system of information for women in Costa Rica) (San José: Fundacion Acción Ya, 1985). Laura Guzmán and Mafalda Sibille, "Situación de las programas, proyectos e investigaciones sobre la mujer en

Costa Rica" (The position of programs, projects, and research about women in Costa Rica), *Seminario de Estudios de la Mujer* (September 1986): 155–58. Centro de Orientación Familiar, *Inventario de Instituciones y Grupos Asociatives Femeninos* (Inventory of women's institutions and associated groups) (San José: Centro de Orientación Familiar, 1986).

13. Alfonso Aguilar Cambronero of the board of directors of the Community of Nazareno in William Vargas, "Mujeres construyen su vivienda" (Women construct their dwellings), *Aportes* (September 1988): 12.

14. This protest had such an impact that the Centro de Estudios para la Acción Social (Center for the Study for Social Action) edited a handbook about it based on information provided by 12 men, with no mention given to female participation. CEPAS, *La lucha en contra del alza de las tarifas electricas: junio 1983* (The struggle against the increase in electrical rates: June 1983) (San José: CEPAS, 1985).

15. Frances Dennis and Dulce Castleton, "Guararí Community Development Project," *Case Studies in Population and Natural Resources: Report of Field Investigations and Workshop Discussion* (San José: IVCN, World Conservation Union, 1990), 16.

16. For an example of a research-action project see Carmen María Romero, "Educación popular y problematica feminina" (Popular education and the feminine problematic), *Seminario de estudios de la mujer* (September 1986): 87–96.

17. Margarita Penón was so popular as Oscar Arias' first lady that her scores on popularity polls were even higher than the president's. She is currently running as a presidential candidate in the primaries of the PLN.

18. Macarena Barahona, *Las luchas sufragistas.*

19. I would like to thank the following people for their assistance with this chapter: Ana Elena Badilla, a member of the Centro Nacional para la Desarrollo de la Mujer y Familia (National Center for the Development of Women and the Family); Marta Trejos, president of CEFEMINA; and Teodora Tsijli, former president and member of the Alianza de Mujeres Costarricenses (Alliance of Costa Rican Women).

▲ Cuba

POLITICS

Type of Political System: state socialist
  Sovereignty: not applicable
  Executive-Legislative System: not
  applicable
Type of State: unitary
Type of Party System: one party
Major Political Parties

Partido Comunista de Cuba (Communist
Party of Cuba): Founded in 1965 as the
vanguard political party with a selective
membership; in power ever since.
Continuation of the Organizaciones
Revolucionarias Integradas, set up in 1961 to
unify various politico-military organizations of
the 1950s insurrection, which culminated in
the 1959 revolution.
Year Women Granted Right to Vote: 1934
*Year Women Granted Right to Stand for
  Election:* 1934
*Percentage of Women in the Unicameral
  Legislature:* 33.9%
*Percentage of Electorate Voting for Highest
  Elected Office in Most Recent Election:* not
  applicable

DEMOGRAPHICS

Population: 10,468,700[a]
Percentage of Population in Urban Areas
  Overall: 71.6%
  Female: 73.1%
  Male: 70.1%
Percentage of Population Below Age 15: 26.4%
Birthrate (per 1,000 population): 17
Maternal Mortality Rate (per 100,000 live
  births): 26[b]
Infant Mortality Rate (per 1,000 live births):
  11[c]
Mortality Rate for Children Under Five (per
  1,000 live births): 18

Average Household Size: 4.4
Mean Age at First Marriage
  Female: 19.9
  Male: 23.5
Life Expectancy[d]
  Female: 76.1
  Male: 72.7

EDUCATION

Ratio of Female to Male Enrollment
  First-Level Education: 89
  Second-Level Education: 102
  Third-Level Education: 123
Literacy Rate
  Female: 80.0%
  Male: 76.0%

ECONOMY

Gross National Product per Capita: U.S.
  $3,164[c]
Percentage of Labor Force in Agriculture:
  19.1%[f]
Distribution of Agricultural Workers by Sex[g]
  Female: 20.0%
  Male: 80.0%
Economically Active Population by Sex
  Female: 30.6%
  Male: 54.0%

a. State Committee for Statistics, *1988 Yearbook*
(Havana: State Committee for Statistics, 1988).
  b. Ibid.
  c. Ministry of Public Health, *Annual Report*
(Havana: Ministry of Public Health, 1990).
  d. State Committee for Statistics, *1988 Yearbook.*
  e. Ibid. Figure is for gross social product per capita
(an old Soviet indicator) in 1988 prices.
  f. Ibid.
  g. Ibid.

Revolutionizing Women, Family, and Power

JEAN STUBBS

Cuba, a Caribbean island of a little more than 10 million people, has built a political presence in the world disproportionate to its size. After a triumphant revolution in 1959 and Fidel Castro's rise to power, the nascent revolutionary government declared itself the first socialist state of the Americas in 1961; set up Communist Party rule in 1965; negotiated "favored nation" status within the Eastern European bloc in 1972; chaired the Non-Aligned Movement from 1979 to 1983; and, through its Africa policy, helped bring the United States and South Africa to the negotiating table over Angola and Namibia in 1988. After three decades of uninterrupted socialist government (and notwithstanding the demise of Eastern Europe), many forces in Cuba still fiercely defended its brand of socialism, nationalism, and internationalism, and the women's movement was strong among them.

This phenomenon can be understood only with reference to the island's history of conquest and rebellion.[1] The Spanish conquistadors all but wiped out the indigenous Indian population through battle and hard labor in the fields and mines. Slaves from Africa were brought to take their place to build a prosperous colony based on the export of coffee, tobacco, and sugar. Fear of slave emancipation and U.S. annexation held back independence, but after a protracted struggle involving armed uprising and the forming of the Cuban Revolutionary Party, Cuba was among the last of Spain's colonies to break free, in 1898.

In so doing, it became the "ripe apple" that dropped into the nearby waiting lap of the United States.[2] Twentieth-century prerevolutionary Cuba established formal political independence with all the trappings of Western democracy: an elected president, a national executive, a legislature, and parties spanning the political spectrum. But two U.S. occupations

(1898–1902 and 1906–1908) and large-scale U.S. investment in sugar and other spheres of the economy conditioned a political structure circumscribed by "the north," where since the late nineteenth century there had been a significant Cuban émigré community. Recurrent political corruption was punctuated by two dictatorships (1925–33 and 1952–58), both of which were seen as servile to U.S. interests. Each culminated in revolutionary uprisings that brought together reformist, anarchist, anarcho-syndicalist, socialist, and communist groupings under a broad patriotic, nationalist, and anti-imperialist front.

One of the least recognized facets of Cuban history is women's active part in shaping the life of their nation, including those activities more narrowly defined as political, from the abolition of slavery and the forging of nationhood to electoral politics and revolution.[3] Legendary slave women and *mambisa* (women independence fighters) who took up arms and first spoke out for women's emancipation at the 1869 Constituent Assembly, along with women in émigré revolutionary clubs, were forerunners to twentieth-century women's movements. These movements included such organizations as the more middle-class and white Comité de Sufragio Feminino (Women's Suffrage Committee, founded in 1912), Club Femenino de Cuba (Women's Club of Cuba, 1917), Federación Nacional de Asociaciones Femeninas (National Federation of Women's Associations, 1917), Partido Democrata Sufragista (Democratic Suffragette Party, 1927), and Alianza Nacional Feminista (National Feminist Alliance, 1927); the working-class, predominantly black Gremio de Despalilladoras (Tobacco Stemmers' Guild, 1923), Comité de Defensa de la Mujer Trabajadora (Working Women's Defense Committee, 1926), and Union Laborista de Mujeres (Working Women's Union, 1930); and the broader first and second National Congresses of Women (1923 and 1925) and Union Nacional de Mujeres (National Union of Women, 1934), renamed Federación de Mujeres Democraticas (Federation of Democratic Women) in 1946 and banned in 1953. Through these organizations women petitioned, formed coalitions, demonstrated in the streets, developed women's health and education programs, and used the press and radio to bring about a legal reform movement that included family, property, divorce, and labor protection laws in 1917–18; the vote for women in 1934; and, in 1940, some of the most forward-looking labor and maternity legislation, along with other provisions for women, in one of the most progressive constitutions in the hemisphere.[4]

A country with a Hispanic African heritage until the late nineteenth century, and a highly Americanized one in the twentieth, Cuba presented many contradictions in terms of race, color, and gender. By the twentieth century there was a broadly established correlation between class and color, with whites at the top end of the scale, blacks at the bottom, and those of mixed race in between. There was a roughly equal population distribution across the three color groupings, though whites were more predominant in the west and blacks in the east.[5] The Spanish Catholic tradition (a largely white, middle-class to upper-middle-class, urban phenomenon) established a rigid *casa/calle* (home/street) division, confining women to the inner spaces of the home and the sanctity of marriage. There was a marked duality of standards for men and women. But there were women of that tradition who rebelled, and for the majority of women—both white and black, whether of the city working class and slums or the peasantry and rural poor—reality was far removed from the normative, dominant ideology. Consensual unions prevailed. More than a reserve army of labor, women and children were integral to work processes and individual, family, and community survival.

Those women who considered themselves feminists and were in contact with U.S. and Latin American feminist movements were predominantly white, middle-class to upper-class women whose strength and purpose of mind did not preclude notions of femininity, motherhood, and complementarity with men; it was *marianismo* alongside *machismo*.[6] The feminists were set apart from poorer women and women of color, whose struggle was defined more along class and race lines than along gender lines. Black and mulatto women, since slave times, had rebelled against racism and discrimination. Women tobacco and garment workers had a history of staging strikes and joining labor unions.[7] Although statistics show that women accounted for no more than 17 percent of the twentieth-century, prerevolutionary labor force, women worked regularly and casually in great numbers in the extensive subcontracting system, in outwork, and in the informal sector. They were drawn into broader movements over labor issues and community survival. A coalition of women from all classes and races was brought together under the 1930s and 1950s insurrectional umbrella—the Rebel Army that included the Mariana Grajales battalion, the urban underground, and myriad support activities.[8]

THE CUBAN REVOLUTION AND ITS AFTERMATH

The 1959 revolution was one of those moments in Cuban history when high levels of unity and social cohesion were achieved. It was a period when deep regional, class, cultural, religious, and gender cleavages were subsumed in a national project, paralleling the late-nineteenth-century struggles for the abolition of slavery and for independence from Spain. The revolution combined features of political centralism and grass-roots democratization that took as much from earlier Cuban thinkers like José Martí and Antonio Maceo as from Marx, Engels, and Lenin.[9] It consolidated a corporate polity for "populist" ends, whose main ideologues were Fidel Castro and the Argentine-born Ernesto ("Che") Guevara, and which placed great emphasis on building the socialist society and the "New Man."[10] The essential ingredients of the political corporatism that evolved were a strong state and strong leadership to push through change, as well as an electoral system of government and strong mass organizations.

Within two years the revolutionary government had effected a major land reform and nationalized the greater part of the island's economic and financial structure. Such changes created a mass exodus of the propertied and professional classes but also established the basis for wiping out extremes of wealth and poverty by effecting a radical redistribution of income.[11] This, in turn, paved the way for a homogeneous middle-ground support for revolutionary change, even when the combination of internal upheaval and external reprisals, especially the U.S. trade embargo, caused shortages and a rationing system that is still in place.

The various politico-military organizations that fed into the 1950s revolutionary movement were brought together as the Organizaciones Revolucionarias Integradas (ORI, or Integrated Revolutionary Organizations) in 1961, renamed the Partido Comunista de Cuba (PCC, or Communist Party of Cuba) in 1965. Fidel Castro Ruz, who led the rebel army insurrection, became general secretary of the party, as well as president of the country. Since then Castro, the party, and the revolutionary government have spearheaded state-led socialism, with a sweeping social reform program that resulted in education, health, and nutrition indicators that have put Cuba on par with the developed world.[12]

The revolutionary government adopted mainstream socialist thinking on the "woman question." A basic tenet was sexual equality, mainly identified in Engelsian fashion. It was firmly believed that the precondition for women's equality was the destruction of private property as the basis for state and family. Women would be liberated, it was argued, through policies that would guarantee state fulfillment of basic needs (food, shelter, health, education), bring women into the public sphere on a par with men (legislation, job availability, equal pay), socialize traditional women's responsibilities such as child care, and provide sex education.[13]

The tightly knit polity that advocated this social reform program was the single-party system under Castro's charismatic leadership. An attempt to broaden the base of legal and political institutionalization in the early 1970s, however, culminated in the constitution of 1976 and a significant change in electoral government that combined multicandidate, secret-ballot, direct elections for municipal People's Power Assemblies with indirect elections for the provincial and national assemblies. Simultaneously, state administrative agencies were streamlined for more efficiency, and mass organizations were politically strengthened in terms of their own grassroots activity and by gaining representation in the party Political Bureau, the Council of State, and the People's Power Assemblies. The mass organizations included the neighborhood Comités de Defensa de la Revolución (CDRs, or Committees for the Defense of the Revolution); the national worker organization, Central de Trabajadores de Cuba (CTC, or Confederation of Cuban Trade Unions); the organization of smallholders in private (i.e., nonstate-owned) agriculture, Asociación Nacional de Agricultores Pequeños (ANAP, or National Association of Small Farmers); and the sole women's organization, Federación de Mujeres Cubanas (FMC, or Federation of Cuban Women). While this process was imbued with Marxist-Leninist notions of democratic centralism and sought ideological and political legitimacy for the revolutionary government and party, it also involved institutional channels for representation and accountability that often allowed challenges to conventional ideological and political wisdom.

The government envisioned an economic system based on decentralization, enterprise autonomy, worker participation, and residual free-market operations in an otherwise heavily state-controlled economy. These elements were encapsulated in the System of Economic Management and Planning, modeled along the lines of the Soviet reforms of 1965 and introduced in 1976. The program was stepped up after the 1980 Mariel exodus,[14] the result of a combination of political, social, and economic factors—

including what has been called the "shortage economy," which guaranteed a minimum of social and economic well-being to all through the social wage but failed to provide a choice of consumer goods.[15] The System of Economic Management and Planning was called into question under the "rectification of errors" campaign that began in 1986. This campaign called for renewed revolutionary consciousness in the face of state inefficiency, bureaucratism, and corruption on the one hand and emerging inequalities through free-market operations on the other. These problems were not acute but were perceived to be growing. The mass appeal of the rectification campaign lay in challenging political and economic elites, but its chances of success were circumscribed by international events.

Rapid radicalization of the regime in the 1960s had led to its equally rapid isolation in the Western Hemisphere. Into the vacuum left by a particularly hostile United States stepped the Soviet Union and Eastern Europe. The Cuban economy and polity were drawn into a new form of dependence, but one that was beneficial enough to allow Cuba to invest heavily at home (social investment was a case in point) and abroad.[16] Cuba supported Third World liberation movements and nonalignment, and in the 1970s and early 1980s it saw a pragmatic foreign policy encompassing growing Third World and Western (excluding U.S.) links. Such ties were not able to compensate, however, for the disruption caused by the disintegration of the Eastern bloc in the late 1980s.

The revolution's initial blend of social justice and political idealism, national liberation, and anti-imperialism had merged into a political and ideological espousal of Marxism-Leninism that took its cue from the practice of existing socialism. The political and economic shortcomings of this model began to be questioned in the mid-1980s. But while much of Eastern Europe rejected communist rule and the Soviet Union attempted to introduce economic and political liberalization, Cuba embarked on a path of "rectification" that reaffirmed socialism, rejected neoliberalism in the form of a market economy and political pluralism, and stressed nationalism and Third Worldism. Rectification, launched with the slogan *"Atención al hombre"* ("Attention to man"), was reminiscent of the 1960s New Man—referring to the primacy of people and to collective voluntarism and political consciousness in solving problems.

The Cuban leadership pointed to some obvious differences between the realities of contemporary Cuba and Eastern Europe: the relatively recent history of mass revolution, the considerable social gains of the revolution, and the strength of the mass organizations within the Cuban political structure.[17] The revolution and socialism derived great legitimacy from all three, and all three help to explain its mass support, including that among women. The history of Cuban women's struggles, the benefits accruing to women from basic needs and welfare programs, and the channels for women's participation have all contributed to this support.

FORMAL PARTICIPATION: THE FEDERATION OF CUBAN WOMEN

The channels for Cuban women's participation in politics have been varied. Although weaker in the formal political structures of party and government, women have mobilized with the population in general, from the grass roots up, in mass organizations. Women have been active in neighborhood cleaning, recycling, vigilance, and donating of blood through the local CDRs; as workers in unions affiliated with the Confederation of Cuban Trade Unions, which set up a women's section in 1969 to address the problems of women workers; as members of the National Association of Small Farmers; and as participants in the Young Communist League and various student organizations.[18] They have also mobilized through the FMC, which has worked closely with other mass organizations; a case in point is the ANAP-FMC brigades that organized women in agriculture.

Because the mass organizations are integrated into a corporate political structure based on notions of "democratic centralism" (which arguably functions more centrally than democratically), it is not always easy to differentiate the policies and actions of the grass roots from those set by the wider political agenda. Within a broad platform of social equality and justice, the party and state—the predominantly male peak of the corporate pyramid—espoused women's emancipation, pushing through policies and political change. Corporatism has to be seen as a two-way process, however.[19] Through their capacities at work and in the mass organizations women from all walks of life helped set the agenda, addressing political, developmental, and other societal considerations as they mobilized for production, education and training, health, and general welfare gains.[20]

The FMC played a vital though increasingly less exclusive role in this process. A small group of young women who had been involved in the 1950s insurrection set about rallying women en masse, and though the national leadership has tended to be professional, white, and Havana based, membership rapidly broadened across class, race, and nation, and today more than 80 percent of Cuban women over the age of 14 belong to the federation. The agenda of the federation soon went beyond enlisting the support of women for "the revolutionary cause" to lobbying the state and mass campaigning on issues of particular concern to women. Organized in a pyramidal structure reflecting that of the state, the FMC functions at the national, provincial, municipal, block, and delegation levels in urban and rural areas. It is primarily a voluntary organization, and only from the municipal level up are there paid cadres; all cadres are elected by the membership. Though initially supported by the state, it is now largely financed through membership dues.

This structure has permitted the federation to become a major force in Cuban political and social life, enabling the leadership to communicate policy decisions to the rank and file while tapping their concerns. Within its Marxist-Leninist orientation it has been essentially pragmatic, responding to issues as they arise. Major policy questions have been aired at its national congresses, to which member delegates are elected from all over the country. Prior to the congress, documents known as theses are drawn up by the national office and modified after discussion in the local organizations. The credibility and prestige of the federation were at their height in the late 1970s and early 1980s, a time of relative economic boom and flourishing political activity both nationally and internationally. Since then the economic and political downturn has been accompanied by structural constraints on the internal life of the organization and on the leaders' responsiveness to the rank and file, as well as by the failure to deliver on an ambitious program, all of which have helped sow the seeds of disillusionment and indifference. In the context of broad complaints about the functioning of the overall political structure voiced in the pre-congress debates in summer 1990, the federation came under particular criticism. Many of its constituents said the FMC was out of touch with the problems of Cuban women today, and now the federation is rethinking its political role within the theory and praxis of gender and patriarchy under socialism.

It is impossible to predict either the broad sweep of changes in Cuba or the form they might take for women. But it is a timely moment to reflect on how the issues and mobilization effort changed over the past three decades. The process can be broken into two broadly sequential but overlapping phases: the "mobilizing for revolution" and "revolution within the revolution." The strains and limitations of both are the issues most in question today.

MOBILIZING FOR REVOLUTION

In November 1959 seventy-seven Cuban women traveled to Santiago, Chile, to attend the First Latin American Congress of Women. The nucleus of women involved in this congress were to found the women's movement in Cuba under the revolution. The impetus for creating the movement came with the threat of counter-revolution in 1960 and 1961. The revolutionary government appealed to all women to join the militias and the Committees for the Defense of the Revolution. In May 1960 the Congress of Cuban Women for Latin American Liberation was held, and that August the Federation of Cuban Women was established, bringing together existing women's groups under a unified revolutionary mass organization affiliated with the Soviet-backed World Federation of Democratic Women. Membership ran to 17,000 within a few months, and by 1962, at the time of the First National Congress, there were almost 400,000 women members.

The 1962 FMC Statutes do not mention women's equality as a goal but rather emphasize "the effective and full incorporation of Cuban women from all sectors of the population in the construction of the socialist state." According to Vilma Espín, the founder and only president of the FMC, there were no clear goals at the outset except in that "the objectives we pursued were not oriented to gain partial revindications for women alone, but to unify them, and to mobilize them, so we could constitute a powerful force that could defend, support and fight for the revolution, which had by then defined its populist and anti-imperialist character."[21] Espín says it was Castro himself who asked her to form the FMC.[22] In 1977 she recalled, "I asked precisely why do we have to have a women's organization? I had never been discriminated against. I had my career as a chemical engineer. . . . I was very poorly read in politics. Fidel was different. He was much more prepared than any of us. I was only beginning to be a revolutionary."[23]

Members of the FMC went from house to house recruiting women. Beyond the more overtly political issues, mobilization centered around education, health, and child care. The Ana Betancourt Schools were set up in February 1961 to bring young peasant women from all over the island to Havana to give them sewing skills and the foundation of a broader education.[24] The FMC mobilized 100,000 women to join the volunteer brigades going out to the countryside in the National Literacy Campaign; they included young middle-class and upper-class women from the cities who were radicalized by learning first-

hand how poor rural women had to live. The federation ran adult education classes, including courses for housewives, domestics, and prostitutes, and provided training in a range of skills, from clerical work, car mechanics, agronomy, primary healthcare, and child care to political leadership. It organized women as teachers' aides and auxiliary staffers in the new primary and secondary schools, and as workers in the new health posts and day-care centers. As a result of the six-month campaign illiteracy dropped from 23 percent to less than 5 percent, and women constituted 55 percent of those who had been taught to read and write. By 1970 young women made up 55 percent of high school students and 40 percent of those in higher education. Nearly half of Cuba's medical students in the mid-1960s were women.

Federadas (women members of the FMC) also organized on a politico-military basis to defend the nascent revolution from sabotage, counter-revolutionary bands, and invasion. There was a women's platoon fighting back the Bay of Pigs invasion in 1961 and at the ready in the 1962 Missile Crisis. As men went into military service and were mobilized into agricultural work in the countryside, the rear guard comprised women in the civil defense and staffing factories, as well as in hospitals and schools, where they have predominated ever since. This was the backdrop to Cuba's hosting the All-American Congress of Women in January 1963, attending the 1963 Moscow (and 1969 Helsinki) World Congress of Women, and having observer status in the Pan African Organization of Women and the Afro-Asian Organization of Women. Two leading women from the insurrection, Melba Hernández and Haydée Santamaría, were key international figures, Hernández in the Tricontinental Movement of Asia, Africa, and the Americas, which held its first conference in Havana in 1966; and Santamaría in chairing the first conference of the Latin American Solidarity Organization in 1967. Tamara Bunke, a Cuban resident of German-Argentinean background, became a revolutionary legend, dying along with Che Guevara in the guerrilla force in Bolivia.

Throughout the 1970s the FMC did not see itself as a feminist organization: "Feminine, not feminist," Espín declared mid-decade. "We never fought for partial demands, we were always conscious that the problem of women is a part of the whole society and integrally related to the struggle of all the people for their liberation, to men and women together sweeping aside the very foundations of capitalist society to build a new life."[25]

For two decades the FMC tried to juggle the specifics of women's needs and demands within the broader framework of revolutionary change. Thus the 1975 Main Report to the second FMC Congress listed three of its main objectives: to make women aware of the value of their participation; to raise the ideological, political, and cultural level of women so that they would be able to play a role in building the new society as workers, mothers, and educators of new generations; and to raise the problems, concerns, and difficulties of women to the party and state organs, in search of solutions, in some cases material, in others legal, political, or ideological.

On the eve of the second FMC Congress in 1974 Espín said, "Total incorporation of women in the political, social and economic life of the country in conditions of equality with men has not been achieved in its entirety."[26] At the congress, party central committee members Blas Roca and Antonio Pérez discussed male attitudes toward women. In Castro's closing speech he observed that Cuba had developed a "party of men and a state of men and a government of men" and gave new meaning to the term "revolution within a revolution." All of this was taken up by the party, which attacked "backward ideas that we dragged with us from the past."[27]

Over the next decade (1975–85) the FMC developed a three-directional program: a sex education campaign designed to foster parental, especially male, responsibilities in familial and couple relationships; a campaign for the political advancement of women; a framework for the monitoring and legal arbitration of cases of discrimination against women in work placement and promotion. The campaigns were partially successful, resulting in an increasing number of women achieving leadership positions. A quota system was established for women in political office, and 22.6 percent of the National Assembly was made up of women by 1980, though the figure was considerably lower (11.5 percent) at the municipal level, and the highest levels of government continued to remain a male preserve. Women's membership in the party, which had increased from 10 percent in 1967 to 15 percent in 1974, rose to 22 percent in 1984.[28] That year, women represented some 30 percent of managers and 40 percent of assistant managers and administrators. In the trade union federation, the CTC, women held 17.7 percent of the leadership posts at the national level but more than 45 percent at the local level. Women also directed offices in government commissions on foreign relations; in constitutional and judicial affairs; in economic, scientific, and technological collaboration; in industry, construction, and building materials; and in health, ecology, culture, education and science, labor, and social security. Nora Frómeta became the first woman minister, heading the food ministry. When the labor courts started, a point was made of having 71 female judges to handle women's cases.

Participation in leadership positions was not without problems for women, however. There were negative consequences to wielding power. "A woman in power is not easily forgiven: if she makes a mistake, it's attributed to her being a woman, whereas if a man makes a mistake, it's just one of those things that happens."[29] And then there's the loneliness of women who have "made it." In the words of television and film scriptwriter Maité Vera: "The Revolution created an explosion of consciousness in Cuban women. Men had to lose some 'rights' and take on some responsibilities to even out the situation, because before men had all the rights and women had all the responsibilities. . . . Women have advanced incredibly over these past 30 years. Men have been left behind. . . . There is no correspondence, no understanding. Many women lead lonely lives."[30]

Notwithstanding these drawbacks Cuban women continued to organize. Having participated in the U.N. Commission on the Legal and Social Condition of Women, Espín became vice-president of the U.N. International Research and Training Institute for the Advancement of Women (INSTRAW). The FMC was active in many international forums and was instrumental in its support for the Intercontinental Women's Front for Latin America. Many women volunteered for the education and health brigades working abroad. When in the early 1980s the Cuban government suspected renewed threats of U.S. military intervention, a regular women's platoon was formed in the army and women were reviving the militia; there were also women among the Cuban troops abroad. For example, the women's antiaircraft artillery unit played a decisive part in the Angolan-Cuban victory over South Africa in the late 1980s.

Yet Cuban women still wonder, as Georgina Rey, head of the Havana development group, asked, "Why aren't there more women in positions of responsibility? This may sound like a declaration of principles, but I think that it is not for lack of ability and intelligence on the part of women. I think there are social conditioning factors that carry a lot of weight, for both men and women. However, I insist it is women who have to take the first step. I know extremely intelligent women, with tremendous ability, who when I have approached them about accepting a certain responsibility, have refused."[31]

Noelia Fuentes, a member of the CTC Secretariat and a National Assembly deputy since 1986, elaborated: "As women have never held key posts, at first they think the responsibility is too much. You've got to work and study a lot, spend more time than a man might, get support from people around you, listen to people with more experience. I was a union leader at the provincial level and they tried to get me on the National Executive several times. . . . I always refused, because I didn't think it would be possible for me."[32]

Rosario Fernández, a party Central Committee member who for ten years was the only woman on the 15-member CTC Secretariat, echoed this: "It hasn't been easy, I myself don't know how I've been able to do it all, but I have. . . . Progress has been made, although there is still underestimation. I would say not so much as regards ability as opportunity. . . . Men worry about women's family ties, they doubt that they will be able to meet their responsibilities in a post given the domestic problems that may come up."[33] Alejandrina Herrera, on the National Assembly since 1986, added that "I have never felt limited because of being a woman. We ourselves have to break with all those things that tie us down and educate the family in the concept of sharing domestic responsibilities."[34]

REDEFINING POLITICAL PARTICIPATION

The 1980s closed on a critical moment in the practice of socialism in Cuba, not only as experienced by policy makers or planners but in every arena of life, on the streets, and in homes. The era closed not only with the macro-level geopolitical strains and tensions of the times but, where women were concerned, with an arguably reinforced patriarchal state power and a potentially more democratic family in crisis.

Prior to its fifth congress in March 1990, the FMC launched a new campaign platform, from the grass roots up, around women's political promotion and the family. As with earlier campaigns, this cut into politics on every level, from the obstacles to women's advancement in the formal political structure to a reaffirmation of women's politics, family politics, and the politics of sexuality. Discussion was stymied at the congress when the FMC leadership shifted from an exciting gender agenda to one of defense and production for reasons of national political expediency. Many women accepted the policy decision at the time, though with mixed feelings, but the grass-roots work was not lost.

Defense was the operative word, however, as Cuba was coming under siege as perhaps never before in its revolutionary history. The East-West roller coaster preempted North-South dialogue, Cuba's erstwhile partners became more engrossed in an essentially Western venture of "democratization and capitalization," and the noose of a U.S.-spearheaded war of attrition through blockade and threat tightened. Many women viewed the revolution and its rectification program as a humanitarian option that, for all its contradictions, provided the basis for an alternative agenda.

The 1990 FMC Congress exemplified the complex relationship between women and the state in revolutionary Cuba. It testified to the strong identification of women with the state but also to the growing disjuncture between formal and informal politics. Looking beyond the congress, the picture was more complex still. As Cuba entered the 1990s the FMC constituency was very different from that of three decades before. The first difference was its enormous size. From a membership of about 400,000 at the first congress in 1962 it had grown to 1.9 million at its second congress in 1974; to 2.4 million at the third congress in 1980; to 2.8 million at the fourth congress in 1985; and to 3.2 million by the fifth congress in 1990. The organization had become a pro forma part of women's lives.

The second change in the FMC was in composition. Between 1974 and 1990 the percentage of housewives in the membership had dropped from 54 percent to 40 percent, whereas the percentage of women working full time in the paid work force had increased from 26 percent to almost 40 percent—and to 45 percent in Havana. In terms of 1989 work-force composition, women were overrepresented in clerical work (85 percent) and in the services (63 percent), and underrepresented in the manual trades (19 percent). They comprised 58 percent of skilled technical workers, 27 percent of managerial workers, and 57 percent of higher education students. These changes put their own strains on the organization beyond the strains and tensions of the times.

At the 1990 congress political tasks were seen to hinge on women's analysis, participation, and *concientizacion* (consciousness-raising). Again

there were no political prescriptions in the theses drawn up for discussion prior to and at the congress. The questions asked were: How do you, as a woman in Cuba today, see the FMC? What do you think needs to be done to further promote women in economic, political, and social life? How do you think the family can be revolutionized?

In effect, FMC leaders endorsed a rethinking of the organizational form and membership. They recognized that the organization influenced national policy but felt that the federation had lost its functional impetus at the local level, where change on a community, familial, or personal level had to take place. The membership included women who were pioneering new professions and those with solid political experience, as well as women on the margin of change. The FMC hoped that women would explore their commonalities and differences in women's drop-in centers and through courses in women's studies and in gender and development.

WOMEN'S EMPLOYMENT

In keeping with its commitment, the FMC was particularly interested in women's experiences in the paid labor force. The great surge in women's employment in Cuba came in 1969 during the mass drive for a 10-million-ton sugar harvest when a record 100,000 more women joined the labor force. Yet about 76 percent of those entering the work force dropped out again the same year. An FMC survey highlighted the reasons given by women: inability to cope with domestic and family chores, which were particularly laborious because of shortages of goods; lack of domestic appliances, and so on; lack of services to lighten the domestic work load; lack of economic incentives (goods were scarce, hence the money earned could buy few extras); poor working conditions; and lack of understanding on the part of managers of women's specific problems.

In 1969 Espín articulated the belief that "to the extent that women incorporate themselves into the work force, so they find realization as social beings, creating the new society together with men."[35] She was correct in that the involvement of women in social production and political life certainly developed its own impetus, wearing down some of the old prejudices. Castro extrapolated from this when he addressed the Fifth FMC Plenum in Las Villas province:

If we were to be asked what is most revolutionary about the revolution, we would have to say that it is the revolution taking place among women in our country. . . . There is within women in society a potential force and extraordinary human resource for a revolution. . . . This phenomenon of women in the revolution is a revolution within another revolution. . . . If women in our country were doubly exploited, doubly humiliated, this simply means that in a social revolution women have to be doubly revolutionary. . . . It is the social base that goes to explain Cuban women's firm support for the Revolution. . . . [But, he warned,] the conditions for women's liberation, the conditions for women's full development in society, the conditions for truly equal rights, for true equality of women and men in society, depend on the material base, on the economic and social development of the country.[36]

The burden of building the material base of the economy fell heavily on women. Rapid social change placed great strain on the family. Men and women left home to work in distant provinces; they were studying at night and doing volunteer work on weekends. An increasing number of children were away at school. Many Cuban homes were literally crumbling as construction materials were prioritized for public works. At the same time the collective marriage policy—a practice adopted in the early 1960s through which collective marriage ceremonies were performed in rural and marginal urban areas where consensual unions had prevailed—dissolved in the face of a soaring divorce rate in the 1970s and 1980s. Other concerns were the high number of teenage pregnancies and single-mother families, though the overall female fertility rate dropped below replacement level. Talk about the "crisis" of the family was heard for the first time, though Espín denied this vehemently, claiming that "the family is not in crisis but rather in the process of change," and that there are many stresses and strains, but the progression is toward a more democratic family form, one that demands greater male involvement rather than women's "return."[37]

This view had found resonance over the years, especially among working women. In the late 1960s many women workers had militantly opposed a suggested reduction of the workday for women, asserting their right to work a full day and demanding more services. They were instrumental in forming the Women's Section of the CTC in 1969 and in campaigning for more nurseries, work and school canteens, after-school programs, boarding schools, special shopping facilities for working women, labor legislation for women, and for better husbands and fathers. When the CTC held its 13th congress in 1973 under the slogan "Rights and duties of workers must go hand in hand," a leading women's magazine published an article entitled "Rights and Duties Must Go Hand in Hand in the Home, Too."[38]

The CTC Congress was grounded on the socialist principle of "to each according to his [or her] 'work'" rather than the communist principle of "to each according to his [or her] 'need'"—and work was defined as full-time paid labor. The reward system to supply scarce housing, cars, and appliances was operated mainly through the CTC and ANAP for those who were outstanding in their "work" effort. By excluding domestic labor and many other forms of work undertaken informally in society by women of the popular classes and women of color, this system contributed to the devaluation of women's labor, despite exhortations to the contrary. Since the reward system operated on an individual basis, women were at a distinct disadvantage. Most disadvantaged of all was the single working mother, but the pressure was also on couples for one person (logically the man) to excel at "work" and the other (the woman) to look after the home. This again ran counter to desired policy. The household was not recognized as being integral to the political economy or as having its own needs, interests, and values. Only now is it being recognized by the FMC leadership and in political circles that women who may not have direct economic integration into the formal work force may play a much more active part in the broader civil society than women or men who work formally.[39]

The debate on women within the trade union sector was extended to the national political arena the following year. In the 1974 trial-run People's Power elections in Matanzas province —the first experiment in electoral democracy since the 1959 revolution—only 7 percent of the nominations and 3 percent of those elected as candidates were women. An FMC survey pointed to the double day and the average 25 hours per week women spent on housework in addition to all the other demands made on them. Given the limited material development of the country and the resulting unavailability of services and labor-saving devices, housework shared among all family members—female and male, adults and children—was proposed as the revolutionary, "political" solution. As Cuban poet Milagros González put it in First Dialogue, "Where are you, spirit of man of my times . . . / You make Revolution / shirt starched / refrigerator clean / beds made / pans polished . . . / Revolution is more than / Party / Congress / Meeting."[40]

In its first lobbying campaign during the Women's Decade (1976–85) the FMC focused on discrimination against women in work placement and promotion. This was seen to be important on two counts. First, it acted as a check on the decentralization and profit mechanisms involved in the System of Economic Management and Planning, which, it was feared, would lead managers to prefer not to take on the extra liabilities of women workers given the maternity and other social benefits to which they were entitled. One of the criticisms of the system was the extent to which the profit motive had taken hold, creating a "male technocrat" syndrome of downplaying anything that might affect profits. This included a reluctance to hire women and a decrease in such provisions as child care, along with the concurrent spinoff in interpersonal relations. Then, as economic dislocation set in, women feared they would be the ones made redundant and that there might be a backlash of pushing women back into the home as a solution

to the crisis in the family—two trends later observed with perestroika in Eastern Europe.

The FMC's lobbying on discrimination issues was also important for drawing attention to the obstacles women faced when they entered nontraditional careers. One nontraditional sector to which women were recruited was construction, part of a public works and public housing drive that also mobilized thousands in volunteer brigades.

By 1980 the percentage of women in paid employment had risen to 30 percent of the work force; it reached 36 percent in 1984. In keeping with these statistics, the issue of women's participation in the work force continued to be an issue for the FMC throughout the 1980s. The draft thesis circulated for discussion prior to the fifth FMC Congress in March 1990 continued to see participation in formal, paid work as liberating, inasmuch as it opened up new horizons for women. The fruits of that labor were seen as beneficial to society as a whole. But was it fair, the document asked, that domestic responsibilities should still naturally fall to the woman? Aside from the double burden this entailed for working women, acceptance of this division of household labor led to the acceptance of women's absence from work as natural and to the preference for men when it came to training and promotion, both professional and political. For instance, by 1989 women held 35 percent of the seats on the National Assembly of People's Power and only 17 percent on the municipal assemblies, an inverse relationship to that of the trade union movement, in which women constituted 51.4 percent of local leaders (significantly higher than their work force participation). Women, however, accounted for only 11.3 percent of the leaders in management and politics.

FAMILY LIFE AND SEXUALITY

The FMC focused its political and educational campaign in 1974 and 1975 on the draft family code, the draft theses for the December 1974 second FMC Congress, the Thesis on the Full Exercise of Women's Equality for the 1975 First

Party Congress, and the 1976 constitution, which provided that "all citizens have equal rights and are subject to equal duties. . . . Discrimination because of race, color, sex or national origin is forbidden and will be punishable by law." The documents were debated fiercely in study circles, in work centers, and in mass organizations throughout the country amid a barrage of media coverage. All suggestions were recorded and voted on.

The family code was part of a wider legal overhaul involving mass discussion of new legislation in tune with a society in transition to socialism. The code defined the family as "the elementary cell of society" and was a legal prescription for greater equality within the family regarding property rights and responsibilities to be shared by family members. It was described by Blas Roca, head of the Law Studies Commission, as a contribution to the strengthening and development of the socialist family on the basis of respect and mutual help. The preamble to the code stated: "Obsolete judicial norms from the bourgeois past, which are contrary to equality and discriminatory with regard to women and children born out of wedlock, still exist in our country; these norms must be replaced by others fully in keeping with the principles of equality and the realities of our socialist society." Articles 27 and 28, stipulating shared housework and responsibilities, were among the more controversial; subsequently read to couples at marriage ceremonies, they could be legal grounds for divorce.[41] The code represented a political shift in focus from "the continuing inequality of women" at work and in the power structure, to looking more closely at the family and dual standards of morality and sexuality that "held women back." The code, therefore, had the backing of the state, but it also implied a challenge to the state.

Cuba's family code became law on 8 March 1975, International Women's Day. The code signified a return to the notion of the family as a major arena of child socialization, which had disappeared from the policy sphere in the first decade of the revolution. It also, perhaps more crucially, represented an attempt to prescribe a particular concept of family—the nuclear family—that was arguably not the dominant family type in Cuba. Moreover, sexual policy was overwhelmingly moralistic in its model of appropriate sexuality, geared more to social stability than to sexual fulfillment, with a substantial gap between sexual knowledge, behavior, and values on the one hand and policy aspirations on the other.[42] Seen in historical and contemporary perspective, the ideal family and sexual type is more of a white, middle-class to lower-middle-class phenomenon, which again raises fundamental conceptual questions concerning race, gender, social provision, and sociocultural values within a national policy prescription inscribed in revolutionary ideology. Single mothers and single-mother-headed households have only recently become a national policy concern, but they are certainly not an emerging phenomenon.[43]

Ignoring this fact in the revolutionary period has contributed to a process wherein the "nonnormative" families of the popular class and of people of color have found themselves on the margins of change. Thus, for example, single-parent households headed by women, which constitute 40 percent of total households, are overrepresented in run-down city neighborhoods. Not until the mid-1980s was self-help housing extended beyond work-center-based brigades to the community, whereby "nonworking" female heads of households stood a greater chance of contributing and also being allocated homes.[44]

Just as politics affected the family, family life affected women's participation in politics. As laid out in various FMC documents, including the theses to the 1980 and 1985 congresses, the changing consciousness of men and women on the political, work, and home fronts was viewed as an anchor in improving the status of women. Thus, the 1985 theses on the causes of women's continuing inequality in work and political advancement refer to the underestimation of women and misguided protectionism or paternalism: "In many homes there still exist archaic and profoundly unjust concepts leaving women shouldering the burden of domestic work that should be shared by family members. . . . Child care . . . is the responsibility of father and mother, *men and women are to blame for such habits continuing*" (emphasis in original).[45] The FMC took on the responsibility for social work with "problem" families and children. Violence, domestic or otherwise, was not seen as an issue, but the high proportion of teenage pregnancies, multiple abortions, and young single-mother families were singled out for special attention.[46]

The draft thesis at the fifth FMC Congress in 1990 accorded particular recognition to women in the paid work force, who are socially and politically active in the mass organization at the community level. For the 1990s the *ama de casa* (housewife) played a fundamental, voluntary, politico-ideological role at the activist grass-roots level, though, as in the case of the trade unions, women's roles diminished with their movement higher up the hierarchy of any given organizational structure. The FMC continued to see the family as the most important factor in preventing women from taking a more active political role in the running of the country at all levels. The family, it was recognized, could be extremely varied. There were nuclear, extended, and single-parent (mainly single-mother, though some single-father) families. Whatever the type, however, the brunt of household labor and care of family members, especially children, fell to women.

In seeking to ascertain women's perceptions of family life, the FMC document asked its members such personal questions as: Do your son and daughter do the same jobs at home? Does your son clean the house and wash the clothes? If he doesn't, are you not reproducing an unjust order in which this is considered women's work? Do you think you are preparing your son well for the future? Yet the document also raised wider societal concerns: Have you asked why men rarely request family leave of absence from work, even when the legislation permits, and why, when they do, hurdles are often placed in their way? How can this be changed?

WOMEN'S REPRESENTATION IN THE MEDIA

Campaigning for change inevitably involved the media and highlighted the latent tension between political project and sociocultural reality. Numerous feature films and documentaries about women have been produced for both film and television—the epic, the propagandistic, and those with a perceptive and sensitive approach to women's struggle. The first major feature was *Lucía* (1968), a three-part film dealing with women's struggle in key periods of Cuban history: an upper-class white woman embroiled in the 1868–78 First War of Independence, a working-class white woman in the 1930s revolution, and a mulatto peasant woman in the 1960s agricultural work drives. *One Way or Another* (1974) is the story of a young white middle-class teacher who goes into the barrio and a mulatto worker fighting his proletarian background. *Portrait of Teresa* (1979) is about a woman textile worker's struggle to juggle work, amateur dramatics, and family. The crunch comes when a defiant Teresa is separating from her macho husband and her mother philosophically declares: "A man is a man and a woman, a woman. Not even Fidel's going to change that." Teresa questions why "it's not the same." Other films include *Up to a Point* (1983), a film within a film about the machismo of the crew shooting a movie about machismo on the docks; *Cecilia* (1982), an interpretation of the classic nineteenth-century novel about a beautiful, poor, free mulatto woman caught up in the race web of slavery; and *María Antonia* (1990), about a twentieth-century equivalent of Cecilia.[47] Whether historical reconstruction or contemporary critique, the films were political statements on discrimination and prejudice against women but open-ended in their attempt to highlight societal contradictions in a way that invited reflection and change.

All were made by men and with an element of autobiography, except for *One Way or Another,* and even that was finished by men after the untimely death of its maker, Sara Gómez, Cuba's only woman feature filmmaker to date. With the exception of Gómez and the director of *María Antonia,* the filmmakers were also all white, a bias that was reflected in their choice of protagonists. Black women have yet to come into their own in feature films.

There are a number of women documentary makers, but the issues they address have been less overtly political and more racially heterogeneous. The subjects of these documentaries range from a mulatto woman engineer who loses her job and ends up selling homemade candies, to the training of women of varying ages, colors, and backgrounds for the volunteer militia; from black Olympic women's volleyball champions reflecting back ten years on the trauma to their bodies and personal lives, to a leading white ballerina who wrestles with her choice to have a baby and her determination to continue to dance. The films also pay homage to women internationally, from a Hollywood star to a South African civil rights fighter to a Latin American peasant leader.

In spite of the positive elements of such films and documentaries, three women authors of a 1990 study on the overall role of the media were pessimistic in their conclusions, calling on the media to become an ally of change. "The role of second fiddle is nearly always reserved for women. . . . When fictional characters come to a crossroads, the men nearly always know what to do, while women reel in a neurotic tailspin." Sociologist Marta Nuñez elaborates, citing an example from a recent popular novel: "There was one woman who was positive as a worker but a terrible mother. In fact, she despised her son. The only woman technician in the novel was wrapped up in an extramarital love affair. She was played in a very bad light, so audiences didn't like her, either. And the only professional—a doctor—had hysterical relations with her patients."[48]

Notwithstanding such critiques, the films show how rural and urban, class and race differences, in their most blatant forms, have broken down enormously, not least because of explicit state policies to that end. But differences among women, as well as between men and women, must of necessity continue to find their way into discourse and be addressed. To look at Cuban women today is to be like the camera with myriad angles, seeing women—and men—in all their contradictory strengths and weaknesses, juggling many realities.

PROSPECTS

From a gender perspective, the contemporary world crises of both socialism and capitalism demand a clarity of thought and action—pressingly so in the sphere of daily life, where democracy becomes practice rather than mere form. The collapse of "really existing socialism" in Eastern Europe has had both negative and positive implications for women. As the state has retreated from its self-designated role as "emancipator of women" to be replaced by market forces, civil society, and new political groupings, vulnerable social groups such as women are threatened by an abandoning of old commitments and a deepening of social divisions and political tensions. Women have been adversely affected as unemployment has risen and social provisions have eroded. With the quota systems gone, new groups can now form their own organizations and challenge previously limited concepts of citizenship.[49] In Cuba this has not happened. Few illusions are held about a switch to Western-style market democracy or Eastern-style perestroika-glasnost, each being seen as a potential threat to women's gains. No oppositional groupings of import have emerged within the broader political structure, either to the party or to the mass organizations; there is no rival to the FMC, feminist or otherwise.

In reflecting on existing socialism in Eastern Europe and in the Third World, what becomes most clear is that there have been enormous limitations and differences in praxis circumscribed much more by the historical, developmental, and sociocultural legacy of the countries in question than by any national political project.[50] The resurgence of ethnic and racial issues is one manifestation of having tried to subsume such issues and, so to speak, sweep them under the carpet. Another crucial area concerning women entails rethinking the Engelsian paradigm that has provided the theoretical underpinnings for state policy on "the woman question."[51] Engels's service in his time was to take the family out of the realm of timeless nature, situate it in history, and tie its evolution to changes in production. Nonetheless, his vision, like that of Marxism in general, was bound by a nineteenth-century Eurocentrism. The linear progression from barbarism to civilization had much in common with mainstream Western development thinking on modernization. The two combined in twentieth-century revolutionary experience to create serious obstacles to the depth of analysis not only on gender and patriarchy, but also on race, ethnicity, and social and cultural value systems, as class took precedence within the socialist experiment.

What has this legacy of revolutionary struggle meant for Cuban women? I leave the last word with Mavis Alvarez. She was a woman of peasant origin, mixed race, and Catholic upbringing who trained as an agronomist and economist, joined the insurrection, gave out credit and land titles in the agrarian reform, and headed the National Association of Small Farmers' agricultural extension team. "I broke into a world of men where I wasn't wanted or understood. A woman like myself is often alone with her solitude. I admire my life and respect it. I know now that I must have been a rebel among rebels."[52]

NOTES

1. There is a vast historiography on Cuba. A good general overview of the prerevolutionary twentieth century can be found in Louis Perez, *Cuba: Between Reform and Revolution* (London: Oxford University Press, 1989); for the revolutionary period see Max Azicri, *Cuba* (London: Pinter, 1988).

2. The U.S. statesman John Quincy Adams likened nineteenth-century Cuba to a "ripening apple."

3. A first general documentation of this history was produced by the Federación de Mujeres Cubanas (FMC, or Federation of Cuban Women) to mark 100 years of struggle: *La mujer en los cien años de lucha, 1868–1968* (Women in the hundred years of struggle, 1868–1968) (Havana: Communist Party of Cuba, 1968). A more recent perceptive questioning can be found in Johnetta Cole, "Women's Collective Actions in Cuba: Struggles That Continue" (Paper presented at the Mijas Conference, 1985).

4. A detailed study can be found in K. Lynn Stoner, *From the House to the Streets: The Cuban Women's Movement for Legal Reform* (Durham, N.C.: Duke University Press, 1991).

5. There were also poor whites and a sizable white working class and, conversely, wealthy mulattoes and blacks, though the last two groupings had been seriously diminished in number with the massacres of the 1843 Ladder Conspiracy and the 1912 Race War.

6. Machismo refers to male chauvinism; *marianismo* is its female equivalent. The term comes from María, the Virgin Mary.

7. On the women tobacco workers see Jean Stubbs, "Gender Constructs of Labour in Pre-Revolutionary Cuban Tobacco," *Social and Economic Studies* 37, nos. 1 and 2 (1988); and *Tobacco on the Periphery: A Case Study in Cuban Labour History* (Cambridge: Cambridge University Press, 1985). Reference to the textile workers can be found in Helen Safa, "Women, Industrialization and State Policy in Cuba" (Gainesville, Fla., 1990, Mimeographed).

8. Fidel Castro and his followers called themselves the Generation of the Centennial, the centennial being that of the birth of independence leader José Martí, a figure they much revered. The battalion was named after Mariana Grajales, a hero of the independence wars in her own right and mother of Generals Antonio and José Maceo.

9. There are 20 volumes of José Martí's political and poetic writing, and he has been the object of considerable study. A recent collection of essays is Christopher Abel and Nissa Torrents, eds., *Jose Marti, Revolutionary Democrat* (Durham, N.C.: Duke University Press, 1986). A three-volume study of Antonio Maceo is Philip S. Foner, *Antonio Maceo: The "Bronze Titan" of Cuba's Struggle for Independence* (New York: Monthly Review Press, 1977).

10. Fidel Castro, a lawyer, gave his own defense plea at the trial for the 1953 attack on the Moncada Barracks. See Martin Kenner and James Petras, eds., *Fidel Castro Speaks* (New York: Monthly Review Press, 1969). For Che Guevara's writings on the "New Man," see "Man and Socialism in Cuba" in David Deutschmann, ed., *Che Guevara and the Cuban Revolution: Writings and Speeches of Ernesto Che Guevara* (Sydney: Pathfinder, 1987).

11. The second wave of Cuban immigrants during the 1960s (the first was during the late nineteenth century) went largely to the United States and formed the basis of the wealthy Miami Cuban enclave and the influential Cuban American community.

12. The Cuban revolution has generated a wealth of studies by Cuban, Cuban American, and foreign scholars. Recent anthologies in English are Sandor Halebsky and John Kirk, eds., *Transformation and Struggle: Cuba Faces the 1990s* (New York: Praeger, 1990); and Philip Brenner, *Cuba Reader* (New York: Grove Press, 1989).

13. Crucial political options taken within this frame-

work as steps in women's march to equality in Cuba proved narrowly circumscribed developmentally and culturally, thereby excluding many women.

14. Described as the Mariel boatlift in the Western press, this exodus ran to 150,000. Subsequent studies conducted by Cubans and Cuban Americans show that Marielitos formed a cross section of Cuban society and left for a host of personal, socioeconomic, and political reasons. The Marielitos were seen in their majority as undesirables by the established exile community. Today the Cuban American community is estimated to equal one-third of the island Cuban population, and about one in three Cuban families on the island has at least one family member abroad. This made the attempted dialogue between the two communities and the family visits of the late 1970s and 1980s so important.

15. The concept of the social wage includes a broad package of state-provided services and benefits, including the free national health service and education system, social security provisions, and subsidized food and housing. This is explained in greater detail in Jean Stubbs, *Cuba: The Test of Time* (New York: Monthly Review Press, 1989).

16. The estimates vary wildly, but there is general agreement as to the beneficial nature of Soviet aid and subsidies to Cuba through the special pricing agreements on sugar and oil. It is hard to imagine that Cuba could have done much of what has been done without that relationship.

17. The importance of mass politics in Cuba is recognized by detractors as well as supporters of the Cuban revolution. For a projection of its continuing importance in a post-Castro Cuba see Jorge Domínguez, "Testimony on Cuba to the U.S. House of Representatives Subcommittee on Western Hemisphere Affairs," 30 April 1991.

18. The student organizations included Federación Estudiantil Universitaria (FEU, or Federation of University Students), Federación de Estudiantes de la Ensenanza Media (FEEM, or Federation of Secondary Students), and the younger Unión de Pioneros de Cuba (UPC, or Union of Pioneers).

19. I discuss corporatism and the corporate polity in Cuba in "State vs. Grassroots Strategies for Rural Democratization: Recent Developments among the Cuban Peasantry," *Cuban Studies,* no. 21, Spring 1991. For an account of rural women's mobilization see Jean Stubbs and Mavis Alvarez, "Women on the Agenda: The Cooperative Movement in Rural Cuba," in Carmen Diana Deere and Magdalena León, eds., *Rural Women and State Policy: Feminist Perspectives on Latin American Agricultural Development* (Boulder, Colo.: Westview, 1987); and Mavis Alvarez and Nurka Pérez, "La mujer campesina en Cuba" (Peasant women in Cuba) (Havana, 1986, Mimeographed).

20. Germaine Greer, in her chapter on Cuba in *Women: A World Report* (New York: Oxford, 1985), 271–91,

states: "In all Cuba's struggles women have been in the front line . . . The female network which contributed so much to the rebel effort was officially instituted as the Federation of Cuban Women, the FMC. . . . [Women] were to consolidate the revolution by convincing the passive and fearful that they could construct a new society . . . politicising women. . . . [Theirs] is real power, unlike the authoritarian fantasies that pass for power in most of the world. And the women of Cuba struggled for it, defined it and exercise it on their own behalf." Max Azicri in "Women's Development Through Revolutionary Mobilization," *International Journal of Women's Studies* 2, no. 1 (1981): 457, writes, "Cuban women have struggled for their emancipation, and scored substantive gains, within the parameters of a socialist society whose goals are actually prescribed by an almost all-male leadership. Consequently, the regime supports the Federation of Cuban Women and its work by encouraging, requesting, and/or inducing women to comply with modernizing policies which have been decided by the government. However, operating within the context of the revolution's egalitarian and collectivist values, the government allows and expects rank-and-file participation in the decision-making process." The primary and secondary documentation of this includes FMC Congress documents printed at the time as discussion documents, reproduced in whole or part in the press, and often later published in pamphlet or book form; the published speeches of Castro; articles in women's magazines and the popular press; and academic studies written by Cuban, Cuban American and foreign scholars. Overview accounts of the 1980s are Rita Pereira, "La mujer en Cuba: realidades y desafios" (Women in Cuba: Realities and challenges) (Paper delivered at the 30th Anniversary of the Cuban Revolution Conference, Halifax, November 1989); Virginia Domínguez, "Sex, Gender and Revolution: The Problem of Construction and the Construction of a Problem" and Marifeli Pérez-Stable, "Cuban Women and the Struggle for 'Conciencia,'" both in *Cuban Studies,* 17 (1987); Isabel Larguía and John DuMoulin, "Women's Equality and the Cuban Revolution," in June Nash and Helen Safa, eds., *Women and Change in Latin America* (South Hadley, Mass.: Bergin and Garvey, 1986); Debra Evenson, "Women's Equality in Cuba: What Difference Does a Revolution Make?" *Law and Equality: A Journal of Theory and Practice* 4, no. 2 (July 1986); *Women: A Revolution Within the Revolution* (Havana: Orbe, 1982); Elena Díaz, "La mujer y las necesidades básicas" (Women and basic necessities), *Economía y Desarrollo,* no. 64 (September–October 1981); and Lourdes Casal, "Revolution and Conciencia: Women in Cuba," in Carol Barkin and Clara Larett, eds., *Women, War, and Revolution* (New York: Holmes and Meier, 1980). Extensive interviews with Cuban women can be found in Inge Holt Seeland, *Women of Cuba* (London: Zed Books, 1983); and Margaret Randall, *Cuban Women*

Now: 20 Years Later (New York: Smyrna Press, 1981). See also Vilma Espín, *Cuban Women Confront the Future* (Melbourne: Ocean Press, 1991).

21. Quoted in *La mujer en los cien años*, 43.

22. Outside accounts acknowledge Espín's own role in the insurrection but also play on the fact that she is married to Fidel Castro's brother Raúl Castro, head of the armed forces.

23. Sally Quinn, "Vilma Espín: First Lady of the Revolution," *Washington Post*, 26 March 1977, sec. B, p. 1.

24. The schools were named after Ana Betancourt, who spoke out for women's emancipation at the 1869 Constituent Assembly.

25. Vilma Espín, *Cuban Women*, 57.

26. Vilma Espín, "La mujer como parte activa de nuestra sociedad" (Women as an active part of our society), *Cuba International*, Special Issue (November 1974): 70.

27. The 1975 congress documents are reproduced in Elizabeth Stone, *Women and the Cuban Revolution* (New York: Pathfinder, 1982).

28. Espín became an alternate member of the Politburo. Marta Deprés sat on the Council of State, whose secretary was Celia Sánchez. Digna Cires headed the Women's Affairs Bureau.

29. Patricia Grogg, "A Woman's Work," *Cuba International*, April–May 1989, 12–16, quoted in *Mujeres*, December 1984.

30. Quoted in Esther Mosak, "Helping Machismo Out," *Cuba International*, March 1989, 40–44.

31. Ibid.

32. Ibid.

33. Ibid.

34. Ibid.

35. Quoted in *La mujer en los cien años*, 78.

36. Speech reprinted in Elizabeth Stone, *Women and the Cuban Revolution*.

37. Interview with Vilma Espín in *Bohemia*, 10 March 1989, reprinted in Vilma Espín, *Cuban Women Confront the Future* (Melbourne: Ocean Press, 1991), 43.

38. For a discussion of the household in rural context see Jean Stubbs, "The Rural Household in Transition, 1940–1990," in Janet Momsen, ed., *Women and Change in the Caribbean* (London: James Currey, 1992). Given the size of the Cuban American community and mobility on the island, the split household is another understudied area.

39. I develop the point that civil society is the crucial and often-neglected arena of politics that is proving all-important in the current capitalist and socialist rollback of the state in *Cuba: The Test of Time*.

40. Included in Margaret Randall, *Breaking the Silences: An Anthology of 20th Century Poetry by Cuban Women* (Vancouver: Pulp Press, 1982). See also Nancy Morejon, *Where the Island Sleeps Like a Wing* (San Fran-

cisco: Black Scholar Press, 1985); and poems of Reina María Rodriguez in Phyllis Janik, "Reading Cuba, 1984," *Another Chicago Magazine* 13 (1985).

41. Article 27 reads: "The partners must help meet the needs of the family they have created with their marriage, each according to his or her ability and financial status. However, if one of them only contributes by working at home and caring for the children, the other partner must contribute to this support alone, without prejudice to his duty or co-operating in the above-mentioned work and care." Article 28 reads: "Both partners have the right to practice their profession or skill and they have the duty of helping each other and co-operating in order to make this possible and to study or improve their knowledge. However, they must always see to it that home life is organized in such a way that these activities are coordinated with their fulfillment of the obligations posed by this Code."

42. It was called family education policy in Cuba. For a fuller discussion see Lois Smith and Fred Padula, "Twenty Questions on Sex and Gender in Revolutionary Cuba," *Cuban Studies* 18 (1988); and Lois Smith and Alfred Padula, "Gender and Sexuality in Contemporary Cuba," in Sandor Halebsky and John Kirk, eds., *Cuba in Transition: Crisis and Transformation* (Boulder, Colo.: Westview, 1992).

43. An up-to-date account can be found in Marguerite Rosenthal, "Single Mothers in Cuba: Social Policy for an Emerging Problem," in Halebsky and Kirk, eds., *Cuba in Transition*.

44. This point is made in Jill Hamberg, "Cuban Housing Policy," in Halebsky and Kirk, eds., *Cuba in Transition;* and in Kosta Mathey, "Self-Help Housing in Cuba: A Reappraisal," ibid.

45. Draft thesis to the fourth FMC Congress, FMC Study Material, September 1984.

46. Although not seen as a major problem, there are cases of domestic violence to which oblique reference can occasionally be found in the press. One reference is "Absolute Confidence," *Granma Weekly Review* (30 August 1987) about a young woman graduating from military school who referred to her childhood as "a nightmare" of beatings and "going without." She and her brothers were taken into care after their parents left the country in 1980.

47. For a fuller description of women in Cuban feature films see *Jump Cult*, nos. 19 and 20 (1980).

48. Quoted by Gail Reed in "The Media Caught Napping," *Cuba Update* (Summer 1991), 15.

49. An analysis of this can be found in Maxine Molyneux, "The 'Woman Question' in the Age of Perestroika," *New Left Review*, no. 183 (September–October 1990). A good earlier overview is Sonia Kruks et al., eds., *Promissory Notes: Women in the Transition to Socialism* (New York: Monthly Review Press, 1989).

50. See Maxine Molyneux, "Mobilization Without Emancipation? Women's Interests, State and Revolu-

tion," in Richard Fagen et al., eds., *Transition and Development: Problems of Third World Socialism* (New York: Monthly Review Press, 1986); Maxine Molyneux, "Family Reform in Socialist Societies: The Hidden Agenda," *Feminist Review*, no. 21, 1985; and Maxine Molyneux, "Women in Socialist Societies: Problems and Theory and Practice," in Kate Young et al., eds., *Of Marriage and the Market* (London: Routledge, Kegan, and Paul, 1984).

51. For good theoretical critiques see Gayle Rubin, "The Traffic in Women," in R. Reiter, *Toward an Anthropology of Women* (New York: Monthly Review Press, 1975); and Karen Sacks, "Engels Revisited: Women, the Organisation of Production, and Private Property," in M. Rosaldo and L. Lamphere, *Women, Culture, and Society* (Stanford: Stanford University Press, 1974). For Cuba see Carolee Bengelsdorf, "On the Problem of Studying Women in Cuba," *Race and Class* 27, no. 2 (1985).

52. Quoted by Mirta Rodríguez Calderón in "Huele a tierra mojada" (Trample the wet earth), *Bohemia* (1990).

▲ Czechoslovakia (former)

POLITICS

Type of Political System: democracy
  Sovereignty: republic
  Executive-Legislative System: mixed
Type of State: federal
Type of Party System: multiparty
Major Political Parties

Občanská Demokratická Aliance (ODA, or Civic Democratic Alliance): Supports economic liberalism and resembles Western political conservatism.

Liberalně Demokratická Strana (LDS, or Liberal Democratic Party): Supports the transition from a communist to democratic political system but wants to ensure citizen participation in the process. Favors structuring the state as a union between Czechoslovakia and Slovakia or declaring the independence of both republics.

Křesťanskodemokratická Strana (KDS, or Christian Democratic Party): Strongest proponent of a market economy.

Ceskoslovenská Strana Lidová (CLS, or Czechoslovak People's Party): Small Catholic group; joined the Communist-dominated National Front in 1948. Policies have been significantly revised since 1989.[a]

National Front: Coalition of noncommunity political groups under the communist regime.

Občanské Hnutí (OH, or Civic Movement): Center party that strongly supports democratic changes being implemented in the political system.

Komunistická Strana Ceskoslovenska (KSC, or Communist Party of Czechoslovakia): Formed in 1921; the only Communist formation in Eastern Europe to operate legally before World War II.[b]

Veřejnost Proti Nasiliu (VPN, or Public Against Violence): Initially an umbrella group in Slovakia; now fragmenting into smaller parties and movements.

Krestanskodemokraticke Hnutie (KDH, or Civic Democratic Movement): Primarily active in Slovakia; developing a pro-reform stand.

Konservativní Strana–Svobodný Blok (KS-SB, or Conservative Party–Free Bloc): Right-wing, conservative party; advocates a reduction in state power and a reform program of government.

Ceskoslovenská Socialistická Strana (CSS, or Czechoslovak Socialist Party): Supporter of economic reform; advocates a stronger state role during the transition period.

Zemědělská Strana (ZS, or Agrarian Party): Represents the interests of farmers and criticizes the farm policy offered by the government.

Klub Angažovaných Nestraníků (KAN, or Club of Nonaligned Activists): Rightist party; argues for a quick transformation of the economy.

Hnutí za Ceskoslovenské Porozumění (HCP, or Movement for Czech/Slovak Accord): Advocates a unitary state and unconditional economic reform.

Leva Altraeira (LA, or Left Alternative): Supports democratic and self-governing socialism.

Romanská Občanská Iniciativa (ROI, or Romany Civic Initiative): Rightist group; emphasizes the rights of Romanies as citizens.

Romský Národní Kongres (RNK, or Romany National Congress): Center-left party; demands that Romany nationality be recognized in the constitution.

Asociace Sociálních Demokratů (ASD, or Association of Social Democrats): Advocates renewal of social democracy.

Národně Sociální Strana (NSS, or National Socialist Party): Positioning itself to be on the left of the emerging rightist block.

Hnutie za Demokratické Slovensko (HZDS, or Movement for a Democratic Slovakia): The most dominant party in Slovakia; rejects the government's economic reform program and wants a strong state role in the economy.

Komunistická Strana Cech a Moravy (KSCM, or Communist Party of Bohemia and Moravia): Considers itself to be "constructive opposition" to the current government.

Slovenska Narodna Strana (SNS, or Slovak National Party): Rejects economic and political reform under way.

Občanská Demokratická Strana (ODS, or Civic Democratic Party): A rightist, strongly anticommunist party supporting a rapid move to a market economy.

Ceskolovenská Strana Socialní Democracie (CSSD, or Czechoslovak Social Democratic Party): Reformulated from the interwar party of the same name, it was forcibly incorporated into the Communist Party in 1948. It reemerged as an independent party in 1989. Seeks a federative system based on an agreement between the two republics—the Czech Republic and Slovakia—created from the former Czechoslovakia.

Hnutí za Samosprávnou Demokracii–Společnost pro Moravu a Slezko (HSD-SMS, or Movement for a Self-Governing Democracy–Society for Moravia and Silesia): Slovak-based coalition advocating a federal setup for a state comprising three equal lands—Bohemia, Slova, and Moravia-Silesia.

Strana Zelených (SZ, or Green Party): Small, environmentally oriented party; more active in Slovakia.

Year Women Granted Right to Vote: 1920
Year Women Granted Right to Stand for Election: 1920
Percentage of Women in the Legislature
  Lower House: 25.4%[c]
  Upper House: 29.3%
Percentage of Electorate Voting for Highest Elected Office in Most Recent Election (1990): 96.0%[d]

DEMOGRAPHICS
Population: 15,671,000[e]
Percentage of Population in Urban Areas
  Overall: 74.1%
  Male: not available
  Female: not available
Percentage of Population Below Age 15: 24.5%
Birthrate (per 1,000 population): 13[f]
Maternal Mortality Rate (per 100,000 live births): 8
Infant Mortality Rate (per 1,000 live births): 13[g]
Mortality Rate for Children Under Five (per 1,000 live births): 15[h]
Average Household Size: 2.9
Mean Age at First Marriage
  Female: 21.6
  Male: 24.7
Life Expectancy
  Female: 74.3
  Male: 67.1

EDUCATION
Ratio of Female to Male Enrollment
  First-Level Education: 97
  Second-Level Education: 170
  Third-Level Education: 73
Literacy Rate
  Male: 99.0%
  Female: 99.0%

ECONOMY
Gross National Product per Capita: U.S. $5,820
Percentage of Labor Force in Agriculture: 14.0%
Distribution of Agricultural Workers by Sex
  Female: 41.0%
  Male: 59.0%
Economically Active Population by Sex
  Female: 62.1%
  Male: 77.6%

a. Arthur S. Banks, ed., *Political Handbook of the World, 1991* (Binghamton, N.Y.: CSA Publications, 1991), 175.
b. Ibid.

c. Sharon L. Wolchik, *Czechoslovakia in Transition* (New York: Pinter, 1991), 71.

d. Jan Obrman, "Civic Forum Surges to Impressive Victory," *Report on Eastern Europe,* vol. 1, no. 25 (Radio Free Europe, 22 June 1990), 13.

e. "Vzhledem kubytku" (With respect to the decline), *Lidové noviny,* 5 January 1991, p. 3, cited in Wolchik, *Czechoslovakia.*

f. *The Europa World Yearbook, 1991* (London: Europa Publications, 1991), 1:859.

g. *Social Indicators of Development, 1989* (Baltimore: Johns Hopkins University Press, 1989).

h. Ibid.

Women's Issues in Czechoslovakia in the Communist and Postcommunist Periods

SHARON L. WOLCHIK

This chapter was completed prior to the June 1992 elections, which presaged the division of Czechoslovakia into two states, the Czech Republic and the Slovak Republic, in 1993. The split of the country into two independent states will have a number of important implications for women as well as men. But change in this aspect of political structure is unlikely to have a major impact on women's opportunities for political expression and activity. Similarly, though the economic policies of the Slovak and Czech republics may diverge to some extent, women in both will face many of the same constraints and hardships.

The political system of Czechoslovakia has changed several times during the twentieth century. Part of the Austro-Hungarian Empire until World War I, the Czechoslovak Republic came into being as a unified state in 1918. The country was established as a parliamentary democracy through the efforts of such leaders of the independence movement as Tomaš G. Masaryk, who became the country's first president. In general, the postwar democracies set up in Eastern and Central Europe by the Allies to fill the vacuum created by the demise of the Austro-Hungarian Empire were quickly replaced by autocratic governments. But the Czechoslovakian democratic

government survived until World War II, when the country was invaded and dismembered.

A parliamentary system was restored in 1945 after the country was liberated. Given the proximity of Soviet troops and the fact that many prewar political parties were outlawed, the Communist Party had many advantages over its democratic opponents. But pluralistic politics continued until February 1948, when Communist Party leaders forced a crisis that led to the establishment of a government dominated by the communists. Party leaders then reoriented Czechoslovakia's political structure and values to parallel those of the Soviet Union. Except for the brief period of political reform in the late 1960s known as "Socialism with a Human Face," the communist system prevailed until November 1989.

At that time, hundreds of thousands of Czechoslovakians staged demonstrations that brought down the communist regime. Although political change came late to Czechoslovakia, the process of reestablishing democracy moved quickly once the Communist Party surrendered its leading role in late 1989. The changes in political structure and values had a major impact on the ways citizens could participate in politics and on how policies are made and implemented.

Political life in Czechoslovakia has always been shaped by the ethnic composition of the country. Conflict between the two main groups—the Czechs and the Slovaks—and the situation of the large Sudeten German minority colored the politics of the democratic interwar republic and helped lead to its breakup. The country's ethnic composition was simplified somewhat after World War II, when many Germans and Hungarians were forced to leave, but tensions between the Czechs and Slovaks continued throughout the communist period. Slovak dissatisfaction with the unitary state system adopted after 1945 and lower levels of development in Slovakia compared with the Czech Lands helped to spark the political reforms of the 1960s. Although the federalization of the political system adopted at that time survived the changes that followed the Soviet invasion of 1968, tensions between the two groups grew. With the end of censorship and the restoration of pluralistic political life, both sides have aired their grievances more openly. Conflict between Czechs and Slovaks has led to several political crises in the postcommunist period, and it continues to complicate both the writing of new constitutions for the federal and republic governments and the process of economic transformation.

Women's political roles in Czechoslovakia and the way women's issues emerge as subjects of political debate and decision have been profoundly influenced by the changing political structures and values of the state. From 1948 to late 1989 these structures and values resembled those in other communist countries. But since the demonstrations that sparked the "Velvet Revolution" ended the Communist Party's monopoly on power, the political system has undergone a radical transformation in its effort to recreate democratic political life. In this chapter I explore the impact that the organization and values of the state in both the communist and postcommunist periods have had on policy making in areas that are particularly important to women: demographic policies, employment policies, and policies regarding religious groups and practice.

CHARACTERISTICS AND IMPLICATIONS FOR POLICY MAKING

The areas on which I focus in this chapter have certain similarities that have had important implications for policy making, particularly during the communist period. In fact, the Communist Party elite eventually identified each of these areas as problematic. In each case, women were crucial to the success or failure of the policies adopted and, to varying degrees, the issues under discussion were related to other top-priority elite goals.

At the same time, the three issues differ in important ways. Although Marxist-Leninist ideology had certain implications for policy making generally, demographic and employment policies could more easily be presented as technical problems—that is, problems that required specialized expertise to resolve. Furthermore, most issues concerning demographic and employment policies were not sensitive politically in that they did not challenge the leading role of the Communist Party or contradict the tenets of Marxism-Leninism. Policies regarding religious groups and practices, however, were fundamentally related to official communist ideology.[1]

These differences influenced the number and kind of actors other than top party and government officials who helped formulate policies and, therefore, the likelihood that women's views would be considered. The kind of issue under consideration and its relation to the prevailing ideology also determined how to analyze a policy problem and the range of solutions that could be considered and adopted.[2]

From 1948 to November 1989 the way these issues emerged politically was influenced by the rule of a communist government. The system was characterized by the monopoly of power by one political party; censorship; a central planned economy; reliance on the secret police to maintain political order; subordination of government and mass organizations to the Communist Party; and prohibition of independent organizations. There was also a single official ideology: Marxism-Leninism.

The political structure and values associated with communist systems had a profound impact on all aspects of politics and policy making. They also determined the opportunities available to women, as well as other citizens, to raise issues or otherwise participate in politics. Thus, channels of political influence were more limited than in democratic political systems and access to the policy-making arena more restricted. The monopoly of power by the Communist Party meant that political recruitment was carefully controlled by a single political force. Large time commitments were required of party activists, and lengthy apprenticeships were demanded of those who sought promotion to positions of real influence. Within the party were further factors limiting women's participation in the exercise of power. Opportunities to challenge existing policy orientations or to get issues onto the political agenda from outside the party were limited, given restrictions on forming independent organizations and party control of the media, means of socialization, and culture. Neither women nor most men had many opportunities to influence policy making.[3]

Although its influence on the content of policies decreased over time, the ideology of the state shaped public issues, including those of importance to women, and how they were discussed. There was ample evidence, including survey research results released prior to the 1989 demonstrations, of widespread disaffection from Marxist-Leninist values.[4] Furthermore, ideology had ceased to serve as a guide to action or policy making for some time. Even though women's equality was officially supported by the state ideology, protected by constitutional guarantees, and reflected in certain policies that benefited women, the commitment to achieving equality was often less important than other considerations in determining policies. And the existence of an official ideology made it difficult to consider certain policies that would have contradicted the ideology.[5]

The direct political role played by women has been limited throughout the history of Czechoslovakia. Women supported the national move-

ment in the Czech Lands in the nineteenth century and were active in a variety of community organizations. They were enfranchised in 1919, soon after Czechoslovakia was created as an independent state. Individual women made crucial contributions to Czech and Slovak society during the interwar period, and most women, as well as men, were literate; educational levels approached those in the more developed Western European states. Although most of the population was nominally Roman Catholic, the lack of more restrictive religious traditions—such as those in the Muslim or Orthodox areas of the Balkans that prescribed markedly subordinate roles for women—created more favorable conditions for women's participation in public life.[6] Women also were active in a number of women's, charitable, and partisan organizations during the interwar period. But women had only a small role in the leadership of the country's many political parties, and few were elected to office.[7]

This pattern persisted after the communist system was established in Czechoslovakia in February 1948. But as a result of policies designed to further women's equality and to meet the need for change in certain women's roles so that other, higher-priority elite goals could be reached, roles changed in important ways, particularly concerning educational access and participation in paid labor outside the home increased considerably. But significant inequalities remained in both areas. Although girls and young women entered vocational or technical training in greater numbers than before, most continued to choose or be channeled into fields considered appropriate for women or into medicine, which was feminized after 1948. Differences in educational specialization were in turn reflected in occupational segregation in the labor force, in the lower wages that women received, and in the small numbers of women chosen to fill top economic positions.[8]

There was little change in women's exercise of political power during the communist period. Though women were exposed to more political information than previously, and many rural women were drawn into the national political community for the first time, women played a far smaller role than men in the effective exercise of political power. As the 99 percent voter turnout figures that were common for elections during the communist period attest, the vast majority of eligible women and men voted in the single-slate manipulated elections. And women also participated in other symbolic political activities designed to demonstrate support for the regime. They were mobilized to demonstrate on major holidays, required to participate in "volunteer" labor brigades, and encouraged to attend citizens' meetings. Women were well represented among the symbolic governmental elites, but at the mass level they were less likely than men to be members of the Communist Party, despite the growth in their educational and employment opportunities.[9]

Women were rarely found among the leaders of the Communist Party at any level, but their representation in party membership and leadership was greatest just before and after the communists took power.[10] As the Stalinist system was consolidated, the number of women leaders decreased. The women leaders in both the government and the party also tended to differ from their male counterparts in terms of social backgrounds and career routes, as well as in tenure and turnover rates. Women legislators, for example, were far more likely to be workers or peasants than were the men, who were largely drawn from party and government ranks. Women in party leadership were more likely than male leaders to have had careers with such mass organizations as the trade unions and women's organizations.[11]

Women were also less likely than men to participate in unauthorized activities or to become dissidents in the communist period. But in contrast to the situation in Poland, for example, where few women held leadership positions in Solidarity, women were represented in the leadership of Charter 77, the main dissident organization. The group, founded in 1977, played an important role in keeping independent thought alive in the last decade of communist rule. Charter activists provided the core of those who formed Civic Forum, the organization that led the spontaneous demonstrations that toppled the Communist Party. Many women signed the charter, and one of the group's spokespersons was always a woman. Although the charter did not devote a great deal of attention to issues directly related to women's status, its documents reaffirmed the principles of women's equality and right to work.[12]

Women became somewhat more active in dissent in the last years of communist rule. Young women, in particular, emerged as leaders of several of the independent groups that formed between 1987 and 1989 and took the lead, along with their male counterparts, in organizing demonstrations to mark significant anniversaries or to protest regime actions.[13]

With the fall of communism, the policy-making process has changed fundamentally. There are now numerous channels through which citizens may articulate their interests, voice political views and demands, organize with others of similar perspectives, and pressure political leaders to take action. The existence of a free press, the end of the political control of culture by one party, and the reemergence of a private sector in the economy have further increased the opportunities for independent political action.[14]

Nonetheless, women's direct role in policy making as political leaders or citizens continues to be modest. Women professionals who had pushed for reform from within the system, accompanied by dissident writers, artists, and others who had been unable to work because of their political activities or involvement with the reforms of 1968, were actively involved in forming Civic Forum in the Czech Lands and Public Against Violence in Slovakia in November 1989. As in other contexts, women provided many of the support services during this period. But most of those who emerged as leaders in the chaotic days following the brutal beating of student demonstrators by police on 17 November 1989 were men. Women remained marginalized as the situation stabilized in Czechoslovakia, with few exceptions: in 1989 and 1990, Rita Klimová, the dissident economist who became ambassador to the United States, and Jana Ryšlinková served as spokespersons for the Civic Forum. Women also continued to play important support roles as secretaries and in public relations in both the Forum and in Public Against Violence.[15]

But there were few women in the national or local leadership of the Forum and Public Against Violence. Dagmar Burešová, a lawyer who defended many dissidents during the communist period and became the chair of the Czech National Council in 1990, and Daša Havlová, a former dissident activist who played a key role in Civic Forum, were exceptions to this rule in the Czech Lands. Soňa Szomolyaňiová, a sociologist, was one of the few women in the top circles of Public Against Violence in Slovakia in 1990. Helena Woleková, also active in Public Against Violence, became minister of labor in the Slovak government in April 1991. Several women were among those appointed to positions vacated by discredited communist legislators. But Eda Kriseová, the dissident writer, and Vera Caslavská, a former gymnast, were the only women among President Václav Havel's top advisers in 1990 and 1991. Similarly, few women leaders emerged in the approximately 100 other political parties that have developed since November 1989. The trends continued in the June 1990 elections, with women making up only 10.7 percent (32 of 300) of the deputies elected to the Federal Assembly.[16] The majority of these women ran as candidates of the Civic Forum and Public Against Violence.

Women's underrepresentation in politics is questioned occasionally in the media. But many women whose primary political experiences had occurred while they were mobilized participants in symbolic activities organized by the communist leadership welcomed the opportunity to withdraw from forced activism.[17] Such attitudes were part of a more general reaction to the fact that women's equality was, to a large extent, a goal imposed on the population from above, as well as disappointment with the uneven pattern of gender role changes that resulted in the communist period.[18]

Given the limited influence of women and most men on policy making through direct political participation during the communist period,

how did issues of special concern to women get onto the political agenda? As I discuss below, there are important differences and similarities in the way the three sets of issues discussed in this chapter reached the policy-making arena.

Common to all three issues is the important role played by specialists and professionals in policy making. Despite the Communist Party's domination of political life, policy making in Czechoslovakia was a complex, multilevel process in which a variety of actors, each with his or her own personal, occupational, institutional, and situational perspectives took part. But the party had a good deal of control over who entered the process and how an individual contributed. Large numbers of individuals were involved in the making and implementing of policies.

It was often specialists and professionals who first noticed new public issues—often as part of their routine occupational duties—and brought them to the attention of political leaders. And, as members of government commissions, study groups, and professional associations, they helped to articulate and evaluate policy approaches. In many cases they also affected the success of particular measures during implementation of policies adopted by central political bodies. The political leadership, particularly mid-level party bureaucrats attached to the central party bodies, played an important gatekeeping role in this process and controlled which specialists and professionals were asked to help formulate policy and which were allowed to enter on their own.[19]

The degree of political control, as well as the amount of influence the specialists and professionals had on policy making, varied with the issue being considered. In general, they had a greater role when issues were not ideologically sensitive or could be presented largely as technical issues. Their impact also varied with the changes in the broader political climate. The influence of these actors was greater when political controls were relaxed somewhat, as during the brief thaw that followed the death of Stalin and in the period leading up to the reforms of 1968.[20]

Because political leaders had a great deal of

control over their working conditions and career advancement, specialists and professionals were reluctant to press for political change. Toward the end of the communist period, however, many of the specialists and professionals who remained part of the official world grew increasingly alienated from the regime. In the Czech Lands these actors began to support some of the initiatives of longtime dissidents; in Slovakia they also joined those who had used opportunities created by the somewhat more lenient regime to work for change from within official institutions.[21]

Specialists and professionals affiliated in many cases with the Communist Party played a key role in translating the demands and concerns of women regarding demographic and employment policies to the political leadership. Because those concerns could be presented as largely technical, nonideological issues, broader groups of people were allowed to take part in formulating policy. But in the sensitive area of religious rights, there was little room for anyone outside political leadership to be involved.

The opportunities for women, as well as for men, to voice opinions on these issues or to get them onto the political agenda also varied with the political climate. But in all cases women specialists and professionals, as well as women members of the political elite, were allowed a greater role in the process than were ordinary women. Similarly, aside from highly unusual political times, such as the mid to late 1960s, women at all levels had more influence on the implementation of policies than on their formulation.

DEMOGRAPHIC POLICIES

Prior to the late 1950s, discussion of demographic trends and policies was colored by the expectation, derived from the writings of Marx, that there would be an increase in population under socialism after the negative aspects of capitalist systems—private property and economic uncertainty—were removed. Thus, early discussions by specialists of the fact that the population had been declining since 1953 were circumspect and indirect. Specialists and professionals affili-

ated with the State Statistical Office continued to monitor population trends, and researchers began to investigate the causes of the decline. But there was no public acknowledgment of the seriousness or even the existence of the declining birthrate.[22]

The change in the political climate in Czechoslovakia following the 22nd Party Congress in 1961 in the Soviet Union allowed more open discussion of the fall in the birthrate and its implications for the size of the labor force and for economic development. Demographers and sociologists linked the drop in the birthrate to both the type of economic development and to the uneven pattern of change in women's roles that occurred during the communist period. The high employment rates of women of prime childbearing age and the stress created by the lack of change in gender roles in the home contributed to the decline.

Discussion of women's situation remained at the elite level until the late 1960s, however, when the changes in the political and intellectual climate that prepared the way for the political reforms of 1968 allowed more open debate and discussion. Until 1950 the official party-controlled women's organization, the Svaz československých žen (Union of Czechoslovak Women), provided a controlled mechanism for women's participation. But when communist leaders declared that the organization was superfluous because equality for women had been achieved, ordinary women had virtually no opportunities to participate in political debate. A decade later more varied groups of women became involved in policy making by expressing their opinions in the mass media and by responding to surveys concerning women's roles, childbearing, and possible measures to encourage couples to have more children. Once the connection between women's lives and population trends was made, experts began to address, in journals and at conferences, other problematic aspects of women's situation.[23]

Throughout 1967 and much of 1968 demographic issues were discussed in the context of a freewheeling debate about women's roles and the impact on women of the economic and social policies adopted after 1948. Women intellectuals who were leaders of the Výbor československých žen (Czechoslovak Committee of Women), an official organization that existed primarily to represent Czech and Slovak women in international gatherings, began to criticize the way the government approached women's issues. It called for a rethinking of public policies that affected women, as well as for the elaboration of new models for women. As evidenced in the mass women's magazines and in the broader media, these discussions filtered down to local branches of the Union of Czechoslovak Women, which was reestablished in 1967. Although it continued to be led by party-affiliated intellectuals, the organization began to operate as an interest group in the Western sense of the word. Thus, rather than serving largely to mobilize women to support elite-determined objectives as it had prior to 1950, it began to defend women's interests vis-à-vis party and government officials. Their views also were transmitted to political leaders through the results of public opinion polls and survey research.[24]

The open debate over women's issues and roles was suppressed after the Soviet invasion in August 1968. But a reevaluation of women's maternal roles—urged by demographers and such women intellectuals as Irena Dubská and other leaders of the women's organization—led to improvements in reproductive policies and in the overall approach of the communist leadership to women's issues.[25]

As a result of these debates and the continued decline in the birthrate, political leaders began to give greater emphasis to women's material situation in the early 1970s, adopting a number of policies designed to ease the burdens of bearing and raising children, including extended paid maternity leave and mothers' allowances that paid women with two or more children to remain at home to care for them until the youngest turned three.[26] But, for the most part, women's impact on the making of demographic policies was indirect. Policy changes came about not because women organized to pressure the govern-

ment and party on their own behalf, but because experts in demographics, as well as party intellectuals on the Women's Committee, saw the connection between the problems facing women and the higher-priority policy goals of maintaining a stable population and continuing economic development and brought that connection to the attention of policy makers. Women's action in inaction—their decision not to have more children—also contributed to change.[27]

Another example of women's indirect impact on policy making concerns the government's decision to eliminate abortion commissions, whose approval women were required to obtain before having an abortion. Women's persistence in reapplying for permission for abortions—or in resorting to illegal abortions when their demands were denied—eventually prompted the professionals who worked in this area to urge political leaders to eliminate the commissions, which consisted of local leaders, medical personnel, and social workers. Because abortion was the main form of birth control, this change affected many women.[28]

The end of communist rule has changed policy making in many areas, including demographic policies. Women now have far greater opportunities to organize and to make their views known to policy makers. Recent discussions of maternity leave and abortion rights, for example, have been influenced by such newly relegitimated political actors as churches and religious groups, and by women themselves. In extending mothers' allowances to broader groups of women, specialists in the Ministry of Health were responding to a general feeling that women should be allowed to stay at home with their children and out of the labor force for longer periods of time. The new policies thus were informed by the broader backlash against many of the changes in women's lives that occurred during the communist period. But the new legislation for the first time also allows fathers to remain at home to care for small children and receive parental allowances. No information is yet available concerning the number of men who have used them. Given the disparity in wages between men and women and the popular perceptions concerning family roles, it is still likely that the mother rather than the father will stay at home with young children.[29]

The sharp debate over abortion rights reflects disagreement in public opinion concerning what public policy on the issue ought to be. Opinion polls conducted in April 1990, for example, found that 56 percent of the population thought that women should have the right to decide whether to have an abortion. Only 6 percent wanted abortion to be completely illegal. But about 27 percent felt that abortion should be permitted only when justified by considerations for the health and social prospects of the child; 11 percent accepted abortion only when the pregnancy threatened the woman's life. Women were significantly more likely than men (61 percent versus 51 percent) to support women's right to choose.[30] Church groups have sought to mobilize public opinion to press for greater restrictions, and their position is supported by some of the new groups established by Christian women, including several that had been active in the dissident movement. Medical experts have also entered the debate and, for the most part, continue to support free access to abortion.

EMPLOYMENT POLICIES

As with demographic policies, changes have occurred in the options available to women to participate in the making of employment policies. During the communist period women were largely the objects of such policies, not the formulators—with the exception of some specialists and professionals. The majority, however, had little input into many of the decisions that affected them at work.

During the early years of communism the official women's organization provided a forum for raising problematic issues. Leaders of the organization arranged for programs to make shopping easier for employed women and for lectures on topics related to work and home. The group also helped organize women who volunteered their labor to address community problems. These ef-

forts paralleled those of the other mass organizations, such as the trade unions and youth leagues, and they reflected the attempt to politicize all areas of life, including leisure. They also were part of the effort to substitute labor for state financial resources to deal with community issues. But even though the women's organization served largely to mobilize women toward fulfilling objectives determined by the elite, it allowed its activists to propose solutions for some of the problems created by the influx of women into the labor force.[31] Once the organization was disbanded in 1950, these possibilities were lost, as there were no mass-membership women's organizations of any kind from 1950 to 1967.[32]

But the Communist Party allowed loyal party intellectuals who had been members of the Committee of Czechoslovak Women to re-create an organization with mass membership in 1967. The Union of Czechoslovak Women began acting as an interest group in the Western sense of the term and raised such issues as occupational segregation, gender-related wage differentials, the widespread violation of regulations designed to protect women's health in the workplace, the lack of support services for working women, the barriers to career advancement for women, and the conflicts between economic and family roles.[33] Although the organization survived the reimposition of censorship and the return to political orthodoxy, it renounced its role as an interest group for women and reverted to its mobilization and support functions. The leaders who replaced the reformists of the 1960s continued to discuss the need to reduce the conflict between women's economic and domestic responsibilities, and they called for differentiated approaches to women's needs at various stages of the life cycle.

As indicated by the bitter critiques of the organization's activities that were made publicly after November 1989 and the virtual disintegration of the organization in its old form in early 1990, most women perceived the Union of Czechoslovak Women as a tool of the communist leadership. Women intellectuals, including several who had been opposition activists, denounced the organization and noted that it had not served women's interests. Other women, including several in Prague who broke from the organization to form an independent group in early 1990, argued that the older organization should be dissolved. Although the women elected to replace those who had led the Union of Czechoslovak Women during the last years of communist rule decided not to disband the organization, the group has lost most of its members. The new government required the group, along with the remnants of the other communist-sponsored mass organizations, to relinquish part of its assets and property to the state.

Despite constitutional and legal guarantees to the contrary, many inequalities between men and women continued to exist in the workplace.[34] Even though women's presence in the labor force grew rapidly during the early communist period, and ideological support existed for women's equality, many of the options present in other economies—such as flex time and part-time work—were not available. In part, the lack of such options reflected the value that Marxist-Leninist ideology placed on work for all citizens and the importance that party theoreticians assigned paid employment outside the home and the elimination of private property, in fostering gender equality. The lack was also consistent with the party's tendency to see labor as a cheap resource that could be easily manipulated by central economic authorities with little regard for the impact of such actions on workers themselves.

Women also received little help from government or party leaders in the area of wage inequality. Researchers who examined the remaining disparity in wages between men and women found little progress during the course of the communist period. They pointed primarily to structural factors, including occupational segregation, to explain the lower incomes of women.[35] Women tended to be concentrated in low-priority areas of the labor force with lower-than-average wages. They also tended to be assigned to and accept positions that did not utilize their qualifications. But women did not take the obvious next step—determining why wage

scales, which were established to a great degree by central authorities, were lower in areas in which women predominated.

Similarly, little action was taken in regard to violations of regulations that prohibited women from being required to carry loads above certain weight limits. Nor did women openly challenge the protective regulations that prevented them from entering certain well-paying but potentially hazardous occupations while they were allowed to enter low-paying unskilled positions that posed equal health hazards. In each of these cases, women's ability to pressure leaders for policy change was limited by the Communist Party's control of political life, as well as by an official value system that did not recognize that the interests of particular social groups might diverge from those of other groups. Thus, the subordination of the unions and official women's organization to the Communist Party, the restrictions on independent organizations, and the risks inherent in openly opposing existing policies help to explain why women did not challenge these policies during the communist period.

The employment policies that benefited working women developed not as the result of women's direct political actions, but because of other factors. Thus, guarantees of women's right to work incorporated in the constitution of the communist system were part of the general copying of Soviet institutions and policies. In addition to reflecting the commitment to women's equality in the new official ideology, such guarantees furthered higher-priority goals, including rapid economic development, by use of all available labor resources. As in the case of demographic policies, modifications in this area occurred largely because political leaders came to perceive a connection between some aspect of women's work and other elite goals.

Since the fall of the communist government, women have also utilized newly available tools to make their preferences known in this area. In reaction to the enforced high levels of women's employment during the communist period and the resultant burdens on women and their families, many women and men feel that current levels of women's employment are too high. These attitudes have been voiced in the mass media and in the speeches of political candidates and officials.[36] They are reinforced by the movement toward radical economic reform, which places greater pressure on managers and economic officials to cut labor costs.

There are several limits on the extent to which Czech and Slovak women will be able to leave the labor force for anything other than brief periods. The shift to a market economy creates new pressures on working women and on their employers. As in other formerly socialist countries, women have been the first to lose their jobs when state subsidies for unprofitable enterprises are eliminated. As the effort to privatize some 100,000 enterprises continues, employed women—as well as men—are feeling the pressure of the new expectations to take profit considerations into account in the workplace. Because women continue to bear primary responsibility for household management and child care, they especially feel the burden of the marked price increases that followed price liberalization.[37]

The main advocates of measures to deal with inequality in the workplace and elsewhere are leaders of the successor to the official women's organization, which now comprises separate Czech and Slovak groups. Experts who have worked on women's issues or are officeholders themselves have also drawn attention to how economic and political changes have affected women.[38] But few of the women leaders actually identify themselves as women's advocates, and most have given little attention to women's issues.[39] This lack of interest reflects the postcommunist backlash against the goal of sexual equality, and it reflects the perception, common in many other crisis situations, that women's issues are low-priority concerns that should not deflect attention from the multitude of more serious tasks ahead.[40]

It is likely that additional advocates will emerge as workplace inequality persists and new problems arise in a market economy. These individuals will have many more opportunities to mobilize public support and to pressure political

officials than existed under the communist regime. At present, however, the main emphasis of public discussion concerning women's employment is on reducing the number of women in the work force.[41]

RELIGIOUS RIGHTS

The antipathy of Czechoslovakia's communist leaders to religion was evident from the outset of communist rule. Leaders enacted policies to reduce the influence and economic power of organized churches. They also mounted campaigns against reliance on religion and encouraged the acceptance of Marxism-Leninism as a worldview.

Church property was confiscated, and many religious orders were dissolved. The government allowed seminaries to train only a few new priests and ministers and required that clergy be licensed by the state. Political leaders also enacted other restrictions on the operation of churches. To counteract the influence of religion, political leaders established museums of atheism that depicted the abuses and misdeeds allegedly perpetrated by organized religion. Measures were also taken to force individuals to leave the church: practicing believers were penalized economically; many who refused to renounce their beliefs were denied career advancements or lost their jobs altogether. The religious background or affiliation of an individual or an individual's parents was also a handicap in receiving permission to seek higher education. And individuals who openly practiced their religion in this climate were seen as politically suspect.

These antireligion measures and campaigns were carried out most crudely in the Stalinist period, and they were pursued most vigorously in Slovakia, where the Catholic church had played a larger role in politics in the interwar period and had been more important at the individual level throughout the communist period. The apparent success of these policies was evident in a rapid fall in church attendance and in a decreasing number of individuals openly identifying themselves as believers. In contrast to the situation in Poland, the church in Czechoslovakia was successfully neutralized politically. Although courageous individual religious leaders attempted to retain some independence from the state, most members did not contest the limitations.[42]

Beginning in the early 1980s, however, the Catholic hierarchy began to challenge the regime more actively. Cardinal František Tomášek, despite his advanced age, emerged as a strong popular leader and spokesman for those whose human rights had been violated. Lay people affiliated with the Catholic and Protestant churches also became more active. The number of people attending unauthorized services and participating in other illegal religious activities increased, especially among Catholics, as did the number of people making pilgrimages to shrines in Moravia and Slovakia. In the early and mid 1980s such pilgrimages were estimated to have been made by 100,000 people per year; in 1989 an estimated 600,000 took part. During the communist period primarily older people openly practiced their religions. As the period waned many young people became more actively involved in religious activities.[43]

Decision making in regard to religion was confined to a smaller group of political leaders, and women were virtually excluded, particularly in the early communist period. Women leaders and activists at lower levels of the Communist Party and in the official women's organization (when it was permitted to exist) helped to implement measures that were part of the antireligion campaign, but the main outlines of the policy were set without active input from women.

At the same time, women, particularly in rural areas and in Slovakia, played an important role in resisting the campaign. Surveys conducted in the mid-1980s found, for example, that significantly more women than men identified themselves as religious believers.[44] Resistance took the form of open attendance at church and observation of other religious practices. Women were active in unofficial, or underground, religious groups that emerged in the late communist period. Women also played an important role in keeping religious belief alive through discussion and teaching within the family.

Most women, as well as men, who wished to practice their religion throughout the communist period did not attempt to use official channels to influence policy making. Instead, they joined other independent activists who spoke out in defense of human rights, including the right to practice one's religion, or, more frequently, quietly continued their religious observances, irrespective of the costs.

The Catholic hierarchy and laity were more active politically than were the smaller Protestant denominations, which included the Slovak Evangelical Church of the Augsburg Confession, the Evangelical Church of Czech Brethren, the Silesian Evangelical Church of the Augsburg Confession, and the Reformed (Christian) Church in Slovakia. Given the more traditional attitudes toward gender roles fostered by the Catholic church and the fact that many Catholic activists disagreed with the communist regime's focus on women's equality, it is not surprising that few women were among those who openly challenged religious policies in the 1980s. Women who did participate in unauthorized activities tended to engage in small-group endeavors focused on preserving and propagating religious belief and strengthening the ties between parents and children. This response, which paralleled in many ways the differences in the styles and actions of men and women in other dissident groups,[45] also reflected women's alienation from politics, an attitude that appears to have continued after the fall of the communist system.[46]

The fall of communism and the repluralization of political life has had a dramatic impact on this policy area. Restrictions on religious organizations have been lifted, and some property has been returned to church control. Political and economic sanctions against those who practiced their religion openly have been eliminated, and people may freely attend church and participate in activities organized by religious groups. Parents may enroll their children for organized religious study. Some Czech and Slovak women have formed women's groups, similar to those that exist in other countries, that are designed to foster Christian attitudes in the home and society.[47] Others have become active in new Christian organizations that encourage lay people to become involved in church activities. Many women, however, remain active largely through personal religious observances and such routine family events as weddings, baptisms, and funerals.

Under the new political conditions, churches and other religious groups have become more involved in addressing public policy issues, particularly reproductive rights. Even though the polls indicate that most women and men want to preserve women's right to choose abortion, the issue continues to be controversial. Catholic activists have emerged as the leaders in groups seeking to restrict women's right to abortion and in groups promoting a return to more traditional arrangements in the home. Women are less likely than men to support the communist parties that continue to exist in both the Czech Lands and Slovakia after the end of communist rule and more likely to support the Christian parties.[48]

THE CHARACTER OF WOMEN'S POLITICAL ENGAGEMENT IN CZECHOSLOVAKIA

In contrast to the situation in the communist period, women can speak openly on specific issues and on politics in general. But most women appear to regard politics as something that is not truly appropriate for women. This attitude, which is reflected in public opinion research, is also heard in conversations with women, including many who hold or have held leadership roles in the new government and political parties. It is also reflected in statements from the leaders of the new, independent women's organizations. This attitude is part of what appears to be a broader rejection of elite policies toward women during the communist period and toward the goal of gender equality itself. Women were told for four decades that they had achieved equality, yet they were forced to live daily with the contra-

dictions that were created by continuing inequalities. The loyalty of women elites to the communist regime during the late communist period and the subordination of the women's organization to the Communist Party further discredited the notion of women as political activists.[49]

Although they do not see themselves as activists, many women today are involved in activities that have a political dimension. Several of the new women's groups have demonstrated against the contamination of Czechoslovakia's food supply (by heavy metals and other pollutants) that occurred during communist rule. Others have asked their members to work at the local level to resolve such problems as the need for child care and facilities for handicapped children and abused women, and to provide other services that affect women's lives.[50] Although almost all of these new groups eschew the label "feminist," they nonetheless bring women together to discuss issues of common concern and sponsor lectures and seminars on the changed political and economic situation.[51] These organizations may well serve to increase women's political awareness and consciousness.

At the same time, there is little indication that the broader political organizations or most of the country's new leaders will be any more receptive than their communist predecessors to efforts to remedy continued gender inequality. Many appear to share the popular reaction against the form of gender-role change imposed during the communist period, and most give women's issues a far lower priority than those related to economic and political transformation. As it did during the communist period, women's responsibility for the care of home and children will limit the time and energy they have available for political activity. The shift to a market economy may in fact increase the demands on women as it creates greater pressures to perform at higher levels at work.[52] Thus women's political engagement may continue to reflect the legacy of the communist period for some time, despite the new opportunities for independent activism available to women. But women now have far greater numbers of channels through which to have an impact on policy making should they choose to do so and to defend their interests openly in the political realm should they perceive them to be challenged.

IMPLICATIONS FOR THE STUDY OF POLITICS

Women's political activities and women's influence on policy making in areas with a central impact on their lives were mediated to a large degree during the communist period. To some extent, the same can be said of all political activities under communist rule. Given the uneven pattern of change in women's roles during communist rule, however, the persistence of traditional values concerning the appropriateness of women's political activism, and the lack of energetic efforts on the part of the political elite to overcome these hindrances, women had fewer opportunities for influencing policy formulation than men. From the late 1960s to the end of the communist period, the renewed emphasis on women's domestic roles resulted in a certain congruence of views between the population and the leadership concerning gender roles. This agreement gave women greater freedom to express what was undoubtedly a more general alienation from politics by taking part in as few political activities as possible. Because they were less interested than men in career advancement, and because most officials and administrators, as well as most ordinary people, continued to define women primarily in terms of their domestic roles, women were able to avoid many of the tedious, time-consuming political activities required of men who wanted to keep their positions or advance professionally. Thus, although men and women both were mobilized to participate in mass demonstrations and to vote, women faced fewer pressures to become party members or to participate in other forms of activism. The lower activity levels of women in these areas limited their career advancement and their role in policy making during the communist period; certain women who wished to be more active politically undoubtedly encountered barriers. But for many women, the ability to argue that domestic responsibilities and a resultant lack of free time prevented them from being politically active provided a welcome excuse.

Examining how policies were made and implemented reveals the largely indirect ways citizens could affect policy making during the communist period. It highlights the importance of looking at mediated responses to politics and indirect, informal methods of influencing policy. Focus on policy making in the three issue areas examined also demonstrates the importance of developments at the implementation stage in determining the success or failure of policy measures as well as the impact that unorganized individuals can have on policy outcomes through the sum of their individual response or lack of response to elite-initiated measures.

The fact that women continue to be marginalized from politics in the pluralistic political system that replaced one-party rule in Czechoslovakia raises a number of interesting questions. Many of women's current actions and attitudes with regard to politics undoubtedly are influenced by the general reaction to the policies of the communist period. Thus, women's lack of interest in being politically active beyond voting and the view that politics is somehow not an appropriate field for women may well be transitory. As political life stabilizes and as the need to reject the mobilized activism of the communist period fades, more women may use the far greater opportunities available in democratic states to make their views known to policy makers and to be active in politics. The shift to a market economy will affect the living standards of families as well as women's opportunities in the workplace, creating new problems for women. A serious challenge to the right to abortion or the introduction of other measures designed to reduce women's reproductive freedom may also mobilize women. The general exclusion of women from positions of power in the new democratic political order may set a pattern that will be difficult for women to break should they want to be more active. The prevalence of conservative attitudes concerning women's roles and the lack of change in the division of labor within the home will continue to pose barriers to women's political participation. But, given the new political climate and current guarantees of freedom of expression and association, women who desire to be active politically or to mobilize support for positions promoting their interests will find it easier to do so than they did during the communist period.

Although focusing on women's political engagement regarding demographic, employment, and religious practice policies illustrates some of the ways in which politics and policy making in communist political systems differ from those in democratic states, it also demonstrates the importance of factors other than political structure and values in shaping women's relationship to politics. Women's experiences with politics in Czechoslovakia during the communist and early postcommunist periods highlight how gender roles in other areas, patterns of social and family relations, and economic policies have affected women's political activities and how women use existing political resources. Although there are profound differences between democratic and communist regimes, the existence of democratic institutions alone does not automatically lead to equal participation by all groups in the exercise of political power or in equal access to policy makers.[53]

NOTES

1. The importance of these factors in shaping the policy-making process and the number and kinds of groups that will be included is suggested by Donald R. Kelley, "Toward a Model of Soviet Decision Making: A Research Note," and William Zimmerman, "Issue Area and Foreign-Policy Process: A Research Note in Search of a General Theory," both in *American Political Science Review* 67, no. 4 (1973). See also Donald R. Kelley, "Environmental Policy Making in the USSR: The Role of Industrial and Environmental Interest Groups," *Soviet Studies* 28 (1976): 570–89; and Sharon L. Wolchik and Jane Curry, "Specialists and Professionals in the Policy Process in Czechoslovakia and Poland," *Report to the National Council for Soviet and East European Research,* 1984.

2. See Wolchik and Curry, "Specialists and Professionals." See also Kelley, "Toward a Model" and "Envi-

ronmental Policy"; and Thane Gustafson, *Reform in Soviet Politics* (New York: Cambridge University Press, 1981).

3. For earlier discussions of the impact of these factors see Barbara Jancar, *Women Under Communism* (Baltimore: Johns Hopkins University Press, 1978), 105–18; Alena Heitlinger, *Women and State Socialism: Sex Inequality in the Soviet Union and Czechoslovakia* (Montreal: McGill-Queen's University Press, 1979), 136–38; Sharon L. Wolchik, Introduction to Section 3, in Sharon L. Wolchik and Alfred G. Meyer, eds., *Women, State, and Party in Eastern Europe* (Durham, N.C.: Duke University Press, 1985), 115–20, and "Women and the State in Eastern Europe and the Soviet Union," in Sue Ellen M. Charlton, Jana Everett, and Kathleen Staudt, eds., *Women, the State, and Development* (Albany: State University of New York Press, 1989), 48–52; Mary Ellen Fischer, "Women in Romanian Politics: Elena Ceausescu, Pronatalism, and the Promotion of Women," in Wolchik and Meyer, eds., *Women, State, and Party,* 127–35; and Daniel N. Nelson, "Women in Local Communist Politics in Romania and Poland," in Wolchik and Meyer, eds., *Women, State, and Party,* 153–62.

4. See Anton Jurovský, *Mládež a spoločnosť* (Youth and society) (Bratislava: Věda, 1974); Ladislav Macháchek, "Hnutie mládeže a formavanie jej socialistickej hodnotovej orientacie" (The youth movement and formation of its socialist value orientation), *Sociológia* 20, no. 2 (1988): 129–40; and Ivan Tomek, "K problematice výskumu světového názoru a svetonázorové orientace československé mládeže" (Regarding the problem of research on the worldview and worldview orientation of Czechoslovak youth), *Sociologický časopis* 21, no. 2 (1985): 539–51.

5. Wolchik, "Women and the State," 47–48.

6. For an overview of these factors see Sharon L. Wolchik, "The Precommunist Legacy, Economic Development, Social Transformation, and Women's Roles in Eastern Europe," in Wolchik and Meyer, eds., *Women, State, and Party.*

7. See Sharon L. Wolchik, "Elite Strategy Toward Women in Czechoslovakia: Liberation or Mobilization?" *Studies in Comparative Communism* 14, (Summer/Autumn 1981): 127–29, and "Women in the Czech Lands," in Helen Tierney, ed., *Women's Studies Encyclopedia* (Westport, Conn.: Greenwood Press, 1989). See also Bruce M. Garver, "Women in the First Czechoslovak Republic," and Karen J. Freeze, "Medical Education for Women in Austria: A Study in the Politics of the Czech Women's Movement in the 1890s," both in Wolchik and Meyer, eds., *Women, State, and Party.*

8. See Wolchik, "Elite Strategy," "Women and the State," and "The Status of Women in a Socialist Order: Czechoslovakia, 1948–1978," *Slavic Review* 38, no. 4 (December 1979): 592–95; Jancar, *Women Under Com-*

munism, 12–28; and Heitlinger, *Women and State Socialism,* 147–65.

9. See Sharon L. Wolchik, "Status of Women," 592–95, and "Ideology and Equality: The Status of Women in Eastern and Western Europe," *Comparative Political Studies* 13, no. 4 (January 1981): 457–58; see also Jancar, *Women Under Communism,* 92–96.

10. For discussion of these trends in Czechoslovakia see Wolchik, "Status of Women," 594–95; "Ideology and Equality," 460–62; and "Women and the State," 50–51. For information about similar trends in other communist countries see Gail W. Lapidus, *Women in Soviet Society: Equality, Development, and Social Change* (Berkeley: University of California Press, 1978), chap. 6; and Jancar, *Women Under Communism,* chap. 5.

11. For further information see Wolchik, "Status of Women," 595–96; and Lapidus, *Women in Soviet Society,* chap. 6. See also Sharon L. Wolchik, *Czechoslovakia in Transition: Politics, Economics, and Society* (London: Pinter Publishers, 1991), chap. 4.

12. See Barbara Jancar, "Women in the Opposition in Poland and Czechoslovakia in the 1970s," in Wolchik and Meyer, eds., *Women, State, and Party,* 169–72, 177–81.

13. For further information on these activities see Sharon L. Wolchik, *Czechoslovakia in Transition,* chap. 2, and "Women and the Collapse of Communism in Central and Eastern Europe" (Paper presented at the World Congress of Slavic Studies, Harrogate, England, July 1990).

14. Sharon L. Wolchik, "Women in the Transition to Democracy in Central and Eastern Europe" (Paper presented at annual meeting of the American Political Science Association, San Francisco, September 1990).

15. Renata Siemieńska, "Women and Social Movements in Poland," *Women and Politics* 6, no. 4 (Winter 1986): 20–33; and Wolchik, "Women in the Transition to Democracy."

16. See "Volby 1990," *Hospodářské noviny,* 14 June 1990.

17. Interview with Eva Bártová, Institute of Sociology, Prague, March 1990; and jul, "Kolotoc bez legrace" (A merry-go-round without happiness), *Mladá fronta,* 5 April 1990, p. 4. See also "Zeny rokovaly" (Women discussed), *Zemědělské noviny,* 28 September 1990, p. 2; and interview with Dagmar Burešová, "V parlamentě pískat nebudu" (I won't whistle in Parliament), *Rudé právo,* 7 July 1990, p. 1.

18. See Sharon L. Wolchik, "Women and Work in Communist and Postcommunist Central and Eastern Europe," in Hilda Kahne and Janet Z. Giele, eds., *Women's Work and Women's Lives: The Continuing Struggle Worldwide* (Boulder, Colo.: Westview Press, 1991), 119–39.

19. See Wolchik and Curry, "Specialists and Professionals"; and Sharon L. Wolchik, "The Scientific-Technological Revolution and the Participation of Specialists in the Making of Public Policy in Czechoslovakia,"

in Sharon L. Wolchik and Michael J. Sodaro, eds., *Foreign and Domestic Policies in Eastern Europe in the 1980s* (New York: St. Martin's Press, 1983).

20. Wolchik, "Scientific-Technological Revolution," and Wolchik and Curry, "Specialists and Professionals." See also Kelley, "Toward a Model," and "Environmental Policy Making"; Zimmerman, "Issue Area"; Peter H. Solomon, Jr., *Soviet Criminologists and Criminal Policy: Specialists in Soviet Policy-Making* (New York: Columbia University Press, 1979); Andrzej Korbonski, "Bureaucracy and Interest Groups in Communist Societies: The Case of Czechoslovakia," *Studies in Comparative Communism* 4 (January 1971): 57–79; and Philip Stewart, "Soviet Interest Groups and the Policy Process: The Repeal of Production Education," *World Politics* 20 (October 1969): 29–50.

21. See Sharon L. Wolchik, "Czechoslovakia in Transition" and "Central and Eastern Europe in Transition," in Young C. Kim and Gaston Sigur, eds., *Asia and the Decline of Communism* (New Brunswick, N.J.: Transaction, 1992).

22. See Sharon L. Wolchik, "Demography, Political Reform and Women's Issues in Czechoslovakia," in Margherita Rendel, ed., *Women, Power and Political Systems* (London: Croom Helm, 1981).

23. See Alena Heitlinger, "Pro-Natalist Population Policies in Czechoslovakia," *Population Studies* 30, no. 1 (March 1976): 122–36; and Wolchik, "Demography," 139–45.

24. See Hilda Scott, *Does Socialism Liberate Women?* (Boston: Beacon Press, 1974), 100–116; Heitlinger, "Pro-Natalist Population Policies," 122–36; and Wolchik, "Elite Strategy," 134–39, and "Demography," 139–45.

25. For discussion of these issues see Wolchik, "Demography," and "Scientific-Technological Revolution."

26. See Heitlinger, "Pro-Natalist Population Policies"; and Henry P. David and Robert J. McIntyre, *Reproductive Behavior: Central and Eastern European Experiences* (New York: Springer, 1981), chap. 11.

27. For more detailed information on demographic trends and policies see Wolchik, "Scientific-Technological Revolution"; Heitlinger, "Pro-Natalist Population Policies"; Alena Heitlinger, *Reproduction, Medicine, and the Socialist State* (Houndmills, England: Macmillan, 1987); and David and McIntyre, *Reproductive Behavior.*

28. See Heitlinger, "Pro-Natalist Population Policies," 122–36; David and McIntyre, *Reproductive Behavior;* and Wolchik, "Scientific-Technological Revolution."

29. See ha, "Ne mateřský, ale rodičovský příspevek" (Not mothers' but parents' allowances), *Hospodářské noviny,* 21 September 1990, p. 2; and Alena Kroupová, "Komu, kdy, jaký mateřský příspevek" (To whom, when, and what kind of mothers' allowances), *Hospodářské noviny,* 6 June 1990.

30. See the results reported in Vladimíra Kobyklová, "Informace pro novináře—názory občanu na interrupci" (Citizens' views on abortion), Institut pro výzkum veřéjného mínění, 24 April 1990, p. 2.

31. See Sharon L. Wolchik, "Politics, Ideology, and Equality: The Status of Women in Eastern Europe" (Ph.D. diss., University of Michigan, 1978), and "Women and Work."

32. See Wolchik, "Politics, Ideology, and Equality," and "Elite Strategy."

33. See Scott, *Does Socialism Liberate Women?* 126–37; Heitlinger, *Women and State Socialism,* 68–72; and Wolchik, "Women and Work."

34. See Jancar, *Women Under Communism,* 25–28; Heitlinger, *Women and State Socialism,* 153–57; and Wolchik, "Women and Work."

35. See Jiří Fremr, "Rozdily ve mzdach mužu a žen" (Differences in the wages of men and women), *Statistika* 11 (1965): 506; "Dopis CSSZ vladě," *Funkcionářka* 4 (1968): 3; and Wolchik, "Women and Work."

36. See Wolchik, "Women and Work."

37. See Silva Meznaríc, "Theory and Reality: The Status of Employed Women in Yugoslavia," in Wolchik and Meyer, eds., *Women, State, and Party,* 216–19; Susan L. Woodward, "The Rights of Women: Ideology, Policy, and Social Change in Yugoslavia," in Wolchik and Meyer, eds., *Women, State, and Party,* 244–46; and "Record Low Birthrate, High Death Rate Reported," 24 August 1990, as reported in FBIS-EEU-90-166, 27 August 1990, p. 10.

38. See "Hovoříme s představitelkámi politické strany žen a matek v CSFR" (We talk with representatives of the political party: Women and mothers in the CSFR), *Rudé právo,* 30 July 1990, p. 4; and "Strana žen" (The party of women), *Mladá fronta,* 9 April 1990, p. 2.

39. For an exception see Burešová, "V parlamentě pískat nebudu," 1.

40. See Wolchik, "Women and the Collapse of Communism," and "Women and Work."

41. For more detailed information see Wolchik, "Woman and Work."

42. See Pedro Ramet, "Christianity and National Heritage Among the Czechs and Slovaks," in Pedro Ramet, ed., *Religion and Nationalism in Soviet and East European Politics,* 2nd ed. (Durham, N.C.: Duke University Press, 1989), 264–85. See also Wolchik, *Czechoslovakia,* chap. 3.

43. See Ramet, 264–85; and Wolchik, *Czechoslovakia,* chap. 2.

44. See Richard Scheuch, "Religiozita okresu CSSR" (Religiosity of districts in the CSSR), *Duchovní pastyř,* May 1989, p. 97.

45. See Jancar, "Women in the Opposition," 177–81.

46. Interview with Tereza Sladková, Prague, June 1990.

47. Wolchik, "Women and Work."

48. See Marek Boguszak, Ivan Gabal, and Vladimír Rak, "Ceskoslovensko—Leden 1990" (Czechoslovakia—January 1990) (Prague: Skupina pro nezavislou sociální analyzu, 1990); "Nezaměstnanost u nas," *Mladá fronta,* 21 March 1990, p. 3; and "Ceskoslovensko—Listopad 1990" (Czechoslovakia—November 1990) (Prague: Skupina pro nezavislou sociální analyzu, 1990). See also Hana Navarová, "Impact of the Economic and Political Changes in Czechoslovakia for Women," 1990; and Jiřina Siklová, "Are Women in Middle and Eastern Europe Conservative?" 1990.

49. Interviews with Eda Kriseová, Prague, 1990; and Daša Havlová, Prague, June 1990.

50. Kamila Jasková, "Rozhovor mezi plenkámi" (Conversations among the diapers), *Rudé právo,* 6 April 1990, p. 6. See also M. Panková, "Spojuje nás nejen víra" (We are united not only by faith), *Lidová demokracie,* 19 March 1990, p. 1.

51. See Jasková, "Rozhovor mezi plenkámi"; Panková, "Spojuje nás nejen víra"; and interview with Jitka Havlová, Prague, 13 June 1990. See also Wolchik, "Women and the Collapse of Communism."

52. Wolchik, "Women at Work."

53. Part of the research for this article was conducted with the help of grants from the George Washington University's Research Council and the International Research and Exchanges Board, whose support is gratefully acknowledged. I would also like to thank Michael Kienbaum, Dominic O'Brien, Susan Oh, and Tereza Platzová for their help with this project.

▲ Egypt

POLITICS

Type of Political System: democracy
  Sovereignty: republic
  Executive-Legislative System: presidential
Type of State: unitary
Type of Party System: multiparty
Major Political Parties[a]

Al-Hizb al-Watani al-Dimuqrati (National Democratic Party, NDP): Official government party, led by the president of Egypt, Muhammad Husni Mubarak. Organized by former President Sadat in July 1978.

Hizb al-Wafd al-Gadid (New Wafd Party, NWP): Formed in 1978, reviving the most powerful party in Egypt before 1952. The only opposition party to support the Egyptian commitment of troops to Saudi Arabia during the Persian Gulf war.

Hizb al-'Amal al-Ishtiraki (Socialist Labor Party, SLP): Officially recognized as an opposition party in 1978. Boycotted the 1990 Assembly elections, calling for a more democratic regime. Members believe that Egyptian law should be based on Islamic principles.

Hizb al-Ahrar al-Ishtiraki (Liberal Socialist Party, LSP): Formed in 1976 from the right wing of the Arab Socialist Union; advocates a greater role for private enterprise in the Egyptian economy.

Hizb al-Tajamu' al-Watani al-Taqaddumi al-Wahdawi (National Progressive Unionist Party, NPUP): Officially recognized as the party of the left in 1976. Opposed the Egyptian-Israeli peace treaty and U.S. military involvement in the Persian Gulf. Unlike other opposition parties, it did not boycott the November 1990 elections.

Year Women Granted Right to Vote: 1956
Year Women Granted Right to Stand for Election: 1956
Percentage of Women in the Unicameral Legislature: 3.9%

Percentage of Electorate Voting for Highest Elected Office in Most Recent Election (1990): not available

DEMOGRAPHICS

Population: 50,740,000
Percentage of Population in Urban Areas
  Overall: 43.8%
  Female: 43.4%
  Male: 44.1%
Percentage of Population Below Age 15: 39.6%
Birthrate (per 1,000 population): 36
Maternal Mortality Rate (per 100,000 live births): 80
Infant Mortality Rate (per 1,000 live births): 88
Mortality Rate for Children Under Five (per 1,000 live births): 131
Average Household Size: 5.2
Mean Age at First Marriage
  Female: 21.4
  Male: 26.8
Life Expectancy
  Female: 59.5
  Male: 56.8

EDUCATION

Ratio of Female to Male Enrollment
  First-Level Education: 76
  Second-Level Education: 65
  Third-Level Education (excluding al-Azhar University): 50
Literacy Rate
  Female: 29.0%
  Male: 57.0%

ECONOMY

Gross National Product per Capita: U.S. $610
Percentage of Labor Force in Agriculture: 44.2%
Distribution of Agricultural Workers by Sex
  Female: 3.7%
  Male: 96.3%

a. All political party information is from Arthur S. Banks, ed., *Political Handbook of the World, 1991* (Binghamton, N.Y.: CSA Publications, 1991), 200–201.

The Paradoxes of State Feminism in Egypt

MERVAT F. HATEM

Egypt, located at the northeastern tip of Africa, was for centuries part of the Ottoman Empire. Made part of the British Empire in 1882, it became legally independent in 1923, though it continued to be a British colony in all but name for the next 30 years. In 1952 the Free Officers, an organized group recruited by Gamal 'Abdul Nasser from the middle military ranks, overthrew the Muhammad Ali dynasty, which had ruled the country since 1810, and declared Egypt a republic. In 1954 the Free Officers negotiated an evacuation treaty with the British, and independence became real.

Since then, the national government has consisted of a president and a unicameral legislature, the People's Assembly. In practice, however, because of the personalities of its presidents and the degree to which state powers are centralized in the chief executive office, presidents have held the reins of power. Since the 1950s, Egyptian politics has been dominated by the initiatives of its three presidents: Gamal 'Abdul Nasser, Anwar Sadat, and Husni Mubarak. The People's Assembly is made up of 448 members representing political parties or elected as independent candidates. It functions primarily as a consultative body for the president. The presidents have generally turned to the people through referenda, not to the People's Assembly, when they have felt the need for a mandate. Although the powers of the assembly are subordinate to the president's, the role that it plays in keeping the political system functioning smoothly makes it in some ways equal to the president. By providing a forum for the presentation of dissenting opinions and the

representation of diverse interests, the assembly functions as a safety valve, softening the impact of the authoritarian rule of the president. Thus, even though the presidents have been the primary rulers for the past 40 years, the interplay of politics has centered on the People's Assembly.

The political party system is fairly new. From 1952 through 1976, when Egypt had a one-party system, the state attempted to create a large state-controlled, class-based mass organization or state party. In 1976, after the last of these attempts was declared a failure, a multiparty system was instated. Currently there are five major political parties—Hizb al-'Amal al-Ishtiraki (Socialist Labor Party), Hizb al-Wafd al-Gadid (New Wafd Party), Hizb al-Ahrar al-Ishtiraki (Liberal Socialist Party), Hizb al-Tajamu' al-Watani al-Taqaddumi al-Wahdawi (National Progressive Unionist Party), and al-Hizb al-Watani al-Dimuqrati (National Democratic Party)—as well as several minor parties on both the right and the left. But politics is dominated by one party, the National Democratic Party (NDP).

Although all the political parties claim to have social and political agendas that are sensitive to women, it is the National Progressive Unionist Party that has a well-developed program. Its Federation of Progressive Women is committed to defending women's right to work, to raising the political consciousness of women so that they emerge as responsible and active citizens, and to eliminating any forms of discrimination against women in the work, legal, and political arenas.[1]

Misr (Arab Socialist Party of Egypt), established in 1976 as the official government or state party, was transformed into the National Democratic Party as a base for the Sadat regime in 1978. Since then, the NDP has regularly captured a comfortable but declining majority of the seats in the People's Assembly. Because of the power of the NDP, the multiparty system has, despite the number of parties, only lately begun to take on its historical role of interest intermediation.

Another reason that the multiparty system has met with difficulties may lie in the preeminent role that long-existing class cleavages, along with the more recent religious strife, have played in shaping society and politics. Even before independence, society was sharply divided along class lines. During the first 30 years of formal independence, Egypt was dominated politically, economically, and socially by a small group of rural landowners. Since Nasser and his Free Officers (all from the middle class) took power, Egypt has been politically, economically, and socially dominated by the middle class. That class has not ruled without challenge but has faced strong countervailing pressure from the large and powerful working class.

The societal division along class lines has had two effects on Egyptian women. The material circumstances of their lives and thus the issues that concern them have significantly differed by class. At the same time, because of the important role that bourgeois and then middle-class women played in the history of the Egyptian women's movement, women's political engagement has been directed by the agendas and the activities of women from these social classes. The bourgeois women, led by Huda Sha'rawi, who founded the Egyptian Feminist Union—an organization that shaped the social agendas of women from 1923 to 1947—were the wives and daughters of large landowners.[2] Through familial relationships, they had access to economic resources. Like Sha'rawi, who was one of the wealthiest women of her time, they could also independently own large farms, palaces, and other real estate.[3] These women considered it their social obligation to help needy families and helpless women. In contrast, middle-class women, who eventually challenged the leadership of the older generation,

contended that their own professional education and positions made them better representatives of Egyptian women. As active participants in the social and economic arenas, they were able to offer strong arguments to support women's rights to economic and political equality.

Religious cleavages have also shaped politics. Though less a religious battleground than many of its neighbors, Egypt has faced religious conflicts since the 1970s. Over 90 percent of the population of over 50 million is Sunni Muslim, and the majority of the remaining 10 percent is Coptic Christian. As in many countries in that part of the world, society and thus politics and women's experiences have been influenced by the spread of Islamism, that is, new conservative political and economic interpretations of Islam that have been adopted by large social movements. The struggle between secular and Islamist groups in the middle class divided middle-class women and undermined their capacity to confront the conservative assault on women's rights in the 1970s and 1980s.

Although the unabashed dominance of the rest of society by the military ended with the death of Nasser in 1970, the military, both as a part of the middle class and as one of the most powerful interests in the nation, has continued to play an important role in politics. It has not stepped into the civil political arena, but the possibility of such intervention has been politically significant. The authoritarianism associated with the military ascent to power in 1952 affected the political engagement of men and women, especially the existence of independent organizations and groups. Rather than risk instability and thus military intervention, the state has followed a strategy of minimizing dissent, using carrots—in the form of its welfare state programs—and sticks, which have ranged from bans on political organizations to internment.

All of these factors have helped structure politics and thus women's political engagement, but by far the most consequential political actor since 1952 has been the state. Through the creation of an enormous bureaucracy, growing control over the private sector, and a corporatist approach to rule, the state has shaped Egyptians' lives and political engagement in crucial ways.

Not only has the state become the largest employer of women, but it has supported women's right to work and to vote. It has also attempted to represent women through the creation of a state women's organization, which it has used to mobilize women in support of its development policies, notably birth control. The political engagement of Egyptian women, whatever their class, cannot be understood without examining their relationship to the state and the dramatic reversals that have occurred in this relationship since the 1950s.

The increased political representation of women, initiated by the Sadat regime (1970–81), and reforms in personal status laws (regulating marriage, divorce, and custody of children) in the late 1970s were at first hailed as significant advances for Egyptian women.[4] The changes reinforced the transformation of both working-class and middle-class women into dependent clients of the state, a process started in the 1960s. Meanwhile, these formal and legal changes, once established, also gave the Islamist opponents of women's rights the opportunity to counterattack.

In the 1980s social pressure by Islamists to encourage women to return to the home and international pressure by the International Monetary Fund and the World Bank to dismantle the welfare state as part of a structural adjustment program made the Mubarak regime adopt a new hands-off policy vis-à-vis women. To avoid political and economic instability, the state abandoned its commitment to advance women's rights in return for the social, economic, and political support of conservative forces and international patrons.

Even under the most hospitable conditions, gender issues present states with serious dilemmas, particularly when the interests of men and women clash. In Egypt the key to the alliance between women and the state and the result of that alliance—state feminism as an institutional and ideological system—has been economic growth. Economic downturns have severely

tested this alliance and shown its fragile and transitory nature.

This analysis of Egyptian women's political engagement begins with a brief discussion of the similarities and differences of state feminism as an ideology, a strategy, and an institutionalized system. State policies concerning women's employment, political representation, and organization during the 1970s and 1980s are then analyzed to understand how changes have been affected by different groups and classes of Egyptian women and how Egyptian women have, in turn, been affected by them.

THE PHENOMENON OF STATE FEMINISM

Most theoretical discussions of state feminism are made in the context of the development of the welfare state, especially as it has occurred in the Scandinavian countries. There the welfare state presides over an advanced industrial capitalist economy characterized by prosperity and abundant resources. The welfare state is hence able—as part of its social contract with the citizens—to supply social services and programs to organized interests and social classes, including women. In return, the state can claim a base of popular support. The end result of this relationship in an advanced industrial capitalist society is that the welfare state is a significant social actor similar to other civil institutions, such as the family and private capital, in regulating aspects of the lives of citizens.

The unique development of the Egyptian state and the ways it has affected Egyptian state feminism present a thought-provoking contrast to these standard understandings of the development of state feminism. Egypt traditionally had an underdeveloped, largely agrarian economy; the state had limited resources. Shortly after the 1952 revolution the state began a drive toward economic development and the cultivation of an egalitarian postcolonial citizenry that would provide the state with broad social and political support. Owing to the reluctance of those with private capital to invest in industrialization, the state took the lead with centrally planned capitalist growth. The ideology that accompanied this model of economic development proposed the socialist transformation of society.

With the emergence of an economically active state came the creation of a state sector that provided employment and many social services—including education, health, and social security. The state began to compete with other institutions of civil society, such as private businesses and the family, in satisfying economic and social needs. Sexual discrimination in the workplace was outlawed. To reconcile women's work inside and outside the family, the state required the provision of day-care centers in any facility that employed more than 100 women, and laws made it easy for working mothers to take leave without pay or to work part-time to care for their children. The state also facilitated the economic and social integration of particular sectors of the working population, including women. In short, the middle class, which had been squeezed and excluded by the pre-1952 regimes, became key signatories and partners of the state in a new social contract.

In return for a commitment to the ideal of social justice and inclusion in the corporatist one-party system, these sectors gave up political liberalization. Because the state now controlled political representation and political organization, it could develop new bureaucratic elites who were more loyal to the state than to their own constituents. The state recruited the leaders of these groups, judged their success, and determined the length of their political careers. Women's political representation and participation thus was artificial to some extent, especially because women were the last group to be included in the political system.

Even though Egyptian state feminism developed in a different material and political context than its European counterparts, in both cases the state helped secure women's rights and used the feminist ideology to garner national and international legitimacy. By hiring women for state jobs and by making efforts to reconcile mothering with work outside the home through laws giving women three months of paid maternity leave, al-lowing nursing mothers one paid hour during the workday to feed their children, and providing day-care centers at the workplace, the state led the way toward integrating women into the work force outside the home. More important, the welfare states of Egypt and the advanced industrial societies passed laws that improved working conditions for all sectors of their societies.[5] As a result, both kinds of welfare states enjoyed a progressive image nationally and internationally.

Image and benefits notwithstanding, it is inaccurate to assume that the welfare states were non-patriarchal. Rather, programs and policies either left the old patriarchal forms standing or recreated them in new forms. Despite progressive labor laws that protected women against discrimination in the state sector, Egyptian women were seldom promoted to supervisory positions until they reached their 50s, that is, until close to retirement.[6] In other words, men monopolized leadership positions at every level of the work hierarchy.

The state did not challenge other patriarchal practices in the private sector or in the agricultural work force, where the wage differentials between men and women were large and where women were the last hired. Nor did it challenge the patriarchal character of the family in any way. Instead, even during the period of the most dramatic social and economic changes (1962–66), the state left the patriarchal family mostly untouched: presumably the husband-father was the breadwinner even in two-income families, and housework was the responsibility of the working woman. Instead of letting autonomous women's organizations develop, the state co-opted and incorporated middle-class women's groups into its own corporatist structure, as well as nurtured its own political elite of women to preempt the rise of other autonomous organizations, which would be primarily responsive to women's needs and priorities.[7] In short, state feminism in Egypt, as in the advanced industrial states, replaced the old form of patriarchy based on the family with a new form of patriarchy originating in state control—a state patriarchy.

In welfare states, economic crises seem to have

an impact on the state's commitment to the groups that support it. In particular, a slowdown in economic growth tests the commitment of the welfare state to women and leads to a serious challenge for state feminism. When a conservative social climate prevails during periods of economic downturn and social retrenchment, the state's capacity to continue its commitment to welfare programs is strained. State feminism faces hostile economic criticism (and is accused of contributing to the high cost of labor in the state sector), withdrawal of political support, and social pressure for women to return home. What becomes apparent during economic crises is that state feminism is the proverbial darling daughter, happy and doted on only during times of economic expansion and planned social change.

Confronted with worsening economic, social, and political conditions, different groups and classes of women have been affected by and have responded to them in unique ways. The development of Egyptian state feminism is a study in contrasts. In the 1950s and the 1960s, when the progressive credentials of the state were established through its commitment to public employment and education for women, women made impressive gains in these two areas. Their numbers in the labor force increased by 31.1 percent from 1961 to 1969.[8] Illiteracy among women dropped from 88.2 percent in 1947 to 78.9 percent in 1966. Enrollment gains by women and girls at all levels were equally impressive. Women were 7.5 percent of university students in 1951–52 and 40 percent by 1970–71.[9]

Women's political rights were also expanded. In 1956 the state granted women the right to vote and the right to run for public office. In 1964, in an effort to compensate for its political authoritarianism, the state passed a law guaranteeing jobs in the public sector for all holders of intermediate college diplomas and university degrees.[10] This law was accompanied by the institution of a host of social services that enabled working mothers to remain employed in the public sector. As a result, unemployment reached its lowest levels ever in the first half of the 1960s. The overall unemployment rate was 2.2 percent in 1960. As the state sector continued to enlarge, this rate declined even further, to 1.3 percent in 1966.[11] The 1950s and the 1960s were the golden decades of Egyptian state feminism.

Even in this progressive social and economic period, however, women's unemployment was three times higher than men's. Economic and political crises, manifested in increased national indebtedness and violent clashes between the state and underground Islamist groups, unfolded during the Sadat regime beginning in the mid-1970s. The crises, which are still unresolved, have contributed to conservative social pressure for working women to return to the home.[12]

In developing societies like Egypt, aid-granting nations and international institutions also have an influence during crises. Because state programs and services that benefit women are viewed as an economic burden, these external actors exert pressure on the state to dismantle them, thus participating actively but indirectly in creating conditions that disadvantage women.

External actors have been the most important factors affecting the commitment of the Egyptian government to state feminism and women's employment programs. Since 1978 the International Monetary Fund and the World Bank have exerted pressure on the state to withdraw from the economic arena and to accelerate privatization.[13] As a result, the state reneged on its commitment to employment as an intrinsic part of the social contract that it had agreed on two decades earlier. The reversal of policy continued under Mubarak and shook the official commitment to state feminism in the late 1970s and 1980s. Because of the economic crisis and the ensuing social and political upheavals, significant changes occurred in women's relation to the state in the key areas of employment, political representation, and organization.

WOMEN'S EMPLOYMENT

To correct the inefficiencies of state-led economic development, there was a shift from the centrally planned economy of the 1960s to *infita* (economic openness) and a reliance on local,

Arab, and international private capital in the place of state investment. With an annual inflation rate of over 20 percent, Egypt ended subsidies on some basic goods (flour, sugar, and rice) in 1977.[14] This decision provoked large-scale riots in all major cities in the country.

The economic crisis that has prevailed since the mid-1970s has had several contradictory effects on women's employment. Inflation pushed women into the work force as two-income families became the only means of avoiding downward mobility. The percentage of women in the work force (outside agriculture) nearly tripled, from 4.2 in 1966 to 11.2 in 1986. The economic need to work increased in the 1980s, but pressure on the state and society from both internal and external forces nevertheless led to marked decline in the rate of increase in women's participation in the labor force from 1960–76 to 1976–86.[15]

Economic liberalization in the mid-1970s was accompanied by a new alliance between the state and the Islamist groups who had been the political foes of Nasser and his regime. The political purpose of the alliance was to undermine the power of the former president's political and social supporters—the secular sectors of the middle class—in important institutions like universities and professional associations, thus facilitating the planned economic changes.

In a so-called effort to reduce surplus labor, the state slowed down the pace of hiring new graduates in the state sector. Now graduates of universities and intermediate schools must wait six and five years, respectively, before they can be offered a job there. The state hoped that young job applicants would use the waiting period to find jobs in the private sector. Unfortunately, it misjudged the capacity of the private sector to absorb more educated workers. In 1976, when liberalization accelerated, total unemployment shot up to 7.7 percent: 5.5 percent for men and 29.8 percent for women. By 1986 the overall unemployment rates had doubled to 14.7 percent: 10 percent for men and 40.7 percent for women.[16] The end result of this retreat on the part of the state has been a high level of unemployment among men and an unemployment crisis for women. Because of the particular policies that the state has adopted in the process of structural adjustment, a disproportionate number of the 40 percent of women who want to join the formal labor force and cannot are young graduates. Closely intertwined with the effect of the state retreat up to now has been the resurgence of political groups who use Islam to contest the legitimacy of secular values and roles.

Although Islamist groups have encouraged women's education, they have frowned on women's participation in the economy outside the home, arguing that it contravenes their primary role as homemakers and mothers. The Islamist groups accept public work by women only in cases of economic necessity.[17]

The impact of the high rate of unemployment on middle-class women has been disturbing, especially in terms of the consciousness of the younger generation. The unemployment of younger women enhances their dependence on their families and encourages them to accept their future role as dependent housewives. Meanwhile, because unemployment also affects the prospects of young men, it has effectively raised the marriage age for both men and women. The result is a generation of men and women who experience high levels of frustration and emotional stress, and the women find it difficult to develop an interest in larger social and political issues.

Working-class women have faced an equally trying situation. With the retreat of the state, the working conditions of working-class women have deteriorated in both the private and the state sectors. Private-sector businesses often stop just short of hiring 100 women workers to escape the legal requirement of providing day-care centers. In addition, they often hire women on a contract basis for long periods to avoid paying social security benefits to them. Then, too, they can fire them easily, without the need for documentation.

In the state sector promotions are rare for women workers. Even when a promotion is given, the salary does not increase. Instead, women are given less demanding work away from machines.[18] Managers have recently adopted practices used in the private sector, ignoring the age requirement stipulated by labor laws and hiring girls. Because the girls work on a contract rather than a permanent basis, the employer (in this case the state) does not have to pay pension benefits.

Conditions for child care in the state-run Helwan textile mills show the changes brought about by the state's retreat from economic liberalization. Children used to be provided with a meal of milk, chocolate, and biscuits at the day-care center; now they are given only biscuits. Children used to be given two uniforms to wear on top of their clothes; now they are given only one. Formerly doctors examined the children twice a week, but examinations have been discontinued. The present day-care center does not have enough workers, nor is any type of instruction given to the children. Instead, the children are left in front of a television set. Previously the center admitted all children a year and a half old and older. Now it accepts only those who are at least two years old, and it can refuse to take hyperactive children. Conditions for infant care have deteriorated as well: Where working mothers were entitled to one paid hour a day to breast-feed their children, the hour is now deducted from their pay. Many women no longer make use of this hour and instead wean their children early or switch them to dry milk.[19]

The retreat from liberalization has led to a decline in other social services, especially in the public school system. Because of the fiscal restraints dictated by the International Monetary Fund, public schools operate two half-day school sessions instead of one full-day session. As a result, many working-class women have been forced to put their children in private schools that keep the children until late in the afternoon, when the mothers leave work. The mothers must give their children additional private lessons to compensate for the poor instruction given in the very large classes.[20]

In short, many of the laws and programs that gave Egyptian state feminism a socially progressive image have been undermined since 1974 by the state itself in the switch to economic liberalization. To make the public sector more profitable, the state is hiring girls, paying them less than the women they replace, and cutting off the benefits formerly given to women workers to help them reconcile the tasks of motherhood and work outside the home.

POLITICAL REPRESENTATION

The campaign for equal political representation for women commenced in the early 1920s, when a young Wafdist woman, Munira Thabit, framing the issue in terms of national independence, criticized the constitution of 1923 because it denied women the right to vote and to run for public office. In 1936, when Egypt was acquiring more political autonomy from Great Britain, the Egyptian Feminist Union, headed by Huda Sha'rawi, began to lobby for women's suffrage.[21] Feminists believed that an independent Egypt would give women equal rights in emulation of European states. The Feminist Union, formed in response to an invitation sent by the International Alliance for Women's Suffrage to attend an international conference in Rome, adopted the social and political agenda of the alliance and its role as a lobbying group on behalf of all women—all Egyptian women in the case of the Feminist Union. In the 1920s the major concerns of the union were social. It supported many charitable activities that provided working-class women with jobs and literacy. In the 1930s Sha'rawi, in her arguments in favor of women's suffrage, emphasized the political absurdity of denying educated and well-informed women of the bourgeois and middle classes the franchise while illiterate men were given the right to vote.[22] Although the particular approach to women's equality used by the union gave bourgeois women a certain degree of confidence in their organizational skills and capacities and created a base of support among them, the union was unable to effect any real changes on the question of suffrage.

The struggle for suffrage entered a new stage in the 1950s. The death of Huda Sha'rawi in 1947 contributed to the weakening of the Egyptian Feminist Union, whose organizational cohesion was undermined by feuding among its factions. Duriya Shafiq, representing a new generation of feminists, formed a new organization called Bint al-Nil (Daughter of the Nile) in 1949, which organized young middle-class women around the women's suffrage issue. Using a much more confrontational strategy than the Feminist Union did, they engaged in a series of protests, including storming Parliament in 1951 to protest the exclusion of women from membership and launching a hunger strike in the reporters' syndicate in 1954 to object to the Free Officers' exclusion of women from membership in the Constituent Assembly that was writing a new constitution.[23]

These actions captured the public imagination with their militancy and personal commitment and mobilized a large number of bourgeois and middle-class women in the campaign for women's political equality. The protests contributed to a social climate that made it difficult for the state to skirt the views of women on all important social and political issues. Although men and women disagreed over the tactics used by Bint al-Nil, Shafiq succeeded in moving the public debate beyond the point reached by the earlier feminists with their tactic of gentle persuasion. Equally important, the activism showed the zeal of a core group of women for the cause of women's equality and their capacity to mobilize a much larger number of women around the issue.

Meanwhile, by 1956 it had become clear to the Nasser regime that the issue of women's political rights had developed broad-based support among the diverse and well-organized women's groups of the bourgeois and middle classes and that it was not going to go away. In January 1956, a few days before the announcement of the 1956 constitution, the representatives of 20 women's associations formed a federation "to concentrate the efforts of the different women's associations through the establishment of a larger organization which would serve as communica-tion link among the member associations."[24] These member organizations were voluntary associations whose largely social activities were dominated by bourgeois women. Although the federation was ostensibly apolitical, because some members' charters prohibited political involvement, its formation was a key stepping-stone in the struggle for women's political equality.

During the same week Amina al-S'aid, the editor of *Hawa'* (Eve)—the first women's magazine published by a major publisher—and a newly elected member of the reporters' syndicate, the professional association that represents reporters' views and concerns, gave a lecture in which she defended women's right to vote.[25] Until then, al-S'aid, a pioneering middle-class professional like Shafiq, had been one of Shafiq's critics, a supporter of the new regime and one of its shining role models. Her lecture was a response to news that the 1956 constitution was not going to grant suffrage to women. The ambivalence of the regime transformed her into one of its critics, as her presentation at the syndicate indicated.

Responding to the growing restiveness within these influential sectors of society and trying to defuse the suffrage issue, which split men and women, families, and political groups, the state granted women the right to vote and to run for political office in the 1956 constitution. Yet the constitution also placed limits on women's equality: "All men who have the right to exercise their political rights must be registered to vote. It is also necessary to register those women who request [that right]."[26] The memorandum accompanying the law explained that "the law observed the principle of equality between men and women in registering to vote as part of its recognition of the important role played by women in public life for a long period of time and the manifest impact that this has had on the development of the state. In view of the prevailing Egyptian customs, however, the registration of women to vote is left as a *choice* to be decided by each individual woman."[27]

To be registered, women had to petition the state to recognize and include them as registered voters—a requirement that disadvantaged rural women, a large number of whom were illiterate. This bureaucratic hurdle also discouraged many women from voting and neutralized women's numerical and electoral impact. More important, by creating the registration prerequisite, the state was able to split the women's movement. The issue of women's suffrage was portrayed as the concern of a small minority of privileged women who were isolated from the majority of illiterate and depoliticized women.

If bourgeois and middle-class women noted the limits placed on their exercise of political rights, they were not critical of them. Capable themselves of dealing with the bureaucratic hurdles set up by the state, they did not care about the problems posed for working-class women. Their campaign for political equality had emphasized the absurdity of giving political rights to illiterate men and denying these rights to the educated middle-class women. This may explain why they did not oppose placing restrictions on illiterate women.

Over the next 20 years the requirements prevented all but a very few women from registering to vote. In 1956–57 only 1 percent of the total number of registered voters were women; in 1972, 12 percent.[28] Not surprisingly, the number of women elected to Parliament during this period was also negligible: two in 1957, less than 1 percent of the total membership; six in 1960 (1.7 percent); eight in 1964 (2.2 percent); only three in 1969 (0.8 percent); and nine in 1971 (2.5 percent).[29]

In the corporatist and authoritarian political system, state support was crucial for election. Women were seen as political novices, but because the state was interested in some representation of women in Parliament, which would help it maintain its feminist credentials, it cultivated a new generation of women to serve among the political elite.[30] Both the minister of social affairs—women had filled the position since 1962—and women parliamentarians were members of that elite. Most of the women in Parliament were elected because the state supported them, not because women voted for them. They did not see themselves as representing a gen-

dered constituency and consequently defined their role in terms of the needs of a broad constituency of women and men.[31] The regime's attempt to form its own women's organization was largely unsuccessful, so the political mobilization of women in support of the regime and its policies remained very modest.

From 1950 to 1970 both the bourgeois women and the middle-class women within the political elite adopted as their starting point the importance of gender equality as a part of national development. The early bourgeois feminists, like Shafiq, thought that political equality and women's participation in the government would eventually translate into social equality. As women became part of the legislative process, they were expected to push for state policies that would protect the interests of women as wives, mothers, and working women, and those policies would eventually bring about women's full equality. The assumption was that political powerlessness was a function of illiteracy—not of poverty or systematic social and economic inequality. Education was seen as the most effective means to political empowerment.[32]

In the intolerable economic and social conditions of the 1950s working-class women's priorities were very different. For them, poorly paid and overworked as they were, survival outweighed the need for education, suffrage, and representation. Bourgeois women's attempt to gain influence in the governmental power structure could not succeed, for they did not have the numerical strength of working-class women supporting them.

The socialist approach of the state to the problem of women's subordination identified working-class women in relation to working-class men and focused on the economic hardships that arose from class circumstances. In the late 1950s and the 1960s the state's response to working-women's concerns was to raise the wages of working-class men. Though addressing some survival needs in doing so, the wage policies did not challenge the principle of lower wages for women and certainly did not address the issues of women's equality or self-empowerment.

Rather, the state asserted the dependence of working-class women on men as part of their way of life.[33]

The Sadat regime (1970–81) had contradictory effects on women's political representation. The state's alliance with Islamist groups—concluded to defeat the Nasserites in the early 1970s—contributed to the development of a new constitution in 1971 that was a setback for women. The constitution specified that the national commitment to gender equality applied only in cases where it did not contradict the rules of the sharia (Islamic law), a provision that opened the door to further discussions about whether or not women's rights to work and participate in politics clashed with literal readings of Islamic texts.[34] By widening social and political divisions among women and men, the constitution thereby undermined the security of these important rights.

The economic liberalization that began in 1974 was accompanied by a controlled political liberalization beginning in 1976 and redefinition of the social contract that the state had worked out with the middle classes in the 1960s, giving the middle class increased freedom of political expression in exchange for a lessening of state commitment to the goal of social justice—which had until that point taken the form of a guaranteed right to work and the provision of key social services. Yet the state did not withdraw from the political arena completely. It continued to exercise control over which and how many political parties were allowed to operate and to play off sectors of society against each other. Thus, when the state clashed with the Islamist groups in July 1977 after the assassination of Sheikh al-Dahabi, the minister for religious endowments, it attempted to distance itself from the Islamist groups by asserting a renewed commitment to women's rights.

In the early 1970s Jehan Sadat, the wife of the president, revived the pre-1952 bourgeois feminist approach to women's concerns. She emphasized the importance of the charitable activities of the old bourgeois women's associations in providing badly needed services. In addition to relying on the resources of the old bourgeoisie to ease the state out of the social arena, she appealed to the charity of the Arab, European, and U.S. bourgeoisie and their representatives in financing some of her ambitious projects for physically disabled veterans of the 1973 Egyptian-Israeli war.[35]

Unfortunately for Jehan Sadat, her financial mismanagement of these projects brought them into disrepute with large sections of the population and created serious doubts about the reliability of this approach for the provision of vital social services.[36] More important, the use of charity from the wealthy as the solution to major social problems facing working-class women (such as unemployment) represented a return to the old piecemeal patronization of the poor. The notion of poverty as a social problem and thus the state's responsibility was abandoned in favor of a laissez-faire state attitude toward the poor as merely the object of wealthy people's humanitarian concern.

Jehan Sadat also adopted a superficial bourgeois approach to women's struggle for political equality. Her solution to the problem of the small number of women representatives in Parliament was to lobby her husband to give women their rights through a presidential decree. The prominence of Jehan Sadat and her bourgeois political agenda, in conjunction with the state's break with the Islamist groups, led to a renewed commitment on the part of the state to women's concerns. On 20 June 1979, President Sadat issued a decree that added 30 seats in Parliament for women and specified that 20 percent of the seats in the 26 government councils around the country would also go to women.[37]

Unlike in 1956, when public opinion was mobilized by feminist groups in the campaign for women's political rights, in 1979 the presidential decree sought to force the issue upon a hostile public successfully mobilized by the Islamist groups to oppose further progress on gender issues. In the long run, the attempt to transform relations between the sexes from the top down by authoritarian means (a decree by the president instead of debate in the People's Assembly) rendered a disservice to the cause of women's rights by transferring the people's anger against the regime to the cause.

Political opportunism on the part of Jehan Sadat and the feminists working with her thus resulted in the association of the women's rights movement with a corrupt and unpopular regime in return for increased formal representation, as well as for cosmetic changes in the personal status laws.[38] The latter gave women the right to divorce if the husband took a second wife and gave a divorced wife with children the right to the family home. Short-sightedly, the opportunists apparently did not mind the costs involved either in the identification of women's equality with an unpopular government or in the regime's exploitation of the cause to project a progressive image.

The result was a backlash from the public. Judges refused to implement the new personal status laws, claiming that they contradicted the sharia. The women's rights movement hence found itself in an awkward position: while condemning the way the laws were passed, it also praised the regime for the changes introduced.

In the 1984 elections all 31 seats reserved for women were occupied by members of the NDP (a seat for the Cairo district was added to the 30 seats originally reserved for women). The government appointed two more women to the People's Assembly from the opposition, the New Wafd Party. Dependence on the state for political representation undermined public confidence in the viability of women's candidacy. Without an independent political base of support, women had no power to determine state policies regarding their political representation. Policies were determined by the whim of the state and political expedience.

The laws increasing women's political representation and changing aspects of the personal status laws did not enhance the legitimacy of the cause of women's rights but instead strengthened its enemies. At the same time, women candidates were transformed from independent political actors into dependent clients of the governing regime and its party, the NDP.

The presence of 36 women in Parliament in 1984 (33 in seats reserved for women and 3 elected in their own right) did not make it any easier to get such women's concerns as day-care centers and better working conditions on the legislative agenda. Many of the women who were elected felt that they were bound to toe the party line in the selection of issues to be discussed as well as in the positions taken.[39] The feminist rationale for increasing women's representation in Parliament to create a bloc that would represent women and protect their interests was rendered meaningless. Instead, the law gave a group of women in the ruling party the chance to improve their individual prospects within the system of partisan politics. In return, the presence of these women and the role that they played in the debates on women's issues allowed the NDP to claim that it was the legitimate heir of state feminism.

ALTERNATIVES TO STATE FEMINISM: WOMEN'S NONGOVERNMENTAL ORGANIZATIONS

Since the mid-1970s an intriguing paradox of the state-led democratization in Egypt has been state control over the establishment and recognition of independent social and political groups. Although women's creation of nongovernmental associations has increased significantly, state power to restrict the political organization and activities of women has been a serious obstacle for women from both the middle and working classes and has profoundly shaped the forms that their political organization has taken.

The state has recognized and encouraged the formation of welfare associations sponsored by bourgeois women to provide the services and income-generating activities for the needy that the state is no longer willing to supply.[40] Thus, after 30 years of officially deemphasizing the significance of such social activities, the Ministry of Social Affairs began aggressively supporting them. The minister has attended social functions of the welfare associations, and state-run newspapers publish their news as human interest items. They serve as loyal allies of the state, enjoy official support and approval, and seldom criticize social policies. Bourgeois women, like their entrepreneurial husbands, support the withdrawal of the state from the social arena, which leaves them with socially worthwhile causes (such as adult literacy, healthcare for women and children, and orphaned children) that fill up their leisure time and enhance their social image.[41]

In contrast, the state has been strongly opposed to the formation of middle-class feminist organizations, viewing them as potentially critical and also likely to bring about a confrontation between the state and Islamist groups. The original impetus for the formation of (feminist) nongovernmental associations for women came from the failure of the "official" representatives of women—the members of the NDP in Parliament and in the state-sponsored women's organization, the National Commission for Women—to represent women and protect their interests in the political arena against the attacks of Islamist groups.

The effort to organize independent nongovernmental women's associations began in 1977 with small informal groups of women who came together to discuss women's issues, especially the formation of a national organization of women. Soon, formal committees on women were being set up in existing professional associations and political parties. The first was established in 1979 by women artists and reporters. Luckily, because these formal committees originated as additions to already existing associations, forming them did not require the permission of the state. They were semi-independent (nongovernmental) women's groups whose major activity was the organization of debates and symposia every year to celebrate International Women's Day and Egyptian women's contributions to society.[42]

The activities and mobilizing efforts of the women's committee in the reporters' syndicate encouraged some political parties and other groups to create feminist organizational wings. For example, the Constituent Congress of the Federation for Progressive Women (an organization of the National Progressive Unionist Party) met in January 1982 to discuss its program and its links with the party.[43] In 1984 the Arab Lawyers' Federation set up a permanent committee on women's concerns. The committee was seen as a "natural extension of the federation's interest in the discussion of human rights. . . . It also allowed women to have their own committee within the organization and hence pay special attention to [a group that] makes up half of humanity and whose rights are largely ignored."[44]

The Cairo drive to organize nongovernmental associations for women encouraged activists outside the capital to form their own associations. In 1984 in Mansura, a town in lower Egypt, Jami'yat Bint al-'Ard (Daughter of the Land Association) asked for and got permission to start some cultural activities, largely discussions of Egyptian women's contributions to society. This was the first completely unaffiliated nongovernmental women's organization in Egypt, and its formation demonstrated the existence of a strong feminist awareness among geographically scattered women. Until then, women from Cairo had been the dominant participants in the Egyptian women's movement.

Although Bint al-'Ard shared the middle-class feminist perspectives of other organizations that were coming together then, it did not meet with the same opposition from political authorities. In contrast, Nawal El-Saadawi's controversial reputation and the location of the headquarters of her proposed organization in Cairo caused the state to view Tadhamun al-Mar'at al-'Arabiya (Solidarity of Arab Women's Association) suspiciously. In the early 1970s El-Saadawi's books on male and female sexuality led to her dismissal from the Ministry of Health, where she had been employed as a physician. The state refused to grant official recognition to her association. Eventually El-Saadawi mobilized key liberal (male) public figures, who pressured the state to grant permission for its establishment.

Even though the two organizations do not work together, Bint al-'Ard and Tadhamun al-Mar'at al-'Arabiya have both been primarily concerned with the increasing social conservatism of Egyptian society and its implications for Egyptian women. They are attempting to establish a separate voice for women on the major issues of the day. Both have recently published magazines—for members only, because of the state refusal to allow such publications to circulate among a larger audience. State hostility has been even more marked because the magazines, which are directed first and foremost to the literate urban public, are raising middle-class women's consciousness of the structural forces that oppress them and of their own differences. Thus both organizations, in opposition to Islamist groups, advocate less rigid interpretations of Islamic gender roles and emphasize the importance of women's organizing around issues that unite them while also acknowledging their divisions.[45] They are also concerned with raising public awareness of the role that Egyptian women have played in the history, culture, and society of their country.

Working-class women's efforts to organize have met with state opposition, too. Labor unions have been their vehicle for presenting bread-and-butter issues. The unions do not have a feminist orientation, but at least they deal with the interests of working-class women. The state has repressed women who engage in labor union activities; it views them as a serious threat because they may effectively reach other working-class women—a group that is largely ignored by middle-class organizers. For example, when women workers at the Mahalla Textile Company struck in 1986 in support of their male colleagues, as well as in support of their own demands—to be paid for the weekly day off; to be paid more owing to the "special [stressful] nature of their work"; and to improve the quality of the meals to which they were entitled at work—they were interned by the police.[46] Internment, the harshest response to women's activities, was understandable on one level. The state saw union members' collective action as a potential threat against the state. Working men and women were for the first time united in a single cause, and working-class women, previously assumed to be passive, had become politicized.

THE FUTURE

The prospects for increased employment for Egyptian women are dim. Privatization is presenting women with fewer employment opportunities and deteriorating work conditions. The capitalist model of development, adopted since the mid-1970s, is not woman friendly and has, in practice, undermined the state's commitment to the employment of young people. Because the state still voices the rhetoric of employment opportunities for women, activists can use this avowal in their struggles to address the serious problem of structural unemployment.

The prospects for the quest for equal representation are also unclear. In 1987 the high Constitutional Court ruled that reserved seating for women was unconstitutional, arguing that the special treatment of women undermined the constitutional principle of gender equality.[47] The effect of this ruling on the 1987 election was mixed. On the one hand, limited public support for the women who were identified with the NDP and depended on the state for electoral support became apparent when fewer women parliamentarians (14, down from 36 in 1984) were voted in. On the other hand, the minister of social affairs (a woman) had worked for women's registration to vote, with the result that the proportion of those registered who were women increased to 18 percent.[48]

The ruling seems designed by the women within the regime's political elite to create an outside base of support. But although large numbers of women participated in the 1990 election campaigns and voted, only seven women were elected to the People's Assembly: four from the NDP and three independents. Three were also appointed by the president, bringing the total to ten, a decrease from the fourteen elected in 1987.[49] The president usually appoints some members of the assembly to assure the balanced representation of certain groups (like women and Coptic Christians) whose elected representation may be disproportionately low. In other words, increased voter registration and participation by women did not lead to the election of more women, pointing to women's lack of confidence in women candidates.

How successful the existing independent women's organizations will be in protecting women's interests will depend to a great extent on both the development of their capacity to represent the diversity of Egyptian women and on the state's attitude toward them. Unremitting hostility on the part of the state will affect their articulation of the interests of middle-class women as an important constituency. A more tolerant attitude may make them vital institutions of civil society. Although Bint al-'Ard seems to have been successful in its effort to represent and allocate power to a cross section of middle-class women, Tadhamun seems to be mainly under the sway of the towering figure of El-Saadawi and other members of her family, so it may have less potential to develop as a viable institution that can accommodate women with diverse ideals and approaches.

Working-class women seem more likely to participate in their labor unions than in the feminist organizations of middle-class women. The attempt by some of the working-class women to make the labor unions responsive to their interests is a promising development, despite the state's hostility to their increased activism.

The possible formation of a national organization for women, a goal that is often discussed by middle-class women's groups as a means of bargaining with the state over the personal status laws, child-care policies, and political representation, may be desirable when new working-class women's organizations have materialized or when their struggle to make labor unions sensitive to their needs has succeeded. Only then will such an organization represent the interests of different classes and not just those of bourgeois and middle-class women, the historical leaders.

If the state's hands-off policy has hurt young lower-, working-, and middle-class women, it has also been an impetus for the formation of numerous nongovernmental women's organizations among better-off middle-class and bourgeois women. The result has been a new public debate on gender relations and gender roles and a split among women of different classes along conservative and feminist lines. This split is not likely to disappear in the near future, for it also reflects some fundamental disagreements among middle-class women on the kind of society that they desire and the role that they should play in it.

The legal and institutional framework associated with state feminism has recently come under increasing attack. The ideology has until now shown itself capable of accommodating progressive as well as conservative strategies for change. The state's commitment to women has been affected by changes in its resource base, as well as in its political alliances. In the transition from socialist development to capitalist development the state has adopted ambiguous positions regarding women. Whatever their class, women have been neither passive in accepting state policies nor unified in defining their interests or their coping strategies.

Numerous paradoxes are associated with state feminism at this transitional stage. First, the economic and ideological desire to expel women from the labor force coexists with increased resistance by women of all classes to leaving the labor force at a time of serious economic crisis. Second, the rise of Islamism as a powerful force with an appeal to the victims of the economic crisis has precipitated the organization of independent women's associations. Third, economic and political liberalization has shattered the myth that there are undifferentiated women's interests. The economic and political crises have magnified the differences that exist in the way women of different classes define their interests, their allies, and their relation to the state.

In spite of the unwillingness of the state to defend women's rights after the 1970s, women's organizations will inevitably continue to pressure the state to respond to their needs. As independent constituents, no longer clients of the welfare state, women's organizations may explore strategies to influence national social and developmental policies. Still, women's political engagement, whatever direction it may take, will be determined to a great extent by the state, for women's lives are an arena where many constituents compete for the limited existing resources.[50]

NOTES

1. Al-Mu'tamar al-Ta'ssisi li Itihad al-Nis'a al-Taqaddumi (The founding conference of the Federation of Progressive Women), *Al-Birnamaj, al-La'iha, al-Bayan al-'Am, Qararat Tanzimiya* (The program, the charter, the general statement, executive decisions) (Cairo: Al-Tajamu'a al-Watani al-Wahdawi, 1982), 13–16.

2. Huda Sha'rawi's papers at the American University in Cairo, Special Collections.

3. "'Ihtijab 'Awal Misriyat Rafa'at al-Hijab" (Veiling: The first Egyptian woman removes the veil), *Al-Mussawar*, 18 December 1947, p. 169.

4. Earl Sullivan, *Women in Egyptian Public Life* (Syracuse: Syracuse University Press, 1986).

5. Ahmed Taha Muhammad, *Al-Mar'at al-Misriyat bayn al-Madhi wa al-Hader* (The Egyptian woman between the past and the present) (Cairo: Matb'at al-Ta'lif, 1979), 187, 189.

6. Majmu'at al-Muhtamat bi Shu'un al-Mar'at al-Misriyat (The Group of Women Concerned with the Affairs of the Egyptian Woman), *Al-Huquq al-Qanuniya lil Mar'at al-Misriyaty* (The legal rights of the Egyptian woman) (N.p., 1988), 16.

7. Mervat Hatem, *State Feminism in Nasser's Egypt* (forthcoming).

8. Al-Jihaz al-Markazi lil Ta'bi'at al-'Amma wa al-Ihsa' (The Central Agency for Public Mobilization and Statistics, or CAPMAS), *Al-Mar'at al-Misriyat fi 'Ishrin 'Am: 1952–72* (The Egyptian woman over 20 years: 1952–72) (Cairo: Markaz al-Abhath wa al-Dirasat al-Sukaniya, 1972), 51.

9. CAPMAS, *Al-Mar'at,* 42–45; Arab Republic of Egypt, *Al-Mar'at wa al-T'alim fi Jumhuriyat Misr al-'Arabiya* (Women and education in the Arab Republic of Egypt) (Cairo: Al-Markaz al-Qawmi lil Buhuth al-Tarbawiya, 1980), 76.

10. Heba Handoussa, *The Burden of Public Service Employment and Remuneration: A Case Study of Egypt* (Geneva: Monograph commissioned by the International Labor Office, 1988), 32.

11. Wedad Morcos, *Sukan Misr* (The population of Egypt) (Cairo: Markaz al-Buhuth al-'Arabiya, 1988), 45.

12. Mervat Hatem, "Enduring Alliance of Nationalism and Patriarchy in Muslim Personal Status Law: The Case of Modern Egypt," *Feminist Issues* 6, no. 1 (1986): 19–43.

13. Ibrahim Helmy Abdel-Rahman and Muhammed Sultan Abu Ali, "The Role of the Public and Private Sectors with Special Reference to Privatization: The Case of Egypt," in Said El-Naggar, ed., *Privatization and Struc-*
tural Adjustment in the Arab Countries (Washington, D.C: International Monetary Fund, 1989), 173.

14. Ibrahim Oweiss, "Egypt's Economy: The Pressing Issues," in Ibrahim Oweiss, ed., *The Political Economy of Contemporary Egypt* (Washington, D.C.: Center for Contemporary Arab Studies, 1990), 20–21.

15. Morcos, *Sukan Misr*, 42–43.

16. Nader Fergani, *Tabi'at Mushkil al-Tashghil fi Misr* (A characterization of the employment problem in Egypt) (Unpublished paper, September 1988), 22.

17. Ibid.

18. Fardus Bahnasy, "Humum Imra't 'Amila: Hiwar ma' 'Amilat Nasij" (The worries of a working woman: A dialogue with a female textile worker), *Al-Mar'at al-Jadida* 20 (July 1986): 34.

19. Ibid., 33–34.

20. Ibid.

21. Munira Thabit, *Thawra fi al-Burj al-'Aji* (A revolution in the ivory tower) (Cairo: Dar al-Ma'rif, 1945), 19, 13.

22. Huda Sha'rawi, "Wajib al-Mar'at ba'd al-Mu'ahda" (Women's duty after the treaty), *Al-Misriya,* 15 February 1937, p. 15.

23. Duriya Shafiq, *Al-Mar'at al-Misriya* (The Egyptian woman) (Cairo: Matb'at Misr, 1955), 205–8, 255–61.

24. *Al-Ahram,* 13 January 1956, p. 3.

25. Interview with Amina Shafiq, December 1989.

26. Muhammad, *Al-Mar'at*, 73.

27. Majmu'at al-Muhtamat, *Al-Huquq*, 30.

28. Muhammad Farghali Farag, "Tatawur Musharakat al-Mar'at al-Misriyat fi al-Hayat al-'Amma" (The development of the participation of Egyptian women in public life), in *Taghiur al-Wadh al-Ijtima'i lil Mar'at fi Misr al-Mu'asarat* (Cairo: Al-Markaz al-Qawmi lil Buhuth al-Ijtima'iya wa al-Jina'iyat, 1974), 207.

29. Ibid., 211.

30. Ibid., 211–13.

31. Nahid al-Shafi'i, "'Ashhar Muhamiya Tarwi Qisataha Ma' al-Intikhabat: Mufida Abdel Rahman" (The best-known woman lawyer tells her story of the elections), *Sabah al-Khayr,* 12 March 1987, pp. 22–23; Maha 'Omran, "'Awal Na'iba Barlamaniya fi Misr: Rawiya 'Atiya" (The first woman parliamentary representative in Egypt: Rawiya 'Atiya), *Sabah al-Khayr,* 12 March 1987, p. 25.

32. Shafiq, *Al-Mar'at*, 191, 196.

33. Sa'd Hagras, *Al-Islah al-Zira'i* (The agrarian reform) (Cairo: Maktabat 'Ain Shams, 1970), 238–39.

34. Muhammad, *Al-Mar'at*, 75.

35. Ibid., 301–3.

36. Abdallah Imam, *Jehan: Syidat Misr al-'ula wa al-Akhira* (Jehan: Egypt's first and last lady) (Cairo: Rose al-Yusef, 1986), 60–69.

37. Jehan Sadat, *A Woman of Egypt* (New York: Simon and Schuster, 1987), 364.

38. Ibid., 356–62.

39. The only exception to this general rule was their opposition to the government's effort to eliminate the seats earmarked for women. The elimination would have affected the government's own interests. See Sullivan, *Women in Egyptian Public Life,* 66–68.

40. Magda Mehana, "Qarinat al-Ra'is fi Mu'atamar al-Tanzimat al-Ahliya al-'Arabiya" (The president's wife at the conference of Arab private organizations), *Al-Ahram,* 1 November 1989, p. 5.

41. Alice al-Malakh, "Haw'a Tusehim fi Himayat al-Biy'at" (Women participate in protecting the environment), *Al-Ahram,* 23 March 1990, p. 11; Soheir al-Kayal, "Suq Khayriya min ajl al-Yatimat" (A charitable market for orphaned girls), *Hawa',* 24 January 1987, p. 12.

42. Iqbal Baraka, "Ba'd 'Ashr Sanawat: Maza Qadamat al-Mar'at lil Mar'at?" (After ten years: What have women achieved?), *Saba al-Khayr,* 8 March 1982, pp. 22–23.

43. National Progressive Unionist Party, *Al-Mu'tamar al-Ta'ssisi li Itihad al-Nis'a al-Taqaddumi* (The founding conference of the Federation of Progressive Women) (Cairo, 1984), 24.

44. Ingie Rushdy, "Al-Lajnat al-Dai'mat li Awdah al-Mar'at bi Itihad al-Muhamin al-'Arab Tatlub" (The demands of the standing committee on women's conditions in the Arab Lawyers' Federation), *Al-Ahram,* 30 November 1984, p. 12.

45. Angela Davis, "Women and Sex: Egypt," in *Women: A World Report* (London: Oxford University Press, 1985), 338–42.

46. Bahnasy, "Humum Imra't 'Amila," 37.

47. *Al-Ahram,* 1 January 1988, p. 11; Majmu'at, *Al-Huquq,* 30–31.

48. Majmu'at, *Al-Huquq,* 30.

49. Zakaria Abu Haram, "Fazat al-Dimuqratiya wa Khasirat al-Mu'aradha" (Democracy won and the opposition lost), *Akhr Sa'a,* 12 December 1990, pp. 6, 8–9.

50. The author wishes to acknowledge the financial support of the National Endowment for the Humanities and the American Research Center in Cairo for the research that was done on the early stages of state feminism in 1988–89.

▲ France

POLITICAL INFORMATION

Type of Political System: democracy
  Sovereignty: republic
  Executive-Legislative System: parliamentary
Type of State: unitary
Type of Party System: multiparty
Major Political Parties[a]

Le Parti Socialiste (PS, or Socialist Party): Formerly the French Section of the Workers' International; reorganized in its present form in 1971. Led by François Mitterrand, president of the Republic, since May 1981.

Le Parti Communiste Français (PCF, or French Communist Party): Founded in 1920; remains powerful in local government elections.

Le Rassemblement pour la République (RPR, or Rally for the Republic): Rightist party founded in 1976. Led by Jacques Chirac; includes followers and political heirs of Général Charles de Gaulle, first president of the Fifth Republic.

Union pour la Démocratie Française (UDF, or Union for French Republic): Center-right collection of republicans and liberals.

Les Verts (The Greens): Organized in 1984; focuses on environmental issues.

Le Front National (FN, or National Front): Established in 1972; extreme-right, fascist party that is anti-immigration.
Year Women Granted Right to Vote: 1944
Year Women Granted Right to Stand for Election: 1944
Percentage of Women in the Legislature[b]
  Lower House: 5.8%
  Upper House: 3.4%
Percentage of Electorate Voting for Highest Elected Office in Most Recent Election (1988): 84.2%[c]

DEMOGRAPHICS

Population: 55,996,000[d]
Percentage of Population in Urban Areas
  Overall: 73.4%
  Female: 74.0%
  Male: 72.6%
Percentage of Population Below Age 15: 21.3%
Birthrate (per 1,000 population): 14[e]
Maternal Mortality Rate (per 100,000 live births): 13
Infant Mortality Rate (per 1,000 live births): 8
Mortality Rate for Children Under Five (per 1,000 live births): 10
Average Household Size: 2.8
Mean Age at First Marriage
  Female: 24.3
  Male: 26.4
Life Expectancy[f]
  Female: 80.3
  Male: 72.0

EDUCATION

Ratio of Female to Male Enrollment
  First-Level Education: 94
  Second-Level Education: 102
  Third-Level Education (1980/1984): 97
Literacy Rate
  Female: 97.0%
  Male: 97.0%

ECONOMY

Gross National Product per Capita: U.S. $9,540
Percentage of Labor Force in Agriculture: 8.9%
Distribution of Agricultural Workers by Sex[g]
  Female: 37.0%
  Male: 63.0%
Economically Active Population by Sex
  Female: 44.2%
  Male: 71.2%

a. Arthur S. Banks, ed., *Political Handbook of the World, 1991* (Binghamton, N.Y.: CSA Publications, 1991), 232.
b. Institut National de la Statistique et des Etudes Economiques (INSEE, or National Institute of Statistics and Economic Studies), *Données Sociales, 1990* (Social statistics, 1990) (Paris: INSEE, 1990).
c. Ibid. d. Ibid. e. Ibid.
f. Ibid. g. Ibid.

The Same or Different?
An Unending Dilemma
for French Women

JANE JENSON AND
MARIETTE SINEAU

The revolution of 1789 marked France's first effort to make a political break with a monarchical form of government. The Fifth Republic, established in 1958, confirms this commitment to republican political forms, including a directly elected president and two legislative bodies—the National Assembly and the Senate. It now seems unlikely that the 56 million inhabitants of France would ever abandon this commitment. Nevertheless, controversy raged over institutional arrangements throughout the nineteenth century, and several efforts were made to reestablish the monarchy and even to create an imperial government. By the end of that century, however, the republican principle was firmly established with the creation of the Third Republic (1870–1939).

In all these years of controversy over the form of government—which generated passionate debate over "first principles"—women were excluded. Beginning in the fourteenth century, the *loi salique* (Salic law) prohibited women from inheriting the crown. Even in 1789, when the revolutionaries proclaimed the equality of all individuals in the Declaration of the Rights of Man and the Citizen, women gained no new political rights. Subsequent republics continued this tradition of conferring popular sovereignty only on men. After being the first nation to grant universal suffrage to all male citizens (1848), France was one of the last to give the vote to its female citizens (1944).

Legacies of this exclusion survive. In the election of 1988 women won only 5.8 percent of the seats in the National Assembly. After the senatorial elections of 1989, only 3.4 percent of the seats in the upper chamber were filled by women. Although the percentages were somewhat higher in the 1989 municipal elections (16.5 percent),

only 6 percent of mayors are women, and only one large city is headed by a female mayor.[1] In the bodies elected by proportional representation the statistics are somewhat higher, but never extraordinary. For example, 23.4 percent of the French delegation to the European Parliament, elected in 1989, was female.

With the electoral route seemingly barred to women, there has been a tendency to rely more on appointment to office for access to political power. If, in the 1980s, women still held only 7 percent of the positions in the high civil service, their presence in appointive positions has been greater.[2] Therefore, about a quarter of the ministerial staff is female, and about 13 percent of recent cabinet appointments are women.[3] The most dramatic evidence of this "co-optation from on high" is provided by the appointment of Edith Cresson as prime minister in May 1991.

Any international comparison quickly demonstrates that France lags behind many countries. Of the countries in the Council of Europe, France ranks only 17th in women elected to national office. Even other Roman Catholic and Latin nations, like Portugal, Italy, and Ireland, have more elected women—as does Switzerland, which was also very late to grant women access to electoral politics.[4] In these comparative terms, then, we might say that the French system of liberal democracy has not granted full and equitable access to politics for the female half of the population. Moreover, this absence of women from elite politics is one of the factors contributing to the relative silence in many realms of politics about women's particular situation and specific policy requirements.

During the two centuries that followed the French Revolution, two types of cleavages shaped French politics. The first divided a lay and republican left from a right that was a longtime supporter of expanded rights for the Catholic church and restoration of the monarchy. The second political cleavage was one of class, organized by political parties inspired by Marxist analysis.

Political alignments along these cleavages affected the situation of French women and the character and timing of their acquisition of civil and political rights. For example, the Radical Party believed that women were overwhelmingly under the influence of the church, and throughout the Third Republic it raised the threat of clerical domination if women were given the vote. This argument, phrased in terms of the "danger to the Republic," was completely self-serving in that it meant the Radicals would retain their own political power. In the Fourth Republic (1946–58) the cold war in France pitted the Parti Communiste Français (PCF, or French Communist Party), supported by almost 25 percent of the electorate, against the still-powerful Catholic church. This confrontation contributed to a postwar political discourse of ideological conflict between a Marxist left and a Catholic right, and almost all the strongest women's organizations after 1945 were linked to one of these ideological camps. Women on the right were active in Union Féminine Civique et Sociale (UFCS, or Women's Civic and Social Association), Ligue Féminine (LF, or Women's League), or Action Catholique (AC, or Catholic Action), and women on the left were active in Union des Femmes Françaises (UFF, or French Women's Association). All worked within an ideological framework that identified women's needs and interests in traditional ways. The church promoted traditional family values more than equality within the family and opposed any efforts by women to control reproduction, whether with contraception or abortion. The left-wing organizations never completely succeeded in challenging these visions of gender relations.

The development of the modern state also affected the ways women's politics took form. The state developed in a centralized form that was dependent on the translation throughout the governmental structure of decisions made in Paris. This level of political control from the center, as well as the concentration of cultural and educational institutions in the capital, meant that politics revolved around the actions of Parisians, modified only slightly by the events and needs of the provinces. This legacy of centralization—called Jacobinism to indicate its origins in the French Revolution—has marked all political action. Happenings in Paris have thus profoundly shaped women's politics too. For example, in spite of its outposts in many provincial cities, the radical feminist movement of the 1970s was overwhelmingly Parisian. The capital housed the most visible theoreticians and was the site of the most important demonstrations in the 1970s.[5]

In this chapter we argue that French women's political participation in elections, inside political parties, and in the women's movement has been overdetermined by partisan conflicts. The way women have sought greater space for representing an identity of their own has thus been a reaction to the conditions of party politics. Moreover, the forms that women's politics has taken in France reflect constant tension between a politics of equality and one of difference. This tension, apparent since the French Revolution, has been translated in recent years into a strategic dilemma. Women could claim their place in one of two ways: they could be "different" because of their biology or maternity or they could be "the same" and thereby disappear into an ungendered discourse that granted them little specificity.

The tension between two understandings of women's social and political possibilities has deep roots not only in the political history of France but also in its broader culture. For example, women were much involved in the first social policy initiatives, which culminated in France's version of the welfare state. Acceptance of this role, however, often depended on a clear distinction between politics and philanthropy, the latter of which was interpreted for and by bourgeois women as simply an extension of their traditional domestic responsibilities. Thus, new power granted to mothers inside the home might translate into more public responsibility for mothering, through philanthropy, but it did not necessarily mean that women made any gains toward achieving full civil and political rights—and therefore equality. Indeed, the feminist movement of the late nineteenth century in France only reluctantly came to a pro-suffrage position because it feared the consequences of challenging the division between public and private.[6]

Since the late nineteenth century France has had one of the highest rates of female labor-force participation and until recently one of the smallest gaps between women's and men's wages. It is, however, also a country where the vision of wives as totally subordinate to husbands was not modified in the Napoleonic Code until the middle of the twentieth century and where everyday language celebrates the difference between women and men. In the preamble of the Constitution of the Fourth Republic, women were granted civil, economic, and political rights equal to men.[7] The first election of the Fourth Republic brought a level of female participation in the National Assembly unequaled until the 1980s, in large part because the Communist Party endeavored to have the most women in its parliamentary delegation.[8] At the same time, reforms to establish equal pay for equal work were instituted. But serious limitations on the civil rights of married women embedded in the Napoleonic Code were not removed until the mid-1960s.[9]

It is this ambiguous legacy of political discrimination and everyday sexism that women's movements have had to combat since the nineteenth century. Indeed, all women seeking to participate in politics have faced a choice, albeit a constrained choice, over whether to emphasize the similarities or the differences between women and men.[10]

WOMEN AND ELECTORAL POLITICS

The legacy of the Fourth Republic, the first in which women could vote, was mixed for French women. The era brought new rights and permitted women to enter the political institutions—both elections and parties—in ways never before possible. Further, women's participation in the Resistance and liberation lent new visibility to and revitalized political activity among women's groups associated with the Catholic and Protestant churches and the trade unions.[11] Nevertheless, in their voting behavior and attitudes toward politics, many women confirmed the fears of those who thought that women's suffrage would reinforce the right wing of the political spectrum. Women tended to vote with the right more often, and they had more conservative ideas about social relations and the role of the state.[12] In the 1950s, women still had not developed the habit of electoral participation, and they tended to abstain at a higher rate than men and to describe themselves as disinterested in politics.[13] Much of this difference in attitudes and behavior was associated with women's greater religiosity and their age, which was older on average than that of French men, a generation of whom had been much reduced by the destruction of the World War I.[14]

These factors tended to reinforce a political discourse of difference, in which women were seen as a group separate from men, subject to their own political rhythms and requiring mobilization separately from men. Studies of this right-tilting gender gap and the higher rates of female abstention produced popular and academic discourses emphasizing women's alienation from politics, their lack of support for republican institutions, and their conservatism. Reinforcing these notions of their particularities was the relegation of high-level women politicians to parliamentary commissions dealing with matters considered typically "feminine."[15] This division of labor in the National Assembly also reinforced the sense of gender difference.

Even organizations that sought equality between women and men—like unions and many women's organizations—tended to argue for equality with a discourse of difference. They stressed the need for women to move into public life and break away from the influence of the church. They also pointed to the burdens of maternity and housework, which meant women needed special treatment to overcome structural biases and discrimination. Such claims tended to reinforce rather than dissipate the long-standing theme of women's difference.

For example, the largest trade-union confederation, the Confédération Générale du Travail (CGT, or General Confederation of Work), in the 1950s argued strongly for women's right to work. Its analyses stressed the benefits to children of having a working mother while many other groups claimed that having the mother at home was necessary to family well-being. Nevertheless, in its discourse on women and work, the CGT never separated women from their maternal functions. Working women were always described as mothers, and it was their maternal responsibilities that justified special protections for them. Men, of course, were simply workers; their private lives were considered irrelevant for union politics. Thus, even while making strong claims for new and expanded rights for working women, the CGT did so from a stance that emphasized the particularities of women.[16]

The party system of the Fourth Republic did not encourage much change in these habits. The system was exceedingly fragmented, and only the Communists and to some extent the Socialists maintained a regular party organization. Parliamentary parties rather than mass parties were the norm in this republic, and political formations were small and temporary, often simply a grouping around an individual and his "friends."[17] But the electoral system of proportional representation meant that there was certain depersonalization of politics that benefited female candidates. Thus, despite the decline in the number of women candidates during the 1950s, the total never fell much below 10 percent.[18]

The Fifth Republic was created in 1958. The preamble of its constitution reaffirmed gender equality, but it was the political and social changes provoked by the new institutions that really began to alter the ways French women participated in politics. Two were of fundamental importance, and the first involved an institutional change. With the establishment of a presidential system and an electoral law that discouraged party fragmentation, the party system began to consolidate and to become more regularized and stable.[19] The fragmented multiparty situation of the Fourth Republic quickly became a stable four-party system, with two large umbrella groupings on the right and the left. There were two left-wing parties: the Communists and the new Socialist Party, which organized in 1971 to bring together a wide range of noncommunist leftists. The Gaullists began to solidify as a party and were joined later in the 1970s by a second large formation of the center-right, the Union pour la Democratie Française (UDF, or French Democratic Union). Therefore, if the parties had wished, these stronger organizations could have begun to encourage women candidates.

Unfortunately, the new electoral system, based on single-member constituencies, discouraged such an increase. Between the last election of the Fourth Republic and the first of the Fifth Republic, the percentage of female candidates declined 7 percent, and in 1958 only 2 percent of all candidates were women. Constituency-based elections encouraged candidates with strong local ties that were often strengthened by allowing them to hold several offices simultaneously (e.g., mayor, departmental counsellor, and deputy). A consequence of this type of party system was that candidates for the National Assembly tended to be local notables who had built up political followings in their own region over many years. Few women had had such an experience.

An additional factor of some importance was that governmental appointments in the Fifth Republic tended to come from the senior ranks of the civil service, especially from those educated in the very prestigious *grandes écoles*—Ecole Nationale d'Administration (National School of Administration) and Ecole Polytechnique (the Polytechnic)—which at the time took very few women students.

But by the 1970s pressure for change began to mount. That pressure came from and interacted with other changes that occurred during the Fifth Republic. By the early 1960s it was clear that female participation in the labor force was rising, changing especially rapidly among married women with children. By the end of the

1980s, the model of labor-force participation displayed by women was much closer to that of men than it had been previously, especially among younger people.[20] Female and male rates of participation were drawing closer together and, even more important, women were increasingly likely to stay in the labor force after their children were born.[21]

One political result of these changes was that the electoral participation of women—including their interest in politics and their voting rates—rose rapidly. The difference in voting rates, which had been 7 to 9 percentage points in the 1950s, disappeared completely in the late 1970s and 1980s, as did the gender bias in reported disinterest in politics.[22] The right-leaning gender gap disappeared by the end of the 1970s, and by the end of the 1980s a new gender gap had appeared, with women more likely than men to support the Socialists.[23]

A study of this process of behavioral and attitudinal change shows that the factor most able to produce such a change is active participation in the labor force. Women in paid employment were much more likely than other women to participate in elections and to vote for the left, especially the Socialists. Moreover, the effects of labor force participation persisted even when women were temporarily out of the labor force; such women behaved more like those currently employed than like full-time housewives.[24]

While these two changes—one institutional and one socioeconomic—contributed to a shift in the ways that ordinary French women have participated in politics over the past 30 years, changes in elite practices have been slower in coming. Although the stabilization and polarization of the party system made it easier for women to become candidates, and their labor force participation encouraged their integration into the public world, socioeconomic and institutional barriers remained.

Although economic modernization in the 1960s and restructuring in the 1970s and 1980s has created more jobs for women, those jobs have not always been high-paying full-time occupations. Ironically, women workers as a group are becoming more than ever a central pillar of the national economy at the same time women as individuals are finding themselves in an increasingly precarious position in the labor force.[25] Nor has the wage gap in France closed substantially over these decades. Full-time salaries for men are 25 percent higher than those for women, and the gap is greatest among senior managers and professionals. Even though women are now overrepresented in the higher levels of the school system, they tend to earn less from their education. For example, a man with a degree from one of the grandes écoles will earn 3.5 times more than a man with no recognized training credentials; a similar comparison of women's incomes displays a gap of only 2.7.[26] As a result, those factors so often necessary for a successful career in politics—a prestigious occupation and high income—are in shorter supply for women than for men.

Ways to compensate for such socioeconomic differences have always existed, however. Political parties might *choose* to support women candidates and to encourage their political advancement. In liberal democracies we expect parties to be open to and even to engage in the "formation" of politicians. How they do this, however, involves strategic choices. In France the parties continue to be clubbish and oligarchic institutions that are closed to women in particular. And although they certainly pay attention to the voting power of women, the parties continue to neglect them as candidates for elected office. This reaction is in part still possible because the largest and most visible wings of the contemporary women's movement in France have never focused on the feminization of elected institutions. Thus, the parties remained relatively free to ignore the issue of promoting women and to continue to make decisions for women.

There are some differences among the parties, however. A statement made in 1985 by Jacques Chirac, the leader of the Gaullists, to the women's wing of his party, sums up the situation on the right: "Be among the best, and you will be among the candidates." This attitude serves not only the right-leaning Rassemblement pour la République (RPR, or Rally for the Republic), but also the UDF and the other smaller groupings of the right.

Since World War II the PCF has often behaved differently from the other parties. The Communists have presented themselves not only as the party with the most female candidates and deputies, but also as the one best able to bring about the liberation of women. In spite of this position, the PCF has never accepted a quota that would lead to the feminization of the party hierarchy,[27] and as electoral support for the Communists has collapsed over the past decade, so has their contribution to the representation of women in the National Assembly. In the legislature elected in 1988 the Communists had only 25 deputies (4 percent), and only one was a woman.

In the end, the Socialist Party was the only one to use a quota system to promote women. Party statutes stipulate that the proportion of women on all internal governing bodies match the proportion of women in the party membership. The quota was set at 10 percent in 1974, rising to 20 percent in 1979 and 30 percent in 1990. The quota is also applicable to candidacies, but only for those elections decided by proportional representation. In other words, legislative elections are excluded.

Given this commitment to the promotion of women—and the fact that the Socialist program borrowed certain feminist analyses—many people expected that the election of the Socialists in 1981 would bring some change.[28] Ten years later their record had lived up to none of these hopes, however. The quota has not been respected inside the party organization, nor has much effort been made to elect women to the National Assembly.[29] From the low level of 5 percent in 1978, the percentage of female Socialist candidates had risen in ten years to only 9.4 percent. Moreover, the party's "success rate" is even lower; only 6.2 percent of its delegation in the National Assembly is female. Thus, in this lack of change on the part of the Socialists, who form the majority of the National Assembly, we find much of the reason for the low overall participation of women in the most important elected body in France.

Given the unchanging attitudes of the parties and other actors toward women in politics, it is not surprising to observe that elected women find themselves in the situation of being "different" politicians. According to a recent study of the female politicians in the Assembly and the Senate and others holding party membership or high party positions, male politicians have an image of women politicians as constituting a tiny minority. Teased about being different, women politicians are reduced to their sex and considered inferior because of it.[30]

These elected women often feel themselves being closed out by their "otherness," by those who consider them capable of filling only the role attributed to traditional femininity. In reporting how they undertake their political activities, they describe themselves as being permitted only to occupy the roles of mother, social worker, mistress, assistant, secretary, or confidante.

In spite of being considered different, and therefore inferior, these women politicians do not reject completely the notion of their otherness. Whether they celebrate it or simply note it, they recognize that women's lives differ from men's. Rather than seeking simple assimilation to the world of male politicians, they aspire to change the acceptable ways of doing politics. In particular, women's responsibilities for managing daily life mean they bring a different dimension to the political realm. A majority of the women politicians believed that they represent a group capable of instituting substantial change if they have 50 percent of the seats in the legislature.

One thing they believed would change, for example, is the language of politics. It would become more relevant to everyday life—and truer. Other innovations would appear in the ways politics is done. Political activity could be separated from time-wasting and fruitless ideological quarrels and made more pragmatic and efficient; politics would no longer be a domain of hollow words but one of useful action. The boundaries of legitimate politics would also be expanded by adding to the political agenda issues considered private or unimportant.

In these ways, the female politicians studied not only criticize the words, styles, and practices of their male colleagues, but they also propose an alternative approach to politics. In this hope for an improvement in national politics, women, with their different experiences and relationship to everyday issues, become the hope for the future. Indeed, because of their perceptions of women as profoundly nonviolent, some women politicians believe that a female counterculture is the only one that can guarantee a future.

THE CONTEMPORARY WOMEN'S MOVEMENT

In the first decades after 1945, the situation of women remained one of limited civil rights and a popular discourse of not simply difference but also inferiority. But by the 1970s this situation was openly contested. A vibrant feminist movement appeared, and it has affected the lives of women in France, as well as women's studies far beyond the borders of the country. Yet the influence of the movement was quite limited and its message on the dimensions of similarity and difference ambiguous.[31] Indeed, the character of the contemporary French women's movement, out of which some of the elected women discussed above have come or with which they have been engaged in a 20-year dialogue, helps to account for not only their minority experience but also the meanings they attach to it. Part of the reason for the relative absence of women in the institutions of electoral politics lies with the strategy followed by the contemporary women's movement and with the experience that movement has had with party politics. The history of the women's movement closely followed the changing fortunes of the French left as a whole. It rose to prominence with the reconstruction and the improving electoral position of the left in the 1970s, and it lost strength as economic crises and restructuring undermined anticapitalist social forces in the 1980s.[32] Even though the women's movement was much influenced by the ebb and flow of the whole left in France, it was *gauchisme* (the far left) that had the greatest influence within the movement. Weighted toward the politics of this part of the left, the women's movement eschewed ordinary electoral politics. Indeed, major parts of the movement rejected electoral politics altogether. Within the movement there was little agreement about how to make claims for change, including whether women's needs should be represented in a language of equality or one of difference.

The arrival of what came to be known as the movement for women's liberation was announced by a symbolic act in August 1970 that attracted the attention of the press, especially the leftist Parisian press. A small group of women placed a wreath on the Tomb of the Unknown Soldier in the Arc de Triomphe in Paris. This wreath was placed in honor of the person who was even more unknown than the soldier: his wife. The movement expanded. At first it was unstructured and unorganized, but three major wings emerged quickly: revolutionary feminism, syndicalist feminism, and egalitarian feminism. The first of these was the most visible and came to be labeled French feminism. Because of the links this wing had to gauchisme, revolutionary feminism provided the center of gravity of the women's movement. The other two wings have also exerted an important influence on women's lives in the past two decades. And by the 1990s, these two wings were the only ones to maintain any presence in French society; revolutionary feminism had all but disappeared.

From the beginning the revolutionary feminist mainstream of the movement was labeled Mouvement de Libération des Femmes (MLF, or Women's Liberation Movement). Even this label was much contested, however. In 1979 an organization called Psychanalyse et Politique (Psychoanalysis and Politics) appropriated the label MLF as its exclusive trademark. The action was decried by other groups, who accused Psychanalyse et Politique of attempting to present itself as the sole expression of the movement and the only legitimate position. Other currents in revolutionary feminism have continued to refer to themselves as the MLF, and we follow that practice here.[33] This controversy was only one of the many that were perhaps inevitable for a movement born of sectarian politics like those of France's gauchistes.

Revolutionary feminism from the start displayed many legacies of its gauchiste origins and had a major impact on the far left. Indeed, the weakening of the far left, especially after 1975, both contributed to and in some cases followed from debates over how to respond to feminist demands and politics. Overall, the French women's movement was undermined by the internal conflicts and then severe weakening of the far left in the late 1970s and 1980.[34]

Influenced by Maoism and Trotskyism in the 1970s, the revolutionary wing of the women's movement was far less reformist in its goals than much of second-wave feminism in other industrialized countries. Improved state policies never served as the primary goal of the movement, and fewer reforms resulted from this movement. Instead, revolutionary feminists concentrated on politics intended to transform relations between women and men through cultural change and the construction of new social relations.

The activities by which such transformations were to be achieved also reflected the effect of far left politics. Symbolic assaults on the centers of power, disruption of public events, and intellectual work remained the forms of choice. Particularly important in forging the MLF's identity were the public meetings held in the early 1970s. At these meetings feminists debated, at length and with passion, the major alternative strategies that the MLF might follow.

One subcurrent of revolutionary feminism proposed an essentialism that coupled a version of Marxism with a version of psychoanalytic theory to produce a woman-centered, sexually defined notion of women's difference. This analysis came to inform the position of Psychanalyse et Politique, which published an influential magazine called *Des femmes,* owned a publishing house, and ran a bookstore. Adherents of this analysis rejected the label of feminist altogether, claiming that to be feminist meant to be reformist, assimilationist, and accepting of the terms of male power. This theoretical stance culminated in a rationale for separatist politics, including nonparticipation in electoral politics, as well as for the creation of a sect within revolutionary feminism.[35]

The second important current in revolutionary feminism was less essentialist and more social in its understandings of the oppression of women. For this group, sometimes labeled nonaligned feminism, there were specific societal mechanisms that constructed women as the other and as the inferior of men.[36] While not directly active in far left parties, such feminists were much influenced by the understandings of social change and the possibility for transformation that such formations had developed.[37] Indeed, feminist and leftist analyses were often in direct competition, because nonaligned feminists disputed gauchiste notions of how to define politics, of the revolutionary actor, and of the sources of political knowledge.[38] In doing so, they entered into debate and effective alliance with the third major current of revolutionary feminism, that of the *lutte de classe* (class struggle).

Class struggle feminists came directly from Trotskyist and Maoist organizations, which recognized the mobilizational power and importance of the women's movement and therefore delegated women to survey the movement for their organizations. Within the MLF these women were suspiciously regarded as the outreaching arm of male politics even as they were embraced because they had much better contacts with "ordinary women" than did many other MLF feminists.

These three currents within revolutionary feminism all stressed the differences between women and men, arguing either from a position of essentialism or from one stressing the social construction of difference. They did so to overcome the invisibility of women and their needs within traditional leftist politics. Conflicts with left-wing groups demonstrated the influence of far leftist ideas within the MLF. The birth of revolutionary feminism, in the aftermath of the political and cultural revolution of May 1968 and on the fringes of gauchiste politics, had several consequences. Revolutionary feminism rejected ideas of statist change and sought to develop more spontaneous and less hierarchical forms of organization. As a result, it made few efforts to engage with the French state, while also privileging the idea that societal transformation would come from mass actions against organized capitalism and patriarchy. Moreover, the MLF shared the far left's aversion to large organizations that claimed to speak for and in the name of the oppressed. It remained suspicious of trade unions, of political parties—even those on the left—and of groups that engaged in reformist efforts.[39]

Such suspicion, as well as its organizational links to gauchisme, meant that it was sometimes hard for revolutionary feminists to undertake alliance politics with other wings of the women's movement. Nevertheless, such alliances did occur, especially with syndicalist feminism, the second major wing of the movement.

The greatest change that syndicalist feminism brought to French unionism was a representation of the *specificity* of situation of the working woman in capitalism. In particular, syndicalist feminism pushed unions to consider women as more than—or other than—mothers and to acknowledge their sexuality and the impact it had in the workplace. Wider access to contraception and abortion became a goal of the unions, which sought to give women control over their reproductive capacities. In addition, syndicalist feminism began to analyze the weight of ideas about women and families that contributed to the experiences that women confronted in society as a whole.[40]

Once women were depicted as workers with specific needs, a discourse of difference emerged. Although unions had tended to promote universalistic assumptions about the identity of the working class, they now began, prompted in part by syndicalist feminism, to recognize the specificity of several categories of the labor force, including women and immigrants. With this change in social maps, the unions expanded their definition of what constituted legitimate union practice. In doing so they extended the range of their habitual actions to include matters previously considered within the realm of private life and beyond the reach of union politics.

The most important of such matters was the reform of the law regulating abortion, and syndicalist feminists played a major role in the movement to reform that law. The reform was the most important accomplishment for the whole of the French women's movement in these years.

Syndicalist feminism, like the revolutionary feminism of the MLF, was subject to the pressures of partisan and intersyndical politics. The high point of feminist success within the union movement came with a swing toward unity of action for the two union confederations. This change depended in part on the march toward unity by the forces of the partisan left.[41] When this union agreement broke down at the end of the 1970s, interunion collaboration also came apart. Most critical for syndicalist feminism was that feminists were often caught out on a limb, having supported not only unity of action but also forms of union politics that were defeated in internal union battles.[42] These conflicts, in turn, led to the substantial decline of the union movement as a whole. By the end of the 1970s it was difficult to find more than traces of syndicalist feminism in either of the two major union confederations, a loss that had consequences for the ways in which reforms were finally instituted in the 1980s.

In this movement toward reform, an additional crucial actor was the third wing of the women's movement: egalitarian feminism. Long before the emergence of the MLF in 1970, organizations actively promoted equality for women workers, citizens, and mothers. In the 1970s such groups multiplied, ranging from one created to wage the battle for abortion reform (Choisir la cause des femmes, or Choose the Side of Women, formed by lawyer Gisèle Halimi) to associations of female lawyers (such as the Ligue du Droit des Femmes, or League for Women's Rights, in which Simone de Beauvoir was active) and women's groups and currents within the political parties.

Because there were so many groups it is impossible to give a complete account of them; their very strategy of focusing on specific reforms caused them to multiply in step with the changing agenda of politics. But it is possible to describe their basic positions. Demanding women's equality via legal reforms, egalitarian feminists did not necessarily represent women as a collectivity nor did they assume that women alone would bring about change. Rather, they tended to assume that gender inequalities could—and would—be overcome through the actions of informed and active women and men, primarily in mixed organizations. The discourse of egalitarian feminists represented women as disaggregated into specific functions—as mothers, citizens, workers—and such women could find allies and supporters among those concerned about the family or among male citizens and workers.[43]

The reluctance of egalitarian feminists to identify women as a fundamentally different social category requiring separate mobilization marked a basic difference of principle between egalitarian feminists, revolutionary feminists, and syndicalist feminists. For egalitarian feminists, women-only groups might be useful at times as places where women might feel more comfortable speaking, where they could take up women's issues and where they could practice citizenship. Women's commissions had, indeed, always been important for political parties and for religious groups.[44] But this separate politics was one of convenience and not of principle, as it was for the revolutionary feminists.[45] Thus egalitarian feminists never accepted the first principle of revolutionary feminism, and they continued to define themselves and their actions primarily in terms of the needs and strategy of their larger organizations. This conflict over notions of mobilization became particularly controversial when the campaign to reform the abortion law got under way.

An even greater disagreement between egalitarian feminists and the MLF came over the issue of reformism. The only issue for which most of the MLF was willing to turn to the state and upon which it was willing to organize was that of abortion; all other areas were controversial and divisive. A consequence was that the terrain of reformist action was most often left to egalitarian feminist groups, often in alliance with syndicalist

feminists. As a result, the pressure for reform of the laws and the situation of women in electoral politics was somewhat weakened. Many self-identified feminists and those recognized as such—by the media especially—remained aloof from actions they termed reformist. The efforts of the others were thereby weakened, even delegitimized.

In spite of this weakness in the 1980s, women's applying pressure on the state and within state institutions affected two major realms of policy: reproductive rights and access to economic independence. The story has not always been a positive one, but an exploration of these two policy realms does reveal some of the effects of French women in politics.

THE POLITICS OF REPRODUCTIVE RIGHTS

The only policy realm in which French feminists can point to a clear victory is reproductive rights. Throughout the 1970s the women's movement used mass demonstrations, public law-breaking, institution building, and legislative lobbying to campaign for legal abortion. They achieved partial victory in 1975, and a final law was passed in 1979.[46] The legislation reflected a compromise between right-wing and Catholic deputies who opposed abortion, and progressive ones who advocated abortion on demand, reimbursed by the social security system. The central actors in constructing this compromise, representing pressure from outside the legislature for reform, were the Mouvement Français pour le Planning Familial (MFPF, or French Family Planning Movement), the Mouvement pour la Liberté de l'Avortement et la Contraception (MLAC, or Movement for Free Abortion and Contraception), and Choisir la cause des femmes.[47]

MFPF was the oldest, created in 1956 under the name Maternité Heureuse (Joyful Motherhood) by Andrée Weill-Hallé, a medical doctor. It was also the largest, with 100,000 supporters and 180 family planning centers throughout France at the beginning of the 1970s. Its earliest supporters were a coalition of feminist intellectuals and left-leaning doctors. At first the MFPF focused on providing contraceptive advice and devices. After legislation in 1967 legalized contraception for adult women, the MFPF increasingly turned its attention to reforming the law that restricted abortion services, though this shift prompted the departure of many of the medical personnel who had been important in representing the MFPF. It became a more women-centered, women-run, and feminist organization in these years.

MLAC, founded in 1973, quickly became visible in the debate over reform of the abortion legislation. Militants challenged the old law directly by providing illegal abortions in many urban areas and by organizing bus trips to England and the Netherlands for women seeking abortions. Choisir undertook similar illegal actions, as well as providing free legal defense to those charged under the old law. Some of the trials became major political events, publicizing the opposition of many political groups and figures to the prohibitions on abortion.

Such organizations brought to the parliamentary debate a position that clearly represented feminists' understandings of women's need to control their own reproductive capacities. This stance marked a move away from earlier discourses, which had stressed family planning aspects in the 1960s legislation that broadened access to contraception. This shift would probably not have occurred if not for the presence of some revolutionary feminists who were willing to participate in MLAC, MFPF, and Choisir. Yet both these organizations performed a critical task in parliamentary commissions and by lobbying legislators: they represented the demands of feminists and other reformers for a new and more liberal law. Thus the willingness to lobby and negotiate were also due to the presence of syndicalist and egalitarian feminists in the group, who brought the political expertise and connections necessary for conducting negotiations around a bill.

But beyond legislative lobbying, and as a crucial element contributing to its effects, were the actions organized by other groups in support of reform. In 1971 a petition signed by 343 women—including many famous literary, media, and political personalities—announced that they had had illegal abortions. This was followed by a petition from 331 doctors who admitted having performed such abortions. MLAC was created out of the agitation around these two petitions and was supported by many different associations of doctors, women, and workers. For example, the Confédération Française des Travailleurs, the second-largest union confederation in the country, did not officially back the group but did permit Jeannette Laot, its highest ranking female official, to play an active and visible role in the movement. At the same time, many local unions undertook joint initiatives with MLAC to establish neighborhood counseling centers for women seeking abortions and contraceptive information, as well as to organize trips to countries where abortion was legal. This public law-breaking constituted a threat to the authorities and provided a strong incentive for the state to amend the law. Nevertheless, the reform was grudging, and the law was passed originally for five years only. Throughout the 1970s, until the law was confirmed in 1979, activists had to mobilize both to put pressure on clinics, hospitals, and local authorities to provide services, as well as to achieve the law's final passage. In addition to pressuring local hospitals and clinics, for example, several demonstrations by a variety of autonomous feminist groups, unions, and left-wing political parties were organized. The March of Parisian Women, which took place in October 1979, put 50,000 women into the streets. A similar demonstration the next month put both women and men under the banners of women's groups, left-wing parties, and unions.

The pressure has been successful, and there seems little threat in France that access to safe, legal, and subsidized abortions will be reduced. Indeed, in 1988 the minister of health pressured the company producing the "abortion pill," RU486, to continue distribution in France despite threats of an international boycott made by pro-life activists.

THE POLITICS OF EQUAL EMPLOYMENT OPPORTUNITIES

Less encouraging is the status of equality between women and men in paid employment. In 1983, in a first wave of reformism two years after the election of a left-wing government, an important new law on *égalité professionelle* (equality at work) was passed. This legislation, known as the *loi* Roudy, was named after Yvette Roudy, the then minister of the rights of women, who was instrumental in its design and passage. The law continued the postwar tradition of promoting measures for formal equality, based on an analysis of the discriminatory effects of laissez-faire labor markets.[48] But given the failure of earlier efforts to effect change, the loi Roudy was intended to be more comprehensive and powerful.

The principle of the law is that women may not, simply on the basis of their sex or its supposed characteristics, be excluded from a job. All workers must be treated equally (though provisions for pregnancy and maternity leave and facilities for breast-feeding are permitted for women only). Under this law and another that overhauled collective bargaining arrangements, unions were given the major responsibilities for monitoring and implementing workplace equality plans. The unions are empowered to make complaints about discriminatory practices and to participate in designing programs to remedy those practices. The weight of identifying and overcoming discrimination thus was never left only to individual women.

This law, together with steps taken by the Ministry of the Rights of Women in the first half of the 1980s, reflected an egalitarian feminist discourse that identified educational and training deficits, as well as popular attitudes, as the main factors directing women into low-paying, dead-end jobs. This emphasis on training was also a continuation of practices initiated in the 1970s under the right-wing governments of President Giscard d'Estaing. One of the most important elements of the 1983 law was the provision encouraging companies to set up training programs and to follow hiring practices that identified women interested in and capable of upgrading their skills, thereby allowing them to break away from the bottom end of the wage and skill hierarchy.[49]

Yet these measures to foster equality were hindered by another vision of women's work that informed the state's economic policy at the same time. In the restructuring of the economy provoked by the post-1974 global economic crisis, women, along with young people and immigrants, were designated in much economic discourse as a group on the margin whose relation to the labor market was different from that of full-time, skilled, or well-paid workers. As a notion of a dual society began to take hold in France—as part of the neoliberal restructuring in the name of economic flexibility—marginal workers who might take temporary and part-time jobs became a more desirable category of employee. They were attractive for a number of reasons: they were less likely to make militant demands for improvements in working conditions; their schedules could be adjusted to the needs of the company; and they could be hired and fired more easily as company needs changed.

While companies had many reasons to prefer marginal employees, a certain amount of rationalization was needed before the supposedly left-wing government could share this opinion. The rationale was found in the notion that women, especially married women, supposedly used paid work to meet different needs than did men. According to such reasoning, it was acceptable for women to serve as a more temporary, disposable, and less well-paid labor force. Therefore, after initially resisting the use of such contracts, the Socialist government moved in the mid-1980s to regularize and even encourage these new employment statuses.[50]

The results are striking. In 1989 women made up 85 percent of part-time workers. Only 12 percent of all workers were employed part time, but 23.7 percent of women and only 3.5 percent of men were in this category. In 1989, 8.8 percent of the labor force was in a category of "precarious" work (which includes workers with limited-term contracts or without full employment rights), an increase of 2.2 percent in five years.

Only one-tenth of working men fell into this category, while fully one-quarter of women did. Even in the public service, the use of temporary employment contracts expanded in these years, and 70 percent of them went to women.[51]

Thus, in an overview of the first five years of the law on workplace equality, which Roudy presented to the National Assembly in 1989, the results were found to be much less than had been hoped.[52] The restructuring described here had weakened women's position in the labor force so that there had been no progress made on closing the wage gap. Women's unemployment rate was twice that of men. Few agreements with companies had been signed, and those that did exist often affected only a small number of women. Girls continued to pursue studies in areas that were not preparing them for the high-paying jobs of the future. And most telling, according to Roudy's report, the state seemed to have abandoned any commitment to advancing equality between women and men workers. The discourse of flexibility and difference thus combined to block any improvements in women's situation, and the state confirmed its lack of interest in such matters by substantially downgrading the status of the ministry responsible for monitoring the situation of women.

PROSPECTS

We have described the situation of French women in politics as being balanced between two tendencies—one stressing equality and one emphasizing difference. Sometimes the tendency toward equality dominates, and the situation of women imitates that of men. More common, however, is the emphasis on simple difference that has often worked to the detriment of women. In the area of work, long-standing notions of women as different were employed to justify a form of flexibility in restructuring that worked against the removal of labor-market discriminations and inequities and overwhelmed the efforts of the Ministry of the Rights of Women to push for a more egalitarian position.

In the recent past, however, it is not just the stress on difference that has undermined efforts to improve the situation of French women. Even a language of equality can have such effects. For example, another innovation of Roudy's ministry was to push for a quota of 25 percent women on the lists of candidates for municipal elections. This plan came to an abrupt end in November 1982 when the Constitutional Council—composed of nine men—found the initiative contrary to the principle of equality of all citizens before the law, as guaranteed by the Declaration of the Rights of Man and the Citizen of 1789. That the same declaration had not until 1944 been considered fully applicable to all citizens, irrespective of sex, did not count as evidence of any need for affirmative action measures. In the name of formal equality, the idea of a positive quota was abandoned. And as we demonstrated in this chapter, parapublic institutions like the political parties have not yet taken up the challenge.

There are signs that women will no longer consent to being excluded from so many areas of politics. Some evidence shows that the volatility of women's electoral support, which produced a tilt toward the Socialists in the 1980s, may result in a move away from that party in the future. The Greens, who decided to run an equal number of women and men candidates for the 1989 European elections, benefit from a gender gap as well, and recent survey results indicate this gap may increase as women abandon the Socialists to support the more feminist ecologists. Therefore, the electoral pressure that encouraged left-wing parties to become more feminist in the 1970s may come into play again in the future.

In addition to these signs of change among the electorate and the parties, women's groups continue to be politically active, taking up issues long ignored in France. For example, new attention to the situation of women at work has begun to include—at last—the impact of sexual harassment. This theme, elaborated into initiatives directed at violence against women, provides a focus for mobilization that may revitalize in the 1990s a women's movement that lost so much energy in the 1980s.

Another important source of new energy is the

change that all of Europe is experiencing. Both the collapse of the communist regimes in Eastern Europe in 1989 and the rapidity with which new political arrangements are paralleling the economic unification of the European Community encourage French women to join with women from other countries to ensure that the new societies of Eastern Europe and those of the 12 European Community members will become more woman-friendly. The threat to reproductive rights in parts of Eastern Europe provides an issue with great mobilizational potential for the 1990s, as it did in so many Western European countries in the 1970s. In addition, the added weight of the institutions of the European Community, which have been willing to go quite far toward recommending gender equality, helps women in member countries make claims on their own states and in their own societies. They might even hope for a harmonization of equality provisions that could substantially improve the guarantees of workplace and social equality provided to French women.

Although the balance sheet of women in French politics has often been in the red, there are signs that the 1990s may bring new mobilization and moves toward recognition of *both* real equality *and* difference.

NOTES

1. Catherine Trautmann is the socialist mayor of Strasbourg and the only woman heading a city with a population greater than 100,000.

2. These civil service positions include 7.4 percent of directors and 7.9 percent of the Grands Corps. For a discussion of the development and history of women's employment in the civil service, see Marie-Ange Moreau-Bourles and Mariette Sineau, "Les femmes et le statut des travailleurs: Les discriminations au niveau de l'elaboration des normes" (Women and workplace statutes: Discrimination in the specification of norms), *Droit Social* 12 (December 1983): 697.

3. Such appointments are not always to the most powerful positions. Under the last government of Prime Minister Michel Rocard (appointed October 1990), 13 percent of the ministers were women, but they were all either *ministres délégués* (junior ministers) or *secretaires d'état* (assistant ministers). The government of Edith Cresson,

appointed in May 1991, broke with this treatment of women. While she had the same number of women ministers (six), three of them held full ministerial responsibilities.

4. Mariette Sineau, *Ways and Means of Improving the Position of Women in Political Life* (Strasbourg: Council of Europe, 1989), 4.

5. It is interesting to note, however, that many of the leaders of radical feminism actually were of non-Parisian origin. See Nadja Ringard, "Itinéraires de femmes à Paris" (The experience of Parisian women), in Groupe d'études Féministes de l'Université du Paris VII, *Crises de la société, féminisme et changement* (Paris: Revue d'en face-Tierce, 1991), 158.

6. On the women's movement and its lack of attention to suffrage see Karen Offen, "Depopulation, Nationalism and Feminism in Fin-de-Siècle France," *American Historical Review* 89 (1984): 652; and Jane Jenson, "Paradigms and Political Discourse: Protective Legislation in France and the United States Before 1914," *Canadian Journal of Political Science* 22 (1989): 247–51.

7. This grant was purely a statement of principle. It did not mean that the real inequalities—in civil rights, for example—were immediately abolished.

8. More than one-fifth of the Communists nominated in 1946, and 16 percent of those elected, were women.

9. For details of change in the civil code on labor law see Odile Dhavernas, *Droits des femmes, pouvoir des hommes* (Women's rights, men's power), (Paris: Seuil, 1978), part 1, chap. 3; part 4, chaps. 3–4.

10. On this dilemma, as experienced even in the first half of the nineteenth century, see Michèle Riot-Sarcey, "Différence et exclusion: Ou l'histoire impossible de l'égalité" (Difference and exclusion: Or, the impossible history of equality), *Les Temps Modernes*, February 1987.

11. See Martine Muller et al., *Etre féministe en France: Contribution à l'étude des mouvements de femmes, 1944–67* (Being feminist in France: A contribution to the study of the women's movement, 1944–67) (ATP Recherches sur les Femmes et Recherches Féministes, 1987). Groups associated with the Parti Communiste Français (PCF, or French Communist Party) were particularly important. After the war the Union des Femmes Françaises (UFF, or Association of French Women) was established. It was designed as a wide-ranging association of women working for peace, economic security, and civil liberties, as well as for institutions of particular interest to women. The UFF, for example, was much involved in popularizing natural childbirth techniques in the 1950s. Although intended to be nonpartisan, UFF was always close to the PCF. Similarly, the largest trade-union confederation, Confédération Générale du Travail (CGT, or General Confederation of Work) maintained women's commissions at all levels, established a special publication for women workers, and held national-level conferences of women

workers throughout the postwar years. The CGT was also close to the PCF.

12. In May 1946 the constitutional referendum, which the Catholic church opposed because of its fears for parochial schools, was rejected much more massively by women than by men. In subsequent elections women voters were much less likely to support the Communist Party and more likely to vote for right-wing parties, for the Gaullists, or for Christian democratic parties than were men. Indeed, the Christian democratic Mouvement Républicain Populaire (MRP, or Popular Republican Movement) counted on women a great deal. As its leader said in 1945, "with the help of women, the bishops and the Holy Spirit, we should get one hundred deputies." Mariette Sineau, "Gender and the French Electorate: An Historical View," in Mary F. Katzenstein and Hege Skjeie, eds., *Going Public: National Histories of Women's Enfranchisement and Women's Participation in State Institutions* (Oslo: Report of the Institute for Social Research, 1990:4), 81–82.

13. Janine Mossuz-Lavau and Mariette Sineau, *Enquête sur les femmes et la politique en France* (A study of women and politics in France) (Paris: PUF, 1983), 25–28.

14. For the classic examination of this question see Andrée Michel, "Les Françaises et la politique" (French women and politics), *Les Temps Modernes* 20 (July 1965).

15. On the theme of alienation and conservatism, as well as on female deputies' concentration in the commissions of the National Assembly dealing with social questions see Maïté Albistur and Daniel Armogathe, *Histoire du féminisme français du moyen âge à nos jours* (A history of French feminism from the Middle Ages to the present) (Paris: des femmes, 1977), 408–10.

16. The CGT continued to confound sex and maternity until well into the 1970s, when it finally began to address women simply as working women. For a consideration of the politics of these years and the effects of such discourse in the union movement see Jane Jenson, "The 'Problem' of Women," in Mark Kesselman and Guy Groux, eds., *The French Workers' Movement* (London: Allen and Unwin, 1984).

17. François Borella, *Les partis politiques dans la France d'aujourd'hui* (Political parties in contemporary France), 5th ed. (Paris: Seuil, 1990), 8.

18. In the elections after the war and until the 1970s women's representation in the National Assembly actually declined. In 1945, 6.9 percent of the deputies were women. The corresponding statistic in 1951 was 3.5 percent, and in 1973 it was 1.6 percent. See Interparliamentary Union, *Distribution of Seats Between Men and Women in National Assemblies* (Geneva: International Centre for Parliamentary Documentation, 1987), 51. The number of candidates remained higher, however. Between the legislative elections of November 1946 and January 1956, the percentage of female candidates fell from 13.5 percent to 9.7 percent. The percentage for all parties declined, but the dropoff was particularly marked for the Christian Democrats and the Socialists. The Communists continued to run the most female candidates, but even they dropped from 19.7 to 14.3 percent.

19. The presidential system encouraged the formation of two camps: the supporters of the president and his opponents. In the 1960s—during the presidency of General Charles de Gaulle—these groups came to be designated the right and the left, with the Gaullists the major group in the former and the Communists, Socialists, and diverse leftists forming the latter. The electoral system, with two rounds of voting, encouraged parties to make coalitions for the second round to be sure that candidates from each large group would be present in all constituencies.

20. For a discussion see Jane Jenson and Ruth Kantrow, "Labor Market and Family Policy in France: An Intersecting Complex for Dealing with Poverty," in G. S. Goldberg and E. Kremen, eds., *The Feminization of Poverty: Only in America?* (New York: Greenwood, 1990), 108ff.

21. This pattern varied with the number of children. Women with three or more children still tended to interrupt their work to look after their children. For those with two or fewer children, however, interruptions have become increasingly rare. Institut National de la Statistique et des Etudes Economiques, *Données sociales 1990* (Paris: INSEE, 1990), 42–44.

22. Mossuz-Lavau and Sineau, *Les femmes et la politique,* 25–27.

23. Sineau, "Gender and the French Electorate," 99ff, in Katzenstein and Skjeie, eds., *Going Public*. In the 1988 presidential election the actual left-right gender gap was relatively small (51 percent and 49 percent). But for Mitterrand and the French Greens, it was a positive situation. The overall difference between women and men was about 6 percent in favor of Mitterrand, with young women being much more likely than young men to support him. But women rejected the neo-fascist and sexist candidate, Jean-Marie LePen; he received 17 percent of men's votes but only 10 percent of women's. See Jane Jenson, "Representations of Difference: The Varieties of French Feminism," *New Left Review* 180 (1990): 158–59.

24. Mossuz-Lavau and Sineau, *Les femmes et la politique,* 28.

25. Jane Jenson, "The Limits of 'and the' Discourse: French Women as Marginal Workers," in Jane Jenson et al., eds., *The Feminization of the Labour Force: Promises and Prospects* (London: Polity, 1988), 160.

26. Jenson and Kantrow, "Labor Market and Family Policy in France," 109–10.

27. One result of this reluctance is the slow rate at which women moved up the ladder of power inside the

party. It was not until 1973 that more than ten women were elected to the Central Committee. From 1950 until 1968 Jeannette Thorez-Vermeersch, the wife of Secretary General Maurice Thorez, was the only woman in the Politbureau. It was not until 1979 that the first women joined the Secretariat.

28. For example, Socialist documents and publications began to use the concept of patriarchy to describe the situation of women and especially the role of the family in the reproduction of women's oppression. See, e.g., *Le poing et la rose* (The fist and the rose) 66 (supplement, December 1977): 5. This material was developed in preparation for the Socialists' national convention on the rights of women.

29. In 1990 only 21.4 percent (28 of 131) of the largest internal body (Comité Directeur) was female. The numbers fall off dramatically at each step up the hierarchy. Merely 7 percent of the members of the Secretariat were women.

30. Mariette Sineau, *Des femmes en politique* (Women in politics) (Paris: Economica, 1988). The study consisted of interviews with women deputies, senators, national leaders of the parties, and mayors of several large cities.

31. French feminist theorists have influenced feminist thinking about difference and deconstructionism, particularly in the field of literary studies. These individuals, to the extent that they undertook any political activity, would most probably have found themselves aligned with revolutionary feminism. As theorists for feminist practice, they have been most influential elsewhere, especially in the United States and Italy. For a discussion of this theoretical approach, which locates theorists politically to some extent, see Toril Moi, *French Feminist Thought: A Reader* (Oxford: Basil Blackwell, 1987).

32. On the women's movement in France see Danièle Leger, *Le féminisme en France* (Feminism in France) (Paris: le Sycomore, 1982); Claire Duchen, *Feminism in France: From May '68 to Mitterrand* (London: Routledge and Kegan Paul, 1986); and Jenson, "Representations of Difference."

33. These groups also label Psychanalyse et Politique the MLF *déposé*, playing on the double meaning of déposé, which means both deposed and registered trademark.

34. For a discussion by several participants in this rupture see Marie-Claire Boons et al., *C'est terrible, quand on y pense!* (It's terrible when you think of it!) (Paris: Galilée, 1977).

35. Until the elections of 1981, many revolutionary feminists in this current refused to accept that electoral participation was consistent with their brand of women-centric and separatist politics. In effect they counseled abstention.

36. Duchen, in *Feminism in France*, uses this term to distinguish such feminists from those who practiced a double militancy inside far left parties and in the MLF.

37. They were also much criticized by existing left formations, who accused them of being *petit bourgeois* and not sufficiently attuned to the importance of class relations. For a good discussion of the question of left credentials, see Françoise Picq, *Le mouvement de libération des femmes et ses effets sociaux* (The women's liberation movement and its social consequences) (ATP Recherche Féministes et Recherches sur les Femmes, 1987), 35.

38. Jenson, "Representations of Difference," 134–37.

39. One of the most extreme examples of this aversion was the refusal of Psychanalyse et Politique to participate in the campaign for reform of abortion law in the early 1970s. The group eschewed the mass mobilization for a new and more liberal law in which other feminists and many mixed organizations participated. Jenson, "Representations of Difference," 144.

40. For the best overview of the impact of feminism within the union movement see Margaret Maruani, *Les syndicats à l'épreuve du féminisme* (The unions confront feminism) (Paris: Syros, 1979).

41. A formal agreement among several leftist parties, the most important of which were the Communists and Socialists, was signed in 1972.

42. For details see Jenson, "The 'Problem' of Women," 168ff.

43. For an analysis of this process before 1968 see Muller et al., *Etre féministe en France*.

44. Before the development of syndicalist feminism in the two large union confederations in the 1970s the usual position of the unions was one of egalitarian feminism, and women's commissions were a usual element of such feminism. For a discussion of how this egalitarian feminism became syndicalist see Jenson, "The 'Problem' of Women," 166.

45. For Françoise Picq the principle of women-only groups and action was a defining characteristic of the MLF. See Picq, *Le mouvement de libération des femmes et ses effets sociaux*.

46. The legislation is termed the Veil Law, named after Simone Veil, the minister of health who sponsored the law in 1974–75. For details of this campaign see Jane Jenson, "Changing Discourse, Changing Agenda: Political Rights and Reproductive Rights in France," in Mary F. Katzenstein and Carol Mueller, eds., *The Women's Movements of the U.S. and Western Europe: Political Opportunity and Public Policy* (Philadelphia: Temple University Press, 1987). See also Janine Mossuz-Lavau, *Les lois de l'amour: Les politiques de la sexualite en France 1950–1990* (Laws about love: Policies dealing with sexuality in France, 1950–1990) (Paris: Payot, 1991).

47. On the history of MFPF and the creation of MLAC see MFPF, *D'une révolte à une lutte: 25 ans d'histoire du planning familial* (From revolt to struggle: 25 years of history of planned parenthood) (Paris: Tierce, 1984).

48. See Jenson, "Representations of Difference," 155–56.

49. For a detailed discussion and assessment of the loi Roudy, see CFDT, *Femmes: Clés pour l'égalité* (Women: The keys to equality) (Paris: CFDT Information, 1990), 72–88.

50. For details see Jenson and Kantrow, "Labour and Family Policy in France."

51. For details of these patterns see *Rapport d'information sur l'égalité professionelle entre les femmes et les hommes* (International report on workplace equality between women and men), Assemblée Nationale 1161 (20 December 1989): 98–102.

52. Ibid.

▲ Germany

Type of Political System: democracy
  Sovereignty: republic
  Executive-Legislative System: parliamentary
Type of State: federal
Type of Party System: multiparty
Major Political Parties

Christlich-Demokratische Union Deutschlands and Christlich-Soziale Union Deutschlands (CDU and CSU, or German Christian Democratic and Christian Social Unions): Based on an alliance of conservative Catholic and Protestant forces; catchall party of the center right. Supports a social market economy and has a strongly pro-Western foreign policy orientation. Has governed West Germany in coalition with Freie Demokratische Partei since 1982. Its strong support of immediate German unification brought victory in all-German elections of 1990. CSU is the conservative Bavaria-based ally of CDU; it had 183,000 members in 1988, of whom 14.2 percent were women. In 1988, CDU had about 677,000 members, of whom 22.5 percent were women. Since unification, membership is estimated at 800,000.

Sozialdemokratische Partei Deutschlands (SPD, or German Social Democratic Party): Dating from the nineteenth century, the oldest party in Germany and largest in terms of membership. Founded as a Marxist party of the working class; dropped the more radical aspects of its program in 1959 and has since become a catchall party of the center left. Has generally supported social equality and a greater measure of redistributive welfare state measures than the CDU and took the lead in renewing contact with East Germany in the 1970s. Governed West Germany in coalition with the Freie Demokratische Partei 1969–82. In 1988, had 912,000 members, of whom 25 percent were women; since unification its membership is about 944,000.

Freie Demokratische Partei (FDP, or Free Democratic Party): Centrist party committed to free enterprise, a secular state, and protection of individual liberty. Has participated in governing coalitions with both SPD AND CDU/CSU. In 1988, had 65,000 members, of whom 24 percent were women; membership has increased considerably since unification and was estimated at 2 million in November 1990.

Die Grünen (Green Party): Coalition of environmentalist, pacifist, and left-wing groups. In addition to environmental issues, has supported feminist causes, disarmament, and radical economic restructuring. Represented in the Bundestag 1983–90. In 1990, estimated to have 40,600 members.

Bündnis 90/Die Grünen (Alliance '90/Green Party): Electoral alliance formed in 1990 in the former GDR. Based on the major oppositional civic groups that toppled the Communist regime, such as the New Forum, the Independent Women's Association, and the Green Party (East).

Partei des Demokratischen Sozialismus (PDS, or Party of Democratic Socialism): Former ruling Communist Party of East Germany, founded in 1946 as the Socialist Unity Party and renamed for all-German elections of 1990. Now sees itself as an oppositional party with a Democratic Socialist program. Membership dropped from 2.1 million in 1989 to 345,000 in November 1990.

Nationaldemokratische Partei Deutschlands (NPD, or German National Democratic Party): Espouses a right-wing nationalist program; has yet to reach the 5 percent quota of votes required for representation in the Bundestag. Has about 15,000 members.

Die Republikaner (REP, or Republicans): Extreme right-wing party formed in 1988; has a xenophobic platform and antifeminist stand. Has so far failed to attain the 5 percent quota of votes at the national level, but is represented in some local and state parliaments. Estimated membership is 25,000.

Year Women Granted Right to Vote:
1919

Year Women Granted Right to Stand for Election: 1919

Percentage of Women in the Legislature
Lower House: 20.5%[a]
Upper House: 2.2%

Percentage of Electorate Voting for Highest Elected Office in Most Recent Election (1990): 76.3%[b]

DEMOGRAPHICS

Population: total, 77,812,000; old FRG, 61,171,000; former GDR, 16,641,000

Percentage of Population in Urban Areas
Overall: old FRG, not available; former GDR, 76.6%
Female: old FRG, not available; former GDR, 77.0%
Male: old FRG, not available; former GDR, 76.2%

Percentage of Population Below Age 15: old FRG, 15.4%; former GDR, 17.8%

Birthrate (per 1,000 population): old FRG, 10; former GDR, 14

Maternal Mortality Rate (per 100,000 live births): old FRG, 5;[c] former GDR, 17

Infant Mortality Rate (per 1,000 live births): old FRG, 7;[d] former GDR, 9

Mortality Rate for Children Under Five (per 1,000 live births): old FRG, 9;[e] former GDR, 13

Average Household Size: old FRG, 2.5; former GDR, 2.4

Mean Age at First Marriage
Female: old FRG, 23.6; former GDR, 21.5
Male: old FRG, 27.9; former GDR, 25.2

Life Expectancy
Female: old FRG, 78.1; former GDR, 75.4
Male: old FRG, 71.2; former GDR, 69.5

EDUCATION

Ratio of Female to Male Enrollment
First-Level Education: old FRG, 96; former GDR, 94
Second-Level Education: old FRG, 100; former GDR, 92
Third-Level Education: old FRG, 72; former GDR, 114[f]

Literacy Rate
Female: old FRG, 99.0%; former GDR, 99.0%
Male: old FRG, 99.0%; former GDR, 99.0%

ECONOMY

Gross National Product per Capita: old FRG, U.S. $10,940; former GDR, U.S. $7,180

Percentage of Labor Force in Agriculture: old FRG, 0.4%;[g] former GDR, 4.9%

Distribution of Agricultural Workers by Sex
Female: old FRG, 44.0%;[h] former GDR, 38.7%
Male: old FRG, 56.0%;[i] former GDR, 61.3%

Economically Active Population by Sex
Female: old FRG, 34.0%;[j] former GDR, 60.1%
Male: old FRG, 57.0%;[k] former GDR, 82.3%

a. Political information is for the united Germany; however, all other data are given separately for the old Federal Republic of Germany (West Germany) and the former German Democratic Republic (East Germany). New data for the united Germany were not available from the German Statistical Federal Office at time of publication.

b. Statistisches Bundesamt (Federal Statistical Office), Wiesbaden, 1991.

c. *Statistical Yearbook* (New York: German Information Center).

d. Statistiches Bundesamt, series 12, no. 4 (1989).

e. Ibid.

f. Ibid.

g. Including evening and correspondence courses.

h. Statistisches Bundesamt, Microcensus Results, April 1989.

i. Ibid.

j. Ibid.

k. Ibid.

l. Ibid.

Women and Politics: The New Federal Republic of Germany

CHRISTIANE LEMKE

Much of modern German political history can be read as a history of discontinuity, dramatic turns, and forced reorientations. The women's movement in Germany, which dates to the early nineteenth century, has been shaped by these overall political changes, and women's voices reflect a history of conflict, struggle, and diversity. The unification of the Federal Republic of Germany (FRG) and the German Democratic Republic (GDR) on 3 October 1990 was yet another watershed for German women, creating a brand-new framework for women in both parts of the country. The merging of advanced, industrialized, democratic western Germany with the formerly communist-ruled eastern part of the country is unique in modern political history. Likewise unprecedented is the merging of two countries in which women had assumed very different social and political roles.

In this chapter I address women's political engagement in the new Germany, officially known as the Federal Republic of Germany. Political engagement is defined with reference to the basic issues for women, as well as to women's activities and participation in politics. Although German women have participated in politics previously, it is only in the past two decades that women in the Federal Republic have sought to speak out on their own behalf and to gain visibility in the political realm. In the communist-ruled part of Germany, women's political engagement was dependent on the "leading role" of the Communist Party and was shaped by the powerful state.[1]

THE POLITICAL FRAMEWORK

Germany was divided for 45 years, an era that began in the aftermath of World War II. The new Germany is the most populous state in Europe,

with 78 million inhabitants; 61 million live in the old Federal Republic and 17 million in the former GDR. It is the leading economic power in Europe and one of the wealthiest nations in the world in terms of per capita income. West Germany joined the European Community in 1957 and has been a member of the North Atlantic Treaty Organization. The population of the united Germany is 42 percent Protestant and 35 percent Catholic.

There are about 5 million foreign nationals living in Germany today, about a third of them women. Some 4.9 million foreigners live in the territory of the old FRG, and 120,000 live in the former GDR. More than half of the foreigners come from nations within the European Community, but the largest group—about 1.5 million—is made up of Turkish citizens who were invited to work in the FRG as so-called guest-workers in the 1960s. The majority of the Turkish citizens are second- and even third-generation Turks, who usually do not have German citizenship. In the former GDR, foreign workers came primarily from Vietnam, African countries like Mozambique, and Poland. Foreigners have never been fully integrated into the Federal Republic, and hostilities toward non-Germans have increased since unification.

Women's political struggle and their engagement in the new Germany are shaped by its much-troubled history as a nation-state. Following prolonged dispute and conflict among the numerous kingdoms and principalities in the German-speaking heartland of Europe, a united Germany was forged in 1871 by the influential chancellor Otto von Bismarck. Germany rapidly industrialized and became one of the major powers next to Great Britain and France. The country lagged in political modernization, however. Feudal structures, authoritarianism, and militarism persisted, and the country remained fragmented.

During the first half of the nineteenth century, women in Germany began to demand rights and more opportunities in the social and cultural realm. Especially after the 1848 revolution, women demanded access to education and gainful employment and participation in public life. The first General German Women's Society was formed in 1865. But compared with the women's movements in other industrializing nations, the women's movement in Germany was particularly weak, reflecting the state of political liberalism in general. Women were excluded from politics almost entirely, and women's rights activists remained isolated.[2] A serious, lasting constraint was the internal division of the women's movement. From an early stage the movement was divided into a proletarian wing and a bourgeois wing.

After World War I the monarchy was abolished in Germany, and the democratic Weimar Republic was established in 1918. Women were granted the right to vote and the right to be elected to political office. In the first elections to the Reichstag (the German national Parliament) voter turnout among women was as high as that among men, but only 8 percent of the members elected were women.[3] Gaining the right to vote was a political breakthrough for women; moreover, women were able to address publicly such social and political issues as abortion, better healthcare for women, and support for children and youth. But their political struggle was overshadowed by conflicts within the women's movement that grew bitter as fragmentation of the political culture increased toward the end of the Weimar Republic.

The young republic rapidly lost popular support as economic conditions worsened at the end of the 1920s, helping the leader of the National Socialist Party, Adolf Hitler, gain strength and finally seize power in 1933. With its outrageous racist ideology, expansionist doctrines, and totalitarian style of rule, National Socialism (Nazism) became the most brutal regime in Europe in the twentieth century. The National Socialists barred women from parliamentary bodies and public offices and restricted their access to higher education and the legal profession. Dividing society along gender lines became one of the pillars of Nazism. Women were locked into what the Nazis perceived as the proper place for women; motherhood was glorified and mystified. At the same time, racism provided a ground for policies that were pro-natalist for one group of women but strictly anti-natalist for others.[4] Even though more than two-thirds of Germans today were born after the Nazi period, this troubled past—and especially the genocide of millions of Jews, Slavs, gypsies, and others—is crucial for the understanding of gender politics, since this legacy still overshadows debates about reproductive rights, abortion and genetic engineering in Germany.

The unconditional surrender of Germany on 8 May 1945 offered the chance for a new beginning in gender politics. The war had been devastating; with millions of men killed in battle or interned as prisoners of war, women outnumbered men three to two. Thus it was the women who tried to organize survival after the war, clearing rubble from the cities and taking care of children, orphans and the millions of refugees from the eastern parts of Germany that were placed under Soviet and Polish administration after the war.[5] Large numbers of women were recruited by the Allies to replace men in factories, administrative positions, and voluntary organizations. But women's activities and achievements were not matched by an increase in their political engagement. A small wave of women, most of whom had been active in the Weimar Republic, entered politics after the war. The percentage of female representatives in the first postwar Parliament in 1949 reached only 6.8 percent, as low as in the Weimar Republic 30 years earlier. The division of Germany into two states during the cold war—the FRG, shaped by the three western Allies (the United States, Britain and France), and the GDR, formed under the hegemony of the Soviet Union—set the stage for two very different political and social environments for women.

In the unification process following the "peaceful revolution" in East Germany in 1989–90, the political structure and laws of the old Federal Republic of Germany provided the blueprint for the new political setting.[6] The new Germany, like the old FRG, is a federal parliamentary democracy with a multiparty system. The political power lies with the freely and directly elected federal Parliament—the Bundestag, which has members from several political parties. A sophisticated electoral system combines proportional representation and majority vote; half of the seats are allocated according to proportional representation and the other half according to the winner-take-all system. To limit fragmentation of politics, parties must have the support of at least 5 percent of the electorate to be represented in Parliament. In the election held 2 December 1990—the first all-German election after unification—a special law allowed parties to enter Parliament with at least 5 percent of the votes in either the old FRG or the old GDR; it also allowed parties to form alliances for these elections.[7]

The major political parties are the left-of-center Sozialdemokratische Partei Deutschlands (SPD, or Social Democratic Party); the center-right Christlich-Demokratische Union (CDU, or Christian Democratic Union) and its regional Bavarian counterpart, Christlich-Soziale Union (CSU, or Christian Social Union); Freie Demokratische Partei (FDP, or Free Democratic Party); and Die Grünen (Green Party). The SPD, founded in 1871, is the oldest party in Germany; today it is the largest party in terms of membership. The SPD stands for workers' rights, state regulation of the economy, comprehensive social policies, and progressive reforms, including equal rights for women. Its traditional core constituency includes manual workers, but in recent decades the party has gained support from white-collar workers and from employees in the large public sector, many of whom are women. In 1990 the SPD merged with the newly refounded SPD in East Germany, but support for social democracy in the east has been significantly lower than in the west.

The CDU, formed in 1946 and merged in 1990 with its counterpart in the GDR, is a typical catch-all party. It represents Catholics and Protestants, middle-class citizens, farmers, some members of the business community, and conservative elements of the working class. In the first two postwar decades, the CDU enjoyed wide support from women, but as more women entered professional life they have moved away from the party. CDU policies traditionally were grounded in a conservative approach to the roles of women in society and in the family, but recently the party has "modernized" its stand on women's issues, as outlined in its party congress in the city of Essen in 1985. The CDU/CSU formed a coalition government with the FDP following the elections in December 1990.

The FDP, which was formed in the aftermath of World War II, is one of the smaller parties, but it has been an important player in German politics because of its role as coalition partner for one of the larger parties. Its primary constituency comes from the middle class and the business community; in 1990 the party merged with the Liberals in East Germany. The party advocates a free-market economy, as well as civil rights; the latter includes, for example, a prochoice stand on abortion. However, women's policies are not a core issue in the party, even though prominent individual female politicians have come from the ranks of the FDP.

The Greens formed as a national political party in 1980. In spite of its status as Europe's first and most prominent Green party, it failed to surpass the 5 percent hurdle in the first all-German national elections. The West German Green Party is rooted in such citizen initiatives as the peace and ecology movement; one of the most important bases for the party is the new feminist movement. Supported mainly by the well-educated, younger, urban strata of the population, the Greens advocate left-libertarian policies with a radical, grass-roots approach to democracy, environmental protection, and the equality of citizens. The Greens have been most radical and outspoken on issues of women's rights and self-determination. After unification, the Greens formed an association with the East German Alliance '90, a coalition that came out of the civic movement opposing the communist regime in the fall of 1989. Because of the special electoral law passed in 1990, the East German Alliance '90/Greens is represented for a four-year term (1990–94) in the national Parliament.

The Partei des Demokratischen Sozialismus (PDS, or Party of Democratic Socialism), the reform-socialist successor of the Communist Party of East Germany, won representation in the national Parliament as well. To overcome its discredited past and to gain voter support, the party quickly picked up some of the demands of feminists and women's rights activists, such as the "right to work" for women and the preservation of some of the social policies of the former communist regime. These efforts met with limited success, however, and today the PDS plays only a marginal role in German politics.

Coalition governments are the rule in German politics; from 1949 to 1966 the coalition was led by the conservative CDU/CSU; from 1966 to 1969 the two major parties, the CDU and the SPD, governed. From 1969 to 1982, during the social reform era, a social-liberal SPD/FDP coalition was in power. Since 1982 the government has been controlled by the CDU/CSU and FDP. This coalition also constituted the first government of the united Germany, elected in 1990 under Chancellor Helmut Kohl, a member of CDU. The chancellor, who is also the head of the cabinet, usually comes from the strongest party in Parliament and is politically the most powerful person. The president, who is elected by both houses of the Parliament, has limited power and is primarily a political—and often moral—figurehead of the nation. Neither the president nor the chancellor in postwar Germany has ever been a woman; but the current president of the federal Parliament, who ranks second in the political hierarchy after the president, is a woman: Rita Süssmuth of the CDU. She is the second woman to occupy the position since 1949.

Federalism, which decentralizes political power in the nation, is an important feature of German politics. Above all, the *Länder*, or states, are responsible for education, police protection, cultural affairs, sectors of regional planning, and some of the welfare programs. There are 16 states in the new Federal Republic. Eleven are from the old Federal Republic, including united Berlin, which now forms one state. The five newly recreated states of the former GDR joined the federation under article 23 of the German constitution, known as the Basic Law, the legal arrangement chosen for unification.

The states vary greatly in size and population: the smallest is the city-state of Bremen, with only 600,000 inhabitants; the most populous is North Rhine–Westphalia, with 16 million inhabitants; the largest in territorial size is Bavaria, with 11 million inhabitants. There are great regional variations, as well. The north is mostly Protestant; the south is predominantly Catholic. The southern states have generally been more prosperous in the past decades than the northern states, which tend to be burdened with higher unemployment rates. A sharp difference also exists between the affluent states in the west and the poor new states in the east.

The states are represented in the Bundesrat, or Federal Council, in which each state holds seats according to its population. Since unification, the Federal Council has had a total of 69 seats. The members represent the ruling party or coalition of each state Parliament—and include the states' minister-presidents—and are thus indirectly elected. The Federal Council can be dominated by the same parties that have a majority in the Federal Parliament, though this is not necessarily the case. In fact, after several state elections, the majority shifted from the CDU/CSU to the SPD in spring 1991. Nine of the 16 states were governed by the SPD or SPD-led coalitions in 1991. Politically, the upper house has played a lesser role than the lower house, but most legislation has to pass both houses. Differing majorities make governing a more difficult task.

The federal structure leads to large variations with respect to policies affecting women. In the past decade, some states, especially those governed by the Social Democrats or left-of-center coalitions, have enacted legislation promoting women's rights. Also, wide variations exist in policy practices concerning abortion, which is easier to obtain in some states than in others.

WOMEN AND UNIFICATION

German unification was the originally unintended result of the peaceful civic revolution in East Germany in fall 1989. Women played an important role in prerevolutionary and revolutionary upheaval. Several of them—like Bärbel Bohley, Ulrike Poppe, and Vera Wollenberger—had been active in the pacifist group Women for Peace that formed in 1982–83 or were members of the small human rights, environmental, and women's groups that formed mostly under the shelter of the Protestant church in the 1980s.[8] Because of the rigid policies under the communist regime, several of these activists were expelled from the country or imprisoned. Though few in number, some of the women later took leading roles in the movement that toppled the communist regime.

In fall 1989, shortly before the Berlin Wall opened on 9 November, several women's groups sprang up. Women activists have described the mood of this period as euphoric, and mobilization was highest in the months shortly before and after the regime collapsed.[9] Early in December an umbrella organization called Independent Women's Association was founded, pulling together a range of small, diverse women's groups.[10] Opposition women sharply criticized the failures of the communist regime and set themselves apart from the official Communist Party-dominated Women's Federation. They claimed that the communist regime had failed to establish gender equality. Instead, they argued, the regime had strengthened male-dominated power relations in society. In their first statements, the women demanded that a democratic, separate East German state embrace some of the achievements of the former regime, in particular, the right to work and the provisions for public child care. Because of their criticism of Western capitalism, the new Independent Women's Association rejected the idea of German unification, favoring instead an ecologically concerned,

grass-roots-oriented democracy with communitarian values.[11]

Because of mounting popular pressure in November and December 1989—demonstrations drew up to 500,000 participants—the Communist Party finally agreed to enter talks with the opposition. Following similar arrangements in Poland and Hungary during the transition from communist rule, a "roundtable" was established in Berlin. Fourteen groups and parties met from 7 December until the freely elected GDR government was formed the following spring to discuss and prepare the transition. A major success of the Independent Women's Association was its representation at this roundtable after having protested its exclusion. The association and other grass-roots and opposition groups, such as the prominent New Forum, helped to draft a constitution for a new, reformed East German state. But because of unification, this constitution never went into effect. One of their demands, the establishment of *Gleichstellungsstellen* (equal rights offices) on the local level, was nevertheless met by the first freely elected GDR government, and *Kommunalverfassungsgesetz* (constitutional law of the communities) was passed in May 1990. These equal opportunity offices, which had existed in the old FRG, were later expanded.

The euphoria of grass-roots mobilization was followed in the early 1990s by distress, disappointment, and increasing political marginalization. There are at least three reasons for this marginalization of the women's movement in the former GDR. First, its marginal position reflects the legacies of communist rule. After all, feminism had been silenced under the communist regime, and the concept of an independent women's group did not enjoy widespread support. In a society that had been gender-blind under communism, feminist consciousness was largely absent. Therefore the association never had mass appeal but represented an avant-garde group of women concentrated in Berlin and other major cities. Typically, several activists of the association had been outsiders in their society before the collapse of the communist regime.

Another reason for the increasing marginalization may be seen in the unfavorable climate for maintaining a separate GDR state. Given the squeeze placed on the country by a failing economy, women found it nearly impossible to argue convincingly that their demands were not only desirable but also workable. Economic and ecological problems had been covered up by the regime over the past decade, and a government report published in December 1989 revealed some of the failures in the economy of the GDR. Contrary to widespread assumptions, the state was basically bankrupt. Many East Germans thus viewed unification with the wealthy and powerful Federal Republic as the only way to cope with these problems.

A third reason may be seen in the increasing domination of the political discourse and process by established parties and elite-level politics. In the months before the first free elections, West German parties strongly influenced the agenda-setting, as well as the electoral campaign. The Independent Women's Association and other prominent opposition grass-roots groups that lacked support from the west became increasingly marginalized.

On 18 March 1990 the first free elections were held in the GDR. The results were above all a mandate for unification. The CDU-led conservative Alliance for Germany, which received 48 percent of the votes, had forcefully argued for quick unification with the Federal Republic.[12] It was especially disappointing for the women who had been active in the opposition women's groups that the Independent Women's Association, which ran with the Green Party, received only 2 percent of the votes. Because women had failed to press for top ranks on their coalition party list, they were not even able to send one of their representatives to Parliament. As a result, many activists of the association have questioned the significance of national and party politics and have shifted their attention to local projects. As was the case in the first free elections in other Eastern and Central European countries in 1989–90, women's representation in the national Parliament decreased after quotas were abandoned; in

the case of the GDR, women's representation fell from 32.5 to 20.5 percent.[13]

Following the March elections, unification took an irreversible path at rapid speed under the CDU/SPD coalition government of Lothar de Maiziere (CDU). Unification became primarily a matter of elite-level politics. Policy making was now being shaped by the institutions of the new government, and the civic groups represented at the roundtable were largely marginalized. Following the West German model, the GDR government established a Ministry for Family and Women. Even though the ministry was not well funded or powerful, it gave women some public visibility and support. In its short existence, the ministry addressed several issues relevant to women, such as shelters for battered women, women's studies, and other projects.

In the first treaty of unification, which established the economic, social, and currency union between the states on 1 July 1990, the focus was on fiscal and economic policies; the policies centered around women's roles in society were barely touched upon. The second unification treaty, known as the Unity Treaty, which was to establish the political unification of the GDR and the Federal Republic, finally included an article addressing women and families because of public pressure from women in both parts of Germany.[14] The major point, though, was the abortion law. In a remarkable interparty cooperation, women in West Germany were able—with the wide public support of East German women—to establish that the existing abortion laws remain in effect until the end of 1992. The abortion law in the former GDR was less restrictive than the law in the old FRG. Women hoped that unification would enable them to introduce a less restrictive abortion law.

In spite of this achievement, unification was highly controversial among women.[15] Although East German women welcomed the fall of the authoritarian regime, many have remained critical of the rapid pace and the policies of unification. The speed of the unification process left women little time to evaluate the options. Women in the west—including prominent West

German Social Democrats, Greens, and leaders of the influential West German unions—who were critical about the rush to unification pointed to the mounting social tensions and economic hardships devolving from the crash course of the currency union, increasing unemployment, potential cuts in social programs, and fiscal constraints. Moreover, West German feminists were concerned that the government emphasis on nationalism would strengthen conservatism and paternalism and divert attention from gender issues.

Controversies over the policies of unification were not merely a result of different political affiliation. They also reflected contrasting experiences in the past 40 years and different expectations of women in both parts of Germany. Unification has created new and different lines of dispute among women themselves, some of which are deeply rooted in the history of the German women's movement and in the relation between the two states in the postwar period.

The division of Germany in 1949 during the height of the cold war had split and weakened women as a political force. Communist-ruled East Germany laid claim to the traditions of the proletarian women's movement. The regime incorporated the rhetoric of social equality and implemented some of the policies the socialist movement had demanded in the past—in particular, access to gainful employment. Politics remained a male-dominated sphere, however, and authoritarianism prevailed. In West Germany, on the other hand, the women's movement was not grounded in one particular ideological concept. Since part of the bourgeois women's movement had been co-opted by the Nazi regime, West German women did not simply pick up where middle-class and liberal women had left off before the Nazis seized power.

Given the pluralist structure in the new democratic state, diverse approaches to women's issues were taken.[16] The conservative political environment in the FRG in the first postwar decades provided limited space for the emergence of a women's movement, and it was not until the early 1970s that such a movement took shape. Throughout the past four decades, the German states influenced each other, including their policies toward women. The hostile ideological confrontation of the states was an additional constraint for the women's movement. The Social Democratic Party reclaimed the issue of social equality of the sexes only reluctantly, for example, whereas the conservative and liberal parties would use the GDR as a negative example to undermine strides for equality. In the former GDR, on the other hand, feminism was officially taboo, since the government feared the spillover effects of Western feminism.

In the late 1940s, women's policies in East and West Germany took different roads. In the east, the focus was on incorporating women into the labor force. Because of the chronic labor shortage, policies to provide access to employment, to improve women's qualifications, and to provide public child care were rapidly implemented and enforced. The employment rate of women steadily increased, and with 83 percent of all women between the ages of 16 and 60 working outside the home in 1989, the country ranked among the highest in the world in terms of women's employment rate; in the same year, the rate in West Germany was 57 percent. Women in East Germany contributed 40 percent to the household income; women in West Germany contributed 18 percent.[17]

Although access to gainful employment for women was promoted in the former GDR, their participation in politics was confined to the structure of the bureaucratic, authoritarian regime and subordinated to the general cause and the goals of Marxist-Leninist ideology. According to this ideology the "women's question" was secondary; class dominated over gender. Even though formal political participation was higher in some areas than in West Germany, women in the former GDR did not speak out on their own behalf, nor could they do so under the rigid authoritarian regime, which prevented the formation of new or independent organizations or interest groups. In the East German People's Chamber, for example, women held nearly twice the proportion of seats held by women in the West German Bundestag, mainly because a certain number of seats were assigned to the official Women's Federation. But women's numerical representation did not enhance their voice or power. Feminism was openly rejected even by women who were in charge of women's affairs and those who conducted research concerning women in society. This was especially the case in the past decade, when GDR state officials feared the influence of a radical new women's movement in West Germany. The state's prime concerns were economic modernization and political stability, as well as fertility of women because the birthrate had declined sharply in the late 1960s and early 1970s. Thus the state provided for women in a paternalistic manner, and women themselves remained politically powerless. So, paradoxically, women formally enjoyed equal rights and generous welfare benefits, especially as mothers, but politics continued to be dominated by men; women literally had no voice. As a result, East German society was strangely gender blind, and women themselves often were not interested in emancipation and equal rights.

In contrast, women in the old Federal Republic embarked in the 1970s on radical efforts to publicly claim women's rights. Much as in other Western European countries and in the United States, a second-wave women's movement evolved. Women gained public visibility, and more women entered politics in the subsequent decades. By the second half of the 1980s, established institutions, the state, and political parties had been forced to adapt, at least partially, to this change in the political culture.

In the FRG women had become more demanding, assertive, and professional in politics. In the GDR women had been forced to adapt to the paternalistic, rigid political system or to meet in the privacy of their homes. The radical feminist approach that had become part of the discourse among women in the FRG was confusing for many East German women, and, in turn, women in the FRG found it difficult to relate to the experience of GDR women and to their demands. East German women took pride in their participation in the civic revolution and sought to "bring something into united Germany," but West Ger-

man women often criticized their sisters' lack of experience and their gender blindness.[18] Conflicts also arose over the evaluation of life experiences. For example, motherhood was an essential part of the lives of East German women activists, most of whom had children early in their lives; their demand to secure and improve child care was rooted in their experience as working mothers. While that demand was widely supported by Social Democratic and union women in the FRG, West German feminists often shunned the emphasis on motherhood and family life.

The social life of women in the former GDR changed dramatically with unification. Large-scale plant closings in the GDR followed the currency union with West Germany and the transition to a market-based economy. East German women were hit first because they were more often employed in the least efficient and competitive industries, such as textiles and food processing, or worked in less socially secure positions. Industrial production fell off by 40 percent in the first half of 1990, and unemployment skyrocketed. Early in 1991 about 40 percent of the area's work force of about 8.5 million were unemployed or on "short work with zero hours," meaning that they reported to work to draw part of their wages for a few months.[19] In December 1990, 54 percent of the unemployed in East Germany were women. Single mothers were harmed the most, along with mothers with small children; such women often had difficulties finding new jobs.

Women in West Germany did not experience this sudden process of change. In fact, the West German economy received an unexpected push from unification. Production was expanded to meet the demands of citizens in the east. The gross national product of West Germany increased by 4 percent in 1990 and was expected to grow by 3 percent in 1991, whereas the East German GNP declined by 10 percent.[20] Understandably, women in East Germany were more concerned with jobs and family income and with trying to organize their new lives in a market-based economy.

Women in both parts of Germany still find it

difficult to "speak the same language" because of their different experiences, expectations, and political cultures. This "wall in the head," as it is called, will continue to influence women's political thinking.[21] At a time when women in the former GDR were confronted with dramatic change and a rapidly deteriorating economic situation and social status, women in West Germany were more concerned with the political implications of unification. Not surprisingly, prejudice often turned into mistrust, alienation into frustration.

In spite of these difficulties, women's rights activists try to use the momentum of German unification to push for effective political improvements. Given the need for new policies during the integration of the East German states, politically active women have tried to defend and even expand policies promoting women's rights. In fact, the coalition agreements of the CDU/FDP government of united Germany include several such statements.[22] For example, the agreements, which outline the direction of policies in this legislative term, call for a law on *Artikelgesetz* (equal rights) to regulate the promotion of women, the competence of equal rights officers in the federal administration, and other mechanisms to promote women in industry. According to their share among the unemployed, women are to be included in programs to retrain workers and create jobs. The governing parties also intend to work with the states on regulations to establish a right to public child care. Providing such care has been particularly pressing in East Germany, where the percentage of working mothers has traditionally been higher than in the FRG. It remains to be seen how these statements of intention will be transformed into policies. Nevertheless, the new and challenging situation resulting from unification has obviously led to some policy statements responding to women's demands, at least symbolically.

EQUAL OPPORTUNITY POLICIES

The inclusion of an equal rights article in the 1949 Basic Law was a big step forward. Article 3 (2) states that "men and women shall have equal rights."[23] In spite of the legal provision, women's social, economic, and political situation does not meet the goal of equality; specific legislation to support the guarantee laid down in the Basic Law has been lacking. Cross-national surveys indicate that West German women feel less liberated than other Europeans, that discrimination in Germany is pertinacious, and that German males are more chauvinist than the average European male.[24]

The notion that women and men are distinctly different, play different roles, and live in different spheres of life is particularly prominent in German political thought. Beginning in the early nineteenth century influential political philosophers like G. W. F. Hegel, Karl Marx and Max Weber adhered to and theorized this notion. Child rearing and family were defined as private spheres, and politics, the state, and law were public. Woman's greatest value and esteem was attributed to her role in the private sphere, and man's value was thought to flourish in the public sphere.[25]

The notion of difference created a significant barrier to women struggling for equal rights. Ironically, one of the most progressive early packages of social reform, which proved to have an ambiguous legacy, was based on women's roles as mothers. Germany was among the first European countries to stress state responsibility for the social welfare of its citizens in the nineteenth century. To undercut the potential rise of labor unrest, social policy programs to protect and appease workers were designed under Bismarck. An important part of this parcel was aimed at supporting mothers and children, but such protective legislation was a mixed blessing for women. They enjoyed some support and benefits, but protective legislation provided for differential treatment of men and women, defining women above all as mothers and with respect to their family "duties." Moreover, women were excluded from entire industries, such as mining and construction. Differential treatment allowed employers to restrict women to so-called light (low-paying) work.

In the decades after the founding of the old

Federal Republic in 1949, several laws that discriminated against women had to be changed in accordance with the constitution. A so-called Equality Act of 1957 curtailed the patriarchal power of men as husbands and fathers. The right of the husband to make the final decision in all matrimonial affairs was deleted; in particular, his right to terminate his wife's employment without notice was repealed. It was not until passage of the Reform of Marriage Law and Family Law in 1977, however, that women's equal status was acknowledged. The social-liberal government of the 1970s was more open to redefining women's status as part of its reform package than was the previous conservative government. With this law, the so-called housewife-marriage was discarded, and nonemployed women were to receive social security in case of divorce.

Although equal rights for women in the family were finally acknowledged, women still face discrimination in the workplace. Even in 1987 the average weekly wage of female industrial workers was only 70 percent of the wage earned by men. Women's unemployment rate was higher than that of men (10 percent compared with 7 percent).[26] Minority women, especially the half-million Turks, face the greatest obstacles in finding a job or building a professional career, even though many of them are second-generation foreigners. Two-thirds of the non-German students living in Germany never enter vocational training, and 80 percent of employed women are manual workers.[27]

Mainly in response to European Community directives of 1975 and 1976 that advocated equal pay for work of equal value and equal treatment of women and men regarding access, training, promotion, and working conditions, rather weak antidiscrimination legislation was finally passed in 1980 in the form of an EEC-Adaption Act. In a 1984 ruling the European Court of Justice criticized this legislation for its lack of enforcing provisions. In 1985 the federal government provided guidelines, which were improved in 1990, for promoting women in recruitment, training, continued education, and employment, but again they were weak.

The federal government and several Länder have introduced directives to increase the number of women in higher positions, but they have been reluctant to establish enforcing mechanisms or quotas. Also, some firms have used the guidelines to implement policies favorable to women. But women still find it very difficult to advance in higher-status professions, especially in banking, business, universities, and the corporate world. Discrimination persists, both openly and subtly.[28] Organized pressure to cope with the discrimination against women in the workplace—wage discrimination in particular—came from the influential labor unions and from women in the Social Democratic Party. But it was not until feminists from the new women's movement publicly addressed such issues as sexual harassment that the debate broadened to embrace various forms of discrimination.

In spite of the official governmental rhetoric of equal rights, discrimination against women existed in the GDR as well. Recently released data collected when the GDR was still under communist rule reveal that women's wages among industrial and construction workers were 12 percent lower than those of men even if they performed the same tasks.[29] Extra benefits and wage supplements for overtime additionally increased male workers' income. A significantly higher proportion of women were grouped in the lower and lowest wage groups, and as a result, women's average pensions were lower than those of men. The report also points to a number of discriminatory procedures in hiring and promotion.

Aside from discrimination, one of the major difficulties for women in the Federal Republic has been insufficient child care. Contrary to widespread belief about the advanced German welfare state, the Federal Republic provides fewer facilities and favorable institutional arrangements than other EC countries. Although maternity and parental leave regulations are generous—up to 18 months after the birth of a child—child-care facilities are insufficient.[30] As more and more women entered the labor force, the country fell behind in meeting the child-care needs of working women. Only 3 percent of the children up to two years of age are in nursery schools, and 60 percent of the three- to five-year-olds are in preschool. There are regional differences, but long waiting lists exist in most cities. Also, unlike France, Britain, and Spain, for example, public schools are in session only half a day, making it difficult for women to work full time or to pursue a professional career. In 1991 the CDU/FDP government finally stated in its coalition agreement a goal of working with the states to establish a right to child care.

Frustration with the slow pace of change and the lack of improvement led to sustained questioning of the approach taken by parties and unions. Radical feminists from the Green Party and women activists in the Social Democratic Party have called for policies—similar to those adopted in Sweden and the United States—that would not only ban discrimination but also effectively promote women in job recruitment, training, and employment procedures. So far, Germany has not enacted an affirmative action policy. According to the argument, preferential treatment of women contradicts the principle of freedom of contract guaranteed by the Basic Law to both employers and workers. Powerful interest groups supporting this view of the freedom of contract, as well as traditional thinking and the rigidity of large social organizations, have so far blocked innovative legislation promoting women.

In 1986 an expert opinion delivered by a prominent lawyer for the equal opportunity office in the city of Hamburg argued that the state has the right and even obligation to compensate for the traditional discrimination against women.[31] This argument has been carried further by feminists and women's rights activists—especially those in the Social Democratic and Green parties and in the unions. They insist that the constitution not only provides for equal rights but that it requires action to end traditional discrimination against women in the public and working world. This view is supported by the constitutional demand in the Basic Law that Germany be a "social" state striving for the well-being of all of citizens. Women argue that the state—according to the *Sozialstaatsprinzip,* or welfare state principle—has a responsibility to see to it that discrimination is ended. Following the state responsibility argument, much of the German debate about affirmative action and the preferential treatment of women is centered around fixed or flexible quotas.[32]

Some political and women's groups demand much more effective policies to establish equal opportunities. The most radical approach was taken by members of the Green Party, who set an example in 1983 by introducing a 50 percent quota for candidate selection on their party list. In 1988, the Green Party submitted a far-reaching Antidiscrimination Law proposal to the national Parliament, only to have it rejected in June 1990.[33] One of the main points was a controversial call for a 50 percent quota in training, hiring, and promotion processes in the public sector, as well as in private business. In particular, the latter provision was sharply rejected by the business community, as well as by the governing parties.

Although it has been difficult to achieve effective affirmative action legislation on the national level, women have been slightly more successful on the state level, particularly in states with a left-of-center majority. The state of North Rhine–Westphalia was the first to introduce an anti-discrimination law in the late 1980s. States like Hamburg and Bremen have similar legislation, and in Berlin (West), a law was passed in fall 1990 under the Social Democratic/Green coalition government to ban sex discrimination and establish a 50 percent quota in hiring and promotion in the public sector.[34]

The demand for a fixed quota is highly controversial, even among professional women. As the prominent women's rights lawyer Heide Pfarr (SPD) has warned, such a quota could work against women if they focused their equal opportunities policies primarily on quotas ("crutches") without tackling the general patterns in inequality.[35] The major threat, however, comes from groups and individuals who oppose the promotion of women.

ABORTION AND REPRODUCTIVE RIGHTS

Women's struggle for a liberal abortion law after unification presents an open-and-shut case. At the time of unification there were two laws concerning abortion in united Germany. In the old Federal Republic, abortion was a criminal offense under clause 218 of the criminal code adopted in 1871, except for clearly defined medical, ethical, or social reasons, which were introduced in 1975 *(Indikationslösung,* or indication model). In the former GDR, abortion was legal in the first three months of a pregnancy *(Fristenlösung,* or periodic model). Because of public and political pressure from women, the more restrictive law of the old Federal Republic did not go into effect in all of Germany with unification. Rather, the unification treaty provided for a two-year interim period in which both laws coexisted in the two territories. In May 1993 the Federal Constitutional Court ruled that the more liberal law for all of Germany that was passed by the Parliament in 1992 was unconstitutional. The Court declared abortions *rechtswidrig* (against the law) and severely restricted access to them.

Abortion was the focus of public and political attention in the old Federal Republic in the early 1970s. Public campaigns, such as confessions of prominent women who had undergone abortions and demonstrations against the infamous clause 218, were the catalysts for the new radical women's movement. The reform-oriented social-liberal government finally drafted new regulations. But the law of 1974, which legalized abortion in the first 12 weeks of pregnancy, never went into effect. The opposition CDU/CSU parties turned to the Federal Constitutional Court, which in 1975 decided that the 1974 Amending Act conflicted with the Basic Law of the Federal Republic. The court acknowledged the conflicting interests but argued that because of the Nazi past the protection of human life was more important. Thus in 1976 the penal regulations about abortion were changed again. Under these regulations, abortion basically remained a criminal offense in the Federal Republic except in the following circumstances: if the pregnancy would

considerably endanger the life or health of the woman (medical grounds); if the child's mental or physical health was seriously damaged (eugenic grounds); if the pregnancy was caused by rape (criminal or ethical grounds); and if the abortion would avert serious damage to the pregnant woman's physical or mental health that could not be averted by any other reasonable means (social grounds).[36] If the abortion was not indicated on medical grounds, the pregnant women was also obliged to seek counseling at a recognized counseling center or from a second physician within 12 weeks of conception.

The indication allowing an abortion on social grounds has been the most frequently contested. In several states this indication has been handled favorably for women seeking help. In other states, mostly in the Catholic-dominated south, pressure on doctors and counseling centers has been so strong that it is almost impossible for women to obtain an abortion without leaving the state. Factions of the CDU/CSU parties repeatedly attempted to restrict access to abortion. Stricter counseling laws were suggested in the late 1980s, for example. Attempts to restrict abortion provisions were mainly led by the Catholic church and Catholic politicians, who argued on normative and ethical grounds. Organizations for the "protection of the unborn life" have sprung up in recent years, but they are less militant than similar organizations in the United States, for example.

In the GDR abortion was legalized in 1972. Women were able to decide for themselves whether to terminate a pregnancy during the first 12 weeks; after this period abortion was permitted only under special circumstances. Abortions were performed in a hospital, and the costs were covered by the socialized medical system. Abortion, however, was never an issue of public interest. Instead, communist government leaders decided to legalize abortion while discouraging any public debate. According to GDR sources, the number of illegal abortions had increased sharply in the late 1960s, posing health risks to a larger number of women. Pointing to the example of the Soviet Union and other countries in the Eastern bloc, the government legitimized its decision and tried to picture itself as progressive, but it was obvious that it was seeking to prevent public campaigns like those in the FRG. Even though abortion was legal, it remained a taboo issue in public and even among women. Statistics and other information about the number of or reasons for abortions were not published until 1989 because the government feared they would be interpreted as a sign of social discontent.[37] For women, abortion was seen not so much as a right but as a way to terminate an unwanted pregnancy. Abortion was seen as another method of birth control even though other methods of birth control, such as the pill, were widely available in the GDR.

In 1991 several proposals for a new law were debated in Germany. There were five major approaches: the abolition of clause 218, including abolition of mandatory counseling for women (Greens), thus abandoning the criminalization of abortion and restrictions; the periodic model, which legalized abortion within the first 12 weeks of a pregnancy (a measure endorsed by the SPD and FDP; the latter sought to combine the periodic model with mandatory counseling); the indication model, which left the final decision to the pregnant woman and made counseling mandatory (favored by some CDU members, such as Rita Süssmuth); a revised indication model that turned the decision over to a doctor or a committee (supported by some in the CDU, such as Family Minister Helga Rönsch); and an indication model restricted even further by removing the social grounds, for example (which some CDU politicians and the CSU supported). The CDU/CSU clearly did not wish to legalize abortion, but the party was divided. Moreover, its FDP coalition partner had a prominent and vocal prochoice wing, and thus the government was not united. A poll conducted by Emnid, a public opinion and marketing research firm, in spring 1991 showed that 55 percent of West Germans supported either a complete decriminalization of abortion or legalization during the first trimester. Even in the former GDR, two-thirds of the citizens favored legal abortion.[38] Therefore,

when the German Parliament liberalized the abortion law in June 1992, it had the support of a majority of the German public.

Passed after intense debate—mainly within and among the political parties—the 1992 abortion law left the final decision about an abortion to the woman and decriminalized abortion during the first 12 weeks of pregnancy. The law mandated counseling, which feminist groups had opposed, and included provisions for social policies that encouraged the pregnant woman to bear the child. The *Gruppenantrag* (draft law) was prepared by an interparty group of parliamentarians and was strongly supported by the SPD, FDP, and some progressive, dissident CDU women. The clearly more restrictive proposal by the governing CDU/CSU—supported by the Women's Ministry—failed to find a majority. Shortly after the decision, however, a group of conservative politicians appealed to the Federal Constitutional Court to overturn the decision.

This temporary compromise, which reopened the parliamentary debate on abortion, followed weeks of intense debates that preceded the signing of the unification treaty. The West German government under Kohl, supported by anti-abortion groups and the Catholic church, had no intention of considering a revision of the regulations concerning abortion. In one of the rare cases of interparty alliance, however, women from all political parties opposed the extension of the West German law into East Germany.[39] It was this interparty alliance that finally led to the landmark decision to legalize abortion in 1992. Women saw unification as a chance to decriminalize abortion and to empower themselves to decide about childbearing in consultation with their doctor.

Although the unification treaty left the door open for a prochoice law, the 1993 ruling of the Federal Constitutional Court effectively closed that door. Under this ruling the state must protect the "rights of the unborn life"; pregnant women, however, have no right to determine whether they will bear the child. The ruling, which basically adopts the anti-abortionist position, overturns the comparatively liberal abortion law passed in 1992. It puts an end to the prochoice regulations in the former East Germany, a severe setback for women there. The ruling restricts access to abortion even more than the law in preunification West Germany because mandatory counseling will have to stress "the protection of the unborn life" and because health insurance will no longer cover abortions performed under the social indication (which make up 90 percent of all legal abortions in Germany). As a result, the Federal Republic will have one of the most restrictive regulations on abortion in Europe. The decision, which received broad public attention in Germany, was widely opposed by women from all political parties, feminists, and women's rights activists.

WOMEN'S POLITICAL REPRESENTATION

In recent years the marginalization of women's voices in the political system has itself become a policy issue. Since the channels of access to positions of power have been prestructured by the male-dominated political organizations—especially parties, unions, and business interest groups—the questions for women have been whether to infiltrate these organizations, to form new organizations, or to eschew organization all together.[40]

German women traditionally have aligned with organizations that press for social reforms, particularly with parties on the left and with unions, but Nazism had eradicated the socialist, liberal, and radical roots of the women's movement and left a generation of women more concerned with rebuilding their shattered lives than with organizational or elite-level politics. Several women's organizations were revived after World War II. In the GDR, the Democratic Women's Federation soon was dominated by the Communist Party. In the FRG, several groups merged in 1951 to form the German Council of Women. The women's council, which has about 10 million members, has acted mainly as a lobby group, but it never gained much influence in public life. Throughout the 1950s and 1960s only a few women were active in political parties, unions,

and parliaments. Conservative thinking confined women mainly to the Ks—*Kinder, Küche, Kirche* (children, kitchen, church).

As in other Western European countries, the United States, and Canada, the early 1970s saw an increasing mobilization of women—most prominently in the new women's movement, which evolved from the student movement in the late 1960s.[41] A new reform space was opened when the SPD/FDP government came to power in 1969 and encouraged grass-roots mobilization with its slogan, "Dare more democracy." But frustration about the failure to legalize abortion, the overall slow pace of change, and the inflexibility of large, traditional organizations led many women to believe that only independent new organizations could enhance women's influence and status in society. Fundamental conflicts arose between those activists who sought political change through institutionalized politics—in particular through the Social Democratic Party, the unions and some professional organizations—and radical feminists striving for autonomy. The term *autonome Frauenbewegung* (autonomous women's movement) reflects the anti-statist and anti-institutional approach of radical feminists, who saw the movement as different and independent from conventional political institutions.

Radical feminists concentrated on grass-roots activism and local projects such as shelters for battered women, cultural centers, bookstores and cafes, and summer universities for women. Radical feminism flourished in particular in the university environment, in urban areas, and among well-educated women, but it found little support from working-class and immigrant women. Because the movement was prone to splintering throughout the 1970s it remained a weak national political force. But some support was mobilized from those employed in the educational, health, and cultural sectors as well as in public administration. Several projects and initiatives that originated in the radical feminist counterculture of the autonomous women's movement—such as the shelters and self-help groups—managed to become part of German public life. Even government officials today recognize the innovative capacity of these projects, half of which are run by autonomous groups. Feminists have generally rejected the control and regulation of state bureaucracies, but to survive financially they had to work with state authorities. Most of the projects and centers receive some local and state funds, but they are often not well funded or financially secure.[42]

The ascendancy of the Greens—in 1983 it became the first new party to enter the national Parliament for decades—provided new opportunities for women in the 1980s. Radical feminists and women's activists were major supporters of the grass-roots-oriented Greens. Along with the environmental and peace movements, second-wave feminism was a driving force in the Green Party. Women have been particularly receptive to the "anti-party" approach, as well as to the emphasis on new politics based on non-hierarchical, communitarian philosophies. The Greens have been instrumental in generating public discussion on feminist issues. They were the first to openly address sexism in Parliament, for example. Antidiscrimination legislation has been another major issue of the Greens. Moreover, their bold approach to increasing the political representation of women in parliaments has had a major impact on the German party system because other parties were forced to adopt similar policies. So despite the overall conservative political climate on the national level throughout the 1980s and early 1990s under the CDU/FDP coalition government, women's public visibility increased and feminist politics was professionalized. But division within the Green Party among various groups and on different levels of the organization—which greatly contributed to the disappointing election results in 1990, as well as continuing distrust of institutionalized politics—hindered the consolidation of a strong women's movement. Decentralized grass-roots activities remain crucial for radical feminists, and many women have shifted their attention to peace and environmental activities. Occasional alliances were formed between Green, Social Democratic, and Liberal women on the anti-discrimination law or the abortion issue, but there is no coherent, organized, independent women's movement on the national level.

One of the major results of women's increasing mobilization and political engagement is the establishment of a network of political institutions pursuing women's policies. A new generation of women, influenced and often trained by their experience in the women's movement, has entered politics in the 1980s, in particular on the state and local levels. Women became more visible and influential through women's ministries or offices. At the local level, there were about 900 equal rights offices in 1991 in the old Federal Republic; by March 1991 about 330 such offices were established in the new eastern German states.[43] Women's offices, initiated in 1979, existed in all Länder by the end of the 1980s. In the new states such offices were created along with the reestablishment of the Länder in 1990. Even though the institutional arrangement varies—some states established ministries for women (Schleswig-Holstein, Berlin), some acted as independent authorities (Hamburg, Bremen, Brandenburg), others opened women's offices assigned to the minister-presidents (Baden-Württemberg, Bavaria)—they have given women more voice in policy making and some resources for pursuing women's rights policies, even though many feminists feel that their power and influence are not sufficient. At the federal level, a Ministry for Women was finally established in 1986 (from 1979 to 1986, it was the Directorate on Women's Affairs) as part of the Ministry for Youth, Family, Women, and Health. After the 1990 elections the ministry was restructured to become the Ministry for Women and Youth.

Because of the dominant role of political parties in the German parliamentary democracy, the primary access to decision making in politics is through parties. Party membership is not required for many forms of political participation, such as voting, but it is essential for acquiring a position in the political decision-making process. Women's representation in political parties almost doubled between 1971 and 1981, but it is still significantly lower than that of men.[44] In

1988, women made up 25.6 percent of the members of the Social Democratic Party (1976: 19.9 percent); 22.5 percent in the Christian Democratic Party (1976: 18.5); 14.2 percent in the Christian Social Union (1976: 11.1); 24.0 percent in the Free Democratic Party (1976: 19.1); and 37.5 percent in the Green Party. The number of women on the executive committees of the Social Democratic Party and the Green Party has increased because of quotas. Women are still underrepresented in leadership positions in other parties, however. In the parties' executive committees at the federal level, women's representation is largest in the Green Party (1988: 54.5 percent), followed by the Social Democratic Party (35.0 percent), the Free Democratic Party (21.2 percent), the Christian Democratic Party (20.0 percent), and the Christian Social Union (9.7 percent).

Pressure to increase the number of women at decision-making levels in political parties and in parliaments came in particular from such intra-party women's groups as the Working Group of Social Democratic Women (ASF) in the SPD and the Women's Union in the CDU.[45] Much of the debate is centered around the introduction and implementation of quotas within the parties. The Greens were the first to introduce a 50 percent quota as early as 1986. They implemented the so-called zipper principle, meaning that all odd numbers on a party list had to be filled by women. In the 1987 national elections, the Greens were the only party sending more female than male representatives to the national Parliament (25 of 44).

Their radical approach to increasing the number of women in Parliament influenced other parties because of competition in the parliamentary system. With few exceptions, such as that of the conservative Bavarian Christian Social Union, the parties started to take measures to increase the number of women in political bodies. Women's representation in decision-making bodies became an issue itself, with much of the debate centered around hard, inflexible quotas or soft goal quotas.[46] Under the pressure of women, the parties favored different measures and policies, often

reflecting their ideologies and traditions. The large Social Democratic Party decided in 1988 to establish an initial quota of 33 percent, followed in 1992 by a 40 percent quota for candidacies and offices. In 1988, the Christian Democratic Union introduced a flexible goal that women be represented in offices and mandates proportionate to their membership. The Free Democratic Party adopted a similar resolution under which women were to be represented at all levels from 1988 to 1993 according to their membership proportion, even though the party has been reluctant to introduce ways to enforce this policy.

Thanks to the mobilization of women in the past decade, women's political representation in Parliament has increased. While the proportion of female delegates in the Bundestag had fluctuated between 6.8 percent in 1949 and 9.8 percent in 1983, the proportion jumped to 15.4 percent in 1987 thanks to the high proportion of women in the Green faction in Parliament.[47] Even though the West German Greens are now no longer represented in the national Parliament, the first all-German elections to the Bundestag brought the highest number of women into the legislature of the Federal Republic since the postwar years, owing to the party's strategies to increase the number of women on party lists. Women now comprise 20.4 percent of the representatives in the national Parliament (135 women).[48]

Studies have shown that women are confronting both individual and institutional barriers to their participation in conventional forms of politics.[49] Even though public attitudes toward women in politics have changed significantly, women find it much harder to engage in politics. Marriage and especially motherhood are the most influential factors hindering women who seek political careers, and women in higher political positions are often single, though few of the men are not married. Women find it almost impossible to be politically active while raising children and holding a job, especially since the general conditions for making work and family life compatible are worse in the Federal Republic of Germany than in other European countries.

In recent years, institutional barriers have become another focus of attention. The organization, structure, and political life in parties make no allowances for the specific living conditions of women; parties were structured during the period when women were largely absent from these institutions, and female lifestyles are usually not 280taken into consideration. Women are drastically underrepresented in the leading bodies of the political parties, posing a number of implications for decision making and party politics. In the centralized selection procedure, for example, the party elite has the last say in drawing up the list of candidates, and women are often not nominated because of their marginalization. Therefore, a quota regulation is widely supported by women in the parties, demonstrating the increasing impatience of women. Women have established that democracy implies an equal share of political power, at least on the symbolic level. But for years to come women will struggle to implement policies that will increase their share of power and political representation.

Even though political parties in the Federal Republic were forced to respond to women's demands for equality and self determination, the current conservative government is less favorable to women. Elite politics is a good example. Even though the new cabinet of united Germany includes four women—the highest number in postwar history—the women all fill low-prestige ministerial posts (family and the elderly, youth and women, health, housing).

Politics within the EC has become another area of women's political engagement in recent years. The creation of the barrier-free internal market by 31 December 1992 and the move toward further political integration within the EC drew considerable attention in the FRG. With the push toward integration, significant changes in national political economies, labor markets, career profiles, and social mobility are expected to take place. Recently the EC has drafted several directives that affect women, including regulations about part-time work, shift work, and maternity leave. Through cooperation on the EC level and lobbying at the community's commis-

sion, political groups such as the German Council of Women seek to ensure women's representation and voice in European policy making, an arena that has so far been dominated by bureaucrats and lobbyists from the agricultural, business, trade, and financial worlds.[50]

Because of unification, women in the Federal Republic are facing a number of immediate challenges. Unification has created a new urgency to push for policies—social, economic, and equal rights—to cope with discrimination. Over the past decade, women in the old Federal Republic have had some success on the symbolic level of politics. Not only has their participation in conventional forms of politics increased, but more importantly women have been able to gain public visibility through a new network of institutions such as the women's offices and ministries on the local and state levels. Women's current political participation can best be summarized as a dual system: an increasing number of women are engaged in institutionalized politics today, often as feminists or women's rights activists, but for a considerable group of feminists, grass-roots activities—including some of the new projects in East Germany—based on communitarian and non-hierarchical values remain essential. Thus Germany may not have a coherent, nationwide movement, but women will continue to play a significant role in politics.

The progress made on the symbolic level of politics is, however, not matched on the material stage of policy implementation and in particular the redistribution and allocation of resources. Here women are confronted with tremendous obstacles. Given the constraints on the national economy as a whole resulting from the immense task of shaping up the economy in East Germany, women are facing tough times. One of the major current challenges is the restructuring of the new states of former East Germany. It is particularly the women who face the uncertainties of this socioeconomic transformation.

Just as unification greatly affected women, so will the process of European integration change their social and political environment. Although the main thrust of the project—to create a single

European market—is economic, important areas of the social and political order in European countries are beginning to change as well. In the past, European Community directives, in particular on equality in the workplace, offered women in a number of European countries, including the FRG, a chance to push for woman-friendly policies. Whether this will hold true for the new era in European integration—when market liberalism is dominant—remains to be seen. In any case, women's future political struggle will more and more be influenced not only by the national setting but also by the framework of the European Community.

NOTES

1. For a general overview of the situation of women in the old Federal Republic and the former German Democratic Republic see Federal Ministry for Youth, Family, Women, and Health, ed., *Frauen in der Bundesrepublik Deutschland* (Women in the Federal Republic of Germany) (Cologne: Kölnische Verlagsdruckerei, 1989). See also Hanna Beate Schöpp-Schilling, ed., "Change and Continuity in the Roles of Women in Post-War Germany" (Keynote address presented at the Women in Post-War Germany conference, North Carolina State University, Raleigh, September 1989). In English see Eva Kolinsky, *Women in West Germany* (Oxford: Berg Publishers, 1989). The situation of women in the German Democratic Republic is documented in Gunnar Winkler, ed., *Frauenreport '90* (Report on Women: 1990) (Berlin: Die Wirtschaft, 1990).

2. Women's history has slowly become a research field in Germany. See, e.g., Karin Hausen, ed., *Frauen suchen ihre Geschichte. Historische Studien zum 19. und 20. Jahrhundert* (Women in search of their history: Studies in the history of the 19th and 20th centuries) (Munich: Beck, 1983); Annette Kuhn, ed., *Frauen in der Geschichte* (Women in history), several vols. (Düsseldorf: Schwann, 1979). In this article I use the term *feminist*, in accordance with the German discourse, for the radical feminists of the new women's movement who emphasize women's personal autonomy and self-determination; the term *women's rights activist* is used more broadly for those women fighting for equal rights.

3. See, e.g., Joachim Hofmann-Göttig, *Emanzipation mit dem Stimmzettel. 70 Jahre Frauenwahlrecht in Deutschland* (Emancipation through the voting ballot: 70 years of voting rights in Germany) (Bonn: Verlag Neue Gesellschaft, 1986).

4. Women under National Socialism have received some scholarly attention in Germany. One of the most prominent works is Gisela Bock, *Zwangssterilisation im Nationalsozialismus. Studien zur Rassenpolitik und Frauenpolitik* (Forced sterilization under national socialism: Studies in race policy and women's policy) (Opladen: Westdeutscher Verlag, 1986).

5. See, e.g., Hanna Schissler, "Women in West Germany" (Paper presented at the Women in Post-War Germany conference, North Carolina State University, Raleigh, September 1989).

6. For a general introduction to the Federal Republic's political system see Russell J. Dalton, *Politics in West Germany* (Glenview, Ill.: Scott Foresman, 1989); and Russell J. Dalton, "Politics in the New Germany" (Manuscript, 1991).

7. In the most recent national elections on 2 December 1990—the first to elect an all-German postwar Parliament—the parties received the following share of votes: Christlich-Demokratische Union Deutschlands and Christlich-Soziale Union Deutschlands (CDU/CSU), 43.8 percent (319 seats); Sozialdemokratische Partei Deutschlands (SPD), 33.5 percent (239 seats); Freie Demokratische Partei (FDP), 11.0 percent (79 seats); Alliance '90 / Greens (East), 1.2 and 5.9 percent in the East (8 seats); Partei des Demokratischen Sozialismus, 2.4 percent and 9.9 in the East (17 seats); Greens (West), 3.9 percent (no seats); Republicans, 2.1 percent (no seats); other parties, 2.1 percent. The number of seats in the national Parliament has increased from 496 to at least 656. Since the CDU won six extra seats through its district victories, the Bundestag was expanded to include these extra mandates, adding up to 662 total seats. Not represented is the Women's Party, which has played a marginal role in German politics (a total of 12,110 of the votes in 1990). The right-wing extremist party (the Republicans), which is known for its an antifeminist stand, failed to gain representation. *Das Parliament* 40, no. 50 (1990): 1; "Election '90," *The Week in Germany,* the German Information Center, 7 December 1990, 1. The share of female voters was highest among SPD voters: women made up 54.5 percent of all SPD voters; 53.6 percent of CDU/CSU voters; 52.2 of Green voters; 40.1 percent of FDP voters; and 39.4 percent of all PDS voters. Dalton, *Politics in West Germany,* 29.

8. Bärbel Bohley ("mother of the revolution") became the major spokeswoman for the New Forum, the most popular opposition group. Ulrike Poppe is an active member of "Democracy Now." Vera Wollenberger is a founding member of the East German Green Party and member of the German Parliament for the Greens. Opposition women often did not see themselves as women's rights activists or even feminists. Rather, gender issues were intertwined with human rights and peace issues. Some feminist thinking was expressed in the former GDR in women's

literature, which served as a kind of public voice of women. On feminism in the GDR see Christiane Lemke, *Die Ursachen des Umbruchs. Politische Sozialisation in der DDR* (The causes of radical change: Political socialization in the GDR) (Opladen: Westdeutscher Verlag, 1991), chap. 4.3.

9. This was clearly expressed by Tatjana Böhm and Petra Streit, both active members of the Independent Women's Association, at the Harvard Workshop "Women and Unification," Harvard University, Center for European Studies, 18–19 May 1991. Böhm was one of the two representatives at the roundtable in East Berlin in 1989–90.

10. Unabhängiger Frauenverband (Independent Women's Association) was founded on 3 December 1989 in Berlin. See "Aufbruch der Frauen gegen die 'mittelmäßigen Männer" (The rise of women against "medicine men") *Tageszeitung,* 4 December 1989; "Die Frauenbewegung braucht einen groen politischen Anspruch" (The women's movement needs great political aspirations) (interview with Ina Merkel), *Tageszeitung,* 6 December 1989. The history of the women's movement in the former GDR has yet to be written. Some activists have claimed that it started as early as 1978, with the emerging peace movement. Clearly earlier activities— often severely curtailed by the Stasi (secret police)—fed into the movement of 1989–90. In September 1989 a group called Lila Offensive had published a statement in a church-sheltered gathering, criticizing the failures of the regime. In respect to the emergence of an informal network of women in the academia in the GDR see "Atemschwelle. Versuche, Richtung zu gewinnen" (Breathing threshold: Attempts to find a direction) *Feministische Studien,* no. 1 (1990): 90–106. Professional women in academic institutions published a statement in an official journal in November 1989; "Geht die Erneuerung an uns Frauen vorbei?" (Is renewal passing women by?) *Für Dich* 46 (1989). A Center for Interdisciplinary Women's Research was also established at the Humboldt Universität Berlin. See Irene Dölling, "Situation und perspektiven von Frauenforschung in der DDR" (Situation and perspectives for women's studies in the GDR), in Zentrum für interdisziplinäre Frauenforschung, *Bulletin No. 1* (Berlin: Humboldt Universität Berlin, 1990), 1–25. The feminist journal *Ypsilon* emerged from the mobilization of women in the former GDR.

11. When it became obvious in early 1990 that the GDR would move toward closer cooperation with the FRG, the association defined itself as a women's organization in "Germany," in Winkler, ed., *Frauenreport,* 204. For an elaboration on the early goals and policies of the new association see, e.g., Ina Merkel, "Frauen in der DDR: Vorschläge für eine Kultur der Geschlechterverhältnisse" (Women in the GDR: Proposal for a culture in gender relations), in Hubertus Knabe, *Aufbruch in eine andere DDR* (Reinbek: Rowohlt, 1989), 90–97.

12. The first free elections in the GDR brought the following results: Alliance for Germany (CDU, DSU, DA), 48 percent; SPD, 21.8 percent; PDS, 16.3 percent; Liberals, 5.3 percent; Alliance '90 (New Forum and other civic groups), 2.9 percent; Greens (with Independent Women's Association), 2.0 percent; others, 3.2 percent. A simple proportional system was used in the elections.

13. In other former communist countries in Eastern Europe the decline was even more drastic. Women's share in the Hungarian Parliament fell in 1990 from 20.9 to 7 percent; in Czechoslovakia, from 29.5 to 6 percent; in Bulgaria, from 21 to 8.5 percent; in Romania, from 34.5 to 3.5 percent. "Weniger Frauen in den Parlamenten" (Fewer women in parliaments), *Das Parlament,* no. 32 (1990): 13. The major reason the decrease is less dramatic in the former GDR is that several parties, including the Social Democrats and Democratic Socialists, used quotas in placing women on their lists.

14. "(1) It shall be the task of the all-German legislator to develop further the legislation on equal rights for men and women. (2) In view of different legal and institutional starting positions with regard to the employment of mothers and fathers, it shall be the task of the all-German legislator to shape the legal situation in such a way as to allow a reconciliation of family and occupational life. (3) In order to ensure that day care centers for children continue to operate in the territory specified in Article 3 of this Treaty the Federation [the former GDR] shall contribute to the costs of these centers for a transitional period up to 30 June 1991. (4) It shall be the task of the all-German legislator to introduce regulations no later than 31 December 1992 which ensure better protection of unborn life and provide a better solution in conformity with the Constitution of conflict situations faced by pregnant women—notably through legally guaranteed entitlements for women, first and foremost to advice and public support—than is the case in either part of Germany at present. In order to achieve these objectives, a network of advice centers run by various agencies and offering blanket coverage shall be set up without delay with financial assistance from the Federation in the territory specified in Article 3 of this Treaty. The advice centers shall be provided with sufficient staff and funds to allow them to cope with the task of advising pregnant women and offering them necessary assistance, including beyond the time of confinement. In the event that no regulations are introduced within the period stated in the first sentence, the substantive law shall continue to apply in the territory specified in Article 3 of this Treaty." *Treaty Between the Federal Republic of Germany and the German Democratic Republic on the Establishment of German Unity* (Unification Treaty), trans. German Information Center, Article 31, "Family and Women," 1990.

15. In fact, there was widespread feeling among women in the east that they would be the losers in German

unification and that East Germany was being annexed or occupied by the FRG. Thus the impact of unification was hotly debated by women in summer 1990. See, e.g., Christiane Lemke, "Frauenpolitische Optionen und Kontroversen im deutschen Vereinigungsproze" (Options and controversies in women's politics during German unification), in Ulrike Liebert and Wolfgang Merkel, eds., *Die Politik zu deutschen Einheit* (Opladen: Leske und Budrich, 1991).

16. See, e.g., Ute Gerhard, "A Hidden and Complex Heritage: Reflections on the History of Germany's Women's Movements," *Women's Studies International Forum* 5, no. 6: 561–67; and Myra Marx Ferree, "Equality and Autonomy: Feminist Politics in the United States and West Germany," in M. Katzenstein and C. McClurg, eds., *The Women's Movements of the United States and Western Europe* (Philadelphia: Temple University Press, 1987), 172–95. With respect to women's organizations see also German Women's Council, ed., *Handbuch deutscher Frauenorganisationen* (Handbook of women's organizations in Germany) (Bonn: Bad Godesberg, 1989).

17. The different lifestyles and expectations are well documented in "Frauen in den neuen Bundesländern," the first empirical survey by Institut für angewandte Sozialwissenschaft (INFAS). See also Bundesministerium für Frauen und Jugend, ed., *Materialien zur Frauenpolitik 11/1991, Dokumentation* (Materials concerning women's policy 11/1991, documentation) (Bonn: Bundesministerium für Frauen und Jugend, 1991).

18. One example of the different approaches is the debate over *Berufsbezeichnungen* (male and female nouns and professional titles). Because of the feminist critique and pressure from women's groups in the old FRG, job advertisements have to address both male and female candidates (e.g., *Professor, Professorin*) and there is a greater sensitivity toward women in addresses, newspaper articles, and the like regarding use of male nouns. In the former GDR, only male titles were used. Women lecturers refer to themselves as *Dozent* (not *Dozentin*); mechanics call themselves *Mechaniker* (not *Mechanikerin*). West German feminists and women's rights activists criticized this practice, but East German women regarded the debate as superficial.

19. Dalton, "Politics in the New Germany," 30; *Wirtschaftswoche,* no. 52–53, 21 December 1990, p. 52. See also "German Privatization in East Mired in Hard Times," *New York Times,* 12 March 1991, p. 1. The significance of paid employment for East German women is well documented in the first comprehensive survey of women in the new East German states: INFAS, *Frauen in den neuen Bundesländern im Proze der deutschen Einheit* (Women in the new German states during the process of German unification) (Manuscript, 1991).

20. *Wirtschaftswoche,* no. 52–53, p. 52.

21. Language interpreted in a different cultural and political context is often telling. One example is the different perception of the term *Pflichtberatung* (mandatory counseling) in the abortion debate. As one East German feminist explained, many East German women perceive the term as an obligation for the state to offer women counseling about abortion, something they did not have under the communist regime. West German women read the term as *Zwangsberatung* (forcible counseling), which they see as patronizing to women.

22. See "Auszüge aus der Koalitionsvereinbarung. Schwerpunkte der Politik in den nächsten vier Jahren" (Excerpts of the coalition agreement: The main political issues during the next four years), *Das Parlament,* no. 6, 1 February 1991, pp. 7–8. There has been increasing public pressure to enhance women's status and rights. For example, the meeting of 500 professional women in Germany, sponsored by the Frankfurt Commission for Women in October 1990, called for a revised constitution for united Germany along the lines of "freedom, equality, and sisterhood." "Women Seek More Rights Through New Constitution," German Information Center, *The Week in Germany,* 2 November 1990, p. 6.

23. This article was included in the Basic Law only because the four female members of the Parliamentary Council, the 61-member body that drafted the constitution, had forcefully argued for it. Political parties in the Federal Republic held different views of women's roles in society and politics. See Birgit Meyer, "Frauenpolitiken und Frauenleitbilder der Parteien in der Bundesrepublik" (Women's policies and images of women in political parties in the Federal Republic), *Aus Politik und Zeitgeschichte: Beilage zur Wochenzeitung das Parlament,* no. 34–35 (1990): 16–28.

24. Kolinsky, *Women in West Germany;* and Commission of the European Communities, *Eurobarometer* 19 (Brussels: Commission of the European Communities, 1983).

25. On the split in women's life see Elisabeth Beck-Gernsheim, *Das halbierte Leben: Männerwelt Beruf: Frauenwelt Familie* (The Divided Life: Men's world work, women's world the family) (Frankfurt am Main/M: Fischer Verlag, 1985).

26. Women are highly concentrated in so-called female jobs, which are often low-paying because they are performed by women. Three-fourths of girls and young women concentrate in only 20 professions out of 350 tracks offered in vocational training. And despite women's skills professional opportunities often remain inaccessible. Studies show that doors that have been opened for women in the educational sector are slammed shut in the labor market. Federal Ministry, *Frauen in der Bundesrepublik,* 32–38.

27. In 1988, about 2 million girls and women living in the Federal Republic were *Ausländerinnen* (non-German

nationals). The federal government has supported a number of projects to improve girls' education, their job chances, and their social integration, but with limited success. Federal Ministry, *Frauen in der Bundesrepublik*, 73.

28. In spite of pressure from professional women, students, and some professional organizations, German universities continue to be male-dominated. The number of female students in universities and colleges in the (old) Federal Republic increased to 38 percent in 1987, but the share of female professors remains low. Only some 5 percent of all university and college professors are women. The situation in the former GDR was not much better: though about 50 percent of the students were female, only 4.3 percent of the professors were women. Federal Ministry, *Frauen in der Bundesrepublik*, 28; "Deutsch-deutsche Gemeinsamkeiten: Kaum Frauen an der Spitze: Frauenanteil an den Universitäten der Bundesrepublik und der DDR" (German-German commonalities: Few women in top positions: Women's share at universities), *Der Spiegel*, no. 8 (19 February 1990): 150.

29. Winkler, ed., *Frauenreport*, 121.

30. See Hanna Beate Schöpp-Schilling, "Women's Employment and Family Issues: The European Experience" (Paper presented at Managing in the Nineties conference at the Singapore National Employers Conference, Singapore, 26–27 June 1990).

31. See Ernst Benda, *Notwendigkeiten und Möglichkeiten positiver Aktionen zugunsten von Frauen im öffentlichen Dienst* (Necessities and opportunities for positive action in favor of women in the public service sector) (Freiburg: Institut für Offentliches Recht, 1986); Camilla Krebsbach-Gnath and Ina Schmid-Jörg, *Wissenschaftliche Begleituntersuchung zu Frauenförderungsmaßnahmen* (Research survey about positive action on behalf of women) (Stuttgart: Kohlhammer, 1985).

32. Proponents of quotas point to the U.S. and Swedish examples. See Anneliese Lissner, Rita Süssmuth, and Karin Walter, eds., *Frauenlexikon* (Women's handbook), "Frauenquotierung," 374.

33. *Entwurf eines Gesetzes zur Aufhebung der Benachteiligung von Frauen in allen gesellschaftlichen Bereichen, insbesondere in der Erwerbsarbeit (Antidiskriminierungsgesetz)* (Draft law on the removal of discrimination against women in all sectors of society, especially in the job sector [antidiscrimination law]) (Bonn: Bundestagsdrucksache 11/3266, 1988).

34. The law was vehemently opposed by the CDU in the Berlin Parliament. See Gabriele Riedle, "Die Dummen wären wider die Damen" (The ladies will be the cheated ones again), *Die Zeit*, no. 46 (9 November 1990): 24.

35. For a detailed and differentiated approach see Heide Pfarr, *Diskriminierung im Erwerbsleben. Ungleichbehandlung von Frauen und Männern in der Bundesrepublik* (Discrimination in work life: Unequal treatment of women and men in the Federal Republic), Gutachten im Auftrag des Bundesministeriums für Jugend, Familie, Frauen und Gesundheit (Baden-Baden: Nomos, 1989).

36. There were 83,684 registered legal abortions in the Federal Republic in 1988; more than half of the women were between 18 and 30 years old, and only 2.6 percent were under the age of 18. Experts estimate that the actual number of abortions is about 200,000 per year. Federal Ministry, *Frauen in der Bundesrepublik*, 95.

37. According to a recently released statistic, there were 80,000 abortions in the German Democratic Republic in 1989. Winkler, *Frauenreport*, 27.

38. *Der Spiegel* 45, no. 20 (13 May 1991): 71. Because abortion is still a criminal offense, women are frequently subjected to criminal investigations. Some recent reports revealed that data about women who had undergone abortions were registered by the criminal police. According to a report by the weekly political magazine *Der Spiegel*, a woman had even been subjected to forced gynecological examinations because border officials suspected that she had traveled to Holland to obtain an abortion. See "Abtreibung: Zwangsuntersuchung an der Grenze" (Abortion: Forced examination at the border), *Der Spiegel* 45, no. 10 (4 March 1991): 64–72.

39. "Abtreibung: Wirklicher Durchbruch" (Abortion: A real breakthrough), *Der Spiegel*, no. 36 (3 September 1990): 22–23; and Margit Gerste, "Gerechtigkeit für die Frauen" (Justice for women), *Die Zeit*, no. 37 (7 September 1990): 1.

40. Since German political science is a latecomer in incorporating feminist scholarship there are only few studies analyzing women's role and voice in the institutional political arrangement of the Federal Republic from the perspective of women. Rare exceptions are Beate Hoecker, *Frauen in der Politik. Eine soziologische Studie* (Women in politics: A sociological study) (Opladen: Leske und Budrich, 1987); Meyer, "Frauenpolitiken"; and Barbara Schaeffer-Hege and Heide Kopp-Degethoff, eds., *Vater Staat und seine Frauen* (Father state and his women), vols. 1 and 2 (Pfaffenweiler: Centaurus Verlag, 1990).

41. One of the best-known German radical feminists is Alice Schwarzer; see her *Der "kleine Unterschied" und seine große Folgen* (The "small difference" and its big consequence) (Frankfurt: Fischer Taschenbuch Verlag, 1977). For other writings by German feminists see E. Altbach, J. Clausen, D. Schultz, and N. Stephan, eds., *German Feminism: Readings in Politics and Literature* (Albany: State University of New York Press, 1984).

42. Of about 200 shelters for battered women in the old Federal Republic, more than half are run by autonomous women's groups; the others are supported by welfare or church organizations. After the collapse of the communist regime, several shelters were opened for women in the territory of the GDR. In the old Federal Republic, an estimated 4 million women per year are abused by their husbands. According to one survey, rape

occurs at least once in one of five marriages. Matrimonial rape is not yet a criminal offense in the Federal Republic. See Federal Ministry, *Frauen in der Bundesrepublik,* 69.

43. *Pressemitteilung des Bundesministeriums für Frauen und Jugend* (Press report by the Federal Ministry of Women and Youth), no. 32 (18 April 1991). See also "Gleichstellungspolitik in der DDR und der BRD" (Equal opportunity policies in the GDR and FRG), report on conference held at Humboldt Universität Berlin, 17–19 September 1990.

44. Federal Ministry, *Frauen in der Bundesrepublik,* 80. Some 460,000 women in the Federal Republic were members of one of the parties before unification, or about 1.7 percent of the female population older than 18.

45. Rita Süssmuth, a university professor and current president of the federal Parliament, built her political career through the CDU's Women's Union. In 1986 she became chairperson of the Women's Union; in 1987, the minister for Youth, Family, Women, and Health in the Kohl cabinet; and in 1988, president of the Federal Parliament, a position she continues to hold in the new Bundestag. As a representative of the left wing in the CDU and advocate for women's rights, Süssmuth is a controversial politician even in her own party. As president of the federal Parliament she has a prestigious position, but one that offers limited influence on actual policy making. Her suc-

cessor as federal minister, Ursula Lehr (CDU), was less forceful in supporting women's rights. In 1991 Angela Merkel (CDU) from East Germany became the minister for women and youth.

46. Federal Ministry, *Frauen in der Bundesrepublik,* 80.

47. Ibid., 79.

48. The largest share are Social Democratic women with 64 members (27 percent of the party's faction); followed by the CDU/CSU, the strongest faction in Parliament (44 women, or 14 percent of the faction): the FDP (16 women, or 18 percent), and the two small parties, the PDS (8 women) and the Alliance '90/Greens (3 women). In Länder or state parliaments, the proportion of women varies between 9 and 29 percent. It is usually higher in states with a left-of-center majority (SPD, Greens), such as Hamburg or Schleswig–Holstein, whereas in the CDU- and CSU-governed states such as Baden–Württemberg, Saxony, and Bavaria, the proportion is smaller.

49. The most comprehensive discussion is by Hoecker, *Frauen in der Politik.*

50. To lobby more effectively in the European Community, women's associations from the member states— including the German Women's Council—decided in fall 1990 to establish a joint office in Brussels. So far, women have been severely underrepresented. For example, only one of the 16 EC commissioners and two of 25 department heads are women.

▲ Ghana

POLITICS

Type of Political System: authoritarian
  Sovereignty: not applicable
  Executive-Legislative System: not
  applicable
Type of State: unitary
Type of Party System: no parties
Major Political Parties: not applicable
Year Women Granted Right to Vote: not
  applicable
*Year Women Granted Right to Stand for
  Election:* not applicable
Percentage of Women in the Legislature: not
  applicable
*Percentage of Electorate Voting for Highest
  Elected Office in Most Recent Election:* not
  applicable

DEMOGRAPHICS

Population: 14,900,000[a]
Percentage of Population in Urban Areas
  Overall: 32.0%[b]
  Female: 32.4%
  Male: 31.6%
Percentage of Population Below Age 15: 46.8%[c]
Birthrate (per 1,000 population): 44[d]
Maternal Mortality Rate (per 100,000 live
  births): 700[e]
Infant Mortality Rate (per 1,000 live births):
  86[f]
Mortality Rate for Children Under Five (per
  1,000 live births): 140[g]
Average Household Size: 4.9
Mean Age at First Marriage
  Female: 19.4
  Male: 27.1

Life Expectancy
  Female: 55.8
  Male: 52.2

EDUCATION

Ratio of Female to Male Enrollment[h]
  First-Level Education: 81
  Second-Level Education: 63
  Third-Level Education: 25
Literacy Rate
  Female: 18.0%
  Male: 43.0%

ECONOMY

Gross National Product per Capita: U.S.
  $390[i]
Percentage of Labor Force in Agriculture:
  59.3%[j]
Distribution of Agricultural Workers by Sex
  Female: 42.4%
  Male: 57.6%
Economically Active Population by Sex
  Female: 45.8%
  Male: 44.9%

a. *World Development Report* (Washington, D.C.:
World Bank, 1992).
  b. Ibid.
  c. Ibid.
  d. Ibid.
  e. *Human Development Report* (New York: U.N. Development Program, 1992).
  f. Ibid.
  g. Ibid.
  h. Ibid.
  i. *World Development Report.*
  j. Ibid.

Women and the Evolution of a Ghanaian Political Synthesis

KAMENE OKONJO

In 1957, after only 55 years of formal British rule, the Republic of Ghana, located on the south coast of West Africa, became the first colony in Africa to gain its independence. Some 15 million Ghanaians live in a country consisting mainly of tropical plains in the south, semi-arid plains in the north, and savanna. The economy is a mixed one, with foreign exchange earned through a small range of exports, the most important of which are cocoa, gold, timber, diamonds, aluminum, and manganese. The government derives most of its income from taxes on exports and imports, customs, and excise duties. More than half the population is engaged in agriculture.

Half of the population practices various indigenous religions, another quarter is Christian, and one-quarter is Muslim. Akan is the most widely used language, spoken by 40 percent of the population as a first language and by a considerable number of the rest as a second language.

WOMEN IN THE INDIGENOUS POLITICAL CONTEXT

Particularly in Akan society, the family is the bedrock of the lineage, settlement, village, village group, and state. Most families have a male head. The head of the family that first settled in an area had precedence over other family heads. He took possession of the land, allocating it to members of his family and families that later joined them. As the settlement grew and became a village, the authority of the head of the first family of settlers increased, and he became an *odikro* (village head). As the village grew, the younger generation moved out and formed a new village, with the originator of the migratory movement becoming the distributor of land and odikro of the new village. As many more villages were established, the ancestral village head became an *ohene* (chief). At a later stage, village groups formed an *oman* (state), and the head of the state became an *omanhene* (king). These leaders were not autocrats and had no absolute powers. Their conduct was expected to follow the laws and customs of the group as sanctioned by the ancestors. This political framework exists in modified form today, renewing itself by recruiting distinguished persons trained in the Western tradition to important positions.

The power of the leaders was tempered not only by custom but also by the significant role played by women. At the highest level of the state, the *omanhemaa* (queen mother) was the counterpart of the omanhene. The queen mother was elected by a council of chiefs, and she exercised considerable authority. The conduct and welfare of the girls and women in the state were her direct responsibility, especially in matters related to birth, puberty, marriage, and family life. She settled quarrels among women and held court the same way the king did. As the authority on kinship relations, she determined the legitimacy of an aspirant to the royal stoolship, or throne, and had the prerogative of nominating the omanhene, subject to ratification by a council of elders.[1] When her nomination was not approved, she nominated another chief. If her nomination was accepted, it was her duty to advise the new omanhene about the rights and obligations of his exalted office and also to act as the accepted authority on ritual and genealogy. If the king had to leave his throne to make war, the queen mother ruled the state until his return.[2] She was supposed to be the reincarnation of the feminine aspect of Nyame, the Supreme Being, whereas the omanhene represented the masculine aspect.

Women distinguished themselves in many other ways. Some Akan women even served as rulers of states, and on occasion women went to war and fought alongside their men. All schoolchildren in Ghana learn that Yaa Asantewaa, queen mother of the town of Ejisu, a suburb of the Ashanti capital, Kumasi, led the Ashanti warriors to battle in the final Anglo-Ashanti war of 1900–1901.

Women were largely responsible for the socialization of the young, giving them an understanding of and respect for tradition. Because these customs were first formulated in the family, then extended to other families, and finally codified into prescriptions and laws, women were best placed by their familial role to be the interpreters of the ancestral obligations by which the moral restrictions on the head of the family were sanctified.[3]

In traditional Ghanaian societies women could own and keep property—no matter how extensive—in their own right. Both husbands and wives were expected to be economically active and to contribute to the upkeep of their families. Men and women farmed independently, with women growing crops like corn, cassava, pepper, vegetables, and spices. It was the duty of husbands to help their wives with the crucial work of clearing plots for farming. Women also engaged in trading and in the manufacture of such local goods as pots and mats. All the proceeds from women's economic ventures were theirs to keep or to dispose of.

Thus, in spite of sex-segregated roles and male political dominance, women held posts and played roles that were socially, economically, and politically significant. The position of women in the indigenous states of Ghana was neither superior nor inferior to that of men; it was simply different and complementary.

COLONIALISM AND WOMEN'S STRUGGLE IN NATIONAL POLITICS

It is unusual to think of political development in states like Ghana in terms of the evolution of the formal structures of a Western liberal parliamen-

tary democracy. For several reasons, such an approach to the Ghanaian political system and the role that women play in it is bound to lead to difficulties.

First, British authority was imposed on 200 or so existing indigenous states. The creation of the territorial unit known as the Gold Coast—now Ghana—did not abolish these states. Rather, under the British system of indirect rule they continued to run their internal affairs.[4] The states still exist in modified form within the national boundaries of Ghana.

Second, the majority of the societies of the Gold Coast and the states that evolved from those societies have communal, not liberal, political structures. The values and principles that underlie their operation, though valid in their own right, are not the same as those underlying Western liberal societies and political structures. Their internal logic and social grammar differ. For example, political decisions in communal societies are taken not on the basis of a majority vote but on the basis of a consensus.

Third, in most Ghanaian societies roles are sex segregated; and in the evolution of the Ghanaian political system, participation in national politics has been cast as a male role. The political system must thus be seen as composite, rather than integrated and unified. Within it, modified communal and Western liberal structures operate side by side, and the political scene is a fractured one. The continuing task of politics is to fuse the imported system with the indigenous ones and to achieve an acceptable political synthesis that can lead to greater freedom and justice in the country, as seen through Ghanaian eyes.[5]

Women's position within the political structure of the indigenous states contrasts sharply with their position in national politics, for that can be traced to the colonial experience. Although formal colonial rule began with the British in 1902, European contact started with the Portuguese in 1471. By 1488 the Portuguese had received permission to build a fort at Elmina, which stands to this day. Joined later by the Dutch, the Danes, the British, and the Germans, the Portuguese were forced out by the middle of the seventeenth century by rivalries among the respective merchant companies.

The overriding interest of Europeans in the Gold Coast, and the impetus for their rivalry, was trade. As the Europeans expanded their sugar cane, tobacco, and cotton plantations in the Americas, and the indigenous American populations began to die off, a triangular trade sprang up. In an organized, unequal exchange, Europe exported tawdry manufactured goods and rum to West Africa and in exchange received slaves, who were transported to work on the plantations in the Americas, the produce of which was shipped to the European metropolitan powers. The slave trade lasted for four centuries and had terrible demographic, social, and human consequences for sub-Saharan Africa.

By the middle of the nineteenth century the slave trade had become unprofitable. In a new twist on mercantilism, Africa was conceived of as one vast plantation producing raw agricultural materials and minerals for European factories in exchange for manufactured goods. The trade ensured a continual flow of resources from African territories to European countries. This new international economic order, "colonialism," was guaranteed politically by the selective physical occupation of the territories. Although Britain claimed political suzerainty over Gold Coast, extensive British settlement of the area was out of the question. Diseases like malaria killed off white men, and the indigenous people stoutly resisted any attempts to annex their land. White women were not normally seen in these areas. For more than four hundred years the merchant companies remained within their forts, functioning as armed trading organizations that interfered in the internal politics of the coastal states in order to protect their interests.

The colonies were thus military societies in which European women had no place, whereas in the indigenous societies around them African women ran a political structure parallel to men's. Formal contact between the indigenous states and the Europeans was between Black and white males. Because the British operated under the system of indirect rule, the colonial government

did not interfere unduly with the internal governance of the local states, which continued to include a place for women in their political structures.

British colonial officials had sexist Victorian attitudes and biases, seeing women as politically incapable and good only for minding the home, the children, and the kitchen. Adult suffrage was still a dream in Europe; and being unfamiliar with the internal workings of the local states, the British looked down on the sociopolitical structures of the subject peoples, which included a legitimate place for women, and were unable to recognize how superior the structures were.[6] Consequently, the colonial government structure that evolved reflected prevailing European attitudes toward women and had no place for women.

It remained for the nationalists and the supporting women's organizations to remind the colonizers that women could be mobilized to act as a political force. Kwame Nkrumah, who later became independent Ghana's first prime minister and elected president, realized from the very start of the nationalist movement that women, if effectively mobilized, could constitute an enormous power bloc for his party—the Convention People's Party (CPP), founded in 1949. He made every effort to secure their support, especially as he found that women were useful in the fight against colonialism. Women were already organized into market women's associations, singing bands, dance societies, and various other voluntary units. Many women functioned as chief field organizers for the party and were responsible for bringing about its solidarity.

The tasks facing the CPP changed when political independence was achieved in 1957. It was imperative to restructure the colonial economy for national development, to replace those British professionals in the top echelon of the civil service who refused to serve under the nationalist government, and to reorient the population from consumption based on external trade to production for national development. All of these objectives required closer cooperation between the government and the people and more emphasis on the building of human capacity. Accordingly, in a bid to strengthen the CPP's position with women and to assure their loyalty, the party inaugurated the National Council of Ghana Women in 1960.

The council was charged with the establishment of day nurseries, vocational centers for mothers, and education programs. Although there were considerable problems, including lack of effective leadership, poor organization, inadequate resources, and lack of explicit directions from the CPP, several women earned acclaim for their political activities, which belied the colonial prejudice against women's political capability.[7] A number of measures initiated by Nkrumah's government benefited women, including the expansion of the educational system and the abolition of school fees. The immediate result was an increase in the enrollment of girls in schools. Although women were better situated than men to participate in policy making at the national level, because they were a majority of the population, the centralizing tendencies of the party meant that power became increasingly concentrated in the hands of the men nearest Nkrumah.

In spite of periodic efforts by the Nkrumah government and the CPP to ensure the involvement of women in the national government, their inclusion was very limited indeed. This was partly due to the nature of the CPP and its constituency. It was a party avowed to serve the masses, not the party of the educated elite. Consequently, its higher echelons contained very few women from the educated elite. As political cronyism became more prevalent in the CPP from 1954 onward, the party overwhelmingly chose men for the many posts it had to fill. Furthermore, most market women, the traditional allies of the CPP, were illiterate in English and so could not easily be incorporated into the government or Parliament, participation in which required a high level of sophistication in English language, politics, and culture.

The inclusion of women in government therefore amounted to tokenism, and their participation in government from the beginning of Nkrumah's rule in 1951 until his overthrow in 1966 was very limited. Some women, however,

did participate in the legislative branch and thus in the discussion of national affairs at the highest level. A few were even appointed ministers in the executive branch. Notwithstanding the unisex character of the structure of government that Ghana was forced to adopt in order to achieve independence and notwithstanding the centuries of contact with Europeans, within three years of independence Ghanaians unconsciously recognized the sex bias of the received political institution, and women were added to Parliament by appointment.

Yet the experiment that was the First Republic soon failed. Nkrumah initially tried to push national economic development along orthodox liberal lines, following some of the best liberal economic advice available.[8] When this failed in practice, he leaned leftward and introduced a Seven-Year Development Plan that sought to promote industrialization and to restructure the neocolonial economy. But the increasing economic difficulties and sacrifices required to implement the plan became important causes of the military coup in 1966, which was prompted also by the illegal but widely tolerated political cronyism and nepotism of the CPP and the continued domination of the minds of the leaders of the armed forces and the educated class by external political and economic forces and ideas.[9] The coup toppled the Nkrumah regime, brought the one-party state to an end, and broke up the CPP. The National Liberation Council, the military junta that took over the reins of government, banned all party political activity and ruled for a little over three years. During this period the military leaders prepared to transfer power to their "educated" civilian counterparts. Women were therefore not involved in the council government.

For the 16 years after the transfer, control of the government alternated between civilian republics and a series of five military juntas. The women's wings of the political parties that succeeded the CPP were occasionally revived during periods of civilian rule, only to pass into oblivion once the votes had been counted and the men for whom the women campaigned had been duly elected. A coup on 4 June 1979 brought Flight Lt. Jerry John Rawlings to power. He pledged to clean up the government, remove the "economic saboteurs," and return the country to civilian rule.[10] Rawlings remained in office for only four months; an elected civilian government under Harry Limann and his People's National Party then took office under a new constitution in the Third Republic.

Political corruption and the mounting economic problems of Ghana could not, however, be arrested by the Limann government. The unicameral National Assembly became a talk shop; members discussed and approved programs and projects for development that everyone knew could not be implemented. As Ghana slid toward economic bankruptcy, relief came in the form of a second coup on 31 December 1981. Rawlings became head of state and chair of the eight-person military-civilian junta, the Provisional National Defence Council (PNDC), which had full executive and legislative powers. Of the 84 people who constitute the government, 76 are men, and 8 are women (9.5 percent), with 1 woman serving on the PNDC itself.

Thus, in the regimes that followed Nkrumah's ouster, women played even less significant roles in national politics than was the case under Nkrumah. The political framework should not therefore be regarded as appropriate for ensuring the adequate representation of women in national politics. Women's noninvolvement in politics after Nkrumah's regime is usually ascribed to four main factors. Political posts tended to be filled by people educated in English customs, language, and political practice, and these individuals were invariably men. In a holdover from the precolonial era, when men played prominent roles in warfare, men also continued to dominate political affairs. The armed forces were mainly male, and women's participation in government during military regimes fell to zero. Meanwhile, women's organizations were oriented toward religious, economic, or social goals, not political engagement. The best known of these organizations, the Nanamei Akpee (Society of Friends), was a mutual benefit society whose aim was to

assist women with loans and to enable them to start businesses, mostly in trading.[11]

These reasons for low levels of participation by women after the fall of Nkrumah are not fully convincing, however, and smack of blaming the victim. Most of these conditions already existed during Nkrumah's government. The autocratic governments that dominated politics after Nkrumah had much less interest in popular participation, particularly women's participation. The nondemocratic rulers ignored the Nkrumah government's example of including women in the various branches of government.

But beyond failing to take easy measures, most Ghanaian governments have not confronted the structural issues that limit women's participation. Leaders have ignored the sex bias and class stratification of the imported political system, as well as the dual-sex nature of local societies. Ghanaian women already run their own affairs and occupy responsible positions. By 1984, 14 percent of all university graduates employed in Ghana were women.

Finally, the definition of political issues should reflect the expressed needs and wishes of the people. In a country where 4.1 million Ghanaians, or 36 percent of the population, were at risk for malnutrition in 1980, it is not surprising that women's first concern is the welfare of their family.[12] Women's entrepreneurship, which would result in national development, should be recognized as an appropriate political concern and supported with government funding. The interest of women in trading and mutual aid programs is a sign of the importance of such programs for restructuring the neocolonial economy. Where social security is limited to workers in government and commercial firms, the abiding interest of women in their family's welfare and in the economy is understandable.

CONCERN FOR FAMILY WELFARE
AND SOCIAL SECURITY

Women constitute approximately half the labor force, and within the system of sex-segregated roles, all women are expected to be productively employed. Because they help to support men who can no longer find work in government and commercial establishments in the urban areas, they also provide the central government with a hidden social welfare subsidy. Women farm, dominate the food distribution network and food processing, and lend political backing to persons and parties that represent their economic interests. The support given by women to Nkrumah and the CPP during the struggle for independence stemmed from crucial questions about the operation of the colonial economy and its effect on the people of Ghana.

The foreign trade of the colonial economy of the Gold Coast consisted mostly of the export of cocoa and a few minerals and the import of manufactured goods. Export-import and shipping were the monopoly of a few British firms, led by the United Africa Company, a branch of the multinational corporation Unilever. The European firms operated on a wholesale basis and employed indigenous people, mostly women, as their trading agents and distributors. These agents were excluded from the lucrative business of importing manufactured goods and exporting agricultural raw materials.

In 1945, when the Labour Party was elected in Britain, agitation against the monopolistic tendencies of the British firms broke out in the Gold Coast. As a consequence of Labour Party policy, a Cocoa Marketing Board was set up for the Gold Coast, ending the British monopoly over the export of cocoa. Imports still remained a British monopoly, however, and firms issued passbooks and chits entitling their mainly female Gold Coast trading agents and distributors to purchase limited quantities of desired imports. There was considerable dissatisfaction with the system, particularly among women, because it was also bound up with "conditional sales," which had the effect of forcing the women to buy and sell lines of goods that they knew were not fast moving.

At the same time, the Gold Coast was a member of the West African Currency Board, along with Nigeria, Sierra Leone, and Gambia.[13] West African pounds in circulation could not be ex-

changed for British pounds sterling, even though they had been earned by exporting primary commodities. In consequence, as the population grew and the domestic market economy expanded, up to 5 percent of the annual gross domestic product of these colonies was given as a perpetual loan to Britain through unfair monetary and trade policies. Moreover, the issuing of West African pounds for circulation in the Gold Coast and its neighbors meant that the colonies were not able to conduct an autonomous monetary policy.

There was thus a coincidence of interest between the women traders, who were dissatisfied with the import and distribution networks dominated by the British firms, and the nationalist CPP, which was fighting for an autonomous and convertible currency. Accordingly, market women and the CPP joined forces against their common enemy—the British—to free themselves from the British business monopolies, as well as the impositions of the West African Currency Board.

Nkrumah reportedly found his firmest support among the market women who, as party activists, sold imported manufactured goods through the chit and passbook systems. That support was utilitarian and conditional on the government's readiness to keep granting patronage to the women. As soon as shortages became a regular feature of the economy, market women became disenchanted with the CPP and its leadership and withdrew their support. During the latter part of the Nkrumah regime and subsequent regimes, when cutting the demand for imports became a national priority, market women were no longer a base of support but rather a source of opposition to the government. The economic interests of market women were thus a significant factor in the movement for national autonomy and in the subsequent demise of the Nkrumah government. With the aid of the officer class in the armed forces, the educated elite, and professionals, foreigners were then able to intervene openly in domestic affairs and overthrow Nkrumah and the CPP government. The same phenomenon occurred under later regimes when market women added to the general dissatisfaction with these regimes and rejoiced when they were overthrown.

Finance and trade remain strong interests of Ghanaian women. Serious reorganization of the banking system began in 1981, and a woman, Teresa Owusu, was appointed deputy governor of the Bank of Ghana, the central bank of the country. The bank is paying particular attention to the expansion and development of the rural banking system. One function of this system is to mobilize local savings for investment by local entrepreneurs, many of whom are women, especially in the farming and food-processing industries. Small-scale industries like the processing of fish, cassava, coconut, and palm oil, as well as soap making, are expected to benefit from funds made available by the rural banks. Mutual aid societies, *susu* (thrift) organizations, and other financial institutions are being encouraged to mobilize domestic resources for capital formation. As a result, the activities of women in forming mutual aid groups will now be supported by the government. More women are becoming bank managers and are setting higher standards of probity in their work.

Guidelines for the operation of credit institutions outside banks have also been issued. The Bank of Ghana has encouraged the development of the financial institutions of the domestic market sector of the economy and has issued operating licenses to Resource Pool and Women's World Banking Ghana Mutual Assistance Susu, two financial institutions that specifically support investments by women. These new institutions will make credit available at much lower interest rates and to many more people without collateral than would otherwise have been the case. Bank credit will be available to the poor and to women.

If women's entrepreneurship is dedicated to improving their family's welfare, much of their anxiety revolves around the simple survival of their children. Tropical sub-Saharan Africa is the most disease-ridden area of the world and child survival cannot be taken for granted. The high death rates from the six major childhood diseases and the unsettled social conditions in the eigh-

teenth, nineteenth, and twentieth centuries all contributed to a female ideology that values the survival of children above all else. At the same time, women's own health status has been perilous, though it has improved gradually. Life expectancy for Ghanaian women at birth, which was on the order of 25 years in the precolonial era, climbed to 35 or more in the 1950s and now stands at 56. Although men have primary responsibility for the socialization of boys, it is to their mothers that children turn when they are ill. In Ghana children are the greatest object of parental and societal love and the center of their mothers' attention.

Not surprisingly, the populist Acheampong government that ruled Ghana between 1972 and 1978 responded positively to the initiative of the U.N. General Assembly—which had passed the Declaration of the Rights of the Child in 1959— to mark 1979 as the International Year of the Child. The Ghanaian government followed the example of the United Nations in declaring 1979 the Year of the Child, and in 1977 it set up an ad hoc committee to prepare. A recommendation of the committee implemented by the Rawlings regime in 1979 was the establishment of a commission on children.

The Ghana National Commission on Children is a corporate body with a membership of 19: the chair, 12 nonaffiliated members, and 6 institutional representatives. The institutions represented are the Ministry of Foreign Affairs, the Ministry of Local Government's Department of Social Welfare and Community Development, the National Youth Council, the Ghana Assembly of Women, the National Council on Women and Development, and the Ministry of Education's Ghana Education Service. The National Council on Women and Development is in effect the government ministry that deals with women's affairs, but the Ghana Assembly of Women, a private organization, receives public support. Although both men and women serve on the commission, it has a built-in majority of women. Since its inception, the commission has had women as its chair and executive secretary.

The commission has worked to advance the

general welfare and development of children, as well as to promote the rights of the child as declared by the United Nations. It is expected not only to ensure the cooperation and collaboration of the agencies responsible for implementing programs, policies, and essential services for children but also to help establish, regulate, and run crèches, day-care centers, homes for disabled children, facilities for gifted children, and diagnostic and welfare services in all ten regions of Ghana. The commission ensures the use of research data on children and has sole responsibility for making proposals to the government on the enactment or review of legislation regarding children's rights, privileges, and benefits.

In spite of the very difficult economic situation between 1979 and 1986, the commission undertook its responsibilities. From 1979 to 1983 it established an office, assembled staff, and sponsored the first National Workshop on the Status of Women and Their Role in Better Child Care. It even arranged a holiday program for children between the ages of 7 and 13, which enabled them to spend their holidays with families in parts of the country other than their regions of birth or residence.

From 1984 to 1989, with its financial allocation from the government reaching as much as 22 million cedis (U.S. $120,000) in 1988, the commission showed great ingenuity in persuading nongovernmental and foreign agencies to provide in-kind donations, which the commission was able to convert into cash for its multifaceted work. For example, donations of canned fish helped finance essential and fundamental research on child psychology and the child's place in the family in African cultures.[14] All the laws affecting children have been collated in a report, "Laws Affecting Children in Ghana," and a legal research unit on the child, as well as a child education fund, have been set up. A Sociology and Child Research Group was also formed in the universities. Preschool services for children have been surveyed, work continues on the study of child labor, and the informal education of school dropouts is being promoted. In addition, the commission is establishing complexes containing parks and libraries in each national, regional, and district capital and in urban, rural, and neighborhood centers in the smaller communities.

Some of the proceeds from donated gifts converted into cash have been used to finance a sustainable child-nutrition project that encourages local production of weaning foods derived from local materials. Because the youngest children in most homes are likely to receive the least nutritious fare, the commission cooperates with the Ministry of Health and UNICEF Country Program in the Sustainable Child Nutrition Project, which promotes better child nutrition, child health, and overall development of the child.[15] In this connection, the commission has established 32 corn mills and is constructing another 24 mills that use corn and a large variety of legumes to produce food of high nutritional content for children from birth to age five. The work of the commission, which revolves around the survival and proper development of the child, has been greatly supported by women, who dominate not only the commission itself but also its various working committees.

Restructuring the neocolonial economy to provide a higher quality of life for both children and adults requires the full cooperation of all women, and such cooperation can only be obtained by actively removing the socioeconomic disabilities of women and promoting women's economic interests. On coming to power in 1981, Rawlings and the Provisional National Defence Council government therefore set themselves the goal of securing the cooperation of women in the task of first revitalizing and then restructuring the economy. National policy was promulgated in a series of laws issued by the initially all-male PNDC, which subsequently broadened its base by appointing Aanaa Enin, a widely traveled former teacher and businesswoman, to the council. She was later joined for a short while by Susana Alhassan, who had served in the government under Nkrumah. Committees for the Defence of the Revolution, to which all Ghanaians could belong, were formed in each ward and organization of the country to articulate the needs and wishes of the people, to fight political corruption and other ills, and to promote the efficient allocation and use of resources, as well as accountability in the use of these resources.

Revitalizing the economy was the highest initial priority. Because government income from taxes and excise duties did not cover expenditures, efforts were made to expand the tax base, cut down on government spending, reduce waste, squeeze out excess personnel, improve efficiency in operations, and eliminate ghost workers (nonexistent personnel maintained on the rolls). The education sector received particular attention as not only one of the largest government agencies but also one of the biggest spenders. The most urgent task that the government would have to deal with after rehabilitating the economy would be building human capacity.

The PNDC government moved quickly to associate women with its work and appointed more women to high office than had any previous government. Ama Ata Aidoo, the writer and university lecturer, was appointed PNDC secretary (minister) for education. Gertrude Zakariah-Alli, a demographer, became the deputy secretary for local government; later she became the executive secretary of the National Council on Women and Development. Joyce Aryee, a public relations consultant, was made PNDC secretary for information; she subsequently headed the Ministry of Education, replacing Ama Ata Aidoo. Mary Grant, a medical practitioner who became PNDC regional secretary for Accra, is the only woman serving on the PNDC itself in 1993; she oversees the educational and health sectors. Two more women hold office as deputy secretaries in the Ministry of Education. Vida Yeboah, a former headmistress of a girls' secondary school, is in charge of both primary and secondary school education, while Esi Sutherland-Addy, a university lecturer, is in charge of higher education. Teresa Owusu, who used to be PNDC deputy secretary for finance and economic planning and then for fuel and power, is deputy governor of the Bank of Ghana.

Apart from affiliating women with the government, the PNDC has tried to improve the status of women generally. In 1985 it passed the Intestate Succession Law and the Customary Marriage and Divorce (Registration) Law. A woman whose customary marriage is registered can expect to inherit one-third of her husband's estate, and so can their children. The husband's family likewise receives one-third of the estate, rather than, as before, the whole estate. The laws also make provision for widows to be protected from humiliating practices on the death of their husbands. Local governments, like the Kumasi Metropolitan Assembly, are now moving to register all imams (spiritual leaders) in their area of jurisdiction and to have them licensed by the Ministry of Justice, so that they can conduct marriage ceremonies and handle divorce cases, thus regularizing marriage and divorce among Muslims.

The greatest long-term impact on the status of women has been caused by the reform of the pre-university school system. Under the supervision of PNDC deputy secretary for school education, Vida Yeboah, pre-university schooling is being reduced from 17 years to 12, and greater emphasis is being placed on curricula relevant to everyday life. All children are now required to attend at least nine years of basic school. Teaching time in all segments of the school system has been increased, and the school year has been extended from 36 to 40 weeks a year at the primary level and from 33 to 40 weeks at the junior and senior secondary levels, each of which lasts three years.

The new system has already affected school enrollment positively. At the primary level, total enrollments have increased by 12 percent. Gains in the enrollment of girls has been modest, but, much more important, the dropout rate for girls is decreasing. The reduced number of years spent at school, coupled with increased teaching time, has led to a vast number of girls going on to the junior level. Many of these girls can now also proceed to the senior level, because they can complete secondary school at 18 instead of 23, as was previously the case, so fewer need to drop out because of pregnancy.

Rather than opening elitist secondary boarding schools, the central government has encouraged towns and villages to build their own day schools, with the government supplying the teachers. This has lessened the government's financial burden while encouraging self-help and self-reliance in the countryside. Secondary school entries have increased immensely; instead of only 26,000 pupils going on to do secondary school work each year, now 200,000 pupils enter junior secondary school each year. Furthermore, the dropout rate has decreased dramatically.

The establishment of day schools has meant that the government does not have to build boardinghouses for secondary school students or subsidize their feeding. These schools are thus less costly—not only to the government, in financial terms, but also to parents, in emotional terms, for they now have their children living at home. Girls have benefited most. The government is also working toward ensuring the equality of women's participation in the school system and toward removing gender biases from the curriculum. Promoting mixed secondary schools instead of elitist, sex-segregated boarding schools has relieved the government of building more boys' schools. With more schools for girls and a diminished dropout rate, Ghana can look forward to the proportion of girls in school more closely approximating their proportion in their respective age-groups. Ministry of Education officials expect that by the year 2000 women will constitute far more than the 14 percent of university graduates employed in Ghana in 1984.

WOMEN AND THE EMERGING POLITICAL SYNTHESIS

In 1988 women made up less than 10 percent of the people holding national office. If the PNDC slogan "Power to the people" is not to be mere rhetoric, means must be found to increase the representation of women in all branches of government. Given the sexual division of roles in society, there needs to be a sex segregation of representation if matters of interest to women are to be discussed by their representatives. Thus, the imported Western political instruments must be modified. Even the more common Ghanaian practice of inserting women into the political

structures that formulate policy at the local level has not been able to correct the sex biases of these structures. By current definition, the needs of women are not political.

The 1989 district elections are a case in point. After eight years in power, the PNDC started treading the path toward constitutional rule and devolving more power to the local level. First, 110 districts were created out of the 64 that had existed in 1978. This redivision tended to make the districts coincide with the indigenous states or to combine two or more states whose citizens spoke related languages. The discussion of problems of government and development became easier because it could be conducted in a common local language in addition to English, enabling everyone to participate.

Legal backing was given to the 1989 district elections through the passage of the Local Government Law of 1988. The districts elected 4,840 members to the district assemblies, or parliaments, in as many electoral areas. The national government, as in previous district elections, reserved the right to appoint one-third of the members of these assemblies (2,420 people). The electorate nominated 9,280 people, 350 of them women, to run for the contested seats. Altogether, women made up 3.8 percent of the contestants and 2.7 percent (131) of the elected parliamentarians; 37 percent of the women who contested seats were elected. The government, in good measure, nominated 349 women and 2,071 men, mostly technocrats, to serve in the assemblies. The result is that women now constitute 480 (6.6 percent) of the 7,260 members of these assemblies. Considering how the elections were carried out, this representation cannot be considered satisfactory. It contrasts strongly with the total strength of women's organizations; the 31st December Women's Movement, for example, has more than a million women members.

The elections were conducted by the National Commission on Democracy, which is expected to help Ghana find its way to true democracy. By providing a forum for the discussion of the individual manifestos of the candidates, the commission tried to ensure that the elections were conducted on a nonparty basis and at a minimum personal cost. The elections were held in this manner in the hope that political opportunism would not need to arise among successful contestants, who might otherwise have tried to recoup their election expenses in unwelcome ways. The elections were simple and devoid of the fanfare that had characterized party-based elections in the past. In the discussions about a return to constitutionalism, public opinion has overwhelmingly advocated that future local elections be conducted in the same way—even though women ended up being grossly underrepresented in each district.

A way forward is indicated by the character of Ghanaian society and the political developments of the past. Strong and interested women's wings of parties, including ruling parties, have campaigned for the election of men in electoral constituencies: politics is considered a man's job. Given the sexual division of roles, the consciousness-raising efforts of the PNDC have led to the emergence of not one but two organizations—the 4th June Movement and the 31st December Women's Movement. The first organization, which is primarily male, commemorates the formation of the PNDC headed by Rawlings, whereas the second exists solely for women.

In the preconstitutional discussions, people thought that the 31st December Women's Movement should be retained. It serves as a catch-all organization for women, and its agenda consists mostly of matters of interest to women. It organizes women to cooperate in the building of day-care centers, nurseries, and kindergartens, and helps to arrange training for those who run them. It promotes women's cooperative societies and the use of appropriate technologies by women to lessen the burdens of running their homes and earning income to support their families. The movement backs the withdrawal of women in the rural areas from dependence on imported goods, and it tries to mobilize savings and outside funding for rural capital formation and the engagement of women in income-generating ventures to improve their standard of living.[16] It is headed by Nana Konadu Agyeman Rawlings, wife of the PNDC chair.

Essentially, the 31st December Women's Movement recognizes that men and women have differing interests. It also recognizes that women and their needs are simply not political in the commonly understood meaning of the term. The way forward for the Ghanaian polity may thus lie in the sexual division of political representation in local and national government, whereby each electoral constituency elects a man and a woman to the requisite parliament. Such sexually segregated representation would eliminate the sex stratification and role biases in current political arrangements. It would also encourage an ongoing political dialogue and ensure a political synthesis of the imported and indigenous forms of political expression.[17]

NOTES

1. In Ghana kings sit on stools, not thrones. Each stool is believed to hold the spirit of the king or chief sitting on it. Thus, the most famous stool, the Golden Stool of the Ashanti, encapsulates the spirit of the Ashanti Confederacy. When a king or chief dies, his stool is blackened and put away.

2. Although a male regent usually acted for the omanhene while he was away, the queen mother often took on the omanhene's duties until he returned safely from war with another state.

3. For example, in these structurally communal societies the head of the lineage was the ancestors' representative on earth and was responsible for seeing to (or at least inquiring about) the welfare of members of the lineage and their families. Family members who felt neglected could complain to the odikro and receive satisfaction. They could, however, also complain to the ancestors before witnesses while pouring liquor on the ground in a libation. Witnesses would endeavor to dissuade the complainants from taking such drastic action, and the head of the lineage would be appalled that his behavior had led to such bitterness. Normally, advised by the older women that matters were building to a flash point, the head would take preventive action. Women were regarded not as restrictors of opportunity but rather as a help in the smooth functioning of society.

4. In the political system of indirect rule invented by Fredrick Lugard (later Lord Lugard of Abinja) for the governance of indigenous states incorporated into the British colonies, states were allowed relative freedom in the management of their internal affairs. Defense, foreign

affairs, and territorywide concerns were reserved for the colonial power and came under the authority of the secretary of state for the colonies in London.

5. The motto of the Republic of Ghana is Freedom and Justice.

6. In *Ashanti Law and Constitution* (Oxford: Clarendon Press, 1929), R. S. Rattray, the distinguished British anthropologist, described the matrilineal system as unnatural and grotesque.

7. See the observations of Emily Watts Card, "The Politics of Underdevelopment: From Voluntary Associations to Party Auxiliaries in Ghana" (Ph.D. diss., Columbia University, 1972). The rhetoric of the CPP promised power to the people, but the method by which this power could be exercised was not specified. Rather, power was gradually centralized in the person of Kwame Nkrumah. The expected blossoming of this and other organizations did not therefore take place among the people.

8. Arthur Lewis, the West Indian liberal economist, later a Nobel laureate in economics, was a special adviser to the newly independent government. He sold a liberal economic policy to Nkrumah and recommended inviting the investment of foreign capital. These measures did nothing to lessen the dependence of the economy, and foreign financing of industrialization did not materialize.

9. There is evidence to show foreign involvement in the overthrow of Nkrumah. Western readers will find Richard Mahoney's *John F. Kennedy: Ordeal in Africa* (New York: Oxford University Press, 1983) of interest. Mahoney is the son of the American ambassador to Ghana in the early 1960s.

10. Economic saboteurs were persons who either benefited from the prevailing political cronyism and nepotism or employed sharp practices like underinvoicing exports or imports to avoid their obligations to the state. The Ghanaian word *kalabule* (high inflation) is used to cover such practices. A new "people's court" system was introduced to ensure quick dispensation of justice by avoiding the slowness of the imported legal system and its many technical loopholes. The courts, introduced by the Provisional National Defence Council, are still boycotted by members of the Ghana Bar Association.

11. See Audrey Chapman Smock, "Ghana from Autonomy to Subordination," in Janet Zollinger Giele and Au-drey Chapman Smock, eds., *Women: Roles and Status in Eight Countries* (New York: Wiley, 1977), 207.

12. See, e.g., Kamene Okonjo, *Women and Fertility Among the Ewe of Ghana and the Igbo of Nigeria* (Nsukka: Hansberry Institute of African Studies, University of Nigeria, forthcoming).

13. The French still operate a currency board—the CFA franc zone—in their former colonies in West Africa.

14. Of the 3,000 preschool service units that existed—day-care centers, crèches, nurseries, and kindergartens—61 percent (1,822) were outside the control of the Department of Social Welfare and the Ghana Education Service, which are the government agencies responsible for preschool services. These preschool services were established on the initiative of, and are still being run by, private persons and communities.

15. In the Ghanaian family, children either eat together or with their parents, boys with their father and girls with their mother. In either case, the protein foods are shared by the children after the staple has been eaten, and the children take their shares according to age, so the youngest child gets the least. Kwashiorkor, the medical name for malnutrition caused by protein deficiency, was borrowed from a Ghanaian language.

16. In the neocolonial state of Ghana the middle-class and urban population consumes 85 to 90 percent of the services of the state—mainly water, electricity, fuel and transportation, roads, telephones, police protection, law and order, health facilities, and education. The miners and the rural population together consume only about 12 percent. See Kofi Nyidevu Awoonor, *Ghana: A Political History from Pre-European to Modern Times* (Accra: Sedco Publishing, and Woeli Publishing Services, 1990), 252. Awoonor, a professor at the University of Cape Coast, Ghana, is the U.N. representative from Ghana. Following Chukuka Okonjo, we call this consuming sector of the economy that transports value from Ghana abroad and imports goods in exchange the "parasitic enclave sector." The complementary sector of the economy, which produces value for export, is the domestic market sector, which is coterminous with the rural areas.

17. The author acknowledges the support received in the preparation of this chapter from Reginald Sam of the Balme Library, University of Ghana, Legon.

▲ Great Britain

POLITICS

Type of Political System: democracy
  Sovereignty: constitutional monarchy
  Executive-Legislative System: parliamentary
Type of State: unitary
Type of Party System: two party
Major Political Parties

Conservative Party (National Union of Conservative and Unionist Associations): Party of the center-right and right; successor to the Whig Party and Tory Parties of the nineteenth century. Led by Prime Minister John Major.

Labour Party: Party of the center-left and left; a "broad church" party containing affiliated trade unions and cooperative branches. Led by Neil Kinnock. Since 1945, the Labour Party and the Conservative Party have been the governing parties.

Liberal Democratic Party: An amalgam of the Liberal Party and a majority of the Social Democratic Party that merged in 1988; party of the center. Normally has a small representation in Parliament. Led by Paddy Ashdown.

Social Democratic Party: Formed by right-wing Labour members of Parliament in 1981; center party. Had some initial success, but by 1988 retained only a "rump" of four MPs. Led by David Owen.

Plaid Cymru (Party of Wales): Welsh nationalist party; favors greater autonomy for Wales. Tends to support the Labour Party in parliamentary votes.

Scottish Nationalist Party: Favors Scottish independence and Labour politics on other issues. Normally comes in second in Scotland, after the Labour Party.

Northern Ireland: Maintains a separate party system. Main party is the Unionist Party, which favors union with Britain. Until direct rule in 1972, was part of the Conservative Party; then split into Official Unionists and Democratic Unionists (Protestant parties). Catholic parties are the Social Democratic Party, the Labour Party, and Sinnfein (the political wing of the provisional Irish Republican Army). The Alliance Party attempts to bridge the two communities.

Year Women Granted Right to Vote:
  1918/1928[a]
Year Women Granted Right to Stand for Election: 1919
Percentage of Women in the Legislature
  Lower House: 9.2%
  Upper House: 5.5%
Percentage of Electorate Voting for Highest Elected Office in Most Recent Election (1991): 87.7%[b]

DEMOGRAPHICS

Population: 56,891,000
Percentage of Population in Urban Areas
  Overall: 87.7%
  Female: not available
  Male: not available
Percentage of Population Below Age 15: 19.5%
Birthrate (per 1,000 population): 13
Maternal Mortality Rate (per 100,000 live births): 9
Infant Mortality Rate (per 1,000 live births): 9
Mortality Rate for Children Under Five (per 1,000 live births): 11
Average Household Size: 2.7
Mean Age at First Marriage
  Female: 23.1
  Male: 25.4
Life Expectancy
  Female: 77.2
  Male: 71.4

EDUCATION

Ratio of Female to Male Enrollment
  First-Level Education: 95
  Second-Level Education: 99
  Third-Level Education: 81

Literacy Rate
Female: 99.0%
Male: 99.0%

ECONOMY
Gross National Product per Capita: U.S.
$8,460
Percentage of Labor Force in Agriculture: 2.4%
Distribution of Agricultural Workers by Sex
Female: 20.2%
Male: 79.8%

Economically Active Population by Sex
Female: 45.4%
Male: 77.2%

a. In 1918 women 30 years old and older gained the right to vote; in 1928 women's suffrage was granted on the same terms as men's suffrage.
b. Information supplied by the British Embassy of the United States in 1993.

The Rules of the Political Game: Feminism and Politics in Great Britain

JONI LOVENDUSKI

Great Britain, an island country consisting of England, Scotland, and Wales, is a tiny country in terms of area, but its 57 million inhabitants make it the 12th most populous in the world. Its previous role as the cornerstone of a global empire has been replaced by a more modest economic leadership: it is one of the 20 wealthiest countries in terms of per capita income and the fourth largest trading nation in the world. The British population is renowned for its virtually universal acceptance of the constitution and government—a constitutional monarchy—since the seventeenth century. The Parliament consists of a strong House of Commons, whose 650 popularly elected members produce the bulk of the legislation, and a nonelected House of Lords, whose more than 1,000 members can delay nonbudgetary legislation for up to a year but hold little additional power. The executive power is embodied in the cabinet, headed by a prime minister who is appointed by the monarch but who is in practice the head of the majority party in Parliament. The majority party or coalition controls the cabinet, while the opposition party from the House of Commons serves as a check on the authority of the executive body.

Great Britain and Northern Ireland together make up the United Kingdom, which functions as a two-party democracy. There are actually many parties in the United Kingdom, including the Conservative Party (the National Union of Conservative and Union Associations) and the Labour Party—which between them normally win more than 90 percent of the seats in the House of Commons—two centrist parties, as well as Scottish and Welsh nationalist parties. A separate five-party system exists in Northern Ireland.

The individual countries are incorporated into the U.K. political system in varying ways. Since 1707 the Scottish Parliament has been assimilated into the English House of Commons; it holds 71 seats. Wales was absorbed into England in 1535 and is allocated 38 seats in Parliament; Northern Ireland has 17 seats. Because the politics surrounding relations between Northern Ireland and the rest of Britain are well beyond the scope of an essay of this length, I will concentrate on the diversity of politics in Great Britain.

Among European societies, Great Britain has most resisted including women in the political elite. By 1990, after two decades of second-wave feminism and more than 60 years of women's suffrage, women made up only 6 percent of the membership of Parliament and were scarcely to be found in ministerial office, in the senior ranks of the higher civil service, in the higher judiciary, in the corporate bodies of government and industry decision making, or even on the boards of major corporations. This exclusion probably is more attributable to the social closure practiced by the male elite as part of British class politics than it is to the simple-plurality single-member constituency electoral system, which is widely considered a barrier to women's political representation.

Bids to reconstruct this gendered order of power have met effective and entrenched resistance. Although women are entering many sections of the political elite, their rate of entry is so slow that their socialization into the initial norms and practices of elite bodies takes place on practically a one-by-one basis. This ensures that their political influence as women is minimal. Thanks to traditional recruitment practices, women's rates of entry to the appointed arenas of power continue to be low. These practices, which are structured to exclude, involve lengthy, continuous apprenticeships with considerable weight given to seniority in key institutions such as the judiciary, the civil service, the universities, and the trade union hierarchies; geographical mobility as a means to advancement; implicit qualification criteria that, in practice, are male oriented; and a tradition of official secrecy, including the widespread practice of nominating through undisclosed channels, thereby obscuring the discriminatory nature of recruitment and promotion practices. Such devices, which might be called the "chap" strategy, mean that promotion panels, search committees, and nominating bodies are able to recruit in their own image—a predominantly male, upper middle class, and white image. Chaps are especially good at looking after other chaps, a fact reflected by the institutions of state power and reinforced by the rules of the political game.

Because class has been so important to British politics, it has been difficult for women to argue successfully the political significance of gender divisions. The two main political parties traditionally divide along class lines. The Conservatives, or Tories, are typically middle-class and better off; Labour is the party of the working class and the less well off. Both experience some cross-class support, but class lines and images are durable and significant.

Of course the political elite consists of more than party elites. Those in powerful positions throughout British society are protected by a system whose implicit rules, implemented informally by nonaccountable officials working through undisclosed channels, are notoriously difficult to challenge. The requirements for a judgeship, for example, reflect the mechanisms of elite protection in a variety of ways. To become a judge, one must have practiced law for at least ten years. In addition, one generally must sit as a recorder or as an assistant recorder, appointments that normally go to individuals in their late 30s or older. In short, a long and continuous apprenticeship is necessary before one may be appointed to the judiciary by the lord chancellor. Selection procedures are obscure, and suitable individuals are expected to "emerge." An employee of the lord chancellor's office identifies promising individuals by mixing socially with people in the legal profession. There are few formal procedures for nomination, and self-nomination procedures normally require that at least one judge be named on the nomination form as a referee. Thus the judiciary in many respects resembles a self-recruiting oligarchy. Although this structure was not devised to exclude women, women have never been well represented in the British judiciary, and they are nonexistent at the top echelons. In January 1990 there were no women among the ten Lords of Appeal, the highest appeal court in Britain. At the next level, the court of appeal, there was one woman, Elizabeth Butler Schloss, among 28 lord justices. One woman and 81 men were high court judges, and 17 women and 434 men were circuit judges.[1] This apparatus of closure is particularly well suited to excluding women whose lifestyles and child-rearing responsibilities make it difficult for them to fulfill long apprenticeships and keep them out of the networks through which the chaps emerge.

Because it lacks a theory of political power, the women's movement has been slow to acknowledge the importance of Britain's apparatus of closure. When feminists began to work in the Labour Party during the early 1980s, for example, many were horrified by the long apprenticeships and elaborate procedures that were a required part of influencing the party. Autonomous radical feminists involved in movements against male sexual violence consistently underestimated the power of administrators and were regularly outmaneuvered by welfare bureaucrats who had a professional interest in cases of domestic violence, rape, and child sexual abuse. During the 1980s radical feminists tended to regard political institutions as undifferentiated manifestations of male domination, and socialist feminists were often suspicious of women who sought public office and were unsympathetic to those who achieved it.

Some feminists sought public office nevertheless, challenging the secrecy among appointed elites and organizing to secure a presence among elected elites. But elite and institutional responses to their efforts have been ponderous, grudging, and slow to result in real change, evidence that the rules of the political game in Britain were established long before women attempted to secure a political voice.

THE RULES OF THE POLITICAL GAME

In British politics, the majority party appoints the government (which is confirmed by the monarch, de jure head of state) from its ranks and draws up the parliamentary timetable. The majority party relies on strict party discipline among its MPs for support of its legislative program. Political engagement in the United Kingdom is a matter of coming to terms with institutions that are notably unreceptive to the self-organization of emergent groups. Only when activists infil-

trate, replicate, or outmaneuver the established structures of politics are their politics acknowledged. When their representatives are admitted and allowed to participate, their policy demands are included on the political agenda and in negotiations about policy. It is at this stage that political activity becomes visible. The political process was designed to maintain a civilized but ruthless closure by elites. Britain's political institutions were designed by men; they are comfortable for men and unwelcoming for women. But they were not designed with the exclusion of women in mind. For most of the twentieth century, political conflict has centered on class. The British establishment sought to exclude first the bourgeoisie and later the working class. Excluded groups sought entry by founding and supporting mass political parties, professional organizations, trade unions, and other representational organizations.

The patterns of class politics have a territorial dimension. The political system in the United Kingdom reflects largely English political traditions, and Scotland, Wales, and Northern Ireland—home to significant cultural minorities represented in English institutions—are rarely able to pursue their separate national interests. The constitutional position of Northern Ireland is unresolved, and in 1990 none of the national minorities had its own representative institutions. The issue of separate representation for Scotland was on the political agenda, however, and of the main British political parties then in Parliament, only the ruling Conservatives were not publicly committed to including a form of Scottish assembly on their political manifestos. The conservative reluctance to devolve power is longstanding, but it was a particular hallmark of the government of Prime Minister Margaret Thatcher, which consistently reduced the powers of local government vis-à-vis central government.

That policy may be related to the geography of class politics. England itself is not culturally uniform, and the main regional divisions closely follow the class divisions of British politics. Northern English constituencies, like their Welsh and

Scottish counterparts, are the heartland of the Labour Party's electoral support, and the south of England is Tory. This territorial element produces a cultural map that has significance for women. In the north, Labour is less likely to nominate women candidates for the winnable Parliamentary seats in the region, undermining efforts by the party leadership to elect more women to Parliament. The most plausible explanation for this syndrome is that the traditional industrial and trade union cultures of the northern constituencies are traditionally hostile to women. But a similar syndrome is apparent in the safe Conservative seats of the south, suggesting that the desire to exclude women politically may be more universal than class analysis allows. Class politics may be important at the margins, however. Some evidence suggests that the Conservatives are less willing than Labour to make such nominations.[2] Yet it is the Conservatives whose stronghold is in the south, where more women seek political posts and where it is easier to combine domestic life with a political career if only because these southern constituencies are closer to the seat of government in Westminster.

Along with class and region, race is an important factor in British politics. Two "racialized" black ethnic minorities exist in Britain: those from or descended from Indian subcontinent populations and those from or descended from African and Afro-Caribbean populations.[3] There are also significant Cypriot, Iranian, and Chinese communities in Britain. All of these groups experience considerable oppression, but there is little doubt that "an overwhelming level of racism is directed explicitly at black people."[4]

The significance of race to party politics typically is assessed in terms of the number of wards, boroughs, and parliamentary constituencies in which an ethnic community holds a majority or is judged to hold the balance of power. Although both the Labour and Conservative leaderships aim to appeal to a class-differentiated black electorate, the Labour Party normally receives the support of politicized black communities. Members of Britain's ethnic minorities generally are less well off than the dominant population, and

their political power is constrained because they constitute a small proportion of the total population (less than 5 percent in 1985). The black communities are concentrated geographically, however, and they are of strategic electoral importance in many inner-city constituencies. In 1987 four of Labour's elected MPs were black; one of them, Diane Abbot, is a woman. She and the other black MPs were successful at the game of party politics. During the 1980s there was a running debate within the Labour Party about the most appropriate organizational vehicle for representing the minority races. Black activists opted to form black sections within each constituency, but by the end of the decade those sections had not been accepted by the party leadership. But blacks are organized within the Labour Party, and for most practical purposes black sections exist. The Labour Party has become increasingly responsive to its black electorate and membership, and in 1989 Paul Boteng, a black MP, joined Labour's front-bench team (the shadow cabinet). There are no black Conservative MPs, hence Labour's commitment appears to be more substantive at the level of political representation.

Although the electoral implications of race and ethnicity in Britain are well understood, the wider political implications only now are being investigated. Issues of race and gender caught up with British feminism at the beginning of the 1980s as black women asserted their differences from a mainly white and largely ethnocentric women's liberation movement. At both the theoretical and strategic level differences are still being articulated and discussed. The key issue might best be described as the meaning of difference: the experiences of black women are different from those of white women, and the experiences among black and ethnic minority communities are also different. Race and ethnicity mediate the gendered meanings of work, family, reproductive rights, male violence, citizenship, and the state in ways that challenge a feminist discourse that tended to regard women as a unitary category. One result of that challenge is that the British feminist literature of the 1980s reflects the diversity of women's politics and acknowledges at least the significance of difference.[5] Black women have tended to focus their strategic energies on the struggle against racism, which is perceived in the black communities as the primary struggle. Although there are many black feminists, there are many more black women who regard overcoming widespread hostility toward the black communities as their political priority and who would not countenance politics that demanded public criticism of black men.

For one to understand the political engagement of British women, gender, race, and class must be addressed together. Gender and race are mediated by class in ways that sometimes exaggerate and sometimes conceal political differences. The interplay takes place in a set of circumstances, institutions, and political rules devised by middle-class white men. In short, feminist politics are played out on a terrain colonized by class politics. When women have tried to gain political access, either to the agenda or to the powerful institutions of state and society, they have done so in circumstances conditioned by earlier attempts. Access to positions of power has been pre-structured by the male-dominated organizations of class politics (unions, parties, and so on) that were designed to put male outsiders into office. Strategically, the question for women has been one of whether to infiltrate or to ally with the parties and associated pressure groups, to form new organizations, or to eschew organization altogether.

The development of the political engagement of British women has been conditioned by the socialist domination of the political left. During the 1980s the rise of the New Right altered the political opportunity structure first by polarizing and later by shifting the entire political spectrum to the right. Ironically, the triumph of the New Right was presided over by Thatcher, Britain's first woman prime minister, who was elected in 1979. Although her several terms of leadership provided a powerful female image and presence at the head of government, Thatcher was disinclined to devise policies to assist women in political or professional careers, and she did not promote other women politicians, although she could easily have done so.[6]

These new political circumstances also involved the rise, split, merger, and decline of a new center party and a shift by the Labour Party. The single-member simple-majority electoral system in Britain tends to deliver absolute parliamentary majorities to one of the two main national class-based parties. Other parties have been able to offer successful challenges in the post–World War II period only where they have a concentrated regional base, as with the Scottish National Party and the Welsh National Party. The Liberal Party held on to a small number of constituencies during these years, but its position was always fairly marginal. During the 1980s a gap appeared between a rightward-shifting Conservative Party and an apparently leftward-moving Labour Party. This precipitated a nationwide challenge from the Social Democrats, who at times rose to second place in the public opinion polls. Electoral success eluded the Social Democrats, however, and the party merged with the Liberal Party after the 1987 general election. But the period of increased party competition alerted all parties that women were a significant electoral force.

The overall effect on women's political engagement was mixed. The increased competition brought about a new recognition of the potential of the women's vote. But the damage the Thatcher government did to the public sector—the main site of training and employment for British women—could not be ignored. Party politics were making a gendered difference, and feminists began to reconsider their strategies of avoiding established political mechanisms.

Even by the beginning of the 1990s clear patterns of women's political involvement had not emerged. Two-party class politics has created a political arena in which only limited entry is available for issues that cut across or are not influenced by class considerations. National divisions follow the geography of class divisions in the sense that Wales and Scotland belong to the less prosperous and Labour-voting north of the country. Similarly the black communities and the ethnic minorities are largely concentrated in Labour-voting urban areas.

The rules of the political game have affected not only how British women address political issues but also the specific issues they choose to address. To illustrate these points I have chosen four policy areas that have affected women's interests and mobilized women in the 1980s: political representation, equal opportunities, reproductive rights, and male violence.[7] Each of these is affected in different ways by the class politics on which the political system is based, but none divides opinion into the convenient class camps that the system was designed to negotiate. Moreover, all divide the women's movement.

POLITICAL REPRESENTATION

The early, bourgeois feminists of Britain were at the forefront of the struggle to win the vote and to establish an independent political voice for women. The vote was secured for women older than 30 in 1918 and for women on the same terms as men in 1928. But the expected surge of women into local government councils and Parliament did not occur, despite the presence of women activists in all the major political parties. Neither the Labour nor the Conservative Parties paid much attention to their women members or voters until the beginning of the 1980s, when several changes took place. These changes included the apparent increase in party competition after the Social Democratic Party was founded in 1980; the concerted efforts by feminists to organize within the Labour Party as a way of gaining access to the political agenda and of obtaining political representation; and the disappearance of the gender gap in British voting whereby women were more likely to vote conservative than men.[8] This meant that women became a constituency for which parties might compete, a fact not lost on the new Social Democrats, whose pledges to achieve equality of the sexes prompted such competitive bidding.

There have always been feminists in the Labour Party, but in the 1980s there was an increase in the number of women who had been politicized by the social movements of the 1970s and who were prepared to prioritize feminist issues. They organized within the party and in 1981 set up the Women's Action Committee, which launched a campaign to seek political equality for women in the party. The project was assisted by a feminist presence in the trade unions that would ultimately affect Labour Party policy.

The political representation of women was officially accorded high priority by all three parties—Labour, Liberal and Social Democratic—and throughout the 1980s progress toward increasing women's representation was apparent. All three parties introduced quotas for women on parliamentary shortlists. In the 1987 election, manifestos featured commitments to positive action, contract compliance, and an array of equal opportunity policies. The Labour Party committed itself to establishing a Ministry for Women with cabinet status. In the 1989 shadow cabinet elections Labour brought four women onto its front benches to increase women's leadership profile. The Conservatives, previously content to express their concern for women's issues through their interministerial committee on women, raised their profile in the summer of 1990 by making Angela Rumbold a home office minister (number two in the Home Office and therefore not in the cabinet) responsible for women's affairs. So feminist organization, party competition, and perceptions of a gendered electorate produced change across the political spectrum.

There was considerably less activity on the right, however. In spite of considerable dissatisfaction on the part of many Conservative women, the Tories had no policies to promote women and made no special appeal to the female electorate in their 1987 election manifesto. No women were appointed to Thatcher's cabinet. Women made up only 6.6 percent of Conservative candidates in comparison with 15 percent of Labour candidates and 16 percent of the Alliance (Liberals and Social Democrats) candidates.[9] Although the right has been prepared to engage some women's issues, it does not ease the way for women to enter politics.

Obtaining political representation has not been a priority for all feminists; neither has it won the wholehearted support of other groups of organized women. Many feminists believe that attempts to join male elites only harm women and that the women who obtain entry will become more like the men who have constructed the relevant arenas. At least this was the view until 1978, when the last of Britain's national women's liberation conferences was held and the movement split, never to come together again at the national level. Since then it has been impossible to know whether any individual or collective statement by women represents the views of anyone other than the individual or group making the statement. Radical and socialist feminists divided, and major tensions arose between heterosexual and lesbian women. Some evidence indicates that many radical feminists have a separatist political orientation but that they prefer cultural and small group activities to more traditional political organization. Socialist feminists have increasingly, if reluctantly, learned to play the political game and moved into the Labour Party after the Conservative electoral victory of 1979.[10] Many members of traditional women's organizations object to the idea that special treatment is required for women to be represented in legislatures and councils in proportion to their presence in either the general population or even the politically active population. But in Great Britain virtually all the obstacles to women's political representation are not legal but informal, structural, or cultural. For elected office the gateway is nomination for a winnable seat by one of the major political parties; for appointed office in one of the influential public bodies, the government often seeks party recommendations along with those of trade unions, business and professional associations, and other established organizations.

Practice must first change in the political parties themselves. This change is more advanced in Labour than in the Conservative Party, perhaps because the period of rising feminist activism in the Labour Party coincided with a long and painful period as the political opposition. The resultant remodeling of party policy and organization

provided an unusual opportunity for women's voices to be heard.

Issues of women's political representation are good indicators of a society's commitment to gender equality. They are crucial to the changing context in which other gendered issues are treated. Thus it is important to consider the issues that engage women politically in a manner sensitive to the gendered order of formal political power. The presence of women is not enough, however. A pro-woman policy commitment must also be present if gender politics is to be reconstructed. In considering the formal political arena, with its traditional practices of politics, one confronts the problem of maintaining the commitment to sex equality provided by the women's movement while operating within the male-dominated state. The tension that results comes from many sources. Not only is the gendered order of power under threat, but many of the structures designed to provide democratic access for the working class are being pressured to change. As a result, many of the changes necessary to empower British women are resisted by the very trade unions and parties that were established to empower outsiders. In the Labour Party, for example, the traditional industrial trade unions have nominating rights and, as such, a great deal of influence over the choice of parliamentary candidates. Many unions continue to support candidates that come from their ranks; those candidates typically are white men. During the 1970s many unions and their umbrella organization, the Trades Union Congress, resisted the implementation of equal pay and employment legislation because it was perceived as usurping their collective bargaining prerogatives. This resistance to women's entry and to the consideration of women's issues by patriarchal organizations is an obvious obstacle to women's demands for equitable participation in democratic organizations. Such obstacles are to be expected as a part of the normal self-insulation strategies pursued by elites, which happen to be male.

Less predictable are divisions that arise among women. Although one can argue that all women have an interest in the increased presence of women in political elites, it is not so easy to contend that every woman requires similar family or reproductive policies. Nor do all women have the same transportation, tax, or housing needs. But British women are more likely than men to be users of certain services—they are more likely to be poorer, to be single parents, and to use public transportation. The gender blindness in politics that favors men and penalizes women will be alleviated when the variety of women in society is as well represented in policy making as the variety of men.

Until then British women are disadvantaged in the political game, and their policy-making successes depend to a large extent on their ability to make political alliances. Given the current labor shortage and the need to bring more women into the paid labor force, the opportunity to make such alliances is good. These alliances will be able to build on the policy successes of the 1970s and 1980s. Not only were party decision-making structures influenced and infiltrated by organized women, but government policy was also influenced. Equal opportunities policy, abortion policy, and policy about pornography show the kinds of political alliances women form, the effectiveness of those alliances, and the effect of the imperatives of the particular political climate in which explicitly gendered issues are addressed.

EQUAL OPPORTUNITIES POLICY

The campaign to put equal opportunities policy on the British political agenda was one of a variety of early feminist campaigns to equalize women and men's social, political, and economic positions. Leaders of the women's movement organized traditional campaigns for change, making alliances with male power holders and using established parties and interest groups to bring about a number of important changes. The 1882 Married Women's Property Act recognized a wife's property and income as distinct from that of her husband; in 1888 the Trades Union Congress first voted in favor of equal pay. In 1919 the Sex Disqualification (Removal) Act opened the professions and the higher grades of the civil ser-

vice to women. In 1946 equal pay for women was instituted in schools, local government, and the civil service. The struggle for equality in Britain is largely conducted in accordance with the rules of the political game. As each new law is passed, party, union, and professional associations are mobilized. Members of Parliament are lobbied, media support is generated, and informed opinion is cultivated. It is slow work. The Equal Pay Act did not become law until 1970, and even then firms were given five years to bring wage policies into line. The Sex Discrimination Act, which introduced the notion of equal opportunities into employment, education, and the provision of goods, facilities, and services, and established the Equal Opportunities Commission, did not become law until the end of 1975. Only in 1988 did the government propose independent taxation for married women, a measure finally implemented in 1990. Various amendments sought to bring pension and social security for men and women into line, sometimes resulting in lowered benefits for men. Legislating equal opportunities involved forming cross-party alliances and working at a pace that did not offend the most cautious of party supporters. The Treaty of Rome required such legislation, prompting support from various governments. The treaty, which founded the European Economic Community, created three European Commission Directives during the 1970s that obliged member states to provide for equal pay, employment, and social security for men and women.[11] Improvements to the Equal Pay Act came about after the European Court of Justice found that Britain had breached the equality directives 13 times during the 1980s.

A large number of women were engaged in getting the equality legislation on the statute books. The group was made up of women who had influential positions in the unions, the universities, the parties, the media, and the women's organizations and who were committed to the cause of equal rights. They were, in short, the traditional women's movement. Their work was undoubtedly assisted by the second wave of British feminism, but alliances between the established organizations and the new feminists were still relatively minor. A tacit division of labor—sometimes accompanied by hostility—informed the different types of women's political engagement. Second-wave feminists were, at first, more impressed by the failures of sex equality policy than by its successes, regarding the failures as the expected outcomes of a strategy of working in male political structures.

ABORTION AND REPRODUCTIVE RIGHTS

Policy making in areas concerning sexuality has followed a less traditional pattern and mobilized women in a greater variety of ways. Feminists have always been interested in reproductive rights, but policy demands have changed over time. Many feminists of the late nineteenth and early twentieth centuries who campaigned for the vote also sought the general availability of birth control. But birth control was an issue that cut across the class lines of British politics and divided feminists. Many socialist women objected to what were seen as Malthusian threats to reproduction in the working class. Religious differences also cut across the political spectrum and were especially important on the left, where a significant Catholic working-class community was a natural ally for the anti-Malthusian socialists. These divisions reappeared every time an issue of reproductive rights was raised.

The issue of abortion has given the women's movement and the political system their most sustained, varied, and comprehensive interaction. The movement to decriminalize abortion had its start when the Abortion Law Reform Association was founded in the 1930s. The association, organized by women's rights activists, lobbied and formed alliances with the medical profession, gradually gaining support from the professional associations and such traditional women's organizations as the Townswomen's Guild in their effort to decriminalize abortion.[12] In 1967 Parliament passed David Steel's Abortion Law Reform Act, a private member's bill (as opposed to party legislation) introduced by a Liberal MP in what was in effect an extra-party

procedure. Party discipline was lifted for the parliamentary vote on abortion, which was typed a moral question. Whenever reproductive rights cases come before Parliament, members continue to be allowed this free vote. The party system clearly cannot accommodate the issue.

Steel's bill, one of the first proposals to decriminalize abortion, preceded the second wave of feminism and its demands for a woman's right to choose. The changes the bill brought were extremely beneficial, allowing virtually anyone to get an abortion in Britain—provided she is determined enough.[13] But it does not make abortion a matter about which the pregnant women herself decides. Instead, the law legalizes abortion only if two doctors agree that the risk of continuing the pregnancy is greater than if it is terminated. Doctors consider whether an abortion would pose any risk to the woman's life and health, whether the fetus is developing abnormally, and the well-being of the woman's other children. The law has been interpreted more liberally than its drafters had foreseen or its supporters had hoped but does not empower the woman who is making the decision. Moreover it has been regularly contested in Parliament and on occasion in the courts ever since it was passed. By 1990 Parliament had considered 15 bills that sought to reduce the provisions of the 1967 act, and each bill had been contested by organized women inside and outside Parliament. Even though by the end of the 1970s the Labour Party was committed officially to the defense of the act, the party whips did not require Labour MPs to vote the party line on this issue.[14] In spring 1990 a government amendment to another bill produced a majority for change in which the permissible abortion time limit of 28 weeks was reduced but the enabling conditions for termination of pregnancy were somewhat extended. This was also decided on a free vote.

The attempts to restrict the provisions of the abortion law to recriminalize abortion were mainly the work of such organizations as LIFE and the Society for the Protection of the Unborn Child, groups that had at their disposal the communications resources of many of the nation's churches. The 1990 amendment represented both successes and failures for the movement. The initial law and the parliamentary maneuvering that has protected it are evidence of the skillful activities of organized pressure groups with access to informed medical and administrative opinion. Public mobilization, support by trade unions, and organization within the parties have in part been the result of activity by second-wave feminists whose political experience emanates from the politics of new social movements. They have altered issue definitions and gained agenda status for reproductive rights in new arenas. The result is not only a mobilization of support by both men and women but also the introduction of a new kind of discourse into politics, one that recognizes that issues involving reproduction are also issues of rights, as relevant in the workplace as they are in the home. The political alliances that have protected the 1967 act connected a range of networks—from groups within the Conservative Party to branches of the National Union of Mineworkers. The issue brought even separatist feminists into the arena of conventional politics.

But it also caused divisions. Black women, who found that it was only too easy to get abortions, felt they were being pressured by medical practitioners not to have children and believed that campaigns to defend the provisions ignored their interests. And feminists interested in a more comprehensive strategy to secure reproductive rights increasingly worried that the need to defend the act was preventing real progress in changing attitudes about whose decision an abortion should be. Meanwhile, large numbers of women continue to oppose legal abortions and campaign to rescind liberalizing laws. Activity over this issue is perhaps the most sustained and widespread of all women's political participation in Britain.

MALE VIOLENCE AND PORNOGRAPHY

It is around the question of male violence toward women that the meaning of male power is most systematically, painfully, and comprehensively addressed. Since 1970 British women have concerned themselves with a number of issues of this kind, including domestic battery, rape, pornography, and child abuse. Pornography has recently sparked a new kind of feminist political engagement that contrasts sharply with the more traditional and sedate styles of women's politics.

Pornography is an issue that has often been on the political agenda, but its return because of feminist concern reflects the development of feminist politics during the 1970s and 1980s. Pornography is a classic feminist issue in that it cuts across the main lines of political cleavage, reveals the contradictions in a liberal insistence on a public-private divide, divides feminists, and cannot be resolved within existing political structures. The key devices of social control, the law, the police, and the courts are unable to solve the problem.

Feminists agree that pornography eroticizes power and domination and therefore makes power sexual. They also agree that violent, sadistic pornography, which shows women and children raped, bound, mutilated, chained, gagged, murdered, and so on, is objectionable. The divide comes over what it means. One perception is that pornography expresses men's true sexuality, that it causes men to rape, and that it is a significant social device for subordinating women. Taken to its logical conclusion, this view holds that pornography is an expression of male power that simply reflects the violent sexuality by which men dominate women. Another dimension stems from the view that the problem with pornography is not its literal effect, but its crucial role in establishing codes by which women are increasingly perceived and understood. Such codes, or "regimes of representation," as they are sometimes called, are socially situated—they have different meanings in different social contexts. A major intellectual project of British feminism in the 1980s was to deconstruct these codes and to demonstrate their pervasiveness in the representation of women in a variety of popular outlets.[15]

A new debate began in 1988 when Claire Short, a feminist Labour MP, raised the matter of pornographic representations of women in the popular press. She met with no success in the House of Commons but generated discussion in the feminist and left-wing political press. There was widespread popular revulsion against what was perceived to be a growing problem. By the end of 1989 two new feminist campaigning groups had emerged. Most conspicuous is Off the Shelf, a direct-action group coordinated by the Campaign Against Pornography. Its primary tactic is to gather as a group, then remove clearly pornographic magazines from a news agent's shelf and picket the shop. Because the only legal restriction on selling pornographic magazines is that they be displayed above eye level, most news agents carry them. The shelf-clearing and picketing strategy is clever, gets attention, and appears to mobilize local and national opinion. But many feminists are uneasy about it, fearing a backlash from anticensorship campaigns. They also dislike the alliances that are forming between feminist and New Right groups. As a result, a group of feminists who were prominent in the 1970s and early 1980s have begun Feminists Against Censorship, a countercampaign whose central objective has been to generate debate within the Campaign Against Pornography. Drawing on the work of the women's studies movement about regimes of representation, they seek to convince women that the crucial point about pornography is not its content but how it is understood. They argue that the strategy to combat it must address how women are perceived throughout society. Politically, an attack on pornography as a specific object is easier to make than one that regards pornography as a manifestation of the prevailing discourse. This is especially the case in the British political culture, which, at the best of times, regards intellectuals with some hostility.

Two styles and strategies compete here: the direct-action mode of the new social movement and the intellectual attack by several well-known feminist intellectuals. Both groups have resources, both have access to the media, and both have members who are part of well-organized political networks. But many others are contending to define policy about pornography. Senior

clergy from the Church of England and establishment figures are all engaged, as are a number of ad hoc pressure groups, such as the Festival of Light. As late entrants to this policy arena, feminists must contend with a variety of definitions of the problem and its solution in their efforts to be influential. Divisions in the movement impair its political effectiveness as does confusion about what, precisely, the preferred policy outcome is.

Each of these four policy areas exemplifies the extent to which women's politics in Britain is both embedded in and at odds with political culture and tradition. The established women's organizations have the skills but not the access to alter the political agenda. The new feminists brought new ways of working into the political arena, but these methods have proved costly in terms of time, personnel, and commitment. What might once have been reasonably regarded as two separate and sometimes opposed women's movements have, through the experience of numerous tactical alliances, developed into two wings of essentially the same formidable movement. Each wing has been altered and influenced by the other. But political effectiveness and the more certain status of being political insiders continue to elude British women.

NOTES

1. Joni Lovenduski, *Women and European Politics* (Amherst: University of Massachusetts Press, 1986), 217–19; and *The Report of the Hansard Society Commission on Women at the Top* (London: Hansard Society, 1990).

2. Joni Lovenduski and Pippa Norris, "Selecting Women Candidates: Obstacles to the Feminisation of the House of Commons," *European Journal of Political Research* 17 (1989): 553–62.

3. Colin Brown, *Black and White in Britain: The Third Policy Studies Institute Survey* (London: Policy Studies Institute, 1984), 2; and Zig Layton-Henry, *The Politics of Race in Britain* (London: Allen and Unwin, 1984). At the time of writing, the issue of whether it is preferable to be regarded as black was the subject of heated debate among U.K. citizens of Asian descent.

4. Michele Barrett, *Women's Oppression Today*, rev. ed. (London: Verso, 1988), viii.

5. Floya Anthias and Nira Yuval Davies, "Contextualising Feminism—Gender, Ethnic and Class Divisions,"

Feminist Review 15 (1983): 62–75; J. Bhabha, F. Klug, and S. Shutter, eds., *Worlds Apart: Women Under Immigration Law* (London: Pluto Press, 1985); B. Bryan et al., *The Heart of the Race: Black Women's Lives in Britain* (London: Virago, 1975); Michele Barrett and Mary Macintosh, "Ethno-Centrism and Socialist Feminist Theory," *Feminist Review* 20 (1985): 23–48; KumKum Bhavnani and Margaret Coulson, "Transforming Socialist Feminism: The Challenge of Racism," *Feminist Review* 23 (1986): 81–92; Shabnam Grewel et al., *Charting the Journey* (London: Sheba Feminist Publishers, 1988). See also Barrett, *Women's Oppression Today,* intro.; and V. Amos, G. Lewis, A. Mama, and P. Parma, eds., "Many Voices, One Chant: Black Feminist Perspectives," *Feminist Review* 17 (1984) (special issue).

6. Beatrix Campbell, *The Iron Ladies* (London: Virago, 1987).

7. Two other areas of women's activism significant in the 1980s were the women's peace camps, which began at Greenham Common as a demonstration against cruise missiles, and Women Against Pit Closures, which supported the 1984–85 miners' strike. Both generated mass movements, but neither achieved real integration into national or local political structures. They are, however, important to the women who participated and as examples of women's self-organization. See Vicky Seddon, ed., *The Cutting Edge: Women and the Pit Strike* (London: Lawrence and Wishart, 1986); Jean Stead, *Never the Same Again: Women and the Miners' Strike* (London: Women's Press, 1987); B. Hartford and S. Hopkins, ed., *Greenham Common: Women at the Wire* (London: Women's Press, 1984); and Jill Liddington, *The Long Road to Greenham* (London: Virago, 1989).

8. Pippa Norris, "Gender Differences in Political Participation in Britain: Traditional, Radical and Revisionist Models," *Government and Opposition* 26 (1991): 56–74.

9. Nor did Prime Minister John Major appoint women to his first cabinet in 1990. When Thatcher was ousted she was the only woman member of the cabinet, and she was not replaced. At the time of writing there are no women in the cabinet.

10. Sheila Rowbotham, Lynne Segal, and Hilary Wainwright, *Beyond the Fragments* (London: Merlin Press, 1979); Lynne Segal, *Is the Future Female?* (London: Virago, 1986); Sarah Perrigo, "Socialist Feminism and the Labour Party," *Feminist Review* (1986); Liddington, *The Long Road to Greenham.*

11. The Treaty of Rome is the founding treaty of the European Economic Community. The United Kingdom became a signatory upon its entry into the EEC on 1 January 1973. Community law is constitutionally superior to the law of the member states.

12. K. Hindell and M. Simms, *Abortion Law Reformed* (London: Peter Owen, 1971).

13. Abortion was not decriminalized in Northern Ireland, and no equivalent of the 1967 act was passed there, a decision made to avoid offending the Dublin government.

14. Joni Lovenduski, "Parliament, Pressure Groups Network and the Women's Movement: The Politics of Abortion Law Reform in Britain," in J. Lovenduski and J. Outshoorn, eds., *The New Politics of Abortion* (London: Sage, 1986), 49–66.

15. Annette Kuhn, *The Power of the Image* (London: Routledge and Kegan Paul, 1985); Carol Smart, *Feminism and the Power of Law* (London: Routledge, 1989), chap. 6; Segal, *Is the Future Female?* 105–15; Suzanne Kappeler, *The Pornography of Representation* (Cambridge, Eng.: Polity Press, 1986); and Sheila Jeffreys, *Anticlimax* (London: Woman's Press, 1990).

▲ Greece

POLITICS

Type of Political System: democracy
  Sovereignty: republic
  Executive-Legislative System: parliamentary
Type of State: unitary
Type of Party System: multiparty
Major Political Parties

Nea Demokratia (ND, or New Democracy): Founded in 1974 during the *metapolitefsi* (political reform) following the fall of the military junta. Led by Constantinos Mitsotakis. Platform publicly subscribes to the politics of *phileleftherismos* (liberalism) conceived in terms of a balance between freedom and state intervention. Not typically centrist. In 1990 was the governing party in Greece with a slight majority of deputies in Parliament. Supported by economically prosperous groups, including doctors, lawyers, and university professors.

Panellinio Socialistiko Kinema (PASOK, Panhellenic Socialist Movement): Founded by Andreas Papandreou in 1974 during the period of political reform. Governing party in Greece 1981–89; committed to *allaghi*, a change of social, economic, and political structures within a socialist democratic framework. Relies on a semipopulist rhetoric recalling the virtues and rights of the Greek "folk" and the nation. Draws support from civil servants (active and retired) and agricultural workers. Was the major opposition party in Parliament in 1990.

Synaspismos tis Aristeras kai tis Prodhou (Coalition of the Left and Progress): Formed in the late 1980s by two key left parties, KKE and KKes. Major spokespersons are Harilaos Florakis, general secretary of Kommunistiko Komma Ellados (KKE, or Communist Party of the Exterior), and Leonidas Kyrkos, leader of Kommunistiko Komma Esoterikou (KKes, or Communist Party of the Interior). Created to strengthen electoral forces and parliamentary presence of the political left in Greece; a uniform program is in the making. Recent record on promoting Greek women in politics is the best of major parties so far (lesser left-wing parties have an even better record); first woman vice-president of Parliament came from KKE. Largely supported by intellectuals, students, and lower economic groups. Its few deputies are seated on the left of the president of Parliament, PASOK deputies are in the center, and the ND deputies are on the right.

Year Women Granted Right to Vote: 1952
Year Women Granted Right to Stand for Election: 1952
Percentage of Women in the Unicameral Legislature: 5.3%[a]
Percentage of Electorate Voting for Highest Office in Most Recent Election (1990): 77.4%[b]

DEMOGRAPHICS

Population: 9,966,000
Percentage of Population in Urban Areas
  Overall: 58.0%
  Female: not available
  Male: not available
Percentage of Population Below Age 15: 21.5%
Birthrate (per 1,000 population): 13
Maternal Mortality Rate (per 100,000 live births): 9
Infant Mortality Rate (per 1,000 live births): 13
Mortality Rate of Children Under Five (per 1,000 live births): 18
Average Household Size: 3.2
Mean Age at First Marriage
  Female: 22.5
  Male: 27.6
Life Expectancy
  Female: 76.4
  Male: 72.2

EDUCATION

Ratio of Female to Male Enrollment
  First-Level Education (1980/1984): 94

Second-Level Education (1980/1984): 92
Third-Level Education: 94
Literacy Rate
Female: 76.0%
Male: 93.0%

ECONOMY
Gross National Product per Capita: U.S.
$3,550
Percentage of Labor Force in Agriculture:
40.6%

Distribution of Agricultural Workers by Sex
Female: 35.7%
Male: 64.3%
Economically Active Population by Sex
Female: 24.8%
Male: 73.6%

a. Greek Ministry of the Interior, 1990.
b. Estimates by T. Cacoullos, Greek Statistical Institute, based on figures from the Ministry of the Interior.

Women Confronting Party Politics in Greece

ANN R. CACOULLOS

Greece, located in Southern Europe on the Mediterranean Sea, has experienced political upheaval, civil war, and military coups, most blatantly during the praetorianism of the military junta of 1967 to 1974. Since the adoption of a new constitution in 1975, Greece has been a parliamentary democracy governed by a 300-member Chamber of Deputies elected for a four-year term. The president serves in a largely ceremonial position whereas executive power resides in the prime minister, the head of the governing party.

Although Greece acquired the basic structures of parliamentary government early in its modern history, it has developed a corporatist political system, meaning that power is centralized and political participation is channeled through groups authorized by the state. In this system there is a tendency "to inhibit the formation of autonomous interest groups."[1] Further, the turbulence of Greece's history (in the twentieth century alone the nation has been involved in five international wars, two civil wars, three periods of military rule, and ten major military revolts) and a legacy of praetorian politics have reinforced corporatism, especially in the form of a strong political party system. Parties are the sole authorized groups that define and represent political interests.

In spite of the marked advance in democratic government in recent years, modern Greek society still lacks a supportive political culture and a network of autonomous citizens' associations. Although demands for representative government and democracy have been widespread in Greece since the mid-nineteenth century, democracy has been largely "understood as a set of formal institutions undergirded by constitutional provisions and laws. . . . No consideration has been given to the political culture necessary to sustain democracy and freedom."[2] In Greece today, as in the past, political parties are the formal institutions of democracy; with *metapolitefsi*, the return to parliamentary government in 1974, Greek political parties, whether newly formed or realigned, resumed their traditionally dominant role in political life, exercising their usual control over all forms of political activism and issue formation. Moreover, old and much-criticized styles of party politics linger in the practices of clientelism, patronage, and "personalism"—that is, the uncontroverted leadership of the head of the party.

Students of Greek society have observed that apart from Parliament and the political parties, other arenas of activism in Greece—like trade unions and voluntary associations—have marginal political clout, if any. Although citizens' groups are no longer suppressed, they "still face a situation where virtually all forms . . . are infiltrated by party antagonisms, and as a *consequence directly reflect central political contradictions instead of contributing to the shaping of them*. Even today there is a marked hesitation on the part of members of [various] organizations to manifest any kind of conflictual differentiation in relation to central party lines" (emphasis added).[3] Hence political parties control the sphere of activism in Greece and the scenario of political controversy. That is, "whatever pressure groups exist have been created with a strong dose of state activism or through political party initiative for purposes other than the defense of the interests of their members."[4] In addition, the fledgling and largely unworkable arenas of communal, village, or municipal government in Greece do not provide alternative mechanisms of political activism and issue formation.[5] Moreover, the judiciary does not function independently of the state and thus cannot be counted as an effective arena of independent civic or political action.[6]

The first appearance in the mid-1970s of a powerful left-of-center party that challenged the historical rule of the conservative right held out hope for change in the system. In fact, as events have shown, there was greater entrenchment of the old practices. Thus the governing party of the 1980s, Panellinio Socialistiko Kinema (PASOK, or Panhellenic Socialist Movement), "sought to pack the machinery of state with its own supporters and, despite promises to the contrary . . . to subordinate the trade union movement to its party interests."[7] Personalist politics was again reproduced in the unchallenged control of the party's leadership. An all-too-inevitable consequence of party-centered politics in Greece has been the deflection of issues that were independently formed or expressed and a containment of substantive, pluralist controversy.

Greek women have had to face the problems posed by a corporatist party system in their organizing efforts. In the absence of such practices as grass-roots civic action, strong interest groups, independent pressure groups, and lobbies, and in a political ambience defined largely by old-boy patron-client relations, women's issues as originally defined have a low survival rate in a policy cycle controlled by government and parties.[8] Thus Greek women frequently come to adopt a "particized" (*kommatikopoiemeni*, literally, made into a party matter or issue) stance, which has meant an allegiance to a party.

Although 25 parties were represented in the June 1989 elections, Greek politics has been dominated by three political parties since the re-emergence of the Greek Republic in 1975. On the left of the political spectrum is Synaspismos tis Aristeras kai tis Prodhou (Coalition of the Left and Progress) which represents a late 1980s collaboration between Kommunistiko Komma Ellados (KKE, or Communist Party of the Exterior, aligned with the Soviet Union) and Kommunistiko Komma Esoterikou (KKes, or Communist Party of the Interior, aligned with Euro communism). The program of this party is being developed, but a major item on its agenda is the maintenance of a viable third party in the political system. The party is headed by Maria Damanaki of KKE. Numerically larger is PASOK, formed by Andreas Papandreou following the demise of the military junta in 1974. PASOK follows a vague socialist orientation; its major aim is to free Greece from foreign control and economic oligarchies. PASOK was Greece's governing party in the 1980s. Since 1990 the government has been controlled by the center-right party, Nea Demokratia (ND, or New Democracy), the successor of the Center Union Party, which governed Greece between 1975 and 1981. ND is now led by Prime Minister Constantinos Mitsotakis. It favors a free-market economy and limited state control in all sectors. Synaspismos draws its support largely from workers and intellectuals; PASOK relies on the vote of farmers and active or pensioned civil servants; and Nea Demokratia has the support of businesspeople and professionals in medicine, law, and education.

The parliamentary stance of these parties on women's issues generally has been neither strong nor unequivocal. Moreover, the wider juridical guarantees in the new constitution, which established the equality of the sexes, were secured largely in response to another sort of pressure, namely, the need to reestablish the international status and credibility of Greece, which had been undermined by the seven-year military junta. New constitutional provisions were in an important sense inevitable as Greece struggled to demonstrate its capacity for reform and its recommitment to a democratic social polity. The new reforms were supported by all democratic political forces in a brief suspension of party politics and polarization in Greece. No major political party can be credited with initiating constitutional reform regarding women's juridical equality. Rather, the plausible argument is that the important articles affecting women were included in the new constitution as a result of Greece's application for membership in the European Community, which presupposed that Greece honor the international conventions on women's rights that it had ratified.[9]

The new constitution states that Greek men and women have equal rights and obligations (article 4, paragraph 2); article 116 provides for the amendment and modification of all existing legislation contrary to the principle of the equality of the sexes (incompatible laws were to be invalidated after 31 December 1982); and article 22, paragraph 1 secures the right to equal pay for work of equal value irrespective of sex. Thus the constitution secured a de jure equality for women and provided an impetus to reform that was borne mainly by women, whose policy issues were a response to the powerful mandate of article 116. With respect to these issues, some of which I will review, women's organizations addressed the spirit of the law, whereas the male-dominated parties that controlled reform attempted to make the law more vague and ambiguous. ND and PASOK simply set up the government machinery that translated and delegitimized women's issues—consistent with the corporatist framework of Greek politics.

The juridical situation of women in Greece today is one of formal equality. But the Greek recommitment to a democratic polity has not substantially opened the political system to a wider citizenry. For example, the celebration of women's rights by PASOK in the 1980s was largely symbolic.[10] Greek women are still conspicuously absent from influential decision-making posts in the government (women are typically appointed as deputy ministers in education, culture, welfare, and so on, and rarely in the more influential ministries of the exterior, interior, and finance) and have a low representation in the high civil service—for example, the judiciary. The number of women in representative bodies on the national and local-county levels is among the lowest in Europe, about 4 percent in Parliament and 1.6 percent on the municipal level (mayor or president of the municipal council).

The fledgling efforts of some Greek women to organize their demands from the "bottom," eschewing tutelage from the "top," encounter great obstacles from a highly centralized political system and from the absence within the culture of party-independent forms of political socialization and grass-roots organizing.[11] It is in the context of such a closed system that I examine the character of Greek women's political engagement.

Although the women's movement in Greece has drawn women from different geographic, social, and economic areas, it has been largely urban based and generally led by affluent and socially prominent women. Rural women face additional problems that circumscribe their political engagement, given the cultural restrictions imposed on the public movement of women in villages and the dominant view that politics is for men only.[12] The majority of women activists thus organize mainly in Athens and Salonika, and women in smaller cities like Larissa and Patra follow their lead. Women activists are educated, fortified by holding jobs and having some economic independence. They work in such areas as law, banking, civil service, and education. Many women have been attracted to these fields (which provide excellent retirement benefits), but their position in the hierarchies is invariably low.[13] In the late 1970s younger women, university students, and women looking for employment in urban areas became active participants in the

Greek women's movement and provided a new style of political engagement as they articulated the problematics of feminist sexual politics in the Greek social context.

In this chapter I shall illuminate the range of women's engagement, mainly through a review of certain policy issues that emerged on the political agenda in the decade of *allaghi* (change) that was PASOK's great promise for Greek politics. Three issues of great concern to Greek women have already been dealt with by policy makers; these are the 1983 reform of an archaic family law; the demand for a liberalized abortion law, which passed Parliament in 1986; and the 1984 reform of regulations in the penal code regarding sexual violence and rape. The issues have been at the core of Greek feminist demands since the turn of the century, and they are still very much alive.

It is widely acknowledged in Greece that recent reform delegitimized many of the demands made by women's groups and organizations in the sense that issues were transformed and made tractable for government action in the policy cycle. Thus, although women formulated and defined the issues in formal and informal women's groups, the representation and implementation of these issues were effected by government elites who acted according to party instructions. The question for many Greek women today is whether the middle and end of the policy cycle— from whose leadership women are virtually excluded—has any substantive connection to its beginning when interests are articulated and demands are formulated by women.

In the 1920s a militant Greek feminist remarked, "The struggle of women neither begins nor ends with the vote."[14] Given recent reform in the 1980s I would amend the remark: the political engagement of Greek women, for the most part, neither begins nor ends with political representation. The story of what Greek women sought and what they got—from first formulations of demands in a wide scenario of political action to the committees organized by government and the debates in Parliament—can provide an important perspective on the study of politics in Greece.

WOMEN'S GROUPS AND ACTIVISM

The history of activism among Greek women, being investigated for the first time by Greek feminist historians, shows that women in the early 1920s did not limit their struggle to suffrage. The true feminist struggle, it was widely argued at the time, advocated for all the changes in public policy that were preconditions for women to "begin to think with their own heads" and to become self-determined.[15] In a rich program of demands, early Greek feminists (who belonged to a variety of associations, among which there was not always unanimity of opinion) agitated for equal rights for women in the family, legal recognition of civil marriage, protection of children born out of wedlock, abortion rights, and the abolition of prostitution houses—issues that addressed the right to reproduction and sexual self-determination within the framework of the criminal or penal code.[16] In the forefront of women's activism in this period was the League for the Rights of Women, formed in 1920.

In the early 1920s, with neither the right to vote nor the right to stand for election, women were located on the threshold of politics, articulating and promoting issues of concern to them in arenas independent of party programs and ideology. These arenas included woman's humanitarian groups and schools organized by and for women, as well as a variety of craft and literary organizations. Women lectured and wrote in a prose noteworthy for its simplicity and clarity; they used the *demotike,* the spoken version of Greek, in strong contrast with *katharevous,* the formal and highly stylized literary version of Greek used by public officials and male writers, who abused the language in their quest for obscurity.

The league published the periodical *O Agonas tis Gynaikas* (Women's struggle) and organized public forums where women presented their case. It was the only women's group that overtly resisted party interference; not unsurprisingly, its archives were confiscated by the military dictatorship of Ioannis Metaxas in 1936. Its claim of being party-independent is still widely acknowledged, as is the fact that its membership does not have a wide mass base. Other early Greek feminists, however, chose—or perhaps were compelled—to promote their issues within the framework of a political party to make their arenas of activism politically influential (namely, the Socialist Women's Association, established in 1919, which was the first group to raise the issue of abortion rights). This political strategy has been widely adopted by major Greek women's organizations.

Greece's entry into World War II and the aftermath of the country's civil war—which culminated in the almost unchallenged supremacy of a conservative government in the 1950s and early 1960s—effectively erased activism for women's issues; during the years under the junta, political life ceased altogether. In 1975 Greek women formed an organization called *Kinesi Demokratikon Gynaikon* (KDG, or the Movement of Democratic Women), which aimed to contribute to the *themeliosis* (grounding) of a genuine democracy. Women's equality was considered a fundamental component of democratic practices, and a declaration of demands was signed by the members, who included women who had held political office in the 1960s and those who had been active in the political struggles of the civil war and in the first Panhellenic Congress of Women held in May 1945. The KDG, whose aims were integral to the nationwide demand for democratic reconstruction, was the only nonpartisan umbrella group in the first wave of Greek women's activism. It did not last long as a powerful political actor, however. With the realignment and reorganization of political parties after the restoration of parliamentary government, many women withdrew from the KDG to join such newly formed party-aligned women's organizations as Enosis Gynaikon Elladas (EGE, or Union of Greek Women), which leaned ideologically to PASOK; and *Omospondia Gynaikon Elladas* (OGE, or Federation of Greek Women), which espoused the program of the reorganized KKE.[17] KDG today exists with a small membership that often expresses solidarity with the other leftist party in Greece, the KKes; it has also cooperated frequently with non-party-aligned feminist groups in Greece.

Formal women's organizations in Greece each have hierarchical leadership and their own constitution—a *katastiko*, which is juridically required of all associations in Greece; in this formal sense, they are independent. But activism, emergence of issues, and leadership are mainly guided by party strategies and ideology. The EGE stance on abortion illustrates this point. According to a founding and active member of the organization, EGE was late to join the abortion campaign because its leadership had been "advised" by PASOK to hold off until the PASOK government had formulated its policy on abortion. This occurred even though the majority of EGE members wanted to join forces with the autonomous women's groups that had been the standard-bearers of the issue throughout the late 1970s and 1980s. EGE gave its official support to legal abortion in 1984, only two years before the passage of the law.[18]

The question of which women's organizations contributed most significantly to the formulation of issues and to women's activism is hotly debated among women in Greece, as is the matter of individual leadership. The 1980s were characterized by an unfruitful tension between the EGE—the organization that was taken to represent "state feminism," headed by Margarita Papandreou, the wife of Prime Minister Andreas Papandreou—and other women's organizations. Resentment among the latter grew when the former was projected in the mass media as *the* representative of women's issues. In fact, EGE was the most circumscribed group, consistently directed by PASOK; other organizations were less tutored and dependent.

The autonomous women's groups project a different kind of organizing in Greece. They eschew formality, hierarchy, and party tutelage but are extremely knowledgeable about the structure of politics in Greece. Membership of the individual groups is usually small, though it invariably includes the women most responsible for Greek feminism and those who established an alternative activism. They are the out groups from the perspective of party-political practices in Greece, but they seem to be more politically aware than the in groups.

The autonomous groups formulated and promoted the demands with respect to abortion and rape, and the well-established League for the Rights of Women took the lead in the formulation of demands regarding family law. Autonomous groups lost interest in law reform because the legalistic discussion of the topic had transformed the issues.

REFORM OF THE FAMILY LAW

At the outset of the seven-year struggle to reform the family law, women activists employed the one resource available to them: the pen. They wrote articles and issued proclamations to the government. Issues emerged in articles published in such women's periodicals as the league's *O Agonas tis Gynaikas,* OGE's *Synchroni Gynaika* (Contemporary woman) and EGE's *Anoichto Parathiro* (Open window), as well as the short-lived feminist journals *Poli Gynaikon* (City of women) and *Scoupa* (Broom). Women who belonged to KDG organized symposia and published papers on women's problems. The Syntonistike Epitrope Gynaineikon Ekprosopon Syllogon (SEGES, or the Coordinating Committee of Representatives of Women's Organizations), formed by women in 1976 to protest the induction of women in the army quickly became an arena for activism on family law. Women from a wide political spectrum participated in this committee, which was a short-lived but impressive example of coalition building in the history of Greek women's political engagement. It was undertaken shortly after the metapolitefsi, when state power was relaxed and parties were still reorganizing. SEGES exerted a strong influence on the first parliamentary debates on family law reform, though the group ceased to exist by the time Parliament passed the reform in 1983.

The patriarchal society of Greece, fortified by the dicta of Aristotle and Saint Paul, permeates family law.[19] Contesting the "wisdom" of these august figures regarding the essential inferiority of women required all the intellectual and emotional strength women in modern Greece could summon. They were to demand a complete overhaul of the law that for decades had defined their legally and morally subordinate status in society and the family.

The issues for women revolved largely around the abolition of the *patria potestas* (paternal authority) principle under which the father had exclusive rights with respect to children until they reached age 21; the acceptance of women's self-determination of their role in the family and the rearing of children; common property rights (which are important, given the fragile position of women in the labor market); legal recognition of civil marriage and divorce; the right to choose one's surname after marriage; and legal accountability of men with respect to children born out of wedlock. Autonomous groups demanded that the status of the family itself be redefined to reduce the strong social pressure on Greek women to marry and raise families. This issue, important to women university students and unmarried professional women, was articulated in the journal *Scoupa,* published by a feminist collective, and the newspaper of the *Kinesi gia tin Apeleftherosi ton Gynaikon* (Movement for the Liberation of Women), an important autonomous group of women organized in the late 1970s. In addition, the KDG demanded that the new provisions of the law be articulated in a language accessible to a wide Greek public, not simply to those with legal training.[20]

The family law provisions demanded by women were put through the sieve of three government-appointed ad hoc juridical committees between 1976 and 1982. Each was headed by a male lawyer or jurist whose surname identified the committee: the Gazis Committee (liberal and pluralistic), the Michaelidis-Nouaros Committee (conservative and reactionary), and the Manessis Committee (compromising and conciliatory). Only in the Manessis Committee did the number of women (who were lawyers themselves) equal that of men, an achievement that followed demands made by the League for the Rights of Women. The legislature adopted the recommendations of the Manessis Committee, and the law was passed by Parliament at zero hour. The principle of parental care, in which both parents are obliged to care for their children, replaced the principle of paternal authority; the dowry was abolished; and civil marriage was recognized as an alternative to church marriage—though not as the main legal mode as women had demanded and as PASOK had promised in its electoral campaign. There were also provisions dealing with divorce and child custody. Common ownership of property, a major issue for women, was not addressed, and the independent ownership of property under the old law remains valid. Joint ownership of assets may be established under the new law by contract between the spouses, an option not readily available to uneducated or rural women, who cannot maneuver the intricacies of the law and who have no ready access to legal aid.

According to Aliki Marangopoulou, the noted activist, lawyer, and professor of criminology who headed the league in the 1980s, the family law reforms were by no means revolutionary. "Social attitudes had already advanced beyond the old law," she argues.[21] But many of the important issues for women were seriously attenuated during the eight-year legislative battle. Although reform had been initiated by the ND government in 1976, tortuous parliamentary debates and delaying tactics had transformed the issues women had defined, eventually producing the compromises passed by the PASOK government. The law is indeed scarcely revolutionary, but Greek women today wonder why it was so long in the making.

ABORTION

Transformation and reorientation also characterized the reform of abortion legislation. Women in autonomous groups organized activities typically called disorderly politics: protesting at demonstrations, marching with banners, sitting in at government buildings. They changed the traditional style of women's political engagement in Greece. In addition to lecturing, writing, and issuing proclamations, women stormed the streets, asserting the politics of their personal lives.

Women linked the abortion issue to demands for sex education in the schools, for legal distribution of contraceptives and for public information on their use. The campaign for free abortion on demand was launched by the Movement for the Liberation of Women, which on 1 May 1976 issued a manifesto; in July it organized the first exhibition in Greece on contraceptive methods. Until 1986 the campaign remained primarily in the hands of autonomous women's groups: Aftonomi Kinesi Gynaikon (Autonomous Women's Movement), based in Exarchia, Athens; *Dine*, a feminist journal collective; Spiti Gynaikon (House of Women); and Adesmefti Kinesi Gynaikon (Unaligned Women's Movement). All of the groups attempted to expose the hypocrisy of a state and church that had tolerated illegal abortion.[22] In a dramatic move in April 1983, 500 women signed a statement prepared by the Autonomous Women's Movement and attested to having had an abortion. This act made them liable for prosecution. The public challenge went unnoticed until January 1985, when an obscure though conscientious district attorney called in for interrogation seven women who had signed the statement. As the seven included prominent political women and deputies of Parliament, the event was widely publicized. An embarrassed PASOK government quickly intervened to prevent a court case, and the abortion issue went "to committee"—this time one composed of doctors who were asked to provide expertise on women's abortion needs.

The anti-abortion position of the Greek Orthodox church was influential throughout the campaign and directly affected the outcome of the legislation. The church views the reproductive capability of women as defining both their obligations to reproduce and their role in society. The legalization of abortion was resisted in Parliament by the major opposition party, Nea Demokratia, which largely adopted the views of the church and further argued that abortion threatened the effort to increase the birthrate in Greece. KKE and KKes attempted to translate the abortion issue from one of a woman's right to choose to one of family planning. PASOK defended legal abortion on the grounds that it was the obligation of the state to protect the health of women, hence the title of the law: "For the Health of Women and the Technical Interruption of Pregnancy." Thus the issue of a woman's right to decide when and if she will reproduce, which was a main issue for women, was not addressed in Parliament by supporters or opponents of abortion reform. Hybrid legislation, typical of abortion reform throughout Europe, was adopted in Greece as well. Abortion in the first 12 weeks of pregnancy is now legal, but there are no clear provisions for free abortion clinics, and the rules that allow abortion for younger, unmarried women are so convoluted that they almost evoke a nostalgia for the liberality afforded by the illegal though unencumbered abortion practices of the past.

RAPE AND SEXUAL VIOLENCE

When the campaign against rape and sexual violence introduced sexual politics to Greece, previously condoned sexual abuse of women was addressed for the first time. The campaign, conducted by the autonomous feminist groups of Athens and Salonika, also enlisted the women's student organizations, notably the Women of the School of Philosophy, at the University of Athens. Women focused on the "covering" provisions of the penal code whereby rapists could be exonerated and cases ruled out of court on the grounds that the prosecution would involve psychological and public damage to the victim. Women sought an overhaul of the code, demanding that rape be reclassified as a felony against women's personal freedom and dignity (and not simply as a crime "against morals," as it was specified under the existing law); that rape be prosecuted directly, as in cases of murder and manslaughter; that other forms of sexual assault be treated as felonies rather than misdemeanors; that marital rape be punishable; and that representatives of women's organizations be present as civil plaintiffs in rape trials when this was accept-

able to the victim. The main demand was for a new approach to sexual assault legislation so that incidents of rape could be reported and prosecuted without such "leniency windows" as marriage between the victim and rapist (a common practice in village rape cases) or "rape money" paid to fathers, brothers, or husbands of the victim.

Revising the rape and sexual violence provisions of the penal code evoked the strongest kind of containment of women's issues and of the grass-roots leadership attempted by autonomous women's groups in the 1980s. Both the media and parliamentary leadership considered women's demands a matter of sexual freedom for everyone, not one of women's personal freedom and dignity. Newspaper reports of rape in this period were especially demeaning, as they focused not on women victims but on "manly sexual impulses," for which they counseled control. The male-dominated media did not report a problem but rather an embarrassment that could be corrected with due male propriety. Women charged that the media were distorting their issues as they marched in the streets of Athens on the night of 25 June 1981, holding candles and chanting, "Any woman can be raped" and "The press rapes us daily."

The new provisions of law 1419/84, article 336 address rape as alienating the sexual freedom of both men and women.[23] The overriding demand of women that rape charges not be revocable under any leniency considerations was ignored. Gender-neutral language was used in writing the law, partly because rape is a controversial issue in Greek society. It is extremely painful for the male establishment to be confronted with evidence that women are being sexually harassed and raped by men in their immediate family and in the higher political circles and not simply by "deviant freaks" descending upon the city from villages, as popular belief suggested.[24]

ANALYZING WOMEN'S POLITICAL ENGAGEMENT

It has been said that the party affiliation sought by women's organizations "provided the broader male legitimation needed for the women to mobilize throughout the country."[25] This analysis seems to ignore a fundamental historical fact. It is not that women cannot mobilize or organize easily and so seek "male legitimation"; the history of Greek feminist organizations and women's activism today demonstrate that they can, especially because those who organize have been from the educated and prosperous classes. These women do not need special tutoring or permission from their male kin. The fact is that any action women undertake is almost immediately engulfed in the controlling practices of party-dominated politics, which effectively close the political system to all issues but those defined by party ideologies. Greek women know that being politically active and influential means belonging to a party, though they also know that party legitimation contributes to the delegitimation of women's issues—not an unusual paradox.

Yet the political activism and feminist perspectives of Greek women are not clearly illuminated by the liberal-socialist-radical typology widely used in Anglo-Saxon feminist political theory. There are two sides in the evolving politics of Greek women: the incremental side and the radical side. The first views the issues in terms of a just redistribution of rights and goods within the system and includes women of the conservative right, the liberal left, and the far left who mobilize their contests more or less within the framework of party politics while maintaining skepticism with respect to that framework. The radical side views issues in terms of the uprooting and reversal of corporatist, personalistic party politics—itself involving some fundamental changes in the political society—and includes women in the autonomous groups whose political views are not represented in existing party alignments. It is radical women's incisive critique of Greek politics that has presented a major theoretical challenge to existing leadership processes and styles in Greece.[26] Radical activists, viewed as fringe groups within the women's movement, are treated with the suspicion and cynicism that the claim of autonomy evokes in the Greek political culture, where the idea of acting independently

of party associations or of building coalitions has not taken root. Their engagement is thus generally viewed as disorderly politics, given that the orderly form involves party-initiated and -directed activities.

Greek women have in general formulated their own issues, particularly in unconventional arenas where ideas are being formed. But women are largely absent in arenas where demands are represented and implemented. Given the country's corporatist political system, such issues emerge immediately as political demands for government action.[27] Support for and opposition to the issues are invariably expressed within the programs of political parties, which shape the demands in the policy cycle. Outcomes are monotonously predictable to anyone familiar with the ideology of each party.

In this setting of centralized politics, it is difficult to measure the preference for solutions that are not originated by the state, though it is clear that such a preference exists—at least among women, who have trenchantly criticized leadership styles.[28] Further, women are pursuing self-help mechanisms. The League for the Rights of Women has tried to organize free legal counseling for women who are victims of battery in the home, an attempt that is all the more significant given the inability of the Secretariat for Women's Equality, a government organ, to open a shelter for battered women. Such a shelter has been opposed by the ND government on the grounds that it will weaken "family solidarity."[29] The question is whether the league's initiative can survive for long.

Thus the emergence of women's issues in Greece suggests an ultimately lamentable choice between two inadequate arenas: private writing, lecturing, and disorderly politics on the one hand and public party-tutored political strategy on the other. The first is inadequate because the political impact is minimal; the second is inadequate because women's issues are co-opted and delegitimized, and because established political power is exercised to obscure and transform the real social and political challenge posed by the issues. Leadership for women's issues in Parliament is still lacking, a problem cited by women, as well as by several male deputies, in parliamentary debates.[30] Women holding elite positions, parliamentary posts, or appointments to peripheral ministries invariably adopt the party lines of their male colleagues—an important condition for their election or appointment to office. The corporatist and personalistic leadership styles adopted by major male politicians is reinforced in Parliament as deputies discuss and vote on issues in party blocs; deviations from the party line can result in rebuke, demotion, or even expulsion from the party. Disagreement, when it does emerge, comes mainly from the few MPs with the status of elder statesman (like Panayiotis Kanellopoulos, a leading member of the old Center Union Party and former prime minister, in the debates on rape legislation); a national hero (like Manolis Glezos, who risked his life to raise the Greek flag on the Parthenon during the German occupation, in the debates on abortion reform); or an established political personage from an important family (like Virginia Tsouderou, the deputy who worked hardest and earliest for the new family law).[31]

CONSEQUENCES

The recent changes in the political culture of Greece can be attributed in part to the concerns women have raised, especially because women were most visible in the early stages of the policy cycle, when the main aim was to encourage public interest in the issues. A major consequence of bringing these issues to the fore is that mass-level political involvement of women has become an increasingly observable and measurable phenomenon. In a 1988 nationwide study Greek women, especially those who were employed or were seeking jobs, indicated a high level of interest in politics and demonstrated a wide range of efforts to become politically informed.[32] Women are thus being studied as political actors, not solely as homemakers.

Further, women's issues have won extensive media coverage, but the media response was a caricature of both the issues and the activism of women, prompting a homophobia hitherto unexpressed in Greece. Women's demands were characterized by the media and in Parliament as the sexual frustrations of ugly women and, worse, lesbian women (lesbians were in fact among the most influential activists in the autonomous groups organizing the abortion and rape campaigns). This response demeaned women's efforts and inadvertently exposed an essentially homophobic society. But homophobia succeeds—paradoxically, perhaps, in the land of Sappho of Lesbos—as a general, unreflective mistrust of feminism that characterizes the attitudes of Greeks on various social levels today.

Although ordinary Greek citizens argue all the time about political matters (it is the favorite topic of conversation), there is no genuine contestability of issues in Greece. A contest presupposes that one treats the views of an opponent as worthy of response.[33] A major consequence of women's political engagement in Greece has been to make genuine controversy respectable and worthwhile—for women at least. The contests in which women engaged brought to modern Greek political society, perhaps for the first time, a kind of contestability and pluralism, a major condition for what has been called the "open society." This is what women's political engagement is all about in Greece: the widening of arenas of activism, the respect for real controversiality as opposed to party-oriented divisionism over nonsubstantive issues, skepticism about leadership styles, and recommendations for alternative grass-roots modes of organizing and leadership. If my reckoning is correct, women's political engagement is challenging centralized politics in Greece, a challenge that has yet to be assumed by the dominant party-controlled system.

WOMEN'S ENGAGEMENT AND THE STUDY OF POLITICS

In a society where civic culture and modes of political socialization are underdeveloped, determining what is in one's own interests or even what interests one has can be extremely difficult.[34] Women's political engagement focuses attention on the poverty of politics in Greece, especially on the lack of alternative modes to express real grievances and demands, and, more insidiously, on the absence of independent forums for interest and issue formation. Thus women's engagement illuminates and condemns the politics of corporatist systems but also recommends revisiting some abiding models of democratic theory, especially the theory of democratic elitism. The question women's engagement raised in the 1980s was how substantial is political representation in a country where the criteria for representation are still determined by the "mobilization of bias" that universally characterizes politics but is especially forceful in centralized political systems.[35]

In spite of the expressed intentions of a democratically recommitted Greek state, closed politics is exercised as usual, leaving wide political representation hanging not so delicately in the balance. Women's activism has exposed the politics of limitation and the polarized pluralism forged by the parties in Greece. Issues emerge or reemerge in familiar, one-dimensional ways, a limitation that evokes the perverse but constant celebration by specific governments of their own initiatives in launching issues, whereby they also ignore or devalue any mass action that may have been organized. There is a vicious circle here—practically a norm in Greek political culture—in which governments pay populist lip service to emerging issues and at the same time demean any popular, mass attempt toward, or preference for, alternative solutions.[36] In the conjunction "women and politics," the Greek case demonstrates that the most problematic parameter is politics as practiced in Greece.

The political situation is becoming more stable, but the prospects for Greek women's political engagement will not be automatically enhanced. And that is the challenge for the study of politics: to expose and interpret the structural limitations and the false polarities (party divisionism) that obstruct real controversy. Women's political engagement in Greece suggests a need for richer and deeper categories of political analysis.

Feminist political scientists have argued widely and effectively for the expansion of descriptive categories that identify women's political activities worldwide. The goal now is to project and analyze the political change that these activities are proclaiming. Women's political engagement in Greece demonstrates the need to collapse the line between normative theory and descriptive political science in the study of politics.

In Greece women have been trying not simply (though it is not so simple) to engage in politics; some have attempted to alter mainstream theoretical frameworks in their activism and in their use of nonconventional politics. Their experience recalls the warning of the Stagerite in the *Nicomachean Ethics:* when we investigate the world of politics, we do so to learn more about how we can secure a common good, which as the Stagerite was to argue, includes not simply justice but friendship as well. The idea of a common good or public interest—the normative strain—must return to inform political inquiry, otherwise we shall lose sight of a variety of political experiences, especially those of women who are struggling for place in the polis.

NOTES

1. Nicos P. Mouzelis, *Politics in the Semi-Periphery: Early Parliamentarianism and Late Industrialization in the Balkans and Latin America* (London: Macmillan, 1986), 74.

2. Adamantia Pollis, "The State, the Law, and Human Rights in Modern Greece," *Human Rights Quarterly* 9 (1987): 593.

3. Constantine Tsoucalas, "Radical Reformism in a 'Pre-Welfare' Society: The Antinomies of Democratic Socialism in Greece," in Zafiris Tzannatos, ed., *Socialism in Greece* (Hants, England: Gower, 1986), 32. The matter is captured on an informal level during periods of national elections when Greeks ask each other not what or for whom they are voting. They ask instead, "What are you?" implying an almost complete personal identification with one's party.

4. Margarita Dritsas, "Changes in the Character of Greek Parliament," *Greek Review of Social Research* 41 (January–April 1981): 4.

5. The problem of decentralization is complex. Local organizations are hampered by the unavailability of funds; thus, though local government exists (e.g., municipal and

village councils), its efficacy is limited to an advisory (rhetorical) function at best. "Local government has never reached a minimum of financial and political autonomy." Tsoucalas, "Radical Reformism," 32.

6. It has been said that the Greek courts have functioned as "legitimators of the prevailing regime and bulwarks of the status quo, be it dictatorial or parliamentary. . . . Law . . . has been the principal mechanism through which the state co-opts and integrates both individuals and associations into its framework." Pollis, "The State," 596–97.

7. Richard Clogg, *Parties and Elections in Greece: The Search for Legitimacy* (London: C. Hurst, 1987), 144.

8. Politics in the Greek system reproduces that of the nation's first influential political tutor, namely, Great Britain, which in the nineteenth century was a foremost guarantor of Greece's independence from the Ottoman Empire. It has been observed that political power in Britain is "highly centralized—in both the horizontal and the vertical structures of policy making. . . . Grass-roots lobbying . . . has little impact in a system as centralized as that in Britain." Joyce Gelb, *Feminism and Politics: A Comparative Perspective* (Los Angeles: University of California Press, 1989), 16.

9. International conventions ratified by Greece override any contrary national legislative provisions, according to article 28, paragraph 1 of the constitution of 1975.

10. PASOK is "highly traditional again, despite its professed concern with women's rights, in the paucity of women in the parliamentary party." Clogg, *Parties and Elections,* 144.

11. It seems that grass-roots organizing is still a largely unexamined concept in the literature, though the term is widely used. For the argument in this chapter I take it to mean nonparty initiatives that are political in intent. In this sense, there have been attempts at grass-roots organizing in Greece, especially among women who form independent collectives and party-autonomous groups, but these have almost always been unsuccessful as political arenas of action because a highly structured party politics dominates the political life of Greece and provides the main mode of political socialization. In another sense, as I shall try to show, these attempts have articulated an important mode of criticism of establishment politics in Greece.

12. See Ann R. Cacoullos, *Greek Rural Women in Decision-Making Processes* (UNESCO, 1990). In that research study I provide evidence of rural women's politicality as well as the obstacles they face, not the least of which is the charge that they are not educated enough to participate in politics. In general, those few who win a post on the village or communal councils are independently wealthy.

13. For example, there are no women bank directors, and no woman has been appointed to the two highest courts of the land. For a recent analysis of women working in banks and insurance companies see Ann R. Cacoullos, *Gynaikia Apascholisi kai Nees Technologies stin Ellada* (Women's employment and new Technologies in Greece) (Athens: ETEBA, 1988).

14. Avra Theodoropoulou quoted in Efi Avdela and Angelica Psarra, eds., *O Feminismos stin Ellada tou Mesopolemou* (Feminism in Greece in the interwar period) (Athens: Gnosi, 1985), 104–5.

15. A paraphrase of the words of Athina Gaitanou-Giannou, who said, "Feminism is a woman thinking with her own head, determining herself . . . participating with her own self in all of human life . . . understanding that necessarily the State, Society and Governments are male constructions and for the man." Avdela and Psarra, eds., *O Feminismos* (Feminism), 392, 395 (my translation). The Avdela-Psarra study is a breakthrough in the historical investigation of Greek women.

16. For a succinct and sensitive summary of Greek women's concerns in the 1920s see the essay by Artemis Kalavanou, "The Greek Feminist Movement," in the current research on women and politics in Greece directed by Ann R. Cacoullos for the Foundation of Mediterranean Studies, Athens.

17. The leaders of the two formal women's organizations with perhaps the widest mass base (Zeli Sakellaridou, president of OGE in the 1980s, and Margarita Papandreou, president of EGE until 1988) have denied party alignment in public and personal interviews. The fact remains, however, that women belonging to these organizations consistently support the programs of the male-dominated parties.

18. Interview with Katy Lazari, June 1987. Similarly, the position of OGE on abortion reflected the central party lines of KKE, namely that the issue was one of family planning and not the right of women to choose.

19. The provisions of the family law in Greece, until their amendment in 1982, revolved largely around Aristotle's remarks on the inferior nature of women (*Politics* 1.5) and the propriety of their subordination to their husbands as enunciated by Saint Paul (*Epistle to the Ephesians* 5:22–25).

20. The proclamation issued by KDG on 7 March 1980 sums up the demands of this period: the need for a radical reformulation (*riziki anamorphosi*) of the family law and its expression in the language of the people (*na ekphrazetai sti glossa tou laou*). See Kalavanou, "Greek Feminist Movement," 45. The language cited is the demotic form of modern Greek, the spoken language, as opposed to the *katharevousa* form, in which laws and legal documents were framed until the mid-1980s, when the government declared that all official discourse (in the courts, Parliament, and so on) must be in demotike.

21. Aliki Marangopoulou, "Some Aspects of the Legal

Status of Greek Women," in Tzannatos, ed., *Socialism in Greece,* 91.

22. In general, Greek women were able to have an abortion without hassle or great expense, and doctors made a bundle on the side. Illegality posed no practical problems, and even the church remained silent. The key questions raised by women were: Why are abortions tolerated if they are illegal? Whose interests does this tolerance serve?

23. This piece of "asexual justice," as one writer put it, evoked the notorious remark of elder statesman Panayiotis Kanellopoulos, who expressed an inability to understand how it is possible for a woman to rape a man, that is, with force, violence or the threat of violence, and penis penetration. Gianna Athanasatou, "Ena Adikima Eksynchronizetai" (An injustice is modernized), *Dine* 2 (October 1987): 24. Kanellopoulos was not advancing a sophistic argument but rather calling for a rephrasing of the provisions to focus on what are clearly acts of sexual violence against women and not "mankind." His query went by the wayside, and parliamentary debate responded more to the rhetoric of a leftist deputy who argued that the "problem of rape is babies"; such issues as sexual violence, assault, and sodomy were not considered worthy of discussion. *Proceedings of Parliament,* 15 February 1984, p. 4091.

24. The idea that rape is a deviant phenomenon has been challenged by writers in the Dine collective, who have shown that it is a common occurrence, especially among friends, political colleagues, and relatives.

25. Eleni Stamiris, "The Women's Movement in Greece," *New Left Review* 158 (1986): 107.

26. See the published articles and symposia organized by feminist collectives such as Dine in Athens and Katerina in Salonika.

27. This observation is substantiated in the first place linguistically by the wide use of the verb *diekdikoume* ("we demand"), with which all women's petitions, proclamations, and memoranda are prefaced (as opposed to "we are concerned about," which is rarely used) and in the second place by the fact that all demands are directed to the *politeia* (an impossible term to translate as it includes government, the state, and the overall authoritative "whole") for action.

28. A number of issues have been raised by feminist writers in a major feminist periodical. Two issues of *Dine,* 3 and 4 (1988 and 1989), have been devoted to the range of issues concerning women and politics in Greece and address the tensions and contradictions that have arisen in leadership processes. The variety of leadership needs that emerged in the campaigns for legalized abortion and radical reform of rape legislation are still being analyzed and debated among autonomous feminist groups.

29. Interview with Rena Lampsa, who headed the secretariat, "Oramatizomai mia pio anthropini koinonia" (I have visions of a more human society), *Synchroni Gynaika* 64 (1989): 10–13.

30. See especially the remarks of Deputy Manolis Glezos in the abortion debate, who observed that representatives of women's groups should have been present during the debate, and the comments of Panayiotis Kanellopoulos during the review of the penal code in regard to rape and sexual violence. *Proceedings of Parliament,* 5 June 1986 and 15 February 1984.

31. Interview with Deputy Tsouderou, February 1986. Tsouderou remarked on the tight control of pluralist debate in Parliament and accused herself and fellow deputies of simply "playing the musical score" as directed by party-government leadership.

32. See "Politike Symberifora ton Gynaikon" (Political behavior of women), *Greek Review of Social Research* 69A (Summer 1988). See also Roe Panagiotopoulou, "Apascholisi kai Politike Symberifora ton Gynaikon: Merikes Prokatarktikes Skepsies" (Work and political behavior of women: Some preliminary thoughts), *Dine* 4 (June 1989): 55–61.

33. In an interview with Nicos Poulantzas published in the newspaper *TA NEA* in 1975, the influential political theorist asked, "How and why is it that common opinion in Greece views criticism and opposition as a scandal such that the most physiological expression of a social formation is viewed as peculiar, needing special interpretation?" His question addresses the possibility of real controversy in a social formation where consensus is valued above all, whatever the modes of its achievement.

34. Nikiforos Diamandouros, among others, has commented on the lack of civil society in Greece; see his "Greek Political Culture in Transition: Historical Origins, Evolution, Current Trends," in Richard Clogg, ed., *Greece in the 1980s* (New York: St. Martin's, 1983), 43–63. The entire matter of civil society in Greece (for which there is no equivalent term in the modern Greek language) evokes some of the large and hard abstractions of classical liberal political theory, beginning with Thomas Hobbes. The commentators, including Pollis and Tsoucalas, who have lamented the absence of civil society in Greece have not, in my opinion, examined the notion itself, which is one of the most obscure in the literature. I would say that Greeks do not lack a *conception* of civil society but rather a support system for their attempts at civic action. That is, they lack a civic culture and this is largely a function of the unchecked overflow of the state into all areas of human life.

35. This felicitous phrase is taken from E. E. Schattschneider, *The Semi-Sovereign People: A Realist's View of Democracy in America* (New York: Holt, Rinehart, and Winston, 1960), 71. If Americans are a semi-sovereign people, Greeks are a nonsovereign people, democratic rhetoric and symbolic democratic practices notwithstanding.

36. The recent PASOK style of populism has been critiqued by James Petras in "Greece: The Crisis of a Crumbling Populism," *Against The Current* 1, 4–5 (September–October 1986): 17–22. I would argue that all Greek governments in recent decades have pursued a "populist idiom"; all prime ministers and party leaders refer to the "will of the people" in a political culture where no practices exist for the expression of this will. One should treat all populist rhetoric in Greece with suspicion.

▲ Hong Kong

POLITICS

Type of Political System: British colony, to revert to the People's Republic of China in 1997[a]

Type of State: not applicable

Type of Party System: no parties[b]

Year Women Granted Right to Vote: 1985[c]

Year Women Granted Right to Stand for Election: 1985[d]

Percentage of Women in the Legislature
Lower House: 11.5%[e]
Upper House: not available

Percentage of Electorate Voting for Highest Elected Office in Most Recent Election (1991): 39.1%[f]

DEMOGRAPHICS

Population: 5,822,500[g]

Percentage of Population in Urban Areas
Overall: 93.1%
Female: 93.3%
Male: 93.9%

Percentage of Population Below Age 15: 20.9%[h]

Birthrate (per 1,000 population): 12[i]

Maternal Mortality Rate (per 100,000 live births): 6[j]

Infant Mortality Rate (per 1,000 live births): 8

Mortality Rate for Children Under Five (per 1,000 live births): 10

Average Household Size: 3.4[k]

Mean Age at First Marriage[l]
Female: 26.4
Male: 29.4

Life Expectancy[m]
Female: 80.5
Male: 74.9

EDUCATION

Ratio of Female to Male Enrollment
First-Level Education (1980/1984): 91
Second-Level Education (1980/1984): 100
Third-Level Education: 53

Literacy Rate[n]
Female: 83.0%
Male: 94.6%

ECONOMY

Gross National Product per Capita: U.S. $6,230

Percentage of Labor Force in Agriculture: 1.8%[o]

Distribution of Agricultural Workers by Sex[p]
Female: 36.3%
Male: 63.7%

Economically Active Population by Sex[q]
Female: 49.5%
Male: 78.7%

a. Hong Kong will become a special administrative region of the People's Republic of China on 1 July 1997. Until then, it can be described as an administrative no-party state in which the government bureaucracy occupies an important role in policy making.

b. Parties and representational groups are still in a formative stage because limited suffrage was not granted until 1985.

c. An indirect election of less than half the Legislative Council was first held in 1985. Since then, a minority of people of both sexes have been eligible to vote and to stand for election.

d. Ibid.

e. Hong Kong Government, *Hong Kong, 1992* (Hong Kong: Government Printer, 1992), 389–91. The figure is for the Legislative Council.

f. Ibid., 28.

g. Ibid., 364.

h. Ibid.

i. Ibid.

j. Hong Kong Government, *Hong Kong, 1992*, 429.

k. Hong Kong Census and Statistics Department, *Hong Kong 1991 Population Census: Summary Results* (Hong Kong: Government Printer, 1991), 2:58.

l. Demographic Statistics Section, Hong Kong Census and Statistics Department, "Average Age at Marriage, 1971–1988," Internal Department Document.

m. Hong Kong Government, *Hong Kong, 1992*, 429.

n. Hong Kong Census and Statistics Department, *Hong Kong 1991 Population Census.*

o. Ibid.

p. Ibid.

q. Ibid.

The Underdeveloped Political Potential of Women in Hong Kong

FANNY M. CHEUNG,
SHIRLEY PO-SAN WAN,
AND OLIVIA CHI-KIE WAN

Hong Kong is a British colony located on the southern coast of China. Of its 5.8 million inhabitants, 98 percent are Chinese. Originally part of China, Hong Kong became a British colony in 1843 following the first of the Opium Wars between the two countries. Today Hong Kong society is based on, and caught in, the clash between traditional Chinese and contemporary British culture. The lives of women, from their position in the family to the form of their participation in the work force and their engagement in politics, have been shaped by the interplay of these two very different cultures.

British control of the colony depends on a 99-year lease that will expire in 1997. Then Hong Kong will become a special administrative region of the People's Republic of China. The implications of this changeover for Hong Kong are not yet clear. All that is clear is that its approach has been an important influence on Hong Kong society and politics for the past ten years. Although the changeover is not supposed to alter any major aspect of Hong Kong for 50 years, efforts are being made by every group in the colony, including women, to encode legally important social norms and practices so that they are less vulnerable to change. This uncertainty about the future is probably the largest force structuring women's political engagement today.

Hong Kong's system of government is primarily appointive. The colonial government of Hong Kong consists of a British governor appointed by the British monarch, an Executive Council (Exco), and a Legislative Council (Legco). Most council members are Hong Kong Chinese residents. The governor appoints all of the members of the Exco and until recently those of the Legco

as well. The Exco consists of both ex officio members, who are high government officials, and unofficial members, who are generally prominent members of society. The Legco also has official members, usually the same high government officials who serve on the Exco, and unofficial members, who are chosen to represent the interests of different groups within society. The main function of the Exco is to advise the governor on all important matters of policy. It also has the power to make subsidiary legislation under a number of ordinances. The major functions of the Legco are the enactment of legislation and the control of public funds.

Until 1985 the entire Legco, like the Exco, was appointed to office by the governor. From 1985 to 1990, however, 26 of the 46 unofficial members of the Legco were chosen through indirect elections. Twelve of these 26 were elected through an electoral college—composed of the members of the Urban Council (Urbco), Regional Council (Regco), and District Boards (DBs)—as representatives of geographical constituencies. The other 14 were elected by nine functional constituencies to represent the interests of occupational or professional groups.[1] Direct election to Legco was introduced in 1991 but is limited to 18 seats, replacing the electoral college constituencies at the district level. For the most part, then, lawmaking power is highly centralized and rests with the governor and senior government bureaucrats.

The regional and local governing bodies are less centralized and have few lawmaking powers. At the regional level there are two municipal councils, the Urbco and the Regco. They are statutory bodies with financial autonomy, administrative independence, and considerable executive authority for providing municipal services to the population in the urban areas and the New Territories, respectively. The majority of the members of these bodies are elected through 27 geographical constituencies, and the rest are appointed. The Urbco and the Regco also have more independent authority than either the Exco and the Legco. The district-level government, like the Urbco and the Regco, is less centralized, with many of its members elected through a total of 210 geographical constituencies for the 19 District Boards. A DB is a consultative body on local district issues and has no independent policy-making power. Because this appointive system of government is based on old-boy networks and is so highly centralized, women have had a hard time getting their concerns addressed and have often had to rely on better-entrenched interests for help in pursuing women's issues.

Hong Kong has no party system. Instead, voluntaristic associations like neighborhood associations and chambers of commerce provide the interest mediation often provided by parties. Women's engagement has primarily been in the form of these voluntaristic associations or groups.

Women's experience is also shaped by the economic situation of the colony. Hong Kong, with the second-highest per capita income in Asia (after Japan), has become a prosperous and highly industrialized state. The material conditions of women's lives are much better than they are for women in many countries. Nevertheless, not everyone is well off; there are severe income inequalities. Both the overall prosperity and the income inequalities generated by that prosperity have played a significant role in shaping both the actors and the interests involved in politics and thus the political engagement of women.

REPRESENTATION

For over a century the colonial government de-emphasized representative politics on a Western model by filling the power centers with members of the social elite as appointed members or consultants. Policy-making power was monopolized by the elite government bureaucrats, and women's participation and representation in politics were basically nonexistent. In spite of these inequities, Hong Kong was able to maintain a high degree of political stability without suffering from any large-scale political unrest or anticolonial and nationalist challenge. Drastic socioeconomic changes since the late 1960s, together with the scheduled return of Hong Kong to China in 1997, have nevertheless recently led the government to undertake some political reforms in order to develop representative government.

In the absence of a broad electoral system, the people have to rely on the goodwill of the councillors to represent their interests. Probably because of the heterogeneity of women's interests, the incohesiveness and lack of institutionalization of women's power, and the traditional subjugation of women through the political system, women's rights and interests have always been underrepresented.

The introduction of elections to government councils and the broadening of the electoral franchise have opened more channels and greater opportunities for women's political participation. As a result, a few outstanding women politicians have enjoyed a high degree of mass media exposure. The gender disparity in political activities is still great, however, and we would like to focus on the low representation of women in politics and the reasons for this gender disparity.

The distribution of political power between the sexes has always been extremely unequal in Hong Kong. The first Chinese man was appointed to the Exco, the highest decision-making body, in 1926, but the first woman was not appointed until 1976, and the first Chinese woman not until 1982. Throughout the history of the colony, only five women have ever been appointed executive councillors. The figures for the Legco are similar. The first Chinese member—a man—was appointed to the Legco in 1880, but the first woman was not appointed until 1966. Since then, a total of 20 women have served as Legco members, four of them beginning their first terms in 1988 and another two beginning their first terms in 1991. Indirect election of members to the Legco from functional constituencies and the electoral college was first held in 1985. In the 1985 and 1988 elections only two women candidates succeeded in being elected. In the 1991 elections only one woman was elected to one of the 18 directly elected seats, and another woman was elected indirectly through the functional constituencies. The majority of women appointed or elected to these bodies are Chinese.

Women are also poorly represented in regional and local government. The Urbco, which is the oldest part of the elected government, was the first government council to have women members. The first election to the predecessor of the Urbco (the Sanitary Board) was in 1888, but the first woman member was not elected until 1956. The total number of women who have been on the Urbco through 1989 is 17: seven were elected members, nine were appointed, and one was representative. There have also been few women in the Regco, which was set up in 1986. Rural leaders are strongly represented among the elected and appointed members, but only three women have ever served in the Regco, and all of them were appointed. The total number of women who have sat on DBs is larger than for the other government councils because of the larger number of seats on the DBs. Yet the percentage of female DB members has been lower than the percentage of women on the Exco, Legco, and Urbco. In 1989, when there were 50 women DB members, they constituted only 11.6 percent of the total DB membership.

Over the past decade women's access to political power and to higher positions in the political power structure has been growing. Women holding public office have considerably increased in number. The most impressive advance has been at the central level: the percentage of women Exco members has grown from none in 1981 to 28.6 percent in 1989, while the percentage of women Legco members has grown from 4.1 to 17.5 percent during the same time. But because many women politicians serve on more than one council and usually stay in office for more than one term, the actual number of women who have participated in politics is even smaller than it appears. Women's share of decision-making power is still generally minimal.

The sex of government officials is also a significant indicator of the political representation of women. Women administrators were not appointed to sit on the Exco or the Legco as official members until July 1989. The primary reason was and still is that generally only deputy directors of government departments or above are appointed as official members, and only secretaries at the branch level join the councils as ex officio members. Not until 1987 did the first and only woman become one of the 21 secretaries (she was the secretary for economic services). In 1984, Anson Chan was also the first woman to be promoted to the post of department head (she became director of social service). Only five women headed government departments or occupied posts of equivalent status in 1989—a mere 8.5 percent of the department heads. The women department heads were also located in the "soft" government departments (as director of information services, secretary general of the Office of Members of the Exco and Legco, director of broadcasting, director of social welfare, and commissioner for television and entertainment licensing). The words of Elizabeth Wong, secretary of health and welfare and a Legco member, may illustrate how men feel about and respond to women who reach senior positions:

We have a historical link with powerful Asian women who subsequently proved not so good. Women in authority have been shown in a bad light and that has definite effects on the way men see women. They are all right in *certain* jobs only. For instance, the Director of RTHK [Radio Television Hong Kong]: OK. Director of Information: OK. Director of Social Welfare: all right. These are what I call the "softer side" positions. If you have women Directors of Industry, of Personnel, of Civil Aviation, then you'll get a different reaction. I'm talking about perfectly qualified women who are capable and have proven themselves. Then men are going to be suspicious and probably afraid.[2]

Women's concerns have also been poorly represented in the political platforms of candidates.

In the 1988 DB election, 440 men and 53 women contested 264 seats. Thousands of items, from the installment of street lights to the support of political reform, were listed in their political platforms, most relating to the improvement of people's quality of life. The elderly and the young received the most attention; women's interests were not a major concern. Of 440 men candidates, only 33 (7.5 percent) listed women's interests—such as promoting women's welfare and encouraging women's participation in the community—in their political platforms, and 20 (4.5 percent) listed separate taxation (that is, allowing working wives to file tax forms independently of their husbands.[3] The degree of concern for women's interests was significantly higher among women candidates than among men candidates. Of 53 women candidates, 20 (37.7 percent) listed women's interests, and 6 (11.3 percent) listed separate taxation in their political platforms. The more successful women candidates tended to show more concern for women's interests than the unsuccessful ones.[4] Yet the connection is not strong enough to suggest that the advocates of women's interests have been likely to secure the support of women voters.

In the 1986 Urbco election 34 men and 5 women competed for fifteen seats. The success rate of the women candidates was very high: only one failed to be elected. Their political platforms dealt primarily with recreational and cultural facilities and services, the improvement of environmental hygiene, and the need to solve social problems. The interests of young people and the elderly were singled out. None of the men candidates listed any women's interests in their political platforms, and only one woman candidate indicated that she would focus on women's rights if she was elected.

Thirty-eight men and two women competed for 12 seats in the 1986 Regco election. The major concerns listed in their platforms were similar to those listed in the Urbco election. Neither woman candidate included any women's interests in their platforms; yet two men (5.3 percent) did (i.e., to deal with the problems of women workers and to provide for enough child-care

centers to enable women to concentrate on their work). Although half of the eligible voters are women, feminist themes have been included in election campaigns only vaguely, if at all, and women's interests have apparently been a minor concern. Generally candidates at the district level have been more inclined to address women's interests than have candidates at the regional level. Women candidates have also expressed more interest in women's concerns than their male counterparts.

The questions asked and the bills passed during the 1985–88 term of the Legco suggest much the same conclusion. The oral questions asked in the Legco sessions of 1985–86, 1986–87, and 1987–88 numbered 1,093, 711, and 974, respectively.[5] The majority of the issues addressed were gender neutral. Elected members from electoral colleges were more likely to be interested in environmental, traffic, and transportation affairs, and elected members from functional constituencies were more inclined to focus on occupational and professional matters. Among various target groups, women received far less attention than elderly and young people. The total numbers (and percentages) of questions addressed to women's issues in particular were merely 22 (2.0 percent), 28 (3.9 percent), and 30 (3.1 percent) for the respective sessions, with a majority of them related to the problem of personal safety (e.g., sexual offenses against mentally retarded women, indecent and sexual assaults against women, and domestic violence).

On the whole, Legco members tended to be more interested in women's issues than their male counterparts. Although women constituted only 15.2 percent of the total unofficial membership, 45 percent of the women-related questions were asked by women councillors. Generally, women councillors were concerned with manifest women's problems (i.e., sexual assaults and domestic violence) and legislation for women's special needs (e.g., provision of cervical screening tests). On the other hand, it was men councillors who were concerned with sexual inequality in the immigration policy adopted by the government (which was the only equality issue addressed by the legislature in the 1985–88 period). Many questions widely regarded as demands based on women's special needs were asked (e.g., the provision of child-care centers), but the legislators' rationales were rarely based on the benefits to women per se; rather, they were based mostly on children's welfare, family well-being, or the possible contribution of women to solving the labor shortage problem.

Similarly, most of the bills introduced were gender neutral, with only a few having particular relevance to women, and most of those were not concerned just with women. An exception, the Employment (Amendment) Bill of 1987, which focused on the terms of maternity leave, was apparently considered because of women's special interests. Because wife beating is the major form of domestic violence, the Domestic Violence Bill of 1986 can also be regarded as one enacted mainly with women's interests in mind.

Generally speaking, all bills promoting women's interests have been supported by legislators of both sexes with little debate and practically no opposition. Yet a differentiation by sex in the substantive representation of women's interests is discernible. Women councillors have shown a greater tendency to be concerned with women's interests than men councillors have. Yet notwithstanding their "obligation" to represent women's interests, women councillors have been keen on their professionalism and for the most part have refrained from taking up an active feminist role. Therefore, when issues related to women's rights or related indirectly to women's manifest problems have come up, some of the male councillors have been more outspoken and more feminist than women councillors. For example, when discussing the Control of Obscene and Indecent Articles Bill of 1986, seven members presented their views. Four of the five men who spoke out supported the bill by expressing a concern for women's rights and interests. One indicated the correlation between a high circulation of sex magazines and a high crime rate, especially for rape and other sexual offenses. One recommended that "to ensure that the [Obscene Articles] Tribunal can scrutinize pornographic material from the women's point of view and consider whether the female image has been distorted, there should be a fair number of female adjudicators," and another proposed that half of the panel members should be women to reflect the composition of the total population. One councilman even advocated gender equality by quoting and supporting the viewpoints of the Association for the Advancement of Feminism (these include objections to reinforcing the subordinate role of women in the relations between the sexes and objections to the contents of certain magazines that treat women like objects) and urged the government to take these into account in future sex education programs. Conscious of the high turnover rate of political leaders, the torpidity of the feminist movement, and the insecurity of relying on mass support for gaining political power, women politicians are very conscious of sustaining their professional and nonradical roles. Though supporting the bill, neither of the women councillors expressed her concerns from the perspective of women or asked for a fair proportion of women adjudicators on the Obscene Articles Tribunal.[6]

Although socioeconomic developments have liberated women in many ways, and the participation of women is visible in many social activities and local affairs, politics remains a male activity. At all levels and in virtually all channels of access to political power (e.g., government councils, trade unions, pressure groups, and political groups), women are fewer in number and proportion, and most of them play peripheral roles in the political process. In government councils, specific concern for women's interests is scarce, and distinguishable feminist representatives are practically nonexistent. Thus, for example, in the 1985–88 legislature, none of the councillors asked the government to ratify the U.N. Convention on the Elimination of All Forms of Discrimination Against Women even though nearly 100 countries, including Britain and China, had become parties to it. Manifest women's problems that attract public concern may capture politicians' attention; yet many latent women's issues not commonly regarded as social problems have not been placed on the political agenda.

Besides this unfavorable political environment, there are structural constraints, social norms and responsibilities, and gender stereotypes that have also played roles in retarding women's political interests and participation and thus prevented them from assuming positions of political leadership. Until the early 1970s, for example, women were barred from becoming ascriptive representatives by a government policy that reduced the training opportunities, seniority, and promotion prospects for women civil servants. At that time, women civil servants were required to resign from their posts once they got married and were reemployed with temporary contracts only.

Another major reason for women's low level of representation and participation has been their exclusion from both candidacy and voting for the Legco. The Legco system of election through functional constituencies has not just been disadvantageous to women but has actually excluded a majority of women from participation. Because the majority of Hong Kong women are housewives, unpaid family workers, part-time or home-based pieceworkers, or holders of nonunionized jobs, they have been disqualified from Legco candidacy and from voting for Legco candidates from functional constituencies. The result of this policy has been the institutionalization and strengthening of a cumulative gender inequality. At the same time, in spite of the diminishing gender disparity in educational attainment and labor-force participation, women have been and still are generally inferior to men in terms of personal resources, such as educational qualifications, socioprofessional status, and experience, that enable participation in politics. Only three women competed for functional constituency seats in the last Legco election, and all of them failed. Even in "feminized" occupational categories like nursing and teaching, men candidates outdid women candidates.

Part of the reason for women's low involvement stems from Hong Kong's particular political environment and can be understood as one facet of the sociopolitical alienation and apathy of ordinary Hong Kong Chinese citizens. On the one hand, the long-term practice of veiled, yet well-accepted and appreciated, colonial governance has provided little opportunity and incentive for people to participate actively in politics. On the other hand, being afflicted with a pervasive sense of political inefficacy and a widespread distrust of the Chinese government next door, many Hong Kong Chinese who themselves or whose parents fled from their motherland and who remember traumatic experiences are planning to emigrate before 1997 to find stability and freedom elsewhere. Living in uncertain times and in a society with no sovereign power, the majority of Hong Kong Chinese are disinterested in active and systematic political involvement.

The appointment system, a common tool for political co-optation, affects women's participation in politics in a different way. Owing to the implicit old-boy elitism underlying the system of appointment, women have generally been in a disadvantageous position for selection.[7] Old-boy elitism thus legitimizes and perpetuates the unequal distribution of political power between the sexes. Conservatives and conformists tend to be appointed, but aside from that, the selection process itself encourages conformity. As a result, rarely have any women councillors endeavored to play the role of advocate or feminist. The appointment system has been beneficial to women in certain senses, nonetheless. It has facilitated the political involvement of socially elite women who are qualified to hold public office but would not take the initiative to participate in politics through the electoral system, as well as ordinary women who have little chance to succeed in political elections or to participate in the regional and local governing bodies.

WOMEN AND THE FAMILY

Chinese women's roles and social behavior have been entrenched in the family. Women's situation in the family and the changes that have occurred in it should be understood within the context of the interplay of English law and Chinese cultural traditions. According to Chinese custom, the law is despicable, and Confucian ethics and virtues determine the family as a social unit, but according to English law, the courts and the government can determine the nature and existence of the rights and liabilities of members of the family. These parallel social forces have simultaneously propelled women's modernization and weighted women down with conflict and guilt. Changes in women's status in the family have been achieved largely through legislation brought about by the colonial British government, which is heavily influenced by English laws. Some of the protective measures accorded to women were enacted pursuant to similar amendments to the English law. Yet in spite of changes in China in 1911, with the establishment of the Chinese republic, and in 1949, with the establishment of the People's Republic of China, the colonial government has avoided introducing major changes into the local culture. Because traditional Chinese culture has remained strong in Hong Kong, women's roles are still traditionally defined. A woman is supposed to follow her father when she is young, her husband when she marries, and her son when she gets old. Her status is threatened when she is unable to bear a male offspring. In fact, until the 1960s an often accepted reason for a husband to take a concubine or to divorce his wife was the lack of a son. Even today, regardless of a wife's level of education or economic status, the inability to bear a son still weighs heavily.[8]

The struggle for the 1971 Marriage Reform Ordinance and the reforms that followed epitomize both this cultural conflict and the role that legal reform has played in changing the status of women in the family. Prior to 1971 three valid forms of marriage contracts were allowed in Hong Kong. The first, Chinese customary marriage—a legacy of the imperial Qing dynasty that ruled China when Hong Kong became a British colony—allowed the husband to take concubines. The second form, the modern Chinese marriage, or open marriage, was introduced after the Qing dynasty was overthrown in 1911. Polygamy is not permitted in an open marriage.

The third form, specified by the Hong Kong Marriage Ordinance, requires that marriages be registered and be monogamous in nature. Early efforts to eliminate the first form of marriage and its acceptance of polygamy were unsuccessful. In 1953 a Committee on Chinese Law and Custom, set up by the home affairs secretary, recommended a review and reform of the antiquated Chinese marriage laws. But without an organized women's movement there was no strong impetus from the public for changing what many Chinese accepted as the cultural norm. Because of social inertia, the government did not take any action on the Marriage Reform Bill or any other reforms for 17 years, while similar bills related to family law reforms were passed in England.

Following these reforms in England, a series of ordinances giving legal protection to women in the family were passed in Hong Kong: the Matrimonial Causes Ordinance, Married Persons Status Ordinance, Intestates' Estate Ordinance, and the Matrimonial Proceedings and Property Ordinance, as well as the Marriage Reform Ordinance. These legislative changes made Chinese customary and open marriages invalid and made registered, monogamous marriages mandatory. The statute governing divorce was reformed so that divorce would be based on mutual consent and regulated through registration. A daughter's right to equal shares of inheritance and a married woman's independent status—for example, with respect to the right to hold property—were also established. Beginning in the mid-1980s married women were also allowed to retain their birth name for registration, as in applications for passports. Again, these changes did not come from any organized pro-women movement in Hong Kong.

Passage of these laws was not easy. Although the laws were supported by the majority of the legislators because of the changing social climate, the dissenting views of a few men legislators were representative of the underlying social attitudes found then and now in the Chinese community. In a speech against equal pay, one legislator said:

In the case of thousands of clerical workers of government, one must bear in mind that there is an inbuilt factor in a male clerk's salary for him to support his wife and children. . . . This [legitimated] the original differences between the clerical grades of male and female staff. Surely the responsibilities of a male clerk supporting a wife and two children and those of a single young lady are different. . . . The differences . . . originate from the fact that the male clerk must support his wife and family, whereas the female clerk presumably does not. This is the way our society functions. However, if the female clerk can substantiate the contention that she is supporting her husband and children, I think it would be fair to raise her pay to the male clerk's level. There are merits in matriarchy.[9]

Even in the debate on the Marriage Reform Bill a year later, in 1970, one Chinese male legislator objected to the abolition of polygamy by questioning whether monogamy was "so manifestly a superior institution to the traditional Chinese institution of marriage that we should completely deny the right to people to opt out of it if they so wish?" He further challenged his woman colleague who advocated the bill in the legislature by claiming that his intention was to protect all women: "Whereas she would wish to protect the rights of one class of woman, namely those fortunate enough to be principal wives, I would protect all women, including those that do not have the good fortune, who otherwise, if we pass this law, would be deprived of the opportunity of having an honorable and a recognized status."[10] In the end, these laws were passed because of the relentless efforts of the only woman legislator at that time, Ellen Li, who also founded the Hong Kong Council of Women—the first women's organization to promote women's rights and welfare in Hong Kong.

Another source of improvement for women's status in the family has been the successful family-planning campaign since the 1970s. Household characteristics have changed with the drop in the average annual population growth rate (now 1.6 percent). In 1986 the average household size was 3.4, compared with 4.2 in 1976. Large families are on the decline, with a rapid decrease in the proportion of households with six persons or more. Around 60 percent of the households in 1986 were in the form of one unextended nu-

clear family. The median monthly household income has risen from HK $1,425 (U.S. $306) in 1976 to HK $5,160 (U.S. $662) in 1986 (HK $2,255, or U.S. $485, in 1976 prices).[11] This increase may be attributed in part to the greater participation of women in the labor force, but it is also due to Hong Kong's overall prosperity.

Women's status inside and outside the family has also been helped by their growing participation in the work force outside the home. As the economy grew, the percentage of working-age women in active employment increased from 43.6 percent in 1976 to 49.5 percent in 1991. The median age of the female labor force has increased from 28.1 to 30.3, for more women are marrying later in life and continue to work after marriage.[12] As a result of the combined efforts of these legal reforms on behalf of women's interests since the 1960s, the family-planning campaign, the overall economic prosperity that Hong Kong achieved in the 1970s, and the increase in women's participation in the labor force, women's status has improved significantly. Such objective indicators as measures of health, marriage and children, education, employment, and social equality have showed improvement. In a global comparison of 99 countries that use 20 indicators of sexual equality, women in Hong Kong fared in the top half. Among the Asian countries, Hong Kong ranked highest after Japan and close to Singapore and Taiwan, reflecting the overall economic prosperity of these countries.[13]

The objective indicators of women's status in Hong Kong are often cited to prove that equality for women has already been achieved and that there is no need for a feminist movement, but their status within the family has not been wholly transformed. The extension of women's roles into the workplace has not relieved their responsibilities in the household. A number of studies have, on the contrary, pointed to the burden of having two careers: wage earner and homemaker.[14] Many working mothers experience conflicts between work and family life. In spite of more fathers expressing the opinion that child care should be shared, few husbands take responsibility for child care or other family duties. The decision to have children is also directly related to women's choice of work.[15] Having a young child under three years of age decreases the possibility that a married woman can work outside the home. Although she can usually accept take-home work when the child grows older, the strong relation between a limited choice of work and having young children reflects the inadequate social support for working mothers. In much the same way, the lack of low-cost, high-quality child-care facilities restricts women's opportunities to enter paid employment.

Better child-care support is one of the main needs voiced by women's groups in Hong Kong in the 1990s. Several women's organizations concerned with the advancement of women's welfare and status were formed in the 1980s. A coalition of grass-roots women's groups, including the Women's Centre of the Hong Kong Council of Women, the Association for the Advancement of Feminism, and the Hong Kong Women's Christian Council, was formed to lobby the government to provide more state support for quality child care. They held press conferences, made petitions, and organized public rallies, but the campaigns on this and other issues cannot be assumed to be successful.

SEPARATE TAXATION FOR MARRIED WOMEN

Another major women's concern in the 1970s and 1980s was the taxation of married women. Under the Inland Revenue Ordinance (IRO), the income of a wife was considered to be the income of her husband for the purposes of the salaries tax and personal assessment and was chargeable accordingly under his name. It was the husband's obligation to file tax returns for both himself and his wife, and it was also his responsibility to pay the tax. Earned incomes of married couples were also assessed jointly on their aggregate amounts. The effects of joint assessment were different on couples with different combinations of incomes. In general, when only one spouse had gainful employment or both had gainful employment

but one of them had an income less than his or her tax allowance, joint assessment allowed the couple to enjoy their aggregate tax allowances to the full and thus resulted in a smaller tax bill. When both husband and wife had gainful employment and each had an income that reached the level where the standard tax rate applied, the tax bill under joint assessment would be the same as that under separate taxation.[16] For cases that fell between these two groups, the tax bill under joint assessment was larger than that under separate taxation, for the progressive tax rate structure pushed the aggregate income of husband and wife into a higher tax bracket. Therefore, separate taxation was considered a middle-class issue from the beginning.

For over 15 years three main interest groups were engaged in a struggle over this issue. The women's rights groups wanted due recognition of the independent status of women. The middle class wanted separate taxation for reduced tax bills. The government did not want separate taxation, concerned as it was with the revenue loss that would result and with the symbolic attack on the traditional Chinese family. The different ways that these interests approached the issue of separate taxation, along with their successes and failures, show both the barriers and the opportunities that women have faced in Hong Kong.

Although this unfair treatment of married couples had been the subject of much criticism since the enactment of the IRO in 1947, the first significant effort at its reform did not occur until 1967. The second report of the IRO Review Committee of 1967 argued that treating a married woman's income as her husband's was out of step with social developments and the changing status of women. The committee, while retaining the view that the family was the best unit on which ability to pay should be assessed, recommended the introduction of a working wife allowance for families where wives took up paid employment. This recommendation was implemented by the government in the 1970–71 fiscal year. But it was abolished after only three years when the newly appointed financial secretary of Hong Kong, Philip Haddon-Cave, declared it inconsistent with the principle of equity to vary allowances according to the conditions of, and the standard of living expected or enjoyed by, different classes of taxpayers. He also said that the relief given by the working wife allowance for domestic and private expenditure was "specifically forbidden" as a deduction according to the IRO.[17]

In spite of this setback, the public continued to demand measures to mitigate the unfair tax burden on married couples, so the subject of reform was included in the agenda of the Third Inland Revenue Ordinance Review Committee (TIRORC), set up in 1976. The committee, composed of five men and one woman, met between June and December 1976. During this period women's organizations were particularly vocal in pressing for separate taxation for married women. At a women's conference held in 1975 commemorating the U.N. Decade for Women, 25 major women's organizations and over 700 individual women passed the resolution that "a married woman should have the option to be taxed as an individual." Nevertheless, although these women's organizations considered separate taxation an important issue in their fight for equality of the sexes, their stance was not strongly reflected in the Legislative Council debates or report.[18]

The TIRORC report concluded that recognition should be given to married working women for their contribution to society. But because of the loss to the treasury that would result from complete disaggregation of married couples' incomes, the committee recommended the reintroduction of the working wife allowance, set at a fixed percentage of the personal allowance, instead of separate taxation. Repeating its 1973 arguments, the government rejected even this recommendation. When the financial secretary refused to implement the recommendation of the TIRORC, only one woman Legco member expressed disappointment.[19]

This disappointment notwithstanding, women's groups continued their efforts to reform the tax laws. Convinced that it would not be an easy battle, the Hong Kong Council of Women, to-gether with eight other professional women's groups, including the Hong Kong Association of Business and Professional Women and the Hong Kong Federation of Women Lawyers, formed the Ad Hoc Legal Committee on Women's Issues in late 1981 with "the ultimate objective to achieve separate taxation, or if this proves to be unattainable, at least re-wording of these parts of the Ordinance which are currently outdated and offensive."[20] Comparing taxation legislation relating to women in other countries, members of the committee, either individually or jointly, conducted the campaign by directly approaching government officials, contributing to the "letters to the editor" columns of major newspapers, and organizing public seminars.

Meanwhile, other professional organizations and trade unions also joined the fight for separate taxation, but from the start their arguments focused on the unfair treatment of the so-called sandwich class. Tax rates in Hong Kong are progressive until one's income reaches a level where the option for personal assessment—which imposes a flat rate on the aggregate of all sources of income a person receives—is most beneficial. Prior to April 1984 the tax rate for personal assessment was 15 percent. With the low effective tax rate for the rich and the limited provision of social services, the middle-income group complained about paying a disproportionately high tax for few benefits. They are thus described as the sandwich class.

The government continued to emphasize the loss of revenue that a separate tax would bring about and the importance of the family to Chinese society. John Brembridge, in his first budget speech as the new financial secretary to the Legislative Council in 1982, described the issue of separate taxation as "the contentious issue" that had caused him "sleepless nights."[21] In his 1983 budget speech, he argued that separate taxation, even if it could be proved financially beneficial, was not tenable for other reasons as well. "Though I am sympathetic to the women's cause, my sympathy must not be allowed to overshadow wider considerations"—specifically, the "radical departure from our traditional concept of the family as the fiscal unit of charge" and "filial piety and family unity" as integral to the Chinese community.[22] The legislative councillors and the media alike soundly refuted this argument, pointing out that the "marriage tax" actually encouraged people to cohabit to avoid the increased tax burden. The women's groups and the government's differing perceptions are best illustrated in connection with a luncheon meeting held by the Hong Kong Association of Business and Professional Women in March 1983. The association invited the financial secretary to deliver a speech on separate taxation for married couples. He declined to speak on the proposed topic and instead wanted to speak on the situation of the sandwich class. When pressed for his views on the status of women in Hong Kong, he remarked that he had always thought that the status of women was higher than that of men.[23]

In the face of mounting public pressure in 1983, the government was forced to make certain concessions and adopted women's concerns as a shield against the professional middle-class lobby. The sex-discriminatory wording of the ordinance was replaced. The amendments also allowed married couples the option of choosing separate assessments and being charged for their individual shares of the total tax bill. The total amount of tax, however, was still calculated on the aggregate taxable income of both husband and wife, thus bringing no change to the tax bill for the couple.[24] The measure also retained the husband's exclusive right to choose personal assessment. To maintain this right, the amendments made in 1983 contained a new clause, which said that for the purpose of personal assessment " 'individual' does not include a wife unless she is a wife living apart from her husband."

The halfheartedness of the proposed amendments did not bring much credit to the government, but the proposal did help to reduce public pressure on the government for the time being. The subject of separate taxation gained momentum again, however, with the introduction of indirect elections to the Legislative Council in 1985. Many of those elected through the functional constituencies came from the middle class, which stood to benefit the most from separate taxation. When the issue of separate taxation was brought up once again, debate centered on the financial implications of separate taxation for different income groups and not on women's equality.

Unlike before, the battle was characterized by a strong alliance between some legislative councillors and the professional middle-class groups demanding separate taxation. Their collaborative efforts ensured that pressure was exerted on the government both inside and outside the legislature. The rejection of their demand for separate taxation by the financial secretary in 1987 aroused heated debate in the Legislative Council. Although the status of married women in paid employment was among the concerns raised, most of the legislators argued for separate taxation on the basis of the welfare of the middle class and also on the basis of the disincentive that the marriage tax might have on married women to participate in the labor force at a time when Hong Kong was experiencing a labor shortage. Some legislators also proposed the reintroduction of the working wife allowance. With the failure of the reform, dissent was recorded for the first time in the history of the Legislative Council with the passage of the Appropriation Bill. Wah Szeto, the elected member from the education constituency, voted against the Appropriation Bill and the continuing existence of the marriage tax in 1987 to reflect his constituents' "dissatisfaction and to follow their wishes."[25]

Professional associations and trade unions again joined the fray over the tax. Because professionals and workers were affected differently by the tax, their coalition has to be explained by the peculiar sociopolitical setting of the colony. Interest organizations in Hong Kong had been marked by their small size. Many small organizations would ally to strengthen their bargaining power on specific issues vis-à-vis the government. In this case, a coalition of ten professional and trade unions led by the Hong Kong Professional Teachers' Union was formed in late 1987. Members approached the tax issue as an economic question. To accommodate the interests of both the middle and the lower classes, they argued that separate taxation would not benefit those families in which only one spouse worked or in which both husband and wife worked if one of them earned below his or her personal allowance—thereby depriving them of the full benefits of their tax allowances under separate taxation. The coalition suggested that married couples should be allowed to elect joint or separate assessment depending on what was most beneficial financially.

Although women's groups continued to be involved in the issues of separate taxation, they were displaced for the most part by the middle-class groups. When the Association for the Advancement of Feminism, a women's organization set up in 1984, proposed the inclusion of the demand for amending the sex-discriminatory wording in the IRO as a condition for their joining the coalition, their proposal was rejected on the grounds that the coalition did not want to divert the issue, which to them was essentially an economic one. After this rebuff, three women's rights groups—the Association for the Advancement of Feminism, the Women's Centre of the Hong Kong Council of Women, and the Hong Kong Women's Christian Council—formed their own coalition to demand, among other things, the deletion of sex-discriminatory wording.

There has been progress on the issue of separate taxation since then, but it has not been based on women's concerns with the marriage tax. Women's voices have been overwhelmed by the highly organized and vocal professional and trade unions. The Association for the Advancement of Feminism, which initiated the coalition of women's groups, also had to yield to the situation and in their own recommendations to the government proposed that with the implementation of separate taxation, either spouse should be allowed to use the unused tax allowance of the other spouse in order to avoid the tax disadvantage that resulted for the lower-income groups. Their leaders admitted that in view of the low level of feminist consciousness among women and among the public in general, it was extremely difficult to pursue the issue purely from the feminist perspective and hope to succeed.

In the 1988 budget debate more than half of the appointed legislative councillors spoke in support of separate taxation. Several of them also supported the working wife allowance. As a result, the financial secretary was forced to make a commitment to introduce separate taxation for married women beginning in 1990 and to offer a working wife allowance as an interim measure. Thus, the 1989 IRO amendments included separate taxation. At the insistence of the trade unions, a provision was added to the IRO that allows married couples to elect joint assessment. The IRO was also amended to remove the sex-discriminatory provision that had excluded "wife" from the definition of "individual."

In sum, even though separate taxation was achieved, it was not attained because of women's concerns. The campaign for separate taxation marked the triumph of the middle class and its growing political significance. It also demonstrated the second-class status of campaigns for legislative changes affecting women's concerns in Hong Kong. Part of the reason for their relative insignificance may lie in the position of female councillors on issues relating to women. Whereas the middle class had a direct linkage with the legislators, women did not. The majority of the women councillors spoke on the subject; they invariably pointed out the discrimination of the tax system against married women but emphasized its economic effects. Not all women councillors were even this supportive. One voted against the Inland Revenue (Amendment) Bill of 1989 because being a tax professional herself, she did not find the additional costs and the administrative complications involved in the implementation of separate taxation justifiable. In her opinion, the campaign for separate taxation was "an attempt to establish separate and immaterial rights for married women that are not sought by these women."[26]

VIOLENCE AGAINST WOMEN

In Hong Kong, violence against women reflects women's powerlessness. Although special ordinances provide legal protection for women, they place women in the same category as juveniles, who need to be protected because they are powerless and weak, instead of upholding women's rights. Traditionally, violence against women has been accepted as fate or even condoned as befitting punishment for "wayward" women or disobedient wives. Society tends to look down on and blame victims for being at least partially responsible.[27] Although the feminist analysis of sexual violence has approached the issue in terms of sexual politics and the need for women's empowerment, the approach used by Hong Kong women to tackle these problems has focused on women's powerlessness and their need for social support and societal protection.[28] The campaigns against sexual violence in Hong Kong have taken more of a social service than a woman's rights orientation, with a stress on public education and the provision of services for victims. In the past 15 years services for rape victims and battered wives have been set up through the efforts of women's groups that allied themselves with social service agencies. In addition, existing legislation has been amended to protect the victims.

As in other countries, rape in Hong Kong is an underreported crime. The annual number of reported cases varied between 75 and 120 in the 1980s.[29] The actual number of cases was estimated to be four to five times higher.[30] Although rape is classified as a serious violent crime, its relatively low report rate renders it less important to law enforcement agencies than the more frequently reported crimes of physical assault and robbery. Yet women's concerns about rape arose not only because of its rate of occurrence but also because of its long-term traumatic effects on the victims, especially given the social stigma of rape. The first campaign against rape was initiated by a few individuals who worked with rape victims in alliance with a woman's group.

The War-on-Rape Campaign was started in 1977 by the Hong Kong Council of Women, the most active women's organization at the time. Through the initiatives of a few women, particularly Edith Horsfall, a medical doctor, and Fanny Cheung, a psychologist, a strategy was planned to launch the campaign on four fronts:

services for victims, training and public education, advocacy and social action, and research.[31] Four other social service agencies were invited to join the coalition through personal contacts with individual members: the Family Planning Association, the Samaritan Befrienders, the Salvation Army, and the Kwun Tong Community Health Project of the United Christian Medical Service. These voluntary agencies provide important social services that supplement government services in the community.

The campaign took a community approach to the issue of rape and viewed it as a social problem that concerned men as well as women. With the cultural context in mind, the Chinese members rejected the strategy of highlighting the feminist analysis of rape as male oppression in a male-dominated society. Instead, the campaign stressed social service and public education. To provide much-neglected aftercare services for rape victims, the Family Planning Association started a program that included pregnancy prevention, medical examinations, treatment for venereal disease, and short-term counseling. The Samaritan Befrienders trained their telephone volunteers to handle crisis calls from victims. Social workers and nurses participated in training workshops aimed at consciousness-raising, knowledge building, and skills acquisition. Public talks and community meetings were organized to raise social consciousness and to change public attitudes toward rape and rape victims.

Various government departments have cooperated with the War-on-Rape Committee in the care of victims and in public education through the active liaison efforts of the committee members. One of the most important government agencies to become involved was the police force. At the start the committee convinced the Royal Hong Kong Police Force to review the role of the police in the ordeal of a rape victim. As a result, the police set up a working procedure for the intake of rape complainants, with the rape victim being assigned to a woman officer if one was available. In addition, the police mounted a territorywide public awareness campaign on rape to raise public consciousness of the crime, encourage reporting it, and inform the public about services offered to victims. Other government departments have cooperated with the committee, often because of the conscientious concerns of department officials, who contacted the committee following publicity in the press. During the course of this campaign the committee was approached by the Criminal and Law Enforcement Injuries Compensation Board, which was administered by the Social Welfare Department. The board stated that rape victims were victims of violent crime and as such were eligible for monetary compensation. The War-on-Rape Committee promoted public awareness of this eligibility for the sake of providing monetary awards to victims, but more importantly, for the symbolic recognition that rape is a violent crime, like burglary and robbery, in which the victim has been wronged and deserves to be compensated.

The mass media also played a major role in promoting the War-on-Rape Campaign. After consulting with members of the committee, the government television station, Radio Television Hong Kong, produced a three-episode serial on the ordeal of a rape victim, portraying the psychological and social problems that they face and informing rape victims about resources available to them. The publicity activities of the campaign have been well covered by the press, radio, and television. Some of this coverage is due to social consciousness, and some to the sensational appeal of the topic.

All of this publicity provided an impetus for the passage of the Crimes (Amendment) Bill of 1977, which deals with offenses against women and girls, including rape and prostitution, and the Crimes (Amendment) (No. 2) Bill of 1978.[32] The latter bill, which was based on the English Sexual Offenses (Amendment) Act of 1976, dealt primarily with rape, emphasizing lack of consent rather than violence in its definition of the crime. The victim no longer needed to prove severe physical injury to her body before she could prosecute a case. The bill also made the sexual history of the complainant with men other than the accused normally inadmissible in court. In addition, complainants in rape cases were given anonymity to protect them from identification in the mass media. These provisions were extended to cases of indecent assault in the Crimes (Amendment) Bill of 1979.[33]

Because rape victims were portrayed as women who deserved public sympathy and societal protection, little controversy was raised in the debate over these bills in the Legislative Council. Although women legislators pointed out some problems with the bills, legislators of both sexes were supportive on the whole.

Wife beating has been taken for granted in many Chinese families even in modern Hong Kong. Acceptance of this form of violence against women is mainly due to traditional Chinese cultural norms. As a result of long-term societal toleration, there was a lack of social services, economic security, and legal protection for battered wives, which left women helpless and powerless in situations of domestic violence. Prior to 1984 no shelters were provided for battered wives. No official statistics on the problem were kept, other than the few cases that became known to the family service of the Social Service Department. Given the shame in reporting internal family discord to public authorities, the report rate for domestic violence was extremely low. Even when police were called to intervene, the usual outcome was that the couple was persuaded to reconcile and the wife returned to the home with little protection. The issue was a low priority for the government until women's groups organized a campaign on domestic violence in the early 1980s.

The campaign to establish services for victims of domestic violence has been similar to the War-on-Rape Campaign in that women's groups have allied with welfare agencies to push for social services and legal reforms. Members of the Hong Kong Council of Women who were in the medical, legal, and social service professions raised concern about this issue through their contacts with victims of wife battering. They were joined by the Hong Kong Family Welfare Society, a progressive voluntary agency providing family services for a clientele that includes many battered wives. The Hong Kong Federation of Women

Lawyers also announced its strong support for legislation to protect victims of domestic violence along the lines of what had been adopted in England. Shortly thereafter the Hong Kong Council of Women attempted to persuade the government to provide funding for a battered women's shelter.

At the beginning, the Social Welfare Department denied the need for a shelter, basing its argument on the statistics of its clientele. These figures were refuted by the Hong Kong Council of Women. Judith Longstaff, one of its members, conducted a quick study, collecting cases of wife battering at the casualty department of the hospital where she worked as a medical doctor—which showed that the Social Welfare Department figures completely underestimated the size of the problem.[34]

Through these efforts and the ensuing publicity, the Hong Kong Council of Women received support from the Social Welfare Department and the Family Welfare Society to open Harmony House in 1985, the first shelter in Hong Kong for women who are victims of physical violence. Harmony House provides a temporary residential shelter for women with or without children, a hot-line crisis intervention service, counseling, and programs for children.

In 1986 the campaign against domestic violence led to a legislative initiative protecting the rights of battered women. The Domestic Violence Bill of 1986 gave victims the right to claim an injunction from a district court on a simple application. This injunction forbade the molestation of the applicant or a child and excluded the batterer from the woman's home or, if the victim had been shut out, required the batterer to permit the applicant to remain in the matrimonial home. The injunction also allowed for rapid action without the need for divorce proceedings.[35] As one man legislator noted in the debate on the bill, this was "one Bill where the fair sex in this [Legislative] Council have adopted a united front and have received the sympathetic and well considered support of those who are not of the fair sex in this Council."[36]

As with rape, women's groups approached domestic violence for strategic reasons as just another social problem involving both sexes, although women were the chief targets. Portrayed as victims, women received more sympathy than they would have otherwise, and protective measures were enacted quite easily. The community support for protecting women against violence contrasts sharply with the support for efforts to promote women's development, when women's empowerment rather than their victimization has been emphasized. For example, in the campaign to set up a women's center to promote women's self-awareness and development of their potential, much greater skepticism and more difficulties were met in rallying support and soliciting funding than with the campaigns against rape and domestic violence.[37] Even though protection of women as the weaker sex was sympathetically received, promotion of women's rights has not been widely accepted. Similarly, in the attempts to assert women's independence and equality, such as in the campaigns for separate taxation and equal pay, support has been much less forthcoming.

The eventual success of all these campaigns did not derive from the emphasis on women's rights. In the case of separate taxation, support was rallied because of the economic disincentives of existing requirements for the middle class, whereas in the case of sexual violence, support was only a protective measure for women. Even though all of the measures worked to promote the rights of women, they could also have contributed to discrimination against women or the further victimization of women. Furthermore, the legislation may have instituted more permanent forms of protection for women, but it has not changed society. Changes in social attitudes will require continuous advocacy and public education. Legislators and social workers have moved on to other social concerns, but women's groups must continue their advocacy of women's causes, or there will be no more changes.

Although these campaigns for women's concerns have adopted a community approach in which the society as a whole is rallied to protect women who have been treated unfairly, the fact that women's groups came to the fore and championed their own cause expanded the women's movement. More women's organizations concerned with the advancement of women's rights and development were established in the 1980s. These include the Women's Center, a frontline extension of the Hong Kong Council of Women, the Association for the Advancement of Feminism, and the Hong Kong Women's Christian Council. Coalitions have been formed on such issues as maternity leave and benefits, child-care services, sexual harassment, and the Basic Law (the miniconstitution for Hong Kong when it reverts to Chinese sovereignty). The faster pace toward democracy called for by the public and supported ambivalently by the Hong Kong government as 1997 approaches is providing women with opportunities to become more politically involved. In spite of efforts by a few women's groups and political groups to promote civic-mindedness at the grass-roots level, however, women generally remain politically apathetic.

So far the women's movement has not taken center stage in Hong Kong. The image of the women's movement and women's groups suffers from negative stereotypes that alienate many men and women alike. The success of the previous campaigns has been due in great part to the nonfeminist ways the issues have been framed and the patient, dedicated, and persevering efforts of individual women who championed their causes through their professional status, personal contacts, and public appeal. With the political developments in Hong Kong, women's groups need to become more organized, like other political and interest groups, in order to have their voices heard and their concerns taken into account in public policies. In the future the women's movement will not be sustained by individual efforts alone but by the ability of women from different social strata to organize politically and to take center stage in the political arena.

PROSPECTS

In sum, the deep-seated sociocultural bondage and gender stereotypes experienced by women play a critical role in their political alienation and underrepresentation. Notwithstanding women's increasing educational and occupational attainments, their growing involvement in the work force, and their rising socioeconomic status, traditional Chinese values and beliefs regarding the subservient status of women and the sexual division of labor linger on. Owing to differential gender socialization and social expectations, women are generally still expected by both sexes to be responsible for homemaking, domestic organizing, and child rearing. Work and career remain second to the family.[38] Moreover, for the majority of Hong Kong women, social status and worth continue to be derived from their husbands and not from themselves. The family remains their focal concern and major source of life satisfaction.

Culture and law interacted paradoxically in the evolution of women's changing roles in the family and society. Regardless of traditional disdain for the law, especially in the realm of human relationships, the majority of bills passed in the late 1960s and 1970s on women's issues may be viewed as legislation for gender equality—for example, recognizing the legal right of women to hold property, to sue and be sued in tort and in contract, and to inherit property, and making monogamy the only legally accepted form of marriage.[39] On the whole, these bills were supported by legislators of both sexes and were passed with few objections. Since the 1980s the main focus of bills on women's issues has shifted from legislation for gender equality to legislation for women's special needs and interests. Whereas in the past the protection of women was more acceptable as the underlying rationale for such legislation, in the future the recognition of women as individuals with their own rights should be promoted by women's groups in their campaigns for women's causes.

Over the past two decades Hong Kong women have profited from the miraculous socioeconomic development of the territory and from westernization, urbanization, and the slackening of sexism. More women have made it to the top in both the private and the public sectors. In the past, for instance, the proportion of women politicians was smaller at higher levels of the power hierarchy than at lower levels. Yet in 1989, although the proportion of women representatives in various political bodies remained small (ranging from 5.6 to 28.6 percent), the highest proportion of women was found at the top of the political structure, the Exco (where members are appointed by the governor). In contrast, the lowest proportion was found in the political bodies in the rural areas of the territory. Part of the reason is that the Regco and the New Territories DB are politically dominated by the indigenous inhabitants, who tend to be more traditional and patriarchal.[40]

The sociodemographic description of women holding public office has also changed in the past few decades. Before the mid-1970s all of the women who held political office were over 50 at their first appointment or election. They typically came from social service, church, and school-related occupational backgrounds and were more educated than the average citizen. In the 1980s, in contrast, most of the women who held public office were in their mid-30s, and in line with the development of representative government, they came from a broader spectrum of society—they were everything from housewives to professionals and prominent businesswomen. Their education ranged from completion of secondary school to acquisition of a professional degree, yet most were still more educated than the general public. The majority of women who entered the higher echelons of power, that is, the Exco and the Legco, were highly educated, successful career women, whereas women with less education and lower occupational status have tended to hold public offices at the lower echelons of the power hierarchy.

The approach of 1997 gives an impetus for active political participation. Although women's groups would like to promote more female candidates in the upcoming elections, they concede that there are many barriers to women's participation. Accepting the priority of the family and anticipating the heavy duties and time consump-

tion of holding public office, many women may be willing to engage in short-term or issue-oriented sociopolitical affairs only, not those requiring formal or long-term political commitment. Running for public office will require more initiative, self-confidence, and resources than exist among women now. The dearth of female candidates in various elections and the significant gender disparity in the rate of reattempted elections by unsuccessful candidates show women's political aloofness and reluctance to enter the political arena. In the 1982, 1985, and 1988 DB elections, women constituted only 5 percent, 6.2 percent, and 10.8 percent, respectively, of the candidates. And in the 1988 Legco election, women constituted 15 percent and 7.7 percent of the total number of candidates in the functional and electoral college elections, respectively. In spite of the absence of official sex-based voting statistics, empirical studies indicate that both voter registration and voter turnout were significantly lower among women than among men. The major self-reported reasons for women's nonengagement in political activities were their lack of time, the burden of child rearing, and housework.[41] As a woman Legco councillor once commented on women's political participation, "Being single helps, or better still, the children are already grown up and quite independent and the husband is too busy with his own business to miss his better half."[42] In addition to this stereotypical prerequisite for women's political advancement, women's legal right to participate in politics is still denied full social approbation, generating more pressure on or discrimination against women politicians, who often have to answer questions about their family responsibilities and who attract more attention and comments on their appearance (at the expense of performance) than their male counterparts do.

The feminization of the political environment by the increase of women politicians may bring forth a reciprocal effect on the degree of women's participation and the acceptability of women in politics. The prevailing sociopolitical institutions and the dominant cultural values, however, place women at a competitive disadvantage in acquiring the requisite resources for political involvement and gains. Many women's organizations have been formed, and some of them are actively involved in social affairs with politicizing effects. Yet the responses of women in general are neither active nor enthusiastic. Although women have been found to be less satisfied with Hong Kong society and to have adopted a more mistrustful attitude toward government than men, they have been more preoccupied with the importance of social stability than with their own position. They seem to be contented with the sex norms of the status quo.[43] As a result, women's organizations have not yet been successful in uniting women and institutionalizing their presence in the formal political structure, in organizing women as a separate political force with electoral relevance or influence, or in fielding their own candidates. With the introduction of direct election to the Legco in 1991, women had an opportunity to promote public awareness of their disadvantaged position and underrepresentation, to make more use of their political rights, to identify and consolidate their demands and interests, and to coalesce and develop as an electoral and legislative force.

Some women's groups united to formulate a women's political platform for the 1991 election. As in the past few years, however, it is obvious that the significant increase in political interest and participation has primarily focused on issues and strategies related to the decolonization and political transition of Hong Kong in general—for example, localization of political elites, direct election to the Legco, development of democratic government, and the drafting of the Basic Law.

Gender issues have been subordinated to overall concerns about the future of Hong Kong and to the power struggle between the conservatives and the democrats.[44] Without a fundamental change in cultural values and attitudes, the outlook for arousing consciousness and bringing gender issues and women's interests to the top of the political agenda in the transition to 1997 is not bright at all.

NOTES

1. The nine functional constituencies and their respective seats are commerce (2), industry (2), finance (1), labor (2), social issues (1), medicine (1), law (1), education (1), and engineering and associated professions (1).

2. E. Ellis Cushmore, "The Experiences of Successful Career Women in Hongkong: A Study of Strategies for Overcoming Subordination" (Department of Sociology, Hong Kong University, 1989), 16.

3. The target group to appeal to by supporting separate taxation might be the middle class as a whole instead of women.

4. Fourteen successful women candidates (51.9 percent) listed women's interests, compared to eleven unsuccessful women candidates (42.3 percent).

5. *OMELCO Annual Report* (Hong Kong: Government Printer, 1987), 92; *OMELCO Annual Report* (Hong Kong: Government Printer, 1988), 75; and *OMELCO Annual Report* (Hong Kong: Government Printer, 1989), 85. Because asking questions in the Legco is subject to rules (e.g., both the number of questions asked per legislator per sitting and the total number of questions asked per sitting are regulated), it can be considered a limited resource for which legislators compete in order to stage their performances or to pursue their concerns.

6. *Hong Kong Hansard*, 18 February 1987, pp. 842–50.

7. Appointed unofficial members, especially to the Exco and Legco, are usually selected from among prominent members of the business and professional community, particularly those who have proved themselves in public service.

8. Margery Wolf, "Chinese Women: Old Skills in a New Context," in Michelle Z. Rosaldo and Louise Lamphere, eds., *Woman, Culture, and Society* (Stanford, Calif.: Stanford University Press, 1974); Marilyn Young, *Women in China* (Ann Arbor: Center for Chinese Studies, University of Michigan, 1973).

9. Speech by Wilfred Wong, *Hong Kong Hansard*, 13 March 1969, p. 147.

10. Speech by Oswald Cheung, *Hong Kong Hansard*, 17 June 1970, p. 737.

11. Hong Kong Census and Statistics Department, *Hong Kong 1986 By-Census: Summary Result* (Hong Kong: Government Printer, 1986), 84–116.

12. Ibid., 44–82.

13. Population Crisis Committee, *Country Rankings of the Status of Women: Poor, Powerless and Pregnant*, Population Briefing Paper no. 20 (Washington, D.C.: Population Crisis Committee, 1988).

14. Hong Kong Young Women's Christian Association and Hong Kong Shue Yan College, *Report on Working*

Mothers in Family Functioning (Hong Kong: Hong Kong YWCA, 1982); Boys' and Girls' Clubs Association of Hong Kong, *Study on Father's Involvement in Child-Care Activities and Household Chores in the Family* (in Chinese) (Hong Kong: Boys' and Girls' Clubs Association of Hong Kong, 1990).

15. Yue-chim Wong, "Women's Work and the Demand for Children in Hong Kong," *Developing Economies* 25 (1987): 188–200.

16. The salaries tax rate in Hong Kong is progressive, on a sliding scale from 3 to 25 percent for different tax brackets. Taxpayers may also elect for personal assessment, for which all sources of a person's or couple's income are aggregated and taxed at a flat standard rate, which varied from 15 to 17 percent in the 1970s and 1980s.

17. Speech by the financial secretary in moving the second reading of the Appropriation Bill in the Legislative Council, *Hong Kong Hansard*, 28 February 1973, p. 484.

18. Letter to the director of Inland Revenue by the Hong Kong Council of Women, 24 September 1976.

19. Speech by Siu-wah Ko, *Hong Kong Hansard*, 29 March 1978, p. 684.

20. Hong Kong Council of Women, *Annual Report, 1981–82* (Hong Kong: Hong Kong Council of Women, 1981–82), 20.

21. Speech by the financial secretary in moving the second reading of the Appropriation Bill, *Hong Kong Hansard*, 24 February 1982, p. 451.

22. Speech by the financial secretary in moving the second reading of the Appropriation Bill, *Hong Kong Hansard*, 23 February 1983, p. 547.

23. "Issue of Separate Taxation for Married Couples," *Oriental Daily News*, 29 March 1983, p. 3.

24. Ibid.

25. Speech by Szeto Wah, *Hong Kong Hansard*, 19 March 1987, p. 1242.

26. Speech by Nellie Fong, *Hong Kong Hansard*, 19 July 1989, p. 2267.

27. See Fanny M. Cheung and Betty J. Chung, "An Exploratory Study on Attitudes Toward Rape," *Hong Kong Journal of Mental Health* 11 (1982): 7–17; Sheung-tak Cheng, Hung-yuk Ip, and Fanny M. Cheung, "Proclivity to Rape: An Exploratory Study," *Hong Kong Journal of Mental Health* 13 (1984): 45–57; and Betty H. C. Lee and Fanny M. Cheung, "Attitudes Toward Rape Victims in Hong Kong," in Fanny M. Cheung, Robert G. Andry and Roger C. Tam, eds., *Research on Rape and Sexual Crime in Hong Kong* (Hong Kong: Centre for Hong Kong Studies, Chinese University of Hong Kong, 1990).

28. For feminist analyses see Susan Brownmiller, *Against Our Will* (New York: Simon and Schuster, 1975); Diana Russell, *The Politics of Rape* (New York: Stein and Day, 1975); Leona E. Walker, *The Battered Woman* (New York: Harper and Row, 1979).

29. *Royal Hong Kong Police Force Review, 1980* (Hong Kong: Royal Hong Kong Police Force, 1980), 52; *Royal Hong Kong Police Force Review, 1989* (Hong Kong: Royal Hong Kong Police Force, 1989), 68.

30. Fanny M. Cheung and Japhet S. Law, "Victims of Sexual Assault: A Summary of the Crime Victimization Surveys of 1978, 1981, and 1986," *Research on Rape and Sexual Crime in Hong Kong* (Hong Kong: Centre for Hong Kong Studies, Chinese University of Hong Kong, 1990), 1–18.

31. Fanny M. Cheung, "Changing Attitudes: The War-on-Rape Campaign," *Bulletin of the Hong Kong Psychological Society* 19–20 (1987–88): 41–48.

32. *Hong Kong Hansard*, 19 January 1977, pp. 434–36; *Hong Kong Hansard*, 12 April 1978, pp. 766–68.

33. *Hong Kong Hansard*, 11 April 1979, p. 715.

34. Judith Longstaff and George Lo, *Wife Battering in Hong Kong: A Preliminary Survey* (Unpublished report, Department of Medicine, United Christian Hospital, Hong Kong, 1980).

35. *Hong Kong Hansard*, 9 July 1986, pp. 1439–41.

36. Speech by Hilton Cheong-leen, *Hong Kong Hansard*, 23 July 1986, p. 1642.

37. Fanny M. Cheung, "The Women's Center: A Community Approach to Feminism in Hong Kong," *American Journal of Community Psychology* 17 (1989): 99–107.

38. Fanny M. Cheung and Rhoda Yuen, *Psychological and Social Characteristics Related to Social Participation Among Working-Class Housewives in Hong Kong* (Hong Kong: Centre for Hong Kong Studies, Chinese University of Hong Kong, 1987), 1–31; Lau Siu-kai and Wan Po-San, *A Preliminary Report on Social Indicators Research in Hong Kong* (in Chinese) (Hong Kong: Centre for Hong Kong Studies, Chinese University of Hong Kong, 1987), 27–47.

39. Examples are the Matrimonial Causes Ordinance, Married Persons' Status Ordinance, Marriage Reform Ordinance, Intestates' Estate Ordinance, and the Matrimonial Proceedings and Property Ordinance.

40. The indigenous inhabitants are native Chinese residents whose ancestors lived in the New Territories before British occupation. They enjoy a number of institutional privileges in regard to land possession and political representation, among other things.

41. Association for the Advancement of Feminism, *Women's Participation in Public Affairs: A Survey Report* (in Chinese) (Hong Kong: Association for the Advancement of Feminism, 1985), 30–31, 37, 86–87.

42. "Trying Days for the Housewife in Politics," *Hong Kong Standard*, 1 March 1988, p. 17.

43. Lau Siu-kai and Kuan Hsin-chi, *The Ethos of the*

Hong Kong Chinese (Hong Kong: Chinese University Press, 1988), 146–47.

44. The conservatives are mainly the economic elites. Their main goal is to maintain the status quo, and thus they have adopted a pro-China position. The democrats, who are more heterogeneous and have a larger proportion of professionals and intellectuals, are more radical and demand a quicker pace of democratization. They are more reliant on public support and have taken up an anticommunist stance.

▲ Hungary

POLITICS

Type of Political System: democracy
  Sovereignty: republic
  Executive-Legislative System: parliamentary
Type of State: unitary
Type of Party System: multiparty
Major Political Parties

Magyar Demokrata Fórum (Hungarian Democratic Forum): Collective party; deviates decisively from its original objective. Began as a modernizing party, but conservative line of the radical populist wing prevailed. Shows characteristics of a conservative Christian party.

Szabad Demokraták Szövetsége (Association of Free Democrats): Until elections, was an outspoken conservative liberal party. It then assumed more of a socioliberal character.

Független Kisgazda- és Polgári Párt (Independent Smallholder and Bourgeois Party): Party based on historic traditions; appeals to the older age-groups. At the same time, it forms a part of the modern agrarian intelligentsia, which concentrates on the modern farmer economy.

Magyar Szocialista Párt (Hungarian Socialist Party): Began as the successor of the Hungarian Socialist Workers' Party. At the congress of May 1990 the reform wing won; has gradually become a party of the social democratic line.

Fiatal Demokraták Szövetsége (Association of Young Democrats): Originally a youth organization; has become a modern liberal party.

Kereszténydemokrata Néppárt (Democratic-Christian People's Party): Represents European human values and social sensitivity; not based on historic continuity.

Year Women Granted Right to Vote: 1945
Year Women Granted Right to Stand for Election: 1945

Percentage of Women in the Unicameral Legislature: 6.7%[a]
Percentage of Electorate Voting for Highest Elected Office in Most Recent Election (1990): 65.0%[b]

DEMOGRAPHICS

Population: 10,375,300[c]
Percentage of Population in Urban Areas[d]
  Overall: 61.8%
  Female: 62.5%
  Male: 61.2%
Percentage of Population Below Age 15: 21.3%[c]
Birthrate (per 1,000 population): 12[f]
Maternal Mortality Rate (per 100,000 live births): 26
Infant Mortality Rate (per 1,000 live births): 17
Mortality Rate for Children Under Five (per 1,000 live births): 19
Average Household Size: 2.7[g]
Mean Age at First Marriage
  Female: 21.0
  Male: 24.8
Life Expectancy[h]
  Female: 74.0
  Male: 66.2

EDUCATION

Ratio of Female to Male Enrollment
  First-Level Education: 95
  Second-Level Education: 95
  Third-Level Education: 115[i]
Literacy Rate[j]
  Female: 98.2%
  Male: 98.5%

ECONOMY

Gross National Product per Capita: U.S. $2,750[k]
Percentage of Labor Force in Agriculture: 15.3%[l]
Distribution of Agricultural Workers by Sex[m]
  Female: 31.3%
  Male: 68.7%

Economically Active Population by Sex[n]
Female: 36.9%
Male: 49.7%

   a. Calculation by the author using figures from László Medveczky, ed., *Szabadon választott: Parlamenti almanach, 1990* (Freely elected: Parliamentary almanac, 1990) (Budapest: Idegenforgalmi Propaganda és Kiadó Vállalat, 1990), 72–272.

   b. *Választások Magyarországon: 1990. március 25, április 8* (Elections in Hungary: 25 March and 8 April 1990); and *Parlament képviselök* (Members of Parliament) (Budapest: Magyar Távirati Iroda, 1990), 6.

   c. *Evi Népszámlálás. Összefoglaló adatok a 2%-os képviseleti minta alapján* (1990 census: Summary data

based on the 2 percent representative sample) (Budapest: Központi Statisztikai Hivatal, 1990), 7.

   d. *Statisztikai Evkönyv, 1990* (Statistical yearbook, 1990) (Budapest: Központi Statisztikai Hivatal, 1990), 8–9.

   e. Ibid., 10.
   f. Ibid., 7.
   g. Ibid., 44.
   h. Ibid.
   i. Including evening and correspondence courses.
   j. *Evi Népszámlálás,* 19.
   k. Information from Központi Statisztikai Hivatal, 1991.
   l. *Evi Népszámlálás,* 32.
   m. Ibid.
   n. Ibid., 27.

Hungarian Women's Political Participation in the Transition to Democracy

KATALIN KONCZ

Modern Hungarian history is composed of a series of dramatic transformations, from some 40 years of state socialism and one-party rule to a new democratic, multiparty system. Women's political participation may best be understood through a detailed account of the change in representative institutions from the communist era to the democratic regime. While long-lasting dissent was vital in creating the new system, a crucial component of the change was the re-creation of legislatures as democratic arenas. In many ways these new institutions, especially the national Parliament, are leading the process of consolidation of democracy. In the first part of this chapter I recount the changes in the political system and the role women have played in it. I then discuss why formal structural change is not sufficient to guarantee women an equal place in the new democracy. In the last section I speculate on the future of women in a democratic Hungary.

The Republic of Hungary was proclaimed in 1946, but communists took de facto control in 1947 and established the Hungarian People's

Republic in 1949. The constitution of 1949 (amended in 1972) declared that all power in the nation belonged to the working people and that the bulk of the means of production was publicly owned. In reality, communists controlled all levels of society and government through the Communist Party.[1] Under this dictatorship, democracy prevailed in name only. The communist regime enforced the "social interests" of the state while subordinating the individual to the interests of central power. Protection of individual and group interests was feeble, because institutions established for this purpose did not play an important part in society.

The communist regime destroyed communities, as well as social norms and values. The population of 10.4 million is composed mainly of the dominant Magyars, with significant ethnic minority groups totaling about 10 percent of the population.[2] Some two-thirds of Hungarians are Roman Catholic, though religion was suppressed by the communist regime. The people did not accept the declared values of communism, and this crisis of morals and beliefs contributed to the socialization problems of youth, namely to the lack of identification with family, schools, or society. As a result, such social problems as juvenile delinquency, suicide, drug addiction, and alienation increased rapidly. Conditions of daily life were difficult, and people felt they had no say in changing these conditions in the private or public spheres. Every aspect of social life was gravely troubled because of one-party communist rule.[3]

REGIME TRANSFORMATION

Popular resistance to the socialist state steadily mounted, culminating in the widely supported 1956 October Revolution, which was brutally crushed by resident Soviet troops. Economic reforms were gradually begun in 1968, moving the country from a centrally planned economy to the most market-oriented economy in Eastern Europe. The standard of living slowly began to improve.

When the global economic crisis began in 1974, Hungary still had some breathing space. Internal policies kept the crisis outside the country's borders, and measures to prevent economic shocks were not yet necessary. But by 1977 the crisis could not be avoided. By world market standards, the insufficiencies of the Hungarian economy, the structural problems that had accumulated for years, and the lack of progress in economic reform were revealed.

The population's social and economic security was shattered. A rapid increase in prices was followed by stagnation and, later, by a fall in real wages. As a result of years of problems, the rate of inflation is now higher than 40 percent. The current debt of U.S. $20 billion poses nearly insoluble difficulties for stabilizing the economy. One-third of the population lives below the poverty level. In particular, old-age pensioners and families with several children have far worse living conditions than before.

As dissatisfaction among the people increased, the role of the political opposition intensified within and outside the Magyar Szocialista Munkáspárt (Hungarian Socialist Workers' Party),

and the forces of reform became stronger. The dictatorship weakened, and in 1989 it was unable to maintain itself. When the wave of democracy began to sweep across Eastern Europe, Hungary was able to undergo a bloodless revolution.

New parties formed the starting point for the move toward free elections. At the end of 1989, 19 parties were registered; in February 1990 there were 65.[4] On 25 March 1990 the first free elections were held. The number of parties decreased in the election period, when 39 parties reported their intentions to take part in the election drive and 28 parties actually fielded candidates.[5]

As a result of the elections held on 25 March, political events in Hungary took an unexpected turn. The Hungarian Republic was transformed into a multiparty parliamentary unitary state on 8 April 1990. The 386 members of Parliament are now elected to five-year terms.

The new electoral system was built from below, with voters casting ballots both for individuals and for parties instead of choosing from a slate of candidates picked by the central party. Of the total parliamentary membership, 176 members are elected from the same number of individual electoral districts (divided among 19 counties and Budapest); 120 members are elected from parties' territorial lists and 90 from a national party list. Thus the majority of deputies (210 members) have their charge from the parties and the minority (176 members) directly from the voters.

In the first round of elections, 65 percent of eligible voters participated. Only five people were elected because the requirement was for individuals to obtain 50 percent plus one vote.[6] In the second round a simple majority was enough for the person to obtain a mandate. Six parties won representation in the Parliament.[7] The center and right parties did best in the first elections: the ruling center Hungarian Democratic Forum (24.7 percent), the classical liberal Association of Free Democrats (21.4 percent), the rural-based Independent Smallholder Party (11.4 percent), the Hungarian Socialist Party (10.9 percent), the Association of Young Democrats (9.0 percent), and the Democratic-Christian People's Party (6.5 percent).[8] No other parties reached the 4 percent vote necessary for parliamentary participation.

Election of local authorities was held in fall 1990. The first round of voting on 30 September (in which a candidate needed 50 percent plus one vote to win) was decisive only in small settlements and in several cities or districts. The final results, decided on 14 October, thus completed the change of political power.

Women did not fare particularly well in the first democratic elections. Twenty-six women were elected to Parliament, constituting 6.7 percent of parliamentarians. In Europe only nine countries had lower proportions of women in Parliament than Hungary. In contrast, in the early 1980s in Hungary almost one-third of the members of Parliament were women. Even in the last single-party election before the regime change, 21.0 percent of the MPs were women. Only in the 1990 local elections did women begin to approach these levels of representation, with 16.8 percent of newly elected mayors being women.

Women in Parliament do not have positions of leadership. In 1990, during the first period of the democratic regime, there were no female ministers and only three women among the 33 under secretaries. In 1991 there was one female minister without portfolio in the government and one woman among the under secretaries.

Similarly, there is no institution, office, or even expert group within the government to deal specifically with the status of women. More than once the Magyar Nők Szövetsége (Association of Hungarian Women), an umbrella group of new women's organizations, has recommended that an office or expert council be established in or attached to the government. But reducing the national debt and solving economic problems are the priorities for the new government. The recent grave situation of the Hungarian economy makes this understandable to many.

The proportion of women elected in both the old and new regimes must be analyzed not only in terms of numbers but also on the basis of interest representation. Under the old regime, many women were elected only to improve statistics; they did not demonstrate their abilities or their commitment to their electors. The members of Parliament were elected by the public, but the party organization had an important role in the selection of candidates.[9] Therefore loyalty to the party was stronger than loyalty to group interests. The former president of the communist women's group, Magyar Nők Országos Tanácsa (National Council of Hungarian Women), rarely spoke in the Parliament, even though any issue discussed there would involve the interests of women. Under the pressure of the Inter-Parliamentary Union, a women's group of MPs was even established, but it did not actively work for the protection of women's interests.

Whereas the communist system guaranteed the existence of a visible group of women parliamentarians, the system of free elections with competing candidates does not favor women. In the 1985 single-party elections 28 percent of the candidates and 21 percent of those elected were women.[10] In the 1990 democratic elections the proportion of women in the individual electoral districts (where the voters directly elect the MPs) decreased radically to 7.2 percent of candidates and 2.8 percent (a total of five) of those elected.[11] The voters played a more important role in the low proportion of women in Parliament than did the parties. It seems that the parties expected women to be less successful in the individual electoral districts, so (except for the Young Democrats) they presented fewer women candidates in the individual electoral districts than on their national lists. Women were relatively successful in the individual electoral districts in the first round of elections, but in the second round, women were generally defeated.

The parties have shown more confidence in women than the voters.[12] Therefore the probability of getting into Parliament by means of the national party list was slightly better for women than for men. The proportion of women elected to Parliament by local party lists (8.3 percent) and by the national party list (15.5 percent) is greater than that of women elected directly by the voters (2.8 percent).[13] More than 80 percent of female representatives won seats in Parliament by party lists—29.6 percent by local party lists (eight women) and 51.9 percent by national party lists (14 women)—and only 18.5 percent by direct election (five women).[14] Yet in most cases no woman candidate was elected when the other competitors were men. This was due partly to the differences in the hierarchical position of men and women in the economy but also to justifiable reservations and unjustifiable biases on the part of voters.

The meaning of party identification and membership during this early stage of the transition to democracy is uncertain. The proportion of women in the newly established parties ranges from roughly the same to lower than the proportion of women in the Hungarian Socialist Workers' Party, in which 30.5 percent of members were female. Political activities under the one-party system were formalistic, and a significant proportion of party members took little part. The use of passive participants to improve statistics was a product of this political system, which created a favorable appearance without the risk of real activity. The single-party system did not provide an arena for the political participation of the masses, male or female. Even so, women party members in the old regime had little power: no women were secretaries of the Central Committee during the past 20 years, and women comprised fewer than 20 percent of the members of the Political Committee and the Central Committee in 1989. In contrast, the highest proportion of women in the new parties is found in the Democratic-Christian People's Party (37 percent) and the lowest in the Independent Smallholder Party (19 percent) as of March 1991.[15] The proportion of women in the top leadership is low, but there are no specific data available.

In Hungary, popular opinion supports the practices of parties in promoting men in leadership positions. Electors believe that because of practical experience men can perform better as representatives than women, who are too burdened with family affairs and household chores to have enough time left for the tasks expected of

an MP. Such a difference in performance is indeed typical between women with children (especially small children) and men. Electors generalize, however, and their biased image is also used to judge women who are free from such burdens and are able to do the job. Therefore improving women's participation in the political decision-making process requires the creation of conditions to decrease their burdens in the struggle for life. This is the responsibility of political decision makers: the legislature and the government. More favorable conditions would improve women's opportunities so they would be able to prove their capabilities. The successes of women in political life would, in turn, transform public opinion, which would recognize women's aspirations as legitimate. This process will take a long time in the case of a country like Hungary, which is in economic crisis and political transformation.

PARTICIPATION OF WOMEN IN POLITICS

To evaluate female participation in political life, the content of participation should be defined as active, policy-forming contributions. In nondemocratic countries, real participation was replaced by formal participation, and statistics (particularly about women) hid the truth, namely the absence of genuine opportunity.

Four principal factors determine how successful the participation of women will be in Hungary's transition to democracy. First, institutions need to represent women's interests. Second, political leadership needs to be committed to eliminating overt and covert discrimination against women and must act accordingly. Third, social, economic, and cultural conditions must change to encourage women's participation. Fourth, women's political behavior and their demand for participation must be developed. It is evident that significant women's participation in formal representation channels will be difficult to ensure, at least in the short run.

WOMEN'S INSTITUTIONS

The struggle for the emancipation of women was a product of the eighteenth century, when the civil transformation of women's status began. Until World War I the major branches of the women's movement were social democratic, feminist, and Christian. After the war the socialist women's movement began. The movements obtained their most far-reaching results in promoting the education of women. Before World War II, women's suffrage was limited to only one-fifth of women.[16] In 1945 all women in Hungary won the right to vote and to stand for election.

Under the communist regime the women's movement was not organized from below, and the mass of women never had well-developed institutions that represented their interests as women. The Magyar Nők Demokratikus Szövetsége (Democratic Union of Hungarian Women) was formed in 1945 on the initiative of the Magyar Kommunista Párt (Hungarian Communist Party). In 1948 the party united all women's organizations and closed down the noncommunist groups. After the revolution of 1956 the Magyar Nők Országos Tanácsa (National Council of Hungarian Women) took the place of the Union. The National Council of Hungarian Women functioned in the framework of the party-state—that is, the state interwoven with the single party. The council undoubtedly contributed to improved working conditions, and it developed options for childbirth and child care. Nonetheless, the party-state system created a field of action only for a small elite composed of political and economic leaders and the leaders of official women's committees. The political system dictated from above, and its rules had to be followed. It lacked the direct contribution of women and only indirectly protected their interests.

The first new women's group organized, in March 1989, was Esélyegyenlőség Társaság (Society for Equal Opportunity), now a member of the Association of Hungarian Women. Its approximately 100 members are primarily intellectuals. With the democratization of society many independent or party-based women's groups have been founded, such as the Association of Hungarian Girl Scouts, the Group of Greens Against Violence, the Association of Social Workers, the National Association of Entrepreneur Women, and the Democratic-Christian Women's Movement. Little information exists about their activities and size.

In 1989, as a result of the democratization process, the Association of Hungarian Women was established as the legal successor of the National Council of Hungarian Women. The association defines itself as an independent organization with the goal of realizing social emancipation and equal opportunity for women. In 1991, 651 individual members and 22 organizations constituted the association. The main role of the new women's association has been to protect women's interests in the negotiations of the national roundtable that lead to democratic elections and in statements on parliamentary propositions: personal income taxes, family law, and abortion. The association organizes lecture series and makes proposals on family, household, and child-rearing issues. It has also developed informational materials, undertaken publicity campaigns to encourage women's participation in elections, and organized solidarity actions.

The newly organized women's groups remain weak, however, because civil society is reemerging more slowly than are political institutions, which have little commitment to women's presence. These groups are also substantially isolated from one another and they lack a mass base and popular influence. They have yet to find their place in the political arena, and their national outreach and effects are still limited.

Older women's groups, like those associated with the Communist Party and its trade union, have not bridged the two political systems any more successfully. In the former regime, the majority of gainfully employed women were members of the single trade union, Szakszervezetek Országos Tanácsa (National Council of Trade Unions). But within the framework of the system of political institutions ruled by a single party, trade union activities did not offer either a real political arena for the masses or possibilities for validating their interests. The single trade union had no profile independent of the ruling party. In the new democratic regime, three new trade unions have begun to form. The largest in terms of membership is the new Magyar Szakszervezetek Orszagos Szövetsége, or MSzOSz (National Federation of Hungarian Trade Unions), with 73 member organizations (2.7 million members). Next in size are the eight trade unions established after 1987. The smallest are the groups that existed earlier but did not join the MSzOSz.[17]

Looking just at trade union statistics for the old National Council of Trade Unions, women's trade union participation appeared to be similar to that of men. In the leadership, however—especially at the highest levels—their presence was much smaller. Women made up 45 percent of trade union leaders before 1990, but that statistic hides the fact that female leaders worked at lower levels (55 percent of shop stewards were women) while their participation in the top leadership was negligible.[18] In the multiparty system the new independent trade unions are seeking their place, but there are still no women in the top ranks.

POLITICAL LEADERSHIP

In the absence of well-developed institutions representing women's interests, political leadership becomes important in determining women's position in the new political system. The former communist and current democratic constitutions both declared that women and men have equal opportunities and forbade any discrimination based on sex.[19] In practice these provisions have not been enforced, and there are no penalties for discrimination. Theoretically women may turn to the constitutional court for redress, but as yet none have. In practice the disadvantages of women are still being re-created continuously in both open and hidden forms in the spheres of politics, the economy, culture, and the family.[20] This duality perpetuates the contradiction between legally declared equal rights and lack of actual equal opportunity.

The leaders of the old regime took several measures to eliminate these disadvantages. The emancipation of women always constituted part of the communist ideology, based on the economic need for female labor.[21] In 1970 a many-sided party and governmental decision on the position of women outlined what needed to be done.[22] But the success of implementation was limited by two factors. The necessary social conditions linked to the double role of women—like flexible forms of employment and widespread cheap household help—were absent. In addition, the political system did not motivate the executives within institutions or enterprises to implement equal opportunity policies. Without proper enforcement there was an expectation of only formal compliance. Employers did not readily hire women or promote them, citing the frequent absences of women with small children and the career interruptions that arise from women's family obligations.

None of the national leaders, parties, nor broad political institutions like trade unions has provided vigorous leadership on women's issues. None has made a serious policy initiative on women's status in the new political system. Women's issues are considered secondary in democratic politics just as they were in the communist regime. Economic crises preoccupy leaders, and it appears that the new democracy will be established without any strong personal support of women's interests by the men crafting the new political rules.

SOCIAL, CULTURAL, AND ECONOMIC CONDITIONS

Without strong support from leaders or well-developed institutions to represent their interests, women depend on favorable social conditions to overcome their disadvantages in political participation. The most important social preconditions for the political participation of women are their educational and employment levels, infrastructure that coordinates women's double role in employment and household work, division of labor within the family, cultural and religious traditions influencing the possibility of equal opportunity, and the conviction of society—both women and men—that equal opportunity would bring advantages to all. At present many of these preconditions of equal participation are absent or insufficiently developed.

During recent decades the educational level of women has increased significantly, approaching that of men. In 1990, 41.0 percent of men and 38.3 percent of women age 18 and older had finished secondary school.[23] The picture is even more favorable when the employed segment of the population is considered, since here women achieve higher levels of education than men. In 1990, 33.1 percent of employed men and 45.1 percent of employed women had finished at least secondary school.[24] Slightly more women in the work force were university graduates (11.7 percent) than were men (11.5 percent).[25] There were significant differences by generation: the educational level of young women exceeded that of men.

This relatively strong educational background could be expected to create favorable conditions for political activism. But educational achievements do not readily translate into skilled or professional occupational attainments and economic security for Hungarian women, and more than 75 percent of men have some kind of skill qualifications, compared with only 44 percent of women.[26] It is the absence of these practical advantages that more directly limits women's political activism. Women's employment is high (84 percent of women age 15 to 54 in 1990),[27] and the majority of women are employed full time, with 7.6 percent employed part time.[28] Yet women are concentrated in workplaces traditionally considered female—such as the garment, textile, and leather industries, trade, economics, postal services, and some medical fields—and within these occupations the majority of women hold low-ranking jobs.

Because of women's place in the occupational hierarchy, their failure to earn equal pay for equivalent work, and their need to interrupt their employment to give birth and care for young children, women in Hungary earn 20 to 40 percent less than do men.[29] In 1989 white-collar women earned 61 percent of men's salaries, and blue-collar women earned 76 percent. Although the earnings of three-quarters of women are below the national average, this is the case for only one-third of men.[30]

Thus women do not obtain the same place in the social world through their employment as do men. It is in the competitive sphere of high-level positions that men learn the norms and behavior patterns that are indispensable on the political scene. But women are rarely found in these positions. The importance of this preparation can be seen by the occupations of members of Parliament in the last elections of the communist regime and the first elections of the democratic regime. Three-quarters of the members of Parliament elected in 1985 held leading positions in their work.[31] The Parliament elected in 1990 is an "intellectual parliament."[32] The majority of representatives work in arts (24.7 percent), legal (21.0 percent), technical (11.8 percent), and economic (11.5 percent) professions with university graduate education.

But it is not just women's place in the economy that disadvantages them politically. The great difficulty in balancing paid work and domestic work also limits women's participation. The social division of labor, which requires women to play two roles, means that most women carry too great a burden to participate actively. Considering the time they spend commuting between home and work, many women work 12 to 14 hours daily.[33] The two roles—either of which could require full-time work—can be accomplished only with the help of society. In the absence of such assistance, women can fulfill these roles only at the expense of their free time and by neglecting the role they could play in political life.

Hungary provides an inadequate system of supports for women trying to fulfill their double obligations. The economic need to work full time ties down women at the workbench or desk for more than eight hours a day. In 1986, 30 percent of working women spent from 30 to 60 minutes traveling to and from work and 9 percent spent more than 90 minutes.[34] Other unfavorable conditions for reconciling the two roles of women include the lack of choice between paid work and domestic work; lack of flexible employment for women with small children; lack of help with household chores; and high prices. Although the mechanization of households has greatly increased during past decades, the recent decline in living standards has meant that people have more difficulty replacing outdated appliances.

The most important condition of female employment and thus of female political participation is help for child rearing. Mothers are entitled to 24 weeks of maternity leave with full salary.[35] After this period they can take advantage of a wage-adjusted child-care allowance (65 or 75 percent of salary) if they remain at home. Following the child's second birthday women draw a flat-rate child-care allowance that varies with the number of children. The second allowance is significantly lower than the first. Either the mother or father is eligible for both allowances after the child's first year.[36]

After the child reaches three years of age the role of institutions becomes more important. More than half of all children below age four go to a crèche or kindergarten. Three-quarters of four-year-olds and four-fifths of five-year-olds spend the day in kindergarten. Yet child-care centers are responsible only for the physical care of children; they do not assist in a child's successful socialization. The conditions of institutional child care are worsening; crèches and kindergartens are closing down because of financial problems. For school-age children, after-school day-care centers for the hours when parents work have an important role, especially for young children. By age 14, however, only 27 percent of schoolchildren are in day-care centers; 39 percent are without supervision after school.[37] They are the latchkey children, alone at home or gathering in the streets or in subway stations.

During the past decades the entry of women into the labor market has been an especially asymmetrical process. Although the majority of women joined the labor force, their responsibilities inside the family were not reduced proportionately. Men did not take an equal share in the work to be done in the family and the household. In 1986 women age 15 to 69 spent an average of 271 minutes daily looking after their children and working in and around the home, while men spent only 97 minutes on these activities. Women spent an average of 205 minutes on domestic chores and maintenance, 26 minutes on shopping and other errands, and 40 minutes on child care. (Comparable amounts for men were 70, 15, and 12 minutes, respectively.)[38]

In the past, traditions inhibited the transformation of the division of labor in the family. The slowly developing democratization of the family was later halted by economic stagnation and the deterioration of living standards. One salary has always been insufficient to support a family because of the low level of wages. This fact was the most important factor in the extension of female employment. Recently, because of decreasing incomes, men have been compelled to work overtime. It has become the norm for men to work 12, 14, or even 16 hours a day. Consequently, household work and child rearing have again become primarily the responsibility of women, thus limiting their participation in political life.

Traditions in Hungary limit the possibility for women to have equal economic and political opportunities. The majority of Hungarians have conservative views regarding gender issues. Biases against women survive both because of the disadvantages women face over their objective situation and because of their burden of work. Public opinion still holds that the traditional division of labor between the sexes is related to differences in women's and men's abilities. Consequently, many men (and women) believe that women are simply unable to or less able than men to perform certain types of work, especially those tasks that have traditionally been done by men. This is manifested in the career barriers faced by women, lower pay, and mistrust of women political candidates. All these limit women's career ambitions and the establishment of genuinely equal opportunities.

The general public has as yet not realized the advantages of equal opportunities for women and men. Even now equality of the sexes has not been in the interest of either the political or the party leadership, and in the absence of democracy leaders were not compelled to integrate women's specific interests into the world of politics. Equality of opportunity for women has always been dependent on economic interests and requirements. In the past the economy could not function without female labor, but in politics it was not considered important to utilize female capabilities because it would have been necessary to provide women with the missing social supports. This would have required both money and energy, and both are still lacking. Moreover, the existing system of norms in the political world will not easily make allowances for women's responsibilities for child rearing.[39]

WOMEN'S ATTITUDES AND BEHAVIOR

Women's own attitudes are the final precondition for their political participation. In the past most women did not choose to participate actively in political life. The few who wanted to participate often did not have the time and energy, and fewer still finally became part of the political decision-making process. These women had favorable family conditions (like older children or none at all and family or outside help for household chores).

Another reason for the political passivity of women was the masculine world of politics, in which a woman's chances of successful adaptation were limited. It was not that men were more suited to political life; rather, the age-old practices of the division of labor meant that men, not women, learned the skills required for politics. This situation did not change fundamentally over the past 40 years, when women's employment became widespread. The world of politics is ruled by rough rationalities, by interest relations, and by competition, with no room for emotions. The organization and maintenance of the home requires and develops different abilities, which—with a few exceptions—make it very difficult for women to become successful politicians as long as the traditional definitions of politics are the only ones allowed.

PROSPECTS

In Hungary, issues concerning women have not been the focus of the attention or the actions of social leaders. The benefits given to women as employees and as mothers were never initiated by politics but by economic, employment-related, or demographic considerations. In the absence of democracy the single-party dictatorship did not allow the interests of different layers of society to be revealed and addressed. The bureaucratic system, supported by dictatorial methods used to perpetuate political power, lacked human-centered approaches and practices. In the absence of social management centered on people, the one-party bureaucratic system did not solve the problems of women or those of young people, the elderly, or the poor, but it made decisions that were only formally implemented.

The underlying motivation for political decisions regarding women was not improvement of their status but employment compulsion or the desire to affect the size of the population. In the single-party dictatorship there was no place for real social movements. The disintegration of communities (such as fellowships, associations, and clubs), the atomization of society, and the blocking of possibilities for the formation of interest groups were basic preconditions for the operation of the one-party dictatorship.[40] The emergence of a pluralistic and democratic society is a precondition for attention to be paid to the problems of women. However, as a consequence of the practice of the past 40 years, women still remain in the background of the transformation of political and social life, if only temporarily.

The most important political interest of women in Hungary today is the redivision of power. Society, which is becoming pluralistic and democratic, drives women toward the political periphery. In the absence of a real and effective system of safeguarding women's interests, this tendency will increase. Political activities require plenty of time and energy, but in Hungary today women—and men—are busy with the struggle for life and for the maintenance of living standards. The generations of the past 40 years condemned to political passivity are too busy or not in the mood to take an active part in political life. People are disappointed and tired.

Although the newly formed parties have a small number of women leaders, the new Association of Hungarian Women, which declared itself to be independent of the political parties, is finding its place in the changed political battlefield only with difficulty. The present economic conditions and political climate are not favorable for the representation of women's interests. Political activities are concentrated on the elections and on the redistribution of political power, so an organization that declares itself independent of political parties has no place in this political scene.

The political parties did not recognize the significance of the concerns of women, even in the elections. A survey by the Association of Hungarian Women of the 65 political parties found that in 1989 only one had a complex, comprehensive political program on women.[41] At least eight parties had independent women's sections, but none as yet has a special character. None of the parties has even tried to gain the confidence of women, yet representing their interests could perhaps lead to victory. The recent experience with elections suggests that women will be left behind; even women voters were less likely to vote for female candidates. During the elections female solidarity could not be expected to gain ground, but rather the opposite was likely to happen, whether from the ancient sexual rivalry among women, deteriorated human relationships under dictatorship, or envy of successful women.

So long as female interests do not reach the political battlefield through any channel, women will be left out of the redistribution of power. Although the most important issue in the democratization process is to let the interests of many different sectors of society come to the surface and be validated, a society that is becoming democratic paradoxically pushes to the periphery the disadvantaged strata, including women.

The realization of the importance of the concerns of women is not helped by the media, which are not interested in women's issues on their own merits, nor by political scientists, who have become active in Hungary only recently and who have concentrated mainly on the study of the features of the single-party dictatorship. At the time of elections political scientists studied the realities and the consequences of free elections, and now they are interested in the policy of parties and in the competition of power. Only one study refers to the fact that in Hungary women are politically more passive than men.

In Hungary today it is difficult to make even short-term forecasts. The country is facing economic problems: the size of the debt surpasses its load-bearing capacity; inflation seems to be impossible to stop; the unemployment rate is increasing, which may well drive large numbers of women from their jobs; and living conditions and standards are deteriorating. All these factors affect the situation of the family, including women.

The democratization process is charged with the features of the past dictatorship. Strong emotions make people neglect the rules of the democratic game. The debates in Parliament are passionate, and personal remarks are made frequently. The opposition often provokes pseudodebates, thereby slowing legislation; for the most part it favors the overthrow of the new government. However, the more constructive Association of Young Democrats, also an opposition party, proposes a six-party reconciliation instead.[42] A significant proportion of the population does not really understand the rapidly changing events. The power struggles have been concentrated on the elections, then on forming a government. Impatience manifests itself first in opposition to the government, yet the grave problems accumulated during four decades cannot be solved in one year. In these circumstances the problems of women are left in the shadows.

In the long run, the transformation of the political norms, the integration of the interests and values of women, the emergence of social conditions encouraging female participation, and better preparation of women to enter previously male-dominated domains could make for more successful political integration of women. Social support of domestic responsibilities and societal encouragement of women's participation can develop only in tandem; the absence of one would only hamper the other. Politics built on an unchanged system of norms would either continue to leave the majority of women out of the mainstream or would make them adapt to traditionally masculine norms. The absence of social support and of efforts to develop education, skills, and aspirations for women would limit women's integration in politics.

The humanization of politics—a new era in which people are the objectives and not the tool of political actions—can be a long-term goal of a just and peaceful society only, and for its realization an imperative precondition is the increased participation of women.[43] The implementation of change is easier and simpler when approached from the aspects of improving social conditions and developing female talents, skills, and aspirations. Under this policy the examples of successful women—which should be publicized in the media—will be of great importance.

In the next decade Hungarian society and families will face considerable difficulties that will divert attention from women's issues. The conversion to a market economy, privatization, and the repayment of debts all give priority to economic problems. Economic productivity will slowly improve but for the time being the standard of living will decline. Unemployment will rise quickly. In this context the situation of the family—and of individual women and men—will deteriorate. Improvement of the economic situation likely will be achieved no earlier than the middle of the 1990s.

The democratization of society will progress. Different kinds of women's groups (inside parties and as independent movements) will develop to protect women's interests. The women's movement will force the government to create institutional channels for protection of female interests and social conditions for the participation of women in the political decision-making process. The experiences of successful women will increase possibilities and ambitions will grow. By the end of century Hungarian society will discover itself at last, recover from forty years of dictatorship, regain its values, and progress in its development as a nation.

NOTES

1. From 1944–48 it was Magyar Kommunista Párt (Hungarian Communist Party); from 1948–56, Magyar Dolgozók Pártja (Hungarian Workers' Party); and from 1956 on, the Magyar Szocialista Munkáspárt (Hungarian Socialist Workers Party).

2. On the basis of surveys conducted by the nationality organizations 7 to 10 percent of the population belong to ethnic minorities.

3. Katalin Koncz, ed., *Létünk válsága* (Crisis of our life) (Manuscript, 1987).

4. One segment of these parties is the reorganized "historical parties," such as the Social Democrats, the Christian parties, and the Independent Smallholder party. New political parties such as the Hungarian Democratic Forum, the Association of Free Democrats, and the Association of Young Democrats have been formed. Representatives of some social strata define themselves as parties, for example, the Small Pensioners Party and the Party of Generations. Some lobbies have their own parties, including the Greens, the Supporters of the City, and the Health Party. László Medveczky, ed., *Szabadon választott: Parlamenti almanach, 1990* (Elections without restriction: Parliamentary almanac, 1990) (Budapest: Idengenforgalmi Propaganda és Kiadó Vállalat, 1990), 27–34.

5. Ibid., 23, 9.

6. Tibor Császár, György Branyó and Zoltánné Fábián, *Választások Magyarországon (1990. március 25., április 8.)* (Elections in Hungary, 25 March and 8 April 1990) (Budapest: Magyar Távirati Iroda, 1990), 5.

7. Arranging parties according to ideology is difficult. Earlier values have been upset, and all six parties have both left and right elements, as well as a plebeian people's wing and a liberal urban wing. In general, the parties can be loosely arrayed from left to right as follows: the Hungarian Socialist Party, the Association of Young Democrats, the Association of Free Democrats, the Hungarian Democratic Forum (the ruling government party), the Democratic-Christian People's Party, and the Independent Smallholder Party.

8. Medveczky, *Szabadon választott,* 44. The ruling center Hungarian Democratic Forum tries to mix liberal ideas with national traditions. The Association of Free Democrats professes classical liberal ideas.

9. István Kukorelli, *Így választottunk* (So we elected. . .) (Budapest: Eötvös Lóránd Tudományegyetem Allam és Jogtudományi Kar Politikatudományi Tanszékcsoport, 1988), 23.

10. Ibid., 88.

11. Calculation based on information in "Az egyéni választókerületekben a második fordulóba jutott képviselők névsora" (The list of deputies in the second round of elections in the individual electoral districts), *Magyar Hirlap,* 28 March 1990, pp. 3–4; and Medveczky, *Szabadon választott,* 72–272.

12. Calculation based on "Pártok Országos választási listája" (The national electoral list of parties), *Magyar Nemzet,* 2 March 1990, pp. 6–7.

13. Calculation based on Medveczky, *Szabadon választott,* 72–272.

14. Ibid.

15. Information from Ibolya Újváry (Association of Hungarian Women), April 1991. There are no statistics concerning the ruling Hungarian Democratic Forum; I estimate that women make up about 30 percent of its membership.

16. N. Katalin Szegvári, *Út a nők egyenjogúságához* (Way to the emancipation of women) (Budapest: Kossuth Könyvkiadó, 1981), 18–176.

17. Trade union members number about 4 million. After MSzOSz, the most important are the Democratic League of Independent Trade Unions (130,000 members), the National Union of Workers' Councils (106,000), and Solidarity (75,000). The members of the third tier are generally professional groups. Information from Márta Dobos (Central School of National Federation of Hungarian Trade Unions).

18. Communication with the Association of Hungarian Women, April 1991.

19. The new Hungarian Constitution was declared in 1949 and modified in 1972. The new democracy created a constitution in 1990, which has been modified twice. Verbal communication with Vilmos Váradi, constitutional jurist, April 1991.

20. Katalin Koncz, *Nők a munkaeröpiacon* (Women in the labor market) (Budapest: Közgazdasági és Jogi Könyvkiadó, 1987), 392.

21. August Bebel, *A nő és a szocializmus* (The woman and socialism) (Budapest: Kossuth Könyvkiadó, 1976), 385; Friedrich Engels, *A család, a magántulajdon és az állam eredete* (The origin of family, private property and state), in Kossuth Könyvkiadó, ed., *Marx-Engels Selected Works,* vol. 3 (Budapest: Kossuth Könyvkiadó, 1975), 459–571; Marx-Engels-Lenin, *A nőkérdésröl és a családról* (About the woman question and the family) (Budapest: Kossuth Könyvkiadó, 1974), 223.

22. On the party: "A Magyar Szocialista Munkáspárt Központi Bizottságának állásfoglalása a nők politikai, gazdasági es szociális helyzetéről. 1970. februar 18–19" (Position of the Central Committee of the Hungarian Socialist Workers Party on the political, economic and social situation of women, 18–19 February 1970) in Vas Bankóné, ed., *Nőpolitikai Dokumentumok 1970–1980* (Documents of women's policy 1970–1980) (Budapest: Kossuth Könyvkiadó, 1981), 7–33. On the government: "A Magyar Forradalmi Munkás-Paraszt Kormány 1013/1970 (V. 10) számú határozata a nők gazdasági és szociális helyzetének megjavításáról" (Decision 1013/1970 [vol. 10] of the Hungarian Revolutionary Workers-Peasant Government about the improvement of economic and social conditions of women), ibid., 34–40.

23. Központi Statisztikai Hivatal Lakossági adatgyűjtések főosztálya, *1990: évi Népszámlálás: Összefoglaló adatok a 2%-os képviseleti minta alapján* (1990 Census: Survey on the basis of 2 percent pattern) (Budapest: Központi Statisztikai Hivatal, 1990), 24.

24. Ibid., 37.

25. Ibid.

26. Calculation based on data in Központi Statisztikai Hivatal Népesedésstatisztikai Főosztály, *Az 1984: évi Mikrocenzus adatai* (The data of 1984 microcensus) (Budapest: Központi Statisztikai Hivatal, 1985), 139–42.

27. Ibid, 27.

28. The most recent data are from 1982. Katalin Koncz, "Tények és érvek a részmunkaidős foglalkoztatás mellett" (Facts and arguments in favor of part-time employment), *Munkaügyi Szemle* (July 1985):1–6.

29. Központi Statisztikai Hivatal, *Statisztikai Évköyv 1989* (Statistical yearbook 1989) (Budapest: Központi Statisztikai Hivatal, 1990), 53.

30. Ibid. Calculation based on these data.

31. Kukorelli, *Igy választottunk,* 88.

32. Ferenc Pataki, "A rendszerváltás parlamentje" (The parliament of the change of the system), *Társadalmi Szemle* (January 1991):18.

33. Béla Falussy and István Harcsa, *Időmérleg 1977 es 1986 tavasza* (Spring 1977 and 1986 time budgets) (Budapest: Központi Statisztikai Hivatal, 1987), 118–19.

34. Information Department of the Central Statistical Office on Behalf of the Association of Hungarian Women, *Women's Position in Socialist Hungary* (Budapest: Information Department of the Central Statistical Office on Behalf of the Association of Hungarian Women, 1989), 53–54.

35. Ibid., 17.

36. Ibid.

37. Ibid., 21.

38. Falussy and Harcsa, *Időmérleg,* 16.

39. Béla Buda, "Női szerep—női szocializácio—női identitás" (Woman's role—woman's socialization—woman's identity), in Katalin Koncz, ed., *Nők és férfiak: Hiedelmek, tények* (Women and men: Beliefs and facts) (Budapest: Kossuth Könyvkiadó, 1985), 93–110.

40. Elemér Hankiss, *Társadalmi csapdák: Diagnózisok* (Social traps: Diagnosis) (Budapest: Magvetö Könyvkiadó, 1983), 114.

41. In 1989, the Social Democratic Party of Hungary had a complex program concerning women's policy. The

other parties included their women's program in the framework of social policy or concepts on social strata. Magyar Nők Szövetsége, *Tájékoztató a politikai pártok nő- és családpolitikai elképzeléseiről* (Guide to conceptions concerning women's and family policy of political parties) (Budapest: Magyar Nők Szövetsége, 1989), 1.

42. "Kormánybuktatás helyett hatpárti egyeztetést javasol a FIDESZ" (The Association of Young Democrats proposes reconciliation of six parties instead of overthrowing the government), *Esti Hírlap,* 28 March 1991, p. 1.

43. See Inter-Parliamentary Union, *Inter-Parliamentary Symposium on the Participation of Women in the Political and Parliamentary Decision Making Process* (Geneva: Inter-Parliamentary Union, 20–24 November 1989), 4.

▲ *India*

POLITICS

Type of Political System: democracy
  Sovereignty: republic
  Executive-Legislative System: parliamentary
Type of State: federal
Type of Party System: multiparty
Major Political Parties

NATIONAL PARTIES

Indian National Congress–Indira (INC-I), known as Congress (I): A direct descendant of the Indian National Congress founded in 1885 to give dynamism to the national movement for independence. The oldest party in India; in power at the center 1947–89 (except March 1977 to January 1980). Ideology of secularism, socialism, democracy, and nonalignment.

Communist Party of India (CPI): Established in 1925; the second oldest party. Cadre-based with mass fronts of labor, peasants, students, youth, and women. Ideological aim is to establish a socialist and democratic system; has strong links with the international socialist party. Pockets of influence in Kerala, West Bengal, Andhra Pradesh, and Bihar; has a wider base nationally. Tries to offer a left-democratic alternative to the Congress (I).

Communist Party of India (Marxist), or CPI(M): Emerged after the split in the Communist Party of India in 1964. Cadre-based with broad fronts; committed to a democratic socialist ideology. Strong power base in West Bengal, Kerala, and Tripura. Largest parliamentary partner of the left-democratic combination of the CPI(M), CPI, Forward Block, and Revolutionary Socialist Party.

Bharatiya Janata Party (BJP, Indian People's Party): Current manifestation of the former Jana Sangh; founded in 1980 after the breakup of the governing Janata Party coalition. Third largest party in the 1989 general elections. Stands for a liberal, secular, and democratic ideology but has close links with the National Voluntary Organization, Vishwa Hindu Parishad (World Hindu Council), the Bajrang Dal (a militant Hindu group), and Shiv Sena (Army of Lord Shiva).

Janata Dal (People's Party): Became a political party in 1988 with the merger of Janata (People), Jan Morcha (People's Front), and Lok Dal (People's Party). A component of the anti–Congress Rashtriya Morcha (National Front), a 1988 combination of seven opposition parties (four national-level centrist parties—including the three that subsequently joined to form Janata Dal—and three regional groups). Opposes corruption in high places.

Bahujan Samaj Party (BSP, Party of the Majority): An organized force of the most oppressed people in Indian society, the scheduled castes. Formed in 1984; disturbed the traditional support base of the Congress Party. Entered Parliament in the 1989 elections.

REGIONAL PARTIES

Dravida Munnetra Kazhagam (DMK, or Dravidian Progressive Federation): Sprang from the reformist anti-Brahmanical Dravidian movement in 1949. Power base is the state of Tamil Nadu, where it was in power from 1967 to 1977 and again after the 1989 elections. Main plank is anti-Hindu, anti-North, and anti-Brahmanical.

All India Anna Dravida Munnetra Kazhagam (AIADMK, or All India Dravidian Progressive Federation): Leftist offshoot of the DMK; emerged in 1972. In power in Tamil Nadu from 1977 to 1987. Personalized organization founded by the film star M. G. Ramachandran.

Telugu Desam (Telugu Land): Launched in 1982 by N. T. Rama Rave, a film star from Andhra Pradesh. Emphasis on self-determination for 60 million Telugu-speaking Andhraites. Partner of the 1992 National Front center government; in power in Andhra Pradesh from 1983 to 1989 (with a brief break in 1984).

Asom Gana Parishad (AGP, Assam People's Council): Present ruling party of Assam; came into existence in 1985 in the wake of antiforeigner agitation and the Assam accord. Partner of the National Front center government.

National Conference (NC): The All Jammu and Kashmir Muslim Conference, founded in 1931, was converted into the National Conference in 1939; represents the aspirations of the people of Kashmir Valley. In power from 1977 to 1989 and in alliance with the Congress (I) since 1984.

Shiromani Akali Dal (SAD, Akali Religious Party): Formed in 1920; represents the interests of Sikhs. Formed the government on its own in 1985; in power from 1967 to 1969, from 1969 to 1971, and from 1977 to 1980 in coalition with parties like Jana Sangh, CPI, and Janata. Split into various factions; that led by the militant "Mann group" won most of the seats in the 1989 elections to the Lok Sabha.

Year Women Granted Right to Vote:
1929/1950[a]
Year Women Granted Right to Stand for Election: 1929/1950[b]
Percentage of Women in the Legislature[c]
Lower House: 5.2%
Upper House: 9.8%
Percentage of Electorate Voting for Highest Elected Office in Most Recent Election (1991): not available

DEMOGRAPHICS
Population: 844,000,000[d]
Percentage of Population in Urban Areas
Overall: 26.3%
Female: 25.6%
Male: 26.9%

Percentage of Population Below Age 15:
35.6%[e]
Birthrate (per 1,000 population): 27[f]
Maternal Mortality Rate (per 100,000 live births): 340
Infant Mortality Rate (per 1,000 live births): 95[g]
Mortality Rate for Children Under Five (per 1,000 live births): 149
Average Household Size: 5.6
Mean Age at First Marriage
Female: 18.7
Male: 23.4
Life Expectancy[h]
Female: 61.7
Male: 60.6

EDUCATION
Ratio of Female to Male Enrollment
First-Level Education (1980/1984): 65
Second-Level Education: not available
Third-Level Education (1979): 35
Literacy Rate[i]
Female: 39.4%
Male: 63.9%

ECONOMY
Gross National Product per Capita: U.S. $340[j]
Percentage of Labor Force in Agriculture: 72.0%
Distribution of Agricultural Workers by Sex
Female: 30.9%
Male: 69.1%
Economically Active Population by Sex
Female: 30.7%
Male: 84.3%

a. In 1929 women were enfranchised on the same limited terms as men; in 1950 universal adult enfranchisement was granted.

b. See note a.

c. Subash C. Kashyap, "The Ninth Lok Sabha: Socioeconomic Analysis of Membership," *Journal of Parliamentary Information* 36 (1990): 14–43.

d. Barbara Crossette, "India's Population Put at 844 Million," *New York Times,* 26 March 1991.

e. *Report of the Expert Committee on Population Projections for India Up to 2001* (New Delhi: Government of India).

f. Ibid.

g. *World Development Report* (Washington, D.C.: World Bank, 1991).

h. *Report of the Expert Committee on Population Projections.*

i. J. C. Aggarwal and N. K. Chowdhry, *Census of India, 1991* (New Delhi: S. Chand, 1991), 45.

j. *World Development Report.*

Women's Political Engagement in India: Some Critical Issues

HEM LATA SWARUP,
NIROJ SINHA,
CHITRA GHOSH,
AND PAM RAJPUT

India is a nation of 844 million located in the heart of Asia. For approximately 150 years during the nineteenth and early twentieth centuries it was under British colonial rule. Since independence in 1947 the 25 states and seven union territories have been organized into a federal system. In practice, however, the governmental balance of power swings strongly toward the national government, with the states organized primarily on a linguistic basis. The national government has the power to take over state governments if they are not maintaining order to its satisfaction.

The national government consists of a president and a bicameral legislature: the Rajya Sabha (council of states) and the more powerful Lok Sabha (house of the people). The president's role, much like that of the British monarch, is primarily symbolic. The national policy-making executive is the prime minister, the leader of the majority party in the Lok Sabha. If there is no majority party, the prime minister must command majority support in the Lok Sabha. Though formally appointed by the president, the prime minister and the prime minister's advisers (the Council of Ministers) are accountable to the Lok Sabha.

The Lok Sabha has 545 members elected from single-member constituencies based on population. Of these, 119 seats are reserved for members of the "scheduled" tribes and castes, the groups that historically have been the most marginalized members of Indian society. These reserved seats are divided among the states by the proportion of their population that falls into these categories. The majority of the 250-member Rajya Sabha are elected by the state legislatures, with 12 of its members nominated by the president. Although the Lok Sabha and the Rajya Sabha have similar powers, the membership of the prime minister in the Lok Sabha and its control over money bills means that the Lok Sabha is the primary arena of governmental decision making.

Since independence India has mostly been ruled under democratic procedures. The sole exception was from June 1975 through February 1977, when then Prime Minister Indira Gandhi, faced by Jap Prakash Narain's "total revolution" mass movement and the High Court judgment declaring her election null and void, declared a state of emergency.

Although India ostensibly has a multiparty

system, the Indian National Congress, now often called Congress (I)—an outgrowth of the Congress movement that led the fight for independence—has controlled the central government and dominated national politics for most of the period since independence was achieved; only twice, in 1977–79 and 1989–91, has there been a non-Congress government. Currently there are four other major political parties. The Janata Dal, a centrist anti–Congress (I) coalition, is generally regarded as the second most powerful political party. To the left and less influential are two communist parties, the Communist Party of India (Marxist) and the Communist Party of India. The major party emerging on the right is the pro-Hindu nationalist Bharatiya Janata Party (Indian People's Party). There are also several regionally based parties that challenge the Congress (I)'s hegemony at the state level. The most powerful of these are the All India Anna Dravida Munnetra Kazhagam (All India Dravidian Progressive Federation) in Tamil Nadu, Telugu Desam (Telugu Land) in Andhra Pradesh, the Shiromani Akali Dal (Akali Religious Party) in Punjab, the National Conference in Jammu and Kashmir, and Asom Gana Parishad (Assam People's Council) in Assam.

The political parties have for the most part been supportive of women's rights. Congress (I), however—because of the tradition of the freedom struggle and the early liberal leadership of Mahatma Gandhi and Jawaharlal Nehru, as well as because of its greater strength overall—has been more effective both in terms of increasing women's representation in elected positions and in terms of policy initiatives specifically geared to women's interests.

India's status as a developing nation has also played a central role in shaping Indian women's political engagement. The country had a per capita annual GNP of U.S. $340 in 1989; nearly one-third of its population subsists below the poverty line set by the national government; and one in ten infants dies within a year.[1] These statistics present a vivid picture of the human costs of "developing nation" status. Poverty and the high infant mortality rate—together with a rate of population growth that threatens to make India the most populous country in the world by the year 2000, widespread malnutrition, and an economy that is 70 percent dependent on agriculture—have profoundly shaped the daily life experiences of Indian women. For the past 20 years the inclusion of women in governmental development programs has understandably been a primary concern for Indian women.

Society and culture are multilayered, multistructured, multireligious, and multilingual owing to uneven development, incomplete detribalization, and a constant influx of outsiders. Over the centuries a composite culture has evolved, even though fanatics, trying to use religion as a tool of power politics, also try to make religion a point of discord. The Indian population is 82.4 percent Hindu, 11.7 percent Muslim (the fourth largest Muslim population in all the countries in the world), and Buddhist, Jain, Sikh, and Christian in significant numbers. Fifteen constitutionally recognized languages and over 1,600 dialects add to the rich cultural mosaic. Among the Hindus a four-tiered caste system, which has also affected other religious groups, makes for a highly stratified society. Caste and class are inextricably intertwined and complicate simple sociological formulations. The experiences of Indian women and the forms that their political engagement takes have varied according to caste, class, region, and religious and ethnic group. Yet the national tradition of the freedom movement has led in some instances to consensus about certain national objectives and the primacy of certain women's issues.

Cultural diversity has also influenced women's engagement in politics indirectly through its effects on governmental policy. Notwithstanding the Hindu majority, the commonly applicable penal code, and increasingly vociferous demands for a uniform civil code, all religious and ethnic groups and tribes have their own separate personal laws. Though under heavy attack in recent years, this government policy of separate personal codes has minimized open conflict among the different sectors of the diverse population. It has also limited the number of national political issues, often paradoxically shifting the lines of conflict from community against community to conflicts within and across sectors of society, setting progressives in the same or different religious sects against traditionalists or fundamentalists. The state's efforts to defuse violence and tension also have often adversely affected women's efforts to achieve equality, for keeping fundamentalists of the various religions at peace has been important for the state.

The gender relation of dominance and subordination is a political relation that derives material sustenance from conditions and structures of production and that derives its legitimacy from a tradition and culture that uphold subordination. Still, gender relations are only one of several forces that have shaped the context of women's lives. Women's life experiences and their ensuing political engagement must also be understood within the context of a colonial past and a present as a developing nation; a sharply stratified society with ongoing caste and class conflicts; paternalistic religious cultural traditions imposed on the elite class within the heartland but leaving much greater freedom in peripheral territories and among the productive masses (all labeled as lower castes by the dominant Brahmanical tradition), with their mother-cult practices; and the interconnections and conflicts that exist among all these forces. We argue that without first placing Indian women's experiences within the context of these other forces—which have both enabled and constrained women's attempts to better their life conditions through political action—women's oppression on the basis of gender relations can be neither understood nor finally eliminated.

Because of the diversity of their life experiences, Indian women have been politically involved in myriad issues since the 1970s as the women's movement has grown. Three policy questions have become identified as women's issues: women's representation in government; the inattention to women in the development process (widening the chasm between constitutional and legal guarantees and the realities of women's lives); and violence against women, especially in relation to the resurgence of Hindu and Muslim fundamentalism and the concomitant attacks on women's rights. Although Indian women have been involved in many other issues, these have been the primary focus of women's organizations in the Indian women's movement.

WOMEN'S FORMAL AND INFORMAL POLITICAL PARTICIPATION

Indian women's involvement in politics in the modern era started in the late eighteenth and early nineteenth centuries. Although British imperialism profoundly influenced the political engagement of both elite and nonelite women during this period, its impact on the character and purposes of their engagement was very different. Nonelite women fought against the British colonialists. Moved by the hunger of their children, the British confiscation of their land (their means of livelihood), and oppressive British taxes, women, along with men, participated in "famine revolts" in the late eighteenth and nineteenth centuries and other revolts in the nineteenth century.

Elite women were mainly involved in the Indian Renaissance—the social reform movement of the nineteenth century. The main goals were to do away with what were to elite women the most offensive of traditional Indian practices through the abolition of female infanticide, *sati* (immolation of a widow on her husband's funeral pyre), child marriage, and laws prohibiting widows to remarry. The women in this movement also campaigned for women's education. Although high-caste women composed the main body of the movement, high-caste, Western-educated men led it. The emphasis was not on women's equality but, rather, on the separateness and complementarity of the roles of women and men in society. The movement was an attempt to make women into better mothers and wives for progressive, Western-educated men by promoting women's education and eliminating what these men saw as backward and degrading practices like sati.

Because the reforms proposed by the elite

women's movement did not threaten the traditional family structure and the perception of women's role in society and the home, some men supported them, and proponents were able to enact some of the reforms. In contrast, because the political efforts of tribal and peasant women were ranged against the exploitive colonial system, they had no such success.

With the beginning of the twentieth century a number of organizations exclusively for women appeared among high-caste or elite women. Beginning in 1913, Saroj Nalini Dutt, the educated daughter of a high-caste Hindu in the Indian civil service who was married to an officer of the same class and caste, founded *mahila samitis* (women's committees) in many towns. She also started women's institutes in Bengal. In 1910, Sardadevi Choudhurani, also married to an officer of the same class and caste, founded the Bharat Stree Mahamandal (Great Circle of Indian Women) to assert women's independent identity. She explained her frustration with other women's organizations: "They are the so-called social reformers. They advertise themselves as champions of the weaker sex; equal opportunities for women, female education, and female emancipation are some of their pet subjects of oratory at the annual show. They even make honest efforts at object lessons in the above subjects by persuading educated ladies to come up on their platform and speak for themselves. But woe to the women if they venture to act for themselves."[2]

Several other of these new women's organizations were all-India in scope. In 1917 the Women's India Association (WIA) was founded in Madras by Annie Besant, the Irish theosophist who urged Indian women to join the Home Rule League and the Swadeshi movement. The National Council of Women in India was founded in 1925 by Lady Aberdeen, Lady Tata (a Parsee woman from the leading industrialist family of western India), and others; and the All India Women's Conference (AIWC) was founded in 1927 through the efforts of Margaret Cousins (an Irish suffragist-cum-theosophist), and others. Muthulakshmi Reddy, a high-caste highly motivated Tamilan woman doctor, became one of the first female legislators.

As the independence movement moved forward, the elite women's movement stood at a crossroads. Both the WIA and AIWC vacillated on the issue of participation in the freedom movement, even as their activities increasingly addressed political issues. In 1917, when Lord Montague came to India to discuss Indian demands for political representation, the WIA raised the issue of women's suffrage. Its lobbying was somewhat successful and influenced the passage of the 1919 Government of India Act, which granted a restricted franchise to women, such that the right to vote in elections for the provincial assemblies was based on wifehood, property, and education. (In 1935 the act was extended so that women were also allowed to participate in elections to the Central Assembly.)

In response to pressure from women's organizations, the Congress movement pledged itself to principles of sexual equality and adult suffrage after independence at its annual meeting in Karachi in 1931. Many members of the AIWC and the WIA would have liked their organizations to confine themselves to the narrow issues of legislative representation of elite women, property and marriage law reforms, and social and educational reforms specifically geared to the interests of upper-class and upper-caste Hindu women, instead of participating in nonviolent mass movements like the civil disobedience movement (1930–31) and the Salt Satyagraha (insistence on truth) movement of 1931. Kamla Devi Chattophadhya, a socialist and an activist in Gandhi's mass movement, spoke powerfully to the difficult choice then faced by the elite women's movement as represented by the AIWC: "Though the [AIWC] Women's Conference had originally stated it would not participate in politics, it realised that it would have to concern itself with politics in its wider term, without alignment to any particular political party. While it accepted as members women from any party, it took a strong nationalist stand, and demanded equal rights for women to enable them to play their full and legitimate role in the national affairs; otherwise all other rights might become illusory."[3] However, under the leadership of the great patriot Sarojini Naidu, Congress president in 1925 and leader of AIWC, a section of elite women not only built support for their cause of women's equality but also formed an alliance with the nationalist movement for the ouster of the British by linking freedom for women with freedom for India.

The independence movement brought the two streams of politically involved women together—the elite and the masses, who both participated in the struggle for independence. They were nonviolent soldiers in Gandhi's army of liberation in the 1919 protest movements against the promulgation of the Rowlatt Acts—which strengthened control over the press and legalized internment without trial for suspected subversives—and against the Janian Wala Bagh massacre. Their support was vital in Gandhi's 1921–22 Non-Cooperation Movement, the Khalifat Movement (a pan-Islamist protest against the British policy undermining the Turkish Khalifat rule), the civil disobedience movement of 1930–31, the Salt Satyagraha of 1931, the Individual Satyagraha Movement of 1941, and the Quit India Movement of 1942. Women wore the handspun and handwoven *khadi* cloth as a uniform, and they made salt and did not pay salt taxes in defiance of the oppressive Salt Laws. They also picketed liquor and foreign clothes shops, burned foreign clothes, braved *lathis* (long, sturdy batons) and bullets, and went to jail. Nearly 10 percent of the prisoners in the independence movement were women with babies in their arms. Other women who did not go to jail or were not directly involved in the activities of the Congress movement shouldered the burden of supporting their families while their men were in jail. During lulls in the struggle for independence, women devoted themselves to developing alternative lifestyles and socioeconomic structures based on the Gandhian philosophy of sustainable development.

As a kind of continuum from pre- to postindependence and as a bridge between the political and the socioeconomic, some very militant peasant movements of both women and men need special mention. The Tebhaga movement (1946–50) in Bengal and the Telengana (1948–51) movement in Andhra Pradesh were launched to obtain a more equitable distribution of land. In both movements women formed "women's brigades" to protect villages, homes, and children against police atrocities and were given guerrilla training for self-defense. These two movements led to the passing of *zamindari* (landlordism) abolition acts in many states in the early 1950s, which granted some rights to the tillers of the land.

The second and third decades of the twentieth century also saw the emergence of an armed struggle by enthusiastic, patriotic young men and women, mostly belonging to the upper strata of society. They were all labeled terrorists by the British and the historians of their empire. The Chittagong Armoury case—with Kalpana Dutta, Kanaklate Barua, Preetilata Wadedkar, and other women associates—the Lahore and Kakori case, and many others involved women directly as makers and throwers of bombs and indirectly as helpers and givers of refuge to the male patriots.

By the time of independence the elite women's movement had won the battle of the franchise, the partnership of a few women's organizations and the Congress movement had been established, and women from all sectors of society had participated in politics. Direct political participation promoted women's confidence and self-reliance and broke the barriers of the public-private dichotomies in their lives. Yet on the issue of women's roles in society, an ideological conflict continued between those who looked to the pristine purity of an idealized past, when women and men had separate but complementary roles, and those who saw the reality of women's multidimensional roles. In sum, five factors shaped the similarities and differences in the organizational and political form and substance of women's political engagement prior to 1947: colonial exploitation and the early mass protest movements; the primarily elite origins of the leading participants in the women's movement and male leadership of the early social reform movement; the nonviolent national mass movement under Gandhi;

the marginalized militant movement; and the absence of a radical onslaught on the patriarchal basis of Indian culture and society.

Independence brought women constitutional guarantees of justice, liberty, equality, and dignity for the individual in the form of the Fundamental Rights and Directive Principles of the constitution. These guarantees signaled a shift in the emphasis of women's organizations. Underlying the new constitution was the desire of the mostly male framers to create a new sociopolitical order and a liberal, democratic polity. This desire on the part of liberal men like Nehru for a new Indian sociopolitical order was supported by the AIWC and the women who would soon form the National Federation of Indian Women (NFIW).

The NFIW was formed in 1954 by active left-wing members of AIWC, who struggled for egalitarian and socialist structural changes in the socioeconomic sphere, conceptualized women's roles as multidimensional, and demanded a network of support services for working women in urban and rural areas.[4] Women peasants, agricultural laborers, and workers in factories, the service sector, schools, and offices joined in large numbers. Here, too, the leaders were highly educated, progressive-minded elite women, but they were closely connected with the masses of women and vocalized their marginalization, poverty, and oppression through the legislative bodies and protest movements. The NFIW's affiliation with the Women's International Democratic Federation made them aware of global trends and the thrust of the first U.N. Development Decade (1961–70).

Together these women and progressive men lobbied for reform of the personal laws relating to marriage, divorce, and property rights. Their efforts were opposed by Hindu conservatives, as well as by elements within the Congress movement who were hostile to any legislation that threatened male supremacy in personal and familial matters. In spite of this opposition, the efforts of progressive men, the AIWC, and the NFIW eventually led to the passing of the Hindu Code Bills in 1954 and 1956.

After the fierce fight for the Hindu Code Bills, many of the leaders of the established women's organizations turned their focus away from further legislative lobbying for equal rights, settling down instead to implementing social welfare measures created by the Congress government—such as consciousness-raising, skill training, creation of support services, child welfare and nutrition, condensed courses for school dropouts, and working women's hostels.

While these established women's organizations attended to implementation of these programs women's representation in the political power structure remained low. Even though more than 10 percent of the Indians who went to prison in the struggle for independence were women, since 1952, the year women were first allowed to stand for election, women's representation in the Lok Sabha has never risen above 8 percent.[5] The cause of this low level of representation does not lie in women's nonparticipation in politics. Historically men have been more likely than women to vote; but between 1952 and 1984 the difference between men's and women's voting participation was cut in half, from 17.9 to 9.6 percent.[6]

Several factors have contributed to women's low levels of representation. For the most part the women who have been elected to the Lok Sabha have been Congress members. As a result, the defeats of Congress at the polls in 1977 and 1989 led to declines in women's representation in the Lok Sabha. In 1977 and 1989, respectively, only 3.4 and 5.2 percent of the Lok Sabha were women.[7] The paradox of the Indian polity is that with the passage of time rightist parties like the Bharatiya Janata Party (Indian People's Party) and regional ones like the Akali Dal have been fielding and getting more and more women elected while the non–Congress (I) centrist and left parties have successfully fielded negligible numbers. Women candidates have increased gradually in number, from 51 in 1952 to 164 in 1989. With the exception of 1967 and 1977, however, the overall percentage of candidates who are women has remained between 2.7 and 4.3.[8] At the same time, the women's wings of the parties have been marginalized for the most part, leaving women outside the party power structures.

Under the Congress governments of Indira Gandhi (1966–77 and 1980–84), women's lack of formal participation in politics came to be seen as a problem, with the 1971 census revealing the limits to women's gains. A comparative time-series analysis shook the complacency and false optimism generated by the constitutionally guaranteed rights, the legal reforms, the educational advances for women, the entry of women into the public service, and women's token ascension to governmental and elected power in the previous 20 years. In response to these alarming figures, a Committee on the Status of Women was appointed in September 1971 to investigate the condition of women. The committee's report, "Towards Equality," published in December 1974, heralded the International Women's Year, for it showed how far women in India had come toward equality since independence and how much effort was still required to bring Indian women true equality in fact as well as in words.

Reviewing women's political participation in its report, the committee concluded that women had a negligible impact on the political process—that though they constituted a numerical majority, they were slowly acquiring the features of a minority group because of inequalities of status and political power. To make women's political rights more functional and to give women more opportunities to participate in the formal political process, the committee recommended that political parties set a quota for women candidates. In the meantime, as a transitional measure it proposed allotting a block of seats to women in the municipal councils. As a second transitional measure it advocated the establishment of women's *panchayats* (local councils) at the village level, directly elected by village women. These women's panchayats would have autonomy and resources of their own for the management and administration of women's and children's welfare and development programs.

The committee also recommended the creation of permanent independent commissions on women at both state and national levels, with the power to collect information from government agencies on issues of concern to women, to evaluate existing programs and laws that affected women, and to recommend new laws and programs. To ensure that the recommendations would be followed, the committee stipulated that the government would be legally bound to follow its recommendations.

Over the course of the U.N. Decade for Women (1976–85), some of the committee's more general recommendations were taken up. The Equal Remuneration Act, which guarantees women equal pay for equal work, was passed in 1976; and a women's department in the Ministry of Labour and Employment and a Coordinating Bureau for Women in the Ministry of Welfare were created.

The Congress (I) and Janata Dal did set a 30 percent quota in their election manifestos in 1989, but the provision was not implemented. The National Commission for Women Act was passed in 1990; the commission, however, has yet to be set up. The Panchayat Bill has been passed, but the recommendation of a women's panchayat was not accepted. A bill to allot a block of seats to women on municipal boards is still pending in the Parliament.

The very process of writing the report "Towards Equality" brought together many committed academics, administrators, parliamentarians, and others propounding the women's cause. The impact of the International Women's Year and the Women's Decade and the associated imperative for the government to report to the U.N. Commission on Women at Vienna (the coordinating global agency) gave rise to the women's studies movement in India in the mid-1970s, with the establishment of the Centre for Women's Studies at SNDT University, Bombay (1975), the Centre for Women's Development Studies, Delhi (1980), and the Indian Association for Women's Studies (1981). The movement is a vigorous one, combining academism, activism, and commitment. It is a great help to the women's movement and part of it.

An increasing incidence of violence against

women, in spite of the climate of the Women's Decade, caused many new organizations of women to be formed in the late 1970s and early 1980s. These new organizations are affiliated with various political parties. Two important ones are Mahila Dakshata Samiti (Women's Competence Committee, founded in 1977) and the Joint Women's Programme (1981). The All India Democratic Women's Association, another left-wing organization, was founded in 1981 and has been active since then, with more or less the same emphasis as that of the NFIW.[9] Another important women's group, the Working Women's Forum, arose out of concern for women in the unorganized sector.

Many groups that are autonomous from the parties but were also established at this time—like Samata Manch (Equality Forum), Stree Sangharsh Samiti (Women's Struggle Committee), Stree Mukti Sangathan (Women's Emancipation Organization), Feminist Network Collective, Stree Shakti Sangathan (Women's Power Organization), and Purogami Sangathan (Forward-Stepping Organization)—represent a new awareness of the situation of women and the necessity of organized struggle against social injustices to ensure the achievement of the goals of the Women's Decade. Whereas the new women's associations with political party affiliations are mainstream organizations with an all-India scope, the autonomous groups are basically locale-specific, militant groupings of young women fighting oppression and violence against women generated by the system itself. Most of these autonomous groups are led by educated, urban, and vocal young feminists who have worked with women in rural areas, slums, and trade unions and created awareness and organization among them. Some groups, like the AIDWA and Stree Sangharsh Samiti, have concentrated on issues of change in the socioeconomic system and opposed antidemocratic measures like the amendment to the Industrial Disputes Act and to the Hospitals and Other Institutions Bill (1986), which proposed to limit the rights of workers to organize. There has also been an unprecedented flowering of joint actions by women's groups in response to specific actions of violence against women.

These efforts of independent women's groups and the scope of the problems that they have addressed have encouraged some groups to renew the demands made in 1974 for a 30 percent women's quota in the Lok Sabha. Before the 1989 elections all the bourgeois parties promised 30 percent of their seats to women. After the election they reneged. To attain the goal of larger representation, efforts are being made to widen the base of the women's movement through grass-roots organizations and greater participation of women in trade unions. Larger groups of women's organizations such as the All Gujarat Social Organizations Interventionist Central Organization are also being created to build a greater awareness of women's issues among voters and to contest elections on women's issues. They also give financial help to women candidates.

Overall, women still face many obstacles in their fight for representation. No women's organizations specifically focus on getting women elected at the national level. Unlike the earlier elite women activists, most women have not had the economic freedom to choose their life and career. The material circumstances of their upbringing have made their choices for them and inhibited their participation in formal politics. Women's cultural socialization and the fear of unsettling the family and their position in it—the family is considered women's domain—have also lessened many women's desire to participate in politics. Many unattached young women may be politically active, but once married, they disappear from the political scene. In spite of the progress since independence, lack of education and lack of knowledge about the intricacies of party politics among many nonelite women have limited their participation in the formal political arena. The role of money, the corruption of politics, and growing violence against women have also constrained many potential activists.

In numerous ways, Indira Gandhi has been the archetype for women who are trying to obtain not only political representation but also a place in the power structure in postindependence India. A symbol of both accomplishments and contradictions, she represents the tokenism in women's ascent to power and the underlying limits of the efforts of the women's movement to attain equality and political representation. Her rise to power was due less to the strength of the women's movement than to a combination of other factors, such as her family background in the nationalist movement and the Congress (I)'s need for a compromise candidate. Up to now, almost all other women's efforts in the political arena have been affected by similar forces.

BRINGING WOMEN INTO DEVELOPMENT

Since independence national development has been premised on an understanding of development primarily in terms of economic growth. Though achieving a modicum of growth and increased industrialization, India has nonetheless failed to achieve "growth with justice." A central example of growth without justice has been the way that development has totally bypassed the needs of Indian women. While the per capita GNP has risen, the health and educational and economic status of women have remained much worse than men's, or even declined.[10] In response, during the 1980s women, with the help of the government, have organized to create independent local development projects specifically geared both to meeting women's material needs and to increasing women's voices in national development planning and implementation. This approach augments the social service efforts of the government and women's groups to ameliorate the immediate problems of poverty and economic marginality.

Women's generally poor health is indicated by the declining sex ratio and their higher mortality rates. The ratio of women to men has decreased from 972 females per 1,000 males in 1901 to 926 per 1,000 in 1991.[11] In spite of the increase in women's life expectancy from 44.7 years in 1971 to 56.2 in 1981–86, age-specific death rates for female children and young women for every five-year cohort up to 35 years of age are higher for

women than for men.[12] The reasons lie in excessive child-bearing, female infanticide and feticide, and lack of proper nutrition and medical care.

Development has also bypassed women in the crucial area of education. The diffusion of progressive ideas notwithstanding, the majority of the population still consider girls to be unwanted burdens. Among the poorest masses, girls have hence been required to help support their families and look after siblings from an early age. Education has not been considered a priority. As a result, even though the overall literacy rate improved from 28 percent to 52 percent between 1961 and 1991, women's literacy rate rose much less: from 15 percent to only 39 percent. Girls' school enrollment figures partly explain this low literacy rate. Whereas 99 percent of the boys between six and eleven were in primary school in 1981, only 66 percent of the girls in the same age-group were enrolled. Nearly 56 percent of the dropouts at the primary level and almost 78 percent at the middle level (ages eleven to fourteen) were girls.[13]

Women's employment outside the home has also been adversely affected by development. Their participation in the paid labor force, instead of increasing with economic growth, has been on the decline. In 1961, 28 percent of the main workers to total population were women; by 1981 only 14 percent of the main workers were women.[14] A lack of technological education and training means that most women who have jobs are forced to do low-paying manual work. The modernization of agricultural techniques and the rapid growth of the organized industrial sectors of the economy have caused a decline in cottage industries, which are dominated by women. Unskilled women workers have very little place in the technologically advancing economy.

Those women who have been able to work have faced another set of problems as well. Without trade unions or organizations of any kind, the 94 percent of the women in the labor force who are in the unorganized sector of the economy face serious exploitation. They have not been paid wages equal to men's and have often been held in bondage as indentured servants. They also suffer sexual harassment at the hands of their (male) employers. Even the women who work in the organized sectors of the economy have encountered hardships. In spite of the existence of the Equal Remuneration Act, women have generally been paid less than men except in the service sector. In many factories and firms, labor laws have not been followed consistently, nor have the male-dominated trade unions made elimination of discriminatory practices against women workers a priority.

The Committee on the Status of Women concluded in its 1974 report that many of the inequities that women faced in the traditional economy were aggravated by the process of development. In spite of their legal equality and regardless of whether they were far above or far below the poverty line, their status in every sphere of life remained unequal.

In the late 1970s, following the release of the report, many more women's organizations became involved in bringing women into development. Taking a grass-roots approach to the problem, they have focused on the organization and integration of poor rural women—particularly from the scheduled tribes and castes—into development programs. One organization, the Self-Employed Women's Association, a trade union and cooperative for poor working women in the city of Ahmedabad, has provided credit for poor women. Working Women's Forum, with members in many southern states, and Annapurna Mahila Mandal, a Bombay-based organization, both work on behalf of self-employed women and those in the unorganized sector, taking joint economic and social action to win loans, impart entrepreneurial skills, and achieve empowerment for their members.

Since the release of the committee report, the state has also made renewed efforts to bring women into development, urged by the activities and lobbying of all major women's organizations. The government now consults more actively with women's groups and includes them more in advisory activities. Beginning with the framing of the Fifth Five-Year Plan in 1973–74, a central concern of the government's development effort has been an effective attack on the negative side effects of growth: poverty, unemployment, and inequality. Nonetheless, not until the late 1970s did the efforts of women's organizations to shape development programs to meet women's needs bear fruit.

In its Sixth Five-Year Plan (1980–85) the government made a major attempt to improve women's access to existing development projects both symbolically and programmatically. By including a separate chapter entitled "Women and Development," it recognized women as more than just passive beneficiaries of government programs and acknowledged them to be equal partners in national development. The government adopted a grass-roots approach, urging the use of *mahila mandals* (women's groups) and other voluntary women's organizations as intermediaries for government-funded programs providing wages and self-employment for women in rural areas. It recommended the provision of appropriate technology for upgrading women's existing skills, as well as wage law reforms. One radical suggestion was to confer joint titles on both husband and wife for all development activities involving the transfer of assets and the distribution of land and house sites.

Women were also given priority as beneficiaries of government aid programs in rural areas. The Integrated Rural Development Programme accorded preference to women heads of household. Under another program, Training of Rural Youth for Self-Employment Management, over 38,000 women, constituting almost 37 percent of the total number of beneficiaries, were trained in 1986 and 1987. In 1982 and 1983 a Development of Women and Children in Rural Areas project was started as a pilot project in 50 blocks (delineated areas for development within a district) around the country. Women below the poverty line, its special targets, were organized into groups of 20 to 30. Each group was provided training in a chosen economic activity, such as weaving, fish vending, broom and rope making, brick making, and pickle making. Between

1983 and 1985 over 2,772 of these groups were formed and trained, benefiting over 36,000 women.[15]

The Seventh Five-Year Plan (1985–90) had much the same focus as the sixth. It emphasized facilitating women's access to resources like loans, credit, and land. One program set up women's corporations to employ poor women and made women-headed households a priority in the distribution of surplus governmental lands. The plan also focused on upgrading women's skills and at the same time de-emphasized technologies that displaced women in the labor force. It included an important symbolic step forward with the recognition of the worth of women's work within the home: it acknowledged the long hours spent by masses of women in collecting fuel, fodder, and water, as well as their time laboring on the family farm or in family businesses. Supportive services in these essential areas and for maternal and child care were to be offered as a package. Attempts to compute women's hitherto largely invisible labor, however, did not come about until the discussions for the Eighth Five-Year Plan (1992–97) began with women's groups in 1990 and 1991.[16]

In the second half of the 1980s the government began to use other policy mechanisms to promote women's integration into development. Since the middle of the 1960s education had been conceived of as an instrument of social transformation. Not until the debate on the New Education Policy in 1985, however, was the question of education for equality, specifically women's equality, addressed at the national level. Almost all the women's organizations and the women's studies activists worked together to create a new policy document, "Education for Women's Equality." In compliance with this policy there were efforts to implement reorientation programs for teachers and administrators to eliminate sex bias and efforts to redesign courses and curricula. Since 1985 nearly 25 universities and 12 departments or colleges have started centers or cells in women's studies. The thrust of the program was decelerated for political reasons, with the new government in 1990 appointing a "review committee." Women's organizations and groups have thus been able to get the state to acknowledge the importance of bringing women into development, and a small number of women (relative to the size of the rural population) have been affected by the public programs. Advocates of inclusion have been less successful in changing the reality that development bypasses women. Funds earmarked for women's development programs have often not reached the target groups because of governmental and bureaucratic corruption. At the same time, the vicissitudes of the industrial economy have often resulted in a poor domestic market and little export potential for products manufactured by women. The majority of women have consequently experienced little benefit from development programs.

VIOLENCE AGAINST WOMEN

Women in India traditionally have faced, and continue to face, many forms of violence simply because they are women. Among the most extreme forms of violence that arise from patriarchal religious views and economic considerations are sati, female infanticide and feticide, rape, and dowry murders. The secular and liberal state envisioned by the national movement and the constitutional guarantees established in the initial years of Congress (I) rule provide the legal bulwark against culturally condoned violence against women. With the erosion of the leading position of the Congress and the rise of religious fundamentalism, both institutionalized violence against women and public support for it have grown.

In earlier times the practice of child marriage led to early widowhood and the infamous Hindu practice of sati, the burning to death of the widow on the husband's funeral pyre. Although sati has been illegal since 1829, incidents have continued to occur.[17]

Because of the costs of raising and marrying a daughter and the humiliation involved in having a daughter, even well-to-do people have long practiced female infanticide. One reason—lack of food—has disappeared, but the practice continues even today, though with different methods. The modern-day version is the destruction of the female fetus following amniocentesis.

Women and their families, both poor and well-to-do, prefer to pay the short-term cost of the sex-determination test and abort a female fetus than to incur the long-term cost of a girl's upbringing. Some women think that it is better to spend 200 to 800 rupees (U.S. $12 to $40) in the present than to give birth to a female baby and spend thousands of rupees for her marriage when she grows up.[18] Rehana Ghadially has reported that between 1978 and 1983 around 78,000 female fetuses were aborted in India. Older forms of infanticide also continue to be practiced among poor and rural women. Female infants in Tamil Nadu are often either fed poisonous milk from a wild plant or choked to death by stuffing their mouths with tufts of rice plants. From 1976–85 there were 6,000 deaths due to infanticide.[19] Though high, even this figure probably underestimates the true number of deaths, because infanticides frequently go unreported or are reported as normal deaths.

Most women's organizations have been only sporadically involved in this issue, unlike the issue of sati. Because of girls' unwanted position in the traditional Indian family, whether Hindu or Muslim, and the economic reasons for infanticide, these deaths have usually had the sanction of the local community, whether urban or rural. Under pressure from all women's organizations, the People's Science Group, and particularly the Bombay-based Forum Against the Sex-Determination and Sex Pre-Selection Test, the Maharashtra government passed the Maharashtra Regulation of Prenatal Diagnostic Techniques Act in 1988. A bill to bring out uniform central legislation is pending before a select committee in the Parliament and is expected to be passed soon.[20]

The primary foci of women's efforts to end violence against women have been two other throwbacks to the past, rape and dowry deaths. Mass rapes during periods of political instability, like rapes of women as the *devidasis*, or slaves, of the gods used to be common occurrences. Today women face large-scale "eve-teasing" (public sexual harassment) and an increasing incidence of rapes of all kinds—individual, custodial, and gang rapes. According to the minister of state for home affairs, 8,706 rapes were reported in 1988; the number was up to 9,517 in 1990.[21] Sadly the problem of rape is even larger than these figures indicate. Given the symbolic importance attached to women's physical purity among both Muslims and Hindus, rape is incredibly devastating to women and their families. Because of the stigma and social ostracism that rape victims undergo, most rapes go unreported. When cases are reported and heard by the courts, all too often the victim is blamed and the perpetrator(s) go free. The rape of women from the lower classes, the scheduled castes, and tribes is especially common. Because of the increased caste conflict that has come with the end to the formal suppression of the scheduled classes and castes, gang rapes of these women have also been on the increase. The greatest threat of rape for women today, however, is from those who are supposed to protect them—that is, the police and the guardians of girls and women. Police and custodial rapes are among the most common forms of rape in India today.[22]

Civil rights groups began to protest the incidence of custodial rape in 1977, but women's organizations did not initiate the antirape movement until 1980 with the public outcry following a custodial rape. Mathura, a 15-year-old girl and member of a scheduled caste, was raped by two policemen at a police station. The policemen were acquitted by the Sessions Court on the grounds that "there was no rape because there was no proof that Mathura had resisted." Although on appeal the decision was reversed by the Bombay High Court, the Supreme Court again acquitted the policemen, holding that Mathura's story of stiff resistance was false and that the intercourse was a "peaceful affair."[23]

Significantly, an open letter written by four university professors asked for another review of the judgment: a review of a Supreme Court judgment is rarely requested except under extreme provocation. In addition, on Women's Day (8

March) in 1980 thousands of women—groups of women students from major universities, the women's wings of left political parties, housewives, professional women, and women's organizations of varying political traditions—came together in the cities of Ahmedabad, Nagpur, Pune, Bombay, and Delhi to protest the court's decision and demand a reopening of the case. In Bombay and Nagpur a series of rallies, seminars, marches, sit-ins, and street plays by women's theater groups were also held, and a woman's organization that specifically focused on ending rape, the Forum Against Rape, was founded. The Supreme Court took heed and agreed to review its decision, but ultimately stuck to its verdict. Pressure from this campaign meanwhile affected the recommendations of the Law Commission of India, so harsher legal penalties for rape were recommended in the Criminal Law Amendment Bill of 1980, which was passed by the Parliament in 1983. The punishment for custodial rape is now ten years in prison. More important, the onus of proof in rape cases is now on the accused, not the victim.

Marriage without dowry was part of the Gandhian and left ethos during the nationalist movement and continues to be part of the Congress (I) philosophy even today. Though illegal since the passing of the Dowry Prohibition Act in 1961, the practice of dowry is still quite common and increasingly costly. Rising costs have led to an increasing number of "dowry deaths" in the past 15 years (where daughters-in-law are burned to death or otherwise murdered by their in-laws), as well as predowry suicides singly and collectively by young women who are financially unable to marry. Dowry deaths, or more accurately dowry murders, have also mounted because of greed and the desire for status symbols like televisions and VCRs, which grooms and their families demand before marriage. In 1988, according to the minister of state for home affairs, there were 2,209 dowry deaths reported; in 1989, 4,324; and in 1990, 4,952.²⁴

Women's large-scale organizing against dowry began around 1977, when the Mahila Dakshata Samiti organized to ensure prosecution of the Sudha murder case in Delhi: a well-placed government doctor dissatisfied with his wife's dowry, murdered her for another woman and threw his wife's body in the Ganges River in Kanpur. The death remained a mystery for a long time, but the husband was ultimately nabbed and punished. Since then, nearly all women's organizations, both separately and in coalitions in major cities, have been organizing protests against the in-laws, the lawyers, and the police officials involved in arranging, committing, and not investigating dowry deaths. Women's organizations have also engaged in consciousness-raising about the practice.

The efforts of these women's groups and women MPs like Pramila Dandavate and Geeta Mukherjee have brought about the amendment of the Dowry Prohibition Act of 1961 in 1984 and again in 1986. In these amendments the burden of proof was shifted to the accused, and the language prohibiting dowry giving was broadened to include requests for gifts, not just before marriage but also after it. The effects of these amendments on the incidence of dowry and dowry deaths are not yet clear.

From early on, because of the influence of Western education, the social reform movement, and the nationalist reformism of leaders like Gandhi and Nehru, the male elite and the few educated women adopted the cause of women's equality. Set in opposition to this progressive movement since its inception, however, have been the forces of Islamic and Hindu fundamentalism, which have tried to keep traditional patriarchal mores and practices alive.

This conflict between the forces of progress and fundamentalism simmered beneath the surface of the Indian cultural-political life during the nineteenth century and the beginning of the twentieth century; mainly because of the strength of the nationalist Congress movement and the central government, it did not erupt into a visible conflict of interest at any level until recently. Since the nineteenth century, legal reforms of some of the traditional practices most oppressive to women have come easily. Sati was banned in the nineteenth century. The Sharda

Act, outlawing child marriage, was passed in 1929. The Hindu Code Bills were passed in 1954 and 1956 despite opposition. Since roughly 1975, however, the weakness and instability of the national government and the formerly hegemonic Congress party have allowed the resurgence of both Islamic and Hindu fundamentalism and the surfacing of this conflict.

Symptomatic of dangers that resurgent fundamentalism poses to women's rights is the Shah Bano case of 1985 and the attendant furor. A 60-year-old Muslim woman, Shah Bano, was granted alimony by the Supreme Court over the protests of her advocate husband, who had divorced her. The husband, who had already married a much younger woman, appealed to Muslim religious leaders on the grounds that the courts were interfering with Muslim personal law as enunciated in the sharia. Muslim religious leaders raised a hue and cry and threatened the government. In an attempt to appease the Islamic fundamentalist forces and ensure political stability, the Congress (I) government introduced the Muslim Women's (Protection of Rights in Divorce) Act in 1986, confirming the primacy of Muslim personal law for Muslim women.

Women's organizations and activists protested this legislative measure. Educated Muslims demonstrated against it. Over 100 distinguished Indian Muslims from all walks of life, both men and women, petitioned against it together. Arif Muhammad Khan, a Muslim member of the Central Council of Ministers, resigned.

For the sake of political expediency the government passed the act, which pushed Muslim women back by two centuries. For women the danger and the implications of the act were clear, giving as it did a "new lease of life to religious fundamentalists and obscurantists who [could] now perpetrate injustice on women in the name of religion with impunity." Promila Dandavate, president of the Mahila Dakshata Samiti and a former member of Parliament, further warned Prime Minister Rajiv Gandhi when she and a group of Muslim divorcees called on him to plead for the dropping of the bill that "if the govern-ment succumbs to the pressure of the Muslim fundamentalists now, the day is not far when a section of the Hindu fundamentalists will come forward to demand the right to burn widows on the pyre of their husbands in the name of the religious freedom."[25]

Within a year Dandavate's prediction was proven true, for Hindu fundamentalists began to press for their right to practice sati. In September 1987 at Deorala, a young widow, Roop Kanwar, was burned to death on her husband's funeral pyre in the presence of thousands of people. Although there had been other instances of sati prior to this and a number of sati temples still stood in different parts of the country, this incident, coming as it did right at the end of the U.N. Decade for Women and the Shah Bano case, caused a stir.

The response was strong on both sides. Thousands of men and women in Jaipur marched with bare swords in support of sati, treating it as a matter of cultural and family right. Women's organizations and intellectuals condemned it outright as inhuman and culturally oppressive. Many investigative studies were conducted, which led to a nationwide debate on the practice of sati and the sanctity of traditions of cultural groups that were oppressive to other members of society. Mass meetings and marches were held all over the country. The major women's organizations, including the National Federation of Indian Women, the All India Women's Conference, the All India Democratic Women's Association, the Young Women's Christian Association, and the Joint Women's Programme, participated in this movement and together formed the Joint Action Committee Against Sati.

Responding to this pressure from Indian women, the government enacted the Commission of Sati Prevention Act in 1987 not only to provide more effective prevention of sati but to stop its glorification. The act defined sati comprehensively, and the death penalty was prescribed for persons inducing or encouraging it, participating in sati processions, or preventing the widow from saving herself. Persons convicted but not sentenced to death under the act would be disqualified from contesting elections under the Representation of People Act of 1951 from the date of such conviction and would continue to be disqualified for a further period of five years after release.

Act or no act, many attitudes did not change. The Shankrachaya of Puri (one of the four spiritual leaders of the Hindus) came out in defense of sati, saying that a woman who commits sati "earns salvation for the families of her father and her husband."[26] Vijaya Raje Scindia, the queen dowager of Gwalior State, a senior leader of the Bharatiya Janata Party, and a sitting member of the Lok Sabha, strongly defended sati at a function of the BJP Mahila Morcha (the women's wing of the party).[27] The Dharma Raksha Samiti (Save Religion Organization) asserted that sati was part of their traditional Rajput caste culture and identity. Others argued the economic benefits of sati, which frees the in-laws from the burden of supporting the widow and can in fact add to their wealth.[28]

Thus, in the name of supporting traditional law and custom, Muslim and Hindu fundamentalists have tried to reinforce the loosening shackles of medieval paternalistic morality and preserve male supremacy. Although fundamentalists have so far been only somewhat successful, their power is increasing. This resurgence, coupled with the desire of the central government to maintain political stability at all costs, means that the influence of progressive and secular women is likely to be less powerful on this issue than on others.

LESSONS FROM THE PAST AND PROSPECTS FOR THE FUTURE

The Indian women's movement is now in transition. Feminism has not yet become the voice of anger that it has become in other parts of the world. Indian women's reaction to the patriarchal forces in their society is complex. While acknowledging the existence of these forces, most do not view men as their oppressors. They have not yet asserted their right to complete independence from the traditional Indian understanding of women's role.

Although the legal changes of the 1980s have been victories for the women's movement, the outcome of the battle for equality has not been decided. Some trends noticeable today are clear setbacks for the women's movement. Huge processions of Muslim and Hindu women marched in favor of the retrograde Muslim Women's (Protection of Rights in Divorce) Act of 1986 and in favor of sati. Some BJP women leaders have supported sati. The progress of the women's movement toward socioeconomic justice and the end to women's subordinate status are seriously threatened by the fundamentalist and communal backlash. To succeed, the women's movement will have to go beyond fighting for women's issues alone and fight against broader issues like communalism. It will have to fight for distributive justice and the minimum needs of the wider masses of women and men alike.

The success of the Indian women's movement will depend a great deal on the strategy that it adopts. To attain long-lasting structural change, feminist activists need to develop both political visibility, including media exposure, and political clout—the capacity to deliver or withhold a significant block of votes. Dependence on political parties, ideologies of female subordination, the reluctance of male party leaders to include women, and corruption currently limit this approach. Women will also have to give up their reluctance to be involved in party politics as it is practiced and turn the women's wings of the parties into more active participants in party power structures. As the political clout and visibility of the women's movement increase so, too, will its stature and its capacity to initiate long-lasting changes.

Another factor that will help determine the future of the Indian women's movement is the balance of other political forces. If the strength of forces hostile to women, such as Islamic or Hindu fundamentalism, continues to grow, the women's movement will probably be in jeopardy, because these forces divert attention from basic development issues and other issues important to women. On the other hand, if the political balance of power remains the same and women can continue to tie the interests of the Congress (I) and left parties to theirs, they will almost certainly reap benefits. The form that this alliance should take is not yet apparent, but that there must be an alliance is clear: the Indian women's movement cannot and will not succeed unless it is backed by an already established political player.

So far, nonelite women have with virtually no exception stayed out of formal party politics, but there are some signs that this noninvolvement may be coming to an end. In November 1984, disturbed by the decreasing number of women in Parliament and the legislative assemblies, about 150 women's organizations met under the auspices of the Akhil Gujarat Samajik Sanstha Madhyasthta Mandal (All Gujarat Social Organizations Mediation Group) and drew up a manifesto for the 1984 parliamentary elections. The manifesto, which detailed women's political, economic, and social rights and included a list of demands, was sent to all the parties and candidates participating in the election. Meanwhile, these urban women's organizations also made efforts to increase women's political awareness of their rights and their ability to pressure the government by voting for candidates who supported the manifesto.

There is also some evidence that coalition building among different women's organizations is increasing. Coalitions emerged in the 1970s to celebrate International Women's Year and the U.N. Decade for Women and formed around the Mathura rape case in 1979 and the Roop Kanwar sati case in 1987. These coalitions are trying to keep women's issues and their solutions above petty party politics.

What is needed is women's widespread involvement in decision making, both within the family and outside it at all levels of government. The key to the quest for power and equality is the empowerment of the masses—of both women and men. The women's movement cannot cut a furrow on its own but must be part of wider efforts. The basic issues of sustainable development, the nonexploitation of nature and human-

kind, and the prevention of Mother Earth's being blown up are fundamentally linked to women's equal rights, not to mention their very survival.

Above all, if the Indian women's movement is to become a viable, recognized, and important political actor, it must not isolate itself either from the diversity of India or from the myriad other social and political movements within the country. It must find a way not only to respect the diversity of India but also to establish itself as an important part of that diversity.

NOTES

1. Per capita GNP is from *World Development Report, 1991* (Oxford: Oxford University Press, 1991), table 1. Measurements of households below the poverty line diverge greatly. One source reports 48 percent. *A Social and Economic Atlas of India* (Government of India, 1987), table 100. In 1991 about a third of the households were said to be below the poverty line. The final tabulated results of the 1990 economic census are not yet available.
The infant mortality rate in 1989 was 95 per 1,000. *World Development Report, 1991,* 258.
2. Sardadevi Choudhurani, "A Women's Movement," *Modern Review* (1911): 343.
3. Kamla Devi Chattophadhya, *Indian Women's Battle for Freedom* (Delhi: Abhinav, 1983), 98.
4. The NFIW is presently affiliated with the Communist Party of India.
5. D. Butler, Lahiri Ashok, and Roy Prannoy, *India Decides (Elections, 1952–1989)* (New Delhi: Living Media India, 1990).
6. G. N. S. Raghavan and G. Balchandran, *Forty Years of the World's Largest Democracy* (New Delhi: Gian Publishing House, 1990), 2; *Women in India: Statistical Profile, 1988* (New Delhi: Government of India, 1988).
7. *Chandigarh Tribune,* 25 April 1991.
8. *Women in India: Statistical Profile, 1988,* 174.
9. The AIDWA is presently affiliated with the Communist Party of India (Marxist).
10. *Women in India: Statistical Profile, 1988,* various tables.
11. *Census of India, 1991,* series 1: "India: Provisional Population Totals," Paper 1 of 1991 (New Delhi: Registrar General and Census Commissioner), 1.
12. *Women in India: Statistical Profile, 1988,* table 2.6.
13. *Census of India, 1991,* 59; Butler, Ashok, and Prannoy, *India Decides,* 57–58, xxiii.
14. *Census of India, 1991,* 95.
15. Ibid., table 8.45.
16. "New Education Policy" (Government of India Documents, Ministry of Human Resource Development,

1986), sec. 4; and "Programme of Action" (Government of India Documents, Ministry of Human Resource Development, 1986), chap. 2. "Against a target of 30 percent the share of women within the 1.9 million families assisted rose to 21.11 percent by 1988, from 19.53 percent in 1987. The banks were instructed not to ask for collateral in sanctioning the loans." Department of Women and Child Development, *National Prospective Plan for Women (1988–2000 A.D.)* (Government of India, 1988), xiv. "5,545 groups and 96,117 members of DWCRA groups had benefitted by 1986–87. 38,339 women, nearly 37 percent of the total, were trained under TRYSEM [Training of Rural Youth for Self-Employment Management]." *Hindustan Times,* 10 January 1989. Under the Wasteland Development Programmes, a large number of women were employed in social forestry.

17. Incidents are mentioned in sporadic newspaper reports. The government crime statistics do not have a sati category because the crime is rare.

18. Patel Vibhuti, "Sex-Determination and Sex Reflection Tests: Abuse of Advanced Technologies," in Rehana Ghadially, ed., *Women in Indian Society* (New Delhi: Sage Publications, 1988), 181.

19. S. H. Venketramani, "Born to Die: Female Infanticide," *India Today* (June 1986): 26–37.

20. *Jansatta* (Hindi daily), 9 November 1991, p. 27; and Lok Sabha Secretariat, "Violence Against Women," Information Bulletin, September 1991, 1B-6/REF/91, p. 13.

21. Lok Sabha Secretariat, "Violence Against Women," 4. Reply to unstarred question no. 1405 dated 31 July 1991.

22. The statistics on gang rapes are included in the rape statistics; no breakdowns are available. Our comments are based on frequent reporting in all major newspapers.

23. *Tukaram v. State of Maharashtra,* A.I.R. 1974, S.C. 185.

24. Lok Sabha Secretariat, "Violence Against Women," 6. Rajya Sabha unstarred question no. 1391 dated 31 July 1991.

25. Promila Dandavate, "Social Legislation and Women," in Promila Dandavate, Ranjna Kumari, and Jamila Verghese, *Widows, Abandoned and Destitute Women in India* (New Delhi: Radiant, 1989).

26. Ibid.

27. Anand Mulk Raj, ed., *Sati* (Delhi: B. R. Publishing, 1989), 107–9.

28. "It is reported that within three months of the Roop Kanwar *sati* incident her in-laws had collected 9.5 million rupees [approximately U.S. $380,000]." Newspaper reports, 26 December 1987.

▲ Israel

Type of Political System: democracy
  Sovereignty: republic
  Executive-Legislative System: parliamentary
Type of State: unitary
Type of Party System: multiparty
Major Political Parties[a]

Likud-Liberalim Leumi (Unity–National Liberal Party), called Likud: Formed in 1973 under the stewardship of former Prime Minister Menachem Begin; formed when several smaller parties united around the belief that Israel should retain all land between the Jordan River and the Mediterranean.

Mifleget Ha'avoda Hayisre'elit–Mapai (Israel Labor Party, ILP): Founded in 1968; resulted from the unification of the Israel Workers' Party, the Israel Workers' List, and the Unity of Labor–Workers of Zion. Led by former Prime Ministers Shimon Peres and Yitzhak Rabin.

Mifleget Datit Leumit–Mafdal (National Religious Party, or NRP): Formed in 1956 by the merger of two older organizations; dedicated to fundamental tenets of religious Zionism.

Shomrei Torah Sephardiim–Shas (Sephardi Torah Guardians): Orthodox religious party, a 1984 offshoot of Union of Israel. The primary support comes from Jews of Sephardic descent.

Tehiya (Renaissance): Organized in 1979 by dissidents from Likud and right-wing and nationalist groups; advocates formal annexation of disputed territories.

Tzomet (Zionist Revival Movement): Formed in 1988. The leaders defected from the Renaissance party.

Degel Hatorah (Torah Flag): Non-Zionist ultra-Orthodox religious party; captured first Knesset seats in 1988.

Moledet (Homeland): Ultra-Zionist secular party formed in 1988; advocates annexation of occupied territories.

Agudat Israel (Union of Israel): Anti-Zionist Orthodox religious party led by Shlomo Lorincz, Menaham Porush, and Avraham Yosef Shapiro.

Mifleget Hapoalim Hameuchedet–Mapam (United Workers' Party): Formed in 1948; has traditionally endorsed a neutralist foreign policy, greater equality for Arabs, fewer restrictions on labor. Once the second largest party after Labor.

tha-Tenua le-Zechouot ha-Ezrakh–Ratz (Citizens' Rights Movement): Advocates women's rights, electoral reform, reduction of religious power.

Hazit Democratit la-Shalom ve-Shivayon–Hadash (Democratic Front for Peace and Equality, or DFPE): Organized to support 1977 candidates from the former New Communist List, the "Black Panther" movement of Sephardic Jews, and unaffiliated local Arab leaders.

Center Movement (New Liberal Party, or NLP): Formed in 1987 as an alliance of two previous parties and former Likud liberals.

Progressive List for Peace (PLP): Self-identified as joint Jewish-Arab movement, established in 1984 to oppose West Bank Jewish settlement. Advocates a Palestinian Arab state to coexist with Israel.

Darousha (Arab Democracy Party): Formed in 1988; committed to international recognition of Palestinian self-determination.

Kach (Thus): Banned party formerly led by Meir Kahane; advocates forcible expulsion of Palestinians from Israel and occupied territories. Found by High Court of Justice in 1988 to be "racist" and "undemocratic," thus prevented from submitting a Knesset list in 1988.

Year Women Granted Right to Vote:
1948
Year Women Granted Right to Stand for Election: 1948 .
Percentage of Women in the Unicameral Legislature: 9.0%
Percentage of Electorate Voting for Highest Elected Office in Most Recent Election (1992): 76.7%[b]

DEMOGRAPHICS
Population: 4,476,800[c]
Percentage of Population in Urban Areas
  Overall: 89.2%
  Female: not available
  Male: not available
Percentage of Population Below Age 15: 31.7%
Birthrate (per 1,000 population): 23[d]
Maternal Mortality Rate (per 100,000 live births): 5
Infant Mortality Rate (per 1,000 live births): 14
Mortality Rate for Children Under Five (per 1,000 live births): 16
Average Household Size: 3.6
Mean Age at First Marriage
  Female: 23.5
  Male: 26.1
Life Expectancy[e]
  Female: 77.0
  Male: 73.6

EDUCATION
Ratio of Female to Male Enrollment
  First-Level Education: 97
  Second-Level Education: 105
  Third-Level Education: 84
Literacy Rate
  Female: 83.0%
  Male: 93.0%

ECONOMY
Gross National Product per Capita: U.S. $10,300[f]
Percentage of Labor Force in Agriculture: 4.6%[g]
Distribution of Agricultural Workers by Sex[h]
  Female: 21.7%
  Male: 78.3%
Economically Active Population by Sex[i]
  Female: 40.0%
  Male: 74.9%

a. Arthur S. Banks, ed., *Political Handbook of the World, 1991* (Binghamton, N.Y.: CSA Publications, 1991), 334–36.
b. Chen Dagan, "Likud Voters Remained at Home," *Hedashot,* 28 June 1992, p. 8.
c. *Statistical Abstracts of Israel* (Jerusalem: N. HO Central Bureau of Statistics, 1989).
d. Ibid.
e. Ibid.
f. *Facts About Israel* (Israel Information Center, 1992).
g. *Statistical Abstracts of Israel.*
h. Ibid.
i. Ibid.

Women and Politics in Israel

DAPHNA SHARFMAN

The Middle Eastern state of Israel, with a predominantly Jewish population of 4.5 million, is bordered by four Arab states: Lebanon, Syria, Jordan, and Egypt. Its ideological, political, social, and economic foundations were built during the *yishuv,* or prestate era, a period (1882–1948) of Jewish settlement before Israel was established as a Jewish state.

The creation of Israel in 1948 was primarily the result of the Zionist political movement led by the World Zionist Organization, established in 1897. The organization served as an umbrella for a variety of social and ideological groups that argued that the only real solution to the problems of the Jewish people was the re-creation of an independent Jewish state in Eretz-Israel, where the ancient Jewish kingdom had existed until the first century A.D.

The manner in which the nation came into being and the form it took influence the lives of Israeli women today in several ways. For example, their political struggle for status in the emerging society was a part of this nation-building process. In turn, the division of power established then has strongly influenced the current status and power of the women's movement. Religious differences with the rest of the Middle East and the contest over the legitimacy of its territory have caused Israel to spend much of the last 40 years at war. The overwhelmingly Jewish population and the motivation that led to the creation of the country as a Jewish homeland have brought the state and the Jewish religious laws and norms closer together. One outgrowth of this relation is that many issues governing women's personal lives are determined by religious law and courts.

The primary lines of division in society and politics concern religion and, among the Jewish population, one's origin before coming to Israel. The population is 85 percent Jewish with small Christian, Muslim, and Druze minorities. Half of the Jews are of Middle Eastern or North African origin, and half are of European origin. The most significant cleavage in policy making, however, concerns the question of how much the Jewish religion should determine the laws and shape the lives of the people. This division is played out between groups who favor a more secular state and those who want a state that is based to a greater degree on religiosity.

Such cleavages have led to a multiparty parliamentary system where chief executive power is held by the prime minister. The Knesset is a unicameral legislature of 120 members, elected in a national proportional electoral system. The governments have generally been coalitions, yet politics has been dominated by the most powerful party, the Israel Labor Party, for most of the nation's short history. Strong center-right nationalist and religious conservative parties, Likud (Unity) and the Mifleget Datit Leumit–Mafdal (National Religious Party), have also played an influential role. Since the mid-1970s these parties have been increasingly contentious and divided, especially along secular and religious lines.

HISTORICAL OVERVIEW OF THE WOMEN'S MOVEMENT

The Israeli women's movement developed within the Labor Zionist movement, which was inspired by radical socialist ideas gaining momentum in Russia at the turn of the century. Because the Labor Zionist groups professed an egalitarian ideology, women did not organize into separate groups, nor were they assigned specialized roles. Still, women in the Labor Zionist bloc tended to be more active in cultural activities than in politics.[1]

Although Labor Zionists were ideologically committed to social equality, they did not concern themselves with women's emancipation, mainly because they defined the problem of Jewish existence as the fundamental and overriding social issue to which all efforts had to be directed. Because the subordination of women in society was not identified as a condition requiring special action, creating the specialized institutional arrangements necessary to implement changes had no legitimation.[2] In contrast, women in the nonsocialist sector of the Zionist movement, in both Europe and North America, formed separate chapters that engaged in fund-raising, education, and philanthropy.

Palestine—a British mandate from 1923 to 1948—became the nations of Israel and Jordan. As a consequence of their Zionist beliefs, the first women who came to Palestine did not expect to struggle for equality. They thought it would accompany their move to the new homeland, allowing them to participate more fully in Palestinian social life than they had been permitted to in Jewish bourgeois circles in Russia. Sara Malchin, a founder of the women's movement, explained the attitude of the pioneers: "These young Zionist women dreamed of engaging in battle and sacrifice for the ideal of redemption, even while still in the diaspora."[3]

Faced with unemployment and filled with a desire to establish a new type of Jewish society, the second wave of Jewish immigrants to Palestine (1904–14), consisting mainly of socialists, established a new type of communal life—the *kvutza* (group), a small collective settlement in which everyone labored. Two of the guiding kvutza principles were "conquering the land," that is, making it arable for farming, and achieving economic self-sufficiency.

For men and for many of the women, the conscious rebellion against the traditional occupational structure of Jewish society did not extend to women's work, for women were automatically assigned to the kitchens and laundries of the kvutzot.[4] The attitude of the men is described by one of the women pioneers in an article that appeared in the Socialist Party newspaper: "Many [of the male workers] believed that the role of the young female idealist coming to Palestine was to serve them. The young women, who were still inexperienced, submitted to this view and believed that in cooking and serving they were solving most of our questions [concerning our role] in Palestine. The young woman who dared to doubt this assumption was considered strange."[5]

Women were deprived of the opportunity to "conquer new fields of work" through agriculture and to guard the kvutza as the men were doing. Accorded less than full membership in the kvutza, they also resented the restrictions placed on their participation in group decision making about kvutza affairs.[6] These resentments eventually led to a meeting of 17 women in Kineret, near the Sea of Galilee, in 1911—the first step toward the emergence of a women's movement within the Labor Zionist bloc. As a result of this meeting, the problems faced by women workers emerged as a social reality, thus legitimizing the establishment of a segregated women's organization and establishing the need for social action.

This early women's movement emphasized the need for self-transformation, an ideology formulated at Kineret and reiterated at every subsequent conference of women workers. To achieve their goal, namely equal participation, women had to change themselves: "We, the women laborers, like men, aspire first and foremost to rehabilitate our spirit and bodies through work . . . in the field and in nature, and in this way we can rid ourselves of the habits, the way of life and even the way of thinking that we brought with us from the diaspora."[7] By stressing self-alteration, the pioneers adopted a stance that fit well with the dominant Zionist ideology and therefore was politically attractive.

Women believed that they had the same potential as men, though their own had remained dormant for historical reasons. Through training in manual skills, they planned to overturn their image as passive and dependent. As Ada Maimon, a leading figure in the struggle for women's equality, wrote: "At the dawn of the movement we thought that we had only to overcome the barrier of occupational training, and as for equality, it would all follow automatically."[8]

Their strategy was to push for the development of new agricultural specialties, such as vegetable gardening and poultry and dairy farming, that were considered "suitable for women." Women also demanded a monopoly over these areas of work, for, they argued, men had many other jobs to do. The farm at Kineret was to serve as a training center where women could learn technical skills and could begin their personal transformation within a supportive environment, unhampered by the presence of men. These women also decided that in the future women should join only those kvutzot willing to accept at least ten of them, so that rotation between household and agricultural work would be feasible.[9]

The more formal organizational arm of the women's movement was established in 1914. After protesting the failure to invite any women's representative to the fifth conference of the Galilee agricultural union, women decided to convene their own conference of women agricultural workers. Thirty delegates met, representing 209 women workers.

The issues on the agendas of the annual conferences that followed between 1914 and 1918 were similar to those that had been raised in Kineret in 1911. When the pioneers gave birth to their first children, the problem of how to combine child care with work activities outside the home became urgent. Because women accepted child raising as their primary responsibility, the demand that men participate, too, though occasionally voiced, was never seriously considered. Yet if each woman had to care for her own children, she would have to give up many tasks outside the home, and the gains made by the women's movement as a whole would eventually be lost. Miriam Baraz, the first mother in the kvutza, described her resistance to the social pressure: "The general opinion was that I should devote all my time to my child. I objected to this with all my might. I knew that way I would no longer be a part of the community and of everything that was happening in the group."[10] The solution that was eventually adopted was collective child care, with the responsibility rotating among women in the kvutza.

In sum, prior to 1918, the women's movement brought about some important changes in the norms regarding woman's role in society. Yet the movement did not develop an institutionalized structure to serve as a power balance against other organizations in the yishuv or in the World Zionist Organization.[11]

Some change did occur after the occupation of Palestine by the British army in 1918, which occurred when Britain was granted a mandate by the League of Nations to rule Palestine. As democratic institutions were set up in the yishuv, women's right to vote and to participate in government became a major issue. The women of the Labor Zionist movement were joined in this struggle by a new organization of middle-class women, the Hebrew Women's Organization for Equal Rights in Palestine. The strongest opposition to women's suffrage came from the religious sector, which viewed the question of women's right to vote as crucial in determining the basic values of the emerging society in Palestine. Religious leaders were also afraid that allowing women to vote would undermine the political power of the religious sector, because conservative religious women would not take part in the elections.

According to an agreement among political parties, women could participate on a temporary basis in the first elections to the assembly. Officially called the Assembly of the Elected, the body was composed of representatives of various organizations and groups in the Labor movement, the middle class, and religious sectors. To compromise with the religious conservatives, religious men were given a double vote as compensation for their wives, who did not take part in the elections. Women were elected to 14 of the 314 seats, constituting 4.5 percent of the assembly membership. After this, the women's organizations faced continued pressure to give up the fight for the vote, for even the more progressive yishuv Labor leaders were afraid the issue would lead to the disintegration of the newly formed institutions.[12] One leader of the women's movement described the mounting pressure on women representatives in the Assembly of the Elected: "They signaled to the women that their stubborn behavior [would] ruin the organization, and 15 women sat as if on burning ashes and did not leave the hall because they did not believe that they were ruining it."[13]

The question of women's suffrage was finally settled in 1925, when the Zionist religious group Hamizrachi joined the supporters of women's suffrage, and the ultraorthodox were left on their own. In the next election 26 of 221 representatives voted in were women—12 percent of the total.[14]

Meanwhile, the leaders of the Labor movement decided that the women's movement posed a problem of social control. A main organ of the labor movement besides the Labor Party is Histadrut, the major trade union in Israel, which essentially serves as an umbrella organization for numerous sub–trade unions. Labor leaders, headed by David Ben Gurion, felt that women's accusations of discrimination undermined the legitimacy of Histadrut's claim to represent all workers. They described the women's movement as a watchdog guarding the interests of a "minority group," rather than viewing it as the creator of a new cultural image for women in the emerging socialist society.[15]

The conflict came to a head at the third Histadrut convention in 1927. The leaders, all male, passed a resolution supporting appointed women's committees, instead of committees directly elected by women to represent their special interests, as was suggested by the women leaders. The resolution was supported by a group of women who had arrived in the third wave of immigrants (1919–23). These women did not identify with the struggle of the women in the second wave to maintain their separate power or with their claim that Histadrut should not serve as the representative of women.

Soon thereafter, Golda Meir was appointed by the Histadrut leaders to be the new leader of the women's movement within Histadrut. Meir, who had immigrated in 1921 during the third wave, supported the Histadrut position on women's participation in the organization. Since Meir's appointment, women's role in public life has been mainly social service oriented, with attention turned more and more to providing for the welfare needs of mothers and children in urban centers. Women do serve in some political capacity, most importantly by mobilizing support for the Labor Party at general elections among women who utilize the movement's social services.[16] Major political decisions, trade union activities, and economic policy making, however, have been left in the hands of the male establishment. Women lost the struggle for an equal position in public life, and for the next 50 years the women's movement did not make any significant effort to change this basic division of roles in society and politics.

The women's movement lost further ground in the 1950s, when Israel faced great economic and social difficulties following its achievement of independence in 1948. Pressure to absorb a massive influx of immigrants before the state was able to develop the necessary economic structure, together with severe security problems, pushed aside any issue that was not viewed as vital to daily life. In facing the problems of absorption, leaders like Prime Minister Ben Gurion attempted to strengthen the family unit by establishing the ten-child family as an ideal. Women were encouraged to fulfill their time-honored role as childbearers through grants of special stipends to families with ten or more children. The policy supported the preservation of conservative norms that valued the family over the individual and viewed women more as procreational tools than as worthy human beings. The majority of women immigrants in the 1950s and 1960s became housewives or accepted low-paying jobs as factory workers or secretaries in order to support themselves and their families, in lieu of pursuing careers.[17]

To strengthen their political position and to augment their ideological authority, Labor leaders developed a myth of the pioneering years, presenting themselves especially as creators of a new, egalitarian society. In spite of the historical truth, they described women's status as equal. The unique case of Golda Meir, who became a minister of labor and then minister of foreign affairs, helped to perpetuate the unfounded belief that elite positions were open to women—women just did not want them.[18]

Yet women continued to fight to improve their status. From the 1960s to the mid-1970s the struggle for women's rights focused primarily on the need to protect and improve women's position as workers. The Labor-controlled government responded to these demands by enacting protective legislation. In contrast to the other two major issues—personal status and political representation—women have enjoyed the official support of the political elite on employment issues, for these are viewed as an essential part of the Labor social agenda.

The change in attitudes toward women began with the Yom Kippur War of 1973 and the ensuing protest movement. A Commission on the Status of Women was appointed as a result of pressure from women's groups; it was chaired by Ora Namir, a Knesset member of the Labor Party. The commission's report, presented in 1978, publicly revealed and described in detail the situation of women in Israel and the discrimination to which they are subjected. Nevertheless, its recommendations were only partially implemented.

The installation of a new government headed by the Likud Party in 1977 increased the power of the women's movement. For the first time in many decades the Labor Party found itself in opposition, making it easier for the women workers' movement to struggle against the government. The Labor Party was joined by another opposition party, the Civil Rights Movement, which was led by a woman Knesset member, Shulamit Aloni, who had a long history of fighting for civil rights in general and women's rights in particular. As a result of their joint action, women's organizations in Israel today have considerable potential to influence policies concerning women, and in certain respects they have exercised it quite successfully.

WOMEN'S ORGANIZATIONS

Women's organizations can be divided, according to the common denominator of their activities, into two categories: multipurpose and feminist. In general, feminist organizations are considered less established and more radical than the multipurpose organizations. Their fields of activity and the political orientation of their leadership overlap considerably.

There are five major multipurpose organizations. NA'AMAT (Working and Voluntary Women's Movement) was founded in 1921 as the women's arm of the Labor movement. It is the largest women's organization in Israel, with 750,000 members and with sister organizations abroad, and now represents 60 percent of Israeli women, both Jewish and Arab. Unlike the majority of Western feminist organizations, which are based on grass-roots participation outside political parties and other mainstream institutions, NA'AMAT is bound to a framework of political and national interests. Though functioning autonomously, it receives a substantial part of its budget from the Histadrut. Any woman who belongs to the Histadrut, or whose husband does, automatically becomes a member.

NA'AMAT is closely affiliated with the political policies of the Labor Party. Accordingly, it is primarily interested in such party issues as child care, youth education and training, women's and family services, leadership and community involvement, legislation, and legal aid. Since 1977, NA'AMAT has attempted to increase its political activity by lobbying through its Department for the Status of Women. The department holds lectures on legal issues and offers free legal advice on discrimination in the workplace, insurance rights, and other matters. One of its main functions is to undertake legal research and to draft legislation. For example, NA'AMAT sponsored a Status of Women month in 1986 to publicize problems relating to laws of personal status and the status of women in the rabbinical courts. Legal experts were commissioned to suggest changes compatible with halacha (Jewish religious law) or with a combination of halacha and Israeli legal practice. The campaign was successful in promoting public awareness of these issues, but it has not resulted in any major changes.

NA'AMAT's attempts to advance women's rights have met a number of obstacles, including its close Labor Party and Histadrut ties, the party loyalties of members, and women's low representation in mainstream political institutions. In addition, budgetary constraints have forced the organization to rely heavily on volunteers to staff projects. The unpaid and part-time nature of the work may also help to perpetuate the low status of women's activities.[19]

The Women's International Zionist Organization is a voluntary organization of Zionist women founded in 1920. Currently 50 federations from all over the world are affiliated with it, giving a total membership of over 250,000. The main projects operated by WIZO include child care, schools, youth clubs, women's clubs and centers, home industries, and legal advice bureaus. In addition, WIZO includes the Council for the Status of Women, which endeavors to protect the rights of women and to advance their status. The council sponsors information centers that provide legal advice and guidance and is actively engaged in initiating and promoting legislation concerning women's rights, such as the inheritance law of 1965.[20] Still, WIZO's self-description as nonpartisan limits to a great extent its ability to influence the political struggle for women's rights. This is especially true on the national level.

EMUNAH (National Religious Women Organization) operates autonomously, but it also constitutes the women's section of the National Religious Party. EMUNAH, which has more than 70,000 members and sister organizations in 12 countries, strives to promote traditional Jewish values, as well as to improve the status of women and members of their families. Its main projects include child care, boarding schools, vocational training, and women's and family services.[21] Its affiliation with the National Religious Party does not limit its independence. For example, after the party agreed to the ultraorthodox parties' demands not to present women as candidates in the 1989 municipal elections, EMUNAH successfully presented an independent list of candidates in Jerusalem.

The Herut Women's League was founded in 1948 as a branch of the Herut Movement, a historical-revisionist party of the right. (The Herut Movement and the Liberal Party constitute what is now called the Likud Party.) The league continues its political involvement while functioning as an independent voluntary women's organization. With a membership of several thousand women and assistance from sister groups abroad, it operates day-care facilities and boarding schools and provides women's and social services.[22]

One last multipurpose organization, the Israeli Women's Network, was established in 1984 as a nonpartisan association of women from various sectors who wanted to act together to raise public consciousness about issues concerning the status of women and to put pressure on authorities and organizations that are supposed to deal with these issues.[23] The members of the Women's Network include activists from political parties, academics, and professionals. The network is involved in political debates that have a particular impact on the status of women. For example, it

established a special committee of representatives from political parties and political scientists to discuss the influence on women of the proposal to change the electoral system from national-proportional to regional-proportional.

The feminist organizations date from the founding of the Israeli feminist movement in Haifa in 1970, which developed three main centers of activity, in Tel Aviv, Jerusalem, and Haifa, as well as a number of project-oriented groups. Several attempts to unite these centers and groups into one national feminist movement have failed. Instead, the various organizations have been meeting annually at a national conference.

In March 1982 a formal association was registered under the name Israel Feminist Movement. The movement was founded to achieve full equality between the sexes and to eliminate sex discrimination in all facets of life, including the personal status law, employment opportunities, wages, professional advancement, and social security. Although the association is a direct descendant of the Tel Aviv feminist center, its goals and methods of operation are shared by the various sister groups.

The feminist movement as a whole has taken up many issues of concern to women. Feminists have brought rape and wife battery to the public eye and introduced them to the Knesset. In addition to working for improved legislation and more sensitive police handling of victims, feminists have taken positive action themselves to address issues of violence against women. They operate three shelters for battered women (in Haifa, Herzlia, and Jerusalem) and three rape crisis centers. The Center for the Study of Media and the Family and A Different Image, two groups of feminist activists, have been exerting concerted pressure to bar the publication of sexist advertisements. They also focus on women's special health problems, labor legislation, and improving women's personal status, and they publish books and a feminist quarterly.[24]

Feminist as well as multipurpose organizations invest heavily in making women aware of their status as a class, their sex-role socialization, and concerns about individual self-fulfillment. To this end, they conduct courses, workshops, seminars, and lectures on such topics as personal consciousness-raising and group support, women's rights and the assertion of these rights, involvement in community affairs, and preparation for public leadership roles.

To change public attitudes regarding women—the most difficult task—women's organizations have undertaken intensive campaigns: publicizing projects that seek to improve the status of women, stimulating research and data collection and adapting the results for public use, and sensitizing the media to general and specific issues. In addition, women's organizations have publicized sex discrimination policies and cases, written letters to the editor, and published books, periodicals, and newsletters on women's issues.

The extensive social and community work carried out by women's organizations enhances their public image and gives leverage to the positions they advocate. The government regularly earmarks funds for a number of projects conducted by the organizations, mainly day-care centers, thereby supporting and increasing women's activities, which in turn attract members, strengthen organizational structures, and enhance organizational power.

A considerable amount of activity is devoted to lobbying for legislative measures to improve the status of women and to counteract measures adversely affecting it. Women's organizations frequently draft or amend legislation pertaining to women and often submit written and oral positions on pending legislation to governmental and parliamentary bodies. To mobilize public pressure for or against issues, women's groups have also organized demonstrations, held press conferences, met with Knesset members, led letter-writing and phone call campaigns, and published articles in newspapers and magazines.

Yet the organizations' preoccupation with social service activities has been challenged in recent years. Some women have voiced the opinion that many of the services rendered by the organizations, especially day-care centers, should be regarded as the responsibility of the state and should therefore be taken over by the state administration. Women's resources, they argue, should be expended primarily for the promotion of women's status and the attainment of equal opportunity. The ultimate evaluation of these conflicting approaches will depend on the impact of two main considerations: first, the present likelihood of deeper state financial involvement in the services in question and, second, the adverse effect on the power and leverage of women's organizations that might result from the curtailment of these services.

WOMEN'S EMPLOYMENT

Women's status in the labor market has been characterized by incremental change. During the first 15 years of Israel's existence, the government employment policy was directed mainly toward creating jobs for men. Approximately 70 percent of working women were employed in female-dominated occupations; approximately one-third were concentrated in seven traditional occupations.[25] Women's attitudes toward employment correlated with their ethnic origin. Whereas Jewish women from Europe and from English-speaking countries were more favorably disposed toward women's employment because they had fewer children, Jewish women from predominantly Muslim countries, as well as Arab women, tended to follow their cultural traditions by confining their role to the family.

During the 1950s and 1960s a body of legislation created directives for the employment of women. The Women's Work Law of 1954 established regulations concerning maternity leave that included a mandatory leave of 12 weeks with nearly full pay, the right to take up to a year's leave without pay, and shorter working hours in the year following childbirth. It forbade the employment of women in certain jobs (for example, at a zinc kiln) that might be injurious to their health, as well as restricting dismissal of a pregnant woman and prohibiting the dismissal of a woman during maternity leave. In 1959 the Employment Service Act prohibited employment discrimination against women, and in 1964 the Male and Female Workers (Equal Pay) Act established the principle of equal pay for equal work.

A number of developments during the 1970s led to the accelerated entry of women into the labor force. Economic development and the expansion of the financial, insurance, community, and other service industries stimulated the demand for additional workers. Meanwhile, as a result of the extension of army service for men from two to three years, the creation of new military units for service in the territories conquered in the Six-Day War, and the growth of the universities, the available supply of men in the work force was reduced. Between 1964 and 1969, the proportion of men in the civilian labor force dropped from 77 to 70 percent. This shortage of qualified men compelled employers to hire women for jobs that had previously been filled by men.[26]

As the economy expanded, women's position within the family also changed. Women from immigrant families experienced increasing levels of education because of a law establishing mandatory education, and the birthrate among Jewish women from Muslim countries dropped, allowing them to join the labor force. Together with the coming of age of the better educated baby-boom generation and legislation aimed at helping the working family, these developments facilitated the integration of women's work and family life.

Although state leaders still viewed mothers as responsible for the family, their continuing socialist commitment to "work" demanded that women participate in the labor force outside the home as well.[27] One way the state sought to enhance women's employment was to provide day care. The Ministry of Labor and Social Welfare subsidized the building of day-care centers in the 1970s, creating tens of thousands of places for children of prekindergarten age.

Because the government policy was to encourage women to enter the labor force, particularly in factories in the development towns (small towns founded in the 1950s and 1960s, primarily by Asian and African immigrants), day-care fees

were set according to a mother's income and rarely amounted to more than a quarter of her gross earnings. Even though this policy reinforced the view that child care is the wife's responsibility, the low rates also gave women an economic incentive to seek paid employment. The two-income family improved women's situation, and many younger women grew up preparing themselves to join the labor force. During the 1980s, however, unemployment was on the rise, and day-care fees were linked to the per capita income of the total family. This policy did not affect women's labor force participation in the urban areas, but it did make employment less feasible for the low-income women in the development towns.[28]

Legislative efforts to increase women's labor force participation continued in the 1980s. The Equal Opportunity in Employment Law of 1981 prohibited discrimination against women on the grounds of their sex, marriage, or parenthood in employment, vocational training, or advertisements. This law was amended in 1988 by the Equal Opportunity in Employment Act, which prohibits discrimination and sexual harassment and entitles fathers to take parental leave after a new baby is born and to resign from work without losing their compensation rights in order to raise a newborn child.[29]

Since 1948 women's work force participation has been slowly increasing. Between 1954 and 1989 the proportion of women aged 15 and older in the civilian labor force rose from 21 to 40 percent. Women now constitute 38 percent of the total civilian labor force in Israel. Because this growth in their participation came at a time of declining participation for men, over 60 percent of the new workers in the past decade have been women.

In addition, marriage and the presence of small children in the home have become less of a deterrent to women's employment. The proportion of married Israeli women in the work force grew from 26 percent in 1968 to 46 percent in 1988, and in 1987, almost 60 percent of all ever-married Jewish women whose youngest children were between two and four years old were in the labor force. Levels of labor force participation continue to be significantly lower for Arab and Druze women, however, because of traditional norms about women's role as mothers.

Their gains in employment notwithstanding, working mothers have had to develop special strategies to balance work and family obligations. Part-time employment is a popular recourse: 70 percent of part-time workers are women. Women's average workweek is 29 hours, compared to 40 hours per week for men.[30] This strategy limits women's earning power and their chances for promotion because women are perceived as lacking interest in pursuing careers.

Women's increasing levels of education have also contributed to their greater participation in the work force. The more educated a woman is, the more likely she is to be employed. Among women with 16 years or more of education, labor force participation rates are the same as for men (77 percent).[31]

Still, there are significant differences in the occupational patterns of women from different ethnic groups. The service and production jobs at the "bottom" of women's labor market are typically held by immigrant women of Asian and African origin. At the center of the labor ladder is clerical work, mostly held by second-generation Asian and African women. The semiprofessional and scientific occupations at the "top" are typically held by second-generation Ashkenazi (Jews of European and American descent) and to a lesser extent by first-generation Ashkenazi. These differences are mainly the result of a persistent gap in education among ethnic groups. Thus far, women's ability to break out of the confines of the female labor market seems to be dependent on their level of educational achievement, and the second generation of Ashkenazi women is ahead in this respect.[32]

Among Arab women the level of work force participation is 28 percent for Christians, 15 percent for Druzes, and 12 percent for Muslims.[33] Arab women generally have jobs that fall into one of two categories. The first type is primarily taken by village women, who work at service and industry jobs with low wages, no social benefits, little vacation or sick leave, and no job security or opportunity for advancement. Their work is usually arranged through contractors, generally male relatives, and the textile plants where the women work are usually in their own villages or nearby, because it is still considered undesirable for women to work far away from home unless a male relative is working in the plant.[34]

The second type of job is mainly white-collar—teaching, nursing, and social work, the first professions to gain social legitimacy in Arab society. Recently, educated Arab women have begun to work in private offices as doctors, lawyers, and pharmacists. Some have also set up independent businesses, such as boutiques and insurance companies.[35] These women, especially those living in the cities, enjoy modern life together with their family responsibilities, and their education and professional status is very similar to that of Jewish women.

In spite of the increases in women's labor force participation, women face barriers in the workplace. In Israel, as in most industrialized countries, they are still concentrated in a small number of female-dominated occupations.[36] Many women work in academic, semiprofessional, and white-collar occupations, but in all institutional spheres—political, military, economic, educational, religious, and cultural—the higher the position, the smaller the proportion of women. In the civil service, for example, women constitute 51 percent of those employed, but only 11 percent of those in the top five ranks of the administrative hierarchy and only 20 percent of those at the top of the professional (academic) hierarchy.[37]

Yet women have responded to new opportunities created by men leaving an occupation or by rapid expansion of a field, as occurred in personnel management and training, marketing, and public relations. They have also increased their university enrollment in nontraditional fields. Between 1974 and 1988 the proportion of women law students increased from 32 to 41 percent. Similarly, the number of women in business and administration programs rose from 12 to 30 percent, and the number in medical (including dental) programs went from 20 to 41 percent.[38]

Israeli women also earn less than men and face discrimination in the workplace. Although the seniority gap between men and women in the civil service decreased in the 1980s, the earnings gap widened. In 1978 women's hourly earnings were approximately 78 percent of men's, despite laws that guarantee equal pay for equal work. By 1988 women's earnings had decreased to 71 percent of men's. As elsewhere, women are discriminated against in job promotion.[39] Employers also discriminate between men and women in essentially similar jobs by means of differential allocation of fringe benefits, such as overtime payments and telephone and car allowances (which can account for 40 percent of take-home pay), and in the assignment of different job titles for what is essentially the same work (secretary as compared to adviser, for example). This discrimination is perpetuated by a gender bias against women and the diehard opinion that men are heads of households and thus more in need of money than women.

WOMEN AND POLITICAL
REPRESENTATION

The bias against women extends to the arena of politics. In the first three Knessets, elected between 1949 and 1955, women composed 9.1 percent of the total membership. Since then, the proportion of female members has declined and is now between 6.6 percent and 8.3 percent. In the 12th Knesset, elected in 1988, there are eight female members, constituting 6.6 percent of the membership. There has been no woman minister in the government since 1988. The decline in women's representation can be explained by organizational stagnation and the conservative attitude toward women's representation among the majority of the parties and their leaders.

At the local level, women have fared slightly better; the percentage of women elected to local councils has grown from 4.2 in the first elections in 1950 to 8.6 in the 1989 elections. More than one-third of local councils are still all-male pre-serves, however; the average number of women elected to councils stands at 1.8. Only a few women have served as heads of local councils, among them a Christian Arab woman, Violet Khoury.[40]

In 1975 the law controlling local government administration was radically reformed to provide for direct elections of all mayors (council chairpersons) by local citizens, concurrent with the election of local councils. This change made the position of mayor the only directly elected position in Israel, and at the same time it raised the prestige of the position and increased men's competition for it. Since the reform, only one woman has been elected head of a local council (mayor), in the small town of Even Yehuda. Nevertheless, some progress can be noted, for women are now serving as deputy mayors in a number of cities, including Haifa and Jerusalem.

Women constitute between 40 and 50 percent of total party membership. Yet the ratio of their representation at the political decision-making level in both the government and the parties lags far behind. The organizational structure of all the major parties, as well as some of the smaller ones, includes women's departments in one form or another. In principle, these departments, which usually have a small paid staff and elected executive officers, support women's rights and the need to enhance women's political power within the parties. In practice, the actual amount of effort invested by the women's departments to attain these goals has varied.[41]

A circular put out by the Women's Department in the Labor Party illustrates the organizational steps followed to gain influence. An important strategy is securing representation of the female membership in all party institutions, local as well as central, and ensuring women not less than 20 percent of all elected and appointed positions. (The actual level of representation is usually 10 to 16 percent.) To achieve this end, the Women's Department pressures and lobbies party leaders, participates in the constitution committee in order to ensure obligatory representation of women in most elected local and national bodies, and becomes involved in specific cases where women's representation or other interests are at stake. The department also conducts discussions and takes positions on women's issues and defines ways to improve women's status in major fields.

With varying degrees of effort, women's departments in other political parties have implemented similar measures. The need is evident: there are, for example, only one female Knesset member from the more conservative Likud Party and four women members from the Labor Party. Likewise, women are not well represented on the central committees of these parties (which elect representatives to the Knesset in a secret ballot): 13 percent of Likud committee members and 16 percent of the Labor committee members are women.

Nevertheless, none of the women's departments has secured the desired minimum of 20 percent female representation in all elected positions inside their party or in national and local bodies.[42] The low numbers are caused mainly by conservative attitudes among party elites, who ignore the issue of women's electoral power and the gender gap.

Women's position within the Histadrut is similar to their position within political parties. The trade union, because it commands vast economic power, has political as well as economic significance. The members, 80 percent of the Israeli population over eighteen, come from all levels and sectors of the work force. Nearly 50 percent of the Histadrut members are women, yet women lead only a few individual trade unions, all of which are composed primarily of women (e.g., nurses and textile workers). In the Central Committee, the governing body of the Histadrut, five of the forty members are women: three were elected in a secret ballot by the Labor Party Central Committee, one is the elected general secretary of NA'AMAT, and one was nominated by the general secretary of the Histadrut after long service in a previous Histadrut Central Committee. The major activity of these women is working on women's affairs—protection of women's rights in the workplace, consumer protection, and welfare. None has an influential position in the most important part of the organization—the trade union division.

The harmful effects that women's relative powerlessness in the Histadrut has on their lives is illustrated by the recent negotiations over the introduction of a five-day workweek into the civil service. Although the Israeli Women's Network had presented a document containing women's reservations and demands concerning this proposed change, the all-male union delegation of the large white-collar civil service union (whose membership is 50 percent female) accepted the employers' suggestion without discussion, despite the disadvantages for women employees with young children.[43] Constraints on women's power limit their ability to promote their status and employment opportunities, limiting in turn their economic and political influence.

WOMEN, RELIGION, AND THE LAW

Not just the constraints on women's political activity but the centrality of religion in Israeli political life as well has had an adverse impact on civil rights issues. The religious "status quo" agreement that preserves relations established in the yishuv era between the ruling Labor Movement and the religious parties, together with the decision not to adopt a constitution, made on the eve of the founding of the state, led to civil rights issues being pushed to the sidelines, with a far-reaching effect on the basic values in society and on the condition of women. As early as 1951, when the Law for the Equal Rights of Women was adopted, the Knesset supported the proposal that all matters relating to women's matrimonial status should be excluded from the domain of the civil courts. Regardless of the opposition of female Labor representatives, legislation was passed mandating that anything concerning matrimonial status be decided in rabbinical courts, as the status quo obligation of the Labor Party required.

The rabbinical courts' Jurisdiction (Marriage and Divorce) Law of 1953 implemented this decision, vesting exclusive jurisdiction for all matters concerning the marriage and divorce of Jewish citizens or residents of the state in the rabbinical courts. Because the rabbinical courts decide cases according to Jewish law, they do not recognize the equality of men and women in modern society. Non-Jewish Israeli citizens have their own Muslim or Christian religious courts, which are also conservative in their attitudes toward women. The jurisdiction of the rabbinical courts is not absolute in all spheres of family law, however; women do have the right to choose the forum for the trial (rabbinical or civil) in matters not connected with marriage or divorce.[44] That is, if a woman appeals first to a civil court, that court will have jurisdiction. Civil courts usually decide cases based on a modern and egalitarian point of view, compared to the conservative and discriminatory view of rabbinical courts. (Criminal cases and all other matters are under the jurisdiction of civil courts only.)

The enormous political influence wielded by the religious parties has created large normative questions concerning the direction that Israeli society must take—for example, whether to separate state and religion or to continue the current integration. One of the most controversial questions for many years concerns the demand for civil marriage for those who would like to marry without a religious ceremony or who cannot marry according to religious laws. This demand is supported by left-wing and small central parties, the feminist movement, and civil rights organizations. It is opposed by the two largest parties, Labor and Likud, and by the religious parties. Even though NA'AMAT had been reluctant to support this demand, because it is contrary to official Labor Party policy—which was intended to maintain its coalition with religious parties—the women's organization adopted a resolution at its January 1990 congress calling for the legalization of civil marriage for individuals who prefer it. This resolution resulted from the failure of a long-standing NA'AMAT policy to advocate reforms with the cooperation of the religious courts.

On other legal questions affecting women, the impact of this dual legal system has been almost nonexistent because state laws have predominated over religious ones. The Knesset has taken the position that women's rights must be promoted by civil legislation and that the authority of the rabbinical courts should be limited. Laws that protect women include, for example, the Legal Capacity and Guardianship Law of 1962, which explicitly states that both parents are the natural guardians of minors and that there must be full cooperation and agreement between both parents regarding the upbringing, education, and training of children.

The Succession Law of 1965, in contrast to Jewish law, improves the position of widows by recognizing their legitimate rights as heirs and by increasing their share of a husband's estate to 50 percent. The act also recognizes the right of a common-law wife to inherit her partner's estate and imposes on the estate the cost of providing equally for a widow if she is in need of support.

Financial relationships between husbands and wives are determined in the 1973 Spouses (Property Relations) Law, which allows the couple to determine what proportion of their property they wish to share. Their written agreement is confirmed by a civil court. If no such agreement exists, then the property acquired in the course of the marriage is divided by the civil court into two equal parts, and each partner is entitled to half.

The Criminal Law of 1977 provides that an abortion can be carried out on any of the following legal grounds: the woman is under 17 years of age or over 40; the pregnancy is the result of out-of-wedlock or forbidden relations; the newborn may have a birth defect; and the pregnancy endangers the health of the mother. The fifth section, which permits socioeconomic problems to be grounds for abortion, was removed from the law in 1979 because of pressure on the Likud government from ultraorthodox parties.

PROSPECTS

Women in Israeli society have been involved in a struggle for rights and status for 80 years. Their failures and successes can be analyzed only against the background of the development of the Jewish yishuv and the state of Israel—a new society fighting to survive wars, the absorption of huge waves of immigrants, and social and minority problems. The framework that determined women's position in society was established in the 1920s and remained almost unchanged until the mid-1970s.

The political-economic elite functioned to a large extent as a "closed shop." Women were regarded as a marginal, almost nonexistent force. The elite had no inclination to encourage women to receive professional training or to seek advancement in their place of work, nor were women appointed to senior positions in the private or civil sectors. Women's contribution to society was viewed as inherently secondary and supportive. The Labor movement elite saw women as voters, but not as decision makers.

The rise to power of the right-of-center Herut Movement under Menachem Begin in 1977 did not improve this situation, for proponents emphasized tradition and old-fashioned European chivalry. The liberal philosophy of the movement's spiritual father, Ze'ev Jabotinsky, was submerged in layers of conservatism and the zealous patriotism that characterized his followers.[45]

Centralist-conservative developments have constituted a persistent obstacle to the advancement of women's status and the achievement of equality. The political elite and the leaders of the two major parties still do not view women as an essential part of political decision making. Neither Labor nor Likud party leaders chose to include women in the national unity government that was established in 1986, and there was no woman in the Likud government in 1992.

Ultimately, the slow rate of change and occasional reversal of women's political mobility should be seen as the result of a general political stagnation and the permanent national focus on security. After a solution is found to the pressing security problems of Israel, perhaps the political leadership and society will be able to change the order of their priorities and give more attention and support to women's rights and women's equal position.

NOTES

1. Katzir, *Source Reading for the Zionist Movement in Russia* (in Hebrew) (Tel Aviv: Massada Press, 1964).

2. Dafna N. Izraeli, "The Zionist Women's Movement in Palestine, 1911–1927: A Sociological Analysis," *Signs* 7, no. 1 (1981): 89.

3. Sara Malchin, "The Woman Worker in Kineret" (in Hebrew), *Hapoel Hatzair* 11, no. 13 (1912).

4. Izraeli, "Zionist Women's Movement," 90–92.

5. Thia Liberson, "On the Question of the Women Workers" (in Hebrew), *Hapoel Hatzair* 27 (1913).

6. Izraeli, "Zionist Women's Movement," 94.

7. Ibid., 96.

8. Ada Maimon, *Along the Way* (in Hebrew) (Tel Aviv: Tel Aviv Am Oved, 1972), 121.

9. Ada Maimon, *Women Workers' Movement in Eretz-Israel* (in Hebrew) (Tel Aviv: Tel Aviv Hapoel Hatzair, 1929), 23.

10. Miriam Baraz, "How I Conquered Work" (in Hebrew), in Shazar R. Katznelson, ed., *With the Steps of Generation* (Moetzet Hapoalot: Histadrut, 1964).

11. Izraeli, "Zionist Women's Movement," 100.

12. Daphna Sharfman, *Women and Politics* (in Hebrew) (Haifa: Tamar, 1988), 44–48.

13. Maimon, *Along the Way,* 201.

14. Sharfman, *Women and Politics,* 48.

15. Ibid., 56.

16. Izraeli, "Zionist Women's Movement," 106–13.

17. Daphna Sharfman, "The Status of Women in Israel—Fact and Myth," *Israeli Democracy* 3, no. 2 (Summer 1989): 12–14.

18. Ibid.

19. Juliet Pope, "Feminism and Nationalism Within Israeli Women's Organizations: A Case Study of NA'AMAT," in Barbara Swirski and Marilyn P. Safir, eds., *Calling the Equality Bluff: Women in Israel* (New York: Pergamon, 1990), 225–33.

20. "Participation of Women in Political and Social Life" (Israel National Statement to the European Regional Seminar at UNESCO, Bonn, 24–26 October 1982), 14–15.

21. Ibid., 16.

22. Ibid.

23. *The Status of Women in Israel* (Jerusalem: Israeli Women's Network, 1987), introduction.

24. This discussion of multipurpose and feminist organizations draws on "Participation of Women," 12–21.

25. Dafna N. Izraeli, "Sex Structure of Occupations: The Israeli Experience," *Sociology of Work and Occupations* 6 (1979): 404–29.

26. Dafna N. Izraeli, "From Collective to Career: Women in the World of Work," in Swirski and Safir, eds., *Calling the Equality Bluff,* 1–2.

27. Marilyn P. Safir, "Tradition and Public Policy Shape

the Family in Israel," in Swirski and Safir, eds., *Calling the Equality Bluff.*

28. Ibid.

29. *Forty Years of Law* (Prime Minister's Office, Advisor on the Status of Women, March 1988), 5–15.

30. Ibid., 10.

31. Izraeli, "From Collective to Career," 5.

32. Dvora Bernstein, "Together Along Different Routes: Oriental and Ashkenazi Women in the Israeli Labor Market," in Swirski and Safir, eds., *Calling the Equality Bluff,* 5, 8–9.

33. Izraeli, "From Collective to Career," 4–5.

34. Saniya Abu-Rabiya, "Arab Women in the Israeli Labor Market," in Swirski and Safir, eds., *Calling the Equality Bluff,* 3–4.

35. Ibid., 5.

36. Ibid., 4–7.

37. Nina Toren, "The Status of Women in Academia," *Israel Social Science Research* 5, no. 1–2 (1987): 138–46.

38. Izraeli, "From Collective to Career," 8.

39. Ibid., 8–9.

40. Judith Buber Agassi, "Golda Notwithstanding: Participation and Powerlessness," in Swirski and Safir, eds., *Calling the Equality Bluff,* 8–9.

41. "Participation of Women," 11, 8–9.

42. Ibid., 8–9.

43. Buber Agassi, "Golda Notwithstanding," 11–12.

44. *Forty Years of Law,* 7. Much of the following information about specific laws comes from this source.

45. Sharfman, "Status of Women in Israel."

▲ Japan

POLITICS

Type of Political System: democracy
  Sovereignty: constitutional monarchy
  Executive-Legislative System: parliamentary
Type of State: unitary
Type of Party System: multiparty
Major Political Parties

Jiyūminshutō (Liberal Democratic Party, LDP): The ruling party in 1992 and the major conservative political group; formed in 1955 through the merger of two conservative parties founded after World War II. It has governed since 1955. The basic policy planks are (1) to perfect Japan as a cultural and democratic state by enhancing the functions of existing institutions in line with the best principles of democracy; (2) to build a self-reliant and independent Japan; (3) to improve international relations on the basis of universal justice for a humankind that aspires for peace and freedom; and (4) to plan and implement a comprehensive economic program based on individual initiative and free enterprise, keeping in mind the welfare of the public, and to stabilize the people's livelihood and achieve a welfare state.

Nipponshakaitō (Japan Socialist Party, JSP): Formed in November 1945 through a merger of prewar proletarian parties; split into left-wing and right-wing parties in 1951; reappeared as a unified party in October 1955. Its objective is the realization of socialism through a "peaceful and democratic revolution" while upholding the present constitution. In July 1986, Doi Takako was elected chair of the JSP—the first woman to head a major political party in Japan.

Kōmeitō (Clean Government Party): Formed in November 1964, originally as the political arm of the Sōka Gakkai, a lay body of the Nichiren Shōshū sect of Buddhism. In its first general election in January 1967, 25 of its candidates were elected to the House of Representatives. The party has since declared its independence from religion. Its aims include the construction of a welfare society based on the concept of "humanitarian socialism."

Minshushakaitō (Democratic Socialist Party, DSP): Formed by right-wing members of the Japan Socialist Party in 1961; stands against extremist ideologies and is dedicated to the creation of a socialist society through democratic processes. According to its platform, it endeavors to "overcome capitalism and totalitarianism, whether of the left or of the right," and it is not a class party but "a popular party that recognizes the diversity of interests among various social groups and at the same time the existence of common national interests."

Nihonkyōsantō (Japan Communist Party, JCP): Founded as an underground political association in July 1922; became a legal party after World War II. It aims to realize a communist society in Japan through "a democratic revolution of the people and a subsequent socialist revolution."

Shakaiminshurengō (United Social Democratic Party): Officially formed in March 1978 through merger of two minor political groups. Its objective is the realization of a "new and liberal socialism."

Year Women Granted Right to Vote: 1945
Year Women Granted Right to Stand for Election: 1945
Percentage of Women in the Legislature[a]
  Lower House: 2.3%
  Upper House: 14.7%
Percentage of Electorate Voting for Highest Elected Office in Most Recent Election (1990): 73.3%[b]

DEMOGRAPHICS

Population: 122,700,000[c]
Percentage of Population in Urban Areas
  Overall: 76.7%

Female: 76.5%
Male: 77.0%

Percentage of Population Below Age 15:
19.7%[d]

Birthrate: 10[e]

Maternal Mortality Rate (per 100,000 live births): 9[f]

Infant Mortality Rate (per 1,000 live births): 6

Mortality Rate for Children Under Five (per 1,000 live births): 9

Average Household Size: 3.0[g]

Mean Age at First Marriage[h]
Female: 25.9
Male: 28.4

Life Expectancy[i]
Female: 82.1
Male: 76.1

EDUCATION

Ratio of Female to Male Enrollment[j]
First-Level Education: 95
Second-Level Education: 99
Third-Level Education: 67

Literacy Rate
Female: 97.0%
Male: 99.0%

ECONOMY

Gross National Product per Capita: U.S. $11,300

Percentage of Labor Force in Agriculture:
6.4%[k]

Distribution of Agricultural Workers by Sex[l]
Female: 47.9%
Male: 52.1%

Economically Active Population by Sex[m]
Female: 47.1%
Male: 76.1%

a. *Women's Outlook* (Tokyo: Fusae Ichikawa Memorial Association, 1990).
b. Ibid.
c. Asahi Shimbun, *Asahi Almanac, 1991* (in Japanese) (Tokyo, 1991), 438.
d. *Population Census of Japan* (Tokyo: Management and Coordination Agency, 1990).
e. *Vital Statistics of Japan* (in Japanese) (Tokyo: Ministry of Health and Welfare, 1991).
f. Ibid.
g. *Survey of Living Conditions of the People on Health and Welfare* (in Japanese) (Tokyo: Ministry of Health and Welfare, 1990).
h. *Vital Statistics of Japan.*
i. *The Abridged Life Tables* (in Japanese) (Tokyo: Ministry of Health and Welfare, 1991).
j. *Report on Basic School Statistics* (Tokyo: Ministry of Education, 1991).
k. *Population Census of Japan.*
l. Ibid.
m. Ibid.

The U.N. Convention on Eliminating Discrimination Against Women and the Status of Women in Japan

NUITA YŌKO,
YAMAGUCHI MITSUKO,
AND KUBO KIMIKO
TRANSLATED BY
ELIZABETH J. CLARKE

Japan, an archipelago of four main islands and 30,000 smaller ones, is located off the east coast of the Asian continent. It covers a land area of 143,750 square miles and has a population of 122.7 million (50.8 percent female).[1] The governing power rests with the people, but an emperor is the symbolic head of state.

The Meiji Restoration of 1868 brought an end to 250 years of feudal military rule, leading to the formation of a modern nation-state with a constitution. A parliamentary form of representative government was instituted with the opening of the Diet (parliament) in 1890, a year after the constitution was promulgated. The Meiji government, striving to catch up with the technologically advanced Western nations, put its energies into the development of economic and military structures. In 1872 a modern educational system was established as a keystone to national advancement, and compulsory schooling for both boys and girls was instituted. Confucian values, the foundation for a male-dominant society, resulted in an educational policy that trained girls to be "good wives and wise mothers." The 1896 promulgation of the civil law code created a legal system that weakened women's social status, further contributing to male dominance in both the private and the public spheres. A sharp division of roles based on sex placed men in the public domain and women at home.

This social pattern of thought and practice persists today and influences women's participation in the political world. A description of the political system and the status of women since World War II is therefore necessary. Three significant public issues illustrate the barriers to women's participation in the political process. The examples encompass educational, nationality, and employment policies, all of which require government action for change to occur and all of which came to the forefront politically because of the governmental decision, made under pressure from women's groups, to ratify the U.N. Convention on the Elimination of All Forms of Discrimination Against Women. Finally, we will analyze factors that influence women's entry into the formal political system and the obstacles that women confront as they seek elective office.

THE POLITICAL AND ECONOMIC SYSTEMS

The Diet epitomizes the principle of sovereign power residing with the people and is the highest organ of state power, being the sole lawmaking body in Japan. It consists of the House of Representatives, with 512 seats, and the House of Councillors, with 252 seats. The two houses utilize different electoral systems for selecting their members. The members of the House of Representatives are elected in a system of medium-sized constituencies with three to five seats per constituency (except for one constituency with a single seat) for terms of four years, subject to shortening as the result of a dissolution of the Diet. Members of the House of Councillors are elected for terms of six years, half of the councillors (126) being elected every three years. Each voter casts two ballots in upper house elections. One ballot is cast for a candidate from an electoral district. (In the upper house each prefecture or equivalent entity constitutes an electoral district.) Of the 126 councillor seats contested in each election, 76 are elected directly from these local constitutencies in each prefecture. The other 50 councillors are chosen by ballots cast for a registered political party. Before the election each party submits a prioritized list of its candidates. On the basis of the percentage of total votes that each party receives, it is allocated a proportional number of the 50 seats being contested. For example, if the Liberal Democratic Party (LDP) receives 30 percent of the national vote in any given election for the House of Councillors, the top 15 persons on its list are automatically elected.

Japanese citizens 25 years old and over are eligible for election to the House of Representatives, and those 30 years old and over may be elected to the House of Councillors. Japan has universal suffrage for every citizen aged 20 years and above. The five major political parties include the Liberal Democratic Party (in power since 1955), the Japan Socialist Party, Kōmeitō, the Japan Communist Party, and the Democratic Socialist Party.[2]

Executive power is vested in the cabinet, which consists of the prime minister and not more than 22 ministers of state; the cabinet is collectively responsible to the Diet. The prime minister, elected by and from the Diet, has the power to appoint and dismiss the ministers of state, all of whom must be civilians and a majority of whom must be members of the Diet.

Japan is divided into 47 prefectures, including metropolitan Tokyo; and prefectural, city, town, and village governments each have their respective assemblies that act òn local legislative matters. The prefectural governors and city, town, and village mayors, as well as members of local assemblies, are elected by the registered voters within each district.

Japan's political institutions were formed in the aftermath of World War II. So, too, did Japan's unconditional surrender to the Allied powers in 1945 mark a new beginning for Japanese women. There were three periods of major economic and social change from 1945 to 1990: 1945–60, characterized by the change to a new set of values; 1961–74, known for its rapid economic growth; and 1975–90, distinguished by a reassessment of the sex-based division of work. Understanding them will help to explain the status and life of women in Japan within a changing economic and political environment.

While Japan was occupied by the victorious Allies after its surrender, its people suffered extreme hardships—physical and spiritual devastation, a shortage of commodities, severe inflation. Occupation officials aimed to eliminate militarism from Japan and instituted far-reaching changes in economic policy and the public education system to establish democratic structures. Political, social, and educational emancipation for women opened up unprecedented opportunities for new forms of participation.

Women leaders of the prewar movement for women's suffrage—like Akamatsu Tsuneko, Ichikawa Fusae, and Yamataka Shigeri—once again gathered their forces to press the Japanese government to extend full democratic rights to women.[3] They organized the Committee to Formulate Postwar Policy Measures for Women to negotiate with Japanese officials the legal and social reforms needed to remove the limitations that had prevented women's participation in society. On 17 December 1945 the revision of the election law was completed, extending the franchise to women for the first time. The peace constitution promulgated in November 1946 not only stipulated the renunciation of war but also prescribed respect for fundamental human rights and the equality of women and men. In the old constitution women were considered subservient to men, with no political and limited civil rights. The new constitution required the revision of laws to guarantee women property ownership, inheritance, and education rights and equal work rights (tempered by protective labor laws). A new day would dawn for the women of

Japan: they would now have equal rights with men.

Before these new measures became effective in changing everyday practices and attitudes, however, the war in Korea broke out in June 1950, intensifying the cold war between East and West. Security issues resulted in both the United States and the Soviet Union consolidating their military strength, which in turn had a direct impact on occupation planning for Japan. Policies leading to a democratic Japan without a military force were reversed to enable the Japanese government to contribute to the military endeavors of the West. The peace treaty that finally ended World War II for Japan was signed in 1952 and excluded the Soviet Union and other socialist nations. The East-West conflict directly influenced Japan's partnership with the West and its security arrangements. Japanese leaders who had been purged from public life during the occupation had their rights restored, and they once again sought political leadership—bringing traditional attitudes toward women's role in society to their renewed activity, and the effect of this became evident in the formation of post-occupation policy.

Ironically, the Korean War stimulated the Japanese economy and initiated industrial recovery. Rapid economic progress followed during the 1960s, bringing about salient changes in the industrial structure. In particular, the development of the tertiary industrial sector created new employment opportunities for women. A growing number of women found a place in the labor market.

Women's rising interest in activities outside the home could be attributed to several factors: the changing life cycle, represented by the decline in the birthrate and the extension of women's average life expectancy; the increase in leisure time as a result of technological innovations in the home; and equal educational opportunities, which allowed more women to receive higher education. Their life activities, which had hitherto been confined to the home, extended into the industrial sector, and their income began to enrich their families. But society was being distorted by the profit-motive-oriented and production-based industrial policy. The destruction of the environment by industrial pollution and the emission of toxic substances, together with an increase in traffic accidents, steadily undermined the health of the family.

Husbands persisted in placing business first, ignoring the dysfunctional social consequences of basing a society on consumerism; at the same time, wives, conscious of the encroaching dangers to the health and well-being of the family, began to engage in grass-roots movements to protect the environment and their children. Working mothers also recognized their need for child-care facilities. Small groups of women joined together so their voices could reach the government agencies that should have dealt with these issues. Increasing numbers of women realized that without political action their pleas would be for naught, so they began to select and successfully support their own candidates for local legislatures—sometimes women members of their local study and action groups.

In the 1960s the women's liberation movement, with its mounting concerns about discrimination based on sex, came to the forefront in the United States. In Japan the new constitution had declared that "all of the people are equal under the law and there shall be no discrimination in political, economic or social relations because of race, creed, sex, social status or family origin" (article 14). Sexual equality was affirmed in principle but was still far from everyday practice. Only a few scholars, journalists, and activists considered the sharply defined sex-role division of labor a matter of discrimination. The United Nations initiated its effort to raise the consciousness of women about their status in society, designating 1975 as International Women's Year, with a three-pronged emphasis on equality, development, and peace. Women who attended the three international conferences for women, held by the United Nations during International Women's Year and the U.N. Decade for Women (1976–85), called for governments as well as women themselves to increase their efforts to improve women's status. These movements, together with the Convention on the Elimination of All Forms of Discrimination Against Women, adopted by the U.N. General Assembly in 1979, strongly criticized the existing division of labor between the sexes.[4]

The Japanese government established the Headquarters for the Planning and Promotion of Policies for Women in the Prime Minister's Office in 1975, using the World Plan of Action adopted by the first World Women's Conference in the same year. In 1977 this agency announced a National Plan of Action as the government's policy and strategy for initiating change for women throughout Japan. Each prefectural government also established its own structure to implement an appropriate local plan of action.

Leaders of national nongovernmental women's groups mobilized their members to raise public awareness about women's issues and formulate policies that would improve women's status. For the first time, as part of the International Women's Year, leaders of these organizations met to form a coalition that would work independently of the government's program to improve women's status. A new group, which called itself the Liaison Group for Implementation of the Resolutions from the International Women's Year Conference of Japan, organized national conferences every five years beginning in 1975 and at each meeting formulated goals of action for the subsequent five-year period.

Grass-roots organizations sprang up to search for ways to improve women's participation and status by exchanging information and forming study groups. Members did not limit their concerns to problems directly related to the home but enlarged their interests to include community issues, such as healthcare, social welfare, and the tax system. Their voices were heard calling for the amelioration of deteriorating social policy.

Their activity was the result of changes that have occurred since the end of World War II. Women's traditional child-rearing and household duties have changed dramatically. Year by year the number of employed women has increased significantly, as has the variety of jobs in which women work. In 1989 women workers represented 37.4 percent of all employed persons.[5] The number of working married women reached 10.2 million (58.6 percent of all employed women). By the early 1990s women who were full-time homemakers were also active in the public sphere, cultivating new interests in cultural activities, educational concerns, and local citizens' movements. Then or now, it is doubtful, however, whether women's capabilities at the workplace or in the local community are fully recognized, so that women are truly able to influence society as a whole. Although women have become active in their professions and in local movements, their participation in formal decision making is still limited. They are hampered in attaining administrative positions in politics, public office, and business—largely because the sex-role division of labor, which assigns women to a subordinate status, continues to be firmly rooted in Japanese practice and tradition.

POLICY FORMATION ON WOMEN'S ISSUES

A transformation is slowly taking place, however. The national elections of 1989 and 1990 exemplified the heightened awareness of the female electorate, and the 1990s may well be an era of increased direct involvement by women in politics at every level. One major force behind this change is the vigorous activity of women's organizations. We will focus on how these groups have worked within the political system to bring about greater participation by women. Much of this activity was spurred by the efforts of women's groups to get Japan to ratify the U.N. Convention on the Elimination of All Forms of Discrimination Against Women.

In 1946, after Japanese women were legally liberated by the new constitution, those women's organizations that had been forcibly disbanded, or whose function had been severely limited by government decree during World War II, once again became active. New organizations were also formed. The conditions after World War II were such that those women's groups that were able to operate at all focused their energies on finding food and housing. In spite of the exigencies of survival, however, some groups also instituted educational programs to encourage women to become involved in the radically changed political and social environment. The women's sections of the reorganized labor unions concentrated on improving labor conditions for working women.[6] Then, in 1951, with the signing of the peace treaty, an independent Japan returned once again to prewar attitudes and practices, including the establishment of a rudimentary military force. A peace movement emerged to counter this, but doubts that the nation could stem the conservative trends took hold.[7]

In the early 1960s, after the domination of the two big parties (the Liberal Democratic Party and the Japan Socialist Party) gave way to a more vigorously multiparty system, each party formed its own women's section. In addition, the parties separately organized women's groups to enlarge their support base, for they recognized the importance of women as new voters.[8]

In the latter part of the 1960s, when rapid economic growth directly affected all aspects of life, the grass-roots consumer movement expanded into a national movement dominated by full-time housewives. They tackled homemaking problems that had immediate relevance to them, such as the high cost of living, food additives, and false advertising. Their activities directly contributed to democratization at the community level, as well as led to new consumer laws, which in effect reflected women's primary concern with family-related issues. These women, who might have used their energies and organizational skills to advance the status of women, did not; instead, they responded to the pressures of the conservative male forces of business and government to focus on issues related to home life, and raised no objection to the traditional division of work. These pressures were felt quite concretely because decision makers in the consumer movement and women's sections of the labor unions were predominantly male.

For 30 years after World War II some women's groups continued their struggle for equality with little success. Then in 1975 the U.N. International Women's Year created an energetic commitment to reconstruct the women's movement in Japan. The achievement of female and male equality in every aspect of life became the foundation of the new crusade for radical social change. Well-known women's associations formed a loosely structured liaison group to deal specifically with women's issues and plan for concrete unified action. Some women's groups, like the Japan Housewives' Association and the Consumer Science Federation, finally recognized that the deeply rooted sexually based discrimination against women required that women take the initiative in restructuring society; otherwise, nothing significant would happen.

Forty-one women's organizations held the Japanese International Women's Year Conference with the theme of equality.[9] At this historic event the inequalities in politics, education, labor, family, and social welfare were confronted, and resolutions were adopted to achieve full equality for women and men. Participating organizations consisted of women's groups affiliated with political parties, professional groups, religious groups, labor unions, and other women's groups. There were full-time housewives, professional women, ordinary workers, and executives, representing a remarkable range of backgrounds, training, and experience.

All the groups concerned had their own purposes and programs, but they joined in the women's cause. The conference resolved to form a coalition, the Liaison Group for Implementing the Resolutions of the Japanese International Women's Year Conference, which would continue to exchange information and engage in action to eliminate discrimination based on sex. In 1990 the IWY Liaison Group consisted of 50 organizations with 23 million members.[10] Because the group represents a broad spectrum of political views and experiences, gaining consensus for action on specific issues proves to be a slow process. The founding leader and chief advocate of the IWY Liaison Group was the late Ichikawa Fusae, noted for her strong leadership in enfranchising women.

The government also responded to International Women's Year. In 1977, when it drew up a National Plan of Action indicating measures to deal with the problems that women were facing, women's organizations criticized the plan as ambiguous and disappointing and called a nationwide meeting to express their dissatisfaction.[11] Many issues were raised at the conference, including procedures for the selection of women civil servants and the inadequate guidelines for reviewing discriminatory practices in government employment. In the government proposal, no clear-cut procedures were provided to ensure equal opportunity in employment or to legally revise the government employment system. There was no plan to counter prostitution, either. Kubota Manae, director of the Prime Minister's Office for Women's Affairs, explained that the government's plan of action was in the initial stages of preparation and that the specific measures for implementation would be forthcoming. The government's poor start showed that unless the women's organizations closely monitored the government's policy-making and implementation efforts, they could not expect much progress. The IWY Liaison Group undertook this responsibility with a firm resolve to make its objections known to the Prime Minister's Office, each political party, and the Diet.

In December 1979 the Convention on the Elimination of All Forms of Discrimination Against Women was adopted by the 34th General Assembly of the United Nations, with Japan casting its vote for adoption. Japanese policy, however, contradicted the convention in many areas. When government officials had carefully examined the convention in relation to Japanese laws, they found at least 150 items that would have to be changed.

In April, before the opening of the Mid-Decade World Conference in July 1980, the IWY Liaison Group held a conference in Japan, where it passed a resolution urging early ratification of the convention. The group notified the Japanese government of the decision of the conference and demanded action.

Meanwhile, the United Nations had decided to hold a signing ceremony at the world conference in Copenhagen to promote the ratification of the convention in every country.[12] In May the IWY Liaison Group petitioned the minister of foreign affairs, Okita Saburō, to notify the United Nations of Japan's intention to sign. In fact, the Japanese government had decided not to sign because it knew that endorsing the convention would commit the government to working toward its implementation and ratification, a decision that the officials saw as containing serious problems for Japan.

Shocked at learning of the government's position in an article by a woman reporter that appeared in the *Asahi Shimbun* on 8 June 1980, the IWY Liaison Group moved into action. Women leaders immediately conveyed their anger to Prime Minister Itō Masayoshi and Minister of Foreign Affairs Okita, questioning the government's plan to send official delegates to the world conference when Japan had no intention of signing the convention—which would seriously embarrass the Japanese delegates and the nation. The IWY Liaison Group unleashed its indignation to gain the necessary support. Through personal meetings group members urged women Diet members and the Prime Minister's Advisory Council on Women's Affairs to press the government to sign the convention. The group was assisted by the mass media, which publicized the government's reluctance to sign.

In response to the women's strong determination, related government bureaus quickly completed a survey of the legal changes necessary to implement the convention and agreed to promote them during the last half of the women's decade, 1981–85. Upon hearing that report on 15 July, the prime minister and his cabinet decided that Japan would participate in the signing ceremony. Two days later the head of the Japanese delegation, Takahashi Nobuko—Japan's first-ever woman ambassador, who was appointed to Denmark—signed the convention at the world conference in Copenhagen.

Signing the convention and acknowledging the need for changes in the law made it clear that although the constitution guaranteed the equality of women and men, laws did not follow suit. Women's organizations resolved to persuade the government to change laws that perpetuated sex-stereotyped patterns of work and discriminatory attitudes. Their strategy was to encourage women throughout the country to study the convention as an important human rights document and work for its implementation.

In May 1981 the Headquarters for the Planning and Promotion of Policies for Women, a government agency, identified three priorities for action. One, instituting a new high school home economics curriculum for boys and girls, required the establishment of new curriculum guidelines by the Ministry of Education in order to fulfill the provision in the convention that there be the "same curricula for boys and girls." A second priority was revising the Nationality Law, which did not apply equally to women and men. The third required enacting an equal employment opportunity law by the Diet because equality in employment could not be assured under existing labor laws. All this work had to be completed rapidly in order for Japan to ratify the convention by 1985. At the IWY Mid-Decade National Conference of Japan in November 1980 (held after the international meeting in Copenhagen), women's organizations had already resolved to heighten their efforts for early ratification by intensifying their lobbying of the government, political parties, and the Diet. The method most frequently used to achieve policies of equality included continual consultation with ministries and participation in ministerial work groups, along with media campaigns to encourage public support and support among the masses of women in women's organizations.

In the prewar traditional patriarchal family, the woman was expected to take care of household duties and child rearing. Only girls studied domestic science in elementary and junior high schools. In contrast, the postwar education reform conceived of the family as a democratic institution, based on the cooperation of husband and wife, and home economics became a required subject for both boys and girls in the nine years of compulsory education. Prewar domestic

science had taught the technicalities of housework, but with the new program the emphasis shifted to the collaboration of man and woman in the family. In senior high schools, home economics became an elective subject, which both boys and girls were equally free to take.

In 1951, however, when Japan was liberated from the rule of the occupation force and prewar leaders moved back into power, the traditional sex roles for women and men were once again supported. In 1958 the Ministry of Education restructured the curriculum in junior high schools to emphasize the doctrine of separate spheres: females in the home and males in the workplace. Boys were required to take industrial arts, and girls, home economics. In senior high schools, home economics continued to be an elective subject for both boys and girls until a major curriculum revision in 1978 made the subject compulsory for girls but elective for boys. Very few boys selected it. It was clear that the Ministry of Education was committed to reinstituting traditional sex-role concepts into the schools.

Teachers, lawyers, and women activists rose in protest against this infringement on the equality of women and men, which is assured in the constitution and the Basic Education Law. In 1974 they formed the Organization for Promoting Coeducational Homemaking to strengthen their protest movement and call for a revision of the senior high school curriculum. Two years later this organization became a member of the IWY Liaison Group, and the home economics issue gained the support of a wide spectrum of women.

Home economics became a political issue when it emerged as one of the obstacles to the ratification of the convention. As taught in schools at that time, home economics infringed on article 10b of the convention ("same curricula for boys and girls") and article 10c ("elimination of stereotyped concepts of the roles of women and men at all levels and in all forms of education"). In 1984 the Ministry of Education set up a committee consisting of school principals, home economics teachers, university educators, and other leaders to consider the home economics issue. During the discussion many members apparently based their views on perpetuating the division of roles between the sexes. They pointed out that making home economics compulsory for both boys and girls would create severe practical problems, such as the need for new facilities, newly trained teachers, and, most difficult, a fundamental revision of the curriculum to make it appropriate for both boys and girls. The committee nonetheless concluded that "home economics in senior high school should be made compulsory for boys and girls under the principle of equality of sexes." On the basis of this report, the Education Curriculum Council, an advisory committee to the minister of education, made a similar recommendation in 1987. The Ministry of Education is currently preparing a number of elective courses for boys and girls. This revised compulsory home economics curriculum will be introduced in 1994.

In this way, equality of the sexes has been affirmed, at least ostensibly, in school education. Whether or not equality will be guaranteed is a matter of concern, however. Home economics will be compulsory for both sexes, but some courses seem to suit girls and others to suit boys. For example, technical skills involving electricity, machinery, and information science are listed under the title "Technology for Living," and homemaking skills encompassing foods, clothing, and child care will be taught in another course, entitled "Skills for Everyday Life." These courses are likely to attract students on the basis of sex, in effect reinforcing the concept of sex-role division. The Organization for Promoting Coeducational Homemaking is continuing its campaign for sexual equality in education by carefully monitoring the preparations for and implementation of the new home economics curriculum.

Women's organizations and the government followed a similar process in changing nationality and employment laws to conform to the U.N. convention. In October 1981 the Ministry of Justice embarked upon the amendment of the Nationality Law and announced an interim plan in February 1983. The IWY Liaison Group commented on the plan in a hearing and submitted a position paper to the ministry in May. The group was concerned that Japanese women who married foreigners were unreasonably discriminated against.

Two aspects of the Nationality Law were discriminatory. The law stipulated that children born of a Japanese mother could claim Japanese nationality only if the nationality of their father was not known or if he had no nationality, although children whose father was Japanese could always claim Japanese nationality. The law also stipulated that foreign men who married Japanese women could be naturalized only if they lived in Japan continuously for more than three years and if they had sufficient assets and the ability to support a household. No such conditions were required of foreign women who married Japanese men.

In 1985 the revised nationality law was passed with significant changes. Now paternal and maternal family lines are equally respected, and children can claim Japanese nationality if either their father or mother is a Japanese national at the time of the birth (article 2-1). The law was also changed so that the conditions for naturalization are the same for all foreigners whose spouse is a Japanese subject, regardless of sex.

In 1978 the Women's and Young Workers' Problems Council—an advisory organ to the minister of labor consisting of representatives from management, labor, and public interest groups—began studying ways equal opportunity and working conditions could be guaranteed for both women and men.[13] All parties basically agreed that it was necessary to legislate for equal opportunity and equal working conditions, but the preparation of new legislation was delayed until nearly the final deadline for ratification of the convention because the representatives of labor and management were unable to agree on specific matters. They found it necessary to review the Labor Standards Law and reexamine the provisions for the protection of women. The labor members of the advisory council enumerated the issues that needed reconsideration: overtime work, work on days off, menstrual leave, late night work, the handling of dangerous materials, and work in mines—all of which were limited for women by the law.[14] The existing provisions for maternity leave were acceptable to labor.

The opinions of council members were divided on several critical issues. Management members proposed that personnel procedures for hiring, advancement, training, retirement, resignation, and dismissal could be modified through new company policies to bring about equal opportunity for female and male employees without revising the law. Conversely, they also proposed that the special protective provisions for female employees in the labor law be discontinued. The labor members of the council, not at all satisfied with this approach, made a counterproposal, which called for an equal employment opportunity law. Referring to article 4 of the convention, which allows special protective measures for employed mothers, labor members sharply opposed the removal of protective measures under the guise of strict male and female equality. Labor and management members also sharply disagreed on child-care leave, with labor strongly supporting it to enable women to carry their double responsibilities at home and work. Another major disagreement came over labor's insistence that penalties be imposed on companies not complying with the law.

In March 1984 the council submitted its recommendations to Labor Minister Sakamoto Misoji without having agreed on protective measures and penalties for noncompliance. In the end, the management members overrode the labor members' insistence on stronger provisions for full equality. The Equal Employment Opportunity Bill that was submitted to the Diet in May 1984 omitted both the protective measures and the penalties. The law was passed May the following year and took effect on 1 April 1986.

During the three years that the Equal Employment Opportunity Bill was being prepared, the IWY Liaison Group continued to press the minister of labor, the councils concerned, the Diet and its members, management associations, and political parties to consider several key points. The liaison group insisted that the elimination of all forms of discrimination against women should be

clearly stated as a purpose of the Equal Employment Opportunity Law and that a provision for penalizing employers who did not abide by the law should be included to ensure its enforcement. It also supported the creation of an impartial grievance board to which women employees could appeal in cases of sexual discrimination. Because of the extraordinarily long working hours in Japan compared to those in other industrialized countries, the liaison group also recommended improvements in the basic working conditions for both sexes: shorter working hours, a five-day workweek, an increased number of paid holidays, and, more important, that priority be given to reducing the homemaking work load of employed women.[15]

The women's sections of the labor unions, with the support of other women's organizations, played a key role in the passage of the Equal Employment Opportunity Law in 1985. The law was based on the principle that women who are both mothers and members of the work force must be given full respect in both roles. They should be able to develop their skills as employees and enjoy a work environment that will allow them to advance their careers at the same time as they fulfill their family responsibilities. Although the law forbade employers to discriminate against women in ensuring the availability of in-service training, the provision of additional benefits, the determination of retirement age, and retirement and dismissal practices, no penalties were provided for noncompliance. The head of each prefectural Women's and Young Workers' Bureau was supposed to give advice and guidance to employers in implementing the law and assistance in settling disputes. The law included a provision for a mediation board to be attached to each prefectural bureau to monitor the implementation of the Equal Employment Opportunity Law and to mediate in cases where both management and labor agree to consider matters related to working conditions as proposed by either side. (So far this procedure has not been used.) Guidelines were provided for employers regarding their obligation to endeavor to implement the law in order to eliminate discriminatory practices against women. The Labor Standards Law also included some revisions in items related to the protection of women workers. These revisions addressed issues such as extension of the period of leave before and after childbirth (six weeks before delivery, ten weeks in the case of multiple births; eight weeks after delivery); release from overtime work, work on days off, and work after midnight when requested by a female employee who is pregnant; and easing of regulations for the protection of women, such as permitting overtime work, work on days off, and work on holidays and late at night.

The basic principle of the Equal Employment Opportunity Law spoke to the need of women to balance their roles as homemakers and employees—an everyday reality for the women in the work force. Doors were at last opening for women to have wider and more varied work opportunities, if they so desired. Moreover, the severe limitations on women's workhours had been slackened, so women could enter management positions from which they had been excluded, ostensibly by the protective regulations.[16] As a result, employment opportunities have improved, but at the same time the double burden of job and home has become heavier because women are working more hours in the paid labor market with no corresponding reduction in hours of domestic labor. The issues of shorter working hours and more days off have taken on greater importance. At the insistence of management members of the advisory council, penalties for violation of the statute were not written into the Equal Employment Opportunity Law, so the principle of equality in hiring, in-service training, additional benefits, resignation, retirement, and dismissal—all of which were included in the law—could be an empty promise. Compliance with the law depends on the goodwill of the employer or the perception of management that a commitment to sexual equality is advantageous.

In spite of the "equal pay for equal work" provision in article 4 of the Labor Standards Law, women continue to receive 53.4 percent of the average male wage. Because of a growing labor shortage, more women are entering the labor force, but as part-time workers who desire more flexible work schedules.[17] They have no job guarantees, however, and no bargaining base from which to improve their working conditions, and they are subject to economic changes with no recourse to protect their jobs. In sum, the 1985 Equal Employment Opportunity Law represents a modest advance for women in terms of career opportunities that may well have come at the expense of increasing the combined work load at home and on the job.

The change in the home economics education guidelines, the revision of the Nationality Law, and the new Equal Employment Opportunity Law were either completed or in process in 1985, making ratification of the convention possible. The Diet approved the convention on 24 June 1985, making Japan the 72nd nation to do so. Much still remained to be done, however, for Japan to meet its requirements. To this end, the Headquarters for the Planning and Promotion of Policies for Women formulated a New National Plan of Action in 1987 and told each prefectural office to review its local plan of action to bring it into line with the convention.

In 1988 the IWY Liaison Group, working to achieve its goal of full implementation of the convention by the year 2000, also revised its own plan of action independently of the government's plan as a strategy for gaining "equality, development, and peace." It called for women's participation in decision making at all levels of government and for their full involvement in five special areas—education, mass media, family, welfare, and peace and international cooperation—to exert pressure on the government to execute its new National Plan of Action, already formulated but not yet implemented.

The IWY Liaison Group is taking steps to involve women Diet members, women leaders, and journalists directly in a network to influence public opinion, and to urge that the Headquarters for the Planning and Promotion of Policies for Women be entrusted with legal authority and be headed by a woman minister. This was the immediate goal for 1991.

WOMEN'S PARTICIPATION IN POLITICS

Although women have made marked advances in various fields, few are in policy-making positions. The same is true in the political world, where only a few women legislators have been elected. After Japanese women obtained suffrage in 1945, the first election in which they participated was the House of Representatives election in April the following year. From 1945 to 1990 Japanese women have voted in 18 House of Representatives elections, 15 House of Councillors elections, and 11 local elections.[18] Since the mid-1950s not only has the number of women in the electorate exceeded that of men, but the percentage of women voters who have cast their ballots has been greater than that of men, giving women important political power.[19] Women voters have contributed their share of support to keeping the Liberal Democratic Party in power since 1955—which can be seen as testimony to the satisfaction that women feel about their lives as sustained by the political and policy decisions of that party.

A brief explanation of the 1989 House of Councillors election provides insight into the political consciousness and voting patterns of Japanese women. This election campaign was rocked by two political scandals: the Recruit scandal and Prime Minister Uno Sōsuke's sex scandal.[20] These scandals—combined with a revised agricultural policy and a new consumer tax—threw the political world into turmoil.[21] For the first time in the history of the House of Councillors, the Japan Socialist Party (JSP) and other opposition parties captured a majority of the seats. It appeared that the party balance of power was changed by the women voters, who had previously supported the Liberal Democratic Party quite consistently. In this election, however, women voters expressed their disapproval of the government's ambiguous position on the prominent political issues.

A post-election survey of 3,000 voters by the Association to Promote Clean and Fair Elections showed that women's reactions to the elections were both similar to and different from men's.[22]

Women and men were attached to democratic politics, and they evaluated current governmental competence in much the same way. For example, women were slightly more likely than men (26.6 percent compared to 23.0 percent) to report that a strong sense of citizen duty was their major reason for voting. Three-quarters of both groups said that they were not satisfied with current politics, and 70 percent reported that taxes were an issue that they considered important when voting. But the sexes differed somewhat in terms of their responses to personal problems and policy issues. Asked if they were satisfied with their present standard of living, women showed more satisfaction than men (72.5 percent compared to 66.0). But women were much more likely than men (48.2 percent compared to 36.4 percent) to list commodity prices as an important election issue.

In the survey, 38.3 percent of women said that they voted for the Japan Socialist Party (up from 14.2 percent in the previous election), but the proportion of women who said that they voted for the LDP declined sharply—to 28.3 percent (down from 47.3 percent in the previous election). In the proportional representation vote in the election, the results were similar, with 36.9 percent of the women who responded saying that they supported the JSP (up from 12.7 percent) and 27.6 percent saying that they supported the LDP (down from 47.3 percent). In short, the JSP doubled its votes from women while the LDP lost half its votes. (The same tendency was evident among male voters.)

The results of this survey indicate that women are politically motivated by a strong sense of duty to vote and politically interested in issues directly related to their everyday lives. The contradiction between their reported satisfaction with their standard of living and their strong dissatisfaction with current politics reflects a wide distrust of politicians who went against their election promises not to impose a consumer tax—a distrust exacerbated by the political scandals. As long as the populace is content with its standard of living, the conservative forces are likely to continue receiving widespread public support. The swing vote that the JSP received in the 1989 election can be interpreted as a vote against the consumer tax, rather than as wholehearted support for the party itself. The significant proportion of women voters who do not consistently support one political party but vote instead according to the particular issues highlighted in an election campaign tends to change election results unpredictably, making it difficult to forecast the outcome.

The reversal that gave the JSP and other opposition parties a majority in the House of Councillors was not sustained in the 1990 House of Representatives election. The LDP regained its power base and received a public mandate for stability in government and no fundamental change in policy. Women voters who a year earlier in the House of Councillors election had made known their strong and clear opposition to the LDP's consumer tax opted now for continuation of the LDP policies that had brought them prosperity—despite the passage in April 1989 of the consumer tax bill that they had opposed. Perhaps the unexpected changes in the socialist governments in Eastern Europe at the end of 1989 undercut the temporary attraction of the JSP and made it difficult for the opposition parties to advocate a new vision of government under their leadership.

WOMEN ELECTED TO THE NATIONAL AND LOCAL LEGISLATIVE BODIES

Thus, in April 1990 women members of the Diet occupied 12 of 512 seats in the House of Representatives (2.3 percent), and 37 of 252 seats in the House of Councillors (14.7 percent), accounting for 5.9 percent of the combined membership of both houses. In December 1989 women occupied 75 (2.6 percent) of 2,911 seats in the prefectural assemblies, 908 (4.4 percent) of 20,582 seats in city assemblies, and 579 (1.3 percent) of 43,785 seats in town and village assemblies. According to a 1989 survey of all countries with parliaments, Japan stands in 112th place for the number of women members of a "single or lower house of parliament"—lowest among the industrialized nations.[23]

There are a number of structural barriers to women's involvement in the formal political arena. First, when parties choose candidates at the start of an election, they tend to choose men, not women. For example, the number of women candidates in the House of Representatives election in February 1990 was 66 (6.9 percent of all candidates), the largest number ever. The LDP had only 1 woman candidate, and she was not elected; the JSP had 12 women candidates, of whom 7 were elected; Kōmeitō, 1, who was elected; and the JCP, 29, of whom 2 were elected. Only 2 of 23 candidates who belonged to other groups or ran independently were elected. The LDP gave priority to incumbents—men—in party nominations.

Although the LDP has the largest number of women members among the five major parties, that does not pave the way for women to win party nomination. Most of its members, including many women (36 percent of the LDP's 2.2 million members are women), are merely personal supporters of members of the Diet or prefectural and local assemblies—their allegiance is to a candidate rather than to the party—so very few women party members have any ambition to be involved in party affairs, to say nothing of running for national or local office. In the case of the JSP, which depends largely on labor union support, the union officers make the nominations for party candidates. Therefore women, who hold no leadership positions in the unions, have no way to participate in the selection of candidates or to be recommended as candidates.

Competition among the candidates for winning party nomination is severe. It is often said that a candidate cannot win an election without a "base support" (a strong organization of supporters in the electoral district), a well-known name, and money. Women's home-centered life limits their access to and ability to acquire these necessary tools, and their domestic responsibilities mean that they would need extremely generous cooperation from family members in order to run. Women also tend to consider politics corrupt and assume that participation as candidates will taint them by association. In recent years, however, the women's sections of some parties have exerted considerable pressure upon the male party leadership to provide subsidies to encourage women to run for elective office.[24]

What a party does about women candidates may well show how its members regard women. Since 1983, when the proportional representation system was introduced in elections to the House of Councillors, the IWY Liaison Group and other women's organizations have been pressing the political parties to put women candidates high on their lists of candidates.[25] In the 1989 election, when the LDP leadership was under criticism because of the sex scandal, that party made the unprecedented decision to place a token woman candidate at the top of their prioritized list of candidates: Shimizu Kiyoko, director of the Division of Nursing in the Ministry of Health and Social Welfare, was chosen for her government experience. Placing her at the top of the list assured the LDP that a woman would be elected.

In 1987 the JSP made a daring decision to elect a woman chair, Doi Takako—the first time a woman became head of a political party. The party also broke precedent by choosing a constitutional law scholar with a distinguished career in university teaching instead of relying on labor union leadership. Doi led her party to make a commitment to search for new candidates outside the regular party structure. Women leaders were found who had experience in policy formation in the grass-roots consumer movement or who were lawyers, scholars, journalists, or leaders of women's movements. They formed an untapped resource for women candidates. As a result, in the 1989 and 1990 elections more women candidates than ever before entered the campaign.[26]

Although the number of women elected to legislative office is small, those women who have achieved office have contributed to a wide range of policy issues. During the 114th ordinary session of the Diet (held between December 1988 and June 1989), women members of both houses of the Diet sat on the executive committees of the standing committees on education,

social and labor affairs, budget, foreign affairs, communications, and audit, among others. During the legislative session, women members questioned and commented on issues concerning the environment, defense and security, international development, political reform, and the tax system. They submitted several bills—including one that amended the Employment Insurance Law by extending the coverage of employment insurance to part-time workers. It was passed. In addition, women Diet members raised questions about the enactment of a child-care leave law and a law to protect part-time workers. They spoke for the adoption of different surnames by husband and wife and commented on the shortage of brides in agricultural villages, on issues of women and development, on prostitution, and on the prime minister's sex scandal. (Ironically, the Headquarters for the Planning and Promotion of Policies for Women is headed by the prime minister himself.)

Now that women account for nearly 40 percent of the total labor force, one of the most pressing issues is the enactment of the Child-Care Leave Bill.[27] The business community was against the introduction of the bill, which they considered to be premature, for there was not yet widespread public support for it. In contrast, most of the women Diet members elected in the House of Councillors election in 1989 and the House of Representatives election in 1990 had campaigned in favor of the Child-Care Leave Bill, which passed on 8 May 1991 with the support of all women Diet members.

During the 40 years that women have been elected to the Diet they have worked together on many issues related to women's concerns. The Diet Members' Association for Women, a supraparty organization formed in 1953, has focused its efforts on passage of the Prostitution Prevention Bill and the Inebriates' Control Bill and on action to prevent the closing down of the Women's and Young Workers' Bureau of the Ministry of Labor.[28] In 1984 the association's concerted efforts were an important factor in the passage of the Equal Employment Opportunity Bill.

Women voters still find it difficult to see the connection between their daily lives and politics. As long as this view persists, the number of women elected to office will continue to be small. In the 45 years since World War II, however, women have begun to discover the importance of their role in politics and are becoming more aggressive in their participation.

Along with the rapid growth of business and industry in the 1970s and 1980s have come problems with the environment and the educational system. Women have discovered that they can make a difference in confronting these issues through consumer and citizen movements. They have moved from petitioning legislators and governments to running for local legislative office and have worked to assure their own candidates' election. More than ever, they are realizing that in place of male-oriented concepts of production and efficiency, female-oriented perceptions deriving from ordinary everyday experience are needed in the political arena.

This direction became strongly evident with the inordinate interest in the 1989 consumer tax issue, discussed earlier. Public disenchantment with corruption in politics—like the Recruit stock scandal caused by collusion among politicians, government officials, and business leaders—resulted in an upsurge of interest in women entering politics. Women represented the honesty and integrity that was lacking in the political leaders.

Without a doubt, the appearance of Doi Takako on the political scene helped change the image of women politicians. Doi, with her charismatic personality and political skill, challenged entrenched politicians and encouraged women of all political persuasions to overcome the apprehension that being in politics would stain their character—a fear that has held women back from the front lines of government and politics. The network of women's organizations and supporting campaign groups has expanded rapidly; the prospects for the involvement of women is brighter than ever before. Another positive de-velopment was the selection of two women to Prime Minister Kaifu Toshiki's cabinet in 1989.[29] This was the first time that two women served in the cabinet simultaneously. Moriyama Mayumi became chief cabinet secretary, with a responsibility to oversee the proper functioning of the cabinet secretariat, which prepares the agenda for the cabinet. She was the principal political adviser to the prime minister, often making announcements to the press on his and the cabinet's behalf. Takahara Sumiko became director of the Economic Planning Agency, whose portfolio encompasses the formation of national economic policy. These posts, particularly chief cabinet secretary, have high visibility. Seeing women in such places of responsibility gives other women a growing certainty that they can handle these posts as well as anyone; they are more and more challenged to take the risks that public office entails, confident that they have an irreplaceable contribution to make to the nation.

Although the proportion of women legislators in the Diet is still small, it is larger than in city, town, and village assemblies. With the local elections of 1991 lies an unparalleled opportunity to reverse this. It will take strategic planning and joint efforts to increase the number of women in local politics and thereby form a solid base at the local level that will prepare women for greater roles in both local and national politics. Women's participation is essential for setting the policies that will take the nation into the twenty-first century.

NOTES

1. Asahi Shimbun, *Asahi Almanac, 1991* (in Japanese) (Tokyo, 1991), 438.

2. The Japan Socialist Party changed its name to the Social Democratic Party of Japan in January 1991. In this chapter the former name is used.

3. Names in this chapter are presented according to the Japanese custom of putting the family name first.

Akamatsu Tsuneko (1897–1965), a leader in the prewar labor union movement for women, was elected to the House of Councillors in 1947, 1953, and 1959.

Ichikawa Fusae (1894–1981) was a leader in the prewar women's suffrage movement. After the war she was elected to the House of Councillors five times on an independent ticket, first in 1958 and last in 1980. She served as the chair of the Japan Women's Committee of U.N. Non-Governmental Organizations and played a major role in forming the national organization of women's groups in 1974. In 1975 this body successfully planned the Japanese International Women's Year Conference. Ichikawa served as chair of the 1980 IWY mid-decade conference, which took as its theme "No equality without peace; no peace without equality." Her leadership empowered the movement to support Japan's signing the Convention on the Elimination of All Forms of Discrimination Against Women. When she died in February 1981 at 87 years of age, still an active politician and leader, the women's movement of Japan lost a strong ally. She was trusted by all political parties as a person of integrity and probity—a courageous, creative postwar leader.

Yamataka Shigeri (1899–1977), a leader in the prewar women's suffrage movement, established the National Federation of Regional Women's Organizations in 1952 and served as its president. She was elected to the House of Councillors in 1962 and 1965.

4. The convention was adopted by the U.N. General Assembly on 19 December 1979 and came into effect as a treaty on 3 December 1981, thirty days after the 20th member nation ratified it. The convention is essentially an international bill of rights for women and a framework for women's participation in the development process. It spells out internationally accepted principles and standards for achieving equality between women and men.

5. Rōdōshō, Fujin kyoku (Ministry of Labor, Women's Section), *FY1990 fujin rōdō no jitsujō* (1990 report on working women) (Tokyo: Rōdōshō, Fujin kyoku, 1990), 2.

6. The Federation of Japanese Women's Organizations, the League of Women Voters of Japan, and the Japanese Association of University Women were active in these areas. Sōhyō (General Council of Labor Unions in Japan) had a women's section.

7. Hiratsuka Raichō and Ichikawa Fusae were among the women leaders who organized one group, Women Opposing Remilitarization of Japan, on 19 December 1951.

8. The women's support organizations associated with the political parties are the Japan Women's Association (Japan Socialist Party); the New Japan Women's Association (Japan Communist Party); the Japan Housewives' Association (Kōmeitō); and the Japan Democratic Women's Association (Democratic Socialist Party). These are independent from the women's sections of the political parties. The Liberal Democratic Party has no associated women's organization, but it has a loose structure of women's auxiliaries affiliated with each legislator's support group.

9. The 41 member organizations of the International Women's Year Conference were Alliance of Japanese Housewives; All Japan Buddhist Women's Association; All Japan General Federation of Labor, Section on Policy Planning for Youth and Women; All Japan Women's Federation; Consumer Science Federation; Federation of Japanese Women's Organizations; General Council of Labor Unions in Japan, National Conference of Housewives; Japan Association for Women's Education; Japan Association of Retired Women Teachers; Japanese Association of University Women; Japanese Medical Women's Association; Japanese Mothers' Congress; Japanese Nursing Association; Japanese Women's Democratic Club; Japan Democratic Women's Association; Japan Family Life Problem Study Association; Japan Housewives' Association; Japan Women's Christian Temperance Union; Japan Women's Bar Association; Japan Women's Council; Japan Women's Forum; Japan Women's Union; Japan Section of the Women's International League for Peace and Freedom; Kusanomikai; National Federation of Regional Women's Organizations; National Liaison Council of Retired Teachers; National Women's Committee of U.N. Non-Governmental Organizations; New Japan Women's Association; Nomura Center for Lifelong Integrated Education; Society of Japanese Women Scientists; Japan Young Women's Christian Association; League of Women Voters of Japan; Pan-Pacific and Southeast Asian Women's Association of Japan; National Catholic Women's League of Japan; National Federation of Business and Professional Women's Clubs of Japan; Research Institute for Better Living; Single Women's Association of Japan; Women's Association, National Christian Council in Japan; Women's Section of the General Council of Labor Unions of Japan; Women's Democratic Club; and Zenkoku tomo-no-kai (National Friendship Association).

10. These include women's sections of labor unions, the federation of women's cooperatives, and other national women's organizations. The total membership is one-half of the female voting population of 46.6 million. Each of the member bodies has its own program goals, which do not necessarily place top priority on women's issues. Although the IWY Liaison Group receives no government funding, government officials and agencies watch its activities with deep interest.

11. This meeting was called by 34 of the 41 member organizations of the IWY Liaison Group, joined by the Association of Working Women, the Organization for Promoting Coeducational Homemaking, the Association for the Advancement of Good Nutrition, and the Organization to Study Issues of Prostitution.

12. Signing the convention obligates governments to do nothing that contravenes the principles set forth in the articles. Ratification of or accession to the convention, then, obligates the governments to pursue a policy of eliminating discrimination against women and to report on progress in that effort to the U.N. Committee on the Elimination of Discrimination Against Women.

13. Advisory councils are attached to each government ministry to examine and study matters that are assigned to it. The minister of labor appoints the 22 members of the Women's and Younger Workers' Problems Council; 10 members are women.

14. No women or workers under 18 years old could be assigned work from 10:00 P.M. to 5:00 A.M., according to the Labor Standards Law, article 62.

15. In Japan the average worker puts in 2,168 work-hours a year, compared to 1,659 in West Germany. Workers in Japan, both female and male, have made shorter workhours and more paid days off key issues. These changes would enable men and women to share in homemaking responsibilities. At present, the workweek is 48 hours (8 hours per day), with one day off. There are 20 paid days off per year.

16. After the Equal Employment Opportunity Law was passed, some of the protective measures for women were eliminated—for example, the limit on overtime and work on regular days off to no more than two hours per day, six hours per week, or 150 hours per year. The removal of this protective measure has led to the possibility of increased work time for women.

17. In 1960, 8.9 percent of women workers were part-time workers. In 1988 the percentage had increased to 23.6. Rōdōshō, Fujin kyoku, *FY1990 fujin rōdō no jitsujō,* 29.

18. Every four years since 1947 local elections have been held across the nation. Exceptions occur when an assembly is dissolved in mid-term or when a town and village are merged. In 1987 the local elections were held for the 11th time.

19. In the February 1990 House of Councillors election 46,555,038 women voted, about 280,000 more than the number of men who voted. The percentage of women voting was 74.6, which was 2.7 percent more than the percentage of men who voted (71.9).

20. The president of Recruit, a company that helps business and industry advertise for new employees, used his connections to sell unlisted company stock cheaply to politicians, government officials, and business executives to gain their cooperation in advertising for and recruiting university graduates for the company's clients. When this malfeasance was uncovered in 1988, it became a major political scandal, toppling influential political and business leaders. In the *Sunday Mainichi* of 18 June 1989 a former geisha asserted that Prime Minister Uno had given her 3 million yen (about U.S. $26,000) for her services as a companion. Newspapers around the world gave the story front-page coverage. Diet members sharply questioned the prime minister to determine the facts, and women's groups raised indignant voices against him.

21. The government policy of buying up surplus rice and wheat, even though the demand had dropped markedly in recent years, helped hold the domestic prices for these grains high. This policy has protected farmers by preventing the importation of rice and other food products.

To equalize the tax burden, the government decided on a radical reform of the tax system in 1989. A consumer tax of 3 percent was imposed at every level (raw materials, manufactured products, wholesale and retail sales), resulting in price increases across the board. Small business owners, who were especially affected by the new consumer tax, expressed their strong dissatisfaction.

22. Disturbed by the use of money to buy votes and other illegal acts by the candidates running for election in 1976, the Ministry of Home Affairs formed an auxiliary organization of citizens, the Association to Promote Clean and Fair Elections, to educate the populace about election procedures and to monitor the elections. The statistics here are from Zaidan hōjin akarui senkyo suishin kyōkai (Association to Promote Clean and Fair Elections), *Dai 15 kai sangiin giin tsūjō senkyo no jittai* (An analysis of the 15th House of Councillors election) (Tokyo, February 1990).

23. Inter-Parliamentary Union, *Women in Parliament as of June 30, 1989* (Geneva: Inter-Parliamentary Union, 1989).

24. The Japan Socialist Party has provided funds for women candidates standing for election to local assemblies for the first time, as well as funds and personnel to assist women candidates who have children and older parents for whom they must care. The Democratic Socialist Party provides more funds for new women candidates for local assemblies than for men candidates. The Japan Communist Party provides funds and personnel to assist women candidates who have children and older parents for whom they must care.

25. To reduce the high cost of running for election as a candidate from the nation at large, the government instituted the proportional representation election system. One unforeseen result of the new procedures was the unprecedented increase in women candidates.

26. In the 1989 House of Councillors election the JSP had 12 women candidates, compared to 6 in the previous election; 11 were elected, compared to 2 before. In the 1990 House of Representatives election the party had 8 candidates, compared to 3 in the previous election, and 7 were elected, compared to 2 before.

27. In 1987 the opposition parties together submitted a law to the Diet for child-care leave for male and female workers. Since 1975 a law permitting child-care leave had been in force for such women civil servants as nurses, public school teachers, and nursery personnel. Some companies that employed large numbers of women had already made provision for child-care leave for women through their contracts with labor unions. The proposed law was the first one to include men as well as women.

28. In 1956 the Prostitution Prevention Law, in which

prostitution was declared illegal, passed the Diet. Because women prostitutes could be arrested while their men customers were not subject to arrest, the law has been viewed as ineffective. The 1961 Inebriates' Control Law made it possible to arrest drunks who were public nuisances or who were violent. Many incidents of a husband's violence in the family due to the use of alcohol had reached public attention. The law called for short-term care for those who were taken into custody and long-term care for those who were diagnosed as alcoholics. In 1946, when the Ministry of Labor was established, an internal bureau was set up to deal with the problems of women and young workers—specifically, to assist in raising the status of women and to upgrade welfare measures for young workers. By 1951 the administrative reform plan of the government included the disbanding of the bureau, according to behind-the-scenes reports.

29. Within six months of the formation of the first Kaifu cabinet, a House of Representatives election was called. The LDP gained a majority and formed the second Kaifu cabinet, in which no woman was named to any post. It seemed clear that appointing two women to the first Kaifu cabinet had been a ploy to gain the women's vote for the LDP. From 1946 to 1990 only three other women have been named to cabinet posts.

▲ Kenya

POLITICS

Type of Political System: partial democracy
  Sovereignty: republic
  Executive-Legislative System: mixed[a]
Type of State: unitary
Type of Party System: one party
Major Political Parties

  Kenya African National Union (KANU): Formed in 1960; the country's ruling and only party. Supports "African socialism," centralized government, racial harmony, and nonalignment. Only party members can hold civil service positions.[b]

Year Women Granted Right to Vote: 1963
Year Women Granted Right to Stand for Election: 1963
Percentage of Women in the Unicameral Legislature: 1.7%
Percentage of Electorate Voting for Highest Elected Office in Most Recent Election (1992): not available

DEMOGRAPHICS

Population: 24,032,000[c]
Percentage of Population in Urban Areas
  Overall: 22.0%[d]
  Female: not available
  Male: not available
Percentage of Population Below Age 15: 52.5%
Birthrate (per 1,000 population): 47[e]
Maternal Mortality Rate (per 100,000 live births): 170
Infant Mortality Rate (per 1,000 live births): 71
Mortality Rate for Children Under Five (per 1,000 live births): 113
Average Household Size: 4.5

Mean Age at First Marriage
  Female: 20.4
  Male: 25.8
Life Expectancy
  Female: 60.5
  Male: 56.5

EDUCATION

Ratio of Female to Male Enrollment
  First-Level Education: 93
  Second-Level Education (1980/1984): 68
  Third-Level Education: 36
Literacy Rate[f]
  Female: 51.0%
  Male: 30.0%

ECONOMY

Gross National Product per Capita: U.S. $290
Percentage of Labor Force in Agriculture: 78.0%
Distribution of Agricultural Workers by Sex: not available
Economically Active Population by Sex[g]
  Female: 58.0%
  Male: 90.0%

a. The Kenyan president is elected separately from parliamentarians.

b. Arthur S. Banks, ed., *Political Handbook of the World, 1991* (Binghamton, N.Y.: CSA Publications, 1991), 361.

c. *Whitaker's Almanack, 1993* (London: J. Whitaker and Sons, 1992).

d. *World Development Report* (Washington, D.C.: World Bank, 1990).

e. Ibid.

f. Ibid.

g. *The World's Women, 1970–1990: Trends and Statistics* (New York: United Nations, 1991).

Man-Made Political Machinery in Kenya: Political Space for Women?

MARIA NZOMO
AND KATHLEEN STAUDT

Kenya is frequently touted as an African success story. Its economic potential and growth rates are reasonably good; it offers routine elections with candidate choices in the context of one-party rule; and, despite attempted military coups, the country remains under civilian (albeit authoritarian) political control. A parliamentary system when the country became independent in 1963, the government of Kenya now consolidates power in the executive (consisting of the president and cabinet ministers) and the legislature (the National Assembly). Under the broad ideology of "mixed economy," policies support export-oriented agricultural development in the context of state-owned enterprises and patronage politics.

This somewhat typical and seemingly benign appearance notwithstanding, men control Kenya's formal political machinery more thoroughly than elsewhere in Africa. Women now occupy only 1.7 percent of the seats in the National Assembly—they never have held more than 4 percent—and no woman has ever served in the full cabinet.[1] Such gender imbalance is a paradox, for the majority of farmers in this agricultural economy are women, virtually all women are economically active, and women's organizational activities flourish.

Literature on African politics suggests that the nature of the state may be the reason for this paradox. Africanist literature questions the strength, capacity, and legitimacy of the often bloated, arbitrary, and corrupt state. Victor Azarya develops an engagement-disengagement continuum: people "associate with the state and take part in its activities in order to share its resources" or "withdraw from the state and keep at a distance from its channels as a hedge against its instability and dwindling resource base."[2] Given their near exclusion from the formal political machinery, women become politically engaged through women's organizations, which are concerned with poverty and basic survival. Goran Hyden laments the implications for the state that arise from this situation: the state cannot "capture" its inhabitants, who operate in "affective" relations.[3] Thus, although Kenya is considered a relatively "strong" state,[4] when it is examined with a gender lens, a new perception emerges.

The Kenyan state has only belatedly attempted to capture women, who are embedded in material as well as affective kin relations but who are also economic actors central to all aspects of agricultural production, from household to national levels. Until recently women's distance from the thoroughly male-dominated political machinery has meant that they share few of the patronage and distributional benefits that the state offers.

In this chapter we explore women's relationship to the Kenyan state, their activities in local and national organizations and in electoral politics, and the treatment of women in development and health policy implementation. First, we describe women's organizations in Kenya and their interaction with the formal political machinery, paying special attention to the ruling party's takeover of Maendeleo ya Wanawake (MYWO, or Progress of Women), the largest women's organization. Then we examine the limitations of electoral politics in authoritarian regimes, along with women's search for a rights-oriented legal foundation.

Finally, we turn to development policy, an issue crucial to understanding the Kenyan state and women's relation to it. The core of development efforts includes state initiatives and spending to promote economic growth and food self-sufficiency, to build infrastructure, and to improve living standards through education, healthcare, and other social services. We examine in particular the gender-contested terrain of agriculture and reproductive health in the context of structural adjustment programs (SAPs), which aim to change the framework of the economy and improve the efficiency of the state (largely by reducing its size), based on negotiation between Kenyan policy makers and international bankers. Although the process has important gender consequences, women have no voice in negotiation or subsequent policy reform.

We argue that women's centrality to development goals has entered development discourse and practice in a tentative but control-oriented fashion. Stymied by a type of development "integration" that controls rather than empowers them, Kenyan women are politically active at the grass-roots level, where institutionalized male political machinery is weaker, but are co-opted nationally, except for the few courageous women. First, however, we outline gender in Kenya's political machinery in historical context.

GENDER IN KENYAN POLITICAL HISTORY

Located in East Africa, Kenya is a country of more than 24 million people who are divided into more than 40 ethnic groups with their own language and indigenous religion. Over the past few centuries, most Kenyans have come to identify with Roman Catholicism, Islam, or various Protestant denominations. People with primary education and above speak English and Swahili, as well as their regional and local languages.

Kenyan people have a history of movement, trade, and alliance in a wide variety of political structures. In previous centuries, Nilotic-, Bantu-, and Swahili-speaking peoples shared this expanse of arid plateau and rain-fed mountainous terrain, working as farmers and herders. Ethnic labels and boundaries were quite fluid. The British, however, drew Kenyan territorial boundaries at the beginning of the twentieth century and,

with their "thin white line" of force, law, and resources, gradually began the massive colonial social engineering project.[5] Key elements in colonial control included squeezing taxes and low-cost labor from inhabitants, setting aside land (known as the White Highlands) and subsidies for white settlers in areas of high agricultural potential, building transport infrastructure to facilitate extraction and trade, and establishing a public-private distinction in which men were viewed as breadwinners and public spokespersons, and women as domestic helpmates. Christian missionary work, in its ideological, social-welfare, and educational dimensions, also reinforced this public-private distinction.[6]

Kenyan people initially reacted to the structural grid of colonialism in diverse ways, resisting, cooperating, or ignoring new dictates. While women worked extensively in agriculture, trade, and household activities, working-age men increasingly migrated from rural areas in search of wage labor in the cities, on large farms, and on the coast. In accordance with the British principle of "indirect rule" used in African and Asian colonies, colonial officials designated chiefs (invariably men) as local leaders and vested these collaborators with the authority to collect taxes and maintain order.

Under colonial alliances, politics was a male affair, except for several attempts to place a token woman (to "represent women") on local councils. The colonial state had captured large numbers of men, sanctioned male control over women's labor, and interacted with kinship authority. Yet some space still existed for women to exercise their considerable economic influence in ways that thwarted official and male goals, given widespread male out-migration and female dominance in farming. For example, women farmers did not respond to cotton-growing promotions in the 1950s, given cotton production's extensive labor burdens, low prices, and use of land needed for food crop production.[7]

As the colonial state consolidated itself, protests occurred in growing urban centers like Nairobi, beginning in the 1920s. Women were involved in the disturbances, shouting taunts, cheers, and *ngemi* (high-pitched cries) and agitating in the large crowds.[8] Women sometimes demonstrated more courage than men in resisting colonial rule, as in the 1922 Harry Thuku riots. But much of Africans' political voice was raised within internal territorial boundaries, at the provincial level and especially in district-level units and below—boundaries that loosely corresponded with the previously fluid ethnic and kinship boundaries. This internal territorial grid, along with the co-optation of "chiefs," helped give a lasting ethnic cast to politics.

Although coalitions constantly shifted, the major political players came from the three largest ethnic groups—Kikuyu, Luo, and Luyia—until they were joined more recently by the loose collection of people now known as Kalenjin. Moreover, what was to become a patron-client orientation in politics encouraged the distribution of goods and services based on regional or ethnic ties, ignoring gender equity. Even today such "cultural" politics frequently strengthens male dominance and pits ethnic localism against progressive nationalism.[9]

In most of Kenya's ethnic groups, both historically and currently, women marry outside their lineage and join that of their husband. A husband and his male relatives have important material stakes in their control over female labor. They acquire rights to the wife's labor and custody of their children, a relationship solidified with the exchange of bridewealth from the husband's to the wife's family. In her husband's home, a woman produces and reproduces on land to which she acquires user rights as a wife and mother. Structurally, this puts a woman in a tenuous position, dividing her loyalties between her own family and other women.

In the colonial era, as today, the Kenyan economy depended heavily on agricultural production, but only a fifth of the country's landmass is suitable for rain-fed farming. As Kenya's population grew in middle and later colonial years (1930–63), fierce competition ensued over densely settled land in African areas and the huge farms and ranches in the White Highlands, on which settlers—a mere 2 percent of the population—made their livelihood. Land density was acute in the "African Reserves," particularly in the Central Province among the Kikuyu people, on whose shoulders the lengthy and violent nationalist struggle of the 1950s primarily rested. When it became clear that the white settlers would not give up control without a struggle, African guerrilla fighters took to the forest and began a decade-long resistance movement that threatened settlers, divided the Kikuyu people (some loyalists supported the British), and created the opportunity in 1955 for greater African political representation and ultimately for independence negotiations. Women went to the forest, provided food to the fighters, and converted homes into armories for storing guns.

As the physical conflict drew to a close, colonial policies established the framework for land reform to provide what were termed "progressive farmers" with legal title and thus a stake in the land and the incentive to pursue commercial agriculture. The Swynnerton Plan of 1955 was gradually implemented in African areas throughout the late colonial period and continued after independence in 1963. After that, with the departure of some settlers from the White Highlands, the new government sponsored resettlement schemes to respond to ongoing land hunger. Not surprisingly, land reform was largely focused on men, dispossessing all but a minuscule number of women.[10]

Independence was achieved, under the leadership of President Jomo Kenyatta of the Kenya African National Union (KANU), a party that prevailed over the Kenya African Democratic Union (KADU). Political analysts interpret this party competition in different ways. One analysis suggests that the parties were divided by organizational principles—KANU supported unitary rule whereas KADU supported federalism. Another view suggests that the parties were organized around ethnic alliances: the Kikuyu and Luo coalesced in KANU and the Luyia and Kalenjin formed KADU.[11] Despite differences in outlook, with KANU in the majority at independence, KADU parliamentary representatives (including current President Daniel arap Moi) crossed party lines to join KANU. At present, KANU's skeletal countrywide structure allows the party to recruit candidates, but the party has no meaningful role in articulating programmatic ideology, in contrast with the personal networks of powerful men in favor with the president. More important, the dominant class interests of large landowners and businessmen permeate the political machinery, including the Parliament, the office of the president, and the government bureaucracy. Such elites have been challenged occasionally by leaders of other parties, such as the Kenya Peoples Union, or KANU colleagues who—at great risk—used populist rhetoric to promote redistributive policies. The assassinated populist J. M. Kariuki, whom E. S. Atieno-Odhiambo calls the "millionaire rhetorician for the poor," cautioned the regime against "building a country of '10 millionaires and 10 million poor people.'"[12]

During Kenya's early years of independence, an ascending class of wealthy men gained considerable economic and political power. Men with positions inside or with close access to insiders in government ministries accumulated great wealth through state subsidies, state licenses, and employment contacts, among other means.[13] In addition, the 1971 Ndegwa Commission gave official endorsement to civil servants' commercial activities and to conflicts of interest.[14]

Women's isolation from the state establishment excluded them from such politically tinged economic opportunities, and this distance still influences women's personal choices and political engagement today. Women's ability to access men's resources is tempered in several ways. First, women head a third of rural smallholdings, according to the 1979 census; among many, a feminization of poverty exists.[15] Second, despite romanticized myths about household income pooling, the reality is far more complex, with women's access to family or male income uncertain.[16] The majority of households depend upon women's income and resourcefulness. Third, polygamy is still practiced in Kenya, dividing a husband's loyalty among wives. The 1984 Kenya Contraceptive Prevalence Survey indicates that a quarter of married women aged 15 to 49 are in polygamous unions.[17] The harshness of this reality of limited access to economic resources merits a closer examination of women's engagement with the state and of specific policies that embrace women unevenly.

POLICIES: GENDER EQUITY?

Until recently, women in Kenya have not been viewed as an important social stratum or even as a population base that politics ought to address. The 1965 *Sessional Paper on African Socialism* (written by Kenyan policy makers to establish a rhetorically acceptable vision of a mixed-economy, welfare, and self-reliant society) is silent on gender, as have been subsequent policy documents. Yet this silence exists side by side with highly gendered policies. In addition to land dispossession, women farmers have been routinely excluded from the distribution of agricultural benefits, especially the credit that is guaranteed with land title deeds. Until recently, educational disparities have existed, with glaring gaps at secondary and university levels that have obvious implications for women's employment in the formal labor force and civil service.[18] In addition, women's few rights under the law are not easily exercised in this largely rural country in which customary practices often prevail.

Although not part of the official political agenda, reallocation of male preference in the distribution of government resources and patronage (what we view as gender redistributive issues) is certainly political to the core. As Kenyan scholar Achola Pala Okeyo remarks, "For African women the subject of women's advancement is highly political because it is an integral part of our quest for justice not only at the household level but all the way within the local, national and world economic order."[19] Gender politics threatens male interests and hence is perhaps more easily accommodated through the technical, seemingly neutral language of policy discourse.

The issue of women's place in the economy and society entered the policy discourse through an influential International Labour Organization (ILO) report on *Employment, Incomes and Equal-*

ity in Kenya, published in 1972, which elicited questions about access and equity in women's educational enrollment, low employment rates, and burdensome responsibilities in rural agriculture.[20] In its retort, the government declared that it was "not aware of overt discrimination against women in the country. Women are employed in important positions in the armed forces, in the police, in the prisons and in government as well as the private sector." Yet the government realized that more than equal employment opportunity and legal statutes were at issue, as reflected in new phrases and figures in subsequent development plans that claimed to recognize women's economic activity.[21]

In present-day Kenya, women are increasingly acknowledged in public policy; they are also well organized and positioned to assume a larger share of official political space, should Kenya move toward democracy. To preempt that possibility, in 1987 KANU took control of the largest national women's organization, Maendeleo ya Wanawake, and party leaders chronically meddle in its affairs. As opposition forces now call for a multiparty system, human rights, and constitutionalism to challenge one-party rule, their leaders experience the same exclusion, intimidation, and official silence that women have undergone.[22] While women's organizations avoid the political fray, individual women challengers make transparent the practices of the male political machinery.

GROUP POLITICS

Two women's organizations have achieved national prominence in Kenya. One of the oldest national women's organizations, Maendeleo ya Wanawake, formed under colonial rule in 1952 but soon Africanized with dynamic leaders, achieved reasonable success in mobilizing women during its first decade.[23] It underwent a period of decline and then revitalization in 1975; by 1985 it comprised 8,000 groups with 300,000 members. Local and regional chapters mobilize and train women in domestic and income-generating activities. By 1987 the resources,

membership, and international fame of the organization made the government seek to control its activities.

The other major women's organization, the National Council of Women of Kenya (NCWK), was founded in 1964 to coordinate women's organizations and was long headed by the dynamic and controversial Dr. Wangari Maathai, an internationally known environmentalist. Maathai is the founder of the Greenbelt movement, which sponsored an environmental program of tree-planting in an increasingly deforested Kenya. The role of NCWK diminished after MYWO withdrew in 1981 because of personality conflicts, though it is the primary independent forum for articulating women's interests. The NCWK is unpopular with the government owing to its attempts (unusual among women's groups in Kenya) to take a position on such issues as the infamous Otieno burial case discussed below. Personality conflicts and power struggles have been common among national-level organizations, limiting effective coalition building for legislative and policy change. Leaders vary in ideology and tactics, and the government exploits these differences to marginalize its female critics and opponents.

After the 1975 U.N. International Women's Year Conference, the government established the Women's Bureau in the Ministry of Culture and Social Services in 1976. The calls of U.N. women's advocacy units for "women's machinery" in government finally paid off—and at minimal cost to the government. The bureau aims to promote awareness of women's work and needs among policy makers, compile and disseminate information, train women leaders, and promote income-generating projects. It registers women's groups, which numbered 4,300 (156,892 members) in 1976 and 26,000 (1.4 million members) in 1988. Registered organizations sit atop a pyramid of informal women's groups in rural areas that exchange agricultural labor, provide mutual support and religious fellowship, contribute to community development efforts, accumulate savings for distribution on rotational bases, and occasionally voice women's views in electoral campaigns. As for political priority in the national budget, though, women's programs accounted for only 0.1 percent of total government expenditures between 1978 and 1982. Government grants to women's groups have dropped from 3.3 million shillings (U.S. $206,250) in 1986, to $162,500 in 1987, and to $100,000 in 1989.[24] Nevertheless, the establishment of the Women's Bureau has had a significant effect on changing the perception of gender politics, supporting local community politics and chipping away at the consistent male preference that operates in all government activity except primary education.

Seed money from the Women's Bureau provides leverage for grass-roots women's leaders to participate in the District Development Committees (DDCs) that plan, coordinate, and manage government and community development efforts. The bureau also provides group leaders with "insider" brokers (community development assistants, field agents for the Ministry of Culture and Social Services) who connect them with other possible sources of assistance.

Contradictory effects are also in evidence, however. In some instances, coastal women's "front" organizations have been mobilized by local men to tap money from the government and international organizations. Male patrons provided women with contacts and access to money, and in return, women earned income that served as an incentive for husbands' acquiescence to their wives' group participation. Other political patrons compete for women's support, a process through which women secure some gains. Community development assistants have established criteria that now reduce groups' dependency on local male patrons, who cannot so easily embezzle funds because of financial accounting requirements.[25]

Although the Women's Bureau seeks to influence policy makers, it lacks the authority to do so. No presidential authorization or official policy gives it leverage in interaction with other ministries. The closest thing to a national policy on women is a chapter devoted to women in President Daniel arap Moi's book, *Kenya Africa Nationalism: Nyayo Philosophy and Principles*, which is the most detailed statement of government policy, amid numerous documents that now routinely, but rhetorically, mention women. After outlining women's accomplishments, Moi draws several conclusions, among them that women should "build upon their achievements . . . by continued cooperation with the Government, in faith, loyalty and co-action with the leadership from the grass roots to the top."[26] The political situation thus invites loyalty, not voice.

In a rare show of solidarity in September 1984, leaders of women's groups made modest demands to advance women's interests, including calls for all unionizable women workers to join trade unions, for women to be involved in decision-making processes, and for discriminatory practices against women in employment to be corrected. The participants, who included women leaders representing various women's organizations, were preparing for the 1985 U.N. International Women's Year Conference in Nairobi. The government responded with a strongly worded warning to Kenyan women "to avoid making statements and demands that could create problems for them." They were also cautioned against "talking about their rights, as indeed all Kenyans have their rights but do not talk about them." Women were also reminded that they "had little to complain about as they were adequately represented in various fields in the country."[27] Women were intimidated, and a few disassociated themselves from the demands.

The dominant male ideology upholds the view that if women have anything to complain about, they should blame themselves and not the government or society. Thus, for example, in 1985 a government minister felt no compunction in addressing a seminar by saying: "I am forced to believe that the woman is lazy in her mind. She is too lazy to think. You women think and believe that you are inferior to men."[28] In this way, the burden of responsibility has often been shifted to women; by working harder or developing the right attitude, they will move forward. The structure, meanwhile, remains blameless.

Despite these drawbacks, women's organizations have been somewhat more tolerated than ethnic organizations, which the government has banned since 1980 because of perceived threats to political stability.[29] Women's organizations remain "legal" as a result of their distance from the intrigues associated with those who gain or lose favor with the president, but they lack the independent ability to criticize policies or advocate change. Yet the organizational base for women's groups is huge, only partly because of the registration process for the Women's Bureau. It is therefore not surprising that KANU moved to take control of Maendeleo ya Wanawake in 1987 on the pretext of financial mismanagement. The government's objective, however, was to strengthen its own base and further fragment the fragile and divided women's movement with these females who seemed to be insiders. Alternatively termed a merger, marriage, or co-optation, the newly labeled KANU-MYWO inspires much debate on the extent of its independence and the implications for women's empowerment. Maendeleo's conservative leaders have worked closely with government and benefit from the relationship; critics of the merger said these leaders have long been co-opted. Almost no one, except the government, has spoken in favor of the merger. Several women spoke against it during the 1990 KANU Review Committee. In 1989 a director of women and youth was put on KANU's Executive Committee; women await action on a 1990 pledge to add a place for MYWO.

In the 1989 Maendeleo election, Kenya's cautious press reported that men were squabbling over candidates, advice, and issues in this women's organization. One district officer revealed a "well-organized plot by some men" to "pose as women" in order to vote, though no impersonators were arrested. President Moi even commented that women ought to run their own affairs, though he changed rules several times about voter eligibility. In the end, the elections provided the opportunity for key male politicians to ensure that their wives and sisters captured leadership positions. As such, the process reinforced the class and male dominance of Kenyan politics. Hilary Ng'weno, *Weekly Review* editor, called the affair a "sorry statement . . . on the status of Kenya women in politics."[30]

Thus, on the national level, official intervention co-opts and manipulates women's groups to support and legitimize the man-made political machinery. At the grass-roots level, where stakes are smaller, women have more room to maneuver.

ELECTORAL POLITICS

Kenya's de facto one-party rule under KANU provides considerable competition among candidates, leading to its characterization as clientelist politics, with voters exercising accountability based on whether politicians can deliver goods and patronage to their districts. Elections are held every five years, and incumbents are turned out of office in sizable numbers: in 1983, 43 percent of backbenchers (junior MPs), 41 percent of assistant ministers, and 19 percent of ministers lost their seats. Frontbenchers constitute a majority of the 188 National Assembly members.[31] In addition, election rigging is quite common in Kenya. Usually those who enter Parliament are not necessarily those who received the most votes, but rather those preferred by the key players in the political establishment. Few women present themselves as candidates, for they face sociocultural prejudices, encounter fund-raising constraints, and experience considerable resistance from men who employ diverse strategies, including the control of KANU recruitment machinery, to exclude women. No woman currently serves in the 12 parliamentary-nominated positions. One woman currently serves as assistant minister in the Ministry of Culture and Social Services.

Competition among candidates declined after a controversial queuing system was installed in 1988 in which KANU party members queued publicly behind a picture of their preferred candidate to cast their vote. (Since KANU is the only legal party, all candidates represent KANU.) Such public declaration of voter preferences clearly violates the democratic notion of secret balloting. It poses political, and possibly physical, risks for supporters of the losing candidates; thus it is not surprising that 65 candidates ran unopposed in the 1988 elections. Competition was low in part because queuing made it easier for husbands to monitor wives' votes. One of the two elected women MPs, Mrs. Ndetei, said, "A woman was battered by her husband and she had to run away from him simply because she was going to vote for me. . . . I confronted many other cases where women were not free." Male MPs responded that women's representation was good enough; some questioned Ndetei's capacity to discharge her duties.[32] As on other political issues, few women participated in pressuring the government to abolish queue voting.

As a majority of voters, women have carved out some political space for themselves in clientelist politics, although it is limited to non-programmatic patronage. During the mid-1970s candidates courted women's groups in western Kenya with matches and small bags of sugar. In the mid-1980s women's groups in Kiambu District developed a mutually supportive relationship with the local MP and other power brokers. Women's group support, or the lack thereof, can mean success or failure for candidates: "The decision of a group of women to 'get up and dance' for a candidate means that they intend to vote for the person in question. This is how these women express their political preferences."[33]

Once in Parliament, however, men ignore women's issues, and women's groups disdain political advocacy because of co-optation, their organization's apolitical stance, or harassment. The two women MPs shoulder the enormous responsibility of enlightening colleagues and building coalitions in an atmosphere where it is "politically correct" to applaud male dominance. Former MP Phoebe Asiyo's account of the two-time failure to pass the Law of Marriage and Divorce tells the grim story well.[34] The law fully addressed household relations; it strengthened women's rights to own property, to be protected from corporal punishment, and to avoid polygamy. Asiyo quotes from the parliamentary debate: MPs said corporal punishment was necessary to discipline wives, and wives should be

beaten, for it is "a pleasure to her . . . a way of expressing love in Luhya custom." A woman MP's query on why women providers did not have the right to punish their husbands invoked a defense of bridewealth: "because she has not bought [her husband]." The most vigorous debate occurred over polygamy, with lengthy rationales being offered in support of the practice: what if the first wife was childless, old, or rude? What if a man needed a nurse in his old age?

Participants at the 1987 seminar on Women and the Law in Kenya, sponsored by the Women's Bureau and Public Law Institute, identified Kenya's multiple legal systems as crucial to understanding men's layered legal and social control of women.[35] Culture is also often invoked in defense of male privilege, and, in such circumstances, challenges by courageous individuals occupy important political space. In a dramatic example of cultural revivalism, for example, Wambui Otieno was denied the right to bury her husband according to his wishes and hers and sought relief from her husband's Luo relatives in the courts. Hers was a cross-ethnic (Kikuyu-Luo) marriage; they were professionals who resided in Nairobi, and Otieno had had suspicions of his relatives' intentions to dispossess his spouse materially after his death. The male-dominated judiciary manipulated the contradictory customary and common laws of Kenya to malign Wambui Otieno and pass judgment against her claim. She retained control over household property, however. The implications of this case for women are mixed, given the compromise decision that included burial and property rights issues, but the courtroom process underlined men's dominance of legal and political machinery. It also demonstrated the general lack of gender awareness among women and their inability to unite on issues of common concern. The leadership of the NCWK did try to organize a petition drive in support of Wambui, but it was neither packaged in a politically acceptable way nor made easy for women politicians to support; MP and Assistant Minister Grace Ogot, a Luo, disassociated herself from the petition drive.[36]

More recently, Wangari Maathai challenged

KANU's plan to build a skyscraper in Nairobi's Uhuru Park.[37] To be funded with external loans at the cost of 7 percent of Kenya's budget, the complex would destroy greenbelt (parks) and remove recreational space for the city's poor. When Maathai sought a high court injunction on the project, the entire membership of Parliament descended on her, attacking her personally as a "sentimental, frustrated divorcée" who had no credentials or mandate to challenge a state decision. KANU-MYWO demonstrated against Maathai and her actions, helping the government to legitimize the subsequent harassment and ostracism she suffered. Maathai was intimidated, and the Greenbelt movement was investigated. After international lenders refused to support the skyscraper, however, the government finally scaled down the complex.

As these examples illustrate, men's tight control over the political process narrows the political arena and reduces the number of political voices, especially those of women. Ironically, though, this atmosphere shifts opposition to new forums that embrace women and to the fluidity of cultural interpretations and inventions, as the Otieno case demonstrates. As Patricia Stamp says of the mechanisms used to influence and criticize an authoritarian regime: "Kenyans turned to every nonpolitical forum available in order to express opposition or fight for their interests."[38] As government critics and supporters line up on formerly nonpolitical gender issues, gender enters mainstream politics in more central ways.

DEVELOPMENT POLICY

In electoral politics as well as for women's groups, much of the contest of Kenyan politics is over economic development policy, the role of agricultural policy within development plans, and the extent of state spending on social services. In these as in most policy areas, the Kenyan government and the bureaucracy long have had tremendous influence in making and implementing policy.[39] Although the colonial law-and-order mentality still imbues organizational culture somewhat, development ideology overlays

that culture as well. Development ideology supports a proactive role for state intervention toward change, economic growth, and (occasionally) equity. The ideologues are ranking bureaucrats and their expatriate advisers. Women rarely reach such ranks, but when they do, they confront organizational cultures with long legacies of male preference that resist transformation. Whatever the policy rhetoric, the *practice* of development ideology often takes a top-down, control orientation. As E. S. Atieno-Odhiambo would interpret it, an "ideology of order" influences administrative practice, with loyalty to President Moi's ruling coalition reigning supreme.[40]

"Orderly" development struggles to keep pace with community self-help, known as *harambee* (pulling together), in which people contribute money and labor to build schools, clinics, and the like. Scholars like Gideon Mutiso and Frank Holmquist view self-help, estimated at 30 percent of development spending, as rural efforts to squeeze complementary resources from the center and to pre-empt top-down planning.[41] Women are certainly a strong part of harambee,[42] but the number of officially registered women's groups surpasses the number of officially registered harambee groups.[43] The government's obsession with registration, traced back to colonial times, goes beyond the ability to maintain an accurate count of organizations.

Government officials have made various attempts to contain self-help efforts by planning, coordinating, and managing these endeavors. The most recent reincarnation of this policy of central control is the establishment of District Development Committees (DDCs), on which a majority of civil servants sit.[44] On DDCs, field staff from diverse ministries are supposed to meet with political and organizational leaders to coordinate development planning, spending, and activities. Yet considerable economic activity and initiative continue to occur outside government control. In the following section, we focus on agricultural and reproductive health programs within the market-driven structural adjustment policies, an orientation that necessarily affects employment as well. By looking at Kenya through this "bureaucratic lens," we can address the extent to which man-made political machinery extends into the very heart of bureaucracy in the language and activities used to embrace clients.[45] We will examine how far the bureaucracy will go to include or empower women in the name of "sound policy." Kenyan women react to this by distancing themselves from further male appropriation of their labor and earnings. Yet this distance frequently excludes women from significant support, subsidies, and patronage readily provided to men.

AGRICULTURAL POLICY

As women make up a majority of Kenya's farmers, head households in sizable numbers, and are responsible for family food supplies, they are greatly affected by agricultural policies. Problems in the implementation of agricultural policy include a bias in the delivery of resources and technical support toward rich, large landowners and toward men; an emphasis on export-oriented cash crops that detracts from food crop production (maize is a major exception); and marketing difficulties.

Agricultural production has long been central to Kenya's economy, both in colonial and contemporary times, as Kenya is 80 percent rural. Colonial policies were designed to serve the settler population in the large farm sector in maize, export crops, and dairy products through subsidies, marketing boards, and research-extension services. Once confronted with racially based restrictions on participating in certain spheres of agriculture, African farmers began growing crops like coffee and tea for an export market in the 1950s. Throughout the twentieth century, women have shouldered major labor burdens for food and cash crop production, from preparing soil and planting to weeding, harvesting, storing, and marketing crops—without benefit of advanced technology. Short-handled hoes remain their main tools.

Independent Kenya's first development plan,

promulgated in 1964 by the planning ministry, advanced few agricultural priorities and took heed instead of the development "expertise" of the time, which stressed industrialization. Subsequent development plans gave priority to agricultural development for export, national food self-sufficiency, and increased income for the largely rural population. Unlike many African countries, Kenya has not extracted excessive hidden tax from its farmers through artificially low agricultural prices, though the government does control some agricultural marketing through parastatal agencies of mixed efficiency and through officially registered cooperative societies.[46] Male control of these institutions undermines women's ability to profit from the fruits of their labor by extending men's control to incomes as well. Thus the multiplication of parastatal agencies is in part a multiplication of male patronage positions and control opportunities.

Kenya's political-economic elite has a strong stake in a healthy agricultural economy. They are among Kenya's largest farmers and ranchers (termed the landed gentry in some analyses), a pattern that accelerated following the sale of significant tracts in the White Highlands after independence. The large farm sector is less productive economically than the small farm sector, but large farm owners are politically powerful.[47] This political-economic elite, consisting of agro-businessmen, commercial investors, and managers and civil servants, represents 2.6 percent of landowners but controls half of the land under cultivation. Absentee ownership has earned many the dubious distinction of "telephone farmers," according to S. E. Migot-Adholla.[48] Agriculture constitutes a third of the gross domestic product and nearly three-fourths of export earnings. Tourism, coffee, and tea are the top three foreign exchange earners.[49] This reliance on agriculture means that Kenya's overall economy could benefit if women farm workers— the majority of all agricultural workers—had incentives to be more productive. Yet institutions and agricultural services in Kenya often serve to restrict women in the agricultural economy.

Under colonialism, the Ministry of Agriculture established a gendered organizational culture based on ideological conceptions that men were the appropriate recipients of agricultural extension advice delivered by male field agents. Kenya's 1929 *Annual Report* quotes historian Lord Lugard: "Since men alone tend oxen in Africa, the result, as I have elsewhere said, will be to replace female labor in the fields to a large extent."[50]

Through the agriculture extension service, farmers learn recommended agricultural practices and gain contacts about other services. Studies in the mid-1970s documented a pervasive and persistent bias against women farm managers, who constituted nearly two-fifths of households sampled.[51] Male agricultural extension agents concentrated their visits on farms where a man was present. The male farmers were four times as likely to receive training at Farmer Training Centers and ten times as likely to know about credit. Government-subsidized credit, tied to land title deeds and waged salaries, was overwhelmingly distributed to men. Agricultural credit disparities linger into the 1990s, with women receiving less than one-tenth of loans.[52] Women continue to feed and support their families, but without the structural advantages of men, who are the preferred administrative clientele. Wary of political rhetoric, women rely on themselves and women's groups.

After independence, a separate home economics unit focusing on women was established in the Ministry of Agriculture. Home economics agents represented a mere 2 percent of field staff in the ministry but worked in such areas as child care, cooking, knitting, sanitation, and gardening. Clearly, the home economics unit promoted a domestic ideology and had questionable links to production.[53] After a brief period of "integration," the unit is again separate.

Since Kenya's independence, massive investments have been made in training an expanded field extension staff, using public revenue and external loans and grants. In a sense this is a job subsidies program for men. Evidence from the 1970s indicates that general agricultural field staffers did a poor job of communicating accurate agricultural research recommendations to farmers.[54] Moreover, their "advice" often had the effect of hooking farmers into such expensive purchases as fertilizers. Staff members visited, at most, 20 farm households per month, but they were especially attentive to what David Leonard calls the "political squawk" factor: well-off farmers with the clout to complain to field staff supervisors received greater attention. Few women, save those linked to a petit bourgeois rural elite, were squawkers, in the 1970s or now. Furthermore, women are wary of investments that they can neither afford nor necessarily profit from, given that men mediate payments in cooperatives, marketing structures, and households. Coffee and tea, for example, are marketed through male cooperative members and registered farmers, authorized through the visible hand of bureaucracy.[55]

Both 1979 and the mid-1980s were catalyst periods in agricultural policy change. Kenya experienced two institutionally fueled food crises that were aggravated by drought, rising oil prices, and increases in the prices of manufactured goods, with which agricultural prices did not keep pace.[56] Without adequate space in government marketing-board buying centers and storage facilities, agents stiffened quality standards and rejected locally produced maize (Kenya's food staple) in large quantities. These actions complicated the district-level marketing restrictions faced by farmers, including women, and limited the amount of maize they could sell without bribing or sneaking past police officers posted at district boundaries. Not surprisingly, farmers cut back production, and the government was forced to use precious foreign exchange to import maize.

Other constraints on women's agricultural activities existed, many of them documented under the auspices of local research institutes like the Institutes for Development Studies and African Studies at the University of Nairobi, the Kenya Agricultural Research Institute, and international and national nongovernmental organizations. The translation of these findings into action is an inherently political process. With this research as a base of support, extension reforms to benefit more women farmers were proposed in the 1980s. Curriculum changes integrated training in agriculture and nutrition for prospective agricultural and home economics extension staff members, and agricultural colleges recruited more women as prospective agricultural agents. Male extension staffers were encouraged to work with the many grass-roots women's agricultural groups. Patrick Muzaale and David Leonard document successes from this reform, though women's groups earned paltry sums and poor women did not participate because they lacked funds to contribute to group projects.[57] These and other reforms strengthened the quality and control of the extension staff instead of empowering women farmers, demonstrating that lack of political will in the male-dominated political machinery rather than lack of information hampers change.

Conceptualized and supported by the World Bank, the new extension model, "Training and Visit" (T&V), aims to improve training and supervision of extension agents. In a two-stage model of disseminating agricultural information, extension agents work with "contact farmers," who constitute about 10 percent of farmers. Contact farmers are then supposed to work with "follower farmers" to disseminate information between extension visits. Kenya's Ministry of Agriculture adopted T&V in 1983 and temporarily integrated agricultural and home economics extension. These bureaucratic reforms have improved the quality of extension personnel and reduced prejudicial attitudes about women farmers: a World Bank country study declared that Kenya's "achievements in bringing agricultural extension services to women farmers are outstanding." T&V was designed and implemented with the "deliberate intent" of reaching women as well as men.[58] The consequences of these changes for women have been limited, as studies by the government and the World Bank demonstrate. Staff logs show overwhelming incidence of contact with men farmers, but in the field itself, more than half the agents say they see a majority of women, either contact farmers or their wives. Internal ministry and bank reports reveal that contact farmers are prosperous older farmers who, in practice, work with only one or two "followers," well below the official aim of five to eight followers.[59]

More emphasis will be placed on extension officers' contacts with existing women's agricultural groups in the 1990s. Nzomo's study of a U.S. Agency for International Development project documented the shift away from T&V's biased interaction with better-off farmers toward *myethya* (self-help) groups in the delivery of agricultural inputs, such as seedlings and hoes.[60] T&V's primary legacy for women seems to involve more labor on their part in order to adopt extension agents' recommendations. Agricultural extension efforts directed toward women's groups that do not make a serious attempt to empower women will mean only more of the same.

The intensification of agricultural production invariably results in increased labor burdens, and women's gains from additional labor depend on their husbands' goodwill. The extent to which women can control earnings from their produce appears to be linked to the profitability of the enterprise, with men taking over profitable "family" income.[61] How can women gain access to income and control production assets and the land they till? Strategies to overcome gendered marketing obstacles and unequal household relations require political support because of the threat they pose to male interests, the base on which the current regime rests.

INCOMES AND INCENTIVES

Scholars and practitioners have long recognized the importance of providing incentives and stakes to those who are responsible for agricultural-driven economic growth. Land reform programs routinely use such rationales but consider households the final unit of analysis—as though households were equitable structures in which incomes are pooled. Drawing on Amartya Sen's terminology, households are better conceptualized as situations of "cooperative conflict."[62]

As previously mentioned, land reform in Kenya puts title deeds in men's names. Although complicated institutional procedures are involved, widows can gain title, and women can purchase land if they have sufficient cash. Yet gender disparities in access to capital have a long history in Kenya, given patriarchal systems of property ownership and inheritance, as well as decades of educational inequality between girls and boys and thus differences in credentials needed to gain lucrative wage employment.

Under this system, wives have less secure access to land than under the traditional user rights, for husbands can now sell their land without informing their wives. Fiona Mackenzie reports that after numerous complaints from women in the Murang'a District, the MP "instigated a process whereby it became mandatory for the spouse of the landowner (and, if adult, the children) to appear before the Land Board, where a sale was to be heard, in order to indicate their knowledge of the matter and their agreement." Afterward, land sales dropped dramatically.[63]

Land is not the only resource that is officially controlled by men through bureaucratic registration and licensing procedures. The Kenya Tea Development Authority (KDTA), a "success story" in international agency and development management literature, registers male landowners, who usually receive payments for plucked leaves as well as bonuses deposited directly in their bank accounts. In the view of KDTA agents, a woman's access to tea income would threaten her husband's dominance and weaken his control over female labor. According to the KDTA, husbands who share their income with wives and children can usually expect cooperation from their wives. Not all husbands regularly share income, however, and women respond accordingly in the form of "direct negligence of the tea or a low productivity level," according to research from Kericho District.[64] In this way, women use their autonomy politically: they withhold their labor.

In Central Province, women tea harvesters, resentful of the male-only tea bonus award, organized a successful protest. "A group of the most outspoken women went to the local committee of the KDTA, angrily protesting that they rarely saw the annual bonuses because their husbands spent the cash on beer, meat and other items for their exclusive use." Women celebrated their success at a community meeting "with ululations and impromptu dancing."[65]

Women's "everyday forms of resistance" are replicated in production of other crops.[66] Development project managers, disappointed with the amount of rice marketed in a rice settlement scheme, learned that women diverted rice to unofficial markets to gain income for their numerous household responsibilities. Payments to husbands were not pooled in these households.[67] In another case, the production of the pyrethrum plant plummeted when men received payments for their wives' labor.[68] Coffee cooperatives pay men for joint labor. Joint bank accounts in the names of husbands and wives, which are more common in areas with extensive male out-migration, do not guarantee women's control over income, but as Fiona Mackenzie concludes, "it may be seen as a step in that direction."[69] Women realize small victories in local action, where they sometimes influence change in how policy is implemented.

Many analysts interpret the income-generating activities of women's groups as attempts to earn independent incomes outside husbands' control.[70] Government promotions of such activities, like those subsidized by the Women's Bureau, can thus be viewed as a potential threat to a nearly unassailable male-dominated bureaucratic machinery that directs resources to men. Yet it must also be understood that government seeks to use many women's group income-generating projects as international showpieces, though few produce significant earnings for women.[71] Studies that query whether women's agricultural productivity equals men's miss the mark, for they neglect women's intentional resistance to structures from which they derive no benefit. Moreover, women's economic response amid authoritarian household relations borders on compulsion—caused not only by hunger, but also by male dominance. In essence, women's resistance to development interventions that increase labor without concomitant payoff demonstrates that Kenyan women are politically engaged in ways that mainstream developmentalists are only beginning to fathom.

The question remains as to whether women's situations would improve if they took their produce directly to market, free from all the institutional tentacles of man-made political machinery. After all, bureaucracies harm women in numerous ways: patronage appointments, usually from men to men; gender ideologies that justify male preference in service delivery; and seemingly neutral subsidies to the wealthy that nonetheless benefit men disproportionately. As a result of pressure from internal market advocates in the bureaucracy and of external pressure from structural adjustment agreements, Kenya is gradually lifting severe district-level marketing restrictions. Women farmers and traders may thereby benefit from direct payments and less police harassment. Yet international capitalism's history has rarely been favorable to women or to countries of the Southern Hemisphere like Kenya. In addition, the feminization of poverty makes many women easily exploitable as cheap labor. Women still face appropriation of their income by husbands when these earnings become sizable, requiring that attention be paid to securing equity in household relations.

Extension integration strategies are not the same as empowerment strategies that would assure women's access to income and control over land through the law, political voice, and reconstructed marital relations. Beyond that, women's development prospects do not stop at national borders. Kenya's men and women are constrained in an international political-economic environment that disempowers African states. Kenyan women are especially affected by this arrangement, since state officials are more apt to accept the conditions of structural adjustment agreements that affect weak political constituencies such as healthcare clients.[72]

REPRODUCTIVE HEALTH AMID STRUCTURAL ADJUSTMENT PROGRAMS

Kenya has made remarkable progress in healthcare since independence; life expectancy has lengthened, and infant and maternal mortality rates have dropped. In two decades, the number of hospitals has increased from 148 to 218, health centers from 160 to 274, and dispensaries from 400 to 1,184.[73] Structural adjustment agreements threaten these gains.

The Kenyan economy's annual growth rate in the first decade since independence was an impressive 6.5 percent. But this economic performance could not be sustained during the 1970s when the economy experienced three externally derived economic crises: the oil price increases of 1973–74 and 1979–80; deteriorating terms of trade for primary commodity exports; and rising interest rates. These crises forced Kenya to turn to the International Monetary Fund and the World Bank to finance its balance of payments deficits and to accept the economic and policy conditions imposed by them.[74] Such conditions, which reduce government spending, the size of the civil service, and deficit spending, promote budgetary redistribution at the expense of politically marginal constituencies. Thus, structural adjustment burdens fall heavily on women.

To raise additional state revenue, new taxes and user fees have been imposed for various social services. Some fees are linked to healthcare, a sector not particularly well endowed, consuming just 5 percent of recurrent budgetary expenditures during the 1980s. Cutbacks have caused drug shortages in Kenyan hospitals, and high costs deter use of medicine outside hospitals. Crowding in public hospitals has forced some birthing women to share beds or to sleep on the floor. In addition, the government requires that if maternity fees are not paid before a woman leaves the hospital, she may be detained there. Such conditions discourage the already minimal deliveries at hospitals, and maternal mortality now accounts for 40 percent of female deaths among 15- to 35-year olds.[75]

Higher healthcare costs are not necessarily disastrous, but fewer people, especially women, have the resources to pay. Government employees' real wage rates declined by more than a third from 1974 to 1988; in some cases there were more than 200 percent increases in the compulsory National Hospital Insurance Fund and cuts in the number of personnel. Women's unemployment and general welfare is disproportionately affected because the services cut are more likely to be staffed by women. Furthermore, demands on women's time and labor increase to fill the gaps in services.

At the same time, work in the informal sector expanded, and real minimum wages in the formal economy fell. Women constitute three-quarters of the informal sector, working as hawkers, traders, prostitutes, and brewers, occupations with unpredictable and generally low incomes. The government licenses better-paying informal sector work like vehicle repair and small appliance manufacturing, in which men predominate and where startup capital and credit are easier to acquire. Women's "illegality" makes them subject to persistent harassment, penalties, and confiscations of their goods.

Structural adjustment policies in the manufacturing sector propose Export Processing Zones, which are likely to affect women's prospects for formal employment, their marginalization, and their exploitation. A World Bank report estimates that women will constitute at least three-fourths of EPZ employees: in other words, cheap labor.[76] Here again, international and national bureaucrats rhetorically "recognize" women, but politics and dominant global economic forces will determine whether greater integration into the formal wage sector translates into improvement in welfare and status.

Economic instability, for individual women and for government, ripples through health priorities and associated family planning efforts. For a time, Kenya ranked highest in the world in population growth rates, at 4.1 percent annually, with a total fertility rate of eight children per woman. Such growth places extraordinary pressures on arable land, school buildings, and the job market. At current growth rates, Kenya's population of 23 million may surpass 30 million by the year 2000.

Kenya was the first sub-Saharan African country to declare support for family planning in 1966, but the government itself now concedes "limited program success." Only 17 percent of reproductive-age Kenyan women use birth control, and within that group, only half use such "modern" methods as pills, IUDs, or sterilization. In the eyes of population technicians, the government responded to this dilemma with the right kinds of programmatic moves. It elevated bureaucratic coordination of family planning to the Office of the Vice-President and Home Affairs; it integrated family planning and health programming; its largest women's organization distributes contraceptives; and it built clinics strategically to lessen the distance women have to walk for services.[77] Kenyan culture, however, is strongly pronatalist and women receive far stronger cues to reproduce than to use contraception. Surveys in the early 1980s reported that on average, women desire 6.2 children and men desire 8.7.[78] Child care complicates women's multiple roles and hampers their participation in public decision-making positions.

In sum, agriculture and reproductive policy strategies and reforms do not yet recognize women's concerns. This lack of recognition limits policy achievements and endeavors to control women rather than empower them. Although a far-reaching family planning program could allow women to make their own choices, the current Kenyan government is unprepared to take such steps. In essence, male control of female productive and reproductive labor is more important to national politics than overall economic productivity or women's reproductive health.

PROSPECTS

"If the men worked as hard as the women, Kenya would be developed by now."[79] This quote from a community development officer reminds us that development is not the sole purpose of the state. Kenyan political machinery is concerned with power and control, and its base is men, whose control over women remains unthreatened. It is therefore not surprising that development policy discourse and practice reaps such meager results in the area of women's empowerment.

Although development policies rhetorically "recognize" women's work, policy practice seeks to ensnare women in a web of control. It succeeds only in part. On paper, agricultural extension and reproductive health reforms seem advanced, but in practice they make minimal progress toward the economic empowerment of women. States, of course, are not impermeable monoliths; tiny cracks may appear at the center, through Women's Bureau activities, for instance, and especially at the edges, where women seek to act in ways that advance their interests. In the meantime, development policy goals cannot be realized unless women share economic assets and political voice.

At the national level, women's groups are cautious. The grand scheme in which they have a role pitifully and temporarily shores up the regime. Locally, women use whatever means possible to augment their meager incomes and to extract goods and services from MPs. At the same time, women seek a stronger legal foundation for their claims to equal rights so that discretionary cultural traditions do not control their lives. Yet women also recognize the lengthy struggle associated with enforcing more substantive legal foundations. Just as cultural constructions are not gender-neutral in their allocation of power, so the state is far from neutral, notwithstanding Kenya's signature to the U.N. Convention on the Elimination of All Forms of Discrimination Against Women.

In the meantime, women work, extract resources as best they can, and build ties with others. They resist unfair practices when possible and use their political space wisely until democratic accountability finally exists for women in Kenya.

NOTES

1. For figures on elected and nominated members, see Maria Nzomo, "Women in Politics and Public Decision Making in Kenya" (Paper presented at the U.N. Expert Group Meeting on the Role of Women in Public Life and Decision Making, Vienna, 21–24 May 1991). On cabinet-level women, 1989 figures, see table 1 in Kathleen Staudt, "Women in High-Level Political Decision Making: A Global Analysis" (Expert Group Meeting on Equality in Political Participation and Decision Making, Vienna, 18–22 September 1989), 28–40. As of 1989, in sub-Saharan Africa, there were no women in the cabinets of Kenya, Angola, Cape Verde, Congo, Djibouti, Equatorial Guinea, Ethiopia, Malawi, Mozambique, Nigeria, Sierra Leone, Somalia, and South Africa. A majority of sub-Saharan countries have women in their cabinets, with Ghana and Ivory Coast the highest at four and five women, respectively. For an excellent treatment of "high politics" in Kenya, see David W. Throup, "The Construction and Destruction of the Kenyatta State," in Michael G. Schatzberg, ed., *The Political Economy of Kenya* (New York: Praeger, 1987), 33–74. Throup discusses intrigues that span the Kenyatta and Moi regimes, naming more than 100 elite figures, only one of whom is female. Chelagat Mutai, a radical populist on land issues, was jailed on seemingly trumped-up charges in the mid-1980s and lived in exile in Tanzania ("Chelagat Mutai Returns to Kenya," *Weekly Review,* 27 April 1984, pp. 4–7).

2. Victor Azarya, "Reordering State-Society Relations: Incorporation and Disengagement," in Donald Rothchild and Naomi Chazan, eds., *The Precarious Balance: State and Society in Africa* (Boulder, Colo.: Westview, 1988), 6–7.

3. For a gender-blind analysis, see Goran Hyden, *No Shortcuts to Progress: African Development Management in Perspective* (Berkeley: University of California Press, 1983). Also see Jane Parpart and Kathleen Staudt, eds., *Women and the State in Africa* (Boulder, Colo.: Lynne Rienner, 1989).

4. David Leonard, *African Successes: Four Public Managers of Kenyan Rural Development* (Berkeley: University of California Press, 1991), 124.

5. A. H. M. Kirk-Greene used the term "thin white line." Also see analysis in Kathleen Staudt, "The State and Gender in Colonial Africa," in Sue Ellen Charlton, Jana Everett, and Kathleen Staudt, eds., *Women, the State, and Development* (Albany: SUNY Albany Press, 1989), 66–85.

6. Also see C. M. Clark, "Land and Food, Women and Power in Nineteenth Century Kikuyu," *Africa* 50, no. 4 (1980): 357–70; and, more generally on African women's economic contributions and organizational activity, see Karen Sacks, *Sisters and Wives: The Past and Future of Sexual Equality* (Westport, Conn.: Greenwood, 1979).

Although men controlled public authority in indigenous societies, women's group activities and economic contributions were considerable and recognized as such, as in Staudt, "State and Gender," 79–84.

7. Hugh Fearn, *An African Economy* (London: Oxford University Press, 1961), 77.

8. Audrey Wipper, "Kikuyu Women and the Harry Thuku Disturbances: Some Uniformities of Female Militancy," *Africa* 59, no. 3 (1989): 300–337; Cora Presley, "Labor Unrest Among Kikuyu Women in Colonial Kenya," in Claire Robertson and Iris Berger, eds., *Women and Class in Africa* (New York: Holmes and Meier, 1986), 255–73; and "Kikuyu Women in the 'Mau Mau' Rebellion," in G. Okihiro, ed., *In Resistance: Studies on African, Afro-American and Caribbean Resistance* (Boston: University of Massachusetts Press, 1986), 53–70.

9. The patron-client approach is most often articulated by Joel D. Barkan, "The Electoral Process and Peasant-State Relations in Kenya," in Fred Hayward, ed., *Elections in Independent Africa* (Boulder, Colo.: Westview, 1987), 213–38. On the "invention" of tradition see Margaret Jean Hay and Marcia Wright, eds., *African Women and the Law: Historical Perspectives,* Boston University Paper on Africa no. 7 (Boston: Boston University, 1982); Martin Chanock, *Law, Custom and Social Order: The Colonial Experience in Malawi and Zambia* (Cambridge, Eng.: Cambridge University Press, 1985); Staudt, "State and Gender"; and the gender-free analysis in E. Hobsbawn and Terence O. Ranger, eds., *The Invention of Tradition* (Cambridge, Eng.: Cambridge University Press, 1983). Patricia Stamp's work on cultural revivalism is superb; see "Burying Otieno: The Politics of Gender and Ethnicity in Kenya," *Signs* 16, no. 4 (1991): 808–45. In *The Comforts of Home: Prostitution in Colonial Nairobi* (Chicago: University of Chicago, 1990), 39, Luise White says, "Africans did comprehend these forces; in fact, they manipulated them."

10. Studies put women's ownership at zero to 17 percent of land titles. See Achola Pala, "Daughters of the Lakes and Rivers: Colonization and the Land Rights of Luo Women," in Mona Etienne and Eleanor Leacock, eds., *Women and Colonization: Anthropological Perspectives* (New York: Praeger, 1980), 186–213. On history, see Margaret Jean Hay, "Women as Owners, Occupants, and Managers of Property in Colonial Western Kenya," in Hay and Wright, eds., *African Women and the Law,* 110–23; Jean Davison, "Who Owns What? Land Registration and Tensions in Gender Relations of Production in Kenya," in Jean Davison, ed., *Agriculture, Women, and Land: The African Experience* (Boulder, Colo.: Westview, 1988), 157–76; Bonnie Kettel, "The Commoditization of Women in Tugen (Kenya) Social Organization," in Robertson and Berger, eds., *Women and Class in Africa,* 60; World Bank, *Kenya: The Role of Women in Economic Development* (Washington, D.C.: World Bank, 1989),

which estimates five percent based on a review of studies; and U.S. Agency for International Development, Staudt personal communication, 12 June 1991, which estimates 15 percent, based on a baseline survey for a maize market development program in six districts.

11. See selections in Schatzberg, ed., *The Political Economy of Kenya,* and in Joel Barkan, ed., *Politics and Public Policy in Kenya and Tanzania,* rev. ed. (New York: Praeger, 1984).

12. E. S. Atieno-Odhiambo, "Democracy and the Ideology of Order in Kenya," in Schatzberg, ed., *The Political Economy of Kenya,* 199.

13. Leonard, *African Successes,* chap. 4.

14. Gelase Mutahaba, *Reforming Public Administration for Development: Experiences from Eastern Africa* (West Hartford, Conn.: Kumarian Press, 1989), 50.

15. From the 1979 Kenya Census, Nadine R. Horenstein, "Women and Food Security in Kenya," World Bank Population and Human Resources Working Paper (Washington, D.C., 1989), 24. World Bank, *Kenya: The Role of Women* (xiii, 9–11), estimates 40 percent and draws on government sources and income differential studies to make the women's poverty case.

16. Horenstein, "Women and Food Security," 13–16; E. Kennedy and B. Cogill, *Income and Nutritional Effects of the Commercialization of Agriculture in Southwestern Kenya,* International Food Policy Research Institute Report, vol. 3 (Washington, D.C.: International Food Policy Research Institute, 1987); Frank Odile and Geoffrey McNicoll, "An Interpretation of Fertility and Population Policy in Kenya," *Population and Development Review* 13, no. 2 (1987): 209–43. See discussion below on income and incentives. On the material stakes wealthy women share with husbands, and thus implications for class politics, see Staudt, "Women's Politics, the State, and Capitalist Transformation," in Irving Leonard Markovitz, ed., *Studies in Power and Class in Africa* (New York: Oxford University Press, 1987), 193–208. On the educated elite, see Bessie House-Midamba, "The United Nations Decade: Political Empowerment or Increased Marginalization for Kenyan Women," *Africa Today* 37, no. 1 (1990): 37–48.

17. See The World Bank, *Kenya: The Role of Women,* 65.

18. Education is not addressed in this paper. See Florida A. Karani, "Education Policies and Women's Education," in Mary Adhiambo Mbeo and Oki Ooko-Ombaka, eds., *Women and Law in Kenya: Perspectives and Emerging Issues* (Nairobi: Public Law Institute, 1989), 23–28; George S. Eshiwani, "Kenya," in Gail P. Kelly, ed., *International Handbook of Women's Education* (Westport, Conn.: Greenwood, 1989), 25–42; World Bank, *Kenya: The Role of Women,* chapter 2. The tragedy at St. Kizito coeducational boarding school in July 1991, with the mass rape of 71 schoolgirls and deaths of 19 other girls,

has produced some soul-searching about glaring gender inequalities, even among the mainstream press in Kenya.

19. Cheryl Johnson-Odim cites Pala Okeyo in "Common Themes, Different Contexts: Third World Women and Feminism," in Chandra Talpade Mohanty, Ann Russo, and Lourdes Torres, eds., *Third World Women and the Politics of Feminism* (Bloomington: Indiana University Press, 1991), 317–18.

20. International Labour Organization, *Employment, Incomes and Equality in Kenya* (Geneva: International Labour Organization, 1972), chap. 18 especially.

21. For example, the ILO criticized the 1971 *Kenya Statistical Digest* for its estimate that 45 percent of women are economically active. According to the government's development plan for the period 1984–88 most rural women are economically active, and 87 percent report being employed (Nairobi: Government Printer, 1983), 91. The retort is in Republic of Kenya, *Sessional Paper No. 10 of 1973 on Employment* (Nairobi: Government Printer, 1973), 64, as cited in Maria Nzomo, "The Impact of the Women's Decade on Policies, Programs and Empowerment of Women in Kenya," *Issue* 17, no. 2 (1989): 9–17.

22. *Africa Report* provides sustained coverage of trials, detentions, and assassinations over the past five years. Also see Patricia Stamp, "The Politics of Dissent in Kenya," *Current History* 90, no. 556 (May 1991): 205–9, 227–29; "1990: The Year That Was," *Society* (January 1991): 8–17; Michael Paul Maren, "Kenya: The Dissolution of Democracy," *Current History* 86, no. 520 (1987): 209–12, 228. For theoretical treatment, see selections in W. Oyugi et al., eds., *Democratic Theory and Practice in Africa* (Portsmouth, N.H.: Heinemann, 1987).

23. On Maendeleo ya Wanawake, see Nzomo, "Impact of the Women's Decade"; Audrey Wipper, "Equal Rights for Women in Kenya?" *Journal of Modern African Studies* 9, no. 3 (1971): 429–42; and Audrey Wipper, "The Maendeleo ya Wanawake Organization: The Co-optation of Leadership," *African Studies Review* 18, no. 3 (1975): 99–120. Founded by the colonial government, MYWO has a complex history of official alignments, including its attempt to win over "loyalists" during the 1950s resistance.

24. Nzomo, "Impact of the Women's Decade," 15, and "Women in Politics," 18.

25. Monica Udvardy, "Women's Groups Near the Kenyan Coast: Patron-Clientship in the Development Arena," in David W. Brokenshaw and Peter D. Little, eds., *Anthropology of Development and Change in East Africa* (Boulder, Colo.: Westview, 1988), 229.

26. As quoted in Nzomo, "Impact of the Women's Decade," 15. Also see World Bank, *Kenya: The Role of Women,* 163–68. "Nyayo" initially meant "following in Kenyatta's footsteps"; it has more recently taken on the meaning of "loyalty."

27. Maria Nzomo, "Women, Democracy and Development in Africa," in Oyugi et al., eds., *Democratic Theory and Practice in Africa,* 124.

28. *Sunday News,* 25 May 1985, p. 1.

29. Both Kenyatta and Moi railed against "tribalism." Until 1980 many ethnic interest groups organized themselves as welfare organizations, but were finally deemed threatening and divisive, especially the powerful Gikuyu, Embu, and Meru Association, which appeared to be seeking a Kikuyu successor to Kenyatta. See Dirk Berg-Schlosser and Rainer Siegler, *Political Stability and Development: A Comparative Analysis of Kenya, Tanzania, and Uganda* (Boulder, Colo.: Lynne Rienner, 1990), 47–48.

30. Letter from the editor, *Weekly Review,* 3 November 1989, p. 3.

31. Barkan, "Electoral Process," 230. On appointive majorities and queuing see Todd Shields, "The Queuing Controversy," *Africa Report* (1988): 47–49. Queuing was later abolished.

32. Nzomo, "Women in Politics," 9.

33. Ibid., citation to Betty Wamalwa, 22; Kathleen Staudt, "Administrative Resources, Political Patrons, and Redressing Sex Inequities: A Case from Western Kenya," *Journal of Developing Areas* 12, no. 4 (1978): 398–414.

34. Phoebe M. Asiyo, "Legislative Process and Gender Issues in Kenya," in Mbeo and Ooko-Ombaka, eds., *Women and Law in Kenya,* 41–49. Noteworthy are two male supporters, former Vice-President Mwai Kibaki and former Attorney General Charles Njonjo, considered by many analysts as crucial supporters of President Moi's power consolidation, who were later discarded by him.

35. See especially Ooko-Ombaka, "The Kenya Legal System and the Woman Question," in Mbeo and Ooko-Ombaka, eds., *Women and Law in Kenya,* 31–39.

36. Ibid., 35; Stamp, "Burying Otieno"; Nzomo, "Women in Politics." See also David W. Cohen and E. S. Atieno-Odhiambo, *Burying SM: The Politics of Knowledge and the Sociology of Power in Africa* (Nairobi: Heinemann, 1992).

37. Stamp, "Politics of Dissent," 228–29; Nzomo, "Women in Politics," 16–17.

38. Stamp, "Politics of Dissent," 208.

39. Emphasized in classic studies of Kenya, such as Cherry Gertzel, *The Politics of Independent Kenya* (Nairobi: East African Publishing House, 1970); Henry Bienen, *Kenya: The Politics of Participation and Control* (Princeton: Princeton University Press, 1974); Leonard, *African Successes,* 6. The one permanent secretary who is a woman is in the Ministry of Commerce.

40. Atieno-Odhiambo, "Democracy and the Ideology of Order," 188–92.

41. See the review in Frank Holmquist, "Class Structure, Peasant Participation, and Rural Self-Help," in Barkan, ed., *Politics and Public Policy,* 171–97. See Leonard, *African Successes,* 228ff. on harambee as a partial redistributive mechanism.

42. Barbara Thomas, *Politics, Participation, and Poverty: Development Through Self-Help in Kenya* (Boulder, Colo.: Westview, 1985).

43. Nzomo, "Impact of the Women's Decade"; discussion above on group politics; Joel D. Barkan and Frank Holmquist ("Peasant-State Relations and the Social Base of Self-Help in Kenya," *World Politics* 41, no. 3 [1989]: 360), whose estimate is based on review of district-level registration rolls.

44. John M. Cohen and Richard M. Hook, "District Development Planning in Kenya," Harvard Institute for International Development Discussion Paper no. 229 (Cambridge, Mass., 1986). Leonard (*African Successes*, 203–9) cites a 75 percent civil service participation rate. Udvardy ("Women's Groups Near the Kenyan Coast," 229), reports that through party elections, three women sit on DDCS.

45. Leonard's phrase, *African Successes*, as applied to gender, see Kathleen Staudt, ed., *Women, International Development, and Politics: The Bureaucratic Mire* (Philadelphia: Temple University Press, 1990).

46. Kenya is 80 percent rural. On pricing policy, see Michael F. Lofchie, *The Policy Factor: Agricultural Performance in Kenya and Tanzania* (Boulder, Colo.: Lynne Rienner, 1989), and "Kenya: Still an Economic Miracle?" *Current History* 89, no. 547 (1990), where he reports that the government passed 70 percent of world coffee and tea prices on to producers, after deducting transport and processing costs, but 61 percent of maize prices. Most farmers do not sell maize to the government marketing board, even after it established (and then closed) hundreds of new buying centers. Barbara Grosh reports on the efficiency and profitability of 17 government marketing operations (half performed adequately) in "Performance of Agricultural Public Enterprises in Kenya: Lessons from the First Two Decades of Independence," *Eastern Africa Economic Review* 3, no. 1 (1987): 51–64. Also see Leonard, *African Successes*, 209ff.

47. On elite stakes see Robert Bates, *Beyond the Miracle of the Market: The Political Economy of Agrarian Development in Kenya* (Cambridge, Eng.: Cambridge University Press, 1989); Lofchie, "Kenya: Still an Economic Miracle"; Leonard, *African Successes*, chap. 4. On productivity see Leonard, *African Successes*, 92; World Bank, *Kenya: The Role of Women*, 2, 4–5, in a review of government and scholarly studies.

48. Land figures from Berg-Schlosser and Siegler, *Political Stability and Development*, 37. S. E. Migot-Adholla, "Rural Development Policy and Equality," in Barkan, ed., *Politics and Public Policy*, 213.

49. World Bank, *Kenya: The Role of Women*, xiv, 1. Seventy percent of export earnings are thereby earned (excluding refined petroleum).

50. Lugard is quoted in Staudt's "Women Farmers and Inequities in Agricultural Services," in Edna G. Bay,

ed., *Women and Work in Africa* (Boulder, Colo.: Westview, 1982), 211.

51. See Staudt, "Women Farmers," and Staudt, *Agricultural Policy Implementation: A Case from Western Kenya* (West Hartford, Conn.: Kumarian Press, 1985) for fuller exposition.

52. World Bank, *Kenya: The Role of Women*, 23–27. Yet large-scale farmers have dismal repayment rates, another example of male class preference.

53. Staudt, *Agricultural Policy*, 5. On the ubiquitous home economics curriculum—time-consuming, with few income-earning payoffs—as an example of what Ian Dey calls "male bias" in adult education, see Dey, "The Failure of Success and the Success of Failure: The Youth Polytechnic Programme in Kenya," *Public Administration and Development* 10 (1990): 179–98. After a brief integration between home economics and agricultural extension, the Home Economics Branch separated itself again and organized into four sections: food utilization, home management, population education, and home economics training. See Horenstein, "Women and Food Security," 19ff., on how home economics headquarters believed its mission was shortchanged under integration, with insufficient training time and disinterested male staff, who were unable to handle food preparation and home management topics. On the perils of separate bureaucratic strategies see Staudt, *Women, International Development, and Politics.*

54. David Leonard, *Reaching the Peasant Farmer: Organization Theory and Practice in Kenya* (Chicago: University of Chicago Press, 1977); Jon Moris, "Extension Under East African Field Conditions," in Nigel Roberts, ed., *Agricultural Extension in Africa* (Washington, D.C.: World Bank, 1989). The linkage of extension to productivity increases is difficult to establish, due to the multiple factors (education, wealth, and so on) that affect farmer performance. Even cutbacks in the much-applauded KDTA's separate extension service (see below) had little impact on performance (Leonard, *African Successes*, 135).

55. Dorthe von Bulow and Anne Sorensen, *Gender Dynamics in Contract Farming: Women's Role in Smallholder Tea Production in Kericho District, Kenya* (Copenhagen: Center for Udwiklingsforskning, 1988); Fiona Mackenzie, "Local Initiatives and National Policy: Gender and Agricultural Change in Murang'a District, Kenya," *Canadian Journal of African Studies* 20, no. 3 (1986): 386, examined coffee cooperative records spanning three decades and found female membership to be one tenth of the total, though women's participation increased in later years. In a multipurpose cooperative society, Staudt found only 7 percent female membership, mostly widows ("Administrative Resources," 411).

56. Bates, *Beyond the Miracle of the Market.*

57. Patrick J. Muzaale and David K. Leonard,

"Kenya's Experience with Women's Groups in Agricultural Extension: Strategies for Accelerating Improvements in Food Production and Nutritional Awareness in Africa," *Agricultural Administration* 19 (1985): 13–28. By the late 1970s, the U.S. Agency for International Development regularly targeted higher recruitment goals in project funding for agricultural training. See women's internal struggles to achieve these small bureaucratic "victories" in Staudt, *Women, Foreign Assistance and Advocacy Administration* (New York: Praeger, 1985).

58. World Bank, *Kenya: The Role of Women*, 1, 15.

59. Ibid., 16–21 on studies. World Bank staff, interviews with Staudt, June 1991.

60. Nzomo, "The Impact of Foreign Aid on Women Projects in Kenya: Some Preliminary Findings" (Paper presented at the African Studies Association Annual Meetings, 19–23 November 1987). "Myethya" is a term for self-help groups among the Kamba ethnic group; their membership is predominantly female but has some male participation, mainly at leadership levels.

61. This is documented in Regina Oboler, *Women, Power, and Economic Change: The Nandi of Kenya* (Stanford: Stanford University Press, 1985).

62. Amartya Sen, "Gender and Cooperative Conflicts," in Irene Tinker, ed., *Persistent Inequalities: Women and World Development* (New York: Oxford University Press, 1990), 123–49.

63. Mackenzie, "Local Initiatives," 388.

64. Von Bulow and Sorensen, *Gender Dynamics*, 77. Tea farmers grow in a less regulated but capital-intensive environment. KDTA's supporters have ranged from the World Bank to scholars like Leonard (*African Successes*, 1 and chap. 6).

65. Davison, "Who Owns What?" 168.

66. The term is originally from James Scott. See his and other selections in Forrest D. Colburn, ed., *Everyday Forms of Peasant Resistance* (New York: M. E. Sharpe, 1989).

67. Jane Hanger and Jon Moris, "Women and the Household Economy," in Robert Chambers and Jon Moris, eds., *Mwea: An Irrigated Rice Settlement in Kenya* (Munich: Weltforum Verlag African Studien, 1973), 209–44.

68. Raymond Apthorpe, "Some Evaluation Problems for Cooperative Studies, with Special Reference to Primary Cooperatives in Highland Kenya," in Peter Worsley, ed., *Two Blades of Grass* (Manchester: Manchester University Press, 1971).

69. Mackenzie, "Local Initiatives," 391.

70. Patricia Stamp, "Kikuyu Women's Self-Help Groups: Toward an Understanding of the Relation Between Sex-Gender System and Mode of Production in Africa," in Robertson and Berger, eds., *Women and Class*, 27–46; Henrietta Moore, *Feminism and Anthropology* (Minneapolis: University of Minnesota Press, 1988), chap. 5.

71. Nzomo, "Impact of Foreign Aid."

72. On structural adjustment, new euphemisms ("with a human face," "human dimensions of," "poverty alleviation"), and negotiations see Staudt, *Managing Development: State, Society, and International Contexts* (Newbury Park, Calif.: Sage, 1991), chap. 8.

73. Republic of Kenya, *Development Plan*, 35.

74. This and the next three paragraphs from Maria Nzomo, "Beyond the Structural Adjustment Programmes: Democracy, Gender Equity and Development in Africa" (Paper presented at the International Studies Association Annual Meeting, Vancouver, 20–23 March 1991).

75. World Bank, *Kenya: The Role of Women*, 70. Less than 20 percent of women now deliver at hospitals.

76. *Daily Nation*, 7 December 1990, pp. 23–30.

77. Republic of Kenya, *Development Plan*, 145; Shanyisa A. Khasiani, "The Family Planning Programme in Kenya: Current Impact and Future Prospects," in S. Ominde, ed., *Kenya's Population Growth and Development to the Year 2000* (London and Nairobi: Heinemann, 1988), 40–47; World Bank, *Kenya: The Role of Women*, chapter 3.

78. Odile and McNicoll, "An Interpretation of Fertility," 1987.

79. Barbara P. Thomas-Slayter, "Politics, Class and Gender in African Resource Management: Examining the Connections in Rural Kenya," Boston University African Studies Center Working Paper no. 140 (Boston: Boston University, 1989), 9.

▲ Korea, Republic of (South Korea)

POLITICS

Type of Political System: democracy
  Sovereignty: republic
  Executive-Legislative System: presidential
Type of State: unitary
Type of Party System: multiparty
Major Political Parties

Democratic Liberal Party (DLP): Formed in 1990; represents the merger of the party of then President Tae-Woo Roh and two parties previously in opposition. The merger gave the Democratic Liberal Party control of the legislature.[a]

New Democratic Union (NDU): Established in 1991 when two parties combined: the Peace and Democracy Party (PDP) and the smaller Party for New Democratic Alliance (PNDA). Supports a market economy and increased morality in public life.[b]

Democratic Party (DP): Organized in 1990 by people opposed to the merger that formed the Democratic Liberal Party.[c]

Year Women Granted Right to Vote: 1948
Year Women Granted Right to Stand for Election: 1948
Percentage of Women in the Unicameral Legislature: 2.0%[d]
Percentage of Electorate Voting for Highest Elected Office in Most Recent Election (1987): 89.2%

DEMOGRAPHICS

Population: 41,975,000[e]
Percentage of Population in Urban Areas
  Overall: 65.4%
  Female: 65.7%
  Male: 65.0%
Percentage of Population Below Age 15: 27.3%[f]
Birthrate (per 1,000 population): 21
Maternal Mortality Rate (per 100,000 live births): 34

Infant Mortality Rate (per 1,000 live births): 25
Mortality Rate for Children Under Five (per 1,000 live births): 33
Average Household Size: 4.6
Mean Age at First Marriage
  Female: 24.1
  Male: 27.3
Life Expectancy
  Female: 69.1
  Male: 62.7

EDUCATION

Ratio of Female to Male Enrollment
  First-Level Education: 94
  Second-Level Education: 88
  Third-Level Education: 43
Literacy Rate
  Female: 81.0%
  Male: 94.0%

ECONOMY

Gross National Product per Capita: U.S. $4,968[g]
Percentage of Labor Force in Agriculture: 18.7%[h]
Distribution of Agricultural Workers by Sex
  Female: 43.9%
  Male: 56.1%
Economically Active Population by Sex
  Female: 40.0%
  Male: 77.4%

a. Arthur S. Banks, ed., *Political Handbook of the World, 1991* (Binghamton, N.Y.: CSA Publications, 1991), 374.

b. Ibid.

c. Ibid., 375.

d. General Office of the National Assembly, *History of the National Assembly (Kukhoe-Sa)* (Seoul, 1950–90).

e. *Whitaker's Almanack, 1993* (London: J. Whitaker and Sons, 1992).

f. *Demographic Yearbook, 1988* (New York: United Nations, 1990).

g. National Bureau of Statistics, *Korea Statistical Yearbook, 1989* (Seoul, 1990).

h. *Demographic Yearbook, 1988.*

Women's Political Engagement and Participation in the Republic of Korea

BONG-SCUK SOHN

The Republic of Korea has a population of 42 million, with 25 percent residing in the capital city of Seoul. Korea was an independent state spanning the entire Korean Peninsula until 1910, when it was occupied by Japan. After the Japanese occupation ended with the close of World War II, the peninsula was occupied by U.S. and Soviet military forces. At the close of a bloody war brought on by superpower tensions and by conflicts between domestic forces in the north and the south, the peninsula was officially divided along its 38th parallel. The Republic of Korea was established in the southern half of the peninsula, the area formerly controlled by the United States; the Democratic People's Republic of Korea in the northern half, the area formerly controlled by the Soviet Union.

The experience of the Korean War has profoundly affected the form of the political system in the Republic of Korea and the nature of Korean politics. As a result of the war, millions of South Koreans became refugees, creating a constant threat of political instability. Since the war South Korea has also faced a continual threat from North Korea. For the past 40 years, therefore, South Korea has been politically unstable, with right-wing repressive regimes in power. Since 1948 Korea has officially had a presidential system of government and a unicameral legislature, the National Assembly. In practice, the governmental structure has been less democratic. An initial period of highly centralized but democratic rule ended with a military coup in 1961, led by Maj. Gen. Chung-Hee Park, and the institution of martial law.

Immediately after coming into power the military revolutionary government dissolved the national and local assemblies. The National Assembly was reestablished in 1963 after the transfer of power from a military to a civilian administration, but the government postponed the establishment of local assemblies on the grounds that a strong central administration was necessary to pursue economic development. The Park regime, which lasted until his assassination in 1979, was a period of severe repression during which thousands of Koreans were arrested and imprisoned. After a brief spell of democracy, when labor and student unrest and party activity increased, the military again intervened in 1980 and once more established martial law. Since 1982, under Gen. Doo-Hwan Chun, one of the leaders of the takeover, South Korea has been gradually and tentatively inching toward democratization and decentralization of the president's powers.

Officially, the National Assembly shares power equally with the president. In practice, however, its power has been severely curtailed because of the centralization of power in the presidency over the past 40 years. Since 1972 the National Assembly has been a handmaid of the administration: two-thirds of the members have been elected from single-member constituencies, and the remaining one-third have been nominated by the president.[1] In 1992 the percentage of nominated members in the assembly declined from one-third to one-quarter as part of the move toward greater autonomy.

The political party system also reflects four decades of political instability. Even though political parties have been important political actors, they have not shared power equally. The dominant party through 1980 was the Democratic

Republican Party, the government-sponsored party that was formed under the Park regime. The major opposition party in the 1960s and 1970s was the New Democratic Party. In 1980 the Democratic Justice Party (DJP) replaced the Democratic Republican Party as the government-sponsored party. Similarly, the New Democratic Party was eclipsed when the opposition split into the Party for Unification and Democracy and the Party for Peace and Justice. After the election in 1988—when the opposition won the majority of the seats in the National Assembly for the first time—four different parties shared legislative power. The ruling Democratic Justice Party first governed through a political structure called "little government party, big opposition." Then President Tae-Woo Roh launched a re-formation of the governing party, merging his own DJP with former opposition parties to create the Democratic Liberal Party. He orchestrated this change because he felt that a strong opposition would be a heavy burden in running the administration.

The instability of South Korean politics is also evident in the tension between centralized political control and local autonomy. Two levels of local assemblies exist: those at the big city and provincial level and those at the small city and town level. The national government assumed tasks previously taken by the local assemblies before their dissolution. The opposition seized every opportunity to bring up the issue of local government, arguing that "no democratization is complete without local autonomy." This, along with the president's commitment to democratization, resulted in an agreement to reinstate local autonomy after 1990, and local elections were held in 1991.

Like the political system, the South Korean economy has also experienced instability, but in a different sense. Until the mid-1970s nearly 50 percent of the population was involved in agriculture—the primary sector that dominated the national economy. Light and heavy industry and the service industry—the secondary and tertiary sectors, respectively—were dramatically expanded after a series of successful five-year economic development plans in the 1970s. In the last 20 years rapid economic growth has changed an agriculture-oriented economy to an expanding urban industrial economy. Because of industrialization under the authoritarian regimes of the 1960s and 1970s, the tertiary sector composed 46 percent of the national economy in fiscal year 1984. Moreover, per capita GNP increased at the same time, from U.S. $594 in 1975 to $4,968 in 1989.[2]

The proportion of women in the work force in the secondary and tertiary sectors increased remarkably with industrialization: 85.6 percent were agricultural workers in the 1960s; 57.2 percent were in the 1970s; and 38.9 percent were in the 1980s. In contrast, the percentage of working women in heavy or light industry was 4.9 percent in the 1960s, 12.2 percent in the 1970s, and 22.5 percent in the 1980s. The figures for the service sector are 9.5 percent, 30.6 percent, and 38.6 percent, respectively.[3] Women's wages, however, were very low owing to a labor surplus.

The economy of the Republic of Korea was, and still is, characterized by the leading role of the state in economic development, and the power of the administration has been strengthened to control industry effectively. The highly centralized government stressed "development first, distribution later"—a policy that forced female workers to sell their labor cheaply. People believed that economic development would result in equal distribution. When distribution did not occur, labor stopped withholding its demands and became more vocal. The idea of equal wages for equal work spread as the democracy movement focused on the issue of fair distribution, along with human rights problems. It is against this background of political and economic change that women's political participation and representation are entering a new phase in South Korea.

WOMEN'S MOVEMENTS

Women's movements in South Korea have evolved along three ideological lines. The established line follows an incremental approach. The women in this group work within the political system and seek expanded roles for women in politics by working in legally and politically accepted ways. Their efforts do sometimes benefit South Korean women as a whole; yet because of their obligations to traditional-minded male party leaders, there are great limitations to what this approach can accomplish.

Another approach to reform is adopted by women who work outside the established political structures. They are dissatisfied with the existing pro-government approach. One wing of this group formed a coalition of women's groups known as Korean Women's Associations United, which aims at achieving democratization and women's liberation simultaneously and often joins with dissident groups and opposition parties in pursuit of this goal. These dissident women's groups have taken part in the democratization struggle. KWAU, for example, has fought for the rights of workers, farmers, and working women and criticized the repressive labor control of the authoritarian government. Other campaigns have focused on human rights, pollution, and consumer protection, as well as issues of sexual equality.

The third form of women's political involvement is more radical. The participants—who are mostly young, urban, educated, and single—adopt a Marxist stance and advocate fundamental changes in the existing social structures, calling for an entirely new solution to the problem of sexual discrimination. They regard the relationship between men and women as that of exploiter and exploited and argue that equality will come when women's oppressed status is overcome. Adherents are neither numerous nor influential enough to bring about real changes. Nevertheless, radical women play an important role by shocking traditional women's circles and occasionally facilitating cooperation among less radical groups.

REPRESENTATION OF WOMEN IN POLITICS

Even though over 50 percent of the eligible voters in the Republic of Korea are women, women have not been equally represented in politics. Since the first National Assembly in 1948 the proportion of legislators who are women has remained quite constant and low, ranging from 0.5 percent to 5.5 percent (from one to twelve in number). It is much the same story for women's representation in the government bureaucracy. Since 1948 there have been only eight women cabinet ministers, and four of them served for less than one year. Few women have attained positions high in the government bureaucracy or anywhere influential on the hundreds of government advisory committees to which members are appointed.

Underlying this continuity, however, have been important changes in the nature of women's political participation and the form of their representation in politics. In fact, their participation in politics can be divided into three different phases: the nation-building period of 1948 to 1961; the modernization period of the 1960s and 1970s under the Park military-authoritarian regime; and the period of democratic transition since the mid-1980s. During the first phase a few women pioneers took part in politics without a clear awareness that they were representing women. In the second phase some notable women were co-opted by the government to play the role of supporting the authoritarian government. In contrast, women's awareness of the importance of their political participation strengthened in the 1980s in conjunction with the acceleration of the democracy movement. In this phase—especially in the early 1990s when the country moved closer to the implementation of local autonomy—the struggle to increase women's political representation became a vital part of the women's movement.

During the nation-building period women's opportunities to participate in politics were extremely limited. Women were held back not only by legal and institutional barriers but by sociocultural practices and beliefs as well. In addition to the limits on political participation, women were also discouraged from participating socially by the Confucian tradition that stigmatized even their casual outings as unfeminine. Men were encouraged to go into politics because Confucianism taught that the eminent man should succeed as a scholar-bureaucrat. The only politically active women were the highly educated superwomen who were well known to the public by virtue of their privileged family, social, and professional backgrounds. A small number of these elite women were appointed to prominent public positions by the government.

In the 1950s only two women, Young-Shin Lim and Helen Kim, were appointed ministers. They were famous, having earned doctorates in the United States and served as presidents of major universities. Both were close friends of President Sung-Man Rhee. Given their reputation and celebrity, their appointment to important posts in the government was looked on as a matter of course. Yet women politicians did not play an active role in political parties at that time. Most of them were not career politicians and returned to their original professions after short periods in political posts. Only Sun-Chun Park remained in politics for a lifetime—as a leading opposition party member. It was difficult for only two or three women politicians to form a political alliance of their own. Moreover, because the superwomen enjoyed their status as exceptions, their involvement in politics did not make them role models for other women. In fact, they mostly allied themselves with their male colleagues, rather than actively working for women's issues.

During the 1960s and 1970s, as South Korean society underwent an unprecedented period of rapid social change, modernization occurred in every facet of society, including women's lives. As industrialization proceeded, social participation increased both for low-wage-earning women and educated professional women. But these socioeconomic changes in women's roles were not accompanied by an increase in the number of women entering politics. The successive authoritarian regimes, exclusive of all but a small elite and dominated by men, contributed little to the improvement of women's political position. Only one or two women were sent to the National Assembly from local constituencies. There

were only two assemblywomen in 1963, and the number reached a maximum of twelve assemblywomen in 1973. Generally speaking, women who entered politics during this time were passive regarding women's issues.

Like many politicians of the time, women assembly members were not freely elected by the people but achieved office under the national constituency system, introduced in 1963. The national constituency seats are filled by indirect election in proportion to the percentage of seats that each party wins by direct election. If, for instance, a party wins 60 percent of the directly elected seats, it then gets 60 percent of the national constituency seats, which are filled from a ranked list of candidates prepared by the party. Through this members-at-large electoral system, the authoritarian regime selected leading women in the civilian sector for legislative seats. Women's participation in the government essentially served to show that the government was concerned about women's status.[4] A total of 38 women served in the National Assembly as members-at-large between 1963 and 1988. Four were from the opposition, and the rest were from the government party. Thus, although there were more women politicians than during the preceding period, for the most part they were not effective transmitters of women's policy demands. Those individual women who were co-opted into politics did not represent any social force or interest group. Instead, they were used by a government with weak legitimacy for political window dressing, that is, to demonstrate that the government was supported by diverse strata of society. These women's major concerns were limited to women's education and the equal rights campaign.

In the late 1970s the women's movement in the Republic of Korea was influenced by the global tide of women's organizing, like the United Nations proclamation of International Women's Year in 1975, which boosted women's issues around the world. From that time on, the organized women's movement in South Korea became more active. Assemblywomen took a growing interest in women's issues as women in the general public pressed them to represent women as a whole, rather than simply acting as agents of the government. This prompted the assemblywomen to formulate various bills and policies related to women.

The radical political transformation from authoritarianism to a more open democratic political process and the continuing economic growth that South Korea experienced in the 1980s also affected the nature of women's political participation. Although politics still tends to be repressive, public participation in politics has increased and has become more visible than ever before. The uprising on 10 June 1987 was not just a student demonstration; more precisely, it was a citizens' resistance movement against the authoritarian regime. The students and citizens together stood against the authoritarian regime that wanted to keep the existing constitution to secure its power. This civil uprising forced the government to promise to bring about a transition to democracy, which included changing the presidential election law to provide for direct, not indirect, elections. The government also promised the revival of local autonomy, which had been suspended for the previous 30 years.

Although the power of the National Assembly and the political parties increased with the movement toward democracy, women's representation improved only slightly. The Sixth Republic, established in 1988, did not bring an immediate increase in the number of women in the National Assembly: not a single woman was elected to the National Assembly by direct popular vote in 1988.[5] Because competing with men in direct elections is still extremely difficult for women who want to enter the political arena, some women politicians continue to take the easy route to the National Assembly and cooperate with the male-dominated party system. Still, the parties chose women to fill only 6 of 299 seats in the at-large selection of members of the National Assembly.

In spite of these drawbacks, the momentum toward women's involvement in politics has continued to grow, partly because of changing attitudes. Traditional social norms blocking women's participation in politics have been eroding. Media coverage of women's political standing elsewhere in the world has also helped to mute the hostility toward women's political involvement at home. Women politicians who reached national leadership positions in the 1980s have also inspired South Korean women to become more active. As a result, both men and women are now more likely to accept women's political participation, which has now entered a new stage.

WOMEN'S REPRESENTATION IN THE GOVERNMENT BUREAUCRACY

During the nation-building period there were also serious obstacles to women's appointment to and retention in high positions in the government bureaucracy. The key role players in economic development were high-ranking bureaucrats, who served as a leading force for modernization and had close relationships with politicians. The male monopoly of crucial national affairs was never challenged; it was accepted in principle that women should stay home. Even when women did participate in public life, they were considered supplementary or less important. Male politicians regarded women not as political partners but as token presences.[6]

At the end of the 1970s the women's movement became more active, and the government-financed Korean Women's Development Institute was established to conduct research on women's issues. In 1988 the Ministry of State became the Second Ministry of Political Affairs and was given full responsibility for women's issues. The government also opened family welfare bureaus in 15 cities to deal with women's concerns. Still, in 1990 only one woman, Kye-Sun Lee, head of the Second Ministry of Political Affairs, served in the cabinet.

At the end of 1990 women accounted for 24 percent of the public service personnel. Of those, 1.4 percent (162 of 11,512) ranked above the fifth grade as section chiefs in state offices, and 1.5 percent (144 of 9,303) ranked above the fifth grade in regional offices. (Grade refers to ranks in the civil service; there are nine grades, with one through five being the higher levels.)[7]

Advisory committees within each government department—such as those on health and welfare, agriculture, and youth and crime—consist of specialists in various fields who give advice on policy issues. These specialists wield some influence over government decisions. It is desirable for more women to participate in these committees, for with more representation, a stronger voice for women will probably be heard. Women's participation in these policy-making committees never exceeded 2.2 percent before 1984. Since then, it has been gradually expanded, reaching 8.1 percent in 1989.[8]

For women, the South Korean judicial system remains one of the least representative in the world. The knowledge that law school and legal practice are men's endeavors deters women from taking the law school entrance exam. As of 1990 only 57 women in the entire country had passed the national bar examination, the sole channel for recruiting judges and lawyers. As a result, the Republic of Korea has just 35 judges, 2 district attorneys, and 18 defense attorneys who are women.[9] Until the beginning of the 1980s there were no more than a total of 10 female district attorneys and defense officers.

REVISION OF THE EQUAL EMPLOYMENT AND FAMILY LAWS

In spite of the still-existing constraints, political awareness among women and the desire to participate in politics have grown rapidly in recent years. Even with only a few women in the National Assembly, women have made gains—through, for example, amendments to the Equal Employment Opportunity Law and the Family Law. The idea for an equal employment opportunity law was first brought up in 1982 by Song-Ja Kim, the manager of the women's division in the Ministry of Labor. Activity on this issue was partly the result of a court case begun by another woman, Young-Hee Kim, who had been retired unwillingly from the Korean Electric and Communication Company at the age of 43. Young-

Hee Kim filed a suit charging that a mandatory retirement age of 43 for women was unconstitutional. Women's groups and the media took up the cause, prompting hearings by the ruling Democratic Justice Party in 1986. Although Song-Ja Kim attempted to submit an equal employment opportunity bill at the time, consideration of the bill was postponed because some departments did not see the need for such a bill.

In 1987 the bill was again proposed to the National Assembly, and assemblywomen had great influence in lobbying for it. Song-Ja Kim, as one of the highest-ranking women in the government, played an important role in the passage of the legislation. The equal employment bill also won support from male assembly members, but only because the men thought that the legislation for women was insignificant and that the new law would have little impact.

The Equal Employment Opportunity Law passed in the National Assembly in December 1987 and was further revised in April 1989 to improve its effectiveness. For example, the government prohibited sex segregation in government employment beginning in June 1989. All women employees are now guaranteed rights equal to their male counterparts. Employers are prohibited from discriminating against women in hiring, dismissal, or retirement. The law guarantees special protection for pregnant women and mothers, with provisions for one-year child-care leaves as well as 60 days of paid maternity leave. The law also requires employers to provide child-care facilities in the workplace. It has made a significant contribution to abolishing discrimination against women.

The amended Family Law, which became effective in January 1991, was finally revised in December 1989 after a 37-year struggle. Several major amendments were passed: First, the revised law entitles a woman obtaining a divorce to seek a share of the couple's property in proportion to her contribution to its accumulation. Second, upon divorce, child custody is no longer automatically granted to the father. Rather, this right is determined either by the couple's mutual agreement or by the court. Third, women's right to inherit property has also been expanded. The revised law eliminates discrimination against daughters, but it falls short of abolishing the controversial head-of-family system that requires the oldest son to become the head of the family.[10]

Although the bills were passed, efforts to emend the Family Law and the Equal Employment Opportunity Law met the barrier of the male-dominated National Assembly every time that women sought a legislative mandate. Women realized that the shortcut to upward political mobility was to send more women representatives to participate in the decision-making process. Thus, they held seminars emphasizing women's increased political participation, on the one hand, and pressured political leaders to increase the number of women candidates for elected positions in political parties, on the other. Women mounted various attacks to open up more political positions for women and to challenge the domination of the political system by men. Assemblywomen started to pay more attention to women's issues and tried harder to persuade their male colleagues to pass bills related to women. But because most of these men were from the government party, they approached women's issues by defending the basic policy objectives of the government.

ACTIVISM ON THE LOCAL LEVEL

As women's self-awareness and interest in political participation grew, discussions of how to increase women's representation in government developed. Currently there is a wide consensus among various women's groups that previously had different ideological orientations—the Korean League of Women Voters, the Korean National Council of Women, and Korean Women's Associations United, for example—that to improve the status of South Korean women, more women should take political posts and participate in policy making. The trend is natural considering that the extent to which women's interests are recognized and acted on in the policy process is closely related to the number of political positions that women hold in the national and local governments.[11]

Local assembly elections were held twice in 1991. Members of the lower-level city, county, and district assemblies were elected in March. Elections for the higher-level provincial and metropolitan assemblies were held in June. Both elections were considered golden opportunities to expand women's political lot. Because local elections require less costly campaigns and less organizational skill than national elections, women have more strength as candidates in this arena. In addition, because local autonomy means management of community living, women's participation at the local level is better received by the general public than women's participation in national politics. Until the 1991 local elections, the 299 popularly elected seats in the National Assembly were the only popularly elected legislative seats in the country. The local elections opened 866 new positions at the higher level and 4,304 at the lower level.

Yet it was extremely difficult for women to compete against men for these seats. Even in local elections women face many barriers and disadvantages. As a result, some women's groups wanted a fixed proportion of seats in the National Assembly to be reserved for women, although how women were to be elected to these seats was not specified. Other women's groups pushed for quotas on political party lists for the national constituency seats and in nominations for single-member district seats.

The question of quotas was partially addressed in partisan debates during the preparation of the electoral law. The Party for Peace and Justice, the women's division of the former Democratic Justice Party, and Korean Women's Associations United proposed a proportional representation system in 1990. The opposition Peace and Democratic Party, or PDP (which took the same name as the Democratic Party in 1992), insisted on the proportional representation system in local elections because party leaders felt that it would not only extend women's participation but would also increase the number of representatives from groups like labor or education. The government party rejected the opposition's argument and charged that the proportional representation system of the PDP was a pretext for obtaining political funds.[12] KWAU insisted on the proportional representation system to promote women's participation, but it did that partially because it ordinarily shares the PDP line.

During the initial legal preparation of the bill, the Policy Evaluation Committee of the ruling Democratic Justice Party was led by women members who supported the proportional system. But later on, the DJP killed the idea of a proportional system, because it was seen to conflict with the party line.[13] Eventually, in March 1990, the PDP submitted a bill requiring the local election law to allow one-fourth of local assembly members to be elected under a proportional system that would permit parties to nominate candidates from various professions. KWAU and other women's groups supported this proposal and also demanded an institutional guarantee that a certain proportion of women be elected under the proposed system. Women's groups also suggested a male-female ratio of 50-50 on each party's list of candidates for local legislatures.[14]

Some women's groups promoted the idea of affirmative action or a quota system in the distribution of seats, just as others suggested a quota system in candidacy. The Korean League of Women Voters, for example, suggested giving 20 percent of seats to women. Because women could reach the national or a local assembly through election only with difficulty, it was argued, a quota system had to be adopted for a certain period. The Center for Korean Women and Politics proposed a quota system in candidacy designed to ensure that a certain portion of the candidates nominated by political parties would be women. The advantage was that women candidates who win party endorsement can more easily win elections than those without party support. For instance, in the local assembly election of June 1991, five of the eleven women candidates with government party backing won seats (45 percent), whereas only two of the twenty independent candidates were able to win seats (10 percent). Two-thirds of the National

Assembly members are from the government party, which indicates that nomination by the government party is the surest way to be elected. In addition, party nomination promises organized support and increased funding. Different reasons for and methods of promoting women's representation have been offered, but the final goal has been the same—to improve the status of women in political life.

The support of political parties for the proposals of women's groups was not solely based on a true concern for women. The opposition Peace and Democracy Party supported the proportional representation system because it needed women's votes if it was ever to unseat the governing Democratic Liberal Party (the former Democratic Justice Party). Meanwhile, the Democratic Liberal Party was indifferent to the quota system because it did not want to risk its dominant position by having political parties become involved in local elections.

In spite of various moves and pressures, the case for sending more women to local assemblies was not very successful. Proposals for proportional representation or a quota system met with considerable opposition from the beginning. Most male politicians and legislators were opposed to any local election law that allowed a "special premium" for women. The argument was the typical one: because the constitution guarantees equality between the sexes, a quota system is unconstitutional. The executive committee of the ruling party also barred the adoption of any reform proposed by the circle of women's organizations.

One of the main problems that women had to face in their battle to get proportional representation was women themselves. The ruling party, which could swing the passage of proportional representation for women, did not show particular interest in this issue because up to this time women voters have failed to form an effective and powerful voting bloc. The Democratic Liberal Party thus had no reason to think that it needed women's support to win.

In the end, none of the schemes for proportional representation was adopted. Because the government party had an absolute majority in the National Assembly, no bill that the government opposed could pass. The opportunity to improve women's chances in the local political arena was eliminated when the proportional system was rejected.

Meanwhile, because of the pulling and hauling among political parties, the local autonomy program that was scheduled to begin in early 1990 was postponed until 1991. At last a compromise was made between the government party and the opposition on the timetable, with the nonpartisan elections for smaller units of local assemblies being held separately from the partisan elections in larger communities. In these local elections, revived after 30 years of suspension, women candidates had to compete with male rivals without proportional representation or a quota system in seats or party nominations.

In city, county, and district elections, 122 women (of 10,120 candidates, or 1.8 percent) ran for seats, and 40 of the 4,304 seats went to women (0.9 percent). In the elections for provincial and metropolitan council members, 63 of 2,877 candidates were women (2.2 percent), and they won 8 of 866 seats (0.9 percent). The results attest to how tough it still is for women to succeed in South Korean politics.

Most of the women who ran in the last two local elections had to rely on whatever support they could get from women's groups, family, and volunteers. They admitted that their male counterparts had better access to money, networks, and organizations, more systematic campaigns, and better-paid campaign aides. Although the general public is becoming less hostile to politically engaged women, many people still believe that women should stay home to do the housekeeping and not involve themselves in politics. In addition, presenting strong and electable female candidates is not easy, for many prominent women are reluctant to enter "the dirty world of politics."

Though small in number and disappointingly low in seat returns, most of the female candidates showed that their campaigning styles were models for fair and democratic electoral behavior. The spirit of cooperation among diverse women's organizations that was achieved during the campaigns is a promising sign. Some of these groups have already joined in pressing the government to amend laws and regulations regarding election management and in planning joint political education programs to strengthen the power of women.

PROSPECTS

Women in the Republic of Korea have been underrepresented in both elected and appointed political positions for many reasons.[15] Prominent among these are family responsibilities, discriminatory legal and social practices, difficulties in raising money, lack of organizational skills and resources, women's own attitudes, and the nature of the governing regime and political process in South Korea.[16]

Elections in South Korea have always been costly, and financial resources have been an important factor in winning elections. Women do not have the same connections to industry and other sources of funds that men have, so raising money to run for office has always been more difficult for women than for men.[17] Nor in many cases do those who contribute to campaigns regard women as the kind of candidates that they want to support. In a political system where quid pro quo for campaign contributions has been a fact of life, women have been viewed as incorruptible, and therefore contributions to women have not been regarded as good investments. Recruitment channels and political networks have been informal and very much closed in South Korean society. Getting to know the top politicians and party leaders who select candidates for election has been crucial for those who want to launch political careers. Women politicians, no matter how able, are accustomed to being excluded from the major channels of political recruitment.[18] Women's groups believed that local autonomy would help women's political participation considerably. But given the poor electoral results for women, it does not appear that progress will necessarily be smooth or automatic.

On the whole, however, an assessment of the prospects for women's political engagement points to guarded optimism. Paramount among the many factors that will affect the task of promoting participation are the progress of democratization and economic development.

During the last decades, with the dramatic social changes that have occurred in South Korea, women's lives have been transformed. Sexual discrimination is prohibited by the constitution, but legal and institutional discrimination still exist. The 1987 Equal Employment Opportunity Law and its subsequent revision ensured women equal opportunities for employment, at least legally. The amendments to the Family Law in 1989 have further contributed to improving women's legal and economic status. It is thus expected that women's status in politics will be promoted accordingly in the course of overall democratization.

Women have played an important role in economic growth. Women's labor, which constitutes 41.1 percent of the labor force, was an essential element in the amazing economic development of the country. Most women who hold jobs earn low wages as unskilled laborers.[19] As industrialization and economic development continue, the demand for skilled women will increase in the various sectors of the economy. This, in turn, will enhance their economic and political standing. Women's social status will also be improved as the number of educated women increases. In 1989 women constituted 29.5 percent of all college students. The number of women students in the humanities, law, business and management, and engineering (traditionally men's fields) has also increased, showing that the preferential choice of major according to sex is also changing.[20] These trends are additional evidence for optimism.

Meanwhile, to speed up the pace of political change for women, women's organizations need to pool their strength and work together on the following projects.

- They need to prepare and implement cooperative electoral management plans to find able candidates and help ill-funded, less-experienced candidates. The plans should include reaching out to voters to encourage them to elect women.
- It is necessary to politically educate women candidates, campaign managers, and volunteer workers on women's issues. Doing so would help raise the political consciousness and competence of women who want to engage in politics.
- Women's groups should encourage more women to participate in various community services—an area in which women's contributions are badly needed. Through such efforts, women can enhance their leadership skills and win the minds of people.
- Women's groups should make joint efforts to change the provisions of the election law that create barriers to women's participation in formal politics. For example, the restrictions on citizens' speaking out in support of candidates should be removed or relaxed, for women candidates depend heavily on volunteer assistance. Likewise, women's groups should press for the adoption of electoral reforms that improve the likelihood of electing women, such as quota systems for women on the party lists for the national constituency seats and in nominations for the single-member districts. Encouraging the government to place women in appointed positions would also increase women's formal participation.
- More active participation of women in party politics is recommended in order to increase the number of women candidates, particularly because parties are the primary channels for recruitment to all political positions.
- Women need to help the nation achieve speedy democratization. If ongoing democratic experiments in the Republic of Korea falter, the momentum and unity that have been achieved so far can easily be eroded.

NOTES

1. The vast proportion of constituencies in the Republic of Korea elect only one person to the National Assembly. A few constituencies, however, defined in conformity

with historical boundaries, elect more than one member because they have large populations.

2. National Bureau of Statistics, *Korea Statistical Yearbook* (Seoul, 1990), 579.

3. National Bureau of Statistics, *Korea Statistical Yearbook* (Seoul, 1961), 229; *Korea Statistical Yearbook* (Seoul, 1974), 66; *Korea Statistical Yearbook* (Seoul, 1983), 74.

4. Robert Darcy and Sunhee Song, "Men and Women in the South Korean National Assembly: Social Barriers to Representational Roles" (Seoul, 1985, Mimeographed), 5–7.

5. During the past 40 years only seven women have been sent directly to the National Assembly by popular vote: Young-Shin Lim, Sun-Chun Park, Chul-An Kim, Hyun-Sook Park, Ok-Sun Kim, Yoon-Duk Kim, and Chung-Rye Kim.

6. Haingja Kim, "A Comparative Study of the U.S. House of Representatives and the National Assembly of Korea: A Cross-Cultural Study Focusing on Role Analysis of Female Politicians" (Ph.D. diss., University of Hawaii, 1975), 155–63; Darcy and Song, "Men and Women in the South Korean National Assembly," 16–18.

7. Ministry of Government Affairs, *Yearbook of the Ministry of Government Affairs* (Seoul, 1991), 166.

8. Second Ministry of Political Affairs, *Women in Korea: Current Status and Future Prospects* (Seoul, 1991), 3.

9. *Law Daily Newspaper,* 17 March 1991, p. 3.

10. Second Ministry of Political Affairs, *Women in Korea,* 4.

11. Susan J. Carroll, *Women as Candidates in American Politics* (Bloomington: Indiana University Press, 1985), 138–56. For an empirical study on this in South Korea refer to Bong-Scuk Sohn, *A Study on Women Legislators in the South Korean National Assembly* (Seoul: Center for Korean Women and Politics, 1992).

12. The proportional representation system not only works for women but also benefits those in the party list who have donated large amounts of funding to the party. Also, because party discipline is strong in the National Assembly, party members must follow the official party line even if they disagree with it personally.

13. Bong-Scuk Sohn, *Local Autonomy and Women's Participation* (Seoul: Center for Korean Women and Politics, 1990), 64–65.

14. According to my calculations, 16.6 percent of the seats can go to women if one-third are elected under proportional representation *and* a 50-50 male-female ratio is maintained. If one-fourth are proportionally elected with the same sex ratio, the number of seats going to women will be 12.5 percent.

15. The same phenomenon has occurred in the United States. See Irwin N. Gertzog, "Changing Patterns of Female Recruitment to the U.S. House of Representatives," *Legislative Studies Quarterly* 4 (August 1979): 41.

16. In telephone interviews conducted by Korea Gallup Poll right before the local election of March 1991, 46 percent (1,021 people) answered that the primary reason for women's low participation rate in politics was the negative social response to women politicians. Center for Korean Women and Politics, *Survey Report on Local Elections* (Seoul, 1991).

17. Ruth B. Mandel, *In the Running: The New Woman Candidate* (New York: Ticknor and Fields, 1981), 155–201; Jeane J. Kirkpatrick, *Political Woman* (New York: Basic Books, 1974), 85–105.

18. Sohn, *Study on Women Legislators,* 23–26.

19. National Bureau of Statistics, *Annual Statistics* (Seoul, 1989), cited in Ministry of Political Affairs, *Women in Korea: Current Status and Future Prospects* (Seoul, 1991), 2:7–8. In 1988 women constituted 51.6 percent of the workers employed in wholesale and retail business, 44.6 percent of the workers in the agricultural and fishing industries, and 42.1 percent of manufacturing workers. Ibid., 8.

20. Ibid., 6–7.

▲ *Mexico*

POLITICS

Type of Political System: democracy
  Sovereignty: republic
  Executive-Legislative System: presidential
Type of State: federal
Type of Party System: multiparty
Major Political Parties

Partido Revolucionario Institucional (PRI, or Institutional Revolutionary Party): Founded in 1929 as Partido Nacional Revolucionario (National Revolutionary Party); renamed Partido de la Revolución Mexicana (Party of the Mexican Revolution) in 1938; in 1946 became PRI. Made up of three sectors: workers; *campesinos* (country people, or peasants); and *popular,* or "people's" sector. Has "won" (often fraudulently) all presidential elections since 1917.

Partido de Acción Nacional (PAN, or Party of National Action): Founded in 1939 by Manuel Gomez Morin; to the right of PRI and composed mainly of large and small entrepreneurs, people in business, and conservative professionals.

Partido de la Revolución Democrática (PRD, or Party of the Democratic Revolution): Founded in 1989 by a coalition of groups. Made up of dissidents who left the PRI, headed by Cuauhtemoc Cardenas (unchallenged leader of the party and its secretary general) and Porfirio Muñoz Ledo; past members of the former Mexican Communist Party; ex-members of Trotskyite and socialist parties and groups; and independents. Represents the Mexican left.
Year Women Granted Right to Vote:
  1947/1953[a]
Year Women Granted Right to Stand for Election: 1953
Percentage of Women in the Legislature[b]
  Lower House: 8.6%
  Upper House: 4.7%

Percentage of Electorate Voting for Highest Elected Office in Most Recent Election (1988): 51.6%[c]

DEMOGRAPHICS

Population: 82,739,000
Percentage of Population in Urban Areas
  Overall: 66.3%
  Female: 67.2%
  Male: 65.3%
Percentage of Population Below Age 15:
  40.2%[d]
Birthrate (per 1,000 population): 33
Maternal Mortality Rate (per 100,000 live births): 82
Infant Mortality Rate (per 1,000 live births): 46
Mortality Rate for Children Under Five (per 1,000 live births): 68
Average Household Size: 5.4
Mean Age at First Marriage
  Female: 20.6
  Male: 23.6
Life Expectancy
  Female: 66.0
  Male: 62.1

EDUCATION

Ratio of Female to Male Enrollment
  First-Level Education: 95
  Second-Level Education: 95
  Third-Level Education: 66
Literacy Rate[c]
  Female: 79.9%
  Male: 86.2%

ECONOMY

Gross National Product per Capita: U.S. $2,080
Percentage of Labor Force in Agriculture: 24.0%[f]
Distribution of Agricultural Workers by Sex
  Female: 14.2%
  Male: 85.8%

Economically Active Population by Sex
  Female: 30.1%
  Male: 82.4%

a. In 1947 women voted for the first time in *municipal* elections. Julia Tuñon, *Mujeres en México* (Women in Mexico) (Mexico: Planeta, 1987).

b. Information from the Mexican Embassy of the United States, for 1991–94.

c. Comisión Federal Electoral (Federal Election Commission), *Elecciones federales 1988: Cómputo distrital* (Federal elections 1988: Calculations by district).

d. Teresita de Barbieri, "La subordinación de las mujeres en una sociedad desigual. Notas para un diagnóstico de la condición de la mujer en México" (The subordination of women in an unequal society: Notes toward a diagnosis of the position of women in Mexico) (Manuscript, 1988).

e. Ibid.

f. Ibid.

The Struggle for Life, or Pulling Off the Mask of Infamy

ELI BARTRA

TRANSLATED BY JOHN MRAZ

If our lives have been confined primarily to the "private" sphere and our problems of gender are dismissed as "personal," then . . . let the personal be political!

In 1821 Mexico became politically independent from Spain. It was not until 130 years later that women became political actors by law by winning the right to vote. Since 1917 Mexico's government has consisted of a president and a bicameral legislature. Although the nation is formally a multiparty democracy, Mexico has been ruled by only one party since the Mexican revolution in 1917, the Partido Revolucionario Institucional (PRI, or Institutional Revolutionary Party). There have been other political parties on both the left and the right, but it was not until the 1988 presidential campaigns that a strong challenger to the PRI emerged: the left-wing coalition Partido de la Revolución Democrática (PRD, or Party of the Democratic Revolution). At present, three parties struggle for power in Mexico: the PRI, the PRD, and the conservative Partido de Acción Nacional (PAN, or Party of National Action).

The PRI is a descendant of the bourgeois faction that triumphed in the revolution. Today this party is directed by the bourgeoisie but rests on a base of organizations composed of workers, peasants, and the middle class. This corporatist structure also includes a women's sector, some members of which are sensitive to feminist issues.

The PRD was created by dissident members of the PRI and various militants of groups and political parties on the left. The PRD's membership is primarily middle class but also includes peasants and workers. Among PRD's members are some feminists long involved in movements to transform the situation of women.

The PAN is made up of people from the upper industrial and financial bourgeoisie, as well as the *petit* commercial bourgeoisie. Although women in this party tend to be conservative and religious, PAN congresswomen have joined the struggle to change laws relating to rape and sexual abuse.

Even though the Roman Catholic church has been formally separate from the state since 1859, Mexico remains heavily influenced by Catholicism in both the private sphere and the public political arena. About 93 percent of the population is Catholic.[1]

With a per capita GNP equivalent to U.S. $2,080, Mexico is an underdeveloped capitalist country. Thus, in addition to any barriers that Mexican women face on the basis of gender, they are also confronted with the problems of underdevelopment, such as poor healthcare and an inadequate food supply. Moreover, Mexico faces the ramifications of developing its economy in a world system that is structurally biased against it. As a result of its efforts to catch up with the advanced industrial nations of the world over the last 40 years, Mexico has incurred an enormous debt, which has devastated the country's economy.[2] The state's attempts to placate such creditors as the International Monetary Fund and U.S. banks have led to high unemployment and rampant inflation. This debt crisis profoundly affects women in specific ways. Because housewives confront the cost of living directly in their purchases, they are acutely aware of inflation and frequently participate in public demonstrations against price increases. The economic crisis has also forced large numbers of women to enter the formal labor market and, in even greater numbers, the informal economy.

Although no one can escape the effects of the country's underdevelopment, not all women face these difficulties to the same degree. The particular barriers that a Mexican woman faces and her immediate concerns are shaped by her socioeconomic class and where she lives—in the city or countryside—and the way these cleavages intersect. The minimum salary in Mexico City today amounts to little more than U.S. $3 a day. This is not enough to live on, as is also true of the salaries of many jobs that pay more than minimum wage. Domestic workers earn the equivalent of U.S. $10 per day—about U.S. $240 a month for a domestic servant who works six days a week. An associate professor at a university earns the equivalent of U.S. $600 a month. One of the survival strategies that Mexicans have developed to contend with the high cost of living is moonlighting in two or more extra jobs.

THE WOMEN'S MOVEMENT

Historically, Mexican women have been politically marginalized. Their situation did not change appreciably during the revolution or in the political system established afterward. Large numbers of peasant women accompanied the revolutionary armies, providing food for their husbands, brothers, and fathers. A few women entered the struggle as soldiers, and several attained the rank of general or colonel in the rebel armies. But the chapter of Mexican history describing the precise role of women in the revolution has yet to be written. Despite their participation at every level in the revolutionary struggle, no women were invited to attend the Constitutional Congress of 1917. The result of this exclusion was that, even though progressive laws were passed regarding the rights of workers and favoring land reform, the laws relating to the status of women were profoundly sexist. Professor Luz de Lourdes de Silva, a sociologist from the Colegio de México, sums up the discussion of women's rights at the Constitutional Congress in the following way: "Although the campaign in favor of women's suffrage had counted some small gains prior to 1916, it did not become a subject of official debate until the petition was made by Hermilia Galindo to the Constitutional Congress. There it was argued that not all women have the capacity to exercise those rights, and the Congress decided against the inclusion of women in political life."[3]

In the absence of female suffrage during the first half of the twentieth century, Mexico's public politics and policy-making process were clearly and completely controlled by men. Although women were not allowed to participate formally in the country's governing institutions on any level, some were politically active. These early activists, like the suffragists, were primarily from the middle classes. They organized and struggled in a multitude of ways; one early example is the Feminist Congress of Yucatan, held in 1916. The Ligas de Orientación Femenina (Leagues of Feminine Orientation) were created to fight for equality of salaries and within unions, but they had other concerns as well. Prostitutes played an important role in the renters' movement in Veracruz during 1922. In 1935 the Frente Unico Pro Derechos de la Mujer (Single Front for Women's Rights) was created by women representing all social classes. The group's principal concern was obtaining the right to vote.

In 1947 women were given the right to vote and to run for office in municipal elections. Enriqueta Tuñón has described how Mexican women received that right at the national level: "Doña Amalia Caballero de Castillo Ledón, President of the Interamerican Women's Commission, met with Adolfo Ruíz Cortines, then the PRI candidate for president [1951], and asked him to give women the right to vote in national elections. The candidate offered his assistance on the condition that he was provided with the signatures of 500,000 women asking for such a right."[4] The population of Mexico at the time was 30 million.

Doña Amalia brought together various groups of women and created the Alianza de Mujeres Mexicanas (Alliance of Mexican Women), which obtained the required signatures. This anecdote also shows the "Mexican style" of doing politics, through personal connections.

Thus women took the necessary—but by no means sufficient—first step toward political equality in 1953 when they won the right to vote and to run for national office. Since then women have begun to enter public politics little by little and to participate in the higher circles of leadership. Between 1953 and 1970 Mexican women did not really organize or struggle for their emancipation, however. Their participation in politics was principally confined to membership in political parties, though some parties had women's organizations—for example, the Mexican Communist Party's Unión Nacional de Mujeres Mexicanas (National Union of Mexican Women).

The percentage of women in the higher circles of political leadership remains grotesquely insignificant. In 1982–83 women constituted only 8.6 percent of the members of the lower house of the legislature and 4.7 percent of the upper house. The women elected to office generally come from the urban upper-middle class and the urban bourgeoisie. Nor has male dominance of the political sphere been limited to participation in the governing institutions. With very few exceptions, Mexican women have until recently been excluded from both public politics and public life.

The feminist movement in Mexico both reflects and responds to these conditions. Although suffrage movements and struggles to better women's living conditions existed in Mexico throughout the first half of the twentieth century, they were essentially isolated battles and challenges. Then the so-called new wave of the feminist movement erupted onto the Mexican political scene at the beginning of the 1970s. In my view, the universe of public politics has been transformed since then. The feminist movement began with the creation of Mujeres en Acción Solidaria (Women Acting in Solidarity). In 1974 the Movimiento de Liberación de la Mujer (MLM, or Women's Liberation Movement) was formed. Slowly new groups were created, sometimes through splits in existing organizations and sometimes in answer to new needs and concerns. I started my own feminist activism in Mexico in the MLM.

To unify efforts regarding specific issues, six of these groups joined together in 1976 to create the Coalición de Mujeres Feministas (Coalition of Feminist Women). The group was formed by the MLM, the Colectivo de Mujeres (Women's Collective), the Movimiento Feminista, the Movimiento Nacional de Mujeres (National Women's Movement), Lucha Feminista (Feminist Struggle), and the Colectivo La Revuelta (Collective "The Revolt"), of which I was a member. The members of all of these groups were middle-class women from urban areas.

The coalition's political agenda focused on the right to free, legal abortion; the struggle against rape; and the defense of battered women. The coalition was the dominant feminist organization in Mexico until 1979, when the Frente Nacional de Lucha por la Liberación y los Derechos de las Mujeres (National Front in the Struggle for Women's Liberation and Rights) was created. The group was composed of women from such leftist political parties as the Mexican Communist Party and the Partido Revolucionario de los Trabajadores (PRT, or Revolutionary Workers' Party, a Trotskyite organization), and from such independent unions as that of the Universidad Nacional Autónoma de México (National Autonomous University of Mexico). Also joining the group were three groups from the coalition: the MLM, the Women's Collective, and Feminist Struggle. The National Front attempted to co-opt the Coalition of Feminist Women and the rest of the autonomous feminist movement. Although it quickly failed, the previously consolidated Coalition of Feminist Women fell apart as well. In 1982 a new effort was made to create a blanket organization, and the Red Nacional de Mujeres (National Women's Network) was formed. But the network disintegrated without really unifying its member organizations or encouraging the exchange of information at the national level among women's groups.

The 1980s were characterized by the rise and consolidation of numerous women's groups engaged in politico-feminist activities among women of the lower classes—that is, workers, peasants, and housewives in the proletarian communities of Mexico City. These groups include Comunicación, Intercambio y Desarrollo Humano en América Latina (Communication, Interchange, and Human Development in Latin America), Mujeres en Acción Sindical (Women's Union Action), Taller de Mujeres del Chopo (Women's Workshop in Chopo), Mujeres para el Diálogo (Women for Dialogue), and Agrupación Popular para la Integración Social (APIS, or Popular Association for Social Integration).

In 1988 the Coordinadora de Mujeres "Benita Galeana" (Women's Coordination "Benita Galeana") was created by 17 groups. In July 1990 it began publishing the magazine *La Mata Dando*

(The Yielding Bush). In 1990 there was yet another attempt to coordinate the autonomous feminist groups along the lines of the former Coalition of Feminist Women, with the creation of Coordinadora Feminista in the Mexico City area.

Mexico's feminist movement grew out of the women's liberation movement in the United States and Europe, a circumstance that has created some problems for feminists. One of the most facile and recurrent forms of attack against the movement has been to devalue and discredit it as originating from satanic, foreign, colonialist, or imperialist forces. Viewed from this perspective, the problems that Mexican feminists are trying to address are not Mexico's; they were brought in from the outside. The truth is that the ideas of the Mexican feminist movement—like the ideas of the national liberation movements of the late eighteenth century—did come from outside, but the problems that the movement addresses always have been very much those of Mexico's women.

Another difficulty concerns leadership. During the 1970s there was a constant struggle to maintain a non-hierarchical structure within the movement to forestall criticism from both inside and outside feminist circles. But a hierarchical leadership did eventually develop as the groups that did most of the work and received most of the recognition became the voices for the entire feminist movement. This tension between the goal of a non-hierarchical movement and the inevitable existence of leadership continues.

I have based my analysis of Mexican women's political engagement on activities related to the concerns that brought together the Coalition of Feminist Women: free and legal abortion, rape, and domestic violence. These issues best provide a sense of both the continuity and the changes that have characterized the growth of the Mexican feminist movement. Both the similarities and the differences in how these issues move through the policy process are very informative in this regard. Moreover, these issues highlight the crucial interconnections of the state and civil society in Mexico today while they draw out in stark detail both the marginalized status of contemporary Mexican women and the ways women have begun to struggle against marginalization.

The three issues appear to bear little resemblance to what are usually considered political issues. For the most part, abortion, rape, and domestic violence are viewed as private and personal matters, as opposed to such avowedly political concerns as suffrage or participation in political parties. All three issues highlight how the state's framing of an issue affects the policies it creates. Likewise, each issue draws out the implications for state power or a new understanding of what makes an issue political. Although there are class divisions regarding access to safe, illegal abortions, for the most part these three problems affect the lives of all Mexican women—they are often literally questions of life and death for the majority of Mexico's women, particularly in the case of abortion.

In my discussion of women's political engagement on these policy issues I begin by describing the problem and the state's stance on the issue. I then lay out the strategies used and actions initiated by women, and the responses of the state, if any, to these critiques and challenges.

THE RIGHT TO FREE, LEGAL ABORTION

Abortion is illegal in Mexico. The law of the Federal District (Mexico City) states that anyone who practices or aids in the practice of abortion, even with the woman's consent, will be jailed for one to three years. For abortions administered without the woman's consent, the punishment is three to six years; for abortions entailing violence, the sentence is six to eight years. The punishment for a woman who consents to an abortion is six months to one year in prison provided that she does not have a bad reputation; that she manages to hide her pregnancy; and it is the result of an illegitimate union. If any of these conditions is not present, the sentence is one to five years in prison.[5]

The state's official stance is that the need for abortion arises primarily from lack of knowledge about birth control. Thus, the state and the party that controls it, the PRI, have taken the position that the need for abortions can be reduced by offering appropriate sex education in schools. PRD favors decriminalization of abortion, and PAN strongly opposes decriminalization. The government's sex education campaign, though accompanied by the distribution of contraceptives, has not been very successful, however. It is at best basic education about reproduction. The state view is that there are no accidents or errors or fallible contraceptives, and that as long as sex education and contraceptives are provided, there ought never to be a need for abortion.

The moral and religious considerations regarding this issue, voiced primarily by right-wing groups and the Catholic church, combined with the ruling sexist ideology, are probably the primary determinants of the attitude of the state and most members of civil society toward abortion. Although the Catholic church also opposes contraceptive methods other than the rhythm method, it appears that the state has been able to avoid conflict on this issue by ignoring the church's stance. The state has launched birth-control campaigns because lowering the birthrate is of crucial importance to the government. The government has not acted on the question of decriminalization of abortion, however, because of the ferocious opposition of the church and the ultra-right wing.

Furthermore, the state is invested with a patriarchal morality that prohibits abortion. Women may not be permitted to decide anything because it would signify power—especially when they exercise a mass power of decision over their bodies and their lives. The call for abortion rights reveals a rejection of forced maternity. Under any circumstances, then, the demand for abortion in Mexican society signifies a fissure in patriarchal ideology and in men's political domination over women.

Whether abortion law is a matter of politics, education, morality, or piety, it has had little effect on the number of abortions performed and the need for them. There are 14 million women between 20 and 49 years of age in Mexico; according to some researchers, one of every four or five pregnancies ends in abortion.[6] There is no way of knowing the real numbers of abortions or their relative frequency among different sectors of society, given the fact that it is a clandestine practice. But the data that exist suggest that abortions are more common in urban than in rural areas.[7] The data also suggest that the great majority of women who have abortions are Catholics who already have more than three children.

Women's need for abortion is often economically based. The percentage of single mothers in both the cities and the countryside is enormous, for a number of reasons. An extra child is often a financial burden for a single mother, a problem that is made even more acute by the current economic crisis.

Yet obtaining an illegal abortion is not without its own costs. The price of an abortion in 1991 averaged about the equivalent of U.S. $500, though it may be possible to obtain one for less under wretched conditions. Because the minimum salary in Mexico is about U.S. $3 per day, an abortion costs a poor woman something like 150 days' wages. Even for a university professor, an abortion is equivalent to about a month's salary. But an illegal abortion often entails more than financial hardships; illegal abortion costs some women their lives. In 1978 Mexican sources estimated that 78,000 women die each year from illegal abortions. In 1987 it was estimated that 2 million abortions are performed in Mexico every year. If one accepts the World Health Organization's calculation that between 7 and 14 percent of the world's women who abort die from complications, then some 140,000 women in Mexico die each year as a result of clandestine abortions.[8] Whichever estimate one accepts, illegal abortions have high costs for Mexico's women.

The dangers of illegal abortion are not equal for all Mexican women. The risks depend largely on socioeconomic class, and most deaths are of women from the lower classes. Moreover, the actual practice of abortion is a mirror of class differences. A bourgeois Mexican woman can fly to the United States and have an abortion in secure and hygienic conditions or she can get a good—and expensive—doctor in Mexico. For women of limited means the costs of abortion are likely to be measured not only in pesos but also in terms of their health or lives.

Aside from the dangers and costs of illegal abortion, there are other drawbacks to this policy on abortion. Illegal abortions are also an economic burden on the state. Mexico has a social security system that gives every worker the right to free medical care. Therefore, the state must spend millions of pesos annually on the thousands of women who are admitted to government health centers because of problems caused by poorly executed abortions. Denying women the right to abortion also conflicts with the state's 20-year concern with population growth. But the state's campaign to promote birth control—led by slogans like "Responsible parenting" and "The small family lives better"—has not sufficiently reduced population growth.

So far, however, the state has avoided confronting any of the problems resulting from its policy on abortion. The impetus for change has had to come from women. Given the large number of women who have abortions, one might think that this would be a popular cause with them. Unfortunately this is not the case. Although many women do abort, abortion is a private matter in the real and the metaphorical sense. The result is that there has never existed, nor will there exist for a long time, a large grassroots feminist movement capable of putting a million women on the streets to demonstrate in favor of legalized abortion.

Instead, the movement to legalize abortion has concentrated on working within the existing power structure and state institutions to change policy and on attempting to raise women's consciousness in general. Mexican feminists have approached the issue as a question of women's right to control their own bodies. Abortion is not presented as just another method of birth control, but rather as a final recourse for pregnant women, who should have the right to choose. On a personal level many individuals have voiced their interest in seeing abortion decriminalized, including several well-known doctors, both men and women.

The effort to decriminalize abortion began in the mid-1970s, when some members of the Coalition of Feminist Women proposed a law of voluntary maternity. The proposed law legalized abortion but recognized the need for sex education and the importance of a general family planning program. In 1979 the Coalition and the National Front felt that favorable political winds were blowing, and they decided to turn over the proposal to the Grupo Parlamentario Comunista (Communist Group in Congress), a left-wing coalition made up entirely of men. The group presented the proposal to the Chamber of Deputies. But with the death of both the Coalition and the National Front there no longer existed a political pressure group that could push the proposal through Congress.

Meanwhile, right-wing extremists organized the Movimiento Pro-Vida (pro-life movement) and campaigned against the proposal. The Catholic church also continued its attacks on abortion. But even if it had been sympathetic to the proposed law, the Mexican state would not have been ready to engage in direct confrontation with these two forces. And the male members of the Chamber of Deputies who had introduced the proposal did nothing to promote its passage, given the lack of effective lobbying on the part of the coalition and the pressure of the pro-life campaign. The law never passed. The legislation continues to sleep in some drawer of the Chamber of Deputies.

After this setback, almost nothing was done during the 1980s to advance efforts to decriminalize abortion. Some articles were written, some lectures were given, and there were some isolated public protests. But the majority of feminists dedicated themselves to educational or *asistencialista* (assistentialist) tasks, largely at the grass-roots level.

It was not until 1989 that feminist groups resumed their struggle to decriminalize abortion. This concern has remained latent, and at present it is barely beginning to open its eyes timidly, yawn, and stretch, but the issue has not yet really been awakened.

In 1991 the campaign of the pro-life movement continued to be an important factor in preventing legalization of abortion; it also acted as a brake on the development of consciousness in civil society in general and among women in particular. There is reason to hope, however, that the battle for legalization may be swinging in women's direction. For example, the Coordinadora Feminista of the Mexico City area is leading a movement for legalization. Drawing on the lessons learned from the struggles of the 1970s, some groups are using new strategies and tactics. Efforts are being made to conduct a well-organized, unified campaign. At the same time, following the initiative of the Catholics for a Free Choice movement in the United States, efforts are being made to confront the issue of abortion from a religious perspective. Catholic women are speaking out in defense of women's right to decide for themselves about abortion.

The struggle for the legalization of abortion has thus far failed to make a concrete change in state policy. Still, the movement has made other, less tangible progress. In urban areas, there has been a slow growth of consciousness among both men and women on the issue and on its connection to machismo and sexism. People are beginning to consider seriously the use of contraceptives. There has also been a considerable increase in the number of vasectomies.

THE STRUGGLE AGAINST RAPE

The recent history of the struggle against rape differs in certain respects from the movement for the legalization of abortion. The state has been less of an adversary and at least a lukewarm ally of women on the issue of rape. Women's political engagement on this issue is also marked by the use of different strategies and the active involvement of women from the working and lower classes. Further, more battles have been won against rape, and the tangible advances have been greater than in the struggle to legalize abortion.

As it is elsewhere in the world, the problem of rape in Mexico is great. It was estimated that in 1990 there were some 65,000 rapes in Mexico City alone, an urban sprawl containing some 18 million people. Only 2,200 of these rapes would be reported—in other words, a rape would occur every eight minutes, but a rape would be reported only every four hours. From January to April 1988, 407 of the 698 complaints filed in Mexico City for sex crimes were for rape.[9] A major reason for both the problem and its underreporting has been that the dominant attitude toward rape in Mexican society is that it is an evil of little importance.

Until recently, this attitude was evident in the legal treatment of rape. Until 1984, rape was punishable with a prison term of less than five years, and convicted rapists often avoided prison simply by paying a fine. Punishments for gang rape and the rape of minors carried penalties of eight to twenty years and from four to ten years, respectively.[10] Not surprisingly, these penalties did not deter potential rapists.

Feminists have attempted to combat the problem of rape by using three strategies: self-help and support for the survivors of rape from autonomous feminist collectives; organized street demonstrations; and collaboration with state agencies. Since 1979, when a group of primarily middle-class women created the Centro de Apoyo a Mujeres Violadas (CAMVAC, or Center for Aid to Violated Women), feminist collectives using a strategy of self-help have provided support for rape survivors. In 1984 another group was created, the Colectivo de Lucha contra la Violencia hacia las Mujeres (COVAC, or Collective of Struggle Against Violence Directed Toward Women), which provided similar assistance. This strategy remains a significant aspect of the feminist response to the problem. In 1989 a nationwide grass-roots organization against rape was formed, the Red Nacional contra la Violencia hacia las Mujeres (National Network Against Violence Directed Toward Women). The members of the center, the collective, and the network are primarily middle-class feminist women, though COVAC has male participants as well.

These groups were formed in Mexico City and have devoted most of their efforts to the problem of rape.

Although the struggle against violence directed toward women began with these middle-class feminist collectives, it now also includes—and in fact has been largely taken over by—women from the lower classes and the state. It has proved easier to involve the state, on the one hand, and women from the lower classes, on the other, as well as women from reactionary parties such as PAN, in the campaign against rape rather than in the campaign to legalize abortion. This appears to derive from the fact that the struggle against rape is less threatening to the dominant ideology and to patriarchal power. One can even see rape as an extreme form of theft; to take by force what is not yours is a punishable offense according to the ruling morality and the laws that defend private property. A woman always (or almost always) belongs to a man, be he her father, husband, or lover. Thus, rape is a crime committed against men; something is stolen from a man. It is therefore easier to accept punishment for rapists, because rape is a crime against the sanctity of private property.

The expansion of the struggle against rape to working-class and poor women began in Bogotá at the Primer Encuentro Feminista Latinoamericano y del Caribe (First Latin American and Caribbean Feminist Meeting) in 1981. The feminists present established 25 November as the international day of No Más Violencia Contra Las Mujeres (No More Violence Against Women). Activities and street demonstrations have taken place on this day in Mexico ever since. These activities are typically organized by women of the popular sectors and particularly by members of the Coordinadora Nacional del Movimiento Urbano Popular (CONAMUP, or National Coordinating Council of the Popular Urban Movement). However, the street demonstrations also include members of all the feminist groups. Whether or not they belong to CONAMUP or to political parties, women from the lower classes engage in many kinds of activism and street demonstrations: for example, protests against the cost of living, demands for basic services, and requests that titles to their land be regularized.

The third phase of the feminist response to rape got under way only recently. One of the original groups within the Coalition of Feminist Women, the Movimiento Nacional de Mujeres (National Women's Movement), along with other feminist groups, began working with the Secretaría General de Protección y Vialidad (General Secretary of Protection and Road Communications, the Ministry of Police in Mexico City). These women requested the state's help in their efforts to aid rape survivors in a more rapid and effective way. They also wanted the government to assume that responsibility. Together they have created three Centros de Orientación y Apoyo a Personas Violadas (Centers for Counseling and Aid to Violated People), which depend on the government for funding.

The state has also opened three agencies of the Ministerio Público (district attorney) that deal specifically with sex crimes and depend directly on the Procuraduría General de la República (national police force). These agencies are a direct result of the pressure brought to bear by feminist women and represent the first phase of a new state program. The state intends to open more such agencies and is also considering the creation of courts specializing in sex crimes.

This collaboration with the state has had drawbacks, however. The fact that rape almost exclusively affects women has been downplayed. The centers are not limited to aiding and counseling women; they extend their services to anyone who has been raped. It is not possible to open centers that treat women exclusively it seems! Instead the generic term *people* must be used. The 8.3 percent of those treated by the centers who are boys or men serve in a sense to legitimize the treatment of the 91.7 percent of center users who are women.

Nevertheless, the movement against rape has had some success. The national and international feminist movement undoubtedly has contributed to the pressure, as have the United Nations and those groups and organizations that defend human rights around the world. Not only are more facilities now available to victims of rape; there have also been changes in the legal code. Under the 1989 reform, for example, punishment for rape has been increased to a prison sentence of 8 to 14 years, and up to 21 years for gang rape. Moreover, it is no longer possible for a rapist to get out of his sentence simply by paying a fine. Nor is rape any longer considered to be the type of crime that requires the victim to file charges for prosecution to occur. Further, as the considerable rise in the number of complaints filed in Mexico City in the past few years shows, there have been advances in the area of consciousness-raising. Unfortunately, however, neither the reality of judicial practice nor society's attitudes regarding rape has changed as readily. Only 5 percent of the rape complaints filed in Mexico City courts actually result in a trial and sentencing of the rapist. Despite the consciousness-raising, the attitude that rape is a minor evil and, moreover, one that is generally provoked by women themselves, is still voiced on the streets, as well as on radio and television.

THE DEFENSE OF BATTERED WOMEN

Although the struggle against domestic violence was one of the three major causes adopted by the feminist movement when it began in the 1970s, it has had even less success than the struggle against rape or the battle for legalized abortion. Domestic battery is a widespread problem, but I doubt that statistics reflect the total number of complaints or the prison sentences meted out. Battered women must file a complaint. If their injuries heal within 15 days of the assault, the perpetrator is either pardoned or assigned a three- to four-month prison sentence. If the injuries do not heal within 15 days, the sentence is from four months to two years. Thus the length of the sentence is directly related to the injuries incurred and can reach up to 10 years.[11]

Mexican feminists have been much more committed to the struggles against rape and in favor of legalizing abortion than they have been to the defense of battered women. But the slogan "No more violence against women," heard in street protests, has often served to express both the struggle against rape and against domestic violence. In fact, the violence is essentially the same.

The great majority of battered women—and mistreated children—probably come from the poorer classes. Domestic battery is an extreme expression of machismo, aggravated by such social conditions as misery, lack of education, unemployment or underemployment, and alcoholism.

Unfortunately, efforts oriented toward the defense of battered women have been largely unorganized and have not achieved any significant changes. Organized street protests are carried out twice a year, on 8 March (International Women's Day) and 25 November (International "No More Violence Against Women" Day). The participants in these demonstrations include women from popular-sector organizations like CONAMUP and members of feminist groups, as well as independent feminists. Some groups provide legal and psychological counseling for battered women who request it—for example, the Kollantai Collective, made up primarily of women from the urban middle class. There have, however, been neither large numbers nor continuity among those involved in these efforts. Women's groups have also lacked resources for dealing with this issue. To provide adequate aid to battered women would require both an infrastructure and extensive economic resources. In addition to legal advice, psychological counseling, and medical aid, battered women also need shelters in which to live. Another reason for the lack of progress is that the state has made no commitment to ending the problem. As a result of these factors, the shelters for battered women found in many developed countries have never existed in Mexico.

Nevertheless, I do not think one can talk solely in terms of success and failure. I believe that the solution lies in the long, arduous process of eradicating machismo from Mexican society, a process that has only begun in the past 20 years. Time will tell whether the movement against domestic battery is a success or failure.

PROSPECTS

Women's future progress in each area remains unclear. Women have attempted to resolve the issue of abortion through institutional channels but have accomplished nothing. The moral and religious conditioning on this question is so pervasive that even if a referendum on the legalization of abortion were held among women only, it is possible the majority will not come out in favor of legalization. Given these circumstances, the Mexican state will probably legalize abortion only when its own policy priorities of "modernization" require that it do so. This forecast is not as grim as it sounds, however. For, if the politics of demography continue to assume the importance that they do now, such a moment may be close at hand. President Carlos Salinas de Gortari has declared that Mexico's annual population growth rate must be lowered from 2 percent in 1990 to 1 percent by the year 2000. He told such governmental agencies as the Secretaría de Salud (Secretary of Health), the Consejo Nacional de Población (National Population Council), and the Seguro Social (Social Security), as well as the states' governors, that "the government's efforts to reduce the rate of population growth throughout the country must be realized."[12] This increasing concern with population growth, combined with the renewed activism of feminists on the abortion issue, bodes well for change.

The struggle against rape is also moving forward at an increased pace. In July 1990 the Chamber of Deputies approved a legislative proposal submitted by representatives from all of the political parties. This new law contains several important changes: the maximum penalty for gang rape has been increased to 21 years in prison; sexual harassment is now defined as a crime; and it is proposed that the medical examination of raped women be assigned to female personnel, so that what has been described as a "second rape" at the hands of male doctors is avoided. Certain changes can be seen in relation to sexual harassment, where women have begun to denounce perpetrators publicly.

As for battered women, it appears that the feminist movement has not yet developed a concrete strategy of struggle; nor does it appear that there are any satisfactory solutions in the short run. The only real solution is a massive raising of men's consciousness. The policy of creating shelters is a post facto aid to women, which is essentially assistentialist. The true answer lies in men not beating women. Thus, the task of feminists appears to be a slow and long-term, if not infinite, raising of consciousness that would solve the problem at its root.

More generally, whatever Mexican women are able to accomplish in these three policy areas, as well as others, will depend a great deal on the state and how it views the particular issue. The state prohibits abortion, has until recently upheld weak laws to prevent and punish rape, and has taken no part in the struggle against domestic violence. In effect, the state protects fetuses rather than women and believes the position of the church to be more important than either. Neither the right to abortion nor the problem of domestic violence exist in the eyes of the state because they are seen as belonging to the private family realm or as simply a matter of education. As a result, the state shows little concern over how women think or feel about its policies. Nor is it concerned about the conditions in which women live or in what situations they die as a result of its policies. Yet the state has participated in the struggle against rape. How the state frames an issue and whether women are able to make the government see these as "public" political issues will probably continue to play a key role in determining women's success.

Women will also have to decide on the best strategies regarding the use of their own resources. We still have a long way to go to subvert the current power relations of the genders. I would argue that performing abortions and assisting raped and battered women may not be the most effective way to get there. But as long as abortion remains illegal, it is important to have highly qualified people available to perform abortions at low cost in hygienic, safe conditions for women who want the procedure. Obviously, at certain moments—for example, in the case of

rape—it is also important to provide medical, legal, and psychological aid to women who have been victims of violence.

The task of feminists, however, may be more to struggle so that abortion is legalized and rape and domestic violence disappear, rather than to dedicate ourselves to providing "band-aid" treatment to raped and battered women and offering safe abortions. Asistencialismo, essentially a form of charity, may be a means to advance the process of consciousness-raising, but it ought never to become an end in itself for feminism. Because of its resources, the state is better suited than private citizens to the task of asistencialismo, which it should accept as its responsibility. The feminist movement must go beyond asistencialismo, though there are those who would argue, for example, that sending a survivor of rape to a state agency for aid may harm her. Nevertheless, I think the movement is at a point—or will be soon—at which it will be forced to choose priorities and the best strategies for accomplishing them.

Finally, it is clear from this discussion that a fundamental transformation of the androcentric orientation of what are considered public and political issues is required. The transformation will undoubtedly be slow, but as the political engagement of Mexico's women demonstrates, it is necessary if the study of politics is to keep pace with the reality of politics.

NOTES

1. *Information Please Almanac* (New York: Dan Golenpaul Associates, 1988), 229.

2. Thomas E. Skidmore and Peter H. Smith, *Modern Latin America* (Oxford: Oxford University Press, 1984), 250–55.

3. Luz de Lourdes de Silva, "Las mujeres en la élite política de México: 1954–84" (Women in the Mexican political elite, 1954–84), in Orlandina de Oliveira, ed., *Trabajo, poder y sexualidad* (Mexico: El Colegio de México, 1989), 268.

4. Enriqueta Tuñón, "La lucha política de la mujer mexicana por el derecho al sufragio y sus repercusiones" (The political struggle of Mexican women for the right to vote and its repercussions), in Carmen Ramos et al., *Pres-*

encia y transparencia. La mujer en la historia de México (Mexico: El Colegio de México, 1987), 188.

5. *Código penal para el Distrito y Territorios Federales* (Penal code for the Federal District and territories) (Mexico: Ed. Andrade, 1981), 82–83.

6. Amalia Rivera, "Insólita cotidiana" (Daily unusual) *Doblejornada,* Mexico City, 3 January 1990, p. 12.

7. Ibid.

8. Ana María Portugal, ed., *Mujeres e iglesia. Sexualidad y aborto en América Latina* (Women and the church: Sexuality and abortion in Latin America) (Washington, D.C.: Catholics for a Free Choice, 1989), 4.

9. Data provided by the Procuraduría de Justicia del Distrito Federal (Justice Department of Mexico City).

10. *Código penal para el Distrito y Territorios Federales* (Mexico: Ed. Andrade, 1977), 90.

11. *Código penal para el Distrito y Territorios Federales* (Mexico: Ed. Andrade, 1988), 76.

12. "Más de 100 millones, la población en el año 2000" (More than 100 million: The population in the year 2000), *La Jornada,* Mexico City, 7 February 1990, p. 16.

▲ *Morocco*

POLITICS

Type of Political System: partial democracy
  Sovereignty: constitutional monarchy
  Executive-Legislative System: parliamentary
Type of State: unitary
Type of Party System: multiparty
Major Political Parties

Union Constitutionnelle (UC, Constitutional Union): Founded in March 1983 by former Prime Minister Maati Bouabid to create a new conservative center for Moroccan politics. Moderate party that emphasizes economic self-efficiency. Said to have royal support.

Rassemblement National des Indépendants (RNI, National Assembly of Independents): Launched at a constitutive congress in October 1978; branded by the left wing as a king's party. Led by Ahmed Osman, president of the Chamber of Representatives. Designated as official opposition in late 1981.

Mouvement Populaire (MP, Popular Movement): Organized in 1957 as a monarchist party of Berber mountaineers. A major participant in government coalitions of the early 1960s, weakened by later dissension within the leadership. Won second largest number of legislative seats in the elections of June 1977; ranked third in September 1984 elections.

Parti de l'Indépendance (Istiqlal, or Independence, Party): Founded in 1943; provided most of the nation's leadership before leading the struggle for independence in 1956 in close alliance with Sultan Muhammad V. Party policy is strongly nationalist. Members are primarily urban and middle-class, with many religious officials also providing support. The party was forced out of the government in 1963; it reentered the government in 1977 with eight cabinet posts. Notable for a reformist attitude, it supports the king only on selected issues. The leading

party in the election of June 1977, it suffered heavy losses in both the 1983 municipal elections and the 1984 legislative balloting.

Union Socialiste des Forces Populaires (USFP, Socialist Union of Popular Forces): Organized in September 1974 by the Union Nationale des Forces Populaires–Rabat section. (The UNFP, created in 1959, played a leading role in postindependence Morocco.) The USFP calls for political democratization, nationalization of major industries, thorough reform of social and administrative structures, and cessation of what it believes to be human rights abuses by the government. Doubled its directly elected representation in September 1984. Refused to participate in the coalition government formed in April 1985, charging lack of official effort toward economic reform.

Parti du Progrès et du Socialisme (PPS, Party of Progress and Socialism): Formed in 1968 to replace the banned Moroccan Communist Party; obtained legal status in 1974. Criticizes economic liberalization and has endorsed USFP's call for the formation of a national front of opposition parties, which should attract Istiqlal and the Organisation de l'Action Démocratique et Populaire (OADP, Organization of Democratic and Popular Action), composed of former members of the USFP and the PPS). Ali Yata, its leader, won the party's only seat in the 1977 chamber; the party gained an additional seat in 1984.

Year Women Granted Right to Vote: 1959

Year Women Granted Right to Stand for Election: 1959

Percentage of Women in the Unicameral Legislature: 0.0%[a]

Percentage of Electorate Voting for Highest Elected Office in Most Recent Election (1984): not available

DEMOGRAPHICS

Population: 25,100,000[b]

Percentage of Population in Urban Areas
Overall: 47.0%
Female: 42.6%[c]
Male: 57.4%[d]

Percentage of Population Below Age 15:
41.0%[e]

Birthrate (per 1,000 population): 31[f]

Maternal Mortality Rate (per 100,000 live births): 300

Infant Mortality Rate (per 1,000 live births): 58[g]

Mortality Rate for Children Under Five (per 1,000 live births): 76[h]

Average Household Size: 4.2 persons[i]

Mean Age at First Marriage[j]
Female: 23.5 years
Male: 27.9 years

Life Expectancy[k]
Female: 62.5 years
Male: 59.1 years

EDUCATION

Ratio of Female to Male Enrollment[l]
First-Level Education: 66
Second-Level Education: 70
Third-Level Education: 50

Literacy Rate[m]
Female: 22.0%
Male: 49.0%

ECONOMY

Gross National Product per Capita: U.S. $960[n]

Percentage of Labor Force in Agriculture: 51.7%

Distribution of Agricultural Workers by Sex[o]
Female: 42.9%
Male: 57.1%

Economically Active Population by Sex[p]
Female: 19.7%
Male: 80.3%

a. Alan J. Day, *Political Parties of the World* (Chicago: St. James Press, 1988).

b. Ministry of Planning, *Statistics Annual of Morocco, 1990* (Rabat: Centre de Recherche et d'Etudes Demographiques [CERED], 1990).

c. Ministry of Planning, *Femmes et condition féminine au Maroc* (Women and women's condition in Morocco) (Rabat: CERED, 1989), 35.

d. Ibid.

e. Ministry of Planning, *Statistics Annual.*

f. DHS, 1992. Ministry of Health.

g. Ibid.

h. Ibid.

i. Ibid.

j. Ministry of Planning, *La condition de la femme au Maroc* (The condition of women in Morocco) (Rabat: Direction de la Statistique, 1992), 40.

k. Population Division, U.N. Department of International Economic and Social Affairs, *World Population Prospects: Estimates and Projections as Assessed in 1984 as of 1985–1990,* U.N. publication no. E.86.XIII.3.

l. Ministry of Planning, *Statistics Annual.*

m. Ministry of Planning, *Femmes et condition féminine au Maroc.*

n. *World Development Report* (Washington, D.C.: World Bank, 1990).

o. Ministry of Planning, *Enquête sur l'emploi rural, 1986–87* (Study of rural employment, 1986–87) (Rabat: Direction de la Statistique, 1987), 23.

p. Ministry of Planning, *Enquête sur les ménages, 1981–82* (Study of households, 1981–82) (Rabat: Direction de la Statistique, 1987), 54.

Women in Morocco: Gender Issues and Politics

AICHA AFIFI

AND RAJAE MSEFER

The Kingdom of Morocco, a North African country of 25.1 million, is a unitary constitutional monarchy with a parliamentary structure. At present the king, a member of one of the world's oldest reigning houses, appoints a prime minister and other members of the cabinet, or Council of Ministers, without referring to the majority in the Parliament. Two-thirds of the parliamentary deputies are directly elected, with the remainder elected indirectly by local councils, professional groups, and workers' unions. The four conservative parties usually support the monarchy and typically control Parliament by a decisive majority. They are the Union Constitutionelle (Constitutional Union), Rassemblement National des Indépendants (National Assembly of Independents), Mouvement Populaire (Popular Movement), and Parti National Démocrate (Democratic National Party).

The Istiqlal (Independence) Party, which almost exclusively dominated the preindependence political scene, is in the center of the political spectrum between the conservative parties and the leftist and progressive parties. In May 1985 the Istiqlal Party went into opposition (when four Istiqlal Party representatives left the government), joining the Union Socialiste des Forces Populaires (USFP, or Socialist Union of Popular Forces)[1] and two Marxist parties, the Parti du Progrès et du Socialisme (PPS, or Party of Progress and Socialism) and the Organization de l'Action Démocratique Populaire (OADP, or Organization for Democratic and Popular Action) —both of which are increasingly moving away from Marxist dogma. During periods of national emergency, the constitution allows the king to dissolve Parliament and govern by decree. The monarch dominates national politics, making all political appointments and deciding which parties will form a government; members of the government and of Parliament initiate legislation.

In this almost universally Muslim country, the reputed descent of the king from Muhammad lends legitimacy to the monarchical institution. Since the sixteenth century the monarch has maintained both religious and political control over the population, even during the period of French colonization (1912–56). Some scholars claim that the French occupation actually strengthened the monarchy in that it reinforced centralization of political power (*makhzen*) by reducing the traditional autonomy of the tribes, which were sometimes Arab but most often Berber (a non-Arab Muslim and tribal people indigenous to North Africa). The French period left other lasting marks on Moroccan society: not only do governing elites continue to favor the French language over the official Arabic, but the government structures, armed forces, and political parties are all styled on the French model (though much less now than in the early years of independence). Berber traditions are nonetheless very strong in rural areas, especially in the mountains, and the Berber language still prevails overwhelmingly. The collective ownership of land in the rural Berber communities, common until the 1960s, is now moving toward more privatized systems.

Both Arab-Islamic and Western cultures have shaped current Moroccan society, which is characterized by patriarchal structures that enhance the primacy of males. Islamic law, especially in the Malikite version that has historically predominated in the Maghreb region of North Africa, gives males extensive control over key decisions affecting women's lives.

For centuries Arab-Islamic society has emphasized the seclusion of women and the dominance of male rights, although the advent of Islam in 622 A.D. brought about enormous changes in women's status. Prior to Islam, women were treated as slaves and exchanged as commodities. The Islamic code, however, structured the family and codified male-female relationships, enabling women to become active members of the community. The participation of the wives and women disciples of Muhammad in social and political life demonstrates the extent of the changes in women's status.[2] Historically this period extends from the first year of the Islamic calendar (622 A.D.) to the beginning of the Abbasid dynasty (750 A.D.). Gradually, however, women's rights were once again denied and the primacy of males was reimposed. Under the reign of the Abbasids, who controlled the Islamic world until the end of the ninth century, women lost all their prerogatives as active members of society and the superiority of men was reaffirmed.[3] In Morocco the status of Arab women was not different from that of their counterparts in other Islamic countries, even though in Berber areas this status was based on community practice (*orf*) rather than on Islamic law.

The penetration of French colonialism brought about some trivial social changes that partially liberated women from their traditional bondage, especially in urban areas. Nonetheless, society overall continues to discriminate against women. Power remains a male prerogative, with men retaining economic, political, and religious control. Women's space is restricted to the spheres of reproduction and household tasks. Public space is still limited to men and elite women.

At the beginning of the twentieth century, scholars in several Islamic countries debated the issue of modernizing women's roles. Leaders of conservative political and religious groups in Morocco, such as members of the *zawiyas* (monasteries or brotherhoods in which ascetics taught children and adults the rudiments of Islam), rejected the changes called for by the Western model, whereas promoters of change, such as 'Allal al Fassi, Mekki Naciri, and Ben Larbi Alaoui, called for educating women and granting them access to the labor market.

The emergence of the renaissance nationalist movement, known as Nahda, in the late 1920s helped create a countrywide consensus that favored women's participation in different arenas of activism.[4] The reformists (mainly intellectuals) drew on the ideas of *Salafiya*, meaning "returning to the source." The Salafiya movement, which had appeared in the nineteenth century, taught the essence of religion, acknowledged the failure of traditional Islamic societies to face foreign domination, and expressed a desire for radical changes in the intellectual and social domains. The education of women, changes in dress, and literacy campaigns for adult females were among the first signs of change in the condition of women. Moving beyond the traditional role of mother and wife, women became more involved in events outside the domestic realm, first becoming engaged in the national movement of liberation, then in the process of economic and social development. Inevitably women's increased involvement created a new perception of women's role in society. As the Moroccan sociologist Fatima Mernissi attests, "Before these last few decades, women in our Muslim societies were not allowed a future, they only grew old. This change in women's consciousness is the substance of the revolutionary process that [has] taken place in the Muslim world."[5] However, women's new status was more easily welcomed among political elites (including members of political parties, in which some women acquired high positions) than among less educated, average people.

During the postcolonial period, women have seen significant improvement in educational and employment opportunities, and in 1959 they received the right to vote and to be elected to public office. International pressure has encouraged the integration of women into Morocco's social and economic sectors as well. In spite of women's new-found access to the political sector, where their influence remains limited, and to a few economic sectors where they are not yet part of the decision-making process, the integration of issues important to women, such as education, employment, and birth control, into national policies is not the result of women's public efforts or a reflection of widely held views within Moroccan society. Rather, the institutional leadership has taken the initiative, not only selecting which issues will be addressed but also carefully orchestrating their transformation into objectives of national development plans.

This attitude on women's issues is not without its paradoxes. Princesses have held positions of considerable authority, the king having appointed his sister ambassador to Italy and his oldest daughter head of the Department of Social Affairs for Military Troops. At the same time, however, the king has maintained the seclusion of his wife. On a national scale, the institutional leadership has been reluctant to legitimate any legal reforms that are inconsistent with the spirit, if not the letter, of Islam. If supporting economic and social justice (perceived by the masses in terms of employment opportunities, improvements in lifestyle, and the like) increases the popularity of the elites, supporting gender equality and increased public participation for women is of little political advantage. For example, providing access to education and employment for women may serve the interests of the political elite by increasing its international credibility and the support it receives from the upper and middle classes, but an upheaval in the present situation of female subordination would only undermine the sacred legitimacy of the political leadership.

In the past 20 years the practice of veiling, perhaps the most visible symbol of women's seclusion and confinement to domestic activities, has almost disappeared from urban areas and has decreased in rural areas. This evolution is partly due to women's greater access to health services, education, and labor markets. The decision to wear the veil is sometimes the woman's own; others, however, may contribute to or dictate its observance (for example, the father, husband, or in-laws). Recently the expansion of Islamic fundamentalism, which is perceived by many as a reaction against the westernization of Islamic societies, has led an increasing number of young women to veil their faces. These women view the veil not only as a way to follow the precepts of the Quran but as a symbol of freedom from the tyranny of Western culture.

Where traditional restrictions on women remain strong, initiatives by the elite on women's behalf have proven ineffective in several dimensions. First, women constitute a heterogeneous group, reflecting the diversity of Moroccan society. Divergent interests among women reflect the differences among social classes. Whereas wealthy women seek to keep their privileges, poor women—those without education or access to public space—do not have the political consciousness and willingness to adhere to any organized action that would improve their conditions. Only women from wealthy and intellectual segments of the population may be aware enough of the necessity for change in women's conditions to engage in any action to improve them.

The diversity of women's needs and interests, which vary from basic survival to aspirations of power and prestige, hinders their collective participation in national politics and makes it difficult, if not impossible, to implement effective government policies that appeal to all Moroccan women. Because most women often do not recognize given policies as serving their interests, they are unlikely to work to accomplish these goals and may not support government efforts purportedly undertaken on their behalf.

Although under current Moroccan law women are entitled to the same economic, social, and political rights as men, some of these elite-initiated priorities have not necessarily won broad support. Moreover, inequalities remain between these rights and their exercise owing to the slow evolution of most Moroccan men's attitudes toward women and to the low level of commitment by political leaders to enforcing these rights. This rift is revealed in various ways, including discrimination in the labor market. Entrenched patterns of social behavior may explain why women's organizations and nongovernmental organizations should continue to struggle for improvement of women's conditions through education, family planning, and economic participation.

Although both international and local non-governmental organizations (and to a lesser extent the government) continue their efforts to improve women's status, the female population that benefits from these efforts is small, and most women must still struggle privately to improve their own conditions. Given these circumstances, we shall focus on the three policy areas of education, family planning, and economic participation, considering the successes and failures of these programs, particularly in light of the elitist origins of the issues and policies.

WOMEN'S POSITION IN FORMAL POLITICS

Before considering these issues, however, it seems important to discuss how women have participated in public life and how they are incorporated into the elite decision-making structure. The Moroccan woman has always played an important social and political role in society: she has battled colonialism, helped in times of war, and provided a backbone for society during periods of calm and transition.

Women's access to modern opportunities has been strongly influenced by the policies of the government, which define appropriate domestic and public roles for women. The government reflects the nation's Arabic heritage in its caution in attempting to extend to women political responsibilities traditionally held by males. In spite of domestic and international laws that affirm the equality of the sexes in regard to political rights, a deeply entrenched resistance to change permeates society. Even though Moroccan women have in principle been offered political opportunities, their participation in public life has been established gradually by elitist initiatives, not by grassroots struggle or consensus. Women were given the right to vote and to be elected in 1959, at the same time men were, and had this right reaffirmed by the constitutions of 1970 and 1972.

Yet several factors affect women's perception of these policies, including each woman's level of education and participation in social and economic development, which determine her degree of awareness concerning the existence of such rights. Women's political awareness and the likelihood that they will exercise their rights are also related to the degree to which society, particularly men, accepts the practice of women's rights. The majority of men—and of women too, unfortunately—believe that the role of women is at home, not in politics.

Although women's rights have been bestowed from above and have been constrained by social norms and limited opportunities, women have nonetheless played an active role in Morocco's political history. For example, women were active in the struggle against French colonialism; a number of women have recounted episodes in which they concealed weapons in their shopping baskets or hid members of the resistance in their homes. More recently, in 1975, when King Hassan II organized the so-called Green March into the western Sahara—a mass immigration of 350,000 Moroccan civilians into the Spanish-occupied territory then called the Spanish Sahara—the participation of women was vital in preventing Spanish soldiers from firing on the claimants, thereby securing the land for Morocco with minimal bloodshed. And in 1986 several hundred women demonstrated in Melilla to protest a discriminatory law imposed by the Spanish authorities.[6]

Although dramatic, these episodes do not characterize women as consistently engaged in making decisions or involved in movements for change. To a large extent, this is also true in electoral politics. When the first local elections were held in 1960, of the 17,174 candidates for office, only 14 were women, none of whom won. In 1963, during the legislative elections, there were no women among the 414 elected deputies. When the next local elections were held in 1976, women made up 47 percent of the electorate but were represented by only 76 candidates of the 42,638 running. Only nine women were elected. The women who ran for office were handicapped not so much by their lack of political experience as by the commonly held belief that politics is men's business and by the male electorate's lack of confidence in women seeking office.

During local elections in 1983, women won 43 of the 13,358 seats. The Socialist Union of Popular Forces had the highest number of women elected in these communal and municipal elections. In the legislative elections of 1984, 16 candidates were women out of a total of 1,366.[7] Again, no woman was elected to the Parliament, and to date there are no women members of the government. Almost all parties nominate women candidates, but the number presented by the political parties derived from the independence movement (the Istiqlal Party, the USFP, and the PPS) is higher than the number nominated by the progovernment parties (such as the National Assembly of Independents and the Constitutional Union).[8]

The major sources for positions of power remain the monarchy and the political parties—particularly those making up the parliamentary majority.[9] The positions of the National Assembly of Independents and the Constitutional Union constitute the official policy toward women. They are attempting to promote various changes for women, including reforms in labor legislation, a review of women's personal status, and the realization of economic independence for women. The law about family, marriage, divorce, and inheritance is embodied in the Code of Personal Status, passed in 1958, which openly differentiates between men's and women's rights. This code states the dependency of women on men within the family. For example, a husband may forbid his wife to work unless she specifies otherwise in her marriage contract. He may have up to four wives, and he has the right to make decisions regarding residence and children. Moreover, inheritance laws favor male over female heirs, thus limiting women's assets.[10]

The code represents a major constraint to increasing women's participation in development. By emphasizing policy reforms these political parties associate changes in women's conditions with social ascension and the emergence of female elites. The intellectual elites behind these policies, including women, are far removed from the experiences of the majority of Moroccan women, who are more concerned with survival and who struggle to gain a small amount of power in a society dominated by men. Nevertheless, some women activists within these two parties seem convinced that the policies represent women and will promote real changes in women's conditions.

A more aggressive approach to changing women's conditions calls for radical transformation of the political and social structures. This thesis of progressive change is supported by two leftist parties—the Socialist Union of Popular Forces and the Party of Progress and Socialism—which, as minority parties in Parliament, have little influence on official policies. The Socialist Union of Popular Forces has been consistently supportive of improving women's status. It considers women's struggle for a better life as important as men's. Apparently, the government also viewed women as equal partners in this struggle, for when the party was repressed in the 1960s, both male and female party members were affected. The Socialist Union of Popular Forces believes that women's liberation will follow as political and economic structures become more democratic.[11] Because current structures exploit men as well as women, the role of women in the process of change is seen as very important.[12] The Party of Progress and Socialism considers the participation of women essential to achieving real change and is concerned primarily with the situation of women workers.[13]

The heterogeneity of the leaders of Morocco's political parties seriously limits the organizations' ability to implement their progressive intentions. Their contributions and desire for change are also limited by their narrow regional appeal and particularly by the low proportion of women within the parties.[14] Like other efforts to change women's status in Morocco, the parties' elite-driven approach has thus been unable to overcome the numerous obstacles to creating a policy that would effectively change women's position.

EDUCATION

Modern educational policy provides an excellent example of an elite-directed strategy whose successes have been tempered by enduring and widespread sexual discrimination. Conservative social customs maintain that a woman's value depends solely on the number of children she has instead of on her contribution to income-generating activities. This belief may explain the persistence of discrimination within the society and the low level of women's participation in education, employment, and activities outside the household. Within the family the husband has authority over all aspects of the household, including the allocation of income and the education of children. And to a large extent the majority of ordinary, nonelite women passively endure their situation of subordination.

Because political leaders and other Moroccan elites see it as vital for economic development, education has been a priority of the government for several decades. Prior to French colonization, education in Morocco consisted largely of apprenticeship in various guilds and enrollment in traditional or Quranic schools, which emphasized religious education but did not necessarily teach the skills necessary to ensure national development and rarely taught women or girls. Before the arrival of the French, it is estimated that of a population of 4 million, about 150,000 students were enrolled in Quranic schools and 2,500 at higher levels, including the prestigious Quaraouine University in Fez, the oldest university in the world, founded in 857 A.D.[15]

The modern educational system, established during the colonial period, was designed to serve children of the large European community and only a small number of Moroccans. French education policies toward the Moroccan population, though complicated, had a long-term goal: the creation of artificial opposition between Arabs and Berbers.[16] French authorities attempted to popularize the false idea that Berbers were less attached to Islam and refused to acknowledge the authority of the monarchy. In the early years the French set up French-Berber schools in which the Arab language, as well as any reference to Islam, was outlawed.

Thus, throughout the first half of the twentieth century access to education continued to be limited for most Moroccans, particularly females. On the eve of independence girls represented only 10 percent of the student population at all levels of instruction. In 1960 the rate of illiteracy was 87 percent (96 percent for women and 78 percent for men), reflecting the lack of French interest in educating the Moroccan population.[17]

Following independence in 1956, universal education became one of the main demands of the nationalist movement. Initially, volunteer groups spontaneously launched literacy campaigns throughout the country. During the first year of independence, the proportion of children enrolled in school swelled to 18.7 percent, five times the proportion of the previous year. Realizing that modern education was fundamental to economic development, the government soon took over the project, making it a top priority. As a result, education has had a privileged position in every development plan; modern political leaders now perceive it as both a right and a necessity. Illustratively, King Hassan II issued a royal decree in 1963 making education compulsory for all children under the age of 14.

This perspective is reflected in the four principles of the national educational strategy: universal opportunity (to create a tuition-free system open to all students), unification of the system (to simplify the multiple, complex school systems left by the French), Arabization (to replace French with Arabic as the language of instruction), and Moroccanization (to develop a corps of indigenous instructors to replace European expatriates). The Ministry of Education shares responsibility for implementing the educational objectives with other governmental organizations, including two ministries that coordinate special programs for women. The Ministry of Handicrafts and Social Affairs serves approximately 50,000 illiterate and semiliterate women between the ages of ten and eighteen, offering them education and employment through 400 centers. The Ministry of Youth and Sports coordinates preschools, women's centers, and a promotion sector, which carries out public awareness campaigns on health, family planning, and education of girls in the countryside.

The remarkable improvement in educational opportunities for women since independence is illustrated by the increased rate of literacy for urban females, which climbed from 4 percent in 1960 to 42.4 percent in the mid-1980s.[18] Also significant is the rise in school enrollment for girls aged seven to eleven, which leapt from 35 percent in 1965 to 62 percent in 1986.[19] Yet in spite of the implementation of goals, policies, and structures by a government elite, widespread sex discrimination within the household continues to keep girls from attending public schools.[20] This is true particularly in rural areas, where boys are four times more likely to have access to education than are girls.[21] The stark differences in accessibility are illustrated by differences between the rates of primary school enrollment for seven-year-old girls in the countryside (34 percent) and for their rural male counterparts (69 percent) and urban female counterparts (85 percent).[22]

In poor rural areas, families might decide that the costs of educating a daughter will be ill rewarded in that school attendance will not only decrease the child's help within the household (which girls are expected to begin at a much earlier age than are boys) but will also bring the family little gain in the long term (because girls typically leave home to marry at a young age). In addition, because Moroccans often equate the honor of a family with the behavior of its women, parents in rural areas may be reluctant to send their daughters to distant schools, which have predominantly male teachers. The decision to send a daughter to school is the father's prerogative and in urban areas is most often based on economics. In rural areas, conservative social pressures may deter parents from sending their daughters to school. Evidently, the expense of school supplies, the considerable distance from home to school, the low quality of instruction, and the lack of opportunities for educated women all influence the low levels of female enrollment in rural areas.

Although education is compulsory, enforcement by the authorities is minimal. More than that, some rural areas do not even have a sufficient number of schools. A study done in 1979 reported that the inhabitants of several villages built schools but the schools were never used because the Ministry of Education did not supply teachers.[23]

In spite of such obstacles, the educational status of women has improved remarkably since independence, especially in rural areas, where previously almost the entire population was illiterate. Female enrollment in primary schools, however, is still very low. In the school year 1987–88 the rate of female enrollment was 57 percent (of all women in the same age-group).[24] Because most traditional Muslim restrictions on female mobility begin at puberty, enrollment at the secondary level is in some ways a better indicator of changing educational opportunities for young women. The rate of females enrolled at that level is 27 percent of those eligible, compared with 39 percent of eligible males.[25] Only 9 percent of all students who enter elementary school will ever reach the university level. At the university level, however, women represent about 34 percent of the enrollment. These data would indicate that males and females have a more balanced access to advanced education than to primary schooling, although the high percentage of women can be further explained by the lower rate of female dropouts at higher levels. Government education policies of the 1970s and 1980s have also contributed to growing enrollments for both sexes at secondary and postsecondary levels by enabling the Ministry of Education to shift financial resources from primary education to secondary and higher education.

Even with these limited successes, the government has recently recognized a crisis in the educational system, as reflected by the stagnation in enrollment rates (in spite of rapidly increasing numbers of children eligible for school attendance) and by the discovery of severe inefficiencies in the educational system.[26] This failure is due in part to the inequitable distribution of public resources between rural and urban areas, between boys and girls, between rich and poor, thereby resulting in unequal educational opportunities for children. For example, although the poor constitute three-quarters of the population, they receive only 29.8 percent of public outlays for education. Both the middle class, which makes up 18.5 percent of the population, and the upper class, which represents about 6 percent of the population, receive disproportionate shares of expenditures (43 percent and 27.2 percent, respectively).[27] Similarly, although males constitute half the population, they received 72.8 percent of the state's educational expenditures in 1982.[28] Regardless of the official emphasis on increasingly universal and democratic education, strong inequalities still exist. Discrimination particularly affects impoverished, rural, and female children.

Unequal educational prospects have a direct impact on women's lives, as well as on national development. Education not only widens employment opportunities for women; it also creates greater possibilities for women in other ways. An educated woman is also likely to influence the future attitudes of her children—particularly her daughters—in the areas of education, employment, and family planning.

FAMILY PLANNING AND WOMEN'S HEALTH

Moroccan women face many disadvantages related to healthcare, particularly reproductive care. Poor rural women are subject to high fertility rates, inadequate prenatal care, deficient nutrition, and closely spaced pregnancies. A Moroccan woman now bears an average of 4.8 children, a number higher than the averages in Tunisia or Turkey (two other Muslim countries with low to middle incomes), though considerably lower than the 7.2 children borne by a Moroccan woman 25 years ago.[29] Even today only a quarter of all pregnant women receive prenatal care, and the maternal mortality rate is about 0.4 percent.[30] Some reports also estimate that half of all women between the ages of 15 and 49 are undernourished, a fact that affects the health of both women and their offspring.[31]

Although women's high rates of mortality and morbidity during their childbearing years are related to all of the factors mentioned so far, public policy has primarily addressed only one facet of the health problems of women: the high birthrate. Just as the government made education policy a priority, in part to facilitate economic growth, so too did it promote family planning as a means of bringing about greater economic development. By 1964 the swelling population was exerting such tremendous pressure on national resources that the elites became convinced that it was hampering economic development. Taking into account reports by the World Bank and other organizations, Moroccan leaders formulated policies to reduce fertility and consequently the gap between economic growth and population growth.[32]

Family-planning activities could have played a role in increasing the health of both women and children, but economic considerations rather than women's needs were once again the driving force in the construction of this policy issue. This fact, along with objections raised by other segments of the population, limited the effectiveness of this elite-initiated policy.

The government's first family-planning policy, which was introduced in 1966, addressed fertility solely as a development issue, failing even to mention women's health needs. Later, however, the government was forced to adapt the policy to include some mother-child activities in order to lessen the resistance of target groups (in this case, women in their childbearing years) and of public and political powers. Opponents and supporters of the birth control policy were found in both the public and private sectors. This issue elicited a great deal of negotiation between official and unofficial leaders.

Traditional political parties, especially the Istiqlal Party, the most powerful and influential party of that time, were strongly against the proposed policy of limiting births. Some Istiqlal members perceived the policy as immoral in the sense that it conflicted with prevailing social, cultural, and religious values.[33] For most Muslims a child is a gift from God and as such is always welcomed. There is a religious belief that each child will generate his or her own prosperity and that believers must comply with the will of God. The hostility and anger of Muslim political leaders were communicated to the public through the mass media and reinforced by other elite groups and religious scholars. They argued that the policy was alien to Moroccan culture and defined family-planning objectives ambiguously.

Midwives, poorly educated and guided by self-interest, also opposed birth control and spread negative images of modern contraceptive methods. Problems in promoting the government's policy were especially frequent in rural areas, where the illiteracy rate among women was believed to be 95 percent in 1960 and misconceptions about contraceptives were not only shared but spread by service providers.[34] Nurses from the Ministry of Public Health and others working in clinics were convinced that family-planning methods might have hazardous effects on women's health. Lack of training and psychological preparation may explain their negative attitudes.

Meanwhile the government used a variety of means to make the public aware of the policy's importance, including an intense campaign through television, radio, newspapers, lectures, and the like. This campaign seems to have swayed some members of the public, because their subsequent behavior indicates that they came to favor and practice family planning. More and more parents became aware of the benefits, not only for the welfare of the family but also for the mother, whose health might be damaged by successive and close pregnancies. Efforts to promote and implement the plan were supported by such progovernment organizations as the Moroccan League of Children's Protection and the Moroccan Family Planning Association. Additional reinforcement came from some liberal religious scholars, who gained public attention by supporting the policy at a seminar of Moroccan and international religious scholars in 1970.[35] These religious leaders encouraged the public to differentiate between social norms or beliefs and Islamic religious teachings, stressing that the latter did not forbid taking preventive measures.

Clarification of the religious issue has contributed significantly to the use of contraceptives today. Efforts by the Ministry of Public Health, which has been assigned to implement the policy, have also helped spread the word. Family-planning activities are integrated into health services already being carried out all over the country by medical and paramedical public health workers. Rural areas are served by outreach programs of public health nurses, who provide family planning as well as other health services for women and children on a house-to-house basis, with backup provided by clinics.[36] The Ministries of Youth and Social Affairs complement these public health efforts by incorporating information and communication programs into their centers' action plans, especially in urban areas where contraceptive information is widely available.

The private sector and some nongovernmental organizations have also contributed to the promotion of family-planning activities, but their intervention seems to be limited. The most important nongovernmental organization working in this area, the Moroccan Family Planning Association, has worked to promote awareness of the need for population control. The National Union of Moroccan Women, the Family Protection Association, and the League of Children's Protection contribute to the spread of positive information about contraceptives through their respective centers. The Ministry of Health has sponsored sales of contraceptives by the private sector in community-based outlets, kiosks, fairs, and markets, as well as in pharmacies.

Along with urbanization, the delay of marriage, and increases in the number of women working outside the home, family-planning efforts have yielded a negative impact on the birthrate. Nonetheless, examination of the plan's outcomes reveals that it has not been very successful. Profile demographics indicate that annual rates of population growth from 1982 to 1987 averaged 2.7 percent. Only 25 percent of women of childbearing age have visited a family planning center, and of these women only 36 percent practice contraception.[37]

Many social, cultural, and economic factors have contributed to the limited success of governmental family-planning efforts. The desire to have a large number of children is strong, especially in rural areas, for both economic and cultural reasons. In poor households, children's contributions to labor are essential to the survival of the family. For women, large numbers of children are a means of securing economic and decision-making power within the household. Although Morocco is one of the few countries in the region that do not restrict political rights on the basis of sex, the Code of Personal Status does differentiate between the rights of men and women in matters of marriage, family obligations, inheritance, and obedience. This law, which is reinforced by social customs, represents a major threat for Moroccan women, who must look to their children—particularly their sons— as their source of status, assurance, empowerment, and protection against repudiation (dissolution of the marriage solely by the will of the husband).[38]

In the matter of marriage, the legislature allows the husband to have up to four wives, whereas Islamic law allows polygamy only on the condition that the wives be loved and cared for equally.[39] The status of sterile women is very low compared with that of mothers with numerous male children. Customarily, for example, the mother of four or more children cannot be easily divorced, because in the eyes of civil and religious leaders, who oversee divorce proceedings, the children guarantee the woman a high level of security. In this light, women's refusal to limit their fertility is understandable as a deliberate strategy for securing their social and economic position; in Moroccan culture there are few other alternatives for achieving such security.

Women's reluctance to use contraceptives and their misuse of them is also related to education and women's status. Approximately 53 percent of Moroccan women with degrees from secondary schools or higher educational institutions use contraceptives, as compared to 46 percent of women with primary education and 25 percent of women with no education.[40] Considering that Moroccan women have one of the highest illiteracy rates in the world (78 percent in 1982, down from 96 percent in 1960), it hardly is surprising that relatively few women use contraceptives.

All these factors collectively represent the main constraints to the success of family-planning policy in Morocco. The government's efforts to increase primary healthcare—and particularly family-planning services—have not been sufficient either to improve the state of women's health or to decrease their rates of fertility. This policy weakness reflects the gulf that exists between the development goals of government elites and most women's need for security and status. Until the government can somehow influence the demand for children, especially as it pertains to cultural attitudes and women's status, family-planning efforts are unlikely to meet with much success. Although family planning seems to be one of the most important concerns of women and of the population as a whole, its promotion cannot be handled solely by political leaders. Success will require not only policy intervention in different areas, such as improving the living conditions of the poor by fighting malnutrition, ignorance, and poverty but also the provision of a role for women in the family-planning program. Allowing women to become part of the policy-making process would help remove constraints as well as provide support for the government in its efforts.

ECONOMIC PARTICIPATION

The involvement of women in the economy reflects and follows the gender-specific biases already limiting women's access to education, health, and other public services. Since independence, integration of women into the development process has been no more than a theoretical policy of the government. Although some efforts were made to grant women jobs, healthcare, and free formal education, several factors continue to limit their involvement in the economy, as well as their access to specific areas of the economy. The economic activity rate of women has improved over the past 30 years, registering 27 percent in 1986. Although this rate compares favorably with those of other countries in the Maghreb region of North Africa, it remains low in absolute terms and is about half of the corresponding rate for males. Moreover, rates of female economic activity remain particularly low in urban areas, reaching only 16 percent as against 36 percent in rural areas.[41]

The presence of urban and rural women alike is concentrated in informal activities and in a few spheres of work, all of which are marked by low wages. Most rural women work in agriculture, and young and educated women have especially limited opportunities. In 1986, 32 percent of women between the ages of fifteen and twenty-four and 41 percent of women holding baccalaureate degrees were unemployed, compared with only 16.2 percent of women with little education. At the same time, four of five female urban workers held jobs in one of the following economic sectors: textiles, personnel services, social services, or public administration.[42] The contribution of women in these sectors continues to increase primarily because the cost of female labor is cheap but also because some enterprises, as in the textile and leather industries, prefer women workers over men, because women are seen as hard-working, docile, nonunionized, and capable of delivering a higher quality of work.

In urban areas, where 47 percent of the population resides (about 100,000 persons migrate there each year), women's role in the economy is characterized by low participation rates, high unemployment, dense concentration in specific sectors, and low wages. These problems remain serious in spite of the strong improvement registered in the 1970s and 1980s resulting from government initiatives, as well as the inability of an increasing number of households to get by on only one salary. Women's gross economic participation rates in urban areas continue to be particularly low; in 1986 only 16 percent of urban women were economically active compared with 46 percent of urban males. Only in child labor statistics do females balance with males; half of the 800,000 children under the age of twelve who work in urban areas are girls.[43]

The rate of employment for urban females is underestimated by official employment figures, which do not take the so-called informal economy into consideration—a sector in which women's participation is relatively stronger. Women who are workers at home, family helpers, mistresses at public baths, or vendors of bread are included in the informal economy. Within the domestic services sector, composed mainly of rural women who have emigrated to the cities, working conditions are the least desirable. Salaries are usually below the minimum guaranteed interprofessional salary, work hours are long, and the job of maid is socially despised. Moreover, these employees do not benefit from any government, legal, or social protection.

Although the law prohibits discrimination between female and male wages for equal work, women's wages in both the informal and the formal sectors are on the average much lower than men's. The lower wages can be explained not in terms of lower productivity but in terms of the segregation of the labor market. Market sellers, carpenters, and transporters are likely to be men, whereas housekeepers and home-based pieceworkers are generally women, the demand for women workers being limited to a few areas of the economy and to more menial tasks. Moreover, strong all-male labor unions have never been interested in organizing female laborers. Conditions in professional jobs, such as public administration, follow similar gender biases. A professional woman's salary is an average of 15 percent lower than her male counterpart's.[44] This indicator reflects men's higher representation in the better paid and higher-level professions.

In rural areas women's activity rates are high and unemployment is low. Their labor is not, however, allocated through the labor market. In fact about 84 percent of it belongs in the category of nonwage labor. According to a recent study by the Ministry of Agriculture, a high proportion of rural women's work is devoted to fetching water and wood, producing goods for household consumption, and raising children and animals. Only men are directly involved in trading and marketing in the final stages of the production cycle.

Although rural women are involved not only in food production but also in its processing and distribution within the tribe or the family, the magnitude of their labor and the range of their activities have typically been either underestimated or ignored by government record keepers. From 1971 to 1986 rural employment growth rates were much higher for women than for men (13.9 percent versus 1.9 percent); and although the female economic activity rate was as high as 36 percent, much of it fell in the ambiguous category of family labor.[45] These increases may be explained to a great extent by the migration of men to urban areas and abroad (traditionally to the countries of the European Economic Community, mainly France and Belgium) and by the impoverishment of rural areas owing to the combined effects of lack of land, overpopulation, and low productivity. These conditions forced women to add other activities to their household responsibilities, such as temporarily heading households.

Male emigration has mixed effects on the lives of women left at home. Women may take a greater role in making decisions within the household and in managing the money remitted by their husbands. Yet their work load, especially in rural areas, may significantly increase because they may have to take on their husbands' duties. However, it is likely that women left at home are relatively better off, both because of higher European wages and the migration of men from poor areas, where incomes are very low already. Recent patterns of emigration, however, show that young women are migrating and living abroad with their husbands.

Thus, in spite of their numerical presence in the rural work force, women continue to be ignored or to be perceived by society as helpers, never as decision makers. A government survey of 1987 found that 4 percent of employed rural women were educated, 12 percent were classified as independent workers (mostly farmers), and 84 percent of the female labor force were categorized under "unaccounted-for family labor." Women's participation is irrelevant to the rural service sector but is very high in the rural indus-

trial sector, which employs 14 percent of all women who work.[46] Unemployment in rural areas tends to affect educated women in particular; those holding secondary school or baccalaureate diplomas have levels of unemployment over twice as high as those with little educational background.

The life of the working rural woman is rough. She typically works 12 hours a day, though 19-hour days are hardly unusual.[47] A comparison of male and female jobs reveals not only that women's work load is greater relative to men's but also that women's position is subordinate within the family as well. Men work three to four fewer hours a day than women, who must shoulder child-care and household responsibilities as well as their economic roles. Yet men make the most important decisions, such as how much land to devote to different crops, or how much of the agricultural output to market and which inputs to buy. They even handle the selling of handicrafts and other objects produced by women, such as carpets, wool clothes, and blankets, which are sold in the marketplace.

Ignorance, resignation, and passivity toward their social, cultural, and economic conditions constrain women and hinder their progress. In a recent field study of 71 households in the province of Essaouira (on the Atlantic coast of Morocco), women expressed an interest in participating in training activities, especially sewing and embroidering, but all feared their husbands' opposition.[48] Most also seemed to be unaware of the advantages of working within a group or a cooperative and did not wish to be part of such groups.

A large burden of family and household responsibilities, lack of formal and technical education, discrimination in the labor market, lack of access to credit, and discriminatory marketing practices all hinder women's participation in the economy. The removal of these impediments would improve both the welfare of women and the efficiency of the economy. Not all government efforts to remove these impediments have worked, however. Labor laws are still characterized by forms of legal discrimination against women under the guise of protective legislation. Article 6 of the commercial code, for example, stipulates that "women may not be public merchants without the consent of their husbands, regardless of the provision of the Code of Personal Status."[49] Similarly, although government ministries provide vocational training to both sexes, women constitute only 35 percent of all trainees because their lower educational level puts them at a disadvantage.[50]

Certain women—for example, those engaged in the political arena as members of political parties, labor unions, and women's associations and those simply concerned by the precarious situation of women—are aware of the need to improve the employment status of all women. Many feel that the status and submission of poor women prevent them from enjoying the freedom they are entitled to as human beings and constrain their access to social facilities and recreational activities. Such concerns have been and continue to be the priority of many women's organizations in Morocco. Seminars, conferences, and colloquiums have been organized by women's professional organizations and associations to sensitize Moroccan women, their government, and international audiences to women's plight. In the 1980s certain leftist parties, such as the Socialist Union for Popular Forces and the Party of Progress and Socialism, have also designed activities in their respective political programs to promote the economic role of women.

PROSPECTS

Government policies to promote education, family planning, and women's economic participation have not been fully implemented. Women's literacy rate is still only 22 percent, which is low even by global standards. The fertility rates of Moroccan women are an important indicator of their poor physical health and social dependency. Their participation in economic and political activities is limited to the lowest professional positions. Inefficient government attempts to implement public policies also relate to the difficulty of organizing women to voice their

interests in particular issues. Women in Morocco do not constitute a homogeneous group; the diversity of their needs and interests hinders the definition of appropriate actions to encourage their participation in national politics. Rural women are powerless; their main objective is to meet their basic needs and those of their families. Although educated women and the elites look for power and prestige within the society, we believe that the success of any action requires that all women recognize the importance of self-help, especially among poorer women.

Our evaluation of women's current situation leads us to offer a number of suggestions. First, the Code of Personal Status must be reformulated to guarantee social, political, and economic equality to women. Second, all regulations preventing women's access to specific jobs should be removed, and regulations on labor safety should be divorced from gender considerations. Child care as well as healthcare for the old and infirm should be more widely available so that women can turn their attention to the labor market. Furthermore, vocational and training programs should focus not only on educating illiterate women but also on involving them in decision making. Women's voices and needs should be heard at both the community level—within the cooperative, tribe, and village—and at higher levels.

In addition, the government should actively create employment opportunities for female workers, especially educated women. Women must be allowed to become involved in making choices to promote economic growth. The government must integrate women into the national development process and recognize women's economic contributions. It should also make executive administrative appointments on the basis of expertise and experience, not gender. Currently, women do not have access to high public office because only men are appointed, and they by royal decree.

The creation of several women's organizations with specific roles may contribute to a better definition of the needs of various kinds of women. Given the economic and social conditions of Morocco and the persistence of traditional attitudes toward the emancipation of women, the success of implementing egalitarian policies requires that more women and men participate in the decision-making process. The women of Morocco deserve a better level of representation and commitment.

NOTES

1. Until 1972 the name of the Socialist Union of Popular Forces was the National Union of Popular Forces.

2. Fatima Mernissi, Aicha Belarbi, Rahma Bourkia, Zohra Mezgueldi, Mohammed Alayane, Fatima Oulad Hammouchou, and Fatima Zohra Zryouil, *Femmes et pouvoirs* (Women and power) (Casablanca: Editions le Fennec, 1990), 69.

3. For more detailed information on this period see Fatima Mernissi et al., "La Jariya et le Khalife," in Mernissi, *Femmes et pouvoirs.*

4. For more information on this coalition see A. Moulay Rchid, *La condition de la femme au Maroc* (The condition of women in Morocco) (Rabat: Editions de la Faculté des Sciences Juridiques, Economiques et Sociales, 1986), 19.

5. Fatima Mernissi, *Beyond the Veil: Male-Female Dynamics in Modern Muslim Society* (Bloomington: Indiana University Press, 1987), 65.

6. Melilla and Ceuta, two cities on the northern coast, are under Spanish authority. In 1986 the Spanish government enacted a law that calls for the expulsion, without appeal, of any noncitizen in these territories who does not have a work permit. About 100,000 Moroccans were threatened by the enacting of this law. Although most Moroccans living in the two cities were born there, they are not Spanish citizens.

7. The figures on women's political participation are from A. Moulay Rchid, *La femme et la loi au Maroc* (Women and the law in Morocco) (Casablanca: Editions le Fennec, 1991), 98.

8. Rquia El Mossadek, *La femme et la politique* (Women and politics) (Casablanca: Dar Toubkal of Publications, 1987), 29–43.

9. The Istiqlal Party was the first party in Morocco to work actively for changes in women's conditions. It not only created a commission on women's rights, mothers, and children in 1955 but has consistently had the highest number of women among its leaders. At the last national party meeting in 1982, eight women served on the 80-member Central Committee. The party also presented several candidates in the 1977 legislature and at lower-level elections in 1976.

10. A daughter inherits half the share that a son does.

11. The party's commission on women has suggested several changes. In 1975 it proposed a literacy campaign at the national level, improvement of women's status in the labor market, and the creation and extension of vocational training centers. More recently, the party has asked for constitutional reforms, respect for human rights, and the creation of a high council of women. The task of such a council would be to improve women's economic, legal, social, and cultural conditions and to fight any kind of discrimination against women.

12. From time to time the party organizes seminars or roundtables devoted to the analysis of the situation of Moroccan women. However, there are no women in the Political Bureau of the party.

13. Three women are on the Central Committee of the Party of Progress and Socialism, and one woman has been nominated to the Political Bureau.

14. The parties communicate through newspapers, labor unions, and conferences (at the city or district level); regional or national leaders reinforce such efforts. Also important are meetings celebrating special events, such as the death of leaders who have been martyrs in the struggle for democracy.

15. André Adam, *Casablanca: Essai sur la transformation de la société marocaine au contact de l'occident* (Casablanca: Essay on the transformation of Moroccan society upon contact with the West) (Aix-en-Provence: Centre National de la Recherche Scientifique [CNRSS], 1968), 122.

16. In addition to setting up European schools and Jewish schools, the French established Islamic, French-Berber, and French-Islamic schools, as well as schools for the children of the Moroccan elite.

17. Ministère du Plan, *National Census of the Population of Morocco, 1971* (Rabat).

18. Ministère du Plan, Direction de la Statistique, *Femmes et condition féminine au Maroc* (Rabat: Centre de Recherche et d'Etudes Demographiques [CERED], 1989), 56.

19. Ibid., 87.

20. Brief mention must be made of the private school sector. Although it represents only 4 percent of students in the primary and secondary levels, the enrollment rate of girls is significantly higher than in public schools (44.3 percent versus 36.4 percent). Because the private schools students come almost exclusively from the upper classes, they are not likely to face the same economic constraints that would force some families to sacrifice one child's education to guarantee that of another. For more information on the backgrounds of private school students, see Jamil Salmi, *Crise de l'enseignement et reproduction sociale au Maroc* (Crisis in education and social reproduction in

Morocco) (Casablanca: Editions Maghrebines, 1985), 110.

21. Mernissi, *Beyond the Veil*, 45.

22. Ministère du Plan, *Femmes et condition de la femme au Maroc*, 46.

23. Mohammed Behri, "Un primaire encore à généraliser" (A primary schooling yet to be generalized), *El Maghrib*, 9 October 1979.

24. Ministère du Plan, Direction de la Statistique, *Annuaire statistique du Maroc, 1990* (Statistical yearbook of Morocco, 1990) (Rabat), 234.

25. Ibid.

26. In 1980 the king of Morocco convened a conference to seek alternatives for dealing with the crisis and to propose long-term solutions.

27. Salmi, *Crise de l'enseignement et reproduction sociale au Maroc*, 91.

28. Ibid., 93.

29. *World Development Report, 1989* (Washington, D.C.: World Bank, 1989), 288.

30. Ibid.

31. Ministry of Public Health survey related to nutrition (Rabat, 1982). Children also suffer from vastly inadequate medical attention: only 25 percent of children are attended by trained medical personnel, and infant mortality is estimated at 73 percent nationwide, although this rate varies significantly between urban and rural areas. *World Development Report, 1989, 294.*

32. On 21 January 1964, during the opening of the National Commission of Planning, King Hassan II made an official statement recognizing a crisis in the Moroccan economy and the gap between production, which was increasing at the rate of 1.6 percent, and population, which was growing at the rate of 3 percent.

33. The Istiqlal Party is the oldest political party in Morocco. Because of its major role in the fight for Moroccan independence and its well-known leader, 'Allal al Fassi, a famous Moroccan scholar and militant, the party became very influential and powerful at the time of liberation.

34. Aicha Afifi, "Application du marketing social à la planification familiale au Maroc" (Application of social marketing to family planning in Morocco) (Diss., Institut Superior du Commerce et d'Administration des Enterprises, Casablanca, 1986).

35. Ibid., 89.

36. This program was called Visite à Domicile de Motivation Systematique (Systematic motivational domestic visits). The services include oral hydration therapy, nutritional surveillance, breast-feeding promotion, immunization referrals, weaning information, and food and iron supplements. *World Population: Facts and Focus* (Washington, D.C.: Population Reference Bureau, 1988), 34.

37. Afifi, "Application du marketing social," 98.

38. Unlike divorce initiated through the court, which is permitted by Moroccan law (with some restrictions), no motive is required of a husband who repudiates his wife. Repudiation is an important cause of instability in marriages.

39. Article 418 of the penal code stipulates that "murder, injuries and blows are excusable if committed by a husband against his wife as well as her accomplice when he catches them in flagrante delicto."

40. Ministère du Plan, *Femmes et condition féminine au Maroc*, 75.

41. Ministry of Agriculture and Agrarian Reform, "Enquête sur la population active en milieu urbain, 1984–86" (Urban employment survey, 1984–86) and "Enquête sur la population active en milieu rural, 1986–87" (Rural employment survey, 1986–87) (Rabat: Ministry of Agriculture and Agrarian Reform, n.d.).

42. Ministère du Plan, *Femmes et condition féminine au Maroc*, 102, 104.

43. Ministry of Youth and Sports, "The Role of Women in Development" (Rabat, 1988, manuscript).

44. Ministère du Plan, *Femmes et condition de la femme au Maroc*, 111.

45. Ministry of Agriculture and Agrarian Reform, "Enquête sur la population active en milieu urbain" and "Enquête sur la population active en milieu rural."

46. These figures are drawn from a 1987 survey of about 1,500 rural households, which was directed by the Ministry of Agriculture and Agrarian Reform in 1988.

47. Ibid.

48. This survey was carried out by M. Salahidine as part of a regional study: see "Women Economically Active in the Informal Sector of the Economy," in *Europe, Middle East, and North Africa (EMENA) Report, January 1990* (Washington, D.C.: World Bank, 1990).

49. Rchid, *La femme et la loi au Maroc*, 55.

50. Ministry of Agriculture and Agrarian Reform, "Enquête sur la population active en milieu rural."

▲ Nepal

POLITICS

Type of Political System: democracy

  Sovereignty: constitutional monarchy

  Executive-Legislative System: parliamentary

Type of State: unitary

Type of Party System: multiparty

Major Political Parties[a]

Nepali Congress (NC): Founded in 1947; worked for the abolition of the *panchayat* system. In the mid-1980s engaged in a civil disobedience movement for the release of political prisoners and the legalization of political parties. Formed a successful coalition government in 1991 and won a majority of seats in the legislature.

United Nepal Communist Party (UNCP): Formed in 1991 from the merger of two smaller communist parties. Man Mohan Adhikari is the parliamentary leader of the party and the leader of the opposition.

Communist Party of Nepal/pro-Moscow (CPN/M): Established in the early 1960s as a result of the Sino-Soviet dispute. In recent years has experienced severe factionalism.

Communist Party of Nepal-Maoist (CPN-Maoist): A pro-Chinese group that supports China's discredited Gang of Four.

Nepal Mazdoor Kissan Party (Nepal Workers' and Peasants' Party, or NWPP): The only pro-Beijing communist group.

National Democratic Party (NDP): Supports the panchayat system.

Janabadi Morcha (Peoples' Front): A revolutionary, antimonarchist organization; permitted to participate in the 1991 elections even though several of its leaders had been sentenced to death in absentia for a series of bomb attacks.

Year Women Granted Right to Vote: 1951

Year Women Granted Right to Stand for Election: 1951

Percentage of Women in the Legislature:

  Lower House: 3.4%

  Upper House: 5.0%

Percentage of Electorate Voting for Highest Elected Office in Most Recent Election (1991): 65.0%[b]

DEMOGRAPHICS

Population: 18,462,081[c]

Percentage of Population in Urban Areas[d]

  Overall: 17.6%

  Female: 16.7%

  Male: 18.4%

Percentage of Population Below Age 15: 42.3%[e]

Birthrate (per 1,000 population): 38[f]

Maternal Mortality Rate (per 100,000 live births): 850[g]

Infant Mortality Rate (per 1,000 live births): 123[h]

Mortality Rate for Children Under Five (per 1,000 live births): 189[i]

Average Household Size: 5.6[j]

Mean Age at First Marriage[k]

  Female: 17.1

  Male: 21.8

Life Expectancy

  Female: 51.0

  Male: 53.0

EDUCATION

Ratio of Female to Male Enrollment (1980/1984)

  First-Level Education: 58

  Second-Level Education: 42

  Third-Level Education: 25

Literacy Rate (six years old and older)

  Female: 24.9%

  Male: 55.1%

ECONOMY

Gross National Product per Capita: U.S. $170[l]

Percentage of Labor Force in Agriculture: 80.1%[m]

Distribution of Agricultural Workers by Sex[n]
  Female: 44.8%
  Male: 55.2%
Economically Active Population by Sex[o]
  Female: 45.2%
  Male: 68.0%

a. Arthur S. Banks, ed., *Political Handbook of the World, 1991* (Binghamton, N.Y.: CSA Publications, 1991), 476–77.

b. *International Forum,* vol. 51, Nepal, 1991.

c. *Population Census of Nepal, 1991,* vol. 1: *Advance Tables* (Kathmandu: His Majesty's Government/Nepal, National Planning Commission, Central Bureau of Statistics, 1992).

d. Ibid.

e. Ibid.

f. *Human Development Report* (New York: U.N. Development Program, 1992).

g. Ibid.

h. Ibid.

i. Ibid.

j. *Population Census of Nepal, 1991.*

k. *Population Monograph of Nepal* (Kathmandu: His Majesty's Government/Nepal, National Planning Commission, Central Bureau of Statistics, 1992).

l. *World Development Report* (Washington, D.C.: World Bank, 1992).

m. *Population Census of Nepal, 1991.*

n. *Population Census of Nepal, 1981,* vol. 1, part 1 (Kathmandu: His Majesty's Government/Nepal, National Planning Commission, Central Bureau of Statistics, 1984).

o. *Population Census of Nepal, 1991.*

Political Participation of Women in Nepal

MEENA ACHARYA

Nepal is a small landlocked state sandwiched between India and China. Its population of 18 million is predominantly rural. Since its unification 200 years ago Nepal has been a monarchy, though the king's power has varied considerably. For a little over 100 years the king was merely a figurehead, for Nepal was ruled by a succession of oppressive oligarchies of the Rana family. Since 1951, when the last of these hereditary prime ministers was overthrown, Nepal has ostensibly been a constitutional monarchy. In practice, however, from 1960, when the king banned all political parties and introduced the partyless *panchayat* system, until April 1990, when democracy was restored, state powers were increasingly concentrated in the king. In place of political parties, corporatist organizations, representing the interests of women, youth, peasants, laborers, and military veterans, served to counteract potential opposition to the king and the panchayat system. Roughly parallel but with less power than the king were the official cabinet and the Rashtrya Panchayat (National Parliament), a 140-member

unicameral legislature. One hundred twelve of the members were elected at large by the people, with the other 28 chosen by the king. The regional and local governments consisted of popularly elected district panchayats and village or town panchayats.

At the national, regional, and local levels the panchayat government was paralleled by the corporatist organizations. They wielded considerable power in weeding out nonconformist elements throughout the panchayat period, but the precise mechanism of their control varied from time to time. At the final stages of the panchayat system a candidate who wanted election to any of the panchayat bodies had first to join one of these organizations. In addition, there were zonal commissioners who derived their power constitutionally from the king and who served as the crown's liaison to the local panchayats and to the local government administrative bodies. Each candidacy had to be cleared informally with them as well.

This dual power structure enforced a system of

repressive laws restricting all political and social activities not approved by the authorities. The Law on Maintenance of Peace and Security (1989) empowered local administrations to detain and jail people for unlimited periods without filing charges in court. Similarly, even social organizations could not exist without registering with the government and the Social Services National Coordination Council, which was presided over by the queen. A social organization could register only with extreme difficulty unless it was patronized by a member of the royal family. Besides registering, all nongovernmental organizations had to have their programs of action and their budgets approved by the council.

Nepal, whose economy is based primarily on subsistence farming, has a gross national product per capita of U.S. $170. More than 40 percent of the population have an income far less than what is required to meet their basic needs of food, shelter, primary education, and healthcare. Life expectancies at birth—53 years for males and 51 years for females—are among the lowest in the world. Only 40 percent of the population over six years old are literate; female literacy is 25 percent. As a consequence, one of the main goals of the panchayat government, in addition to preserving the monarchy, was promoting economic development.[1]

In April 1990, Nepal's political system underwent a fundamental change brought about by a mass movement initiated by the Nepali Congress Party (a party of social democrats) and the United Left Front (made up of seven communist parties). The movement for democracy and the establishment of a constitutional monarchy started on 18 February 1990 and culminated with the king's 8 April abrogation of many provisions of the panchayat constitution. Subsequently a joint interim government of the Nepali Congress Party and the Left Front was formed, and all restrictions on political parties and fundamental rights were lifted. The position of zonal commissioner was also abolished. The interim cabinet had all the powers of the panchayat cabinet and the National Panchayat combined. Since then a new constitution incorporating funda-

mental rights and limiting the powers of the monarch has been promulgated. The country will now have a bicameral legislature, an executive cabinet responsible to the Parliament, and an independent judiciary. The king's powers have been limited to those of a constitutional head. In May 1991 elections to the lower house were completed. The Nepali Congress Party emerged as the majority party, winning 109 of the 205 seats and forming the government. The leftists together won 81 seats.

Nepali women's lives and the nature of their political engagement have thus been shaped by the objective conditions of underdevelopment, the repressive political system, and the government's formula for development. But a more fundamental factor determining the extent of their political engagement is the cultural environment.

THE CULTURAL MILIEU

In spite of its small size, the population of Nepal is heterogeneous, with more than 75 ethnic groups speaking roughly as many languages. On one level, Nepali women's experiences have been diverse, shaped by their many different unique cultures. At another level, most of the ethnic groups can be classified broadly as either Indo-Aryan or Tibeto-Burman, each with very different understandings of a woman's place inside and outside the home.

Two basic features of the Indo-Aryan culture are the patrilineal inheritance system and the concern over the purity of the female body, which result in severe limits on women's mobility and various forms of female seclusion. Although the social seclusion of women in Nepal has not taken the extreme forms of purdah or veiling, the ideal of virginity is cherished, and any activity that puts women in unconventional situations is suspect. Therefore Indo-Aryan women tend to limit their activities to inside the household. In the Tibeto-Burman groups, on the other hand, much less importance is attached to women's sexual purity, and women can move around freely. The Tibeto-Burman women's sphere of activities is not confined to the household, and their life experiences are not so dominated by the dichotomy of inside-outside or public-private spheres.[2]

Although the influence of the Tibeto-Burman culture on the Indo-Aryan communities is felt at many levels, it is the Indo-Aryan culture that dominates the cultural spectrum, political life, and state policies. In spite of the diversity in culture, then, Nepali women's formal political engagement has been shaped by the commonality of their oppression under the dominant Indo-Aryan culture.

The inheritance system in Nepal, as codified in the Mulki Ain (National Code of Nepal) of 1963, is patrilineal in character and derives from the Hindu system of beliefs emphasizing the need to keep family property within the agnatic group, which, in turn, is related to the need to have a son to continue the lineage and perform religious ceremonies after death.[3] Although the legal system is not explicitly based on any religious scriptures and departs fundamentally from the classical Hindu practice of totally excluding women from inheritance rights, it falls far short of granting equal property rights to women. The whole system of family laws that govern marriage, divorce, property rights, and inheritance reinforces the patriarchy and puts severe limits on women's command over economic resources.

According to the Mulki Ain, as amended in 1975, a woman shares equal rights of inheritance with her husband and, when he dies, with her sons. She is also an equal co-parsoner (one who may claim a share) in the ancestral property if her husband is not alive, provided that she is at least 30 years old or has been married for at least 15 years. She is entitled to equal inheritance rights with her brothers in her parental household only if she is unmarried and is at least 35 years of age at the time of the property partition. The property that she inherits is termed *ansa,* and her rights over ansa are conditional. The most important condition for exercising her right over the ansa that she receives in the husband's household is that she remain faithful to the husband even if he is dead. She forfeits all rights to this ansa upon marrying another person or upon being charged

with adultery. A woman may demand divorce from her husband under certain circumstances, but if she does, she may not claim a share in his property and after five years forgoes even this claim to maintenance. A woman inheriting property in her parental household must return it to her brothers or their direct male descendants if she later marries.

A woman has absolute rights only over *stridhan*—property that originates in the woman's own earnings or in gifts from her parental household, her husband, his household, or any other source. Her access to sources of income are, however, limited by the "family laws," customary laws according to which the husband has the right to decide the place of settlement, and a wife must have her husband's permission to work outside the home. Also, a woman can make legal contracts only in connection with her stridhan.

This system of inheritance puts girls at a disadvantage right from birth. The girl is a guest in her father's household because she will move to another household when she marries. She does not inherit property from her natal household, and she has no concomitant duties toward her parents and this agnatic group. In addition, she is an outsider in her husband's household because she comes from another household, and she has to prove her allegiance to the new agnatic group by giving birth to a son and remaining faithful to the group. These social conditions of existence shape all her aspirations and actions, including her political engagement.

To engage in politics a woman must have a secure economic base, which present laws deny her. Moreover, she can be disinherited by her affinal household on grounds of infidelity, imagined or real. Engagement in politics requires mobility, and mobility entails association with people of one's own sex and the opposite sex. Such association always provides potential grounds for charges of infidelity.

Concern over the purity of the female body in the subcontinental culture not only restricts female mobility but also enhances female seclusion.[4] In Hindu scriptures, virginity and abstinence from sex are highly prized. The highest form of Hindu marriage is *kanyadan,* which literally means "gift of a virgin." Parents who give their daughter in kanyadan gain special merit. A father who gives his daughter in kanyadan opens the path to heaven for himself. Thus, a daughter has to be kept a virgin to be given away. The most powerful goddesses evoked—in times of crisis and in times of stability as the regular family deity—are virgins.[5] Writing about South Asia in general, I have noted that this excessive social concern with purity of the female body

leads to a number of undesirable social practices, such as female seclusion and purdah, child marriages, and mob rapes of women during times of social upheaval. Mass rapes of women during the partition of British India, the Independence War of Bangladesh, or the often reported gang rapes of low caste women by higher caste men in Indian villages, may partly be explained in terms of this exclusive concern over purity of the female body in most South Asian communities. . . . In South Asia women are considered carriers of the family honor in general. Any violation of their bodies is the greatest violation of the family honor. Women thus become prime targets of mob violence.[6]

Apart from the general seclusion of women, this kind of social situation results in severe restrictions on the mobility of adolescent and young girls, even in elite and educated families that do not believe in female seclusion. Girls and young women who try to break the rules of seclusion are faced with the problem of male violence at the societal and individual levels. Young girls and women who move around unescorted are generally considered to be free with their sexual favors or of loose moral character and are subjected to all kinds of harassment, from "eve-teasing"—groups of young men stand on the streets making abusive comments about young women passing by and fondle them in buses and crowds—to murder and rape. Yet it is not the young men who are blamed for this kind of behavior but the girls, who are censured by society and their parents for being unescorted in public.

Unconventional women and girls also face threats of violence within the household. If un-

married girls choose to disobey older members of the household, they are threatened with being given away in marriage immediately. Most often these threats are carried out literally, and the girls are married off before they even realize what is happening to them. Wife beating is a socially accepted practice, too.

This situation, along with women's responsibility for household activities, excludes most middle-class girls and young women from participating in politics. In any case, girls have little opportunity to learn the art of politics while they are in schools and colleges, the places where most boys learn it. Girls and women can hardly expect to be escorted all the time in their political activities or to hire servants to carry out their domestic chores. Only women from rich and upper-middle-class households can afford to move around with escorts and in private vehicles and thus participate in public life. Even so, such activities are possible only if approved by the older men and women in the household. Because men are the heads of the households and generally more educated and more experienced in public life than women, only they can decide what their wives and daughters may do.

The chain of command from the male head of the household down to the youngest female member is, however, broken in the case of older women, particularly mothers and mothers-in-law. These older women have command over the household resources and freedom from household duties, as well as the right to tell their children what to do. When they belong to an elite family that is already in politics, they have even greater mobility because they move among people they already know. Unlike women at other stages of life and from different classes, they are also able to count on the support of the men in their families. As a result, some older women from prominent political families have been able to rise to positions of power.

Given the dominance of the Indo-Aryan culture and its emphasis on women's traditional role within the family, together with the atmosphere of repression and mass poverty, women's participation in the formal political process under the panchayat system and their access to positions of power were low. Lynn Bennett and I found that 5.1 percent of rural women had attended village panchayat meetings only occasionally. Another 3.5 percent attended these meetings once in a while. The rest (91.4 percent) had never gone to a meeting. Thirty-one percent had never voted, 53 percent had voted once or twice, and only 16 percent had voted regularly in the panchayat elections.[7]

In spite of their low participation in formal meetings and elections, 57 percent of the respondents knew the name of their local village panchayat, 82.6 percent knew the name of the *pradhan pancha* (village chief), and 65.1 percent were correct about the number of the ward in which they lived. But only 4.5 percent knew the name of the chief district officer, 2.5 percent the name of the district panchayat chief, and 0.8 percent the name of the prime minister.[8]

Not surprisingly, very few women reached positions of power in panchayat institutions.[9] Of the 140 members in the outgoing National Panchayat, eight (5.7 percent) were women: 109 men and 3 women were elected, and 23 men and 5 women were nominated by the king. Overall, 4.6 percent of the candidates in the last National Panchayat election were women. Only three (4.5 percent) of the female candidates won, whereas the success rate for male candidates was about 8 percent.

Women's participation in local bodies was also minimal. There were 75 district panchayat executive committees in the country with a total of 825 elected members, including chairs and vice-chairs. In 1986, in the last election to these committees, only five (0.6 percent) women were elected. None of the chairs and vice-chairs were women. Similarly, of the 188,564 village panchayat executive committee members, only 1,079 were women (0.57 percent). Among the candidates for these elections, only 0.51 percent were women. Of 4,012 elected village chiefs, 12 were women (0.3 percent). The comparable figure for the *upa-pradhan panchas* (deputy village chiefs) was 7 (0.17 percent). No woman was ever elected to the post of town panchayat chief, and

among 31 deputy chiefs there was only 1 woman (3.2 percent).

Women's access to positions of power in executive bodies and to the courts has also been limited. In the 25-member panchayat cabinet that was dissolved on 8 April 1990, there was 1 female minister, who held the health portfolio. None of the 23 secretarial posts at the top of the bureaucracy was held by a woman in late 1990; and according to a Women's Service Coordination Council study in 1986, very few of the 50,307 government officials were women.[10] Of 64 special class officers (the highest bureaucratic position), none was a woman. Three women were promoted to first-class positions during the last few years of the panchayat system, but under the direct order of the queen rather than on the basis of their work records.

WOMEN'S ORGANIZATIONS AND THE WOMEN'S MOVEMENT

Women in Nepal live in a patriarchal culture that in many ways is oppressive to them, both because Nepal had a repressive political system until April 1990 (except for a relatively liberal period between 1951 and 1960) and because Nepal is one of the least developed countries in the world, and a majority of its people must spend all their time eking out a living. As a consequence, women have been politically engaged mostly with more general issues, like establishing a democratic political order and human rights, eradicating such socially oppressive practices as child marriage, child widowhood, and female seclusion, and increasing women's access to employment, income, and modern channels of information. On these issues there is wide consensus among the elite, both men and women. It has therefore been possible to achieve mass action and some policy reforms on these issues.

The history of women's organizations and the women's movement in Nepal, like the political history of the country, can be divided into four parts: 1917–49, 1950–60, 1961–April 1990, and post–April 1990.[11]

In the early period women's organizations

were formed by the wives, mothers, and daughters of political leaders who were fighting against the Rana regime. Their main objective was to mobilize women against the despotic Rana rule. Sometime in 1917–18 a small group of women led by Dibya Koirala established Mahila Samiti (Women's Committee), formally a Gandhian institution organized with the explicit objective of teaching women cloth weaving. Dibya Koirala was the wife of K. P. Koirala and the mother of B. P. Koirala, both leaders in the democracy movement.[12] In 1947 another women's organization, Adarsha Mahila Sangh (Model Women's Organization), was formed in Jayanagar, a border town in India, with Revanta Kumari Acharya as chair. She is the wife of Tanka Prasad Acharya, who was then serving a life sentence for his anti-Rana political activities in the 1930s.[13] Adarsha Mahila Sangh's objectives were to raise the social and political consciousness of women and to mobilize them against the Rana regime. Its objectives that specifically related to women were to work for ending such social malpractices as child marriage. It established an office in Janakpur, a town in the central Terai, which was also used as a site for covert Nepali Congress Party activities; the party then operated from the other side of the Nepal-India border. In the meantime Nepal Mahila Sangh (Nepal Women's Organization) was established in Kathmandu; it was chaired by Mangala Devi, wife of Ganesh Man Singh, and included several other women—most, but not all, related to prominent male leaders.[14] Several of these women later became prominent political workers. The minister of industry and commerce in the interim cabinet formed in April 1990, Sahana Pradhan, was among its founding members. Besides organizing political agitation against the Ranas, this organization fought successfully for voting rights for women. Similarly, Nari Jagriti (Consciousness of Women), formed in Biratnagar, worked to improve girls' access to education.

In the 1950s and 1960s, after the Rana regime was overthrown, Nepal experimented with democracy, and numerous political parties became active. Many women who had been active in the

anti-Rana struggle under the umbrella of Nepal Mahila Sangh left it to establish or join new organizations. Nepal Mahila Sangh functioned in close collaboration with the Nepali Congress Party, and other women's organizations allied with other political parties were formed. Akhil Mahila Sanghathan (All Women's Organization) was established in 1950. The left-dominated Akhil Nepal Mahila Sangh (All Nepal Women's Association) was established in 1951. Women's Voluntary Services was formed in 1952, primarily as a social service group, with a royal family member as chair.

During 1950–55, although various women's organizations worked with allied political parties on political issues, they worked with each other on issues related to women. In 1951 the Advisory Assembly was formed to assist and advise the king and the cabinet on matters of state and administration. When no women were included among its 35 members, the Nepal Mahila Sangh and the All Nepal Women's Organization jointly sponsored nonviolent protest demonstrations. The composition of the assembly became controversial on other counts as well. In 1954 it was dissolved, and a second Advisory Assembly, with 113 members, was constituted. Four women, two each from Nepal Mahila Sangh and the All Nepal Women's Organization, were nominated as members.

By 1957–58, following cooperative endeavors among the political parties to establish democracy and institute elections to the first-ever Parliament, women's organizations had also united into a Samyukta–Nepali–Nari Samiti (United Nepali Women's Organization). Membership reached about 500, but the unity lasted only a year. As a result, despite women's efforts, only two women were elected to the Parliament in 1959.

In 1960, King Mahendra introduced the panchayat system and banned political parties and organizations. Another new organization, the Nepal Mahila Sangathan (All Nepal Women's Organization, or NWO), was formed as one of the corporatist organizations, deriving both its policy directives and resources from the government. Its major objectives were to work toward the fulfillment of the objectives set by the party-less panchayat system; to supervise, evaluate, and keep watch over the activities of officeholders to ensure their loyalty to the system; and to take action wherever necessary.[15] Thus, it was primarily a policing organization, intended to keep track of the women's movement, though it also conducted some social programs, such as adult literacy classes, income-generation projects, and legal services for women, and acted as a pressure group for bringing about important changes in the legal system.

The legal reforms initiated in the 1980s mostly concerned women's property rights and family laws. Already in the late 1960s, some women leaders both inside and outside the Panchayat Parliament had called for equal inheritance rights to parental properties—notably Kamal Rana, then president of NWO.[16] The idea was ridiculed, however, and the voices were subdued. When Nepal became a signatory to the U.N. Convention on the Elimination of All Forms of Discrimination Against Women in 1975, the government had to do something, and legal reforms were introduced on the explicit initiative of the queen. Subsequent reforms conferred a few more property rights on women. For example, before 1975 an unmarried daughter 35 or older was entitled to only half the share her brothers received upon their parents' death, even if she remained unmarried. Now an unmarried daughter receives a full share, although she can dispose of only half of the immovable property. Some other important improvements in divorce and other family-related laws have been made as well.[17]

A visible women's movement and women's institutions functioning openly under the panchayat system developed along two parallel lines—one within the political and semipolitical panchayat institutions and at various levels of panchayat government. Many women active in pre-1960 organizations joined NWO and became prominent leaders under the panchayat regime. The other, parallel group of activists, composed mainly of intellectuals, tried to influence government policies and programs through research

and lobbying. The concern expressed for gender equality by the United Nations and other multi-lateral and bilateral funding agencies after the International Women's Year of 1975, and the flow of funds for women-related activities therefrom, were instrumental in bringing this group of women to the fore.

Following the U.N. convention of 1975 and an increased flow of external funds for women into Nepal, the government set up the Women's Services Coordination Council in 1977. It was established to coordinate and thus implicitly control activities of various institutions concerning women in public and private sectors. The queen appointed all the officeholders in this council, which operated under her direction. Later, women's cells and divisions were created in several ministries to incorporate gender issues into the planning process and into sectoral programs. The council also encouraged programs directed specifically at women, run by various semi-governmental agencies and foreign nongovernmental organizations.

Notwithstanding its ostensible objectives of vigorously developing and expanding the services and efforts of organizations oriented toward women's welfare and of defending and advancing women's causes in a healthy, decorous, and disciplined manner, the activities of the Women's Services Coordination Council were primarily limited to glorifying the queen and the royal family and controlling the flow of funds from foreign nongovernmental organizations.[18] All social organizations related to women had to get the approval of the Women's Service Coordination Council on all financial matters, including income, expenditure patterns, and government and external funds received. Since April 1990, however, the queen has stopped guiding the council, and its future role is not yet clear.

The Women's Development Division in the Ministry of Labor and Social Welfare was established in 1987 chiefly to serve as a national platform for issues on women and development in the South Asian Association for Regional Cooperation. Women's cells have also been established in the Ministries of Agriculture and Education.

The Ministry of Local Development (formerly the Ministry of Local Development and Panchayat) has a full-fledged Women's Development Division. It is mainly responsible for running a community development and credit program for women called the Production Credit for Rural Women program.[19]

In the meantime, gender-specific institutions and activities have been developed in the private sector. A Business and Professional Women's Club was registered in 1975 with the objective of promoting working women's interests.[20] A few women's research and action groups, such as the Centre for Women and Development, were established; and existing research and action groups, such as the Family Planning Association of Nepal, Integrated Development Systems, and New ERA started paying more attention to gender-specific issues and incorporating women's concerns into their research activities.

All these efforts directed at institution building, however, came from the top and were not able to reach the grass-roots level. At the time of the field studies reported in *The Status of Women in Nepal* (1978), only 6.8 percent of the rural women interviewed knew about the existence of the All Nepal Women's Organization, despite its pretensions of being a countrywide network of women's groups. Similarly, only 2.5 percent were aware of the existence of the Women's Services Coordination Council.[21] The activities of the Business and Professional Women's Club so far have been confined to running one or two child-care centers in the industrial areas and organizing seminars on women's issues from time to time.

POLICY AND PROGRAM INTERVENTIONS

In the mid-1970s, chiefly because of research findings underlining the crucial role of women in Nepal's economy and the consequent pressures from international aid agencies to include women in the development activities that they funded, the government initiated specific policies, projects, and programs for promoting women's equal participation in economic development, along with some legal reforms. Until the beginning of the U.N. Decade on Women, however, no specific efforts had been made to involve women in direct income-generating or productive projects. Newly initiated programs, like Mother and Child Care, and some components of family planning programs were targeted at women with the objective of improving women's general acceptance of these programs. The importance of female education was realized early in the planning process, but no specific programs were designed to induce families to send girls to school. Evaluating the general development programs in 1979, I wrote:

Women as a group did not fare well in the past strategies of development. Many poor women lost traditional occupations and employment in cottage industries, portering, etc., and had to turn to subsistence agriculture. The percentage of women engaged in agriculture increased from 93.5 in 1952–54 to 98.2 in 1971. [The percentage was 96 in 1981.] They were losers in the construction and industrial sectors as well as in the fast-expanding service sector. The minority of women who moved to higher socio-economic strata as members of upwardly mobile households found themselves in an unenviable position because they turned from economically and socially independent members of a family into dependent ones. Although as members of the middle class they were able to reap indirect benefits in the form of increased opportunities in education, a better standard of living, better health facilities, etc., the price they had to pay for this was, to my mind, disproportionately heavy in terms of loss of economic independence and social worth. . . .

Legally Nepalese women have an equal right to avail themselves of government or factory job opportunities, equal political rights to vote and to get elected to any office, and the right to own self-earned property, though they do not have equal rights to the inheritance of ancestral property. Theoretically they have an equal right to credit from the banking sector. However, since the availability of credit is tied up with the ability to produce collateral, the limitation on their rights to inherit ancestral property also effectively limits the opportunity for borrowing. Although women have an equal right to government jobs, the child-care and family obligations of women make them less desirable recruits from the institutions' point of view. They have to perform better than men to gain equal status with their men colleagues.

Thus, on the one hand, the women of lower economic strata have lost out because they are part of the ignored majority, but on the other hand, the women of higher economic strata have not been able to benefit much because of social constraints. However, there is hardly any awareness of this situation.[22]

To a large extent, these conclusions still hold. What has changed is the awareness of this increasing inequality between the sexes; a good deal of theoretical attention is being paid to involving women directly in development—not as passive recipients of the benefits but as active participants in the process.

The extensive studies on the status of women in Nepal, completed in the early 1980s, present a comprehensive account of women's work patterns, economic contributions, and decision-making roles in rural households.[23] The publications underline the crucial role that women played in agriculture in general and in poor subsistence households in particular. Together with brainstorming in seminars and workshops conducted in connection with the International Decade for Women (1976–85), these studies made policy planners aware of the need to involve women directly in the development process, if only to increase the efficacy of the efforts.

Consequently, a specific chapter on women was incorporated into the Seventh Development Plan (1985/86–1989/90).[24] Although the plan did not spell out specific programs for women, it did present policy statements to the effect that quotas would be instituted for women in state-run literacy and training programs in various fields, including health, agriculture, and engineering, and that agriculture and cottage industry training programs would be developed specifically for women. According to the plan, legal reforms were also to be effected to facilitate women's participation in development. Several programs were subsequently developed for women in government and semigovernment sectors.

An important aspect of this campaign to bring women into development programs has been the effort to make credit more readily available through the Small Farmers Development Pro-

gram and the Intensive Banking Program. Both programs facilitate women's participation, and both target lower-income groups; but the most theoretically significant common feature is that both recognize that people without assets need specially tailored programs to enable them to take advantage of opportunities created in the development process. The Intensive Banking Program targets small-scale entrepreneurs in agriculture, industry, and the service sector, and the Small Farmers Development Program small farmers. Attempts are made under these programs to deliver credit—along with other complementary services, such as training, raw materials, agricultural inputs, and extension services—as part of a comprehensive package. Both programs have social-welfare components, such as adult education, access to drinking water, child-care centers, immunization, family planning, and sanitation. Lending is project oriented, at least in theory, and there are mechanisms to lend even without tangible collateral.[25]

Nevertheless, it was realized early on that specific efforts were needed to reach women, even within these programs. The Agricultural Development Bank of Nepal found that even though women's enterprises formed under the Small Farmers Development Program were successful, very few women were participating in these programs. Also, the International Fund for Agricultural Development (FAD), on whose funding the Small Farmers Development Program depended, insisted on having a women's component in the program. Consequently a Women's Development Program has been part of the Small Farmers Development Program since fiscal year 1981–82.[26]

As a result of the efforts of the people who had worked on the *Status of Women* project earlier, the Production Credit for Rural Women Program was designed to run with the Intensive Banking Program. By the end of 1981 the findings of the *Status of Women* studies—that women played crucial roles in the rural economy—the success stories of women's enterprises financed by the Grameen Bank in Bangladesh, the failure of earlier efforts in Nepal to lend to the poor, and the new funding available for women's programs all had psychologically prepared the authorities in the Nepal Rastra Bank (Central Bank of Nepal) and the government for a women's credit program. When UNICEF and the Priority Sector Credit Unit in the bank put together a project proposal on production credit for rural women, it was readily accepted.

Three explicit objectives were set for the Production Credit for Rural Women and the women's component of the Small Farmers Development Program. The first was to increase the income levels of women from poor rural households by drawing them into small-scale production activities with a package of credit, training, and other complementary inputs. The second was to develop self-confidence among rural women so that they would be able to undertake community development activities by themselves. The third was to develop an effective delivery mechanism to channel resources to women at the grass-roots level. Both programs integrated credit, social, and community development and institution-building activities.[27]

These two credit programs have successfully created social and community action groups of women who can articulate their needs and improve their access to facilities and opportunities.[28] They have also set up other trailblazing initiatives for women that are far from the stereotypes of what women's activities, economic or otherwise, should be.

Thus far, economic benefits for women have been on a small scale, but changes in women's attitudes and awareness have been remarkable. Village women have been eager to participate in both these programs, as well as in adult literacy projects. To be able to read and write has increased their self-confidence enormously, as have access to credit facilities and the opportunity to participate in a market economy. Village drinking-water facilities have decreased the time needed for water collection. At the same time, these programs have developed delivery mechanisms to integrate women's concerns into mainstream national credit projects.

But the implementation of programs has not been trouble free. Both the Production Credit for Rural Women program and the Women's Development Program of the Agricultural Development Bank were supposed to be project oriented, and lending decisions were to be based on project viability rather than collateral. In practice, because of the difficulty in enforcing financial discipline, banks require collateral for large loans. Only small loans (5,000 to 30,000 rupees; U.S. $165 to $1,000 at the rate set in July 1991) may be granted under the group guarantee system. Banks are reluctant to increase loans to women beyond 5,000 to 10,000 rupees ($165 to $330), but a good quality cow, for example, costs 20,000 to 25,000 rupees ($500 to $700). Because women have no inheritance rights to parental property and enjoy only limited inheritance and disposal rights to their husbands' property, they own little property. Also, women must get permission from men in the household to undertake any activity, particularly an economic activity; and because they do not have living or business space of their own, they cannot start a business that uses too much house space or family land.[29]

Banks have also usually required parental guarantees of repayment if their clients are unmarried women, because if girls marry they leave the natal household and are hard to keep track of. There is a definite dilemma. This younger generation of women can be educated and quickly mobilized to accept new ideas and ventures, but their mobility is the most strictly controlled. In a real sense, they are the proletariat. Further, illiteracy among poor women has tended to exclude them from group leadership roles, for banking procedures designed even for this group require at least the ability to read, write, and do simple arithmetic.

The government, semigovernment organizations, and various foreign agencies in the private sector have initiated numerous smaller training and income-generating projects for women, in addition to the efforts to increase women's access to the existing banking infrastructure. The government has established special training centers for women. The first Women's Training Centre, established in Kathmandu in 1956, initially ran home economics courses for women. During the 1960s such centers were established in other parts of the country, and their programs were expanded to include training in a few household industries, such as textile and garment making and basketry. Leadership training for women panchayat workers at the village and district levels was also made part of the regular curriculum at the centers. The course, however, was mainly geared to create loyalty to the panchayat system. Currently there are Women's Training Centres at five regional headquarters, and they run courses on subjects like rural development, leadership development, and textile and garment making, in addition to subjects related to home management and family healthcare. In the late 1970s home economics courses began to include elements of agricultural extension and food management.

Many women-specific microprojects have also been implemented within the larger Integrated Rural Development projects and population and family planning programs. A few are separate projects in and of themselves. A review of 17 evaluation reports on both kinds of projects shows that all these projects are tiny in scale, underfunded, and understaffed.[30] All are foreign funded and lack any future independent existence once the foreign funding is withdrawn.

Besides funding and management difficulties, perception-related problems also abound. Most of the activities and training planned and implemented for women are still stereotypically related mainly to home management and family nutrition and health. Even when a project is designed as an income-generating activity, the training does not go beyond the sewing, knitting, weaving, or carpetmaking considered appropriate by the middle class in Nepal or the old-fashioned donors from the West. Trainers and trainees alike seem to prefer these areas for women's projects in spite of their low productivity, market problems, and low income-generating potential.[31] No attention is paid to the opportunity cost of women's labor: it is implicitly assumed to be equal to zero. Given the heavy work load of

women (9 to 11 hours per day) in Nepal's agricultural household economy and the opportunity cost of having somebody else do the work, only a few women continue to practice the skills taught once the training period expires. These skills are particularly useless to poor women, who have to earn a living and who can make more money by hauling a load of wood or brewing liquor for sale or working directly as wage laborers. No wonder few choose to participate in such programs.

TRANSFORMATION OF THE REGIME AND THE WOMEN'S MOVEMENT

While the All Nepal Women's Organization and various other research and action groups were functioning openly to improve women's lives, a parallel underground movement directed at the overthrow of the panchayat system and the establishment of democracy was quietly brewing. Some of the women's organizations existing before 1960 kept themselves politically active underground after that date. A few of the women leaders maintained their political alliances, worked with the respective political parties, and somehow kept their organizations alive. Of special interest are the Akhil Nepal Mahila Sangh and Nepal Mahila Sangh, which helped organize the 1990 mass movement for democracy and which have now come out in favor of equal rights for women in all spheres of life. Some new women's groups and associations formed underground have come out into the open, too. Several women from prominent political families, who had no clear affiliation to any women's groups, also took an active part in organizing the antipanchayat movement.

As a consequence of all this activity, a distinguishing feature of the anti-panchayat political movement of February–April 1990 was the remarkable mass participation of women. The date, 18 February, when the Rana regime was overthrown in 1950, was celebrated as an official Democracy Day by the panchayat government, even though there was no real democracy in the country. The movement for democracy started with the anti-panchayat forces organizing a counterdemonstration of their own on that day.

Most of the pro-democracy leaders had already been placed under house arrest once the plan for such a counterdemonstration was announced. Many of the communist leaders were arrested after 18 February. But several second-rank leaders of both the Congress Party and the Communist United Front had already gone underground. As the movement gathered momentum, the government was determined to use force to repress it. Women played a crucial role in both planning and organizing the demonstration in a way that would confuse the police.

When the panchayat regime responded brutally to the public demonstrations, women with children acted as a shield for the other demonstrators, putting the police in a fix. The police did not want to kill women and children and thereby look repressive to international viewers, so the shield did confuse the powers-that-be to some extent. Still, at least six women and one child (a girl) were killed in police shootings at different places in the country. Hundreds of women were arrested, molested, beaten, tortured, and jailed. Women showed great courage in these demonstrations, facing police squads wielding machine guns. The events that took place in one southern town are illustrative.[32]

Narayanghat is a town in the southern Churia Hills at the intersection of two major highways, one leading north from India to Kathmandu and Pokhara and the other extending to the eastern and western parts of Nepal. The 18th of February started with a demonstration of 50,000 men and women. Police fired to disperse the crowd, and several people, including women, were taken prisoner. In the afternoon a women-only demonstration of 600 to 700 persons proceeded through the town and several women were arrested. On 21 February, angry at the police for their indiscriminate firing and the brutality shown to the crowd, 300 women started a demonstration in front of the panchayat building, with their babies on their backs and with sickles, kitchen knives, and whatever farm implements

they could find in their hands. Police surrounded the demonstrators and fired on them, instantly killing two women. Hundreds were arrested and detained at the local army camp.

On 13 March a massive demonstration started, with 2,000 or so women in front holding red banners and placards denouncing the regime. The demonstrators paraded around the town and surrounded the local police post. The police first fired in the air, but when the women did not retreat, they fired point-blank at the demonstrators. The courageous women still stood their ground. About 200 women were arrested and taken to a jungle camp, where they were kept in the open, starved, tortured, and molested. In recognition of their valor, the local people gave the women of the town the title Tigresses of Chitwan. In all those towns where the protest was particularly strong, women participated in the anti-panchayat rallies.

Since the end of the panchayat regime and the restoration of democracy in April 1990, some previously established women's organizations have been revived, and a number of new ones have been formed. Even though almost all of the women's organizations are informally aligned with one or another of the political parties, all of them have emphasized the need to create conditions of economic equality for women. All of them submitted recommendations to the Constitution Drafting Committee demanding equality for women in all spheres of life. They have raised issues of equal property rights, quotas in education and jobs, and having a voice in political parties and the government, rather than issues of social justice and social welfare reform, as in the 1950s. These organizations, particularly on the left, are mostly led by militant feminists.

The All Nepal Women's Association, the All Nepal National Women's Forum, and the Democratic Women's Association of Nepal are closely aligned with different Communist factions. The All Nepal Women's Association works closely with the strongest communist party, the United Marxist-Leninist Party (UML), which shared power with the Nepali Congress Party in the interim government and is currently the main opposition in the Parliament. UML stands for equality in all spheres of life, including equality in inheritance rights, wages, education, and employment. Its other objectives are to end child marriage, polyandry, inequality practiced in the name of religion and culture, the export of women for prostitution, and all other social malpractices that harm women.[33] In July 1990 it organized a protest against the rape of a 12-year-old girl.[34] It has also organized a seminar on women's rights to discuss recommendations to the Constitution Drafting Committee.[35]

The All Nepal National Women's Forum, on the other hand, is aligned with the more extreme of the Communist factions. The forum is more militant, and in addition to the demands of the All Nepal Women's Association, it wants a 25 percent reservation of positions for women in terms of scholarships, employment, promotions, and admissions to technical institutions. It also demands an end to family planning experiments on women, the establishment of homes for destitute and elderly women, pensions for all people over the age of 60, universal employment, an end to the recruitment of Nepalese Gurkha men into British and Indian armies, and the establishment of special mobile courts for resolving lawsuits filed by women.[36] In July 1990 the forum successfully prevented a beauty contest organized by the Coca-Cola Company in Nepal. Afterward it organized a seminar on the issue in one of the most respected coeducational colleges in the country.[37]

The Democratic Women's Association of Nepal is aligned with the milder of the Communist factions. It was established underground in 1980 and from then on was active in the anti-panchayat movement. The association stands for equal democratic and civil rights for women, children's welfare, freedom for women from all cultural and religious taboos, equal opportunity in employment and wages, and world peace.[38] In August 1990, together with All Nepal Women's Association, it organized a demonstration against inflation and for clean water and better garbage disposal and sanitation facilities in the Kathmandu Valley.[39]

PROSPECTS

The two major tenets of the South Asian (Indo-Aryan) culture—namely, the ideology of virginity, which leads to various forms of female seclusion and restrictions on women's mobility, and the patrilineal inheritance system, which places severe limits on women's access to resources—curtail women's political engagement in Nepal. Politics is concerned with the distribution of resources and power among various ethnic groups, castes, and classes, and the political arena in Nepal has been dominated by the emerging rich, industrial bourgeoisie, the urban middle class, and the rural landed gentry. Against this background, only women from rich households and from rural and urban elites have some scope for active participation, and only they have a chance to rise to positions of power. But even these women are hampered by a lack of economic resources and by restrictions on their mobility during the early stages of their lives. Until April 1990 the repressive political structure presented one more obstacle to women's political activity. In spite of these inhibiting factors, however, women's participation in the recent political movement was remarkable and helped bring the repressive regime to an end.

At this juncture the supreme priority for all Nepalese citizens, men and women alike, is a smooth transition from a system of absolute monarchy to a system of democracy and the rule of law. How the women's movement evolves will depend very much on the alliance of political forces that crystallizes. Like other political forces in the country, women's organizations have strong differences over the role of the monarchy, religion, and the philosophy of political organization. Nevertheless, women's organizations seem to hold similar views on vital issues concerning women. All these organizations and all the political parties have issued statements supporting equal constitutional rights for women in all spheres of life. But only the forces on the left have come out clearly for equal inheritance rights.

The degree of gender equality in the new constitution is not a great improvement over the degree of gender equality in the panchayat constitution. The panchayat constitution (with its amendments) theoretically guaranteed equality to all citizens without discrimination on the grounds of religion, race, sex, caste, or tribe in the application of the law.[40] It also guaranteed freedom and personal liberty and the right to own property (article 15). Article 17 of the constitution, however, empowered the government to regulate and control fundamental rights—to protect the interests of minors and women, for example, thus bracketing minors and women together. The constitution also discriminated against Nepalese women in its treatment of foreign spouses: foreign wives of Nepalese citizens were given preferential treatment in matters of citizenship, but no such preference was available to foreign husbands.[41] The new democratic constitution retains all these features of gender inequity. The only provision added to appease women is the article on election rules (article 114). The constitution now requires that women amount to at least 5 percent of the candidates filed by each political party in the elections for the House of Representatives. At least 5 percent of the members of the upper house must also now be women.[42]

Even though almost all parties supported gender equality in the process of constitution making, all reverted to tradition when this value came into conflict with such entrenched practices as male inheritance rights or spousal citizenship. It is thus difficult to be optimistic for gender equity when women's organizations and the political parties did not think it appropriate to incorporate complete gender equality into the new constitution.

Women do seem to be united on issues related to the integration of women in development and increasing their access to modern avenues of employment. While some organizations seem to be asking for quotas for women in education, employment, and political institutions to achieve this integration, others are just demanding supportive actions.

The third dimension of women's struggle involves action for female education, the use of mass media, and the creation of awareness about gender issues among the masses. Education and the mass media are viewed as necessary instruments for changing traditional conceptions about women.

Women's organizations and the women's movement in Nepal have evolved, the former welfare-oriented approach being replaced by more militant demands for equal political and economic rights for women. What can be achieved and at what speed will depend on the level of mass support for these issues and on the attitudes of prominent male leaders in the political parties. The top leaders of the major political parties are from an older generation and still view women only as the custodians of future generations.

Not much is known about female leadership in the political parties. The only woman visible at the highest levels of the left is Sahana Pradhan, who headed the United Left Front and was a minister in the outgoing interim cabinet. She won a seat in the House of Representatives as a United Marxist-Leninist Party candidate from Kathmandu. Her leadership of the left today, however, may be somewhat accidental. Although she is one of the foremost female leaders in the country and has been an active political worker since the inception of the Nepalese Communist Party in the late 1940s, she may well have been chosen to head the United Left Front because she is the wife of a founding member of the Communist Party, rather than because she is a political worker in her own capacity. Nevertheless, she has headed the Ministry of Industry and Commerce; in the panchayat era, in contrast, women ministers held portfolios only in the welfare sector. There are not many women leaders visible in the Nepali Congress Party, either.

All women leaders make speeches about women's equality, but considerations of party alliance seem to overwhelm their concerns for women's issues when it comes to a fight. No women's organizations mounted protests against the inequitable provisions of the new constitution. In March 1991, when ten women's organizations presented a joint memorandum to the prime minister demanding equal property rights, the All Nepal Women's Organization, aligned with the party currently in power, refrained from signing even this memorandum.[43] In spite of the plethora of women's organizations, women's issues were not put on the political agenda, even in the 1991 parliamentary elections.

In the 12 May 1991 election for the House of Representatives, the Nepali Congress Party had 11 women among its 204 candidates, and the United Marxist-Leninist Party included 9 women among its 177 candidates. The final list of 1,345 candidates included 80 women. Of the 205 candidates elected, 7 were women: 5 from the Nepali Congress Party and 2 from the UML. Because the constitution requires that women make up 5 percent of the upper house, 3 women were also nominated to fill the quota. It is telling, however, that no party thought it appropriate to have more female candidates or upper house members than the constitution requires.

At lower levels of party leadership, however, quite a few women are emerging in both the Congress and the Communist parties. How far they will be able to capitalize on their positions is not yet clear. On the one hand, there is very limited participation by women in the formal political process. Yet women have been mobilized during times of mass movement to fight for general causes. Many authors have noted that in other countries in the subcontinent, women have mobilized on a mass scale in times of crisis, and then once the crisis is over, they have been relegated to exclusively domestic roles.[44] Women must understand that although a democratic framework is a necessary condition for women's advancement, it is not a sufficient condition. Democracy provides only a starting point, and women must fight further to eliminate economic and social inequality. Only the future will tell what will emerge from the present turmoil—whether or not the young women leaders, most of whom are of college age, will survive and be able to bring about substantial change in the status of women in Nepal.

NOTES

1. For estimates of the population below the poverty level see Nepal Rastra Bank, *Multipurpose Household*

Budget Survey (Kathmandu: Nepal Rastra Bank, 1989), 136.

2. For a summary discussion of women's position in these broad cultural groups in Nepal see Meena Acharya and Lynn Bennett, "Women and the Subsistence Sector: Economic Participation and Household Decision Making in Nepal," Staff Working Paper no. 562 (Washington, D.C.: World Bank, 1983), 9–22. For a more detailed account of the lifestyles of various ethnic groups, the reader may refer to the five-volume series *The Status of Women in Nepal* (Kathmandu: Center for Economic Development and Administration, Tribhuvan University, 1979–81), esp. vol. 2, parts 1–3, pp. 5–7, 9. Also see Sidney R. Schuler, *The Other Side of Polyandry* (Boulder: Westview Press, 1987); Nancy E. Levine, *The Dynamics of Polyandry: Kinship, Domesticity, and Population on the Tibetan Border* (Chicago: University of Chicago Press, 1988); and R. L. Jones and S. K. Jones, *The Himalayan Women: A Study of Limbu Women in Marriage and Divorce* (Palo Alto: Mayfield, 1976).

3. Information in this section is condensed from a detailed review in Lynn Bennett, *Tradition and Change in the Legal Status of Nepalese Women,* in *Status of Women in Nepal,* vol. 2, part 2, pp. 11–75; Mahila Nyaik Sewa Pariyojana, *Swasnimanisko Amsa Ma Adhikar* (Women's rights of inheritance) (Kathmandu: Kanuni Shiksya Pustika, 1987); and Sushila Shinha, *Hamra Kanuni Adhikar* (Our legal right) (Kathmandu: Mahila Nyaik Sewa Pariyojana, 1989).

4. See Shahida Lateef, "Ethnicity in India: Implications for Women," in James W. Bjorkman, ed., *The Changing Division of Labor in South Asia* (Riverdale, Md.: Riverdale, 1986), 100–111; P. Manikyamba, "The Participatory Predicament: Women in Indian Politics," in ibid., 112–27; and Scarlet Epstein, "Cracks in the Wall: Changing Gender Roles in South Asia," in ibid., 17–32; David G. Mandelbaum, *Sex Roles in North India, Bangladesh, and Pakistan* (Arizona: University of Arizona Press, 1988); Ranjana Kumari, Renuka Sing, and Anju Dubey, *Growing up in Rural India: Problems and Needs of Adolescent Girls* (New York: Advent Books, 1990).

5. For a detailed description and analysis of the place of virginity among the high-caste Hindus in Nepal see Lynn Bennett, *Dangerous Wives and Sacred Sisters* (New York: Columbia University Press, 1983).

6. Meena Acharya, "Changing Division of Labor and Participation," in Bjorkman, ed., *Changing Division of Labor,* 137.

7. Meena Acharya and Lynn Bennett, *The Rural Women of Nepal: An Aggregate Analysis and Summary of Eight Village Studies,* in *Status of Women in Nepal,* vol. 2, part 9, pp. 199, 198.

8. Ibid., 195, 206.

9. I compiled the information in this section on women's access to positions of power from the 75 detailed

district-by-district election records published by the Election Committee: *National Panchayat Election Results* (Kathmandu: His Majesty's Government Press, 1986) and *National and Local Panchayat Election Results* (Kathmandu: His Majesty's Government Press, 1986–87).

10. Women constituted 1 of 157 first-class officers (0.1 percent), 17 of 659 second-class officers (2.6 percent), 585 of 4,435 technical officers (13.2 percent), and 497 members of the vocational and occupational sections (11.2 percent). *Statistics on Women in Nepal* (Kathmandu: Women's Service Coordination Council, 1986).

11. The historical material presented here is primarily based on personal communications and on Bina Pradhan, *Institutions Concerning Women in Nepal*, in *Status of Women in Nepal*, vol. 1, part 3, pp. 4–8.

12. Krishna P. Koirala was a Gandhian, persecuted by the Ranas for his beliefs. His son, the late Bishesware P. Koirala, is known for his unceasing fight for democracy, both during the late 1940s and after the 1960 coup d'état by King Mahendra. He died in 1982.

13. Tanka P. Acharya established Praja Parishad, the first political party, and initiated the struggle against the Rana regime in the early 1930s. He was elected the first honorary president of the Nepali Congress Party in 1946 while still in jail.

14. Ganesh Man Singh, another founding member of Praja Parishad, who later joined the Nepali Congress Party, was busy organizing the anti-Rana movement from India. He was in the forefront of the February–April 1990 political movement and is currently the supreme leader of the Nepali Congress Party.

15. Akhil Nepal Mahila Sangathan (All Nepal Women's Organization), *Bahu Udeshiya Kendra: Parichaya Pustika* (Multi-Objective Center: An introductory text) (Kathmandu: Bargiya Shangathan Kendriya Salahakar Samiti, 1977).

16. This information is based on personal communications with Kamal Rana.

17. Bennett, *Tradition and Change*, 29–75.

18. Social Services National Coordination Council, "An Introduction to SSNCC," in *SSNCC News* 1, no. 1 (January 1990).

19. Anjali Pradhan, *Women in Development Resource Manual, Nepal* (Kathmandu: U.S. Agency for International Development, 1990), 86, 96.

20. Nepal Business and Professional Women's Club pamphlet (Kathmandu, 1975).

21. Acharya and Bennett, *Rural Women of Nepal*, 208.

22. Meena Acharya, *Statistical Profile of Nepalese Women: A Critical Review*, in *Status of Women in Nepal*, vol. 1, part 1.

23. The *Status of Women* series (1979–81) consists of 12 books divided into two volumes: (1) Meena Acharya, *Statistical Profile of Nepalese Women: A Critical Review*; (2) Lynn Bennett, *Tradition and Change in the Legal*

Status of Nepalese Women; (3) Bina Pradhan, *Institutions Concerning Women in Nepal*; (4) Indira M. Shrestha, *Annotated Bibliography on Women in Nepal*; (5) Pushkar Raj Reejal, *Integration of Women in Development: The Case of Nepal*; (6) Meena Acharya, *The Maithili Women of Sirsia*; (7) Augusta Molnar, *The Kham Magar Women of Thabang*; (8) Drone Rajaure, *The Tharu Women of Sukhrwar*; (9) Sidney Schuler, *The Women of Baragaon*; (10) Bina Pradhan, *The Newar Women of Bulu*; (11) Lynn Bennett, *The Parbatiya Women of Bakundal*; and (12) Meena Acharya and Lynn Bennett, *The Rural Women of Nepal: An Aggregate Analysis and Summary of Eight Village Studies*.

24. Planning Commission, *The Seventh Five-Year Plan, 1985/86–1989/90* (in Nepali) (Kathmandu: His Majesty's Government Press, 1985).

25. Meena Acharya, "Priority Sector Credit Programs and Women's Access to Credit," *Networker* (Kathmandu: Center for Women and Development, May–August 1989), 5–8.

26. Nepal's fiscal year is from mid-July to mid-July.

27. Acharya, "Priority Sector Credit Programs."

28. The findings on the effectiveness and problems in the credit program in this and the following paragraphs are based on numerous evaluation reports, the two latest of which are Integrated Development Systems, *Third Small Farmers Development Project, Nepal: Final Report* (Kathmandu, 1989); and Center for Women and Development, *Production Credit for Rural Women Project: An Impact Evaluation Study, Draft Report* (Kathmandu: UNICEF, 1989).

29. Meena Acharya, "Priority Sector Credit Programs," 5–8.

30. For a summary discussion on these issues from various reports, see Meena Acharya, "Poverty and Women in Nepal" (Unpublished report submitted to the World Bank, 1989). The projects reviewed include His Majesty's Government (HMG) and U.N. Fund for Population Activities (UNFPA), Population Education (1981, 1983); HMG, Women's Training Centres' Programmes; HMG, Panchayat Training Centre in Jiri—Carpet, Clothes, and Bag Weaving for Women (1975–); HMG, Overseas Development Agency/United Kingdom, Koshi Hill Rural Development Project (1973–); SATA/Switzerland, Integrated Hill Development Project (1974–); World Neighbors, Women's Skill Development Project (1973–); International Planned Parenthood Federation (IPPF), Bangdovan Integrated Welfare Project (1983); Ford Foundation and U.S. Agency for International Development, The Legal Service Project (1974–); UNFPA, Nepal Family Planning/Mother and Child Health Awareness Raising Programme (1983–1985); Mahaguthi—A Nepali Trust (private donors), Nepal Charkha Pracharak Gandhi Smarak Mahaguthi (1925–); IPPF, Planned Parenthood and Women Development Project (1983); IPPF, Chitwan In-

tegrated Family Welfare Project (1983); U.S. Agency for International Development, Save the Children (1980–); Private Agencies' Collaboration Together, Education and Income Generation for the Chepang Youth and Women (New York, 1983); Family Planning Association of Nepal (FPAN)/IPPF, Deokhuri Family Welfare Project (1983); USC (Canada)/U.N. Development Program (UNDP)/ Economic and Social Commission for Asia and the Pacific (ESCAP)/Partners in Action Cooperating Together (PACT)/FPAN, Mother's club (1975). See also Bina Pradhan and Indira Shrestha, *Foreign Aid and Women in Foreign Aid and Development in Nepal: Seminar Proceedings (October 4–5),* (Kathmandu: IDS, 1983), 99–154.

31. CERID (Centre for Educational Innovation and Development), *Women's Participation in Nonformal Education Programme in Nepal* (Kathmandu: CERID, Tribhuvan University, 1986).

32. The information on women's participation in the February–April political movement has been obtained from personal contacts, as well as from *Asmita,* vol. 3, no. 8 (Kathmandu: Asmita Prakashan, Vikram Calendar 2047, Ashad/Shrawan), 23–27.

33. Akhil Nepal Women's Association (ANWA), *Constitution and Programme* (Kathmandu: ANWA Central Committee, April 1990).

34. *Gorkhapatra* (Kathmandu), 21 July 1990.

35. *Gorkhapatra* (Kathmandu), 1 July 1990.

36. *All Nepal National Women's Forum (ANNWF) Manifesto* (Kathmandu: ANNWF, Central Ad Hoc Committee, May 1990), 13–16.

37. *Muldhara* (Kathmandu), 10 July 1990.

38. *Democratic Women's Association of Nepal (DAWN) Constitution* (Kathmandu: DAWN, November 1990), 1–6.

39. *Gorkhapatra,* 13 August 1990.

40. Ministry of Law and Justice, *The Constitution of Nepal, 1961 (with Third Amendments Incorporated)* (Kathmandu: His Majesty's Government Press, 1980), 6.

41. Ministry of Law and Justice, *Nepal Ain Sangraha* (Compendium of Nepali laws) (Kathmandu: His Majesty's Government Press, 1988), 136–42.

42. Ministry of Law and Justice, *The Constitution of Nepal, 1990* (Kathmandu: His Majesty's Government Press, 1990).

43. The memorandum and the signatory institutions were published in the *Networker* (Kathmandu: Center for Women and Development, May 1991).

44. P. Manikyamba, "The Participatory Predicament: Women in Indian Politics," in Bjorkman, ed., *Changing Division of Labor,* 136–42; and BANGLADESH.

▲ The Netherlands

POLITICS

Type of Political System: democracy
  Sovereignty: constitutional monarchy
  Executive-Legislative System: parliamentary
Type of State: unitary
Type of Party System: multiparty
Major Political Parties

  Christelijk Democratisch Appel (CDA, or Christian Democratic Appeal): Largest party in the Netherlands, formed by the merger in 1980 of three religious parties (Roman Catholic, Calvinist Christian Democratic, and Dutch Reformed).

  Partij van de Arbeid (PvdA, or Labor Party): The only large, mass-based left-wing party in the Netherlands. Belongs to the mainstream of continental European social democracy.

  Volkspartij voor Vrijheid en Democratie (VVD, or Liberal Party): Self-described as liberal, it has strong conservative tendencies at times and in certain policy areas. Sometimes it is comparable to (the moderate wing of) the British Conservative Party and sometimes to British or German liberal parties.

  Democraten 1966 (D66, or Democrats 1966): Leftist-liberal party founded in 1966. Its aim has been democratic reform.
Year Women Granted Right to Vote: 1919
Year Women Granted Right to Stand for Election: 1917
Percentage of Women in the Legislature
  Lower House: 22.7%
  Upper House: 28.0%
Percentage of Electorate Voting for Highest Elected Office in Most Recent Election (1989): 80.1%[a]

DEMOGRAPHICS
Population: 14,661,000
Percentage of Population in Urban Areas
  Overall: 88.5%

Female: 88.8%
  Male: 88.1%
Percentage of Population Below Age 15: 19.6%
Birthrate (per 1,000 population): 12
Maternal Mortality Rate (per 100,000 live births): 5
Infant Mortality Rate (per 1,000 live births): 8
Mortality Rate for Children Under Five (per 1,000 live births): 9
Average Household Size: 2.8
Mean Age at First Marriage
  Female: 23.2
  Male: 26.2
Life Expectancy
  Female: 79.7
  Male: 72.9

EDUCATION
Ratio of Female to Male Enrollment
  First-Level Education: 97
  Second-Level Education: 93
  Third-Level Education: 70
Literacy Rate
  Female: 100.0%
  Male: 100.0%

ECONOMY
Gross National Product per Capita: U.S. $9,290
Percentage of Labor Force in Agriculture: 6.2%
Distribution of Agricultural Workers by Sex
  Female: 15.6%
  Male: 84.4%
Economically Active Population by Sex
  Female: 30.8%
  Male: 70.2%

a. *Volkskrant,* 7 September 1989, p. 1.

Political Participation of Women: The Netherlands

MONIQUE LEIJENAAR
AND KEES NIEMÖLLER

The Kingdom of the Netherlands, with approximately 15 million inhabitants, is a densely populated, small Western European country. Its highly developed economy, which is based on private enterprise, provides a high standard of living: per capita income is in excess of U.S. $15,000. An unemployment rate of almost 11 percent and a high government deficit, however, are considered serious economic problems. The fully autonomous territories of the Netherlands Antilles are also part of the kingdom.

A constitutional monarchy was established in the Netherlands in 1814 under a multiparty parliamentary system, with a monarch as formal head of state and a prime minister as head of the government. The executive is responsible to a bicameral parliament, the Staten Generaal. Following each election, the leader of the party electing the largest number of candidates is asked to form a cabinet with other parties to reach a majority in Parliament. The Parliament controls cabinet activities and decisions. The 75 representatives of the First Chamber are elected indirectly by the members of the provincial councils. The 150 members of the Second Chamber are directly elected every four years, as are members of provincial and local councils.

Each voter casts one vote, and for all practical purposes the Netherlands as a whole forms one constituency. Ballots contain the names, grouped by party, of all candidates competing for seats. Although citizens may vote for any candidate on the list, most choose to support a party rather than individuals. As a result, only three times since 1945 has a candidate been elected to the Second Chamber because of preference votes (votes not cast for the top-listed candidate).

Given the low threshold for gaining representation (0.67 percent), a relatively large number of parties consistently win seats in Parliament. Yet three parties have dominated parliamentary politics and coalition formation since World War II. The largest, Christelijk Democratisch Appel (CDA, or Christian Democratic Appeal), was founded in 1980 with the merger of three religion-based parties. The Partij van de Arbeid (Labor Party) is the only mass-based left-wing party in the Netherlands. The third of the largest parties, Volkspartij voor Vrijheid en Democratie (Liberal Party), has strong conservative overtones reminiscent of Britain's Conservative Party. Another more leftist-liberal party, Democraten 1966 (Democrats 1966), founded in 1966 on a platform of constitutional reform, has recently been gaining electoral support. In 1991 five additional parties were also represented in Parliament.

The origins of the party system are usually traced back to the mass emancipation movements of the late nineteenth century. These movements were shaped not only by class conflict, as in all European countries, but even more markedly by religious divisions among Calvinist, Roman Catholic, and Dutch Reformed segments of the population. The dominant issues of the time—government funding for private (religiously oriented) schools and the extension of suffrage—reflected and reinforced religious and class cleavages in Dutch society. These issues were resolved in 1917 in a major compromise among political groups. This so-called pacification of 1917 established equal public funding for private and public schools, as well as universal male suffrage. In 1919 suffrage was extended to women.

The nineteenth-century emancipatory movements gave rise not only to political parties but also to an array of other social institutions organized along denominational and class lines. Political, social, cultural, and some economic organizations were largely based on the same cleavages in the population, resulting in the formation of Catholic, Protestant, Socialist, and "Neutral" (secular liberal) subcultures. For many citizens, for example, Catholicism encompassed nearly every aspect of life. If born a Catholic, one went to a Catholic church and attended a Catholic school. When ill, one stayed in a Catholic hospital. One joined the Catholic youth organization, the Catholic trade union, and the Catholic broadcasting organization and, of course, voted for the Catholic Party. This process is generally known as *verzuiling,* the "pillarization" of Dutch society. In the early 1960s some 82 percent of the population was religious, and more than 70 percent of these voters supported their respective religious parties. In recent decades verzuiling has been breaking down as religion has become less important. At present, only 62 percent of the electorate is made up of religious voters, and they are less likely than in the past to vote for religious parties (only 54 percent did in 1992).

Another important characteristic of Dutch political development is the extension of the corporate sector after the war. In the 1950s and 1960s a highly institutionalized network of interest groups was formed, most around such agencies as the Ministries of Social Affairs, Internal Affairs, Culture, and Agriculture. A defining characteristic of the neocorporatist structure was the defense of group interests through representation.

Verzuiling and neocorporatism are both important in explaining the development of women's political involvement in the Netherlands. First, the strong religious overtones in society diminished the possibilities for women to participate in the political arena. In general, the practice of religion encouraged and strengthened the de facto inequality of women in the family and in society by perpetuating the idea that women's proper role is at home. The negative stance of many faiths, especially Catholicism, on birth control also adversely affected women's status. More directly, women's political participation was negatively influenced by the fact that the religious parties did not welcome women into their midst. The Protestant Party, for example, did not allow its women members to stand for election until 1953.

Another consequence of verzuiling was the pillarization of women's organizations. Before the new women's movement of the 1960s, women were organized in so-called traditional women's organizations, such as Katholiek Vrouwen Dispuut (Catholic Women's Club), Nederlandse Vereniging van Huisvrouwen (Dutch Organization of Housewives), Nederlandse Bond voor Boerinnen (Dutch Organization of Farmers' Wives), and Nederlandse Katholieke Boerinnenbond (Dutch Catholic Organization of Farmers' Wives). There also existed (and still exist) separate women's wings in many labor unions and political parties. Apart from these the traditional women's organizations viewed themselves as politically neutral and were not concerned with issues of gender inequality or the oppression of women.

Neocorporatism also discourages women from political involvement. As Joke Swiebel and Joyce Outshoorn point out, newcomers in the policy arena, like the organizations of the women's movement in the 1970s, found it hard to break into the system of close-knit policy networks, which were often formally institutionalized in official advisory bodies. Moreover, the corporatist network is heavily dominated by economic interests and correspondingly tends to ignore women's interests.[1]

It is in this context of a pillarized and corporatist political structure that women have had to fight for their rights. The struggle was originally concerned with the rights to vote and to stand for election. Since achieving these goals in 1919, women have expanded their fight to include the right of married women to work, the right to legalized abortion, and, finally, the right to be treated as individuals, not merely as mothers and wives.

One of the first issues to unite Dutch women was the restriction of women's right to perform paid labor. Between 1904 and 1940 twelve attempts were made in Parliament to ban women from paid employment. A bill proposed in 1904 mandated that women civil servants be fired upon marriage. Although this bill was defeated, others were successful, including the law tabled by a Catholic minister of social affairs and passed by the Parliament in 1937 that forbade the employment of married women (or women who "lived in sin"). Several women's organizations participated in the activities of the Committee to Defend the Right of Women to Paid Labor, founded in 1935. With newspaper advertisements and pamphlets, the committee drew attention to the injustice. Citizens were requested to send postcards to the minister of social affairs asking for women's rights. In addition, female students invited their professors to speak about the historical right to work. In February 1938 there was sufficient financial support to organize a large protest in Amsterdam, followed by meetings in other towns. As a result of this pressure, the next minister of social affairs, a socialist, discarded the contested law.[2]

The new women's movement began with the emergence of two feminist groups in the late 1960s: Man Vrouw Maatschappij (MVM, or Man-Woman-Society) and Dolle Mina (Wild Mina). Members of MVM, both women and men, were primarily leftist liberals in their 30s. They aimed for equal rights and focused on convincing the government and Parliament to pass legislation that guaranteed equality. Members discussed such issues as the double message that girls were given at school (study hard for a future career versus become a mother and housewife who stays at home and cares for the children), the negative aspects of being a housewife (long working hours, dependency, lack of appreciation), the reduction of working hours, and the sexual division of labor. MVM pursued its goals cautiously. To avoid shocking and estranging the public, the group always conducted decorous campaigns. In contrast, Dolle Mina, an offshoot of student and left-wing radical groups, had much stronger views about the oppression of women. Its members, anarchists and Marxists among them, believed that housework was slavery, that motherhood was oppression, and that abortion should be legalized. They used the media expertly by organizing campaigns then considered shocking. For example, women demonstrating for the legalization of abortion displayed their bare bellies with the words "Baas in eigen buik" (Boss in our own belly). The distinctive publicity campaigns were highly successful; wide media coverage encouraged many to join Dolle Mina.

In its first five years, 1967 to 1972, the new women's movement concentrated on the pursuit of equal rights and on increasing public awareness that the societal roles and positions of women and men did not result from "natural inclinations." From 1972 on, political action groups were gradually replaced by consciousness-raising groups, the first step toward developing a critique of patriarchy and power relations between men and women. In the mid-1970s many radical feminist groups were concerned primarily with developing women's culture and with campaigning against sexual violence and pornography. They formed feminist publishing houses, feminist bookshops, women's centers, and women's cafés. Another autonomous movement, socialist feminism, stood for both feminist and socialist change but pursued its goals independently of male-dominated political organizations. Its members were prime movers in the struggle for the legalization of abortion, among other political issues. Radical feminism and socialist feminism differed in the extent of their cooperation with left-wing political groups and men in general and in their views regarding lesbianism.[3] The strength of both types of feminist groups reflects the heterogeneity of the women's movement. Never has one organization represented all women's groups. Joint action has only been possible in pursuit of a specific goal; to achieve that goal, coalitions are set up to overcome the ideological breaches between groups.

An important example is the coalition formed for the campaign to legalize abortion. Laws from 1886 and 1911 prescribed that women who had abortions, as well as their acting physicians, were liable for prosecution. In practice, however, pregnant women could obtain abortions in special abortion clinics. When attempts were made to change this practice, the national committee Wij Vrouwen Eisen (WVE, or We Women Demand) was formed in 1974 with the following demands: abortion should be removed from the penal law; abortion should be available through the National Health Service; and women should be able to decide for themselves whether to choose abortion.

Many women's organizations joined WVE—the autonomous socialist and radical feminist groups, as well as the women's wings of the leftist and liberal parties. The committee organized many campaigns. Activists held large demonstrations and sit-ins in Amsterdam, occupied an abortion clinic when the police threatened to close it, and formulated an alternative abortion law. From 1977 on, the abortion issue was high on the political agenda, almost toppling the government. The coalition cabinet then consisted of the Christian Democratic Party, which opposed a more liberal abortion law, and the Labor Party, which supported such a law. A bill favoring legalization was put forward by socialist and liberal members of Parliament. With the support of several small parties, the bill passed the Second Chamber (lower house) but was rejected by the First Chamber. In 1980 another bill was launched by a coalition government of Christian Democrats and Liberals. Although this bill would have legalized abortion, it seriously threatened the right of women to decide whether to obtain an abortion. It stated that "a pregnancy will be terminated no sooner than on the sixth day after the woman has visited a physician and has discussed her intention with him."[4] In other words, women were to be sent home for five days "to think it over." With left-wing parties and small orthodox Christian parties opposing it and Christian Democrats and Liberals voting for it, the bill passed the Second Chamber 76 to 74.

WVE and other branches of the women's movement were greatly disappointed with the result. A radical women's group organized a women's strike for the day before the vote on the abortion bill in the First Chamber. But not all women's organizations supported the strike; the women's wings of the labor unions and the Labor Party did not join in, even though Labor members had participated in WVE. The unsuccessful strike (few women participated, and the bill was passed the next day) highlights the main division within the women's movement—cooperation versus noncooperation with existing institutions and culture.

Breed Platform voor Economische Onafhankelijkheid (Platform for Economic Independence) also reflects joint efforts to extend and intensify cooperation among political women's organizations, autonomous women's groups, and women trade unionists. It was founded in 1982 when the women's wing of the Labor Party asked many women's organizations to join forces to prevent the worsening of women's economic position during an ongoing economic recession. The Nederlandse Vrouwenbeweging (Dutch Women's Organization), affiliated with the Communist Party, organized a meeting around the same theme. A study group whose common denominator was the economic independence of women resulted. Its goals are the establishment of women's rights to work and to welfare benefits, regardless of marital status or lifestyle; the protection of all the rights that women have fought for and gained; the redivision of paid and unpaid work, inside and outside the home; and the banning of all discriminatory laws and regulations.

The members of the Platform for Economic Independence try to influence policy makers through lobbying. In addition, they organize study meetings and publish reports. At present, more than 40 women's organizations take part. Not only do the women's wings of most political parties and unions participate, but so do many traditional women's organizations and interest groups. Participation is not formal; organizations can choose whether to support each activity.[5]

A final single-issue women's organization is

the Associatie voor de Herverdeling van Arbeid (Association for the Redivision of Labor), founded in 1984. Its goal is a society in which everybody who is able, regardless of way of life or socioeconomic status, can earn a living through paid labor and can combine the work with other (private) tasks. This, however, means structural changes, such as the redivision of paid and unpaid labor between women and men and the shortening of the work week from 40 hours to 25. About 20 women's organizations are members of the association.

Both the Platform for Economic Independence and the Association for the Redivision of Labor challenge the traditional ideology of the one-earner family: a male breadwinner with a wife and children. The success of both organizations in attracting members underscores the importance of this "ideology of motherhood" as a main cause of women's subordinate position in society. Both associations are also unusual in bringing together traditional women's organizations and those of the new women's movement.

These associations, as well as many other women's organizations focusing on such issues as child care, urban planning, sexual violence, incest, income policies, and women's education, have been able to flourish and to create continuity partly because of government subsidies. For more than ten years the government has subsidized women's organizations and activities aimed at strengthening the position of women and developing women's emancipation. In 1990 almost 30 million guilders (U.S. $54 million) was spent for this purpose, distributed along ten funding channels in different departments.[6] Without this support structure many activities would not have taken place and some organizations would have ceased to exist. Conversely, however, this support perpetuates the dependency of women's organizations on government funding and on their adaptation to governmental structures.

The women's movement today is characterized by a multiplicity of initiatives and activities, but it is also more professionalized and institutionalized than ever. That the women's movement receives less publicity than in the days of Dolle Mina does not mean that it has disappeared from the political scene. It has merely changed shape.

WOMEN'S PARTICIPATION IN THE LABOR FORCE

Until recently most Dutch women were not involved in paid employment—one explanation of their lower political participation rate compared to men. Employment gives women not only material independence but also professional skills and greater self-confidence. Women are often unfavorably positioned in the labor market with regard to the skills thought desirable for politics. When in the remunerated labor force, women often focus their education and career development on what are frequently termed nurturing professions, usually not considered good training for political leadership. Women are often concentrated in occupations that allow little flexibility for leaves of absence and work hours—flexibility that is useful for political positions.

In the Netherlands, unlike in other countries of the European Community, women have never been a large part of the labor force. From 1900 to 1960, with slight variation, women formed about one-fifth of the working population. The kind of women who participated in wage labor did change significantly, however. At the beginning of the century women composed 22.5 percent of the work force engaged outside the home. Most working women were working class, and the wives of shop owners and farmers. In the 1950s many married women withdrew from the labor market for several reasons, including a steady rise in the standard of living, a high marriage rate, and Roman Catholic and Protestant dictates that married women belong at home.[7] After 1960, as all these factors changed, the percentage of women in the paid labor force increased rapidly, primarily because of the entrance of married women from all social classes into the labor market. Between 1960 and 1981 the proportion of employed married women rose from 7 to 33 percent.

In spite of this rapid increase, the Netherlands still has one of the lowest participation rates of women in wage labor in the European Community. Of all women aged fifteen to sixty-four, 41 percent participate in wage labor, compared to an average of more than 50 percent in most other EC countries. The late start of industrialization in the Netherlands compared with Britain, France, and Belgium is one reason for this low rate. Male labor was cheap and plentiful, and there was no great need for women and children in the labor force. Because the Netherlands was involved neither in the Franco-Prussian War of 1870–71 nor in World War I, no shortage of men occurred as in other European nations. In addition, Dutch wages and social security benefits were relatively high, permitting married women to stay at home. Finally, the ideology of family and motherhood propagated by Dutch churches fostered unfavorable attitudes toward women who worked outside the home.

The recent increase in the number of working women has not changed the existing segregation of jobs for women and men. The expansion of the service and public sectors of the economy, which hire large numbers of women, is primarily responsible for the rise in women's employment. In 1963, 70 percent of employed women and 41 percent of employed men had jobs in these two sectors.[8] This occupational segregation did not change in the 1970s and 1980s. Of women employed in 1981, 84 percent held jobs in the service and public sectors, compared to 55 percent of employed men. One-third of all employed women worked in sales, secretarial/receptionist, or administrative positions or "caretaking" jobs (e.g., nursing and teaching). In comparison, one-third of all employed men work in fourteen occupations. Women constitute only 7 percent of managerial and executive workers.[9]

The female labor force also differs from the male labor force in the number of hours worked per week. In 1989, 71 percent of all part-time workers (fewer than 40 hours a week) were women. Of those women who worked part-time, 32 percent worked fewer than 20 hours a week. Only 8 percent of male part-time workers were employed fewer than 20 hours a week. That more women than men work part-time is due to the difficulties of combining child care with paid employment. In 1988, 58 percent of all women between the ages of 18 and 37 with no children had full-time jobs, whereas only 5 percent of women in the same age-group with young children worked. Besides the difference in hours worked by women and men, there is a significant earnings differential. In 1986 women received only 76 percent of the gross pay per hour of men.

Overall, family responsibilities still determine the number of women in the paid labor force, as well as the kind and level of jobs that women occupy. This applies to the private as well as the public sector. In spite of activities with regard to affirmative action for women, the increase in the percentage of women employed in the public sector is in most years not even 1 percent.

The still prevalent ideology that young children need their mothers full-time, together with the lack of adequate child-care facilities, discourage many women with small children from taking paying jobs. This situation is changing somewhat, however. Due to an expected shortage of employees (in the 1950s and 1960s fewer children were born than before), the private and public sectors are expanding their facilities in ways that will enable women to combine motherhood and paid employment. The government is also increasing funding for child-care facilities. Given the growing numbers of women who want to be employed, this increased commitment from the government will mean that the percentage of women involved in paid labor will grow steadily.

WOMEN'S FORMAL PARTICIPATION IN POLITICS

Besides the pillarization and neocorporatism of Dutch politics, with their negative impacts on women's political participation, and the strong influence of motherhood ideology and its consequences for women's economic participation, there are many other explanations for the limited formal participation of women in the political process. Barriers related to the organization of society give women little opportunity to emerge from the private, or domestic, domain. Examples include the virtual nonexistence of nurseries, impediments in the labor market, and tax laws that reinforce traditional gender roles and inhibit women's employment. Explanations can also be found in the political system itself. For example, party procedures for recruiting and selecting candidates limit women's opportunities. Recruitment for cabinet officers and representatives (parliamentary, regional, and local) is the sole responsibility of political parties. Because fewer women than men belong to political parties and perform activities within these parties, they are underrepresented in politics—it is from the ranks of active party members that candidates for political office are recruited.

The religious parties have historically been more resistant to women's participation in the public sphere than have the other large parties. In the early twentieth century confessional, or religious, parties opposed women's suffrage because of the traditional view that politics is a man's job. Suffrage was granted to women in 1919 not so much because of a change in attitude but because the majority in Parliament feared a possible revolution of the left wing, as had occurred a year earlier in Germany. Because women were thought to be more conservative in their voting behavior, their participation in politics was expected to be a stabilizing factor. The conviction that women were more likely to vote for the religious parties was another reason why the confessional parties in the Second Chamber generally supported amending the constitution to grant women the right to vote.

After World War II, largely because of pressure by some prominent women members of the Katholieke Volkspartij (Catholic Party), the negative attitude of confessional parties began to change somewhat. As a result of this pressure, the Catholic Party accepted a resolution in 1949 calling for the involvement of more women in party politics. In 1953 the party appointed the first woman junior minister and in 1956, the first woman cabinet minister, Marga Klompé.

Klompé earned her appointment through her hard work in the Catholic Party. She entered the party in 1946 and that year founded the Catholic Women's Club. That she was unmarried and had a doctorate in chemistry were also factors in her cabinet appointment. Before entering politics Klompé had worked as a high school teacher while performing volunteer work in the community. Working in the Resistance during World War II raised her interest in politics. When the war ended, she debated whether to join the Labor Party or the Catholic Party and so went to meetings of both. In those days by custom the Labor Party ended its meetings by singing the "Internationale" (the hymn of the socialist movement, calling on the working class to unite). Klompé did not like this at all, so she joined the Catholic Party. Marga Klompé was an influential member of the party, serving as minister for the Department of Culture and Voluntary Work in five cabinets.

In the quarter-century 1953–77, only one woman served at the level of cabinet minister or junior minister in each cabinet. The 1977 cabinet broke with this unspoken "token woman" rule: that year one female minister and four female junior ministers were appointed. In the third cabinet of Prime Minister Ruud Lubbers, installed in 1989, three female cabinet ministers were appointed, heading the Department of Internal Affairs, the Department of Cultural Affairs, and the Department of Transport; three female junior ministers were also appointed.

From 1953 to 1992 nine women have been cabinet ministers and sixteen have been junior ministers. Most have held a university degree (chemistry, classical languages, law, education, or economics), have been married, and have had one or more children. Their average age on entering the cabinet has been about 50—after their children had grown. All held several other political positions before becoming cabinet minister, including local councillor, provincial councillor, and member of Parliament.

Since 71 percent of the cabinet ministers are recruited from Parliament—the others come from other political positions or from the private sector—one explanation for the low number of women in cabinets is the low participation rate of women in Parliament and in politics in general. The introduction of women's suffrage in 1919 did not lead to women's proportional representation in Parliament. Until the 1970s women made up fewer than 10 percent of parliamentarians in the Second Chamber. The percentage of women representatives has gradually increased; women accounted for 22.7 percent of seats after the 1989 elections.

Before 1956 only two women had served in the First Chamber. In the 1970s the percentage of women rose to 9 and in 1981 to 21. In 1991 the percentage of women in the First Chamber was 28. Among parties, the confessional parties have had the lowest percentage of women parliamentarians. Until 1977 this figure was less than 10, but it increased to 22 in 1989. Labor Party representation of women currently is 31 percent while Liberal Party representation is 18 percent.

An analysis of the backgrounds of all the female (145) and male (1,208) MPs in the period 1918 to 1986 shows that the situational variables for women MPs, such as being married and having children, have shifted. The data suggest that sentiments about the role of married women and mothers have changed over time, even in politics. Between 1948 and 1946 only half of the women MPs were married and most had no children. Yet later, between 1977 and 1986, nearly 75 percent were married and some 40 percent had children, although the children were usually grown by the time these women reached political prominence.

Female MPs are also more likely than their male colleagues to come from better-off families (measured by the father's profession) and from politicized families. In education, female and male MPs differ little: from 1918 to 1986 half the MPs, regardless of sex, had completed university degrees. In contrast to the female adult population at large, however, the majority of female MPs had actively pursued a profession before becoming representatives. These high percentages (in comparison to the electorate) indicate the importance of a good education and professional

experience for selection, and these criteria seem to be more important for women than for men.

Other analysis reveals differences in the parliamentary work performed by male and female MPs.[10] For example, female politicians judged themselves to be more practical, more pragmatic, and more sensitive to their constituents than their male colleagues were. Female MPs were also more inclined to forge compromises and to sustain contacts with MPs from other parties. The women paid more attention than the men to attending party conferences, meetings at party centers, and sessions of the parliamentary party, as well as to answering correspondence and meeting with social groups. Male MPs were more inclined to mention the importance of parliamentary party meetings and maintaining contacts with government members. Several surveys also show that female representatives spend much more time on the job than do their male colleagues.[11] One visible difference between female and male politicians, apparent as soon as the first woman entered Parliament, has been the division of tasks according to gender. Throughout their years in Parliament female MPs have tended to occupy themselves with social issues customarily attributed to women, such as welfare, health, education, and emancipation. In the 1970s and 1980s this division of labor has lost some of its sharpness—some women are now prominent in foreign affairs and defense—but it has by no means disappeared.

Female politicians have made an effort to stand up for women and their particular interests. They are more inclined to notice the disadvantaged status of women in society, and to remedy it they will occasionally form a front, breaching party lines to support an issue favoring women. When the law to ban the right of married women to paid employment was discussed in Parliament in 1937, all women MPs, regardless of political background, voted against it. Usually, however, women MPs vote according to their parties' wishes.

Women's rate of participation in local and provincial government is about the same as within Parliament. In 1919 in the first local elections in which women were allowed to be candidates, 88 women won seats, fewer than 1 percent of positions. Until 1970 fewer than 10 percent of councillors were women. Since then their number has increased every election by 3 to 4 percent; in 1990 their number was 22 percent.

A somewhat higher representation of women at the local and regional level as compared to the national level might have been expected, as in many other European countries.[12] Many policy matters at the local level are especially important for women, such as child care, housing, traffic, schools, and the subsidizing of women's groups. In addition, contacts between local councillor and citizen are more direct and more frequent than the contact of MPs with voters. And council work requires no long-distance travel. Nonetheless, the representation of women was higher at the national level than at the local level until 1986. The main reason is that in most communities the Christian Democratic Party has the majority, and it has not strongly supported the political integration of women. In addition, most communities are rural, places where the effects of the new women's movement have not been as powerful as in the larger cities.

Worldwide, women's rates of participation tend to be higher when political positions are filled by appointment than when they are filled by direct election, the rationale being that those doing the appointing have to account for their nominations and find it useful to balance appointments among social groups.[13] Yet this proposition fails to hold true for the Netherlands; the percentages of women state commissioners and mayors, positions appointed either by the queen or by the cabinet, are much lower than the percentages of women councillors. One reason for the low percentage of women mayors (8 percent in 1991) is a prevailing gender bias of the appointers in favor of male candidates, particularly those already serving as mayors in other cities.

In 1919, after the qualification "male" was erased from the election law, women were able to vote. The struggle for women's suffrage had taken about 25 years. Opposition to the enfranchisement of women had been based mainly on the concept of separate spheres—the belief that women and politics do not mix. In the end, the doubling of the electorate had little effect. The power constellation in the Parliament remained about the same, and women did not vote en masse for women candidates.

Even though Christian parties opposed women's political integration, women in general have voted more often than men for the Christian Democratic Party and its predecessors. Yet the gender difference is not large, nor does it indicate a trend. With the other two largest parties, gender differences in party choice are much smaller. In some elections more women than men vote for the Labor Party; in others, the opposite is true. The same can be said for support of the Liberal Party.

Distinguishing among the parties in terms of "secular" versus "confessional" and "left" versus "right" does, however, point up larger and more consistent differences between men and women in party choice. In four of the six elections for which data are available (1971, 1977, 1981, and 1986) women evidenced a greater preference for confessional parties. The correlation is weaker when the parties are classified as left and right. Women had a greater preference for right-wing parties in two of the six elections. But these gender differences disappear when employment and age are taken into account.[14] One explanation for women's greater preference for religious parties is that for those whose political ideology is right of center, there are only two large parties to vote for: the Christian Democrats and the Liberals. The Liberal Party, which emphasizes policies in support of a free economic market, presents itself much less than the Christian Democratic Party in terms of social policies and values—subjects that tend to interest women more.

Male and female voters also differ in their views on specific issues. When asked about such matters as income differences, nuclear disarmament, or the environment, women are more likely than men to opt for the left-wing point of view. To date, gender-related differences in issue preferences have not affected party choice or the balance among the parties. In a multiparty system like the Dutch one, differences in issue preferences do not always lead to specific differences in party preference, either because the parties themselves do not differ markedly on these issues or because other issues or preferences, such as religious attitudes, have overriding importance.

Few Netherlanders belong to a political party—only 4 percent of the electorate did in 1990. Moreover, of these few party members not even 10 percent can be considered activists, that is, members who attend party meetings, discuss party matters, become members of local party boards, or participate in the selection of candidates. Fewer women than men participate in political parties. There is no overall gender balance among the parties' representatives in Parliament nor in other representative bodies. Thanks to the continuing pressure of women's wings within parties, however, the executives of most political parties now favor the election of more female party officials and representatives. This positive attitude will lead to more gender-balanced party representation in the future. Again, the role of women within political parties needs analysis because of the prominent role that parties play in the Dutch system. Party members help select political personnel and are themselves recruited as candidates.[15]

Although political participation of women was not a major issue in the formation of the Christian Democratic Party, the first draft of the party's rules stipulated that 20 percent of the members of the National Executive had to be women. This proposal was rejected in the discussion of the three "old" religious parties over the rules of the new unified party.[16] Women remain a minority in the Christian Democratic Party. They make up 22 percent of the membership, and their representation in political and party bodies is even lower. In the past decade this low figure has become a concern for the CDA because its electorate consists of more women then men. As early as 1984, the Party Council accepted a report that recommended nominating more women (and

young people) to party bodies and to the lists of candidates.[17]

The share of women has not increased significantly since then, and the party recently examined how women can be encouraged to participate. In 1988 and 1989 the Christian Democratic Party, and other parties, received state subsidies to develop affirmative action policies for female party members. In 1989 the Party Council adopted a resolution supporting a change in attitude toward the participation of women. It was decided to recruit female members, foster the political education of women, and increase knowledge about affirmative action among regional and local party officials. It was also recommended that contracts be drawn up both between regions and local branches and between the National Executive and regions defining targets for the percentage of women participants.[18]

Like most Dutch parties, the Christian Democratic Party has a separate women's wing. About 10 percent of all female party members are united in this women's organization, the CDA-Vrouwenberaad. This organization is represented in party bodies, such as the National Executive and the Party Council. Its main aims are to stimulate the integration of women into the party, to increase the political consciousness of women, and to contribute to the development of party policy.[19] This last objective has brought the Vrouwenberaad into conflict with other party bodies. On several occasions it has voiced opinions on political issues that have differed from the general party view. And it assumes a much more radical stance than the party on issues regarding women.

The Liberal Party, since its foundation in 1948, has always included at least one woman in the National Executive and among parliamentary representatives. From 1965 to 1975 party rules even guaranteed the participation of a minimum of 4 women in the 27-member National Executive. In 1969 it became the first Dutch party to elect a female president. But this does not mean that now as many women as men participate in the party. The share of women in party offices in 1988 was much lower than their share in the membership. In that year about one-third of party members were women; yet women's representation was significantly lower in the National Executive and on party advisory committees. National Executive representatives decided that the participation of women in representative and party offices should be the same as their share in the party membership: 33 percent. The party did not wish to codify this intention, however, because to do so was presumed to be incompatible with party rules and liberal principles. Instead, Liberals argued that the participation of women in the party should increase "naturally."[20]

The women's organization of the Liberal Party, De Organisatie Vrouwen—part of the party structure since 1948—has long emphasized its interest in increasing the number of women in representative and party offices. For example, when the number of seats in the Second Chamber was increased in 1956, the women's wing pleaded for the election of a second woman to the liberal parliamentary party. It has repeatedly tried to recruit women from its ranks for representative and party offices. For more than a decade the organization has administered a data base of qualified women for use by party members when filling positions. This list is rarely consulted, however.

Formal links between the Liberal Party and its women's wing exist at several levels.[21] Since 1953 the women's organization has had two representatives on the Party Council, and since 1963 it has also had official representatives on the National Executive. The party strengthened the influence and representation of regional organizations in 1975, at the expense of its national organizations and centralized regulations. The guarantee of at least four women in the National Executive was deleted from party rules. The women's organization has had an advisory delegate in the Regional Executive since 1977. And since 1986 its local branches have been represented in the party's Local Executive.

The position of the Liberal women's organization has changed thoroughly since 1984. Previously all female party members were presumed to be affiliated with the women's organization; from 1984 on, female members have been required to sign up separately for the women's organization. The organization now has 4,000 members, just 12 percent of female party members. The women's wing can no longer claim to speak for "all liberal women." Liberal ideology in general seems to have been more of a hindrance than an encouragement to women to participate in the party. The notion that all party members already have equal opportunities to participate restrains the party from implementing special measures for the participation of women and obstructs a view of the actual positions of men and women.

In 1946, when the Labor Party was founded, 27 percent of the members were women; in 1990 women made up 38 percent of the membership. Women have always been present in the National Executive and in the parliamentary party, albeit as a minority. The low participation rates of women in representative and party offices became an issue in the Labor Party during the later 1970s. After a lobbying effort by Rooie Vrouwen (Red Women), the women's organization of the Labor Party, the party congress resolved in 1977 that women should occupy at least 25 percent of all seats in representative and party bodies. But sanctions were not established to guarantee the implementation of this resolution. Because the percentage appeared to function as a maximum quota, the party congress decided in 1987 to aim for 50 percent representation of women in all party offices, with a minimum of 25 percent.[22] The goal of 50 percent has not yet been reached in any of the party offices, although the participation of women is growing. By the end of 1990 about 30 percent of the parliamentary party consisted of women, as compared with 19 percent in 1988.[23]

In the 1970s the women's organization of the Labor Party changed in character. The Vrouwencontact, then the official women's organization, consisted mainly of older female party members. Yet more and more often, some women took direct action, such as opposing advertising that discriminated against women and opposing discriminatory hiring practices. These women, most of them young and well educated, called themselves Rooie Vrouwen on these occasions. In practice, two women's groups existed side by side in the Labor Party during the 1970s. The Vrouwencontact group waned, and in 1975 the Rooie Vrouwen became the official women's organization of the Labor Party.

The political activism of the Rooie Vrouwen led to several clashes with the party. The National Executive wanted the Rooie Vrouwen to consult it before undertaking any action or making any political statements. For a short period formal links between the women's organization and the party were abolished. In 1977, however, these links were reinstated because of the Rooie Vrouwen's financial dependence on the party. Since then, a paid member of the National Executive has been in charge of the work of the women's organization. This individual is usually the president of the Rooie Vrouwen. The formerly conflictual relations between the Labor Party and its women's organization have become reasonably smooth.

The Rooie Vrouwen now has a twofold function. It lobbies for the participation of women in party bodies and for the selection of female candidates to representative bodies on the national, regional, and local levels. And it serves as a pressure group within the Labor Party by attempting to place women's issues on the party agenda. Although the results of its efforts vary, the organization has successfully encouraged the discussion of such issues as the reduction of working hours and the introduction of the individual (instead of the family) as the smallest unit in the taxation and social security systems. Occasionally the organization has had to compromise with the party, for example, on abortion. The Rooie Vrouwen supported the legalization of abortion. This issue became the focus of a national demonstration organized by We Women Demand in 1977, but the Rooie Vrouwen did not participate, not wanting to disrupt negotiations on the formation of a new coalition cabinet between the Labor Party and the Christian Democratic Party. The

proposal to legalize abortion was one of the greatest differences between the two parties.

WOMEN AND PUBLIC POLICY

Against the background of the "second emancipation wave" of the late 1960s, the government began in 1974 to adopt policies designed to improve the position of women. As Swiebel and Outshoorn describe it: "The idea that it is part of the responsibility of government to have an overall policy on women was new in 1974–75; it was a deliberately staged innovation. As with other European nations, it can be clearly attributed to the revival of the women's movement at the end of the sixties. At first the movement concentrated on rediscovering and redefining women's issues and on setting up its own mutual support facilities and campaigns. Soon it realized that government was indispensable for tackling many of the issues raised."[24]

To encourage government action, the women's organization Man Vrouw Maatschappij organized a postcard campaign in 1974. Many women sent postcards to the Labor prime minister telling him that it was time for an overall government policy on women. The Department of Culture, Recreation, and Social Work then established two governmental committees: a national committee charged with coordinating activities for the Year of the Woman (announced by the United Nations for 1975) and the Advisory Committee for Emancipation. This marked the beginning of a specific government policy on women—emancipation policy. Previous policies on women were embedded in general welfare provisions developed after World War II.

Amid controversy, the Advisory Committee for Emancipation managed to produce nearly 100 recommendations. Although most of its advice was not solicited by the government, some of its recommendations became policy. These included the appointment in 1977 of a junior minister for emancipation and the formation of an administrative organization to oversee emancipation policy. In 1977 the Department for the Coordination of Emancipation Policy was established, together with intraministerial coordinating committees or advisory groups within several ministries. Moreover, emancipation policy was defined as multidisciplinary, or "facet," policy, meaning that women's issues were not phenomena to be isolated in one department. Instead they were to be seen as an aspect of policy problems in every conceivable field.[25]

In 1981 the Advisory Committee for Emancipation was renamed the Emancipation Council. It serves as an independent advisory body for equal opportunity policy. All ministers of government are required to seek the advice of the council when their plans involve equal rights or equal opportunities for women. The council may also issue advisory reports on its own initiative. For example, the council can draw a minister's attention to the possible effects on women of a specific policy.[26]

From 1974 to 1981 the goal of governmental emancipation policy was to change people's attitudes, opinions, and outlooks concerning the roles of women and men. Education was considered the appropriate weapon to attack current beliefs with regard to men and women and to prevent future prejudice. Courses were organized for women with small children who wished to enlarge their general knowledge. These "second chance comprehensive schools" for mothers attracted many eager students. Meanwhile, sons and daughters were educated using screened teaching materials in which father did not merely smoke a pipe but washed the dishes as well.

In recent years people have increasingly come to realize that the inferior position of women in society is fundamentally rooted in socioeconomic structures. As a result the junior minister for emancipation was moved from the Department of Culture, Recreation, and Social Work to the Ministry of Social Affairs and Employment. This department is generally seen as more important than the Department of Culture, making the move appear political to some. In 1982 a committee consisting of women from the women's movement, as well as civil servants from several ministries, was installed. The committee's task was to draw up an Emancipation Policy Program for the years 1985–90. This program was presented to and accepted by the Second Chamber in 1986, including specific policy initiatives. It forms the touchstone for all government emancipation policy.

The starting point of the Emancipation Policy Program is the recognition of a structural imbalance of power between women and men, resulting in fewer opportunities for women than for men. The main objective set forth in the program is "a pluriform society in which everyone has the opportunity to lead an independent existence irrespective of their sex or marital status and in which women and men have equal rights, opportunities, freedom and responsibilities."[27]

Now the question is how to evaluate the outcome of 15 years of state-sponsored emancipation policy. First, women's policy has been quite successful where it concerns "small" benefits to women. On the national as well as local level, a regular stream of subsidies has been available to finance activities of women's organizations and to set up women's groups, women's health centers, rape crisis centers, and shelters for battered women.[28] Another somewhat positive result is the legalization of abortion. Although the process took about 15 years, owing to vehement opposition by the confessional parties and "prolife" groups, and although some paragraphs of the law are paternalistic toward women, abortion is now legal.

Second, in some areas legislation has been changed. For example, the Equal Pay Act was passed in 1975. Neither it nor the Law on Equal Treatment—passed in 1980 with the intention of ensuring equal treatment of women in the labor market—has been very effective. More recently, social security regulations and fiscal laws have been made less "family oriented." The women's movement has always claimed the right of women to be treated as individuals, regardless of their way of life or family status. As a result of several directives of the European Community, Dutch laws and regulations have been changed so that Dutch women are entitled in their own right to unemployment benefits, pensions, welfare benefits, and medical benefits.

LOOKING AHEAD

More women will eventually gain access to the political arena. The main political parties are now willing to select more women for political posts, although because this entails a redistribution of political power, it will be a very slow process. The recruitment and selection procedures that stand are still biased because they promote the tenure of groups and individuals, predominantly men, who are in positions of power. Incumbents are very difficult to defeat, and open seats for high-level political offices are rare.

Several strategies could be pursued to speed the entrance of women into formal politics. First, the government could place an upper limit on the number of years an individual could serve in offices that are now characterized by low turnover. In addition, the range of criteria used by parties and appointers to select political leaders could be broadened. The characteristics that are most valued now are those mainly associated with men. Similarly, the standards by which qualifications for public office are evaluated are defined by men's experiences. A background in law or business, which is more common for male candidates, is viewed as more appropriate than a background in teaching or social work, which is more common for women candidates. Moreover, unpaid volunteer experience is not accorded the same importance as paid vocational training. Increasing the diversity of characteristics that selectors look for in political leaders would bring more women into public office. A final strategy could be a change in the formal selection procedures. Certain procedures clearly offer better chances for the nomination of women than others. Three possibilities are quotas, centralization of selection procedures, and involvement of more party members in selecting candidates. With such changes, women would soon participate in politics on an equal footing with men.

Women elected officials will be concerned with diverse issues. Of primary importance will be the redistribution of the unpaid labor of women and the paid labor of men. For this, more flexible and shorter working hours, as well as increased child care, are needed. Until recently, looking after children was the sole responsibility of the parents. Neither government nor the private sector spent money for child care. Not until 1990 did the cabinet decide to increase the budget for child care substantially. The provision of more child-care facilities will be an important impetus for pregnant women to keep working. In addition, women's organizations will continue to advocate that women be treated as individuals. In part because of the reduction of government spending, not all laws and regulations have been changed accordingly.

Last, the ongoing political and economic integration of the countries assembled in the European Community will affect women's organizations. Dutch women's organizations will soon face several supranational levels of political decision making. To promote women's interests, they will have to operate on a European level. Only then can women influence policy making in Europe as a whole.

NOTES

1. Joke Swiebel and Joyce Outshoorn, "Feminism and the State: The Case of the Netherlands" (Paper presented at the Annual Meeting of the Dutch Political Science Association, Twente, 12–13 June 1991), 6.

2. W. H. Posthumus van der Goot et al., *Van moeder op dochter: De Maatschappelijke positie van de vrouw in Nederland, vanaf de Franse tijd* (From mother to daughter: The social position of the woman in the Netherlands since the French period) (Sun reprint, 1977), 267–81.

3. Swiebel and Outshoorn, "Feminism and the State," 10.

4. Jeanne de Bruijn and Barbara Henkes, "Women's Strike in Holland," *Feminist Review* (1982): 40.

5. See also Truus Ophuysen and Ina Sjerps, "Van vrouwen en de dingen die haar binden" (Of women and the things that bind them), *Katijf* 21 (July 1984): 19–23.

6. Swiebel and Outshoorn, "Feminism and the State," 14.

7. Centraal Bureau voor de Statistiek (Central Bureau of Statistics), *Statistisch zakboek* (Pocket book of statistics) (The Hague: Staatsuitgeverij, 1979), 5.

8. Centraal Bureau voor de Statistiek, *Statistisch zakboek* (The Hague: Staatsuitgeverij, 1982), 11.

9. Corina Oudijk, *De sociale atlas van de vrouw* (Social atlas of women) (The Hague: Staatsuitgeverij, 1984), 199.

10. Monique Leijenaar, *De geschade heerlijkheid, politiek gedrag van vrouwen en mannen in Nederland, 1918–1988* (The shattered loveliness: Political behavior of women and men in the Netherlands, 1918–1988) (The Hague: SDU, 1989), 174–80.

11. Ibid., 166.

12. Robert Darcy, Susan Welch, and Janet Clark, *Women, Elections, and Representation* (New York: Longman, 1987), 8; Janine Mossuz-Laveau and Mariette Sineau, *Women in the Political World in Europe* (Strasbourg: Council of Europe, 1984), 9.

13. Darcy, Welch, and Clark, *Women, Elections, and Representation*, 111; Mossuz-Laveau and Sineau, *Women in the Political World*, 50.

14. Leijenaar, *De geschade heerlijkheid*, 46.

15. See Hella van de Velde and Monique Leijenaar, "Women's Access to Political Parties" (Paper presented at the Joint Sessions of the European Consortium for Political Research [ECPR], Essex, March 1991), *Nijmegen Political Science Reports*, 12.

16. Report on the development of party rules for the Christian Democratic Party in the archives of the CHU (Christelijk Historische Unie, or Christian Historical Union) (ARA, The Hague, 1978).

17. Recommendation formulated in the general party report *Appèl en weerklank* (Summon and consonance), October 1983, and accepted at the Party Council, 18–19 May 1984.

18. Resolution accepted at the Party Council, 16 December 1989.

19. Annual party report (1987), 57.

20. Note concerning affirmative action accepted by the National Executive, 20 June 1988.

21. Party rules, 1953, 1963, 1966, 1975, 1977, 1986.

22. Article 12 of the party statute.

23. Party note on affirmative action, 1989.

24. Swiebel and Outshoorn, "Feminism and the State," 6.

25. Joke Swiebel, "De vrouwenbeweging en de beleidsorganisatie bij de overheid" (The women's movement and the organization of the government), *Katijf* 45 (1988): 15.

26. See Equal Opportunity Council, The Hague, *Emancipatieraad* (Equal Opportunity Council) (1990): 5.

27. Emancipation Policy Program, 1985, quoted in Saskia Keuzenkamp, "You Cannot Make an Omelette without Breaking Eggs: Emancipation Policy in the Netherlands" (Paper presented at the Fourth International Interdisciplinary Congress on Women, New York, 1990), 2.

28. Swiebel and Outshoorn, "Feminism and the State," 17.

▲ *Nigeria*

POLITICS

Type of Political System: authoritarian
  Sovereignty: not applicable
  Executive-Legislative System: not
  applicable
  In 1993 the government was in transition
to civil rule.

Type of State: federal

Type of Party System: two-party

Major Political Parties

  National Republican Convention (NRC):
Slightly to the right of center; formed by the
Babangida administration.

  Social Democratic Party (SDP): Slightly to
the left of center; also formed by the
Babangida administration.

Year Women Granted Right to Vote:
  1957/1978[a]

*Year Women Granted Right to Stand for
  Election:* 1957/1978[b]

Percentage of Women in the Legislature: not
  applicable

*Percentage of Electorate Voting for Highest
  Elected Office in Most Recent Election
  (1983):* not available

DEMOGRAPHICS

Population: 88,514,501[c]

Percentage of Population in Urban Areas: not
  available

Percentage of Population Below Age 15: 46.4%

Birthrate (per 1,000 population): 43[d]

Maternal Mortality Rate (per 100,000 live
  births): 750[e]

Infant Mortality Rate (per 1,000 live births):
  101[f]

Mortality Rate for Children Under Five (per
  1,000 live births): 167[g]

Average Household Size: 3.9

Mean Age at First Marriage
  Female: 18.7
  Male: not available

Life Expectancy
  Female: 50.2
  Male: 46.9

EDUCATION

Ratio of Female to Male Enrollment[h]
  First-Level Education: 93
  Second-Level Education: 73
  Third-Level Education: 39

Literacy Rate
  Female: 6.0%
  Male: 25.0%

ECONOMY

Gross National Product per Capita: U.S. $378

Percentage of Labor Force in Agriculture:
  44.6%[i]

Distribution of Agricultural Workers by Sex
  Female: 37.1%
  Male: 62.9%

Economically Active Population by Sex
  Female: 48.2%
  Male: 88.2%

  a. Women in southern Nigeria were enfranchised in
1957, and women in northern Nigeria in 1978.

  b. See note a.

  c. *Population and Vital Statistics Report,* series A, vol.
44, no. 4 (New York: United Nations, 1992).

  d. *World Development Report* (Washington, D.C.:
World Bank, 1992).

  e. *Human Development Report* (New York: U.N. Development Program, 1992).

  f. Ibid.

  g. Ibid.

  h. Ibid.

  i. Ibid.

Reversing the Marginalization of the Invisible and Silent Majority: Women in Politics in Nigeria

KAMENE OKONJO

The subtropical West African country of Nigeria, with 115 million citizens, is the most populous in Africa. The area that it occupies has a recorded history of states and empires extending back to the tenth century and earlier.[1] At the confluence of the lower Niger and the Benue rivers is the original homeland of many of Nigeria's ethnic groups. The groups speak 268 languages and have various social structures and religious traditions, with language and religion the principal cleavages.

English is the official language. The three principal indigenous languages are Hausa, Igbo, and Yoruba. Many of the Nigerian languages are in the Benue-Congo family of languages and are mutually intelligible within subfamilies. Some are spoken by fewer than 4,000 people while others, like Igbo and Yoruba, are spoken by more than 20 million people each.

Almost half the population is Muslim, 35 percent is Christian, and the remainder practice traditional African religions. Linguistic, religious, and ethnic differences define the three largest cultures in Nigeria—the Muslim Habe-Fulani to the north, the predominantly Christian Igbo to the east, and the mixed Christian and Islamic Yoruba to the west—who together account for about 56 percent of the population. Although each group has a distinct history and culture with respect to women's role in society, they all share a "separate spheres" approach to male-female relations. This approach may provide a particularly Nigerian solution to the gender bias of democratic institutions, an important issue in making a transition from military to civilian rule and im-

plementing a newly crafted constitution. The societal and religious structures of the Habe-Fulani, Igbo, and Yoruba not only delimit women's positions and options for political action but also complicate Nigeria's efforts at nation building.

A British colony from 1884 Nigeria inherited a bureaucratic organization and the framework of the nation-state when it gained independence in 1960. Along with European political institutions, the British imposed the system of political control known as indirect rule. The country was carved into divisions and districts, each under the supervision of a white official (prefect). Because each native state fell within one of the new political divisions, the Nigerian elite, headed by the kings or chiefs who governed the states, were allowed control of most of their internal affairs, provided that they accepted overall British authority and the advice of the white prefect supervising their area of authority. Many of the indigenous customs and rules concerning women, like those on marriage, divorce, and the possession of children, thus persisted under British rule.

External trade and shipping were the preserves of British merchant traders and companies, with internal trade and distribution left to the natives. The metropolitan power bought raw materials from the colony and sold manufactured goods to it.

Besides the political and trading systems that Britain imposed, the third prong to its attack on local values, traditions, and cultures was religion. The British brought Western religious and educational "opportunities" to select regions of the country. Responsibility for matters involving souls, culture, and education fell to the missionaries. They were not, however, allowed to evangelize in the North, where Western (Christian) religion and secular education could be regarded as a challenge to Islam and Arabic (Islamic) education and would disturb the status quo.

Thus, the new nation inherited not only the many indigenous states but also a federal government and three regional governments—the latter modeled on the British parliamentary system—plus the social and economic legacies of colonialism. Since independence, rapid changes in the form of government, weakness in democratic institutions, and militarism have meant that participation in formal politics has not been prevalent for either men or women.

The massive corruption of members of the federal government in the first postindependence regime, their economic mismanagement, and the political instability caused by the jockeying for positions of influence resulted in a loss of confidence in that government. After a failed military coup in January 1966 civilians relinquished political control to the armed forces. For two of the past three decades since independence, the country has been ruled by a succession of military regimes. It also suffered through a bitter civil war when the eastern region seceded to form the Republic of Biafra in 1967. The war cost more than a million lives and ended with the collapse of Biafra in January 1970.

In some respects the various political experiments with the imported central system of government can be seen as an attempt to govern and administer a heterogeneous group of indigenous states as one entity while trying to transform them into a unified nation state. The experiments started with the British, who needed to create a political framework for governing their new colonial state, and they continue with present efforts to implement the third constitution.

In 1991, Nigeria consisted of 30 states and the Federal Capital Territory of Abuja, and it was ruled by an Armed Forces Ruling Council headed by the president and commander-in-chief of the armed forces, Gen. Ibrahim Babangida.

The country was in the midst of its latest political reorganization of the federal, state, and local governments, with power to be fully transferred to civilians in 1993.

In all these changes in territorial politics, women were only minimally involved, if at all. The colonial dispensation—the system of rules, promises, and values handed down by the British—initially excluded not just Nigerian women but also Nigerian men. As the British formed executive and legislative councils for the central government and later moved from a colonial to a representative type of government, they felt the need to associate Nigerian men with the organizations that they established. From the beginning, they made territorial politics an arena into which only men would be admitted. By 1960, when independence was achieved, it had become accepted in Nigerian societies, where the gender division of roles is normal, that national politicking was reserved for men. Such a division of roles does not, however, characterize the politics of the indigenous states. Both civilian and military governments have therefore tried to obtain legitimacy by associating individual women with their governments.

Such tokenism has not given the postindependence governments the desired legitimacy. What special obstacles, then, do women encounter in trying to participate in national politics, and have the postindependence governments helped or hindered their efforts to participate? To put it differently, Can women come together to act and speak with one voice on matters that affect them? How can women's representation in the gender-biased political system be made effective for quick action on any matters of special interest to women? And, finally, given the gender-biased and stratified nature of the educational institutions, what avenues are open to women to achieve effective representation in the national political arena?

To provide useful answers to these questions, one must first understand the cleavages in the political system and the nature of the variations in the political participation of women in the indigenous states. An examination of the position of women in the three dominant cultures, Habe-Fulani, Yoruba, and Igbo, reveals the formidable obstacles that must be overcome to establish a unified and gender-neutral nation-state.

WOMEN, FALSE CONSCIOUSNESS, AND POLITICS IN MUSLIM HABE-FULANI SOCIETY

Muslim Habe-Fulani (or Hausa) society in Northern Nigeria is feudal.[2] It is founded on inequality, organized hierarchically, and characterized by unequal interaction and service, as well as obedience to superiors.[3] Its most essential feature is its division along gender lines, reflected in everything from household architecture to the rules of public discourse. Because the women in this society are not to be seen by men who are not their husbands, they live their lives separately from men, and even within the household women's activities are confined to special quarters. Buying and selling in the market and the other social interactions necessary to running a household are handled by husbands or children.

In the past, group survival required that women bear numerous children to replenish the constantly decimated population, so women produced children from the onset of puberty to menopause, if indeed they survived that long. Conditioned to accept this duty, girls were married off by their families between the ages of 9 and 14 years (always by puberty). Women thus remained, and were treated as, minors throughout their lives, first as daughters by their fathers and then as wives by their husbands.

The gradual spread of Islam, introduced as a religion of the ruling class and of foreigners as early as the eleventh century, and the change from matrilineage to patrilineage were accompanied by the institutionalization of women's subordination in Hausaland. The predominantly illiterate elite population relied on a cadre of learned *mallams* (Muslim priests) for interpretation of the Quran and guidance on how to achieve everlasting life. Instructed by the mallams to be obedient and submissive to their husbands and conditioned to accept marriage as the only true means of personal fulfillment, women believed that the world was as limited and restrictive as their experience suggested.

Tragically, although women in the Hausa states of Northern Nigeria won limited rights with respect to marriage, inheritance, divorce, and child custody through the introduction of Islam, those rights were negated by other aspects of Islam and the cultural practices of Hausa society. The cultural conventions of patriarchy—the state of social development characterized by the supremacy of the father in the clan or family—patrilocality, child marriage, and polygyny all combined with Islam to reduce the rights granted women. Women were confined to their homes and could not engage in public work, travel, trade, or public roles in government or religion. British imposition of indirect rule institutionalized the feudal state structure. Autocracy reinforced by British Victorian gender biases eliminated whatever minimal political participation remained for women.

With the development of nationalist movements in the Southern regions of Nigeria in 1945, there arose in Northern Nigeria the Northern Elements Progressive Union (NEPU), a radical, populist party of the young intellectual elite. NEPU was based in Kano, the intellectual hub of the conservative, feudal, and Islamized Hausa-Fulani states of Northern Nigeria. Under the patrician but radical leadership of Aminu Kano, NEPU staked out the *talakawa* (masses), including women, as its constituency. It also set out to achieve the ideals of Islam—social justice, equality of rights, and human dignity—for both men and women. In the feudal societies of the North, the appeal to the masses to rid themselves of their oppression by voting for NEPU was bound to fail, because until 1978 only men had the vote in the North. The party needed the votes of women to gain the necessary plurality over its competitors.

Over a period of 29 years the continuous and steady reiteration of Islamic ideals by NEPU—now transformed into the People's Redemption Party (PRP)—had a telling effect, particularly on women voters. The 1979 elections heralded a return to civilian rule and representative government in all parts of the federation and the beginning of the Second Republic. The elections were also the first in which the newly enfranchised Muslim women of the North could vote. "So successful was this campaign that there was a much higher number of women than men voting in the 1979 elections. Even women in purdah insisted on turning out and, if necessary, queuing all day to vote. Campaigners found, somewhat to their surprise, that many women in the rural areas especially were much more politically aware than their husbands. The radio was a particularly important factor in this."[4] The silent and marginalized majority of women spoke at last, and the People's Redemption Party won the elections in Kano State.

The victory was of great political significance. National elements espousing radical programs within the context of Islamic ideals of social justice had been able, with the support of women voting for the first time in the North, to defeat the conservative National Party of Nigeria (NPN) in what was regarded as its home base—the conservative, feudal, and Islamized North.

From the inception of representative government in the 1950s to the enfranchisement of Northern women in 1978, the primary political question for Muslim Hausa women was whether they could participate in public affairs. When only men could vote, both the PRP and the NPN turned to sympathetic women who were not in seclusion to help them woo male voters and entertain them at political rallies. With the enfranchisement of women in 1978, mobilizing women voters became important. In the 1979 elections both the PRP and the NPN resurrected the mechanism of women's wings and for their leaders revived the title *magajiya* (queen mother, "one who speaks for women"), a well-known title for women leaders of women. Before the 1983 elections the PRP moved further and appointed Kande Balarabe, a staff nurse and midwife in a Kano hospital, as secretary of its women's wing in Kano State. After the elections she became deputy national president of the PRP.[5]

But Kande Balarabe was a woman out of step with her culture. In a state where fewer than 1 percent of the adult women over the age of 21 are literate in English and 98 percent of all adult women are still in near-total seclusion, the PRP found it difficult to find women with the political and administrative experience to help implement its programs. Yet the PRP kept faith with the women in Kano State and carried out its campaign promises. It built girls' schools and women's centers, established women-only evening literacy classes, and appointed women to public posts—three women commissioners (state ministers), one permanent secretary (head of a government department), and ten women (one each) to para-statal boards. Thus, women reappeared in public affairs in Muslim Hausa society, although no specific women's agenda emerged until 1983. Even then, the youth of the women appointed to public positions and their relative lack of experience made it difficult for them to carry out their responsibilities. The high visibility of the appointments, however, has meant that for the first time many women and girls have begun to see themselves as having a public life.

The appointment of women to public positions by the PRP also had an effect on the NPN. The Shehu Shagari civilian administration of 1979 appointed Ebun Oyagbola, a Yoruba woman, minister of national planning for four years and Elizabeth Evase, a woman from the North, junior minister for education in the federal government. No fewer than six Northern women were appointed commissioners in their states. The Shagari government was overthrown in December 1983 by the military. General Majammadu Buhari, the new head of state, required all the state governments to include one woman as a member of each state cabinet. This directive was confirmed by Gen. Ibrahim Babangida, who toppled the Buhari government in another military coup in 1985.

YORUBA WOMEN AND THE POLITICS OF TRADE

The Yoruba, numbering more than 20 million people in Nigeria, have a common linguistic heritage. They populate virtually all of the area once known as Western Nigeria, including the states of Lagos, Ogun, Ondo, Oshun, and Oyo, as well as parts of the Delta, Kwara, and Benue states.[6] The portions of Nigeria in which they live include coastal swamps, a dense rain forest, and savanna, which reaches in some places to the banks of the Niger River.

Between the fifteenth and nineteenth centuries the Yoruba country was one of the most fertile sources of African slaves to work in the Americas and so earned itself the name Slave Coast. Perhaps as an adaptation to the insecurity of their existence, the Yoruba evolved a characteristic diplomatic style likely to preserve their way of life; they are typically seen as polite, restrained, cautious, and subtle in their dealings with others.

As with the Hausa in Northern Nigeria, British overlordship in the latter part of the nineteenth century left the indigenous kingdoms much to themselves in their daily political activities. The colonial government was not interested in exerting influence over those matters of greatest concern to women at the time—that is, those involving matters of personal law in activities such as marriage, child custody, and child rearing, as well as health, home maintenance, and the scientific support of agriculture and manufacturing.[7] There was little conflict of interest between the colonial government and Yoruba women in these matters.

In fact, British activities were in many ways useful to women. The Pax Britannica brought internal peace and, with the abolition of the slave trade, greater personal security.[8] Yet women did resist those British-made laws that they felt were inimical to their interests, using all the avenues available to them. Because trade proved to be one such area, the colonial era is marked by actions of women to defend their trade interests. Colonialism thus inspired its own group of women political activists, many of them, like Madame Jojolola, leaders of women's market associations.[9] Allying themselves with the educated elite, they used new techniques to fight for their cause, including press campaigns and petitioning the colonial office and government authorities in Britain.

Militant women's organizations like the Lagos Women's Party and the Abeokuta Women's Union pressed further and asked for female representation in local government bodies and the right to vote in municipal elections.[10] Both organizations sought to establish a broad base of political, social, and economic activity for women, setting up branches throughout the country that linked elite women and traditional market women in a common cause.

With the introduction of party politics in 1950 and representative government in 1951, Yoruba women became politically active, organizing women's wings of political parties. But in the decade of transition to political independence (1950–60), even though women in Southern Nigeria were granted the vote in 1957, not one woman was elected to the national legislature. During the subsequent 20 years Southern political parties were genuinely reluctant to nominate women as candidates.

In the 1979 elections, which ushered in the second instance of civilian representative government (the Second Republic) after 13 years of military rule, not many women ran for political office, and only two were nominated by their parties as running mates to male candidates for governor. Although both women lost their bids for gubernatorial office, Janet Akinrinade, a Yoruba, won the election in her state and was later appointed minister of state in the Federal Ministry of Internal Affairs for a short period.[11] A second woman, Ebun Oyagbola of the NPN, was appointed minister for national planning and served for four years in the Shagari cabinet. Even though a few Yoruba women attained elective or appointive office, their presence in a sea of male legislators was sheer tokenism—as a recapitulation of the 1979 national elections will show.

None of the five political parties that existed in 1979 fielded a woman for the post of president, vice-president, or even governor. The NPN, however, did nominate two women for the office of deputy governor. There were no women in the 95-member Senate and only two women in the 449-member House of Representatives. Of the 45 members of the federal cabinet, only one woman had full cabinet rank, Ebun Oyagbola. There were also three female junior ministers.

In the 1983 elections, according to party sources, fewer than 100 of the 12,000 candidates for political office were women. Two candidates ran for deputy governorships, 4 for seats in the Senate (with one winning a seat), 19 for seats in the House of Representatives, and 71 for seats in state assemblies. The PRP, then led by Aminu Kano, was the only party that nominated a woman, Bola Ogunbor, as a presidential running mate. But the experiment was aborted with the death of the presidential candidate, Aminu Kano, three weeks after he had announced his choice for vice-president.

More than half of the 65 million registered voters in Nigeria were women, but women's presence in national political organs was meager. The women's wings of the political parties worked tirelessly and energetically for their parties but merely to ensure the election of men. If the record of women's participation in national political office was poor under the civilian governments, under the military regimes, which have been in power longer, it has been dismal.

Under military rule not one woman has been appointed to the Supreme Military Council or the Armed Forces Ruling Council. Even the Constitution Drafting Committee appointed by Gen. Muritala Mohammed did not have a single woman member, and the Constituent Assembly that ratified the constitution of 1979 contained only three women members in a country where women make up more than 50 percent of the population. It is therefore not surprising that Yoruba women, many of whom are Muslims, voiced no concern when the 1979 Constituent Assembly ratified the provision for including sharia (Islamic law) in the constitution of 1979.[12]

Thus, for Muslim women the matters that affect them most—marriage, divorce, child custody—are not under the protection of the constitution but under the sole jurisdiction of the states.[13] Yet, barring a few sections of the constitution that were suspended, the post-1983 military regimes allowed the provisions of the 1979 constitution to stand, including the section on "fundamental human rights," which guarantees every citizen equality of rights, obligations, and opportunities before the law. These constitutional guarantees are in conflict with the sharia, which renders a woman's testimony in court equal to half that of a man and her property rights less than a man's.

Yoruba women, like other women in Nigeria, have not awakened to basic flaws and gender bias of the new institutions being offered as models for imitation. Women have yet to realize, for example, that government investment decisions can make the difference between prosperity and poverty and that scientific research can be applied to solve the problems of health and agriculture. When they do, women will react even more vigorously than their 50,000 sisters in the northern Plateau State who "went berserk and took to the streets" to protest the failure of the state government to pay teachers' salaries and make grants to schools.[14]

SAYING NO TO DEMOCRACY: IGBO WOMEN AND POLITICS

The Igbo are a group of 20 million people living mainly in the Abia, Anambra, Enugu, Imo, and Rivers states of Southeastern Nigeria.[15] One million of them, sometimes referred to as the Ika Igbo, live west of the Niger River. Other ethnic groups have joined it on the west side of the river in the Delta State. The Ika Igbo appear to have been greatly influenced by their neighbors farther to the west in the powerful Yoruba and Benin kingdoms. Unlike their kin on the eastern side of the river, whose political system is a republican type of village democracy, they have established a constitutional type of village monarchy. The major difference is that in the village democracy it is not possible to identify a territorial unit in which there is a governmental authority. Leadership is achieved rather than ascribed, and authority is so dispersed within each autonomous unit that it is difficult to point to particular individuals of either sex who play an outstanding role in the community's political life.[16] Both political systems are similar in their dispersal of political authority between the sexes and among lineage and kinship institutions, age-groups, religious leaders, and social organizations and in the small size of their political units.

Among the Igbo, group thought and action take precedence over individual concerns. This strategy has allowed the Igbo to survive the harsh environment in which they live and to guarantee the reproduction of society in a context where individual survival still remains the central question of existence. Because much of the Igbo heartland is in the wet forest zone of Southeastern Nigeria, it is one of the most disease-ridden regions in the world. The prolific insect life and the prevailing ignorance about the causes of most diseases made life in precolonial times precarious. Death rates were high, and, in response, birthrates, sustained by culture and religion, were also high.[17] By 1953, soon after the transition to independence had begun, crude birthrates in the Igbo areas ranged from 51 to 55 per 1,000, with women averaging between 6.5 and 7.3 live births.[18] Life expectancy at birth was somewhere between 25 and 35 years.[19]

The insecurity of living with disease and the five centuries of slavery combined to make the survival of the group important. Individuals see their immortality as guaranteed through preservation of the group, which traditionally acknowledges a community of ancestors who exist contemporaneously with the living; personal and group prospects are conflated. Even today, when life expectancies have improved to about 51 years, other factors have arisen to encourage group values among the Igbo.

Like the Yoruba and Hausa, the Igbo are farmers and traders. Among the Igbo, however, gender roles tend to be the reverse of those in other Nigerian societies. Igbo men engage in trade, while farming has remained a shared responsibility of both men and women, with men clearing the land and tending the yam crop and women doing the other backbreaking work that agriculture entails.

Power is dispersed between Igbo men and women. In both the democratic republican and constitutional monarchic political systems, each sex manages its own affairs, with separate kinship institutions, age grades, and secret and title societies.[20]

Igbo marriages are generally close. Although polygyny is allowed under Igbo custom and Nigerian law, monogamous marriages are far more commonplace. In the home women are subordinate to their husbands and defer to their authority in decision making; outside the home women display a good measure of resourcefulness and courage, tackling issues that men lack the courage to approach. For example, in the past few years village women have been the driving force behind the provision of better water supplies, the building of maternity, health, and day-care centers, the increasing mechanization in processing rice and *garri* (grated cassava that has been dried, allowed to ferment, and then fried), as well as the use of the UNICEF Expanded Programme on Immunization and adult literacy programs for women. It is among the Igbo that one encounters the most illustrative historical examples of Nigerian women's participation in politics.

Perhaps the most memorable of women's mobilizations in the colonial period was the Women's War of 1929.[21] Without consulting the Igbo, the British colonial authorities created a decentralized prefecture system to implement indirect rule and appointed local male agents to act as warrant chiefs. Because the Igbo did not have a chieftaincy system, they were offended not only by the exclusion of women but also by the warrant chiefs' often blatant misuse of power. The Igbo could not even imagine how one man could arrogate to himself the responsibility of speaking for all the people and the white ruler at the same time.[22] When the news spread that women's property (usually livestock) was to be assessed, women assumed that this was an initial move toward female taxation.[23] The prospect of taxation without consultation aroused their fury. Igbo women resisted the census and expressed their dissatisfaction with the native administration, the colonial system, and the exclusion of women from politics by holding demonstrations across the Igbo heartland. They were met with volleys of bullets from the colonial army and police that left more than 50 women dead. A commission of enquiry into the Women's War listed some of their grievances and demands, among them that "the Native Courts no longer hear cases" and that "all white men should go to their own country"—or at least that "women should serve on the Native Courts and a woman [should be] appointed District Officer."[24]

Although such demands may have seemed irrational and ridiculous to the British colonial authorities, they were legitimate in the context of Igbo society, where the sexes could be represented fully in any decisions that affected their lives.[25] In attempting to establish specialized political institutions on the Western model, with participation on the basis of individual achievement, the British created a system in which there was no place for group solidarity, no possibility of shared political authority or power of enforcement, and thus very little place for women.

Interestingly, the demands articulated in the Women's War and other political movements have been met and are no longer vital issues for Igbo women. The white man has gone back to his country (Nigeria is independent), and the Native Court system has been abolished. In the Abia, Anambra, Delta, Enugu, Imo, and Rivers states, as elsewhere in the country, women currently serve as judges and magistrates, as well as lawyers in the courts. In 1976 a woman was appointed attorney general of Anambra State.

The prospects of women's participation in public life in Southeastern Nigeria underwent important changes immediately after the civil war in January 1970, when the unity of the country and the rights of every citizen to live unmolested and earn a livelihood in any part of the country were reaffirmed. Since then there has been an upsurge in the employment of women and in their education. With many men joining the Biafran armed forces, educated women were pressed into service to maintain civilian operations in the rear. When these were efficiently run, attitudes toward the employment of women began to change, and in consequence the education of girls was less likely to be regarded as a waste of resources. The experiences of the war also proved that old people could be maintained just as well by their daughters as by their sons. Only in the two Igbo states of the federation is there a preponderance of girls over boys in primary and secondary schools and an ever increasing number of women in the universities.

Igbo women, conditioned by their culture to expect group solidarity as well as shared political authority, have a history of activism in politics and development. Having also shouldered the burdens of the civil war along with men, they have earned a greater measure of independence in their affairs than have Hausa and Yoruba women, and they serve as models of what Nigerian women can achieve.

WOMEN'S PARTICIPATION IN PUBLIC AFFAIRS

Although women have individually and collectively made great strides toward the ultimate goal of equal rights, obligations, and opportunities before the law, progress has been piecemeal. Only now are women as a group becoming visible; only now is their situation being regarded as a national problem. Unlike three decades ago, women and men now receive equal pay for equal jobs in the formal economy. They no longer have to resign when they go on maternity leave and then reapply for their jobs when ready to return to work. Individual women, like Pamela Sadauki in Kaduna State and Latifat Okunnu in Lagos State, have been appointed deputy governors. But Nigeria remains a male-dominated society, and no specific women's agenda has emerged. As Gambo Sawaba, a Zaria-based political activist with NEPU, has said, "Men simply use women and dump them. . . . We are constantly reminded, directly and indirectly, that because we are women, we cannot partake of the goodies when they become available. . . . I have fought to reform society alongside men. The so-called monolithic north (created as one region dominating the two, later three, southern regions, populationwise and politically) is no longer there. We [Northern Nigerian women] killed it for the sake of the unity of the country. We said no to religious intolerance. We said no to feudalism. But what did we get in the end?"[26]

Part of the problem is that most men are not even conscious of contributions that women make to society and are brought up to think of women simply as appendages. So, for example, it is not well understood that by taking care of sick, injured, retired, and elderly people from the urban areas, rural women are providing social security and thus subsidizing the federal and state governments. In fact, by physically reproducing and nurturing the labor force of the future, women are in effect running a free social security system for the parasitic British-imposed enclave economy, consisting mostly of the urban centers and their associated industrial establishments.[27]

But things are changing fast, and the realization has seeped through the educated male elite that women must be associated with men to build a united country and develop it. Thus, in 1987 the Better Life Programme for Rural Women was started under the auspices of Maryam Babangida, the wife of the head of state. This program is intended to stimulate rural women to achieve a better standard of living and to sensitize the general population to their plight. It is also meant to mobilize women to work toward specific goals in all spheres of national life through collective action, and to raise the consciousness of women about their rights and their social, economic, and political responsibilities. The program has been very popular with the elite in the urban areas and with donor agencies; UNICEF, for example, has tacked onto it a very successful Expanded Programme for Immunization. The Better Life Programme for Rural Women has not, however, evoked much enthusiasm in many rural areas, where it has been nicknamed "the bitter life programme for rural women." Many women contrast the harsh facts of life in rural areas with the meetings and celebrations of the program that feature elite urban women. Whether this highly publicized and visible program has mobilized rural women to support the transitional military regime is questionable, because its expenditures work out at less than one naira (less than U.S. $0.05) per year for each married woman in a country of more than 55 million females.

Women have also set up their own organizations to fight their gender wars. Marginalized as they are, they have established more than 300 nongovernmental organizations nationally, with the National Council of Women Societies (NCWS), founded in 1958, as their umbrella organization.[28] This council, which seeks to promote the welfare of women in various fields, emphasizes education and training for women, and it was recognized by the military government as the representative body for women. A final stone in the foundation upon which women may initiate action to secure their equality in law and in society was laid by the military government on 19 June 1990, when the eleven-member National Commission on Women was inaugurated in response to resolutions 3320 and 3523 of the U.N. General Assembly, made in December 1975. The commission, which includes two men and is chaired by a woman, Bolanle Awe, acts as the coordinating body for programs to facilitate the development of women's potential and to ensure their full integration into socioeconomic development.[29]

The NCWS has adopted a low-key approach to solving the problems of women. As Emily Aig-Imokhude, president of the council, said, "Even though some people say the NCWS is not radical enough, we survive by working hard. I have found that confrontation has negative effects, and you do not get much done that way."[30] This approach has led to the establishment of much more radical groups, like the Federation of Muslim Women Associations in Nigeria and Women in Nigeria (WIN). Founded in 1982 at the Ahmadu Bello University in Zaria, WIN has seen the need for women to "organise and fight for their social and economic rights in the family, workplace and society." It aims at creating non-sexist alternative channels to government, and it has established institutions through a socialist ideology, departing from the traditional social welfare aspect of women's lives and substituting instead a radical democratic feminism.[31] WIN publishes and carries out research on urban and rural women in the fields of health, education, family, law, religion, and the treatment of women in the media.

What chances of success has such an approach in Nigerian society, which is male dominated and in which the sexes are so sharply dichotomized, especially in the North? Given the cultural climate, WIN might be successful in righting minor wrongs. But on major issues that challenge the authority of men over women, it is likely to lose. Although women outnumber men in Nigeria, and women have the vote, the female majority is far from becoming a political majority. As Barbara J. Callaway has remarked, "The vote is not particularly powerful, when power rests and is exercised largely outside the formal political process."[32] Women's progress now depends to a great extent on their finding supportive men in positions of authority and power—which accounts for the low-key approach of NCWS. In a society where men head extended families and where women are regarded as subordinate to men, there is likely to be resistance to any direct challenge to the authority of men over women, such as a radical revision of the family laws on child custody, marriage, and divorce (including the sharia laws). Particularly in Northern Nigeria, a sharp turn to conservative Islamic fundamentalism is a likely consequence.[33]

At this stage of the search for equality, women's way forward seems to be the indirect approach favored by the NCWS, with its emphasis on expanding opportunities in education and training for women, attacking sexually discriminatory absurdities in the application of the laws, and generally creating more elbow room in which women can operate. Women have already had an encouraging experience with education in the states peopled mainly by the Igbo, where there has been a change in social attitudes toward the employment of women. Expanded educational opportunities have led to a preponderance of women in primary and secondary schools in the Igbo states, which will have consequences for women's positions of authority.

In Kano State, the heart of Muslim Hausaland,

education is recognized as the key to the future for women. Because participation in public affairs requires literacy in English, a good general education allied with experience in managing an organization has become a vehicle for the social advancement of women that does not overtly call the authority of men into question. Thus, Alhaji Galadanci has been able to legitimize the expansion of the education by invoking the needs of society and the injunctions of Islam—not, it should be noted, by invoking women's rights.[34] The rapid expansion of the education of girls and women has not yet, however, challenged the position of men in the family and in society.

Western education, with its emphasis on learning to read, write, and analyze, as contrasted with Muslim education, which stresses memorization, cannot of itself change the life prospects or the public and domestic roles of women. Rather, it is a precondition for change, making it possible for qualified women to find careers in an expanding economy as an alternative to marriage, housekeeping, child rearing, and nurturing. To be able to challenge the male domination of society, women require a market for the skills that they acquire through education, as well as changes in the cultural norms that now demarcate the social space within which women can operate. Such changes are apt to come slowly.

As women become more educated and gain mastery over their lives, and as their life expectancy increases—in conjunction with decreases in infant and child mortality—the muted questions now being raised by elite women about the wisdom of having so many children will become the concern of women generally. Programs restricting population growth and promoting family planning will then become more acceptable in this pro-natalist society.[35] Elite women began questioning the sexism involved in the population policy formulated by the military regime of Ibrahim Babangida, which called for "four children to one woman." Women's societies are also seeking legal ways of doing away with polygyny.

In spite of the advances made by women in recent years in their fight for equality with men, one major question remains unanswered: How will women be represented in the system of parliamentary democracy crafted and put into operation by the Babangida military regime? The new parliamentary institutions, like those of the Western world that they replicate, are gender biased and need to be freed from the effects of the powerful class and sex stratification systems inherent in such institutions, which ensure male domination of politics and government. It is already clear that in the government-imposed two-party system, whichever party is voted into power in the 1993 elections—the Social Democratic Party or the National Republican Convention—will pursue a policy of tokenism with regard to women.[36]

The winning party has to set up a government that, while promising to provide social and economic progress, will probably try to guide progress within a framework that does not generate demands for mass political participation, particularly by women. Rather, as before, policy will tend to be agreed on between the party in power and the hidden guarantor of the constitution—the military. As in the past, the important decisions will be made outside the established political framework. Individual women will simply be used by the government to legitimize itself in the eyes of the majority of women voters.

Ultimately, however, genuine democracy and political legitimacy depend on the extent to which a government permits popular control of its basic policies, as opposed to mere tacit assent to or ratification of the policies that it puts forward itself.[37] For control over policy to be popular and genuine, it must include the active participation of the more than 50 percent of the Nigerian population who are women. This means not only that women's political and other organizations must be active at all levels but also that the government must ensure that women and their organizations are constantly informed and educated about matters of policy and issues of particular interest to them. These requirements have not been fulfilled; in consequence, no specific women's agenda has emerged.

Apart, then, from setting up organizations that make possible this flow of information, it is necessary to correct the gender biases of the newly crafted political system consciously. This can be done by changing the current basis of representation in legislative assemblies at all levels to ensure parity of representation in each constituency for both men and women. My proposal would be to have one electoral roll divided into two parts: one for men, the other for women. Each electoral constituency would elect two representatives to any legislative assembly—one a man, the other a woman. All voters in a constituency would vote for one man and one woman to sit on the legislative organs.[38] Such elections would be more in keeping with the indigenous division of roles in Nigerian societies, especially those societies where the male-female dichotomy is sharp and where women preside over their own affairs.

What would then emerge would be legislative assemblies with parity of representation between men and women—a modernized dual-sex system—rather than legislatures with a token sprinkling of women. Moreover, if the convention of equal or nearly equal gender representation in the cabinet is established and maintained, policy matters of particular interest to women can be discussed at the highest levels of policy making. Such representation would also better reflect the gender dichotomy already familiar to Nigerians in the operation of the dual-sex system and would pave the way for the easier attainment of the equal human rights enshrined in the Nigerian constitution.

PROSPECTS

Because the tyranny of a minority (men) is undemocratic and unacceptable, and because women have interests particular to women, a modern version of the indigenous sex-based system could be profitably introduced into the received political and educational systems. No matter how liberal and broad-minded male representatives might be, they cannot fully represent women's interests. No president of Nigeria or commander-in-chief of the armed forces has been pregnant for nine months, delivered a live baby, and then had to watch the baby die in his hands, as many Nigerian women do. Only a woman knows the pain and suffering that attend such unnecessary deaths. The British colonial government and its successor Nigerian governments, both civilian and military, did not achieve this elementary understanding of the interests that motivate women.

The effect of ensuring parity of women's representation in legislative assemblies would be of special benefit at the national and state levels, where societies of different cultural backgrounds meet to discuss policy. Experience in Norway and Sweden has shown that where there is a substantial representation of women in the executive and legislative organs of the state, discussion has become less acrimonious and more fruitful.[39] A parity of representation would also be more in keeping with the "federal" character of Nigeria.[40]

It remains to be seen whether Nigerian women or any other African women can gain political power without the creation of a modern version of the traditional dual-sex system or without drastic changes in economic structures. Economic equality is necessary to support political equality for all men and women, just as economic stratification now supports male domination and female dependence. Whatever the economic or political system, unless the ruling elite institutes parity or near parity in the political representation of women and develops a feminist consciousness, women will remain discriminated against and invisible.

NOTES

1. Northern Nigeria, for example, was peopled by the Hausa (who speak a Chadic language), the Kanuri, the Tiv, the Jukun, and others. The Habe (Hausa) states, whose population now numbers more than 20 million, had a feudal state structure and were trading with Muslim North Africa by the eleventh century. Similarly, the Benin Empire in southwestern Nigeria antedated the tenth century and, along with the Yoruba Empire, traded in slaves with Western Europe as far back as the fifteenth century. In contrast, groups in southeastern Nigeria like the Igbo, Ibibio, and Efik had a communal social structure, whose

gender biases were less marked than those in neighboring precolonial states and certainly than those in twentieth-century Britain.

2. The different migrating peoples who had adopted Hausa as their common language by the sixteenth century are collectively known as the Habe to distinguish them from the Fulani, a nomadic people who conquered the Habe states in the jihad (holy war) of the early nineteenth century. The term Hausa is often used for the Habe and Fulani taken together. Habe is thus used to designate the language of the Hausa-Fulani as one cultural group. The Habe-Fulani now occupy mainly the Jigawa, Kaduna, Kano, Katsina, Kebbi, and Sokoto states of Nigeria, and Hausa-speaking peoples number around 20 million in and outside Nigeria. Independent republics like Niger are mostly Hausa.

3. Johan Galtung, "Perspectives on Development: Past, Present, Future," in Johan Galtung, *Peace and Social Structure: Essays in Peace Research*, no. 3 (Copenhagen: Christian Ejlers, 1978), 315–32.

4. Ayesha Imam, *Women and Politics in Northern Nigeria* (Lagos: Punch, 1981).

5. Kande Balarabe was born and raised in Sierra Leone, where her father was in business. She attended the Freetown Girls' Secondary School, the Hartford Secondary School for Girls, and the Royal School of Nursing in London. In 1977 she became a staff nurse in a Kano hospital, joining the PRP in 1981. Barbara J. Callaway, *Muslim-Hausa Women in Nigeria* (Syracuse: Syracuse University Press, 1987), 119.

6. Yoruba-speaking peoples also live in Togo and Benin, the neighboring countries to the west.

7. The British were very interested in expanding the production of cash crops in the colonies, and they experimented with and gave advice on the production of commodities like cocoa, tobacco, palm produce, and cotton. People were free to accept or reject the advice given. In Northern Nigeria, for example, the farmers preferred growing groundnuts to growing the cotton promoted by the British. The cultivation of groundnuts thus expanded without British scientific support.

8. Although the trade in slaves was immediately abolished upon the imposition of British rule, the abolition of domestic slavery was only gradual. Not until the early 1930s was domestic slavery finally eliminated under pressure exerted on the British in the League of Nations.

9. Madame Jojolola, who died in 1932, was the second *iyalode* (first lady) of Abeokuta. She used her position and influence to promote the interests of the traders and cloth dyers (*adire*) of Egbaland.

10. LeRoy Denzer, in "Colonial Nigeria" (Paper delivered at the Congress to Assess the Impact of Colonial Rule in Nigeria, University of Nigeria, 1989), gives a fuller discussion of the activities of Yoruba women during the colonial era in defense of their trade interests.

11. The other woman gubernatorial candidate, Oyibo Odinamadu, is an Igbo.

12. The 1979 constitution defined sharia to pertain to marriage, divorce, family relationship, or the guardianship of an infant (sec. 242 [ii]); any question of Islamic personal law (sec. 243); any question of Islamic personal law regarding an infant, prodigal or person of unsound mind (sec. 241[4]), as well as establishing sharia courts of appeal in each of Nigeria's ten "Islamic" states, all in Muslim Hausaland (sec. 240 [i]).

13. See below; and Callaway, *Muslim-Hausa Women in Nigeria,* 102–8.

14. *Nigerian Standard,* 9 March 1983.

15. Victor Manfredi, "Igboid," in John Bendor-Samuel, ed., *The Niger-Congo Languages* (Lanham, Md.: University Press of America, 1989), 336.

16. For a further discussion of the political institutions of the Igbo, see Kamene Okonjo, *Nigerian Women's Participation in National Politics: Legitimacy and Stability in an Era of Transition, Women in International Development* series (East Lansing: Michigan State University, 1991).

17. J. C. Caldwell, "The Social Repercussions of Colonial Rule: Demographic Aspects," in A. Adu Boahen, ed., *General History of Africa,* vol. 7: *Africa Under Colonial Domination, 1880–1935* (London: Heinemann, 1985), 463.

18. Ansley Coale, "Estimates of Fertility and Mortality in Tropical Africa," in John C. Caldwell and Chukuku Okonjo, eds., *The Population of Tropical Africa* (London: Longmans, 1968), 182.

19. Etienne Van De-Walle, "An Approach to the Study of Fertility in Nigeria," *Population Studies* 19, part 1 (July 1965): 11.

20. An age-grade society is one whose members consist of persons—girls and boys separately—within three to five years of the same age. For running their affairs women were grouped into the *ikporo-ani* (all adult women in a community), the *umuada* (all married and unmarried daughters of a lineage, village, or village group), and the *unyemedi* (all wives of a lineage, village, or village group). Other effective groups were the *otu-ogbo* (initially play groups of all girls and boys separately in age grades of three to five years) and titled societies like the Ozo title group. See, e.g., A. E. Afigbo, *The Warrant Chiefs: Indirect Rule in South-Eastern Nigeria, 1891–1920* (London: Longmans, 1972); Margaret Mackeson Green, *Ibo Village Affairs,* 2nd ed. (New York: Praeger, 1964); Sylvia Leith-Ross, *African Women: A Study of the Ibo of Nigeria,* 2nd ed. (New York: Praeger, 1965); and Kamene Okonjo, "The Dual-Sex Political System in Operation: Women and Community Politics in Mid-Western Nigeria," in Nancy Hafkin and Edna Bay, eds., *Women in Africa: Studies in Social and Economic Change* (Stanford, Calif.: Stanford University Press, 1976).

21. The word *war* is used in the sense used by the Igbo. "Making war" is an institutionalized form of punishment used by Igbo women and is also known as "sitting on a man." For further details on the custom of sitting on a man see Judith Van Allen, "Aba Riots or Igbo Women's War? Ideology, Stratification and Invisibility of Women," in Hafkin and Bay, eds., *Women in Africa.*

22. It was not necessary in the constitutional village monarchies of the western Igbo to create such warrant chiefs, for the British converted the male chiefs into their local agents. The female chiefs were not incorporated into the local government system.

23. A previous census of men and their property had been followed by the taxation of men in 1926, despite assurances by British officials that this would not happen. In 1925 the British had decided to introduce direct taxation in accordance with their imperial philosophy that the colonized should pay for the costs of colonization. Male taxation was introduced without widespread trouble, although there were tax riots in Warri Province (west of the Niger) in 1927. Van Allen, "Aba Riots or Igbo Women's War?" 71.

24. Ibid., 71–75. The first commission of enquiry, appointed in January 1930 and reporting at the end of the same month, completely exonerated those responsible for the firing. A second commission, which was more representative, was appointed in February 1930 and reported in May of the same year. The second report, with its annexures and minutes, runs to two bulky volumes. For further discussion of the Women's War see Sylvia Leith-Ross, *African Women,* 19–39, 109–10, 163–65, 214; and Margery Perham, *Native Administration in Nigeria* (London: Oxford University Press, 1937); and Afigbo, *Warrant Chiefs.*

25. The colonial government's use of force against the women was excessive and unjustified. Although there were claims before the first commission that the demonstrations of the women were threatening and terrifying, no evidence was produced of one single person being killed or even gravely hurt by the women. The commission did not attempt to find out why the demonstrations in so many dispersed places took the same form, why the demands made at the various demonstrations were the same, or who the leaders of the "insurrection" were. The commission, with its British gender bias, assumed that men were behind it all.

26. Gambo Sawaba, in *Newswatch* (Lagos) 12, no. 24 (1990): 30.

27. The British established many new urban centers and expanded old ones, linking them all together to create a parasitic enclave economy, which they tied to the world capitalist system then dominated by Britain. These centers have served as staging points for the transmission of value from the domestic market economy to the economy of the metropolitan power. The enclave economy imposed by

Britain on the domestic market economy has become part of the Nigerian economic structure and to that extent is indigenous.

28. Prominent among these are societies like Women in Nigeria, the National Association of University Women, the Nigerian Market Women's Association, and the Federation of Muslim Women Association in Nigeria.

29. Bolanle Awe is a professor of history at the University of Ibadan and director of the Institute of African Studies at the university. She has served as a commissioner in Oyo State.

30. Quoted in *Newswatch* 12, no. 24 (1990): 31.

31. Soji Akinrinade, "For Girls Only," *Newswatch* 12, no. 24 (1990): 31.

32. Callaway, *Muslim-Hausa Women in Nigeria,* 124.

33. Radical rhetoric coupled with an appeal to fundamentalist Islam can lead to disastrous developments, as events in Kano at the end of 1980 show. There the fanatical and heretical religious movement—the Maitatsine—took over parts of the city, and the army and police had to be called in to disband it, with a loss of nearly 10,000 lives. Ibid.

34. Alhaji S. Galadanci, "Education of Women in Islam with Reference to Nigeria," *Nigerian Journal of Islam* 1, no. 2 (January–June 1971): 6. When Alhaji Shehu Galadanci wrote this celebrated article, he was vice-chancellor of the University of Sokoto. Ten years later the arti-cle became the centerpiece of the PRP platform in Kano State.

35. For example, in Kano City, the heartland of the Muslim far North and a metropolitan area of some 5 million persons, no family planning office or publicly available information on either family planning or birth control was available as late as 1983. Callaway, *Muslim-Hausa Women in Nigeria,* 28.

36. The two parties are government sponsored, with the SDP slightly to the left and the NRC slightly to the right of center.

37. Victor Wallis, "Two Elections," *Monthly Review* 36, no. 10 (1985): 55–59.

38. A possible variation of this scheme would be for all men to elect one man and all women to elect one woman in each constituency. I prefer the option in which all voters—both male and female—elect a man and a woman.

39. Gun Hedlund, "Women's Interests in Local Politics," in Kathleen B. Jones and Anna G. Jónasdóttir, eds., *The Political Interest of Gender: Developing Theory and Research with a Feminist Face,* Sage Modern Politics Series, vol. 20 (London: Sage, 1988), 79–105.

40. The federal government, in the interests of unity in the country, tries to have all states represented in the bodies that it establishes. This policy is called "maintaining the federal character of the federation."

▲ *Norway*

POLITICS

Type of Political System: democracy
  Sovereignty: constitutional monarchy
  Executive-Legislative System: parliamentary
Type of State: unitary
Type of Party System: multiparty
Major Political Parties

Det Norske Arbeiderparti (AP, or Norwegian Labor Party): Democratic socialist party established in 1887; has dominated politics in Norway since 1927. Leader is a woman, Gro Harlem Brundtland.[a]

Senterpartiet (SP, or Center Party): Founded as the Agrarian Party in 1920; generally conservative on most economic, social, and religious issues but also stresses ecology.[b]

Høyre (Conservative Party): Primarily urban based; emphasizes private investment, limited government control of industry, and lower taxes, especially for businesses.[c]

Kristelig Folkeparti (KrF, or Christian People's Party): Center Christian party formed in 1933; focuses on maintaining the principles of Christianity in public life and has introduced anti-abortion legislation.[d]

Sosialistisk Venstreparti (SV, or Socialist Left Party): Formed in 1973; resulted from the merger of several leftist parties.[e]

Fremskrittspartiet (FrP, or Progress Party): Formerly Anders Lange's Party; founded in the 1970s as an antiestablishment party.[f]

Venstre (Liberal Party): Formed in 1884; moderate on economic policy, occupying a position between the Conservative and Labor parties; stresses ecological issues.[g]

Det Liberale Folkepartiet (DLF, or Liberal People's Party): Formerly the New People's Party; founded after divisions in the Liberal Party in the 1970s.[h]

Norges Kommunistiske Parti (NKP, or Norwegian Communist Party): Has participated in several coalitions of leftist parties but has remained an independent party.[i]

Arbeidernes Kommunistparti (AKP, or Workers' Communist Party): Marxist-Leninist party formed in 1972.[j]

Rød Valgalliannse (RV, or Red Electoral Alliance): Electoral alliance of the Workers' Communist Party and nonaligned socialists.[k]
Year Women Granted Right to Vote: 1913
Year Women Granted Right to Stand for Election: 1907
Percentage of Women in the Unicameral Legislature: 35.7%[l]
Percentage of Electorate Voting for Highest Elected Office in Most Recent Election (1985): 84.0%[m]

DEMOGRAPHICS
Population: 4,273,624[n]
Percentage of Population in Urban Areas
  Overall: 70.7%
  Female: 71.9%
  Male: 69.5%
Percentage of Population Below Age 15: 20.1%
Birthrate (per 1,000 population): 12
Maternal Mortality Rate (per 100,000 live births): 4
Infant Mortality Rate (per 1,000 live births): 7
Mortality Rate for Children Under Five (per 1,000 live births): 8
Average Household Size (1991): 2.1[o]
Mean Age at First Marriage
  Female: 24.0
  Male: 26.3
Life Expectancy[p]
  Female: 79.8
  Male: 73.4

EDUCATION
Ratio of Female to Male Enrollment
  First-Level Education: 96
  Second-Level Education: 100
  Third-Level Education: 113

Literacy Rate
    Female: 99.0%
    Male: 99.0%

ECONOMY
Gross National Product per Capita: U.S.
    $14,370
Percentage of Labor Force in Agriculture: 8.7%
Distribution of Agricultural Workers by Sex[q]
    Female: 26.0%
    Male: 70.7%
Economically Active Population by Sex[r]
    Female: 70.2%
    Male: 82.5%

a. Arthur S. Banks, ed., *Political Handbook of the World, 1991* (Binghamton, N.Y.: CSA Publications, 1991), 506.
b. Ibid.
c. Ibid.

d. Ibid.
e. Ibid.
f. Elina Haavio-Mannila, ed., *Unfinished Democracy: Women in Nordic Politics* (New York: Pergamon, 1985), 171.
g. Banks, *Political Handbook of the World, 1991*, 506.
h. Haavio-Mannila, ed., *Unfinished Democracy*, 171.
i. Banks, *Political Handbook of the World, 1991*, 507.
j. Ibid.
k. Haavio-Mannila, ed., *Unfinished Democracy*, 171.
l. Equal Status Council, "Minifacts on Equal Rights" (Oslo: Likestillings Rådet, 1992).
m. Central Bureau of Statistics of Norway, *Storting Elections, 1989*, vol. 1, table 20.
n. Equal Status Council, "Minifacts."
o. Equal Status Council, "Minifacts on Equal Rights" (Oslo: Likestillings Rådet, 1991).
p. Equal Status Council, "Minifacts on Equal Rights" (Oslo: Likestillings Rådet, 1990).
q. Ibid.
r. Equal Status Council, "Minifacts," 1992. Individuals 25 to 65 years of age.

The State and Women: A Troubled Relationship in Norway

JANNEKE VAN DER ROS

The kingdom of Norway, with 4.3 million people, covers nearly 150,000 square miles of land and consists of mainland Norway—located on the western half of the Scandinavian Peninsula—the Svalbard Archipelago, and other islands in the Arctic. Norway is a constitutional monarchy with executive power formally vested in the king. In practice, power is controlled by the prime minister, the Council of State (cabinet), and the 165-member Parliament (Storting), which is elected for four-year terms. The Storting is divided into two chambers, the Lagting (upper chamber) and the Odelsting (lower chamber).

As in other parliamentary democracies, the prime minister is a member of the Storting and the leader of the party or one of the parties that holds a majority of seats—or most of the seats, in the case of a minority cabinet. The prime minister appoints members of the cabinet, each of whom heads a ministry. Together the ministries constitute the central administration, an important actor in Norwegian politics. From 1986 to 1989 and again since October 1990 a minority government headed by the Labor Party's Gro Harlem Brundtland (the nation's first woman prime minister) has controlled the government.

Norway has a multiparty system organized around several stable cross-cutting cleavages in the political culture.[1] Political cleavages include divisions along the left-right spectrum, as well as conflicts between rural and urban interests, modern industrialism and populism, and secular and religious approaches to politics. Because the cleavages do not reinforce each other, support for particular policies from several parties is often possible. Although the Labor Party has a minority cabinet, the Socialist Left Party ensures this cabinet parliamentary support for forming the cabinet.

The two economically based cleavages—between capital and labor and between producers and consumers of agricultural products—gave rise to Høyre (the Conservative Party), Det Norske Arbeiderparti (Labor Party), and what was originally the Agrarian Party but later became Senterpartiet (Center Party). These parties developed 100 years ago with the creation of increasingly mass-based parliamentary democracy, and they can clearly be identified by their economic, or class, interests. Venstre (Liberal Party) represents old rural-based interests and concerns over political freedoms that first challenged the Conservative Party. The Labor and Conservative parties are the largest political parties, holding 38 percent and 22 percent of the seats in the Storting, respectively.

Religiosity, cultural divisions over language, and differences about Norway's international role are reflected in the party system as well. A commitment to making a place for Christian values in politics gave rise to Kristelig Folkeparti (Christian People's Party) in the 1930s. The conflict over languages, especially the use of old Norwegian versus new Norwegian, is paramount in the cultural cleavage. As a result of controversy on international questions, primarily over whether to join the North Atlantic Treaty Organization, a faction within the Labor Party was thrown out and established Sosialistisk Folkeparti (Socialist People's Party). That faction gained support in another international debate through which Norway suffered in 1972: whether to join the European Economic Community (EEC). In 1973, when the Socialist People's Party combined forces with Norges Kommunistiske Parti (the Norwegian Communist Party), the new party became known as Sosialistisk Venstreparti (Socialist Left Party). During the 1970s Fremskrittspartiet (Progress Party), an antiwelfare state party capitalizing on sentiments against high taxation, overregulation, and

bureaucratization, emerged on the extreme right.

There are two main channels of political influence in Norway: electoral and corporate. The first channel is represented by political parties, their electoral platforms, the nomination of candidates, and voting. It is based primarily on territorial representation. The other channel is represented by the large number of organizations that work to promote specific interests and goals. This channel consists of the many boards, commissions, and councils through which bureaucrats, representatives of important interest organizations, experts, and political parties meet to assist the central administration in preparing legislative reforms. The basis for representation here is primarily functional, and members of these bodies are government appointees. Obtaining access to this meeting ground is of utmost importance for an interest organization's political influence. Women's organizations have found it difficult to gain access to these bodies, that is, to be defined as relevant organizations in this channel.[2]

Three main types of women's organizations exist in Norway: social and humanitarian, political, and economic. The first category comprises many older organizations, like Sanitetsforeningen (Norwegian Women's Public Health Organization), established in 1896. With 240,000 members it is the largest women's organization in Norway. Among the political organizations are women's chapters in the political parties, or auxiliaries, as well as such independent women's rights organizations as Kvinnesaksforeningen (Norwegian Association for the Rights of Women), established in 1884; Stemmerettsforeningen (the Association of Women's Suffrage), established in 1889; and the organizations of the new women's movement from the 1970s, such as Nyfeministene (New Feminists), Kvinnefronten (Women's Front), and Brød og Roser (Bread and Roses). The new women's movement revitalized and radicalized the older organizations.[3] Women's activism on economic issues is found in older labor organizations such as the women's trade unions and in women's organizations based on women's identification as economic actors, such as Bondekvinnelag (Norwegian Country Women's Organization), where women farmers and farmers' wives convene, and Husmorforbundet (Norwegian Housewives' Association), established in 1915, in part in opposition to the working-class Housemaids' Association (established in 1908). It is primarily the long-established women's organizations such as the National Women's Public Health Association and the Norwegian Housewives' Association that have obtained some access to the corporate channel. For the organizations of the new women's movement, with their radical aims, nontraditional methods, and nonhierarchical structures, it has been virtually impossible to access the corporate structure directly.

Helga M. Hernes, feminist political scientist and junior secretary of state, has described the Norwegian social democratic state as a patriarchal guardian state.[4] By this, Hernes means that the state has taken over guardianship of women from individual men. In spite of women's integration in the political system, the state is still male dominated, both with regard to actors and with regard to values and political priorities. As Hernes expresses it, "Women have been the object of welfare policy and not its creators."[5]

The relationship between women and the state had changed considerably over the past 30 to 40 years. Earlier, women's contact with the state had been mediated through men—their husbands, fathers, or legal (male) guardians. With the development of the social welfare state, women's connections to the state became direct: as public employees—in the extensive public sphere where 70 percent of state employees are women, and 45 percent of women who work outside the home are employed; as social clients; as citizens— women vote to the same or to an even higher degree than men do; and as taxpayers.[6] As clients of state-provided social services, women receive paid maternity leave for 30 weeks, paid leave of absence in case of a child's illness (ten days per year for each child under age ten), public funds during a period of transition after a divorce, and other benefits. Millions of Norwegian kroner are allocated yearly to improve the conditions of women in geographically and economically peripheral areas who tend to leave the small villages because of the lack of job opportunities and satisfying service structures.

The welfare state is dependent on women's expertise, their participation in the labor force, and, finally, their contribution as a legitimizing force through their high voting turnout and their political demands. In turn, women depend on the state for their independence from individual men.[7] Political pressure from the right to deconstruct the welfare state represents a serious threat to women as employees and as social clients. The mutual dependency between women and the state is expressed in women's integration in the political system. Both in absolute and in relative figures, women's access to the political and politico-administrative system has increased considerably since the 1970s. Norway is known worldwide for its first woman prime minister and her "women's cabinet," in which women held 40 percent of the posts. In Parliament and in local councils women hold about one-third of the seats. In the 1980s there were a few all-male municipal governments, but none after the 1987 election. After the local elections in 1991, however, women's representation in local councils decreased slightly to 28.4 percent.

In the central administration there are a considerable number of women in the higher levels of the bureaucracy and in many areas of policy implementation. They are often referred to as "state feminists" because many of them were once active in the new women's movement and in women's studies at the universities. Their presence has increased the state's concern for women's situation. Nevertheless, women still constitute a minority among the ruling elites and still face both horizontal and vertical divisions of labor between the sexes. The proportion of women is greatest at the lower end of the political and administrative pyramids and in such soft sectors of the political system as social affairs, education, and cultural politics.

From the late 1960s through the early 1980s the new women's movement managed to politicize the personal—to open the public agenda for women's issues and concerns and thus gradually to gain access to the political agenda. Introducing women's interests in the political sphere has meant and will continue to mean conflict: reprioritizing and redefining reality in response to the entry of new groups of actors and new interests. Three issues are of special interest to women: abortion legislation, the Equal Status Act, and the establishment of crisis centers for battered women.

Abortion has been characterized as a regulative and redistributive type of issue, one that was visible in Norwegian politics and was dealt with in the electoral channel through the parliamentary arena.[8] Women initiated and spearheaded the abortion rights movement, in part because the mainstream political system was uncomfortable with matters of sexuality. Women were eventually able to involve the political parties as actors.

But women's organizations never quite got a handle on the Equal Status Act (ESA), initiated by the Labor Party. One reason for this was that the ESA developed almost exclusively in the corporate arena, where the issue was dominated by labor market interest organizations. The ESA is probably one of the most frustrating topics in Norwegian women's political history, keenly illustrating women's relative powerlessness in a patriarchal guardian state. The ESA, which represents a traditional approach, is different from other legislation because it is primarily meant to work as an agent for changing attitudes. Formally and legally, Norwegian women have the same rights as men; however, legal rights have proved insufficient to ensure women equal status in society, equal access to important societal positions, or an equal share in the distribution of resources. Although the proposed U.S. Equal Rights Amendment was meant to ensure the legal rights of women, the ESA is meant to promote equality of status between the sexes.

The crisis center issue is different from both the abortion rights movement and the ESA because it was dealt with primarily within municipalities. From the beginning, the need for crisis centers for abused women and children was artic-ulated by women and addressed in the voluntary sphere. Like abortion, the crisis center issue was dealt with in the electoral channel.

ABORTION LEGISLATION IN NORWAY

An examination of the abortion issue illustrates the interplay of the Norwegian women's movement with the institutional, political, and cultural domains of the political system. This issue gives a keen illustration of the historical roots of the patriarchal guardian state.

Winning legal abortion has been a long struggle. The actors, arenas, and arguments have changed over the 60 years required to obtain abortion on demand—what Norwegians call free abortion. "Free" here means that during the first 12 weeks of pregnancy women are able to make their own choices on whether to have an abortion, free from physicians' or institutional interference.[9] (Like all medical care in Norway, abortion is free of charge. The cost of abortion has never been an issue in the debates.)

Few issues have gone through as much redefining as the abortion controversy. Indeed, "the major challenge has been over the way in which the issue is defined."[10] Active Christians, including members of the Christian People's Party and officials of the state Norwegian Lutheran Church, tried to make it a moral issue; the medical profession added a purely medical dimension to it. Women and men feminists defined the right to abortion as a political matter; denying women the right to decide was considered sexual power politics, or gender politics. Women and their organizations were divided on the issue. The majority of activists in the new women's movement were prochoice, as were the women, and many of the men, in the political parties on the left. A majority of traditional Christian women, and those in the Christian People's Party, were antichoice, or, as they defined their stand, prolife. In the traditional women's organizations the issue created many conflicts involving generational differences and religious convictions.

Historically, abortion was considered a class issue. In the early twentieth century bourgeois and working-class women had opposing views; they agreed with the men of their own class rather than with other women. Upper-class women were opposed to legislation expanding abortion rights. They could always get a legal abortion or a safe illegal abortion; besides, they had the knowledge necessary to avoid many unwanted pregnancies. Furthermore, women in the higher echelons of society were probably less at risk of unwanted pregnancies because of the double standards of morality, which had gender and class dimensions: bourgeois men's sexual urges could be satisfied by lower-class women, so the purity of upper-class women was retained and the threat of unwanted pregnancy among bourgeois women was diminished.[11] Working-class women were prochoice, but their lack of knowledge about and lack of access to contraception led to many illegal and unsafe abortions. In addition, they risked legal prosecution.

Abortion was defined as a criminal act in Norway in 1687 when King Christian V ordered the death penalty for those who performed abortive acts. The criminality of abortion was reaffirmed in 1902 by paragraph 245 of the penal code, which allowed up to three years' imprisonment for a woman who sought an abortion and up to six years' imprisonment for the person who helped a woman abort.

A penal code commission was appointed by the government in 1934 to prepare a report for the Ministry of Justice on reform of abortion legislation. The commission was established partly in response to pressure from physicians who were performing an increasing number of legal and illegal abortions because of deteriorating social and economic conditions. Interestingly, five physicians were invited to participate in the commission, giving greater representation to the views of the medical profession than to those of the legal profession in the commission's findings.

This perspective influenced the commission's final report, which was "first and foremost an attempt to bring the issue of abortion from the arena of penal code to the arena of social policy."[12] The report recommended that abortion be legalized according to a number of indicators:

medical, in cases where the life or health of the mother were endangered; ethical, in cases where the pregnancy resulted from rape or incest; eugenic: in cases of fetal deformity; and social, in cases where the woman's social and economic situation made abortion an appropriate alternative. The commission's recommendations were not implemented.

After World War II a cooperative women's committee, with representatives from the traditional women's organizations and the Women's Caucus of the Labor Party, started an initiative to get abortion on the political agenda, and in 1951 another commission was formed. This commission included female as well as male physicians and came to the same conclusions.[13] The recommendations from this commission were taken into account in the legislative process and provided the basis for legislation passed in 1960, the first actual abortion law to pass Parliament. This legislation introduced the use of abortion councils to control access to abortion, a recommendation from the 1951 commission. Abortion councils were appointed by the hospitals and normally consisted of two physicians and the hospital's social worker. A woman who wanted to end her pregnancy had to apply to the council for permission to have an abortion; the council then decided whether any of the indicators applied in her case. The final decision to grant an abortion rested with the abortion councils.

The 1960 legislation was significant because it introduced a new form of expert control of abortion. Although earlier the courts had represented society's control mechanisms (albeit after the abortion), the medical profession now became the controller since it was physicians in the abortion councils who determined which indicators were to be validated and when. The physicians basically considered only those social conditions that had possible medical consequences.[14] This practice continued until 1978, when the right to free abortion (during the first 12 weeks of pregnancy) was won.

The early 1970s brought the most success for abortion rights advocates, in many ways because this was also a period of political turmoil. The nation was divided on the question of Norway's relation to the EEC. The Labor Party government, strongly supported in Parliament by the Conservative Party, wanted Norway to seek membership in the EEC. The cabinet had allies in the economic sector in industry, and among trade union leaders. The leftist parties and the small parties in the center, such as the Center Party, the Christian Democrats, and the Liberals, were strongly opposed to membership. The conflict was partly a division along urban-rural lines (though urban intellectuals sided with rural opposition). A clear gender gap arose over the issue in that a large majority of women were opposed. They feared that women's position in Norwegian society with regard to legal equality and the social democratic safety net could be threatened. Women established their own anti-EEC organizations and were active and vocal in the public debate. Norway's economic situation was healthy, and opponents were not willing to lose autonomy over the huge oil resources in the North Sea to Brussels, the site of the EEC headquarters. Two large grass-roots organizations were established, a "No-to-EEC" organization and a "Yes-to-EEC" organization, both partly funded by public grants and private gifts (especially large grants from industry to the Yes-to-EEC organization). Norwegian society was thoroughly politicized, and virtually everybody took a stand. Parties split, new alliances were formed (which created new and unexpected bedfellows), and many grass-roots voter movements developed. Finally, a 1972 referendum on the issue ended in a 51 percent vote against joining the EEC, thereby sending a vote of no confidence to the government. The Labor Party cabinet had to go, and a center cabinet, with a prime minister from the Christian Democrats, was formed.

In the election campaigns of 1973, abortion was an important issue. The political fluidity and the political confidence many women had obtained in the EEC struggle helped to open the political agenda to new issues. The Socialist Left Party increased its representation in Parliament considerably, and women in this party, the Women's Caucus of the Labor Party, and the

New Feminists (the first organization of the new women's movement) were important in keeping abortion on the political agenda. Parties had to announce their stands, and in doing so catalyzed many voters. In this way, women finally managed to attain the power to define the issue by pulling "the issue out of the bureaucratic, corporative structure and [introducing] it into the parliamentary arena."[15] Also critical was the fact that abortion became a common cause in spite of the many disagreements among different groups in the new women's movement. The question became the familiar prochoice versus prolife antagonism. "Between 1973 and 1978, debate was concentrated on the question of whether women ought to have the power to decide to have an abortion, or whether society had a duty to protect the fetus."[16] The debate was played out by women from the new women's movement and their supporters versus church officials and Christian activists, including women and (more vocally) men from the Christian Democratic Party.

Following the election of 1973 the Labor Party and the Socialist Left Party held a majority in Parliament, and both parties advocated free abortion in their political programs. Such programs are important in the Norwegian political culture because they provide clear promises to the voters and party members. Parties, as well as their representatives in elected positions, are held accountable for delivering the program. The Labor Party had held a prochoice position since 1969, when women backbenchers at the Labor Party convention introduced a proposal demanding reproductive freedom. Women backbenchers brought up the issue, for which the delegates had not been prepared. The proposal was strongly supported by the women delegates, and it was passed by a majority vote without any debate. Free abortion suddenly and quietly became part of the party's platform. The ease with which the proposal was accepted probably took even its initiators by surprise.

Although the Socialist Left Party held the same position, it later became divided on the abortion issue, with the Christian Socialist faction gaining a dominant position over the feminist faction, which also claimed the Socialist Left Party as its own. To avoid clashes within the party, legislators used the tactic of depoliticization and permitted legislators the "luxury of voting according to conscience."[17] This tactic broke the back of the liberal, emancipatory abortion law in Parliament in 1975 in that a Christian Socialist vote against such a law was decisive. The proposed law had required the abolition of the abortion councils, eliminating physicians' control over access to abortion. Nevertheless, the 1975 legislation was considerably liberalized, in that it accepted social indicators as grounds for permitting abortion.

In 1978 the Labor cabinet sent a new proposal to Parliament. By then the Socialist Left Party had ceased the tactic of conscience voting; the feminists had won over the Christian Socialist faction on that matter. Women, and especially feminists from the new women's movement, became more important in the Socialist Left Party, not only because they were strong, vocal, and politically experienced, but also because the party had a large segment of women voters to take into account. Being blamed for the 1975 defeat of a central piece of progressive legislation was hard on the party. After parliamentary elections in 1977, the party did not allow candidates to have reservations about the abortion issue; representatives were supposed to vote in line with the party program, as is normal political procedure in the Norwegian system. In 1978 the same arguments were repeated in the parliamentary debate as had been heard 50 years earlier. This time a small majority passed a law allowing women to decide for themselves whether to terminate their pregnancies during the first 12 weeks and to have abortions performed free of charge in public hospitals.[18] The majority consisted of Labor Party representatives, the Socialist Left, Liberals, and some Conservatives. The Conservative Party allowed for conscience voting (the issue not being on the party program) and most of the women representatives from this party voted for the proposal. Since 1978 abortion has been a civil right, a claim pregnant women can make on the state.

Throughout the struggle for abortion rights the actors and their influence changed, as did the arenas for the struggle. Women's organizations, Christian groups, and experts, such as doctors and lawyers, all played important roles. Although Christian groups' influence was strong in the early phases when the Labor Party was new in government, their influence faded when the Labor Party forged strong alliances with other groups, such as the Socialist Left Party. Although Christian bishops had threatened to leave the state church if abortion legislation passed in 1978, their tactic was unsuccessful. By the 1970s women had become a group to be reckoned with—as voters, party members, and officials.

For several years feminists and women in general have considered the abortion rights battle over and won; however, signals from the Christian Democratic Party, persistent prolife activities, worrisome population developments, and economic recession should warn women and feminists to remain alert. The Christian People's Party is considering a kind of equal rights amendment for the unborn. Two former ministers who had left the church in protest over the 1978 legislation have recently used aggressive and illegal forms of action in abortion clinics and hospitals, similar to prolife actions in the United States. The right to free abortion may not have been gained once and for all.

EQUAL STATUS ACT

To explain the importance of the ESA, I first need to emphasize the role of legislation in Norwegian political culture. Political forces organize and transform everyday life to the extent that rules and regulations affect virtually every aspect of life. According to one observer of the Nordic democratic states, "They dreamed of being able to produce the good human being by legislation. They dreamed of legislating evil out of existence."[19]

The pubic debate on equal status has been primarily molded and developed in the corporate channel of the political system, which remained a male-dominated sphere of influence throughout the 1970s. The context in which issues are framed can affect their interpretation, as Swedish political scientist Maud Eduards and her colleagues noted: "The substance of the equality laws, their ideological aims and the tangible means of putting them into effect reflect the way in which the political system safeguards the interests of women. But looking after women's interests is not just a question of the way in which these interests are finally expressed; it is also a matter of how they have been interpreted along the way and by whom."[20]

The institutionalization of equal status policies began in Norway in the early 1970s. The Norwegian Equal Status Council was established in 1972 as an initiative of the Labor Party cabinet. The council replaced and expanded the tasks of the Equal Pay Committee, formed in 1959. Trade unions and the Employers' Federation are represented on the Equal Status Council, as are representatives from women's research from the Labor, Center, and Conservative parties. Women's organizations are not represented. The formal function of the Equal Status Council is to promote sexual equality through advisory, informational, and investigative activities. For the 1990s the council is focusing on equal pay for work of equal value.

Representatives from the Equal Status Council participated in the legislative interministerial committee drafting the Equal Status Act, which passed Parliament in 1978 and was implemented in 1979. Beatrice Halsaa, a feminist political scientist and a long-standing member of the Equal Status Council, describes the aims of the act as follows: "On the one hand, it intended to ensure substantial equality of treatment in all areas of life. On the other hand, the law intended to influence attitudes to sex roles, committing the authorities to work actively for equal status through instruments which were not encompassed by the Act."[21] The new women's movement, the Women's Caucus of the Labor Party, the Socialist Left Party, women in academia, and women officials in the Equal Status Council argued for women-specific legislation. They also argued for an antidiscrimination act and active statutory implementation measures with preferential treatment and quota regulations to ensure equal results regarding the improvement of women's conditions. In addition, they argued for a bill encompassing all spheres of society, including the private family sphere (in cases of battering, for instance).

The final version of the Equal Status Act, the flagship of the Labor government, is gender neutral and in certain situations has led to the advancement of men's conditions. The bill has not resolved the ominous wage differences between the sexes, despite the longevity of this important issue as a political problem. The sanctity of private life and freedom of negotiation between labor and capital have been ensured at the expense of women and their freedom.

To understand how this happened, it is important to examine the legislative process concerning the ESA. The debate illustrated the differences of opinion between the political leadership and women and the relative disempowerment women experienced in the legislative process. This process began during the 1973 election campaign when the Labor Party launched the issue of discrimination against women and promised "measures to abolish discrimination against women in all areas of society, but especially in the labor market."[22] The Women's Caucus of the Labor Party had played an important role as initiator and instigator of this effort, and the caucus' pressure coincided with the party leadership's need for new campaign issues and ideological stands.[23] The traditional dividing lines among parties had become vague, and new issues to demarcate party lines were welcome. Furthermore, "public support for the women's movement made it likely that a party's women's policy could be an important 'vote and membership catcher.'"[24]

The discussion about the ESA unfortunately became to a large degree a discussion within political and administrative establishments, excluding the active groups within the new women's movement. That is, the arena for defining policy measures became exclusive.

Those who assumed leadership roles in the early phases of the policy cycle were the influential organizations in the corporate channel: labor market interests such as the Norwegian Federation of Trade Unions, the Confederation of Employers, and business interests. A political committee was established to lead the legislative process; its members were the secretary of consumer and administrative affairs, the secretary of justice, leaders from the Labor Party, and representatives from the Labor Union and the Confederation of Employers. The two labor market interest groups dominated the policy process and the process of defining the issue. Because the Labor Party had started to draft legislation on discrimination against women, especially in the labor market, the central interest groups in this sphere—the Federation of Trade Unions and the Confederation of Employers—were key actors in the process. The organizations' strong position in the corporate channel is unquestioned. Furthermore, the connection between the trade unions and the Labor Party is close. Women's position in the Federation of Trade Unions was weakened in the 1970s, in that special committees for women's affairs were abolished. A strong, male-dominated, patriarchal leadership aimed to override all women's opposition. Moreover, women are few and weak in the Confederation of Employers.

Because these groups controlled the policy process there was a fundamental change in the substance of the ESA, from a focus on discrimination against women to a focus on equality in general, that is, gender-neutral legislation. "The Federation of Trade Unions would by no means accept a bill prohibiting discrimination against women, not even one restricted to the labor market, if such a bill would imply substantial limitations on the collective negotiations between labor and capital."[25] In the preparation of the legislation, the Labor Party administration was pushed by the Federation of Trade Unions to moderate its orientations as expressed in the act. In fact, the Labor cabinet's proposal found support in the final round in Parliament from the Conservative Party after yet another moderation of the act by the cabinet, which limited differential treatment in access to education and ensured freedom of internal organizational practices for religious groups and the Norwegian church.

During the election campaign of 1973 the Labor Party had explicitly stated that the purpose of the ESA was to eliminate discrimination against women; later, however, the general "passion for equality" (i.e., designing an act for a "future egalitarian society") dominated.[26] Proponents of a "discrimination bill," on the other hand, maintained that the bill ought to take into account the actual situation of discrimination against women rather than a future egalitarian society and thus ought to formulate the unambiguous principle of improving women's situation.[27]

Even following the legislative battle, debate continued on the question of whether the act is aimed at equality in general or whether it is specifically aimed at improving women's subordinate position. Paragraph 1 of the Equal Status Act is aimed at the improvement of women's situation, ensuring women and men equal opportunities in education, work, and cultural and professional development. But the general clause, paragraph 3, prohibits discrimination in general terms. Together, these paragraphs promise a confusing interpretation and implementation. The general clause opens up the possibility of affirmative action through its formulation: differential treatment in order to obtain equality. This may mean differential treatment in the recruitment of men to low-level positions (where men constitute a minority) or it may mean recruitment of women to higher-level positions (where women are a minority). Public administration has accepted affirmative action in its personnel policy rules, but appointment practices show a rather poor record when it comes to affirmative action for women.[28] This type of gender-neutral ban on discrimination practices masks the fact that it is primarily discrimination against women in society that the legislation originally intended to correct.

The issue of preferential treatment of women has given rise to disagreements among parties in Parliament, especially between the Socialist Left Party and the Conservatives and between women and men intellectuals. Preferential treatment of women would bring about improvements specifically for women, most probably at the expense of some individual men. Gender-neutral measures of preferential treatment result in and have actually brought about the advancement of men's positions at the expense of women. "[Gender-neutral] quota regulations in employment may especially in times of recession help to amend gender distribution in lower-level jobs, but they have little or no effect in terms of more senior positions."[29]

ESA formulations regarding wages illustrate some of the problems identified above. The question of wage differences between women and men has a long political history in Norway; as early as the 1940s, a national committee was established to analyze this problem, and in the late 1950s the Council for Equal Pay was established. Paragraph five in the ESA states: "Women and men working for *the same employer* will have equal pay for work of equal value" (emphasis added). This has been one of the most controversial provisions of the ESA. Proposals from the secretary of consumer and administrative affairs originally were aimed at ensuring fair relations in general between women's and men's wages and salaries. The strongly sex-segregated labor market in Norway is simultaneously clearly a wage-segregated market, with women in low-level positions. Thus women are at a disadvantage since equality in general, and equality between women and men in particular, has its basis in economic independence and economic equality.

Because Norway's welfare state is characterized by strong redistributive measures through the proportional taxation system, the concept of a reasonable degree of economic equality is ingrained in Norwegian policies. Nevertheless, the Federation of Trade Unions was not willing to accept such generally stated proposals in the ESA. The unions argued that such proposals would endanger the freedom of wage negotiations between labor and capital. Even the International Labor Organization Convention's paragraph 100, with its broad and more general formulation "equal pay for work of equal value," was not acceptable to the Federation of Trade Unions. As it now stands, ESA's paragraph five is obviously insufficient to reduce wage differences in the sex-segregated labor market.[30] As many as 85 percent of gainfully employed women work in totally or heavily segregated occupations (those in which 60 to 100 percent of those employed are women).[31]

Instead of establishing policies to change the economic consequences of sex segregation in the labor market, the political strategy in recent years has been to change sex segregation itself. Motivational and regulatory policies are mainly targeted to recruit women to the male-dominated sectors and occupations.[32] This may, however, lead to two unwarranted consequences. First, in times of recession women will be first fired because they are last hired. Second, recruitment of new employees to low-paying jobs in the social sector will become even more difficult as there are labor shortages in the sector because many women have left their caretaking functions in the private sphere for jobs in the paid labor market.[33] Men are not easily recruited to these poorly paid jobs.

In practice, then, the ESA has not produced the outcome desired by feminists in the new women's movement. Another problem from women's point of view is that the bill has few statutory implementation measures. It merely prohibits discrimination in general terms. The emphasis is on such voluntary action and attitude-forming measures as education. As such, it indicates the low level attached to the policies in question. Government can enforce legal affirmative action, but considerations of equality have had to yield to other principles, such as the principle of free negotiations. Although a 1980 amendment to the act includes a clause on the nomination of women to public boards, councils, and committees to improve women's representation in the corporate system, this is not an acceptance of women's interests but an acceptance of women in this sphere of influence.

The most controversial dilemma raised by the ESA is the question of private versus public rights. The question concerns whose freedoms are regarded as being most decisive. The seemingly general principle of freedom often implies confinement of someone's particular freedom. In Western patriarchal societies it has meant a confinement of women's freedom. Although we find many instances of government intruding upon citizens' rights, such as mandating use of seat belts in cars, government interference in domestic disputes is possible only when a battered woman asks for assistance.

In the debate over the ESA women's interests have appeared on the political agenda; the problems concern the definition, interpretation, and implementation of women's issues. Women and women's interests have not been considered relevant in their own right, however. Reform policies such as the ESA are considered by many feminists to be preventive measures that divert more radical demands. Feminist scholars argue that the official ideology and institutionalization of equality may contribute to the concealment of inequalities and oppression.[34]

The main frustration many feminists experience with the ESA and the institutionalization of equality policies is the distortion of the ideas of the new women's movement about liberation as understood, defined, and implemented by women themselves. The ESA is an act regarding equality on men's terms, as defined and implemented by mostly male political actors. The merging of organized interests of labor (the Federation of Trade Unions) and capital (the Confederation of Employers) has greatly affected the type of equality legislation Norway has enacted. Conflicting interests between the sexes are not acknowledged in the political culture and thus are not explicitly addressed in the political structures, either in the electoral or corporate channel. In equality policies, however, gender conflicts emerge clearly, and the usual opponents, such as labor and capital, become allies against women, the newcomers in the political arena.

CRISIS CENTERS

The establishment of crisis centers is a practical political consequence of a slogan from the new women's movement, "The private is political."[35] This slogan has particular significance in Norway because of the sharp distinction between the private and public spheres and the absence of pri-

vately funded social service agencies. The idea that social help is first and foremost a public responsibility is deeply ingrained in the Norwegian sociopolitical culture. A problem is either purely private, that is, a family matter in which nobody interferes, or it is a matter to be addressed by government. Once an individual problem has been lifted out from the private realm and defined as a social problem, it is, in the Norwegian political culture, a public affair. Private charity hardly exists in Norway; public concern means that an issue is a welfare state issue.

The Crisis Center movement (CCM) emerged from the new women's movement as individual members from different organizations initiated telephone hot lines for women in crisis. Many of the active members have themselves experienced violence in the family. The initiator of the center in Oslo was a lesbian member of the New Feminists; in other cities, individuals from the Women's Front have been the active force. The CCM perceives itself as an integrated part of the women's movement.

The dual purpose of the movement is first to provide direct help through offering temporary refuge to battered or raped women and children and offering women the opportunity to take an active part in the center's work; and, second, to work to abolish women's subordination/oppression in general and specifically to eliminate those conditions that cause private violence against women and children. Important factors here include educating the public about private violence and helping battered women to become independent.

The first crisis centers were established in Norway soon after the 1977 Brussels Tribunal on Violence Against Women, a convention of women active in crisis centers in Europe. Since the convention, crisis centers have developed quickly and successfully in Norway. In 1978 the first crisis center opened in Oslo, and 47 additional crisis centers were established from 1978 to 1988, as well as about a dozen crisis telephones. There was a boom in the first half of the 1980s when about six new centers were established each year. Since 1986 the pace has been reduced to about one or two per year. Each of Norway's 19 counties now has at least one crisis center, and most counties have several refuges, but there is certainly a tendency toward more centers in the Oslo area, where more than half of the Norwegian population resides. In the northern counties, centers are few and far between, and public transportation is poor.

Through crisis centers, many battered women have found the help and support no other social service agencies have been able or willing to provide. In 1987 about 2,500 women and more than 1,700 children lived for an average of two weeks at one of the 46 crisis centers in operation that year, an average of 55 women per center. The range of use among centers varies from two women using one center to 473 women users in another. In addition, the centers responded to 17,000 requests for help, information, and counseling.[36] Most centers have open channels of communication with public social service agencies, the police, and family centers. Crisis centers have been accepted by public government and public administration and are considered important agencies for serving a group that the traditional agencies could not address appropriately.

Crisis centers depend mostly on voluntary help provided by members of the Crisis Center movement; consequently, the CCM has a slight flavor of the charity performed by the traditional humanitarian women's organizations. With the exception of one crisis center in the northern county of Finnmark, the initiative to establish crisis centers has come from women volunteers. There are about 3,000 volunteers nationwide who help operate the centers in addition to the one or two paid staffers at each center. The CCM has always had as its goal obtaining payment for services: the movement considers violence against women a societal problem and, as such, one that must be addressed and its remedies funded by the political system. In addition, there is a fine line between volunteerism and charity in Norwegian culture. Norwegians are not comfortable with charity; it reminds them too much of unequal conditions. When services are publicly funded, however, the

equality between helper and helped is restored. According to the feminist core in the CCM and socialist women in the leftist parties, payment should be through public funding. "We have accepted private gifts, but we have never gone and asked for such."[37] In other words, the Crisis Center movement has always considered the national and local governments to be its immediate and only paths to funding.

Hence, crisis centers are financed primarily through municipal and national public funds, and they resemble other social service agencies. In 1988 public funding amounted to 41.2 million kroner (U.S. $5.9 million). The average grant level per center was 860,000 kroner ($123,000). The smallest amount granted was 118,000 kroner ($16,900), while one center had financial support of 3.8 million kroner ($0.5 million). An average-sized crisis center with appointed staff and volunteers paid on an hourly basis would require 1.6 million kroner ($228,600). (Although the term "volunteer" is used in Norway, these are nevertheless paid positions.) The total amount needed on a national level would be 76.8 million kroner ($10.9 million).[38] It is not likely that such amounts will be forthcoming from the national budget; signals from the secretary of social affairs imply that about 50 million kroner ($7.1 million) will be the ceiling in national and municipal funds. In contrast, 20.8 billion kroner ($3.2 billion) was budgeted for defense purposes in 1989.[39] In the social welfare realm, the gross public expenditure for kindergartens in 1988 was 3.7 billion kroner ($500 million).[40] According to this formula, the crisis centers would receive about 0.02 percent of the total national budget of 331.3 billion kroner ($51 billion).[41]

To obtain financial support, the Crisis Center movement had to document the need for a refuge, which the Oslo group did by starting a crisis telephone early in 1977. The need for this type of social service was established quickly. In 1982, only four years after the first center opened, the government earmarked funds to stimulate the further establishment of centers around the country. To a large degree it is the municipalities that cover the largest expenditures. Right before the 1982 municipal elections, local politicians influenced the central government in expanding national funding. In that respect, the Crisis Center movement attained easy access to the political and economic agenda, even though the funds were not large. But public funding has also produced conflict because the crisis centers do not want the funding agencies to control how the money is to be used.

This conflict illustrates one way in which crisis centers have forged a difficult alliance between radical parts of the women's movement and the political system. The right to safety and the right to receive help when in need are embedded in the Norwegian sociopolitical culture.[42] As such, it is possible to get political support for crisis center endeavors, though it is not always readily converted into financial support.[43] But such financial support implies the right of the government funding unit to control, regulate, and standardize service. In the crisis centers, however, the principle of creativity, rather than regulation and standardization, is held in high esteem.

Another difficulty lies in the government's principle of nonintervention in family affairs. There is an uneasiness on the part of public officials about interfering in private relations.[44] But the Crisis Center movement is eager to unveil private (male) abuse toward women and children, discrimination against women in general, and the subordination of women within the traditional nuclear family.

These contradictory expectations and needs clearly unleash political struggle. Two different cultures meet and clash: the orderly, regulated social democratic welfare state ideology internalized by mostly middle-aged, male public officials accustomed to pyramidal organizational structures versus the radical feminist ideology borne by young women experimenting with new organizational devices of flat, leaderless, participatory, and democratic models.

The original organizational model of most crisis centers follows the antihierarchical ideas advocated by the new women's movement, with plenary sessions of members and clients/users

the only decision-making body and with the absence of formal leadership. Three groups of actors are important to the operation of a crisis center: members/volunteers, staffers, and users. Internally, the plenary session makes the decisions and divides the tasks among the different groups. Thus, the command lines for staff are flexible and all members can, in principle, give orders. Simultaneously, the staff has the most information about the center's daily routine. Since the staffers are members as well, they have voting rights at the plenary session and thus serve as their own employers.[45]

This type of structure poses problems with regard to external contacts, because increased funding has often been accompanied by claims for political representation within the organization. It means a change in organizational structure as well, as representation presupposes a board. In the past the CCM was vehemently opposed to representation of political officials (such as local council members). Now crisis center members want to ensure such cooperation, and they suggest increased representation. The pragmatic argument is that cooperation most often results in increased economic support. Consequently, most centers have gradually given up the flat structure and task rotation. The more typical structure is now a representative board including external representatives from the funding authorities, an executive committee, a manager, and staff. In other words, the typical structure is hierarchical, with clear lines of control and command.

There have been some positive consequences of the introduction of political representation. Such representation has increased communication with the political arena and furthered the development from "issues" to "troubles," that is, a development from abstract political issues to concrete identifiable human pain.[46] Politicians become more personally involved and politically responsible for the problem of violence. Additionally, this change has increased political and economic support for crisis centers.[47]

Another consequence has been the downgrading of ideological commitment and feminist praxis. There are many crisis center members for whom the aspect of helping individual battered women is central and the feminist ideology secondary or even absent. Several activists in the CCM have complained about the feminist aim of crisis centers being downgraded in favor of daily practical problems—from sexual politics to practical politics. In fact, the movement itself has internalized some of the claims of regulation and standardization (e.g., in terms of geographical distribution), thereby renouncing spontaneity of individual initiators in different areas. In other words, if there are no initiators in an area where a crisis center should be established, the establishment would come from a central authority.

The issue of hourly payment of volunteers introduces further disagreement. On the one hand, such payment may ensure a stable group of volunteers. (Burnout and high turnover have been problems for all centers.) On the other hand, it may recruit women whose primary motive is earning money.[48] One possible implication of this change is that the crisis centers will lose their feminist profile and, as a result, an important part of the centers' mission may disappear.

All crisis centers underline the importance of egalitarian relations between members/ volunteers and users. At one time the Crisis Center movement could have been viewed as having an antiprofessional attitude. Staffers may give advice, such as where to find professional help, but they themselves are not in the helping professions. In this way, they avoid the boundary issues of professional-client relationships and engage in women's situations by taking a stance on the battered woman's side. As such, they often act as advocates for the user vis-à-vis social service agencies.

Now, however, there is a tendency to supply professional crisis center staffers from the established public health sector and to define crisis center staffers as public health employees.[49] This new group of employees is demanding pay and working conditions in line with those of public employees. This too is sexual politics because it is women who provide these services at a low pay level. But this is completely different from the original sexual politics of women taking action against battering and other oppression of women.

After the first enthusiastic phase, then, and despite political struggles and internal problems, the Crisis Center movement became an established part of the Norwegian social landscape. There has been steady development toward the social democratic mind-set. The once-radical Crisis Center movement is gradually becoming a responsible social democratic institution. Yet the political climate in Norway for helping battered women in an alternative way over a long period of time is poor. For one thing, although access to the political agenda (and to the budget process) has been relatively easy, social democratic molding of these radical issues has been relatively easy as well. It is a give-and-take situation: the welfare state gives grants and takes control.

PROSPECTS FOR WOMEN IN NORWAY

The outlook for women in Norway and for the welfare state as a woman-friendly state is somber. The economic recession, with an unemployment rate of about 7.5 percent (which is high, relative to earlier periods), is felt by women as well as men. Many women who are laid off, especially the older women with little education, disappear from labor market statistics and thereby from the labor market agencies. The bleak economic situation threatens women's economic independence. Girls still tend to choose traditional education or vocational training, and thus they risk being "educated for unemployment," because many traditional women's industries (textiles, food processing, and the like) have been moved to other countries, and industries like healthcare and social services are no longer expanding. With Norway's new rapprochement with the EEC and accommodation to EEC principles of free exchange of products, services, labor, and capital, the situation in the Norwegian labor market in general, and for women in particular, is disquieting. The Labor Party government has on several occasions decreased funding to municipal social services. Such reductions are first felt by women who work in the social service area, as their work loads are increased. It is primarily women who suffer the consequences of reduced budgets in the welfare state. Cuts in public programs mean loss of jobs and social services for women, as well as increased family responsibilities for women whose services are being reduced. In a general climate of high unemployment rates, efforts to reduce women's access to the labor market, as well as negative attitudes toward immigrants and refugees, can become more than mere whisperings. Nonetheless, women's integration in the political system and in the central and local bureaucracies will not make it easy for politicians to reverse the hard-won victories of the women's movement.

NOTES

1. Stein Rokkan, "Introduction," in Martin Lipset and Stein Rokkan, eds., *Party Systems and Voter Alignments* (New York: Free Press, 1967), i–xvi.

2. For more information about the legislative system see Jon Gunnar Arntzen and Bard Bredrup Knudsen, *Political Life and Institutions in Norway* (Oslo: International Summer School, University of Oslo, 1980).

3. Beatrice Halsaa, "Policies and Strategies on Women in Norway" (Paper presented at the Workshop on Policies and Strategies Related to Women's Issues, Lima, 1989), 21–23.

4. Helga Maria Hernes, *Staten—Kvinner ingen Adgang?* (The state—no access for women?) (Oslo: University Press, 1982), 85; and Helga Maria Hernes, "The Welfare State Citizenship of Scandinavian Women," in *Welfare State and Woman Power: Essays in State Feminism* (Oslo: Norwegian University Press, 1987), 133–63.

5. Helga Maria Hernes, "Women and the Welfare State: The Transition from Private to Public Dependence," in H. Holter, ed., *Patriarchy in a Welfare Society* (Oslo: University Press, 1984), 26–45.

6. Bernt Aardal and Henry Valen, *Velgere, Partier og Politisk Avstand* (Voters, parties, and political distance) (Oslo: SSB, 1989), 261.

7. For instance, the state can force an ex-husband to pay alimony by deducting the payment from his paycheck.

8. Joni Lovenduski and Joyce Outshoorn, eds., *The New Politics of Abortion* (London: Sage, 1986), 6.

9. After the twelfth week of pregnancy, the decision to abort has to be made by a physician and based on medical indicators.

10. Lovenduski and Outshoorn, eds., *New Politics of Abortion*, 2–3.

11. Christian Krogh eloquently described this double standard in *Albertine* (Oslo: Gyldendal Norsk Forlag, Lanterne, 1967) (first published in 1886). Albertine was a working-class girl who became a prostitute after she was seduced by a young man from the upper strata of Oslo and was disillusioned by his treatment of her. Krogh describes the situation of working-class women and the rules that required physical examinations of prostitutes to avoid their spreading venereal diseases to "important" men and their wives.

12. Brita M. Gulli, "Abortlovgivningens historie" (History of the abortion law), in Anne-Marit Gotaas et al., *Det kriminelle Kjonn* (The criminal sex) (Oslo: Pax Forlag, 1980), 134.

13. Gulli, "Abortlovgivningens historie," 142.

14. Ibid., 149–54.

15. Jorun Wiik, "The Abortion Issue, Political Cleavage and the Political Agenda in Norway," in Lovenduski and Outshoorn, eds., *New Politics of Abortion*, 148.

16. Wiik, "Abortion Issue," 147.

17. Alvin Cohan, "Abortion as a Marginal Issue: The Use of Peripheral Mechanisms in Britain and the United States," in Lovenduski and Outshoorn, eds., *New Politics of Abortion*, 29.

18. Healthcare professionals had used their right to refuse to perform or to assist in the performance of abortions on the grounds of conscience. This created considerable qualms in several hospitals in rural areas of the country.

19. Per Olav Enquist, "On the Art of Flying Backward with Dignity," in Stephen R. Graubard, ed., *The Passion for Equality* (Oslo: Norwegian University Press, 1986), 67.

20. Maud Eduards, Beatrice Halsaa, and Hege Skjeie, "Equality: How Equal?" in Elina Haavio-Mannila, ed., *Unfinished Democracy, Women in Nordic Politics* (New York: Pergamon, 1985), 145.

21. Halsaa, "Policies," 25.

22. Hege Skjeie, Brit Fougner Førde, and Marit Lorentzen, *Forvaltningsansvar: Likestilling* (Administrative responsibilities: Equality), ISF Report 89: 3 (Oslo: Institute of Social Science, 1989), 95.

23. Eduards et al., "Equality," 145.

24. Ibid., 137.

25. Skjeie et al., *Forvaltningsansvar,* 99 (my translation).

26. Hege Skjeie, *Likestillingsloven som Beslutningsprosess* (Equality legislation as a political decision-making process) (Oslo: Department of Political Science, University of Oslo, 1982), 86.

27. Skjeie et al., *Forvaltningsansvar,* 100.

28. Hege Skjeie, "Likestillingspolitikk som Personalpolitikk: Om bruk av kvotering ved ansettleser i staten" (Equality policies as personnel policies: Quotation in public administration) in *Tidskrift for Samfunnsforskning* (Journal of Social Research), vol. 27 (1986): 1.

29. Eduards et al., "Equality," 153.

30. Skjeie, *Likestillingsloven,* 95–101.

31. *Kvinnor og män i Norden: Fakta om Jämställdheten* (Women and men in the Nordic countries: Facts about equality) (Nordic Council of Ministers, 1988), 82–83.

32. Skjeie et al., *Forvaltningsansvar,* 25–26.

33. Ibid., 29.

34. Eduards et al., "Equality," 158–59.

35. I prefer to use the Norwegian term crisis center because it is women in crisis who come to these centers.

36. Wenche Jonassen, *1989 Norsk Institutt for By og Regionforskning* (4) (funded by the secretary of social affairs, 1989).

37. Information brochure from the Krisesentergruppa i Oslo (Crisis Center Group in Oslo), 33.

38. Jonassen, *1989 NIBR Report,* 145.

39. "Stortingsmedling no. 4 (1988–1989) Langtidsprogrammet" (Long-range program: White paper from the secretary of the treasury), 287.

40. *Social Statistics* (Central Bureau of Statistics of Norway, 1988), 106.

41. Ibid.

42. See also Janneke van der Ros, "Equality, Politics, and Everyday Life in Norway" (Lecture at Elder Hostel for Americans, Nansen Skole, Norwegian Humanist Academy, 1990).

43. "One can say that the attitude we have encountered from public officials has been a mixture of interest in the project itself—violence against women is a rather hot political issue just now—and large distrust with regard to the way we think things should be handled. Our organizational form, flat structure, has been looked at with skepticism." (Information brochure from Krisesentergruppa i Oslo), 34.

44. Nevertheless, in 1972 a law was passed denying parents the right to use corporal punishment on their children.

45. Jonassen, *1989 NIBR Report,* 64–65.

46. C. Wright Mills uses this distinction in *The Sociological Imagination* (London: Oxford University Press, 1959).

47. Jonassen, *1989 NIBR Report,* 48.

48. Ibid., 50.

49. Wenche Jonassen, "Vennetjeneste eller offentlig tiltak?" (Friends' help or public policy?), *1987 NIBR Report,* 114.

▲ Palestine

POLITICS

Type of Political System: not applicable

Type of State

Sovereignty: not applicable

Executive-Legislative System: not applicable

Since 1964 the Palestinians have been led by the Palestine Liberation Organization in their search for statehood. The PLO is an umbrella body led by an Executive Committee headed by Yasser Arafat and governed by the Palestine National Council (PNC), which has representatives of various Palestinian parties and groupings.

Type of Party System: multiparty

Major Political Parties[a]

Fateh (Palestinian Liberation Movement): A centrist and mainstream group founded in 1959 and led by Yasser Arafat; dominant in the PLO since Arafat's election as PLO chair in 1969.

Popular Front for the Liberation of Palestine (PFLP): Leftist group established in 1967; supports formation of a Palestinian nation based on scientific socialism and objects to the intermediate strategy of establishing a state on the West Bank.

Democratic Front for the Liberation of Palestine (DFLP): Split from the PFLP in 1969; has in recent years been internally divided regarding its position toward the proposed "two-state" solution.

Palestine Communist Party (PCP): Favors withdrawal of Israeli troops from the occupied territories and creation of a Palestinian state.

al-Sa'iqa (Thunderbolt): Pro-Syrian; believes the PLO is not revolutionary enough.

Arab Liberation Front (ALF): Palestinian wing of the Iraqi Ba'ath Party.

Year Women Granted Right to Vote: not applicable[b]

Year Women Granted Right to Stand for Election: not applicable

Percentage of Women in the Legislature: not applicable[c]

Percentage of Electorate Voting for Highest Elected Office in Most Recent Election: not applicable

DEMOGRAPHICS

Population: 4,490,214[d]

Percentage of Population in Urban Areas: not available

Percentage of Population Below Age 15: 36.0%[e]

Birthrate (per 1,000 population): not available

Maternal Mortality Rate (per 100,000 live births): not available

Infant Mortality Rate (per 1,000 live births): not available

Mortality Rate for Children Under Five (per 1,000 live births): not available

Average Household Size: 6.5[f]

Mean Age at First Marriage: not available

Life Expectancy: not available

EDUCATION

Ratio of Female to Male Enrollment: not available

Literacy Rate: not available

ECONOMY[g]

Gross National Product per Capita: not available

Percentage of Labor Force in Agriculture: 20.0%

Distribution of Agricultural Workers by Sex

Female: 27.0%

Male: 73.0%

Economically Active Population by Sex

Female: 4.0%

Male: 36.0%

a. Arthur S. Banks, ed., *Political Handbook of the World, 1991* (Binghamton, N.Y.: CSA Publications, 1991), 794–96.

b. Women voted in the Palestinian National Council in 1965.

c. Women made up 9.0 percent of the Palestinian National Council in 1989. *UNRWA Statistics of Palestine Refugees* (refugees only), REF. WWR 730/B, run date 11 March 1989.

d. Palestinian population worldwide. See the table in this chapter.

e. *UNRWA Statistics of Palestine Refugees.*

f. Central Bureau of Statistics, *Statistical Abstracts of Israel, 1988*, no. 39 (1988), for the West Bank and Gaza Strip.

g. Ibid.

Women's Participation in the Palestine Liberation Organization

AMAL KAWAR

The Palestinian people have sought statehood since the early 1920s, first in opposition to the British occupation and then in opposition to Israel. Since 1964 the Palestinians have been led by the Palestine Liberation Organization (PLO), now headquartered in Tunis.

The Palestinian aspiration for statehood is contested by the Israeli state, created in 1948 over most of the land of Palestine. Parts of Palestine—the Gaza Strip and the West Bank—fell respectively under Egyptian and Jordanian administrations as an outcome of the armistice agreements that halted the first Arab-Israeli war in 1948. In the Arab-Israeli War of 1967, Israel seized the West Bank and the Gaza Strip, thus extending its rule to all of Palestine. The outcome of these wars was a major demographic dislocation in which over half of the Palestinians were forced to become refugees outside their homeland, and Palestinians everywhere became subjects of other governments (see table). The mobilization of the scattered Palestinian people to establish a state in Palestine is at the heart of the PLO strategy.

The discussion of PLO policies toward women begins in the late 1960s, when an independent Palestinian national movement mobilized the people for an armed struggle. Prior to that, Arab states had taken up the Palestinian cause; indige-

nous resistance, which was negligible, consisted of secret cells organized in the 1950s, mainly among students. The fundamental goal of the movement, as proclaimed by the PLO in the Palestine National Charter of 1968, was a secular democratic state of Palestine to replace Israel.

In the early 1970s the PLO redirected its efforts from an armed struggle toward a compromise political solution: acceptance of a state on any part of Palestine, most logically the more recently occupied West Bank and Gaza Strip. In 1988 the two-state solution, as this compromise became called, was passed by the Palestine National Council, the legislative body of the PLO, in its 19th session. The PLO thus recognized Israel and agreed to settle for a state in the West Bank and Gaza Strip with East Jerusalem as its capital. The conflict between the PLO and Israel persists, for the Israeli government rejects the two-state solution and refuses to negotiate because it does not recognize the PLO as the legitimate leadership of the Palestinians.

PLO policies toward women, which can be traced to these historical developments, need to be examined in three important areas: (1) political participation, (2) political representation, and (3) social welfare. In addition to printed materials, my research relies on taped interviews with

Distribution of the Palestinian Population

	Females	Males	Total
West Bank	418,900	418,800	837,700
Gaza Strip	272,000	273,100	545,100
Jerusalem			120,000
Israel			643,100
Jordan	443,159	470,610	913,769
Lebanon	145,239	150,703	295,942
Syria	136,610	139,593	276,203
Other Arab states			633,400
Rest of world			225,000
Total			4,490,214

Sources and Notes: For the West Bank, the Gaza Strip, and Israel see *Statistical Abstracts of Israel, 1988,* no. 39 (Central Bureau of Statistics, 1988), table xxvii/3. The Israeli statistics include both refugees and nonrefugees but not Arab residents of Jerusalem. For Jordan, Lebanon, and Syria see *UNRWA Statistics of Palestine Refugees,* REF. WWR 730/B, run date 30 November 1989. The UNRWA statistics do not include Palestinians who are not on U.N. refugee rolls, including many of the Palestinians in Jordan. My estimate is that over half of Jordan's population of 3,065,000 is Palestinian. See Bureau of Statistics, Treasury Department, *Statistical Abstract of the U.S., 1990* (Washington, D.C.: U.S. Government Printing Office, 1991), 832. For Jerusalem and elsewhere see Edward W. Said et al., *A Profile of the Palestinian People,* rev. 2nd ed. (Chicago: Palestine Human Rights Campaign, 1987), 14. These estimates are for 1984.

top female and male leaders in the PLO. In most cases, interviewees must remain anonymous for security and political considerations. Secrecy is not altogether foreign to gathering data from political elites, who may not wish to have their views made public. Within the context of a national liberation struggle, secrecy becomes paramount, especially for those whose political roles are clandestine or dependent on the good graces of the country in which they reside.

Use of the concepts of participation, representation, and social welfare presumes a nation-state framework; therefore, their operationalization is difficult when examining a national liberation movement. Uppermost among these problems in the case of the PLO is reaching the Palestinian people. The PLO, with some exceptions—mainly the refugee camps in Lebanon in 1971–82—

does not have direct access to or legal authority over most Palestinians. Through their members and the media, however, PLO factions do have variable, often clandestine access to Palestinians in their different locations, most noticeably the refugee camp populations.

THE PLO AND THE GUPW

The PLO is an umbrella organization for several resistance factions that are unified in support of an independent Palestinian state but that might disagree over tactics and strategies. Of interest here are the three dominant factions that have a long history of popular organizing: Fateh (Palestinian Liberation Movement), the Popular Front for the Liberation of Palestine, and the Democratic Front for the Liberation of Palestine (which split from the Popular Front in the 1970s). Two other factions are worth noting: the Palestine Communist Party, which has identifiable support primarily in the occupied territories, and the Arab Liberation Front, which is affiliated with the Iraqi Ba'ath Party. Support for this group is not readily identifiable but may be mainly among Palestinians in Iraq.

Fateh, headquartered with the PLO in Tunisia, is the oldest and largest faction. Its leader, Yasser Arafat, is the president of the PLO. Fateh is a centrist organization that appeals to the Palestinian mainstream, ranging from conservative Muslims to leftists and socialists. In the latter part of the Nasserist era and following the 1967 Arab defeat, Fateh spearheaded the Palestinian armed struggle against Israel. It grew in strength under the banners of Palestinian armed struggle, national unity, and pragmatic policy. By situating itself at the center of Arab and Palestinian politics, Fateh was able early on to legitimize itself to the Palestinian people and the Arab states and to take control of the PLO and mold its policies. The newly formed Popular Front soon joined the PLO, followed by other factions, mainly groups that split from Fateh and the Popular Front. Fateh is by far the wealthiest faction, with funds that come from friendly states and Palestinians.[1] The Popular Front and the Democratic Front are leftist organizations with very limited financial resources. They make up for that lack, however, with a more disciplined organization that emphasizes long-term goals and programs. Since the 1983 Fateh-Syrian break in relations, the Popular and the Democratic fronts, headquartered in Syria, have continued to have access to Palestinians in the refugee camps there.

The organizational framework for PLO policy making embraces social, political, and economic institutions that have legislative, executive, administrative, and limited judicial functions. The PLO is governed by the Palestine National Council, which consists of four groups: (1) representatives from the resistance factions; (2) representatives of popular frameworks (organizations like women's, students', and workers' unions); (3) representatives of communities outside Palestine; and (4) independents and others. The members of the council share a goal—an independent Palestinian state—and accept the PLO as the legitimate representative of the Palestinian people.

Throughout its history the Palestine National Council has been preoccupied with political programs to achieve statehood, as well as with various crises. The PLO executive functions are held by the Executive Committee, elected by the council from among leaders of the resistance factions and Palestinian communities and headed by President Arafat. The PLO administrative bureaucracy consists of several departments—including the treasury, called the Palestine National Fund. Some PLO offices and programs, such as the Palestinian Red Crescent Society, predate the executive departments and have remained somewhat autonomous. The judicial functions of the PLO are minimal, limited to military and security matters. The PLO also supports various social and economic Palestinian organizations, mainly in the occupied territories. Traditionally, much of the funding to the occupied territories has been channeled through a joint Palestinian-Jordanian committee.

The PLO headquarters have had to be moved several times, to Lebanon after the Jordanian civil war in 1971 and again in 1983 to Tunisia with Israeli occupation of Beirut. The constituent organizations may have headquarters outside Tunisia in other Arab countries, and there are branch offices where concentrations of Palestinians can be found.[2] Although the repeated transfers of the PLO headquarters have had serious and sometimes fatal impacts on program development, the organization itself has engaged in policy formation and implementation over the past quarter-century, with substantive as well as symbolic effects on major portions of the Palestinian people.

The General Union of Palestinian Women, created in 1965 immediately after the birth of the PLO, is headquartered with the PLO in Tunisia. As an official PLO popular framework, GUPW itself acts as an umbrella for women's sectors in the major PLO resistance factions, namely Fateh, the Popular Front, the Democratic Front, the Arab Liberation Front, and a few independents. Seats on the GUPW's 15-member General Secretariat, its leadership body, are apportioned according to factional strength, Fateh having the most seats. The GUPW, however, is headed by an independent, Issam Abdul Hadi, who has led the union from the beginning. The General Secretariat provides the framework for dialogue and coordination among women from the different groups, but the success of this process has depended on how heated the competition is among the factions. In addition to shared GUPW activities, women's sections of the Popular Front, the Democratic Front, and the Ba'athist Arab Liberation Front carry on their own mobilizational activities, much the way other parties do.

The GUPW contrasts with traditional women's social work societies in being openly political and mobilizational, both as the conveyor of women's interests to the PLO leadership and as a supportive popular framework for the statehood cause. The activities of the GUPW rise and ebb with the fortunes of the PLO, and recurrent military crises have caused reverberations in women's programs. As will be discussed later, crises not only politicize women and make the public and leaders more aware of women's contributions, but they also disrupt the creation of programs that are essential for structuring and routinizing women's participation in the political process.

Because the GUPW is illegal in the occupied territories, a number of political activists began in the late 1970s to organize action groups that became known as women's work committees. The groups fit into the strategy of building popular frameworks of women, students, and trade unionists to stand steadfast against the Israeli occupation. The emergence of women's work committees brought to the political arena the outline of an autonomous women's agenda that focused not only on raising the status of women but also on their empowerment. The women's movement, which has become progressively larger, now has thousands of members. By the early 1980s the women's work committees had become identified with different PLO factions. In order of establishment, the four major women's organizations are the Union of Women's Action Committees, identified with the Democratic Front; the Union of Working Women's Committees, identified with the Palestine Communist Party; the Union of Palestinian Women's Committees, identified with the Popular Front; and the Union of Social Work Committees, identified with Fateh. In 1990 a fifth framework—the Union of Women's Struggle Committees, affiliated with the Arab Liberation Front—was announced.

The West Bank also has dozens of social work societies; the largest and most politicized is Jam'iyat 'Ina'sh el-Usra (Society for the Development of the Family) in al-Bireh, founded in 1965 and headed by its founder, Samiha Khalil. In the Gaza Strip the only established social work society is the Palestine Women's Union, founded in 1964 and also headed by its founder, Yusra Berberi. Traditional social work societies have had an enduring presence in Palestinian politics as protectors of Palestinian welfare in both its material and cultural aspects. But they became even more important in the national agenda after Israel occupied the West Bank and Gaza Strip, forcing the Palestinians to rely on themselves for services. During the Palestinian uprising (known by its Arabic name, Intifada), leading societies were subjected to harassment and arrest of their officers, thus bringing them more prominence in the Palestinian political arena.

The Intifada spontaneously began in December 1987, when Palestinians from both the Gaza Strip and the West Bank rose in nonviolent opposition to the Israeli occupation. Since 1967, Israel has governed the occupied territories under military law, suspending civil liberties and causing enormous stress to the social, economic, and educational fiber of the occupied society. The uprising immediately spread to all segments of the population and became organized, with leadership (the Unified Command of the Uprising), popular committees, and other nationalist groups. The existing women's organizations, which have flourished in the 1980s and 1990s, became important support for this ongoing resistance.

Since the turn of the century, the women's agenda and the national agenda have been intricately connected in both the raison d'être of the women's societies and unions and their regular activities. Their sisters in Egypt, Tunisia, and other Arab countries fought for women's emancipation through the abolition of polygamy and summary divorce and through improved educational opportunities for women. In contrast, the purpose of the First Arab Women's Council of Palestine in 1929 was to support Palestinian self-determination by mobilizing existing charity societies to engage in the national struggle against the British mandate.[3] To help orphans, to feed and clothe the hungry, to educate people, and to provide markets for women's crafts are considered part of the struggle for nationhood. In that sense, Palestinian women's organizations have always emphasized an important political objective.

An analysis of prestate policies toward women informs the continuing debate over the effect of national liberation struggles on the transformation of women from obedient subjects, allocated to the social sphere, into active participants in the political sphere. Palestinian women share with many of their sisters elsewhere in the Third World the experience of living with an ingrained patriarchal system that coexists with a mobilizational national liberation movement.

Frantz Fanon's *Studies in Dying Colonialism* first drew a general hypothesis about the effects of resisting colonialism on the politicization of women in traditional societies. Involvement in the Algerian resistance, Fanon argues, meant that women moved out of the sheltered, narrow, private world, where they were constrained by the cultural rules of "honor." The war of independence provided women with opportunities for expressing their individuality and taking on public responsibilities.[4]

The Palestinian struggle mirrors the Algerian revolution in an important way: both show the significance of societal unity in a predominantly traditional Muslim social system and its effects on women's participation in nationalist struggle. Any effort to break the barriers so women can participate fully in the nationalist movement has faced resistance from sizable social forces that adhere to strict patriarchalism. Living in diaspora has had contradictory effects on the social threads of society. On the one hand, living in refugee camps, without national cohesion or authority, has reinforced the traditional behavioral norm of turning to the family for leadership and support. On the other hand, the migration of thousands of men and women away from their families in quest of education and employment has loosened the grip of tradition.[5] As a consequence, many Palestinian women have received unprecedented opportunities for mobility and for educational and occupational attainment.

The experience of the bulk of Palestinian women in the PLO was shaped in the early years of PLO development (the late 1960s to early 1970s) by the few men and women who constituted the Fateh elite. No national women's movement that permeates all the various Palestinian communities exists, either in the Palestine National Council or within any of the resistance factions, to formulate a women's agenda. The role of women in the Palestinian movement emerged in informal discussions inside the highest strata of the mostly male Fateh leadership.

In practice, how women participate in national movements differs little from country to country, and much of what they do is social in character. PLO factions have generally failed to create programs to solve the problem of gender inequality in participation and representation. When women's issues are brought up, debate takes place among women and men in local, regional, and national meetings of various PLO factions. The PLO news media has occasionally addressed the issue of women's role in the national movement, but that was mainly during the first few years. Reviewing various factional official publications for 1968–75, Ghazi Khalili concludes that discussion of women's issues reflects the diverse theoretical orientations of the resistance factions.[6] To maintain national consensus, the PLO has been reluctant to challenge publicly the patriarchal control and sex segregation still practiced by many Palestinians.

When women made inroads in establishing organizations and programs, their efforts tended to suffer from limited public visibility. For example, the mention of women's participation from January 1989 to February 1990 in the Intifada by *Falastin al-Thawra*, official organ of the PLO, focused almost exclusively on demonstrations and sit-ins. The work of the autonomous women's committees and the contributions of the social work societies were not highlighted, yet these organizations provide the main structured ways that women can participate in the Intifada.[7]

The visibility of women's programs is also hampered by conditions limiting women's media outreach. The GUPW itself does not sponsor a periodical, primarily owing to the difficulty in reaching the dispersed population. The Popular Front and the Democratic Front publish newsletters, the *Voice of Women* and *Women's Committees Bulletin*, respectively, but their distribution is limited mainly to the Palestinian camps in Syria, where the two groups are headquartered. The women's committees in the West Bank and Gaza Strip publish their own newsletters, which are irregular, one-time issues to meet the publication restrictions of the Israeli emergency regulations.

Furthermore, the Palestine National Council has been unable to function as a forum for the discussion of women's concerns, apart from GUPW lobbying for more seats. In the absence of statehood and jurisdiction over the Palestinians, domestic legislation has remained in the background, superseded by crises and the fundamental issue of establishing and preserving the liberation agenda.

PLO policies toward women became institutionalized quickly during the early 1970s. The impetus was Fateh's coalitional strategy to mobilize all sectors of the Palestinian society.[8] Also, the various programs were initially funded by Fateh and remained under its control. Fateh leaders, in a calculated response to perceived needs and unhindered by bureaucratic structures, moved freely to set in motion policies that became the basis of its power and legitimacy.

WOMEN'S POLITICAL PARTICIPATION

In democratic states, political participation is a regularized activity whose function is to express public will. In contrast, participation in national liberation movements has two distinct functions. First, it harnesses the resources of the people for the cause of liberation. This inward process finds structure in popular organizations that engage in activities ranging from militarized actions to educational and health services. In this context, participation fulfills the goal of nation building. If the society itself is under threat of destruction, however, as is evidently the case in the occupied territories, then participation also takes the form of a steadfastness that protects societal institutions against destruction. Women's social work societies have played a very important role in this area.

The second function of participation in national liberation movements is confrontation with the occupying forces. Although nation building can be confrontational, the reference here is to activities directed at the enemy, including military attacks, civil disobedience, strikes, demonstrations, sit-ins, and petitions of grievance. The activities tend to be sporadic in response to political events, but they may also be planned.

Since the turn of the century the community-based middle-class societies have been the vehicle of Palestinian women's political action. Opportunities arose mainly during the many political crises, beginning with the much opposed Balfour Declaration of 1917, which supported a Jewish homeland in Palestine. During such times women publicized their concerns to the world community through petitions to diplomatic missions, press releases, attendance at national and international women's congresses, demonstrations, strikes, and sit-ins.[9] These activities continue to be the most visible aspect of women's participation and, since 1948, have encompassed women from every social class. In fact, women from the refugee camps, who tend to be worse off than their town sisters, have become major actors in such public events. They become involved because their families and friends have been injured, imprisoned, and killed and also because the refugee camps are located near urban centers, not isolated like many of the villages.

Before the creation of the GUPW in 1965, Palestinian women did not have a formal national organization to mobilize them for the nationalist movement. In the West Bank and Gaza Strip about 1963, some of the leaders in the social work societies, like Wadiah al-Khartabil and Abdul Hadi, tried to muster women's energy for the national cause.[10] During that period Fateh women in Cairo engaged in covert outreach by opening vocational training classes in the nearby 'Ein Shams refugee camp. Then, in 1965 the Department of Popular Organizations of the PLO invited various women's groups to organize the GUPW as an official popular framework. Since that time, women's organized participation has been channeled through the GUPW and its constituent factions.

The political participation of women in the PLO has undergone three stages: (1) the 1964–70 pioneering period, when the PLO was headquartered in Jordan; (2) the 1971–82 institutionalization period in Lebanon, when the GUPW had free access to a popular base in the camps surrounding Beirut and in the south; and (3) the period from 1983 to the present at the Tunisia headquarters, characterized by skeletal operations primarily in support of the Intifada. Since 1978 the women's committees in the occupied territories have also engaged in separate participatory activities.

In Jordan in the late 1960s the GUPW was still in its infancy, and the members consisted mostly of middle-class women not unlike those typically active in the social work societies. Opportunities opened for women's participation, including the use of arms. Women also entered secret organizations of the various resistance factions, and militant women, some imprisoned or killed, became heroes. Although women continued to experiment with militancy, it became evident that their organized participation paralleled the traditional female occupations: they attended to cooking, cleaning, and nursing. As female and male leaders later reflected, the experience in Jordan brought the problem of cultural resistance to unsegregated militant activities. Because much of women's training with arms was secret at this time, the full impact of family opposition was felt more during the Lebanese period, when the PLO worked openly in the Palestinian community.

During the PLO's 1971–82 stay in Lebanon, militants like Laila Khaled, the well-known hijacker (now head of the women's section of the Popular Front), continued to be seen as role models for young women; however, the male leaders' interest in having women in the military declined, probably in part because of the lack of an urgent need for more fighters. Internally, the PLO channeled much effort into political mobilization and infrastructure building in the refugee camps. By 1974, President Arafat had also begun his diplomatic initiative, known as the Ten-Point Program, to accept any part of Palestine, rather than necessarily the whole territory, for the new state.[11] To some extent, too, dwindling interest in women's armed participation was an accommodation to the stricter traditional social environment of the refugee camps. With loss of country, the family has become a place of constancy and stability, and the traditional patriarchal culture has become entrenched. Consequently, the PLO has tempered its women's mobilization policy in the face of established social traditions that draw different paths for the sexes within the confines of the family honor system.

Women's participation in armed activities also carried some social stigma. Ghazi Khalili notes that female martyrs were revered as heroic, with their pictures displayed on walls, but women commandos were sometimes perceived as deviant and sexually easy—women from whom men found it difficult to receive orders.[12] This bias against women-in-arms has been found in other parts of the world as well.[13]

While women's involvement in the PLO military remained backstage, the activities of the GUPW expanded and became more mobilizational in Lebanon. The key strategy was to provide services through which the PLO could reach women and children in the sex-segregated community of the camps. Kindergartens and vocational centers became the core of the GUPW work in the camps. Women in the various resistance factions, as in the GUPW, had separate educational and political activities to serve the national cause and to recruit members. Women were also able to sit on popular committees in the camps that dealt with such services as sanitation, health, and security.[14]

The GUPW reached a significant number of Palestinian women in Lebanon, where GUPW membership reached its height, yet mainly young and single women joined, because marriage and childbearing often resulted in withdrawal from public life. As Rosemary Sayigh and Julie Peteet have found, motherhood was women's main contribution to the national movement during the prime of their childbearing years.[15]

In my interviews I found that some of the GUPW cadres in Lebanon did seek to persuade their male colleagues to take a more programmatic approach to obstacles to women's participation. Khadija Abu Ali, a member of the GUPW General Secretariat, addressed this issue in her book on the Palestinian women's experience during 1967–71 and made several recommendations. She called on the resistance factions and the GUPW to address the women's question and to encourage fuller participation through slogans, political education, and programs.[16] Although the leadership has been rhetorically supportive, no programs have been designed to attack gender inequality in the resistance. In recent interviews GUPW leaders representing Fateh, the Popular Front, the Democratic Front, and the Arab Liberation Front all concurred that leaders have been made aware of the problems facing women and to a certain degree have been sensitized to the importance of women's work. A poignant example comes from 1982, during the last critical days of the PLO departure from Beirut. The GUPW was entrusted with the final arrangements regarding care of the population but, I was told, not the control of the funds to cover expenses.

The GUPW's power within the PLO is weakened by its lack of independent funding sources. The idea of membership fees was never seriously implemented because of the obvious economic hardships in refugee life. The GUPW's budget comes from the Palestine National Fund—a fact, more than any other, that has led to a centralization in the decision-making process of the GUPW. This is not to say that the GUPW leaders do not have influence within the PLO. Examples to the contrary appear below.

Since the 1983 PLO move to Tunisia, the mobilizational role of the GUPW has become very limited. A consensus exists among observers that crises have acted to politicize Palestinian women.[17] The experience of the GUPW is that the outcome of crises can be catastrophic to women's programs. The pioneering GUPW leaders repeatedly mentioned in interviews that displacement from Jordan to Lebanon and then to Tunisia meant always having to begin again. The wars in Lebanon caused the loss of cadres and the closing of most of the kindergartens and vocational centers (some were destroyed with the camps, and others were taken over by Syria), as well as the destruction of records and files. The GUPW was further weakened by personal and factional conflicts. These problems intensified with the departure from Lebanon when the resistance factions temporarily split the PLO, which resulted in resignations of key cadres.

The most fundamental development for the

GUPW after 1982 was the effective loss of free access to the Palestinian populations in Lebanon and Syria. The women's sections in the Popular Front and the Democratic Front continued to have access to the camps in Syria, where they are headquartered, but their activities are at the prerogative of the Syrian government. Also, the resistance factions have not been permitted to organize openly in Jordan since the 1970 civil war. At its headquarters in Tunisia the GUPW leadership is now distant from all popular bases in the occupied territories and in the bordering Arab states. A review of the meeting minutes of the General Secretariat for the years 1985–89 indicates that the action agenda of the GUPW is now focused on rebuilding its structure and lending support to the Intifada.

In essence, the GUPW is now most visible at the leadership level, where the General Secretariat acts as women's voice. For example, in 1990 it convinced the PLO Executive Committee to halt distribution of a new Palestinian identification card and family book that, among other items, made space available for four spouses (the maximum number of wives permitted in Islamic law). The GUPW memorandum to the Executive Committee noted that Palestinian women everywhere, especially those struggling in the occupied territories, conveyed their concern about the document. The GUPW argued successfully (as I learned later) that the PLO should review the format used in these documents and should guard the principle of cultural pluralism in Palestinian society established in the 1988 Palestinian Declaration of Independence.[18]

In place of the GUPW, which remains illegal in the occupied territories, a number of social work societies and women's committees provide channels for organized participation. Since the Intifada began, the women's committees and the societies have been subjected to closures and harassment. As a result, their leaders have gained visibility as the representatives of Palestinian women and as spokespersons for the uprising. The relation between the GUPW and women's organizations in the occupied territories is difficult to document owing to the sensitivity of the information, but the groups do have informal communications and dialogues.

In the occupied territories, women's committees dealing with specific problems have been established at the local and regional levels. These committees are organized into general unions that are aligned with specific factions: the Union of Women's Action Committees (Democratic Front), the Union of Working Women's Committees (Palestine Communist Party), the Union of Palestinian Women's Committees (Popular Front), the Union of Social Work Committees (Fateh), and the Women's Struggle Committees (Arab Liberation Front). The committees and their general unions constitute a grass-roots movement that has taken shape under the leadership of a new generation of students and professionals. In contrast to the charity-oriented societies of their mothers, the women's committees mobilize members in villages and camps, and their strategies are comparable to those of the GUPW in Lebanon. The idea is to reach women in the traditional communities of the refugee camps and villages through kindergartens, literacy classes, vocational centers, consumer cooperatives, and markets for traditional crafts. The agendas of the different associations of women's committees and the traditional societies do overlap, and all have offered literacy classes and vocational training.[19]

The activities of the five general unions are markedly similar, but the styles of leadership and feminist consciousness vary. Within each union, local committees work on different projects. The Palestine Women's Committees and the Social Work Committees tend to have more centralized planning, whereas the Women's Action Committees and the Working Women's Committees tend to be more autonomous at the local level. All are democratically organized and decentralized.

The women's committees depart from the social work societies and the GUPW in having a more intense commitment to women's self-initiative and autonomy.[20] Evidently, the Women's Action and Working Women's committees in the occupied territories are the most committed vocally and programmatically to feminist agendas. Furthermore, although the GUPW has brought women from the different PLO factions under its umbrella, the women's associations in the occupied territories have kept separate agendas and structures. (For example, the Working Women's Committees are especially interested in women in the labor force, and the Women's Action Committees are concerned with the problems of women at home.) Since 1989, efforts at coordination among all women's groups have intensified. Early informal networking has now led to the establishment of a leadership coordinating council that includes representatives from the women's committees and societies.

In the Intifada the work of women has become more visible as they have provided emergency needs, like food, clothing, education, and health services. Their enterprises also include food-processing cooperatives to help strengthen the economic self-sufficiency of individual women, as well as the area. Preoccupied with the more immediate requirements of the uprising, the women's committees have had to scale down and temporarily halt some of their long-term programs, such as literacy classes.

Members of the women's organizations have also joined with other women in demonstrations and sit-ins. Women's assistance to children who defy the occupation with stones has been noted in Western media coverage of the Palestinian uprising. The stone-throwing image was recalled by Abdul Hadi, the GUPW president, for whom it evoked four generations of participants: the grandmother breaks the stone, her daughter carries the stone, the young one dies as a martyr throwing the stone, and the youngest raises her hand with a victory sign. What is newsworthy, however, is heroism in the streets, not organizational developments. The extent to which women's participation translates into political gain is recognized by the women elite as a major challenge for women's frameworks, both inside and outside the occupied territories.

WOMEN'S POLITICAL REPRESENTATION

Palestinian women have two avenues of political representation, the Palestine National Council and the congresses of the various resistance factions. In the Popular and Democratic fronts, the Political Bureau is the highest executive body, and in Fateh, the Central Committee is. The central committees of the Popular and Democratic fronts and the Revolutionary Council of Fateh are the interim leadership bodies that act for the factional congresses when they are not in session. Little formal record exists of how women participate in PLO and factional decision-making councils. In interviews I found that the women elite can be active in the informal deliberations within the PLO.

Because of the dispersion of the Palestinian people and the inability of the PLO to hold popular elections, representation in PLO bodies generally means that representation of cadres in the militias, factions, and popular frameworks is granted by the leadership. Owing to data limitations, I shall focus only on the progress to elect more women to the leadership bodies.

In the Palestine National Council women participate primarily as representatives of the GUPW, the largest of the popular frameworks in the PLO. The representatives consist of women from the higher tiers of the group, including all 15 members of the General Secretariat. With rare exceptions, like the Palestine Teachers' Union, other popular frameworks and the core resistance factions have failed to send women representatives to the Palestine National Council. The percentage of women in the council has risen gradually from 2 in the early 1970s, leveling out at 9 by the 20th session in 1991. According to the GUPW president, Abdul Hadi, the group continues to lobby for more women's seats. Abdul Hadi also sits on the Central Council, the interim organ of the Palestine National Council.[21]

The general profile of GUPW representatives in the Palestine National Council reveals two types, cadres who have been active in factional politics and those who gained seats in recognition of their roles as wives and relatives of PLO leaders. Some marriages, however, are an outcome of the movement, which provides a meeting ground for activists of both sexes. Abdul Hadi, an independent, is very much an exception to this general

pattern because she first entered the council as a longtime activist in the women's societies. The GUPW leadership, which has little turnover, has incurred criticisms of elitism and stagnation. The counterargument is that the GUPW has had to scale down its activities since 1983 and the departure from Lebanon owing to limited access to a popular base; however, the organization continues to expand its membership.

Women in the Palestine National Council symbolize women's political achievement to the outside world because of their high profile. But many activities within the PLO are carried on within the different resistance factions, which are less open to public view. Women there are leaders who function much as they would in a disciplined political party in a sovereign state. For Fateh, the largest and centrist faction, the rise of women to top posts has been slow, although important gains are being made.

Two Fateh women have held prominent positions in the PLO. Intissar al-Wazir, known as 'Um Jihad, is the wife of the assassinated Fateh leader Abu Jihad.[22] She is president of the Institution of Social Affairs and the Care for Families of the Martyrs and Prisoners (popularly called the Families of the Martyrs Institution), the largest organization in the PLO bureaucracy. 'Um Jihad is also a member of Fateh's highest body, the Central Committee. The other preeminent woman, known by her nom de guerre, 'Um Nasser, was the chief of President Arafat's office for many years before her retirement from that post in 1985. She is currently in charge of the GUPW headquarters in Tunisia, for the president, Abdul Hadi, resides in Jordan.

'Um Jihad has been at the forefront of advances made by women in Fateh. At her initiative Fateh took steps first to integrate women into the core organization and then to have them participate in its national congresses, its Revolutionary Council, and its Central Committee. As the record of the 1980s indicates, progress has been gradual. At the Fourth Fateh Congress in 1980, women occupied 14 of a total 450 seats (3 percent), and 'Um Jihad became the first woman to be elected to the Revolutionary Council. Representation in Fateh congresses is based on geographic as well as institutional affiliations; 'Um Jihad thus attends as a representative of the Families of the Martyrs Institution. At the Fifth Fateh Congress in 1989, 80 of 1,100 members were women (7 percent). The Revolutionary Council gained six women, and 'Um Jihad was finally elected to the Central Committee.

Whether the Fifth Fateh Congress signaled a dramatic change remains to be seen. Both male and female PLO leaders have told me that the highly visible role of women in the Intifada has made men more appreciative of their contributions. Another interpretation given by a participant at the Fifth Fateh Congress was that success in bringing more women to the Fateh Revolutionary Council reflected the electoral system as much as changing norms. She explained that with some 50 open seats, various Fateh factions had to present nomination lists for all of them. Women gained more seats because some factions listed them to reduce the possibility of men from competing factions winning. The assumption was either that women were less likely to win than men or that seating women from rival factions was less objectionable than seating men from rival factions.

Women of the Popular and Democratic fronts, the more leftist factions, have fared somewhat better, although men monopolize the top tier of leadership, the Political Bureaus. Women in the Popular Front constitute about 15 percent of the general membership and 5 percent of the Central Committee (the tier just below the Political Bureau). The Democratic Front appears to be the most egalitarian among the PLO factions: women constitute 28 percent of the general membership and 17 percent of the Central Committee.

Patriarchal attitudes and structural barriers stand in the way of women's rising in the PLO. Male leaders—Fateh's Yasser Arafat, George Habash of the Popular Front, and Nayef Hawatmeh of the Democratic Front—appear genuinely supportive of women.[23] In the late 1980s women made some progress, and two have been appointed PLO ambassadors. Below the top tier,

however, men in the PLO reportedly often discriminate against women, and there is no plan or program to deal with this discrimination.[24] The Popular Front, putting its egalitarian rhetoric into practice, in 1990 changed internal rules to include criteria to evaluate how male cadres treat women and women's issues.

How participation is structured in the PLO has also prevented women's participation in the national liberation movement from being widely noticed. The common reality in such movements is that many of the armed activities are done by men. Women's economic, health, and educational contributions, essential as they are, tend to be played up less in the rhetoric of armed revolution. The PLO began as an armed struggle, and military usefulness has remained the primary criterion for membership in the core resistance factions. Women are much less likely to be fighters, a fact that has worked against raising their proportion in the representational organs. A further structural obstacle to women's achieving the highest level of leadership is that existing seats are occupied by long-time incumbents—the explanation that 'Um Jihad gave when I asked why she has not been elected to PLO's Executive Committee.

Finally, women cadres and leaders keep the representation of women on institutional agendas through informal discussions in PLO circles, but rarely are these issues brought into public debate. Such an occasion occurred in Beirut in 1981, when the GUPW brought leaders of all resistance factions to a conference to listen to experts discuss the social and economic status of Palestinian women. Out of that meeting came a promise to increase the size of women's representation in the Palestine National Council. Nihaya Muhammad, who spearheaded the GUPW work for the meeting, said proudly that in the next council session the GUPW gained 12 seats. Recent conversations with female and male leaders in the PLO indicate that women's involvement in the Intifada is acknowledged and greatly admired, which will strengthen the argument to increase the number of women in the leadership circles of the national movement.

SOCIAL WELFARE PROGRAMS

The social welfare policies of the PLO were defined and formulated by the men leading Fateh. No women or any other group participated in these early decisions. The institutional core of the PLO's approach to social welfare consists of three organizations: the Families of the Martyrs Institution, the Society for Works of the Children of Palestinian Martyrs, known as the Samed (steadfast) Foundation, and the Palestinian Red Crescent Society. The first two were started primarily to benefit women and children; the last provides the PLO's health service, hence will not be discussed here.[25]

In 1965 the Fateh strategy was to enlist the Palestinian people in the nationalist struggle and to provide a sense of national belonging. From the beginning, social services played a key role in PLO outreach. 'Um Jihad has said that because Fateh's resources were limited, the establishment of social services was more a symbolic act than an actual meeting of needs. Fateh women pioneers, led by 'Um Jihad and 'Um Nasser, conceived the idea of providing vocational training and product marketing to help economically destitute wives and sisters of the resistance martyrs and the wounded. This was the seed of both the Families of the Martyrs Institution headed by 'Um Jihad and the Samed Foundation begun by 'Um Nasser.

From this modest beginning, the Families of the Martyrs Institution has grown into an organization with a monthly outlay of U.S. $8.5 million in its budget. The two-pronged program of social care and social insurance covers not only families of those killed but also PLO employees. In 1988 another task was added—payment of public employees' salaries in the occupied territories, salaries that Jordan had previously paid. The yearly budget of the Families of the Martyrs Institution was about $110 million in 1989, with 156,000 receiving some form of payment and three-fourths of this expenditure going to Palestinians in the occupied territories. This outlay is intended to cover various sustenance, health, and educational needs.[26] The proportion of the recipients who are female is not available, but from what I could estimate, the majority are women and children. This institution is the first of its kind in national liberation movements. As 'Um Jihad has recalled, "Even [individuals from] the Iranian revolution, at the beginning, came to learn from our experience."

The significance of having a woman lead the first social program of the PLO cannot be underestimated. 'Um Jihad was especially interested in making women economically self-sufficient by opening doors of employment for them. Women constitute approximately 65 percent of the employees at the Families of the Martyrs Institution;[27] however, none of the sections at the Jordan headquarters is currently headed by a woman, perhaps because administrative responsibilities for the headquarters are not shouldered by 'Um Jihad but by her deputy, a colleague from the days when the program began as a Fateh committee of three. Perhaps 'Um Jihad's greatest contribution to the institution is the early decision to allocate payments to the wife of a martyr as guardian of her children. This policy is a marked departure from the dominant Muslim tradition, in which males (grandfathers or uncles) are considered the guardians of children whose fathers have died.

'Um Jihad's long tenure as chief of the Families of the Martyrs Institution can be attributed to a number of factors. Foremost is her stature inside the Fateh hierarchy as the wife of the co-founder Abu Jihad. As his wife, 'Um Jihad came to occupy highly sensitive posts. Also, her institution has managed to escape dislocation pains and remains intact: it was headquartered in Syria until 1985, when it was moved to Jordan. From my personal observations I would say that 'Um Jihad's interest and participation in the GUPW are appreciated, and she is considered a friend of the women's cause.

The social welfare function of the PLO is also served by the Samed Foundation, created by 'Um Nasser during the late 1960s in Jordan. Samed, like the GUPW, went through three stages of development as the PLO moved from Jordan to Lebanon and then to Tunisia. 'Um Nasser's early vision was for Samed to provide training for the widows of martyrs, as well as to support traditional Palestinian crafts and culture. The purpose of Samed, however, was changed by a decision of Fateh leaders after the PLO moved to Lebanon in 1971. Ahmad Abu 'Ala, who was already in charge of other PLO production activities, took the helm while 'Um Nasser moved on to organize and head President Arafat's first office in Beirut. Samed's new mandate was to be the economic arm of the PLO, focusing on an economic self-sufficiency agenda.

Samed operated several enterprises related to that purpose, including the provision of clothing, shoes, food, and munitions. As in the Families of the Martyrs Institution, the majority of the employees in Lebanon were women, constituting 67 percent of the rank and file and 27 percent of the leaders.[28] Women held only two positions on the 15-seat executive committee, but they held strategically important jobs as the deputy chief and the political officer. At the height of activities in Lebanon, Samed operated 43 factories and employed over 3,000 workers, including many piece workers.[29] Samed followed the general PLO policy of a pay schedule calibrated by position, but married men received additional wife and child supplements. For the most part, women worked in traditionally female crafts, such as sewing, a choice that reflected prevailing norms in the camps. According to a former high-ranking woman, day care for workers' children was needed, though not acutely because of the availability of GUPW-operated kindergartens.

By leaving Lebanon, Samed lost access to the refugee camps, which resulted in another dramatic change in its development and gender makeup. Prior to the move, Samed had established agricultural and other enterprises mainly in Arab but also in African countries.[30] In Tunisia, Samed turned to these projects for income generation, and the workers became primarily male and non-Palestinian. With regard to both Samed and the GUPW, violent conflicts have had detrimental effects on their work and outreach to the Palestinian population.

The historic decentralization of social and economic programs has provided multiple entry points for women as cadres and leaders, thus decreasing the urgency to pressure the PLO decision makers for a more comprehensive approach toward women. In the case of social welfare programs, reorganization is under way. In 1987 the PLO decided to place all offices in a departmental structure with the different departments headed by individual Executive Committee members. The Families of the Martyrs Institution is now formally under the Department of Social Affairs, and Samed Foundation is in the Department of Economic Affairs and Planning; in 1990, however, the Families of the Martyrs Institution still remained quite autonomous under 'Um Jihad's direction.

PROSPECTS

In spite of elitist beginnings, the PLO now provides women with a multiplicity of opportunities and arenas for agenda building in a manner unprecedented in Palestinian history. Like women in other liberation struggles, however, Palestinian women have faced cultural and structural obstacles that continue to limit their political roles.

The Palestinian mobilizational experience conforms to the time-honored truth that the parameters of women's public involvement rarely depart from social, educational, and health services. The heroes—'Um Jihad, the commandos and martyrs, and the committed cadres—are exceptions. Women are expected to draw on their existing, largely traditional resources to serve the statehood cause. Their public roles are drawn outright from their private roles as protectors of children and providers of education, healthcare, and sustenance. Their agendas and programs are casualties of recurrent violent crises. In the 1990s, however, the women's committees in the occupied territories offer renewed hope that a women's movement will rise with a women's agenda.

PLO opposition to a military solution to the Iraqi occupation of Kuwait and the consequent loss of financial support from Saudi Arabia and the gulf states has brought additional hardships to the national liberation movement. Much of the support used to be channeled toward educational, health, and charity work inside and outside the occupied territories. How the drying-up of funds will affect the Palestinian women's organizations and their agendas is yet to be determined, but the Intifada continues the struggle for independence.

Given the history of national liberation movements, one might argue that after independence Palestinian women will be demobilized, and no political gains will become permanent, especially given the rise of Islamic fundamentalism in the region. Without underestimating these forces, let me suggest that the history of the Palestinian women's involvement indicates a departure from prior national liberation experiences. My conclusion is based on two primary observations. First, Palestinian women leaders have the lessons of the past available to them. They know what happened in the Algerian and other national liberation movements—in part because of international women writers investigating women's participation in various revolutionary movements. In a symbolic move, the first of the women's work committees in the occupied territories officially began on 8 March 1978, the International Women's Day, and the committees thrived in conjunction with the U.N. Decade for Women (1976–85).

A more important factor is the organizational effort of the women's committees to create long-lasting structures to formulate and guard a women's agenda. Observers have often shown concern over the preservation of political gains made by Palestinian women.[31] The persistence of national crises has politicized several generations of Palestinian women. Indeed, Palestinian women activists are a better educated and more politically experienced generation than their mothers. The lessons learned from having the pluralistic, democratic structures of the women's committees promise great hopes for a post-independence women's movement. Patriarchal forces will unquestionably fight to return Palestinian women to the private sphere. What is also

evident is that women's organizations are preparing to withstand the challenge.

NOTES

1. Funds from Palestinians working in the gulf area and Saudi Arabia have been collected through employers' deductions from their salaries. These funds were then delivered to the PLO, and President Arafat personally held the key to the purse. Since the beginning of the 1990 gulf crisis, these arrangements appear to have ended.

2. For more detail see Helena Cobban, *The Palestine Liberation Organization: People, Power, and Politics* (Cambridge, Eng.: Cambridge University Press, 1984); and Cheryl Rubenberg, *The Palestinian Liberation Organization* (Belmont, Mass.: Institute of Arab Studies, 1983).

3. Matiel Mogannam, *The Arab Woman and the Palestinian Problem* (Westport: Hyperion Press, 1937; reprint, 1976), 70–72.

4. Frantz Fanon, *Studies in Dying Colonialism,* trans. Haakon Chevalier (New York: Monthly Review Press, 1959), 135–57.

5. Shafeeq Ghabra, *Palestinians in Kuwait: The Family and the Politics of Survival* (Boulder: Westview Press, 1987).

6. Ghazi Khalili, *Al-mar'a al-falastinia wa-al-thawra* (The Palestinian woman and the revolution) (Beirut: Palestine Liberation Organization Research Center, 1977).

7. Highlighting such activities might provide the Israeli government with justification for further harassment and suppression, so the PLO media may prefer not to draw attention to them.

8. Khalil Nakhleh, "Palestinian Intellectuals and Revolutionary Transformation," in Khalil Nakhleh and Elia Zureik, eds., *The Sociology of the Palestinians* (New York: St. Martin's Press, 1980), 176–99; and Cobban, *Palestinian Liberation Organization,* 21–35.

9. Mogannam, *Arab Woman*; Raymonda Hawa Tawil, *My Home, My Prison* (London: Zed Books, 1983); Camilia Odeh, "Palestinian Women in the International Arena," *Palestine Focus* (March–April 1986): 8.

10. Maisoon el-Atawneh Wheidi, "The Women's Movement in Palestine Since the Beginning of the Twentieth Century," (1988), 11–13.

11. Rashid Hamid, *Resolutions of the Palestine National Assembly, 1964–1974,* Palestine Books, no. 64 (Beirut: Palestine Liberation Organization Research Center, 1975), 247.

12. Khalili, *Al-mar'a.*

13. Miranda Davies, *Third World, Second Sex: Women's Struggle and National Liberation* (London: Zed Books, 1983), 29, 67.

14. See also Mai Sayigh, "Choosing the Revolution," in Monique Gadant, ed., *Women of the Mediterranean* (London: Zed Books, 1986).

15. Rosemary Sayigh and Julie Peteet, "Between Two Fires: Palestinian Women in Lebanon," in Rosemary Kidd and Helen Callaway, eds., *Women and Political Conflict: Portraits of Struggle in Times of Crisis* (New York University Press, 1987), 16.

16. Khadija Abu Ali, *Maqadammat hawl waqi' al-mar'a wa-tajribatuha fi al-thawra al-falastinia* (An introduction to the reality of the woman and her experience in the Palestinian revolution) (Beirut: General Union of Palestinian Women, 1975).

17. Khalili, *Al-mar'a*; Julie Peteet, *Women and National Politics: The Palestinian Case* (Ann Arbor: UMI Dissertation Information Service, 1985); Sayigh, "Choosing the Revolution"; Rita Giacaman and Penny Johnson, "Building Barricades and Breaking Barriers," in Zachary Lockman and Joel Beinin, eds., *Intifada: The Palestinian Uprising Against Israeli Occupation* (Boston: South End Press, 1989), 155–69.

18. GUPW, General Secretariat Memorandum to PLO Executive Committee, 24 February 1990.

19. Wadad Ahmad, *Al-mar'a al-falastinia wa-al-intifada* (The Palestinian women and the Intifada) (Tunis: General Union of Palestinian Women, 1988); Alex Fishman, "The Palestinian Woman and the Intifada," *New Outlook* (June–July 1989): 9–11.

20. Zahira Kamal, "Tatawor al-haraka al-nisa'iya al-falastinia fi al-aradi al-muhtala" (Development of the Palestinian women's movement in the occupied territories), *Darb al-Mar'a* (April 1987): 5–13; Giacaman and Johnson, "Building Barricades"; Kitty Warnock, *Land Before Honour: Palestinian Women in the Occupied Territories* (New York: Monthly Review Press, 1990), 158–75.

21. Suha Sabbagh, "Interview: Yasser Arafat on the Role of Palestinian Women," *Return* 3 (April–May 1990): 9–13.

22. For example, 'Um Jihad and Abu Jihad mean mother and father of Jihad. In many Arab countries, parents are called after their eldest son.

23. See also Sabbagh, "Interview."

24. Khalili, *Al-mar'a*; also several interviews.

25. The Red Crescent Society, begun in 1968 as a private organization by its founder, Fathi Arafat, was incorporated into the PLO in 1969 and now runs 45 hospitals and dozens of clinics and rehabilitation centers in several Arab countries. Seventy percent of the employees are women, mainly nurses, and approximately 25 percent of the supervisors and decision makers are women. Abu Ali, *Maqadammat*; see also Ahmad Omar Shahin, "Al-ri'aya al-sihiya lil-sha'ab al-falastini" (Healthcare for the Palestinian people), *Samed al-'Iqtisadi* 12 (January–February 1990): 50–66.

26. See also Yussef Abed al-Haq, "Al-himaya al-ijtima'iya lil-nidal al-falastini" (Social security in the Palestinian struggle), *Samid al-'Iqtisadi* 12 (January–February 1990): 39–49.

27. Khadija Abu Ali "Al-dawr al-siyasi lil-mar'a al-falastinia 'ala al-sa'id al-duwali" (The political role of Palestinian women at the international level), *Samed al-'Iqtisadi* 8 (July–August 1986): 99–109.

28. Ibid., 99–109.

29. Ibrahim al-Jundi, "Tajribat 'ishrina 'aman fi al-'amal al-'iqtisadi al-falastini" (Twenty years of experience in Palestinian economic work), *Samed al-'Iqtisadi* 12 (January–February 1990): 18–38.

30. Ibid.

31. Khalili, *Al-mar'a*, 295–97; Sayigh, "Choosing the Revolution"; Giacaman and Johnson, "Building Barricades," 294.

▲ *Papua New Guinea*

POLITICS

Type of Political System: democracy
  Sovereignty: constitutional monarchy
  Executive-Legislative System: parliamentary
Type of State: unitary
Type of Party System: multiparty
Major Political Parties[a]

Political parties in Papua New Guinea are unlike parties in Western nations. They are institutionally weaker, with few ties to the grass roots and limited organizational capacity. Instead of forming around ideological issues, they are often based on regional concerns or individual personalities.

Pangu Pati (Papua New Guinea United Party): Organized in 1967 and led since that time by Michael Somare; active in the independence movement. Has been the largest party in Parliament since 1977, though it has been unable to attain a majority.

People's Democratic Movement (PDM): Split from the Papua New Guinea United Party; formed by Paias Wingti in 1985.

People's Progress Party (PPP): Viewed as the party of owners of small to medium businesses; established in 1970 by Sir Julius Chan.

Melanesian Alliance (MA): Slightly to the left; created in 1970. More nationalistic than other parties and supports decentralization.

Morobe Independent Group (MIG): Based in the province of Morobe; led by Utula Samana, a leftist politician who supports nonalignment and economic nationalism.

National Party (NP): Slightly to the right; currently led by Stephen Tago. Has joined in coalitions with various parties.

People's Action Party (PAP): Formed in 1987 by former minister of defense, Ted Diro.

Year Women Granted Right to Vote:
  1964/1975[b]

Year Women Granted Right to Stand for Election: 1964/1975[c]
Percentage of Women in the Legislature: 0.0%
Percentage of Electorate Voting for Highest Elected Office in Most Recent Election (1992): not available

DEMOGRAPHICS

Population: 3,502,000
Percentage of Population in Urban Areas
  Overall: 13.1%
  Female: 11.5%
  Male: 14.5%
Percentage of Population Below Age 15: 41.6%
Birthrate (per 1,000 population): 37
Maternal Mortality Rate (per 100,000 live births): 900
Infant Mortality Rate (per 1,000 live births): 57
Mortality Rate for Children Under Five (per 1,000 live births): 81
Average Household Size: 5.0
Mean Age at First Marriage
  Female: not available
  Male: not available
Life Expectancy
  Female: 52.7
  Male: 51.2

EDUCATION

Ratio of Female to Male Enrollment
  First-Level Education (1987): 78
  Second-Level Education: 57[d]
  Third-Level Education: 32
Literacy Rate[e]
  Female: 35.3%
  Male: 54.8%

ECONOMY

Gross National Product per Capita: U.S. $680
Percentage of Labor Force in Agriculture: 83.0%
Distribution of Agricultural Workers by Sex
  Female: 45.0%
  Male: 55.0%

Economically Active Population by Sex[f]
Female: 30.0%
Male: 67.0%

a. Mark M. Turner and David W. Hegarty, *The 1987 National Election in Papua New Guinea* (Canberra: Australian Institute of International Affairs, 1987), 8–12.

b. In 1964 under the Australian administration; in 1975 under the Papua New Guinea constitution.

c. See note b.

d. Eileen Wormald and Anne Crossley, *Women and Education in the South Pacific* (Waigani: University of Papua New Guinea Press, 1988).

e. Eileen Wormald and Anne Crossley, *Women and Education in Papua New Guinea* (Waigani: University of Papua New Guinea Press, 1988).

f. Estimates based on International Labor Organization figures.

Rhetoric, Reality, and a Dilemma: Women and Politics in Papua New Guinea

EILEEN WORMALD

Papua New Guinea is described to tourists as the "last unknown," which might equally apply to its political scene. Although the country has provided fertile ground for the work of anthropologists throughout this century, its distance from most of the developed world, with established structures of research and communication, has militated against investigation by other academic disciplines until recently. In particular, the role of women has been ignored or, it is claimed, misinterpreted, and women's political activity is seen, if at all, as embraced within that of men.[1]

This neglect is not surprising if the history, geography, and physical conditions of Papua New Guinea are taken into consideration. Though inhabited for over 50,000 years, much of this magnificent country was virtually impenetrable until the advent of the airplane. There are over 700 language groups, each embracing several clans, which have their own traditions and which remained isolated not only from the outside world but also from each other until after the first "white men" (mainly Christian missionaries) settled in the 1870s and foreigners began to explore the interior in the 1930s.

Germany and Britain shared control of the territory known today as Papua New Guinea from the late nineteenth century until 1921. In that year the League of Nations gave Australia a mandate to administer the southeastern portion—which Britain had handed to Australia in 1906 and which Australia had renamed Papua—in addition to the former German territory of New Guinea. The Australians governed the country until it won political independence in 1975 with the full cooperation of the Labor government in power in Australia and without the bitter struggle that has characterized many of the bids for freedom by colonial territories. The modern nation of Papua New Guinea is made up of the eastern half of the island of New Guinea and a number of adjacent Pacific islands.

The country still has strong ties with Australia, which contributes some 25 percent of the national budget, and is a member of the British Commonwealth. It also has close relations with Asian countries, and government ministers attend meetings of the Association of Southeast Asian Nations. It remains unaligned, however, except for its membership in the South Pacific Forum, where knowledge about development projects is shared. Indonesia is its nearest neighbor, and there are problems on the border with Irian Jaya, the western New Guinea province of Indonesia, because of the activities of the Organisasi Papua Merdeka, the Irian Jayan independence organization, and the resultant influx of refugees into Papua New Guinea. The two governments maintain friendly relations nevertheless.

The country is a parliamentary democracy, with a prime minister and a National Executive Council that exercise executive power. The 109-member unicameral Parliament is elected from single-member constituencies by simple majority vote every five years. Voters elect one representative from each of the 19 provinces and the National Capital District and from 89 "open electorates," representing geographic and demographic groups and community interests. There are also 19 elected provincial governments and an appointed commission for the National Capital District, as well as numerous "community governments." Adult suffrage is universal.

In 1987, in the third national election since independence, 1,515 candidates competed for the 109 seats, 37 percent with the official blessing of one of fourteen political parties, and 63 percent as independents. Because of the large number of candidates in an election, a winner can receive less than 10 percent of the popular vote. The election process can take as long as three weeks, for some voters must walk many miles to remote voting stations.

Voting is by secret ballot, but illiterate voters are allowed to cast "whispered votes" to election officials, who then mark the ballots, or to have a "witness" accompany them as they vote. Allegations of election fraud are common, yet the population takes the process very seriously, as demonstrated by the high voter turnout: over 74 percent of eligible voters participated in the 1987 election.[2]

The political system is generally characterized as multiparty, but the so-called parties are institutionally weak and have few ties to the grass roots and little organizational capacity.[3] Members of Parliament form clusters during national election campaigns, and these clusters often have personality-driven or regional identities. The oldest party, Pangu Pati (Papua New Guinea United Party), was founded in 1967 (before independence) by a small group of men including Michael Somare, prime minister from 1975 to 1980 and 1982 to 1985; the party was synonymous with Somare until he resigned in 1988 in favor of Rabbie Namaliu. Pangu could be classified as center right, although parties are not specifically ideological in orientation, and policy statements during elections are diffuse and overlapping.

On a hypothetical political spectrum the Melanesian Alliance and Morobe Independent Group would represent the left. Smaller parties would join Pangu and the People's Democratic Movement, the party of former Prime Minister Paias Wingti (1985–88), at the center. The right would be composed of the People's Progress Party and the National Party.[4] Party support is important during campaigns mainly because parties assist with financial support, if only at the level of providing election posters and pamphlets. In the 1987 election only seven of the eighteen women candidates obtained party support, and although one of those lost her deposit, four of the five women candidates polling the most votes were party candidates, each in a different party.

To discuss the power position of women in Papua New Guinea, it is vital to remember local geography, history, and culture. The largest and most populous country (over 3.5 million inhabitants) in the South Pacific region, Papua New Guinea became a nation only recently. Just 1 percent of its land is arable, though its economy is still largely agricultural, with minerals increasing in importance. Its mountainous interior is still so difficult of access that, for example, the only communication between the capital, Port Moresby, and the other major towns is by air. Apart from the east-west highway from Lae to Goroka, most roads are inadequate, and many villages—where more than 80 percent of the population lives—can be approached only by canoe or on foot. English is the official language in education and commerce and Pidgin is the lingua franca, but the hundreds of local languages are still used.

There are three national newspapers (including one in Pidgin); but even if they reached the villages before they were out of date, they could not be read by 65 percent of the women or 45 percent of the men, who are illiterate. Radio is becoming more readily available, but reception in many areas is poor, and the programs directed specifically at women are among the first to be threatened whenever budget cuts are considered.[5]

THE STATUS OF WOMEN

Traditionally the people of Papua New Guinea lived in village groups based on kin and linguistic ties, usually described as clans. Each clan had a chief, or bigman, who presided at village meetings where decisions were made, and he adjudicated on customary law; such leaders are still powerful in the affairs of many villages. Women in village society generally play a subordinate role, though before contact with the West, their role in some clans was complementary to that of men in some aspects of life, such as the economic, which are difficult to distinguish from the political. In such a fragmented country it is not possible to speak of one traditional culture, but in decision making the clans were, and are, male dominated, with women excluded from power and from participation in religious ritual.[6] Yasap Nagari's contemporary description, "In big village meetings [women] are often not allowed to speak," is painfully evocative of an earlier description by the anthropologist Kenneth Read of his main companion: He held "a long cane in his hands, raising it to whip the naked bodies of women who have dared to speak out at a public gathering."[7]

The subordinate role of women was reinforced during the period of colonization, when the Australian patrol officers, all men, appointed *luluais* (village constables) and *tultuls* (interpreters) from among the native men. Christianity further superimposed Western ideas of gender roles, mediated, with a few notable exceptions, through education in the mission schools, while economic changes deprived women of the status that their contribution to the economy through subsistence farming had previously given them. While women continue their work in both subsistence and domestic production, it is largely men who leave their villages for the paid employment that enables them to acquire status, along with the cash to purchase a higher standard of living.[8]

Women were not notably active in the preindependence movement. Only Josephine Abaijah, later a member of Parliament and head of the National District Interim Commission, campaigned for a separate state for Papua and later continued her work for her fellow Papuans, the people of the coastal region, through her own party, Papua Besena. Nor were women among the members, staff officers, or external consultants of the 1972 Constitutional Planning Committee; of the 2,000 submissions made to that body only 3 came from women's groups and 13 from individual women.[9]

Nonetheless, the 1975 constitution went against tradition by unequivocally declaring women the equals of men: "All citizens have the same rights, privileges, obligations and duties, irrespective of race, tribe, place of origin, political opinion, color, creed, religion or sex." This statement, reinforced by the national Goals and Directive Principles, which call for "equal participation of women citizens in all political, economic, social and religious activities," has spurred some women to reconsider their subordinate position and take tentative steps to change it.

Statutory laws, in both their promulgation and their interpretation, have recognized women's equal rights and continue to extend them. (For example, in 1988 an amendment to the Superannuation Act promised full benefits to women in the public service, whether married or not.) Yet the majority of women are either outside the orbit of these laws, as in the matter of equal pay, or fearful to use them because of custom and tradition, as in cases of divorce and domestic violence.

Moreover, even though the rhetoric constantly reaffirms the equality of women, the reality is that women's affairs have a low priority in public expenditure; for example, budgetary constraints led the President's Conference in Manus in 1988 to consider eliminating women's representatives from the 16 community governments in that province, and in that year the Southern Highlands Province cut off funding for district women's officers, who earned the equivalent of U.S. $51 per fortnight and assisted women's groups in projects ranging from a mobile canteen to a stationery shop to several small businesses.

It appears, therefore, that despite the promises, despite the 1989 adoption of a National Women's Policy initiated by the government in 1987 and drawn up by the Women's Division of the Department of Home Affairs and Youth as a basis for allocation of funds to women's projects, and despite aid from governmental and international agencies, it is likely that the majority of women have experienced change as an imposition and not as a benefit and that for those in urban squatter settlements it has been a disaster.[10] That they are not resigned to change as only a negative factor is evidenced by the growth and activity of women's groups throughout the country, which are working on a variety of projects, from literacy campaigns in Simbu in the highlands to making clothes for cash in Manus.

The situation of women is always precarious, with opposition from men or withdrawal of funds constantly threatening the success of their projects. Until recently, lack of communication among women's groups has also meant the replication of mistakes that could have been avoided if the groups had been able and willing to learn from one another. The rivalries among groups, some based on religious affiliation (63 percent of the population is Protestant, including a strong following for the Seventh-Day Adventists, Baptists, and over seventy sects; 31 percent is Roman Catholic; and 6 percent belong to local religions), others on clan or regional differences, have to date militated against cooperative efforts.

Yet when women are brought together, as in the 1982 and 1986 Waigani Seminars—biennial events intended to serve as forums for discussion of national development—and the 1988 Conference on Women and Education, all mounted at

and by the University of Papua New Guinea, they quickly learn that their problems are similar and that there are a number of solutions that can be evaluated for effectiveness. They also perceive a fundamental dilemma common to most development: whether women's interests are best served by the creation of special women's programs or whether women should work through existing institutions and structures. Should women strive for numerical equality with men in power structures, or should they work to change the structures created by modernization that perpetuate the subordination of women by their very existence?

Embedded in this dilemma is the relationship between the educated and the uneducated and between expatriates and nationals—the former in each case often being activists in the women's movement but moving on either domestically or abroad before their agitation has led to successful action. Participants in the East Sepik Women's Development, Documentation and Communication Project who are working to reclaim their own experience rightly say: "Popular development programs which actually work and grow thrive not so much on the basis of brilliant plans as they do on the often accidental or incidental popular products and promotional styles of the people involved at the grassroots."[11] The women in the project are not educated in the conventional sense, but their life experiences have empowered them within their own sphere; they are, however, vulnerable when dealing with the bureaucratic demands of national and international agencies that have project criteria and guidelines and that need submissions, accounts, and records in order to provide assistance.

The constitutional rhetoric is far removed from the reality of women's lives, but it still provides a benchmark against which actions by government and outsiders—international agencies in particular—can be judged.[12] In three areas—education, domestic violence, and rural development—women have attempted to improve their lives with varying success, but their actions pose the question of whether any of their efforts are likely to be beneficial unless women have fuller representation in the government and more women than the current 5 percent hold senior positions in the public service. Participation in political structures is thus discussed here as a fourth public policy issue of particular importance to women in Papua New Guinea.

EDUCATION

The education system is a product of Australian colonialism and the work of Christian missionaries, which was extended by the postindependence governments. It is now administered by the government in consultation with those churches (Catholic, Lutheran, and Seventh-Day Adventist) that fund denominational schools and teacher-training colleges. Schooling is not free: fees have to be paid for those children who attend school from approximately ages 7 to 12 in community schools, from 12 to 16 in provincial high schools, and from 16 to 18 in national high schools. Tertiary education for the few who achieve it is free, and it is available from a number of specialist colleges (for agriculture, fishing, health, and community teaching) and in two universities, the University of Papua New Guinea, founded in 1966, and the University of Technology, founded in 1969. The Department of Education promotes a "national curriculum" in all schools and teacher-training institutions, pays all teachers' salaries, and, through the inspectorate, directs teachers' career paths. Secondary school teachers are trained at Goroka Teachers' College, which is an off-campus part of the University of Papua New Guinea, where postgraduate and inservice work for teachers takes place. Considerable funding comes from the World Bank, and with this aid the stated intention is to introduce free universal primary education (UPE) during the 1990s, though, as the former secretary of education Gena Roakeina has suggested, the goal is not unequivocally acceptable: "Whilst UPE is a highly desirable goal the speed with which it is achieved must be carefully considered to ensure the benefits continue to outweigh the social, emotional and financial costs."[13]

The secretary was speaking at the 1987 Conference on Women and Education, which was financially supported by a number of international agencies so that women from every province could be flown in to the meetings at the University of Papua New Guinea, in Port Moresby. The participants were united on many issues but divided by the knowledge that advance on all fronts simultaneously is not possible and undecided as to which would prove most beneficial to women—UPE, decreased illiteracy, increased high-school places for girls, or more tertiary education.

For many women increased educational opportunity is seen as the key to a general improvement in the quality of their lives. Felicity Dobunaba and others, in their research for the U.N. Decade for Women (1976–85), found that the main constraints on women were social attitudes and the lack of educational and training opportunities.[14] The interplay between these two factors, however, presents problems not easily resolved by simplistic attempts at equalizing opportunity. In the speech quoted above Roakeina said: "In many ways the basic values of the old clan system are an implicit part of our culture or life-style today. These values include care of children, respect for elders, sharing work, gardening routines, marriage obligations and duties to kin. These values we still want to retain. Girls and women traditionally have clearly integral roles in this part of the world. These roles may appear oppressive through modern eyes, but culturally this is not so."[15] That this was an essentially male view was demonstrated later in that same conference when a group of women from the national Department of Education asked themselves why there was unequal educational opportunity for women: "Clearly it is because of social status. The men of this country will have to learn the hard way and that is, in a changing society social status must also change. . . . A rapidly developing society such as ours . . . cannot afford to use outmoded social status as a criterion to select and to provide its work force."[16]

The group that gave this women's view was formalized after the Women and Education Conference by women public servants in the national

Department of Education. Their intention was to act as an interest group within that department to promote the education of women at all levels by, for example, obtaining female representation on decision-making committees such as those that select people for in-service training or endorse or reject curriculum developments. In making these demands the women officers are following in the steps of women in community teacher-training colleges who have examined in their workshops ways in which the National Education Board directive to colleges to discriminate in favor of women could be successfully implemented. As a result of their initiatives the percentage of women students in these colleges, which had increased from 30 in 1978 only to 41 in 1984, was over 50 by 1987. Within the colleges themselves other attempts have been made to change the cultural climate: "At the beginning of the year men are to be seen walking over to the mess carrying their new plate, cup, fork and spoon. After a few months, no man is carrying anything except perhaps a cup. Why? The women have them. They wash them and keep them for the men! In the mornings the men cut the firewood and the women make breakfast. If duty officers are not alert, the women cut the wood and make breakfast. But we are working on the women to say, no wood, no hot breakfast. By the second year, the women feel able to say this."[17]

Increases in the presence of women at teacher-training colleges and changes in social attitudes among teachers in community schools could be important in improving the position of girls in the early stages of education. Although there has been a striking rise in the number of girls in primary education—to 75 percent of the eligible age-group in 1986 (as against 90 percent for boys)—as Lyn Yeoman has shown, parents rapidly become disenchanted when education does not lead to high school entry or to the learning of skills required for community development.[18] With the promised advent of universal primary education women will need to promote the intrinsic value of education; and some moves have been made to that end by women's collectives, most notably in East Sepik, where the members also act

as voluntary truancy officers on a rotating basis. None of this, however, will succeed while fathers, and some mothers, believe that "girls are worse than useless after schooling even if they finish their exams. Their heads are turned, they have no respect for us, they think they are somebody special and won't work with their mothers."[19]

This view is not greatly at odds with that expressed by the male secretary for education. In spite of the presence of a few notable women at the top—such as the sisters Rose and Jean Kekedo, who have each held several of the most senior positions, including secretary of the Department of Employment and ombudsman commissioner, and Mina Siagaru and Naomi Martin, who have successively been heads of the Commission for Higher Education—the public service, like other political institutions, is still male dominated. Educated elite women in Papua New Guinea are few, and many women feel that efforts should be concentrated on raising their number. They believe that many more than the current 36 percent of girls who attend high school should be enabled to do so and that the percentage of women at the two universities (17 percent, of whom 6 percent are at the constituent Secondary Teachers' College) should be rapidly augmented so that women's voices will be heard at the seat of power.

Others fear that more education for girls will only distance them further from the largely subsistence-farming population. Even though unemployment of graduates is not yet a problem, a growing number of secondary school leavers are suffering from the lack of expansion in the economy. An experiment to provide relevant education for high school students who return to their villages has had some success for girls.[20] The diffusion of this scheme may go some way toward resolving the dilemma posed above: the students who return to their villages and utilize their skills there will have studied alongside those going on to further education, for the project was designed to maintain academic standards while providing appropriate education for those who will return to village life in their late teens. There is, therefore, the prospect of informed communication based on shared learning and understanding between rural women and women officeholders.

In spite of, or perhaps because of, education development, women are increasingly questioning whether real improvement in their status is likely unless they are more active in the political sphere, where decisions, pronouncements, and implementation of policies happen.

DOMESTIC VIOLENCE

Questions about the value of political activism came to the fore in Parliament in 1987 when the tabling of a Law Reform Commission Report on Domestic Violence led to a debate in which the minister of housing said, "I paid for my wife so she shouldn't overrule my decision because I am the head of the family." Another member confessed: "Previous speakers . . . talk very strongly about husbands drinking and going home and bashing their wives. . . . I am one of these people." There was, happily, opposition to these views from men, as well as women. The minister of health said: "In my province the Enga Women's Association asked me to say in this Parliament that they do not regard wife-bashing as a domestic matter. They regard it as an offence whether it be an assault or grievous bodily harm."[21] But the minister of labor and employment declared: "I wish to stress that family quarrels and fights are natural behavior." This view has common currency, according to an interim commission report: "The majority of rural husbands, which is 69%, say that it is acceptable in some circumstances to beat a woman; on the same token about 55% of the women in villages agree they expect to be beaten [while] 95% of E. Highlands men think it is acceptable."[22]

Whether expectation is the same as acceptance is doubtful, but if it is, then it can be related to the customary protection of women by men, symbolized today by men commonly walking in front of the women they are with, even in towns. Writing of one small group, the Gainj, Patricia Johnson says: "A man should protect his wife from physical assaults by others and, to some degree,

by himself. Wife-beating is acceptable in Gainj society within limits. . . . If she fails in her duties as wife, mother or gardener or if she exhibits willfulness she can expect to be beaten or even speared by her husband. It is not only his right but his duty to do so."[23] The minister of justice obtained agreement for legislation to penalize domestic violence to be brought into Parliament after the 1987 election, but he was then defeated in the election, and there the matter rests.

Most marriages in Papua New Guinea are traditional, which means that they involve a bride-price. Although some see paying a bride-price as buying a wife, others regard it as a formal recognition of the marriage, and still others look on it as a source of wealth for women's families, particularly where money has replaced or augmented traditional payments of pigs, shells, or food. Many women see it as giving women economic value, as well as cementing family ties, for all kin are involved in amassing the bride-price. Even though it is sometimes suggested that bride-price payment and wife beating are connected, there has been no strong move to end the former custom. Women's associations, on the other hand, constantly press for action on domestic violence.

A wife can, under statutory law, apply to the courts for her husband to be restrained from, but not penalized for, such violence, but under customary law in some parts of Papua New Guinea a husband has the right to beat his wife, just as he may keep the children if the marriage breaks down after the completion of bride-price payments or marry more wives whether or not the first wife consents. Statutory, or written, law is based on English law through the Australian heritage, whereas customary law is traditional and varies among communities.

The written law takes precedence over customary law, but in practice, as Christine Bradley states, "customary law is administered informally by local elders or by magistrates of Village Courts untrained in either the Constitution or the written law, so disputes settled according to customary law are rarely challenged even when they do contradict the principles of the Constitution or the written law."[24] This would be especially true where the adjudication concerns traditional conflicts—over bride-price, custody of children, marital matters, gardens, and the ownership of pigs. Women have, therefore, banded together in the Women and Law Committee, formed to provide legal information to women. It is a voluntary body, and its work is funded by donations, mostly from overseas. The committee has published information on statutory rights in Pidgin and in English and recently made a video on wife beating that may be borrowed by schools, women's groups, and other community organizations. In other areas, such as divorce, maintenance, and child custody, where customary and written laws diverge, the Women and Law Committee is attempting to provide women with basic information on how to use both types of law to protect themselves and their children if their marriage breaks up.

Such work is invaluable, but again there is a lack of educated, qualified women—in this instance, lawyers—to represent and campaign on behalf of all women. Although the number is growing, only 20 or so women have graduated in law from the University of Papua New Guinea, and not all of them practice. Because only 17 percent of all undergraduates are women, the statistic is not surprising, nor is the fact that those who do study law tend to be actively concerned with women's issues. An example is a current attempt to obtain funds for a "women's village" at the university, where women can live—possibly with their children—while studying; a recent investigation found that at the university there was a "generally poor relationship between men and women students, a relationship too often characterized by fear and ignorance on the part of women and traditional feelings of dominance, superiority and ignorance on the part of men."[25]

The need for more highly educated women in the law and elsewhere is considered by some women to be more urgent than the need for universal primary education with its concomitant frustrations. They feel that only a large group or "critical mass" can make a substantial impact on male-dominated institutions. Nevertheless, an increased presence of women as lawyers and as judges might encourage more women to avail themselves of their statutory rights, which—though they do not give women complete equality with men—do give them a legal position that could enable them to improve their immediate situation significantly.[26]

RURAL DEVELOPMENT

Papua New Guinea is rich in mineral resources, particularly copper and gold, which are currently being exploited with international capital. This exploitation is, however, a cause of considerable contention—recently evidenced by the closing down of the Bougainville copper mine in the North Solomons by local "rebels" who feel that their island has received insufficient benefit either from the local activities of the company or from the income that it pays to the national government. Many Papua New Guineans also believe that more emphasis should be placed on small-scale rural development in order to decrease reliance on Australian aid and on mining. Papua New Guinea is still largely a rural economy, with 80 percent of the population dependent on subsistence farming, though most grow some surplus to sell in the local markets for money to buy tobacco, beer, household goods, and supplementary food like canned fish and rice and, in some cases, to pay school fees. On some smallholdings cash crops are grown, particularly coffee in the highlands and cocoa and copra in the lowlands. But subsistence farming is the norm, and women are the mainstay of this activity, which traditionally gave them some economic independence: "They need not ask permission from the men before going to the gardens to collect food and they distribute any surplus to whomever they wish."[27]

With the advent of a cash economy the status ascribed to subsistence farming diminished. Income-generating projects were granted importance, and these were the province of men, for whom leaving the traditional village world to earn cash was seen as appropriate accommodation to a changing world. Women, on the other hand, had to stay home and cope with the additional work and burdens imposed by the absence of their menfolk. Women have also decried the idea that wages from male employment would be shared by the dependent families: "While women contribute a substantial part of the oil palm labor, receipts for their labor go to the husbands and women receive little direct benefit for their contribution. Moreover, the income earned from oil palm is predominantly spent on male pursuits."[28]

Although the government has taken a number of steps since independence to improve the position of women within the changed economic structure, the evidence suggests that these have not benefited the 89 percent of women who live in rural communities, for there has been no clear policy, organization, or evaluation of projects.[29] Even the appointment of female agricultural extension officers to work with women in improving their land cultivation often failed because having been trained by men, they followed the male pattern of traveling and advising on cash, not subsistence, crops. Fungke Samana has suggested that the government should retrain extension officers to assist people in subsistence food production and small-scale livestock production and to be more responsive to community needs.[30] The government spasmodically accepts the failure of its policies to meet the needs articulated by women and sets up another office, such as the Women's Division under the Department of Home Affairs and Youth, or reconstitutes the National Council of Women or allocates money under the national Public Expenditure Plan for projects directly benefiting women.

The Women's Division says it is "the national government's advocate on behalf of women and is responsible for developing women's policies and programmes."[31] Nonetheless, many women believe that the division does not consult adequately with the grass roots or, alternatively, that there are insufficient educated women to set and implement an appropriate women's agenda. The same dilemma appears in relation to the many international aid projects; most of the major aid donors recognize the importance of women in the development process and the particular roles of women in the Pacific, but the need to channel

aid through the government can defeat their objective of improving women's lot.[32] Aid given through nongovernmental organizations appears to be more effective in reaching rural women, but there is still a failure to include women adequately in decision making, so their needs in subsistence agriculture, cash crop production, and village technologies are given inadequate attention.

A frequently investigated area of development throughout the Third World is that of planned agricultural settlement schemes, in which underpopulated areas are opened up for productive use through the resettling of rural people away from their home areas by allocating "settler blocks" of land to them. In Papua New Guinea more and more indigenous women in these settlements speak of the erosion of their subsistence base, the allocation of land only to men, and the nonrecognition of the work done by women. These projects are government initiatives, but they are often devised to attract loans from overseas agencies, which, it is claimed, do not appreciate the impact on women.[33] Elizabeth Cox quotes a 1984 study showing that in the 16-year-old Hoskins Oil Palm Settlement Scheme much of the cash crop income was being monopolized by men and spent on beer, gambling, and other forms of luxury consumption while the income derived from women's food crop production and marketing was providing for most of the basic family purchases.[34] A similar picture emerges at the Gavien Rubber Settlement Scheme; here local and national officials and the international evaluators from overseas banks have dismissed appeals by workers for a review of the way in which the scheme is organized—so that, for example, women would no longer be counted as only half a labor unit in the points-score system for allocation of settler blocks.

Faced with nonrecognition and dismissal women have struggled to set up their own development groups, which survive precariously despite crushing opposition.[35] One woman who started a women's group to share skills in gardening and to produce small crafts encountered first the opposition of members' husbands and "now it was the agricultural officers who became cross, accusing us of delaying their development efforts. Even the little meetings which made our women happy and gave them incentives, ideas and the planting material for good gardens, seemed to make the official managers mad. They made up all sorts of reasons to go against us, to stop or divide the group."[36]

This woman activist is illiterate and would not, therefore, be eligible for training sponsored by the government; only nongovernmental organizations, such as the Van Leer Foundation, have given rural women the chance to travel and train in different provinces and overseas, yet the work the women trainees are doing among the village women's groups makes an incalculable or rather—because it is not included in official budgets—uncalculated contribution to development. The need to be listened to leads to a desire to learn how to communicate and in some cases to a belief that only by gaining access to power structures in local community governments and Parliament will women make men listen to them.[37]

PARTICIPATION IN POLITICAL STRUCTURES

Papi Ogi relates an anecdote about women's efforts to take action:

In one district of the E. Sepik province, several women's clubs wanted to start agricultural and small business projects. After frequent requests for help to the relevant government departments, some received a few, infrequent visits, some none. These calls were not enough to get anything off the ground. Finally women from the Provincial Council (a branch of the National Council of Women) and other development agencies responded to their requests by putting selected members of these clubs through various skill training, leadership and management courses. On [their] return, some of these women started up projects with their own clubs. The government officers of that district did not appreciate this development and the women involved were publicly reprimanded for their presumption and audacity. They were told more or less that they existed to be led, not be leaders![38]

In the face of this traditional stereotyping and the resultant obstructionism it is little wonder that to some women the first-line solution to their problems is to obtain greater representation in government institutions both as elected members and as paid officials.

Although, in the light of their traditional role, it is remarkable that as many as 41 women have fought in the four national elections since independence, still, only 3 have won seats; and in 1987 the only woman MP, Nahau Rooney, who was also the only woman to hold government office, was defeated in her bid for reelection for a third term. It is perhaps noteworthy that apart from their high educational qualifications the common factor among the three successful women, Josephine Abaijah, Waliyato Clowes, and Nahau Rooney, is that each had the encouragement of an expatriate man who may have had a different conception of women's roles from that of men in Papau New Guinea: two were married to men of Australian birth, and the third was the protégée of another.[39]

Education, rather than—for example—village leadership, is increasingly an attribute of all members of Parliament, so educated women may soon be able to compete more equally with men. That old traditions die hard, however, may be evidenced by the possible effect on Rooney's candidacy in 1987 of her failure to abide by traditional gender customs: "The fact that she was a woman was in itself a defiance of tradition, for a lapan (leader) was always a man. It followed from this that she should not have been allowed to hold betel nuts when she spoke at the launching of her campaign, for this was a lapan privilege. The betel nuts were also a source of lapan power. If a lapan held a bunch of betel nuts when talking, he had to be obeyed unquestioningly. However, if a lapan dropped a betel nut during his speech, he would sit down quietly, for his power had temporarily, at least, been sapped. Nahau Rooney, it was claimed, had not only illicitly held the bunch of betel nuts, but had dropped one and still gone on with her speech."[40]

Even education, as currently practiced, may not be appropriate training for aspiring political activists. Girls, here as elsewhere, have been fitted into an education system devised for boys, and although enlightened policies have ensured that political education plays an important part in the school curriculum, that education has been gender biased. Marilyn Brown analyzed the high school social-science textbooks and found that only one of the photographs of political leaders and activities showed a woman, and she was casting her vote. Overall, Brown states: "The 'masculine' behavior and roles implied are: have a trade or skill, earn money, be a leader and make decisions. The 'feminine' behavior and roles implied are: work at traditional tasks, be happy but don't aspire to leadership, leave decision making to the men, and learn such skills as typing, nursing and switchboard operation."[41]

So the schools, while ensuring political knowledge equally for boys and girls, have not abolished the gender divide on political aspirations: a recent survey of high school students showed that one-third of the girls but two-thirds of the boys said that they were interested in becoming politicians one day.[42] In this new state, education has clearly been intended as an instrument of social change, but gender differentiation is nevertheless being reproduced. Would the presence of more women heads, inspectors, curriculum writers, officials, or government ministers make a difference? The activities of the national Department of Education Women's Group, which since its foundation in 1987 has successfully campaigned for women's representation on important committees within the department, suggests that it would, but evidence elsewhere is less positive.

In Parliament, although Clowes was a proponent of women's rights and Rooney saw herself as "automatically the minister determined to do battle on behalf of women," there is little evidence that their presence at the seat of power influenced the position of women.[43] Clowes and Rooney have been lone voices in a world where male dominance is based on long and strong tradition. It has been suggested that women have been more influential at the local and provincial levels. The only published figure from 1978 includes 7 women among the 4,313 local coun-

cillors, but in the 1980s the figure has neared 50, while in the twenty provincial governments women have been elected to office and have taken advantage of the provision in the 1976 Law on Provincial Governments for "appointed or nominated members." Thus a nominated woman became minister for community services in New Ireland; Josephine Abaijah was appointed chair of the body that governs the National Capital District in 1988; and an elected woman, Enny Moaitz, became, albeit briefly, the first female premier of Morobe Province. Moaitz has said: "I have been very concerned, as an individual person over the years, that women leaders have attended many provincial, national and even international conferences, seminars and conventions to discuss women's programmes and problems and acquire knowledge to help mothers, but sadly enough there is very little action taken so far. Why is this? Is it because we women are incapable or is it because the Government at various levels are not co-operating with us?"[44]

The answer may lie in the lack of a policy agenda for women in Papua New Guinea. Many women will enter politics or the public service for their own fulfillment, but given a set of policies that would benefit their "mothers" or their "sisters," it is likely that they would gladly promote these policies whenever appropriate.

The president of Women in Politics, founded in 1986 to assist more women to enter Parliament, has said that "women should work together to achieve one goal—to vote women into Parliament so that issues affecting women can be better catered for."[45] Yet at no point have women articulated the important issues on which they can and will unite. Even at the organizational level there is a divergence of opinion between those who feel the main objective of the group should be to work for the election of women to all levels of government and those who feel its purpose should be to form an electoral lobby to monitor all parliamentary decisions affecting women and to represent their interests—though to do the latter they would need agreement on women's issues, which in a heterogeneous religious and cultural group is not easy to obtain. This body, inaugurated by two women at the University of Papua New Guinea, has been hampered not only by disputes but by a lack of funds and office space, as well as by the other heavy commitments of its officers—who are all volunteers and all educated women pursuing prestigious careers.

Unfortunately, the divisions within Women in Politics are replicated among many women's groups, not least the National Council of Women. A group of women formed the council in 1975 especially to meet the needs of rural women. A nongovernmental organization, it is legally constituted and financially assisted by the government; it has a substructure of provincial councils, though not every province has one, and some councils exist in name only. Its stated aims are to implement proposed projects and programs to follow up on resolutions passed at annual conventions, to encourage and promote the flow of information and services from the national to the local level, to facilitate the articulation of needs from the local to the national level, and to press for greater responsiveness from government departments and the Parliament.[46] Weak organization, lack of clarification about membership, divisions based on parochial issues and regional differences, financial mismanagement, and opposition from other women's groups—such as those attached to churches, community groups, and work cooperatives—have all militated against achievement of these aims. After a checkered and largely fruitless career it was re-formed in 1989 and transferred as a commission from the Department of Home Affairs and Youth to the Department of Personnel Management, but it almost immediately ran into difficulties that have not yet been resolved.

Such experiences suggest that women may find it easier to unite on specific, rather than general, issues, and this may be the way forward when their numbers inside political structures increase significantly.

PROSPECTS

In the short period since independence there have been improvements in the position of some women through increased provision of education, changes in the law, and steps toward equal employment opportunities, but nowhere does the progress made meet the rhetoric of the constitution. Changes in, and from, subsistence farming have even deprived women of status, and women have not been equal partners with men in economic development.

Women are not, however, passively accepting this situation. Organizations like the Women and Law Committee, which has demonstrated how to alert women to their rights and to lobby Parliament to increase those rights, have now been joined by a professional women's group in the Department of Education, determined to improve the position of women in the department and consequently to be able to improve female access to education. If Women in Politics can assist more women candidates to enter political structures, then women may have a much greater impact on policy decisions in areas like education, health, and employment.

Pressure for new economic policies for women seems more likely to be a movement from the grass roots upward; the East Sepik Women's Development Group has shown the way by improving communication and by pressing for funding for their own projects, such as making and marketing handicrafts. These women have shown that small-scale development can succeed, and given the instability of the markets for the primary products of the country and the problems encountered in the exploitation of its minerals, such micro projects may provide a basis for economic stability in Papua New Guinea. Women need strength and determination to overcome opposition if they step outside their traditional roles, but listening to the voices of these women makes it clear that they can and will do this. At the Gavien Women's Development Club, Margaret Apan said (in Pidgin): "We women work together to grow food in our gardens. . . . We grew food and we taught other women how to use that food and how to save their seeds for future gardens . . . and then we decided to build a women's house . . . to meet, talk, sew, make *bilums* [string bags], whatever." They met opposition and had to leave the house, so took further steps. "Because of some financial help we have been able to build four workshops for the four groups that make up our women's club. Many government officers have complained about this building. . . . Some people have threatened to tear these buildings down. We have been very upset. But we are still trying hard, working together."[47]

It is difficult to generalize about a nation with such recent independence and a new sense of national identity, as well as such a varied and dispersed population. Time will be needed to develop national institutions after a long history of colonial administration and missionary work that often conflicted with traditional values. The 1987 national election unseated the only woman MP in her bid for a third term, and in 1992 no women were elected to Parliament. Yet regarding women's broad range of political participation certain themes are already emerging. In particular, all the aspects of women's lives discussed in this chapter—domestic violence, education, rural development, and political activism—demonstrate the impossibility of separating the "personal" from the "political." How to reconcile the rhetoric of the latter with the reality of the former is the dilemma facing women today in Papua New Guinea, thus linking them with women throughout the world.[48]

NOTES

1. Dianne Johnson, "Women and the Constitution of Papua New Guinea," in Ross de Vere, Duncan Colquhoun-Kerr, and John Kaburise, eds., *Essays on the Constitution of Papua New Guinea* (Port Moresby: Papua New Guinea Government, 1985), 68. On misinterpretation of women's political activity see F. J. P. Poole and G. H. Herdt, *Sexual Antagonisms, Gender and Social Change in Papua New Guinea* (Adelaide: University of Adelaide, 1982).

2. E. P. Wolfers and A. J. Kegan, *The Electoral Process in Papua New Guinea: A Handbook of Issues and of Opinions* (Port Moresby: Institute of Applied Social and Economic Research, 1988), app. 3, table 2.

3. Mark M. Turner and David W. Hegarty, *The 1987 National Election in Papua New Guinea*, Occasional Paper (Canberra: Australian Institute of International Affairs, 1987), 8.

4. Ibid., 9–10.

5. *Nius Bilong Meri,* Newsletter of the Women's Division, Department of Home Affairs and Youth (Boroka National Capital District, Papua New Guinea), 1 March 1988, p. 8.

6. Marilyn Strathern, *Women in Between: Female Roles in a Male World* (London: London Seminar Press, 1972), 169.

7. Yasap Nagari, "Women, Education and Development," in Peter King, Wendy Lee, and Vincent Warakai, eds., *From Rhetoric to Reality?* (Port Moresby: University of Papua New Guinea Press, 1985), 116; Kenneth Read, *The High Valley* (London: Allen and Unwin, 1966), 64.

8. Fungke Samana, "Women in Subsistence Agriculture," in King, Lee, and Warakai, eds., *From Rhetoric to Reality?* 159; Stephanie Fahey, "Producers or 'Consumers'? Women's Entry into the Cash Economy in Madang, Papua New Guinea," in *Women in Development in the South Pacific* (Canberra: Australian National University, 1985), 142–45; Penelope Schoeffel-Meleisea, "Women's Clubs and the Sexual Division of Women in Transitional Society," in Susan Stratigos and Philip J. Hughes, eds., *The Ethics of Development: Women as Unequal Partners in Development* (Port Moresby: University of Papua New Guinea Press, 1987), 50–58.

9. Johnson, "Women and the Constitution of Papua New Guinea," 60–61.

10. Sister John Paul Chao (Paper delivered at the 17th Waigani Seminar, University of Papua New Guinea, 7–12 September 1986).

11. East Sepik Women's Development, Documentation and Communication Project, "Doing Our Own Development Documentation," in Stratigos and Hughes, eds., *Ethics of Development,* 8.

12. King, Lee, and Warakai, eds., *From Rhetoric to Reality?* 32–177.

13. Gena Roakeina, "Past and Future for Girls and Women in the Education System: An Overview," in Eileen Wormald and Anne Crossley, eds., *Women and Education in Papua New Guinea and the South Pacific* (Waigani: University of Papua New Guinea Press, 1988), 22.

14. Felicity Dobunaba et al., "Present Status of Women in Papua New Guinea: Constraints and Goals for the Future" (Papua New Guinea Collection, University of Papua New Guinea, Waigani, Papua New Guinea, 1979, Mimeographed).

15. Roakeina, "Past and Future," 14.

16. Women's Education Group, National Department of Education, "Education and Equal Participation," in Wormald and Crossley, eds., *Women and Education,* 41.

17. Community School Teacher Trainers, "Teacher Education for Community Schools," in Wormald and Crossley, eds., *Women and Education,* 76.

18. Lyn Yeoman, "Universal Primary Education: Factors Affecting the Enrollment and Retention of Girls in

Papua New Guinea Community Schools," in Stratigos and Hughes, eds., *Ethics of Development*, 123.

19. Ibid., 153.

20. Pani Tawaiyole, "The Secondary Schools Community Extension Project: Female School Leavers in Their Villages," in Wormald and Crossley, eds., *Women and Education*, 66.

21. Papua New Guinea, *Hansard Parliamentary Debates* (1987), 23:34.

22. Law Reform Commission Interim Report on Domestic Violence, *Parliamentary Debates* (1987), 2:34.

23. Patricia Johnson, "When Dying Is Better than Living: Female Suicide Among the Gainj of Papua New Guinea," *Ethnology* 20 (1981): 331.

24. Christine Bradley, "Some Thoughts on Education and Women's Rights," in Wormald and Crossley, eds., *Women and Education*, 179.

25. Joan Oliver, "Women Students at the University of Papua New Guinea in 1985," in Stratigos and Hughes, eds., *Ethics of Development*, 171.

26. Bradley, "Some Thoughts on Education," 182–83.

27. Nagari, "Women, Education and Development," 115.

28. Samana, "Women in Subsistence Agriculture," 161.

29. Rose Kekedo, "The Role of the Department of Community and Family Services in Women's Advancement," in King, Lee, and Warakai, eds., *From Rhetoric to Reality?* 32–37.

30. Samana, "Women in Subsistence Agriculture," 160.

31. *Nius Bilong Meri*, 1 March 1988, p. 8.

32. Suliana Siwatibau, "Women's Access to Aid Sponsored Training in the South Pacific," in *Women in Development in the South Pacific*, 90.

33. Elizabeth Cox, "Women in Rural Settlement Schemes: Institutionalized Gender Bias and Informal Gender Abuses," in Stratigos and Hughes, eds., *Ethics of Development*, 31.

34. Ibid., 30.

35. Tailepa Samuel, Lusey Goro, and Anna Kimbange, "What Stands in the Way?" in Stratigos and Hughes, eds., *Ethics of Development*, 18–27.

36. Matarina Anjam Wai, "A Difficult Decade: Personal Dilemmas and Decisions in Development Work," in Stratigos and Hughes, eds., *Ethics of Development*, 15.

37. East Sepik Women's Development, Documentation and Communication Project, "Doing Our Own Development Documentation," 7–9; Samuel, Goro, and Kimbange, "What Stands in the Way?" 21.

38. Papi Ogi, "Women in Rural Development: An Anecdotal Account from the East Sepik Province," in King, Lee, and Warakai, eds., *From Rhetoric to Reality?* 152.

39. Eileen Wormald, "Women Candidates in the Election," in Michael Oliver, ed., *Eleksin, 1987* (Waigani: University of Papua New Guinea Press, 1989), 83.

40. Alexander Wanek and Eileen Wormald, "The Manus Vote," in Oliver, ed., *Eleksin, 1987*, 200–201.

41. Marilyn Brown, "Implicit Values in the Social Science Curriculum: Male and Female Role Models," in Mark Bray and Peter Smith, eds., *Education and Social Stratification in Papua New Guinea* (Melbourne, Australia: Longman Cheshire, 1985), 180.

42. Eileen Wormald, "Gender and Political Learning," in Wormald and Crossley, eds., *Women and Education in Papua New Guinea*, 47.

43. Nahau Rooney, "Women and National Politics in Papua New Guinea," in Maev O'Collins, ed., *Women in Politics in Papua New Guinea* (Canberra: Australian National University Press, 1985), 43–47.

44. Enny Moaitz, Keynote address to the annual convention of Women in Politics, Port Moresby, Papua New Guinea, 20 November 1987.

45. Wormald, "Women Candidates," 94.

46. Suzanne Bonnell, "Equal Participation by Women: The Role of Women's Councils at the National and Provincial Level," in King, Lee, and Warakai, eds., *From Rhetoric to Reality?* 57.

47. Margaret Apan, "Gavien Women's Development Club: A Case Study of Rural Women's Participation in Development," in King, Lee, and Warakai, eds., *From Rhetoric to Reality?* 156.

48. The author wishes to thank Orovu Vitaharo of the Politics Department, University of Papua New Guinea, for her helpful comments on this chapter.

▲ Peru

POLITICS

Type of Political System: democracy
  Sovereignty: republic
  Executive-Legislative System: presidential
Type of State: unitary
Type of Party System: multiparty
Major Political Parties

Alianza Popular Revolucionaria Americana (APRA, American Popular Revolutionary Alliance): Center party founded in 1930; led by Luís Alva. After a long period in the opposition, won the 1985 elections with 45.7 percent of the total vote. Alan Garcia was the president until July 1990.

Frente Democrático (FREDEMO, Democratic Front): Right-wing coalition led by Mario Vargas Llosa; formed in 1988. Gathers three main groups: Acción Popular (Popular Action), founded in 1956 (leader Fernando Belaúnde Terry has been president twice, 1965–68 and 1980–85); Partido Popular Cristiano (Christian Popular Party), founded and led by Luis Bedoya Reyes, acted as an ally during the second period of Acción Popular's government; and Libertad (Freedom), organized as an independent movement headed by Mario Vargas Llosa.

Cambio 90 (Change for '90): Formed in 1990 and led by the president of Peru, Alberto Fujimori.

Izquierda Unida (Leftist United): Formed in 1980 with a collective leadership; an electoral front that gathered different groups, including Partido Unificado Mariateguista (Unified Mariateguist Party); Patria Roja (Red Fatherland); Movimiento de Acción Solidaria (Solidarity Action Movement); Partido Revolucionario Mariateguista (Revolutionary Mariateguist Party); Frente Obrero, Campesino, Estudiantil y Popular (FOCEP, or Popular Front of Workers, Peasants, and Students); and Acción Política Socialista (Socialist Political Action).

Izquierda Socialista (Socialist Left): Has collective leadership; began as part of Izquierda Unida in 1980 but split off as an independent electoral front in 1989.
Year Women Granted Right to Vote: 1955
Year Women Granted Right to Stand for Election: 1955
Percentage of Women in the Legislature[a]
  Lower House: 6.7%
  Upper House: 6.7%
Percentage of Electorate Voting for Highest Elected Office in Most Recent Election (1990): 97.0%[b]

DEMOGRAPHICS[c]

Population: 22,332,100
Percentage of Population in Urban Areas
  Overall: 69.9%
  Female: 70.3%
  Male: 69.4%
Percentage of Population Below Age 15: 39.2%
Birthrate (per 1,000 population): 33
Maternal Mortality Rate (per 100,000 live births): 301[d]
Infant Mortality Rate (per 1,000 live births): 81[e]
Mortality Rate for Children Under Five (per 1,000 live births): 128
Average Household Size: 5.6[f]
Mean Age at First Marriage
  Female: 20.5[g]
  Male: 25.7
Life Expectancy[h]
  Female: 65.3
  Male: 61.5

EDUCATION

Ratio of Female to Male Enrollment
  First-Level Education: 93
  Second-Level Education (1980/1984): 83
  Third-Level Education (1980/1984): 53
Literacy Rate[i]
  Female: 82.0%
  Male: 94.0%

ECONOMY

Gross National Product per Capita: U.S.
  $1,010
Percentage of Labor Force in Agriculture:
  37.0%j
Distribution of Agricultural Workers by Sex
  Female: 14.7%
  Male: 85.3%
Economically Active Population by Sex
  Female: 25.1%
  Male: 79.3%

a. Congreso Nacional, Camara de Senadores, Oficina de Relaciones Públicas (National Congress, Senate, Public Relations Office), 1990.

b. Jurado Nacional de Elecciones (National Electoral Council). By law, voting is compulsory in Peru, hence the high voter turnout in the general elections.

c. Richard Webb and Graciela Fernandez Baca, Instituto Nacional de Estadística (ENDES, or National Institute of Statistics) en Perú en Numeros 1990, Almanaque Estadístico (Statistical Almanac) (Cuanto S. A., Editorial Navarrete, 1990).

d. Ministerio de Salud (Ministry of Health), Programa Nacional de Planificación Familiar, 1988–91 (National Family Planning Program, 1988–91) (1989).

e. Instituto Nacional de Estadística, Censo nacional, 1991 (National census, 1991), 1.

f. Instituto Nacional de Estadística en Programa Nacional de Promoción de la Mujer, 1990–95 (National Program for the Advancement of Women, 1990–1995), Presidencia del Consejo de Ministros, Consejo Nacional de Población (Lima, 1990).

g. Ibid.

h. Webb and Fernandez Baca, Almanaque estadístico.

i. Ibid.

j. Instituto Nacional de Estadística, Censo national, 1991. Fishing is considered part of the agriculture industry.

Between Confusion and the Law: Women and Politics in Peru

VIRGINIA VARGAS
AND VICTORIA VILLANUEVA

Peru, which is midway on the Pacific Coast of South America, has a population of more than 22 million. The government is democratic in structure, but truly democratic regimes have been few and weak for the past century—eight military governments have taken power. Some have been more democratic than others, like the military coup in 1968 that was led by Gen. Juan Velasco Alvarado and proposed reforms. Since 1979 and the overthrow of Velasco Alvarado's regime, Peru has held tenuously to democracy.

There are several political parties with different ideologies in Peru. One of the most important is Alianza Popular Revolucionaria Americana (APRA, or American Popular Revolutionary Alliance), which was founded in 1930. After years of operating illegally, it became part of the govern-

ment coalition in 1945. It won the 1985 elections and controlled the government until 1990. A crucial political group on the right until it broke up in 1989 was Frente Democrático (FREDEMO, or Democratic Front), formed by Acción Popular (Popular Action), Partido Popular Cristiano (PPC, or Christian Popular Party), and Movimiento Libertad (Freedom Movement). The most significant political force on the left until its breakup in 1989 was Izquierda Unida (IU, or Leftist United). Its principal members were Partido Unificado Mariateguista (PUM, or Unified Mariateguist Party), Patria Roja (Red Fatherland), Partido Socialista Revolucionario (Socialist Revolutionary Party), Partido Comunista Peruano (Peruvian Communist Party), Partido Mariateguista Revolucionario (Mariateguist Revolutionary Party), and Movimiento de Acción Solidaria (MAS, or Solidarity Action Movement); all now exist as independent parties.

There are also illegal groups on both the left and the right: the left-wing terrorist groups Sendero Luminoso (Shining Path) and Movimiento Revolucionario Tupac Amaru (MRTA, or Tupac Amaru Revolutionary Movement), and the right-wing paramilitary group Rodrigo Franco Command. Members of the new social movements have been the primary targets for Sendero Luminoso's terrorism. Paramilitary groups, like the Rodrigo Franco Command, have carried out countless murders and sent death threats to many union, populist and feminist leaders.

"A country of all different bloods" is possibly the clearest description of the complexity and richness of Peruvian society.[1] This multicultural, multi-ethnic land is to some degree a microcosm of the Latin American reality of cultural, ethnic, and regional differences and of the historical, social, and economic elements that include aspects of the premodern, modern, and postmodern periods. Although the overall rural population has diminished since the 1981 National Census, when it constituted 37.91 percent of the total population, the proportion varies among the country's regions, from Lima (the capital city) to areas where the population is more than 70 percent rural. These differences result in wide regional variations in wealth. For example, 70 percent of Peru's modern industrial production is concentrated in Lima. Language differences also contribute to Peru's diversity, with a significant minority of the population speaking only Indian languages.[2] In spite of profound social and economic changes during the past few decades, these sharp inequities in Peruvian society have not been eliminated.

The complexity of this situation and the inequities that result make it extremely difficult to change society's attitudes regarding women's roles. The fragmentation of Peru's social structure and the profound polarization of society even make it difficult to think of this country as a nation.[3] This fragmentation and polarization has hindered women's efforts to participate in institutions that are capable of responding to conflicts and demands in a democratic way, and it has prevented women from thinking about their own proposals from a women's perspective. Fragmentation and weak institutions have also obstructed the development of political proposals that benefit the different groups of women.

The characteristics of the Peruvian state have not facilitated the integration of the nation or of women into politics. All the historical permutations of the relations between the state and society—patrimonial, representative, and participatory—are still present in some form.[4] None of these three forms of state-society relations leaves space for women. The patrimonial relation of the oligarchical state to society openly denies women's capacity as individuals and their right to citizenship. The representative relation that is traditional to the parties and social classes generally considers women accessories to politics, leaving them in subordinate positions and without representation. The participatory relation of the populist state to society generally manipulates women for its own political purposes or as cost-free labor without recognizing them as autonomous subjects.

Modernization and urbanization, which began in the 1950s, expanded educational and employment possibilities for the population and resulted in the breakup of the traditional oligarchic system of rule. By the end of the 1960s, during the military government of Velasco Alvarado, the oligarchic system had reached its end.

As a result of this modernization, Peru's traditionally weak civil society has become stronger. Social and economic modernization have resulted in the growth of an internal market and in industrialization and urbanization, all of which have caused more economic integration. For women, modernization also meant increased access to education and to the labor market, especially in the cities. Pressure began to build for more democratic decision making at the national level.

This strengthening of society facilitated the emergence of diverse social movements, among them the women's movement, which comprised a feminist stream, a community-based popular stream, and a traditional political stream. The conjunction of state actions and the actions of the many social movements permitted state and society to approach each other, thus diminishing the tremendous historical gulf between the real country and the legal country. More important, the social movements contribute to the democratization of society and state through a process in which the movements themselves have become democratic at the organizational level and in regard to the breadth of their objectives. Most significant is the simultaneity with which these movements have appeared. This simultaneity can produce tension among movements when a specific movement's need for individuality breaks down stereotypes and generates a new political culture from different spaces through the action of multiple subjects. Thus, these social movements do not always recognize the particularity of the problems of the women that participate in them, nor do they recognize the importance of the women's social movement, but women's presence in many of those movements is helping to make demands and proposals more visible than before.

In spite of the influence of the social movements on society, the state has not managed to overcome its historic vices of patriarchy, authoritarianism, and "refined verticality."[5] The modernization of the state has been felt more institutionally and less normatively and culturally.

The return to democracy at the beginning of the 1980s brought to Peru a new constitution that proclaimed equality for all citizens. Participatory and democratic local governments with directly elected mayors and city officials were reinstalled. The new constitution also prompted the political parties to expand their activities beyond a style of struggle that only raised demands for democracy and participation in the formal spaces of power, like the Parliament. The "new" social movements (e.g., the women's movement, the squatters' rights movement, and the regional movement) also started to transform their immediate demands into long-term expectations

within the newly established democracy and into pressure for greater access to the structures of institutional power.

Meanwhile, Peru faces the gravest economic crisis in its history. To the negative effects that the new world economic reorganization brought to the rest of Latin America, Peru added the lack of continuity and coherence among the economic policies of successive governments over the past decade. This crisis worsened between 1985 and 1990 because of a populist economic policy that irresponsibly defended expanding fiscal disbursement while placing severe economic restrictions on the productive apparatus. Together, they have produced hyperinflation of 7,650 percent in 1990, with an average annual inflation rate of 746 percent during the past five years, according to the National Institute of Statistics.

This economic crisis has been accompanied by a deep political crisis that has brought the state and its political institutions to the verge of collapse. The fiscal crisis forced the tax base to fall from 14.1 percent in 1985 to 6.5 percent in 1989, and it has gravely affected the amount of money budgeted for social programs. The Ministry of Education's budget was cut from 18.8 percent of the total budget in 1970 to 11 percent in 1985, with similar cuts occurring in health and housing. New investments have been reduced practically to zero. As the state's inability to heed the most urgent social needs has grown, a crisis of confidence in state administration and leadership has developed.

To approach the question of women and politics in Peru, it is necessary to take into account two fundamental elements of Peruvian life today. The first is the country's political-economic crisis and its wrenching social conditions. The situation requires that all of Peru's citizens work toward building a stable democracy to prevent the country from falling under military rule once more. Women are playing a major role in opening the spaces and consolidating the weak, mistreated, and difficult process of democracy in Peru. The second element is the growth of the women's movement over the past ten years, which has modified the relation between women and politics. It is not only a question of a greater presence of women in politics, or of more laws that benefit women; the change seems to be more qualitative. The development of the women's movement means that women's presence in politics does not remain unseen, and it enables women to try democratic alternatives.

Over the past decade, it has become evident that Peruvian women's struggle transcended a fight for both the immediate necessities of life and for the conventional arenas and channels in politics. In the process, the women's movement has adopted new issues and generated its own arenas and channels for political expression. Explicitly or implicitly, the women's movement has added the demand for gender equality to a set of demands of citizenship. Together these demands have modified and widened the scope of Peru's democracy by incorporating new social and political subjects and by raising new demands and proposals at public and private levels. The diverse streams of the women's movement, which have been consolidating and articulating themselves, contain a plurality of processes that reflect the diversity of women's realities in the country. Peru's women's movement is a heterogeneous movement that recognizes and honors its plurality.

WOMEN AND THE STATE

Until recently both the characteristics of the nation and the historically weak and difficult relations between society and state contributed to women's lack of interest in state policy. Women were thus excluded from the political culture for a long time. Women's relation with the state really began with their attempts to achieve the vote. The struggle for suffrage was initiated in the 1920s by the first feminist groups in the country, but the 1933 constitution incorporated neither women nor peasants' right to vote. Women eventually received the right to vote in 1955, a right that undoubtedly opened channels for greater participation among women. Such participation did not occur automatically, however, as the right to vote was not a result of women's pressure but of the efforts of a military leader, Gen. Manual A.

Odria, to obtain women's votes. So women's political preferences were not their own nor was the system necessarily democratic.

The initial perceptions and activities in the women's movement during the late 1970s were anchored in mistrust and devaluation of formal political arenas and of the state's capacity to ameliorate the condition of women. The different streams of the women's movement shared these perceptions, with the feminists responding to them most strongly. The feminists viewed the state as the quintessence of patriarchy, a view influenced by Marxist and other sometimes sharply conflicting understandings of the relations of state and society. The theoretical tension among these perspectives was eventually mediated by another view of the state, society, and women that originated in the practices and experiences of the women's movement. This view emphasized the legitimation of new spaces and subject areas for policy making by the state, and the relations of the women's movement with the state began to widen both the concepts and the practice of politics.

At the same time, however, an essentialist vision of the capacity of women to make politics "in another way" appeared. Although this vision defended and legitimated the spaces of politics that women were developing, it also reinforced the idea that women's political practice in their organizations and spaces of action was the only valid one, and that women's exclusion from power made them more honest and more ethical than men. This essentialism did not facilitate, in this first stage of the women's movement, the acknowledgment of the complexities of the state as an institution that, far from being a monolithic entity, has presented a series of chinks and cracks, contradictions and possibilities of influence.

The U.N. Decade for Women made visible and widened these chinks and cracks in the state for women. This, together with a certain sensitivity from some sectors in the Velasco Alvarado government, led to the military state of Peru becoming the first to use state policy making to "revalue" women. Thus in 1974, as part of the preparatory activities for the Decade for Women,

Velasco Alvarado's government opened a bureau oriented to the problems of women, the Comision Nacional de la Mujer Peruana (CONAMUP, or National Council for Peruvian Women). The president's wife, technical personnel from different ministries, as well as professional women and representatives of intermediate and grass-roots institutions that served women, all worked together in CONAMUP. The council developed legislation to modify existing labor laws, initiated an investigation of prostitution in Peru, and carried out employment training at a national level.[6] CONAMUP had no time to develop more reforms regarding women's situation and rights, however, nor was it able to abandon its hierarchical characteristics. For all its efforts, CONAMUP did not substantially modify the ideas that women had of the state and of their own status as women. Its most significant success was probably that an important group of professional women got together with feminists and some social leaders. The majority of these women played important roles in the Peruvian women's movement in the late 1970s.

Women's relation to the state began to change and widen only after the defeat of the oligarchy (and the Velasco Alvarado government) in 1975 and the further institutionalization of democracy in 1979 with the Belaúnde government. After the return to democratic rule, cooperation between the women's movement and the state became stronger than ever. Amid important struggles, strikes, and workers' and peasants' mobilizations at a national level, women went to the streets in large numbers, not only to support male workers on strike but also to proclaim their own demands as workers. They began to face as a group the contradictions between their political and union actions and their domestic affairs. Meanwhile, the country was discussing the new constitution, which would consolidate the democratic process that had just begun. The question most women started to ask was, What is our role in democracy? The answer at that moment was not very encouraging, for only two of the 180 representatives elected to the 1979 Assembly for the Constitution were women.

In 1983 Fernando Belaúnde Terry's government developed a new initiative toward women—again in answer to pressure generated by the Women's Decade. The Women's Bureau was created at the Ministry of Justice to coordinate all governmental actions toward women. But the bureau had no human and financial resources, so it achieved little.

It was not until 1986, when the Women's Bureau was replaced by the Special Commission for Women's Rights, that the state backed up with resources its support for women. The special commission's aim was to make known the laws to protect women's rights. Representatives from all government ministries and from nongovernmental organizations (NGOs) participated in the commission. A grass-roots leader was supposed to be part of the commission, but because of the difficulty of naming only one representative and because of the fear on the part of the grass-roots organizations that participation would be seen as collaboration with the government, no one was chosen. Instead, other forms of participation were established for the grass-roots organizations. The commission organized a national conference attended by representatives from all ministries and regional state bureaus, grass-roots women's organizations, and the feminist movement. The conference produced a document diagnosing the situation of Peruvian women.

The special commission also encouraged the creation of the first women's police precinct in 1988. The feminist movement had demanded a Women's Precinct years before, but plans for it had never gone beyond informal discussions in the Women's Rights Commission. The rights commission responded to women's demands this time because of the high rate of sexual assaults on women, who would not come to the police station out of fear or shame. The women's movement responded immediately to the Women's Rights Commission's recommendation, and the Ministry of the Interior and the Ministry of Justice agreed to set up the Women's Precinct. Women from the feminist movement participated as members of the first Support Commission of the precinct, offering legal advice at the precinct, taking on cases through their own law firms, and training policewomen regarding the problems of gender and violence against women. This feminist participation in the Support Commission has had obvious limitations, as the feminists are not allowed to make policy decisions. But the state's decision to establish the precinct legitimated the struggle against violence toward women, not only for the population in general but also for the police forces, one of the sectors that resists the legitimacy of the struggle against violence toward women. The Congress, with the support of feminist groups, is putting together a proposal to increase the number of Women's Precincts nationwide and to include rape as a type of crime attended to by the police. Pressure is also being exerted by women's groups so that policewomen, currently limited to entry-level and noncommissioned ranks, can become officers.[7]

The creation of the Women's Precinct has had a great impact on women's lives and on society more generally. For the first time, the most private aspects of life—rape and domestic violence—have been made public through the mass media. In a society as traditional as Peru's, publicizing this daily violence through official channels has made the problem legitimate. At the same time, it is no longer just feminists but also the state that has become interested in these issues, shocked by the violence against women.

Questions regarding the most appropriate spaces or origins, bearers, and arenas for women's demands have characterized the Peruvian women's movement. These questions initially led to a division between the autonomous women's movement and the women who were active in public and governmental arenas. Because of this demarcation of spaces, both groups lost out in the end. Eventually some of the sensitized women who participated in formal politics saw the necessity of a united front for effectiveness, which led to the smashing of these separatist attitudes among women. The resulting broader movement included a modification of the politicians' vision of the autonomous feminists, and vice versa.

Not until the end of the 1970s and the beginning of the 1980s did the outlines of what we now consider the women's movement, with all three of its streams, become clear. The emergence of the movement was not, however, an easy process. The experience of the struggle for democracy united the streams of the movement initially. The first stage was in 1978–79, when the "feminist coordinating" collective was formed by five feminist groups: Acción para la Liberación de la Mujer (ALIMUPER, or Action for the Liberation of Women), Centro de la Mujer Peruana Flora Tristan (Flora Tristan Center for Peruvian Women), Movimiento Manuela Ramos (Manuela Ramos Movement), Frente Socialista de Mujeres (Socialist Women's Front), and Mujeres en Lucha (Women in Struggle). Together they called on all of the different women's sectors to mobilize for what were then considered the most critical struggles of women. A march against the Somoza dictatorship in Nicaragua was held. Another march was held to protest the murder of Peronist leaders in Peru. The women's groups also held a 48-hour fast in support of striking teachers. None of these mobilizations incorporated the gender perspective, however. It was only after the first mobilization for abortion and reproductive rights—which had incredibly low participation by women and was criticized by all political parties for diverting attention from the most important political issues—that the women's movement and especially the feminist stream realized that this struggle for democracy without attention to gender would have no positive effect on the construction of an autonomous women's movement. Still, these previous actions contributed greatly to the widening of women's perceptions of themselves in relation to society and created a fertile ground for the women's movement to grow.

Each stream of the women's movement has had its own dynamics and has made its own contributions to women and society. The first has been the feminist stream, composed of women who had a great deal of experience with parties of the new left and began to question their situation as women inside these parties. At the beginning of the women's movement, most of these women were middle-class university students and professionals, and only some of them had previous experience working with other women. Distancing themselves from the political parties to which they belonged, they dared to create the autonomous feminist movement. The second stream has been made up of women of the popular classes who, though acting from within the space defined by their traditional roles, began to enter the public sphere and change the content of these traditional roles. This stream has organized around survival problems, healthcare problems, and public services. It has also brought forth a rich nationwide organizational network. The third stream has been made up of women who were already participating in the formal ("traditional") political spaces, such as those of the political parties, unions, and guilds. These women began questioning and organizing from within these masculine spaces. Most of them were also middle-class students or professionals, and a few were union or community leaders who decided to engage in the feminist struggle from inside their organizations. Thus, most of the first feminine commissions, or women's sectors, were formed within parties on the left, as well as in some unions and federations. Over the past ten years, these three streams have become consolidated into the women's movement. Each stream has developed its own objectives, types of struggle, and organization. Nevertheless a decade of crisis and violence and also of great political and civic participation by women has contributed to the merging of the streams around the common problems of violence, crisis, and democracy that they face.

The feminist stream is composed of independent groups and several consciousness-raising groups in Lima, as well as groups in outlying districts linked through local, regional, and national networks. Besides the groups organized around collective political action—with their themes of human and reproductive rights, antiviolence, lesbian rights, and communication—the feminist stream has spurred the formation of feminist institutes and centers that research and edit numerous magazines and books. These centers run

legal aid, health, library, and women's history programs. At the same time, they have been at the forefront of efforts to integrate the feminist sector with other streams of the movement by channeling part of their efforts and resources into collective projects with organizations of women from the marginalized neighborhoods, union organizations, rural and middle-class women's groups, and the like.

The popular stream of the women's movement developed mostly during the early 1980s. In response to the deepening economic crisis, these women generated new arenas and organizations for political action and gave another meaning to the traditional organizations in the popular areas. Thus, the old neighborhood organizations for women, previously clientelistic and assistance oriented, developed new political contents and organized around the needs for health, survival, and education.

Several factors contributed to the expansion of these "new" women's organizations. Because the settlements formed by the "invasion" and expropriation of uncultivated urban property by migrants from rural areas lacked water, electricity, transportation, and other elements of basic infrastructure, the women organized around their need to make these places livable by means of basic services. The government under Velasco Alvarado had created an organizational structure in the popular areas that worked "from beneath" to solve these problems.[8] This structure incorporated women, but only at the bottom and not at the decision-making level. At the same time, the rural origins of the majority of the occupants of these zones facilitated the development of communal projects and cooperation based on the country's Andean tradition. These women had strong solidarity and mutual help networks that, together with the organizing tradition of the 1970s and the effects of the economic crisis, help explain the enormous amount of organizing that they engaged in during the 1980s.

Although they have organized for subsistence items or for basic services, women of the popular classes have had to fight within their own homes for the right to participate in such activities outside the home. Through these community organizations they have begun to confront and reject the domestic violence that affected their home lives. In many popular areas, women have organized a defense against domestic violence (e.g., using whistles to alert other women that one of them is a victim of violence in her home). The uproar caused by these groups has sometimes been sufficient social punishment to end the violence. In the process, they, as well as those in other streams of the women's movement, have discovered that violence is not an individual problem but one shared by many.

This popular current of the women's movement—composed of various types of organizations, each with its own objectives and strategies—is by far the most extensive. Most of the organizations concentrate on tasks linked with daily survival, such as community kitchens, legal defense, or production. There are about 3,000 community kitchens in Peru, with more than 200,000 women participating in them. The various types of community kitchens are organized along more or less the same lines. They are created by zone, and each serves a certain number of families. The women take weekly turns buying and cooking the food. There are also 9,500 Glass of Milk committees with a total membership of more than 300,000 women. The Glass of Milk program began as a functional organization in which women could come together to prepare and distribute one daily glass of powdered milk to children under age seven. Now it is one of the most organized action groups, with a substantial capacity for mobilization. It has exercised political pressure not only to assure the donation of the milk but also to prevent the state and the political parties from manipulating the committees for their own purposes.

The community kitchens, as well as the women from Glass of Milk, have frequently been opposed by the local corporatist popular sector organizations, generally led by men who tend to be manipulative and who refuse to give women representation in the organizational structures. These men also try to generate organizations parallel to the existing women's organizations as a way of assuring their control over women.

There are other types of popular sector women's organizations. One of them is the Federación Popular de Mujeres de Villa El Salvador (Popular Federation for the Women of Villa El Salvador). With a gender-explicit perspective, the leaders of FEPOMUVES express most clearly the political viewpoint and potential power of this stream. In general, all of the organizations in FEPOMUVES are breeding grounds for the new leadership of the women's movement, as well as for women who enter the more formal political arenas. Many women in FEPOMUVES, and in other popular organizations, have had close relations with political parties, especially those on the left. Nevertheless, these women publicly maintain an ambivalent attitude toward the parties. They are constantly confronting them to keep the parties in general—and the ones on the left in particular—from defining and deciding the context of the vindications, struggles, and dynamics of the women's movement. Still, women accept and participate in the representation quotas for grass-roots organizations or labor federations that the parties insist upon for local government and most political campaigns, though there are no women's quotas yet.

The relation of peasant women to the women's movement is complex. As we have noted, Peru is a fragmented country, and Peruvian peasantry is the most clear example of this lack of unity. So the links of peasant women to the other streams of the women's movement or with their own stream are still weak. Peasant women have, however, always had a fundamental role in the development and consolidation of peasant organizations that include men and women. Although other peasant women's organizations have existed for a long time, such organizations did not facilitate an autonomous struggle of peasant women. Thus, the women's organizations that did develop in rural areas did not really favor the creation of a women's movement. Under the traditional and hierarchal conditions of rural Peru, even class organizations, though historically male-oriented, seemed to offer rural women a better vehicle for confronting and questioning their experiences as women peasants than did other traditional women's organizations.

Peasant women's struggle for their rights has thus taken place within the two bigger peasant organizations: Confederación Campesina del Peru (Peruvian Peasant Confederation) and Confederación Nacional Agraria (National Agriculture Confederation). In the 1960s and the 1970s women, side by side with men, participated in major struggles for land. When women's secretaryships were created within the peasant organizations mentioned, however, women were not placed in charge of them. It was not until 1982 that a peasant women's movement developed. The women's goals were to achieve acknowledgment of their own space within the unions, to direct women's secretaryships, to obtain access to land and credit, to have representation in the peasant unions' leadership, and to punish their husbands' violence against them.

The diverse stream of the women's movement within the traditional public space (women from trade unions, professional unions, rural and urban federations, and central unions, as well as women from political parties) has evolved more slowly than the popular stream. Women within traditional political spaces have been the most resistant to changing their points of view regarding social relations and political struggle.

Still, women from the trade unions and federations have had a stronger voice as women in the past few years. The impulse given by the actions of the women's movement on the macro level and the work carried out by feminists who organized working women have been significant influences. By creating nuclei of women within the unions and by sensitizing men, these union women have been able to make women's conditions in the labor force and in unions visible, to form women's secretaryships in many unions, and to be elected to positions of union leadership.

A major effort of this stream in the women's movement, initiated periodically, has been the dissemination of the Female Workers' Petitions (Memoriales de la Mujer Trabajadora). These proposals first appeared within the interunion activities supported by the feminist movement. During the government changeover in 1985, as part of the country's widespread reflection on its general politics, working-class women raised their demands to the state. The initial demands concerned working conditions, salary policies, employment training policies, and social security. Many trade union women lobbied state bureaucrats and the Parliament. This mobilization, which meant actual negotiations between women workers and MPs from different political parties, led to a rich discussion in Parliament. In 1986, after more lobbying, sexual harassment in the workplace was made a legal misdemeanor for the first time. The second petition, in 1989, was more oriented toward women's identity as workers. Some of the earlier demands were included, as well as a proposal for sex-related quotas in each of the industrial branches. These new demands are generating significant discussion and mobilization within this sector of the women's movement.

Another important space gained by working-class women has been the Secretariat of Women's Affairs within the Central General de Trabajadores del Perú (General Central for Workers of Peru), the major workers' union in the country. Even though the union had existed for 50 years, it was not until 1987 that the first Women Workers' Meeting took place. Other unions, like the Bank Employees Federation, also now include women's commissions in their structures as a result of pressure from women. The political parties have also been modified by their women members in the past ten years. In trying to establish some distance from traditional political arenas to create a more autonomous perspective, some women, mostly from the political parties on the left, formed female commissions within their parties. At first, there were two basic objectives with this initiative: to raise consciousness among the party militants, especially males, on the condition of women, and to help lead women's struggles. Their initial efforts brought them together as women and allowed them to modify their a priori view about women's role in the transformation of society and their own role as political militants.

They thus began the intense and fruitful process of seeing themselves as women, not just as political militants of a given cause; they had a gender perspective in their reflections and in their actions. This process, which began with the militants of left-wing political parties, has now extended to almost all the existing political parties. At present, Popular Action, Freedom Movement, and the Christian Popular parties have women representatives in Parliament who, together with congresswomen from APRA and the Izquierda Socialista (Socialist Left) and in coordination with the feminist movement, introduce legislation on behalf of women.

While the women's movement has grown, women's role in society has expanded, and the division that separates the public sphere from the private one has became increasingly questioned; the same public sphere, with its decision-making levels and designation of proposals, has remained in the hands of men. In spite of this, women keep trying to consolidate the weak, mistreated, and difficult process of democracy in Peru. In a country fragmented by special interests and points of view that often seem irreconcilable, it has been a challenge to overcome polarity within the women's movement to work toward the democratization of society. This conjunction of diverse efforts represents women's different though not always successful attempts to build bridges between society and the state.

Until now, these efforts have had positive results for both women and the relation of society to state. Society itself has been enriched and changed through new topics and new sociopolitical perspectives. At the same time, the impulse toward modernization and democratization of both the state and public arenas has forced the state to widen its dialogue, to reorient its meager resources, to change some of its laws, and to open more organic channels of participation. This has been a tension-filled process as women have learned to readjust, to negotiate, to make pacts, to give up, and to remake their goals.[9] At the same time, it has been and continues to be an excellent apprenticeship for democracy, both for women and Peru as a whole.

WIDENING THE RELATION BETWEEN CIVIL SOCIETY AND THE STATE

The issue of representation constituted a fundamental challenge to both the women's movement and society as a whole in the late 1970s and in the 1980s. The women's movement was confronted with the question of attaining power in public spaces and in the state, a question that was evaded by the early feminist movement. As we have noted, women only won the right to vote in 1955 after eight years of dictatorship. The following democratic period lasted 12 years, until Velasco Alvarado's military coup in 1968. The general would rule for ten years. Before the 1980s women's democratic experience had thus been very limited.

The first significant attempt to establish a feminist presence in the formal political space took place in 1985. We, the authors of this chapter, ran as independents in the general elections for the Senate and Congress on the lists of Leftist United.[10] Campaigning was, without doubt, an enriching experience, but it was also full of discouraging ambiguities. On the one hand, we had to face enormous difficulties with regard to the feminist movement that supported us, but we also feared that its autonomy could be damaged if it expressed its support too loudly. On the other hand, people within the Leftist Front regarded us as two parvenus who had criticized political parties but who were now using their space.

We lost the elections, but we opened the way for others. With us as candidates, the distinctiveness of women's gender issues was made visible. The political debate included an agenda that had never been seen before in an electoral campaign. Using the slogan "Vote for yourself, woman" and raising issues previously ignored in a political campaign (sexuality, violence, labor, organization, female representation), we appealed to women's commitment to themselves to transform their subordination. One of our objectives was to be able to watch over women's interests from inside a center of official power. We also hoped to protect women from harmful measures, to develop laws to further women's rights, and to end women's status as "refugees" inside their own country. By appealing to women's rebellious spirit, we tried to raise to the level of politics women's right to know and decide over their own bodies, to live their sexuality with no impositions on it, and to control their own capacity for work.

Our presence as feminists and not as women from parties put the issue of women on the agenda. The appearance of the feminist movement in the public and formal political world also opened doors for other women's more active and dynamic presence in official politics. Many women from political parties felt encouraged to support, at a later date, other initiatives in favor of women. Women from political parties also later designed campaign strategies oriented to women.

Women's entry into the public space has been most apparent on the local level. In 1985, after a feminist councilwoman was elected to city hall in Lima, a new public space clearly different from previous ones was opened. We, along with councilwomen from different political parties, made up the board of directors. The board was basically an advisory commission with a mandate to develop working proposals to benefit the women of Lima. The commission's most important action was creating the Municipal House for Women in Lima's city hall just a few yards from the Government Palace. At the municipal house, legal assistance was given to women who had been raped or mistreated. Films, photographic exhibitions, forums, and panels on women's issues were scheduled each week.

After a year and a half of women's management, a new outlook was stamped into this official space, both in the kind of actions carried out and in the content of the debate. Beginning in 1987, the Mother's Day celebration, traditionally marked by its patriarchal style, gained a feminist content. The city allocated a budget, and free transportation to the celebration was given to mothers from the slums. Held at the Municipal Theater, Peru's biggest and most elite

theater, this celebration was oriented toward strengthening the participants' rights as women and citizens.

The coordination work done by the Municipal House made evident the difficulties of collective and democratic work in the face of political differences. When a particular initiative was proposed by the councilwoman who belonged to the left-wing front, the other councilwomen felt that to support her proposal was to support her political front. Thus, many times indirect or strong opposition appeared, as women did not want to commit themselves to actions that had no party backing or left them without clear political benefits.

Still, this short period of management on the part of women (it ended in 1987) was barely enough to allow women to get to know the unruly bureaucratic world of Lima's municipal government. It was hard to learn how to deal with the entrenched bureaucracy, which had been unknown to women. Thus, every proposed action had to be fought for little by little as women learned to use tradition for their own purposes, to incorporate new contents into old policies.

The Municipal House has continued to function, though with less impact than in its initial years. In spite of being subject to party changes in local government, the Municipal House constitutes an alternative to the specific services for women that the state can offer, which have a political and not necessarily assistance-oriented perspective. All in all, the municipal space has proved to be an important channel for popular expression, especially for the women who are organized in each jurisdiction. City hall has the authority to plan and execute local public services, and its actions have a strong impact on public opinion. In this sense, municipal governments have been the most immediate and direct way of involving women in politics.

In the 1990 election, favorable conditions were created for women's representation on the national level. For the first time, many party lists provided women with increased opportunities for candidacies. During these elections, sixteen parties offered 960 candidates for senator, 129 of whom were women.[11]

Although the women's movement did not field its own candidates, it did manage to generate an important space during the campaign: the Foro Mujer (Women's Forum), which was created as a committee by various feminist organizations to encourage formulation of policies that favor women. The Women's Forum sent an open letter to all the presidential candidates, urging them to incorporate women's interests into their agendas. Even though the letter did not receive much attention from the male candidates, it did have an impact on the women who were candidates for Congress. The first forum was organized with their participation in the middle of the electoral campaign. This was made easier because the candidates in this election had campaigns that addressed women's conditions. Picking up where the "Vote for yourself, woman" campaign left off, these campaigns used slogans like "With me, all women are present in Congress"; "As a woman and a mother, I know your problems"; "Without fear of participating in politics, we women can change them"; and "An open letter to the other half." These slogans suggested that voting for the women candidates should not be done as a favor to women, but as a way of establishing equilibrium between men and women. Four women were elected senators and twelve were elected deputies. Some congresswomen have already become presidents of a few working commissions in Parliament and are presenting bills plainly identified with women's issues.

The space opened by the Women's Forum has had effects beyond the electoral process. It has helped to build bridges among the diverse groups that make up the women's movement and has offered points of union and consensus. It has the support of the congresswomen and the women in the political parties who consider the forum a new way to garner support for their own parliamentary proposals or to increase their power within their party organizations. One of the objectives of the Women's Forum in relation to Parliament is to build a women's lobby, an action previously unheard of in such an unrewarding and polarized environment. In March 1991, as the result of one year's work in the Women's Forum, women in Parliament announced the constitution of a front called Women in Parliament. They meet regularly to exchange opinions in order to undertake joint actions.

A WAY OF BALANCE: THE DIRECTION OF WOMEN'S POLITICAL ACTION

In spite of all we have described, the rich process of all the streams of the women's movement has moved backward and forward at different times. Each stream knows about the difficulty of entanglements, about the effects of social pressure to lessen women's rebellion, about the effects of validating and reinforcing only those aspects of the women's struggle that fit their own interests. These difficulties, which we think of as common to all women's movements, are worsening with the effects of economic crisis and political violence. The economic crisis, more than ever, is constraining the streams from developing more autonomously. The enormous needs that women face, especially in popular and rural areas, are leading them to assume a greater amount of work, sometimes two, three, or four times the usual working day. The popular stream is probably the most vulnerable to these pressures. Until now, these women's organizations have been successful in avoiding the trap of becoming service organizations, fixed to "assistance-ism" and the most urgent and immediate family needs, and have been able to advance on their political agenda.

Because of the political-economic crisis of the state, however, these women's organizations now risk losing what they have achieved. Women's daily workload is increasing, leaving them no time to organize themselves, to value themselves, to dream. The entire burden of the crisis has fallen on their shoulders, and survival has become their main worry. The government has implemented social compensation programs that use the work of women's groups and their organizational capacities to the maximum extent. Yet they take away from women one of the most important achievements of these organizations: the capacity of at least deciding about and controlling their own programs. Most of these organizational programs are now controlled by the church and some government programs in which these women have no representation. Still, the struggle goes on. Not long ago, the Glass of Milk organization carried out a large mobilization demanding, among other things, greater control over the process of distributing the milk. Political parties' attempts to manipulate such organizations have also intensified.

At the same time, the feminist stream of the women's movement must deal with an increased need for resources. National campaigns sponsored by the different women's organizations, including those from the state, to stop violence against women, against the "feminization" of poverty, and in favor of reproductive rights, cultural festivals, publications, and so on, are all at risk because of the lack of resources to carry them out.

Finally, relations among the streams of the women's movement are still sometimes conflictual. At other times it is full of solidarity and creativity. Race, class, geographic region, age, political interests, and other differences exist. All of them, nevertheless, contribute to the construction of a different way of being a woman in Peru. The women's movement, more than any other movement in Peru, has forced a new relationship between society and the state. It has demonstrated that old political paradigms that focus solely on class are outmoded, showing the multiplicity of situations of power and powerlessness in which people are involved. It has demonstrated women's capacity to be social and political subjects who, from their positions of subordination, rebel, shout, strive, and propose changes. The women's presence has opened new spaces anchored in daily life at the same time as it has gone beyond them. It has entered male-oriented spaces, and changed them. The concept of "politics" has gotten a new, broader, and more human dimension as it has incorporated new issues and newly visible social subjects.

This quality of "sheltering plurality" may also explain why the movement has had diverse points of departure (survival, health, political representation, party organization, explicit gender issues). Each of these points has involved a multiplicity of political objectives: the solution to immediate and urgent demands; the development of social practices, and new forms of personal and social relations, anchored more in solidarity and "horizontality"; the possibility of developing a democratic perspective for women's own lives; the conquest of citizens' rights; the legitimation of women's gender-specific conditions with concrete demands; and, most important, the formation of multiple identities as women, which acknowledge the differences and diversity of Peruvian women.

The multiplicity of women's collective action and the difficulties of living in a society so resistant to women's voices and proposals has led to contradictions in women's social practices. These are marked by a continuous, opposing process of both submission and rebellion. Recently, women have discovered the need to find alternative ways of dealing with the world, ways hinged on more democratic values in which women are included and respected and in which they can become more autonomous in their own lives. Still, they continue to be influenced by traditional ideas and practices regarding their role. The traditional contents of women's social and political practices have not been static. On the contrary, they have had creative continuity. Women have given new meaning to their traditional roles and transferred them to the public sphere with a new content of solidarity among women. This may also be why the different streams of the women's movement have a different language, more anchored in daily life and in subjectivity. ("I dream, Mr. President," said one of the new congresswomen during a meeting held between the Parliament and the new cabinet.) While this subjectivity is not necessarily always efficient, it does constitute a sign of how women's political action tends to question the separation between the public and the private.

Is this enough to ensure a change in the political agenda—to generate an irreversible will for the conquest of citizenship for women? The risks are many, both from within the movement and within the political spaces. Opposition by the state and from the formal political spaces is not easily defeated over the long term, much less in the short term. The important thing is that the women's movement is developing and practicing multiple strategies to articulate women's needs and interests; change those needs into political proposals; ensure women's representation without shying away from the different conventional and non-conventional spaces; look for mechanisms to support those in a position to influence the state more directly; and fight to consolidate and build more autonomous spaces for dialogue, interchange, and pressure from and within society.

We believe that in this way Peruvian women—in the women's movement, in their daily lives, and in formal political spaces—are contributing to a qualitative jump toward political citizenship for themselves and for society as a whole. They are influencing, modifying, and widening the contents of the incipient democracy in Peru.

The year 1990 brought new possibilities and greater spaces for women's political action in collaboration with the state. Decentralization and regionalization, initiated in the previous government, may well create a new space for nationwide work. The networks of women that exist in Peru, many of them supported or created by the feminist movement, could reinforce this process.

NOTES

1. Better than any sociolingual study, the novel *Todas las sangres* (All different bloods) (Buenos Aires: Editorial Losada, 1964) by Peruvian Jose Maria Arguedas penetrates the many-hued national identity—the mixture of cultures and peoples, vision and hopes—that exists in Peru.

2. The Quechua-speaking population decreased from 31 percent in 1940 to 6 percent in 1982. The Aymara-speaking population fell from 3.5 to 1 percent in the same period.

3. Sinesio Lopez, "Sociedad y estado en el Perú actual: Patrimonialismo, participación, representación" (Society and state in current Peru: Patrimonialism, participation, representation), in *El Dios mortal. Estado, sociedad y política en el Peru del siglo XX* (Lima: Instituto Democracia y Socialísmo, 1989).

4. Ibid.

5. Julio Cotler, *Clase, estado y nación* (Class, state and nation) (Lima: Instituto de Estudios Peruanos, 1981).

6. Nora Galer, "Mujer y desarrollo: Balance de acciones y propuestas de política" (Women and development: Evaluation of actions and policy proposals), in Patricia Portocarrero, ed., *Mujer en el desarrollo: Balance y propuestas* (Lima: Flora Tristan-IRED, 1989).

7. Policewomen can now enter the ranks, but they cannot be officers, so police stations are headed by male officers.

8. This organizational structure was encouraged to assure a basis of popular support for the Velasco Alvarado government. Though it failed to organize the population for its own aims, this basically corporatist structure did create the foundation for significant participation by women in the organization of the territory.

9. Luis Aguilar, "La democracia civilizatoria" (The civilizing democracy), *Revista Debate Feminista*, no. 1 (March 1990).

10. Because Leftist United was a front formed for the elections, not a political party, there were quotas for each party, as well as a significant quota for independents.

11. The actual legal representation in Parliament achieved by women does not express the role played by many women in the process. The APRA party has five women representatives. CAMBIO '90 also has five women representatives. FREDEMO has four congresswomen. The Socialist Left has two women representatives.

▲ The Philippines

POLITICS

Type of Political System: democracy
 Sovereignty: republic
 Executive-Legislative System: presidential
Type of State: unitary
Type of Party System: multiparty
Major Political Parties[a]

Communist Party of the Philippines–New People's Army (CPP-NPA): Radical underground movement; not a political party in the usual sense.

Moro National Liberation Front (MNLF): Radical underground Muslim movement in Mindanao; founded in 1972.

Laban ng Demokratikong Pilipino (LDP, or Struggle of Democratic Filipinos): Won a majority in the Senate and House of Representatives in the May 1992 elections. Supported Corazon Aquino during her presidency (1987–92).

Partido Demokratikong Pilipino (PDP, or Filipino Democratic Party): Founded by Sen. Aquilino Pimentel. Formed a coalition with some Laban elements to establish PDP-Laban, which fielded Senate candidates in the 1992 elections.

Liberal Party (LP): Founded at independence in 1946. Formed a coalition with the PDP in 1992 to support the presidential candidacy of Sen. Jovito Salonga.

Lakas ng Bayan [People's Power]–National Union of Christian Democrats (Lakas-NUCD): Alliance formed by President Fidel Ramos during his 1992 presidential candidacy.

Nacionalista Party (NP, or Nationalist Party): Oldest major party in the Philippines; formed in 1907 during the U.S. colonial period.

Nationalist People's Coalition (NPC): Alliance organized by Eduardo Cojuangco to support his presidential candidacy in 1992.

People's Reform Party (PRP): Alliance organized by Miriam Defensor Santiago to support her presidential candidacy in 1992.

Kilusang Bagong Lipunan (KBL, or New Society Movement): Party created by President Ferdinand Marcos in 1986 while the Philippines was under martial law. Marcos used this party to run in the 1986 snap presidential election against Corazon Aquino.

Year Women Granted Right to Vote: 1937
Year Women Granted Right to Stand for Election: 1937
Percentage of Women in the Legislature[b]
 Lower House: 8.9%
 Upper House: 8.6%
Percentage of Electorate Voting for Highest Elected Office in Most Recent Election (1992): not available

DEMOGRAPHICS

Population: 60,480,000[c]
Percentage of Population in Urban Areas[d]
 Overall: 42.0%
 Female: not available
 Male: not available
Percentage of Population Below Age 15: 39.0%[e]
Birthrate (per 1,000 population): 35[f]
Maternal Mortality Rate (per 100,000 live births): 80
Infant Mortality Rate (per 1,000 live births): 46
Mortality Rate for Children Under Five (per 1,000 live births): 75
Average Household Size: 5.6[g]
Mean Age at First Marriage
 Female: 22.4
 Male: 25.3
Life Expectancy
 Female: 63.7
 Male: 60.2

EDUCATION

Ratio of Female to Male Enrollment
 First-Level Education: 94

Second-Level Education: 99
Third-Level Education: 119
Literacy Rate[h]
  Female: 82.8%
  Male: 83.9%

ECONOMY
Gross National Product per Capita: U.S.
$590
Percentage of Labor Force in Agriculture:
49.0%[i]
*Distribution of Agricultural Workers by
  Sex*
  Female: 23.5%
  Male: 76.5%
Economically Active Population by Sex[j]
  Female: 46.1%
  Male: 81.7%

a. Political parties in the Philippines are not formal organizations but loose and shifting coalitions without fixed memberships. Party descriptions are provided by the author.

b. Commission on Elections, *1987 National Election Results* (Manila).

c. *Philippines Country Profile, 1991–1992* (London: Economist Intelligence Unit, 1991).

d. *Asia 1992 Yearbook* (Hong Kong: Far Eastern Economic Review, 1992), 7.

e. *National Statistics Yearbook, 1989* (Manila: National Statistics Office, 1990).

f. Ibid.

g. Ibid.

h. *Philippine Development Plan for Women, 1989* (Manila: National Commission on the Role of Filipino Women, 1990).

i. *Philippine Country Profile, 1991–1992.*

j. *Integrated Survey of Households Bulletin,* series 56 (Manila: National Statistics Office, First–Fourth Quarters, 1986).

Philippine Feminism in Historical Perspective

BELINDA A. AQUINO

The Philippines is a tropical archipelago of 7,107 islands—115,781 square miles of territory—on the southeast rim of the Asian continent. Though often considered a small country, the Philippines has a population of 60.7 million, making it the world's 17th largest nation. The great majority of the people are Roman Catholics (82.1 percent), with the rest divided among Muslims, Protestants, Aglipayan (Philippine Independent Church) members, cultural minorities, Iglesia ni Kristo (Church of Christ) members, Buddhists, and others.[1] A relatively poor country, the Philippines has suffered from a deteriorating economy in recent decades, mostly as a result of large-scale corruption during the regime of Ferdinand Marcos.

Long before the islands were colonized by Spain and then the United States, they had their own cultures, which were shaped by indigenous forces, as well as by Chinese, Arab, and Indian influences. In 1521 the Portuguese explorer Fer-

dinand Magellan claimed the islands for Spain and named them after King Philip II. Spanish colonial rule—characterized by cruelty toward and repression of the local population by the friars and civil guards—lasted three centuries, not ending until the proclamation of the first Philippine republic in 1898. But after Spain's defeat in the nationalist revolution another colonial power, the United States, formally took possession of the Philippines at the conclusion of the Spanish-American War in 1898.[2] Filipino nationalist forces resisted the new foreign occupation but were overwhelmed by the superior U.S. troops. In August 1898 the U.S. government instituted a military government that lasted until July 1901, when civilian rule was established in areas controlled by the U.S. military. In 1935 the U.S. colonial authorities set up the Philippine Commonwealth with Manuel Luis Quezon as president.

Commonwealth status was meant to be a transition to the eventual independence of the Philippines, to be granted ten years after the adoption of a constitution and a national election in 1935. But independence was delayed by World War II and the occupation of the country by Japan from 1942 to 1945. United States forces reoccupied the country in late 1945, and on 4 July 1946 the Philippines won its independence from the United States.

Although it is common to characterize politics in terms of form—liberal democracy, one-party rule, military junta, civil-military coalition, social democracy, theocracy, and so on—these labels have only analytical convenience and do not capture the political culture of a country. Political systems in the Third World are especially difficult to fit into the conceptual models that Western social scientists have developed for political analysis.

In the Philippine case, today's political culture has its roots in the hegemonic system established under Spanish rule and monopolized by an elite class known as the *ilustrado* (enlightened). This was a small class of landed gentry that controlled the vast majority of the population. Elite rule was essentially continued by the U.S. authorities in spite of their avowed goals of developing democracy and representative government in the colony that they took over from Spain. Formal mechanisms for citizen participation, such as elections and political parties, were formed, and the concepts of due process and checks and balances of governmental authority were introduced. But no real changes in the highly unequal social structure and benighted economy took place. Economic policies pursued by the U.S. colonial government—free trade, for instance—favored elites and made them wealthier and more powerful. The elite class also dominated electoral contests and positions.

The continuing influence of the United States in Philippine affairs has been another major fact of political life. The presence of two huge U.S. military bases—Clark Air Base and Subic Naval Base—on Philippine territory has long been the subject of contentious debate between the two countries. Per agreements in 1947 and in subsequent years, the lease on the bases has expired. Negotiations for the termination or continuance of the bases are being conducted, and if a new treaty results from these talks, it will have to be reviewed and approved by the Philippine Senate.

The Philippines remains basically agricultural, with two-thirds of its population dependent on agriculture, forestry, and fishing for their livelihoods. The industrial sector, which is located principally in the metro-Manila capital region, has not kept pace with the needs of a poor and rapidly expanding population. The economic growth of the country has been hampered by an onerous foreign debt of nearly U.S. $29 billion, which exacerbates the impoverishment of the people—49 percent are poor according to official estimates, but as many as 70 percent are poor by other estimates.[3]

The political system is anchored in a constitutional democratic form of government, with a president, a bicameral Congress, local governments, a judiciary, and a bureaucracy constituting the basic framework. Except during the nearly 14 years of the Marcos dictatorship, which lasted from September 1972 to February 1986, regular national and local elections have been held since independence in 1946. The 202 members of the House of Representatives are elected by district; 18 of them are women. The 23 members of the Senate are elected at large; 2 of them are women. The country is divided into 13 administrative regions, with metro Manila designated the National Capital Region. Each region is composed of a number of provinces and cities.

Prior to the imposition of martial law in 1972, political power alternated between the Nacionalista (Nationalist) Party and the Liberal Party. There was little difference in the agendas of the two parties, which were controlled by elite interests. Political candidates opportunistically switched allegiances. Candidates from smaller parties, including those supported by the left, rarely got elected. Though democratic in form, Philippine politics was, and still is, substantially a matter of patronage and privilege.

With the overthrow of the Marcos dictatorship

in the now-famous People Power Revolution in 1986, "democratic space" in the country was restored. Corazon C. Aquino, widow of the slain opposition leader Benigno Aquino, Jr., was installed as president. A new constitution was ratified in February 1987, and elections for members of Congress were held three months later. Twenty-two of the winning senators ran as part of Aquino's ruling coalition, which was principally composed of the PDP-Laban (a merger of the Partido Demokratikong Pilipino, or Filipino Democratic Party, and Lakas ng Bayan, or People's Power), the Liberal Party, the United Democratic Nationalist Organization (UNIDO), and other, smaller groups. Only two candidates were elected from groups identified with the opposition.

A communist insurgency led by the Communist Party of the Philippines–New People's Army (CPP-NPA) and Muslim unrest involving the Moro National Liberation Front and other groups pose major problems for the Aquino government. In addition, six coups or attempts at destabilization were either planned or undertaken by disaffected military elements between 1986 and 1989. The most serious of these, the December 1989 coup attempt, nearly toppled the four-year-old Aquino administration. The military has become politicized in some commands, indicating its dissatisfaction with its traditional subordination to civilian authority. A rise in politically motivated killings and common crimes has also been observed in recent years. At best the post-Marcos period can be characterized as that of a restored but unstable democracy. Marcos's plunder and destruction of the political institutions, as well as Aquino's inability to display decisive leadership, combine to create a climate of insecurity.

WOMEN IN PHILIPPINE SOCIETY

It is within this context that the historical role of women in Philippine society can be examined. Although the evidence is fragmented, instances of what is understood in the Philippines as feminism can be seen as early as the eighteenth century. The best known of the early Filipina activists is Gabriela Silang of the Ilocos region in the northern Philippines.[4] She was married to Diego Silang, a rebel leader who was assassinated by a Spaniard in the town of Vigan. Gabriela continued the struggle, setting up a headquarters for the Free Government of the Ilocos in Abra Province to recapture Vigan. When she and her army of 60 entered the town, they were overpowered by Spanish soldiers numbering in the thousands. Gabriela was the last of her group to be hanged in the public square on 20 September 1763.

The political ferment generated by the struggle against Spain opened opportunities for women to go beyond their traditional roles in society. Several women were recruited by the Katipunan—the secret society founded by the revolutionary leader Andres Bonifacio—to enlist mass support against Spanish oppression. Prominent among these women were Melchora Aquino (more popularly known as Tandang Sora, an appellation denoting affection and respect for age), Gregoria de Jesus, Trinidad Tecson, and Marcela Mariño Agoncillo. They came mostly from upper-class families—many of whom had also produced male revolutionaries—but they had limited education. Other Filipinas worked to advance the cause of education while the Katipunan women were busy in the political struggle. Higher education under the Spanish was open only to sons of the elite. Women were sent to convent schools, where they were taught religion, homemaking, the social graces, and the Victorian code of conduct. The famous 21 "women of Malolos" defied the laws prohibiting the opening of schools for women by petitioning the governor general to allow the establishment of a school where they could learn Spanish.[5] From the perspective of the women of Malolos, the school was important to the Filipino struggle for equality because the ability to speak Spanish was crucial to educational mobility.

Women's participation in Filipino movements during the Spanish era was not limited to elite women, though evidence to support that view is sketchy. As will be seen later, women from the grass roots, who did not have as much wealth and social status as their upper-class counterparts, played a considerable role in shaping the course of Philippine history.

THE STRUGGLE FOR WOMEN'S POLITICAL AND ECONOMIC RIGHTS

By the time the U.S. colonial regime began, following the establishment of civil government in 1901, a significant core of educated Filipinas had emerged. Nuns had established a normal school for women—the first of its kind in the country—in Naga, in the Bicol region south of Manila, in 1877. Next came the establishment of the Instituto de Mujeres (Women's Institute) in 1900; an exclusive school for girls, the Centro Escolar de Señoritas (now Centro Escolar University), in 1907; and the Philippine Women's University in 1910.[6] The founding of the University of the Philippines in 1908 and the transformation of the Philippine Normal School and the University of Santo Tomas into coeducational institutions enabled more women to develop careers, not only in the field of education but also in the various professions.

The creation of educational opportunities for women was a landmark development. Women's next logical step was to win the right to vote and run for public office; they could not vote or put up candidates in the first national election for the Philippine legislature in 1907, nor were women well represented in the civil service.

Women's realization that they had second-class status in spite of their increasing sophistication led to the establishment of organizations to fight for women's rights. "Better educated, more articulate, and relatively freed from domestic duties, the women of the middle and upper classes led the way."[7] Elite women also saw the value of organizing and mobilizing support from other women. In time there were a number of women's groups devoted to advancing education, securing better conditions for working women, assisting poor mothers and children, seeking prison reform, and promoting charitable causes and other social concerns. The momentum for this organizational activity may be attributed to develop-

ments that were put in motion by the arrival of the Americans. Thousands of teachers and missionaries found their way from the United States to the new colony. The colonial government soon realized that "one of the best means to secure the cooperation of the townspeople was through women. . . ."[8] A prominent U.S. feminist, Carrie Chapman Catt, organized the Women's Club of Manila. The other major women's organizations were the National Federation of Women's Clubs, the Asosacion de Damas Filipinas (Association of Filipino Women), the Catholic Women's Federation, the Women's Medical Association, and a Philippine chapter of the Young Women's Christian Association. The impetus for this explosion of female energy was the "desire of Filipino women for their complete emancipation, political and civil."[9] The women began to respond to opportunities for work beyond the confines of their homes and churches.

The women involved in the suffrage movement came from a broad spectrum of socioeconomic backgrounds, but the leaders were mostly from the upper class—highly educated women successful in their professions and active in community affairs. They were often the first women to break through the sex barrier in their chosen professions.[10] Some were still students at the time, such as Carmen Planas, who was elected the first councilwoman of the city of Manila in the election after female suffrage was granted in 1937. There were none of the class-based, religious, geographic, and other kinds of cleavages that disrupt political movements after a while. The leaders campaigned across the country and were enthusiastically received wherever they went.

Men in the government and the professions vigorously opposed women's suffrage. They ridiculed it in the Manila press, calling the suffrage movement a consequence of higher education, which tended to limit the birth rate and thus would depopulate the country.[11] Women found this strange logic infuriating, but such resistance was typical of the problems that they confronted in their struggle for political enfranchisement, and the adverse male reactions served to unite them in a common cause.

To appreciate women's struggle to win the vote in the Philippines, it is also important to understand the larger political picture. In the constitution of 1935 the Philippine legislature established the onerous provision that the right of suffrage would be extended to women only if a national plebiscite were held in which no fewer than 300,000 women voted in its favor. This represented roughly one-third of the total number of women eligible to vote on the basis of age and literacy qualifications.[12] Male suffrage was also limited by property (this was later abolished) and literacy requirements, which meant that the great majority of Filipino men could not vote, either. But not one woman could vote. The framers of the constitution, most of whom were opposed to women's suffrage, probably calculated that it would be extremely difficult to meet the 300,000-vote requirement, especially considering that women would be voting for the first time. They were wrong: 447,725 women voted yes for the amendment in the 1937 plebiscite. The total surpassed the mandated requirement by nearly 150,000 votes! The women themselves were surprised but jubilant about the results of their long struggle.

What accounted for their remarkable achievement? Political organization, as well as persistence and determination. A General Council of Women headquartered in Manila directed the plebiscite campaign, relying on women's clubs in the towns for active support. Club members, in addition to their high social status and high level of education, were experienced in political campaigns and were viewed as strong and influential leaders.[13] Hundreds of women's club presidents in the provinces gave stirring speeches at carnivals, fairs, and suffrage rallies. Their followers distributed thousands of pamphlets, leaflets, sample ballots, posters, and calendars from feminist leaders. Two women's magazines, *Woman's Home Journal* and *Woman's World,* and a radio program featured the suffrage issue. Students were mobilized as well.

Women leaders also relied on their personal networks. For instance, one of the foremost feminists, Pilar Hidalgo Lim, was married to Gen. Vicente Lim. As Minerva Laudico narrates: "You will remember that General Lim then was ranking in the Philippine Army, and therefore, he had to make many provincial inspections, so we used to keep track of his schedule and write the clubwomen that General Lim would be there. So Mrs. Lim would be there to organize the women, etc. One day what happened was, a streamer said, 'Welcome to Mrs. Lim and Party.' So poor General Lim became the party of his wife. But he did not mind."[14] Laudico hastens to explain that this did not mean he was "under the *saya*"—an expression loosely translated as "dominated by his wife," *saya* being a woman's skirt. It simply meant that he was secure and supportive of what his wife was doing to promote the political rights of women.

Impressed by the vitality of the suffrage campaign, even President Manuel L. Quezon, the most influential, albeit chauvinistic, Filipino leader at the time, wholeheartedly endorsed the women's cause. When Quezon's full support of women's suffrage was publicly announced, other politicians, even those who opposed it, "ceased their vociferations" and even worked vigorously for the success of the plebiscite "simply because of their desire to please the chief executive."[15]

While middle- and upper-class women were occupied with the struggle for the vote, their counterparts in other sectors were making their own contributions to Philippine society. According to the 1918 census, 696,699 Filipinas were engaged in "industrial pursuits." They constituted 26 percent of the total female population fourteen years of age or older who were employed in gainful occupations (2,690,331). The figure of 696,699 included women who worked at home, for textiles and clothing were still made by piecework; one source lists weaving, dressmaking, embroidery, hatmaking, and shoe- and slipper-making as domestic manufactures.[16] Housewives augmented their family income without going out to work.

Those who worked outside the home were employed by distilleries and laundries and by garment, paper, glass, candy, hemp, tobacco, food, beverage, handicraft, and jewelry makers. They also operated dormitories and worked in pawnshops, bakeries, and business firms dealing with transportation, real estate, and the embroidery of native attire; in some cases, women were the managers of the firms. A 1930 survey showed that as many as 3,721 women were employed in cigar factories, which were concentrated in Manila. Another 5,000 worked in other industries. They joined labor organizations for "mutual protection and benefit." These "mutual benefit societies" were loosely referred to as unions, although they were not such in the Western sense of the word. In 1931 there were twelve such unions, with a national female membership of 5,266—a significant number in the early labor movement in the Philippines.[17]

Wages were most often the issue that motivated women workers to join strikes and mass actions. The highest weekly wage was 16 pesos (U.S. $8) and the lowest, four pesos ($2). Women's wages varied according to skill and type of work. Some women were paid at a piece rate, and others at a daily rate. The need for better working conditions was another major issue. Some tasks required women to remain standing for long hours, if not for their entire working period. There were no separate lavatories and closets for their use. Lighting, ventilation, and sanitation were dismal in many of the factories. Nor were there adequate provisions for disability and health benefits. Health services while on the job were minimal, if not altogether lacking.

In time, many of these issues were addressed and resolved, owing in part to pressure from the labor organizations. By 1933 the Philippine legislature had passed an important law limiting working hours in factories to only eight a day. Several factories had installed better facilities for the health and well-being of their workers.

Women were also active in social movements directed against U.S. colonial rule. In spite of the existence of a sedition law banning nationalist activities, a number of uprisings against the U.S. authorities took place. One of these, the Sakdal (meaning "to accuse, complain, or protest") movement peaked on 2–3 May 1935, when in three Tagalog provinces the Sakdalistas launched a series of uprisings against the Philippine Commonwealth. They wanted "immediate, complete, and absolute freedom" because they realized "that no other kind of freedom can be conducive to the political, economic, and social salvation of the Filipino people."[18]

One of the major Sakdalistas was a woman—Salud Algabre (later Generalla), a tenant on a landed estate in Laguna Province. She considered the government unjust and abusive: "The needs of the laborers were ignored. The leaders paid no attention to the people."[19] Just before the first uprising on 2 May 1935, Algabre was given the task of telling key rebel leaders in each town to organize the people "to march to their municipal buildings, capture them, raise the Sakdal flag, and proclaim independence." The Sakdalistas only had bolos (oversized native knives), clubs, sickles, and a few shotguns and pistols for weapons. On the first day of the uprising Algabre's husband, Severo, took charge of capturing the Cabuyao municipal building while Salud led another group to the highway. "We felled several trees across the road. It must have been about six o'clock in the evening when we began to stop the traffic." Although the rebellion failed, Salud Algabre never regretted her Sakdal involvement. Several years later she recalled May 1935 as the "high point of all our lives."[20]

Thus, the period from the beginning of the century to the outbreak of World War II was a moment of history for women in the Philippines. They were launched into a new world altogether after centuries of enforced domesticity, illiteracy, and cruel repression under Spanish rule. Possibilities heretofore denied women were opened up during the four decades prior to the war; more than that, the talents and energies of Filipinas were engaged in a political way. They became not just socially but also politically aware. Present-day feminism in the country draws much of its vitality from this earlier period of political engagement, which transformed the traditional world of Filipinas. A new consciousness evolved from their involvement in the suffrage movement, labor unions, and nationalist movements. Although they differed greatly along class lines, they were brought together by changes in Philippine society and the new or expanded roles for women in it.

THE POSTINDEPENDENCE YEARS

During World War II the Philippines was occupied by the Japanese and became a fierce battleground. By the end of the war the country was almost totally devastated physically, economically, and psychologically. But women—having gained the vote and political experience—were prepared to function in the postwar government that was consolidated by the national elections in April 1946 and the proclamation of the independent Philippine Republic on 4 July of the same year. Remedios Fortich from Mindanao and Geronima Pecson from Luzon were the first women elected—to the Lower and Upper Houses, respectively—in the new independent government. From 1946 until 1971 (the last year of free elections before the declaration of martial law), 11 women were elected representatives and 7, senators. During the same period 6 women were elected governors (heads of provinces) and 2, city mayors. A good number were elected vice-governors, members of provincial boards (legislatures), city and municipal mayors, vice-mayors, and council members.

But in Philippine politics before 1971, this record was not enough to make a dent in the male-dominated circles of political power, even though women voters outnumbered men voters. Statistics from the Commission on Elections show that in eight out of eleven elections during this period, more women than men turned out to vote.[21] Nonetheless, Filipinas never got together in substantial numbers to support women's issues or women candidates. Their political organizing was weak, particularly during the immediate postwar period, when women were largely preoccupied with reconstruction efforts in their houses and lives. Moreover, politics was still seen as a man's domain, and women voters were not necessarily voting as women. In 1951 an attempt to organize a National Political Party of Women to consolidate the women's vote never got off the

ground.[22] Instead, in the same year a separate group launched the Women's Magsaysay-for-President Movement to support the presidential bid of Ramon Magsaysay.[23]

By the late 1960s and 1970s a new generation of Filipino women had emerged, less conservative than their parents in social and political orientation and more inclined to new and progressive ideas. They were marrying later and having fewer children, and greater numbers were choosing to remain single. These changes were more visible among urban-based, educated middle- to upper-class women—in short, among well-off professionals. Many women were also leaving for abroad, mostly to the United States, to take jobs or pursue graduate studies.

Philippine politics itself, though still controlled by elite interests, was also undergoing significant changes. The bourgeois political system, highly dependent on U.S. military and economic assistance for survival and embroiled in corruption over the years, was being challenged by new forces in society.[24] The underground left won adherents among the young, and student activism intensified, particularly at the University of the Philippines, long known for nurturing a liberal tradition in education. The newly reestablished Communist Party of the Philippines joined with the New People's Army in 1969 and set up guerrilla-operations zones in major regions of the country. At the same time, the Muslim secessionist movement gained momentum. With the government increasingly threatened by communist and Muslim insurgents in the provinces and by a declining economy, President Ferdinand Marcos declared martial law on 21 September 1972. Marcos was no longer eligible for a third presidential term under the constitution, and the only way he could cling to power was by installing a dictatorship.

The excesses and repression of the Marcos regime drove more and more young people underground. Newly graduated Filipinas and women students joined the cadres of the New People's Army in increasing numbers to participate in mobilization work in the provinces. These women, primarily from middle-class backgrounds, left the comfort of their homes for an uncertain, if not dangerous, life in the hills. Their tasks in the movement were not much different from the men's. As Clarita Roja (a pseudonym) wrote in a letter from the underground, all "comrades" were expected to conduct political work among the masses and among themselves. "Household chores [were] rotated, assignments going to men and women alike."[25]

At the forefront of the women's struggle during this time of political upheaval and social ferment was the Malayang Kilusan ng Bagong Kababaihan (Free Movement of New Women), whose acronym, MAKIBAKA, stood for "dare to struggle." It was organized by Maria Lorena Barros, a militant student leader who led the first mass action—picketing the Miss Philippines Beauty Pageant in April 1970. MAKIBAKA activists, clearly advocating a Marxist ideology, also did organizing work among the women in factories and barrios. The underground network distributed clandestine publications and sent them to supporters in the United States and other countries either by mail or by courier. MAKIBAKA is described in a mimeographed publication entitled *Filipino Women in the National Liberation Struggle,* probably written shortly after martial law was declared in 1972: "Although the membership of MAKIBAKA in its early beginnings was comprised of students, young professionals, and other sectors of the urban petty bourgeoisie, efforts to promote the national democratic line necessitated the incorporation of women of the working class. Women took to the streets to participate in mass actions, established cottage industries, and formed women's associations to set up day care centers not only to educate the children but to politicize the mothers."[26] MAKIBAKA's platform was considered too radical by other women's groups, which were more moderate in their demands or more oriented to reforming existing institutions than to dismantling them altogether.

Barros, who worked as an NPA cadre in Southern Luzon, was caught and murdered by government soldiers in 1976. Although the movement that she headed functioned within the CPP-NPA

framework, it is difficult to label it Marxist or radical feminist, for it combined elements of both. In Barros's words: "The Filipina, through her militant participation in the revolutionary struggle, has brought to life a new woman. This new woman is no longer a mindless ornament (which she would be if born to a well-to-do family), or a mindless drudge (which she would be if she were the wife or daughter of a peasant or worker). She is a woman fully engaged in the making of history, in the destruction of imperialism and feudalism, and the building of a new society. No longer is she simply a woman-for-marriage; more and more she is a woman-for-action. A comrade."[27]

As the women in the NPA and the MAKIBAKA activists were advocating armed revolutionary struggle, another group of women, inspired by the "theology of liberation," openly defended human rights and exposed military abuses. Called religious radicals or the Christian left, these nuns and lay supporters monitored the arrests of suspected "subversives," made representations with military authorities regarding the disappearance of political activists, helped to rehabilitate released political prisoners, and organized the urban poor. Some of them lived in the slums, devoting themselves to work that they called conscienticization—an attempt to raise the consciousness of the poor and disadvantaged, particularly with regard to asserting and protecting their rights. The activist nuns were instrumental in forming various organizations, the best known of which was the Association of Major Religious Superiors of the Philippines, which documented the arrest, torture, and release of political prisoners in a publication entitled *Philippine Human Rights Update.* This organization also provided data to international human rights organizations like Amnesty International on the abuses of the Marcos regime.

A leader of the religious radicals, Sister Mariani Dimaranan of the Franciscan order, was arrested in October 1973 and detained by the military as a subversive for 47 days—anyone who opposed the government was called a subversive. Sister Mariani headed a group called the Task Force

Detainees of the Philippines, which recorded the torture or "salvaging" of political prisoners and of detained underground activists. *Salvaging* was a term used during the years of martial law to describe the summary execution of radical activists in the military camps and in places known only to the military. Sister Mariani's detention did not deter her from denouncing the Marcos regime and the Philippine armed forces in later press interviews.[28] In 1983, the tenth year of task force activities, Sister Mariani said that the organization had helped thousands of detainees. "We are very clear about our purpose. We help victims irrespective of their ideology. 'Komunista man o hindi, may karapatan yan' [Whether Communist or not, he or she has rights]."[29]

Another activist nun, Sister Christine Tan, was also arrested for subversion for her work in the campaign to terminate the agreement allowing U.S. military bases to operate on Philippine territory. She worked and lived in the slums—and still does. Like Sister Mariani, Sister Christine sought audiences with military authorities on behalf of political detainees and their families. She also petitioned the Supreme Court to abolish Marcos's detested Presidential Commitment Order, under which any citizen could be detained without legal charges.

Not Sister Christine alone but groups of women, in cooperation with their male counterparts, opposed the U.S. bases in the Philippines. The bases—a colonial legacy—were a sore point in Philippine-U.S. relations that antedated martial law and that was exacerbated by U.S. government support for Marcos up to the very end of his stay in power. In fact, the phrase "U.S.-Marcos dictatorship" was used to draw attention to the role of the United States in propping up the regime.

A militant women's group, General Assembly Binding Women for Reforms, Integrity, Equality, Leadership, and Action (GABRIELA)—which drew its name from Gabriela Silang, the eighteenth-century rebel leader—spearheaded the movement against the bases. Formed in 1984 out of several organizations across the country, GABRIELA's membership grew to 50,000 in 1985—cutting across social, economic, religious, and ideological boundaries. But the more articulate and militant members advocated a hard-line anti-U.S., anti-imperialist position. Along with other radical groups, GABRIELA's most common activity was picketing the U.S. Embassy in Manila, carrying streamers or signs with messages like "Down with the U.S.-Marcos," or "U.S. bases, time to go." The rallies were generally peaceful, but the police occasionally arrested protesters. The most prominent GABRIELA leader, Nelia Sancho—a former Miss Asia-Pacific beauty queen—was arrested and detained by the Marcos regime for several months in the late 1970s. In the same period, another GABRIELA leader, Maita Gomez, fled to the hills and joined the resistance.

Another major bases-related activity was the teach-in, organized to educate people, especially students, about the history of the bases, about issues in Philippine-U.S. relations, and about the evils that military base economies spawned—including prostitution, gambling, drug pushing, gunrunning, the exploitation of local residents, killing, and other forms of violence. But the main point that women emphasized was that the continued presence of the bases was an affront to Philippine sovereignty—living symbols of an oppressive colonial past.

The issue of prostitution has to be seen in the context of the U.S. military bases and the Marcos government's acceleration of tourism as a source of foreign exchange. The bases have served as magnets, drawing women to prostitution out of poverty and desperation. It is not known exactly how many women are engaged in the trade in the Clark and Subic areas, but 30,000 would not be an unreasonable estimate. They come mostly from depressed farming, fishing, or industrial areas in the Bicol or eastern Visayas region and are typically young (between 18 and 20 years old). The prospect of earning money that they could then send to their families in the provinces, the possibility of going abroad if they are lucky enough to marry U.S. servicemen, and the simple attraction of city life are some of the pull factors that bring many of these women to prostitution at the bases and urban centers.

The Marcos regime exacerbated the problem of the flesh trade by vigorously promoting "sex tourism" to earn dollars for the ailing Philippine economy. In government policies prostitution was euphemistically referred to as "the hospitality industry." The women were presented as "hospitality girls," "a-go-go dancers," "hostesses," and "masseuses." The Ministry of Tourism regularly conducted sex tours for male visitors, and child prostitution was promoted for pedophiles. Pedophiles were taken directly to Pagsanjan, Laguna Province, which earned the disgusting distinction of being the pedophile capital of Asia. The mail-order-bride business targeted men from the United States and Australia who were looking for wives. The exploitation of women and children reached shameless proportions during the Marcos dictatorship. Never before had Filipinas been so degraded.

The ensuing public outrage was mainly the result of efforts by women's organizations to expose the scandalous operations of the Ministry of Tourism and its allies. The Third World Movement Against Exploitation of Women conducted a media campaign to denounce the hospitality industry, projecting the prostitution issue as symptomatic of the basic problems of Philippine society—particularly poverty and the traditional exploitation of women. Any attempt to reframe the issue of prostitution, the organization argued, would be diverting the issue. "Such treatment is not much different from prescribing aspirin for meningitis."[30]

The Center for Women Resources helped by documenting the extent of prostitution. "As of 1980, there were about 120 flesh shops in Manila's tourist belt, 21 of which were accredited by the Ministry of Tourism and licensed by City Hall. Each shop had 80 to 200 girls employed by accredited tour agencies."[31] In regard to the bases, the center repeatedly made a comparison with Saigon, which had 400,000 prostitutes by the time the Americans left in 1975: it had become a city of prostitutes and pimps. Other women's organizations concentrated on the issue of dislocation should the bases pull out: Where would the no-longer-employed women go?[32]

The repression of human and democratic rights by the Marcos regime and the continuing abuse of the population by its instruments, particularly the military establishment, clearly had a radicalizing effect on many women's groups in society. Another example of how women courageously defied the authoritarian practices of martial law was in the Philippine media. One of the first casualties after the imposition of martial law was freedom of the press. Several of those arrested after Marcos shut down the media in 1972 were journalists, mostly male. Marcos cronies bought existing media to silence critics or set up new media to propagandize the regime. Censorship guidelines were laid down by the Print Media Council: criticism of Marcos and the first family was not allowed, for instance. But Philippine journalism has a long tradition of freedom of expression, which the regime could not eradicate. It took a woman, Ma. (Maria) Ceres P. Doyo of *Panorama* magazine, to test the limits of press censorship under Marcos.[33]

Doyo exposed the murder of a Kalinga tribal leader, Macli-ing Dulag, who led the resistance against the construction of the Chico River Dam project financed by the World Bank. After she wrote a piece on Dulag's killing in 1980, she was interrogated and warned by the military. *Panorama*'s editor, Letty Jimenez Magsanoc, another woman journalist, supported Doyo and in turn wrote an article criticizing the "phony" lifting of martial law in 1981. The publisher of the magazine, under pressure from the regime, asked Magsanoc to resign. Instead of cowering, three more women journalists continued their criticism of the regime. Arlene Babst, Sylvia Mayuga, and Niñez Cacho-Olivares—all *Bulletin Today* columnists—openly deplored the intimidation of their colleagues and the perpetual military atrocities against the people.

"Sensing that these writers were creating a strong impact among the readers, the National Intelligence Board (NIB) under General Fabian Ver, Marcos' Armed Forces Chief of Staff, 'invited' eight women journalists for a 'dialogue.'"[34] From December 1982 to January 1983 the board called in Babst; Olivares; the subsequent *Panorama* editor, Domini Torrevillas Suarez, and the staffer Lorna Kalaw-Tirol; Eugenia D. Apostol, the courageous publisher of *Mr. and Ms.*, another magazine critical of martial law; Doris Nuyda, also of *Mr. and Ms.*; and Jo-Ann Maglipon of *Bulletin Today*. The military sued them for libel, and they promptly fought back. Babst, a member of Women in Media Now (WOMEN), an organization originally set up to publish works by women writers, filed a case before the Supreme Court to stop General Ver and his intelligence agents from harassing women journalists. The move was a bold one, leading to pressure to dismantle the military's Special Media Committee, which had undertaken the writers' inquisition. "It was a signal victory for press freedom, particularly for the women journalists of WOMEN who broke the complacency and sycophancy of the then brow-beaten media."[35] Space does not permit going into the backgrounds of these journalists, who are still active in Philippine media circles. But collectively they recall the Katipunan women and the "suffragettes" who forged a brave new world in Philippine society.

THE AQUINO ASSASSINATION AND FEMINIST MOBILIZATION

The brutal assassination of the opposition leader Sen. Benigno Aquino, Jr., by the Philippine military on 21 August 1983 was the proverbial straw that broke the camel's back. It unleashed a fury among the people that probably surpassed that of the 1896 revolutionaries. Millions poured into the "Parliament of the Streets"; they denounced the assassination and clamored for Marcos to step down. Remarkably, violence did not erupt even though the people were seething with rage. They did not want to provoke a military reprisal. They kept up the pressure on the regime by political mass action and alliance building among key organizations.

Women were in the forefront of postassassination politics. By this time they had created formidable alliances with other organizations that had been protesting the increasing militarization, hu-

man rights violations, repression of civil liberties, and government corruption. Because the economic situation was so dire, family incomes had shrunk to the point where even the heretofore apolitical middle class began to complain. Women, who felt the crunch the most, took to the streets. They joined their more politicized sisters in the nearly 200 mass actions that took place between August 1983 and April 1984 after Aquino was laid to rest. Thus, women from all classes and persuasions worked side by side in challenging the dictatorship. Society matrons in their high heels walked alongside urban poor women in their sneakers or slippers in anti-Marcos demonstrations. As they marched in the streets, women in offices threw yellow confetti from high-rise buildings to signify their solidarity with the protesters. The slain Aquino was to have been welcomed home on 21 August with a display of yellow ribbons.[36]

The involved organizations with the most members were GABRIELA and Katipunan ng Bagong Pilipina, or KABAPA (New Filipino Women's Association). GABRIELA, which took shape in the protest movement against the Marcos regime and became a formal organization in 1984, had mostly urban-based and college-educated women for members. At its first general conference in March 1985, 71 organizations endorsed the GABRIELA manifesto, which called for advancing the women's liberation cause, uniting in the fight against poverty and terrorism under the Marcos regime, exposing the sexual abuse of political prisoners, and dismantling the U.S.-Marcos dictatorship.[37] Their red banners with anti-imperialist slogans made them highly visible in demonstrations.

In July 1985, GABRIELA sent a large delegation to the U.N. International Decade for Women Conference in Nairobi to present a special report on militarization during the Marcos regime and its effects on Filipinas. "Many women detainees have been abused in the course of tactical interrogations, either as a form of reprisal for their involvement in anti-government activities or as a means of ferreting out information on such activities," said the report.[38] The GABRIELA delegation also joined a march taking place on the conference grounds to protest the violation of human rights, apartheid, corruption, and other ills in countries ruled by dictators.

Another umbrella organization, largely composed of farmers and other rural women, was also active in political work. Founded in March 1976, KABAPA focuses on issues of economic and legal equality for women and supports broader concerns: genuine agrarian reform, nationalization of key industries, restrictions on multinational corporate profits, and withdrawal of the U.S. military bases.[39]

KABAPA, which has a national membership of 25,000 women, considers its consciousness-raising work among rural women its major achievement and has developed a packet of question-and-answer material that is used in seminars, workshops, study meetings, and role-playing sessions in local communities. The organization concentrates on consciousness-raising as a way to enable rural women—who belong to the 58 percent of the population living in the countryside—to fully understand the connection between their enduring poverty and the elite social structure. As long as they are exploited by the wealthier and more powerful forces in Philippine society, concepts like democracy and equality have no meaning. They will continue to be dependent on the meager resources accorded to them in the highly unequal economic distribution system. To break the pattern, they have to recast their traditional way of thinking and rely on themselves. In short, according to KABAPA, rural women's oppressed status can be rectified to a certain degree by political education, and this must start with self-reliance.

The question has been asked, Why are there so many women's organizations in the Philippines? One observer counted 171 organizations in metro Manila alone.[40] In view of the geographic, regional, ethnic, religious, class, ideological, and other distinctions in Philippine society, groups of or about women are bound to proliferate. Significantly, in spite of the diversity and differences in perspective, there is a minimum of friction among the various women's organizations. GAB-

RIELA has lost some of its initial members who were of a more moderate ideological persuasion than the leaders. Some of these less radical members have joined other organizations or set up their own. GABRIELA continues, however, to be the voice of militant feminism in the country.

WOMEN AND THE 1986 REVOLUTION

The acceleration of women's activity during the Marcos period and the heightened tension brought about by Senator Aquino's assassination reached a logical conjuncture in the People Power Revolution in early 1986.[41] Played out in four days in February (the 22nd to the 25th) at the center of metro Manila's largest highway, Epifanio de los Santos Avenue, more popularly known as EDSA, it was probably the shortest revolution on record.[42] Marcos had arrogantly called for a snap presidential election on 7 February 1986. The various opposition forces united into one and nominated Corazon C. Aquino, widow of the slain senator, to run against Marcos. The president's monumental cheating and use of violence to win the election signaled his final collapse. The showdown was precipitated by the defection of Defense Minister Juan Ponce Enrile and Armed Forces Chief of Staff Fidel Ramos on 22 February 1986. Two million Filipinos gathered at EDSA to force Marcos to step down. What had started as a military mutiny escalated into a people's uprising. Tanks and armored vehicles came roaring down from the military camps around the area. Although the potential for violence was extremely high, people power turned out to be a peaceful confrontation. Outwitted and facing the wrath of the people, Marcos and his family and associates fled under cover of darkness on the night of 25 February. The U.S. government facilitated his exile to Hawaii the following day.

A vivid image from that time of incredible upheaval was nuns and other women holding up rosaries, banners, and pictures of the Virgin Mary, icons of the Santo Niño (infant Jesus), and other religious objects while men braced their bodies against the tanks that were ready to roll anytime. The religious symbolism was powerful. It stunned and mystified the soldiers. A bewildered marine commander ordered the tanks to retreat. More significantly, the leaders of the various military commands and their troops cast their lot with the people. Four days of quiet rage and courage ousted a formidable dictator, and EDSA is enshrined as the Filipino contribution to the theory of modern revolutions.

The women took part in the whole gamut of activities during the revolution. The nuns were the first to answer Jaime Cardinal Sin's frantic calls for people to proceed to EDSA and give support to Enrile and Ramos. He called the Catholic church convents to send nuns to EDSA. One could argue that the religious women were responding out of obedience to their superior, but considering their long years of struggle against martial law, they could not have passed up the moment that portended the end of the Marcos dictatorship.

Women of all classes—affluent Makati matrons, journalists, poor urban workers, faculty and students from public and private universities and colleges, vendors, and factory workers— massed at EDSA during the four days and nights. Those who could not be at the site prepared sandwiches and refreshments, and those who lived around EDSA made their residences available for people's personal needs. The media heroine June Keithley continuously broadcast instructions and messages over Radyo Bandido, which was transmitting from a clandestine station to escape military detection. Without her expert monitoring and forceful guidance over the airwaves, there might have been large-scale confusion about what was going on.

Women also negotiated with the soldiers not to roll the tanks or fire into the crowd. They brought food, water, cigarettes, cookies, flowers, and rosaries to the beleaguered soldiers, who were just waiting for orders from their superiors. It was a volatile situation. One stone thrown at the soldiers could have set off a bloody confrontation. The women negotiators appealed to the soldiers' sense of compassion and fear of God. The soldiers relented, and the tanks rolled back.

In sum, women played key symbolic and practical roles in an unusual political upheaval that gave Southeast Asia its first woman president.

PRESIDENT AQUINO AND THE POLITICS OF CLASS

Corazon Aquino personified the bourgeois woman in Philippine society: descended from a wealthy landowning family in central Luzon with nineteenth-century roots in the Chinese mestizo class, she was proper in demeanor—a product of convent schools—and educated in the United States. Even though she operated in a political milieu—her father having been a legislator and her husband a politician for all of the 28 years that they were married—Aquino was not a public person. She was extremely reluctant to face Marcos in the 1986 election because she thought that as a "housewife" she did not know anything about politics. She had never worked for a living, much less held public office. To appease her supporters, she said (probably not seriously) that she would face Marcos only if 2 million signatures could be gathered urging her to run. Her supporters, many of them women calling themselves Cory's Crusaders, were fervent about her running. They scoured metro Manila and the nearby provinces to collect the 2 million signatures. Aquino herself went into deep meditation and said afterward, "We had to present somebody who is the complete opposite of Marcos, someone who has been a victim."[43] The rest is history. Emerging from her quiet private world, she crisscrossed the country and caught the imagination of voters from all walks of life. Her popularity during the campaign period and after EDSA is unequaled in the annals of Philippine history.

But her popularity has been diminished by a series of coup attempts and by an inability to exercise decisive leadership—which is needed in a society racked by poverty and inequality. Sorely lacking in political experience when she assumed office, Aquino was slow to exploit the potential of people power. For more than a year, from March 1986 to April 1987, during which she could have launched bold initiatives, such as land reform and a thorough cleanup of the military and bureaucracy, she instead chose to wait until the formal structures of government, including a new constitution and an elected Congress, were in place. Perhaps she failed to appreciate and understand the meaning of the revolutionary situation created after Marcos's downfall. Yet to move toward dramatic reform was not easy, either, because the military and other instruments of authoritarian rule remained.

During the delay, Aquino's ruling coalition began to disintegrate. Enrile and his supporters plotted to oust her, and Marcos loyalists demonstrated in the streets. The New People's Army acquired the capacity for urban terrorism and continued guerrilla operations on the countryside as well. The Moro National Liberation Front went back underground after a proposed peace settlement with the Aquino government failed. Peace talks with the National Democratic Front, the umbrella organization that includes CPP-NPA, collapsed, and a new threat developed as the right-wing faction of the military establishment, the Reform the Armed Forces Movement, engaged in several destabilization efforts.

In June 1990, stung by her deteriorating popularity, Aquino launched a political movement of her own—Kabisig, meaning "arm-in-arm" in Tagalog. According to her, Kabisig is not a political party. It is a movement designed to harness the support of the people for various development programs, especially in depressed provinces. With this program Aquino is doing what many supporters felt she should have done when she assumed power in 1986. Her critics see this as "too little, too late," but others view it as an attempt to recover the people's support.

Some argue—though not openly for fear of being labeled sexist—that Aquino's indecisiveness on weighty issues of state may be attributed to her being a woman in a political world still dominated by men. This does not seem to be the case, for she has stood her ground on many occasions, unfazed by crisis and criticism. Perhaps fatalistic, she has been known to say, "Kung darating ang panahon mo, darating ang panahon mo" (When your time comes, it comes).[44]

The Filipino academic and intellectual Francisco Nemenzo offers a different view of Aquino's political style, arguing that her indecisiveness stems from a fear of confronting either the native elite from whose ranks she comes or the U.S. government: "She has desisted from tampering with structures other than those directly linked with Marcos."[45]

It is too soon to judge the Aquino presidency, but it does appear to embody a politics of class that goes against some of the tenets espoused by feminism: equality and the empowerment of women, for example. Only one of more than 20 cabinet members is a woman—a fact that says much about the Aquino presidency's agenda on women. This lone woman cabinet member's position covers a field traditionally assigned to women: social work and development.

CONCLUSION

The participation of women in the nationalist movement against Spain in the nineteenth century and their protracted struggle for female suffrage in the early decades of this century resulted in their deeper political consciousness. Women's militant opposition to the Marcos regime and their mobilization efforts during the tumult of the Aquino assassination and the EDSA revolution were more recent landmarks in the history of feminism in the society.

Philippine feminism has been discussed here as though it were singular, but it is actually a plural phenomenon—a mixed bag of social, economic, and political women-related initiatives on both the ideological and the practical level. Not one but several women's movements have taken place. These have been influenced by developments in other parts of the world, such as the struggle for women's rights and later the consciousness-raising activities of feminist groups in the United States; yet they have their own unique characteristics. Some have followed a specific ideological tendency; others have been guided by the larger issues that Philippine society as a whole has had to confront. I have thus examined the role of Filipino women in a broader social and political context, rather than in terms of the more specific male-female structure of the society.

Philippine society is undergoing a period of redemocratization following two decades of authoritarian rule. The major problems of government corruption, a huge foreign debt, divisiveness in the population brought about by the continuing presence of the U.S. military bases, insurgencies, and unrelenting poverty remain, however. Much has to be done. Women's groups must deal with these societal issues, as well as with the more specific concerns that affect them, such as child care, reproductive rights, male violence, discrimination in the workplace, sexual harassment, prostitution, and healthcare. Philippine feminism is no longer a matter of expanding women's roles, as in the previous century; indeed, women now have many roles to play and much to do. The question is, How they can accomplish all these things, in addition to competing more successfully with men in the public sphere?

NOTES

1. Muslims, 4.3 percent; Protestants, 3.1 percent; Aglipayan, 2.8 percent; cultural minorities, 1.7 percent; Iglesia ni Kristo, 1.6 percent; Buddhists, 0.1 percent; and others, 4.3 percent. The percentages were calculated on the basis of the 1991 population of 60 million by Pedro S. Achutegui, president of the Cardinal Bea Institute for Ecumenical Studies, Loyola House of Studies, Ateneo de Manila University, Quezon City. The National Census and Statistics Office figures only come up to 1970.

The words Philippine and Filipino are often used interchangeably—e.g., Philippine culture, Filipino food, Philippine politics. Filipino refers to people in general, Filipina to Filipino women. Filipino is also the national language, declared so in the constitution of 1987. The language is largely based on Tagalog, spoken in Manila and the neighboring provinces. Its spelling was changed from Pilipino to Filipino in 1973 to make it more consistent with conventional usage and to be more national—it would evolve from the contributions of the different languages in the country, not just from Tagalog.

2. The Treaty of Paris ceded the Philippines from Spain to the United States for U.S. \$20 million.

3. Unlike in the United States, poverty in the Philippines is not measured strictly by income per four-person family. It is more a qualitative concept, encompassing not only income levels but also illiteracy, disease, nutrition, housing, and the availability of a number of amenities—hence the varying estimates.

4. See Fe C. Arriola, *Si Maria, Mema, Gabriela, Atbp—Kuwentong Kasaysayan ng Kababaihan* (Maria, Mema, Gabriela and others—historical accounts of women) (Manila: GABRIELA and St. Scholastica's Institute of Women's Studies, 4 September 1990), 31.

5. Malolos, a historic town north of Manila, was the site of the revolutionary Congress convened by President Emilio Aguinaldo on 4 September 1898, three months after the proclamation of Philippine independence from Spain.

6. This information was drawn from the Colegio de Santa Isabel's historical marker, which still exists in Naga City. See Liceria B. Soriano, "Women and Education," in Yolanda Q. Javellana, ed., *Woman and the Law* (Quezon City: University of the Philippines Law Center, 1975), 81.

7. Fe Mangahas, "The Status of Filipino Women from Pre-Colonial Times to the Early American Period," in Pennie S. Azarcon, ed., *Kamalayan: Feminist Writings in the Philippines* (Manila: Bureau of Printing, 1928), 39.

8. Maria Paz Mendoza-Guazon, *The Development and Progress of the Filipino Woman* (Manila: Bureau of Printing, 1928), 40.

9. Encarnacion Alzona, *The Filipino Woman—Her Social, Economic and Political Status, 1565–1937* (Manila: Benipayo Press, 1937), 67.

10. The more prominent ones were Pura Villanueva Kalaw (writer), Rosa Sevilla Alvero (educator), Encarnacion Alzona (historian), Maria Paz Mendoza-Guazon (medical doctor), Pilar Hidalgo Lim (social worker), Josefa Llanes Escoda (social worker), Concepcion Felix Rodriguez (social worker, teacher), Natividad Almeda Lopez (lawyer, jurist), and Geronima Pecson (educator, senator).

11. Guazon, *Development and Progress*, 45.

12. According to the 1939 census, the total Philippine population was 16,000,303: 8,065,281 male (50.4 percent) and 7,935,022 female (49.6 percent), with 3,346,260 (both male and female) who were 20 years old and older. Because the total population was almost equally divided between males and females, some 1,673,130 women would have been eligible to vote in the plebiscite on the basis of age. But literacy was also a requirement; and applying the 49 percent literacy rate to the total number of women eligible to vote on the basis of age gives only 937,208. Therefore, 300,000 would be 32 percent of 937,208, the total number of women eligible to vote in the plebiscite. Actually, the number would be slightly lower, for the census-based figure includes 20-year-old women, who were one year short of voting age.

13. Alzona, *Filipino Woman*, 106.

14. Minerva Laudico, "Testimonies from Suffragettes," in *Women's Role in Philippine History—Papers and Proceedings of the Conference Held on 8–9 March 1989*

(Quezon City: University of the Philippines Center for Women's Studies, 1989), 75.

15. Alzona, *Filipino Woman,* 104.

16. Ibid., 129.

17. Ibid., 135.

18. *Memorial* (in Pilipino), a Sakdal document intended for transmission to the U.S. Congress on the issue of Philippine independence. See Benedicto S. Librojo, Jr., "An Episode in the Long Agrarian Saga of the Masses— An Analysis of the Sakdal Movement" (Undergraduate thesis, University of the Philippines, Diliman, Quezon City, 1990), 39.

19. Appendix D, "An Interview with Salud Algabre," in David R. Sturtevant, *Popular Uprisings in the Philippines, 1840–1940* (Ithaca, N.Y.: Cornell University Press, 1976), 290.

20. Ibid., 294–95.

21. Tecla San Andres Ziga, "Women in Politics and Government," in Javellana, ed., *Woman and the Law,* 76.

22. Tarrosa Subido, *The Feminist Movement in the Philippines, 1905–1955* (Manila: National Federation of Women's Clubs, 1955), 54.

23. In the 1987 congressional elections, a small all-female political party, Kababaihan Para Sa Inang Bayan, or KAIBA (Women for the Mother Country), put up or supported women candidates. Ana Dominique Coseteng of Quezon City ran for Congress under the KAIBA banner and won, but she was also endorsed by the PDP-Laban. KAIBA also supported another congressional candidate, Venancio T. Garduce of Samar Province, who also won. The party became largely inactive after the election.

24. The term *bourgeois* is not used here with its classic European meaning of a mercantile or shopkeeping middle class that sprouted from a disappearing feudal society. The Philippine usage refers to those who made their fortunes after the Second World War. Unlike the old aristocracy, the newly rich, pejoratively called *burgis* (a Filipino corruption of *bourgeois*), tend to flaunt their wealth, ill-gotten or otherwise, and affect the lifestyle of high living, respectability, and culture of the original bourgeoisie. Many entered the political arena after the war and have maintained their power or influence.

25. Clarita Roja, "Letter to Mrs. D——" (July 1973). After many years it was revealed that Mrs. D—— was Delores Feria, an English professor at the University of the Philippines who supported radical causes and was underground herself in the early 1970s during martial law.

26. Editorial Collective, Philippines Research Center, *Filipino Women in the National Liberation Struggle* (1972?).

27. Ma. Lorena Barros, "Liberated Women," *Ang Malaya* (13 March 1971), 3, as quoted in Editorial Collective, *Filipino Women in the National Liberation Struggle,* 3.

28. See Robert L. Youngblood, *Marcos Against the Church—Economic Development and Political Repression in the Philippines* (Ithaca, N.Y.: Cornell University Press, 1990), 162.

29. Ma. Ceres P. Doyo, "The Sisters Have Come a Long Way," *Philippine Panorama* 12, no. 22 (29 May 1983): 18.

30. Ma. Ceres P. Doyo, "The Prostitution Problem Must Be Viewed from a National, Even Global, Perspective," *Philippine Panorama* 12, no. 22 (29 May 1983): 38.

31. Ibid., 40.

32. Another organization, Campaign for a Sovereign Philippines, headed by Ma. Socorro Diokno, expressed a similar concern for the women who would be dislocated if the bases were pulled out. "We have been looking into the possibility of putting up cottage industries within the bases and also of alternative education for the women involved." There would be initial dislocation, but if the women were given a chance to do something better and certainly less demeaning than prostitution, they would "knock on it," according to Diokno. See *The US Military Bases and the Filipino Women—Women's Discourse, No. 1* (Quezon City: Center for Women's Resources, 1989), 11.

33. Aurora J. De Dios, "Participation of Women's Groups in the Anti-Dictatorship Struggle: Genesis of a Movement," in *Women's Role in Philippine History,* 101.

34. Ibid.

35. Ibid.

36. It is not possible to mention all the women's organizations whose members filled the streets, but among the major ones were Kilusan ng Kababaihang Pilipino, or PILIPINA (Filipino Women's Movement); Samahan ng Babaing Nagkakaisa, or SAMAKANA (United Women's Association); Katipunan ng Kababaihan Para sa Kalayaan, or KKK (Women's Association for Freedom); Samahan ng mga Mag-aaral na Kababaihan, or SAMAKA (Federation of Women Students); Kapisan ng Madre ng Kamaynilaan, or KAMAY (Association of Religious Women in Metro Manila); Women for the Ouster of Marcos and Boycott (WOMB); Mothers and Relatives Against Tyranny (MARTYR); Alliance of Concerned Women for Reforms (AWARE); Concerned Women of the Philippines (CWP); Association of Women in Theology (AWIT); National Association of Religious Women in the Philippines (NOW); Women in Media Now; GABRIELA, then in its formative stage; and Katipunan ng Bagong Pilipina, or KABAPA (New Filipino Women's Association).

37. GABRIELA, *Convention Proceedings* (Quezon City, Mt. Carmel Community Center, 2–3 March 1985), 19.

38. GABRIELA, *Peace Is an Illusion—Militarization and Its Effects on Filipino Women, a Special Report* (Manila: GABRIELA Women's Coalition, 1985), 76.

39. Its basic mission is "To strive for equality before the law in all fields where it does not exist; equality of eco-

nomic rights, including the right to work and the right to equal pay for work of equal value, non-discrimination in employment opportunities and security of employment after marriage, and equality of rights and responsibilities in the family and home." *KABAPA Primer* (Manila, 1976), 1.

40. Barbara Mahel, *The Situation of Filipino Women—Focus on Women's Organizations Based in Manila* (Manila: Friedrich Naumann Stiftung, 1987), 165–94.

41. Although *people power* is commonly used to describe the EDSA revolution, some observers think that the term sounds like the passive *manpower* and that the more appropriate term, *people's power*, has a more political meaning: "organized by the people and used by the people to advance their own interests." Ponciano L. Ben-nagen, "It's People's Power, Not People Power," *Midweek* 1, no. 17 (26 March 1986): 30.

42. The highway is named after Epifanio De Los Santos, a Filipino writer who wrote patriotic articles in Spanish for *La Independencia* (Independence) in 1898.

43. Sandra Burton, *Impossible Dream—The Marcoses, the Aquinos, and the Unfinished Revolution* (New York: Warner Books, 1989), 302.

44. Belinda A. Aquino, ed., *Presidential Leadership and Cory Aquino* (Quezon City: University of the Philippines Center for Integrative and Development Studies, 1990), 26.

45. Francisco Nemenzo, "A Nation in Ferment: Analysis of the February Revolution," in M. Rajaretnam, ed., *The Aquino Alternative* (Singapore: Institute of Southeast Asian Studies, 1986), 52.

▲ Poland

Type of Political System: democracy

  Sovereignty: republic

  Executive-Legislative System: parliamentary

Type of State: unitary

Type of Party System: multiparty

Major Political Parties[a]

Porozumienie Centrum (Centrum Alliance): A Christian-democratic, center-right party with roots in the Solidarity movement, created in 1980. Its political program includes decommunization of the state through a change of state institutions, economic mechanisms, and social relations; an important role for the Catholic church in shaping policy; and security in Poland before participation in a Western European military organization. Its economic program includes opposition to corruption and recession; privatization; and support for the export of agricultural products. Successfully supported Lech Walesa (leader of Solidarity at the time) in the 1990 presidential elections.

Unia Demokratyczna (Democratic Union): A democratic party created in its present form in May 1991 by former Solidarity supporters of Prime Minister Mazowiecki in the 1990 presidential elections. Consists of liberals, conservative-liberals, and factions that want to protect the natural environment. Politically it supports a republican and democratic political system for an independent Poland; a highly decentralized state with strong local communities, a president above party politics, and a mutually independent church and state. Economically it supports development of the private sector and a market economy, state protection of the development of education and science, and state defense of social interests through the creation of a proper legislative system.

Kongres Liberalno-Demokratyczny (Liberal Democratic Congress): A liberal party created in June 1990 on the basis of economic associations active in the 1980s that propagated a market economy and private ownership. Its political program includes support for the establishment of democratic capitalism, cooperation with neighboring countries to overcome the backwardness inherited from the communist system; counterbalancing the power of Parliament with the power of the president and a strong government. Its economic program supports radical change in the economic structure and privatization on a large scale. Was in temporary coalition with the Centrum Alliance, supporting Walesa in the 1990 presidential elections.

Konfederacja Polski Niepodleglej (Confederation for an Independent Poland): Illegally created in September 1979; reshaped as a national party in 1984. Politically it supports an independent and democratic state; economic and military cooperation with other countries of Central Europe; and reorganization of the military forces and the mass media. Economically it advocates rapid privatization of trade and services, changes in the banking system, and a limited state role in the economy.

Polskie Stronnictwo Ludowe (Polish Peasants' Party, PPP): The largest party in Poland, a transformation of the United Peasants' Party, which cooperated with the ruling Communist Party until the fall of the regime in 1989. PPP supported political forces concentrated around Walesa and Solidarity. It has roots in the pre–World War II peasants' movement. Politically it considers the Seym (lower house of Parliament) the highest authority in the country and emphasizes the role of local governments and the necessity of building a modern, professional army. Economically it supports state control of a market economy, equality of different types of ownership, agriculture based on family farms (the party opposes reconstruction of large capitalist estates), and overcoming a deep recession in agriculture.

Socjaldemokracja Rzeczpospolitej Polskiej (Social Democracy of the Republic of Poland): Social-democratic party created in January 1990 at the last congress of the Polish United Workers' Party. Its political program supports the integration of the left-oriented part of society, acceptance of a parliamentary democracy, and opposition to the influence of the church on the state. Its economic program supports equality of different types of ownership, limited access of foreign capital to the economy, an active role for the state in the creation of a market economy, and vigilance against pollution of the natural environment.

Year Women Granted Right to Vote: 1918

Year Women Granted Right to Stand for Election: 1918

Percentage of Women in the Legislature[b]
Lower House: 9.1%
Upper House: 6.0%

Percentage of Electorate Voting for Highest Elected Office in Most Recent Election (1991): 43.2%[c]

DEMOGRAPHICS

Population: 38,038,000[d]

Percentage of Population in Urban Areas[e]
Overall: 60.3%
Female: 61.3%
Male: 59.2%

Percentage of Population Below Age 20: 32.6%[f]

Birthrate (per 1,000 population): 14[g]

Maternal Mortality Rate (per 100,000 live births): 12

Infant Mortality Rate (per 1,000 live births): 16[h]

Mortality Rate for Children Under Four (per 1,000 live births): 20

Average Household Size: 3.1[i]

Mean Age at First Marriage[j]
Female: 22.9
Male: 24.8

Life Expectancy[k]
Female: 75.5
Male: 66.8

EDUCATION

Ratio of Female to Male Enrollment
First-Level Education: 95
Second-Level Education: 103
Third-Level Education (including evening and correspondence courses): 127

Literacy Rate[l]
Female: 100.0%
Male: 100.0%

ECONOMY

Gross National Product per Capita: U.S. $2,050

Percentage of Labor Force in Agriculture: 26.4%[m]

Distribution of Agricultural Workers by Sex[n]
Female: 46.7%
Male: 53.3%

Economically Active Population by Sex[o]
Female: 43.2%
Male: 54.5%

a. Anita Gargas and Maciej Wojciechowski, *Partie polityczne w Polsce* (Political parties in Poland) (Gdansk: Krajowa Agencja Wydawnicza, 1991), 204.

b. Obwieszczenie Panstwowej Komisji Wyborczej z dnia 31 pazdziernika 1991 (Announcement of the National Electoral Commission, 31 October 1991).

c. Ibid.

d. *Maly Rocznik Statystyczny 1991* (Small statistical yearbook, 1991) (Warsaw: Glowny Urzad Statystyczny).

e. Ibid.

f. *Rocznik Statystyczny 1990* (Statistical yearbook, 1990) (Warsaw: Glowny Urzad Statystyczny).

g. Ibid.

h. Ibid.

i. *Maly Rocznik Statystyczny 1991.*

j. Ibid.

k. Ibid.

l. *Rocznik Statystyczny 1990.*

m. Ibid.

n. Ibid.

o. Ibid.

Polish Women as the Object and Subject of Politics During and After the Communist Period

RENATA SIEMIEŃSKA

TRANSLATED BY

G. DZIURDZIK-KRASNIEWSKA

Women's participation in politics in Poland since the end of World War II has been the result of broadly understood ideological circumstances, former experiences, and the present sociopolitical situation. Fundamental political changes in recent years make it important to understand the sociopolitical mechanisms during the periods of communism, the clear collapse of communism in the 1980s, and postcommunism. The last period began with the downfall of the ruling Communist Party (the Polish United Workers' Party, or PUWP) in June 1989 following the first partially free elections to Parliament since the war.

The form that women's presence in politics takes depends to a large extent on the existing sociopolitical situation. But the behaviors and attitudes that arise in a changed situation can be inconsistent with new democratic possibilities that are a reaction to the nondemocratic past. Therefore, in periods of destabilization or change in a system, when the political struggle is particularly harsh, women are represented in lower numbers than in more stable times. This thesis partially contradicts the sometimes formulated thesis that periods of crisis cause an increase in the political participation of women.[1] Many generalizations from Western countries regarding strategies and tactics for introducing women to active political life are not applicable in a changing political and economic system such as the Polish one.[2]

FROM TOTALITARIANISM TO DEMOCRACY

The communist system established in Eastern and Central Europe after World War II was highly centralized. The center was located at the confluence of the highest organs of party and state structures, with final authority derived from the supremacy of state power and the hegemonic position of the Communist Party. Every political organization, voluntary association, industrial enterprise, or local community was treated as a functional subdivision of this superorganization. The recent transformations taking place in all so-called socialist countries have eliminated the dominant role of the Communist parties.

Poland underwent dramatic political changes in the 1980s. Communist rule was abolished after four decades. Before this happened in 1989, the country experienced political and economic crises in 1956, 1968, 1970, 1976, and 1980 that showed the Poles' growing dissatisfaction with the political system and life conditions. Each crisis was a step forward, raising the social consciousness and political skills of the population. The crisis of 1980 began as a wave of strikes; one, the strike in the Gdansk shipyard, gave birth to the first independent trade union in the communist bloc, Solidarity. Solidarity became a powerful social movement, as well as a legal trade union with 9.5 million members, half of whom were women. But 16 months later, martial law was imposed, in December 1981, ending the period of open struggle between Solidarity on the one side and, on the other, the ruling PUWP and the government that it controlled.

Many Solidarity leaders and activists were arrested, but Solidarity continued its activities underground, an illegal organization until martial law ended in July 1983. Slow reforms undertaken by the Communist Party to introduce elements of a market economy into the centrally planned one (based on state ownership of banks, enterprises, etc.) did not work. Agriculture in Poland, unlike in the Eastern and Central European communist countries, was 80 percent in private hands as a result of promises given by Wladyslaw Gomulka, who came to power as the first secretary of the PUWP during the 1956 crisis. (In the early 1950s he had been imprisoned because of his "national-revisionist deviation.")

Growing dissatisfaction with poor living conditions and a lack of political freedom brought a new wave of strikes in spring 1988. The communist government was not able to stop them without the help of Solidarity and its leader, Lech Walesa. The price was a government agreement to talk with the political opposition. The Roundtable negotiation, which took place at the beginning of 1989, became a model for other Eastern and Central European countries as they set up negotiations between the ruling Communist parties and groups in political opposition. As an outcome of the negotiations in Poland, partially free elections to the Parliament were scheduled for the late spring.

The structure of the Parliament was changed during the Roundtable talks from the one-house Parliament (Seym) that existed after World War II to a new Parliament (now called the National Assembly) consisting of two houses: the lower house (Seym), with 460 seats, and the upper house (Senate), with 100 seats. In the lower house 65 percent of seats were reserved for the PUWP and its old allies (e.g., the Democratic Party, the United Peasants' Party, and the organizations of secular Catholics). In the Senate there were no reserved seats. According to the agreement, the president was elected by the Parliament. All the participants in the negotiations treated the established electoral law as obligatory only in the 1989 election.

The results of the election on 4 June 1989 were a surprise for both sides. The candidates from the Citizens' Committee—the body with local branches created by Walesa, built on the foundation of Solidarity—unquestionably won. They won all seats for which they could run: 161 (35 percent) in the Seym and 99 of 100 seats in the Senate. The election opened the way for the creation of a government headed by a non-Communist prime minister, Tadeusz Mazowiecki, a Roman Catholic intellectual and Solidarity adviser. The government was based on a broad coalition including some members of the Communist Party and its old allies, but their role was minor. The president elected by the Parliament was a Communist, according to the earlier agreement.

The Roman Catholic church played a crucial role in the victory of noncommunist political forces. During the whole communist period, the church was the only legal institution opposing the ruling PUWP. Over 90 percent of the population is Catholic, so the church has been not only a religious institution but a political one, playing an important role in maintaining national integration. It became especially strong during the 1980s as a supporter of Solidarity and is therefore exceptionally influential in the new political situation, backing those solutions in social life that are congruent with its doctrines.

Free elections to local governments were held in May 1990. Presidential elections in the fall of the same year made Lech Walesa president of the country and strengthened the political position of some Solidarity-based parties and groups. The most important of these groups are the Center Alliance, Democratic Union, and Citizens' Movement–Democratic Action. Other visible parties are the three peasant parties of different genealogies: Solidarity of Individual Farmers, the prewar Peasants' Party, and the postwar Peasants' Party. Two parties also have roots in the Communist Party, which was dissolved in January 1990: the Social Democracy of the Polish Republic and the Polish Social Democratic Union. Stanislaw Tyminski, an unknown Polish emigrant in Canada before the presidential campaign in the fall of 1990, created Party X, one of the most visible parties. In 1991 there were 147 political parties. People do not know about all the parties, and, as the elections demonstrated, they do not vote for parties but for politicians. Party programs are not crystallized, and the party structure is changing constantly.

The political parties with roots in the Solidarity movement and the peasant parties are more or less center oriented, usually with some connections to the church. To the left of the political spectrum are the parties considered to be remnants of the PUWP and the Polish Socialist Party, which consist of people who were in opposition under the communist regime. To the right are such parties as the Confederation of Independent Poland and the Union of Real Politics.

After World War II rapid industrialization changed Poland from a mainly agricultural society to an industrial one. The percentage of the population employed in agriculture fell from 54 in 1950 to 26 in 1989, with the main decrease in the 1950s and 1960s. At that time, heavy industry was built up following the Soviet model of industrialization, and its development caused a large migration of people from the countryside to the cities. Women were considered a reserve army of laborers; their percentage among employees grew from 30.6 in 1950 to 46.7 in 1989.[3]

The basic characteristics of Polish industry did not change much even when it was modernized in the 1970s. The mismanagement of the economy, the rise in oil prices in the world market, changes in trade relations with the Soviet Union (including the introduction of the transferable ruble), and high debts to Western banks that Poland was not able to repay—all contributed to the growing economic crisis in the late 1970s. This crisis in turn caused popular dissatisfaction with the economic and political performance of the government and the Communist Party responsible for it. The explosion of dissatisfaction in the summer of 1980, the wave of strikes, and the creation of Solidarity, shook the basis of the communist system.

The significant political changes that took place in 1989 as a result of the Roundtable talks opened the way for major economic reforms designed to wean the Polish economy from central planning and control and give it a market orientation. The process included privatization and reprivatization of enterprises previously owned by the state, creation of new enterprises based on internally available capital and joint ventures with Western capital, restructuring of production and services to make them economically efficient, and new management. This transformation was seen as the only chance for overcoming the economic crisis, which had lasted for more than ten years.

The imposition of such major reforms causes sudden impoverishment in some social groups, a drop in the living standards of a significant part of society, increasing unemployment, and decreasing welfare provisions, but it also brings the appearance of a new group of people benefiting from the changes, mainly those making money in trades. Women are more often victims of the change than are other members of the society.

WOMEN UNDER THE COMMUNIST REGIME

By virtue of its considerable centralization, the socioeconomic system developed in Poland after World War II offered greater opportunities for manipulating society than did many other systems. The concentration of economic planning and decision making at the center made it possible to influence directly the extent of men's and women's participation in different spheres of life by creating employment opportunities; determining the pay structure in the predominant public sector; creating amenities and services for working women, including care and education for children; and providing educational opportunities for women. Images of women appropriate to the state's ends were disseminated through the state-owned mass media and in politicians' speeches.[4]

In the early 1950s industry and construction developed rapidly, creating job opportunities for both men and women, though the latter were mostly employed as unskilled laborers. The growth rate in the number of employed women outstripped that of men. With real income stagnating, families could raise their living standards only if more of their members held a job.

Traditional female occupations became even more dominated by women, although women entered new occupations with relative ease. The number of women in traditionally male occupations, however, increased rather slowly. The structure of women's employment stabilized in the late 1970s.[5] Women's educational attainment has risen faster than men's during the last 40 years. Women now constitute a majority in general secondary schools and universities. Women with higher educations usually stay away from technical occupations and professions, and women in general tend to be concentrated in occupations with low pay and low prestige—mainly because of the traditional pattern of gender roles that exists in the social consciousness.[6] Finance and insurance institutions, schools, and health and social welfare services are the most female-dominated and at the same time the lowest paid sectors. In 1989 women made up 77 to 85 percent of the work force in these fields.

Migration to the cities due to industrialization changed the demographic structure of the rural population. It led to the masculinization of the farmer profession, although women play a particularly important role as producers on small farms (with fewer than five hectares, or 12 acres). The percentage of employed women in rural areas was 64 in 1988; in urban areas it was 53. But for women aged fifteen or older living on farms it was even higher: 75.[7]

Among other things, the new political system established after World War II stressed the political equality of men and women, but the number of women in decision-making positions was slow to rise. The increase was loosely related to changes in the number of employed women and women with appropriate professional backgrounds.

In the period 1944–79 only 13 women held top state positions, and they were members of the Presidium of the State Council (the collective presidency existing until 1989), the cabinet, or chairpersons of permanent or extraordinary commissions of the Seym or its presidium.[8] That eight of these women were on the Central Committee of the PUWP reflected the policy for recruitment to decision-making positions at the time.

In 1987 only one minister and two under-secretaries of state were women. There were 29 women among 533 directors of departments and 76 women among 733 deputy directors of departments. That women were appointed to 32.4 percent of decision-making positions in health-care and 67.8 percent in education showed that a lack of proper education was not a reason for the limited number of women at the higher and highest positions in these feminized sectors. The reasons used to deny women employment in the state administration included such things as officials' unwillingness to appoint women, women's fear of responsibility, and women's heavy family commitments.[9]

Polish women were among the first in Europe to be enfranchised (in 1918), immediately after Poland regained its independence following nearly 150 years of partitioned existence under foreign rule (by Prussia, Austria, and Russia). As in many countries, granting women the right to vote did not automatically lead to their full participation in political life.[10] Before the outbreak of World War II, women constituted only 2 percent of the lower chamber and 5 percent of the higher chamber. After World War II, when the political equality of men and women was being stressed, the number of women in the Seym grew significantly. In the last election before the Roundtable talks, 20.2 percent of the members of the Seym were women.

The process of deciding on the candidate lists, however, ensured the PUWP's control over the final list. The ideological principle was that the Seym should be representative of various organizations, social groups, religions, and generations and both sexes. In practice, the party selected people who belonged to these segments of society but did not represent their respective interests. This phenomenon was more pronounced among female than male deputies. During periods of political destabilization (such as the crises of 1956 and the 1980s), when there was a struggle for power and political influence, women were the first to be deleted from candidate lists.

An analysis of the composition of elective bodies in communist countries has distinguished three basic types of members: "activists," "needed" members, and "fillers."[11] The presence of the activists and needed members resulted from their role in the political, economic, and social life of the country; usually they had performed managerial functions or possessed qualifications necessary or useful to legislative bodies. The presence of filler members, however, depended on political considerations, often of an ideological character—that is, what social groups it was deemed expedient to include at the time. Women were often selected as combining in themselves several characteristics of these filler groups, thereby leaving more positions for people who played an active role in political life. The women selected for the 1985–89 term of the Seym were younger and less educated than the selected men, performed manual jobs with twice the frequency, and were six times more likely to be teachers.[12] After the war women were more heavily represented among nonparty members and members of the Democratic Party in those types of positions in the Seym that until the election of June 1989 served the filler function in the government. Studies conducted on the women and men deputies in the ninth Seym (1985–89) demonstrated that the presence of women was accompanied by gender prejudices and stereotyping on both sides.[13]

Women in Poland tend to hold decision-making positions in the lower levels of local authorities, where the scope of power is smaller, but their numbers have been greater at the provincial level than at the lowest level and in urban rather than rural communes. The reasons for this pattern of representation include greater resistance to women in decision-making positions in more traditional rural areas and women's significantly lower level of education as compared to men's in rural communes.

A study carried out in 1983 and 1984 in two provinces differing in history and socioeconomic development showed that women constituted only 12.4 percent of local leaders, whereas at the end of the 1970s they had constituted around 20 percent.[14] For male and female leaders, patterns of entry into professional careers were clearly different. The most common paths to office for women were through work in education and culture, in administration, and in the party apparatus.[15] Men tended to begin their careers in local government in decision-making positions at least at the intermediate level of services and production. Female leaders worked in institutions with less influence over the allocation and distribution of resources. For example, the percentage of men employed in the local committees of the PUWP (the most influential institutions in local communities) was almost twice that of women. More often than men, women occupied the less influential post of deputy.[16]

Until the downfall of the Communist Party, affiliation with it was the prerequisite for managerial or political careers.[17] A question arises as to the extent to which women tried to attain the resources that would enable them to hold managerial positions. The increase in the number of women among members of the PUWP, the Democratic Party, and the United Peasants' Party was particularly rapid from 1960 to 1970. Women's membership in the PUWP rose by 50 percent, in the United Peasants' Party by almost 100 percent, and in the Democratic Party by about 70 percent. In the next twenty years women's membership in all three parties rose by 5 to 6 percent, reaching around one-third in the 1980s. An analysis of data for different provinces showed that an increase in women's activities in political organizations depended more on an increase in their professional activities than on an increase in their level of education.[18]

Women held decision-making positions in the three parties at only about half their rate of party membership, and in the top political organs it was even lower, confirming the phenomenon observed in many countries that the higher a position in a political party, the less likely it is to be filled by a woman.

Even though women formed a large portion of the labor force, their presence in executive positions in trade unions was also small. Women constituted only 9 percent of the members of the National Agreement of Trade Unions Council—an association of trade unions created after the imposition of martial law in December 1981—

and 8.3 percent of its executive committee. Participation by women in the National Committee of Solidarity, the newly created independent trade union, was also small during 1980–81, although they constituted about half of the members.[19]

After the establishment of the communist system following World War II, organizations with long-lasting traditions from prewar times were not allowed to operate, nor were other political and semipolitical organizations. Therefore, no organized women's lobby existed to voice the interests of women from different social groups. The three women's organizations that did exist under the communist regime—the Polish Women's League, the Rural Women's Circles, and the Association of Women in Cooperatives— mediated between the PUWP and women. Their task was to encourage women to participate in achieving the goals set by the party and the government. The ideals of the feminist movement were viewed negatively by these organizations; feminism itself was, in fact, completely unknown to them. When Poland became the stage for student demonstrations at the end of the 1960s, as did many other European and non-European countries, the feminist movement did not gain any momentum. The postwar professional mobilization of women had caused women to feel overburdened; "equal rights" had in reality brought an increase in their duties as they were forced to combine new roles with the traditional ones. This burden, as in other Central and Eastern European countries, was greater than that of many women in Western countries because of the much poorer quality and limited availability of supplies and the inadequate organization of social life.[20]

Apart from that, the problems besetting Polish society—massive migration, reconstruction of the country after wartime destruction, industrialization involving high social costs, sluggish rise in living standards, recurring societal strains, and political and economic crises—united society more than they divided it along gender lines. The basic division perceived by society was between "us" (the people) and "them" (the authorities). The major problems were articulation of the interests of various social groups, classes, and strata; choice of a model for the socialist system; and in the 1980s the transformation of the system into a democratic free-market economy.

WOMEN ON THE EVE OF THE COLLAPSE OF THE COMMUNIST REGIME

At the onset of Solidarity's confrontation with the authorities in the early 1980s, the trade union's only demands specifically concerning women included three-year paid maternity leave and a guarantee of sufficient places for children in kindergartens and nurseries. These demands focused on creating conditions that would improve women's ability to fulfill their traditional roles. The agreements reached with the government contained no proposals for specifying increased participation for women in political or workplace decisions. All political demands centered on the influence of citizens generally. According to many national surveys and studies of particular social groups, the opinions of women and men generally converged. In the context of a hierarchy of values and life aspirations derived from public polls and the role of the family in that hierarchy (the family ranked highest in 1972 and second highest in 1981), the way in which demands concerning women emerged in August 1980 came as no surprise.[21] Differences of opinion occurred much more frequently among social groups than between men and women of the same group.[22]

At the beginning of the 1980s the images of the family and woman's place in it changed, and society returned to the traditional, albeit slightly modified, family model.[23] A steady improvement in living standards, particularly evident in the early 1970s, may have contributed to the revival of a dilemma: whether both husband and wife should work when the children are small. Propaganda in the late 1970s promoting an increased birthrate—because of predicted labor shortages and demographic miscalculations forecasting a severe drop in the birthrate—triggered a favorable response: the birthrate rose by the end of the decade.

At the same time, the alienation produced by multidimensional economic, political, and moral crises brought about the need for greater support by the family. The increasing influence of the Catholic church coincided with the direction of state propaganda, for the church attaches great significance to the family as the basic unit of social life. One indicator of the importance of the family in Poland is the low rate of divorce, a gradual upward trend notwithstanding (0.5 per 1,000 population in 1960 versus 1.3 per 1,000 in 1988).[24]

Rampant inflation in the early 1980s and the breakdown of the consumer market due to economic collapse did not offer women an incentive to continue working at all costs. The 1981 introduction of the three-year paid maternity leave prompted many women with small children to break out of their professional roles. Thereafter the situation changed. Allowances connected with maternity leave became more and more symbolic. Kindergartens diminished in number and became unaffordable for many families.

Poland's postwar history and the stormy events of the early 1980s did not enhance women's participation in politics or economic management. The proportion of female leaders in politics and the economy was lower in the 1980s than in earlier decades, when people had been picked for certain jobs according to formulas establishing numbers of representatives from various population groups.[25]

WOMEN DURING THE TRANSITION TO DEMOCRACY

In 1990, after years of scarcity in the labor force, reflected in the high ratio of available jobs to people seeking employment, the new economic mechanisms bringing the Polish economy closer to a market economy simply decreased the demand for labor. On average, 100,000 persons have joined the ranks of the unemployed each month. In December 1990, 49.1 percent of the unemployed were men and 50.9 percent were women.[26]

Women's employment situation is much more difficult than men's. In December 1990 the overall unemployment rate in Poland was 8.3 percent. Although the difference in unemployment between men and women was only 1 percent, the structure of unemployment and the demands of the labor market for men and women are different. Men can find jobs much more easily. On average, one of every 40 unemployed women was offered a job in 1990, compared with one of every 14 unemployed men. The picture varies from region to region. Where jobs for women were scarcest, one of every 824 unemployed women was offered a job.[27]

The situation is aggravated by the difference in the type of jobs available to women in relation to their level and type of education. The available jobs are incompatible with the skills possessed by women, for the majority of openings are for manual laborers. Unemployed women have more education than unemployed men, and this difference is especially pronounced among young people. The increasing shortage of kindergartens, especially cheap ones, and families' decreased use of many types of services (e.g., cleaning) because of falling living standards make it increasingly difficult for women to accept many types of jobs even if offered.

Women played almost no active role in the changes taking place at the end of the 1980s. In the 1989 Roundtable talks, for example, neither the opposition (Solidarity) nor the government had any women representing its side's interests. The only woman on the side of the government, a university professor, decidedly renounced any particular association with the problems of women. Later, women did participate in the discussions of experts accompanying the Roundtable negotiations.

In the appointment of candidates to the Seym and the Senate before the partially free elections in June 1989 women constituted a decided minority, for both the government and the opposition. Among 2,500 candidates only some 200 were women. The Citizens' Committee had 16 women candidates for the Seym and 6 women candidates for the Senate. Among the 460 persons elected to the Seym 62 were women (13.5

percent), and among the 100 persons elected to the Senate 6 were women.[28]

The guidelines for selecting and promoting candidates for the 1989 elections stemmed from political agreements about the electoral process.[29] Different election tactics were adopted by the various parties and political forces. Solidarity proposed one candidate for a given seat, whereas other political forces sometimes proposed several persons for a given seat. Solidarity presented women and men in the same way—as people supported by Lech Walesa—which was the most important political recommendation. The remaining women candidates led their own campaigns, stressing the specific women's interests that they wished to represent in Parliament in the framework of party ideology. To a certain extent they were supported by the Communist Women's League.

Being aware of the political game, the PUWP and its allies were more inclined to give their support to their members in the next phase of the election campaign. Among respondents in the survey—women candidates and deputies from the PUWP and its allies—those who received organizational assistance during the second phase of the election campaign were five times the number that the PUWP offered to help with collecting signatures in the first phase.[30]

Women starting political careers in Western countries, particularly in the United States, often take advantage of informal support, especially from members of their families.[31] Although only 5 percent of respondents in the previously mentioned survey stated that family members helped them collect signatures, they stressed somewhat more the family's help in organizing the election campaign. About 15 percent said acquaintances and friends helped them collect signatures, and about 10 percent said acquaintances and friends participated in the election campaign. A small group of candidates (3 percent) were proposed by acquaintances and friends. The decided majority of the respondents spoke of their families and friends as looking favorably on their running in the campaign, but 15 percent met with evident reluctance or criticism.

The respondents who complained about specific difficulties in the election campaign were divided into two almost equal groups: those who believed that women have a more difficult time running a good campaign (52 percent) and those who did not think so (47 percent). The attitudes held in this respect were the result of differing experiences, to a large extent depending on the political groups that they represented (Solidarity, the former government side, or other organizations), as well as the more general attitude toward women's participation in politics. The women candidates and deputies of the former government side felt more often that it was difficult to run a good campaign because in this case women were competing with men.

The generalization that women's participation in politics decreases in periods of harsher political struggle was also observed in the late 1980s. The demographic and social characteristics of female representatives had changed over time. Women elected to the Seym in 1989 were for the first time slightly older (average age, 46.8 years) than elected men (average age, 45.5). In addition, the women were decidedly better educated than their predecessors. In comparison with those elected in the last term of the communist regime, representatives with a university-level education increased by over 20 percent, from 60 to 82 percent in the Seym and from 60 to 85 percent in the Senate. The increase was particularly noteworthy among women: 89 percent of the women deputies had a university education, and 10 percent had a secondary school education, whereas among men the respective percentages were 82 and 11. The 1989 elections, apart from the change in the composition of political forces that was decided beforehand during the Roundtable proceedings, also brought a visible change in the profile of selected persons within the PUWP. The party moved from representation of the so-called socioprofessional composition of society toward selection of candidates on the basis of their competence. Almost all the members of the national congress (97 percent) were there for the first time.[32]

In the first free elections for local representatives, held in late May 1990, even fewer women were elected than in the partially free national elections of 1989. They constituted 15 percent of the candidates and 10.3 percent of the elected deputies. As before, women seldom appeared in the highest administrative positions. At the end of 1990 there were 13 women among 200 ministers, deputy ministers, and general directors of departments in the ministries.[33] Women were also almost absent on the political scene as representatives of larger and smaller parties, political groups, and trade unions.

The various parties and political forces are more or less openly debating the concept of women's role in society, many of them arguing for women's return to the traditional roles of wife and mother. For example, the recently formed Union of Real Politics—a right-wing party—promotes not only this view but also the opinion that women should not even have the right to be elected and that the right to vote should apply only to older women (like men, women are enfranchised at the age of 18). Party members say that by nature, younger women are not competent to comment on politics. The idea of limiting women to traditional roles also appears in the speeches of those representing other political groupings. In February 1989, for example, a deputy of the Citizens' Parliamentary Club (an organization associated with Solidarity), evaluating the budget "in light of the social teachings of the church, postulated the introduction of a family wage, which would enable the Polish woman to stay at home with dignity."[34]

The political scene is at present the stage for diverging opinions on the role and place of women in society. Although the Union of Real Politics is politically and socially marginal, the Citizens' Parliamentary Club was the strongest of the political groups that played a role in toppling the Communist Party in the 1989 elections. On this, as on many other issues, the opinions of members of the various parties are not uniform. Some Poles are attempting to carry out changes modeled, for example, on the solutions found in societies with longer democratic traditions. Others search for answers in the history of their own nation, drawing on traditions that are often completely out of touch with the demands of contemporary times.

The changes taking place in Poland, including the creation of Solidarity, are the beginnings of substantial transformations. What was illegal and impossible before is tolerated now to a greater or lesser extent. The first feminist group, established by students at Warsaw University in the early 1980s, gradually brought in persons not associated with the institution. Its goal was to become acquainted with the ideals of feminist movements in Western countries and to develop women's awareness.

The imposition of martial law, contrary to what might have been expected, did not hinder the process of awakening a feminist awareness. Growing social awareness, and through it the creation of new, illegal organizations of varied character and political orientation, stimulated the formation of feminist groups and associations from the mid-1980s on (mostly after the end of martial law). These were small as a rule (from several members to 200), active mainly in large cities and in student and intelligentsia communities.

In 1986, well after martial law ended, the Warsaw University group organized an international film review, "Women's Cinema," to show films by popular women film directors. Some of the directors spoke about the inspiration for their work. But the attempts at broadening the membership of the group were not successful. Women workers believed that the newly created trade union, Solidarity, would help them solve their problems: in a nutshell, enable them to quit their jobs and stay at home. Women who were successful professionally believed that if a woman was talented and strongly motivated to have a career, then she was capable of doing so. Nevertheless, a few feminist groups were created in the late 1980s.

Feminist organizing increased when a conflict over policies regulating reproductive rights erupted. The announcement in 1989 of the proposed anti-abortion law, officially called the Act Protecting the Unborn, brought into being at least 20 new groups and associations, which worked alongside the feminist organizations created in the mid-1980s. These associations, sometimes informal groups, have different political orientations. Some are left-wing, connected to the Polish Socialist Party, the Polish Social Democratic Union, or the Social Democracy of the Polish Republic. Pro Femina, the Democratic Union of Women, is a formally independent group. Other organizations are tied to the Catholic church—for example, the episcopate's Subcommission on Women's Issues. In addition, some women's organizations are not clearly linked to a given political association but keep in touch and sometimes coordinate their activities with women's organizations affiliated with the left—for example, the Movement for Protecting Women's Rights (from Poznan) or Women's Dignity (from Torun). The tendency is to establish communication and cooperation among the organizations when the majority share a goal, like fighting the proposed act. Some groups have planned broader activities aimed at raising the quality of sex education, fighting discrimination against women in its different forms, and organizing meetings and seminars. However, financial difficulties, small memberships, and changes in membership have prevented the development of a feminist magazine, even though several groups would like to publish one.

The organizations created in academic circles have wished to stimulate studies on the status of women, using feminist theoretical assumptions. But in spite of their broadly formulated tasks, these new organizations have concentrated primarily on opposing the anti-abortion act through street demonstrations, petitions, leaflets, and use of the mass media (which is difficult), not on increasing the political influence of women. Being weak, they did not take part in the campaigns preceding the May 1990 local elections. The situation changed before the first free elections to Parliament in October 1991. Women tried then to become candidates on behalf of various political parties but constituted only 11 percent of the candidates and 9 percent of the elected deputies. The Women's Alliance Against the Difficulties of Life, formed during the campaign, won one seat.

The feminist movement, because of its recent opposition to the implementation of the anti-abortion act, is becoming more visible. Nevertheless, the public assigns a lower priority to the need for women's movements (not only the feminist movement, which some associate with its most radical wing and with rejection of the family) than to many other movements. Studies conducted in 1989–90 demonstrate that the women's movement had one of the lowest levels of strong approval (by 48.7 percent of the respondents). The most strongly endorsed movement, the ecology movement, attained almost twice that level of support (by 80.8 percent of respondents), and the disarmament movement and the human rights movement (at home and abroad) had almost as much approval (about 75 percent each).[35] Many women join ecology movements or form eco-feminist groups, similar to those in Western European countries.[36]

The absence of an organized women's lobby has been felt most profoundly in the past several years of transition, when different social and political groups have tried to influence the future form of political, social, and economic life and to secure their position in the new social order. There have been a number of initiatives to create a women's lobby, the first by the governmental Office of Women's Affairs, whose head is a deputy minister. The Forum, a gathering of various women's groups and organizations, was formed in spring 1990 to give representatives of all the women's and feminist groups and associations, regardless of their political orientation, the opportunity to meet, exchange views, and formulate their expectations of the government regarding women's issues.

Another attempt to create a women's lobby was undertaken by women deputies from the Parliamentary Club of the Democratic Left (affiliated with postcommunist parties). In 1990 and 1991 they organized two conferences, attended by women deputies, scientists, and activists of women's organizations with different political orientations. The same type of initiative to strengthen women's political position came in late spring 1991 from the Parliamentary Club of the Democratic Union (rooted originally in Solidarity). The deputies proposed to establish a Parliamentary Club of Women Deputies of all political affiliations. Two-thirds of the women deputies and senators joined the club. The future will show which of the initiatives will give birth to more permanent institutions and to what extent they will become influential in the promotion of women's interests.

THE ANTI-ABORTION LAW: A SIGN OF COMING CHANGE?

Since 1956 the abortion law in Poland has been very liberal. Abortion has been legal, performed on demand free of charge in a hospital, when pregnancy is the result of rape, when a woman does not want to have a child (for so-called social reasons), when a woman's health is at stake, and when other factors make it desirable.

Proposals were made to change the abortion law before the elections to the Seym in spring 1989, before the 1990 local and presidential elections and, most recently, before the elections to the Parliament in October 1991, when, in addition, the economic situation in Poland became very difficult. This pattern suggests the political character of the abortion issue as a means of deflecting public attention from the systemic changes needed to address the poor economic situation. Meanwhile, the political influence of the Catholic church, as one of the architects of political change in the late 1980s, has been growing.

In 1989, before the elections organized by the Roundtable agreement, a legislative initiative to change the abortion law was presented to the Parliament by the deputy circle of the Catholic Social Union, which had long existed as one of the token organizations representing Catholics in Poland. The draft, worked out under the protectorate of the episcopate, was signed by 79 deputies from various deputy clubs. It made abortion illegal and called for prison sentences for women having abortions, as well as for doctors performing them. The draft act caused an upheaval of public opinion and, on the part of opponents,

gave rise to a series of demonstrations, petitions, and interviews in the mass media to mobilize public opinion against the proposed act. Its supporters were not left behind in organizing actions to gain additional support. Women and men were involved on both sides. Opposition and advocacy on behalf of the act were often interpreted in political terms: opposition to the act was seen as support for the authorities, while support for the act was seen as opposition to the authorities, for the draft came from church circles, which have traditionally provided support for political opposition. The problem therefore became very complicated.

The reconstruction of the political system after the 1989 elections to Parliament postponed discussion of the proposed anti-abortion act for a few months. In autumn 1989, though, the issue reemerged. It was examined by the Commission for Family Problems of the Polish episcopate in September 1989 and then by the diocesan family ministers. In December a group of 37 senators (including three women) approached the speaker of the Senate on behalf of the draft presented earlier, the Act Regarding the Legal Protection of the Unborn Child.

At the beginning of April 1990 the Senate commission examined the draft. The year before, a wide range of feminists, journalists, representatives of women's organizations, and others, in addition to the episcopate representatives and their experts, were present at the proceedings. In 1990 the only persons outside the Senate allowed to attend were the representatives of the episcopate. Women's communities reacted with indignation to this exclusion, both because their representatives were not allowed in and because the Senate commission did not even give them a draft of the act to become acquainted with.

The Second Solidarity Congress, held ten days after the April hearing, voted 248 for and 71 against the draft act, with 57 abstentions, passing resolution 14 on "the legal protection of human life from the moment of conception."

The pressure to pass the anti-abortion law has made women aware that the Parliament can make decisions directly affecting them without consulting women's communities. The existing Women's League, the Rural Women's Circles, and the Association of Women in Cooperatives were against the draft act. With liberalization of the political system enabling the creation of various organizations, women's associations were formed with the goal of fighting the proposed act. Therefore, the threat had an unintentional positive function: it became the stimulus for awakening the initiative of women's communities.

In spring 1990 and in 1991 people opposed the introduction of the restrictive new act with a series of street demonstrations and presented petitions with hundreds of signatures to the Seym. The church and right-wing parties, such as the Union of Real Politics, sponsored actions in support of its introduction.

Many people opposing the draft anti-abortion act are aware that the current situation is far from satisfactory. The unavailability of contraceptives, lack of information about their use, absence of discussion about the moral and health aspects and consequences of abortion, and lack of sex education in schools (any attempts to offer courses in sex education have met with violent opposition from groups associated with the church) contribute to the large number of unwanted pregnancies, many of which are aborted. According to some estimates, approximately 1 million abortions are performed annually, roughly equaling the number of births. Adopting a restrictive abortion law will not solve the problem as such.

At the end of January 1991 a new draft of the anti-abortion law, prepared this time by the Senate, was sent to the Seym. Its main author, Sen. Walerian Piotrowski, presented the draft to deputies, arguing that the "right of man to life . . . is natural. Even a mother may not make decisions about it. The law forbidding abortion is necessary—a conscience is not sufficient protection of our rights in social life."[37] In spite of the many deputies who wanted to discuss the issue, the Seym decided not to review the pros and cons yet again. Rejection of the Senate draft, proposed by a left-wing deputy, was opposed by 213 deputies

and favored by 124 (many of them left-wing), and 12 abstained. Deputies representing Catholic associations and Parliamentary Clubs originating from Solidarity mainly opposed rejection. But neither group of voters was politically homogeneous. President Lech Walesa strongly supported the anti-abortion law. As the daily press reported, the day before the Seym was expected to discuss and eventually vote on the Senate draft, the president publicly prayed in "solidarity with each unborn child."[38] A second reading of the draft was rejected during the same session, so a Seym extraordinary commission was set up to work on yet one more draft of the law. Representatives of all political groups in the Seym took part.

Discussions in the commission and so-called social consultation with various organizations and individuals took place in 1991. The Catholic church organized a campaign to support the anti-abortion law. People whose opinions differed from that of the church also sent letters to the Seym. According to information released by the commission, 81 percent of the public signed petitions demanding that abortion be forbidden. The majority of people supporting the anti-abortion law signed petitions prepared by the church. In May 1991, however, the proposed act was rejected in Parliament. The Parliamentary Club of the Democratic Union offered to prepare a new draft of the law. Later, in summer 1991, it withdrew its draft. The law was discussed again after the elections to the new Parliament. In February 1992, President Walesa signed an anti-abortion law with strict limits and sentences of up to two years in prison for doctors who violate the rules.

The results of the social consultation in 1991 indicating overwhelming support for the anti-abortion act were discongruent with many sociological studies showing that since 1989, when the first draft was read in the Seym, the number of people opposing it has increased. In a study conducted at the end of 1989, several months after the appearance of the draft of the law, respondents in a national random sample were asked whether and in what situations they considered abortion acceptable: 72.7 percent considered abortion unjustifiable under any circumstances. The views of women were stricter than those of men: 77.4 percent, compared to 67.8 percent.[39] Public opinion was divided.

The factors influencing the distribution of the replies were religiosity, socioprofessional group, place of residence, age, and marital status. Persons considering themselves religious (91 percent of Polish society) were against abortion more frequently than others. Young people in their reproductive years (to age 30) approved of abortion less frequently than others. The marital status of the respondents was also significant: divorced or separated people were more inclined to approve of abortion.

Two years later, opinions were different. In a national survey carried out in May 1991, 49 percent of the respondents supported abortion with some limitations, 31 percent supported unrestricted abortion, and 19 percent thought that abortion should be forbidden without exception. The youngest people and the oldest were more often opposed to abortion, while people from 30 to 49 were the least likely to oppose it. Well-to-do people, inhabitants of big cities, nonmanual workers, owners of private companies, and members of trade unions created under martial law (1981–83) supported legal abortion more often than others did. The law prohibiting abortion had more support among women than men and is also supported by farmers, people with lower incomes, and inhabitants of small towns.[40] The pattern of distribution of the answers was unchanged from 1989 to 1991, although the number of supporters of the law prohibiting abortion decreased.

A comparison of these studies with studies made in 1981–83 in 22 European and non-European countries shows that Poles justify abortions less frequently than citizens elsewhere.[41] Poland appears among countries with an intermediate level of acceptance of abortion when the life of the mother is threatened and among countries with a low level of acceptance in the remaining cases. The level of acceptance is similar to that found in the United States and slightly lower than in many Western European countries, particularly in Scandinavia. The level of acceptance of abortion is considerably higher in Hungary and the former Soviet Union than in Poland. This finding supports the view that the Catholic church dominates the social life of Poles in their attitudes toward both abortion and the role of the family. Another influence to consider is the meaning attached to the family in the survival of the Polish nation in times of partition, as well as during and since World War II. The family has been a bastion of national identity, a means of passing on knowledge about the nation's history and its system of values.

PROSPECTS

The absence of strong women's organizations is one reason for the lack of attention to women and their problems and a reason for their underrepresentation and minimal participation in political decision making. To a large extent, this situation is also the heritage of the entire communist period, when no organizations other than those fitting into the communist ideological framework could be formed. And it is the result of the model used to persuade women to start professional work and of the character of cyclical crises in Poland, which have tended to unite rather than divide society. Division according to the criterion of sex seemed irrelevant in times of upheaval.

Women's motivation for activism on their own behalf is complex. But women are increasingly aware that they must unite to defend their basic rights and to resist forces that try to diminish their legal status and limit their options.

NOTES

1. Vicky Randall, *Women and Politics* (London: Macmillan, 1982).

2. Ibid.; Cynthia Fuchs Epstein and Rose Laub Coser, eds., *Access to Power: Cross-National Studies of Women and Elites* (Boston: Allen and Unwin, 1981); Renata Siemieńska, "Women's Political Participation and the 1980 Crisis in Poland," *International Political Science Review* 3 (1985): 332–46.

3. *Statistical Yearbook 1990* (Warsaw: Glowny Urzad Statystyczny, 1990), xxxii–xxxiii.

4. Aleksandra Jasinska and Renata Siemieńska, *Wzory Osobowe socjalizmu* (Personality patterns of socialism) (Warsaw: Wiedza Powszechna, 1978); Jasinska and Siemieńska, "Rola rodziny w propagowanym wzorze osobowosci socjalistycznej a jej miejsce w hierarchii wartosci spoleczenstwa polskiego" (The role of the family in the disseminated pattern of socialist personality and its rank in a value hierarchy of the Polish society), *Przeglad Humanistyczny* 11–12 (1980): 75–90; Jasinska and Siemieńska, "The Socialist Personality: A Case Study of Poland," *International Journal of Sociology* 13 (1983): 1–88.

5. Renata Siemieńska, *Plec, zawod, polityka: Kobiety w zyciu publicznym w Polsce* (Gender, occupation, politics: Women in the public life of Poland) (Warsaw: Institute of Sociology, University of Warsaw, 1990), 89–92.

6. Renata Siemieńska, "Women, Work and Gender Equality in Poland: Reality and Its Social Perception," in Sharon Wolchik and Alfred Meyer, eds., *Women, State and Party in Eastern Europe* (Durham, N.C.: Duke University Press, 1985), 305–22; Mino Vianello, Renata Siemieńska et al., *Gender Inequality* (London: Sage, 1990).

7. *Kobieta w Polsce* (Woman in Poland) (Warsaw: Glowny Urzad Statystyczny, 1990), 23.

8. Tadeusz Moldawa, *Naczelne wladze panstwowe 1944–1979* (State authorities, 1944–1979) (Warsaw: University of Warsaw, 1979).

9. Vianello, Siemieńska et al., *Gender Inequality.*

10. Joni Lovenduski and Jill Hills, eds., *The Politics of the Second Electorate: Women and Public Participation* (London: Routledge and Kegan Paul, 1981); Joni Lovenduski, *Women and European Politics: Contemporary Feminism and Public Policy* (Amherst: University of Massachusetts Press, 1986); Randall, *Women and Politics*; and Sharon Wolchik, "Eastern Europe," in Lovenduski and Hills, eds., *Politics of the Second Electorate*, 252–77.

11. Daniel Nelson, "Women in Local Communist Politics in Romania and Poland," in Wolchik and Meyer, eds., *Women, State and Party in Eastern Europe*, 152–67.

12. Tomasz Plonkowski, "Kobiety w Sejmie" (Women in the Seym) (Master's thesis, Institute of Sociology, University of Warsaw, 1987); Renata Siemieńska, "Polish Women and Polish Politics Since World War II," *Journal of Women's History* 3, no. 1 (1991): 108–25.

13. Plonkowski, "Kobiety w Sejmie," 25–42.

14. Jerzy J. Wiatr, ed., *Wladza lokalna w przededniu kryzysu* (Local authorities on the eve of the crisis) (Warsaw: Institute of Sociology, University of Warsaw, 1983), 196; Wiatr, ed., *Wladza lokalna w warunkach kryzysu* (Local authorities in conditions of crisis) (Warsaw: Institute of Sociology, University of Warsaw, 1987).

15. Renata Siemieńska, "Women in Leadership Positions in Public Administration in Poland" (Paper delivered at a conference organized by the Friedrich Ebert Stiftung, Bonn, Germany, 1987).

16. Siemieńska, *Plec, zawod, polityka*, 206–14.

17. Renata Siemieńska, "Local Party Leaders in Poland," *International Political Science Review* 3 (1985): 127–36.

18. Siemieńska, "Polish Women and Polish Politics," 112–14; Siemieńska, *Plec, zawod, polityka*, 172–77.

19. Renata Siemieńska, "Women and Solidarity in Poland in the Early 1980s," in Yolande Cohen, ed., *Women and Counter Power* (Montreal: Black Rose Books, 1989), 33–45.

20. Barbara Tryfan, *Kwestia kobieca na wsi* (Women's issues in a village) (Warsaw: Panstwowe Wydawnictwo Naukowe, 1987), 128–227.

21. Jasinska and Siemieńska, *Wzory Osobowe socjalizmu*, 335–40; Renata Siemieńska, "Women and Social Movements in Poland," *Women and Politics* 6 (1986): 13–41.

22. Vianello, Siemieńska et al., *Gender Inequality*, 240–41.

23. Siemieńska, "Women and Social Movements in Poland," 23–26.

24. *Statistical Yearbook, 1981* (Warsaw: Glowny Urzad Statystyczny, 1981), 638; *Statistical Yearbook, 1990*, 529.

25. Siemieńska, "Women and Social Movements in Poland," 30–33; Siemieńska, "Polish Women and Polish Politics," 121–23.

26. Documents of the Ministry of Labor and Social Affairs.

27. Ibid.

28. *Statistical Yearbook, 1990*, 65–66.

29. The studies carried out by the author encompassed all the women from the Senate, nearly three-quarters of the women deputies, and a third of the women who ran for office but were not elected; half of all the women who ran for election responded (120 women).

30. Ibid.

31. See, e.g., Janet Flammang, ed., *Political Women: Current Roles in State and Local Government* (Beverly Hills, Calif.: Sage, 1984).

32. Documents of the Parliament.

33. *Kobieta w Polsce*, 40.

34. "Report of the Seym Debate," *Gazeta Wyborcza* (Daily), 23 February 1989.

35. The studies were carried out by the author as part of the World Values Survey and conducted on a national random sample of 936 persons from 16 to over 65 years old. The results of these studies have not yet been published.

36. Lovenduski, *Women and European Politics*, 113.

37. Agnieszka Jcdrzejcsyk, "Ustawa do konsultag"

(Law to be consulted), *Gazeta Wyborcza*, 26–27 January 1991.

38. Ibid.

39. See n. 35.

40. Piotr Pacewicz, "Antykoncepcja, karanie, aborcja" (Contraception, punishment, abortion), *Gazeta Wyborcza*, 15 May 1991.

41. *Values on Five Continents, Results from Twenty-Two Societies Surveyed in the 1981–1983 World Values Survey* (Ann Arbor, Mich.: Institute for Social Research, 1989).

▲ Puerto Rico

POLITICS

Type of Political System: democracy

Type of State: U.S. territory with colonial status[a]

Sovereignty: not applicable

Executive-Legislative System: not applicable

Type of Party System: multiparty

Major Political Parties

Partido Popular Democrático (PPD, or Popular Democratic Party): Dominated Puerto Rican politics 1940-68; supports continuation of Puerto Rico's commonwealth status.

Partido Nuevo Progresista (PNP, New Progressive Party): Formed in 1968 by Luis Ferré; advocates statehood.

Partido Independentista Puertorriqueño (PIP, or Puerto Rican Independence Party): Leftist party; militantly supports independence for Puerto Rico.

Year Women Granted Right to Vote: 1929/1935[b]

Year Women Granted Right to Stand for Election: 1929

Percentage of Women in the Legislature[c]

Lower House: 6.0%

Upper House: 15.0%

Percentage of Electorate Voting for Highest Elected Office in Most Recent Election (1988): 83.6%[d]

DEMOGRAPHICS

Population: 3,522,037[e]

Percentage of Population in Urban Areas

Overall: 66.8%

Female: 67.8%

Male: 65.7%

Percentage of Population Below Age 15: 27.2%[f]

Birthrate (per 1,000 population): 19[g]

Maternal Mortality Rate (per 100,000 live births): 40[h]

Infant Mortality Rate (per 1,000 live births): 13[i]

Mortality Rate for Children Under Five (per 1,000 live births): 14[j]

Average Household Size: 3.3[k]

Mean Age at First Marriage[l]

Female: 22.7

Male: 26.0

Life Expectancy[m]

Female: 78.6

Male: 74.2

EDUCATION

Ratio of Female to Male Enrollment

First-Level Education: 91[n]

Second-Level Education: 103[o]

Third-Level Education: 159[p]

Literacy Rate[q]

Female: 89.1%

Male: 90.3%

ECONOMY

Gross National Product per Capita: U.S. $6,961[r]

Percentage of Labor Force in Agriculture: 3.4%[s]

Distribution of Agricultural Workers by Sex[t]

Female: 2.6%

Male: 97.4%

Economically Active Population by Sex[u]

Female: 32.4%

Male: 63.1%

a. Puerto Ricans do not have the right to vote for the president of the United States. Except for a resident commissioner with the right to speak but not vote, they do not have representation in the U.S. Congress. Puerto Ricans elect a local governor and have a local legislature, but Congress retains authority over Puerto Rican defense, laws, communication, and land expropriation.

b. In 1929 women's suffrage was restricted to literate women only; in 1935 universal suffrage was granted.

c. State Elections Council, *Informa preliminar de los resultados de las elecciones en Puerto Rico, 1988* (Preliminary report of the results of the 1988 Puerto Rican elections) (San Juan, 1990).

d. Ibid.

e. U.S. Department of Commerce, Bureau of the Census, *Censo de población y vivienda 1990—Resumen* de características de población y vivienda de Puerto Rico (Census of population and housing, 1990: Review of characteristics of population and housing in Puerto Rico) (Washington, D.C.: U.S. Government Printing Office, 1991).

f. Calculations made by the author from data in ibid.

g. Office of Health Statistics, *Estadísticas vitales preliminares, Puerto Rico, año 1990* (Preliminary vital statistics, Puerto Rico, 1990), Information Bulletin, year 6, series D-6, no. 2 (5 December 1991).

h. A. Comas et al., "Misreporting of Maternal Mortality in Puerto Rico," *Boletin de la Asociación Médica de Puerto Rico* 82 (August 1990).

i. *Estadísticas vitales preliminares, Puerto Rico, año 1990.*

j. Calculations made by the author from data in Office of Health Statistics, Department of Health of Puerto Rico, *Informe anual de estadísticas vitales de Puerto Rico, 1989* (Annual report of vital statistics of Puerto Rico, 1989) (San Juan, 1991).

k. *Censo de población y vivienda 1990.*

l. Jose L. Baszquez-Calzada, *La población de Puerto Rico y su trayectoria historica* (The population of Puerto Rico and its historical trajectory) (Self-published, May 1988).

m. *Informe anual de estadísticas vitales de Puerto Rico, 1989.*

n. Calculations made by the author from data in Department of Education of Puerto Rico, *Informe de matrícula de escuelas publicas y privadas por sexo y grado (DI-1), 1991–1992* (Report of enrollment in public and private schools by sex and level [DI-1], 1991–92) (San Juan, 1992).

o. Calculations made by the author from data in *Compendio de estadísticas* (Compendium of statistics) (San Juan: University of Puerto Rico, 1992).

p. Ibid.

q. *Censo de población y vivienda 1990.*

r. Calculations made by the author from data in Puerto Rican Planning Council, *Informe económico al gobernador, 1989* (Economic report to the governor, 1989) (San Juan, 1989).

s. Bureau of Labor Statistics, Department of Labor and Human Resources, *Encuesta de la población civil no institucional y el grupo trabajador* (Survey of the non-institutional civil population and the working class) (May–June 1990).

t. Ibid.

u. Ibid.

At the Crossroads: Colonialism and Feminism in Puerto Rico

YAMILA AZIZE-VARGAS

According to its 1952 constitution, the Commonwealth of Puerto Rico is "a free state associated with the United States," yet this title does not easily explain the complex relationship between the two countries. A Spanish colony since the late 1400s, Puerto Rico first came under U.S. control in 1898, when troops invaded the Caribbean island at the close of the Spanish-American War. The Treaty of Paris, signed by Spain and the United States in 1898, made Puerto Rico a nonincorporated territory of the United States, and the U.S. Congress retained absolute power over Puerto Rico's political status and the civil rights of its inhabitants. Since then, three acts approved by the U.S. Congress—the Foraker Act (1900), the Jones Act (1917), and Public Law 600 (1950)—have granted Puerto Rico some control over its internal affairs, but the island is still subject to U.S. federal laws. Decisions made by the U.S. Congress and Supreme Court or executive orders from the U.S. president override any legislation passed by the Puerto Rican legislature.

Residents of Puerto Rico are U.S. citizens, but they do not have the right to vote for president of the United States. Puerto Ricans elect their own governor and bicameral legislature—the Senate and House of Representatives—every four years and are represented in the U.S. House of Representatives by a nonvoting resident commissioner. The United States and Puerto Rico share a common defense, market, and currency. The United States controls Puerto Rico's communications system and its sea and air transportation systems, and it administers foreign relations for the island.

The political status of Puerto Rico has been debated for some time, with the political parties endorsing three divergent positions: total independence from the United States; statehood for Puerto Rico; and a continuation of commonwealth status. The party in power since 1988 is the Partido Popular Democrático (PPD, or Popular Democratic Party), which supports autonomy for Puerto Rico "within a permanent union." The major opposition party, the Partido Nuevo Progresista (PNP, New Progressive Party) supports statehood for Puerto Rico. The third largest political party is the Partido Independentista Puertorriqueño (PIP, Puerto Rico Independence Party), which advocates full independence from the United States.

The 3.5 million Puerto Ricans living on the island are primarily *mestizaje,* people of Spanish, Caribbean Indian and African descent. An additional 2.7 million Puerto Ricans live in the mainland United States. The island's relation to the United States has had a profound impact—both negative and positive—on the political rights of women in Puerto Rico. In this chapter we will examine the relation in a historical context and focus on issues of concern to Puerto Rican women: health, employment, family law, and sexual violence.

COLONIALISM, CAPITALISM, AND THE EMERGENCE OF FEMINISM: 1898–1940

The twentieth century brought significant changes to women's status. The invasion and subsequent domination of Puerto Rico by the United States imposed new political and economic relations that allowed women to assert themselves in public life. Their participation in wage labor and formal education and their struggle for political rights, along with the implementation of new health policies, changed women's situation in society.

The influx of North American capital to the sugar and tobacco industries in the early 1900s transformed Puerto Rico's traditional agrarian economy to a capitalist one. Moreover, monopolistic U.S. enterprises accelerated the incorporation of women into the wage labor force on an unequal and sexist basis by taking advantage of the social and economic subordination of women and the political subordination of the country to the United States. With their expanded participation in the economic sector, women no longer were restricted to jobs as domestic servants, agriculture workers, or homemakers. This situation brought conflicting changes for hundreds of women who faced inhumane and unhealthy working conditions on the one hand but who also developed an awareness of gender inequalities, especially in the tobacco industry.

The tobacco sector, one of the largest industries to use a female labor force, hired women to strip and classify tobacco leaves, utilizing their training in manual skills. Women's participation in cigar manufacturing increased from 60 female workers in 1899 to 9,290 in 1930, when women also constituted the majority (53 percent) of all employees in the industry.[1]

Women tobacco workers were subjected to discriminatory working conditions: unequal pay, lack of representation in the labor unions, and sexual harassment. According to the labor press of the period, women workers began to demand the right to organize, to educate, and to protect themselves from such discriminatory practices.[2] Because the organized labor movement initially rejected the incorporation of women into the existing unions, women decided to organize on their own.[3] Demands to include Ladies' Unions in strikes and to educate and organize women workers were discussed and approved in the annual meetings of the labor movement through the initiative of women leaders.[4] Through their unions women started demanding equal pay for equal work, a revision of the minimum wage, compliance with protective legislation for children, and better enforcement of sanitation laws. Other more politically oriented demands followed: recognition of civil rights for women, including their right to vote, and self-determination for the Puerto Rican people.[5]

Although the tobacco industry grew by only 8 percent between 1920 and 1930, the needlework industry registered a 200 percent increase in wage workers and emerged as an important economic activity for women.[6] This increase was a consequence of the U.S. invasion and the development of capitalism in Puerto Rico. World War I accelerated the establishment of the industry by interrupting commercial traffic with the Philippines, an important site for U.S. capital investment in needlework. And Puerto Rico was an attractive production site because the industry there was exempt from federal labor regulations.

The needlework industry was encouraged by a new and more accessible educational system that taught sewing, embroidery, and home economics—along with traditional skills—to satisfy the growing demand for workers.[7] The needlework industry experienced such spectacular growth that during the decade of 1930 to 1940 it became the second most important industry in Puerto Rico (after cane sugar), reaching unprecedented export rates.[8]

Another circumstance that favored the expansion of the needlework industry was the U.S. Minimum Wage Law. In 1919, when the law was enacted, many workshops went underground and home work proliferated.[9] When the U.S. Supreme Court declared the minimum wage law unconstitutional in 1924, the industry contracted even more home workers. The Puerto Rican Bureau of Labor repeated its opposition to home work but declared itself unable to resolve the problem. Legislative initiatives to regulate home work were unsuccessful as well. By 1927 it was estimated that of every ten rural homes and every twenty urban homes, eight were clandestine workshops.[10]

In spite of the drawbacks of home-based work, women's significant participation in the needlework industry allowed them to play a vital economic role in the survival of their families between 1920 and 1940.[11] The home-based nature of most needlework enterprises was an obstacle to organization, however. In fact, the first initiative to organize workers did not begin until the end of the 1920s. Syndicalism, a strategy used by women in the tobacco industry, contributed to the struggle to improve working conditions. In this way, work for wages outside the home and gender interactions within the labor movement encouraged the development of women's activism and the emergence of a feminist labor movement. This proved instrumental in the fight for women's suffrage in the 1920s.

SUFFRAGE FOR WOMEN

Women's participation in the labor movement was critical to making women workers aware of their rights and their place in society. A growing feminist ideology among working women was evident in 1908, when a group of women associated with the Federación Libre de Trabajadores (Free Federation of Workers) voiced the first organized demand for women's right to vote.[12] Their lobbying was successful. Several months later Nemesio Canales presented a bill entitled For the Legal Emancipation of Women to Puerto Rico's legislature. It demanded "all rights, of any kind or nature granted by law to male citizens."

As Carmen Puente, president of the Unión de Tabaqueras de San Juan (San Juan Women's Tobacco Workers Union), stated, "We understand that women's suffrage is not merely the right to vote. . . . Rather, it involves the highest principles of freedom for ourselves."[13] Although the bill was not passed, its extraordinary feminist nature should be underlined.[14]

Before the U.S. invasion, several notable intellectual women demanded more and better education for women, as well as the right to vote.[15] But Puerto Rico's sociopolitical relationship with the United States helped make suffrage one of the fundamental issues among both working-class and upper-class feminists during the 1920s.

Two groups of suffragists coexisted, divided by class issues and by their position on suffrage for women. Feminist working women were protagonists of the 1908 initiative to demand universal suffrage for women and of other labor struggles. Upper-class women organized another suffragist organization, the Liga Femínea (Feminine League) in 1917.[16] Members of the Feminine League included women educated in the United States, where they were influenced by progressive social movements.[17] They published various periodicals and lobbied government officials for restricted suffrage for women.[18]

Bills and petitions presented to the male-dominated legislature by both groups were rejected. Nevertheless, feminist leaders were confident that after universal suffrage was approved in the United States it would be extended to Puerto Rico. The political subordination of the island was made evident, however, when Genara Pagán, a feminist labor leader who had emigrated to the United States, forced consideration of whether the recently approved U.S. suffrage amendment was applicable to Puerto Rico. In 1920 she traveled to Puerto Rico to provoke a test case by registering to vote, citing her U.S. citizenship and the 19th Amendment for universal suffrage.[19] The government of Puerto Rico had to request the opinion of the Interior Department in Washington, which determined that the right of universal suffrage did not apply to the island.[20] The decision clearly demonstrated the colonial status of Puerto Rico and the U.S. government's power to decide whether its laws would apply to "outlying possessions of the United States."[21]

The feminist movement tried other strategies: new organizations, a short-lived coalition between working-class and upper-class feminists, legislative lobbying, and more projects to enfranchise women, as well as work in collaboration with North American feminist leaders. But the controversy over whether to support restricted or universal suffrage was a major obstacle to the passage of legislation. Several legislators were opposed to universal suffrage in particular, fearing that poor women would prefer the Socialist Party.[22] Other conservative leaders opposed women's suffrage as well.

Between 1917 and 1927 ten bills demanding suffrage were presented to the legislature. None was approved.[23] Nevertheless, the public strongly favored women's suffrage, and networking and lobbying by Puerto Rican and U.S. feminist leaders was fruitful. The U.S. National Women's Party lobbied the U.S. Congress, and after two bills were presented, the Committee on Territories and Island Possessions recommended universal suffrage for Puerto Rican women.[24] Before the law could be enacted, the Puerto Rican legislature approved a bill in 1929 that granted suffrage to literate women only. Labor leaders and feminists denounced the proposal, which would exclude most working-class women from the polls, as unjust and discriminatory. With the support of the Socialist Party, working-class women campaigned vigorously to denounce the discrimination. A bill demanding universal suffrage, submitted by Bolívar Pagán, the president of the Socialist Party, was finally approved in 1935.

From the perspective of the upper-class suffragists, who were educated and professionally trained, enfranchisement promised greater participation in public life and incorporation into the country's decision-making bodies. For working women, winning suffrage was a step in their struggle to overcome the terrible circumstances in which they lived. Women's participation in the elections was massive, but it was also evident that enfranchisement could not solve all of women's problems.[25] Nor did the election of women's representatives automatically help in the promotion of women's issues. For instance, the first woman legislator, María Luisa Arcelay, had not been involved in the feminist struggle and did not view the interests of women workers as a priority. Her economic interests in several needlework shops interfered with her consideration of the needs of women in the industry, and she failed to endorse universal suffrage for Puerto Rican women.[26]

Feminist activism did have an impact in other areas. Professional women struggled to gain recognition and empowerment for their professions. Nurses fought constantly—from the formation of the Association of Professional Nurses of Puerto Rico in 1916—for the creation of a Nurses' Examination Board. The board was finally instituted by law in 1930, despite stubborn opposition from the medical sector. Women teachers, who constituted 75 percent of all teachers by 1930 and were excluded from the school hierarchy because of their lack of voting rights, fought for access.[27]

WOMEN'S HEALTH

During the same period, health policies imposed by the United States had serious repercussions for Puerto Rican women.[28] Policies such as prohibition of midwives, population control, and experimentation with contraceptives were not designed to promote women's health but were a response to U.S. political and economic interests. In 1900 the Board of Health, composed mainly of members from the U.S. mainland, outlawed midwives as part of a policy to promote childbirth in hospitals. Although the board acknowledged that infant mortality was a problem, the president of the board said that "the improvement of these conditions will come very slowly and only by a universal raising of the standard of general intelligence" in Puerto Ricans.[29]

But the board's analysis of the problem proved entirely wrong. The majority of the population continued to use midwives for childbirth. By 1928, in fact, statistics showed that 80 percent of women were still using midwives.[30] But a policy developed by a feminist doctor, Marta Robert, proved that intelligence was not the problem. The legalization and training of midwives in 1930—despite the tenacious opposition of the medical establishment—so successfully reduced maternal-child mortality that even former opponents of the policy were willing to recognize its positive impact.[31]

Beginning in the mid-1920s politicians and other professionals promoted population control as a way to solve Puerto Rico's socioeconomic problems, even though other experts stated that "the island's economic imbalances . . . could not be attributed to [an] excess of population."[32] Supporters of population control sought to have

Puerto Rico exempted from the Comstock Act, a U.S. law that prohibited the discussion and distribution of information on sex education or birth control. The depression years of the 1930s aggravated the island's economic situation, and more attention was given to the issue of limiting population growth to reduce poverty. Several reports favored the development of a population control program endorsed by U.S. governors in Puerto Rico and by the directors of the public relief administration.[33]

The socioeconomic and physical health of the Puerto Rican population was not always the priority, however. Clarence J. Gamble of Procter and Gamble, a large U.S. pharmaceutical firm, supported the development of birth control clinics in Puerto Rico in direct violation of the Comstock Act. The firm's support of population control came in part from its desire to experiment with birth control technologies that were difficult to test in the United States but were viewed as suitable for Puerto Ricans, who were seen as an inferior race.[34]

In one of the most extensive experiments in population and birth control ever undertaken, Puerto Rican women became testing subjects for contraceptive foams, birth control pills, and suppositories. Sterilization also was so widely encouraged as a means of contraception that the U.S. demographer J. M. Stycos reported that 17.5 percent of Puerto Rican women of reproductive age had been sterilized by 1954. Studies in the 1980s showed that Puerto Rico has one of the highest rates of female sterilization in the world.[35]

WOMEN'S EMPLOYMENT IN PUERTO RICO AND THE REEMERGENCE OF FEMINISM

As the early U.S. involvement in Puerto Rico demonstrated, the issue of employment was crucial to women's pursuit of equal rights. Women's increased participation in manufacturing and their involvement in labor unions had a direct impact on the adoption of legislation on minimum wage, work schedules, industrial home work, and maternity leave.[36] Several bills were approved but, according to the Puerto Rican Bureau of Labor, owners of industries did not necessarily comply with the law. In turn, the government did not enforce it. In addition, two of the four bills approved had restrictions that made them unenforceable. For instance, the minimum salary law (1919) did not apply to the tobacco industry or to domestic work, the two sectors that employed the most women workers. The U.S. Supreme Court ruled the law unconstitutional. Paid maternity leave, adopted in 1942, was not only an important achievement, but it also demonstrated the importance given by the state to women's reproductive role. Nevertheless, the struggle, recognition, and approval of political and labor rights for women were definite signs of the changes taking place in Puerto Rican society.

Following the depression in the 1930s there was a decline in women's traditional forms of employment (e.g., agriculture, home needlework, and domestic service). In 1942 the Puerto Rican legislature approved an economic development program known as Operation Bootstrap to attract more U.S. capital to the island through tax exemptions and cheap labor. The program opened the way to rapid industrialization and to new occupations for men and women. Although women's participation in the paid labor force did not increase, and women remained in traditional occupations, their participation in the formal economy became more public. In moving from isolated factories or home workshops to jobs as clerical workers, administrative assistants, teachers, and public administrators, women became more visible.

One of the most comprehensive studies of women's economic participation since the initiation of Operation Bootstrap has pointed out that even though there was evidence of "limited improvement" in the quality of women's jobs and that job segregation continued, the "negative growth" of employment in Puerto Rico affected women less than it did men.[37] That is, women were less affected by declining rates of employment than men—a relevant issue when considering the impact that paid work has had on women,

particularly in breaking the men-as-breadwinner myth, as has been pointed out by anthropological research.[38]

It was not until the 1960s, however, that feminist issues were formally raised again in Puerto Rican society. In 1966 a group of professional women appeared before the Puerto Rican Civil Rights Commission to protest discrimination against women in general and women lawyers in particular. The commission opened the way for the legislature to initiate a formal investigation of the matter in 1969. A special legislative commission was established to do research and make recommendations in regard to "alleged cases of discrimination against women workers in different work areas." The commission recommended a broader and more specific investigation, which was conducted by the Puerto Rican Civil Rights Commission.[39]

Diverse sectors of professional women—lawyers, journalists, professors, and the Feminine Front of the Independence Party (the only women's group related to a political party at that time)—presented testimony to the commission. All denounced discrimination in regard to salaries, education, working conditions, family laws, and other areas. In 1972 the commission concluded its report, which became a pivotal starting point for other feminist demands regarding women's situation in Puerto Rico. The study concluded that "there is discrimination against women working outside the home and that discriminatory practices take the most subtle and deceiving forms." It also acknowledged that "legislation and constitutional rights are instruments that may help correct the situation, but they alone do not offer total solutions."[40]

As a result of this study, employment legislation was presented in three areas. First, in 1975 all restrictive and protective legislation—laws regarding physical requirements for a job, for example—was repealed. Such laws had scheduling demands and physical requirements that limited women's participation in salaried work and encouraged job segregation. Many employers used this legislation to avoid hiring women and having to comply with special regulations.

Puerto Rico   631

Second, in 1975 maternity benefits were extended to teachers, municipal employees, and people with adopted children, and women public employees were eligible to receive 75% of their salary during maternity leave. Third, reforms passed in 1985 prohibited sex discrimination in hiring. Some of these regulations were continually disregarded, however. In fact, discrimination against pregnant women is one of the most common grounds for complaints filed at the Anti-Discrimination Division of the Labor Department, which handles its cases in the lengthiest of bureaucratic styles.

DEMOGRAPHIC CHANGE: FAMILY, EMPLOYMENT, EDUCATION

Women's increased participation in the paid labor force was accompanied by great changes in their access to education and in their roles in family life. For instance, women's access to education has been increasing since the 1940s, when women began to surpass men in enrollment at the university level. By 1990 women constituted a record 60 percent of the students enrolled in postsecondary schools. Women received 64 percent of all college degrees awarded that year.[41] The educational background of employed women has also shown significant change, with more than half of employed women holding a university degree in 1990, in contrast with one-third of employed men.[42]

In spite of gender segregation and other kinds of discrimination, women's formal economic participation also influenced authority patterns in the family.[43] Government programs that supported the emigration of Puerto Ricans to the United States to reduce unemployment were partly responsible for changes in the family. Between 1950 and 1960 about 480,000 people had emigrated, and by 1980 the Puerto Rican population in the United States had reached 2 million.[44] By 1990 the figure had reached almost 3 million. Men were the first to migrate, leaving women in charge of the household in most cases. Puerto Ricans of both sexes faced tough living and working conditions in the United States because of discrimination against Hispanics. The current percentage of Puerto Rican women in the U.S. labor force is declining as the number of female heads of household is increasing.[45]

The structure of the family in Puerto Rico has undergone significant changes. Even though Catholics constitute the majority of the population, Puerto Rico has one of the highest divorce rates in the world. In 1978 the rate jumped 10 percent from the previous year to 44 divorces for every 100 marriages, a rate it maintained until 1987. The number of female heads of households increased to 20 percent of all Puerto Rican households in 1980. Women viewed divorce as an explicit way to protest authoritarian and patriarchal gender relationships in the family.[46]

But these changes in employment, access to formal education, and family structure did not give women real access and influence as policy makers. Women's absolute majority in educational, clerical, and health fields, as well as their growing participation in public administration, was not reflected by their representation in decision-making positions.

After universal suffrage was granted, feminist activism in Puerto Rico waned as it did in other countries. However, voting leagues were organized to sponsor female electoral participation, and women began to win positions in the municipal assemblies, as mayors, and in the legislature. Research shows that women voters made up 24 percent of all voters in 1960; in the 1980 and 1984 elections they made up 50 percent of the total.[47] There was not a similar increase in the election of women, however. At the local level, women's participation accounted for only 13.4 percent of municipal delegates and 4.6 percent of mayors from 1932 to 1984. In the legislative branch women held only 3.5 percent of the seats in the House of Representatives and 8.3 percent of the seats in the Senate from 1932 to 1988.[48]

Little is known of the specific issues and legislation presented or endorsed by women in government during these years. One group, made up of militant members of the Nationalist Party, were particularly active during the 1950s. Their fight for independence for Puerto Rico was a political commitment that broke with women's traditional role in politics. Several of these women were imprisoned because of repressive U.S. policies regarding pro-independence groups, but their testimonies and experiences are yet to be fully documented and studied.[49]

WOMEN'S ORGANIZATIONS

The Civil Rights Commission, which had a tremendous impact on fostering legislation for women, also stimulated the foundation of feminist organizations and the discussion of women's issues during the 1972 election campaign. In the mid-1960s, in conjunction with the anti–Vietnam War movement and the demand for civil rights, the feminists arose to combat a social reality that perpetuated and concealed a variety of modes of sex discrimination.

Like feminists in other countries, Puerto Rican feminist groups began to organize within and outside of political parties. The first independent feminist group was Mujer Intégrate Ahora (MIA, or Woman Integrate Now), started in 1972 by five professional women who had made presentations to the Puerto Rican Civil Rights Commission. MIA opened the way for the discussion of such topics as abortion, women in the media, sexism in education, discriminatory family laws, credit, lesbianism, and maternity leave.[50] In collaboration with the government women's commission and other feminist groups, MIA lobbied for a new family code in 1976. The organization folded in 1979 primarily because of pressure from politically oriented factions trying to impose their positions on feminist issues.

Influenced by the report of the Civil Rights Commission and by the coming 1972 elections, the Partido Popular Democrático promised to establish a government women's bureau. After winning the elections, the PPD passed Law 57, approved in 1973, which created the Commission for the Improvement of Women's Rights. The women's commission was linked to the party in power and attached to the governor's office and thus faced restrictions on the topics and strategies it could address. Nevertheless the commis-

sion was successful during its first years in promoting and lobbying for legislation, conducting research on sexism in education, developing alternative educational materials for elementary schools, and providing legal and general counseling to women who were victims of domestic violence, rape, and sexual harassment.

The boom in feminist activities continued through the 1970s. The Federación de Mujeres Puertorriqueñas (Puerto Rican Women's Federation) was originally constituted as a pluralistic, nonpartisan feminist organization. Even though different groups of women began to participate—professionals, workers, students—the federation survived only two years because of differences over its affiliation with the Socialist Party.

Other political parties, following the pattern started by Partido Independentista Puertorriqueño in 1971, organized women's groups. The PPD and the Partido Nuevo Progresista formed women's organizations, but their main concern was not feminist issues. Instead, these organizations sought to use women in such organizational tasks as raising money and working in the electoral process.

Other action groups and activities developed during the late 1970s were concerned with reviewing and rethinking women's historical participation in society. Thus began the rediscovery of the early feminists and their struggles. This research, conducted mainly by women, had some impact but still has not been fully incorporated into the general educational curriculum. On another front, several outreach organizations were founded to deal with the still unrecognized problem of violence against women.

More organizations, formed by middle-class professional women or through government or private institutions, arose during the 1980s. They included Taller Salud (Health Workshop), Organización de la Mujer Trabajadora (Organization of Women Workers), and Feministas en Marcha (Feminists on the March) and have dealt with such issues as health, violence against women, women in the media, and child care. They have also served as pressure groups to demand specific legislation for women. In 1985 the groups were united for these purposes under the Coordinadora de Organizaciones Feministas (Coordinator of Feminist Organizations). Organizations affiliated with educational institutions have focused on research, curriculum work, documentation, and such outreach activities as conferences, symposia, and congresses. Like other groups they have endorsed and lobbied for women's legislation. The groups include Centro de la Mujer (Women's Center), University of Puerto Rico, Aguadilla Campus; Centro de Investigación y Documentación de la Mujer (Women's Center for Research and Documentation), Interamerican University; Centro de Recursos y Servicios para la Mujer (Resources and Services Center for Women), University of Puerto Rico, Río Piedras Campus; and Proyecto de Estudios de la Mujer (Women's Studies Project), University of Puerto Rico, Cayey Campus.[51]

LEGISLATION FOR WOMEN

Since 1952 Puerto Rico has prohibited discrimination based on sex, but in practice this remains a "legal and judicial fiction."[52] Furthermore, almost all the legislation presented or approved concerning women's issues was promoted principally by the feminist movement and some women legislators.

Bills on women's issues have been presented and favored by women legislators from the main political parties.[53] From the family law reform legislation in 1976 to the law criminalizing domestic violence in 1989, the authors of the legislation have been women. Judging from legislative records, male legislators have endorsed women's issues without reservation; however, women legislators have cited tenacious opposition from men, particularly to bills dealing with sexual offenses. Men supported some of the bills because they had promised to do so during their campaigns and because they feared the impact of disgruntled female voters.

Most of the bills concerned with women were related to the family, employment, and sexual of-

fenses. In addition, laws that contradicted the equal-rights principle espoused by the Puerto Rican Bill of Rights—such as the old civil code regarding family laws—were revised.

The family law reform decisively improved women's position in the family by seeking equity in marriage. The reform provided for joint administration of assets accumulated after marriage; recognized both parents as having equal parental authority; eliminated the dowry; considered women and men equally responsible in choosing the domicile of the family; and allowed married women to enter into contractual agreements. Issues such as child support and a woman's use of her maiden name were also addressed in the reform. Although there was little opposition among legislators to the reform, its passage came through the efforts of feminist leaders, the Commission for the Improvement of Women's Rights, and the support and cooperation of Olga Cruz, a House representative at the time.

Violence against women was one of the main legislative concerns of women during the 1980s.[54] The problem has generated the most feminist activism in terms of legislation and public policy, particularly in regard to sexual harassment and domestic violence. The first official recognition of the problem came in 1976 when the Commission for the Improvement of Women's Rights and other support groups won funding for Centro de Ayuda a Víctimas de Violación (Victims' Rape Crisis Center) at the University of Puerto Rico's medical school. In 1982 the legislature approved funding for the Julia de Burgos Shelter for Battered Women.

Statistics continued to show a dramatic increase in the harassment and abuse of women, however. In 1986 about 75 percent of salaried women were victims of sexual harassment on the job, 60 percent of married women were victims of physical or emotional abuse by their husbands, and an average of 50 women died each year after being assaulted by their husbands. Through the persistence of women legislators and feminist lobbyists, the groundwork was laid for tougher legislation. And despite the initial opposition of several male legislators, two bills were passed. The first, sponsored by Sen. Velda González, prohibited sexual harassment on the job. The bill, introduced in 1985 but not approved until 1988, had been endorsed by the executive branch. But the House of Representatives introduced an alternate version that sought to minimize the employer's responsibility in sexual harassment cases and to grant the authority in deciding sexual harassment cases to the head of the Labor and Human Resources Department. The alternate bill also attempted to exempt members of the legislature from the prohibitions against sexual harassment. With the help of lobbying by the women's commission and several feminist groups, however, the original legislation was approved in 1988.

The second bill concerning sexual offenses was passed in 1989 to protect women from physical, emotional or sexual abuse by their spouses. It also established criminal sanctions for certain acts of domestic violence and encouraged the establishment of programs to aid victims and strategies to prevent domestic violence. It was only through the pressure of feminist groups and several women legislators, notably Rep. Zaida ("Cucusa") Hernandez and Sen. Velda González, that the legislation was approved.

Statistics show that the laws are being enforced. Nevertheless, the task of implementing the legislation fully—especially in regard to domestic violence—has been difficult because of the lack of trained personnel at police stations, in the courts, and in social services offices. Police officers, judges, and prosecutors must still be sensitized to the problems of marital abuse and violence.

Puerto Rican women have benefited from several U.S. laws that guarantee sex equity, even though the laws are not always fully enforced. The most conflicting legislation concerns the right to abortion because a majority of Puerto Rican legislators are opposed to abortion rights. Nevertheless, the legislature has not confronted federal legislation on this issue because it would mean raising the issue of Puerto Rico's colonial situation vis-à-vis the United States.

PROSPECTS

The political mobilization of a range of women's groups—labor, suffragist, professional, feminist, and so on—has been important in calling attention to the ways in which women have been kept in an inferior position in Puerto Rico. With the support of women legislators and activist groups, legislation has been passed to improve women's situation. Because almost all legislation related to women's issues has been presented by women legislators, it is clear that women need to achieve greater access to the legislature, as well as to other decision-making positions, even though their presence does not necessarily guarantee a commitment to women's issues.

The written law is not a guarantee that discrimination against women will be eliminated, but it is a basic instrument to study, promote, and use. So it is important to strengthen the belief that women's groups and organizations, feminist and nonfeminist alike, are essential for improving women's lives. Women's struggles throughout history have proved that organization is the most effective tool in attaining the most cherished goals. Suffrage for women, professional recognition, and legislative reforms were all achieved through militancy and collective commitment.

The eradication of sexism in all areas of education should become a priority. Sexism persists in the curriculum, in academia, in the classroom, and in the careers open to women. Because education is one of the fundamental sources of identity formation, a transformation of the educational system would help build a gender-balanced society.

Puerto Rican women's participation in the labor force as salaried workers has affected their gender ideology, raising their consciousness of discriminatory practices and empowering them to break the myth of the man as the exclusive breadwinner. This empowerment has been fundamental for the development of the feminist movement in Puerto Rico. But in a society of high consumerism and technological development it is important to insist that authentic social progress is much more than pseudo-economic prosperity. True development and democracy cannot exist where there is discrimination against women and an absence of political independence. Urgent issues are still to be addressed, including child care, access to credit for women, tax reform for women heads of household, and sexism in the media, as well as women's appointment to policy-making positions.

Puerto Rico's political subordination to the United States has created contradictory situations for women. It has facilitated oppressive and racist health policies, such as sterilization and experimentation with contraceptives. It has undermined possible alliances among feminists from different political parties.[55] But U.S. feminism also has advanced such issues as suffrage, abortion, and some educational equity policies, and it has demonstrated the importance of international solidarity among feminists.

Colonialism, as patriarchy, is rooted in domination and oppression. In this sense the authentic political freedom of Puerto Rico should be on the agenda of both Puerto Rican feminists and U.S. feminists. It would seem fruitful at this time to rethink possible issues of collaboration between North American and Puerto Rican feminists, just as more than 60 years ago the suffrage issue contributed to the attainment of justice for Puerto Rican women.[56]

NOTES

1. U.S. Department of Labor, *The Employment of Women in Puerto Rico* (Washington, D.C.: Government Printing Office, 1934); and Marcia Rivera, "The Development of Capitalism in Puerto Rico and the Incorporation of Women into Labor Force" in Edna Acosta Belén, ed., *The Puerto Rican Woman* (New York: Praeger, 1986), 1935.

2. Yamila Azize, *La mujer en la lucha* (Women in the struggle) (Puerto Rico: Editorial Cultural, 1985), chaps. 1–3. In an eloquent testimony made in June 1904, Josefa Pérez, a tobacco worker, questioned Ramón Romero Rosa, leader of the Free Federation of Workers: "If you lend your assistance to organize men workers, why not do the same with women?" *La Democracia*, 24 June 1904.

3. Union leader Prudencio Rivera Martínez captured this process succinctly: "Since it is impossible to totally impede women's access to the industry, we should adopt easy and practical resolutions to organize them in all of those centers where they are working and to impede as much as possible the increase in the number of women in the cigar industry in Puerto Rico. The unionized woman, together with us and trained by us, is nothing to fear, and should not be our enemy." Federación Libre de Trabajadores, *Actuaciones de la segunda y tercera asambleas regulares de las Uniones de Tabaqueros en Puerto Rico* (Proceedings of the second and third regular meetings of the Tobacco Workers Unions in Puerto Rico) (San Juan, 1914), 49. See also Igualdad Iglesias, *El oberismo en Puerto Rico* (The labor movement in Puerto Rico), 323–27. In 1908 the union directory of the Free Federation of Workers registered eight women's unions, representing about 500 unionized women. That same year three women figured among the directors of the Free Federation of Workers.

4. Azize, *La mujer en la lucha*, 61–78.

5. The resolution approved by the First Congress of Women Workers, held in September 1919, speaks for itself. In addition to their demand for the right to vote, the participants recorded their commitment to struggle to "give personality and international meaning to the Puerto Rican working woman and to interest her in the great struggle for the emancipation and the promotion of the labor that is realized in all parts of the world, to labor for the establishment of equal rights and privileges for women, as well as for men . . . and the enjoyment of suffrage and the self-determination of the people of Puerto Rico." Igualdad Iglesias, *La mujer obrera en las primeras décadas del siglo 20* (The working woman in the first decades of the 20th century) (Mimeographed).

6. Percent of increase was calculated by author. Data available in Marcia Rivera, "Incorporación de las mujeres al mercado de trabajo en el desarrollo del capitalismo" (Incorporation of women into the labor market in the development of capitalism), in *La mujer en la sociedad puertorriqueña* (San Juan: Huracán, 1980), 52.

7. Report of the Commissioner of Education, *Report of the Governor* (Puerto Rico, 1919), 378. Between 1898 and 1925 the illiteracy rate was reduced from 85 to 45.5 percent. Thousands who had been forbidden from attending school were admitted to the public school.

8. María del C. Baerga, "Hacia una reevaluación de la contribución femenina a la sociedad puertorriqueño: El caso de la industria de la aguja" (Toward a reevaluation of the contribution of women to Puerto Rican society: The case of the needlework industry), in Yamila Azize, ed., *La mujer en Puerto Rico* (San Juan: Huracán, 1987), 98. See also Lydia Milagros González, *Una puntada en el tiempo: La industria de la aguja en Puerto Rico, 1900–1929* (A stitch in time: The needlework industry in Puerto Rico, 1900–1929) (Puerto Rico: CIPAF, 1990).

9. *Informe anual del negociado del trabajo* (Annual report of the bureau of labor) (San Juan: Negociado del Trabajo, 1921), 18–19. The annual report of the Bureau

of Labor of 1920 revealed that 98 percent of those employed in needlework were home workers and that 30,000 to 40,000 women earned wages so low "that they did not even deserve to be called as such."

10. Ibid., 13.

11. Baerga, "Hacia una reevaluación," 108.

12. At the annual assembly of the Free Federation of Workers in 1908, three women delegates presented a motion mandating that the federation's legislative committee introduce a bill in the Puerto Rican Legislature that would concede women's right to vote. Federación Libre de los Trabajadores, *Procedimientos del sexto congreso de la FLT de Puerto Rico* (Proceedings of the sixth congress of the FLT of Puerto Rico) (San Juan: Federación Libre de Trabajadores, 1910), 151.

13. *Unión Obrera*, 7 February 1920.

14. "Proyecto de ley de canales sobre los derechos de la mujer" (A project of law of channels for women's rights), *Indice*, 13 September 1929, p. 84.

15. Ana Roqué de Duprey, Lola Rodríguez de Tió, Patria Tió Rodríguez, and Carmela Eulate are among the best-known feminist writers of late nineteenth century. See Azize, *La mujer en la lucha*, 15–30.

16. Ibid., chap. 4.

17. Indeed, seven of the first eight Puerto Rican women doctors—all graduates of U.S. universities—were noted leaders in the women's suffragist movement in Puerto Rico. Luis A. Avilés and Yamila Azize, "Los hechos desconocidos: Participación de la mujer en las profesiones de salud en Puerto Rico, 1900–1930" (Unknown facts: Women's participation in the health professions in Puerto Rico, 1900–1930), *Puerto Rico Health Science Journal* 9, no. 1 (April 1990): 13.

18. Isabel Andreu Aguilar, "Reseña histórica del movimiento sufragista en Puerto Rico" (Historical summary of the suffragist movement in Puerto Rico), in *Revista de la asociación de mujeres graduadas da la UPR* (Puerto Rico: Universidad de Puerto Rico, 1941), 33.

19. *El Mundo*, 3 September 1920. See also Azize, *La mujer en la lucha*, 180–82.

20. *El Mundo*, 6 January 1921.

21. Memorandum for the Chief, Bureau of Insular Affairs, Record Group 350, file 27260–4, box 1217, National Archives, Washington, D.C.

22. Azize, *La mujer en la lucha*, 110–53.

23. Ibid.

24. House of Representatives, *Confer the Right to Vote to Women of Puerto Rico*, 70th Cong., 1928, H. Rpt. 1895; Senate, *Conferring the Right to Vote upon Puerto Rican Women*, 70th Cong., 1929, S. Rpt. 1454.

25. *Porto Rico Progress*, 26 May 1932, 5.

26. Sonia Torres, "María Luisa Arcelay" (1984, Mimeographed).

27. Avilés and Azize, "Los hechos desconocidos," 11; and Nydia Marini, *The Role of Women Administrators in*

the History of Puerto Rican Education (Ph.D. diss., New York University, 1983).

28. Blanca Silvestrini, *The Impact of U.S. Public Health Policy in Puerto Rico: 1898–1913* (1982, Mimeographed), 9.

29. Ibid., 11.

30. Annete Ramírez de Arellano and Conrad Seipp, *Colonialism, Contraception and Catholicism in Puerto Rico: A History of Birth Control in Puerto Rico* (Chapel Hill: University of North Carolina Press, 1983), 57.

31. José Belaval, *Declinación da la mortalidad puerperal en Puerto Rico de 1933–1943* (The decline of mortality during childbirth in Puerto Rico from 1933–1943) (Puerto Rico: Puerto Rico Public Health Tropical Medicine School, 1945), 520–28.

32. Ramírez de Arellano and Seipp, *Colonialism, Contraception and Catholicism*, 26.

33. Ibid.

34. Ibid., 27.

35. A 1965 study found that one-third of women of reproductive age had been sterilized. The most recent statistics indicate that in 1982, 39 percent of women of reproductive age had been sterilized and that 30 percent of all births were done by caesarean. José L. Vásquez Calzada, *La población de P.R. y su trayectoria histórica* (The population of Puerto Rico and its historical trajectory) (Puerto Rico: José L. Vásquez Calzada, 1988).

36. Juan S. Bravo, *Leyes y organismos para la protección de la mujer en la industria* (Laws and organizations for the protection of women in industry) (San Juan: Departamento del Trabajo, 1944), 3–14.

37. Luz del Alba Acevedo, "Industrialization and Employment: Changes in the Pattern of Women's Work in Puerto Rico," *World Development* 18, no. 2 (1990): 231–55.

38. Helen Safa, "Women and Industrialization in the Caribbean," *Anales del Caribe* 7–8 (1987–88): 382–404.

39. Comisión Derechos Civiles, *La igualdad de derechos y oportunidades de la mujer puertorriqueña* (San Juan: Estado Libre Asociado, 1973), 1.

40. Ibid.

41. Marcia Rivera, "El proceso educativo en Puerto Rico y la reproducción de la subordinación femenina" (The educational process in Puerto Rico and the reproduction of female subordination), in Azize, ed., *La mujer en Puerto Rico*, 135.

42. Evelyn Otero, "Las mujeres en Puerto Rico" (Women in Puerto Rico) (1991, Mimeographed).

43. Safa, "Women and Industrialization," 402.

44. Palmira Ríos, "Women Under Colonialism: The Case of Puerto Rico," *TransAfrica Forum* (Summer 1983): 14.

45. Edna Acosta Belén, "Puerto Rican Women in Culture, History and Society" in Belén, ed., *Puerto Rican Woman*, 23.

46. Marya Muñoz and Erwin Fernández Bauzó, *El divorcio en la sociedad puertorriqueña* (Divorce in Puerto Rican society) (San Juan: Huracán, 1988).

47. Isabel Picó, "La mujer y la política puertorriqueña" (Women and Puerto Rican politics), Technical report to the National Foundation of the Sciences (Puerto Rico: Center for Social Research, University of Puerto Rico, 1983), 53–54.

48. Margarita Ostolaza Bey, *Política sexual en Puerto Rico* (Sexual politics in Puerto Rico) (San Juan: Huracán, 1989), 137–41.

49. María Agosto of North Adams State College in Massachusetts started research on this topic in February 1992.

50. Ana Irma Rivera Lassén, *La organización de las mujeres y las organizaciones feministas en Puerto Rico, 1930–1986* (The organization of women and feminist organizations in Puerto Rico, 1930–1986) (Mimeographed).

51. Ibid.

52. Ana Irma Rivera Lassén, *La ley no cambia la mujer, pero la mujer si cambia la ley* (The law does not change women, but women do change the law) (1991, Mimeographed).

53. Ostolaza Bey, *Política sexual en Puerto Rico*, 150.

54. Yamila Azize, "Cronología: La mujer y el cambia social en el Puerto Rico del siglo 20" (Chronology: Women and social change in 20th century Puerto Rico), in Azize, ed., *La mujer en Puerto Rico*, 40–47.

55. Ostolaza Bey, *Política sexual en Puerto Rico*, 153.

56. My gratitude to Margarita Benitez, chancellor of the University of Puerto Rico, Cayey Campus, for her support for this project; to Xaé Reyes and Lanny Thompson, who helped with the English translation; and to all the members of the Colectivo of PRO MUJER, Ana Raquel Collazo, Aixa León, Anabel Rodriguez, and Luisa Torres. My love and gratitude to Evelyn Otero and Luis Alberto Avilés, who provided excellent critiques and support.

▲ South Africa

POLITICS

Type of Political System: partial democracy
  Sovereignty: republic
  Executive-Legislative System: parliamentary
Type of State: unitary
Type of Party System: multiparty
Major Political Parties

African National Congress of South Africa (ANC): Nonracial, extraparliamentary national democratic movement. Unbanned in 1990.

Democratic Party: Liberal, white, middle-class party with representation in Parliament. Formed in 1989 by the merger of several smaller moderate parties; has experienced several splits.

Inkatha Freedom Party: Extraparliamentary centrist party that is Zulu-based.

Conservative Party: Official parliamentary opposition party; white and right-wing in orientation. Members tend to be working class. Opposes sharing power with blacks.

National Party: Ruling party; white. Moving from the right wing to the center under the leadership of F. W. de Klerk. Membership tends toward the middle class.

Pan African Congress of Azania: An extraparliamentary, Africanist national movement, unbanned in 1990. Believes that only armed force can end minority rule and seeks to unite all black South Africans.

South African Communist Party: Unbanned in 1990. Has often supported efforts of the ANC.

Year Women Granted Right to Vote: 1930/1983[a]
Year Women Granted Right to Stand for Election: 1930/1983
Percentage of Women in the Legislature
  Lower House: 3.5%
  Upper House: 2.8%

Percentage of Electorate Voting for Highest Elected Office in Most Recent Election (1989)[b]
  House of Assembly (white parliament): 69.5%
  House of Delegates (Asian parliament): 23.7%
  House of Representatives (coloured parliament): 20.1%

DEMOGRAPHICS

Population: 37,533,000[c]
Percentage of Population in Urban Areas
  Overall: 52.6%
  Female: 51.8%
  Male: 53.5%
Percentage of Population Below Age 15: 41.0%[d]
Birthrate (per 1,000 population): 32[e]
Maternal Mortality Rate (per 100,000 live births): 83
Infant Mortality Rate (per 1,000 live births): 71
Mortality Rate for Children Under Five (per 1,000 live births): 95
Average Household Size: 4.4
Mean Age at First Marriage: not available
Life Expectancy
  Female: 63.5
  Male: 57.5

EDUCATION

Ratio of Female to Male Enrollment[f]
  First-Level Education: 97
  Second-Level Education: 115
  Third-Level Education: not available
Literacy Rate
  Female: 57.0%
  Male: 57.0%

ECONOMY

Gross National Product per Capita: U.S. $2,010
Percentage of Labor Force in Agriculture: 28.0%

Distribution of Agricultural Workers by Sex[g]
Female: 27.0%
Male: 73.0%
Economically Active Population by Sex
Female: 26.7%
Male: 47.9%

a. In 1930 the right to vote and the right to stand for election were given to white women; in 1983 the rights were given to coloureds and Indians. All Africans are disenfranchised.

b. Carde Cooper, Colleen McCaul, Robin Hamilton, I. Delvare, J. Moonsamy, K. Mueller, *Race Relations*

Survey, 1989/90 (Johannesburg: South African Institute of Race Relations, 1990).

c. Laetitia Rispel and Graham Behr, *Health Indicators: Policy Implications*, Centre for Health Policy, Department of Community Health, University of Witwatersrand, Paper no. 27 (Johannesburg, June 1992).

d. Ibid.

e. Ibid.

f. Kate Truscott, *Gender in Education* (Johannesburg: National Education Policy Investigation, Gender in Education Sub-Group, June 1992).

g. Moira Macomachie, "Looking for Patterns of Women's Employment and Educational Achievements in the 1985 Census," *Agenda*, no. 5 (1989), 80–92.

Women in Politics Under Apartheid: A Challenge to the New South Africa

BARBARA KLUGMAN

Wathinth' abafazi, wathinth' imbhokoto, basopha uzokufa! (Now you have touched the women, you have struck a rock, you have dislodged a boulder, you will be crushed!) This is the anthem of the anti-apartheid women's struggle in South Africa, and it aptly reflects the role of the politically engaged women of South Africa.[1] Although women, on the whole, are not on the front lines of political activity, they have shown extraordinary tenacity in the face of continued oppression and poverty. In the words of an African woman whose relative was detained by the security police: "I feel that women in the township are very strong—the men in contrast are lazy and unreliable. I think that women become strong because they have to cope with so much—home, job, families and how to make the money last."[2]

In this chapter I discuss the ways in which South African women have been politically engaged, with particular focus on the 1980s, which marked the development of a radically new form of politics and of women's engagement—a period characterized by mobilization, organiza-

tion and repression. It stands distinct from the politics of the 1990s—the politics of transition.[3]

South Africa is known internationally as the country of apartheid—the system in which blacks are denied political, economic, and social freedom by a minority white ruling class. The population is legally divided into different "race groups," known as Asian (primarily people of Indian descent, 3 percent), African (the indigenous population prior to colonization, 75 percent), coloured (people of mixed-race origins, 9 percent), and white (primarily people of European descent, 13 percent).[4] The race groups have differential access to political power and to economic and social rights, and they are segregated in terms of housing settlement, land rights, and schooling. Even television programs are directed at different race groups. White South Africans control the political system and until 1982 were the only group eligible to vote or hold office. Under the 1982 constitution people defined as coloured and Asian were given the vote, but in parliaments separate from the white parliament. They could consider only issues of relevance to their "population group." This tricameral constitution was accompanied by legislation that set up so-called community councils in the African townships, which the township dwellers considered illegitimate. The constitution still denied Africans the vote and representation in any of the parliaments.

The official languages in South Africa are Afrikaans (a derivative of Dutch) and English, but Africans speak a range of indigenous languages. The Republic of South Africa officially consists of four provinces—the Transvaal, Natal, the Cape, and the Orange Free State—as well as ten "homelands" designated for the African population. These homelands cover a mere 13 percent of South Africa's territory but are meant to be occupied by 87 percent of the population. Four of these homelands were made "independent" by the South African government, which set them up with puppet leaders. They do not have international recognition, nor are they recognized by the majority of South Africans.

South Africa was originally inhabited by the nomadic Khoi and San peoples. Thereafter, Bantu-speaking peoples moved down from areas further north and settled in South Africa. The country experienced its first contact with the Dutch in 1652; British colonial rule began at the end of the eighteenth century. Its early colonial history set the stage for the formal imposition of apartheid in 1948, when the (White) National Party gained power. With colonization the native populations were forcibly removed from their land and compelled to seek employment on white farms or in cities as part of the growing industrial economy. Rural African women were prohibited from migrating with their men and were not allowed to settle permanently with their families in white areas, which led to the destruction of the social and economic life of precolonial African society. African women found employment mostly as domestic laborers in white homes and as such have remained the most exploited and oppressed women in the country.

With the start of National Party rule, apartheid laws became entrenched. The Group Areas Act ensured that African men and women who came to "white" towns lived in separate, adjacent townships. Coloured and Asian people were likewise forced to live separately. During the 1950s there were a number of forced removals of people within cities as nonracial areas were divided and black people were transported to townships outside the white cities. With apartheid came the imposition of the infamous Pass Laws, which required all Africans over the age of 16 to carry a pass when they ventured into white cities to work.

From the earliest period of colonization, the African population fought against white settlement and for the right to their land and citizenship. The National Party's coming to power provoked a major coordinated national protest through the 1950s, particularly around the Pass Laws. The central actors were the African National Congress (ANC), which, along with allied white, coloured, and Indian organizations, called for equality of all races in a united South Africa; the Pan African Congress (PAC), a black Africanist offshoot of the ANC; and the South African Communist Party (SACP), a mixed-race body with ties to the international communist movement. During the 1950s the ANC mobilized women through its Women's League, which with other anti-apartheid women's groups set up a broad federation called the Federation of South African Women (FEDSAW).[5]

The protests of all these organizations were met with brutal repression, including the massacre of 76 anti-pass protesters in Sharpeville in the Transvaal in 1961 and the banning of the ANC, PAC, and SACP. The popular anti-apartheid resistance collapsed.[6] Many people, both men and women, were jailed, including ANC leaders Nelson Mandela and Walter Sisulu, who were sentenced to life imprisonment. Many others were exiled, including well-known women leaders like Gertrude Shope, the head of the ANC Women's League, and Barbara Masekela, a member of the ANC National Executive Committee.[7]

In the 1970s political resistance resurfaced when African students, under the banner of the Black Consciousness movement, which called on black people to stand together and fight their white oppressors, protested the compulsory use of the Afrikaans language in their schools. These protests began a long struggle against inferior and inadequate schooling known as Bantu Education. They also resulted in the deaths of hundreds of people, beginning with a massacre in Soweto on 16 June 1976. Again, women students participated in the resistance. Other student initiatives to organize women into the Black Women's Federation and into a women's wing under the Black People's Convention were defeated with the 1977 banning of all the organizations involved in the uprising. By detaining people without trial, charging others, torturing many, and preventing any meetings from taking place, the iron rod of the apartheid government again smashed mass political protest.

People continued to struggle against the system in their own ways, in particular by defying the Pass Laws and moving to the cities to find work and, in the case of women, to join their husbands. There were also isolated community struggles around specific problems. On a national level, a few organizations that had not been banned continued to speak out against the system. Most notable of these were the National Union of South African Students, based on the campuses of white, liberal universities, which spawned some powerful women leaders over the years, and the Black Sash, an organization of middle-class white women formed in 1955 to protest the removal of mixed-race people from the voters' roll in the Western Cape—the step taken by the National Party to entrench minority rule.[8] Workers' strikes in Durban in 1973 heralded a process of rebuilding black working-class trade unions that had begun in the 1950s. It was the first hint of the period of political challenge that was to transform South Africa in the 1980s.

Although a new chapter of South African history is unfolding in the 1990s, this new history is the result of the political challenges of the 1980s that led the National Party government to agree to work toward developing a negotiated constitution.

In the early 1980s the face of South African politics changed. The National Party realized

that it could not continue with its racist policies and had to acknowledge that millions of black people had settled permanently in urban (white) areas. Yet the 1982 tricameral constitution offered only cosmetic changes to the system of apartheid. Anti-apartheid individuals of all races in South Africa started to mobilize against the legislation and implementation of this constitution, unleashing a national political protest largely under the umbrella of the United Democratic Front, which would affect politics for the remainder of the decade.

WOMEN'S POLITICAL ENGAGEMENT IN SOUTH AFRICA

It is a rather complex task to study the way in which women were politically engaged in this struggle during the 1980s because South Africa's history has created vast schisms among women. The wide disparity between rich and poor and the fundamentally different experiences of people legislated into "race groups"—into positions of domination and subordination—make it impossible to generalize about women in South Africa. Moreover, patterns of protest and anti-apartheid ideologies differ across regions, as does the makeup of the poor in terms of ethnic and religious interests. The right wing also differs regionally, and its response to protest has been more severe in some regions than in others.

Given this context of interweaving cleavages, I have decided to focus predominantly on the majority of women in South Africa—those who are poor and African. Although the most complex terrain of women's political struggles is perhaps the home, I have chosen to look at political struggle in organizational terms, thus limiting discussion to a definition of politics in terms of organized struggles of groups of people for power. I concentrate mainly on anti-apartheid activity, giving less moral weight to other political positions. In addition, I approach the question by focusing on a number of issues on which women engage politically: anti-apartheid politics, women's rights as workers, forced removals, Afrikaner nationalism, and women's representation in political parties. I use specific examples and therefore do not take account of regional diversity. Moreover, in seeking to describe the forms of women's political engagement, I mention successes more often than failures, and one should not assume that specific organizational descriptions can be generalized nationally.

It is too easy to give the impression that women are indeed substantially involved in the political process in South Africa. If this were an article on the nature of political participation generally in South Africa, women would barely be mentioned. *Who's Who in South African Politics*, for example, mentions only seven women among 122 entries.[9] Although this might reflect the bias of the author, it also reflects social reality. Patriarchal attitudes keep most women—across racial divisions—under the control of their fathers or husbands. Moreover, poor women tend to carry primary responsibility for providing for their children both materially and domestically, and they are left with little time and energy to be politically active. The interaction of gender, race, and class oppression means that most women are unable to challenge their situation.

In South Africa, then, the majority of women are engaged in a daily struggle for survival and have not participated in organizational politics. Forty-eight percent of working-age African women are not economically active, and 50 percent of adult African women are either divorced or widowed or have never married.[10] Women are locked into a struggle to obtain food and shelter, to educate their children, to cope with violence in their homes, and, in certain parts of South Africa, to protect themselves and their families from police or vigilante violence.

Women of all races and classes who do get involved in women's organizations tend to choose apolitical service groups, helping poorer people or working within their communities. In addition, there are a few, but significant, rural women's cooperatives: vegetable-growing groups, craft-making groups, or bulk-buying schemes. These sorts of initiatives give women the opportunity to take more control over their lives.

Few women's organizations in South Africa focus on women's rights, except for a number of middle-class, predominantly white organizations in the political center. For example, the Women's Legal Status Committee lobbies, particularly through the legal profession, to improve the legal status of women across racial lines, and it has played a significant role in influencing pro-women changes in South Africa's marriage and divorce laws. The Abortion Reform Action Group lobbies for reform of the abortion law. The National Council of Women, a white middle-class group, and the more conservative, predominantly white Women's Bureau both see their task as providing their members with information about women's rights. The Housewives League (white) and the Black Housewives League address consumer issues, which affect women most directly.

The most vocal of all women's organizations in South Africa, the Black Sash, was not specifically concerned with women's issues from its beginnings, however. As a political protest organization, it has focused on human rights questions—abolishing capital punishment, unbanning organizations, opposing detentions without trial and forced removals of blacks, and fighting the demolition of squatter camps. The members of the Black Sash have engaged racial politics by using their whiteness where it is most powerful—in challenging the white minority government by showing that not all whites support apartheid and by standing between African communities and members of the South African Defence Force or its puppet vigilantes, with the knowledge that their white skin protects them from attack.[11]

Although the Black Sash recognizes that women have specific problems and even employs an organizer to work with rural women, only at its 1990 national conference did its members agree to incorporate women's issues into its human rights focus. This came partly as the result of pressure from young white feminists who were frustrated at the lack of concern for women's rights in other anti-apartheid organizations and felt that the Black Sash would be receptive to their argument.

On the whole, the conservatism and deep patriarchal tradition among the majority of the population and the overriding concern with race oppression among most blacks meant that feminism passed South Africa by. Many black activist women were suspicious of it, and in the 1980s the view that "feminism goes hand in hand with capitalism and imperialism" was often voiced by black women who were involved in organizing other women against apartheid.[12] Feminism was understood in terms of European and North American women's demands for increasing independence from men and from being tied to the home. In South Africa, however, predominantly black organizations used motherhood as their rallying cry against injustice.[13] Indeed, a central concern was to end migrant labor and reunite families. Moreover, in the words of ANC leader Ruth Mompati, "How can women demand to leave the kitchen sink when they are struggling for the right to housing and indeed to have a kitchen sink?"[14] This powerful imagery of women's burden as mothers dominated the ideology of the anti-apartheid women's organizations throughout the 1980s, reflecting the major concerns of most women.

The European and North American feminist movement of the 1970s touched only those women, mostly white, who were students in the few liberal universities. While some of these women did become active in the United Democratic Front and trade unions, their feminist values and lifestyle marked them as different from most women; their approach to women's rights was not accepted into the mainstream national liberation ideology. Because most white activists were particularly sensitive to the need not to impose their value systems on the body politic, and few black women had access to feminist thinking, feminism thus remained within the terrain of personal politics on the white left, and no national feminist movement developed.

Feminism did, however, make one significant impact. It led to the establishment of the first rape crisis center in Cape Town in 1975, and a number of similar organizations sprang up during the 1980s. Using the services of volunteers and some paid employees, the Cape Town center offers a counseling service and housing to battered women and rape survivors. Although originally set up by white feminists, it now has members of all races and actively works with community-based organizations across racial lines to provide support services as well as workshops and training to fight violence against women.

On the whole, then, questions of women's rights have not been central political questions in South Africa, and women have not mobilized around them. Women in general are not active in women's rights groups or other political organizations. Rather, they are involved in their daily lives and in social groups that give them personal support. To the extent that women have been involved in political activity, it has been in anti-apartheid politics (or pro-apartheid politics) rather than women's rights.

ORGANIZING AGAINST APARTHEID

During the early 1980s many people of all races banded together to take up local problems and political issues arising out of the 1982 constitution and apartheid in general. In 1983 these local-level organizations united under the banner of the United Democratic Front (UDF), which sought a nonracial, democratic, united South Africa (without homelands) based on the principles of the Freedom Charter, a document written at the ANC's Congress of the People in 1955.[15] The UDF was not a political party; it was a form of political organization very different from anything before it, primarily because it focused on the development of grass-roots organizations and a system of participatory democracy in which representatives of the member organizations met regularly to plan strategies and work out national campaigns.

The campaign slogans of the UDF were "From mobilization to organization" and "Organizing for people's power"—themes that emphasized the desire to get as many people as possible involved in the struggle. The people's power theme caused outrage in the government. The UDF publicly acknowledged its intention to make it impossible for apartheid structures to function, and in some places it set up alternative systems of local government based on the concept of participatory democracy. The assumption underlying the UDF was that the struggle could only be won through the participation of people at the grass-roots level. This approach held that people develop confidence and political skills by taking up issues that are of immediate concern to them in a collective manner. As a result, UDF affiliates developed by focusing on local issues of concern to their particular constituencies.

The membership of the UDF included residents' associations (known as civics), regionally based women's organizations, youth groups united under the South African Youth Congress, student groups, political groups like the Release Mandela Committee, and human rights anti-repression groups like the Detainees Parents' Support Committee. The UDF incorporated people of all race classifications, another trait that made it different from previous organizations. Some organizations in the UDF were racially mixed, such as the Detainees Parents' Support Committee, which gave assistance to detainees of all races and their families. Other organizations, such as the Federation of Transvaal Women, were organized with a branch structure. Because of the separation of races through the Group Areas Act, most members of each branch were of one race classification, but regional meetings did bring members together across racial lines.

There was a strong ideological push to build nonracialism to prove in practice that the majority of South Africans did not want an ethnically based political system.[16] This was not always easy. White people tended to have more resources in terms of education and confidence, as well as practical advantages like owning cars. In most cases whites felt privileged to be allowed to participate in this political movement after their exclusion from participation during the Black Consciousness era. A fairly strong practice developed in which white activists took care not to dominate meetings and to be circumspect about their input because their experience was very dif-

ferent from that of most other people in the UDF. But their involvement was not always unproblematic. Tensions arose most notably among people of a similar class background, with an anti-white sentiment surfacing among middle-class black activists. On the whole, poor black people tended to be amazed and delighted by the fact that some, albeit few, white people were on the side of the majority, though they, too, expected these white activists to adjust their behavior and approach to fit the majority view. This applied both in women's organizations and in other UDF affiliates. There was little discussion about difference and little sharing about how it felt to be black or white or rich or poor, let alone male or female.

One particularly interesting dynamic developed, which I have called the "honorary man" syndrome. The vast majority of white activists, aside from students, were middle-class, university-educated, single women, probably because, in part, they were less driven to enter into the career trajectory and felt more able to work outside the white establishment and because thousands of anti-apartheid white men left South Africa to avoid compulsory conscription into the army. The majority of black activists were men, because patriarchal attitudes discouraged women's participation. As a result, white women often found themselves working with groups of black men. In this context, they were often treated as honorary men—that is, men found it easier to act as if these women were asexual because the white women's independence from men and from family ties, their ability to make decisions as they pleased and to move around at night, and so on were completely alien to the men. Yet sexual relationships inevitably developed, some of which were lasting but many of which were fleeting, leading the wives of the men concerned to feel threatened and angry toward those women.[17] This type of situation, however, was largely confined to a few cities.

Women were involved in all of the UDF affiliates, but (except in women's organizations) they tended to be active only at the grass-roots level and seldom held positions in the leadership. In the movement to set up civics in black townships, for example, women would be found knocking on doors, persuading neighbors to join, and mobilizing householders (especially other women) for local protests, such as those against high rents. But the power of patriarchy meant that these women did not get elected to the civics' leadership. (On the whole, women themselves did not support women who were nominated.) As a result, though many competent women organizers developed, women had little education, little experience in strategy, and little confidence to speak publicly, let alone in English (the common language). In addition, many women shied away from leadership because of the burden of their domestic responsibilities.

Women were also active in UDF organizations that were specifically organized around women's issues. The regionally based women's organizations in the UDF included the United Women's Organization (which later became the United Women's Congress in the Western Cape), the Federation of Transvaal Women, the Natal Organization of Women, and the Port Elizabeth Women's Organization. All of these groups aimed to incorporate women into the antiapartheid struggle. Prominent among them was the United Women's Organization (UWO), which was started in 1979 by eight African women who lived in a township of Cape Town called Guguletu. They had been involved in the Federation of South African Women in the 1950s and felt that they could mobilize women by setting up a women-only organization. They knew that mixed-sex organizations did not promote women's involvement and leadership. In keeping with the ideology of nonracialism, over time they endeavored to get women of all races involved. They did this by creating branches in different parts of Cape Town and by drawing the women together to plan and run campaigns and to take part in educational events. Members of the UWO Executive Committee described their activities as follows:

In 1982 we chose two themes for the year— "Childcare" and "High prices." On child care, each branch investigated ways of taking up the issue. We

started play groups, and organized around International Children's Day and the United Nations Declaration of Children's Rights. . . .

We held a mass meeting around the issue of high prices and especially the cost of bread. There was a resolution not to buy bread for a week. We also had plays and a procession. . . .

At the end of January in 1984 we . . . agreed to concentrate on drawing working women and church women into the UWO. Also the threat of removal to Khayelitsha [a township far on the outskirts of Cape Town where many African squatters were forced to move] is being taken up in the UDF area committees. The organizations involved in this campaign are the UWO, Cape Youth Congress and the Civic, because the issue affects everyone and we must fight it together.[18]

These kinds of activities typify those of the women's organizations affiliated with the UDF. They focused on mobilizing women around issues of immediate concern to them. Aside from the question of child care, these issues were related to socioeconomic problems and political rights rather than to the oppression of women.

In general the women's organizations were not particularly powerful in the UDF, and their leadership was not taken very seriously by the UDF leadership as a whole. This was partly because of women's lack of experience in developing political confidence and action strategies, but it was mostly because of male arrogance. In fact, the one exception of all the regional women's organizations was the UWO because, unlike the other women's affiliates, the UWO had existed long before the UDF, and the UWO women played a major part in planning and setting up the UDF in Cape Town. As the UWO Executive Committee put it, "Having the experience of how to structure and run the UWO, we have had a lot to contribute to the UDF. When it started, the UWO was the most high profile political organization in Cape Town. So the men would come to us and ask what they could do. Our history has been a big factor in causing a strong relationship between us and other organizations. It has given women's organization a legitimacy."[19]

Probably because of the length of its existence

and the recognition of its leadership by the UDF, the UWO was also the most successful of the UDF women's organizations in training women in organizational and leadership skills. Most of the women in leadership positions in other UDF affiliates in the Western Cape were originally "trained" in the UWO. Women's organizations of the UDF in other regions were just finding their feet when in July 1985 the National Party government cracked down on the popular uprising that the UDF had consolidated.

THE POLITICS OF WOMEN'S ALLIANCES

Under the state of emergency declared by the government in July 1985, the UDF and a number of its affiliates were "restricted," meaning that the organizations were banned from any organized activity. The Congress of South African Trade Unions (COSATU) was also restricted from political activity. The press was not allowed to report activities of the police or army, restricted organizations were not permitted to hold meetings or carry out any other activities, and the government sought to destroy the entire fabric of the UDF by detaining successive levels of leadership—from national UDF leaders to ordinary members of grass-roots organizations. June Mlangeni, an activist in the Federation of Transvaal Women and wife of Andrew Mlangeni, who was serving a life sentence along with Nelson Mandela, described the situation as follows:

This way of life which forces us to live like caged animals in our own homes is called a State of Emergency. As women we have to put up with our homes being raided by strangers. We constantly wait for the knock on the door at ungodly hours, that knock which will take yet another child.

We sit in our homes day after day wondering what is happening to our children who are in prison and those who live as moles underground because they must continue with our struggle. The effect of this type of worry causes the worst heartbreak any person can endure.

At another level, women, like all other sectors in our country, face exactly the same forms of repression meted out by the government; women are detained and kept away from their families for months on end.

At home their absence as mothers creates problems for the family and the daughters who are detained create worry because of the constant fear that they may be raped or killed by the police. The fear that other children may be accused by a legal system which protects the rights of a minority is always there. . . . Do you know . . . this government has robbed us of everything we hold dear.[20]

From the night of the declaration government forces detained thousands of activists, holding them without trial, some for weeks, some for years. Others were questioned, tortured, and tried for a range of acts that were construed as endangering the state. The most well known of these trials concerned members of the national leadership of the UDF who were accused of treason but were found not guilty four years later—thus effectively removing them from leadership for that time. Many women were immobilized by having to leave their homes and hide, and of about 52,000 people detained over three years, 12 percent were women.[21]

Most organizations worked in an underground manner. The Executive Committee of the Federation of Transvaal Women, for example, had to search for sympathetic but uninvolved people to offer their homes for meetings and for housing people on the run. One could not use telephones or cars that were owned by activists or use familiar venues for meetings. The net result was that political activity became a dangerous and frightening business, and organizations floundered, including those of women.

At the same time, anti-apartheid organizations not in the UDF rallied around the crisis. Between 1986 and 1989 an increasing number of organizations started to work in alliances against the emergency specifically and apartheid generally. This loose interaction of groups became known as the Mass Democratic movement (MDM), which united across ideological differences and racial lines to challenge the legitimacy of the ruling National Party and the entire system of government at both the national and local levels. It had at its core COSATU, the UDF, and the South African Council of Churches (SACC), which took on a very public political role when the emergency started.

In addition to the broad MDM, a number of specific alliances developed. One of the early women's alliances was the "Free the Children" campaign initiated by the Black Sash, which drew together human rights organizations and individuals to protest the detention of children. The campaign also included groups with specific interests, such as children's welfare, medical ethics, and law. Although it was not specifically a women's campaign, the majority of participants were women, again across racial lines. One aspect of the campaign was to encourage people who were opposed to the detention of children to send Christmas cards about the detentions to the president of South Africa. Cards were sent from all over the world, and the international pressure on the government and the embarrassment it suffered contributed substantially to the rapid release of many of the children who had been detained.

In 1989 an alliance specifically of women's organizations, Women Against Repression (WAR), was set up in Johannesburg on the initiative of the Federation of Transvaal Women. Its aim was to publicize repression and put pressure on the government to lift the state of emergency. The alliance, like others within the MDM, was known as a "single-issue" alliance—it made no attempt to get agreement of all participants on political solutions, only on the problem of repression. The participants included women's organizations from a range of political positions.[22] For some groups, like Women for Peace and the National Council of Women, contact with the MDM on the question of repression was a step into new political territory, a definite shift into taking a stand on human rights because of the extent and horror of government repression under the state of emergency.

On a practical level, WAR organized workshops that brought together members of its organizations to discuss and debate the escalating violence and what to do about it, and they produced a memorandum demanding responsible policing in a context of increasing township violence and accusations of police bias. In 1990 they went to the executive capital of South Africa, Pretoria, and met with the minister of law and order, Adriaan Vlok, to put forward these demands.

The enormous amount of time WAR spent talking about what was happening in the country created a forum in which all the organizations could share their experiences and debate their interpretations of the events. In particular, given that the press could not report any activities of the police and army, the WAR forum allowed white participants to get firsthand information about what was happening in the black townships. Moreover, as the violence escalated and the government accused UDF supporters of creating the violence, WAR offered the opportunity for debate across ideological positions about self-defense and about strategies for ending the emergency and bringing about peace. This approach was not without its difficulties. Overall, however, the alliance was successful both in publicizing the nature of the repression and in opening up space for people with different views to share them and to find some points of consensus even under such strained conditions.

There is little doubt that WAR was maintained by the shared horror of the violence and the recognition on all sides that women were having to hold together the social fabric and their family lives in the face of a war that was not of their making. For African women, WAR provided an opportunity to talk face to face with women from the oppressor group, and one theme repeatedly surfaced, expressed here by Albertina Sisulu, a patron of the UDF and a leading activist in the development of women's organization in the 1980s: "I have been talking to people in the white suburbs. Some of them don't know what is happening in our townships. Some white women shake their heads and whisper to each other, 'Is she telling the truth?' My approach to the white sisters is, 'Our children are dying in the townships, killed by your children. You are mothers, why do you allow your children to go to train for the army? There is no country that has declared war on South Africa. Do you want your children to come and kill our children?' Because this is what is happening. How can they, as mothers, tolerate this? Why don't they support us?"[23]

As a result of these kinds of initiatives, the pressure remained on the government. This form of politics was basically concerned with creating public awareness of issues and lobbying those in power, however. It did not overcome the obstacles set by the emergency to organizing people at a grass-roots level.

FEDERATION OF SOUTH AFRICAN WOMEN

The most effective of the women's alliances was again in the Western Cape, doubtless because of the relative strength there of the UWO, the number of trained women leaders it had developed (which meant that the detention of a few did not destroy the organization), and because the state of emergency was not as severely implemented in the Western Cape as in other parts of the country. By 1986 the UWO had united with a similar but predominantly African group, the Women's Front, to form the United Women's Congress. The UWCO set about forming an alliance of women's groups in the Western Cape; it came together in the second half of the 1980s as the Federation of South African Women (FEDSAW)— the name of a similar alliance formed in the 1950s that had been inactive since the early 1960s. It included the same mix of organizations as WAR but was broader, drawing in women from rape crisis centers as well as from local conservative women's groups. FEDSAW, unlike WAR, focused on mobilizing women around women's issues in addition to issues of general political concern.

The main aim of FEDSAW was to draw women together around specific events like cultural festivals that focused on women's issues. A conference in August 1989 aimed at exploring what problems women faced and what women could do about them.[24] It explored topics that included work and unemployment, housing, health, education, children and the family, violence against women, culture and the media, repression, and religion. About 300 women, including those from farming areas, came together from 40 different organizations. Perhaps most significantly, the conference incorporated women who had not been active within the MDM, such as women from independent churches, rotating credit associations, and the Taverners (an organization of women who run home-based bars, known as *shebeens*).

The FEDSAW leadership in 1990 decided to organize marches to draw attention to the problem of violence against women, particularly rape and assault. This focus arose in part out of the participation of women from rape crisis centers and their ability to build enthusiasm for taking up this typically feminist issue. Members of FEDSAW distributed pamphlets in the areas where the marches were to happen, and on 30 November 1990, eight nighttime marches were held in different parts of the Western Cape, in both city centers and black townships, calling on women to "take back the night." The size of the marches ranged from 100 to 2,000 women.[25]

With regard to women's rights, FEDSAW can claim two specific achievements. First, it brought together women from a broad spectrum of political opinions and interests and contributed to breaking down the mistrust that exists between feminist and more politically oriented women and also between liberal and left-wing women. Again, this was achieved in part because the forming of an alliance around one issue, in this case women's rights, allowed people who were broadly anti-apartheid but had different ideologies and organizational experiences to act jointly on an issue of shared concern without having to resolve questions of a national political nature that might have destroyed the alliance.

The federation also made a contribution toward training women in leadership by, for example, showing women how to facilitate groups so that they could run the conference workshops— no mean task when workshops are run in three languages simultaneously (Afrikaans, English, and Xhosa). It followed the UWCO system of placing two people in each executive position, with one having explicit responsibility to help train the other, thus giving women practical experience and support in organizational and leadership skills.

It is these "traditions" from UWCO and their influence on FEDSAW and MDM politics generally that have created a situation in which the Western Cape can boast more participation by women in anti-apartheid politics than any of the other areas of South Africa, as well as more consciousness among anti-apartheid activists about women's specific problems and needs.

Members of FEDSAW also participated in campaigns with men and women from other MDM organizations. These campaigns included giving support to detainees during a national hunger strike in 1989. Aided by pressure from the international community, this action led to the release of hundreds of detainees. The other significant campaign was the defiance campaign that challenged the existence of racially segregated "separate amenities" like hospitals and schools. This national campaign, in which FEDSAW was again one of many participating MDM organizations, involved black people arriving en masse at hospitals designated for white people. Again, the publicity embarrassed the government, which agreed to desegregate hospitals and to move toward resolving the education crisis.

These campaigns were the nails in the coffin of apartheid. They showed the government that even from inside the jails and under a state of emergency people would not tolerate repression and disenfranchisement any longer. On 2 February 1990, President F. W. de Klerk announced the unbanning of the African National Congress, the South African Communist Party, and the Pan African Congress, and his willingness to negotiate with all the people of South Africa for a new constitution. This announcement inaugurated a new form of politics and a new era in South Africa's history, cautiously termed "transition." The campaigns of the UDF and the MDM and their tenacity under severe repression, coupled with the economic impact of international sanctions, were certainly the major factors forcing the government to move toward negotiations. Although women were not the major public figures in this campaign, they did make an important contribu-

tion in grass-roots organizations and in public campaigns toward a process of ending minority rule in South Africa.

ORGANIZING FOR WORKERS' RIGHTS

Although direct action against apartheid by an increasing number of women was a feature of the 1980s, direct action by women in support of their own needs was evident in a number of organizations as well. Women's issues and organizations have increasingly been taken seriously by trade unions and, in particular, by the Congress of South African Trade Unions (COSATU), which is a socialist-oriented federation of trade unions committed to the principle of nonracialism (though it still has a predominantly black membership).

In the early 1980s the Commercial, Catering, and Allied Workers Union (CCAWUSA), an affiliate of COSATU, began to fight for maternity rights for working women. This service industry has mostly women employees, and the members of the union are mostly black women. A few men organizers are also committed to maternity rights, and with women members and organizers they have won a number of agreements in negotiations with the management of chain stores, guaranteeing women the right to keep their jobs after maternity leave.[26] The first company to make such an agreement thought that doing so would contribute to its image as a business that took its social responsibility seriously. After one company had agreed, other companies felt pressure to concede.

The decision to negotiate for maternity rights was unprecedented, and few unions believed CCAWUSA would be successful. Most men in the other trade unions did not consider the demand for maternity rights a high priority. But after CCAWUSA's success, women in various other unions raised the question of maternity rights when workers discussed what they wanted to take to the annual union negotiations. Slowly, more unions took on the challenge, and by the late 1980s all unions included maternity rights as a basic demand in their negotiations, and some were winning paid leave, too.

During the 1980s a number of other issues were taken up, including protection against hazardous working conditions for pregnant women and sexual harassment at work, as well as demands for equal pay for work of equal value.[27] These issues have been addressed primarily by women organizers committed to women's rights. In some unions women have managed to win the support of their male counterparts by the moral strength of their arguments, but it is still an uphill battle. An underlying problem for women workers is that the law does not support their demands, so they have very little recourse in the courts.

Another issue that women in the unions have taken up is child care, and COSATU declared 20 September 1990 National Day of Action Around Child Care as part of its National Child Care Campaign. Workers took their children to work to make employers aware of the lack of child care facilities and to demand that both employers and the state take more responsibility. Interestingly, many workers argued that the campaign had another target: men. One shop steward, Templeton Namdo, said, "I think that today's action will lead men to be more interested in our kids in the future. As men we don't know how to raise children. We have a lot to learn." Another shop steward, Patrick Khumalo, added, "Men have realized that child care is also their responsibility. . . . Our struggle is not just with the bosses. It is also about changing backward attitudes in the home."[28]

Since the mid-1980s women in the unions have begun to set up separate women's forums to discuss issues of concern to women—primarily work and union dynamics. There has been much hostility from men to this move, however. Fortunately, certain unions have insisted that separate meetings are necessary in order for women to build their confidence and their ability to take up general worker issues in union meetings on the one hand, and on the other hand to give women the opportunity to discuss issues of particular concern to themselves and then to raise these issues within the unions as a whole. There is no doubt that these women's forums, even though some men have continued to challenge them, have been central to raising the consciousness of both women and men about women's rights, and to the development of women with organizational experience and leadership skills. In 1990 COSATU passed a number of resolutions on women, including a resolution to build women's leadership within the unions, that served to consolidate women's position.[29] Nevertheless, discussion of women's issues still causes a snicker among most men and many women still complain bitterly of sexual harassment by male unionists.

In the mid-1980s some UDF women's organizations felt threatened by the proposal to build women's forums and a national women's coordinating structure within the unions. This was articulated in terms of a broader debate about the relationship between the workers' struggle (presumed to be left wing and committed to socialism) and the national struggle (which incorporated both middle-class and working-class people and was primarily concerned with political rights). The conflict reflected unarticulated anxieties that the trade union movement would be sold out by, or would sell out, community-based politics. The disunity caused by these tensions contributed to undermining women's organizing efforts at a time when union women, who were not as affected by the repression of the state of emergency and who had more organizational experience, could have joined forces with community-based women's organizations to form a national women's movement.[30]

FORCED REMOVALS

Although the UDF affiliates and the organizations within the MDM have included women, and some have focused on organizing women, they are largely urban organizations. Likewise, the trade unions, while reaching out to many towns beyond the major city centers, nevertheless remain primarily urban. Moreover, they organize people who are in some ways a class above the majority because they have jobs in the formal sector. The majority of South African women, however, are

African women living in rural areas. They have barely been touched by the massive political advances of the 1980s.[31]

The system of apartheid has trapped rural African women in a situation in which they have very little infrastructure in terms of access to resources like water and fuel or to services like clinics and schools for their children, let alone access to employment. Moreover, African women are subject not only to the impact of apartheid but also, and arguably more seriously, to a tremendously conservative patriarchy. They are permanently subject to men; in the words of Lydia Kompe, a rural African woman who has played a major part in organizing rural women in the Transvaal, "Women in the rural areas experience a triple oppression—by their husbands, by their sons and by the traditional society."[32]

Land rights, housing rights, and family decisions ultimately belong to men. Lydia Kompe speaks of the frustration of women who, having cultivated food, must cope with their husbands' deciding how that food should be used. Another example of the effect of patriarchal relations is described by Thabi Masia, an African woman involved in supporting rural women's cooperatives.[33] It is the duty of women to gather water in the villages; thus even if a woman has just given birth, she must fetch the water because fetching water is women's work. The men of the household will not even consider doing it. In many ways, it is their gender, rather than class or race, that makes the lives of women so hard.

The contradictions between race and gender oppression can be clearly seen in the struggle of the Mogopa people against forced removal from their land. For more than 70 years, about 500 families of the Bakwena ba Mogopa people lived on two fertile farms in the Western Transvaal on land that belonged to the community.[34] Women, who were responsible for most of the farm work, only had access to the land of their fathers, husbands, or sons. They could not inherit land.

In October 1981 it became clear that the government had decided to remove the Mogopa people because their land was a "black spot" in an area designated white. In 1983 the government began the removal, knocking down the school, churches, and the medical clinic when the families refused to move.[35] The bus service was stopped, and the water pumps were removed. The people were issued a "removal order" stating that they had to leave Mogopa within ten days or be forcibly removed.

On 14 February 1984, the government proceeded with the removal even though the "petition for leave to appeal" was before the Appeal Court, the highest court in the land. The removal came without warning. The area was cordoned off, phone service was cut, and the police moved in. In one day, the remaining families were moved. In September 1985 the Appeal Court found that the removal was illegal, yet the Mogopa people could not return to their land because in the interim the government had expropriated the two farms.

Throughout this period, the people returned on occasion to maintain the graves of their ancestors at Mogopa. Slowly they started to resettle there under the guise of maintaining the graves. They were charged with trespassing and once again appealed to the Court. In August 1990, in an unprecedented move, the judge said that in keeping with the new political era, the situation should be negotiated, and he gave the two sides until November 1990 to resolve the problem. The representative of the relevant government ministry agreed to do so and said that he was prepared to consider restoring their title deeds. In the meantime, the people continued to return illegally to Mogopa, and on 14 February 1991, although they did not have any legal right to do so, they celebrated their return to their land.

The story of the removal of the Bakwena ba Mogopa people is typical—3.5 million people in South Africa have been removed—except that in the Mogopa case the people's tenacity was successful. But one significant and unusual aspect of this story is the way it had an impact on the position of women in the community.[36] As with most rural communities, women in Mogopa had no political power whatsoever. Decisions were made by adult men in a forum known as the *kgotla*, which was responsible for such matters as allocating land, resolving petty disputes, and meting out punishment. Women were not allowed to attend *kgotla* meetings unless called upon to give evidence, and even then they could only speak when spoken to, kneeling as a sign of respect for the men. But when the community was faced with removal, it was the women who were at the front line because most men were away, working as migrant laborers in cities.

As in many similar cases, the women reacted to white government officials in a vocal and aggressive way, not at all in keeping with their "traditional" roles. Their openly confrontational style was both a strategy and an emotional response to the crisis. The women in Mogopa dug open graves and warned officials that their dead bodies would have to be thrown into the graves before they would agree to be moved. Often, after facing "hysterical," angry women, the officials gratefully dealt with male representatives of the community, who presented themselves as reasonable and compromising negotiators. Although the women's responses were based on real fear and anger during the crisis, both they and the men recognized the strategic value of these different approaches. Because their material well-being was more directly affected than that of men, who had made alternative homes in the cities, women were more likely to defy government orders in the face of serious danger.

Given this situation, it was ridiculous for the *kgotla* to meet and discuss strategies for the community's survival without having women present to inform the men about what had happened in their absence. In Mogopa, it was the intervention of fieldworkers like Lydia Kompe, who pointed out the absurdity of relying on indirect reports from women, that persuaded the kgotla to allow women to be present. At the moment, the kgotla has been expanded to include five women (in addition to the twelve men), but many of the older men see this as a temporary arrangement necessary to deal with the crisis. It is unlikely, however, that the men will be able to reestablish the old order, as women's access to this power has boosted their self-confidence and expectations.

As this example demonstrates, the relationship between property rights and power is very close and has a major impact on African women's position in rural areas. In most places women are landless and powerless, and in the very few areas where women do own land their ability to engage politically seems to be curtailed more by their own lack of confidence and acceptance of "tradition" than by men. This is reflected in a comment by a 61-year-old woman landowner: "Women have two lives—old and new. In Soweto, women have a different life. Here in Driefontein, the old life is strong and men look after all the problems. . . . Women here are not educated and we live in the old times. . . . Women feel they have no right to speak when men are talking."[37]

In a significant step, in May 1990 rural African women's groups in the Transvaal, whose membership includes many women who have struggled against forced removals, formed the Rural Women's movement. The movement's aim is to empower rural African women, specifically, so as to ensure that their voices are heard in the debate on a new constitution. They plan to organize discussion groups and to teach rural women how to lobby on issues of concern to them.

AFRIKANER NATIONALISM

While oppressed women were increasingly involved in anti-apartheid struggles throughout the 1980s, the right wing did not go unaffected by this surge in political activity. A range of women's organizations support the cause of Afrikaner nationalism, such as the Suid-Afrikaanse Vroue Vederasie (South African Women's Federation) and the Suid-Afrikaanse Landbou Unie (South African Agricultural Union). These organizations can be understood as backup groups for the ruling National Party. Although their activities reflect an attempt to respond to women's immediate interests, by talking about their roles as mothers, for example, their overarching intent is to bring women into the broader Afrikaner Nationalist movement[38]—a role very similar to that undertaken by the UDF women's organizations on the left. They appear to be fairly successful, because there has been no mass movement of

Afrikaner women distancing themselves from the ideology and practices of the right wing.[39]

The far right wing, as reflected in the Conservative Party, the official opposition in the white parliament, and the Afrikaner Weerstandsbeweging (AWB, or Afrikaner Resistance movement), a paramilitary movement, mobilizes its membership in defense of the status quo. In addition, a small number of people are demanding an independent *volkstaat,* or homeland, for Afrikaners. Women have been a particular focus of organization within these movements. One example is the Afrikanervroue Kenkrag (AVK, or Afrikaner Women Having the Power of Knowledge). Kobie Gouws, "chairman" of the AVK, presents its members' philosophy as being based on Calvinism and, arising from this, on Christian nationalism. "We aim on having an Afrikaner *volkstaat.* We believe that is the only way we'll have peace."[40]

The organization's main role is to empower women with knowledge and to evaluate information in light of Calvinism. To this end it prints newsletters and runs discussion groups. Issues are always tackled from the point of view that what women want for themselves they should want for others. This does not, however, lead to the notion that all people in South Africa should develop a common nationhood. Rather, AVK women argue, for example, that just as they want a particular kind of education for their children, so other "nations" should be able to make the same choices for themselves.[41]

In relation to feminism, Gouws has said that the philosophy of Calvinism holds that women should take their rightful place in the world. Although they believe that men are the head of the family, in practice the principle of self-sufficiency (not depending on black domestic labor because there will not be blacks in the *volkstaat*), has meant that women do not employ domestic workers. Since many women are working outside the home, their husbands are increasingly accepting substantial domestic responsibility. But Janis Grobbelaar, a sociologist who has studied the movement, suggests that this is unlikely to have taken hold among more than a few hundred people.[42]

What is significant is that, like the national democratic organizations such as the UDF, organizations such as the AVK are concerned not with feminism, but with incorporating women into the overall struggle. Although right-wing organizations do not fundamentally challenge women's subordination, they nevertheless contribute to the development of powerful women leaders within the Afrikaner nationalist movement. In some cases, the position of women as subordinate to men is explicitly maintained: the AWB, for example, has an official policy that no woman shall be in charge of men.[43] But on the whole there is simply an implicit understanding that men are at the head of the household and the movement.

Right-wing women from both the National Party and the Conservative Party also support men in the police and the armed forces, whether through the Southern Cross Fund, which provides material aid to members of the South African Defence Force, or through the Support the Police Action Group, which provides ideological support to the police, by, for example, defending their role in quelling protests in the black townships.

WOMEN'S POLITICAL REPRESENTATION

The idea that women should work in support of men seems to be carried to extremes in the system of incorporating National Party women into political leadership. All women members of the National Party are part of what is known as Women's Action. From the constituency to the national level, women meet to discuss politics and to raise funds. The "chairlady" of Women's Action at each level is the wife of the male leader at that level, and she attends the Party Council. It appears that underlying this situation is the view that one should "ask men to say something in politics but ask the women to do something."[44] Grobbelaar argues that many Afrikaner women are indeed the driving force behind their husbands' political achievements, but that the patriarchal values of this community ensure that men remain in public leadership positions. In Parliament itself, only three out of 103 National Party members are women, and only one member of the National Party's cabinet is a woman.[45]

The official parliamentary opposition, the Conservative Party, has made a massive effort to bring women into the party. Its constitution insists that one of the two deputy chairmen of the party must be a woman and that in all decision-making structures 30 percent of the people must be women. The role of the female deputy chairman is to politicize women in the party. Each geographical constituency has a Ladies' Action Committee, which mobilizes women in support of the party by organizing forums to teach women how to write letters to the press, by training women in how to deal with an attack, and by discussing the policies of the party.[46] Given its conservative nature, however, the party has mobilized women not in order to pursue their rights as women but rather to gain their support for a patriarchal and racist ideology. It has no women MPs.

The middle-ground Democratic Party, also in the white parliament, has two women MPs out of 34 and two women on its 37-member parliamentary caucus. It has small regional women's forums and has appointed a women's rights spokesperson and a spokesperson on women's issues.[47] Thus stands the position of women in the legislative body that controls the making of the laws that affect all South Africans.[48]

In terms of the other major political forces in South Africa, the African National Congress, unbanned in February 1990 and at present the major extraparliamentary oppositional force, has three women on its 30-member National Executive Committee, and one-fifth of the representatives at its first internal consultative conference in December 1990 were women. In exile the ANC developed a very strong policy on women's emancipation. It organized a Women's Section to look after the interests of women members and to act as a lobby within the movement to build a nonsexist culture.[49] The Women's Section set up branches in 17 countries for women in exile. These branches forged close relationships with women's organizations in their host coun-

tries. The Women's Section also developed links with U.N. agencies and addressed the United Nations every year on 9 August, a date adopted in 1984 as a day of solidarity with women of South Africa and Namibia. In mid-1990 five of the chief representatives of diplomatic missions of the ANC were women.

In addition, women have been active in the armed wing of the ANC, Umkhonto we Sizwe (MK, or Spear of the Nation). The ANC has a conscious policy of deploying women in positions of responsibility within MK.[50] Women are not constrained to service roles, as in the South African Defence Force, though they do play less of a combatant role than men. The number of women involved in MK is not widely known, as it is an underground structure, but since the arrest of Thandi Modise, the first woman guerrilla to be imprisoned, a number of other women have been charged with high treason, arson, and terrorism arising from their work in MK. Even though few women have been caught working for the ANC and MK and therefore have not entered into public consciousness, they have offered a powerful symbolic message to oppressed women in South Africa.

Overall, the ANC in the 1980s pursued a commitment to building women's equality in the organization and to eradicating sexism, though policy was not always matched by practice. The leadership remains overwhelmingly male, and issues of women's rights tend to be passed on to the ANC Women's League rather than be taken up by the ANC itself. Thus, while the ANC has a policy to promote the development of women's leadership, it has taken no steps to implement this.

The Inkatha Freedom Party, a more conservative, tribally based organization centered in the province of Natal, relates to women in a fairly contradictory way, arguing for women's equality with men but also insisting that the women's organization of the party should be under the direct authority of Inkatha's leader, Chief Mangusuthu Buthelezi, just as women should be under their husbands' authority at home.[51] The party, with predominantly Zulu members, has one woman,

Elizabeth Bhengu, the chairperson of the Inkatha Women's Brigade, on its Central Committee. The Inkatha Women's Brigade was set up in May 1977 to promote economic development and has focused on establishing women's self-help groups. In 1979, however, this aim took on political overtones, and the brigade was seen as a means of getting more people to join Inkatha. Although women are regarded as political activists, this role does not transform their role within the family or give them more power within Inkatha as a whole. Indeed, when asked how women can unite for peace, Elizabeth Bhengu argued that their major role lies in setting an example as educator, helper, and adviser in the home.[52]

The Pan African Congress, which has an almost exclusively black membership, has been silent on the question of women. Patricia De Lille, PAC secretary of foreign affairs, argues that the PAC is anxious not to marginalize women by focusing on them separately from the overall population. It did nevertheless encourage the development of an organization called the African Women's Organization, and since its unbanning in February 1990 the PAC has set up a women's wing that will be represented in the National Executive.[53] The party has two women on its 18-member internal executive and three out of 20 externally.

PROSPECTS

Within this fairly bleak scenario of women's political engagement in South Africa there are a number of positive elements. First, the new period of transition offers a great sense of movement and space for women to push for legal and constitutional changes that would at least support their struggles. In addition, and related to this, the ANC is likely to be the majority party, or at least a major party, in the new government, and it is taking on the woman question fairly seriously. The 2 May 1990 Statement on the Emancipation of Women by its National Executive Committee commits the ANC to ensuring the development of women within the movement and argues for the promotion of women's rights in the broader society: "The only way to solve the problem of women's oppression is to take it up seriously as a campaign in its own right, within ANC structures, and in relation to the process of transformation in South Africa."[54]

Furthermore, the ANC has put forward constitutional proposals with a preamble that reads, "The constitution must be such to promote the habits of non-racial and non-sexist thinking." The ANC's proposed Bill of Rights also addresses women's rights, and women have been canvassed for their criticisms and suggestions in relation to these documents.

No parties other than the ANC have shown a similar commitment to women's rights, but women in many organizations are starting to recognize that now is the time for them to mobilize. Because South Africa is almost certainly moving toward developing a new constitution, there is an opening for women to ensure that the new constitution reflects their visions of a new South Africa. On the other hand, legislation does not alter people's lived experience, and women have a long way to go in terms of building a political base and challenging their subordination to men.[55]

NOTES

1. Literally translated, "You strike the women, you strike a rock, beware you'll die!" these words come from a song sung originally on 9 August 1955 when 20,000 women of the mixed-race Federation of South African Women marched to the seat of the white government's power, the Union buildings in Pretoria. That date is celebrated by anti-apartheid women every year as National Women's Day.

2. Sue Middleton, Julia Segar, Rosemary Smith, and Glenda Morgan, "The Hidden Burden: The Impact of Detention on the Women Left Behind" (Paper presented at Black Sash National Conference, Cape Town, March 1991), 16.

3. It is impossible to give a full historical overview in the space available here, particularly because I want to give the reader a fairly detailed sense of the texture of women's activities in the 1980s. On women's resistance in South Africa see Cheryl Walker, *Women and Resistance in South Africa* (London: Onyx Press, 1982); Jenny Schreiner, "Working for Their Freedom: FCWU and AFCWU and the Woman Question" (Master's thesis, University of Cape Town, 1986).

4. Much as I would prefer not to have to do so, I use these terms to refer to specific race groups because the South African reality is shaped by these classifications. It has become common practice to use the term black when referring to Africans, Asians, and coloureds as a group, all of whom suffer some race discrimination. At times I differentiate among them, since for historical reasons and through apartheid legislation they differ in certain social, economic, and political experiences.

5. This organization is remembered primarily for the women's march to Pretoria on 9 August 1955, when leaders such as Lilian Ngoyi, Helen Joseph, and Francis Baard gained their fame.

6. When an organization is "banned," it is declared illegal. Belonging to and meeting with other members of such an organization, possessing its literature, talking positively about it in public, and even promoting it in informal discussion are illegal. Because banned organizations went underground, the past few decades have seen hundreds of South Africans of all races jailed for illegal membership or activities in support of these organizations. In one well-known but not unique case, a man was jailed for six years for having "ANC" written on his tin tea mug. As a result of the bannings, political activity subsided, and these organizations were not spoken of by ordinary members of the public except in secret, underground contexts until the late 1980s, when political protest and calls for the unbanning of the organizations gained momentum. The practice of banning organizations was repeated again in 1977, with similar effect. The government made another attempt with the "restriction" of organizations in the 1980s, but this time it was not fully successful in quelling popular protest.

7. Although the number of women jailed for subsequent underground activities is small, their presence is nevertheless felt. Among them are Dorothy Nyembe, an African woman sentenced to fifteen years in prison in 1969 when convicted of terrorism and communism, and Barbara Hogan, a white woman sentenced to ten years' imprisonment for sending political information to the ANC. She was the first person in South Africa to be convicted of high treason on purely political grounds rather than on military grounds.

8. In addition, Helen Suzman, who for many years was the only woman member of Parliament and the only parliamentary member of the liberal opposition (the Progressive Party, now known as the Democratic Party), spoke out and took up the causes of the disenfranchised majority. For example, she visited political prisoners and fought to improve their conditions; she argued against the forced removal of black people from their homes and land; and she attempted to improve women's legal status.

9. Sheilagh Gastrow, *Who's Who in South African Politics* (Johannesburg: Ravan Press, 1990).

10. Debbie Budlender, *Women and the Economy* (Jo-

hannesburg: Community Agency for Social Enquiry, 1991), 8, 11.

11. For example, members have attended funerals that the police were expected to break up. The presence of some white women tends to dampen the enthusiasm of the police.

12. Interview with Amanda Kwadi in Beata Lipman, *We Make Freedom: Women in South Africa* (London: Pandora Press, 1984), 130.

13. There has been some academic debate in South Africa about the effect of the focus on motherhood for the liberation of women. See, for example, Debbie Gaitskell and Elaine Unterhalter, "Mothers of the Nation: A Comparative Analysis of the Nation, Race and Motherhood in Afrikaner Nationalism and the African National Congress," in N. Yuval-Davis and F. Anthias, eds., *Women—Nation—State* (London: Macmillan, 1989); and Jo Beall et al., "African Women in the Durban Struggle, 1985–1986: Towards a Transformation of Roles?" in Glenn Moss and Ingrid Obery, eds., *South African Review* 4 (Johannesburg: Ravan Press, 1987), 93–103.

14. Comment made in a talk to the Women and the Law in Southern Africa Conference, Lawyers for Human Rights, Johannesburg, November 1990.

15. While the UDF was not formally related to the illegal ANC, it stood for the same principles, and as the decade progressed, the ANC, in exile as an underground organization, developed increasingly closer links in terms of consultations and strategy with the UDF.

16. The term *nonracial* and the strategy of "nonracial organization" are used in South Africa to mean multiracial or antiracist. This use is intended to challenge the government's strategy of racial segregation.

17. I am not suggesting that white women were any more open sexually than their black women counterparts. But in the context of a ban on sexual relationships and marriage across race lines, such relationships were not common and so were more visible.

18. Jane Barrett et al., *Vukani Makhosikazi: South African Women Speak* (London: Catholic Institute for International Relations, 1985), 241–46.

19. Ibid. Part of the problem in winning legitimacy for women's organizations within the UDF was that there was a very strong ideological argument against mobilizing women as women for any reason other than to further the struggle for national liberation. The argument went that women's liberation would follow after national liberation and that it was damaging to threaten the solidarity in national oppression of men and women by challenging men's oppression of women. This position has been substantially challenged only since the start of the "transitional" period in February 1990, with the unbanning of the ANC. While the ANC's practice is not particularly feminist, in the late 1980s it developed policies that argued that there could not be freedom without women's eman-

cipation, and that the struggle for women's emancipation should occur simultaneously with the struggle for national liberation. For a discussion of the debate see Tessa Marcus, "The Women's Question and National Liberation in South Africa," in Maria van Diepen, ed., *The National Question in South Africa* (London: Zed Books, 1988), 96–109.

20. Detainees Parents' Support Committee, *Cries of Freedom: Women in Detention in South Africa* (London: CIIR, 1988), 11.

21. Ibid., 7.

22. These organizations included Women for Peace (racially mixed, apolitical, and middle-class), the Black Sash (liberal), the University of Witwatersrand Women's Group (white, socialist/feminist), the Federation of Transvaal Women (FEDTRAW, mixed-class, mixed-race, and socialist), the SACC women's desk (predominantly African and mixed-class), and the National Council of Women (white, middle-class, and apolitical), as well as women from mixed-sex organizations like the Five Freedoms Forum (white, middle-class, and liberal), the Human Rights Commission (a mixed-race service group), and the Detainees Aid Center (a mixed-race service group). At the time, all of these groups, except Women for Peace and the National Council of Women, defined themselves as part of the MDM.

23. Diana Russell, *Lives of Courage: Women for a New South Africa* (New York: Basic Books, 1989), 151–52. While many white women engaged politically through giving their support to the SADF, a small but vocal group of white women has campaigned against the compulsory conscription of white men, again through the formation of an alliance. Inspired by the 1983 Black Sash conference, which demanded that the government abolish military conscription, the End Conscription Campaign (ECC) developed as a coalition of more than 50 church, student, women's, and human rights organizations with a large preponderance of women activists. It ran very public and innovative campaigns, ranging from giving support to conscientious objectors (who faced long prison terms) to the "Working for a Just Peace" campaign in 1986, which involved about 600 ECC members working on projects in black communities to demonstrate constructive alternatives to military service. More than 6,000 people attended mass meetings at the end of this campaign. Like most of the very vocal anti-apartheid organizations of the 1980s, however, the ECC was banned during the state of emergency, its leaders were harassed, and about 70 women and men were detained. Laurie Nathan, "Resistance to Militarization: Three Years of the End Conscription Campaign," in Moss and Obery, *South African Review* 4, 104–16.

24. United Women's Congress Education and Training Subcommittee and Media Subcommittee, "A Woman's Place Is in Her Organization," *Speak* 26 (1989): 12–13.

25. Protest against sexual harassment and rape was scarce in South Africa during the 1980s, with few noticeable exceptions. In 1984 the Congress of South African Students ran a campaign against the Department of Education and Training, which is responsible for African education. Demands of the campaign included an end to sexual harassment of schoolgirls by teachers. "Year of Struggle, Time of Learning," *Saspu Focus* 3 (1984): 5. In 1986 women in the small town of Port Alfred in the Eastern Cape stayed away from work in protest against police refusal to charge a known rapist. Franz Kruger, "Women's Stay-away in Port Alfred," *South African Labour Bulletin* 11 (1986): 53–56. In 1990 two small marches against rape—particularly the rape of schoolgirls by teachers—were held by a number of women's organizations, including the ANC Women's League and the Black Sash, and a number of churches in Soweto. The issue promises to be on the agenda of the 1990s.

26. See Barbara Klugman, "Maternity Rights," *South African Labour Bulletin* 9 (1983): 25–51; and Colette Markham, "Maternity Agreements," *South African Labour Bulletin* 12 (1987): 26–32.

27. See Adrienne Bird, "Organising Women Workers," *South African Labour Bulletin* 10 (1985): 76–91.

28. Both quotes taken from "Workers are Parents Too!" *Speak* 32 (1990): 4–7.

29. Barbara Klugman, "Women Workers in the Unions," *South African Labour Bulletin* 14 (1990): 13–35.

30. It was only later in the decade that the UDF and COSATU formed a closer alliance against the repression of the state of emergency, and after this the potential for joint action among union women and women in community women's organizations increased, although actual cooperation remained limited.

31. For more insight into the position of rural women see Barrett et al., *Vukani Makhosikazi*; Joanne Yawitch, "Tightening the Noose: African Women and Influx Control in South Africa 1950–1980," Carnegie Conference Paper 82 (Cape Town: Saldru, 1983); Hannelie Griesel, *Simbambene: The Voices of Women at Mboza* (Johannesburg: Ravan Press, 1987); and Lydia Kompe and Janet Small, "Demanding a Place Under the Kgotla Tree: Rural Women's Access to Land and Power" (Paper delivered at the Conference on Women and Gender in Southern Africa, Natal University, Durban, 30 January to 2 February 1991).

32. Lydia Kompe of Transvaal Rural Action Committee of the Black Sash, interview by Janet Small, 4 August 1990.

33. Personal communications to the author, 1991.

34. Transvaal Rural Action Committee, *Mogopa: And Now We Have No Land* (Johannesburg: Black Sash, 1987).

35. The description of the Mogopa removal is taken

from Transvaal Rural Action Committee, "An Update on the Struggle of the Mogopa People," *TRAC Newsletter* 13 (published by the Black Sash, August 1987).

36. My reflections on the impact of the Mogopa removal on women are taken from Kompe and Small, "Demanding a Place," 7–9.

37. Ibid., 10.

38. Janis Grobbelaar, Sociology Department, University of South Africa, interview with the author, 28 January 1991.

39. This is not to imply that all Afrikaners are right wingers. There is a long liberal history among certain Afrikaners in the Cape, and, in addition, many younger Afrikaans people have rebelled against all of the tenets of Afrikaner society. This is reflected in the work of many Afrikaans musicians, artists, and writers. In the 1980s there were some political initiatives by Afrikaners to mobilize Afrikaners to join the Mass Democratic movement, such as a Johannesburg-based organization called Afrikaans Democrats.

40. Information on the AVK is drawn from my interview with Kobie Gouws on 22 January 1991.

41. This approach has a strong moral flavor and is rather different from the fascism underlying such right-wing groups as the AWB.

42. Grobbelaar, interview.

43. Charles Leonard, "Cooking Comes Naturally to These Warriors: The AWB's First Female Commandant Keeps a 'Beautiful' Shotgun in her Home and Feels that Women are Born Cooks," *Weekly Mail*, 25–31 January 1991, p. 11.

44. L. Geldenhuys, secretary to the chief secretary of the National Party in the Transvaal (Dr. Koornhof), interview with the author, 28 January 1991.

45. Figures on members of Parliament are taken from *Hansard Debates of Parliament* 23 (Government Printer, 1990).

46. Gay Derby-Lewis, Conservative Party, interview with the author, 26 November 1990. I was not altogether sure what sorts of attacks this training had in mind. But the notion of being attacked—the idea that its culture and children are under attack—is central to the mythology of the right wing. For example, 16 June is remembered by people in Soweto as the day that children were massacred in 1976. Most Sowetans treat that day as a public holiday and attend church services. Yet I have heard a number of white people warning that on 16 June blacks are going to march into the (white) suburbs.

47. Dene Smuts, member of Parliament for the Democratic Party, interview with the author, 25 November 1990.

48. The House of Representatives (for coloureds) has one woman out of 85 MPs; the House of Delegates (for Asians) has two women out of 45 MPs.

49. Returning women exiles from the ANC have expressed shock at how sexist local activist men are relative even to those men in exile whom they considered chauvinist.

50. Umkhonto we Sizwe was formed in 1961 as a last resort after the banning of the ANC the previous year.

51. This interpretation of the position of women in Inkatha is taken from Shireen Hassim, "Reinforcing Conservatism: An Analysis of the Politics of the Inkatha Women's Brigade," *Agenda* 2 (1988): 3–17.

52. Reply to a question at an event held by the Institute for Democratic Alternatives in Southern Africa, *Women Facing the Future Together*, Johannesburg, 23 February 1991.

53. Patricia De Lille speaking at *Women Facing the Future Together*. I obtained some information during informal discussion after this speech.

54. "Statement of the National Executive Committee of the African National Congress on the Emancipation of Women in South Africa," *Agenda* (1990): 19–23.

55. I would like to thank the women I interviewed and the following people for commenting on the manuscript: Jacklyn Cock, Shireen Hassim, Beatie Hofmeyr, Moira Maconachie, Mavivi Manzini, Nonqaba Mosunkutu, and Cheryl Walker. Aside from pure description, the approach and views expressed reflect my experience as a white woman anti-apartheid activist in the 1980s.

▲ Spain

POLITICS

Type of Political System: democracy

   Sovereignty: constitutional monarchy

   Executive-Legislative System: parliamentary

Type of State: quasi-federal

Type of Party System: multiparty

Major Political Parties

   Partido Socialista Obrero Español (PSOE, or Socialist Spanish Workers' Party): Founded in 1879; has held government since 1982. Membership ranges from the socialist left to moderate social democrats. Belongs to the Socialist International.

   Partido Popular (PP, or Popular Party): Reorganized since 1977 as the Popular Alliance, Democratic Coalition, and finally Popular Party. Considered of Francoist heritage until its recent attempt to become a moderate right wing party; attached to the European Popular and Christian Democratic groups.

   Izquierda Unida (IU, or United Left): Includes several groups and has federal organization. First formed around the old Communist Party (founded in 1921); divided in the 1980s and became a socialist group separate from the Socialist Spanish Workers' Party and members of social movements.

   Centro Democrático y Social (CDS, or Social and Democratic Center): Formed around the first elected president, Adolfo Suarez. After the dissolution of his heterogenous party, Unión de Centro Democrático (Union of the Democratic Center), many members went to the Socialist Spanish Workers' Party or the Popular Party. Member of the Liberal International.

   Convergencia i Unión (Convergence and Union): Main party in Catalonia; has held government there since 1979. Christian Democrat–oriented.

   Partido Nacionalista Vasco (PNV, or Nationalist Basque Party): Main party in the Basque Country; held the government there during the Second Republic and again since 1979. Divided in the 1980s; Euzkadiko Ezquerra (Basque Left) is a smaller Basque nationalist party. Christian Democrat–oriented.

   There are regionalist parties in almost all of the 17 autonomous communities. These do not hold government regionally and, in the late 1980s and early 1990s, had less than 1 percent representation in the Spanish Parliament.

Year Women Granted Right to Vote: 1931

Year Women Granted Right to Stand for Election: 1931

Percentage of Women in the Legislature[a]

   Lower House: 13.4%

   Upper House: 11.8%

Percentage of Electorate Voting for Highest Elected Office in Most Recent Election (1989): 69.9%[b]

DEMOGRAPHICS

Population: 38,997,000[c]

Percentage of Population in Urban Areas

   Overall: 91.4%

   Female: 91.6%

   Male: 91.2%

Percentage of Population Below Age 15: 24.3%

Birthrate (per 1,000 population): 12[d]

Maternal Mortality Rate (per 100,000 live births): 11

Infant Mortality Rate (per 1,000 live births): 9

Mortality Rate for Children Under Five (per 1,000 live births): 11

Average Household Size: 2.8

Mean Age at First Marriage

   Female: 23.1

   Male: 26.0

Life Expectancy

   Female: 78.6

   Male: 72.5

EDUCATION
Ratio of Female to Male Enrollment
First-Level Education: 93
Second-Level Education: 101
Third-Level Education: 96
Literacy Rate[c]
Female: 92.1%
Male: 96.8%

ECONOMY
Gross National Product per Capita: U.S.
$4,290
Percentage of Labor Force in Agriculture:
13.7%[f]
Distribution of Agricultural Workers by Sex[g]
Female: 27.0%
Male: 73.0%

Economically Active Population by Sex
Female: 16.5%
Male: 52.1%

a. *La mujer en España: Política* (Women in Spain: Politics) (Madrid: Instituto de la Mujer, 1990).
b. Ibid.
c. *Anuario el país* (Country yearbook) (Madrid: Ed. El País, 1991).
d. *La mujer en España: Situación social* (Women in Spain: Social situation) (Madrid: Instituto de la Mujer, 1990).
e. *La mujer en España: Educación* (Women in Spain: Education) (Madrid: Instituto de la Mujer, 1990); and *La presencia de la mujer en el sistema educativo* (The presence of women in the educational system) (Madrid: Instituto de la Mujer, 1988).
f. *La mujer en cifras* (Women in brief) (Madrid: Instituto de la Mujer, 1991).
g. Ibid.

Women's Political Engagement in Spain

MARIA TERESA GALLEGO
MENDEZ
TRANSLATED BY
MARGARITA GOMEZ-REINO

The southern European country of Spain has a modern industrialized society with a democratic system. From 1939 to 1975 the country was under the dictatorship of Gen. Francisco Franco, whose Fascist forces had defeated the republicans in a three-year civil war. The Franco regime, with the support of the army and the Catholic church, abolished rights and liberties and ended only with the dictator's death in 1975.

The political system established by the 1978 constitution defines Spain as a social and democratic state governed by a parliamentary monarchy. The Spanish Parliament (Cortes Generales) consists of the Senate, or upper house, and the Congress of Deputies. The constitution guarantees popular sovereignty, separation of powers,

and a range of rights and freedoms geared toward achieving an advanced democratic society. The constitution also established territorially what is called an *estado de las autonomías* (state of autonomies), a quasi-federal structure under which there are 17 autonomous communities with their own executive and legislative bodies. There is a single nationwide judiciary.[1]

The multiparty system in Spain has been shaped by the transition to democracy that began after Franco's death. Spain has a multiparty system with little parliamentary fragmentation, as the major parties—Unión de Centro Democrático (UCD, or Union of the Democratic Center) and Partido Socialista Obrero Español (PSOE, or Spanish Socialist Worker's Party) until 1982 and

PSOE and Partido Popular (PP, or Popular Party) since then—have occupied 80 percent of the seats in the lower house. There are also regional party subsystems in Catalonia and in the Basque Country. PSOE has been the ruling national party since 1982.

In the general elections held in October 1989 women were elected to 13.4 percent of the 350 seats. In the Senate women make up 11 percent of the membership. When PSOE shuffled the cabinet in March 1991 women were appointed to two of the 17 ministerial posts. Of the high-level positions in the central administration, 10 percent are held by women.[2]

The transition to democracy has greatly influenced women's political engagement. A dilemma for Spanish women has centered on whether to join formal political organizations or whether to act only within autonomous women's organizations. In the arena of formal politics there is a lack of well-developed civic structures and an absence of a well-established democratic political culture—the result of almost 40 years of authoritarian rule. In the feminist arena there remain grave suspicions about the propriety and effectiveness of working in a closed, patriarchal political system. In this chapter I describe this dilemma, emphasizing the transition to democracy, the politics surrounding abortion, institutional capacities, and party governance.

Achieving democracy in Spain was not easy. Since the first liberal constitution in 1812 conflict has existed between new values and social and economic principles on the one hand and a traditional social and economic structure strongly influenced by the Catholic church on the other. Since the restoration of an absolutist government in 1814, all attempts to introduce liberal constitutionalism have quickly failed.

A revolutionary period that began in 1868 led to the formation of the federal system and the progressive First Spanish Republic, which ended in a military coup in 1874. This period was followed by the Bourbon Restoration, which lasted until 1923; the constitution developed in 1876 remained in force for 50 years. A two-party system based on the British model and divided

among liberals and conservatives was workable because politicians agreed to rotate offices and because of electoral corruption. In spite of this official political stability, social and political forces like the anarchist movement and, to a lesser extent, socialism emerged. An organized Spanish women's movement did not yet exist, as it did in other Western countries. But individuals like Emilia Pardo Bazán and Concepción Arenal articulated the situation of women and defended measures to improve it, particularly in regard to education.[3]

The two-party system of the Restoration was overthrown in 1923 in a coup led by Gen. Miguel Primo de Rivera, beginning a decade of dictatorship during which women had a presence in political institutions for the first time. The Consultative National Assembly (whose members were appointed by Primo de Rivera through a bizarre corporative system) had 385 seats, 13 of which were assigned to women, all of whom were from the bourgeois and aristocratic classes. The dictatorship of Primo de Rivera ended in 1930.

The 1931 municipal elections brought republican parties to power in almost all provincial capitals. After a spontaneous popular movement the Second Spanish Republic was proclaimed, abolishing both the dictatorship and the monarchy. It introduced a secular, liberal, and progressive regime. Three women were appointed to the 1931 Constituent Assembly, as the election system introduced by decree in May 1931 did not exclude them from being appointed to office, even though they still lacked the right to vote.

During the drafting of the 1931 constitution there was bitter debate over women's right to vote. The strongest defender of women's suffrage was Clara Campoamor, a lawyer and member of the Partido Radical (Radical Party) who had to face the opposition of parties on both the left and right. Finally, after a controversial struggle over the so-called conservatism and Catholic political attitudes of women, a constitution granting suffrage and sexual equality was passed, and women voted for the first time in 1933.

A number of problems—the division between church and state, regionalism, agrarian reform—

led to a three-year civil war that began in July 1936. The insurrection was initiated by Franco, who was supported by a small part of the army, the oligarchy, and the Catholic church. Later he was helped by Italy and Germany. The Loyalists who supported the Republic included progressive forces helped by the Soviet Union, the military forces of the International Brigades (which proved mostly symbolic), and intellectuals from all over the world. The conflict centered on the debate between the economic and ideological interests of the oligarchy on one side and the aspirations for freedom and egalitarianism on the other.

Spanish women fought in the army to defend the Republic and worked in the health system and in almost every field of production in unprecedented numbers. And several left-wing women's organizations mobilized against Fascism. On Franco's side were Catholic women's groups, particularly the Sección Femenina (Feminine Section) of Franco's Falange Española Tradicionalista y de las Juntas de Ofensiva Nacional-Sindicalista (Spanish Falange Party). Sección Femenina glorified women's traditional roles, defended Catholic womanly virtues, and viewed women as absolutely dedicated to family and motherhood.

Franco's rule, though Fascist-inspired, was an authoritarian and intensively personalistic regime serving conservative socioeconomic groups and supported by the Catholic church. Franco's Movimiento Nacional (National Movement), composed of small right-wing parties, including the Falange, was combined into one party whose ideology was expressed in the slogan "Family, municipality, and trade union."

The dictatorship passed through different stages but never led to a real extension of rights and freedoms. The first Francoist acts "kept women away from the workshop and the factory" so they could devote themselves to motherhood, wifehood, and support of the country. Sección Femenina, the first mass organization for women, became the sole outlet for women's voices in the Franco regime.[4] Franco appointed two leaders of the group to the first Francoist

parliament, a consultative body formed in 1943; 13 women had been appointed deputies by 1975. Beginning in 1968 women were being named to mayoral posts by the provincial governors.

Economic growth during the 1960s and other factors changed the narrow perspectives of Spanish society. Women participated in the clandestine political struggle to recover democracy and political freedoms, though to a lesser extent than men. Women's associations—most of them culturally or professionally oriented, like those for businesswomen, lawyers, or sociologists—played an important role at the time. They introduced and spread, to a limited extent, new ideas and values to counteract the supremacy of Francoist national-Catholic ideology about women and the family. Those ideas and values appealed to traditional stereotypes and were imposed obsessively for four decades.[5]

FEMINISM AND THE TRANSITION TO DEMOCRACY

On 20 November 1975 Franco died. Two weeks later, from 6 to 8 December, the first feminist meeting—planned in secret—was held in Madrid. More than 500 women from all over the country met to assail governmental positions on the International Women's Year. The women opposed the Spanish government's official celebration. The political context was one of great agitation and of doubt, fear, and uneasiness. Although Franco died quietly, his regime finished as it had begun, in blood and death. At the end of September five people were sentenced to death for political reasons and eventually were executed.

There was uncertainty about the reactions of the army and Francoist elites to the general's death. In accordance with the Francoist 1947 Succession Act, Spain became a monarchy with the ascension of King Juan Carlos. Political priorities for the majority of the Spanish population were centered on the possibility of achieving a democratic system. Left-wing parties such as Partido Communista de España (PCE, or Spanish Communist Party), Partida Socialista Popular

(PSP, or Popular Socialist Party), PSOE, and many others demanded a break with the Francoist regime, the immediate legalization of all political parties, and general elections so that a constituent assembly could be established. Political forces of the center and the moderate right such as the Union of the Democratic Center, whose leader Adolfo Suarez is the current president of Spain; Alianza Popular (AP, or Popular Alliance), whose leader Manuel Fraga Iribarne was a longtime minister under Franco; and others preferred slower reform, the gradual shift from the Francoist system to democracy.

In spite of the political repression—including the September executions—and the atmosphere of uncertainty, other factors were present in Spanish society. They produced the "consensus," the most distinctive attribute of the Spanish political transition to democracy. The consensus was a general attitude articulated by political elites that helped decrease political polarization. Among the most important aspects of the consensus were a general feeling of reconciliation and a repudiation of civil war, with people shouting, "Civil war, never more." Political leaders—including the king—were 35 to 40 years of age and members of a generation that had not lived through the civil war and wished to reform political, economic, and social structures. Indeed, economic growth during the 1960s had softened class conflicts despite the absence of rights and freedoms. It has been said that the initial process of political transition took the form of a "hidden rupture" that broke fully with the Francoist regime and led to the 1978 constitution.

Franco's opponents—including communists, socialists, liberals, and Christian Democrats—gathered at an assembly called Coordinación Democrática (Democratic Coordination) in March 1976. Many political activities, strikes, and demonstrations were held that year to demand amnesty for political prisoners. These activities were suppressed by the police as they were still illegal. Spanish women took part in these events spontaneously or as members of political parties or unions, though they had a lower level of participation than men.[6]

The feminist conference in Madrid was the first political meeting to be held after Franco's death, but this fact is ignored in the literature about the transition to democracy, demonstrating analysts' lack of interest in women's politics.[7] In 1976 the Frente para la Liberación de la Mujer (Women's Liberation Front) was created by a few professional and feminist women; the same year the I-Jornadas de la Doña (First Conference of Women) for women from Catalonia was organized in Barcelona. Three hundred women were expected to participate, but about 4,000 women attended the meeting. Other new feminist groups created in the following months were affiliated with parties on the left even though these groups proclaimed themselves to be autonomous. They included the Asociación Democrática de Mujeres Republicanas (Democratic Association of Women for the Republic), Mujeres Libres (Free Women), Unión Popular de Mujeres (Popular Union of Women), Mujer y Socialismo (Women and Socialism), and Movimiento Democrática de Mujeres (Democratic Movement of Women).[8] These groups were mainly composed of feminist women who were also members of left-wing parties.

The national political situation provided the framework for this newborn feminism. At this point the fight for women's rights had become inseparable from the fight for democracy and universal civil rights. Political spaces were gradually opening, and women's demands, especially those dealing with gender oppression, were being addressed in part because the parties on the left were controlled by men who had an interest in receiving and articulating such demands. Between January 1976 and June 1977 a range of new radical feminist groups called *colectivos* (collectives) began focusing on consciousness raising. These small, active groups of artists, lawyers, lesbians, and so on had an intellectual background and extensive knowledge of feminist experiences in other countries.

The outbreak of Spanish feminism took place in a very short period of time. A great amount of political activity during the transition to democracy provided an environment for the diffusion of feminist programs. The common agenda of women's groups included immediate demands: decriminalization of birth control, divorce and abortion; equal wages for equal work; and the provision of social services, mainly child care. In spite of this consensus, from the beginning there was much debate among feminists on whether to pursue single or double militancy—whether to be a member of a formal political organization or of a feminist organization or of both. Advocates of single militancy considered it possible to achieve women's liberation through the work of their own organizations. They regarded the fight for women's liberation as one of gender, not class. The first feminist meeting for women nationwide was held in December 1975. One of the groups that attended did not agree with the common conclusions supporting double militancy declared to the press "the necessity of creating an autonomous feminist movement, revolutionary and independent from any political party. Women's oppression does not end with the establishment of a democratic regime."[9]

Those who accepted double militancy were seen by single-militancy feminists as instruments of men's political power. Women supporters of double militancy were usually affiliated with left-leaning parties and had gained experience in the fight for democracy during Franco's time. Many were affiliated with or were supporters of the PCE, the PSOE, or other parties on the extreme left; some were close to social democratic parties and even Christian Democrats, but they declared themselves feminist oriented, at least concerning equal rights for women.

Ideological, political, and feminist differences could be found among supporters of double militancy, but on the whole they declared that the main goal was democracy, a sine qua non to demand specific rights and freedoms for women. Political resolutions in *I-Jornadas* declared that "women assume the necessity of defining their own interests and participating actively in their defense, to be co-protagonist of the important duty of bringing about a democratic change in Spain, winning a real presence in this alternative which all Spanish citizens are facing today." The

supporters of double militancy also viewed "the necessity of a revolutionary and autonomous feminist movement . . . [and] the autonomy of feminism as a vindicative organization [as] being out of the question. Only through the active and theoretical presence of women in structures and programs devoted to guiding social demands will they achieve their goals."[10]

They had a more realistic view of how the political system worked, though they were also gullible and utopian. They did not establish structures, nor did they lobby to assure an advantaged position on electoral lists, in which candidates are arranged in numbered order. Women most often occupy the last positions on the list, from which they have no possibility of being elected.

The Spanish feminist movement ultimately split over the differing attitudes of these groups toward institutional politics. At a national feminist conference held in Granada in December 1979 the gap between political feminism and autonomous feminism grew wider than ever. The conference, attended by 4,000 women, ended without any compromise or even a clear strategy for the future and pointed toward the end of the period of expansion in the feminist movement. The debate between single and double militancy is alive in Spanish feminism, though some changes in attitude have appeared.

The controversy helps explain the patterns of women's political participation in Spain. The creation ex novo of the democratic system could have led to greater incorporation of women into politics—no one had political experience, but no one had to be removed from office. This incorporation did not occur, however, in part because the Spanish feminist movement was immature and utopian (its most famous slogan was "Say no to power; feminism is autonomous").

The sociopolitical conditions in Spain at the beginning of the transition affected women's political behavior as well. The negative Francoist political culture had created a general lack of confidence in political institutions and a rejection of the state and political power. Because of this distrust, and because citizens knew little about political parties (except for those individuals attached to clandestine political organizations), parties have had difficulty establishing themselves. There were no public rights and freedoms; sexual segregation, common in every sphere, was supported by the sweeping influence of the Catholic church, particularly in regard to moral, family, and women's issues. The negative political culture also influenced the feminist debate over institutional politics. Younger women, the most active members of the feminist movement even though they considered themselves left wing, regarded new political organizations as the most clear example of patriarchal power.

THE FIRST GENERAL ELECTIONS

At the same time that feminists were organizing, political parties were being established openly. Parties were legalized in March 1977, and the first general elections were held on 15 June 1977. There was an obvious lack of experience in democratic procedures among the party electoral committees, which were set up to prepare the lists of candidates. Surveys and opinion polls were undertaken, but their returns did not seem trustworthy because voters did not feel confident enough to express freely which party they would support. Thus every political party speculated about its possible success.

Under these circumstances women did not ask for a representative quota within their organizations. They had neither experience in fighting for power nor, as was typical of their gender, the personal motivation to attain office. Women wanted to change social reality, and they knew political institutions were necessary instruments, but they had not yet learned how to identify the mechanisms used to restrict access by outsiders to the power networks—mechanisms more familiar to men.

A great number of parties, most of them of recent creation, competed in the 1977 elections. More than 5,000 candidates ran for 350 seats in the Congress of Deputies. Only 653 (13 percent) were women, twenty-one of whom (6 percent) were elected. The first elected Senate had 248 seats, of which only six (2.4 percent) were held by

women. The elections did, however, provide the best possible time for feminist demands to reach the public ear. Activism was almost frantic; with declarations, cultural activities, demonstrations, and so on, feminists engaged in a politics of gestures and symbols full of imagination.

The mass media were eager to show these events that, to some extent, put forward the idea that Spanish society was as free as that of its European neighbors. When the euphoria subsided a large part of the feminist movement found it difficult to continue its militancy in a routine milieu. Nevertheless the first electoral platform of the political parties included the most urgent demands of feminism. Women who were affiliated with political parties took advantage of the public presence of feminism to incorporate into party programs a range of issues to be addressed by Parliament and the government. Most parties sought legal equality and suppression of discrimination in employment and in the civil and criminal spheres. Other issues, like equality within marriage, the right to divorce, and protection for unmarried mothers, appeared gradually in the political discussions of the left. In addition, women's demands usually included legal equality for children regardless of their parents' civil status.

The 1978 constitution was agreed upon by the parliamentary parties and the Spanish citizens, who ratified the constitution in referendum. The constitution established equality of the sexes, equality for children, the future regulation of divorce, and the prohibition of discrimination within marriage or employment. Thus the constitution guaranteed legal equality, but the reform of existing legislation and the adoption of new legislation to implement this guarantee would take longer.

The more radical sectors of the feminist movement were disappointed in the lack of real improvement in women's rights and in their situation in the recent Spanish democracy. But until 1979 feminists continued to have a public presence. In March 1979 women were again elected to fill 6 percent of the seats in the Congress of Deputies. At the end of that year the feminist conference in Granada was held, and the split between political and autonomous feminism widened.

At this point a debate on equality versus difference was added to the debate on single or double militancy and the rejection or use of institutional channels. The new debate centered on whether to demand the same rights and opportunities for men and women or to emphasize the different essential qualities of the two. Such ideological cleavages and progressive fragmentation prevented a mass mobilization within the feminist movement. Since then feminist groups have worked together only on such specific issues as sexual violence or abortion rights.

Although qualitative changes in social reality are difficult to achieve in the short run, through legislation women's most urgent demands were answered, though with limitations.[11] Attempts to organize a left-oriented feminist movement in 1981 failed because the many groups were unable to negotiate a common program and organization.[12] The same year there was an attempted coup d'etat whose failure strengthened democratic values in Spain.[13]

The victory of the PSOE in 1982 with an absolute majority of seats in both houses has been viewed by many scholars as the end of the transition period. In that election the Socialist Party presence increased from 120 to 202 seats in the Congress of Deputies. Communist party seats fell from 23 to 4, and the Union of the Democratic Center, a heterogeneous party that held power during the transition, went from 166 seats to 12. A great change had occurred in the party system, yet it did not affect the political presence of women, who maintained 6.5 percent of the seats in every legislature until 1989.

Postelection surveys reveal a differentiated growth in the women's vote for the Socialist Party, though it does not seem that this growth was related to public expression of feminist demands. Even so, new expectations for women were created during the first period of socialist rule. In the following years these expectations were not fulfilled, and the autonomous feminist movement was unable to form an alliance with socialist women.

WOMEN'S CLAIMS IN THE SOCIALIST GOVERNMENT PERIOD

These drawbacks aside, the Socialist government did produce important legislative and political reforms for women. But suitable regulation of abortion remains the most difficult of the Spanish feminist demands to satisfy because the issue continually revives deep dilemmas regarding human life, freedom, and women's self-determination. As the parliamentary debates suggest, because abortion concerns morality and the rights of women to control their own bodies and to choose whether or not to reproduce, it strengthened the ideological conflict among different sectors in Spanish society. The issue of abortion is normally used as a political weapon, generally excluding women from the debate and the political interests in view.

Although decriminalization of abortion was included in the reform of the penal code passed in February 1983, fifty-four members of Parliament appealed the issue to the Constitutional Court. In April 1985 the measure was declared a violation of the constitutional right-to-life guarantee because it did not provide enough protection for the fetus or for the physical integrity of the pregnant woman. The justices declared that the right-to-life rule would allow abortions under three circumstances only: rape, malformation of the fetus, and risk to the mother's life. A new text reflecting the decision was approved in June 1985. During the parliamentary debates on abortion, conservative organizations and the Catholic church expressed opposition to the new law, but the PSOE used its absolute majority in both houses to get the bill passed. The law allows abortions to be performed in the public health system and takes into consideration the mental and physical health of the mother. The difficulties of implementing the law have been enormous, however, and women have censured the government for its inability to resolve the problem.

Political groups on the whole, but particularly pressure groups like pro-life associations and a great number of doctors and judges, are opposed to abortion. Some of these groups make it extremely difficult to apply the current legislation, and the judges' interpretations of the law vary from one autonomous community to another.[14]

Abortion cases that are brought to court mobilize different social groups. The feminist movement is supported by progressive sectors in the health system, young people, members of left-wing parties, and some trade unions. In March 1991 the Comisión Pro-Derecho al Aborto (Committee for the Right to Abortion) was transformed into the Coordinadora Cívica por Derecho al Aborto (Civic Coordination for the Right to Abortion), which comprises a dozen organizations whose members include feminists, civic leaders, and defenders of public health.

Recent events illustrate the contradictions that exist on the issue of abortion.[15] The Catholic church hierarchy rejects abortion absolutely and identifies the practice with terrorism and genocide. The most conservative forces are mobilizing—targeting young students in particular—to develop intensive public opinion campaigns and to exert strong pressure on clinics and people who take part in abortion practices.

In early 1991 there was a dispute over whether to modify the abortion law by introducing a time limit for aborting. The controversy over abortion continues to divide the Socialist government. The minister for social affairs, the feminist and former union leader Matilde Fernández, declared her support of such a time limit. At present, however, the problem is not so much the arguments for or against the time limit but rather that the law itself has proved ineffective in Spain because of the hostile attitude of those expected to put it into practice and the serious risks taken by the minority who do so.

The minister of justice is opposed to a time-limit abortion act, as he does not believe the decision on abortion should be left to the woman. His argument deals with the conflict that arose during the drafting of the 1978 constitution. Article 15 establishes that "all have a right to life," wording that was more widely endorsed than "all *people* have a right to life." The constitutional court interpreted that "all" means that unborn children are constitutionally protected. This con-

flict is difficult to resolve through consensus, but there is a possibility of broadening the consensus on the meaning of democracy itself—that is, on the individual right to abortion and not on the criminalization of conduct that is not a crime for the majority.

INSTITUTIONAL CAPACITY

Abortion politics demonstrates the power of conservative institutions like the church, which was apparent throughout the Franco regime, as well as the lack of equally powerful civic institutions. This imbalance has had special meaning for the development of democracy and for the representation of women's interests. With the exception of traditional women's groups, women have had to develop the institutions that would promote their demands, and neither parties nor the feminist movement have been particularly successful in this regard. Although the number of women's groups has increased rapidly in the first decade of democracy and has expanded women's sphere, these groups have had little effect on governmental institutions.

Women's overall participation in civic and voluntary associations is very low. Some feminists point to the political dimension of such associations to explain the lower level of women's participation in political parties. While 20 years ago feminists declared that "the personal is political," they now assert that politics includes those spheres in which women develop their own activities. But this assertion can be a trap, even though it is important to extend the definition of politics and the traditional forms of political practices.

Notwithstanding these drawbacks, participation in civic and social groups has grown in the democratic period following the Franco era. In 1991 the government's Instituto de la Mujer (Institute for Women) published a list of 1,300 diverse women's associations or groups. This record lists women's associations only, not the neighborhood associations, school councils, or antidrug organizations that draw significant participation from women.

Only 60 of the 1,300 groups describe themselves as national; about 20 are professionally oriented. Some have political orientations, and others define themselves as feminist—the Committee for the Right to Abortion, Comisión contra los Malos Tratos (Commission on Women's Abuse), and Comisión de Asistencia a Mujeres Violadas (Committee for Assistance to Raped Women).[16]

The feminist movement nevertheless has been fragmented and scattered in recent years, incapable of creating dialogues or strategies. Its most radical sector continues to reject institutional political participation. Even so, feminists have developed specific campaigns, particularly in regard to sexual violence, and they have helped to obtain more severe penalties for rape, which is regarded as a crime against sexual freedom. Feminist organizing has also resulted in improved legislation regarding job discrimination, especially the "inversion of proof" statute, which says that when a woman worker cites job discrimination, it is up to the accused to disprove her.

The decline of the visible feminist movement since 1982 has also coincided with the gradual consolidation of the state of autonomies, which facilitated the creation of new regional and local feminist groups with particular national and cultural identities. These groups dealt with their demands in their own legislative and executive bodies, though the situation is different in each community. The majority have an administrative organ dedicated to improving women's rights as part of the autonomous communities' executive branch.[17]

The second half of the 1980s was also characterized by the gradual political institutionalization of women's issues. Even though the autonomous feminist movement itself has become less prominent, its propositions have been introduced into public opinion to some extent, and many of the movement's former members defend the majority of its goals in other ways. There are departments or commissions for women in the central government, the autonomous governments, town halls, private corporations, and public or private institutions (particularly those that are educationally and culturally oriented), as

well as at universities. It is difficult to evaluate the political dimension of all the activities developed in these organizations, but they certainly have had an influence. This period also saw the creation of a network of information centers and shelters for battered women, though there are not enough of these facilities.

The socialist government has also added to this growth of infrastructure. In addition to its support of abortion rights, the PSOE increased women's status, establishing the Institute for Women in 1983 as part of the Ministry of Culture and later the Ministry of Social Affairs. The institute's aim is to develop policies to improve women's situation in many spheres and to promote women's groups through subsidies.[18] In 1990 a total of 375 women's projects were financed with a total sum of 1.366 million *pesetas* (about U.S. $13.6 million). The institute not only works on research and specific policy and educational campaigns, but it has also established an Equal Opportunity Plan for Women, the implementation of which had many effects on various ministries. The plan was inspired by the Plan for Equality from the European Economic Community, of which Spain has been a member since 1986.

There are many women in organizations outside feminist circles, groups about which there is little information. Some organizations were formed by women from disparate professions: engineering, music, law, management. The number of these groups is growing, thanks to the subsidy policy, but no data exist about their social basis, membership size, activities, or goals.

The work of all these groups has introduced changes in public opinion: more respect for women and social condemnation, at least formally, of sexual discrimination. The specialization of these groups helps to define the needs of each one, and it is assumed that they have some influence on political power. But on the whole a great part of this heterogeneous associative network remains outside institutional politics or even rejects it. So while Spanish women are increasingly participating in civil life, civil life itself remains undernourished.

Without denying the political dimension of social movements and atomized associations, it seems clear that such associations do not influence power structures and that they remain outside policy-making processes. Their localism, discontinuity, and lack of structure prevent them from being part of any political agreement. In contrast, the women's movements—including the weak feminist movement—can play an important role in the eventual transformation and development of the political culture and in the search for a new political paradigm. Indeed, the political overvaluation that some people (particularly feminists) make of women's political participation in associations pretends to compensate for their limited participation in institutional politics.

POLITICAL PARTIES

Spain's weak political culture has also influenced women's membership in political parties. Most Spaniards feel alienated from the parties, and their affiliation is low, especially compared with that in other European countries.[19] They are increasingly disappointed with political elites, and they regard parties as power instruments that fight on the elites' behalf.

In a 1984 poll by the Center for Sociological Research 92 percent of women and 85 percent of men said they had never been affiliated with a political party.[20] Twenty-one percent of the people affiliated with political parties were women, but the percentage of women's membership varied widely from one party to the next. In this context it is important to examine women's motivation to participate in party politics. In 1987 nearly 40 percent of women said they will work in politics for "the possibility of doing something useful," though only 3 percent will do it "because of the opportunity to achieve office."[21] This pragmatic feeling and their general lack of interest in power define women's motivation to engage in politics.

Women also find that the language and method within the parties, which reflect the "masculine way of doing things," make it difficult for women to integrate themselves into the

power structure and into the committees and groups where power is distributed.[22] On the whole they find established rules of the game that they cannot remove because they lack sufficient support.

These rules of the game have to be analyzed not only by themselves but also in relation to women's ways of life, which affect their interest in participating in politics.[23] The interest is greater among younger women, particularly if they are professional, single or divorced, and urban. Women's interest in institutional politics and in their affiliation with political parties has increased in recent years, though many factors may be responsible, including the introduction of quotas and some changes in the former feminist debate about single or double militancy.

It was in this context that 1986 general elections were held; the results indicated that the political landscape had not changed. The Socialist Party held the majority again, but its representation fell from 202 to 184 seats in the Congress of Deputies, and the seats appointed to women fell from 18 to 13. The Popular Party fell from 108 to 105 seats, and seats held by women increased from 2 to 8. On the whole, women MPs in Congress maintained 6 percent of the seats. In the Senate the percentage of women grew from 4.3 to 5.6 percent.[24]

During the 1980s it seemed that women's representation in Parliament was unchangeable: since 1977 women had won 6 percent of the seats. But in 1987 at its party congress the Socialists introduced a suggested quota of 25 percent for women. Socialist women had to overcome strong resistance from inside and outside the party to achieve the quota—even though it was suggested, not compulsory. At that moment women made up less than 17 percent of Socialist Party members. Those opposed to the quota included radical feminists who argued instead for a quota of 50 percent.

Notwithstanding feminist concerns, women's representation within the Socialist Party increased astonishingly when the quota system was introduced. Because the party organization is federal, the change has occurred in all the autonomous communities. The percentage of women in regional executive committees has increased on average from 8.1 to 22.4 percent. Indeed, the quota system has caused an increase in women's affiliation with the Socialist Party: when the system was introduced women constituted 16.1 percent of the party; in June 1990 their membership reached 20 percent.[25]

Another party, Izquierda Unida (IU, or United Left), introduced a women's quota of 35 percent in 1988. This coalition party had only seven seats in the Congress of Deputies at the time, and none were held by women. IU's proportion of women members was 12.4 percent. The agreement did not produce a conflict, however, mainly because a large part of the most active sector of the feminist movement supports IU because of its radicalism and interest in social change.

The quota system had an obvious effect on the returns of the 1989 general elections, particularly in the case of the Socialist Party. The returns were: PSOE, 176 seats, 31 of them for women; Partido Popular (Popular Party), 106 seats, 10 for women; Convergencia i Unión (Convergence and Union), 18 seats, 1 for a woman; IU, 18 seats, 2 for women; Herri Batasuna (The United People), 4 seats, 1 for a woman; and Euskadiko Ezquerra (Left of Euskadi), 2 seats, 1 for a woman. The remaining 13 parties with parliamentary representation do not have women MPs. Although the quota system was not a complete success, for the first time women's presence in the Parliament was doubled from one election to the next, giving women 13.4 percent of the seats in the Congress of Deputies and 11 percent in the Senate.

The results of introducing the quota system were not as evident in the autonomous communities. On average, women's seats in the autonomous parliaments increased from 6.4 to 7 percent, though there were great differences among the communities. In Madrid women held 16.7 percent of the seats; in Galicia they occupied only 1.4 percent. There is no comparative research on women's political participation in the communities that analyzes the relations among eco-nomic development, female employment rate, the presence of the feminist movement, and women's attainment of political power. But broadly speaking it seems that increasing these factors does not increase women's representation in regional parliaments.

The increased number of women MPs and the presence of two women ministers in the Socialist government have received mixed reactions from the feminist movement. Feminists are critical not only toward political institutions but also toward women who participate in politics. They argue that women's participation in positions of political power does not change the pattern of politics itself and that women politicians assume the masculine model and engage in politics on their own behalf. In other words, many feminists expect that when women participate in spheres of responsibility they should instantaneously change reality with a magic wand.

Only recently has there been some change in the pattern of the feminist debate about politics. Participants at a feminist workshop in 1990 in Madrid stated,

We consider that the feminist movement should be transformed into a political voice, because it is the only way equality of rights and opportunities will reach every woman. . . . Feminism cannot stop at the frontier of the small self-conscious group, but must expand to more open spheres in which women can walk quietly, express ourselves, be in contact with each other, and participate without the need of heroic efforts, breaks or extraordinary tensions. To be capable of acquiring this social presence the feminist movement needs to develop structures of consensus and coordination . . . and discern what kind of political rules we should learn to use rationally and what kind we should regret and change.[26]

It seems possible that a dialogue between the fragmented feminist movement and the women's sectors working in different institutions will soon be developed, leading to agreements among women again. But there are also many difficulties. The feminist movement split, and adequate channels of communication between women and the representatives of the political parties do not exist. The electoral act in Spain permits only closed and blocked candidate lists, in which voters may indicate their preference for a list only, not for a particular candidate. This prevents the use of the principle "women vote women," with the exception of the Senate, whose electoral system is more open.

Although women are no longer content to occupy a token position in Spanish politics, they lack the support to participate significantly in power structures. So in the meantime it is important to develop theories about women's participation in politics that take into account its normative aspects. It could prove beneficial to find adequate mechanisms for the defense of individual rights, based in equity and respect for diversity, to deepen democracy. This is inseparable from the normalization of equal and free gender relations.

PROSPECTS

If Spanish women do not renounce their intention to change society, a new drive toward women's political participation, especially in spheres of political power, seems essential. Although there is legal equality and a charter of freedoms, the subjects of these rights must be committed to exercising them and to overcoming the obstacles that prevent them from exercising those rights fully.

Feminism as a political movement has answered many women's demands, but problems remain. In 1991, 65 percent of workers were men and, on average, women's wages were 20 percent lower than those of men. The overall unemployment rate is 16 percent, though the rate of unemployed women is double that of men. At the university level women represent 55 percent of those receiving higher degrees and 64 percent of lower degrees but less than 15 percent of those receiving degrees from technical schools. Women are still victims of rape and abuse.

A diffused feminism exists in Spain alongside a structure of relations characterized by gender discrimination in all spheres, private and public. Women's action in society is political as long as women argue about existing relations and pursue

important goals for society as a whole—goals related to equality; to sexual, racial, social, and economic issues; to freedom (the individual right to diversity); and to the maintenance of life (reproduction, ecology, peace). The practice of citizenship demands women's political participation sooner or later to maintain institutional structures, to criticize them, or to change them.

NOTES

1. Between 1979 and 1983 the Spanish Parliament passed the Acts of Autonomy of the 17 communities. Only Catalonia, the Basque Country, and Galicia have a tradition of political autonomy and their own language, as well as a higher level of political responsibilities.

2. During the transition only one ministry was headed by a woman. Beginning in 1982 women became civil governors in charge of security forces at the provincial level.

3. Geraldine Scanlon, *La polémica feminista en la España contemporanea, 1868–1974* (The feminist polemic in contemporary Spain, 1868–1974) (Madrid: Akal, 1986), 23–50.

4. In 1940 Sección Femenina had 600,000 members. See Maria Teresa Gallego, *Mujer, Falange y Franquismo* (Women, the Falange, and Francoism) (Madrid: Taurus, 1983), 73–74.

5. See Concha Borreguero, *La mujer española: De la tradición a la modernidad* (The Spanish woman: From tradition to modernity) (Madrid: Tecnos, 1986).

6. Andrés de Blas, Ramon Cotarelo, and Jose Felix Tezanos, eds., *Las transición democrática española* (Madrid: Sistema, 1989).

7. See Monica Threlfall, "Women's Political Participation," in Christopher Abel and Nissa Torrents, eds., *Spain, Conditional Democracy* (London: Croom Helm, 1984).

8. These groups were created mainly by feminists who were also members of left-wing parties—Maoists, anarchists, republicans. Some small groups were engaged in terrorism. Among the largest and best organized group was the Democratic Movement of Women, founded in 1965 and attached to the Communist Party. In 1975 it added the Women's Liberation Movement to its name and pretended to be an independent group. From 1976 to 1986 it worked with the Women and Socialism group within PSOE.

9. Anabel Gonzalez, *El feminismo en España hoy* (Feminism in Spain today) (Madrid: Zero-Zyx, 1979), 145.

10. Ibid., 144.

11. The Spanish Parliament did not decriminalize the use of contraceptives until 1979.

12. A conference was held in Madrid to organize the

socialist feminist stream. A number of groups attended from all over the country, but the attempt failed. The works presented at the conference were published as *Jornadas de feminismo socialista* (Journeys of socialist feminism) (Madrid: 1984). No author or editor is listed for this book, known as the "yellow book."

13. The Spanish Parliament was held captive by a Civil Guard colonel. Only a fraction of the armed forces was engaged in the attempt, and the situation ended in 24 hours.

14. According to surveys, Spaniards can accept abortion when the circumstances are restricted to those accepted by the 1985 law. The problem is that the application of the law has been impeded. The Ministry of Health reports that through December 1989, 73,353 legal abortions were performed. The real figure is much higher, however, with some sources estimating the number at 100,000 every year though there are no reliable data. Many abortions are obtained clandestinely or abroad. One of the serious issues is that the decriminalization of abortion does not address the socioeconomic reasons for abortion. What constitutes risk to the mother has also been interpreted restrictively, and many cases go to court over the question. In Catalonia, most of the cases concerning risk to mothers are dismissed for lack of evidence. The cases tend to go to trial in Andalucía and other communities.

15. In April 1991 a gynecologist convicted of performing an illegal abortion on a 14-year-old was sentenced to four years in prison. The judge had decided that the sexual abuse the girl had experienced was not rape. A similar case in Valencia ended with the acquittal of the gynecologist.

16. *Guía de asociaciones de mujeres y centros de interés* (Guide to women's associations and information centers) (Madrid: Instituto de la Mujer, 1989).

17. Data and research on women's political behavior in these spheres is lacking.

18. Every year the institute convokes women's organizations to present projects in many different fields, including cultural and assistance programs and educational activities. The institute gives partial or complete financing. Petitioners may not be individuals, only women's organizations.

19. José Ramon Montero and Mariano Torcal, "La cultura política de los españoles: Pautas de continuidad y cambio" (The political culture of the Spaniards: Agendas of continuity and change), *Sistema,* no. 99 (November 1990): 39–74.

20. Center for Sociological Research, December 1984. In Spain members of political parties must join the group formally; there is no breakdown by sex in every party.

21. *Las Españolas ante la política* (Spanish women and politics) (Madrid: Instituto de la Mujer, 1988). Data are from 1987. The next year the percentages were 44.7 percent and 2.5 percent, respectively.

22. Dolors Renau i Manen, "Política, mujer y vida cotidiana" (Politics, women, and daily life), *Sistema,* no. 90 (May 1990): 77–85.

23. Society is hierarchically organized and, despite recent developments, women still perform duties that are considered subordinate to those of men. Family and domestic duties prevent women from having opportunities in every sphere, especially in self-promotion. Women's values and self-esteem are different. See Drude Dahlerup, "Confusing Concepts—Confusing Reality: A Theoretical Discussion of the Patriarchal State," in Anne Showstack Sassoon, *Women and the State: The Shifting Boundaries of Public and Private* (London: Hutchinson, 1987). See also Concepción Fernández and Maria Teresa Gallego, "Exercising Rights: Obstacles for Women," in Fanny Tabak, ed., *The Implementation of Equal Rights for Men and Women* (Onati Proceedings 7, 1991).

24. Data collected in *La mujer en cifras* (The woman in brief) (Madrid: Instituto de la Mujer, 1990).

25. Internal memorandum, "Feminismo y socialismo" (Feminism and socialism), Secretaria de Participación Ciudadana, PSOE, Madrid, June 1990.

26. *Por una política feminista* (For a feminist politics), Foro de Política Feminista, Madrid, 1991. This document summarizes the seminar of the same title held in Madrid in November and December 1990. There are no other works published by the feminist movement that deal with the current debate over institutional politics. Many of the perspectives in this chapter come from personal experience as a feminist and socialist during the past 20 years.

▲ Sudan

POLITICS

Type of Political System: authoritarian
   Sovereignty: not applicable
   Executive-Legislative System: not
   applicable
Type of State: unitary
Type of Party System: no parties
Major Political Parties

Sudan has a military regime that draws
support from the former Islamic Front Party,
one of the dominant political parties during
the democratic era.

Year Women Granted Right to Vote: 1953
   (graduates of secondary school or above),
   1965 (all women)
*Year Women Granted Right to Stand for
   Election:* 1965
*Percentage of Women in the Unicameral
   Legislature:* 0.6%
*Percentage of Electorate Voting for Highest
   Elected Office in Most Recent Election
   (1986):* not available

DEMOGRAPHICS

Population: 24,000,000[a]
Percentage of Population in Urban Areas
   Overall: 20.2%
   Female: 19.2%
   Male: 21.1%
Percentage of Population Below Age 15: 46.0%
Birthrate (per 1,000 population): 45
Maternal Mortality Rate (per 100,000 live
   births): 660

Infant Mortality Rate (per 1,000 live births):
   107
Mortality Rate for Children Under Five (per
   1,000 live births): 181
Average Household Size: 5.1
Mean Age at First Marriage
   Female: 18.7
   Male: 25.8
Life Expectancy
   Female: 51.0
   Male: 48.6

EDUCATION

Ratio of Female to Male Enrollment
   First-Level Education: 68
   Second-Level Education: 73
   Third-Level Education: 68
Literacy Rate
   Female: 4.0%
   Male: 25.0%

ECONOMY

Gross National Product per Capita: U.S. $300
Percentage of Labor Force in Agriculture:
   66.4%
Distribution of Agricultural Workers by Sex
   Female: 24.1%
   Male: 75.9%
Economically Active Population by Sex
   Female: 22.7%
   Male: 87.2%

a. Population Census Office, Department of Statistics, Khartoum, 1989.

The Women's Movement, Displaced Women, and Rural Women in Sudan

MAGDA M. EL-SANOUSI AND
NAFISA AHMED EL-AMIN

Political participation is a difficult challenge for women in Sudan. Civil war has ravaged the country for two-thirds of the time since independence in 1956. At least 500,000 civilians have been killed by war and famine since 1986, and as much as one-third of the population of the south has been displaced. Huge numbers of people have flowed toward the north. Since 30 June 1989 the country has been ruled by a military government, headed by Lt. Gen. Omer al-Bashir, which has abolished the democratic institutions that once flourished.

Colonized by Britain and Egypt, Sudan won independence in 1956—the first African country to do so. Since then, the government has alternated among military regimes (beginning in 1959, 1969, and 1989) and civilian regimes (beginning in 1957, 1964, and 1985). At one time many political parties competed in democratic elections, and a large number of newspapers represented the freest press on the continent. The Bashir government accelerated the process of Arabization and Islamization already under way.

The current military government is headed by the National Salvation Revolutionary Command Council (NSRCC), consisting of 15 members. The NSRCC functions as the collective head of state, with the head of the council, Lt.-Gen. Bashir, acting on its behalf and issuing presidential decrees accordingly. A Council of Ministers, or cabinet, appointed by the NSRCC, has mostly civilian members. The Bashir regime has dissolved the Constituent Assembly (Parliament), suspended the constitution, and banned all political parties, as well as virtually all secular organizations, such as trade and professional unions. Indeed, most of the regimes to date have severely controlled all political participation.

The political engagement of Sudanese women falls into two major categories: the activities of the elite and the experiences of the mass of poor, rural women. Although elite women represent a small minority of the female population, they have played a major role in the women's movement; most of them are literate, and they constitute a strong pressure group. Though economically more secure than other Sudanese women, they experience crises because they must always strive to maintain the rights they gained after long years of struggle under changing regimes. Rural women compose the bulk of the female population. Almost all are illiterate. They also experience crises repeatedly; they suffer from economic disasters, famine, and war. This chapter outlines three major policy issues that have emerged in recent years in light of the current political situation in Sudan and in response to the differences among women: women's political engagement, the problems of displaced women, and the role of rural women as a tool for economic development.

BACKGROUND

Sudan, which covers 1 million square miles, is the largest country in Africa and a bridge between Africa and the Middle East. It has about 400 miles of coastline on the Red Sea, plus common borders with eight other African countries.

The country has 12 distinct geographic regions, from the vast plains that characterize most of the country to volcanic uplands to the highlands in the south. The White and Blue Niles traverse the country, joining at Khartoum, the capital, then continuing north as the Nile River.

Sudan is also divided into eight political regions, in addition to Khartoum: three in the south and five in the north. Following the now failed Addis Ababa peace agreement to end the civil war in the south, the three provinces that existed in the south before 1972 were amalgamated into one region with its own legislative and executive organs and budget. In 1983 the south was divided again into three regions.

The geopolitical diversity is accompanied by cultural diversity: there are more than 300 ethnic groups speaking about 115 languages. Arabic, the official language, is spoken in the north. In the south, where tribal groups are numerous, English is the common alternative. About 70 percent of the population is Muslim. The majority of northerners are Muslim, and most of the Muslim men have only one wife. In the south a significant proportion of the population is Christian, but many people follow traditional African religions and customs, and polygamy is widespread. The Dinka are the largest tribe in the south, and the north contains a large number of non-Arab Sudanese immigrants from western Africa, known as *fellata*.

Sudan's first census was conducted in 1955. According to 1989 figures, the population numbers 24 million, and the fertility rate is high, with women bearing nearly seven children each. All other factors aside, if that rate of growth (3.1 percent in 1983) continues, the population could double by the year 2003. Average household size grew from 5.0 in 1956 to 5.7 in 1983, with larger households in urban areas. The population is overwhelmingly young; 46 percent are under age fifteen, 51 percent are between fifteen and sixty-four, and only 3 percent are over sixty-five. A majority of the population is illiterate; illiteracy rates are higher in the south and among women.[1]

Twenty percent of the population live in urban areas and 69 percent in rural areas; 11 percent are nomads.[2] Although the country is sparsely populated, an increasing flow of rural to urban migration due to inadequate resource allocation and civil war, along with high birthrates in the cities, is responsible for the expanding urban population, especially in the north.

In 1983 the population of refugees in Sudan, who were not included in the official census, was estimated at 1 million or more.[3] Regional famine and war have increased the number of refugees, as has Sudan's liberal refugee policy. Since the 1980s war and drought have displaced as many as 6 million Sudanese from their original homes and communities. Natural disasters, too, play a role in population movement; flooding in 1988 left more than a million Sudanese homeless. Refugee populations are the responsibility of the Refugee Council, which has regular statistics on the arrival of refugees based on the issuance of residence permits. This council has many offices at the different refugee camps.

ELITE WOMEN'S POLITICAL ENGAGEMENT

The Mahdiya era (1881–98) is central in Sudanese history. In 1881 a religious leader in the far north of the country, Muhammad Ahmed al-Mahdi, born to a poor family, incited a nationalist revolution against the Turko-Egyptian colonial government. Women played an important role at the beginning of the Mahdist revolution and during the period when it was a secret movement. The Mahdi chose seven women and entrusted them with the task of delivering letters, hidden in their clothes, to other parts of the country. History records the name of a leading woman, Raba al-Kanania, who changed the course of events in a decisive battle in western Sudan. She discovered a plot against the Mahdi's army and walked a long distance to reach his camp and inform him. He changed his strategy and was victorious over the Turkish army.

The Mahdi showed the importance that he accorded women in several of his written works, which taught that women should be protected and educated and their rights upheld, but only as stipulated in the Quran and the tradition of the Prophet Muhammad. Several women became prominent in the field of religious education, setting up *khalwas* (places where the Quran and Islamic lessons are taught), giving women religious instruction, and swearing allegiance to the Mahdi.

After the fall of the nationalist Islamic Mahdist state in 1898, Sudan was colonized under the Anglo-Egyptian Condominium government. Although there were two condominium powers, nationalist opposition was directed at the British because of their almost complete control over Sudan. Organized nationalist resistance began in 1921, when the Sudanese Unity League was formed. The White Flag League, established three years later under the leadership of Ali Abdul Latif, was responsible for the unsuccessful 1924 revolution, led by officers of the Sudan defense forces. No women were members of either league, but women encouraged the men in their struggle. Because the White Flag League resisted the British and supported Egyptian nationalist ambitions in Sudan, its leaders were persecuted and even killed.[4] During the 1924 revolution al-Azza, the wife of Ali Abdul Latif, became a national hero because of her firm stand against the British; she became a symbol both for contemporary Sudanese women and for future activists in the women's movement.

After the British suppression of the 1924 revolution, nationalist activities lessened for a time but reappeared among groups of intellectuals, who formed literary societies and discussion groups. The Graduates' General Congress, formed in 1938, "was a pioneer, because after its establishment the contemporary nationalist movement in Sudan was born. The congress continued to spread nationalist ideas and fight colonialism until the country was finally liberated."[5]

No women were members of the Graduates' General Congress because of cultural and traditional constraints against women's participation in the public domain. Women had no organization or platform, but they supported the work of the congress by donating jewelry and money. They also held bazaars in aid of private schools in order to increase educational opportunities. These activities were led by teachers, nurses, and housewives in urban areas.

At the end of World War II political parties were established, followed by organizations for workers, farmers, and students. In addition to social and cultural organizations, women's orga-

nizations were begun during this period. Some educated women, through their work with the Graduates' General Congress, were influenced by the intensification of the international movement to emancipate women, particularly in the Arab world. The need for women's organizations became compelling, and some were established, the most important being the Young Women's Cultural Society, the Sudanese Women Teachers' Union, the Society for the Advancement of Women (in Omdurman), and the Sudanese Women's Union.

The first Sudanese women's organization, the elite Young Women's Cultural Society, was set up in Omdurman in 1948 by Fatima Talib, who was preparing to enter the university, and Khalida Zahir, a first-year student in the Faculty of Medicine. Both of their fathers were officers in the Sudan defense forces and members of the White Flag League.[6] There were nine other cultural society members, most of whom had received their education in foreign schools.

For the society to be registered officially by the British authorities, its constitution had to show that it was a social and cultural organization. Although founded in response to educated women's need to organize and unite their efforts, the society ceased its activities after about two years because of differences among its leaders. In 1953 the name was changed to the World Women's Union, and women in the diplomatic corps were the main members.[7] This society still exists as a group of charity volunteers under the name Group of the Diplomatic Corps.

The Sudanese Women Teachers' Union, founded in 1949 ostensibly as a social and cultural organization, later became a nucleus of the trade union movement led by Nafisa al-Mileik and Su'ad abdel Rahman. The teachers' union became a trade union in 1951, and in 1965 women and men teachers' unions joined together to form the present Teachers' Trade Union.

Another women's association dating back to 1949, the Society for the Advancement of Women (in Omdurman), was a social and cultural society established by the Mahdi family under the leadership of Rahma Ali Jadalla, the wife of Siddiq al-Mahdi (father of the late prime minister). Because the British authorities were on good terms with the Mahdi family, they did not oppose this society. Yet the society became less and less effective, despite the enthusiasm of its members, because the majority of Sudanese women were excluded and only the Mahdi's family and friends were allowed to join.

The emergence of the Sudanese Women's Union in 1952 marked a turning point in the women's movement in Sudan. A number of activist teachers at al-Mileik Girls' Intermediate School became its founders. On 17 January 1952, Aziza Mekki invited her colleagues to her home in Omdurman to discuss the idea of forming a new popular women's organization. Nafisa Ahmed el-Amin was among its ten founding members.[8]

Those at Mekki's house decided to hold an open public meeting for women on 31 January 1952 at al-Mileik school to explain the pioneering idea of the union and to set up a preparatory committee. About 500 women attended, in addition to students who were under 16 and too young to become members. The students came from various intermediate and secondary schools, motivated by the idea that a new women's organization could introduce programs related to youth. The women in attendance constituted the general assembly and elected a committee composed of the ten founders, other prominent women, and representatives of working women. The chair was Fatima Talib, who had cofounded the Young Women's Cultural Society four years earlier.

The goals of the Sudanese Women's Union went beyond youth programs. The four main aims were to raise the national and cultural standard of Sudanese women, to propagate national awareness among women, to struggle for women's rights—social, economic and political—and to participate in all types of charitable work.[9] Given such far-reaching ambitions, the founding of the union was warmly supported by other militant movements—those of intellectuals, students, farmers, and workers—as well as leftist groups, especially the Communist Party. The support took different forms—for example, defending the existence of the union in the mass media and motivating women to join.

The Communist Party, which played a major role in the struggle against British colonization and in the achievement of national independence, played a significant role in supporting the Sudanese Women's Union and the independent press. The party was opposed, however, by the two traditional Muslim groups: the Ansar, who had backed the Mahdi and who now constitute the majority of Muslims in Sudan, and the Khatmia, the second largest group of Muslims. The groups support the two traditional political parties, the Umma Party and the Unionist Party, respectively. The Ansar and the Khatmia both thought the Communist Party would call for an overthrow of traditions and values. Other groups raised religious objections, too—for example, the Muslim Brothers, forerunner of the National Islamic Front, and Ansar al-Sunna, a conservative nonpolitical Islamic group.

The Sudanese Women's Union joined a number of international organizations, including the Arab Women's General Union, which had its headquarters in Cairo; the All African Women's Congress, located in El Gezira; and the World Democratic Union of Women. The Women's International Democratic Federation (WIDF), located in East Berlin, provided valuable support for Arabic and African regional and national organizations. Its support for the Sudanese Women's Union, and hence the feminist movement in Sudan, came in the form of sending and exchanging women's publications, encouraging the women in their anticolonialist struggle for political independence and social rights, and recognizing the similarity of Sudanese women's experiences to those of women all over the world.

The Sudanese Women's Union was based on a foundation laid by women trade unionists, as well as by women in the fields of health and education, and was led by a group of teachers from the middle class, some of whom are still taking part in women's activities. Union members held literacy campaigns, evening classes for uneducated women, and training sessions in handicrafts and sewing and inspired older women's societies to become active. The positive spirit spread, and new women's groups were founded, like the Khartoum Women's Advancement Society, with a branch in Port Sudan, as were new branches of the Sudanese Women's Union in Wad Medani, el-'Obeid, 'Atbara, and many other large towns.

The traditional political parties, based on sectarianism and tribal rule, did not support the union or its activities because women's awareness threatened to disturb their structures. The right-wing Umma and Democratic Union parties aimed to preserve traditional aspects of Sudanese society, particularly the role of women, and disapproved of their participation in the public domain. In contrast, the Communist Party, whose members were educated, endorsed the participation of women in the public domain. It was the first political party to open its membership to women.

The leadership of the Sudanese Women's Union split with each other and the Muslim Brothers over whether the struggle for political rights was a constant duty like other struggles— against illiteracy, for the eradication of customs with a negative impact, and for health education and cultural programs for young women and students. The Muslim Brothers later set up a women's wing of its own. Some leaders of the women's union who were members of the Communist Women's League felt dutybound to solicit union members to join the league and to implement its political line within the union, causing a rupture among the union leadership that reached all the way to the grass-roots level.

In 1953, a year after the Sudanese Women's Union was formed, the self-determination agreement establishing the transition from condominium government to national independence was concluded, and preparations were made for the election of an assembly of deputies within the two-year transitional period. The union committee courageously demanded and won the right to vote for women—but only those women who were graduates of secondary schools and universities could do so. Although those enfranchised were very few, the admission of the principle was in itself a major step forward.

The union continued to lead the women's movement in Sudan, and it achieved many victories. It played a historic role in the attainment of independence in 1956. The union called for women representatives on the constitutional committee of the newly independent nation, to which it presented a memorandum on 7 January 1957.[10] Its most important demands were full voting and candidacy rights for all women; the right to work; equal pay for equal work; and changes in family laws to benefit women. All these demands have been implemented except for the last. The family laws regarding such matters as marriage, divorce, and inheritance, are very complicated and linked to sharia. Still, a final draft proposal on the modification of family law for the protection of women has been approved.

The first military government dissolved the Sudanese Women's Union in 1959 and suspended the constitution, all political parties, and trade unions. (Notably, the society in Omdurman run by the Mahdi family was allowed to continue.) But even without the union as the focal point of their activities, Sudanese women remained active in national politics.

Women took part in demonstrations on an unprecedented scale and in the campaign of civil disobedience that brought the country to a halt in the 1964 revolution. Several women were wounded and one was killed. With the fall of the military regime, the return of democracy, and the formation of the first national parliamentary government, all Sudanese women attained full political rights to vote and stand as candidates.

When women were nominated for election to the Parliament in 1965, Fatima Ahmed Ibrahim was the first Sudanese woman to be elected and the only woman elected from the Graduates' Constituency. Although a leading member of the Communist Party, she ran as an independent candidate because the party was not generally popular. With her success at the polls, political parties like the Umma Party, the Islamic Front Party, and the United Democratic Party, began to compete in setting up women's organizations within their structures.

The army, led by Ja'afar Nimeri, took over once again on 25 May 1969. Because of the general disappointment with the traditional political parties, which failed to meet the national demands for a better economic and social life, the people supported the coup, which became a revolutionary movement with a popular base later on through the efforts of the ruling group. The positive response of the people to the May revolution, especially in the rural areas, was reflected in their widespread participation in the political, social, and economic activities of the movement, as well as in the local and national legislative bodies.

Because the new regime declared its full support for all women's rights and demands, most women supported the Nimeri regime, especially in rural areas, where they came out spontaneously to endorse it. Nimeri made many field trips all over Sudan to investigate the problems of rural populations. He was greatly concerned about the status of rural women and made political decisions in many spheres to aid their development. The leaders of the Sudanese Women's Union presented a memorandum to President Nimeri asking for equal pay for women, women's right to pensions and improved conditions of service for those employed in the formal economy, and divorced women's right to half their husband's salary rather than a quarter. The revolutionary government agreed to all these demands, and the union's support continued until conflicts between union leaders and Nimeri led to its dissolution in 1971. Communist Party leaders were split over support for the regime, and some of the leaders of the union were among those who stood against the regime.

In June 1971 the Sudan Women's Union was established, mostly by leaders of the dissolved Sudanese Women's Union, along with other leaders from trade unions and voluntary organizations. It was built to a large extent on the base of the former Sudanese Women's Union, it was led by some of the same women, and it adopted mainly the same aims. An exception to its similarity was that in 1972 the new union was incorporated into the Sudanese Socialist Union, the single party formed by the Nimeri regime in an attempt to develop vertical political institutions supporting the system.

The achievement of peace in the south in 1972 after 17 years of civil war enabled the Sudan Women's Union to set up branches throughout the south. Rural women, especially in the south, emerged as leaders—a striking new phenomenon. The support of southern women for the May 1969 revolution had been based on the achievement of peace in the south, which led to the return and settlement of many families. This stability had enabled southern women to participate in the public domain and allowed the former Sudanese Women's Union to participate in various governmental institutions. The membership of southern women in the newer Sudan Women's Union enables them to hold decision-making positions at local and national levels.

Women made many gains under the leadership of the Sudan Women's Union and the presence of women in decision-making positions at all levels in the government played a significant role in the achievement of many rights for women. The Labor Act of 1975 provided for equal pay and also improved the conditions of service for women by granting paid maternity leaves of two months; the right to leave a job for up to four years to accompany a husband and have the job upon returning; and the right to one hour off per day to feed their children. The 1973 Pensions Act gave families the right to inherit women's pensions. The Social Security Act gave women healthcare security, legal compensation for in-service accidents, and after-service pension benefits. Several new professional areas were opened for women in the armed forces, police, and security services, as well as in the judiciary and the diplomatic corps.

Women made political gains, not just economic ones, including the right to take a ministerial post (1971). They won a special seat in the Political Bureau, the most powerful organ in the government (1972); allocation of seats for provincial representatives of the Sudan Women's

Union in the Central Political Committee (1972); allocation of a quarter of the total number of seats on the people's local councils and the right to compete for other seats (People's Local Government Act of 1971, amended in 1981); allocation of seats in the People's National Council to women representing the different provinces and the capital, in addition to the right to compete for other seats (1973); and allocation of seats in the regional people's assemblies (1981). The allocation of 25 percent of local council seats for women was especially important, for it enabled women at the grass-roots level to hold decision-making positions.

The Nimeri regime fell in 1985 after a successful popular uprising in which the army sided with the people. Women and trade unions also played a prominent role, mainly through their effective participation in civil disobedience. A new government was elected through universal suffrage, and women were both voters and candidates. The free and fair election was supervised by a commission overseen by a judge. The regime upheld human rights and respected basic freedoms, the rule of law, the independence of the judiciary, and freedom of expression. During this democratic interlude (1985–89) the military was under civilian control.

Trade unions and political parties resumed open activities, as did the former Sudanese Women's Union. In spite of strict bans and dissolution, the union, the predecessor of the Sudan Women's Union, had managed to function underground in opposition to the regime. Although the union once again operated openly, it proved ineffective because the constraints and prohibitions of the Nimeri regime against the continuance of union activities had prevented earlier women's organizations from staying in contact with women. In contrast, the Pioneers of Advancement Society, an Islamic youth organization initiated by the Muslim political parties, served as a counterbalance to the Sudan Women's Union, which had been co-opted by the regime. The society was prominent in social work in the latter 1970s.

In the elections held at the end of the transi-

tional year, in April 1986, two women won seats in the constituent assembly. Both were leaders in the Islamic Front Party, a major party that called for the implementation of sharia. For the first time under a democratic government a woman from the Umma Party, the majority party led by Prime Minister Sadiq al-Mahdi, was appointed to the Council of Ministers—a cabinet post.

During this last democratic period women's activities were uncoordinated, nor were any significant gains made, in spite of the large number of political parties (more than 40) and the many opportunities (including conferences) that women had to meet and present their concerns. The number of nongovernmental organizations for women rose from three to sixteen, and the number of women involved in political parties also increased, effectively dissipating women's solidarity and weakening their concerted action toward one goal.

Although all political parties showed great interest in representing women in their political bureaus and central committees, thus encouraging women to rally round at election time, no positive effect was noticeable because women were for the most part absent from decision-making circles. Prime Minister al-Mahdi tried to set up an organization to unite the activities of all Sudanese women in response to a proposal initiated by a group of women in the Umma Party. These women's main objective was to organize the efforts of women of different parties in one body in order to coordinate their activities for the benefit of women in all levels and classes.

The attempt to unite women in such an organization failed for a combination of reasons, including the ideological and methodological contradictions among women's organizations, which represented fundamentalists, rightists, leftists, conservatives, nationalists, and independents; the exclusion of many women leaders who had worked under the previous regime and enjoyed popular support; and the failure to convince some women leaders of the need for a unified body. The idea did result, however, in the establishment of women's units in the Ministry of Agriculture, Ministry of Social Welfare, Ministry of Economics and National Planning, and other governmental institutions.

The failure is not surprising, for a democratic government, by its nature, will have difficulty creating a centralized antidemocratic peak organization that relies on the uncoerced participation of opponents. The drive to create a coordinated body for the different women's organizations continued, however, ultimately leading to the attempted formation of a unified Sudanese Women's Front. The coup that occurred in 1989 prevented it from fully materializing.

When the army took over again on 30 June 1989, political parties, popular organizations, and trade unions were dissolved, and the constitution was suspended. Still, women have been appointed to and participated in a series of government-sponsored conferences held since then to deal with specific social questions.

According to a decision made on 23 December 1989 by the National Salvation Revolutionary Command Council, the highest authority in the country, a conference was convened on "the role of women in national salvation," or how women could support the regime. A 33-member steering committee chaired by Fatima Talib was appointed to organize the event under the supervision of the NSRCC's political committee. The aims of the conference were to mobilize all women; to broaden the participation of women in public activities; to discuss issues and problems facing women in public life; and to propose guidelines for the establishment of a women's organization.

The conference, held on 20–31 January 1991, was attended by 1,600 government-nominated women representing all the regions of Sudan, including the south, where civil war had begun again in 1984. The papers were prepared to a large extent on a specialized and academic basis, so the final recommendations did not differ much from those of previous women's conferences. The problem of peace and war in the south was the dominant topic of discussion, and the recommendations were mainly educational, cultural, economic, and social. The most significant

recommendation resulted in the establishment of a popular women's organization, called the General Union of Sudanese Women. Its establishment and its ability to take action will determine whether or not the other recommendations can be implemented.

No recommendation was made concerning Sudanese women's relations with other women in the world, nor was the role of Sudanese women in the International Decade for Women or its effect on them evaluated. International contacts among women significantly influence feminist movements, and as women exchange experiences and opinions they become aware of their own status. But international contacts were not discussed, even though there have been no obvious or clear constraints against them. The general orientation of the conference was toward the indigenization of ideas and the combating of foreign cultural influences.

The political agenda of the current regime emphasizes Islamization, and the regime's support for the implementation of the conference recommendations will be based on an important fact: women constitute a large political base that may support the regime. But the actual implementation will rely on the establishment of a successful popular women's organization and on its ability to carry out the recommendations and thereby support women.

In light of the imposition of sharia on 1 January 1991, the further participation of women in the public domain now seems unclear. The political engagement of Sudanese women will take place as all Islamic women participate in supporting the regime, either as members of the Women's Unit (a governmental organization that is the nucleus for establishing other women's organizations) or as members of the public committees that function at the grass-roots level to attract more women to support the regime. The Women's Unit has established the General Union for Sudanese Women, which is the governmental body responsible for women's affairs. Under the current regime women will not occupy formal political positions, such as minister. With the declaration of sharia, which enhanced the *quamma* (superiority) of men, women must always have a lower status.

RURAL AND POOR WOMEN

Aside from the geographic and cultural differences between the north and south, the south is also far less developed. The British colonizers effectively separated the two regions to achieve their own, chiefly economic goal: to exploit the natural resources. Because the north contains rich agricultural lands, as well as water resources, the British concentrated their efforts there, ignoring the south, with its harsh environment. After the British halved the country, a rebel movement emerged to seek southern autonomy; civil war raged from 1955 to 1972 and ignited again in 1984. It still continues.

Instead of bringing autonomy to the south, independence from colonial control led to policies of Arabization and Islamization. The groundwork for the long civil war in the south was laid when the population began to leave the southern provinces. Both educated leaders and thousands of others took refuge in nearby African countries, where several political organizations were established to work for southern autonomy. Success came in 1972 with the Addis Ababa peace agreement, which united the three southern provinces as a semi-autonomous region with Juba as its capital.[11]

The 17-year civil war reshaped the role of women in the south. Because of economic needs, war, and famine, men became long-term migrant laborers in northern industries, usually in towns, or seasonal laborers in the agricultural areas. They sought to earn money, usually to buy cattle or perhaps to set up businesses. Their migration compelled the women left behind to take on more responsibilities.

The renewal of armed conflict in the early 1980s, a decade after the agreement that ended the first civil war, is the original cause of famine and displacement in the south. Factors contributing to the conflict include former President Nimeri's abandonment of the terms of the 1972 peace agreement, the redivision of the semi-autonomous south into three regions, exploitation of southern water and oil resources, and the imposition of sharia. Further regime changes have not resulted in a resolution of these issues.[12]

The millions of displaced people—Sudanese who have left their lands because of the civil war in the south and drought and famine in the west—are one of the country's most serious problems. Accurate statistics on the total number are not available, but according to the Council of the Displaced, located in Khartoum, as many as 3.5 million southerners and 2.5 million westerners have been displaced, mainly women and children, as a result of war and drought.

According to a report by the Ministry of Social Welfare, the physical circumstances in which the displaced people live are wholly inadequate. Permanent shelters and privacy are lacking. Water is often nearly a half-mile away, although some areas are served by water tankers from the Sudan Water Aid Programme.[13]

In many ways displaced women are the ultimate objects of policies and forces far removed from their everyday lives. Their responses to profound upheaval constitute the politics of their everyday lives. When they speak, as did Regina, Helien, and Rose—residents of the Farig Shoak Camp—their plight and their reactions bear witness to the struggles of all displaced women.

The Sudan Council of Churches settled the Farig Shoak Camp in south Khartoum with 156 families in December 1988. By January 1989 there were 276 families, but no extra plastic sheeting shelters. A single primary school serves 103 children from six to twelve years old. The area is in need of a healthcare center, as well as tools for cleaning and upkeep.

Regina, aged 33, is married and has three children. She came to Khartoum from Juba four months before this interview.

I left home because of the horrible war in the south. During my escape from the southern rebels, I lost my way. I was separated from my husband and my three kids. I can't forget the horrible scene when the rebels attacked our village and stole our harvest and all our property and raped the women and girls. At home I used to cultivate my land and take care of my family, collect firewood from the forest, bring water from the well three times a day, and cook for my family. My life was harsh and difficult, but I was satisfied. Now, because of the war, I don't know where my family is. My cousin took me to a tracing agency in Khartoum. They said that in three months' time they may know some news about them.

I don't do anything but live with relatives in this camp. I don't know any work but what I used to do at home. I don't sleep, thinking of my family now and why things are the way they are. But I won't go back home unless peace comes back to my village. I may start doing any laborer job to earn money, but I don't know when.

Helien, aged 40, is a widow with three sons.

I came to Khartoum two years ago from Yai. The war was a bad experience for all southerners, particularly us women and children. I came with my three sons. My husband was killed there. Here I make and sell *marisa* [local beer]. I earn quite a lot of money. Making marisa is not allowed by the law; but tell me what the government has done to save us from this poverty and these bad health conditions? It is better for me to make marisa than to beg or to steal. My eldest son now sells water to the people in the camp; I was able to save money to purchase a donkey and a barrel for bringing the water.

I don't leave the camp unless I feel sick [enough] to go to the hospital. Otherwise I stay home here with my relatives and people from my tribe. I don't know what will happen to us in the future. But we won't leave this camp unless the government presents us with a good solution and gives us replacements for our missing land in the south. I will feel nothing toward the government unless it stops the war in the south. The northerners do not realize how big our problem is. I dream of going back home to my land and my people.

Rose, aged 17, is unmarried and illiterate.

I came here with family because of the horrible war, during which we lost our cattle, our shelters. We stayed at a camp near Wau [a big southern city]. We depended on relief agencies, which provided us with tents and food. Then my parents decided to come to Khartoum. We heard it was full of money, a place where we could have cattle again. We came with relatives to this camp by the river. All our dreams were destroyed—no money and no work.

The shortage of food forced me to do something for myself and my poor family. My cousin told me that he found me work as a maid in a family. I felt terrible about working as a maid for strangers, when I had been free and queen of my own land. I started to work for money. After a few months I couldn't bear to be a servant, ordered about and insulted by my employer. I quit my work. I started to go around with men, and I earn quite a lot of money. My family knows that, but I don't care as long as I can feed my little brothers and sisters.

I miss my home, my clean life with my friends, our laughter, songs, and dreams. It is now a horrible life. I prefer to return home even if there is a war, rather than staying here.

These three stories show that the government has not seriously addressed the plight of displaced women or even tried to develop projects for them. It has not dealt with displacement as a problem that will exist as long as the war continues. Poverty and economic need force women to do jobs that go against custom. The war has left its psychological effects on many displaced women.

In the two regions of western Sudan, Dar-Fur and Kordofan, the family, in both extended and nuclear form, generally maintains the culture—through reproductive, social, and productive functions. Women in western Sudan run both farm and household production and produce a variety of handicrafts from wood, leather, and palm leaves for domestic use and for the local and tourist market.

In 1984, when a severe drought damaged crops and reduced livestock herds, many people were forced to move north to areas close to Khartoum for shelter. Now they live in rough huts made of cartons and sacks and are exposed to high daytime temperatures and sand-carrying winds, which sometimes kill drought victims.

The Abu Zeid Camp is located inside Omdurman, the capital, and houses between 500 and 600 families from western Sudan. No services, such as water or healthcare, are provided by the government. Camp life has disrupted village ways and exposed women to special indignities, as the experiences of Hawa, Gisma, and Nima illustrate.

Hawa, aged 20, is married, has one child, and is illiterate.

I came here with my family five years ago. I married my cousin and we made a hut beside my parents' hut. My husband didn't give me any dowry. He lost all his cattle during the drought in our area. I feel depressed about that, but there is nothing to do. All the tribe lost its cattle and herds. My husband didn't even buy me gold. He doesn't have any money. He is working as a laborer. He is illiterate.

The government doesn't supply us with any of the necessities, like sugar, tea, milk, flour, and so on. For two years we depended on the relief agencies to support us, but now they have stopped. We used to exchange the food of the relief agencies that was not familiar to us for sugar, tea, second-hand clothes, and things like that. Last year many children were poisoned because they ate the powdered soap that mothers thought was a baby food.

I never go outside the camp or mix with the urbans. My husband buys everything for me. For four years I have always been here. I feel secure among my family. I'm not used to civilization. I know nothing about the government, but my husband says the government is intending to send us back home. I don't think we will go back unless the rain falls again in our lands. My life there is full of work, but here my husband takes care of everything. Anyway, we don't have cows to milk or land to cultivate. My little daughter was born into a new culture, but I will socialize her to maintain our customs and traditions till we go back home.

Gisma, aged 16, is married. She has no children, is illiterate, and works as a maid.

We came to Omdurman four years ago. My uncle was already here and sent for us to join him in this camp after we lost everything at home. My father is an old man. He has another wife besides my mother. I have four sisters and three brothers, all younger than me. My father couldn't manage feeding everyone in the family. Besides, the prices are very high. My uncle convinced my father that I had to work as a maid. My father agreed, so I worked with many families. I loved watching TV and looking at the makeup tools of the girls in the city.

I married my cousin. He is a laborer. When he cannot find a job I give him some money. I give my family part of my wages and save some to buy gold. I don't know whether the government will help us to go back home. It used to say that daily on the TV. Anyway, I won't go back; I like to be a city girl.

Nima, aged 45, is married and has six children. She is illiterate.

I came with my husband and children four years ago and settled in this camp with relatives. I gave birth to my last two children here in this camp. I prefer Zeinb, the midwife at my village, to the doctors [hakim] here. Many male doctors came and watched me during delivery. I wished I was dead rather than that a stranger could see my body fully, but I had no other alternative. There is no midwife at the camp, and I can't give birth by myself because I'm circumcised, and I face many difficulties while giving birth. My husband works as a laborer. He works [only] one or two days per week, for he is always drunk. My two older daughters, Zahra and Khadija, are the ones who support the family. Early in the morning they go to the houses in town to search for any work, such as washing dishes, cleaning the grounds, taking out the garbage, cleaning the courtyards [hawsh], and so on. Zahra is only ten years old, and Khadija is nine years old. Neither can read or write. At the end of the day my daughters come with the money they earned, and on their way home they purchase some sorghum to make 'asida [a local food made of water and sorghum flour].

I feel sorry for my two daughters. When their father is drunk he beats them and takes the money they earned to buy marisa. My daughters used to hide the money in their hair, but he always found it.

Sometimes respectable men come to our camp, have a look at it, argue, look at our children and the huts, and then go away with a lot of promises for a better future. At the beginning we used to feel happy that they were going to help us in improving our situation, but so far they have done nothing other than give us food from time to time, so we don't care any more. I pray every day. God is the only one who can help us to go back home; he can make the rain fall.

RURAL WOMEN AS A TOOL FOR ECONOMIC DEVELOPMENT

The collapse of rural social and economic life because of war and famine has not only created the pathos of displaced persons but has also made sustained development infinitely more difficult. Development of the rural economy is vital, and women are extremely important in subsistence agriculture and sometimes in small-scale production. The official labor force participation figures only begin to tell the story.

The 1983 census reported that 6.3 million persons ten years old and over were in the labor force, of whom 663,000 (10.5 percent) were unemployed. Males constituted 4.5 million (70.9 percent) of the total labor force, and females, 1.8 million (29.1 percent). The overall crude labor force participation rate was 36.1 percent: 51.4 percent for males and 20.9 percent for females.

For men the difference between the urban and rural crude participation rates was slight: 50.6 percent in urban areas, 51.6 percent in rural areas. But the corresponding rates for women were significantly different: 9.2 percent in urban areas and 24.1 percent in rural areas. These figures vastly underestimate the productive work that women do, ignoring their labor on family farms and their other traditional sector activities—not all of which are measurable by conventional methods but which do contribute to the economy. The labor of women in the rural areas has been overlooked in the controversial debates and research on how labor is measured, evaluated and incorporated into per capita income. Official statistics underestimate the participation of rural women in the labor force and hence the economic development of the country as a whole. In fact, 95 percent of rural women are engaged in agricultural activities, and the remaining 5 percent work as laborers, service workers, professionals, and traders. This unacknowledged labor by women is missed by such measures as national accounts, the census, and the social and economic indicators used in assessments and planning.[14]

An assessment of women's participation in economic production cannot be made without understanding the socioeconomic role of the family—typically, an extended family, especially in rural areas. The family provides both personal and economic protection to its members, becoming in effect a unit of production, and family members are workers within it.[15] Women in rural areas do not have one major activity and one secondary activity, as reported by most censuses but in fact carry out multiple economic activities for varying lengths of time. They work both in subsistence agriculture and in market production to increase the family income.

The economic activities of women in rural areas are shaped by the overall socioeconomic conditions of the country. Yet there are also other factors that directly affect the rate of women's participation in economic production, the kinds of activities they undertake, and their continuity in economic production. Profound regional differences in agriculture and production set the stage for the interplay of factors that affect economic development. These include the economic conditions of the family, group attitudes toward women's economic participation, the out-migration of men, the quality of educational facilities, and the growth of urban centers.

For instance, women in the most northern region do a substantial share of the traditional farm work, as well as help water crops and care for livestock. In private and government large-scale irrigation schemes, however, few women engage in farming activities. This magnifies how women are ignored when mechanized schemes are introduced. With the high percentage of out-migration from the far northern region, northern women have abandoned farming; they no longer even plant trees or cultivate kitchen gardens. Although some women are also involved in cottage industries and the production of handicrafts, either for their own use or for sale, well-off families may prohibit women from undertaking income-generating activities because they associate such work by women with need. Women's participation in economic activities is constrained by this attitude, which persists even among some poor groups.[16]

The central and eastern regions, comprising Khartoum, El Gezira, Kassala, and the Red Sea area, have a different agricultural base. In these regions women work in irrigated agricultural schemes on their husbands' tenancies. Few women own tenancies. Women are excluded from mechanized rain-fed farming, but they help pick cotton in Gezira and fruit and vegetables in the Kassala region.

Agriculture in the poorer western and southern regions is less mechanized and more dependent on erratic rainfall, and a greater proportion of the population drive or follow their herds from pasture to pasture. In the west, in Kordofan and Darfur, the rural population has both settled and nomadic elements. The major economic activities are rain-fed farming and pastoralism. Here, where the production unit is the extended family, women run farm and household production. They may generate additional income by annually migrating to work on mechanized schemes. They also produce handicrafts and trade in the urban centers.

The economy of the Equatorial, Upper Nile, and Bahr el-Ghazal regions in the south is based on rain-fed agriculture and traditional animal husbandry. Women in the south control the agricultural activities on the small individual farms. In many pastoralist groups women have recently settled down to farm while most of the males manage the group's livestock. Southern women are also responsible for many physically demanding tasks, such as water carrying and fuel gathering.

According to Judy Bushra and her colleagues at the Women in Development research project at the University of Khartoum, once Sudan became involved in the international monetary system, there were repercussions in local communities all across the country, specifically for women. Their participation in labor in the new development schemes has been the result, not of a changing ideology about work, but of material changes dictated by outside forces affecting land allocation and the use of natural resources. In the new era of mechanized and irrigated farming, community survival depends on women's added labor.[17]

Political plans may change the structure of the communities to achieve national goals. A major economic goal of the current regime is reflected in the slogan "We eat what we plant, and we wear what we manufacture." The policy, adopted to encourage food production and minimize food imports, may have a positive influence on the status of rural women and better integrate them more fully into the economic development plans.

The disruption of rural life by war and famine works against its success, however.

The previous regime encouraged both governmental and nongovernmental organizations (NGOs) to establish development projects involving rural women and all their activities. The issue of rural women and their role in economic development became very popular. Because Sudan is considered one of the poorest countries in the world, many U.N. agencies and international NGOs have been active in introducing development projects including community development efforts funded by the International Fund for Agricultural Development (1989), the U.N. Development Programs (1987), and Save the Children Federation (1986). Specific programs like poultry production, funded by the Food and Agricultural Organization in 1984, are now run by local governments. A health and literacy campaign with an income-generating component was supported by the Dutch government in 1983.[18]

These organizations have worked under severe economic handicaps, including the unfavorable exchange rate for hard currency donations and high Sudanese prices for project activities. Donors may have to give large amounts for small projects, knowing that the actual beneficiary is the government. Unfortunately most development projects have failed disastrously or at least had very little success—mainly because their sponsors do not give full consideration to the cultural factors that may hinder the development of rural women at the micro level and the economic development of the nation at the macro level.

For the last two years the regime has restricted the activities of many NGOs; some have stopped their work, and others have reduced their donations. Many are discouraged, too, by the civil war in the south and the economic crisis because the continuity of their projects under the supervision of the government cannot be guaranteed. Women are the main victims of the restrictive government policies toward NGOs—policies that have deprived women of development projects.

Both Sudanese government efforts and international development programs have generally failed to reach rural women. The government is burdened with many political as well as economic problems, so the needs of rural women are not likely to be a priority. What rural women need if they are to benefit from economic development are leadership positions in a national women's organization. To date, women's organizations have all failed to reach out to women at the grassroots level, because the leadership has always been dominated by urban women.

The approach that well-integrated rural economic development plans that incorporate women might take has been discussed at many seminars and workshops. The recommendations, not unlike the approaches that other countries with subsistence economies have found successful, are based on several key assumptions. First, rural women will develop through simultaneously integrated training, education, and income-generation projects. Their forgotten labor constitutes a major pillar of development that has to be measured properly. Next, appropriate technology for rural women will enhance the utilization of available resources. Third, improving women's socioeconomic conditions helps to increase their awareness of their rights, both those in the personal status laws and other civil rights. Fourth, the lack of organizational structures reduces the communication among women and the participation of women in development. Founding a central developmental unit for women should be a first step in raising their organizational, communicative, participative, and leadership abilities. The agency should function at the central and grass-roots levels. The absence of such an organized governmental body for women lessens the benefits that rural women obtain from international agencies.

THE FUTURE

Women's political engagement should be directed toward combating the threats that Sudanese society faces on the social, political, and economic fronts: civil war in the south, famine and drought in the west, inflation, illiteracy, the health crisis, the displacement of hundreds of thousands of people, the lack of food and other essential commodities. Women must be present at the decision-making and policy-formulating levels if these problems are to be faced and alleviated.

The current regime does not aim to isolate women from the public domain, for women constitute a large productive base. Indeed, units concerned with women's affairs have been established in some governmental institutions. Women also participated in achieving the recently modified Family Law and Criminal Law. But when it comes to selecting members of political committees to, say, oversee the reconstruction of the trade unions, women are ignored. Most of the women who do participate in politics within the current regime represent a specific ideology, that of the Muslim Sisters and Supporters. Most of the conservative Muslim women who believe in the creation of an Islamic nation and the implementation and enforcement of sharia law (particularly the *higab*, or the requirement that women wear Islamic clothes), are participating in regime-supporting politics.

Women's political engagement in Sudan must be directed toward maintaining the gains made after long years of struggle and sacrifice, as well as toward pursuing new goals that are consistent with the rapidly changing circumstances. Women must resist all attempts to reverse their progress. If they act with unity and solidarity, they can constitute a strong power base. Women's resistance can be in the form of strikes, demonstrations, and other appropriate actions.

Given the realities of Sudan, elite women should raise other women's awareness of their status and rights. Women's organizations have mainly been urban based and elitist, a problem for rural women. But these urban organizations also have the continuity and often the resources to contribute to enhancing the awareness of and improving conditions for rural women. Still, women's participation in decision making and policy formulation cannot be achieved unless a national popular women's organization can be established to shoulder the responsibility of guarding women's achievements and moving forward with new ones. Such an advance is possible only in a free democratic society, where women can exercise their rights as human beings.

NOTES

1. Population Census Office, Department of Statistics, Khartoum, 1989; *Population and Housing Census of the Sudan,* 1983; Sudan National Population Committee, 1983; Population Office, Department of Statistics, Khartoum.

2. Population Census Office, Department of Statistics, Khartoum, 1989.

3. International Labor Organization, *Employment and Economic Reform: Towards a Strategy of the Sudan* (Geneva: ILO, 1987), 32.

4. Nafisa Ahmed el-Amin and Mahassen Gillani, "Development of Political Status of Sudanese Women" (in Arabic) (Paper presented at a seminar on the changing status of Sudanese women, Ahfad University, 1979).

5. Ahmed Diab, *History of the National Movement in the Sudan (1952–1978)* (in Arabic) (Baghdad: UNESCO, Institute for Arabic Research and Studies, 1984), 63.

6. Institute for Social Studies, *The Women's Movement and Organizations in Historical Perspective* (Khartoum: University of Khartoum, 1985).

7. Hagga Kashif Badri, *The Women's Movement in the Sudan* (Khartoum: University of Khartoum, 1984), 109.

8. Nafisa Ahmed el-Amin, "Progress of the Sudanese Women's Movement" (in Arabic) (Paper presented in the cultural festival held in Sudan House, London, 1954).

9. Institute for Social Studies, *Women's Movement and Organizations in Historical Perspective.*

10. El-Amin and Gillani, "Development of the Political Status of Sudanese Women."

11. Ibid.

12. Lona Wilson, *Report on Visited and Registered Displaced People in the Khartoum Area* (Oxfam, 1989).

13. Ministry of Social Welfare, *Report on the Physical Environment of Displaced People* (1989).

14. Asha Abdalla Muhammad and Elsham Mohamed Hamidan, "Women's Employment and Development" (Paper presented at the Tripartite National Seminar on Labor Market Information, Sudan, April 1989).

15. Ibid.

16. Samia al-Hadi al-Nager and 'Alawia Osman Salih, "Women in Production: An Attempt at Curriculum Development" (Paper presented at a workshop on women's studies in Khartoum, February 1989).

17. Judy Bushra et al., "The Human Environment: Socio-Economic Development and Women's Changing Status" (Paper prepared by the Women in Development research project of the Development Studies and Research Centre, University of Khartoum, and presented to the workshop on Women and the Environment organized by the Institute of Environmental Studies, University of Khartoum, 4–8 April 1981).

18. Ministry of Finance and Economic Planning, Department of Regional Planning.

▲ Switzerland

POLITICS

Type of Political System: democracy
  Sovereignty: republic
  Executive-Legislative System: parliamentary
Type of State: federal
Type of Party System: multiparty
Major Political Parties

Freisinnig-Demokratische Partei (FDP), Parti Radical-Démocratique (PRD) (Radical Democratic Party): Right- and center-spectrum party with two seats in the Federal Council and 22.0 percent of the seats in the National Council in 1991.

Sozialdemokratische Partei (SPS), Parti Socialiste (PSS) (Social Democratic Party): Left-spectrum party with two seats in the Federal Council and 21.5 percent of the seats in the National Council in 1991.

Christlichdemokratische Volkspartei (CVP), Parti Démocrate-Chrétien (PDC) (Christian Democratic People's Party): Right- and center-spectrum party with two seats in the Federal Council and 18.5 percent of the seats in the National Council in 1991.

Schweizerische Volkspartei (SVP), Parti de l'Union Démocratique du Centre (UDC) (Swiss People's Party): Right-spectrum party with one seat on the Federal Council and 12.5 percent of the seats in the National Council in 1991.

Grüne Partei der Schweiz (GPS), Parti Ecologiste (PES) (Green Party of Switzerland): Center- and left-spectrum party. Not represented on the Federal Council; had 7.0 percent of the National Council seats in 1991.

Liberale Partei der Schweize (LPS), Parti Libéral Suisse (PLS) (Liberal Party): Right- and center-spectrum party similar to the Christian Democratic People's Party with no representation in the Federal Council and 5.0 percent of the seats in the National Council in 1991.

Unabhängige and Evangalische (UE), Groupe Indépendant et Evangélique (IE) (Independent and Evangelical Group): Coalition of two right-spectrum parties. Not represented on the Federal Council; had a total of 4.5 percent of the seats in the National Council in 1991. The Landesring der Unabhängigen (LdU), or Alliance des Indépendants (AdI) (Independents' Alliance), has six seats, and the Evangelische Volkspartei der Schweiz (EVP), or Parti Evangélique Populaire Suisse (PEP) (Evangelical People's Party), had three seats.

Schweizerische Partei de Autofahreren (SPA), Parti des Automobilistes (PSA) (Swiss Car Party): Far-right party not represented on the Federal Council; had 4.1 percent of the National Council seats in 1991.

Schweizer Democraten (SD), Démocrates Suisses (DS) (Swiss Democrats): Right-spectrum party with no representation on the Federal Council and 2.5 percent of the seats in the National Council in 1991.

Unaffiliated Members: Not represented on the Federal Council; had 2.5 percent of the seats in the National Council in 1991. Three of these members are from the Partei der Arbeit der Schweiz (PdAS), or Parti Suisse du Travail (PST) (Swiss Party of Labor), a left-spectrum party.

Year Women Granted Right to Vote: 1971
Year Women Granted Right to Stand for Election: 1971
Percentage of Women in the Legislature[a]
  Lower House: 17.5%
  Upper House: 8.7%
Percentage of Electorate Voting for Highest Elected Office in Most Recent Election (1991): not available

DEMOGRAPHICS
Population: 6,673,900[b]
Percentage of Population in Urban Areas
  Overall: 60.5%

Female: 61.5%

Male: 59.5%

Percentage of Population Below Age 15: 17.6%

Birthrate (per 1,000 population): 12[c]

Maternal Mortality Rate (per 100,000 live births): 5

Infant Mortality Rate (per 1,000 live births): 7

Mortality Rate for Children Under Five (per 1,000 live births): 8

Average Household Size: 2.8

Mean Age at First Marriage

Female: 25.0

Male: 27.9

Life Expectancy

Female: 80.5

Male: 73.8

EDUCATION

Ratio of Female to Male Enrollment

First-Level Education: 97

Second-Level Education: 104

Third-Level Education: 47

Literacy Rate

Female: 100.0%

Male: 100.0%

ECONOMY

Gross National Product per Capita: U.S. $16,370

Percentage of Labor Force in Agriculture: 5.7%[d]

Distribution of Agricultural Workers by Sex

Female: 22.8%

Male: 77.2%

Economically Active Population by Sex

Female: 36.0%

Male: 63.2%

a. Regula Stämpfli and Claude Longchamp, "Wie wird die Zukunft weiblich? Frauenförderung bei Wahlen und darüber hinaus: Bestandesaufnahme und Strategieformulierungen" (How will the future be feminine? Women's advancement through election and beyond: Taking stock and forming strategy), *Zukunft des Staates,* SVPW-Jahrbuch 30/1990 (Bern: Haupt, 1991); and Bundesamt für Statistik (Federal Bureau of Statistics), *Statistisches Jahrbuch der Schweiz* (Statistical yearbook of Switzerland) (Basel: Birkhauser, 1991).

b. *Taschenstatistik der Schweiz* (Pocketbook of statistics on Switzerland) (Bern: Bundesamt für Statistik, 1990).

c. Ibid.

d. Ibid.

Direct Democracy and Women's Suffrage: Antagonism in Switzerland

REGULA STÄMPFLI

I remember well a weekend in spring 1971. The three generations of women in my family were gathered for the traditional lunch get-together at my grandmother's farm. My grandmother, born in 1899, had worked the farm with the help of her sons since the death of her husband. My mother, born in 1926, was a cashier at a grocery store and the wife of a butcher; for most of the time she supported the family. My sister, born in 1954, had just returned from her one-year household stay in the French-speaking part of Switzerland (a tradition by which young Swiss women train to become good housewives). And I, born in 1962, was a good student at the public school. Together we celebrated the historic introduction of women's suffrage in Switzerland, approved in a national referendum in which the men in the family had just voted.

This personal example shows many of the diversities that exist among Swiss women: age, region, education, and economic status. In addition to language, cultural and religious differences, and political preference, these are the main diversities that can separate one Swiss woman from another. The distinctive rural or urban regions and the various languages complicate communication among different groups and act as a constraint on the development of nation-wide movements like the women's movement. In this chapter I consider two questions that arise when talking about women and politics in Switzerland: Why did it take so long for women to become full citizens? And how has women's representation in politics evolved since 1971?

DIRECT DEMOCRACY AND FEDERALISM

Switzerland, which borders France, Germany, Austria, Liechtenstein, and Italy, has been politically stable and economically prosperous for a long time. It has not been involved in a war for the past 150 years, is highly industrialized, and offers its citizens one of the highest standards of living in the world, and thus has not faced the difficulties of a nation struggling for political and economic independence that often block the integration of women's interests into the political system.

The country has four official languages: 70 percent of the population speak German, 20 percent French, 10 percent Italian, and fewer than 1 percent Romansh. About half of the Swiss are Protestant and half Roman Catholic. Geographic regions vary from isolated mountain valleys to cosmopolitan cities like Zurich and Geneva. All this diversity occurs within a population of only 6 million crowded into a small area.[1]

Switzerland is a confederation of autonomous cantons, which is one of several institutional features that have influenced the way the political system functions, and have affected women's struggle to acquire the vote and to become politically integrated. Other dominant characteristics include the role of direct democracy, the importance of interest groups, and the principle of collegial agreement.[2]

On three levels—federal, cantonal or state, and communal or local—citizens can exercise direct political power through initiatives (to propose changes to the constitution) and referenda (to vote on constitutional changes and laws proposed by the legislature). Citizens employ these means of direct democracy extensively. More than two-thirds of all the national referenda held in Western democracies since World War II have been conducted in Switzerland.[3] The electorate's ability to define or block the decision-making process through the use of initiatives and referenda competes with the use of national legislation. The provisions of direct democracy affect all levels of political opinion formation and all the actors involved.

The popular initiative offers citizens the right to raise issues concerning partial or total revision of the constitution if they can obtain the signatures of 100,000 eligible voters. The direct success of initiatives is limited, but their existence affects agenda setting. (Among 187 initiatives proposed, 105 have been voted on but only 10 were adopted.) An initiative puts pressure on the established powers and raises new political questions, thus is used mostly by opposition groups. In the 1980s and 1990s initiatives have often been used by emergent social movements.

Two types of referenda exist: the mandatory referendum deals with amendments concerning the constitution and urgent federal decisions; the optional referendum can be used when 50,000 eligible voters register their signatures to protest federal laws. The referenda thus raise the possibility of a popular veto. The government must therefore consult with various interest groups before any new bill is introduced. Well-organized and well-funded interest groups clearly have an advantage in organizing referendum campaigns.

Swiss federalism can be compared to federalism in the United States. The building units of the society are the 23 autonomous regions, or cantons, not the linguistic communities. All but four of the cantons are linguistically homogeneous. Although language itself is not always significant, dialect may well be. For example, German speakers, despite their majority, rarely function as a unified bloc in Swiss politics, perhaps because of the large number of distinctive German dialects.[4] Equally significant, the Catholic-Protestant division cuts across the borders between German- and French-speaking cantons. Because linguistic, economic, and religious regions crosscut one another in a very complex way, Swiss politics is characterized by constantly shifting coalitions.

The strong federalism limits the power of the Swiss Federal Assembly, which consists of two chambers (councils) with identical powers. The 200-member National Council represents the people. Elections to the council bear the imprint of federalism, for the cantons serve as constituencies from multiple-member districts. The Council of States has 46 members who represent the cantons. The voters in each canton elect two members; the majority system is generally used in single-member districts. The system of two chambers with identical powers demands considerable cooperation between the federal and regional powers. The Federal Council is the executive power and consists of seven members representing the four major parties.

Party autonomy in the cantons is high because the cantons function as constituencies. The national parties, which have had difficulty organizing themselves efficiently on the federal level, remain relatively weak and function as umbrella organizations for various regional interests. In addition, Switzerland has a functional federalism, with federal laws and policies usually implemented by cantonal governments. Thus the cantons gain a substantial maneuverability with regard to the application and realization of federal laws, the so-called *Vollzugföderalismus* (federalism of implementation). In several spheres (education, health, and energy) the cantons have jurisdiction over the formulation and the implementation of policies; in others (culture, construction, planning, and waste disposal) the communes (municipalities) have jurisdiction.

Owing to a combination of direct democracy and federalism, an elaborate system of prelegislative procedures exists. These include the collaboration of the cantons and interest groups, as well as consultations to prepare bills in a system called *Vernehmlassungsverfahren* (consultation of interests). The Zentralverband Schweizerischer Arbeitgeber (Central Union of Swiss Employers), the Schweizerischer Bauernverband (Association of Swiss Farmers), and the Schweizerischer Gewerkschaftsbund (Swiss Association of Trade Unions) participate on each level of the decision-making process. The hearings, preparatory meetings, and federalist consultations in the implementation process highlight the weakness of the Federal Assembly in the face of the greater influence of different interest groups.

Switzerland is not a parliamentary democracy, which means that the Federal Council (the seven-member executive) cannot be overruled by the Federal Assembly, nor can the Federal Assembly be sustained by the executive. Nor is Switzerland a presidential democracy, which means that the federal councillors are elected by the Federal Assembly, not by the people. Switzerland has a nonparliamentary system of government characterized by *Kollegialprinzip*, or collegial agreement. The equal status of the seven members of the executive means that if a consensus cannot be reached, none of the seven is able to issue general instructions.

The country has been governed by a right-wing conservative majority over the past 30 years. Since 1959 the Federal Council has consisted of two Free Democrats, two Christian Democrats, two Social Democrats, and one representative of the Swiss People's Party. In this way the government represents more than 80 percent of the voters.

It is an unwritten rule that at least two federal councillors represent the language minorities (French and Italian). Proportional representation of language and region is also frequently applied in the federal administration. This constellation of government and legislature, of integrated opposition and ruling majority, has to be considered when talking about parties, issues, and decision making. Collaboration at each level contributes to a pattern of opinion formation that can be called *Konkordanzprinzip*, or consociationalism, which is an amicable agreement among various political parties and policies. Compromise plays an important role in avoiding confrontation. Party discipline does not have a great impact on elected representatives.

Elections take place every four years, and incumbents usually retain their jobs. Many lawyers, farmers, teachers, and local government officers sit in the Federal Assembly. In the Swiss *Milizsystem* (a system of semiprofessionals), politicians continue to practice their professions, rather than becoming professional politicians. The chambers meet four times a year for three-week periods. The decisions are initially drafted by standing or select committees. Members can submit amendments to draft bills during debates, as well as table proposals and question the government by means of interpellation.

One may wonder how political decisions are reached at all, given the complexity of the political system and the way women are involved in Swiss politics. Even politically talented Swiss have trouble explaining the system to foreigners, and in a discussion among feminists from various countries the explanations get more complicated. Often women from other countries focus on the question of how it was possible for one of the world's oldest democracies not to grant half its citizens the right to vote until the late twentieth century.

No existing publication sufficiently answers this question. I explain the late introduction of women's suffrage in Switzerland by examining the distinctive features of the Swiss system as they affect the political situation of Swiss women. Some concrete examples illustrate the difficulties that women face.

THE STRUGGLE FOR WOMEN'S SUFFRAGE

The history of Swiss women's struggle for the right to vote is filled with deceptions, frustrations, and prevention tactics initiated by men and by the state. In a political system where the citizens can express their political wishes by voting and by signing initiatives and referenda, women have long resented depending on men to express their own concerns and interests politically.

In the struggle for suffrage Swiss women were forced to ask their husbands and progressive-thinking men for help. Women's right to vote was not introduced by a constitutional change but by a plebiscite held among men in 1971. The dependence on a majority of men may well be a reason for the late introduction of women's suffrage in Switzerland. But if we examine the many petitions, motions, and postulates concerning women's suffrage, we realize the importance of direct democracy and federalism in hindering the attainment of women's rights in general.

The first National Congress of Women took place in Geneva in 1896 on the occasion of the Swiss National Exhibition.[5] The women's organizations of Geneva, Lausanne, Bern, and Zurich founded the Bund schweizerischer Frauenorganisationen (Union of Swiss Women's Organizations, or USO), which included 17 organizations in 1900 and 23 the next year.

The USO understood itself as a merely patriotic association that offered its help to government officials. The main goal of its members was to influence the contents of the new civil code, which was being formulated in 1912. The women asked for separation of property in marriage, guardianship of children by their unmarried mothers, and equality in parental responsibility for children, instead of the father's predominance. In addition, the women tried to influence the development of a new health insurance bill that would have provided maternity care and leave for women, plus equal insurance costs for women and men. None of the demands of the USO was granted, and some of the discriminatory determinations in the health insurance bill (such as unequal admission procedures) remain today.

The failure of the USO had to do with its structure: the demands and claims of the different member sections were heterogeneous, as were the regional and class-specific claims of the different member unions. The first national organization for women did not focus on egalitarian goals but promoted acceptance of the equivalence between female achievements and values and those of males to show the importance of women's participation at all social and political levels. Gender-specific discrimination was not an issue in the USO, and the main goal was more to show the men how important women were for society as "real women"—as mothers, wives, temperance campaigners, and people socially engaged in the question of pauperism.

The Schweizerischer Frauenstimmrechtsverband (National Organization for Women's Suffrage) was founded by a number of cantonal suffrage organizations in 1909 to organize the cantonal suffrage efforts in order to promote the issue of women's suffrage at the national level. It was very federalized, however, and provided little assistance in cantonal suffrage campaigns. It did not establish a clear policy, nor did it attempt to mobilize the population in cantons without cantonal suffrage organizations. For votes within cantons, the cantonal organizations were largely on their own; the National Organization for Women's Suffrage did not want to interfere. Clearly, cantonal autonomy is a powerful force in Switzerland.

The National Organization for Women's Suffrage soon divided itself into three sections: the traditional USO, the Arbeiterinnenvereine (Working Women's Organization), and the Katholischer Frauenbund (Catholic Women's Organization). The lack of consensus within the national organization hurt the goal of improving women's status more generally.

During World War I the traditional USO alleviated the distress of the war. Women helped the government organize "war aid" without ever mentioning the discrimination they experienced or their own underprivileged situation. Unlike the women of Germany, the Swiss women never dared to ask for suffrage as compensation for the work they did during the war. After the war only the Social Democrats demanded women's suffrage during the general strike in 1918. One Radical and one Social Democrat formulated a motion in 1919 asking for a constitutional change. The government's prevention tactic was to sim-

ply ignore this motion; finally in 1957 both the National Council and the Council of States dealt with the suffrage motion of 1919.

In 1921 there were popular votes on women's suffrage in six part-industrialized, part-rural cantons: Neuenburg, Geneva, Basel-City, Zurich, Glarus, and St. Gall. Suffrage came to a vote only in these cantons because a few women in the cantons were interested in women's issues. Suffrage was rejected in all the cantons, especially in several where the Social Democrats had strong organizations. In spite of the official doctrine of the party, the members, all men, were not in favor of women's suffrage. Swiss men generally were not yet ready to grant women the right to vote.[6]

Another form of organization for women's interests was the professional union, which took shape after World War I. Primarily better-educated women organized unions by occupation (midwives, teachers, female academics, and farmers). At the same time, the trade unions for blue-collar workers underwent a marked decline in female membership because of the resistance that women felt to organizing themselves within the trade union structure.

A nationwide exhibition on female professions (Schweizerische Ausstellung für Frauen-Arbeit) took place in 1928. Its success led to a petition to the Federal Assembly for women's suffrage, signed by 250,000 people—a large number for Switzerland. The Federal Council ignored the petition, this time until after World War II. This petition had an important political effect on the women who organized it, but it failed to put pressure on the parliamentary debates.

Women's demands for suffrage seemed unimportant when compared with World War II. Moreover, fascism in Europe reinforced the ideology of traditional gender values. After the war two ideologies influenced women in Switzerland: the American ideology of growth and industry, and the traditional ideology of women as housewives and caring mothers. In the political agendas of both men and women, women's emancipation and women's suffrage were not the top priority. The skilled women with jobs had learned in the 1930s that they were the last to be hired and the first to be fired.[7] Men, because of their strong organization within the trade unions, were always in a better position to retain their jobs.

Shortly after the war eight cantons again rejected women's suffrage in cantonal referenda.[8] In 1951 the postulates from 1919 were considered in a report by the Federal Council. The breakthrough came in 1957, when the Federal Council scheduled a national referendum—for the first time in the history of the drive for women's suffrage. The National Council and the Council of States both had to discuss the Federal Council's proposal, for giving women the vote required a change in the Swiss Constitution.

Why did the Federal Council so easily endorse women's right to vote in 1957, when it had previously ignored the petitions, motions, and postulates? In 1951 the Council of States had rejected the idea of an elaboration of an amendment for women's suffrage, but since then the international pressure for women's rights had intensified. The U.N. charter and the conventions of the International Labor Organization both called for equal rights and equal pay. The report of the Federal Council was prepared by an outstanding professor of law who was active in Swiss center party politics. Regardless of strong resistance to changing the constitution, both chambers accepted women's suffrage in 1959. If Switzerland had not been a direct democracy, women's right to vote would have taken effect immediately. Given the obligation of a mandatory referendum, the people (that is, the male population) had the final say. But 69 percent of the male voters voted against the amendment—a percentage that corresponds to the cantonal average of all the popular votes on women's suffrage over the previous 30-odd years. Swiss men did not change their attitude toward women's suffrage during this time.

A new women's organization was founded shortly before the vote in 1959. Called the Arbeitsgemeinschaft der schweizerischen Frauenverbände für die politischen Rechte der Frau (Working Group of the Swiss Women's Association for the Political Rights of Woman), this umbrella organization encompassed most of the women's groups in the country and enabled groups on the left and the right to work closely together.

In spite of the defeat in the national referendum, women won the right to vote on cantonal and communal affairs in the canton of Geneva in 1959 and in Vaud and Neuenburg in 1960. The first German-speaking canton to introduce women's suffrage was Basel-City in 1966. Because some women had the right to vote on the cantonal or communal level, women's suffrage seemed increasingly "normal" as the years passed.

In 1963, Switzerland became a member of the European Council and in 1968 wanted to sign the European Human Rights Convention. Because Switzerland did not allow women to vote, it tried to sign the convention with a separate clause allowing an exemption for women's suffrage. Women's organizations across the political spectrum protested, and organized a march to Bern in 1969 with the slogan "Women's suffrage is a human right." The state was forced to respond, for the European Council did not accept the proposal for exemption. Finally, in 1971 a majority of Swiss men voted to support women's suffrage in a national (mandatory) referendum, making women their formal political equals at last.[9]

How did the various women's organizations react to the long wait for suffrage? They were nonaggressive and diplomatic, and the predominant tactic within both the USO and the National Organization for Women's Suffrage was collaboration, rather than confrontation. None of the local women's organizations ever used more aggressive lobbying tactics, such as demonstrations of strength in legislative galleries or verbal denunciations of antisuffrage legislators. Women did not even publicize candidates' positions on suffrage. Instead, they focused on petitions or general letters to the government asking for support on the issue and never used tactics designed to embarrass government officials. The women who favored suffrage were economically and socially integrated and did not want to be mixed up with left-wing parties and progressive ideas. And the left-wing parties were concerned with issues other than women's suffrage.

It was difficult for women to speak out in favor of women's suffrage and feminism. Iris von Roten, for example, published *Frauen im Laufgitter* (Women in a children's prison) in 1958, a ten-year writing project comparable to Simone de Beauvoir's *Second Sex*. Since 1944 von Roten had also been the editor of the women's suffrage paper *Schweizerischen Frauenblatt* (Swiss women's paper). She had studied law, practiced as a lawyer, and formulated in her book a feminist critique that anticipated that of the 1970s. She understood her book as a contribution to the national campaign in 1959, but she was far too modern for her times, her generation, and the population at large.

The male typesetters initially refused to set such an outrageous lampoon of men. Once published, the book created a scandal. Even though the first edition sold out within a couple of weeks, the book was soon forgotten. Even the women in the National Organization for Women's Suffrage rejected any further collaboration with von Roten. She retreated from politics after publishing another small brochure and continued her life, painting and traveling around the world.[10] The example of her life shows well the enormous pressure against freethinking women, suffragists, and feminists in Switzerland—a pressure that was and is consistent with a society and culture dominated by the strong belief in nonconfrontation on all levels.

Because of the political importance and sanctity of federalism (article 74 of the constitution), the state did not want to interfere with the canton's right to grant suffrage.[11] So until 1990 it was possible for the German-speaking canton of Appenzell to refuse to grant women suffrage. Although the women of Appenzell were able to vote on federal affairs, they still could not vote on communal or cantonal affairs, nor could they be elected in the community or canton. They tried petitions and motions—like the earlier suffragists—but failed every time. One Appenzell woman brought the issue to the Supreme Court in Lausanne. The judiciary has jurisdiction only over civil matters, and therefore had no history of considering cantonal bills and political matters. Nevertheless, in 1990 the court accepted the woman's civil appeal and declared that cantons may not restrict women's right to vote at the cantonal and communal level because of the Equal Rights Amendment. For the first time in the history of Switzerland, the Supreme Court restricted cantonal political authority.

This episode was both judicially complicated and embarrassing for the people involved—with the exception of the men from Appenzell, who were proud of their action. It is still not very clear which judicial procedure would have been the correct one to use, for the men in Appenzell had rejected women's suffrage in cantonal referenda every year. The result, in any case, is that since 1990 *all* Swiss women can vote and hold office on the federal, cantonal, and communal levels.

The introduction of women's suffrage in 1971 changed many policies within the federal administration. In 1976, as a reaction to the National Women's Congress in 1975, the state introduced the Eidgenössische Kommission für Frauenfragen (National Commission for Questions Concerning Women). It has its own secretariat and is located in the Department of Culture, which comes under the jurisdiction of the minister of internal affairs. The goal of the commission is to promote women's interests and to advance scientific research on the implementation of women's rights.

THE EQUAL RIGHTS AMENDMENT

Since 1981, when the people of Switzerland voted in favor of the Gleichstellungsartikel (Equal Rights Amendment, or ERA), initiated by the Neue Frauenbewegung (new women's movement), the National Commission for Women has been charged with formulating a catalog of laws that conform to the ERA in order to fulfill the demands stated in the constitution: "Men and women are equal. The law has to guarantee equal rights, especially in the family, education, and work. Men and women are entitled to equal pay for equal work."[12]

It was clear from the beginning that the constitutional amendment did not guarantee equal rights for women and men, but stated a general, symbolic principle. How the Federal Assembly implemented the ERA in bills was and is still the key point. Since the ERA was passed, nothing much has happened. Switzerland—unlike many other countries—has no means to implement the equal pay provision of the ERA. The bills on equal pay proposed in the Federal Assembly have not obtained the needed majority for passage. Discrimination remains, despite the ERA.

The state began to discuss the introduction of an equal rights office within the federal administration in 1982. Both chambers welcomed the Federal Council's 1987 proposal to set one up. The government was influenced here by the success of the U.N. World Women's Conference in Nairobi in 1985 and the new women's movement.

Even though there has been a Büro für die Gleichstellung von Mann und Frau (Federal Office for Equal Rights for Men and Women) in the Department of Culture since 1988, the demands of the National Commission for Questions Concerning Women regarding implementation of the ERA have not been met. The state has fulfilled the wish for an equal rights office without allocating adequate financial resources or personnel for it to carry out its constitutional charge. Its establishment may be a step toward improving women's situation, but the step is tiny, given the huge task of eliminating the overall discrimination against women by the state, employers, schools, and other organizations.

The federal model of an equal rights board has been followed in some cantons (Basel, St. Gall, Geneva, Bern) and in some universities (Geneva, Lausanne, Bern). All the boards suffer from limited financial resources and have little influence in the legislature. The statement by a Green Party member of the Federal Assembly applies nationwide: "Equal rights in general, yes, but not today and at no cost."[13]

THE GENERAL POSITION OF WOMEN IN SOCIETY

A small though important improvement in the situation of women came with the revised marriage law. Since 1988 wives have had greater financial independence from their husbands. Both parents are responsible for their children, and in case of a divorce or the death of the husband, the wife can now legally benefit. But injustices remain. Almost nothing has changed in the social security system, which defines public pensions according to civil status, which means for married women that the husband's salary is the only standard of measurement, even if she has also been employed. Obligatory maternity protection has still not been implemented. Women are not protected during pregnancy or old age, and inequalities in the income tax system still exist. Married women may not fill out their own income tax forms; their husbands must do it for them.

The higher one goes in the political and economic hierarchy, the fewer women can be found. Women are generally less integrated into the trade unions and professional organizations. They cannot count on the help of the trade unions to get equal pay because every woman must plead her legal case on her own under federal law; if she asks the courts for equal pay, she can be fired immediately, for there is no protection against unlawful dismissal. Swiss women are generally less skilled than Swiss men. For example, although 44 percent of gymnasium graduates (secondary school graduates who have access to the universities) were women in 1986, women were only 32 percent of those who received a university degree—and only 20 percent of women with a university degree received a doctoral degree. Among the professors at the universities only 2 percent are women.[14]

Because the division of labor is still very much determined by sex, fewer women than men have jobs, and women are strongly affected by the phenomenon of *Neue Armut* (new poverty).[15] In addition, women earn on average one-third less than men, when both full-time and part-time work are considered.

In Switzerland, as in most Western countries, women's rights organizations have been struggling for a century and a half to redefine women's proper place not only in the family but also in public life. With the beginning of the new women's movement in the 1970s the old "justice" arguments gave way to arguments concerning the social and political relevance of gender. The new women's movement consists of various political women's groups, university women, grass-roots intellectuals, and professional organizations for the improvement of women's situation in general. It is considered a minority movement because its issues are not in the consciousness of most Swiss women. Feminism lives on harsh ground in Switzerland.

The new women's movement was influenced by American and German feminist literature and started out as a women's liberation movement, also referred to as an organization for the women's cause. Since the late 1980s some new feminist women's associations have also been founded, such as the Verein feministische Wissenschaft Schweiz (National Association of Feminist Research). With the formation of the new women's movement, arguments about the differences in the life situations of women and men, and about how their different preferences have produced different and sometimes conflicting interests, have become important. Although heterogeneity still characterizes the movement, it is—at least among Swiss intellectuals—much stronger than any women's movement before.

Although the traditional women's organizations usually addressed their demands to politicians in a nonaggressive way, the new women's movement is more reluctant to play the old power games and more willing to provoke conflicts. But sometimes the new women's movement and such traditional women's organizations as the USO work together during federal elections in campaigns to increase the number of women representatives. The left-wing parties all started their own women's organizations in the 1980s. These are often used as channels whereby the ideas and the demands of the new women's movement can be added to the general political agenda. Since the movement has been active, the mobilization for increased representation of women in politics has become more clearly based on arguments stressing gender as a social and thus politically relevant category. And when such an argument is accepted, it is difficult for most party leaders to ignore women's claims to political representation.[16]

Compared to the feminist demands of the Swiss intellectual elite, progress toward the broad goals of women's emancipation and equality has been slight since 1971. There have been some successes, but in some fields there have been setbacks, even since 1981, when the ERA was introduced. Some political groups want to profit from the amendment that they initially fought against. For example, in addition to granting women equal rights, the amendment has initiated, among other things, discussions of proposals to raise the retirement age for women from 62 to 65 to match the retirement age for men; to grant a widowers' pension analogous to the widows' pension; and to require women as well as men to meet military obligations. Women now serve in the army on a voluntary basis only. The draft applies to all men, who must serve in the army three weeks a year until age 32. Most such proposals are being made by the right-wing parties, which have a chance of obtaining the necessary political majority in the Federal Assembly. Switzerland is an example of how men can profit from an amendment that was introduced for the benefit of women. The ERA made women's position formally equal without locating that formal equality in an unequal society, one measure of which is the use of the law for men but not for women.

INTEREST GROUPS

Given the history of the Swiss confederation and the special diversities of direct democracy, the integration of interest groups occurs at most levels of the decision-making process. Legislators must integrate the views of all interest groups that are capable of initiating a national referendum and thus capable of using their influence to block decisions. The interest groups with strong memberships and centralized organizations have the power to decide—only 50,000 signatures are needed—whether a proposed bill has to pass a popular vote or not. Bills subjected to popular votes are difficult to pass, for the Swiss people tend to say no more often than yes.

A shared gender has not been sufficient to build an economically and politically powerful interest group to promote women's issues. The possibility of collective action by women—despite the known and objectively stated inequalities—is very limited, considering their heterogeneous biographies, age and class characteristics, and linguistic, regional and cultural affiliations.

The lack of a strong women's interest group has two major consequences. First, women's specific interests are not discussed in the preparliamentary stages of creating and passing laws. Second, because interest groups promote the concerns of large groups, the concerns of less-organized groups, such as women, are underrepresented. In times when financial resources are limited, organized economic interests other than women's come into the political debate.

The influence of interest groups does not stop with the preparliamentary consultations. Interest groups also directly influence members of the Federal Assembly. Having a semiprofessional parliament, whose members earn their income not only in their political posts but also through separate professions, allows for the multiplication of functions. The result is legislators with a combination of professional and political interests that are connected with the goals of various interest groups. A member of the Federal Assembly may at the same time represent a party and a large professional interest group, which in effect pays his or her salary as a member of that profession. Owing to the nonexistence of strong women's organizations and women's interest groups, women cannot afford to pay Federal Assembly members a good salary and thus influence them directly.

COLLEGIAL AGREEMENT AND THE POSITION OF THE PARTIES

Women's success in politics often has to do with the formal mechanism of the electoral system. In general, multiparty systems using the electoral principle of proportional representation produce more women representatives than, for instance, two-party systems. In multiparty systems, each geographically defined electoral unit (in Switzerland, the canton) will send several representatives to the legislature, normally from more than one party and normally more than one from each of the largest parties. This way, a woman candidate will not be a political party's only candidate from a given electoral unit. The regional aspect in the electoral units cannot be underestimated. The commune in which a candidate lives may be more important to the party than his or her political profile. Potential candidates often fail to be nominated because their families live in the "wrong" commune. For elections to the Council of States, women often face a no-win situation, where two parties compete for the two seats in a constituency, and both parties have male candidates in the leading position.

Political parties within a democracy are those instruments that enable citizens to articulate interests and preferences and that simultaneously provide the means by which the few can represent the many.[17] Parties in Switzerland cannot be compared in importance to those in Western countries where elections are the most important vehicle the citizen has to express political ideas and where the ruling and opposition parties are in strong competition with one another. Swiss parties are different because of direct democracy and because of the system of collegial agreement among the major parties.

During the 1970s and 1980s established party loyalties began to break down. Class-structured voting is declining, and allegiances are shifting. The parties now compete for the same voters. From a theoretical point of view it would seem easy to attract the least bound party voters—women—by using party strategies and tactics for their benefit. Any party could aim to strengthen its position among women voters in order to strengthen the party as a whole. This has happened to a degree among the parties on the left, which have tried to gain voters through elaborate attempts to represent women's interests.

But the competition among the parties on the left and the right is lessened by collegial agreement, which is strong enough to make it unnecessary to mobilize more women. This amicable agreement among the four major parties, which together propose the seven councillors in the Federal Council, prevents any of the four from becoming a powerful, issue-oriented party with a distinctive competitive image. Until now there has been no real need for one party to obtain a positive profile among women through its policies. Because the major parties make decisions together on all federal policies, why integrate the needs and demands of an intellectual minority, like feminists? Other political issues dominate election campaigns, such as the question of European integration (Switzerland is not a member of the European Community) and the problems of immigration from poor countries. As long as there is no real outburst from the women themselves, the major parties in Switzerland do not need the women's vote to hold or regain political power. The issue of women's representation must be politically relevant before it can affect competition among the parties.

Why is the issue of women's representation being neglected in Swiss politics? One reason could be the short history of political rights for women. Another reason may well be the political culture.[18] Traditionalism, conservative values, and a slow decision-making process are consistent with the Swiss mentality. Swiss in general are not progressive. History has taught them to keep still and stand neutral to avoid becoming involved in great conflicts. Gender politics generate strong conflict and are thus to be avoided.

ELECTIONS

Numbers tell the story of women's representation in Switzerland. In 1971, the first year that women were allowed to run for election, 11 women were elected to the National Council. This number increased to 21 in 1979 and to 29 in 1987. Five women were elected to the Council of States in 1987 (10.5 percent of the seats). The political representation of women has thus changed slowly over time—rising from 5.5 to 14.5 percent of the seats in the National Council over sixteen years. In other Western countries, with the exception of the Scandinavian countries, the rate remains stable at about 15 percent. Without special measures and positive actions—such as quotas—Swiss women are unlikely to exceed the 15 percent barrier, unless a miracle occurs. For what reasons, besides political structure and history, are women still so underrepresented in Switzerland?

In general, Swiss women are underrepresented whenever power is distributed. Men come first; women stay behind.[19] Women still vote less frequently than men; in 1987 the difference was 10 percent. The political parties nominate women less frequently; in 1987 only 29.5 percent of all candidates on party ballots were women. The people elect women less frequently; every 10th male candidate is elected, but only every 25th female candidate. Thus both women and men elect fewer women.[20]

Cantonal elections do not show results any more encouraging than the federal elections do. Five cantons have women ministers in their executive branch, but most of these women serve for only one term and have more difficulty than men in being reelected.

The situation in the Federal Council is particularly bad for women: the seven councillors are all men. The first woman elected (in 1986) to the Federal Council, Elisabeth Kopp, a conservative Free Democrat, had to resign in 1989 because of her husband's business activities; he was reportedly involved in a money-laundering scandal.[21] She was active on several women's issues, but she herself said that she was far from being a feminist. As a councillor, she promoted the revision of the marriage law and the establishment of the federal office for equal rights. As the head of the Justice Department, she introduced the study of the equal pay question, but as soon as the report was finished, she distanced herself (along with her party) from the contents of the report, saying it was too left-wing and counterproductive. Women's issues were not among her main interests. As a young politician, she never engaged in the struggle for women's suffrage. Her resignation was caused by the only real gender-related event during her term as councillor. A male councillor would never have been held responsible for his wife's professional activities in the way that Elisabeth Kopp was held responsible for the business affairs of her husband. The entanglement of the first female councillor in Switzerland in her husband's scandal harmed women's interests enormously, and the women of Switzerland may wait many years until another female councillor is elected.[22]

Both men and women elect women less often to political office for reasons that apply not only to Swiss women but also to a large majority of women elsewhere in the world. Like many women around the globe, Swiss women are socialized at home and at school to fulfill their duties at home and not to engage in public affairs. Regardless of the equal rights postulates of the political elite, the cliché of the politically incompetent woman persists over generations. Swiss women are generally isolated from informal political networks, such as the large interest groups, so they have fewer opportunities to influence policies. The definition of political engagement poses another problem for women, who are involved in voluntary work in schools and in the community. Many women participate almost solely in women's organizations and have a more collective approach to solving problems than men do. In politics, women are often alone in a male-dominated group, which does not help them to build their self-identity and self-confidence. Often the stereotype of women's emotional approach to politics is held up against the standard of political rationality. Swiss women feel that they are viewed as ridiculous and often complain about their feelings of insecurity.

What about the new women's movement in Switzerland? How do members react to the continuing discrimination against women? The movement does not have the financial resources or the organizational structure to promote women's interests fully. Women do not compose a forceful, unified group. The women in the center and right-wing parties still fight for equal rights without big social changes. The women in the left-wing parties and the new social movements are better organized, but politically they—like all the left parties and new social movements—are marginalized and overruled by the conservative majority.

In addition to the divisions among different cantonal and political groups within the new women's movement, there is also a division (mainly in the big cities) between the more academic and intellectual feminists and the feminists of the grass-roots counterculture. Although the more academic and intellectual feminists pursue careers within society, grass-roots feminists do not want to participate within prescribed limits and thus remain radical. Their differences hurt the women involved as well as women's interests in general, but despite their diversity feminists must define the position of the new women's movement in this male-dominated society. The stronger the opposing pressure from society, the more radical the feminist theories become.

On 14 June 1991 all the women's organizations and the new women's movement participated in a surprising and unprecedented collective action. Women trade union members persuaded the unions to proclaim a general "women's strike" for that day to demonstrate how far Swiss women still must go to get equal pay and equal rights. Some 500,000 women participated nationwide, and the strike was a great success. Since 1937 strikes have been forbidden in many institutions, so the action was not technically a strike but a day of consciousness-raising and sharing of experiences by and for women. The state and large employers were careful to use the day to promote many activities within their institutions. It was typical of Switzerland that opposition groups did not demonstrate against the government on the day of the women's strike. Nevertheless, for all the women who participated it was an overwhelming experience, and it revealed a solidarity among women that cannot be underestimated.

REFLECTIONS ON THE FUTURE

In Switzerland the success or failure of women's interests has been influenced by direct democracy. Women's suffrage was established by popular vote and not by constitutional change—an important reason for its late introduction. In writing about the struggle for suffrage, I have concentrated on the political failures and achievements of women's interests within the political system, restricting the discussion to the political system because of the connection between women's interests and the distinctive features of the Swiss confederation.

The Swiss experience shows the importance of numerical strength for women in political positions. The unequal distribution of positions of power between women and men in Switzerland calls for strong corrective action. At the same time, strength in numbers does not guarantee the triumph of feminist issues. Feminization of political power requires much more than increased representation of women; it requires a reconsideration of values within society that would force the integration of women's interests. But after viewing the history of the various women's movements and women's organizations in Switzerland, one has to wonder whether societal values concerning women will ever change.

Women's issues will certainly be influenced in the future by the general political discussion of the connections between Switzerland and the European Community. Swiss women could profit from the progressive social and political rights in the EC. Yet active feminists express many doubts concerning women's political influence and the distribution of positions of power in the so-called *Herrenhaus Europa* (men's parliament of Europe). The decision-making process in the EC is bureaucratic and hierarchical. Most of the decisions about the EC are made by the political elite of the member countries. Because men form the political elites of these countries, there is little hope that women's interests will receive serious consideration. Only the collective action of women across Europe—of different cultures, colors, languages, educational levels, and social backgrounds—could perhaps change this situation. The difficulty of organizing such a collective action can be seen in the history of women's interests in Switzerland and even in the history of a project such as Women and Politics Worldwide. Communication among women of different races and cultures will always present challenges to the advancement of women's interests.

NOTES

1. Jurg Steiner, *European Democracies* (New York: Longman, 1986), 167.
2. Ulrich Kloti, "Vorwort" (Foreword), in *Handbuch politisches System der Schweiz* (Handbook of the political system of Switzerland), vol. 2: *Strukturen und Prozesse* (Structure and processes) (Bern: Haupt, 1984), 39.
3. Steiner, *European Democracies*, 156.
4. Ibid., 168
5. Elisabeth Joris and Heidi Witzig, eds., *Frauengeschichte(n): Dokumente aus zwei Jahrhunderten zur Situation der Frauen in der Schweiz* (Women's history: Documents from 200 years on the situation of women in Switzerland) (Zurich: Limmat, 1986), 449.
6. Susanna Woodtli, *Gleichberechtigung: Der Kampf um die politischen Rechte der Frau in der Schweiz* (Equal rights: The fight for the political rights of women in Switzerland) (Frauenfeld: Huber, 1975), 141ff.
7. Beatrix Mesmer, "Vom 'Doppelten Gebrauchswert' der Frau—Eine Einführung," in Marie-Louise Barben and Elisabeth Ryter, eds., *Verflixt und zugenaht! Frauenberufsbildung—Frauenerwerbsarbeit, 1888–1988* (Zurich: Chronos, 1988), 15ff.
8. Defeat (canton, year, and percent): Basel-Land, 1946: 73.5; Basel-City, 1946: 62.9, 1954: 54.9; Bern, 1956: 54.4; Geneva, 1946: 56.3, 1953: 57.2; Neuchatel, 1948: 67.2; Solothurn, 1948: 50.5; Ticino, 1946: 77.2; Zurich, 1947: 77.5, 1954: 71.3.
9. The vote was 621,109 to 323,882.
10. Joris and Witzig, eds., *Frauengeschichte(n)*, 470.
11. Katrin Holenstein, "Das Engagement für die Gleichstellung von Mann und Frau im eidgenössischen Parlament: Eine Untersuchung über die Legislaturperiode 1983–1987" (The commitment to equality of men and women in the federal Parliament: An examination of the legislative period 1983–1987), in Peter Hablutzel, Hans Hirter, and Beat Junker, eds., *Schweizerische Politik in Wissenschaft und Praxis: Festschrift für Peter*

Gilg (Bern: Forschungszentrum für Schweizerische Politik [FSP], 1988), 127.

12. Swiss constitution, Art. 4, Abs. 2 BV.

13. *Amtliches Bulletin* (1987), 445 (Parlamentarische Initiative Fetz).

14. Brigitte Studer, "Frauen an den Universitäten in der Schweiz" (Women in the universities in Switzerland), in Dokumentationsstelle für Wissenschaftspolitik, ed., *Wissenschaftpolitische Infos* (Bern, 1988), 9ff.

15. Labor force participation rate in 1990 (ratio of economically active population plus unemployed persons to the total population): women, 37.5 percent; men, 62.0 percent; total, 49.5 percent. Federal Statistical Office, Bern, 1992. Unemployment rate (annual average in 1989; only full-time unemployed): women, 0.6 percent; men, 0.4 percent.

16. Hege Skjeie, *The Feminization of Power: Norway's Political Experiment (1986–)* (Oslo: Institute for Social Research, 1988), 25.

17. Ibid., 15.

18. Regula Stämpfli, *Keuchhusten in der direkten Demokratie: Die Banalität des politisch Außergewöhnlichen* (Sickness in the direct democracy: The banality of political abnormality), Teilstudie im Rahmen des Nationalen Forschungsprogrammes 21, Kulturelle Vielfalt und nationale Identität (Bern: FSP, 1990), 172ff.

19. In 1989 only 3 percent of chief business executives were women.

20. Regula Stämpfli and Claude Longchamp, "Wie wird die Zukunft weiblich? Frauenforderung bei Wahlen und darüber hinaus: Bestandesaufnahme und Strategieformulierungen" (How will the future be feminine? Women's advancement through election and beyond: Taking stock and forming strategy), *Zukunft des Staates,* SVPW-Jahrbuch 30/1990 (Bern: Haupt, 1991), 29ff, 35.

21. Catherine Duttweiler, *Kopp und Kopp, Aufstieg und Fall der ersten Bundesratin* (Rise and fall of the first Federal Council) (Zurich: Weltwoche-ABC-Verlag, 1990), 158ff.

22. Ibid., 130ff.

▲ Turkey

POLITICS

Type of Political System: democracy
  Sovereignty: republic
  Executive-Legislative System: parliamentary
Type of State: unitary
Type of Party System: multiparty
Major Political Parties

Anavatan Partisi (ANAP, Motherland Party): Right-wing party founded in 1983; main opposition party in 1992. Won 24 percent of votes in the 1991 national election and 115 seats in Parliament. Led by former Prime Minister Mesut Yilmaz.

Sosyal Demokrat Halkçı Parti (SHP, Social Democrat Populist Party): Center-left party founded in 1986 when the Halkçı Parti (Populist Party) and the Sosyal Demokrat Parti (Social Democrat Party) merged. Coalition partner with the Doğru Yol Partisi since 1991, winning 20.8 percent of votes in the 1991 national election and 88 seats in Parliament. Led by Erdal İnönü (son of İsmet İnönü, second president of the republic), who is deputy prime minister of the Süleyman Demirel cabinet.

Doğru Yol Partisi (DYP, True Path Party): Right-wing party founded in 1983; won 27.0 percent of votes in the 1991 national election and 178 seats in Parliament. Led by Prime Minister Süleyman Demirel, head of the 1992 DYP-SHP coalition government.

Demokratik Sol Parti (DSP, Democratic Left Party): Center-left party founded in 1986. Won 10.8 percent of votes in the 1991 national election and 7 seats in Parliament. Led by Bülent Ecevit, prime minister of several governments before 1980.

Refah Partisi (RP, Welfare Party): Fundamentalist party established in 1983. The Welfare Party, Nationalist Work Party, and Reformist Democracy Party formed a coalition before the 1991 election and entered the election on the Welfare Party ticket. After the election, the coalition dissolved. Won 16.9 percent of votes in the 1991 national election and 62 seats in Parliament. Led by Necmettin Erbakan, deputy prime minister in the coalition governments before 1980.

Milliyetçi Çalışma Partisi (MÇP, Nationalist Work Party): Extreme-right party founded in 1983. Has 13 seats in Parliament. Led by Alparslan Türkeş, deputy prime minister in the coalition governments before 1980.

Islahatçi Demokrasi Partisi (IDP, Reformist Democracy Party): Right-wing party ideologically similar to the RP and the MÇP. Two party leaders serve in Parliament, where they are technically considered independents.[a]

Halkın Emek Partisi (HEP, Populist Labor Party): Formed in 1990 by former members of the SHP. Despite being barred from taking part in the 1991 election, won 22 seats in Parliament on a joint list with the SHP.[b]

Year Women Granted Right to Vote: 1934
Year Women Granted Right to Stand for Election: 1934
Percentage of Women in the Unicameral Legislature: 1.8%[c]
Percentage of Electorate Voting for Highest Elected Office in Most Recent Election (1991): 83.9%[d]

DEMOGRAPHICS

Population: 56,473,035[e]
Percentage of Population in Urban Areas
  Overall: 59.0%[f]
  Female: not available
  Male: not available
Percentage of Population Below Age 15: 37.5%[g]
Birthrate (per 1,000 population): 28[h]
Maternal Mortality Rate (per 100,000 live births): 210
Infant Mortality Rate (per 1,000 live births): 74

Mortality Rate for Children Under Five (per 1,000 live births): 93
Average Household Size: 4.7[i]
Mean Age at First Marriage[j]
Female: 21.8
Male: 24.6
Life Expectancy
Female: 65.8
Male: 62.5

EDUCATION
Ratio of Female to Male Enrollment
First-Level Education: 89
Second-Level Education: 55
Third-Level Education: 50
Literacy Rate
Female: 43.0%
Male: 77.0%

ECONOMY
Gross National Product per Capita: U.S. $1,080
Percentage of Labor Force in Agriculture: 64.0%

Distribution of Agricultural Workers by Sex
Female: 51.6%
Male: 48.4%
Economically Active Population by Sex
Female: 45.3%
Male: 84.2%

a. Arthur S. Banks, ed., *Political Handbook of the World, 1992* (Binghamton, N.Y.: CSA Publications, 1992), 783.
b. Ibid.
c. *Results of General Election of Representatives*, no. 1511 (State Institute of Statistics, Prime Ministry, 20 October 1991).
d. Ibid.
e. *Census of Population: Summary Tables, 1990*, no. 1458 (State Institute of Statistics, Prime Ministry, 1991).
f. Ibid.
g. *Census of Population, 1985: Socio-Economic Tables*, no. 1237 (State Institute of Statistics).
h. *1989 Population Survey of Turkey* (State Institute of Statistics, forthcoming).
i. Ibid.
j. Ibid.

Turkish Women as Agents of Social Change in a Pluralist Democracy

NERMIN ABADAN-UNAT
AND OYA TOKGÖZ

The Republic of Turkey, Türkiye Cumhuriyeti, with a population of 57 million, is located in Asia Minor, with Europe to the north and west and the Middle East to the south and east. Turkey is the geographic border between these two vastly different regions of the world and is the only country to belong to both OPEC and NATO. Its location is fundamental to understanding Turkish politics and the situation that Turkish women face today.

Critical to understanding women's political status and engagement in Turkish society is the deeply embedded conflict of secularism versus religiosity. This conflict imperfectly overlaps and reinforces other political cleavages, such as urban and rural divisions and class differences. Although 98 percent of the population is Muslim, Turkey has had no state religion since 1924, when the constitution defined the country as secular. One principle of the secular state has been equality between the sexes. As a result, for much of this century Turkey has had its own form of state feminism, or support for state-enforced legal equality between men and women, buttressed by a secularism that stands apart from traditional Islamic views of gender relations. Strong religious forces led by the Refah Partisi (Welfare Party) and represented by an electoral alliance of three conservative parties in 1991 presented a platform in the general elections to modify the secular, egalitarian quality of public life.

The situation of women in Turkey can be studied from several perspectives. Most common are the political socialization and structural approaches. The political socialization approach merely verifies rather than explains the existence of a sex-differentiated culture. The structural approach offers a power- and position-based explanation for gender differences in political participation. Marxist structural explanations, for example, focus almost exclusively on economic factors. More useful than the limited structural approach, however, is the patriarchal-structural approach, which uses structural insights to focus on the male-female power dynamics within a society. As Yeşim Arat has written, "The asymmetrical power relations between men and women help to explain women's socially inferior status and lower level of political participation."[1] In examining Turkey, the roles of historical development and state policy must also be incorporated into any patriarchal-structural model. This historical approach helps to explain how in the later years of Ottoman society the status of women was used as a criterion of Westernization and modernization, culminating in the reforms of Mustafa Kemal Atatürk that created an early state feminism.[2] That Turkey is the only Muslim country to adopt secularism as a constitutional principle demonstrates the importance of studying Turkish women in politics with a historical patriarchal-structural approach.

HISTORY AND POLITICS

The modern nation of Turkey was formed from the heart of the Ottoman Empire. When the empire was broken up after World War I, Allied forces occupied part of the country. A successful war of independence, Kurtuluş Savaşı, was waged between 1919 and 1922, and the Republic of Turkey was founded, on the model of parliamentary democracy, in Ankara on 29 October 1923. A transitional one-party government ruled the country until 1946. The party, Cumhuriyet Halk Partisi (Republican People's Party), was founded by Mustafa Kemal Atatürk, victorious leader of the war of independence and first president of Turkey. Atatürk set out to modernize the country with a series of radical reforms.

Atatürk granted women full rights of citizenship in the decade after independence. Except for a group of influential women professionals in Istanbul, Turkish women did not organize nationwide to struggle for their political rights because Atatürk, aiming to establish a modern, secular republic, assumed the leadership in enfranchising Turkish women. Beginning in 1926, leaders who supported modernization granted women social and political rights. Western systems of law—the Swiss civil code, Italian penal code, and German commercial code—were adopted in toto, eliminating the discrimination against women embedded in Islamic law. These political rights encompassed the rights to vote and to stand for election. Atatürk realized that democracy depended on the active participation of female and male citizens alike, and because he had a personal interest in women's rights, he promoted them for their own sake.

Turkish women received political rights much earlier than many of their counterparts in Europe. Through a constitutional amendment in 1930, they gained the right to vote and to stand for elections in municipal councils; women were first elected to local offices in 1933.[3] On 5 December 1934 the Türkiye Büyük Millet Meclisi (Turkish Grand National Assembly) adopted a proposal by İsmet İnönü, Turkey's second president, to confer on all male and female citizens aged 22 and older the right to vote in national elections, and all men and women aged 30 and older the right to hold office.[4]

Yet Turkish women entered a political arena

set in a patriarchal society. The founding fathers of the republic provided at the macropolitical or legal level a framework for individual women, if they were encouraged at the micropolitical or family level, to participate in formal politics. Yet, once in politics, women faced (and still face) limits to male support. Political life continues to be dominated by parties only sometimes interested in or friendly toward women.

Since 1946 Turkey has had a multiparty parliamentary system. Three times in the postwar era political crises have occurred with the military taking power: 1960–61, 1971–73, and 1980–83. Each time the armed forces have returned to their barracks and the multiparty system has been restored. This repeated militarism has, however, undermined democratic stability and made many people wary of political activism.

The Parliament, originally unicameral, was bicameral between 1961 and 1980. With the adoption of the constitution of 1982 the unicameral system of the 1924 constitution was reintroduced. Members of the Parliament are chosen by a proportional electoral system. Executive power is vested in the office of the prime minister, although the president, despite his legal position of neutrality, has occasionally played an important role in politics in recent years.

The Republican People's Party governed uninterruptedly for the first 27 years of the republic. Since 1950, except for periods of military rule, a succession of conservative rightist parties has governed alone or in coalition with smaller parties. The conservative Anavatan Partisi (Motherland Party), currently the major opposition party, controlled the government from 1983 to 1991. At present a coalition government composed of the Doğru Yol Partisi (True Path Party) and the Sosyal Demokrat Halkçı Parti (Social Democrat Populist Party) governs under the leadership of Prime Minister Süleyman Demirel. Two other powerful conservative parties are the Refah Partisi (Welfare Party) and the Milliyetçi Çalışma Partisi (Nationalist Work Party). The other left-wing parties are the Demokratik Sol Parti (Democratic Left Party) and the Halkın Emek Partisi (Populist Labor Party).

WOMEN'S ACTIVISM

The legal, economic, and social status of Turkish women has been discussed since the late nineteenth century, and in the twentieth century conflicts between secularism and religiosity as state policy and personal experience have never been far from the surface. According to Şirin Tekeli, four major forces have influenced the present position of Turkish women: the structure of Ottoman society in the period before the Tanzimat reforms, the process of Westernization starting with the reforms and lasting until the end of World War I, the establishment of the republic and early years under a single-party regime, and the period of fast social change since 1950.[5]

In pre-Tanzimat Ottoman society people were segregated not by class but by religious or ethnic affiliation and sex.[6] Jews, Greeks, Armenians, and Arabs, among others, were considered autonomous and distinct ethnic and religious groups, and within each group the sexes were segregated. Under Islamic law, a woman was worth half a man in matters concerning testimony before courts and inheritance. Under family law, which permitted men four wives, a woman was worth even less. Rural and urban women alike were subjected to the absolute authority of men through the institutions of the state, religion, and family. Although this approach to relations between women and men has been abolished legally, social traditions still reflect its legacy. The Tanzimat reforms, introduced in 1839, defined minority citizenship rights and instituted a period of reforms.

At the turn of the century, Westernization led to changes that deeply affected the status of women, including the establishment of girls' schools, teacher's colleges for women, and midwife training centers, the founding of women's magazines, and the spread of welfare organizations run by women.[7] At the end of the process of westernization—and particularly during the revolution of 1908—women's associations began, for the first time, to protest the rule of patriarchy.[8]

Women entered politics during the ensuing

period of crisis. Following the collapse of the Ottoman Empire, women organized public meetings, addressed the masses, and fought actively in the war of independence.[9] In 1919, after British forces had occupied Istanbul, an internationally known novelist, Halide Edip Adıvar, addressed a crowd of unparalleled size at Sultanahmet, a large square near the palace of the sultan. Inspired by her civic courage, other women leaders started to participate in resistance movements and joined the newly formed national army.[10]

After the republic was founded in 1923, what is perhaps the most far-reaching women's revolution ever realized in a Muslim Mediterranean society took place. Such radical innovations as making religious marriages illegal, establishing compulsory civil marriage, abolishing polygamy, and granting women and men equal rights to divorce, equal shares in inheritance, and equal rights in custody over children became the law. At no time were women legally banned from wearing veils, however.[11]

The growing desire of women to obtain political rights in the second half of the 1920s culminated in the founding of the Türk Kadınlar Birliği (Turkish Women's Union) under Nakiye Elgün. This association dissolved in 1928 after its brief struggle for suffrage.[12] The transformation in the status of women between 1924 and 1934 was primarily accomplished by the state, and women were thus discouraged from taking the political initiative. Therefore, one may conclude that prompt state support can sometimes lead to a decline of political interest and participation.

As a result, beginning in the 1930s, the new female elite—an increasing number of highly skilled professional women—acknowledged the contradictions in their political position. While considering themselves the vanguard of state feminism, they recognized that years would pass before awareness of the rights that women had been granted pertaining to education and to equality before the law permeated the fabric of society. Consequently, these elite women felt a deep commitment to promoting Atatürk's reforms for women.

Many structural and ideological obstacles have delayed the full incorporation of the Kemalist legacy and the later acceptance of feminist ideas.[13] Structural obstacles have included underdevelopment, the strong dependency of women on the patriarchal family structure, and the meager opportunities for women's education beyond primary school. In the 1960s the growing importance of leftist ideologies became a significant intellectual barrier to ideas of women's liberation, for orthodox leftist views considered any kind of feminism a "bourgeois deviation."

Equality before the law and open channels for education have remained the privilege of those who are conscious of existing opportunities. High rates of illiteracy among women and the impact of the current Islamic revival limit how women can use formal equality to better their lives. The Islamic revivalists have started a campaign to control women's sexuality and life opportunities that stresses their role as wives and mothers as the basis of society. The emphasis on domesticity prevents any large-scale rooting and spreading of political awareness among women.[14] Most women are still unwilling or unable to assess objectively their lives as women in a man's society.

Those women who participate today in associational activities are found in feminist groups, women's professional and social service groups, and in (or at least as the focus of) fundamentalist Islamic groups dedicated to traditional roles for women. Both the new feminist groups and the older women's professional and social service groups support secularism and women's rights.

Feminism and the ideology of women's liberation movements reached Turkey in the 1970s and became instrumental after 1980. Ironically, various forms of feminist thought became influential after the military intervention of 1980. While openly political issues with right or left tendencies were prohibited under martial law, women's issues were not considered subversive, and so they were able to spread through informal meetings, press commentaries, the publication of reviews and magazines, and the creation of informal groups.

From the beginning, three types of women's

groups could be distinguished: reform-oriented secular groups, purely feminist consciousness-raising groups, and socialist feminist groups. Reform-oriented secular groups predominantly embrace middle-aged urban professional women and housewives, whereas the consciousness-raising and socialist feminist groups recruit their members from among young professional, often single, women. The second and third types are active primarily in Istanbul and Ankara, but the first has connections throughout Turkey. At the Second Women's Convention, held in Istanbul in May 1989, about 2,500 liberal, socialist, radical, and independent feminists presented more than 70 papers.[15] The platform adopted at the meeting contained many demands, most of them for enactment by the legislature. Participants requested the introduction of sex education in schools, the abandonment of compulsory religious instruction, the modification of discriminatory articles in the penal code, and the abolition of institutionalized prostitution and the bride price.

Beyond the call for fundamental legal changes, feminists are involved on several fronts. Recently they initiated a well-publicized action to combat sexual harassment and assault through the sale of large pins, adorned with a purple bow, to be used as a new type of self-defense "weapon" in such public places as ferryboats. To deal with other types of violence against women—e.g., wife battering—a group of female lawyers in Istanbul established the Mor Çatı Kadın Sığınağı Vakfı (Foundation for the Creation of a Shelter). The experiment is called the House with the Purple Roof. At present the foundation owns no building; it only offers consultative services. This model has been copied by a number of Social Democrat Populist municipalities in Istanbul, Ankara, and other large cities.

The Kadın Eserleri Kütüphanesi ve Bilgi Merkezi (Foundation for the Establishment of a Library of Women's Works and Data Bank) was established by Şirin Tekeli, a professor of political science who resigned in protest over the creation of the Higher Education Council, a supervisory body that has eliminated academic autonomy. Tekeli's foundation actively promotes the trans-lation and publication of recent feminist literature and organizes lectures and seminars on women's rights and feminism. Likewise, the newly founded Kadın Sorunları Araştırma ve Uygulama Merkezi (Women's Research and Education Center) at Istanbul University, headed by the philosophy professor Necla Arat, conducts a graduate program in women's studies, as well as applied programs.

These feminist-inspired organizations and efforts are part of a wider array of women's organizations dedicated to defending the principles of Kemalism, including a secular public life. The major women's associations active in this direction include the Türk Kadınlar Birliği (Turkish Women's Union, established in 1950), the Söroptimist (Association of Professional Women, founded in 1948), the Türk Üniversiteli Kadınlar Derneği (Turkish University Women's Association, founded in 1952), particularly its Ankara branch, the Türk Anneler Derneği (Turkish Mothers' Association, founded in 1982), the Türk Kadın Hukukçular Derneği (Turkish Women Lawyers Association, founded in 1948), the Ayrımcılığa Karşı Kadınlar (Association Against Discrimination Against Women, founded in 1982), the Sosyal Feministler (Social Feminists, founded in 1983), and finally the recently established Çağdaş Yaşamı Destekleme Derneği (Association for the Promotion of Modern Living, founded in 1989 by the psychiatrist Aysel Ekşi). These organizations cite the defense of secularism and women's rights among their major aims.

A number of additional organizations have actively dissented against a return to traditional Islam. All of these groups, together with the support of the newly created Kadının Statüsü ve Sorunları Genel Müdürlüğü (General Directorate for Women's Affairs) in the Ministry of Labor, headed by the only female cabinet member at that time, İmren Aykut, expressed their concern over the backlash against secularism and women's rights. A new Ministry of Women, headed by one of the two female cabinet members, a pharmacist from the province of Tokat, Güler İleri, was recently established.

Even the financially well-endowed, politically right-oriented Türk Kadınını Güçlendirme ve Tanıtma Vakfı (Foundation for the Empowerment and Promotion of the Turkish Woman)—established in 1983 by Semra Özal, wife of then Prime Minister, now President Turgut Özal—has recruited many wives and daughters of upper-middle-class businessmen in the defense of secularism in Turkish public life. The foundation, assisted by the prestige provided by Semra Özal, has launched a nationwide campaign in favor of civil marriages—religious marriages are not legally valid—as well as efforts to promote health for mothers and children. Abroad, the foundation sponsors exhibits demonstrating the modernization of Turkish women. Semra Özal has repeatedly stated that Western dress and habits are perfectly compatible with the requirements of Islam.

The openness during and after the military regime that encouraged the growth in women's organizing and activism has coexisted with a growth of religious fundamentalism in society and in the state that limits the success of egalitarian and feminist efforts. The 1982 constitution made religious education in primary and secondary schools compulsory as part of an effort to implant a new state ideology: the Turkish-Islam synthesis. The ideology rests on a strong belief in pan-Turkism, combined with a reliance on tradition and the strength of Islam.

The Motherland Party has not openly adopted the Turkish-Islam synthesis as its ideology, in part because it claims to be part of a coalition of four conservative parties. Nonetheless, its tacit support of the ideology while it was in power enabled partisans in the Motherland Party to introduce proponents of the Turkish-Islam synthesis into government service, particularly in the Ministry of Education. Members of the public service thus find themselves involved in various political controversies, such as the debate over a required dress code, which, among other things, prohibits men from having beards or women from wearing headscarves in government offices and at public universities.

The fierce debate over Islamic dress that began in 1983 has not diminished. On the contrary, it has polarized public opinion.[16] Adherents of Atatürk's legacy of secularism and equality between the sexes vehemently defend the changes introduced in Turkish life through legal reforms and policies since the founding of the republic. Fundamentalists of different orientations, buoyed by a general growth of religiosity, have vigorously mobilized their forces and have trained and paid militants to work for a return to tradition and Islamic morality in the name of democracy and civil liberties. Supporters of religious fundamentalism have developed a conscious policy espousing the view that women should give up equal status with men and should conform in dress and headcover and obey a rigid rule of seclusion.

Many fundamentalist reviews—among them a woman's magazine, *Kadın ve Aile* (Women and family), with a circulation of approximately 100,000—support this view. Fundamentalism is also promoted by numerous audio and video cassettes sold at mosques in almost every city and distributed in rural areas by imams. The message expressed in these media, as well as in weekly sermons transmitted by state-operated television and promoted by the newly founded Aile Araştırma Kurumu (Family Research Institute), is that women should return to their homes, that their only and most sacred function in life is to bear and raise children.[17] As Günseli Berik has put it, "These attempts represent the efforts of antisecular forces in Turkish society to implement an agenda in which segregation of the sexes in public life and women's confinement to the domestic sphere and to reproductive responsibilities is emphasized. The goal of Islamic fundamentalist groups is to transform the Turkish State from within, and women's status and place in society is the major weapon they use."[18] The Ministry of Women and its representatives, however, are counteracting these efforts, encouraging women to acquire new skills and enter politics.

REPRESENTATION

Few women are in formal politics in contemporary Turkey, but their value far exceeds their numbers. In infiltrating a monopoly of male power, these women have an important democratic mission: to uphold the idea that democracy can be a practice and an opportunity for all. They realize their responsibility to enlarge the scope of civil liberties and to maintain democratic stability in a country that has faced the antidemocratic forces of militarism and the ideology of unequal separate spheres promoted by religious fundamentalists. The instabilities of democratic politics have created conditions that have hindered women's particular experiences in formal politics as well as the political experiences that men and women share. It is difficult for women to hold public office in a patriarchal society like Turkey— competition for party support is sharp and winning elections not easy.

Since 1935 the proportion of female deputies and, in the bicameral period, senators has never been greater than 4.5 percent of the members of Parliament. This zenith occurred in the fifth Parliament (1935–39), to which 18 women were elected.[19] During the single-party era the Republican People's Party, which granted women suffrage, was also responsible for the relatively high percentage of female MPs.

As Turkey moved into the multiparty era in 1946, the number of female MPs declined steadily. The introduction of the multiparty system brought more competition to politics—and against women running for office. Female candidates found it difficult to be ranked in the first rows in the party lists.

Few women served on municipal councils in the years 1933–46.[20] And as with parliamentary representation, the transition to a multiparty system resulted in fewer women being elected to local governments. Women were occasionally elected as mayors, however. The first woman to become mayor, Müfide İlhan, took office in 1950; only ten women were elected mayor between 1950 and 1980.[21]

From 1946 to 1960 and 1961 to 1980 the percentage of female MPs ranged from less than 1 percent to 2. Women's electoral chances depended heavily on their status in their respective parties. Female political representation must therefore be analyzed in terms of the party frameworks in operation during the four distinct periods of contemporary Turkish political history.

The first period, 1935–46, reflects a voluntary commitment on the part of the ruling party to enhancing democratic practices by strongly endorsing women's political representation. This commitment explains the "high" percentage of female MPs (1935–39, 4.5 percent; 1939–46, 3.7 percent). The second period, 1946–60, encompasses the beginning of the competitive multiparty system. The decline in female MPs began during this era (1946–50, 1.9 percent; 1954–57, 0.6 percent; 1957–60, 1.3 percent). In the third period, 1961–80, the Parliament was bicameral. Women served in the Cumhuriyet Senatosu (Senate), as well as in the Millet Meclisi (National Assembly). In the face of similar party constraints, bicameralism did not increase the percentage of women in Parliament. In the National Assembly 0.8–1.3 percent of MPs were women; in the Senate, 1.3–2.0 percent.

In the fourth period, the 1980s, national elections were held in 1983 and 1987. In 1983, 12 women were elected as MPs (3.0 percent). Their number dropped to 6 in the 1987 elections (1.2 percent). The reason for this dramatic decline was that during the first election after the return to democratic rule in 1983, brand-new political parties anxious to defend the principle of equality entered the political scene. But four years later, two of these new parties, the Halkçı Parti (Populist Party) and the Milliyetçi Demokrasi Partisi (Nationalist Democracy Party), had dissolved themselves, leaving the field to the remaining two strong political parties—the Motherland Party and the Social Democrat Populist Party. These parties were involved in fierce intraparty struggles and were not particularly interested in promoting female representation. Further, the constitution of 1982, unlike its predecessor of 1961, prohibited the establishment of women's and youth organizations within the parties, thus depriving women of a platform from which to articulate their special demands. The ostensible reasons for prohibiting their establishment were to avoid intraparty conflicts and to discourage too much political participation. The decision, taken by the military government, has been heavily criticized and will soon be reversed by constitutional amendment.

In the 1991 elections the number of female MPs rose from six to eight of 450. This minor increase is due to a change in the electoral system permitting preferential voting, which generally favors men. Five of the female MPs represent constituencies in large cities, like Istanbul and Izmir; three represent rural communities.

In 1984 women constituted only 0.6 percent of representatives in municipal councils, and most of these were in large cities.[22] For example, some women were elected to municipal councils in Ankara and Istanbul, but none in Izmir. No women were elected mayor in 1984. The local elections of 1989 deviated little from the trend of 1984. In Istanbul only one woman (Fatma Girik, a movie star), on the Social Democrat Populist ticket, was elected.

The educational level of female council members equals that of their male counterparts—some educated housewives do get elected to local councils.[23] Likewise, since 1935, female MPs have had backgrounds similar to their male colleagues. Both tend to be lawyers, doctors, teachers, economists, and the like. Female MPs constitute a social minority among women; women generally are less educated and less professionally qualified than men in Turkey. Women's lack of qualifications has been a major obstacle to their success in politics.[24]

Few women have been party leaders. After being elected to Parliament, Behice Boran became the first female party leader, heading the Türkiye İşçi Partisi (Turkish Labor Party) in 1965. Rahşan Ecevit, wife of former Prime Minister Bülent Ecevit, founded the Democratic Left Party in 1985. After Bülent Ecevit regained his political rights following the referendum of 1987, Rahşan Ecevit turned the leadership of the party over to her husband. Since 1980 a number of female politicians have helped establish new political parties, such as the late Bahriye Üçok, cofounder of the now defunct Sosyal Demokrat Parti (Social Democrat Party), and Günseli Öz-kaya, cofounder of the since-dissolved Populist Party.

In spite of traditionalist social pressure, women have faith in their capacity to participate in formal politics. Female voters consider parliamentary representation and cabinet membership suitable for women. As many as 73 percent of female voters believe that a woman can act as a successful mayor, and 64 percent believe a woman could be a successful prime minister. Still, women are anxious to prevent members of their family from entering politics. Forty-one percent of female voters find it undesirable for their sons to be active politically. This percentage rises to 79 for daughters.[25]

The main reason that women are unwilling for their family members to be politically active is the recurrence of military interventions, each leading to political trials. Political corruption cases have also reinforced the image that politics is a dirty business. Women are further discouraged by the necessity of combining the obligations of married life with the exigencies of a political career.

Men are more informed about and interested in politics than women in Turkey, as research in urban Ankara by Oya Tokgöz shows. Even the mass media do little to promote women's involvement. Women lag behind men in their knowledge of political parties and political leaders. Women are generally less educated than men, and their exposure to mass media and political discussion is less than men's; this is true both among immediate family members and in other settings.[26]

Women's political activities generally take two forms. In small towns and rural areas, women actively diffuse useful, informal political information and party propaganda. These mostly unseen activities are based on women's placement in various social networks—predominantly extensive relationships with kin. Information is also shared at social affairs like engagements, weddings, and religious ceremonies. These women consider their participation not political engagement but support for their menfolk. Their involvement focuses on such "feminine" issues as family and child care. These women are usually between 25 and 40 years old and are almost always controlled by their male relatives.[27]

Independent female politicians are the other sort of politically active women. They come almost exclusively from middle-class families, have completed higher education, and usually have successful careers. They are generally over 45, do not accept male protection, and exhibit a rather asexual appearance and behavior.[28]

The first group is usually chaperoned to and from the gathering places where women congregate; the second group engages independently in political actions. They may, for example, ask their voters to meet them in a coffeehouse and address them there. Yet almost no one from this second group would qualify as a deliberate feminist. These professional women consider politics in exactly the same light as men, accepting it as a game to be played according to certain rules. When an issue that concerns women arises, they tackle it as their male colleagues would. Feminist thought has so far had limited impact on their political discourse.

A striking development in women's political involvement was recently reflected in a conflict in the Motherland Party over the candidacy of Semra Özal, President Özal's wife, who ran for head of the Istanbul Motherland Party organization in 1991. The convention that would have elected her and her followers produced unexpected turmoil, as well as a protest action against her candidacy on the part of three cabinet members. The more conservative opposition wing of the Motherland Party launched the slogan "We don't vote for atheists and women."

At first glance, the clash appeared to be a form of resistance against women's involvement in politics. But it was Semra Özal's use of all the prerogatives due to a president's wife that aggravated the situation. Leftist, not just rightist, opposition parties charged the president in summer 1991 with acute nepotism: he had encouraged his wife, daughter, son, daughter-in-law, and members of his inner circle to run for election as delegates to the national convention. It seems clear, however, that moderates have used the feminist dimension to bring about an ideological realignment in the Motherland Party in order to strengthen the party's image of progressiveness.

To describe and assess Turkish voters is difficult; patterns of male and female voting behavior are not known. According to Ayşe Güneş-Ayata's comprehensive survey, most female voters shun the right-wing fundamentalist Welfare Party and the right-wing extremist National Labor Party. In the national elections of 1987, women voters favored the center-right Motherland Party: 53 percent of women cast their votes for the Motherland Party, but only 34 percent of men voted for it. The survey also found that the personalities of (male) leaders and their wives affected the women's choices considerably. The activities of Semra Özal, which focused on interfamily relations and women's private problems, had a significant impact on female voters.[29]

Güneş-Ayata also found that the most important issues for male voters were inflation (82.1 percent) and unemployment (8.8 percent), whereas female voters cared most about economic dependency (24.5 percent), social control (10.4 percent), bad treatment by spouses (8.8 percent), and inequality before the law (4.6 percent). Interestingly, female voters generally cast their votes independently of marital and family bonds. Pressure on women to make specific political choices seems to be low. Even the political choices of formally passive housewives are not influenced much by new external relationships. The membership of the average female voter in such formal organizations as consumer associations, social welfare organizations, and teacher-parent associations is minimal, which may explain the women's freedom to make political choices.[30]

Although women and men have ostensibly been political equals from early on, it has taken a long time for political parties to incorporate women's policy needs into their platforms. The founding party of the Turkish Republic, the Republican People's Party, lacked a clearly established women's program, for legal reforms were considered sufficient to implement full equality in social life. This picture did not change between

1945 and 1960. The Republican People's Party and the Democratic Party did not adopt special policies for women.[31]

The programs of governments and political parties in power between 1960 and 1980 began to contain some women-related policies because of directives in the three development plans and pressure from nongovernmental organizations. These policies were limited and mostly trivial. Women were mentioned in party programs only in regard to their role in the family—or not at all. Because these programs mirrored conventional thinking about women, they reinforced women's secondary role in society and politics.[32]

With the adoption of the 1961 constitution, political parties were permitted to establish women's and youth branches. The two large parties of the 1960s and 1970s, the Republican People's Party and the Adalet Partisi (Justice Party), made extensive use of this organizational opportunity until the new constitution of 1982 abolished it.

In the 1970s the Justice Party, the Republican People's Party, and the coalition governments touched on the problems of working women and women's and children's healthcare to an extent.[33] Rightist parties, especially the religiously oriented ones, countervailed. According to the dominant Islamic approach, particularly the fundamentalist one, the division of tasks and responsibilities in society ought to be based on gender. Men are responsible for the activities of public life, women for the private sphere of family affairs. Keeping women out of the labor market became a major goal for Islamic parties.

In the 1970s the party programs of the religiously oriented Milli Selamet Partisi (National Salvation Party) frequently cited women's rights but made no serious policy efforts regarding women's needs.[34] Other conservative parties used the women's issue as a tool to enhance their ideologies. The leftist parties of the 1970s also gave little attention to women's issues. In sum, women were given a secondary place in all party policies.

After the return to the multiparty system in 1983, almost all parties incorporated women into their elected organs. Following European practice, the Social Democrat Populist Party modified its bylaws in 1989 to introduce a quota of 25 percent in favor of having women at all levels of the party organization and on candidate lists in future elections. The introduction of the quota system has apparently begun to increase the political participation of women in rural areas.

WOMEN IN PUBLIC SERVICE AND THE HEADSCARF CONTROVERSY

In the past half-century, in accordance with major reforms encouraging emancipation, women have been especially successful in the civil service, where they make up 29.4 percent of workers. Indeed, government service was to be the model for modern egalitarian relations in the work force.

The legacy of secularism in the public service is evident from the number of women employed and the variety of policies that govern their employment. Whereas the number of male civil servants rose sixfold between 1936 and 1976, the number of female civil servants increased nineteen times in the same period. Equal pay for equal work has been the rule for all civil servants since the time of Atatürk. This principle was endorsed at the foundation of the republic and has never been contested. It permits full equality for women and men in government service and also applies to pensions. As a result, approximately 423,000 of the 1.4 million civil servants in 1986, or 29.4 percent, were women.[35]

Most women employed in government service work in the female-dominated fields of education, health, and tourism. In spite of the ability to retire after 15 years in salaried work or 20 years in the civil service, women generally remain in the work force until 55, the age of retirement for women.[36] In such nontraditional fields as postal administration, traffic control, and police work, affirmative action has been implemented to attract more women. Women are being recruited to become police officers because of the growth of new tasks deemed especially suitable for women, such as monitoring juvenile delinquency programs and controlling female passengers in airports. Women were admitted to the armed forces in the 1950s and have achieved the rank of colonel. In recent years they have been recruited by the military for such professions as medicine, nursing, teaching, and librarianship.

Women have also held high positions within the judiciary: Melâhat Ruacan was nominated in 1954 to the High Court of Appeals.[37] Several female judges have also chaired and served on the State Council and Constitutional Court. In the field of diplomacy, a female ambassador has been appointed spokeswoman for the Ministry of Foreign Affairs. The only public function to which women have been denied access is district administration. The refusal to appoint women to district positions has frequently been protested. The argument that these positions require a constant presence at work and service in remote areas is not convincing, for nurses and midwives are sent to such places and called to duty day and night.

Female civil servants still espouse the dominant values of Turkey's patriarchal society. In conflicts between home and work, they prefer to smooth the functioning of family life. Some groups of professional women in both metropolitan areas and small towns also give priority to family life over careers.[38]

The job status of female officials does not automatically increase democratic values within the family or political participation. Marital status and class affiliation produce diversified patterns. For professional women who belong to the upper-middle and wealthy classes, availability of paid domestic help plays an influential role in their motivation to pursue a career. Although they, too, have placed great importance on harmonious family life, adequate domestic service enables them to follow their professions.[39] For salaried women of the lower-middle and upper-lower classes, child care is the crucial factor in the decision to work outside the home. Because child-care centers and kindergartens are few and too expensive for most families, salaried women often confront the choice of turning over all their income for child care or staying at home.[40]

In recent years public opinion has been severely divided over the headscarf controversy. The resurgence of fundamentalism has led, among other things, to a general increase in the number of women wearing a certain type of headscarf, known as a turban. The headscarf publicly represents a traditional Islamic view of the need for women to dress modestly in public and not to "encourage" men's gaze. Law and custom require women and men who work in the public sector or attend public universities to dress secularly and observe a modern outlook. Men cannot wear beards or dress sloppily, and women must abstain from exaggerated makeup, blue jeans, and, in the summer, low-cut dresses. This dress code has not been followed strictly since the return to multiparty politics in 1983.

The movement for Islamic dress has been violently criticized by reform-minded secular feminists and defended by liberal and religious circles.[41] This dispute exemplifies the deep conflict between the two asymmetrically opposed political systems, the secular and the Islamic, which has shaped Turkey for the past century and has profound implications for Turkish women.[42]

The headscarf dispute reflects a multitude of individual, societal, and political demands that have culminated in a nationwide ideological controversy. Proponents present the debate as the struggle for recognition of the constitutionally guaranteed right to worship. They argue that the right to cover oneself and to espouse the so-called Islamic dress code is an indivisible part of religious identity; to deny it is a flagrant violation of democratic practice. Religious sects like Nakşibendi and Nurcu Süleymancı, as well as political parties like the Welfare Party, have repeatedly used this argument.

How women dress in public has thus become the focus of a political fight to abolish secularism in favor of an "Islamic way of life." That a considerable number of female university students have become activists in favor of diminishing their rights is significant. Many of them appear to support clear-cut political programs, such as the leadership of the late Ayatollah Khomeini in Iran or the fundamentalist interpretation of the Quran accepted in Saudi Arabia, the gulf states, and Pakistan. Some of these students, however, act individually, looking to religion to overcome a feeling of alienation.

Since 1988, sympathizers with the new "Islamic order," particularly headscarf-wearing university students, have repeatedly engaged in lobbying, public demonstrations, sit-ins, and hunger strikes. The Motherland Party decreed the right to wear Islamic dress in public institutions of higher education. The Social Democrat Populist Party, which opposed the decree, took the matter to the Constitutional Court, which abolished the provision by stating that the wearing of a uniformlike dress is a political symbol; a change in dress would suggest a change in the political regime and would thus be incompatible with the aims of the constitution. This decision has caused further controversy and has been interpreted variously by university administrators. Not to be defeated, the Motherland Party, supported by the right-wing True Path Party, reintroduced the right in another decree. For the time being, therefore, there is liberty in dress. But the Social Democrat Populist Party has again appealed the decree to the Constitutional Court.[43] Since the formation of the latest coalition government, a new policy of tolerance has been tacitly accepted.

Although the Constitutional Court has so far upheld the requirement of secular dress in public service, the constitution of 1982 is also a source of the controversy. While maintaining the principle of secularism, the constitution has made primary and secondary school instruction in "religious culture" compulsory for the first time. This was originally meant to be a comparative history of religion, but it has meant de facto compulsory instruction in Sunni Islam, thus creating two opposed models of socialization: traditional and secular in primary and secondary schools and secular in institutions of higher learning. This conflict seems unlikely to abate in the near future.

FAMILY PLANNING AND ABORTION

Policy on family planning and abortion has been controlled by the state, not state feminism. From the state's perspective, the issue is population size more than women's health or family relationships. Turkey's population stood at 14 million at the 1928 census. A series of wars during the late nineteenth and early twentieth centuries had decimated the male population. For this reason, until 1961 all governments endorsed pronatalism. Family planning first appeared in public discussion during the debate over the First Five-Year Development Plan for 1961–65. The penal code was then modified to legalize a medically authorized abortion in the case of danger to the mother's life.

The right of abortion until the tenth week of pregnancy without the need to prove an absolute medical justification was granted by the outgoing military government in 1983. If a woman is married, the notarized consent of her husband is required. Abortion and information on contraceptives are provided in all public hospitals. They are still underused in less developed areas but are in great demand in large cities, particularly by people of low income.

The right to abortion was not granted as a result of a continued struggle by women's associations. In fact, in the final parliamentary debates on the issue almost no woman member took the floor. Because these debates took place under martial law, no associations—neither women's groups nor those composed of both sexes—tried to influence legislation. Women's associations could afford to be disinterested; the law was passed with great speed, and the bill received little publicity. The liberalization in abortion represents one aspect of the state's ongoing efforts to slow the rapid growth in population. Although infant mortality in the first year of life has declined from 30 percent in 1940 to 10 percent in the 1980s, the figure remains high and translates into early marriages, marriages between close relatives, and, most importantly, high fertility.[44]

Government agencies have been trying to establish well-functioning family planning since the early 1960s with little success. One reason for the failure is that effective family planning is less the result of media-diffused publicity and associational activities and more a deliberate choice by the potential mother. In this respect, however, little progress has been recorded. The traditional glorification of motherhood and the lack of substantial social security continue to induce Turkish families to produce numerous children, with birthrates higher in rural than urban areas.[45] Although the issue is not generally controversial, in the eastern provinces, most probably for ethnic reasons, family planning is resisted and abortion is considered sinful.

PROSPECTS

Turkey is one of the most visible examples of state feminism translated into innovative legislation and public policies in favor of women. These roots go back to the first half of the nineteenth century and climaxed with the radical reforms undertaken by Mustafa Kemal Atatürk and his followers. Since 1980 a new, associationally based component of activism for women's rights has developed. The groups and their activities have broadened the scope and impact of women's empowerment.

The prospects for Turkish women are likely to be shaped by the country's current secular and religious dualism, which rests largely on a given pattern of social stratification: progressive ideas are espoused more by the educated upper-middle class, and fundamentalist Islam is increasingly the dominant ideology of the marginalized low-income and lower-middle classes. While increasing numbers of better-educated young women will accede to decision-making positions, a mass of newly mobilized, religiously active women may retain the traditional Islamic ways as a protection against modernization, which they perceive as happening too rapidly. These women will opt for seclusion in the roles of housewife and mother. The wide gap between these two groups may be reduced with increasing urbanization, industrialization, and mass education, especially with a political program based on equity and democratic rights for all. The recent changes in government, the creation of a Ministry of Women, the restitution of greater liberties in public life, and an anticipated move for more effective mass education will probably reduce the tension between the two approaches.

NOTES

1. Yeşim Arat, *The Patriarchal Paradox: Women Politicians in Turkey* (London: Associated University Presses, 1989), 119–20.

2. Deniz Kandıyotı, "Ataerkil Örüntüler: Türk Toplumunda Erkek Egemenliğinin Cozumlenmesine Yonelik Notlar" (Patriarchal patterns: Some notes on solutions to male dominance in Turkish society), in Şirin Tekeli, ed., *Kadın Bakış Açısından 1980'ler Türkiye'sinde Kadınlar* (Women in Turkey in the 1980s from the feminist point of view) (Istanbul: İletişim Yayınları, 1990), 351. See also Deniz Kandıyotı, "Women and the Turkish State, Political Actions or Symbolic Pawns?" in Nira Yuval-Davis and Floya Anthias, eds., *Woman, Nation, State* (London: Macmillan, 1988).

3. Nermin Abadan-Unat, *Women in the Developing World: Evidence from Turkey*, Monograph Series in World Affairs, vol. 22 (Denver, Colo.: University of Denver Press, 1986), 137. See also Yeşim Arat, "The Private to the Political Realm: Women Parliamentarians in Turkey," in Ferhunde Ozbay, ed., *The Study of Women in Turkey: An Anthology* (UNESCO, forthcoming).

4. The proposal that enfranchised women was supported by 191 deputies. Abadan-Unat, *Women in the Developing World*, 137.

5. Şirin Tekeli, "Women in the Changing Political Associations of the 1990s," in Andrew Finkel and Nükhet Sirman, eds., *Turkish State, Turkish Society* (New York: Routledge, 1990), 268–74.

6. Nora Şeni, "Ville ottamane et représentatives du corps feminin" (An Ottoman city and representations of the female body), *Les temps modernes* (July–August 1984): 67.

7. Tezer Taşkıran, *Cumhuriyetin 50. Yılında Kadın Hakları* (Women's rights in the 50th year of the republic) (Ankara: Başbakanlık Basımevi, 1973), 37–52.

8. Bernard Corporal, *Kemalizmde ve Kemalizm Sonrasında Türk Kadını* (Turkish women during and after Kemalism) (Ankara: İş Bankası Yayınları, 1982), 78–84.

9. Afet İnan, *Tarih Boyunca Türk Kadınının Hak ve Görevleri* (Turkish women's rights and duties throughout history), 3rd ed. (Ankara: Milli Eğitim Basımevi, 1975), 104–20.

10. Taşkıran, *Cumhuriyetin 50. Yılında*, 74; İnan, *Tarih Boyunca Türk*, 108.

11. Nermin Abadan-Unat, "Women's Movements and National Liberation: The Case of Turkey," *Journal of the American Institute for the Study of the Middle East Civilization* 3, no. 4 (1982): 4–32. The Swiss civil code,

adopted in 1926, replaced Islamic law (*şeriat*), and women were encouraged to discard their veils. The Swiss civil code was adopted in its entirety, in part as a strategy of opposition against a more traditional bill proposed by a legislative committee and in part because of the positive model offered by the Swiss code in dealing with a heterogeneous culture.

12. Nükhet Sirman, "Feminism in Turkey: A Short History," *New Perspectives on Turkey* 3 (Fall 1989): 1–34.

13. Şirin Tekeli, "The Emergence of the Feminist Movement in Turkey," in Drude Dahlerup, ed., *The New Women's Movement* (London: Sage, 1986), 195–97.

14. Kandıyotı, "Ataerkil Örüntüler," 343–44.

15. Şirin Tekeli, "1980'ler Türkiye'sinde Kadınlar" (Women in Turkey in the 1980s), in Tekeli, ed., *Kadın Bakış Açısından*, 23.

16. Feride Acar, "Türkiye'de İslamci Hareket ve Kadın" (Women and the Islamic movement in Turkey), in Tekeli, ed., *Kadın Bakış Açısından*, 69.

17. Whereas the secularist movement exhibits a great number of associations, foundations, and periodicals and represents institutional efforts, the Islamic movement is characterized by its rejection of formal organizations. It operates predominantly through such sects as the Nakşibendi, Nurcu, and Süleymancı. Its most effective method of mobilizing women is by using religious rituals to create informal networks within family structures.

18. Günseli Berik, "The Social Condition of Women in Turkey in the Eighties and the Migration Process," *New Perspectives on Turkey* 3 (Fall 1989): 89.

19. Arat, *Patriarchal Paradox*, 52. See also Yeşim, "Obstacles to Political Careers: Perceptions of Turkish Women," *International Political Science Review* 6 (1985): 355–66.

20. Oya Çitçi, *Yerel Yönetimlerde Temsil: Belediye Örneği* (Representation in local governments: The case of municipalities) (Ankara: TODAİE Yayınları, Üçler Matbaası, 1989), 105. See also Oya Çitçi, "Representation of Turkish Women in Local Government," in *Proceedings of the Conference on Women in Local and Regional Life, Athens, 10–12 September 1986* (Strasbourg: Council of Europe, 1986), 113–20.

21. Çitçi, *Yerel Yönetimlerde Temsil,* 105, 173.

22. Ibid., 173.

23. Ibid.

24. Arat, *Patriarchal Paradox,* 118.

25. Ayşe Güneş-Ayata, "Türkiye'de Kadının Siyasal Katılımı" (Political participation of women in Turkey), in Tekeli, *Kadın Bakış Açısından,* 18, 274–75.

26. Oya Tokgöz, *Siyasal Haberleşme ve Kadın* (Political communication and women) (Ankara: Sevinç Matbaası, 1975), 18, 213–14.

27. Güneş-Ayata, "Türkiye'de Kadının Siyasal Katılımı," 280–81.

28. Ibid., 282.

29. Ayşe Güneş-Ayata, "Türkiye'de Kadının Siyasal Katılımı" (Political participation of women in Turkey) (Paper presented at a conference on the status of women in Turkey in the 1980s, Kassel, 17–21 April 1989).

30. Ibid.

31. Eser Köker, "Türkiye'de Kadın, Eğitim, ve Siyaset: Yüksek Ö'retim Kurumlarında Kadının Durumu Üzerine Bir İnceleme" (Politics, education, and women in Turkey: An analysis of women working in institutions of higher education) (Ph.D. diss., Ankara University, 1988), 137.

32. Ibid., 205.

33. Ibid., 224–25.

34. Ibid., 223.

35. Oya Çitçi, "Türk Toplumunda Kadın Görevlilerini Sosyal Görünümü" (The social outlook of female civil servants in Turkish society), *Amme İdaresi Dergisi* (Local government magazine) 21 (September 1988): 56, 42.

36. Ibid. See also Mohini Sethi, *Modernization of Working Women in Developing Societies* (New Delhi: National Publishing House, 1976), who reports that 61 percent of the Turkish women employed in government agencies who took part in her study would prefer to continue working after marriage. See also Oya Çulpan and Toni Marzotti, "Changing Attitudes Toward Work and Marriage: Turkey in Transition," *Signs* 8 (1982): 337–51; and Janet Browning, "Atatürk's Legacy to the Women in Turkey," Occasional Papers 27 (Durham, Eng.: University of Durham, 1985).

37. Nermin Abadan-Unat, "Women in Government as Policy Makers and Bureaucrats: The Turkish Case," in Margerita Rendel, ed., *Women, Power and Political Systems* (London: Croom Helm, 1981), 94–115.

38. Çitçi, "Türkiye'de Kamu Görevlilerini Sosyal Görünümü," 58.

39. Ayşe Öncü, "Turkish Women in Professions, Why So Many?" in Abadan-Unat, ed., *Women in Turkish Society* (Leiden: Brill, 1981), 181–93.

40. Çiğdem Kağıtçıbaşı, "Value of Children: Women's Role and Fertility in Turkey," in Abadan-Unat, ed., *Women in Turkish Society,* 74–95.

41. Emelie A. Olson, "Muslim Identity and Secularism in Contemporary Turkey: The Headscarf Dispute," *Anthropological Quarterly* 58 (October 1985): 161–71; Fatma Mansur Coşar, "Women in Turkish Society," in Lois Beck and Nikki Keddie, eds., *Women in the Muslim World* (Cambridge, Mass.: Harvard University Press, 1978), 137.

42. For a discussion of women's status in Islam see Barbara Freyer Stowasser, "Liberated Equal or Protected Dependent? Contemporary Religious Paradigms on Women's Status in Islam," *Arab Studies Quarterly* 9 (Summer 1987): 260–83. See also Binnaz (Sayarı) Toprak, "Religion and Turkish Women," in Abadan-Unat, ed., *Women in Turkish Society,* 281–92; and P. Yorgun, "The Women's

Question and Difficulties of Feminism in Turkey," *Khamsin* 11 (1985): 78–83.

43. Feride Acar, "Women in the Ideology of Islamic Revivalism in Turkey: Three Islamic Women's Journals," in Richard Tapper, ed., *Islam in Modern Turkey: Religion, Politics, and Literature in a Secular State* (London: St. Martin's Press, 1991).

44. Sabahat Tezcan, "Health Problems of Turkish Women," in Abadan-Unat, ed., *Women in Turkish Society,* 96–106.

45. Çiğdem Kağıtçıbaşı, "Intra-Family Interaction and a Model of Change," in Türköz Erder, ed., *Family in Turkish Society* (Ankara: Maya Yayıncılık, 1985), 149–63.

▲ Union of Soviet Socialist Republics (former)

POLITICS

Type of Political System: state socialist
  Sovereignty: not applicable
  Executive-Legislative System: not
  applicable
Type of State: unitary
Type of Party System: multiparty
Major Political Parties

Communist Party of the Soviet Union
(CPSU, Kommunisticheskaya Partiya
Sovyetskovo Soyuza): For decades the only
legal party in the Soviet Union; founded by
Lenin in 1903. At the 28th party congress,
held in 1990, the party recognized in its
platform that the Soviet Union was now a
multiparty state and that the CPSU no longer
controlled the government or administrative
employment.[a] Since then the party has
experienced numerous splits. Among the
main subgroups within the CPSU one has a
Marxist platform, which advocates a return to
the basic teachings of Marx, and one a
democratic platform, representing
communists who support democratic
transformations in the party.

Communist Party of the Russian Soviet
Federated Socialist Republic: An orthodox
Communist party based in Russia; led by Ivan
Polozkov.

Russian Communist Bolshevik Party: An
orthodox Communist party.

Communist Parties of Latvia, Estonia, and
Lithuania: Orthodox Communist parties.

Constitutional Democrats: Based on
prerevolutionary party of the same name and
platform.

Socialist Revolutionaries: Based on
prerevolutionary party of the same name and
platform.

Anarchists: Based on prerevolutionary party
of the same name and platform.

Monarchists: Based on prerevolutionary
party of the same name and platform; support
the return of the descendants of the Russian
royal family.

Social-Democratic Party of Russia: Based
on prerevolutionary party of the same name
and platform.

Other movements and organizations:
Nationalist political organizations, or ethnic
and people's fronts—such as Pamiat
(Memory)—have developed in many regions.
In addition, thousands of informal political
associations have been formed.[b] Among these
are the Democratic Party of Russia, Liberal
Democratic Party of the Soviet Union,
Christian Democratic Party, Democratic
Union, Free Democratic Party of Russia,
United Front of Working People, and Green
Alternative.

Year Women Granted Right to Vote: 1917
*Year Women Granted Right to Stand for
  Election:* 1917
Percentage of Women in the Legislature (1989)
  Lower House: 15.7%
  Upper House: not available
*Percentage of Electorate Voting for Highest
  Elected Office in Most Recent Election
  (1989):* not available

DEMOGRAPHICS

Population: 286,700,000[c]
Percentage of Population in Urban Areas
  Overall: 65.7%
  Female: 65.9%
  Male: 65.4%
Percentage of Population Below Age 15:
  27.0%[d]
Birthrate (per 1,000 population): 20[e]
Maternal Mortality Rate (per 100,000 live
  births): 48
Infant Mortality Rate (per 1,000 live births):
  25

Mortality Rate for Children Under Five (per 1,000 live births): 32

Average Household Size (1987): 3.5[f]

Mean Age at First Marriage
Female: 21.8
Male: 24.2

Life Expectancy
Female: 73.3
Male: 64.2

EDUCATION

Ratio of Female to Male Enrollment: not available

Literacy Rate
Female: 100.0%
Male: 100.0%

ECONOMY

Gross National Product per Capita: U.S. $4,550

Percentage of Labor Force in Agriculture: 19.0%[g]

Distribution of Agricultural Workers by Sex[h]
Female: 45.0%
Male: 55.0%

Economically Active Population by Sex
Female: 61.3%
Male: 76.8%

a. Arthur S. Banks, ed., *Political Handbook of the World, 1991* (Binghamton, N.Y.: CSA Publications, 1991), 707.

b. Ibid. Although the informal organizations have different goals and tasks, they share a complete disregard of women as a political force, a denial of women's political interests, and an acceptance of the ideology that "women are predestined to keep the hearth."

c. National Economy of the USSR, *Statistical Yearbook* (in Russian) (Moscow: Finances and Statistics, 1989).

d. Population of the USSR, *Statistical Yearbook* (in Russian) (Moscow: Finances and Statistics, 1988).

e. National Economy of the USSR, *Statistical Yearbook*.

f. Population of the USSR, *Statistical Yearbook*.

g. National Economy of the USSR, *Statistical Yearbook*.

h. Ibid.

Soviet Women and Politics: On the Brink of Change

OLGA A. VORONINA

TRANSLATED BY

ANATOLII SMIRNOFF

This chapter was written between August 1991 and November 1991, a time of both uncertainty and hope in the Soviet Union. The August coup against the government of Mikhail Gorbachev had been unsuccessful, and Gorbachev had declared socialism a failure. The future of the Soviet Union, though brighter than it had been since the 1920s, was still unsure. After the coup the Congress of People's Deputies of the USSR proposed a Union of Sovereign States that would keep the countries emerging from the Soviet Union closely bound to one another. By December 1991 the Soviet Union had ceased to exist, replaced by the weak federation of the Commonwealth of Independent States. At this time, the states in the commonwealth were Armenia, Azerbaijan, Belarus, Georgia, Kazakhstan, Kyrgyzstan, Moldova, Russia, Tajikistan, Turkmenistan, Ukraine, and Uzbekistan. Estonia, Latvia, and Lithuania did not join.

In 1991 the Union of Soviet Socialist Republics was the largest country in the world, stretching across parts of Europe and Asia. It had a population of 287 million. Founded in Russia in 1917, following a revolution that overthrew the czar, the Soviet Union became a federal system of 15 republics, each named after the ethnic or national group that was most numerous. Of these, Russia was the largest and most powerful.[1] Overall, the USSR was home to more than 100 ethnic and national groups that spoke 200 languages and practiced six religious faiths. Numerous other ethnic groups also lived in the Soviet Union: Germans, Jews, Poles, Tartars, Bachkirs, Mordvinians, Chuvashes, Yakuts, Nenets, Nanays, Chukchis, Adygeans, Balkars, Chechens, Ingushis, Karachayevs, and Circassians, among others. Many of these groups were governed by semiautonomous structures within individual republics.

According to the constitution, the Soviet Union was a socialist republic governed by a bicameral legislature, the Supreme Soviet. The two bodies of the Supreme Soviet, the Soviet of Nationalities and the Soviet of the Union, were directly elected by the people. Because the Supreme Soviet met only twice a year, however, an executive committee, the Presidium, carried out most of its functions. The chairperson of the Presidium was officially considered the head of government.

For most of the country's history, however, the Communist Party of the Soviet Union (CPSU) functioned as the actual executive, legislative, and legal decision-making structure. Although homage was routinely paid to the principles of democracy that underlay the structure of the government, it was not complemented by representative democracy or the election of deputies to the Supreme Soviet who expressed the will of the electorate. In the early years the soviets, or councils, were to a certain degree organs of direct democracy, through which representatives of all classes expressed the demands of the voters. But from the 1930s on, the Communist Party in reality monopolized all power and acted as the state. Article 6 of the Soviet constitution said: "The Communist Party of the Soviet Union is the ruling and guiding force of Soviet society, the core of its political system and its state and public organizations."[2] The party controlled practically every aspect of Soviet life, from foreign policy to agriculture. Although officially the Supreme Soviet elected the chair of the Presidium, in practice the Supreme Soviet merely seconded decisions made by the party's highest body, the Politburo. Ostensibly, members of the Supreme Soviet were chosen by the people in free elections, but in fact the Communist Party's control of the election process and its refusal to allow other political parties even to exist meant that usually only one candidate, the party candidate, was nominated for each seat in the Supreme Soviet.

The policy of the party and of the Soviet state toward the issue of nationalities was aimed at the forcible formation of the so-called new historical community of the Soviet people. The cultures of the nationalities within this "community" were deprived of their distinctive features and transformed into a "Soviet culture" that was permeated by communist ideology and dominated by the totalitarian state. National groups, including the Russians, lost the values and traditions—and sometimes even the language—that had made them distinct.

The difficult and controversial process of rejecting old dogmas and concepts began in 1985. The gradual failure of the state-run economy led to the demise of the state-controlled political system. The growing visibility of the failure of the Soviet political system and its eventual destruction inspired nationalist movements among the country's ethnic and national groups. The Baltic states, which Stalin had forcibly and unlawfully included in the USSR, were pioneers on the path to freedom. Their struggle for independence was rewarded in 1991, when the USSR recognized their autonomy. That year all the Union Republics proclaimed their sovereignty and independence from the USSR. With the dissolution of their old ties, many autonomous republics, the once semiautonomous territories, and governing structures for minority groups within each Union Republic now also seek to establish their independence. Thus, although the Soviet Union has ceased to exist, ethnic conflicts between groups like the Georgians and Abkhazians, Moldavians and Gagauzes, Balts and Poles, continue.

National struggles have been only one part of larger political struggles. In 1989 the People's Deputies of the USSR were elected in a new way. The election was based on the principles of universal, equal, and direct suffrage, and the voting was secret. For the first time there were alternative candidates in many constituencies. As a result, representatives of different strata of the population, different public movements and organizations, and different views and opinions entered the highest legislative body in the state.

The Communist Party continued to control the state, however, and dictated how many seats the new organizations could have in the Supreme Soviet—after reserving 100 of 2,250 for itself. As it turned out, the deputies who were elected in 1989 proved rather incapable of handling state affairs. Because of incompetence and conservativism, they rejected many progressive programs aimed at restructuring the society, thereby intensifying the socioeconomic and political crisis.

In spite of all their problems, the deputies nonetheless managed to make certain positive contributions to the progressive cause. One of their most significant acts took place in the spring of 1990. The deputies abolished the notorious article 6 of the constitution, which stated that the party is "the ruling force" of Soviet society. For months afterward the party structures sought revenge, going so far as to attempt a coup d'état in August 1991. But their moment in history was almost over.

The botched coup, intended to prevent a new Union Treaty from being signed, turned out to be the catalyst for numerous changes.[3] The subsequent decrees of President Mikhail Gorbachev and the resolutions of the Congress of People's Deputies proclaimed an end to the control and activities of the Communist Party within the territory of the USSR and ordered the "departization" of the state structures, the military, the KGB, and the police.

The attempted coup revealed the utter inability of the state structures to counter lawless acts. Furthermore, by aborting the treaty that might have preserved the union, albeit with more autonomy, the putsch precipitated the disintegration of the USSR. Following the failed coup, all republics proclaimed themselves independent of the center, and the emergency Congress of People's Deputies proclaimed a "transition period for the shaping of a new system of state relations."[4] A new Union of Sovereign States has been proposed. It is hard to foresee which of the republics will remain members of the new union and what their internal political structures will be.

The law entitled On the Legislative and Executive Bodies of State Power During the Transition Period was passed by the Congress of People's Deputies in September 1991, making the Supreme Soviet the highest representative institution of power in the USSR (as the country remains named). The Supreme Soviet consists of two houses: the Soviet of Republics (formerly the Soviet of Nationalities) and the Soviet of the Union. The terms of membership in the Soviet of the Union are the same as those of 1989, when deputies were elected to represent constituencies with equal populations. The Soviet of Republics includes several People's Deputies of the USSR who were elected in 1989, as well as deputies representing each of the Union Republics, who are chosen by the highest bodies of state power in each republic. Those Union Republics that include autonomous republics or any other autonomous structures send extra deputies to the Soviet of Republics because of the provision that every autonomous formation be represented by one delegate. At the same time, to safeguard the republics' electoral equality within the Soviet of Republics, every Union Republic, whatever its size, has only one vote. Together, the Soviet of the Union and the Soviet of Republics have the power to make laws. Individual republics have the right to suspend any law passed by the Supreme Soviet if it contradicts the constitution of the republic.[5]

The State Council of the USSR functions as the executive of the new union. It coordinates the resolution of questions concerning both home and foreign policy, as well as problems affecting the interests of all the republics. The State Council is based upon the interrepublican principle and includes the president of the USSR and the highest state officials of each of the Union Republics. The work of the council is supervised by the president of the USSR, and its decisions are binding on the Union Republics.

Thus, the presidential decrees concerning the cessation of CPSU activities, the departization of the state structures, and the abolishment of political organs in the military, the KGB, and the Ministry of Internal Affairs have been harbingers of countrywide changes. The separation of state structures from Communist Party structures and the liquidation of party control over the power and activities of the state are both unprecedented events in the history of the USSR.

The Declaration of Human Rights and Freedoms in September 1991 was of no less historical and political importance. In it, the Supreme Soviet proclaimed that "no group, party or State interests may prevail over human interests," that "everybody has freedom of speech and the right to express opinions and beliefs freely, as well as to propagate them both orally and in written form," that "no State ideology may exist that is obligatory for citizens," and finally that "no one can be persecuted for his or her beliefs."[6] Still, in spite of the trend toward rebirth, one problem remains unexposed: the socioeconomic discrimination against women and their permanent alienation from politics.[7]

For 70 years the Communist Party dominated Soviet society as its "leading and guiding force."[8] This is why, in discussing women in politics, I stress the ideology, policies, and activities of the party regarding women, despite the changes that have recently occurred.

Although Marxist-Leninist thought is based on a class analysis, the ideology was not created by members of the class as a whole.[9] The living conditions of a class are apt to generate spontaneously not an ideology but a social psychology. The ideology is created by the propagandists of a given class, the party in this case. Once the party proclaimed itself the representative of the vanguard of society (the working class), the only possible outcome of its "highly scientific" reasoning was the usurpation of the right of actual workers and peasants to decide what was truth. I there-

fore consider the analysis of Marxist-Leninist and party ideology to be an important key to understanding Soviet politics and women's issues in the USSR. I shall dwell on two functions of this ideology mentioned by Western scholars: the way it disguises the true ends of party politics and the way party politics affects women.[10] By looking at facts and figures and analyzing state and party documents, I seek to draw an objective picture of how female citizens were virtually cut off from politics and government.

But this is not my only task. In my opinion, it is far more important to demonstrate why Soviet women—who for more than 70 years have enjoyed the same constitutional rights as Soviet men in every domain, who make up more than half of the working population, who constitute 60 percent of educated professionals like doctors, engineers, teachers, and lawyers—have been alienated from the decision-making levels of Soviet government and from "big politics." I want to demonstrate the hows, whys, and therefores of the Soviet suppression of women and the causes of their exploitation. I hope to show how women became political outsiders in a country that was guided by an ideology preaching equality of the sexes and that proclaimed this equality as an element of the progressive changes necessary in every society.

WOMEN AND POLITICS AT THE TIME OF THE OCTOBER REVOLUTION

The position of Marxism on the problem of discrimination against women provided the ideological basis for Bolshevik political activity concerning women. The main points put forward in the works of Karl Marx, Friedrich Engels, Vladimir Lenin, and others can be summed up as follows. First, discrimination against women was considered merely one instance of the socioeconomic oppression faced by all members of society. It was class, not gender, that brought about women's oppression. Overcoming socioeconomic discrimination against women therefore necessarily entailed the revolutionary transformation of society through class struggle. Once the socialist revolution succeeded and the new society was built, there would no longer be social grounds for the oppression and exploitation of women. Second, for the social condition of women to change, it would be necessary for women not only to enjoy political and civil rights equal to those of men but also to be economically independent from men. Women could obtain their independence by working for pay outside the home. Third, because the traditional family, headed by a male, served as a stronghold of patriarchy and because exacting domestic labor from women was the most efficient means of oppressing them, it was deemed necessary to make into a social responsibility such activities as child rearing and the paltry but burdensome domestic labors usually described by the Russian word *byt*. The system of relationships associated with marriage and the family would also eventually be liberalized under socialism. The framing of this problem played a prominent part in the women's movement, both before and after the Revolution of 1917.

The intensive industrial development in Russia at the beginning of the twentieth century led to women's widespread employment in factories and plants. The extremely low wages for women, the total lack of rights, and the difficult working conditions quickly gave rise to a women workers' movement. As activists in the Russian Socialist Democratic Labor Party propagated their ideas among female workers (instilling in them such notions as the need for women to struggle for the proletarian revolution) they clashed quite unexpectedly with liberal feminists. The latter, who had begun by organizing various philanthropic societies to help working women, had by this point moved on to creating political clubs that called upon women workers to unite and fight for the political, economic, and educational rights of all women. The mere possibility that women would unite under the standard of their sex and not under the banner of class struggle scared the Russian Socialist Democratic Labor Party activists, for the party might lose its influence on the women workers' movement. No wonder that in 1906 at the first All-Russian Congress of

Women, Alexandra Kollontai, then head of the women workers' delegation, castigated "bourgeois feminists."

Bolshevik ideologues had proclaimed the development of an independent feminist movement and women's struggle for human rights a "purely bourgeois whim," serving only to distract the female masses from the real struggle for socialism, thus driving a wedge between feminism and the women workers' movement that was to last for almost a century.[11] In fact, after 1917 the feminists' attempts to single out specific women's interests and to understand specific features of women's position within the traditional patriarchal society came only from abroad. Within the USSR, the Communist Party and state denied the objective development of specific female social interests, thereby depriving the women's movement of its raison d'être. The class approach to discrimination against women led to the absorption of the women workers' movement into the general proletarian movement. As a result, the aims of the former were subsumed by the ends of the latter, and the mission of female emancipation became subordinated to the more global political tasks of accomplishing a revolution. The movement to liberate women was labeled the "female issue."

Following the Revolution of 1917, the Bolshevik-controlled government demolished the old social framework and erected a new society and new state structures based on its own ideology. Some of the government's political and socioeconomic reforms concerned women. According to the constitution of 1918 and to laws enacted at that time, women were given equal rights with men in political, social, economic, and family matters.[12] By themselves, these measures were clearly progressive and showed promise for expanding women's horizons.

Even though the party altered some aspects of the traditional position of women, it was not about to abandon its leadership of the women's movement. After all, a struggle for power involving armed opposition continued against the Bolsheviks until 1922. Other political parties offering alternatives in the search for new concepts of social life might also have gained women's support. The Bolsheviks, trying to widen their popular support, therefore made rhetorical efforts to recruit women. Male leaders of the party claimed, however, that women's oppression by men at home and at work was not as important as the opportunity to participate in the building of a brave new world. The Bolsheviks wished to bring women into the party for both patriarchal reasons (to use them as subordinate workers holding insignificant offices) and political reasons (to further class goals).

Although the party proclaimed the inclusion of women in political life as a central principle, party leaders were in no rush to offer women high party offices. Such rhetoric notwithstanding, in 1920 (the year of the first official party census) female party members totaled no more than 45,000, or 7 percent of the membership, and none were on the party's Central Committee. By 1924 women made up about 10 percent of the Communist Party but only slightly more than 2 percent of the Central Committee—specifically, 2 of the 87 members. The figures for the 1930s were similar, with women making up 13 percent of the party but only 3 percent of the Central Committee. The situation was similar in government bodies. In the first Soviet government there was only one woman, the people's commissar (minister) of social security, Alexandra Kollontai. In local politics, women made up only 1 percent of People's Deputies in 1922, 10 percent in 1926, and 27 percent in 1934. Although the corresponding percentages for cities and towns were slightly higher—5.7, 18, and 32 during the same years—they were still low.[13] Even when women were included in political organizations, their roles were often minor or purely nominal.

In 1918 the Central Committee of the Russian Communist Party (the Bolsheviks) introduced a commission responsible for propaganda and agitation among women attached to the Secretariat of the Central Committee. As part of this effort, *zhenotdels* (women's sections) of local party organizations were created. The main tasks of the zhenotdels were to spread the party ideology among female workers and peasants by means of political work, to draw women into the party, trade unions, cooperative organizations, and soviet bodies, and to cooperate with other organizations like trade unions in such tasks as the creation of kindergartens and community canteens.[14]

Although it is not easy to evaluate the effects of the zhenotdels on women, it is evident that the groups spread the party norms and standards, forced Marxist-Leninist ideology upon the female masses, and exerted ideological control over women. Yet, the first leaders of the *zhenotdel* system (Inessa Armand, 1919–20; Alexandra Kollontai, 1920–22; Sophia Smidovich, 1922–24) were sincerely carried away by the revolutionary romanticism of Marxism-Leninism and by their belief in the need to liberate female workers from the patriarchal family institutions that oppressed them. Their fervor brought energy to the activities of the zhenotdels.

On the crest of the wave of enthusiasm for restructuring, many aspects of family life were liberalized. In 1920 various laws were passed that permitted divorce, gave equal rights to children born in and out of wedlock, and legalized abortions. Widespread discussions also took place over such matters as freedom of love and the future of the family and marriage as institutions.

Although some leaders, like Alexandra Kollontai, eagerly fought bourgeois feminism and worked within the system, they also began to look at the problem of female liberation through the eyes of women. This outlook, however, went beyond the limits of the Marxist ideology and could have threatened the party with the loss of its sway over the female masses. Consequently, party leaders were not in the least interested in the issues that these women raised, such as woman's self-awareness, the problems of housekeeping, and the submersion of the woman's personality in family. Their interest in the emancipation of women went as far as necessary to marshal women to carry out the party's political and economic directives, and no further.

The party ideology also encouraged another form of political activity by women—*zhendele-*

gatskiye sobraniya (meetings of female delegates). During these conferences, the delegates, who had been selected by workers and peasants, discussed various problems arising during zhenotdel activities. In my opinion, zhen-delegatskiye sobraniya turned out to be another way in which women were isolated from the major political arena. The number of female delegates continually increased and by 1927 totaled 620,000, although this figure corresponded to a mere 0.9 percent of the adult female population. The main programs of the zhenotdels were always discussed and decided at party conferences and congresses ahead of time. Moreover, the main task of the zhenotdels was always formulated as the "drawing of women into the building of a new society," not as a struggle for real sexual equality in society. Under Stalin even this puppet form of women's political activity was eventually considered undesirable.

STALIN: "THE FEMALE ISSUE IS SOLVED"

As soon as Joseph Stalin became general secretary of the Communist Party in 1922, the totalitarian system began to take shape. All political parties and public organizations were abolished, with the exception of the Communist Party; and all dissent therein was prohibited. The soviets came increasingly under party control until at last they were nothing more than nominal entities that executed every party decision. The party itself went through significant changes. Rank-and-file members were eliminated from participation in party affairs, and even the central bodies of the party lost power, becoming little more than a sort of deceptive show. Stalin ruled the country on his own. The extermination of any unorthodox thought became the prevailing feature of political life and brought about a series of disastrous purges intended to destroy those whom Stalin decreed enemies of the people.

In the economic sphere, industrialization and the intensive development of the defense industry were proclaimed as goals, to the detriment of other aspects of industry and the economy. The agricultural sector underwent collectivization,

which meant that plots of land that had belonged to the peasants immediately after the revolution were confiscated. Small peasant households and landholdings were forcibly amalgamated into *kolkhoz*es (large collective farms) where farmers were obliged to sell their crops to the state at extremely low prices. Party ideology became a means to extol both Stalin and his lawless methods as part of the historical development of Marxism.

As for women, the old official opinion that they had been liberated by the October Revolution persisted. Stalinist propaganda averred that woman had been given the opportunity "to stand cheek by jowl with her husband, father, or brother in the struggle for a new life."[15] From the viewpoint of Stalinist ideology, women had also gained one more guarantee of their equality with men: Stalin's policy of industrialization and collectivization provided extra jobs for women outside the home and an opportunity for them to work on equal terms with men.

As Soviet society developed under Stalin, women's *opportunity* to participate in non-domestic labor was transformed into their *duty* to work in state-owned enterprises. But women's economic independence was no longer discussed as an indispensable condition for their emancipation. On the contrary, from the 1930s on, women were considered only from a functional point of view; they were valued only as "the great army of labor," as the "colossal reserve of the work force."[16] Because industrialization was carried out by the use of labor-intensive rather than capital-intensive methods, it required an incredibly vast and cheap work force. Stalin's campaigns against the enemies of the people provided many such workers, because those who were not shot were sent to hard-labor camps, known as the "building-sites of communism." One researcher, I. A. Kurganov, estimates that in the 1920s and 1930s about 5 million women were forced to work at the building sites of the Stalinist empire.[17] Women also constituted a considerable part of the labor force that had not already been "taken into custody"—the so-called free Soviet citizenry. During Stalin's rule, the number of women in the work force steadily increased. In 1928, 3 million workers, or 24 percent of the industrial work force, were women. By 1940 that number had risen to more than 13 million, representing 39 percent of the work force.[18]

Women's increasing participation in the industrial work force was "encouraged" by cruel measures. Workers received meager wages, hardly enough for one person to make ends meet, let alone an entire family. Special cards were distributed to exchange for food and clothes. Because a worker's card bought more food than a dependent's, office worker's, or clerk's card, women had to work at the most strenuous jobs to support their families.

The collectivization and mass destruction of the kulaks (wealthy peasants) led to the extermination of the individual peasant household, which in turn undermined the economic foundations of the patriarchal rural family. As a result, rural women had to go to town or to the collective farm to eke out a living. Pushed into an occupational framework that had traditionally been male, women had to accept any job and work on any terms. Thus, women frequently ended up doing the kind of work that male workers avoided, work that was hard, scantily paid, and looked down on.

The establishment of the totalitarian regime meant that citizens also lost their economic rights when they lost their civil ones. The right to work implied the choice of a wide range of jobs, as well as adequate material security and the possibility of professional growth. In practice, however, the principal of equality between men and women—when both men and women were totally deprived of their civil rights—was, for women, transformed into the right to work for minimum wages. In addition to being coerced by economic means into taking up employment, women, like other workers in the 1930s, were legally prohibited from leaving their places of work. Stalin's bequest of the right to work to women thus became an extra device contrived to exploit them. To their traditional domestic duties was added the duty of working at state-owned enterprises. This right to work could not be used by women to gain their economic independence.

In the 1930s the conservativism of official ideology and state policy concerning family issues also increased, adversely affecting women's position in the family. The numerous social and economic upheavals during the first two post-revolutionary decades (including civil war, industrialization, collectivization, the witch-hunt for enemies of the people, and party purges) undermined the family. This in turn threatened the machinery of labor-force reproduction, which was indispensable to Soviet rule. And because all solutions to social problems in a totalitarian society are unavoidably repressive, the policy of the Stalinist state concerning women became increasingly strict. During the mid-1930s, for example, the right to divorce was abolished completely. In 1936 abortions were banned, and contraceptives ceased to be available. Stalin's party-state enthusiastically presented the abortion ban as "one of the most vivid manifestations of the cultural and educational function of the socialist state."[19]

Beginning in the early 1930s, then, state policy concerning women became openly utilitarian. Women were considered no more than a resource for the production of goods and for reproduction of the work force. In the propaganda, this approach toward women was presented as the final solution of the female issue in the USSR and became the pretext for the abolition of the zhenotdels. Under the Soviet variety of patriarchy the ever increasing exploitation of women was called equality.

THE POLITICAL THAW OF KHRUSHCHEV

The policies of Nikita Khrushchev, in power from 1953 to 1964, were motivated primarily by his desire to de-Stalinize society and to revitalize the Communist Party and the soviets. To accomplish this, new forces were brought into action, and new actors appeared on the political stage. Yet even as the question of the political activity of various social strata came to life again after Stalin, it was clear that women hardly participated in politics. In 1956 women were 19.7 percent of party members and only 4.1 percent of the Central Committee (10 of the 244 members). There were no women in the Politburo nor, until 1957, in the Council of Ministers.

These facts did not go unnoticed by Khrushchev. In his famous speech to the 20th party congress in 1956, a speech devoted to criticism of Stalinism, as well as to an analysis of the party's proper role, he drew attention to women's small part in the work of the party and the soviets. "It should not be overlooked that many party and state organs put women forward for leadership posts with timidity. Very few women hold leading posts in the party and the soviets."[20] After long years of propaganda extolling the supposed triumph of the state in the solution of the female issue in the USSR, Khrushchev's statement sounded somewhat promising.

That year the state created the Soviet Women's Committee (SWC), a nongovernmental public organization whose mission was to raise the level of women's labor and social activity. In reality, it soon was busy doing something else: disseminating to other countries lies about the successful Soviet solution of the female issue and fighting bourgeois feminism. The problems that truly bothered Soviet women were of so little concern to this "public" organization that a policeman standing at the front of the SWC's magnificent mansion had orders to admit only the "chosen ones."

In spite of such window dressings of socialism as the SWC, some criticism concerning the position of women was allowed. At the 22nd party congress in 1961, for instance, it was stated that "remnants of inequality in the position of women in everyday life must be completely eliminated. Conditions must be created for the harmonious combination of motherhood with a more active participation of women in the labor force, society, science, and the arts."[21] Consequently, during the years of Khrushchev's rule family law was once again liberalized with the lifting of the bans on abortion and divorce.

The political role of women remained much the same. In 1961 women had virtually the same low levels of representation in party and state organizations as they had in 1956. Only 19.5 percent of the party's membership was female. The percentages of women in the Central Committee and in the Supreme Soviet were 3.3 and 28.0, respectively.[22] Under Khrushchev, however, the phrase "inequality in the position of women" was used in party materials, and some acknowledgment of the phenomenon was thereby legalized. As a result, discussion of the female issue became theoretically possible. But society was not ready for such a discourse. In the powerful outburst of social activity by the intelligentsia during the Khrushchev years, known in Russia as *shestidesyatnichestvo* (the movement of the 1960s), there was no place for a discussion of women's position.

THE EPOCH OF BREZHNEV

From the beginning of his rule (1964–82), Leonid Brezhnev faced a series of worsening socioeconomic problems, such as the drop in labor productivity, the considerable decline in the birthrate, and the work-force shortage that resulted from both these factors.[23] Yet government leaders did not veer from the well-trodden path of the traditional Soviet economy, with its requirement of cheap, widely available manual labor. Rather than restructuring the economy or introducing progressive technology, the party and state saw the problem as how to find extra reserves of workers. An increase in the birth rate was proposed as one possible solution.

Under Brezhnev's administration, women, as 51 percent of the work force, were critical to the economy but were also expected to bear more children. This double burden was discussed in the party and in scholarly literature. The debate elicited the unwilling admission that certain hardships and "nonantagonistic" contradictions existed in the position of women and that in fact the female issue had not been altogether resolved. Almost no one, however, addressed the question of women's equality in all spheres of life, because the equality problem had become less and less popular in discussions of the female issue. The main emphasis was instead on how to combine women's dual roles as workers and mothers and how the party could help women. The utilitarian approach of the Stalin era was thus revived. At the 25th party congress in 1976 the party stressed "its duty to continually protect women, to improve their position as workers, mothers, child rearers, and housewives."[24] At every party congress thereafter, it became a tradition to emphasize certain hardships faced by women as mothers and workers and to issue endless resolutions about improving conditions at the workplace and in the home. No one, however, including the party-state machine, rushed to carry out these resolutions.

As for women's participation in political activities, the party's attitude was both ambiguous and traditional. The official propaganda never denied the importance of their participation as an aspect of sexual equality, but it stressed that the real degree of their participation depended on the level of development of the general social structure, on economic conditions, and on residual attitudes that still lurked in some people's minds. Unwilling to admit that Soviet society and its power structures were not prepared for women in posts of political leadership, the party justified women's absence by citing their extreme economic burden as producers and reproducers and their political passivity. Moreover, the party assumed no responsibility for the socioeconomic practices that created women's double burden and denied any connection between the totalitarianism of the state and political apathy in women. On the contrary, the official propaganda called attention to the "untiring care" and efforts of the party and the government to draw women into sociopolitical activities. The much-talked-about 33 percent of females in the Supreme Soviet was used as proof of its caring.

Any reasonable person, however, could easily comprehend that the strictly observed quota for women in the tame and passive Supreme Soviet (as it was under Brezhnev) fell far short of proving women's participation in managing state affairs. Besides, the party and the soviets artificially preserved the quota by filling it at every election.

Other, more telling statistics testified to women's absence from the middle and top levels of the state structures. Between 1917 and 1967 only 77 of the 2,100 individuals representing the upper political elite of the Soviet Union were women—that is, 3.7 percent. The figures for the middle level of the state-political hierarchy were much the same: only 109 of the 2,500, or 4.4 percent, were women.[25]

The party hierarchy was similarly dominated by men during Brezhnev's 18-year rule. Although 25 percent of party members were women, no women sat on the Politburo, and only one on the Central Committee. Women held no leading posts in regional party organizations and only 4 percent of the top offices in district organizations. Only on the local level were they strongly represented; in the primary party organizations, women held about one-third of the leading posts.[26]

But the scarcity of women among the political elite was, to my mind, not the only problem. Equally important, the women within the political structures did not speak on behalf of the female population. They served merely as symbols for the ideological myth of the Soviet political system, wherein the rights of all social groups and strata were supposedly safeguarded by quotas for those groups in politics and in the management of state affairs. Although women were physically present in state structures, their plenary powers were nominal. All decision making was carried out in the deepest recesses of the *nomenklatura* machine (the party's system for controlling appointments to important positions), not in the representative institutions.

The continued absence of a women's mass movement in the country undoubtedly contributed to this situation. The officially approved swc continued to carry out its propaganda functions and engaged in contacts with foreign women's organizations, but just those untouched by the "sin" of feminism.

Nevertheless, in 1979—and for the first time since the 1920s—an independent religious-feminist group called Maria sprang up in Leningrad. By the end of that year, the group managed to issue an almanac entitled *Woman and Russia* by the *samizdat* route of self-publication. Members of the group, like Tatiana Goricheva, Natalia Malakhovskaya, Tatjana Mamonova, and Julia Voznesenskaya, had a view of women's position that differed significantly from the official one. They protested against the exploitation of women in the Soviet Union, against the suppression of their personalities and the humiliation of their dignity, against the inhuman conditions in hospitals where abortions were carried out, and against the ideological totalitarianism in the public education system. Through the almanac, they were also the first in the country (preceding Andrei Sakharov and other dissidents) to condemn the Afghan war as unjust. Shortly after the group appeared, its members were arrested by the KGB and were either deported or imprisoned. Copies of their book were confiscated.

Such was the way of the Brezhnev administration—to point out demagogically that the political activity of women should increase, yet to trample down the young shoot of an independent women's movement, to willingly recognize the double economic burden of women but do nothing about it.

GORBACHEV AND PERESTROIKA

The party leader who took power in 1985 and who initiated major political and economic reforms, Mikhail Gorbachev, expressed his views on the female issue in two statements. In the first, made at the 27th Congress of the CPSU in 1986, he asserted that it was necessary to revive the *zhensoviets* (women's councils). He was unwilling to let slip the Soviet tradition of party leadership over the women's movement. The second appeared in his book *The Meaning of My Life: Perestroika*, where he wrote that women's "truly feminine predestination should be returned to women completely."[27] Both statements have been echoed in state policy making.

By 1987 the government had created 240,000 zhensoviets across the country, most of which were attached to the party committees of indus-trial enterprises. The SWC assumed the role of organizational center and issued its "Regulations concerning the Zhensoviets," which declared that the organizations would "unite all Soviet women . . . for the good of the cause of communist development" and "work under the leadership of the CPSU."[28]

Thus, the women's organizations created under perestroika were placed under party control, and their activities completely regulated. This did not mean that the party continually meddled in the affairs of the zhensoviets or that the Central Committee strictly supervised every step the SWC took. Yet by establishing the zhensoviets as part of the official political sphere and by assuming leadership over them, the party achieved its goal of transforming them from what could have become a real political force into a nominal one. The party's success was complete, for the overwhelming majority of the zhensoviets proved utterly ineffective and went out of business quite peacefully. The SWC lingers on, pretending to be active, to be a principal center of women's movements, and to speak on behalf of Soviet women. In reality, even before the disintegration of the Soviet Union, the SWC had almost no support among the public.

During Gorbachev's tenure, the attitude of the CPSU toward the promotion of women to high political posts was direct proof of its continued patriarchal stance. Among the 100 People's Deputies of the USSR elected from the Communist Party, only 11 were women. Although in 1990 women accounted for 30 percent of the party, they made up just 6 percent of the Central Committee.[29] Not until 1990 was a woman, Galina Semenova, appointed to the Politburo. Even then, she held the typically female office of chairperson of the Central Committee's Commission on the Status of Women.

Women's representation in the legislative bodies of the state was similarly poor. Although procedures for the 1989 election were for the first time more or less democratic, women did not do well. Only 352 of the 2,250 People's Deputies elected were women—15.7 percent. Within the Supreme Soviet only 18.5 percent of the deputies were women.[30] In addition, all the top offices in the Supreme Soviet continued to be held by men. In the cabinet there were no women. The situation in the governments of the republics was much the same.[31] Thus, under perestroika women were still almost completely absent from all levels of decision making and power, even though they made up 53 percent of the population and 51 percent of the work force.

The reinvigoration of the zhenotdels might have changed this. However, the treatment of women as a resource for production and reproduction, rather than as independent individuals who should enjoy all human rights, became even more apparent during the early years of perestroika and democratization. All the measures supposedly meant to improve the position of women, which were discussed and passed between 1986 and 1991, were really aimed at strengthening the traditional female role in the family. By pursuing a policy of privileges, of various pensions and allowances, the state sought to keep women in the position of social invalids and political outsiders. Stressing the "protection" of woman as mother, the state's program said nothing about measures for incorporating women into the decision-making levels of political structures or for protecting them from unemployment.

Meanwhile, women's employment continues to follow the traditional Soviet pattern. In "male" spheres, women are usually hired for hard, monotonous, and unprestigious jobs that are poorly paid. Wages and prestige are also low in the so-called female professions. "Female" jobs, for example, pay an average of 30 percent less than "male" jobs.[32] At the same time, according to Z. A. Khotina at the Center for Gender Studies, unemployment rates for women are three to five times higher than those for men.

Women have nevertheless become active in the new political parties, public movements, and organizations that emerged in 1990. They make up 30 percent of the membership in such groups as the Memorial, the Greens, the Transnational Party, the Christian Democratic Union of Russia, and the Dark Blue Movement for Human Ecol-

ogy and 50 percent of the membership in the Committee of Social Protection. In other words, women are choosing to participate in parties and organizations that fight to reestablish justice and that stand for the protection of human life and the environment and for nonviolent social transformation. These new democratic movements either remain silent about the problems of women or demand protection for women as mothers and "maintainers of the hearth." They stress that the upbringing of the next generations is the honorable civic duty of woman as mother. At present the programs of only three political movements— the Estonian Popular Front, the Latvian Popular Front, and the Committee for the Liberation of Russia—contain demands for women's equality. But even these groups lack specific plans for attaining this goal. Nor are any of them willing to follow the principle of proportional representation of women and men at the decision-making level of their organizations. The new democrats are quite content to use women in the old conservative way—simply as performers of minor tasks.

So far, women do not have any political parties of their own that reflect and defend female interests in the socioeconomic and political spheres. Two fledgling women's parties exist, the Female Party, in the Siberian town of Tomsk, and the United Party of Women, in St. Petersburg, but they cannot be viewed as serious political organizations. They are too small in terms of membership, are not supported by the general female public, and lack any specific political programs.

I must also mention the somewhat unusual phenomenon of an "interethnic coordination center" called Woman, which was created by an engineer, Evgeni Pilshchikov. The main task of this center is to carry out a special program that includes training a female presidential candidate and running her election campaign. Pilshchikov is convinced that certain "peculiar features" inherent in the feminine psyche are likely to create a new type of president capable of stabilizing the political situation and consolidating society. This supposedly stable society would be based on the principles of national harmony, the preservation of family, and the renewal of the union. Although the idea of a woman president may be politically attractive, women have been reluctant to support the project because of its mechanistic and, in the long run, masculinist nature. The candidate's training, according to Pilshchikov, would be conducted by "learned men." Pilshchikov does not truly address women's interests in this program in the least.

Although women continue to be excluded from big politics, certain changes in the public sphere inspire hope, particularly the development of nonofficial (i.e., independent of the state and party) public organizations of women. The Soviet scholar Valentina Konstantinova, of the Center for Gender Studies, distinguishes three such kinds of organizations: democratic, feminist, and conservative. Among the organizations pressing for democracy are the Committee of the Soldiers' Mothers, which stands for the depoliticization of the military and the introduction of an alternative, nonmilitary national service; the Interregional Political Club, in the town of Zhukovsky (in the Moscow region); the Committee for Equal Opportunities; the Independent Female Democratic Initiative, whose Russian acronym, NEZHDI, could be translated as "don't wait"); and the magazine *Female Reading,* established in St. Petersburg by Olga Lipovskaya. Organizations that focus on feminist issues are the Free Association of Feminist Organizations (SAFO) and the League for Liberation from Societal (Public) Stereotypes (LOTUS), a group of women scientists and scholars who are pushing for the development of women's, gender, and feminist studies in Russian science and are at the same time working generally to draw more women into the struggle for equal rights. Conservatively oriented women's organizations are represented by the SWC and the Union of Women of Russia and also by the renamed network of zhensoviets. Besides these, there are a women's movement called For the Socialist Future of Our Children and various women's religious groups.

Frequently, women's organizations (even those working on similar problems) are separated from, and know little about, each other. To overcome their isolation, members of LOTUS and SAFO, together with research workers from the Center for Gender Studies, organized the First Independent Women's Forum in March 1990. The conference took place in Dubna (near Moscow) under the slogan "Democracy minus woman is not democracy." The main concept was a roll call of women's organizations—an inspection of the forces as they were. Representatives of 48 women's organizations from different regions of the country took part. The female press, as well as female researchers, also attended, as did women who had not yet joined an organization but who felt the urgent need to fight for their rights. Approximately 200 women participated and discussed such issues as women and politics, problems of an independent women's movement, women and the free market economy, women as entrepreneurs, discrimination against women in the patriarchal culture, and violence against women. Those present decided to create the Women's Information Network and to continue the collaboration. They hoped that the work at the forum would help consolidate and develop an independent women's movement in the country.

PROSPECTS

I can give a more exact answer to the question with which I began this chapter: Why were and are Soviet women—who for over 70 years have formally enjoyed rights equal to those of men in all spheres of life—political outsiders? The reasons are deeply rooted in the practice of how the female issue has been framed and is being solved in the Soviet Union.

Marxism has all along viewed the emancipation of women as the gift to women of all the rights of men. This conceptualization smacks of patriarchalism because it implies that men and everything pertaining to men should be taken as a model.

The problem of equality also contains a lot of contradictions. Simply granting women their political rights cannot make them political insiders. Additional measures must be taken in the field of social policy to create true socioeconomic equality. By this I mean that certain political and social privileges such as affirmative action should be granted to women, at least in the beginning, and that public consciousness must be raised. Neither has existed in this country. In addition, formal equality of rights is not sufficient for actual equality of the sexes. In the family, women have traditionally been placed below men. Thus, the entire system of the social functions of the sexes needs to be revamped. Rather than aim at this social revision, however, the state has maintained a functional and utilitarian view of women. The notion of woman as worker and mother was a distinctive feature of the Soviet regime while it existed, and has continued since then.

Another important obstruction to women's emancipation has been usurpation of the leadership of the women's movement by the party and the state. If state social policy had been guided by democratic and humane values, the resolution of women's problems by the state might have been fittingly and efficiently achieved. But in a totalitarian society dominated by ideology, the situation was very different for many years. Having seized the initiative in solving women's problems, the party and the state offered social policies that suited the party, not women. They controlled and suppressed the women's movement all over the country while hypocritically citing the noble paternalism of the Soviet state with respect to women. The lack of an independent women's movement could not help but play a part in the alienation of women from politics. Although women have begun to overcome this alienation, they still do not feel that they are an active political force, and they remain unaware of their political interests as women. They are prepared to fight for the newborn Soviet democracy but not for themselves within the democracy.

One more question is worth mentioning. The myth of the emancipation of Soviet women, which has been skillfully perpetuated by the state machine—together with discrimination, exploitation, and the patriarchal stereotyping of women by the mass media—has somewhat warped women's thinking about emancipation. The average Soviet woman thinks of her emancipation in terms of her present position—namely, as a lot of work disguised as equality with men. No wonder that she is not overly happy about becoming emancipated. Soviet women often see the solution to problems not in a struggle for equal rights—for they think that they have too many rights—but in the rejection of any more sociopolitical activity, which they view as further burdensome business.

The country has entered a new stage in its history, a stage marked by the rejection of the state's Marxist ideology, rejection of the party's control over state and society, rejection of a planned economy, and rejection of the totalitarian suppression of the diverse original ways of life of different nationalities. Although the future shape of the country is unclear, the awareness of the problems resulting from the political, economic, and national life of the former Soviet Union instills hope that sooner or later hardships can be overcome.

A peculiar kind of patriarchy took shape during the 70 years of Soviet rule. Women formally enjoyed many rights and privileges, had a high level of education, actively participated in the economy, and earned independent livings. For all that, even during perestroika the state still considered women to be merely a resource for society's system of production and reproduction. The totalitarian patriarchal state did not need women's voices. All it wanted was the products of their hands and the children of their wombs. And as long as this attitude persists, there will be no real democracy.

NOTES

1. The republics were the Russian Soviet Federated Socialist Republic and the Ukrainian, Byelorussian, Latvian, Lithuanian, Estonian, Moldavian, Georgian, Armenian, Azerbaijan, Kazakh, Tadjik, Uzbek, Turkmen, and Kirghiz Soviet Socialist Republics.

2. *Constitution of the USSR* (in Russian) (Moscow: Politizdat, 1988), 7.

3. This treaty would have given the republics far more autonomy than before.

4. "Resolution of the Congress of People's Deputies of the USSR Concerning the Measures Ensuing from the Joint Declaration of the President of the USSR, and the

Leaders of the Union Republics, and from Decisions Made by the Urgent Session of the Supreme Soviet of the USSR" (in Russian), *Izvestia* (Daily), 6 September 1991.

5. "The Law of the USSR on the Legislative and Executive Bodies of State Power of the USSR During the Transition Period" (in Russian), *Izvestia,* 6 September 1991.

6. "The Declaration of Human Rights and Freedoms Passed by the Congress of People's Deputies of the USSR on 5 September 1991" (in Russian), *Soviet Culture* (Newspaper), 7 September 1991.

7. The term *politics* implies a wide range of meanings. I use it here to refer to any activity that has as its main and ultimate end the seizure and retention of power in the state or the exercise of that power.

8. *Constitution of the USSR,* 7.

9. By ideology I mean the system of views and concepts in which human attitudes toward reality are understood and interpreted. The system also includes the interpretation of social problems and conflicts, along with the aims of social activities directed at either conservation or transformation of the existing social system.

10. Daniel Bell, "Ideology and Soviet Politics," *Slavic Review* 24 (1965): 591–603; and Richard T. De George, *The New Marxism* (New York: Pegasus, 1968).

11. Friedrich Engels, letter to August Bebel, 1 October 1891, in *Marx K., Engels F.: Collected Works* (in Russian), 2nd ed. (Moscow, 1965), 38: 141.

12. Women of the working classes enjoyed the vote, just as men did. Women of the exploitive stratum of society, however, were denied that right, as were the men of that stratum. Thus, the architects of a just, new society introduced a kind of civil rights restriction that depended on social extraction instead of on the property qualification existing in czarist Russia.

13. Gail Washafsky Lapidus, *Women in Soviet Society* (Berkeley: University of California Press, 1978), 210–19.

14. "Communist Party of the Soviet Union," in *Resolutions and Decisions of the Congresses, Conferences and Plenary Meetings of the Central Committees* (in Russian) (Moscow: Politizdat, 1984), 3:285.

15. *Pravda,* 8 March 1936.

16. Ibid.

17. I. A. Kurganov, *Women and Communism* (Germany, 1968), 85–87.

18. *National Economy of the USSR, 1922–1972* (in Russian) (Moscow: Central Statistics Board, 1972), 348.

19. G. M. Sverdlov, *Soviet Family Law* (in Russian) (Moscow: Politizdat, 1958), 78.

20. N. S. Khrushchev, *Summary Report of the Central Committee of the CPSU to the 20th Congress of the Communist Party of the Soviet Union. Verbatim Report* (in Russian), vol. 1 (Moscow: Politizdat, 1956).

21. *Materials of the 22nd Congress of the CPSU* (in Russian) (Moscow: Gospolitizdat, 1961), 393.

22. Lapidus, *Women in Soviet Society,* 210, 214.

23. In 1960 the increment of population growth was 17.8 per 1,000, whereas in 1970 it had dropped to 9.2 per 1,000. See V. I. Perevendentsev, *Demographic Problems in the USSR* (in Russian) (Moscow: Znanjye, 1979), 6.

24. *Materials of the 25th Congress of the CPSU* (in Russian) (Moscow: Politizdat, 1976), 85.

25. Lapidus, *Women in Soviet Society,* 219.

26. Ibid.

27. M. S. Gorbachev, *Smysl moyey zhizni: Perestroika* (The meaning of my life: Perestroika) (Moscow: Politizdat, 1990), 117. The book has been published in English with the title *Perestroika: New Thinking for Our Country and the World* (HarperCollins, 1987).

28. *Regulations Concerning the Councils of Women (the Zhensoviets)* (in Russian) (Moscow: Molodaya Gvardia, 1987), 1.

29. *Arguments and Facts* (in Russian) (Weekly), no. 5 (1990): 6.

30. *Women in the USSR: Articles and Materials* (in Russian) (Moscow: Financy Statistika, 1990), 21.

31. Ibid., 27.

32. N. Zakharova, A. Posadskaja, and N. Rimaschevskaja, "How We Are Solving the Women's Question," *Communist,* no. 4 (1989): 57.

▲ *United States*

POLITICS

Type of Political System: democracy
  Sovereignty: republic
  Executive-Legislative System: presidential
Type of State: federal
Type of Party System: two party
Major Political Parties

Democratic Party: Center or liberal party; has controlled both houses of Congress for 32 years between 1952 and 1992.

Republican Party: Party of the right; has controlled the presidency for 28 years during the same period.

Year Women Granted Right to Vote: 1920[a]
Year Women Granted Right to Stand for Election: 1788/1920[b]
Percentage of Women in the Legislature[c]
  Lower House: 10.8%
  Upper House: 6.0%
Percentage of Electorate Voting for Highest Elected Office in Most Recent Election (1992): 55.0%[d]

DEMOGRAPHICS

Population: 248,709,873[e]
Percentage of Population in Urban Areas
  Overall: 73.7%
  Female: 74.5%
  Male: 73.0%
Percentage of Population Below Age 15: 21.9%
Birthrate (per 1,000 population): 16
Maternal Mortality Rate (per 100,000 live births): 8
Infant Mortality Rate (per 1,000 live births): 10
Mortality Rate for Children Under Five (per 1,000 live births): 13
Average Household Size: 2.2

Mean Age at First Marriage
  Female: 23.3
  Male: 25.4
Life Expectancy
  Female: 78.3
  Male: 71.3

EDUCATION

Ratio of Female to Male Enrollment
  First-Level Education: 94
  Second-Level Education: 97
  Third-Level Education: 110
Literacy Rate
  Female: 99.0%
  Male: 99.0%

ECONOMY

Gross National Product per Capita: U.S. $16,690
Percentage of Labor Force in Agriculture: 3.5%
Distribution of Agricultural Workers by Sex
  Female: 16.3%
  Male: 83.7%
Economically Active Population by Sex
  Female: 50.2%
  Male: 76.5%

a. Women won partial or full suffrage in a number of states before winning national suffrage.

b. The federal constitution did not bar women from running for office, though many state constitutions limited office seekers to electors, eliminating most women's ability to run for office until national suffrage was won in 1920.

c. "Women Candidates and Winners in 1992" (New Brunswick, N.J.: Center for the American Woman and Politics, 12 November 1992).

d. "Voter Turnout Rates for Presidential Elections Since 1932," *Congressional Quarterly* 3553, 7 November 1992.

e. *Census of Population and Housing, 1990* (Washington, D.C.: Bureau of the Census, 1991).

Many Voices But Few Vehicles: The Consequences for Women of Weak Political Infrastructure in the United States

BARBARA J. NELSON
AND KATHRYN A. CARVER

Although a great variety of intellectual traditions and political practices sustain the United States, the country is best described as a liberal democracy. The successes and limits of liberal democracy are thus a prism through which to analyze women's political engagement.

The place of women in America's liberal democracy has routinely been evaluated from three perspectives. The first assesses U.S. programs for women—especially mothers—against those in Western Europe. By comparison, the U.S. programs are meager and not widely available. Limited state support for women is consistent with the nature of the American liberal social contract, which values freedom above reducing inequality through universally available guarantees of economic citizenship. The liberal social contract has special meaning for women, however. Without equal access to the market and without state assistance in meeting the child-rearing obligations that fall disproportionately to women, liberal democracies require women to reconcile their economic dependency through bargains made with individual men.[1]

The second assessment focuses on women's equivocal status in the law. From the earliest days of the republic, legal liberalism, with its emphasis on the freedom of contract between equal individuals, has characterized the rights-based legal system that structured legal relationships among the elite. The legal position of many other groups—women (especially married women), slaves, servants, apprentices, the very poor, and the mentally deficient—was located in an older,

status-based system founded on hierarchical personal and social relationships.[2] After decades of struggle, the most notorious status-based category—slavery—was outlawed, and other status-based groups were brought into the rights-based arena of the law. Nonetheless, the freely contracting person at the root of the law continues to be a particular kind of person. We only have to imagine what labor law would be like if the universal worker were a pregnant woman to see that the unstated universal worker is really a man, who cannot become pregnant and who does not routinely have major responsibility for rearing children.[3] The supposedly universal person of liberal legal doctrine remains a white heterosexual able-bodied Christian man.[4]

The third assessment examines women's position in communal and civic life. One strand of liberal democratic philosophy promotes freedom from governmental interference. It is comparatively easy in the United States for like-minded people to form groups representing their views and hopes.[5] Women engage in a remarkable diversity of communal and civic activities that have greater or lesser democratic content depending on the purposes of the groups. For instance, women have established their own ethnic associations whose goals have been sociability and self-help but whose outlooks have often been exclusionary. Likewise, women have created diverse, inclusionary social movements that are schools for democratic practice and arenas of public discourse and problem solving.[6]

These routine analyses lack an important component, however. Although the system of government and the outward form of institutions have remained remarkably stable in the United States, the functioning of formal political institutions has changed measurably over the past 30 years. Similarly, the relations among formal institutions, communal participation, and civic activities have also changed. The meaning these changes have for women has received little attention.[7]

We suggest that the political milieu in which all women's political engagement has occurred has changed fundamentally since the onset of the contemporary women's movement in the 1960s. Traditional mass-based political institutions like parties and unions increasingly fail to provide an organizational home for the discussion of issues, the development of agendas, and the formulation of strategic alliances. Legislatures have become arenas for free-spending interest-group politics, especially at the national level. Paradoxically, the partisan character of the more neutral branches of government—the courts and the bureaucracy—has intensified. The political information available to the citizenry is dominated by 15-second sound bites on television news. All of these changes occurred during a significant movement to the right, meaning that the state became less receptive to feminist demands at the same time popular institutions were less able to affect the state.

This rightward movement is usually ascribed to the policies of Republican presidents Ronald Reagan (1980–88) and George Bush (1988–92). But cultural changes of the 1950s and 1960s, with their emphases on equal rights for people of color and women, and the economic uncertainties of the 1970s and 1980s, with their lack of good jobs for many workers, left many Americans with the sense of losing ground.[8] The election of Democratic President Bill Clinton in 1992 reflected the desire for a political life open to everyone and the frustration of politics dominated by elites of both parties.

The decline in the effectiveness of official political institutions has been accompanied by changes in communal and civic life. The general retreat from formal politics has extended to nonpartisan civic groups with political purposes, as declines in membership in groups like the League of Women Voters attests. Although participation in service and charity organizations has grown, these groups routinely define their missions as alternatives to politics. Advocacy is on the rise as well, often polarizing political discussions into struggles between good and evil. The number of community action groups is finally rebounding from a decline throughout the 1980s.[9]

Because of these changes women's political engagement needs to be understood not only in light of the traditional evaluations of liberal democracy but also as regards the current democratic crisis brought on by weakened political infrastructure. In the current context, women's organizing—especially feminist organizing—has many voices but few vehicles for translating demands into sustained action. The attenuation of processes that link people with their government has meant, paradoxically, that feminists have needed to give more of their attention to formal politics while sustaining autonomous activism.

In this chapter we examine three areas of vital concern to women's political engagement: democratic representation, abortion policy, and universal health insurance. These issues deal with the effects on women of failing political infrastructure. Democratic representation, with its emphasis on formal politics, examines the place of women in formal political institutions during this period of institutional change. Abortion policy illustrates the rise of interest group politics as well as the unspoken maleness of the supposedly universal person of the liberal polity. Universal health insurance exposes the difficulty of structural political change and the economic vulnerability of women and men of varying backgrounds.

POLITICAL STRUCTURES

In the United States the ideal of equal opportunity and social sameness confronts the reality of contentious social differences and inequalities. The country is a multiracial, multiethnic society with growing class divisions. The population of

249 million is 80 percent white, 12 percent Black, 3 percent Asian, 1 percent American Indian, and 4 percent "other" races. Hispanics, who may be of any race, form 9 percent of the total population.[10] Race and ethnicity are the more visible political cleavages, gender and class the less visible ones. Women experience their lives at the intersections of these political cleavages. Being poor or a woman of color multiplies a woman's political and economic marginality.

The constitution established a political system with significant separation of power among the branches of government and considerable dispersion of responsibility through a federal system. The United States has a two-party presidential system with a separately elected chief executive, the president, and a bicameral legislature, the Congress, whose members are elected from single-member districts. Since World War II it has been the exception rather than the rule for the same party to control both the Congress and the presidency. The Republicans, the party of the right, have controlled the presidency for 28 years between 1952 and 1992. The Democrats, the center or liberal party, controlled both houses of Congress for 32 years during the same period. The same party has controlled both branches of government only 14 of these years. There is no large-scale social democratic or other left party in the United States.

Power is further decentralized through a federal system of 50 states with substantial independent powers. Decentralization extends far beyond the states, however. There are about 83,000 subfederal jurisdictions—including 38,000 cities and towns, 3,100 counties, and 15,000 school districts—most of which have the power to tax, make policy, and spend.

Political organizations respond to and further shape the decentralized political system. In reality, there are 102 party structures in the United States: independent Democratic and Republican organizations in each state, as well as a national structure for each party. The party organizations are inherently weak and loosely linked, operate with enormous independence, and have experienced the same loss of public confidence as most other public institutions over the past two decades. The result is an electoral system based increasingly on candidates' personalities and less on party affiliation or loyalty.

The deterioration of the links between the governed and the government extends well beyond the shriveling of party capacities. Voting, party identification, feelings of political efficacy, and trust in public officials have all declined. In the 1968 presidential elections 61 percent of those of voting age cast a ballot. In 1988 the figure dropped to 50 percent, rebounding to 55 percent in 1992, but still registering the lowest voting rate of all industrialized democracies. From 1968 to 1988 identification with the Democratic Party declined from 46 to 36 percent, and nonpartisanship grew. Belief that government pays attention to "people like me" declined from 43 to 30 percent.[11] Positive feelings about members of Congress were found in 41 percent of the population in 1968 but 35 percent of the population in 1988.[12]

At the same time, the cost of running for office increased at more than twice the rate of inflation. The average campaign for the lower house of Congress, the House of Representatives, has risen more than 500 percent since the numbers were first collected in 1974. The average campaign for a House seat cost just under $270,000 in 1988. Of this, 80 percent is spent producing campaign advertisements and paying commercial television stations to run them. Senate (upper house) campaign costs have escalated even more rapidly, with average costs per candidate growing from $423,000 in 1974 to close to $3 million by 1988. Most of the money for campaigns comes from individual or group donations, and the percentage of funds coming from organized interests in the form of political action committees (PACs) has increased. By 1988 PACs were contributing in excess of $151 million to congressional candidates, and 210 of the 435 House winners acquired at least half of their campaign funds from PACs.[13] The consequence of this financing system is the perfectly legal dependency of candidates, especially incumbents, on organized special interests.

While citizen attachment and institutional responsiveness were declining in the realm of formal politics, grass-roots social action was also under attack. President Reagan, representing the mood in the country and in the Republican Party, initiated a policy of reduced social spending that was continued by President Bush. This policy not only undercut the economic security of millions of poor Americans, it also imperiled the organizations that represented their interests, many of which had come to depend in part on public funds to be able to undertake their missions.[14] In addition to a partisan opposition to social spending, the Reagan and Bush presidencies promoted many of the other economic policies associated with conservative parties: lower tax rates, especially for the rich, and deregulation of industries like banking and air transportation. With an eye toward their chances for reelection, Republicans (with the assistance of a good many Democrats) failed to implement the last tenet of laissez-faire economic policy: fiscal responsibility. The United States now has a $3.5 trillion national debt, which acts as a brake on future social spending, as indeed conservatives planned it would.[15]

In contrast, promotional interest groups have always been strong and have recently gained more power. For example, in 1988 there were 4,800 registered PACs donating money and influencing legislators, a number that has grown 860 percent since 1974.[16] In a political system with weak parties and strong interest groups, social movements feel pressure to develop organizations that take on interest group activities, there being few other effective ways to transmit preferences to public officials. This in turn creates structurally based tensions in social movements between those groups that are antistatist and those that use the dual strategy of state action and independent grass-roots organizing.

Although bureaucracies and the judiciary are indirect links between citizen preferences and public policy, they are traditionally quite important to shaping the content of public policy in the United States.[17] In these areas the Reagan administration also initiated an assault on governmental capacities that had significance for women. Believing correctly that the federal civil service was more committed to social programs than he himself was, Reagan dramatically reduced the federal work force in departments that administered health, social, economic, and consumer programs. Some agencies lost as much as 25 percent of their personnel.[18] A visible group of employees committed to improving women's status had developed in the middle ranks of the domestic policy departments in the 1970s, and the Reagan cutbacks significantly reduced their input into policy formation. At the state and local level, however, the higher ranks of the civil service remained more open to feminist policy making, especially in traditionally progressive states like New York, Minnesota, and California.

Half of the appointments to the federal bench—approximately 400 judgeships, including four seats on the Supreme Court—became vacant between 1980 and 1991. All federal judgeships carry lifetime tenure, and Presidents Reagan and Bush used their appointment powers to pack the trial and appellate courts with judges favoring judicial orthodoxy, a practice that will keep the courts tilted toward conservative views on women well into the next century. The Democrats also want congruence with party policies in their judicial appointments, but they have been less insistent about single-issue litmus tests.

WOMEN'S MOVEMENTS

Feminist and antifeminist activism in the United States is shaped by the nature of the liberal state and the color and class divisions of society. During the past three decades thousands of formal and informal women's groups have emerged in response to the needs and interests of women of different beliefs, races, ethnic heritages, sexual identities, classes, religions, and regions. Women, and sometimes men, move in and out of these organizations, often taking their social movement experiences and skills into other arenas in their lives. Feminist and antifeminist activities in the 1990s are as likely to occur in conventional organizations, like churches or even the army, as they are in autonomous social movement groups.[19]

The contemporary feminist movement that began in the mid-1960s was rooted in the civil rights movement and the New Left.[20] In this period the feminist movement was composed of three somewhat separate efforts: mostly white radical feminists; mostly white reformist feminists; and feminists engaged in antiracist struggles, most of whom were women of color. Radical feminists bequeathed to feminist organizing a tradition of consciousness-raising. In their political activism they concentrated on developing woman-centered, locally rooted politics. Radical women started most of the free-standing rape crisis and domestic violence centers in the United States, though many now receive government funds. Reformist women started organizations like the National Organization for Women (NOW, founded in 1966) and the Women's Equity Action League (founded in 1968), groups that tried to influence public policy and provide forums where women could develop a consciousness about their places in society. Reformist feminists brought new perspectives to established women's organizations, like the League of Women Voters. In the 1970s and early 1980s reformist feminists engineered the monumental but unsuccessful effort to pass the Equal Rights Amendment to the federal constitution.[21]

One of the differences between radical and reformist feminists was in their approach to policy change. In general, radical feminists were distrustful of government action in liberal patriarchal political systems. Reformist feminists were more willing to work within the existing system for political change that would help women and perhaps change the contours, if not the basic structure, of U.S. politics.[22]

The writings and practice of some white feminists articulated a universalistic view of women's interests that masked the privileges of white middle-class experience. This feminist universalism had elements of thoughtlessness and racism, but universalism was also a prominent characteristic of most of the social movements of this era. New and old left movements, Black national-

ism, and feminism all drew sustenance from theories of social change that emphasized one master oppression—class, race, or sex—and imagined a transformational period that would profoundly reconfigure society.

Women of color began the effort to articulate a more socially encompassing and complex picture of women's places in society. Black women became active in contemporary women's issues at the same time as white women, but their experiences were often different, and the documentation of their efforts appeared later. Black women were frequently active in such antiracist social movements as the civil rights movement, the welfare rights movement, and the Black nationalist movement. In some of these movements, especially in Black nationalist organizations, women's demands were viewed as secondary to racial struggles. Experience within these movements led African American women to a critique of the hierarchical approach to oppressions.[23] In the late 1960s and 1970s, independent women's organizing increased among Black, Hispanic, Asian, and American Indian women.

Among women of color, two types of groups developed. The first type was made up of informal groups who wanted a safe social space to explore how gender and color intersected. The Bay City Cannery Workers Committee, which eventually became a labor organization for Mexican American women cannery employees, began this way, with friends and coworkers socializing at breaks and lunchtime.[24] The second type comprised groups that focused more immediately on solving public problems and used more coalitional strategies. The National Black Women's Political Leadership Caucus (founded in 1971) and the Organization of Pan Asian American Women (founded in 1976) are examples of this type of group.

Feminist thought and practice of the 1990s is increasingly multicultural, seeing gender-based inequities as inextricably linked to racial, ethnic, and class divisions. This approach recognizes that women simultaneously share the similarities and experience the differences of a socially grounded womanhood. This recognition—honed in conflict and coalition and embraced in friendship, anger, and hope—has made feminist movements important arenas for antiracist, multicultural activism.[25]

Feminist theorizing and activities focus on respect for differences, recognition of similarities, and the necessity of alliances to solve social problems. Nora Hall, a Black feminist and journalist, describes the practice of multicultural feminism when she connects the independent work of a group she founded, Leadership for Black Women, and its coalitional efforts with other groups: "The leader as mediator, negotiator and visionary [is] a role often modeled by African-American women. Since we have been among the initiators of these styles, it seems appropriate for African-American women to further develop them through alliance work and programs that challenge us to merge and stretch our ideas into new forms that will assist us and the rest of humanity. African-American women, interested in building strong alliances, must commit to a process of candid dialogue."[26]

Similarly, Caryn McTighe Musil, a white feminist and the former executive director of the National Women's Studies Association, describes U.S. feminism in the 1990s in this way: "The challenge of the nineties is to hold on simultaneously to these two contradictory truths: as women, we are the same and we are different. The bridges, power, alliances, and social change possible will be determined by how well we define ourselves through a matrix that encompasses our gendered particularities while not losing sight of our unity."[27]

The interest in diversity by feminists has little appeal to the white women of the New Right, a loose coalition of social conservatives who support Victorian moral values and laissez-faire conservatives who oppose communism abroad and big government at home. Using public forums opened by the feminist movement, socially conservative white women attack feminism as antithetical to their fundamental beliefs. Antifeminist organizing began in the early 1970s in response to the proposed Equal Rights Amendment and the Supreme Court decision that made abortion legal. For white social conservatives, feminism is a self-centered attack on traditional patterns of mothering, a denial of the value of homemaking, an encouragement of government neutrality on issues like abortion and gay and lesbian rights, and an unwelcome supporter of extending governmental authority into realms where the church and family should predominate.[28] Little is known about right-wing women of color, who are not prominent in national right-wing women's groups. The vast majority of Christian African Americans (about 80 percent) belong to the seven denominations of the historical Black church, which, though theologically conservative, are not fundamentalist in their teachings.[29]

The Eagle Forum, an anticommunist and conservative women's organization founded in 1975, and the National Right to Life Committee, an anti-abortion group founded in 1973, are two of the major women's organizations of the socially conservative right, though scores of informal groups have sprung up around issues like the ERA and abortion.[30] Beyond obvious differences in ideology, the principal distinction between nationally based, socially conservative women's groups and nationally based feminist organizations is that right-wing groups are often tied to the larger, wealthy, male-controlled political organizations of the New Right. Socially conservative women have access to the finances of these larger organizations, permitting the larger organizations to draw on right-wing women's groups in political mobilizations.[31] Most feminist organizations—the exceptions being the few within labor unions—are independent and do not have access to the same level of resources.

Social conservatives have not undertaken a widespread grass-roots effort to think about their racial ideologies and practices. Within conservative social activism there is a current of racist expression that has not received much attention. For example, in a 1982 speech at a family conference, Ronald Godwin, vice-president of the fundamentalist religious group Moral Majority (renamed the Liberty Federation in 1986), warned the audience not to accept arguments for family diversity, invoking images of the "uncivilized dark savage" that resonate on racist themes in U.S. political life. "You'll hear many, many feminists and anti-family spokesmen today talking about history. . . . They'll tell you that down on the Fiji Islands, somewhere down on an island of Uwunga-Bunga, there's a tribe of people who have never practiced family life as we know it. But they also have bones in their noses and file their front teeth. . . . [The feminists and anti-family spokesmen will] try to build a historical case for the proposition that the traditional family never was traditional and never really was a dominant force in all civilized societies."[32] Socially conservative women are not the source of these ideas, but neither have they critiqued them.

Laissez-faire conservative women, who are much less visible than social conservatives, are not necessarily opposed to feminist demands for reproductive freedom, day care, or a non-discriminatory workplace. They prefer that government neither regulate nor finance such activities and that policy efforts begin at the state level rather than the national level. Their emphasis on individualism and achievement do not lead to an idealization of motherhood and homemaking. There are no large formal groups of laissez-faire women, and the number of laissez-faire and socially conservative women is unknown.[33]

The beliefs of most American women lie somewhere between the ideologies of feminists and antifeminists. Feminists are winning the struggle to shape public opinion, and the feminist movement—together with changes in the economy, employment, and birth control—has transformed women's expectations about how they will live and work. Between 1970 and 1985 *all* groups of women increased their support for efforts to strengthen women's status. For example, 60 percent of Black women and 37 percent of white women supported greater efforts to improve women's status in the United States in 1970. By 1985, 78 percent of Black women and 72 percent of white women favored more efforts to improve women's status. These changes suggest that, contrary to popular belief, African American women have always been strong supporters of improving women's position. Other

data show that resistance to feminism has been most evident among white working-class women.[34]

Changes in women's abstract views about their status do not tell the whole story, however. Men's support for the changes necessary to improve women's status barely increased at all. Between 1972 and 1982 the proportion of men strongly supporting equal roles for women and men improved only slightly—from 33 to 37 percent. By 1990 only 40 percent of men supported more equal sex roles.[35] Research on the division of household tasks shows that even though women do less housework now than a decade ago, they still do a great deal more than the men in their households. Interestingly, a major increase in household labor comes from children taking more responsibility for household maintenance.

DEMOCRATIC REPRESENTATION

As in most countries, American women are not particularly visible in formal politics, an unsurprising situation given the history of democratic institution building. The extension of formal democratic rights to increasing numbers of men during the seventeenth through nineteenth centuries, welcome though it was as a democratic advance, also strengthened the patriarchal character of formal politics through the exclusion of women from political citizenship. There were other notable exclusions from political citizenship at the founding of the republic. At best, American Indians were treated as foreign nationals and excluded from political life. African American slaves were not considered people, let alone citizens, and they had no political rights. After a civil war of unimaginable carnage, slavery was abolished in 1865. In 1870 male former slaves were enfranchised. But both before and after abolition most women were denied the full range of political and civil rights because the law, public philosophy, and social mores said women lacked the economic independence and innate capacity for independent political judgment. That reasoning failed to acknowledge that first white men's, and then all men's, political participation was not truly independent, based as it was on the unacknowledged domestic, reproductive, and social contributions of women. When women won national suffrage in 1920, the laws about electoral participation changed but not the public philosophy of men's superiority or the gender division of labor on which democratic institutions are based.

Because of this history and, until recently, the active opposition of political parties to women candidates, few women hold elected or appointed office or have careers in the high civil service. They are most visible in local and state offices. In 1990, 16 percent of mayors, 14 percent of other municipal officials, and 17 percent of state legislators were women. Only a tiny percentage of female officeholders were women of color. For example, Black women constituted fewer than 8 percent and Hispanics fewer than 1 percent of women state legislators.[36] In 1992 only 10 percent of the members of Congress were women (forty-seven representatives and six senators), only thirteen of whom were from racial or ethnic minorities.[37] The figures for the meritocratic branch of government were no better. In 1988 only 9 percent of the Senior Executive Service, the highest rank of the federal bureaucracy, were women.[38] A handful of women have been appointed to cabinet offices, but never as secretaries of defense, treasury, or state, where power is concentrated.

The percentage of women holding elected and appointed offices has grown slowly, with most of the growth occurring since the creation of the contemporary women's movement. But the pace of improvement is excruciatingly slow, punctuated by occasional bursts of dramatic improvement like the 1974 and 1992 congressional elections. If the percentage of women sitting in Congress continues to increase at its long-term rate, it will take another 300 years for Congress to be composed equally of women and men. The rise in the number of women holding office is due primarily to the climate of acceptance created by the feminist movement and the efforts of individual women candidates who struggle against the fraternalism and discrimination in political life.

The transformational potential of conventional politics, and thus the propriety of engaging in it as candidate or voter, was greatly debated by feminists in the early years of the contemporary women's movement. Feminists whose beliefs were rooted in radical or socialist thought often viewed elections as instruments of social control and co-optation by a state whose interests were antithetical to those of all oppressed people. In contrast, feminists whose beliefs were rooted in liberal thought viewed elections as a way for women to advance their interests. Increasingly, feminists see these approaches less oppositionally, espousing what in Europe and elsewhere has been called double militancy, a strategy of using state-directed as well as autonomous activities as the basis for individual and social change.

The increasing acceptance of women's participation in formal politics as a feminist goal has many sources. The most immediate was the rightward movement of politics during the Reagan and Bush presidencies, which heightened the practical necessity of working to retain the imperfect state supports for women that feminists had already won.[39] But the acceptance of formal politics as an important realm of feminist activism also grew out of the recognition of the complex experiences and meanings of formal democratic participation. Women candidates, officeholders, bureaucrats, and judges—even women voters—passionately described their struggles to participate in a politics where the unmentioned sex of leaders is always male and where the barriers to even routine political engagement are high.[40] Women's participation in politics repudiates the "natural" division between female reproductive efforts in the private sphere and male civic efforts in the public sphere. If women participate in politics, the public-private division is not natural in the sense of being inevitable, and the sphere of reproduction is not "pre-political," to use the phrase of philosopher Hannah Arendt.[41] The understanding and practice of both family and political life are thus transformed by women's political engagement.

Although there is increasing agreement on the importance of political participation, feminists continue to disagree on what women bring to formal democratic politics if they do participate. Are women more sympathetic to the poor? Are they more peace-loving and more concerned about the environment? Polls show these kinds of differences exist between women and men, differences that are popularly called the gender gap. The reasons for these differences are also the subject of fierce disagreement. Is it an essential female quality, like the capacity to bear life, that makes women empathetic? Or is their compassion primarily a result of analogizing from their social positions to the status of other people? Survey research on attitudes and policy preferences shows that feminist ideology, rather than female sex, distinguishes women and men in the electorate. In terms of ideology, feminist women are more egalitarian, more liberal, and less symbolically racist in their beliefs than are nonfeminist women and all men. In terms of policy, feminist women are less hawkish and more likely to support egalitarian policies for women and Blacks, guaranteed jobs, affirmative action, and aid to big cities than are nonfeminist women and all men.[42]

Because the views of women and feminists are closer to the positions held by Democrats, it would appear that Democrats would be greatly strengthened by the rise of feminism. The reality is more complex. Since the 1980s Democratic presidential candidates have needed to do especially well among women to win, but that support alone could not assure victory. For instance, in the three-way presidential race in 1992, Bill Clinton did better than George Bush and independent millionaire Ross Perot in winning the votes of women. Clinton won with 43 percent of the popular vote, but 46 percent of women compared with 41 percent of men voted for him.[43] This election, with its strong showing by an independent whose support came from election committees with no interest in forming a party, also demonstrates the primacy of candidate image in presidential elections.

Even a woman in the presidential race could not overcome this dynamic of presidential elections. When Geraldine Ferraro ran as the Democratic vice-presidential candidate with Walter Mondale in his 1984 bid for the presidency, such groups as the National Organization for Women thought that the Democrats could capitalize on the attachment of women and feminists to the party. But President Reagan, the enormously popular Republican incumbent, won with 59 percent of the popular vote. The majority of women voted for Reagan, though a lower proportion of women than men voted Republican. In other contests in the 1980s, however, the greater identification of women and feminists with the Democrats acted like a sea-anchor for the party in municipal and state elections. Without these voters, the Democrats would have lost more offices as the rightward tide of politics pulled voters away from their candidates.[44]

Until the 1990s parties had made only desultory efforts to recruit more women, and then often in districts that were considered unwinnable or safely liberal. In an era of disaffection from political institutions, parties recognize that the public sees women candidates as upright outsiders who will clean up government. Such expectations may limit women's effectiveness when they face the legislative norms of compromise and reciprocal support.

Women candidates routinely report that parties are less likely to give funds to female candidates.[45] Similarly, political action committees are less willing to give to female challengers than to male challengers. PACs support incumbents regardless of sex, however. Women also have fewer personal contacts with wealthy interests and less experience raising large amounts of money. Their ability to bypass unsupportive parties and go directly to the voters through television is limited by their inability to raise the large sums necessary to compete politically in the media age. If campaign financing laws were reformed to cap total spending and further limit PAC contributions, it would be much easier for women candidates of both parties to be elected.

In Congress and state legislatures women of both parties take more liberal stances than the men of their parties. Democratic and Republican women vote more frequently for social spending, equal rights, and government regulation than do their male counterparts. (In Congress, women of both parties lend less support to military spending than do men.) But even though women are more liberal within their parties, Democratic women are considerably more liberal than Republican women.[46]

ABORTION POLICY

The most volatile difference between men and women legislators is on the issue of abortion, which does not fit into the traditional partisan issue configuration in the United States. This configuration represents the economic and race politics of the Great Depression, patterns that only partially accommodate gender differences. Women legislators of both parties tend to support legal abortion more than the men of their parties, and Democratic women are the most active supporters. Catholic and fundamentalist Protestant legislators of both sexes and legislators who have many Catholics or fundamentalist Protestants in their districts give less support to abortion, however.

Members of Congress and their counterparts in state legislatures are under intense pressure over their votes on abortion legislation. The pressure comes mainly from a well-financed and well-organized set of conservative religious groups that want to limit or eliminate access to abortion. These groups have been successful in restricting abortion over the past several decades even though most Americans support abortion. The issue demonstrates how a disciplined minority can affect politics when parties do not effectively broker packages of issues and when small changes in voter preferences can alter the outcome of the elections in single-member districts. Paul Weyrich, director of the Committee for the Survival of a Free Congress, a right-wing interest group, summed up this approach to politics at a meeting of 50 leaders of anti-abortion groups in January 1980. "It doesn't matter what the majority of American people think on a poll. What matters is the perception members of Congress have about your issue and their future."[47]

Abortion has been legal nationwide since the *Roe v. Wade* Supreme Court decision in 1973. In that opinion the Court ruled that state laws restricting abortion to a limited number of circumstances or forbidding it altogether were unconstitutional.[48] In essence, the decision reasoned that abortion was covered by an implicit constitutional right to privacy until a fetus was viable under ordinary conditions outside the womb. The success of *Roe v. Wade* depended not only on legal precedents decriminalizing birth control, but also on the crucial support of Roman Catholic Supreme Court Justice William Brennan who, though personally opposed to abortion, felt that the Supreme Court should recognize that religious traditions differed in their views about when personhood begins. The decision occurred during a period when feminists were organized in support of abortion and anti-abortion forces had not yet coalesced.

Public opinion on abortion is divided among those who support it under a wide variety of circumstances, those who are willing to permit it in more restricted circumstances, and those who reject it in all or nearly all circumstances. A woman's reasons for having an abortion are important to public support of the choice. More than 80 percent of the population supports abortion if the woman's health is seriously endangered, the pregnancy was the result of rape, or if there is a strong chance of serious defect in the baby. Only 40 percent of the population supports abortion if the family cannot afford more children, the woman is not married and does not want to marry the man, or the woman is married and does not want any more children.[49]

Those who reject and support abortion, called prolife and prochoice activists, respectively, have fundamentally different views on women's relation to sexual activity, motherhood, and citizenship, and they argue from incompatible philosophical positions. Arguing from a deontological ethical stance—that is, from an unbending set of universal ethical standards—opponents of abortion assert that the embryo is a fully human person from the moment of conception and, therefore, that abortion is murder and not allowable.[50] Because the embryo is regarded as a fully human person, it has a moral standing equal to that of the woman who carries it, and the law and social action must recognize the equal standing of both people and the vulnerability of the less powerful person, the embryo.[51] In general, the fundamentalist Protestant denominations and the Catholic church hold this position, though individual congregants may differ from the position of their church.

The clarity and universal application of the prolife position make its message easy to convey politically. The prolife label encapsulates this moral certainty and represents the resistance of grass-roots prolife women to what they view as utilitarian notions of human relations. For many prolife activists, this moral certainty takes abortion out of the realm of practical politics, where compromise is permissible.

Those who are prochoice offer a more complicated and contingent view of the relationship between the embryo, and later the fetus, and the woman who carries it. Arguing from a teleological ethical position, that is, from an ethics based on ends or consequences, supporters of abortion assert that a pregnant woman should be allowed to weigh the circumstances leading to her pregnancy and the consequences that derive from it. Specifically, in the months before an embryo or a fetus is able to live outside the womb without extraordinary intervention, a woman should be able to end her pregnancy if it was the result of physical or social coercion, or if it will impair her physical or mental health, or if the woman cannot in her own judgment sufficiently care for the child because of serious personal, social, or financial problems.[52] In the main, Reformation-era Protestant denominations and the various branches of Judaism view abortion in this manner, though, again, individual congregants may differ.

In this view of abortion human personhood necessarily has both a biological and a social basis. Fully human life does not begin with conception. The embryo and fetus are interdependent with the woman who carries them, gradually attaining independent and equal moral status. Women supporting access to abortion feel that actions aimed at ending legal abortion force women to complete pregnancies regardless of the circumstances of their lives, treat women as the vessels for fetuses, and privilege one religious viewpoint over others.[53] This more complex view of abortion does not lend itself to easy political campaigns or slogans, however. The prochoice label, adopted to counteract the powerful prolife label, demonstrates the problem of conveying the ethical stance of supporters. The *choice* in prochoice resonates with other uses of *choice* in everyday life, suggesting that supporters of abortion take a consumerist approach to having children rather than disagree with their opponents about when human personhood begins.

Immediately after *Roe v. Wade*, opponents of abortion—first the National Conference of Catholic Bishops and later fundamentalist Protestant organizations like the Moral Majority—began working to limit the availability of abortion and to criminalize it through a Human Life Amendment to the federal constitution that would state that human life begins at conception. Millions of dollars have been channeled into anti-abortion efforts by the Catholic church, fundamentalist Protestant organizations, and concerned laity in both religious traditions. Both groups have extraordinarily well-developed media resources. The evangelical Christian Broadcast Network even has a communication satellite of its own.[54]

The anti-abortion lobby has effectively used contributions to candidates, television advertising campaigns, grass-roots mobilizations, and legislative initiatives in its efforts to reverse the *Roe* decision. As a result of targeted spending in the 1978 and 1980 elections, the anti-abortion lobby helped to defeat four prochoice Democratic senators.[55] While there have been fewer dramatic successes since that time, anti-abortion forces have made abortion an issue on which every elected official must have an opinion and a strategy. The major parties also have official positions on abortion: the Democrats support a woman's right to choose, and the Republicans are opposed to abortion. The extreme anti-abortion stance taken by religious fundamentalists at the Republican Party Convention in 1992 contributed to George Bush's defeat and damaged the party's ability to draw new members in its years out of power. Because of the absence of legislative party discipline in the United States, this damage affects the public's view of the Republican Party more than it limits individual Republican candidates who increasingly make independent judgments about abortion.

Through several pieces of legislation and Supreme Court decisions anti-abortion forces have chipped away at *Roe* by making abortion much more difficult to obtain for poor and young women. In 1980 the Supreme Court's *Harris v. McRae* decision eliminated public payments for abortion for poor women whose healthcare was governmentally financed, even though the government fully funded prenatal care for poor pregnant women who carried their pregnancies to term.[56] In 1989 *Webster v. Reproductive Health Services* allowed states to reduce the time period during pregnancy when abortion is legal and to limit further the use of public facilities and state (as opposed to federal) revenue sources in performing or financing abortions.[57] As a result of *Webster* supporters of abortion feared that the Supreme Court, which had been packed with justices opposing abortion during the Reagan administration, would eventually remove the constitutional zone of privacy protecting abortion, thus allowing each state to regulate it. Supporters redoubled their efforts, holding mass rallies and putting pressure on legislators to keep abortion legal and uniformly available.

In 1991 both abortion opponents and supporters were disappointed by the *Hodgson v. Minnesota* decision, which allowed states to require parental notice of a minor's plan to have an abortion if the state also provided a judicial override for minors who could not or did not want to involve their parents.[58] But supporters of abortion were stunned in 1991 when the *Rust v. Sullivan* decision upheld Department of Health and Human Services regulations—called the gag rule—that forbade personnel in clinics that received any public family planning funds to mention abortion or to make referrals to abortion services unless a pregnant woman faced a medical emergency that might require an abortion.[59] This ruling went so far as to prescribe what doctors and nurses could say if a pregnant woman asked about abortion in all other situations. The required response was, "The project does not consider abortion an appropriate method of family planning." Planned Parenthood announced that it would give up government funds before it would withhold full medical information from patients. Supporters of free speech were appalled that the government was, for the first time, forbidding recipients of government funds from expressing views different from those held by the government.[60]

In 1992 opponents and supporters of legal abortion waited for the Court's ruling in *Planned Parenthood v. Casey*, which many thought might reverse *Roe v. Wade*.[61] Although the Court continued to extend limits on abortion, it did not overturn *Roe*, nor did it permit a husband to veto the abortion of his wife. The conservative court uneasily found support for abortion in the penumbra of privacy.

The weight of the federal government shifted to the prochoice position when President Clinton took office in 1993. He lifted the gag rule. With the retirement of an anti-abortion Supreme Court justice, he appointed a prochoice person to the high court. He began the process of evaluating the safety of the abortion pill, RU 486, for sale in the United States.

Simultaneously, anti-abortion activists stepped up protests outside clinics, even circulating wanted-for-murder posters with the names and pictures of doctors who performed abortions. On March 10, 1993, an anti-abortion activist shot a doctor to death outside a Florida abortion clinic. Fundamentalist Protestant and Catholic groups responded differently to the shooting: "Many abortion opponents, whose movement had been built on appeals to morality, showed palpable anguish at an act of violence in the name of their cause. This anguish was less evident in the earliest reactions from [mostly fundamentalist Protestant] groups such as Operation Rescue,

Rescue America, and Missionaries to the Pre-born, which mixed pallid condemnations of the slaying with calls for cash contributions for the family of the accused killer. . . . By contrast, the U.S. Catholic Conference and some other abortion opponents reacted with rage and sorrow at an act that some say threatens to diminish their cause."[62]

The grounds of the abortion debate are likely to shift as the century closes. Historic animosities between fundamentalist Protestants and Catholics could well create stress in the prolife camp. Prochoice activists will increasingly challenge the claim by prolife adherents that theirs is the only valid religious interpretation of abortion. Supporters of legal abortion will frame abortion rights as an issue of religious liberty, as well as women's rights, with all the attendant problems that may cause.

The availability of RU 486 will also reshape the contest. Most abortions are performed in free-standing clinics, which are easy to picket. With the availability of an abortion pill, abortion decisions will be integrated more fully into the general heathcare of women, abortion activity will be profoundly decentralized, many abortions will occur even earlier in pregnancy, and costs will decline markedly. Each of these changes strengthens the opportunities for individual women and their doctors to make decisions about completing or terminating a pregnancy. Each poses interesting questions about the applicability of judicial limits to abortion promulgated when it was performed only as a surgical procedure.

The changes in abortion policy and practice will have less impact on the overall organization of prochoice and prolife activism. Prochoice activity in groups like the National Abortion Rights Action League and Planned Parenthood Federation of America is organized very differently from prolife efforts. Prochoice organizations, mostly feminist in character, have fewer resources, are more likely to be independent organizations, and are often strategically isolated from other progressive organizations.

The reason for this division of work within the feminist community is that single-focus, prochoice organizations relieve pressure from general-purpose feminist organizations like NOW (which also supports legal abortion). The general-purpose feminist organizations can then pursue a variety of issues without the constant attack of anti-abortion forces. For feminist organizations, and for most individual feminists, access to abortion is one component of full reproductive healthcare that would include sex education; safe contraception; prenatal care; maternal, infant, and child health services; and universally available health insurance. Together these services would acknowledge that the private sphere of family life is constructed by individual and public choices and that without this larger definition of reproductive healthcare women's reproductive activities are in constant tension with their economic and political activities.

UNIVERSAL HEALTH INSURANCE

The election of President Clinton was a watershed in health policy. By the late 1950s the United States was the only industrialized democracy without either universal health insurance or a national health service. In the 1970s and 1980s healthcare financing became a more serious and obvious problem. The juxtaposition of two facts—that the United States had the highest healthcare costs in the industrialized world (14 percent of GNP) and that almost 40 million people were without health insurance—revealed a healthcare sector in crisis.

Clinton campaigned on healthcare reform, promising healthcare cost containment and universally available health insurance. He appointed a large task force chaired by his wife, Hillary Rodham Clinton, a distinguished lawyer, to present a legislative plan to accomplish these goals. The shape the new healthcare policy will take is not known, but its existence is welcome to feminists. Few changes will improve the material conditions and the individual freedom of women more than universal health insurance.

The system that the task force wants to reform is imbued with the values of laissez-faire economics and political decentralization. The United States has a mixed public-private system for healthcare financing. Two-thirds of the population are in the private system: 57 percent of the population are covered by employer health plans, and 9 percent are covered by individually purchased insurance. Nineteen percent of the population are covered by the two big public programs: Medicare (13 percent), which provides health insurance for the disabled and for those over age 64 and is financed by payroll taxes on employers and employees, and Medicaid (6 percent), which provides payments to healthcare providers for about half of the poor under age 65 and is financed through the general revenue. Fifteen percent of the population are uninsured and likely to receive little or no medical care if sick or injured or to be wiped out financially if serious illness occurs.[63]

Women are more vulnerable than men in each sector of the healthcare financing system. The privately financed sector of healthcare was founded on a model of providing benefits to male workers and their dependents. Healthcare benefits are thus more available and more extensive in the heavily capitalized sectors of the economy that traditionally employ white men.[64] Many married women—both homemakers and those employed in service jobs providing limited or no health insurance—can lose access to health insurance through divorce or widowhood. This model undervalues unpaid care giving and builds into public policy the traditional assumptions about women's natural capacities, family obligations, and dependency on individual men.

Women predominate as the beneficiaries of the publicly financed portion of the healthcare system. Two-thirds of Medicaid recipients are women, mostly poor mothers who get Medicaid and small public welfare grants from Aid to Families with Dependent Children. In most instances, the jobs available to women who might leave AFDC do not carry health benefits, and women must choose between low-paying work without health insurance and low public assistance benefits with health insurance. Older women, who constitute almost 60 percent of the Medicare

rolls, face a different dilemma. Often poor, widowed, and without the pensions that men have, many women on Medicare have difficulty making the insurance copayments or buying the extra insurance that would cover them fully.

Even when obstetric and gynecological treatment are removed from the analysis women are more likely than men to report illness and use health services.[65] As Irene Trowell-Harris of the American Nurses' Association reports, it is not clear whether "these statistics reflect real differences in morbidity or some combination of gender-related differences in income and age structure, illness behavior, access to care, and response of the health system."[66] The consequences are clear, however. In the face of greater demand, lower access to healthcare and more uncertain financing make women's health more precarious in the United States. Women of color, who have a more tenuous place in the economy, are particularly vulnerable. For example, maternal mortality rates are four times higher for Black women and three times higher for Hispanic women than for white women.[67]

The opportunity to change healthcare financing and to extend coverage came about when the Democrats harnessed popular dissatisfaction with the existing system. During the Reagan and Bush presidencies, the problem was seen as affecting a Democratic rather than Republican constituency. Republican presidents elected in an era of small government, low taxes, and high debt had few incentives to spend money on working-class and poor people, not their constituency in any event. But Democrats understood that the problem was also the increasing inability of many middle-class people to obtain and maintain health insurance through their employers. They saw universal access to health insurance as a way to woo middle-class voters to their party and to build the cross-class and cross-color coalitions that had been difficult for the party to maintain. Their efforts did not depend solely on the 1992 presidential elections. Democrats in a number of states had also developed state plans for greater access to health insurance.

Popular interest in healthcare financing reform

did not translate into popular participation. Healthcare politics are rarely amenable to popular control. The iron triangle of Congress, the regulatory bureaucracies, and the big providers and insurers shapes policy making on this issue. Thus the dimunition of popular control of political institutions has not been as noticeable in healthcare financing as in other areas.

The Clinton task force did not change this approach. For the first ten weeks of its existence, the identities of the task force's members—who came from every part of the healthcare financing and delivery system—were kept secret. The nationwide hearings held by Hillary Rodham Clinton were input, not participation. The objective of this closed system was to bring all the players to the table to devise a plan and then to offer the complete plan to the public for comment and political debate. The administration argued that a more open process would have let special health interests pick apart the plan during its preliminary stages.

Prior to the Clinton administration, there had been several unsuccessful efforts to develop a form of universal health insurance. None managed to bring together a winning coalition, and the effects of these proposals on women of different social positions were rarely considered. In the 1930s, when Democratic President Franklin D. Roosevelt initiated the national legislation that became the foundation of the modern social contract in the United States, national health insurance was not included, in large measure because the American Medical Association, the professional association of physicians, opposed any government interference in healthcare. Rather, the Great Depression saw the initiation of group-based "nonprofit" insurance plans. Hospitals and doctors, whose revenues had fallen drastically, reluctantly supported these plans. After World War II labor unions withheld their support for national health insurance initiatives in an effort to make union-provided health plans a tool for organizing and rewarding workers.[68]

Each of these efforts compounded the structural bias toward a male model of paid employment as the basis for benefits. By the 1960s most people employed in the primary economy had health insurance paid for wholly or in part by their employers, so families with at least one securely employed member were no longer deeply concerned about the availability of health insurance. Moreover, private health insurers came to have a vested interest in providing insurance through employment, which gave them a generally healthy population to cover. Veterans always had a special class of publicly provided health services available to them and thus were out of the coalition as well. (The small percentage of female veterans were excluded from most benefits until well into the 1970s.) The objections of veterans' groups to universal health insurance voiced in the language of anticommunism and fear of socialized medicine were anomalous at best, because veterans were the greatest beneficiaries of publicly funded healthcare until the enactment of the Medicaid and Medicare programs in 1965. Medicare lessened the pressure from the elderly for universal health insurance, and Medicaid provided a minimum level of service for half of the very poor, with the other half so politically marginalized that they were unable to mobilize. Medicaid also reaffirmed the male work–female dependency approach to healthcare payments by making the health care needs of poor, publicly dependent women visible and by sexualizing the public perception of their motherhood.

In the early 1970s a variety of plans for universal health insurance designed to rationalize this system were proposed by people and groups as different as Republican President Richard Nixon, Democratic Sen. Edward Kennedy, the American Medical Association, and representatives of the hospital and insurance industries. Women's voices and a multicultural gender analysis were only a small part of these policy efforts, even though the women's health movement was in its heyday, with an estimated 1,200 groups across the nation.[69] These groups dealt by and large with improving the treatment of women patients, supporting local clinics for women, criticizing sexist medical textbooks, and lobbying for better working conditions for women in the healthcare sector. The problems addressed by these groups had an immediacy and urgency that motivated direct action. In the early 1970s, for example, the Women's Community Health Center in Cambridge, Massachusetts, initiated what became a national movement to educate women about their own bodies by teaching them to do pelvic self-examinations. The center also worked to end the use of prostitutes as the women on whom medical students were taught to do gynecological examinations.[70] In 1971, Estelle Ramey, a physician, instigated a successful campaign to halt the printing of a general medical textbook that had illustrations of "provocative showgirl-type models and did not show anatomy properly [and had a text that] contained many small and large errors and many jocose references to sexually attractive patients."[71]

A small number of groups undertook direct lobbying on health insurance and on legislation giving patients more rights in the medical process, activities that were themselves controversial in a feminist movement divided over whether to participate in conventional politics. For instance, in 1974 Carol Burris, president of the now-defunct Women's Lobby, testified before Congress on how the various bills proposing national health insurance affected women. Burris expressed concern with bills that relied on full-time work as the basis of access to health insurance because they left many women uncovered or dependent on the employment of the men in their families. She also spoke in favor of greater direct federal government provision of health services.[72] Women's lobbying may have educated some members of Congress, but it was sporadic and uncoordinated and did not create interest in the problem among ordinary grass-roots feminists.

Nothing came of these initiatives for universal health insurance in the 1970s, in part because no plan commanded majority support, and interest groups on all sides were reluctant to compromise. The efforts also foundered because of rapidly rising costs in the existing publicly funded health programs; the poor economy; the scandal swirling around President Nixon, who ultimately left office for sanctioning the burglary of the campaign office of his opponent in the presiden-

tial election; and a growing belief among political analysts that competition would reduce healthcare costs and increase services.[73]

The movement to the right in the 1980s kept national health insurance off the public agenda for a decade. But increasing healthcare costs for middle-class voters and the obvious decline of medical services for the working poor, as well as publicly dependent poor, created a shift in public opinion. National surveys undertaken in 1990 revealed that 55 percent of the population were very satisfied with their own and their families' healthcare, but only 10 percent were satisfied with the current healthcare system. Support for universal health insurance coverage, even if it meant increased taxes, was found in 72 percent of the public, 67 percent of corporate executives, and 92 percent of labor union leaders.[74] In May 1991, the *Journal of the American Medical Association* devoted an entire issue to the question of universal health insurance, announcing in its editorial that "there are signs of a broad consensus that some type of major reform is now required."[75] The interest of physicians in universal health insurance was a significant step toward building a coalition that could pass legislation. Insurance companies were much more reluctant to join the call for significant reform, knowing that their practice of excluding from coverage individuals with medical problems would come under attack.

The insurance companies will nonetheless be powerful players in the Clinton reforms. It is unlikely that any administration in the United States could easily go to a primarily publicly funded healthcare system. Private health insurance is an enormous industry. In 1988 healthcare expenditures financed by private insurers totaled almost $315 billion.[76] Work-based coverage will remain at the center of the reform. Mostly likely the new policy will mandate a basic set of benefits in all health insurance policies, extend employment-based coverage to workers in small businesses, and guarantee coverage of dependents in employment-based programs. The insurance needs of those not in the work force pose different kinds of challenges. Perhaps an enlarged and less stigmatizing public system for the non-elderly poor will be developed. Or perhaps healthcare premiums for the nonelderly poor will be paid fully or partially by the government to private health insurance companies. The Medicare program might be retained for the elderly and disabled or it might also be disbanded in favor of the government paying all or part of the premiums for beneficiaries.

Just as there may be many points of access into the health insurance systems, there will be many sources of financing. Employer-based coverage will continue to be financed by employer and employee contributions. For the first time, workers may have to pay income taxes on the value of their employer's contributions to their health insurance. Partial public financing or tax credits may be needed to assist small employers provide health insurance. The funds for the complete set of reforms may come from some combination of higher payroll taxes, more contributions from the general revenue and thus higher income taxes, and increased taxes on cigarettes and alcohol. Rationing of specific health services and managed competition among providers have been discussed as methods to check rising costs.

Feminists face the same difficulties in contributing to the healthcare financing debate as they do in contributing to many other policy problems. The issues are complex, and the specifics are not well known in the general population, including in the feminist community. Feminist policy expertise is not strong in this area, and the few groups active in the field differ in the extent to which they are willing to compromise. Feminists will confront imperfect policy choices. The new system will provide health insurance with basic benefits for everyone, but the well-to-do will most likely have much better options. Employment-based health insurance will keep many of the characteristics of the male worker model on which these benefits have always been based. And women, by virtue of their place in the economy, will most likely predominate in the basic benefits or publicly financed sectors of the new system. Similarly, the place of abortion in the new system is uncertain. Early comment from the Catholic church expresses support for healthcare financing reform but strong objections to the inclusion of abortion services.

Notwithstanding these considerations, universal health insurance is a good issue around which to raise feminist voices—one that brings women together to work for improvements in their place in society while improving society as a whole. The vehicles for action are the same as for many issues: grass-roots education and mobilization, strategic alliances, thoughtful use of the mass media, and a seat at the bargaining table. There are many challenges, but feminists and their movements are more experienced and more skilled than ever before.[77]

NOTES

1. See, e.g., Helga Hernes, "The Welfare State Citizenship of Scandinavian Women," in Helga Hernes, ed., *Welfare State and Power: Essays in State Feminism* (Oslo: Norwegian University Press, 1987), 133–63.

2. Martha Minow, *Making All the Difference: Inclusion, Exclusion, and American Law* (Ithaca, N.Y.: Cornell University Press, 1990), 124, 148–52.

3. This example derives from Zillah R. Eisenstein, *The Female Body and the Law* (Berkeley: University of California Press, 1988), 1–5.

4. Iris Young, *Justice and the Politics of Difference* (Princeton, N.J.: Princeton University Press, 1990), 96–121; and Minow, *Making All the Difference,* 148–52.

5. We do not mean to suggest that the U.S. government never interferes with the formation of groups. Government surveillance of the civil rights movement and to a lesser extent of the women's movement is well known. See "As the FBI Saw It . . . " in Suzanne Levine and Harriet Lyons, eds., *The Decade of Women: A Ms. History of the Seventies in Words and Pictures* (New York: Paragon, 1980), 29; and *Hearings Before the Select Committee to Study Governmental Operations with Respect to Intelligence Activities* (Washington, D.C.: Government Printing Office, 1976), 6: November–December 1975, 98–103, 360–66, 540–85.

6. Sara M. Evans and Harry C. Boyte, *Free Spaces: The Sources of Democratic Change in America,* 2nd ed. (Chicago: University of Chicago Press, 1992), vii–xxiii; and Jane J. Mansbridge, *Beyond Adversary Democracy,* 2nd ed. (Chicago: University of Chicago Press, 1983).

7. For an initial analysis of this problem see Barbara J. Nelson and Nancy J. Johnson, "Political Structures and Social Movement Tactics: Feminist Policy Agendas in the

United States in the 1990s," *National Women's Studies Association Journal* 3, no. 2 (Spring 1991): 199–213.

8. Katherine S. Newman, *Falling from Grace: The Downward Mobility of the American Middle Class* (New York: Free Press, 1988).

9. Harry C. Boyte, "Civic and Community Participation," in Charles F. Bahmueller, ed., *Civitas: A Framework for Civic Education* (Calabasas, Calif.: Center for Civic Education, 1991), 73–83.

10. Racial and ethnic figures are from U.S. Census, table 2, "Sex, Race, and Hispanic Origin: 1990," in *1990 Census of Population and Housing: Summary Population and Housing Characteristics, United States* (Washington, D.C.: Government Printing Office), 1. We refer to the indigenous people of North America as Indian rather than Native American because we believe that name most accurately reflects the wide practice of indigenous people in collectively naming themselves beyond their self-designated tribal and band names. For an elaboration see Kathryn A. Carver, "The 1985 Minnesota Indian Family Preservation Act: Claiming a Cultural Identity," *Law and Inequality: A Journal of Theory and Practice* 4 (July 1986): 327–54. We refer to Americans of African descent as Black or African American, both terms that are used for self-identification. See Lisa Albrecht and Rose M. Brewer, eds., *Bridges of Power: Women's Multicultural Alliances* (Philadelphia: New Society Publishers, 1990). "Hispanic" is a term used by the government and often by individuals to describe people who identify themselves as being of Spanish origin or descent, or from Spanish-speaking Central or South American countries. Members of these groups also describe themselves as Latinos or Latinas or by the Spanish terms for their country of origin or the name of their people. For an explanation of the definition used in the Census see U.S. Department of Commerce, Bureau of the Census, *1980 Census of Population and Housing: User's Guide,* part B, glossary (Washington, D.C.: Government Printing Office, November 1982).

11. The figures on voter turnout, partisan identification, and external political efficacy come from M. Margaret Conway, *Political Participation in the United States,* 2nd ed. (Washington, D.C.: Congressional Quarterly Press, 1991), 7, 48, and 46, respectively.

12. The questions in this comparison are not fully comparable. In a 1968 Harris poll, 41 percent of those polled gave Congress a positive rating and 59 percent gave it a negative rating. A 1988 Gallup poll contained the question: "Please tell me how much confidence you yourself have in Congress." Of those polled, 35 percent answered "great" or "quite a lot."

13. Larry Makinson, *The Price of Admission: An Illustrated Atlas of Campaign Spending in the 1988 Congressional Elections* (Washington, D.C.: Center for Responsive Politics, 1989), 9–10. See also Frank J. Souraf, *Inside*

Campaign Finance: Myths and Realities (New Haven: Yale University Press, 1992).

14. Frances Fox Piven and Richard A. Cloward, *The New Class War: Reagan's Attack on the Welfare State and Its Consequences* (New York: Pantheon, 1982), 1–39; and Mayer Zald, "The Trajectory of Social Movements in America," *Research in Social Movements, Conflict, and Change,* vol. 10 (Greenwich, Conn.: JAI Press, 1988), 19–41.

15. *Budget of the United States Government, Fiscal Year 1993* (Washington, D.C.: Government Printing Office, 1992), part 1-288; Kevin Phillips, *The Politics of Rich and Poor: Wealth and the American Electorate in the Reagan Aftermath* (New York: Random House, 1990), 130; and E. J. Dionne, Jr., "Reagan Debt Legacy," *New York Times,* 2 December 1988, p. A-11.

16. Larry Makinson, *Open Secrets: The Dollar Power of PACs in Congress* (Washington, D.C.: Congressional Quarterly, Inc., 1990), 16, 163–70.

17. Joyce Gelb, *Feminism and Politics: A Comparative Perspective* (Berkeley: University of California Press, 1989), 5–18.

18. On the policy outlook of federal bureaucrats see Joel D. Aberbach and Bert A. Rockman, "Clashing Belief Systems Within the Executive Branch: The Nixon Administrative Bureaucracy," *American Political Science Review* 70 (June 1976): 456–68. On the personnel cutbacks in federal domestic agencies see Edie Goldenberg, "The Permanent Government in an Era of Retrenchment and Redirection," in Lester M. Salamon and Michael S. Lund, eds., *The Reagan Presidency and the Governing of America* (Washington, D.C.: Urban Institute, 1984), 381–404. Increases in civilian personnel in the Department of Defense offset cuts in domestic agencies. As a result, the total number of federal employees increased during the Reagan administration.

19. Mary Fainsod Katzenstein, "Feminism Within American Institutions: Unobtrusive Mobilization in the 1980s," *Signs* 16, no. 1 (Autumn 1990): 27–54.

20. Sara M. Evans, *Personal Politics: The Roots of Women's Liberation in the Civil Rights Movement and the New Left* (New York: Knopf, 1979).

21. This was the second time an Equal Rights Amendment to the federal constitution had been proposed. The first version, proposed in 1923, split feminists, some of whom opposed it because it would revoke protective labor legislation. See Jane J. Mansbridge, *Why We Lost the ERA* (Chicago: University of Chicago Press, 1986), 8.

22. Nelson and Johnson, "Political Structures and Social Movement Tactics," 199–213. For a discussion of the differences between radical and reformist feminism see Judith Hole and Ellen Levine, *Rebirth of Feminism* (New York: Quadrangle, 1971); Jo Freeman, *The Politics of Women's Liberation* (New York: McKay, 1975); and Anne N. Costain, "Representing Women: The Transition from

Social Movement to Interest Group," in Ellen Boneparth, ed., *Women, Power and Policy* (New York: Pergamon, 1982), 19–37.

23. bell hooks, *Ain't I a Woman: Black Women and Feminism* (Boston: South End Press, 1981), 181–90; and Paula Giddings, *When and Where I Enter: The Impact of Black Women on Race and Sex in America* (New York: Morrow, 1984), 414–35.

24. Patricia Zavella, "The Politics of Race and Gender: Organizing Chicana Cannery Workers in Northern California," in Ann Bookman and Sandra Morgen, eds., *Women and the Politics of Empowerment* (Philadelphia: Temple University Press, 1988), 202–24. Chicanas are women of Mexican heritage who were born or reared in the United States.

25. The other arenas for antiracism work in the United States include progressive religious congregations, neighborhood activism, and university settings. Interestingly, conservatives have targeted universities in their attack against multiculturalism.

26. Nora Hall, "African-American Women Leaders and the Politics of Alliance Work," in Albrecht and Brewer, eds., *Bridges of Power*, 92.

27. Caryn McTighe Musil, Foreword, in Albrecht and Brewer, eds., *Bridges of Power*, vii.

28. Rebecca Klatch, *Women of the New Right* (Philadelphia: Temple University Press, 1987), 119–47.

29. Nancy T. Ammerman, "North American Protestant Fundamentalism," in Martin E. Marty and R. Scott Appleby, eds., *Fundamentalisms Observed* (Chicago: University of Chicago Press, 1991), 3; and C. Eric Lincoln and Lawrence H. Mamiya, *The Black Church in the African American Experience* (Durham, N.C.: Duke University Press, 1990), 1–19.

30. It is important not to confound anti-abortion supporters and social conservatives. They do not totally overlap. See Rosalind Pollack Petchesky, *Abortion and Women's Choice: The State, Sexuality, and Reproductive Freedom* (Boston: Northeastern University Press, 1984), 254ff.

31. Mansbridge, *Why We Lost the ERA*, 173–77.

32. Ronald Godwin, "The Family and the Law" (Speech presented at the Family Forum II conference, Washington, D.C., 27 July 1982), quoted in Klatch, *Women of the New Right*, 126. See also George Gilder, *Wealth and Poverty* (New York: Basic Books, 1981), 70.

33. Klatch, *Women of the New Right*, 147–53.

34. Ethel Klein, "The Diffusion of Consciousness in the United States and Western Europe," in Mary Fainsod Katzenstein and Carol McClurg Mueller, eds., *The Women's Movements of the United States and Western Europe* (Philadelphia: Temple University Press, 1987), 26–28.

35. Keith T. Poole and L. Harmon Zeigler, *Women, Public Opnion, and Politics* (New York: Longman, 1985),

184; and Susan Faludi, *Backlash: The Undeclared War on Women* (New York: Crown, 1991), 59.

36. Susan J. Carroll, "Women State Elected Officials: Problems, Strategies, and Impact" (Paper presented at the State of the States Symposium: Women, Black, and Hispanic State Elected Leaders, Charlottesville, Va., 6–7 December 1990), 26.

37. "Women Candidates and Winners in 1992" (New Brunswick, N.J.: Center for the American Woman and Politics, 11 November 1992).

38. U.S. Office of Personnel Management, *Annual Report on the Status of the Senior Executive Service, 1988* (Washington, D.C.: Government Printing Office, 1989).

39. For an elaboration of feminist interpretations of voting in the United States, see Mary Fainsod Katzenstein, "Feminism and the Meaning of the Vote," *Signs* 10 (Autumn 1984): 4–26. More recently, feminists have also viewed elections from a populist or mobilization perspective. In this view, the value of elections is in participating fully in them, thereby creating a richer civic life.

40. See, e.g., Geraldine A. Ferraro with Linda Bird Francke, *Ferraro, My Story* (New York: Bantam Books, 1985).

41. Hannah Arendt, *The Human Condition* (New York: Doubleday, 1959), 29.

42. Pamela Johnston Conover, "Feminists and the Gender Gap," *Journal of Politics* 50 (November 1988): 985–1010. The design of this survey did not permit men to be categorized as feminist or nonfeminist. Neither did the design distinguish between nonfeminist and antifeminist women.

43. Howard Fineman, "The Torch Passes," *Newsweek*, November–December 1992, special election edition, 6, 10.

44. Klein, "The Diffusion of Consciousness," 30.

45. Ann W. Richards, "Fund-Raising for Women Candidates: All the Equality You Can Afford," *Journal of State Government* 60 (1987): 216–18.

46. Poole and Zeigler, *Women, Public Opinion, and Politics*, 154–74.

47. Quoted in Joyce Gelb and Marian Lief Palley, *Women and Public Policies* (Princeton: Princeton University Press, 1982), 141.

48. *Roe v. Wade*, 410 U.S. 113 (1973). In 1972, the year before *Roe v. Wade* was decided (when legal abortion had been made more available in a number of states), about 590,000 legal abortions and an estimated 1 million illegal abortions were performed. In 1987 about 1.3 million legal abortions were performed, or 356 for every 1,000 live births. The typical woman who has an abortion is unmarried, white, Protestant, under 25 years of age, and has no other children. But this pattern, as always, masks important variations. African American women tend to have abortions after they have established a family of the size they want, and white women tend to have abortions

to delay their child-rearing years. Even though the Roman Catholic church strongly opposes abortion, 31 percent of women who have abortions are Catholics, roughly the same proportion as self-designated Catholics in the population. See "Abortion Surveillance: Preliminary Analysis—United States, 1986 and 1987," *Journal of the American Medical Association* 262 (20 October 1989): 2076; Deborah L. Rhode, *Justice and Gender: Sex Discrimination and the Law* (Cambridge, Mass.: Harvard University Press), 207; and "Facts in Brief: Abortion in the United States," Alan Guttmacher Institute, 1 June 1991.

49. "Abortion: Rights and Wrongs," *Public Opinion* (May–June 1989), 37.

50. Randall A. Lake, "The Metaethical Framework of Anti-Abortion Rhetoric," *Signs* 11 (Spring 1986): 488. See also Clifford Bajema, *Abortion and the Meaning of Personhood* (Grand Rapids, Mich.: Baker Book House, 1974). Some anti-abortion activists grant an exception to this logic in the case of rape, but the exception, while politically useful, fails their moral test.

51. Gary Leber, "We Must Rescue Them," *Hastings Center Report* (November–December 1989): 26–27.

52. Petchesky, *Abortion and Woman's Choice*, 326–63, and Kristin Luker, *Abortion and the Politics of Motherhood* (Berkeley: University of California Press, 1984), 192–215.

53. Katha Pollitt, "'Fetal Rights': A New Assault on Feminism," *Nation* 26 (March 1990): 409–18.

54. John B. Donovan, *Pat Robertson: The Authorized Biography* (New York: Macmillan, 1988), 120.

55. Gelb and Palley, *Women and Public Policies*, 138–39. The four senators who were targeted by anti-abortion forces were Democrats Dick Clark, Birch Bayh, George McGovern, and Frank Church.

56. *Harris v. McRae*, 448 U.S. 297 (1980).

57. *Webster v. Reproductive Health Services*, 492 U.S. 490 (1989).

58. *Hodgson v. Minnesota*, 119 S. Ct. 2926, 2928 (1990).

59. *Rust v. Sullivan*, 111 S.Ct. 1759 (1991).

60. Linda Greenhouse, "5 Justices Uphold U.S. Rule Curbing Abortion Advice," *New York Times*, 24 May 1991, pp. A1, A12.

61. 505 U.S., 120 L. Ed. 2nd 674, 112 S.Ct. (1992)

62. "Slaying Has Abortion Providers Up In Arms—Literally," *Star Tribune* (Minneapolis), 12 March 1993, p. 16A.

63. Karen Davis, "Expanding Medicare and Employer Plans to Achieve Universal Health Insurance," *Journal of the American Medical Association* 265 (15 May 1991): 2525.

64. U.S. Commission on Civil Rights, *Health Insurance Coverage and Employment Opportunities for Minorities and Women* (Washington, D.C.: Government Printing Office, 1982), 21, 40.

65. Lois M. Verbrugge, "Gender and Health: An Update on Hypotheses and Evidence," *Journal of Health and Social Behavior* 26 (September 1985): 156–82; and U.S. Department of Health and Human Services, *Women and National Health Insurance: Where Do We Go From Here?* (Washington, D.C.: Government Printing Office, 1980), 4.

66. Irene Trowell-Harris, "Assessing the Health Care Cap for Women and Minorities and their Families," in Women's Research and Education Institute of the Congressional Caucus for Women, *Who Cares? The Health Care Gap and How to Bridge It* (Proceedings of the 30 April 1986 Conference) (Washington, D.C.: Government Printing Office, 1987), 58.

67. Ibid., 57.

68. Marjorie Lightman, "The Past Still Haunts Us," in WREI, *Who Cares?* 41–45.

69. This number included multi-issue groups that had a health component. Helen I. Marieskind, *Women in the Health System: Patients, Providers, and Programs* (St. Louis: C. V. Mosby, 1980), 291.

70. Sheryl Burt Ruzek, *The Women's Health Movement: Feminist Alternatives to Medical Control* (New York: Praeger, 1978), 151.

71. Marieskind, *Women in the Health System*, 299.

72. Ruzek, *The Women's Health Movement*, 152–57.

73. Paul Starr, *The Social Transformation of American Medicine* (New York: Basic Books, 1982).

74. Robert J. Blendon and Jennifer N. Edwards, "Caring for the Uninsured: Choices for Reform," *Journal of the American Medical Association* 265 (15 May 1991): 2563–65.

75. Ibid., 2563.

76. "Profits Continue to Rise," *Industry Surveys: Insurance and Investment* (5 December 1991), p. I-33.

77. We would like to thank Sarita Ahuja, Gülhan Ovalioglu, Whitney Thompson, and Nancy Vivian for research assistance. Ragui Assaad, Carolyn Ban, Eli Bartra, Sylvia Bashevkin, Richard Bolan, Harry Boyte, John Brandl, Nora Hall, Nancy Johnson, Jane Mansbridge, and Paula O'Loughlin made helpful comments on earlier drafts. Earlier versions of this chapter were presented at the September 1990 American Political Science Association meetings, San Francisco, and in the Hubert H. Humphrey Institute's Dilemmas of Democracy Work Group.

▲ Uruguay

Type of Political System: democracy
  Sovereignty: republic
  Executive-Legislative System: presidential
Type of State: unitary
Type of Party System: multiparty
Major Political Parties

Partido Colorado (Colorado Party): Formed in 1836; follows a liberal-urban-modern direction. Has won almost all general elections in this century.

Partido Blanco o Nacional (White or National Party): Also formed in 1836; has a rural and more conservative profile. Has formed the central government only twice during this century.

Frente Amplio (Broad Front): Leftist coalition formed in 1971.

Year Women Granted Right to Vote: 1932
*Year Women Granted Right to Stand for
  Election:* 1932
Percentage of Women in the Legislature[a]
  Lower House: 6.1%
  Upper House: 0.0%
*Percentage of Electorate Voting for Highest
  Elected Office in Most Recent Election
  (1989):* 84.0%[b]

DEMOGRAPHICS
Population: 3,058,000
Percentage of Population in Urban Areas[c]
  Overall: 87.3%
  Female: not available
  Male: not available
Percentage of Population Below Age 15: 26.9%
Birthrate (per 1,000 population): 19
Maternal Mortality Rate (per 100,000 live
  births): 56
Infant Mortality Rate (per 1,000 live births):
  27
Mortality Rate of Children under Five (per
  1,000 live births): 31

Average Household Size: 2.9
Mean Age at First Marriage
  Female: 22.4
  Male: 25.4
Life Expectancy
  Female: 72.4
  Male: 65.6

EDUCATION
Ratio of Female to Male Enrollment
  First-Level Education: 95
  Second-Level Education (1980/1984):
  112
  Third-Level Education (1980/1984): 130
Literacy Rate[d]
  Female: 96.2%
  Male: 95.2%

ECONOMY
Gross National Product per Capita: U.S.
  $1,650
Percentage of Labor Force in Agriculture:
  15.9%[e]
Distribution of Agricultural Workers by Sex[f]
  Female: 9.2%
  Male: 90.8%
Economically Active Population by Sex[g]
  Female: 32.9%
  Male: 71.3%

a. Electoral Court Statistics, 1989.
b. Ibid.
c. Calculations made by Grupo estudios de la condición de la mujer en el Uruguay (GRECMU, or the Study Group on the Condition of Women in Uruguay) based on *Population Census, 1985* (Dirección General de Estadísticas y Censo).
d. Calculations made by GRECMU based on the University Census, 1988; and statistics of the Ministry of Culture and Education.
e. Calculations made by GRECMU based on the Population Census, 1985.
f. Ibid.
g. Ibid.

Uruguay: A Recent History of a Subject with a History of Its Own

GRACIELA SAPRIZA
TRANSLATED BY
INÉS TRABAL

Compared with its South American neighbors, the República Oriental del Uruguay is a small country of 68,536 square miles. Its population of about 3 million people, virtually all of whom are white and well educated (literacy is currently reported at above 95 percent), is largely urban, with more than half the population living in the capital city of Montevideo and only 18 percent located outside urban centers of 5,000 or more. Uruguay became a Spanish colony at the beginning of the seventeenth century and achieved its independence from Spain in 1817. In 1830, following a struggle against, and negotiation with, powerful Portuguese-Brazilian authorities, the country became an autonomous republic. The early years of independence were unstable owing to a weak state and continuous battles between opposing factions, which in 1836 were organized into two major political parties, the Partido Blanco o Nacional (White or National Party) and the Partido Colorado (Colorado Party).

Except for the period of rule by the National Party from 1959 to 1966 and the military rule of 1973 to 1984, the Colorado Party has dominated the executive and legislative branches of government throughout the twentieth century, with the National Party, perpetually in opposition, consistently receiving a minority portion of the vote for important offices. The survival of the two traditional political parties since independence is proof of their resourcefulness and enormous capacity to articulate an infinity of nuances and tendencies in response to changing political conditions. The Colorado Party presents a liberal-urban-modern profile, whereas the National Party has been built on rural and more conservative solidarity.

These differences are the outcome of history rather than of programmatic and electoral definitions. Sophisticated electoral legislation has permitted the survival of these two forces over the past decades in spite of opposing tendencies in the political system. Although Uruguay has experimented with a number of executive arrangements during its lengthy democratic history, the system of a president with a bicameral legislature has been the most common and was in effect under the constitution of 1966 until the military suspended it in 1973; it was reinstituted in 1985 following the return of civilian rule.

A SEARCH FOR PATTERNS

In this chapter, I focus on the recovery of women's historical memory—because women, and other groups excluded from the power system, are invisible to official history. The attempt to make women's protagonism and participation in the country's political life visible without artificial distinctions between what is public and what is private forms part of a process of recovery of our identity as historical subjects. Oral sources are among the richest methodological tools for reconstructing a polyphonic history inscribed in everyday life—where women have historically occupied a privileged position, unlike their position in the public sphere.

Examples of the political involvement of Uruguayan women during the twentieth century may appear disparate and intermittent. Yet several important events involving women in the public sphere reveal possible patterns in their political engagement. I consider how certain women in Uruguay managed to be politically active in spite of the repressive regime of Gabriel Terra (1933–37) and the later military dictatorship. I also look at how, during Uruguay's transition to democracy (1985–89), women led a movement for a referendum that would deny the military immunity for violations of human rights during the previous regime. These episodes demonstrate that in Uruguay, as elsewhere, resistance to state terrorism and the state's unjust use of authority in other forms constitutes a core of women's political engagement.

I contend that these episodes suggest three patterns of women's political activity. First, Uruguayan women's political engagement appears to have a characteristic feature: the women who are engaged in political action, as well as other individuals in major sectors of society (particularly the popular sectors), assume that women are capable of regenerating a political system or situation that is widely viewed as perverse. Second, women's activism has been in general perceived favorably not only because their projects have been proposed while the country has been in the process of being rebuilt but because their recommendations have been seen as appropriate for women. These recommendations appeared either as responses to ethical concerns or as manifestations of women's responsibility to create a society in which future generations could thrive. Finally, I suggest that women became activists not only out of concern for the needs of home and children but also in response to perceived obligations concerning the democratic norms attendant to their new status as citizens.

In searching for these patterns, I shall join other scholars who use the feminist slogan "Everything personal is political" as an analytical instrument for demonstrating how women's identity as politically active individuals is created.[1] This approach demonstrates the necessity of establishing links between culture (in the sense of a way of living) and a rather unorthodox concept of the political, grounded in the belief that "the arena of the political sphere cannot be determined in an abstract, generalized way, [because] it is related to the daily reality of the affected."[2] Rather than aim at depoliticization, this statement centers on "politicization of the private," recognizing that reproduction of the daily sphere forms part of political life and that everything that presents itself to us as private and personal is and has been the object of politics.[3]

To reconstruct women's political participation, one must consider the dimension of solidarity as well as of emotion and daily life, which are commonly excluded from political analysis because they are not defined as important events. Women have historically played the principal role in complex social relations, made decisions about whether to have children, and taken on responsibilities linked with the development and education of new generations and with all aspects of daily life. Together these factors constitute a central complex in which contradictions and possibilities of change are tied together and untied, where identities and persons are formed and reformed, and where old and new generations converge. Social transformations operate through this sieve by transmitting and changing customs, habits, and expressions of relations. The lives of particular women can serve as a point of departure for reflecting on what different types of resistance meant to them and for understanding how these acts gained political meaning in the broadest sense of the word. Although the commitment of these women was often incomplete and even contradictory, it undeniably led to political change.

During the first three decades of the twentieth century, Uruguay attempted to establish itself as a modern capitalist society. Although Uruguay had been a republic since 1830, the state did not consolidate its dominance until the early twentieth century, during which time the government enacted such a broad range of social reforms (including universal free education, affordable healthcare, and labor legislation) that the country was considered a model for other Latin American states and even labeled the first American welfare state.[4] The political atmosphere, grounded in a tradition of individual liberties and democratic institutions, allowed a variety of issues and reforms to be debated and addressed. Although the ethnic homogeneity of the society precluded concerns over racial differences common in many Latin American states, by the turn of the century the issues of women's subordination as a whole and the condition of working-class women in particular were central to the heated discussions of politicians, trade unionists, suffragists, and anarchist and socialist intellectuals. In 1932, through the struggles of working-class women and middle-class suffragists, women won the right to vote, even though the economic crisis of 1929 had changed the political climate in Uruguay by threatening prospects for stability based on its growing middle class.

During the economic depression that followed the 1929 downturn, many attractive features that had characterized Uruguay disappeared. Once renowned as a welfare state and a country that welcomed immigrants and gave refuge to exiles, Uruguay was transformed. In March 1933 the country experienced its first institutional breakdown as President Terra dissolved the Parliament and the National Council of Administration without the participation of the armed forces, receiving active support only from the fire brigade. In a gesture that became for many a symbol of the defense of democracy, Baltasar Brum, president of the Council of Government, surrounded himself with friends and sympathizers and publicly committed suicide to protest the "Fire Brigade Coup."

The years 1934 to 1936 were difficult for Terra's opposition. The regime tempered the original sin of the coup by quickly building political alliances and implementing economic policies that gave impetus to industrial development, even as its call for elections ensured that the party watchwords of the most conservative sectors would continue to be used. Although broad segments of public opinion were united in opposition to the March Regime, their heterogeneity made it difficult to identify common concerns that might serve as the foundation of a united front, much less evoke fractures in the regime's power. The Batllistas (a faction of the Colorado Party), the Independent Nationalists (a faction of the Nationalist Party), the Socialist Party, and the Communist Party all opposed the Terra regime. Internal rifts often made the opposition ineffectual, as when conflict within the graphic workers' union derailed preparation of a large demonstration by the opposition in 1934. In the pages of his weekly *Acción*, Carlos Quijano, a member of the Social Democrats (one of the groups attempting to set up a united oppositional front), analyzed the situation this way: "The dictatorship is the ultimate expression of the bourgeoisie at its most rancid and conservative defense against bankruptcy. The opposition also forms part of this bourgeoisie that fights for the recovery of lost positions. . . . It's not yet possible for all of us to march in the same line. . . . The meeting would have been a signal of opposition, but never of unity in protest. And the demonstration, though large in number, would have had little impact."[5]

Further obstacles prevented opposition unity, including 100-year-old partisan prejudices that cut across geographic, class, and occupational lines, separating the Uruguay populace into two major groups: the Colorados ("Reds," often called Batllistas after former party leader José Batlle y Ordóñez), who had held power since 1865, and the National Party ("Whites" or Blancos), the perpetual opposition party. The decentralized nature of the party system also meant that a number of long-standing intraparty divisions thwarted the prospects of forming a united opposition.

In spite of the lack of common identification, opponents of the regime did attempt some joint political strategies, including abstention by the various sectors from the 1933, 1934, and 1938 elections. Other, more radical actions (such as the multiparty revolution of 1935) did create links among factions of the opposition, but even such coalitions failed to affect the monopolization of power. The greatest obstacle to unity among the opposition, however, continued to be mutual distrust, not only between Colorados and Blancos but also among groups to the left, whose relations have been described as "everybody against everybody."

In 1936 events outside Uruguay significantly changed the organization of the opposition. The well-educated Uruguayan population had no doubt followed with interest the recent reforms that accompanied the end of dictatorship in Spain in 1931: the new constitution called for establishment of a workers' republic, separation of church and state, secularization of schools, and division of the large estates. When Francisco Franco led a revolt against the new government five years later and attempted to reestablish fascism and monarchy, Spain erupted in a civil war that lasted three years and cost nearly a million lives.

In Uruguay, the onset of the Spanish civil war created an environment in which greater political unity was finally possible. Newspapers recorded various perceptions of the Spanish Republic and the diverse expressions of Uruguayans' solidarity with the Spanish people. Front-page headlines, photographs from fronts of the civil war, and articles analyzing various positions and forces allow us to reexamine Uruguayans' interest in these events.

Several contemporary testimonies indicate that women may well have been the first to abandon the political prejudices that had immobilized so much of Uruguayan politics throughout Terra's rule. Newspaper reports prove that women from diverse social sectors—for example, middle-class educators and professionals, as well as working-class women from the capital and other important cities—were capable of overcoming their mutual distrust to work with other women with advanced ideas, whether Socialists, Communists, Colorados, or Blancos. By mobilizing in solidarity with republican Spain, these women gave new impetus to anti-Terra efforts. For, in defending the cause of the Spanish Republic, these activists were demanding the recovery of liberties lost not only in Europe but in Uruguay as well. Testimonies of those engaged in the pro-republican movement verify the significance they attached to their actions. As one activist later recalled, "We were opposing Terra through our activities for Spain."[6]

Frente Popular, a weekly publication, became the voice of the most pluralistic movement of the time, uniting representatives of the Colorado and National groups (and the factions within each) with Socialists, Communists, and the Democratic People's Group. Committees to support the Spanish people's struggle against war and fascism formed throughout the country. Women activists participated in this new pluralism, redefining political activity by acting outside conventional party boundaries and participating in groups that kept Terra's government under pressure. One of the supra-partisan groups formed during this period was the Women's Union Against War. Founded in 1936 as a pluralist association of 28 women's organizations and incorporating diverse cultural, social, and political orientations, the Women's Union Against War was directly connected to the Popular Front affiliated with the Communist Party. Given the diversity of political views among these women and the geographical remoteness of their cause, one wonders how they were able to unite.

One could say that Uruguayan women were caught in a contradictory situation. With their enfranchisement in 1932, they had come of age politically in the legal sense. Yet, because Terra's dictatorship followed almost immediately, they remained unable to exercise their rights in anything resembling a free election. The plight of the Spanish Republic not only gave many of these women a flag behind which to rally, it also allowed them to participate on equal terms with men. As advocates for the republic or true revolutionaries, they could no longer be accused of making claims specific to women or be made to feel embarrassed by being identified as feminists. Paulina Luisi, perhaps the most representative feminist of the period, repeatedly described being made to feel the fool when she introduced herself as a feminist.[7] For some women, the Spanish civil war may have served as a projection of their ideologies because anarchists, communists, and socialists were all part of the struggle for control of Spain. For Uruguayan women identifying with these ideologies, Spain must have seemed a laboratory in which revolutionary experiences were developed and tested.

For many women the struggle against war and fascism also had a deeper, more intrinsic meaning that addressed questions about life itself and the survival of human values. Because such questions are personal (and therefore outside the realm of public politics), they posed a particular challenge to women, both as keepers of the private realm and as new citizens. In fact, one might speculate that a number of women translated the abstract political discourse of the time in such a way as to incorporate emotion and bring new meaning to their own everyday experiences under Uruguay's fascist regime, thereby highlighting the need for participation and the importance of achieving solidarity against the regime on their home front.

Would the practice of women voting, the historical landmark implemented in 1938, following the ouster of Terra, put an end to the debate on women's equality? We could ask whether women, by virtue of this first electoral experience, were able to perceive the contradictions and frustrations they would endure when faced with the rigidity of a political system planned and established on male terms.

In answer to this, let us refer to the philosophical matrices that underlie Western political ideas. As is clear, our political and philosophical tradition has been based on the "writings of men, written by men, and on the subject of men."[8] One might therefore ask if it is possible to support equality between the sexes with the arguments offered by philosophers concerning the true nature of woman. As the bases of their political theories, the great philosophers—Plato, Aristotle, Rousseau, Mill—posed the questions "What is man? What is he capable of?" When thinking of women, however, they shifted their view and asked, "What is woman for?" and defined her according to her functions—sexual, reproductive, and educational—within the family. According to these traditional Western philosophical views, female nature was determined by her specific functions within society, and biological inequality was assumed as a condition necessary for the functioning of society as a whole.

Uruguayan women's political activity challenged those ideas. Using the phrase "the personal is political" as a point of departure, analysis of women's testimonies and documents unearths evidence of women's presence in political life during the selection of a government to replace the Terra regime. For activists of the time, a formal election was not the only means of intervening in the decision-making process. Yet women's formal entrance into political life was significant. This single event, which enabled women either to vote (thereby supporting continuation of the existing political system) or to abstain from voting, reveals some of the complexity of the subject.

Although women had been enfranchised six years earlier, they voted for the first time in 1938. Fundamentally conservative political leaders tried to capture the female vote, resting their hopes on assumed female conservatism. These leaders probably believed that the "natural" roles of women in preserving and conserving life would be transferred to their political options.

This prejudice regarding female voters also prevailed among progressive politicians, who feared that the female vote might cause a political regression. Results of the 1938 and 1942 elections clarify the question of the electoral behavior of Uruguayan women (though electoral records do not report votes according to sex).

Although women's initial experience with voting was full of contradictions (in that the elections were not truly democratic), one can nonetheless assess the choices some women made and the strategies employed by the male-led parties in addressing this novelty. The attitude of women toward voting in these circumstances appears to be characterized by a sense of civic responsibility or by a desire to inject a renewed spirit into politics to correct its vices. These considerations characterize women more so than the question of conservative or progressive tendencies. For example, Sara Rey Alvarez of the Independent Democratic Feminist Party (the only party with exclusively women candidates), described the proposed contribution of a woman candidate and the principles the party would adopt: "It is necessary for women to enter parliament so their voices will be heard in defense of women's and children's rights and of economic equality. Still . . . to achieve this it is indispensable that those women who wish to enter parliament shouldn't be representatives of any particular party, through which men may impose certain rules of conduct on them. Instead, they should be women who know how to defend their rights, who are representatives of the women and spokeswomen of their economic and social needs and thus open the way toward a broad movement of women's solidarity, the result of which should be the parliamentary representations of their sex."[9]

In contrast, the conservatives' expectations of capturing the majority of female votes and thereby securing the status quo also became more apparent. One enlightened woman, expressing her frustration with this possibility as she faced the 1938 elections, commented that "in the present political situation it would be better for women not to vote," because women's votes would merely support male-dominated parties that demanded unquestioning obedience. Thus "women who follow these men won't be anything else than sheep of the same breed."[10]

Coverage of the 1938 election in *Mundo uruguayo* included interviews with women whose impressions of the voting experience diverged widely because of their varied backgrounds yet still reflected the themes mentioned above. Mrs. America M. de Tronconi, a laborer in an Impresora Uruguaya workshop, was reportedly "very happy to vote, but very calm." Being careful to vote correctly, she reported that she "brought the list in my handbag, and as I had read the instructions very well, I tried not to leave any rouge on the envelope when I closed it."[11] Margarita Borche de Bentancourt, a physician, described the feeling of being an active participant rather than a spectator: "Just imagine you had never been allowed to do something you had every right to [do], and that finally one day you achieved the recognition of justice of this wish and were able to fulfill it."[12] Maria Angelica Napoli de Fernandez, a housewife, is described as "sitting on a rocking chair with her children nearby, happy to have voted. She also had the satisfaction of complying with a duty, so what else do you want me to tell you?"[13]

These reports reveal not only women's different interpretations of the voting experience but a variety of expectations resulting from the event. One might ask if, before entering the political arena, women activists (and women in general) could possibly have been aware of the male domination of the political scene, which had been not only reserved for men historically but also dominated by the hegemonic state. We can speculate that both the political and electoral behavior of Uruguayan women reflects variables other than sex, including educational level, employment, geographical distribution, and family situation. But we might add that certain circumstances serve to unite a broad group of women in the need to rescue ethical values sustaining civic life—whether in the defense of liberties and life or in the necessity of political and judicial openness—and to generate a political movement through their actions.

It is significant that the journalist covering the election in *Mundo uruguayo* concluded his article with the comment that "the women have joined the exercise of sovereignty without any difficulty at all. What else could you ask for?"[14] His question is still valid and constitutes a challenge for anyone interested in the results of women's struggle, for it is by now indisputable that giving women the vote did not protect them from other types of discrimination. In fact, the extension of suffrage may even have veiled other injustices by strengthening the myth of equality. As seems evident today, women of this period were subject to many other injustices, and securing the vote was but a small opening in the wall of a secular oppression. Perhaps only now—with experience and historical distance—can the observer recognize that women activists endeavored not only to include women's issues in formal politics but to transform the concept of politics "by employing the weight of their common experience as women."

Notwithstanding these contradictions, the myth that Uruguayan women had achieved equality with men prevailed for years, sustained not only by the events of 1932 and 1938 but also by the passage in 1946 of a bill on women's civil rights, which brought changes in the civil code. Married women became free to administer and dispose of their possessions. In the case of the breakdown of a marriage, the husband's earnings were to be divided equally between husband and wife. Real property acquired during married life was not alienable and could not be indebted without the express consent of both parties. The conjugal address was to be fixed by the shared consent of the husband and wife. Both parents were to exercise authority over children. Widowed and divorced women who remarried continued to have authority over their children, as well as the right to administer the corresponding property, and these rights were independent of their new marriage partners. At all times one or both partners were able to demand the dissolution of the marriage without having to detail the reasons.

In spite of these apparent gains, women's participation in the formal political sector remained minimal. It was not until 1942 that four women deputies were elected (one of whom sponsored the bill on women's civil rights). In fact, for the first 50 years of suffrage, women never constituted more than 4 percent of politicians and members of Parliament at any one time. In the 1984 elections, which began the process of re-democratization, no women were elected; in the 1989 election only six women were voted in as deputies in a 132-member Parliament. Poor results at the polls contrasted sharply with women's increasing educational levels and levels of employment (they represented close to 38 percent of the work force in 1986).

For a long time, Uruguayan citizens viewed their country as an exception among Latin American countries. Until the 1940s and 1950s the state's success at development had allowed it to cover the costs of social programs, particularly in the areas of health and education. In the early 1960s, however, this welfare state, characterized by a large middle class, was threatened by an economic crisis that plunged the country into ever-increasing social conflict. Many women, espe-

cially young university students, actively participated in the political and social protests of that decade. Urban guerrillas, known as Tupamaros, included women in their ranks, as did other revolutionary groups. Women later came to realize that being *compañeros* in the struggle did not signify equality with males. They were primarily "queens of the printing presses" (in the sense that they were responsible for minor tasks) even though they used arms.

The coup of 27 June 1973 destroyed yet another social myth: that of unalterable political stability. President Juan Maria Bordaberry, a member of the most conservative sector of the Colorado Party, staged a coup d'état with the backing of the commanders-in-chief of the three branches of the army. The two houses of the legislature were dissolved immediately, political meetings were prohibited, classes were suspended, and censorship of the press was established. Central de Trabajadores (Central Workers' Union) challenged the dictatorship by declaring a general strike that lasted 15 days—the most important act of resistance against the coup. From the beginning, statements against the dictatorship from the university community and the Catholic and Protestant churches indicated the isolation and reduction of the dictatorship's social base.

Throughout the Southern Cone of Latin America institutional breakdown had become a necessary precondition for applying so-called adjustment policies. Following the coup of 1964 Brazil became the first country in the region to function under a military government; the 1973 Uruguayan coup was quickly followed by the overturn of the Chilean government of the Union Popular (Popular Unity). Finally, in 1976, the Argentine military took control of the Argentine state. The military regimes made these countries laboratories of terror, embarking on the destruction of civil society's political organizations and trade unions in pursuit of their ultimate objective: the application of the neoliberal economic model required for technological and industrial conversion of these countries.

These bureaucratic-authoritarian processes

developed according to specific conditions within a country. In Uruguay, the weight of political tradition and the importance of democratic consensus forced the military regime to call for a referendum on a new constitution in 1980. After seven years of authoritarianism and corruption, the dictatorship, troubled by its narrow base of power, needed to legitimate its authority. To the surprise of the regime, the electorate resoundingly rejected the new constitution, in spite of official propaganda pressing for its approval. Even though the media had offered no information concerning the right to reject the constitution, 53 percent of the electorate voted no. Not since the French Revolution had a dictatorship organized and lost a plebiscite. This result confused even Latin American intellectuals, who could not grasp how it had come about.[15] In the case of Uruguayan citizens, the years of democratic stability, together with the educational level of broad sectors of the populace, probably proved decisive. These ingredients yielded a deeply politicized society in which political parties as well as personal and family associations were of fundamental importance. In 1980, what had been a muted resistance to the regime emerged. The agents of this resistance—among whom women were prominent—acted from below, from the everyday spaces of the private sphere of family, community, social class, sports centers, and parishes.

In 1982, in conjunction with these changes, internal elections were held within the National and Colorado parties, while the Frente Amplio (Broad Front) coalition of the left was prohibited from holding elections. The 1984 general elections, from which various political elements and personalities were barred, marked the beginning of the transition toward democracy.

During the 12 years of military rule, the entire Uruguayan population lived in a state of terror. From 1972 to 1984 about 60,000 Uruguayans were detained, kidnapped, tortured, and "processed" by military justice. More than 6,000 were made political prisoners—a remarkably large number in a country of only 3 million people. As the result of raids by collaborating Argentine and Uruguayan forces, 120 Uruguayan citizens disappeared, many of them kidnapped from locations in Argentina, where they had sought refuge. Thirteen children were missing for a decade, and four more were presumed to have been born in captivity.[16]

The systematic use of fear and its "confirmation" in prisons and barracks full of political prisoners operated on the social corpus as a panopticon of control and terror. As former women prisoners testified in November 1985, "We thought that the two prisons were a sort of laboratory, aimed at generating fear both outside and inside."[17] Uruguayan psychologist Enrique Sobrado holds that "torture gradually began to leave hell and enter everyday life. Instability at work and in all other instances of life was a constant feature. Mistrust was at the other end of the yarn. Its objective [was] to dismember groups, separate friends."[18]

This sense of pervasive threat became endemic throughout society, producing psychological conflicts detrimental to the daily coexistence of citizens. The regime damaged the fabric of society by creating mistrust and by increasing solitude, insecurity, and depression.

To understand the impact of the military takeover, one must bear in mind that for several generations Uruguayans had lived under normal conditions within a lawful, democratic state. The rupture of institutional life, however, had traumatic consequences for the nation as a whole. Diverse and numerous sectors of the population suffered under this repression and terror. Undoubtedly Uruguay experienced a sort of social and human alteration in the life of the nation, the consequences of which have spanned many years.

In addition to the institutional disruption and political repression, economic and social developments also dramatically transformed Uruguayan society. Salaries decreased by 50 percent, and expenditures for social programs in health and education were reduced.[19] In response to the crisis, more members of the popular sector families sought work, and those already employed worked longer hours. In each case, women played the central role.

In 1973 women made up 32 percent of the economically active population in Montevideo; by 1987 they represented 47 percent. This shift affected the public and the private spheres, for women were forced to assume the double role of wage earners and homemakers. The practice of manufacturing in the home and participating in an informal market, where the feminine qualities that supposedly made women unqualified for the formal labor force, were suddenly in demand. In addition, the composition of the female labor force also changed to include a greater number of married and divorced women and female heads of households. A double system of exploitation—patriarchal and capitalist—was thus expressed in all its crudeness.

All these changes affected intrafamilial relationships, including the division of labor in the home, the use and administration of resources, and the exercise of power. A study by Suzana Prates and Silvia Rodriguez Villamil demonstrates that "this process had undeniable implications in the appearance of new demands, not only in the public domain but also in the private sphere, which conditioned the presence of women as new social and political actors."[20]

Such a situation favored the appearance of women's movements, which became more evident during the transition to democracy as "the whole system of domination suffer[ed] a legitimacy crisis." The period was a critical juncture between two political moments: in the former, nondemocratic situation, citizens were denied their political rights; in the latter, democracy became a possibility but not a reality. Both were fundamental to increasing women's awareness of their subordinate conditions. As a document on the violation of human rights stated: "This is due to the break in the legitimacy of the Public Authorities, which transferred politics to the home and to the community where primary social relations are structured. And this not only enabled women to participate in politics from their own sphere, but, with the rupture in formal politics, the primary roles of women were likewise lost: the responsibility of reproducing citizens capable of granting political legitimacy to the system of domination. This denied the gender condition which served to justify their alienation from the public world confining women to the historical and prioritized domestic sphere."[21]

The assault on institutions and the banning of political parties and labor unions all combined to limit women's political participation to the home and neighborhood. The public world of men also disappeared; the household became the only place in which men could exercise power—as fathers, husbands, and brothers. This testifies to the power of a patriarchal system with no more legitimacy than that of gender hierarchy.

During the period following the 1980 plebiscite, women's movements were organized around the defense of basic needs, the reproductive sphere, and the struggle against the dictatorship, specifically in defense of human rights. In line with the new emphasis on gender-related problems throughout the world, the new feminist impulse and the impact of the United Nations Decade for Women, initiated in 1976, were felt in Uruguay, which had previously remained isolated from many of these issues. Many of the groups formed—such as local community organizations, human rights committees, cooperative movements, and the like—began without making gender-specific demands, pointing instead toward the formation of the social order that would benefit society as a whole.

During the period preceding the transition toward democracy, women participated as a group in the Concertación Nacional Programática (CONAPRO, or the National Agreement Program), the organization in which political parties met with social-pressure groups; the aim was to reach a consensus on the criteria for democratic reconstruction during the transition from military regime to civil government. In 1984 and 1985, five documents related to education, work, health, judicial order, and the political participation of women were discussed and approved. I should stress that although the groups participating were heterogeneous—composed of women from different political parties and with differing occupational status—they managed to subscribe to common objectives by acknowledging their subordination as women. Nonetheless Uruguay still has nothing that could be called a real women's movement, much less a feminist movement.

Finally, and paradoxically, one should note that in spite of the growing participation of women in the political life of the country, they were still largely excluded from political life in the 1984 elections. Immediately after democracy was reestablished, only a few women were elected as councillors in local governments, and no women deputies were elected to the 134-member Parliament. This was the smallest representation of females in elective office since 1932.

The process begun in March 1984 continued with negotiations that sought to obtain a peaceful transition to democracy. Agreements reached by consensus among all political and social factions incorporated this goal but held that certain principles should be respected, among them the elucidation of the violation of human rights. On 26 October 1984, "The Elucidation of Human Rights Violations," a document drawn up by CONAPRO, was signed by representatives of all political parties, the Central Workers' Unions, the students' union, social movements, and the entrepreneurial sectors of Uruguay. The signing took place one month and two days before the first national democratic elections following the dictatorship. General Liber Seregni and Wilson Ferreira Aldunate, the opposition leaders, were prohibited from participating in the election, however. Thus it was established that "keeping Uruguayan society in ignorance in relation to the truth of accusations made and leaving unpunished certain penal unlawful deeds, constitutes a severe risk to the real standing of Human Rights in the future."[22] Meanwhile hundreds of political prisoners remained in Libertad, the men's prison, and in Punta Rieles, the women's.

Ten days after becoming president, Julio M. Sanguinetti signed the amnesty decree for political prisoners still in captivity, and in the first two weeks of 1985 the prisons were emptied. Throughout 1984 Uruguayan citizens had maintained a tolerant attitude toward those who had violated human rights. The executive declared that the problem of members of the military and the police accused of violating human rights was a judicial matter and rejected all political discussion of this problem. At the same time, however, state officials resorted to a variety of legal tricks to obstruct and delay legal processes and investigations of those accused. On 27 October 1985, the president publicly discarded the possibility of an "Argentina-style" judgment of the Uruguayan military, while asserting that this by no means implied that he had granted them amnesty. Yet less than a year later, on 28 August 1986, the executive carried a proposal to Parliament requesting amnesty for offenses committed by the police and military during the period of military rule. The whole society stood impotent in the face of this palace intrigue and the high-level meetings of political leaders of the two main parties, unable to express an opinion on a subject that surpassed all others in importance—as evidenced in the opinion polls and in the political fervor that characterized those days.

Again, women were the first to express this discontent publicly through a demonstration called and organized by all the women's groups active during the period. On 3 October 1986, about 20,000 women picketed in front of Parliament, demanding truth and justice. After reading the group's manifesto, Matilde Rodríguez Larreta de Gutiérrez Ruiz, the widow of a legislator murdered in Buenos Aires, emerged as the emblem of what soon would turn into a national political movement.

On 22 December 1986 the Uruguayan Parliament approved by a majority of votes (the only opposition coming from representatives of the left, some National Party legislators, and one Colorado Party representative) a law granting immunity to those who had violated human rights—in the form of torture, kidnapping, and killing—during the military period. The contradiction between ethical values and political practice thus became evident. Because a high-level political decision transformed the rules of the game concerning democracy and justice (these rules being one of the powers of the state), both the law and all citizens lost their trust in universal values through the protection of torturers and murderers. This exceptional situation was perceived as extremely violent. According to Dr. Jorge Gamarra, one of the most renowned scholars on national civil law, "In all of Uruguayan history there is no law such as this Immunity Law, approved under military pressure, with the prepotency of boots and guns on its back."[23] With the approval of the Immunity Law, the violence initiated under the dictatorship continued.

The passage of the Immunity Law and its effort to confiscate the "memory of the people," had several effects. The Immunity Law affected the process of historical synthesis by distorting references within society's collective conscience and negating critical versions of the recent past. The law diminished the emotional charge of the people's memory of past democratic efforts by trying to break the link between the people and the victims of the regime—the martyrs, the prisoners, and the disappeared. The law also stopped the incorporation of the people's memory into national historic awareness, trying to limit the attempts to incorporate the popular epic or locate its conclusions regarding the past in academic works or curricular programs.[24]

The Immunity Law also sparked opposition. On 23 December 1986 the mothers of detained and missing Uruguayans—along with Matilde Rodríguez de Gutiérrez Ruiz and Elisa Dellepiane de Michelini (the widow of another legislator murdered in Buenos Aires in 1976)—announced a campaign to collect signatures for a referendum to annul the law approved by Parliament on the previous day. This proposal received an immediate response; later that afternoon 50,000 people, summoned by the Central Workers' Union, met in the center of Montevideo.

The Uruguayan constitution stipulates that in order for a referendum to be held, 25 percent of those registered to vote must request such an election. (In many other legislative systems, the requirement for a referendum is 10 percent.) In Uruguay this requirement translated into 550,000 signatures of qualified voters with appropriate identification. The three presidents of the National Pro-Referendum Commission

(NPRC)—Michelini, Gutiérrez Ruiz, and Maria Esther Gatti de Islas, grandmother of Mariana Zaffaroni (who along with her parents had disappeared in Buenos Aires)—headed the effort.

Thousands of Uruguayan men and women crossed the country, campaigning door-to-door, and obtained the required signatures during a period of two years without a single violent incident. Matilde Rodriguez Larreta, commenting on the lengthy referendum campaign, suggested that "all the bad aspects of the delays in the definition of the topic were compensated by the depth of increasing awareness on the human rights issue in the people. Today we can say that [concern about] the problem is not limited to those who feel touched by it."[25]

There were, however, obstacles to the campaign. Members of the NPRC complained that the mass media, particularly television, had offered only partial support, tending to downplay or deride the referendum movement. With only minimal media coverage, the referendum campaign had difficulty getting publicity. The media even prohibited the screening of a video in which Sara Méndez demanded the return of her son, who was born in jail and then kidnapped by members of the Uruguayan armed forces when he was 20 days old.

Obstacles also came in the form of orders imposed by the Electoral Court, which went to absurd lengths to verify signatures. The abrogation stage began once the NPRC submitted the 637,617 signatures to the government. Annulled signatures included those of General Liber Seregni (president of the broad left coalition front) and of National Party Sen. Carlos J. Pereyra, leader of the party sector supporting the referendum. The reasons given for nullifying citizens' signatures were as diverse as they were false. Only a few days before the final date set by the constitution for submission of signatures, the Electoral Court informed referendum supporters that 30,000 signatures had to be verified or replaced to meet the minimum required for consideration. Racing the clock in an extraordinary effort, supporters gathered the needed signatures.

The plebiscite was held on 16 April 1989.

More than 52.5 percent of the country (1.2 million people) voted for the Immunity Law; 40.2 percent (800,000 citizens) cast their ballots for truth and justice. Although opponents of the law did not win the election, the large vote against amnesty for human rights violators reflects a new reality in the political environment and opens a promising stage in Uruguayan democracy. Women, whether in positions of leadership or working at the grass-roots level, assumed major roles in this fight for truth and justice. Women—as mothers and wives deprived of rights first by the dictatorship and then by the Immunity Law—became national symbols. Their courage represented the capacity of society to preserve life and human rights.

The mobilization for the referendum has been one of the most significant episodes in Uruguay's political history and undoubtedly the most extraordinary event in the transition toward democracy. Two hundred years after the French Revolution, a country influenced by Western tradition and imbued with the spirit of democracy carried out the first plebiscite on human rights in history. In 1980, the Uruguayan people also became the first to defeat a dictatorship through a plebiscite.

During the two years following the plebiscite that ousted the military regime, civil society was immersed in a conflict between truth and justice, and oblivion and pardon. This debate took place through the democratic institution of referendum, which, remarkably, was possible without undermining the existing government's legitimacy. The referendum campaign permitted the recouping of the memory of the recent past, along with a more explicit reminder of the state's culpability in human rights violations.

According to Francisco Weffort, political transitions in the Southern Cone have traditionally been uncertain because of the high degree of control exercised by those taking over a regime, the heterogeneous character and disorganization of popular sectors, and the continuation of patriarchal, clientelistic practices.[26] Although the Uruguayan truth-and-justice movement embodied these generalizations, it also refuted them by

calling for judgment of the previous regime, raising a claim for a "controlled democracy," demonstrating a capacity to organize an important sector of civil society, and questioning a regime characterized by vertical functioning and party obedience, all the while searching for new ways of acting outside syndical or party organizations.

The democratic content of the proposal and women's participation in it deserve further mention. I contend that the contradiction between the ethical principles valued by society and the actual political practices of the authoritarian regime and its heirs shaped the widespread participation of women, both in collecting the last-minute names that would ensure the plebiscite and in casting votes for truth and justice when the election was finally held. As the female president of a borough committee in favor of the referendum so aptly said in an article published by *La República de las Mujeres* on 22 April 1989, "I got into this because it was something that hit the eyes. . . . You simply couldn't be out. I think that every moderately well-informed person felt something moving inside. I don't mind being out of party politics because I am so permeated with the subject as to work efficiently."[27]

I have argued that throughout the twentieth century women's participation in political movements in Uruguay has had a characteristic feature: the assumption that women's actions contribute to the regeneration of a morally bankrupt political system. I have further suggested that women became protagonists—and may have been accepted as such—because their entrance into the public sphere and their proposals for change came at a time of national regeneration, when the country was in the process of being rebuilt. Thus, women not only mobilized out of concern for their offspring ("When you have children you ask yourself in what sort of society will I make them grow up?")[28] but may also have felt and have been seen by others as responsible for the growth of the country at large. This sense of responsibility for societal welfare was accompanied by a sense of challenge—"You begin to feel that we are all equal before the law and that we have to participate." Although the initiative was seen as a matter of ethics ("to leave crimes unpunished reflects on the morals of society"), it highlighted a need for open discussion and negotiation of conflict, elements essential to democratic life.[29] As Tapia Valdés said, "Democratic organization is . . . characterized not by its capacity to suppress conflict, but rather by its capacity to regulate it."[30]

In summary, I think the pluralist integration and practices and contents of the grass-roots movement for democracy cleared the way for a high level of participation by women. The acknowledgment of women's presence in the democracy movement, and of the reasons behind it, introduces us to the complex analysis of how women are accepted as historical subjects.

To assume the political importance of women in the transition to democracy also implies accepting the premise that their participation ends soon after the circumstances that gave rise to it are resolved. Women have not generated a solid political presence in the formal political sphere. It has proved difficult to translate the democratic protagonism of women to the established political arena. "This field seems to be forbidden to women. . . . Maybe men didn't exert much resistance, but the political area seems to belong to them."[31] Nonetheless, the historical persistence of women's efforts to give moral content to politics, and thus to revitalize it, ultimately projects their desire to transform the social order, thus joining the private and the public spheres.

NOTES

1. Verena Radkau, "Hacia una nueva historiográfia de la mujer" (Toward a new historiography of women), in *Nueva antropología. Revista de Ciencias Sociales. Estudios de la mujer: Problemas teóricos* 8 (special double issue) (November 1986).

2. Alf Ludke, "Reconstruktion von Alltagswirklichkeit Entpolitisierung der Sozialgeschichte?" (Reconstruction of the everyday depoliticization of social history?), in Berdhal et al., *Klassen and Kultur;* quoted in Radkau, "Hacia una nueva historiagráfia," 90.

3. Susan Moller Okin, *Women in Western Political Thought* (London: Princeton University Press, 1979).

4. The export of agricultural and cattle products

brought about a period of economic expansion in Uruguay that, with the exception of brief recession following World War I, lasted from the beginning of the century until 1930. Society was extremely polarized, with a small upper class and a large popular sector, until the end of the 1930s, when a middle class emerged. This stage is often called "Batllista Uruguay" owing to the strong influence of José Batlle y Ordóñez, a statesman celebrated for his political ideas and work. During this period the state assumed a leading role in economic life, communications, and the educational system, bringing about advanced social legislation, the secularization of public and private life, and a tutoring program for women. The ambitious Batllist project was designed to benefit urban groups, specifically an emerging middle class and an industrial proletariat, and facilitate the integration of European immigrants and their descendants. The result of all this was the transformation of Uruguay, which became the first welfare state on the continent.

5. Carlos Quijano, "La manifestación que nunca fue" (The rally that never was), *Acción* (Montevideo), 14 August 1934; cited in Frega, Maroma, and Trochón, *Frente popular y concertación democrática: Cuadernos de CLAEH (The popular front and democratic reconciliation: Notebooks of CLAEH),* no. 34 (Montevideo, 1984).

6. As told to Dinorah Echániz, educator, professor of philosophy, feminist, and Socialist Party activist.

7. Paulina Luisi, teacher, first woman physician in Uruguay, founding member of the Socialist Party and feminist leader, founded the Consejo Nacional de Mujeres (Women's National Council) in 1916. Archivos Paulina Luisi, Biblioteca Nacional (Paulina Luisi Archives, National Library), file 1, originally I (probably corresponding to 1942).

8. Okin, *Women in Western Political Thought,* 5.

9. *Mundo uruguayo,* 17 March 1938, p. 8.

10. Ibid., interview with Paulina Luisi, p. 9.

11. *Mundo uruguayo,* 7 April 1938, p. 8.

12. Ibid.

13. Ibid.

14. Ibid.

15. Gabriel García-Márquez, "The Generals Who Believed Their Own Story," *Diario el país de Madrid,* December 1980; quoted in a underground bulletin published during the dictatorship without editing or date.

16. Only four children were returned to their relatives. Although other children have been located, efforts to return them to their families have been unsuccessful.

17. The testimony was delivered at the Symposium on Consequences of Torture, organized by several human rights organizations—one of which was the World University Service. It was held in Piriapolis, Uruguay.

18. Citizens were classified as A, B, or C, according to their previous behavior. Category A included those who,

according to the dictatorship, merited the label democrat. Those in categories B and C were denied their rights or had to delay the expression of them. They could be processed and expelled from their work places or held back in their studies and professions; many of them never obtained passports or other official documentation. In many cases, this "disqualification" ended in imprisonment or other forms of legal action.

19. The quality of life in Uruguay has worsened since the welfare state period. The stagnation apparent since the 1960s has created an increasing concentration of income, which explains the abrupt fall of salaries. During the dictatorship, an even sharper fall in salaries occurred when the state stopped applying redistributive policies and repressed the unions, which might have questioned these measures.

20. Suzana Prates and Silvia Rodríguez Villamil, "Los movimientos sociales de mujeres en la transición a la democracia" (Women's social movements in the transition to democracy), *Serie documentos ocasionales,* no. 9 (Montevideo: GRECMU, 1986), 19.

21. Ibid.

22. Document of the Concertación Nacional Programática (CONAPRO) entitled "Esclarecimiento de las violaciónes a los derechos humanos" (Explanation of the violations of human rights), 26 October 1984.

23. Jorge Gamarra, interview in *La razón,* 12 April 1989, p. 4.

24. Alvaro Rico, "Los usos de la historia y la racionalidad liberal en el tercer batllismo" (The uses of history and liberal rationality in the third Battlist period) (Montevideo, 30 May 1989, Mimeographed).

25. *La república,* 24 December 1988.

26. Francisco Weffort, "Incertidumbres de la transición democrática en América Latina" (Uncertainties in the Latin American democratic transition), *La ciudad del futuro journal,* no. 16 (April–May 1989): 7.

27. Margarita Percovich, "La experiencia de muchas voces" (The experience of many voices), *La república de las mujeres,* 22 April 1989, p. 4.

28. Interview published in *La república de las mujeres,* 22 April 1989, p. 5.

29. Percovich, "La experiencia."

30. J. Tapia Valdés and Pax Castrense, "¿La legitimización de la violencia política?" (The legitimation of political violence?) *Revista nueva sociedad,* no. 92 (Caracas, 1987).

31. Interview in *La república de las mujeres,* 22 April 1989, p. 5.

APPENDIX

LIST OF CONTRIBUTORS

INDEX

Appendix: Selected Information from the Country Charts

	Politics								
Country	Political System*	Sovereignty†	Executive-Legislative System‡	Type of State§	Number of Parties	Year Women Granted Right to Vote	Year Women Granted Right to Stand for Election	Women in Lower House	Women in Upper House
Argentina	D	R	Pr	F	3+	1947	1947	5.9%[a]	8.9%[a]
Australia	D	CM	Pa	F	3+	1894/1902[a]	1894/1902[a]	6.7%[b]	25.0%[b]
Bangladesh	D[a]	R	Pa	U	3+	1947[b]	1947	10.3%[c]	—
Bolivia	D	R	Pr	U	3+	1953	1956	3.8%	7.4%
Brazil	D	R	Pr	F	3+	1932	1932	6.0%	0.4%
Canada	D	CM	Pa	F	3+	1917	1920	13.2%[a]	12.5%[a]
China	SS	—	—	U	1	1949	1949	21.3%[a]	—
Costa Rica	D	R	Pr	U	3+	1949	1949	12.3%[a]	—
Cuba	SS	—	—	U	1	1934	1934	33.9%	—
Czechoslovakia (former)	D	R	M	F	3+	1920	1920	25.4%[a]	29.3%
Egypt	D	R	Pr	U	3+	1956	1956	3.9%	—
France	D	R	Pa	U	3+	1944	1944	5.8%[a]	3.4%[a]
Germany	D[a]	R	Pa	F	3+	1919	1919	20.5%[b]	2.2%
Old FRG	—	—	—	—	—	—	—	—	—
Former GDR	—	—	—	—	—	—	—	—	—
Ghana	A	—	—	U	0	—	—	—	—
Great Britain	D	CM	Pa	U	2	1918/1928[a]	1919	9.2%	5.5%
Greece	D	R	Pa	U	3+	1952	1952	5.3%[a]	—
Hong Kong	—[a]	—	—	—	—[b]	1985[c]	1985[c]	11.5%[d]	N/A
Hungary	D	R	Pa	U	3+	1945	1945	6.7%[a]	—

Country									
India	D	R	Pa	F	3+	1929/1950[a]	1929/1950[a]	5.2%[b]	9.8%[b]
Israel	D	R	Pa	U	3+	1948	1948	9.0%	—
Japan	D	CM	Pa	U	3+	1945	1945	2.3%[a]	14.7%[a]
Kenya	PD	R	M[a]	U	1	1963	1963	1.7%	—
Korea, Republic of	D	R	Pr	U	3+	1948	1948	2.0%[a]	—
Mexico	D	R	Pr	F	3+	1947/1953[a]	1953	8.6%[b]	4.7%[b]
Morocco	PD	CM	Pa	U	3+	1959	1959	0.0%[a]	—
Nepal	D	CM	Pa	U	3+	1951	1951	3.4%	5.0%
Netherlands	D	CM	Pa	U	3+	1919	1917	22.7%	28.0%
Nigeria	A[a]	—	—	F	2	1957/1978[b]	1957/1978[b]	—	—
Norway	D	CM	Pa	U	3+	1913	1907	35.7%[a]	—
Palestine	—[a]	—	—	—	3+	—[b]	—	—[c]	—
Papua New Guinea	D	CM	Pa	U	3+	1964/1975[a]	1964/1975[a]	0.0%	6.7%[a]
Peru	D	R	Pr	U	3+	1955	1955	6.7%[a]	8.6%[a]
Philippines	D	R	Pr	U	3+	1937	1937	8.9%[a]	8.6%[a]
Poland	D	R	Pa	U	3+	1918	1918	9.1%[a]	6.0%[a]
Puerto Rico	D[a]	—	—	—	3+	1929/1935[b]	1929	6.0%[c]	15.0%[c]
South Africa	PD	R	Pa	U	3+	1930/1983[a]	1930/1983[a]	3.5%	2.8%
Spain	D	CM	Pa	F[a]	3+	1931	1931	13.4%[b]	11.8%[b]
Sudan	A	—	—	U	0	1953/1965[a]	1965	0.6%	—
Switzerland	D	R	Pa	F	3+	1971	1971	17.5%[a]	8.7%[a]
Turkey	D	R	Pa	U	3+	1934	1934	1.8%[a]	—
USSR (former)	SS[a]	—	—	U	3+	1917	1917	15.7%	N/A
United States	D	R	Pr	F	2	1920[a]	1788/1920[b]	10.8%[c]	6.0%[c]
Uruguay	D	R	Pr	U	3+	1932	1932	6.1%[a]	0.0%[a]

(continued)

Appendix (continued)

Country	Politics		Demographics						
	Year of Last Election	Electorate Voting for Highest Elected Office in Most Recent Election	Total Population	Population in Urban Areas	Women in Urban Areas	Men in Urban Areas	Population Below Age 15	Birthrate (per 1,000 population)	Maternal Mortality Rate (per 100,000 live births)
Argentina	1989[b]	85.0%[b]	31,497,000	84.7%	86.0%	83.3%	31.0%	23	85
Australia	1990[c]	95.8%[c]	16,532,000	85.7%	86.6%	84.8%	23.6%	15	8
Bangladesh	1991	N/A	109,877,000[d]	15.7%[e]	14.0%[e]	17.0%[e]	40.9%[e]	32[f]	600
Bolivia	1985	N/A	6,797,000	47.7%	48.3%	47.2%	43.8%	42	480
Brazil	1989	86.2%	150,368,000[a]	70.8%	71.9%	69.6%	36.4%	29	154
Canada	1988[b]	75.3%[b]	25,652,000	75.7%	76.8%	74.7%	21.5%	15	3
China	–	–	1,100,000,000[b]	20.6%[c]	20.3%	20.8%	28.7%[d]	21[a]	44
Costa Rica	1986[b]	82.2%[b]	3,015,000[c]	44.5%	46.4%	42.6%	36.7%	29	24[c]
Cuba	–	–	10,468,700[a]	71.6%	73.1%	70.1%	26.4%	17	26[a]
Czechoslovakia (former)	1990[b]	96.0%[b]	15,671,000[c]	74.1%	N/A	N/A	24.5%	13[d]	8
Egypt	1990	N/A	50,740,000	43.8%	43.4%	44.1%	39.6%	36	80
France	1988[a]	84.2%[a]	55,996,000[a]	73.4%	74.0%	72.6%	21.3%	14[a]	13
Germany	1990[c]	76.3%[c]	77,812,000	N/A	N/A	N/A	N/A	N/A	N/A
Old FRG	–	—	61,171,000	N/A	N/A	N/A	15.4%	10	5[d]
Former GDR	–	—	16,641,000	76.6%	77.0%	76.2%	17.8%	14	17
Ghana	–	—	14,900,000[a]	32.0%[a]	32.4%	31.6%	46.8%[a]	44[a]	700[b]
Great Britain	1991[b]	87.7%[b]	56,891,000	87.7%	N/A	N/A	19.5%	13	9
Greece	1990[b]	77.4%[b]	9,966,000	58.0%	N/A	N/A	21.5%	13	9
Hong Kong	1991[d]	39.1%[d]	5,822,500[d]	93.1%	93.3%	93.9%	20.9%[d]	12[d]	6[d]
Hungary	1990[b]	65.0%[b]	10,375,300[c]	61.8%[d]	62.5%[d]	61.2%[d]	21.3%[d]	12[d]	26
India	1991	N/A	844,000,000[c]	26.3%	25.6%	26.9%	35.6%[d]	27[d]	340
Israel	1992[a]	76.7%[a]	4,476,800[b]	89.2%	N/A	N/A	31.7%	23[b]	5
Japan	1990[a]	73.3%[a]	122,700,000[b]	76.7%	76.5%	77.0%	19.7%[c]	10[d]	9[d]
Kenya	1992	N/A	24,032,000[b]	22.0%[c]	N/A	N/A	52.5%	47[c]	170
Korea, Republic of	1987	89.2%	41,975,000[b]	65.4%	65.7%	65.0%	27.3%[c]	21	34

Mexico	1988[c]	51.6%[c]	82,739,000	66.3%	67.2%	65.3%	40.2%[d]	33	82
Morocco	1984	N/A	25,100,000[b]	47.0%	42.6%[c]	57.4%[c]	41.0%[b]	31[d]	300
Nepal	1991[a]	65.0%[a]	18,462,081[b]	17.6%[b]	16.7%[b]	18.4%[b]	42.3%[b]	38[c]	850[c]
Netherlands	1989	80.1%[a]	14,661,000	88.5%	88.8%	88.1%	19.6%	12	5
Nigeria	1983	N/A	88,514,501[c]	N/A	N/A	N/A	46.4%[d]	43[c]	750[c]
Norway	1985[b]	84.0%[b]	4,273,624[a]	70.7%	71.9%	69.5%	20.1%	12	4
Palestine	—	—	4,490,214[d]	N/A	N/A	N/A	36.0%[c]	N/A	N/A
Papua New Guinea	1992	N/A	3,502,000	13.1%	11.5%	14.5%	41.6%	37	900
Peru	1990[b]	97.0%[b]	22,332,100[c]	69.9%[c]	70.3%[c]	69.4%[c]	39.2%[c]	33[c]	301[d]
Philippines	1992	N/A	60,480,000[b]	42.0%[c]	N/A	N/A	39.0%[d]	35[d]	80
Poland	1991[a]	43.2%[a]	38,038,000[b]	60.3%[b]	61.3%[b]	59.2%[b]	32.6%[c]	14[c]	12
Puerto Rico	1988[c]	83.6%[c]	3,522,037[d]	66.8%	67.8%	65.7%	27.2%[c]	19[f]	40[g]
South Africa	1989[b]	see note b	37,533,000[c]	52.6%	51.8%	53.5%	41.0%[c]	32[c]	83
Spain	1989[b]	69.9%[b]	38,997,000[c]	91.4%	91.6%	91.2%	24.3%	12[d]	11
Sudan	1986	N/A	24,000,000[b]	20.2%	19.2%	21.1%	46.0%	45	660
Switzerland	1991	N/A	6,673,900[b]	60.5%	61.5%	59.5%	17.6%	12[b]	5
Turkey	1991[a]	83.9%[a]	56,473,035[b]	59.0%[b]	N/A	N/A	37.5%[c]	28[d]	210
USSR (former)	1989	N/A	286,700,000[b]	65.7%	65.9%	65.4%	27.0%[c]	20[b]	48
United States	1992[d]	55.0%[d]	248,709,873[c]	73.7%	74.5%	73.0%	21.9%	16	8
Uruguay	1989[a]	84.0%[a]	3,058,000	87.3%[b]	N/A	N/A	26.9%	19	56

(continued)

Country	Demographics							Education	
	Infant Mortality Rate (per 1,000 live births)	Mortality Rate for Children Under 5 (per 1,000 live births)	Average Household Size	Mean Age at First Marriage, Female	Mean Age at First Marriage, Male	Life Expectancy, Female	Life Expectancy, Male	Ratio of Female to Male Enrollment, 1st-Level Education	Ratio of Female to Male Enrollment, 2nd-Level Education
Argentina	33	39	3.8	22.9	25.3	72.7	65.5	97	112
Australia	9	10	3.1	23.5	25.7	78.8	72.3	95	99
Bangladesh	114[g]	180[g]	5.3[d]	18.1[f]	25.2[f]	55.4[e]	56.4[e]	79[h]	44[h]
Bolivia	113	179	4.0	22.1	24.5	55.4	50.8	88	86
Brazil	65	89	4.9	22.6	25.9	67.6	62.3	95[b]	N/A
Canada	7	8	3.0	23.1	25.2	76.0	72.7	93	95
China	31	43	4.2[a]	22.4	25.1	69.0[e]	66.0[e]	82	69
Costa Rica	18	22	5.7	21.7	25.4	75.7	70.5	94	104
Cuba	11[b]	18	4.4	19.9	23.5	76.1[a]	72.7[a]	89	102
Czechoslovakia (former)	13[c]	15[c]	2.9	21.6	24.7	74.3	67.1	97	170
Egypt	88	131	5.2	21.4	26.8	59.5	56.8	76	65
France	8	10	2.8	24.3	26.4	80.3[a]	72.0[a]	94	102
Germany	N/A	N/A	N/A	N/A	N/A	N/A	N/A	N/A	N/A
Old FRG	7[d]	9[d]	2.5	23.6	27.9	78.1	71.2	96	100
Former GDR	9	13	2.4	21.5	25.2	75.4	69.5	94	92
Ghana	86[b]	140[b]	4.9	19.4	27.1	55.8	52.2	81[b]	63[b]
Great Britain	9	11	2.7	23.1	25.4	77.2	71.4	95	99
Greece	13	18	3.2	22.5	27.6	76.4	72.2	94[c]	92[c]
Hong Kong	8	10	3.4[e]	26.4[f]	29.4[f]	80.5[d]	74.9[d]	91[g]	100[g]
Hungary	17	19	2.7[d]	21.0	24.8	74.0[d]	66.2[d]	95	95
India	95[c]	149	5.6	18.7	23.4	61.7[d]	60.6[d]	65[f]	N/A
Israel	14	16	3.6	23.5	26.1	77.0[b]	73.6[b]	97	105
Japan	6	9	3.0[e]	25.9[d]	28.4[d]	82.1[f]	76.1[f]	95[g]	99[g]
Kenya	71	113	4.5	20.4	25.8	60.5	56.5	93	68[d]
Korea, Republic of	25	33	4.6	24.1	27.3	69.1	62.7	94	88

Mexico	46	68	5.4	20.6	23.6	66.0	62.1	95	95
Morocco	58[d]	76[d]	4.2[d]	23.5[c]	27.9[e]	62.5[f]	59.1[f]	66[b]	70[b]
Nepal	123[c]	189[c]	5.6[b]	17.1[d]	21.8[d]	51.0	53.0	58[c]	42[c]
Netherlands	8	9	2.8	23.2	26.2	79.7	72.9	97	93
Nigeria	101[e]	167[e]	3.9	18.7	N/A	50.2	46.9	93[c]	73[c]
Norway	7	8	2.1[c]	24.0	26.3	79.8[d]	73.4[d]	96	100
Palestine	N/A	N/A	6.5[f]	N/A	N/A	N/A	N/A	N/A	N/A
Papua New Guinea	57	81	5.0	N/A	N/A	52.7	51.2	78[b]	57[c]
Peru	81[e]	128	5.6[f]	20.5[f]	25.7	65.3[c]	61.5[c]	93	83[g]
Philippines	46	75	5.6[d]	22.4	25.3	63.7	60.2	94	99
Poland	16[c]	20[c]	3.1[b]	22.9[b]	24.8[b]	75.5[b]	66.8[b]	95	103
Puerto Rico	13[f]	14[h]	3.3[d]	22.7[i]	26.0[i]	78.6[i]	74.2[i]	91[k]	103[l]
South Africa	71	95	4.4	N/A	N/A	63.5	57.5	97[d]	115[d]
Spain	9	11	2.8	23.1	26.0	78.6	72.5	93	101
Sudan	107	181	5.1	18.7	25.8	51.0	48.6	68	73
Switzerland	7	8	2.8	25.0	27.9	80.5	73.8	97	104
Turkey	74	93	4.7[d]	21.8	24.6	65.8	62.5	89	55
USSR (former)	25	32	3.5[c]	21.8	24.2	73.3	64.2	N/A	N/A
United States	10	13	2.2	23.3	25.4	78.3	71.3	94	97
Uruguay	27	31	2.9	22.4	25.4	72.4	65.6	95	112[c]

(*continued*)

Country	Education				Economy					
	Ratio of Female to Male Enrollment 3rd-Level Education	Literacy Rate, Female	Literacy Rate, Male	GNP per Capita (U.S. $)	Labor Force in Agriculture	Agricultural Workers, Female	Agricultural Workers, Male	Economically Active Population, Female	Economically Active Population, Male
Argentina	113	92.0%	94.0%	$ 2,130	14.8%	6.4%	93.6%	26.6%	81.4%
Australia	111^d	100.0%	100.0%	$10,830	6.9%	27.5%	72.5%	52.3%^e	75.4%^e
Bangladesh	24^h	21.8%^f	36.1%^f	$ 180^i	73.8%^j	50.7%^j	49.3%^j	61.6%^j	80.9%^j
Bolivia	N/A	51.0%	75.0%	$ 470	46.9%	13.4%	86.6%	24.6%	84.1%
Brazil	100^b	63.0%	69.0%	$ 1,640	46.0%	13.2%	86.8%	30.3%	81.7%
Canada	113	98.0%	98.0%	$13,680	5.7%	23.0%	77.0%	49.9%	78.2%
China	42	54.8%^c	80.9%^c	$ 310	71.0%^c	47.4%^c	52.6%^c	69.5%	87.0%
Costa Rica	N/A	93.0%^c	93.0%^c	$ 1,300	38.3%	11.5%	88.5%	21.2%^d	53.9%^d
Cuba	123	80.0%	76.0%	$ 3,164^c	19.1%^a	20.0%^a	80.0%^a	30.6%	54.0%
Czechoslovakia (former)	73	99.0%	99.0%	$ 5,820	14.0%	41.0%	59.0%	62.1%	77.6%
Egypt	50^a	29.0%	57.0%	$ 610	44.2%	3.7%	96.3%	7.8%	79.7%
France	97^b	97.0%	97.0%	$ 9,540	8.9%	37.0%^a	63.0%^a	44.2%	71.2%
Germany	N/A	N/A	N/A	N/A	N/A	N/A	N/A	N/A	N/A
Old FRG	72	99.0%	99.0%	$10,940	0.4%^c	44.0%^c	56.0%^c	34.0%^c	57.0%^c
Former GDR	114^f	99.0%	99.0%	$ 7,180	4.9%	38.7%	61.3%	60.1%	82.3%
Ghana	25^b	18.0%	43.0%	$ 390^a	59.3%^b	42.4%	57.6%	45.8%	44.9%
Great Britain	81	99.0%	99.0%	$ 8,460	2.4%	20.2%	79.8%	45.4%	77.2%
Greece	94	76.0%	93.0%	$ 3,550	40.6%	35.7%	64.3%	24.8%	73.6%
Hong Kong	53	83.0%^d	94.6%^d	$ 6,230	1.8%^c	36.3%^c	63.7%^c	49.5%^c	78.7%^c
Hungary	115^c	98.2%^d	98.5%^d	$ 2,750^f	15.3%^d	31.3%^d	68.7%^d	36.9%^d	49.7%^d
India	35^g	39.4%^h	63.9%^h	$ 340^e	72.0%	30.9%	69.1%	30.7%	84.3%
Israel	84	83.0%	93.0%	$10,300^c	4.6%^b	21.7%^b	78.3%^b	40.0%^b	74.9%^b
Japan	67^g	97.0%	99.0%	$11,300	6.4%^c	47.9%^c	52.1%^c	47.1%^c	76.1%^c
Kenya	36	51.0%^c	30.0%^c	$ 290	78.0%	N/A	N/A	58.0%^c	90.0%^c
Korea, Republic of	43	81.0%	94.0%	$ 4,968^d	18.7%^c	43.9%	56.1%	40.0%	77.4%

Mexico	66	79.9%[d]	86.2%[d]	$ 2,080	24.0%[d]	14.2%	85.8%	30.1%	82.4%
Morocco	50[b]	22.0%[c]	49.0%[c]	$ 960[g]	51.7%	42.9%[h]	57.1%[h]	19.7%[i]	80.3%[i]
Nepal	25[c]	24.9%[f]	55.1%[f]	$ 170[g]	80.1%[b]	44.8%[h]	55.2%[h]	45.2%[b]	68.0%[b]
Netherlands	70	100.0%	100.0%	$ 9,290	6.2%	15.6%	84.4%	30.8%	70.2%
Nigeria	39[c]	6.0%	25.0%	$ 378	44.6%[c]	37.1%	62.9%	48.2%	88.2%
Norway	113	99.0%	99.0%	$14,370	8.7%	26.0%[d]	70.7%[d]	70.2%[a]	82.5%[a]
Palestine	N/A	N/A	N/A	N/A	20.0%[f]	27.0%[f]	73.0%[f]	4.0%[f]	36.0%[f]
Papua New Guinea	32	35.3%[d]	54.8%[d]	$ 680	83.0%	45.0%	55.0%	30.0%[c]	67.0%[c]
Peru	53[g]	82.0%[c]	94.0%[c]	$ 1,010	37.0%[h]	14.7%	85.3%	25.1%	79.3%
Philippines	119	82.8%[e]	83.9%[b]	$ 590	49.0%[b]	23.5%	76.5%	46.1%[f]	81.7%[f]
Poland	127[d]	100.0%[c]	100.0%[c]	$ 2,050	26.4%[c]	46.7%[c]	53.3%[c]	43.2%[c]	54.5%[c]
Puerto Rico	159[l]	89.1%[d]	90.3%[d]	$ 6,961[m]	3.4%[n]	2.6%[n]	97.4%[n]	32.4%[n]	63.1%[n]
South Africa	N/A	57.0%	57.0%	$ 2,010	28.0%	27.0%[e]	73.0%[e]	26.7%	47.9%
Spain	96	92.1%[e]	96.8%[e]	$ 4,290	13.7%[f]	27.0%[f]	73.0%[f]	16.5%	52.1%
Sudan	68	4.0%	25.0%	$ 300	66.4%	24.1%	75.9%	22.7%	87.2%
Switzerland	47	100.0%	100.0%	$16,370	5.7%[b]	22.8%	77.2%	36.0%	63.2%
Turkey	50	43.0%	77.0%	$ 1,080	64.0%	51.6%	48.4%	45.3%	84.2%
USSR (former)	N/A	100.0%	100.0%	$ 4,550	19.0%[b]	45.0%[b]	55.0%[b]	61.3%	76.8%
United States	110	99.0%	99.0%	$16,690	3.5%	16.3%	83.7%	43.1%	57.2%
Uruguay	130[c]	96.2%[d]	95.2%[d]	$ 1,650	15.9%[b]	9.2%[b]	90.8%[b]	32.9%[b]	71.3%[b]

*A Authoritarian
D Democracy
PD Partial Democracy
SS State Socialist
‡Pa Parliamentary
Pr Presidential
M Mixed

†R Republic
CM Constitutional Monarchy

§F Federal
U Unitary

(continued)

ARGENTINA [a]Chamber of Deputies, 1989. [b]Ministry of Home Affairs.

AUSTRALIA [a]In 1894 women in South Australia gained the right to vote and stand for election; in 1902 the federal franchise was extended to all women over 21 years of age. [b]Department of the Parliamentary Library Information Service, Parliament House, "Current List of Women Members of Federal and State Parliaments" (Canberra, July 1992). [c]Australian Electoral Commission, *Election Statistics, 1990* (Canberra: Australian Government Publishing Service, 1990). [d]Commonwealth of Australia, *Women in Australia: Australia's Second Progress Report on Implementing the United Nations Convention on the Elimination of All Forms of Discrimination Against Women* (Canberra: AEPS, 1992). [e]Australian Bureau of Statistics, *The Labour Force, Australia: April 1991*, no. 6203.0.

BANGLADESH [a]Although the constitution embodies democratic principles, the military intervened in politics twice between 1971 and 1990 and governed the country under martial law. Both times the military regimes initiated a process of civilianization that led to the election and functioning of the legislature. [b]An extremely limited franchise was granted to women in 1920s; universal adult franchise was granted after independence from British rule in 1947. [c]The figure given reflects the results of the 1991 election and includes reserved seats. The constitutional provision for 30 reserved seats for women lapsed in 1987 but was restored in June 1990. [d]Bangladesh Bureau of Statistics, *Statistical Pocket Book of Bangladesh, '92* (Dhaka: Bangladesh Bureau of Statistics, 1992). [e]Calculations are based on Bangladesh Bureau of Statistics, *Statistical Yearbook of Bangladesh, 1991* (Dhaka: Bangladesh Bureau of Statistics, 1991). The preliminary report of the 1991 census does not include data on urbanization. [f]Bangladesh Bureau of Statistics, *Bangladesh Demographic Statistics, 1992* (Dhaka: Bangladesh Bureau of Statistics, 1992). [g]*Human Development Report, 1992* (New York: U.N. Development Program, 1992). [h]Computed from data in Bangladesh Bureau of Statistics, *Bangladesh Education in Statistics, 1991* (January 1992); and Bangladesh Bureau of Educational Information and Statistics (BANBEIS), Ministry of Education, *Bangladesh Educational Statistics, 1991* (March 1992). First-level education includes ages 6 to 10 years; second-level, ages 11 to 15 years; and third-level, ages 16 to 25 years. [i]Computed from Bangladesh Bureau of Statistics, *Statistical Yearbook of Bangladesh, 1991*, 523; and the corresponding official exchange rate for 1989–90. [j]Bangladesh Bureau of Statistics, *Report on Labour Force Survey, 1989* (April 1992).

BRAZIL [a]*Whitaker's Almanack, 1993* (London: J. Whitaker and Sons, 1992). [b]1980/1984.

CANADA [a]Both houses had vacancies at the time of publication. These percentages represent 13 of 104 Senate members (eleven vacancies) and 39 of 295 House members (one vacancy). [b]Appendixes to the *Report of the Chief Electoral Officer* (Ottawa: Elections Canada, 1989).

CHINA [a]China National Statistics Bureau, *China Statistics Yearbook, 1989* (in Chinese) (Beijing: China Statistics Publishing House, 1989). [b]"Congress Held to Mark the Population Day of 1,100,000,000 in Beijing" (in Chinese), *People's Daily*, 14 April 1989. [c]People's Republic of China Yearbook Editing Office of XinHua News Agency, *People's Republic of China Yearbook* (in Chinese) (Beijing: Beijing XinHua Publishing House and Hong Kong New China News Company, 1988). [d]China National Statistics Bureau, *China Statistics Yearbook, 1988* (in Chinese) (Beijing: China Statistics Publishing House, 1988). [e]Population Statistics Department, China National Statistics Bureau, *China Population Statistics, 1988* (in Chinese) (Beijing: China Expectations Publishing House, 1988).

COSTA RICA [a]The Costa Rican legislature has 57 seats, seven of which are held by women. [b]Tribunal Supremo de Elecciones (Supreme Electoral Tribunal) (San José, 1990, Mimeographed). [c]United Nations, *The Situation of Women 1990, Selected Indicators* (New York: United Nations, 1990). [d]Ministerio de Planificación (MIDEPLAN, Ministry of Planning), *MIDEPLAN: Estadísticas de empleo por regiones* (MIDEPLAN: Statistics of employment by region) (San José: MIDEPLAN, 1989).

CUBA [a]State Committee for Statistics, *1988 Yearbook* (Havana: State Committee for Statistics, 1988). [b]Ministry of Public Health, *Annual Report* (Havana: Ministry of Public Health, 1990). [c]State Committee for Statistics, *1988 Yearbook*. The figure is for gross social product per capita (an old Soviet indicator) in 1988 prices.

CZECHOSLOVAKIA *(former)* [a]Sharon L. Wolchik, *Czechoslovakia in Transition* (New York: Pinter, 1991). [b]Jan Obrman, "Civic Forum Surges to Impressive Victory," *Report on Eastern Europe* 1, no. 25 (Radio Free Europe, 22 June 1990). [c]"Vzhledem kubytku" ("With respect to the decline), *Lidové noviny*, 5 January 1991, p. 3, cited in Wolchik, *Czechoslovakia*. [d]*The Europa World Yearbook, 1991*, vol. 1 (London: Europa Publications, 1991). [e]*Social Indicators of Development, 1989* (Baltimore: Johns Hopkins University Press, 1989).

EGYPT [a]Excluding al-Azhar University.

FRANCE [a]Institut National de la Statistique et des Etudes Economiques (INSEE, or National Institute of Statistics and Economic Studies), *Données Sociales, 1990* (Social statistics, 1990) (Paris: INSEE, 1990). [b]1980/1984.

GERMANY [a]Political information is for the united Germany; however, all other data are given separately for the old Federal Republic of Germany (West Germany) and the former German Democratic Republic (East Germany). New data for the united Germany were not available from the German Statistical Federal Office at the time of publication. [b]Statistisches Bundesamt (Federal Statistical Office), Wiesbaden, 1991. [c]Old Federal Republic of Germany, *Statistical Yearbook* (New York: German Information Center). [d]Statistisches Bundesamt, series 12, no. 4 (1989). [e]Former German Democratic Republic. Statistisches Bundesamt, Microcensus Results, April 1989. [f]Including evening and correspondence courses.

GHANA [a]*World Development Report* (Washington, D.C.: World Bank, 1992). [b]*Human Development Report* (New York: U.N. Development Program, 1992).

GREAT BRITAIN [a]In 1918 women 30 years old and older gained the right to vote; in 1928 women's suffrage was granted on the same terms as men's suffrage. [b]Information provided by the British Embassy of the United States in 1993.

GREECE [a]Greek Ministry of the Interior, 1990. [b]Estimates by T. Cacoullos, Greek Statistical Institute, based on figures from the Ministry of the Interior. [c]1980/1984.

HONG KONG [a]Hong Kong is a British colony and will become a special administrative region of the People's Republic of China on 1 July 1997. Until then, it can be described as an administrative no-party state in which the government bureaucracy occupies an important role in policy making. [b]Parties and representational groups are still in a formative stage because limited suffrage was not granted until 1985. [c]An indirect election of less than half the Legislative Council was first held in 1985. Since then, a minority of people of both sexes have been eligible to vote and to stand for election. [d]Hong Kong Government, *Hong Kong, 1992* (Hong Kong: Government Printer, 1992). [e]Hong Kong Census and Statistics Department, *Hong Kong 1991 Population Census: Summary Results*, vol. 2 (Hong Kong: Government Printer, 1991). [f]Demographic Statistics Section, Hong Kong Census and Statistics Department, "Average Age at Marriage, 1971–1988," Internal Department Document. [g]1980/1984.

HUNGARY [a]Calculation by the author using figures from László Medveczky, ed., *Szabadon választott: Parlamenti almanach, 1990* (Freely elected: Parliamentary almanac, 1990) (Budapest: Idegenforgalmi Propaganda és Kiadó Vállalat, 1990). [b]*Választások Magyarországon: 1990. március 25, április 8* (Elections in Hungary: 25 March and 8 April 1990); and *Parlament képviselők* (Members of Parliament) (Budapest: Magyar Tavirati Iroda, 1990). [c]*Évi Népszámlálás. Összefoglaló adatok a 2%-os képviseleti minta alapján* (1990 census: Summary data based on the 2 percent representative sample) (Budapest: Központi Statisztikai Hivatal, 1990). [d]*Statisztikai Evkönyv, 1990* (Statistical yearbook, 1990) (Budapest: Központi Statisztikai Hivatal, 1990). [e]Including evening and correspondence courses. [f]Information from the Központi Statisztikai Hivatal, 1991.

INDIA [a]In 1929 women were enfranchised on the same limited terms as men; in 1950 universal adult enfranchisement was granted. [b]Subash C. Kashyap, "The Ninth Lok Sabha: Socioeconomic Analysis of Membership," *Journal of Parliamentary Information* 36 (1990). [c]Barbara Crossette, "India's Population Put at 844 Million," *New York Times*, 26 March 1991. [d]*Report of the Expert Committee on Population Projections for India Up to 2001* (New Delhi: Government of India). [e]*World Development Report* (Washington, D.C.: World Bank, 1991). [f]1980/1984. [g]1979. [h]J. C. Aggarwal and N. K. Chowdhry, *Census of India, 1991* (New Delhi: S. Chand, 1991).

ISRAEL [a]Chen Dagan, "Likud Voters Remained at Home," *Hadashot*, 28 June 1992, p. 8. [b]*Statistical Abstract of Israel* (Jerusalem: N. HO Central Bureau of Statistics, 1989). [c]*Facts About Israel* (Israel Information Center, 1992).

JAPAN [a]*Women's Outlook* (Tokyo: Fusae Ichikawa Memorial Association, 1990). [b]*Asahi Shimbun, Asahi Almanac, 1991* (in Japanese) (Tokyo, 1991). [c]*Population Census of Japan* (Tokyo: Management and Coordination Agency, 1990). [d]*Vital Statistics of Japan* (in Japanese) (Tokyo: Ministry of Health and Welfare, 1990). [e]*Survey of Living Conditions of the People on Health and Welfare* (in Japanese) (Tokyo: Ministry of Health and Welfare, 1991). [f]*The Abridged Life Tables* (in Japanese) (Tokyo: Ministry of Health and Welfare, 1991). [g]*Report on Basic School Statistics* (Tokyo: Ministry of Education, 1991).

KENYA [a]The Kenyan president is elected separately from parliamentarians. [b]*Whitaker's Almanack, 1993* (London: J. Whitaker and Sons, 1992). [c]*World Development Report* (Washington D.C.: World Bank, 1990). [d]1980/1984. [e]*The World's Women, 1970–1990: Trends and Statistics* (New York: United Nations, 1991).

KOREA, REPUBLIC OF [a]General Office of the National Assembly, *History of the National Assembly (Kukhoe-Sa)* (Seoul, 1950–90). [b]*Whitaker's Almanack, 1993* (London: J. Whitaker and Sons, 1992). [c]*Demographic Yearbook, 1988* (New York: United Nations, 1990). [d]National Bureau of Statistics, *Korea Statistical Yearbook, 1989* (Seoul, 1990).

MEXICO [a]In 1947 women voted for the first time in *municipal* elections. Julia Tuñon, *Mujeres en México* (Women in Mexico) (Mexico: Planeta, 1987). [b]Information from the Mexican Embassy of the United States, for 1991–94. [c]Comisión Federal Electoral (Federal Election Commission), *Elecciones federales 1988: Cómputo distrital* (Federal elections 1988: Calculations by district). [d]Teresita de Barbieri, "La subordinación de las mujeres en una sociedad desigual. Notas para un diagnóstico de la condición de la mujer en México" (The subordination of women in an unequal society: Notes toward a diagnosis of the position of women in Mexico) (Manuscript, 1988).

MOROCCO [a]Alan J. Day, *Political Parties of the World* (Chicago: St. James Press, 1988). [b]Ministry of Planning, *Statistics Annual of Morocco, 1990* (Rabat: Centre de Recherche et d'Etudes Demographiques [CERED], 1990). [c]Ministry of Planning, *Femmes et condition féminine au Maroc* (Women and women's condition in Morocco) (Rabat: CERED, 1989). [d]DHS, 1992. Ministry of Health. [e]Ministry of Planning, *La condition de la femme au Maroc* (The condition of women in Morocco) (Rabat: Direction de la Statistique, 1992). [f]Population Division, U.N. Department of International Economic and Social Affairs, *World Population Prospects: Estimates and Projections as Assessed in 1984 as of 1985–1990*, U.N. publication no. E.86.XIII.3. [g]*World Development Report* (Washington, D.C.: World Bank, 1990). [h]Ministry of Planning, *Enquête sur l'emploi rural, 1986–87* (Study of rural employment, 1986–87) (Rabat: Direction de la Statistique, 1987). [i]Ministry of Planning, *Enquête sur les ménages, 1981–82* (Study of households, 1981–82) (Rabat: Direction de la Statistique).

NEPAL [a]*International Forum*, vol. 51, Nepal, 1991. [b]*Population Census of Nepal, 1991*, vol. 1: *Advanced Tables* (Kathmandu: His Majesty's Government/Nepal, National Planning Commission, Central Bureau of Statistics, 1992). [c]*Human Development Report* (New York: U.N. Development Program, 1992). [d]*Population Monograph of Nepal* (Kathmandu: His Majesty's Government/Nepal, National Planning Commission, Central Bureau of Statistics, 1992). [e]1980/1984. [f]Literacy rate for those six years old and older. [g]*World Development Report* (Washington, D.C.: World Bank, 1992). [h]*Population Census of Nepal, 1981*, vol. 1, part 1 (Kathmandu: His Majesty's Government/Nepal, National Planning Commission, Central Bureau of Statistics, 1984).

NETHERLANDS [a]*Volkskrant*, 7 September 1989, p. 1.

NIGERIA [a]The government is now in transition to civil rule. [b]Women in southern Nigeria were enfranchised in 1957, and women in northern Nigeria in 1978. [c]*Population and Vital Statistics Report*, series A, vol. 44, no. 4 (New York: United Nations, 1992). [d]*World Development Report* (Washington, D.C.: World Bank, 1992). [e]*Human Development Report* (New York: U.N. Development Program, 1992).

NORWAY [a]Equal Status Council, "Minifacts on Equal Rights" (Oslo: Likestillings Rådet, 1992). [b]Central Bureau of Statistics of Norway, *Storting Elections, 1989*, vol. 1, table 20. [c]Equal Status Council, "Minifacts on Equal Rights" (Oslo: Likestillings Rådet, 1991). [d]Equal Status Council, "Minifacts on Equal Rights" (Oslo: Likestillings Rådet, 1990).

PALESTINE [a]The Palestinian people have sought statehood since the early 1920s, first in opposition to the British occupation and then in opposition to Israel. Since 1964 the Palestinians have been led by the Palestine Liberation Organization (PLO). The PLO is an umbrella body led by an Executive Committee headed by Yasser Arafat (as of the time of publication) and governed by the Palestine National Council (PNC), which contains representatives of various Palestinian parties and groupings. [b]Women voted in the Palestinian National Council in 1965. [c]Women made up 9.0 percent of the Palestinian National Council in 1989. UNRWA *Statistics of Palestine Refugees* (refugees only), REF. WWR 730/B, run date 11 March 1989. [d]Palestinian population worldwide. [e]UNRWA *Statistics of Palestine Refugees*. [f]Central Bureau of Statistics, *Statistical Abstracts of Israel, 1988*, no. 39 (1988), for the West Bank and Gaza Strip.

PAPUA NEW GUINEA [a]In 1964 under Australian administration; in 1975 under the Papua New Guinea constitution. [b]1987. [c]Eileen Wormald and Anne Crossley, *Women and Education in the South Pacific* (Waigani: University of Papua New Guinea Press, 1988). [d]Eileen Wormald and Anne Crossley, *Women and Education in Papua New Guinea* (Waigani: University of Papua New Guinea Press, 1988). [e]Estimates based on International Labor Organization figures.

PERU [a]Congreso Nacional, Camara de Senadores, Oficina de Relaciones Públicas (National Congress, Senate, Public Relations Office), 1990. [b]Jurado Nacional de Elecciones (Electoral National Council). By law, voting is compulsory in Peru, hence the high voter turnout in the general elections. [c]Richard Webb and Graciela Fernandez Baca, Instituto Nacional de Estadística (ENDES, or National Institute of Statistics) en Perú en Numeros 1990, *Almanaque estadístico* (Statistical almanac) (Cuanto S.A., Editorial Navarrete, 1990). [d]Ministerio de Salud (Ministry of Health), *Programa Nacional de Planificación Familiar, 1988–91* (National Family Planning Program, 1988–91) (1989). [e]Instituto Nacional de Estadística, *Censo nacional, 1991* (National census, 1991). [f]Instituto Nacional de Estadística en Programa Nacional de Promoción de la Mujer, 1990–95 (National Program for the Advancement of Women, 1990–95), Presidencia del Consejo de Ministros, Consejo Nacional de Población (Lima, 1990). [g]1980/1984. [h]Instituto Nacional de Estadística, *Censo nacional, 1991*. Fishing is considered part of the agriculture industry.

PHILIPPINES [a]Commission on Elections, *1987 National Election Results* (Manila). [b]*Philippines Country Profile, 1991–1992* (London: Economist Intelligence Unit, 1991). [c]*Asia 1992 Yearbook* (Hong Kong: Far Eastern Economic Review, 1992). [d]*National Statistics Yearbook, 1989* (Manila: National Statistics Office, 1990). [e]*Philippine Development Plan for Women, 1989* (National Commission on the Role of Filipino Women, 1990). [f]*Integrated Survey of Households Bulletin*, series 56 (Manila: National Statistics Office, First–Fourth Quarters, 1986).

POLAND [a]Obwieszczenie Panstwowej Komisji Wyborczej z dnia 31 października 1991 (Announcement of the National Electoral Commission, 31 October 1991). [b]*Mały Rocznik Statystyczny 1991* (Small statistical yearbook, 1991) (Warsaw: Glowny Urzad Statystyczny). [c]*Rocznik Statystyczny 1990* (Statistical yearbook, 1990) (Warsaw: Glowny Urzad Statystyczny). [d]Including evening and correspondence courses.

PUERTO RICO [a]Puerto Rico is a U.S. territory with colonial status. Puerto Ricans do not have the right to vote for the president of the United States. Except for a resident commissioner with the right to speak but not vote, they do not have representation in the U.S. Congress. Puerto Ricans elect a local governor and have a local legislature, but the U.S. Congress retains authority over defense, laws, communication, and land expropriation. [b]In 1929 women's suffrage was restricted to literate women; in 1935 universal suffrage was granted. [c]State Elections Council, *Informa preliminar de los resultados de las elecciones en Puerto Rico, 1988* (Preliminary report of the results of the 1988 Puerto Rican elections) (San Juan, 1990). [d]U.S. Department of Commerce, Bureau of the Census, *Censo de población y vivienda 1990—Resumen de características de población y vivienda de Puerto Rico* (Census of population and housing, 1990: Review of characteristics of population and housing in Puerto Rico) (Washington, D.C.: U.S. Government Printing Office, 1991). [e]Calculations made by the author from data in ibid. [f]Office of Health Statistics, *Estadísticas vitales preliminares, Puerto Rico, año 1990* (Preliminary vital statistics, Puerto Rico, 1990), Information Bulletin, year 6, series D-6, no. 2. (5 December 1991). [g]A. Comas et al., "Misreporting of Maternal Mortality in Puerto Rico," *Boletín de la Asociación Médica de Puerto Rico 82* (August 1990). [h]Calculations made by the author from data in Office of Health Statistics, Department of Health of Puerto Rico, *Informe anual de estadísticas vitales de Puerto Rico, 1989* (Annual report of vital statistics of Puerto Rico, 1989) (San Juan, 1991). [i]Jose L. Baszquez-Calzada, *La población de Puerto Rico y su trayectoria histórica* (The population of Puerto Rico and its historical trajectory) (Self-published, May 1988). [j]*Informe anual de estadísticas vitales de Puerto Rico, 1991–1989.* [k]Calculations made by the author from data in Department of Education of Puerto Rico, *Informe de matrícula de escuelas públicas y privadas por sexo y grado (DI-1), 1991–1992* (Report of enrollment in public and private schools by sex and level [DI-1], 1991–92) (San Juan, 1992). [l]Calculations made by the author from data in *Compendio de estadísticas* (Compendium of statistics) (San Juan: University of Puerto Rico, 1992). [m]Calculations made by the author from data in the Puerto Rican Planning Council, *Informe económico al gobernador, 1989* (Economic report to the governor, 1989) (San Juan, 1989). [n]Bureau of Labor Statistics, Department of Labor and Human Resources, *Encuesta de la población civil no institucional y el grupo trabajador* (Survey of the noninstitutional civil population and the working class) (May–June 1990).

SOUTH AFRICA [a]In 1930 the right to vote and the right to stand for election were given to white women; in 1983 the rights were given to coloureds and Indians. All Africans are disenfranchised. [b]Carde Cooper, Colleen McCaul, Robin Hamilton, I. Delvare, J. Moonsamy, K. Mueller, *Race Relations Survey, 1989/90* (Johannesburg: South African Institute of Race Relations, 1990). [c]Laetitia Rispel and Graham Behr, *Health Indicators: Policy Implications*, Centre for Community Health, Department of Community Health, University of Witwatersrand, Paper no. 27 (Johannesburg, June 1992). [d]Kate Truscott, *Gender in Education* (Johannesburg: National Education Policy Investigation, Gender in Education Sub-Group, June 1992). [e]Moira Macomachie, "Looking for Patterns of Women's Employment and Educational Achievements in the 1985 Census," *Agenda*, no. 5 (1989).

SPAIN [a]Quasi-federal. [b]*La mujer en España: Política* (Women in Spain: Politics) (Madrid: Instituto de la Mujer, 1990). [c]*Anuario el país* (Country yearbook) (Madrid: Ed. El País, 1991). [d]*La mujer en España: Situación social* (Women in Spain: Social situation) (Madrid: Instituto de la Mujer, 1990). [e]*La mujer en España: Educación* (Women in Spain: Education) (Madrid: Instituto de la Mujer, 1990); and *La presencia de la mujer en el sistema educativo* (The presence of women in the educational system) (Madrid: Instituto de la Mujer, 1988). [f]*La mujer en cifras* (Women in brief) (Madrid: Instituto de la Mujer, 1991).

SUDAN [a]In 1953 the vote was given to women graduates of secondary school or above; in 1965 it was given to all Sudanese women. [b]Population Census Office, Department of Statistics, Khartoum, 1989.

SWITZERLAND [a]Regula Stämpfli and Claude Longchamp, "Wie wird die Zukunft weiblich? Frauenförderung bei Wahlen und darüber hinaus: Bestandesaufnahme und Strategieformulierungen" (How will the future be feminine? Women's advancement through election and beyond: Taking stock and forming strategy), *Zukunft des Staates*, SVPW-Jahrbuch 30/1990 (Bern: Haupt, 1991); and Bundesamt für Statistik (Federal Bureau of Statistics), *Statistisches Jahrbuch der Schweiz* (Statistical yearbook of Switzerland) (Basel: Birkhauser, 1991). [b]*Taschenstatistik der Schweiz* (Pocketbook of statistics on Switzerland) (Bern: Bundesamt für Statistik, 1990).

TURKEY [a]*Results of General Election of Representatives*, no. 1511 (State Institute of Statistics, Prime Ministry, 20 October 1991). [b]*Census of Population: Summary Tables, 1990*, no. 1458 (State Institute of Statistics, Prime Ministry, 1991). [c]*Census of Population, 1985: Socio-Economic Tables*, no. 1237 (State Institute of Statistics). [d]*1989 Population Survey of Turkey* (State Institute of Statistics, forthcoming).

USSR (FORMER) [a]As of 1991. [b]National Economy of the USSR, *Statistical Yearbook* (in Russian) (Moscow: Finances and Statistics, 1989). [c]Population of the USSR, *Statistical Yearbook* (in Russian) (Moscow: Finances and Statistics, 1988).

UNITED STATES [a]Women won partial or full suffrage in a number of states before winning national suffrage. [b]The federal constitution did not bar women from running for office, though many state constitutions limited office seekers to electors, eliminating most women's ability to run for office until national suffrage was won in 1920. [c]"Women Candidates and Winners in 1992" (New Brunswick, N.J.: Center for the American Woman and Politics, 12 November 1992). [d]"Voter Turnout Rates for Presidential Elections Since 1932," *Congressional Quarterly*, 3553, 7 November 1992. [e]*Census of Population and Housing, 1990* (Washington, D.C.: Bureau of the Census, 1991).

URUGUAY [a]Electoral Court Statistics, 1989. [b]Calculation made by Grupo Estudios de la Condición de la Mujer en el Uruguay (GRECMU, or the Study Group on the Condition of Women in Uruguay) based on *Population Census, 1985* (Dirección General de Estadísticas y Censo). [c]1980/1984. [d]Calculation made by GRECMU based on the University Census, 1988; and statistics of the Ministry of Culture and Education.

Contributors

KATHRYN A. CARVER. *See* United States

NAJMA CHOWDHURY. *See* Bangladesh

NANCY J. JOHNSON is associate director of the Center on Women and Public Policy, Humphrey Institute of Public Affairs, and associate director of the Center for Advanced Feminist Studies, both at the University of Minnesota. A former teacher and editor, she specializes in issues related to women and public policy, especially income support, maternal and child health policy, healthcare delivery to low-income populations, and gender-inclusive, multicultural approaches to teaching and research.

BARBARA J. NELSON. *See* United States

PAULA L. O'LOUGHLIN is a Ph.D. candidate in political science at the University of Minnesota. Her research interests include feminist theory and comparative methodology, political psychology, and political economy.

WHITNEY THOMPSON is planner and program director for the Arrowhead Economic Opportunity Agency in northern Minnesota, one of the largest community action programs in the United States. Her interests include welfare policy reforms, child support and its enforcement, healthcare, child care, tax policy, educational opportunity, and the relation of all these to the attainment of self-sufficiency.

Argentina

MARÍA DEL CARMEN FEIJOÓ, sociologist and senior researcher at the Center for the Study of State and Society (CEDES) in Buenos Aires and professor at the University of Buenos Aires, was formerly an executive member of the Council of Women in Buenos Aires Province. In 1992 she was appointed vice-minister of education in the same province. Since 1981 she has been conducting research on women from popular sectors and has coedited several books on Argentine and Latin American women. Among the most recent are *Our Past, Our Future* (1988) and *Life in the Cities* (1991), both in Spanish.

Australia

MARIAN SAWER, senior lecturer in management at the University of Canberra, is former president of the Australasian Political Studies Association and cofounder of its women's caucus. Her books include *A Woman's Place: Women and Politics in Australia* (2nd ed., 1992, with Marian Simms), *Sisters in Suits: Women and Public Policy in Australia* (1990), and edited volumes on the New Right and on affirmative action. She has been active in women's affairs inside and outside government.

Bangladesh

NAJMA CHOWDHURY, professor of political science at Dhaka University, was president of Women for Women, a Research and Study Group, in Bangladesh from 1988 to 1992. From 1988 to 1991 she was chair of Women, Politics, and Developing Nations, Study Group 30 of the International Political Science Association. Among her publications are *The Legislative Process in Bangladesh: The Politics and Functioning of the East Bengal Legislature* (1980) and "Women in Politics in Bangladesh" (1988).

Bolivia

GLORIA ARDAYA SALINAS is a sociologist specializing in social movements, democracy, and political systems. Her publications include *The Army: Crisis in the Transition, Democracy and Poverty in Latin America*, and *Women and Politics: Parties and Labor Unions in Bolivia* (all in Spanish). From 1982 to 1985 she was a member of the Bolivian Parliament, and from 1983 to 1987 she was director of the Latin American College of Social Sciences' (FLASCO) Program in Bolivia. She has also been a consultant for UNESCO and UNICEF.

Brazil

FANNY TABAK is professor of political science and director of the women's studies center at Pontifícia Universidade Católica in Rio de Janeiro. She has written on women and the law and women's political participation. Her books in-

clude *Brazilian Women in the National Congress* (1989), *Women in Politics* (1982), *A New Legal Order: Women and the Constitution* (1989), and *The Profile of the True Brazilian Woman* (1987), all in Portuguese.

Canada

SYLVIA BASHEVKIN is professor of political science at the University of Toronto, with major research interests in comparative political behavior and public policy. She is the author of *Toeing the Lines: Women and Party Politics in English Canada* (1985, 1992) and *True Patriot Love: The Politics of Canadian Nationalism* (1991) and the editor of *Canadian Political Behaviour* (1985) and *Women and Politics in Western Europe* (1985). She has been active in multiparty efforts to improve women's representation in the Canadian political process and is president of the Canadian Political Science Association.

China

YUE DAIYUN is professor of Chinese literature, director of the Institute of Comparative Literature at the University of Beijing, and president of the Chinese Comparative Literature Association. She is the author of *Comparative Literature and Modern Chinese Literature* (1987), *A Course in Comparative Literature* (1988), *Intellectuals in Chinese Fiction* (1987), and *To the Storm* (1985), all in Chinese, and the editor of numerous books on modern Chinese literature and research in comparative literature.

LI JIN is a researcher at the Chinese Modern Literature Museum in the Chinese Writers' Union. She is the author of *Individualism and the New Literature of the May Fourth Movement in China, 1917–1927* (1992), the coeditor of *A Study of Ba Jin Abroad* (1986), both in Chinese, and the author of numerous articles on modern Chinese literature.

Costa Rica

MIRTA GONZÁLEZ-SUÁREZ, professor at the University of Costa Rica, is a psychologist specializing in research on gender issues. Her publications include many articles and three books in Spanish: *Women's Studies: Knowledge and Change* (1988), *Sexism in Education* (1990), and *Latin American National Identity* (1990, with Daniel Flores). One of her most cherished publications is a magazine entitled *Learning to Be a Woman,* developed for grass-roots women's organizations. She chaired the organizing committee for the Fifth International Interdisciplinary Congress on Women, 1993.

Cuba

JEAN STUBBS, a social historian from Britain, coordinates the Caribbean Studies Program at the University of London Institute of Commonwealth Studies and Latin American Studies and lectures in Caribbean Studies at the Polytechnic of North London. She lived and worked in Cuba from 1968 to 1987 and is married to the Cuban writer Pedro Pérez Sarduy, with whom she edited *AfroCuba: An Anthology of Cuban Writing on Race and Integration.* She is the author of the volume on Cuba in the *World Bibliography Series* (1992) and of *Cuba: The Test of Time* (1989), as well as academic and popular articles.

Czechoslovakia (former)

SHARON L. WOLCHIK is director of Russian and East European Studies and associate professor of political science and international affairs at George Washington University in Washington, D.C. She works on issues of gender in Central and Eastern Europe and on nationality relations in communist and postcommunist states. The author of *Czechoslovakia: Politics, Economics, and Society in the Transition to Post-Communist Rule* (1991) and coeditor of *Women, State, and Party in Eastern Europe* (1985), she is president of the Washington chapter of the American Association for the Advancement of Slavic Studies.

Egypt

MERVAT F. HATEM, associate professor of political science at Howard University in Washington, D.C., has been a member of the council of the Women and Politics Section of the American Political Science Association. She is working on a comparative study of state feminism in Egypt and the Scandinavian states. Her article "Economic and Political Liberalization and the Decline of State Feminism" appeared in the *International Journal of Middle East Studies* (May 1992).

France

JANE JENSON is professor of political science at Carleton University in Ottawa, Ontario, and fellow of the Royal Society of Canada. Her recent studies have dealt with the impact of the state on gender relations; the political economy of Canada; and the politics of social movements. Her most recent book is *The Politics of Abortion in Canada* (1992), and she has written frequently on French women's movements, the Left, and state policy.

MARIETTE SINEAU, researcher at the National Center for Scientific Research in Paris, is a political scientist affiliated with the Center for the Study of French Political Life of the National Foundation for Political Science. She has written several books and articles about women's participation in French and European politics. Her latest book is *Women in Politics* (1988, in French), and she is a contributor to *A History of Women in the West* (1992).

Germany

CHRISTIANE LEMKE teaches political science at the Freie Universität Berlin. She was a visiting associate professor of government at Harvard University in 1991–92 and DAAD German Studies Professor at the University of North Carolina at Chapel Hill in 1988–91. Her research focuses on German and European politics, political culture, and policies concerning women, and she has written articles on women in the Federal Republic and the former German Democratic Republic. Her books include *The Causes of Radical Change: Political Socialization in the German Democratic Republic* (1991, in German). She is a founding member of the working group on gender and politics in the German Political Science Association.

Ghana

KAMENE OKONJO received a master's degree in economics from the University of Erlangen, Germany, in 1961 and a Ph.D. in sociology from Boston University in 1976. She has been a Ford Foundation research fellow at the University of Ibadan, an African Studies Center fellow at Boston University, and a professor of sociology at the University of Nigeria. Her research interests include the family, economic and social development, and women in politics.

Great Britain

JONI LOVENDUSKI, reader in politics at the Department of European Studies at Loughborough University, England, convened the Standing Group on Women and Politics of the European Consortium for Political Research and codirects the British Candidate Study. She is the author of *Women and European Politics* (1986), the coauthor of *Contemporary Feminist Politics* (1993), and the coeditor of *The Politics of the Second Electorate* (1981) and *The New Politics of Abortion* (1986).

Greece

ANN R. CACOULLOS, associate professor of philosophy at Paterson College in New Jersey, also teaches in the Department of English Studies at the University of Athens. She specializes in ethics and social and political philosophy. Her books include *Thomas Hill Green: Philosopher of Rights* (1974), *Women and New Technologies in Greece* (1988, in Greek), and *Greek Rural Women in Decision-Making Processes* (1990), a UNESCO study. She is now promoting women's studies programs in the university curriculum in Greece.

Hong Kong

FANNY M. CHEUNG is senior lecturer in the Department of Psychology at the Chinese University of Hong Kong and program director of the Gender Research Programme of the Hong Kong Institute of Asia-Pacific Studies at the university. She spearheaded the War-on-Rape Campaign and founded the first women's center in Hong Kong. Her publications include works on gender roles and attitudes toward rape. As a member of the editorial team of the Committee on Women's Studies in Asia, she has collaborated with women's studies scholars in seven Asian countries to compile a sourcebook on women's studies in Asia.

SHIRLEY PO-SAN WAN is research officer at the Hong Kong Institute of Asia-Pacific Studies at the Chinese University of Hong Kong and program director of the Social Indicators and Social Development of Hong Kong Research Programme at the institute. Her research interests include gender issues, quality of life, social problems, and patterns of social change in Hong Kong. She is coauthor or coeditor of *Indicators of Social Development: Hong Kong* (1988, 1990), *The Development of Social Indicators Research in Chinese Studies* (1992), and *The Chinese Family and Its Changes* (1991).

OLIVIA CHI-KIE WAN is acting director of Meeting Point, a democratic political party in Hong Kong. A political scientist, she is concerned with the representation of women's interests and the policy-making process. She has been active in the women's movement and the democratic movement in Hong Kong.

Hungary

KATALIN KONCZ is associate professor of human resources at the Budapest University of Economics. A specialist in research on women's questions, she is the author of *Women in the World of Labor* (1982) and *Women in the Labor Market* (1987), the editor of *Women and Men—Beliefs and Facts* (1985), all in Hungarian, and the author of more than 100 studies. She is the technical consultant for the Association of Hungarian Women and the national contact for and board member of the European Network for Scientific and Technical Cooperation on Women's Studies.

India

HEM LATA SWARUP, former vice-chancellor of Kanpur University and former professor of political science and English and Indian literature, is also the founding principal of Acharya Narendra Dev Mahapalika Mahila Mahavidyalaya, an education institution in Kanpur. She is president of the Indian Council of Education and the All India Women's Studies and Development Organization and served as chairperson of the Sex Roles and Politics Research Committee of the International Political Science Association from 1985 to 1988. She has carried out research on the political socialization of women and men and on the process of development in India with respect to women. She is coeditor of *Women, Politics, and Religion* (1991) and *Environment and the Disinherited Half: Some Third World Perspectives* (1992).

NIROJ SINHA, professor of political science at Magadh Mahila College, Patna University, specializes in modern political theory, political sociology, and some aspects of public administration. She is the author of "University Administration in India, with Special Reference to Bihar" and two dozen research papers and the editor of *Women and Violence* (1989). A founder of the Centre for Women's Development Studies, a research and action organization in Bihar, she is engaged in research on issues related to women in India.

CHITRA GHOSH, chair of the Political Science Department at Lady Brabourne College, Calcutta, and professor of social and political history at Netaji Institute for Asian Studies, Calcutta, specializes in social history and women's studies. Her publications include *Naari* (Woman, 1989), a special publication on women of Calcutta issued for the Calcutta tercentenary; *Women's Studies in India* (1990) and *Women's Movement Politics in Bengal* (1990). She is president of the International Federation of University Women (1992–95).

PAM RAJPUT, professor of political science and director of the Centre for Women's Studies at Punjab University, is also chair of the Research Committee on Women, Politics and Developing Nations of the International Political Science Association from 1991 to 1994. In 1992 she participated in an international conference on women and the environment in Egypt and organized a roundtable on gender dimensions of the environment and development at the U.N. Conference on Environment and Development in Rio de Janeiro. She is the coauthor of *Constitution of India* (1979) and *Environment and the Disinherited Half: Some Third World Perspectives* (1992).

Israel

DAPHNA SHARFMAN, a writer, teaches political science at Haifa University, where she cofounded the women's studies program. She is the author of *Women and Politics* (1988, in Hebrew) and *Civil Rights in Israel: Living Without a Constitution* (1993). She chairs the Civil Rights and the Human Rights committees in the International Department of the Israel Labor Party.

Japan

NUITA YŌKO, a freelance journalist, was formerly a radio and television news commentator for the Japan Broadcasting Corporation. She is chief editor of the monthly *Women's Outlook* (in Japanese) and the English-language newsletter *Japanese Women*, both published by the Fusae Ichikawa Memorial Association. She has served as a member of the U.N. Commission on the Status of Women and as a delegate to the U.N. world women's conferences in 1980 and 1985. She chairs the Advisory Council on Women's Affairs, which reports to the prime minister.

YAMAGUCHI MITSUKO, secretary general of the Fusae Ichikawa Memorial Association, is engaged in the political education of women, research and publication on women's issues, and international exchange. As executive assistant to the late Ichikawa Fusae (a member of the House of Councillors), she worked for political reform and encouraged citizens' movements, and she continues to be engaged in these activities. She is a member of the Tokyo Metropolitan Committee on Women's Issues, which speaks on behalf of citizens, and is the coauthor of *Politics and Women* (1984, in Japanese).

KUBO KIMIKO is chief of the Research and Publishing Section on Women's Issues for the Fusae Ichikawa Memorial Association. While assisting Ichikawa Fusae, she volunteered in former U.S. Congresswoman Bella Abzug's campaign for mayor of New York City in 1977. She gave presentations on Japanese women's participation in politics at seminars in Seoul in 1989 and New York in 1990. She is the coauthor of *Report on Citizens' Action Against Corrupt Candidates* (1978) and *Clean Elections by Ichikawa Fusae and Her Followers* (1990), both in Japanese.

Kenya

MARIA NZOMO, senior lecturer in the department of government and in the Institute of Diplomacy and International Studies at the University of Nairobi, specializes in political economy, international relations, and gender studies. She has been the research coordinator of DAWN (Development Alternatives with Women for a New Era) in eastern and southern Africa and a member of the executive of AAWORD (Association of African Women for Research and Development), Kenya chapter.

KATHLEEN STAUDT is professor and chair of the political science department at the University of Texas at El Paso. Her research has focused on agricultural policy, development strategies, women in politics, and state-society relations. Her latest books include *Women, International Development, and Politics: The Bureaucratic Mire* (1990) and *Managing Development: State, Society, and International Contexts* (1991).

Korea, Republic of (South Korea)

BONG-SCUK SOHN is director of the Center for Korean Women and Politics, Seoul. A specialist in Korean politics, local politics, and

women's studies, she is the author of *Local Politics in South Korea* (1985, in Korean) and "Political Women in South Korea" (1990) and a coauthor of *Contemporary Korean Politics* (1986, in Korean), *Party Politics in Korea* (1987, in Korean), and *Women in North Korea* (1991, in Korean). She initiated a women's political caucus to help women candidates run for the 1991 local assembly elections—the first such women's effort in Korea.

Mexico

ELI BARTRA is chair of women's studies and professor in the Division of Social Sciences at the Universidad Autónoma Metropolitana-Xochimilco in Mexico City. A member of the Mexican feminist movement since 1974, she specializes in the feminist theory of art, as well as in political philosophy. She is the author or coauthor of *Women, Ideology, and Art* (1987), *The Return: Reflections, Testimonies, and Reports of Women in Mexico, 1975–1983* (1983), *Women: A Bibliography, Mexico* (1984), and *Proceedings of the Latin American and Caribbean Fourth Feminist Meeting* (1988), all in Spanish.

Morocco

AICHA AFIFI is an administrator in the Ministry of National Education and a translator of official documents. She holds a Ph.D. in development economics with a specialty in women and development. The author of "Arab Women and Development: The Case of the Moroccan Women" and *Application of Social Marketing to Family Planning* (1986, in French), she has been active in women's organizations and associations, especially the League of Women in the Public and Semi-Public Sector in Morocco.

RAJAE MSEFER is assistant professor of economics at the National School of Public Administration in Rabat. A specialist in health economics, she studies the impact of mothers' education on child mortality. She has been active in the promotion of women's participation in Moroccan politics.

Nepal

MEENA ACHARYA, an economist, is executive director of the Institute of Integrated Development Studies in Nepal. She has a history of service with policy-making departments at the Central Bank in Nepal. Since 1975 she has concurrently worked on women's issues. She is the coauthor and a major architect of the voluminous study *The Status of Women in Nepal* (1979) and the coauthor (with Lynn Bennett) of "Women and the Subsistence Sector: Economic Participation and Household Decision Making in Nepal" (World Bank Staff Working Paper no. 562, 1983).

The Netherlands

MONIQUE LEIJENAAR is associate professor of political science at the University of Nijmegen. She has published several articles and books on local politics, election studies, and women and politics, including *Gender and Power* (1990, coedited with Kathy Davis and Jantine Oldersma), and *The Shattered Loveliness: Political Behavior of Women and Men in the Netherlands, 1918–1988* (1989, in Dutch).

KEES NIEMÖLLER is senior lecturer in the department of methodology and statistics at the University of Amsterdam. He specializes in election studies, market and opinion research, and data bases and is a coauthor, with Cornelis van der Eijk, of *Electoral Change in the Netherlands* (1983).

Nigeria

KAMENE OKONJO. *See* Ghana

Norway

JANNEKE VAN DER ROS is assistant professor at Oppland College and senior researcher at the Eastern Norway Research Institute. A political scientist, she specializes in women in politics, equality policies, and regional development policies. Her current research project is "A Feminist Perspective on Democracy in Norway." She has contributed to *Unfinished Democracy: Women in Nordic Politics* (1985), coauthored *Norwegian Local Councils: Room*

for Women? (1985, in Norwegian), and compiled bibliographies, including *Women in Politics: Does It Make a Difference? Women's Impact on the Public Agenda* (1989).

Palestine

AMAL KAWAR, associate professor of political science at Utah State University in Logan, is engaged in research on women and politics. She is the author of "Women in the Utah Executive Branch" (1989) and "The Intersection of Gender and Politics: Revising a Political Science Course" (1982). A Palestinian Arab, she has lived in the United States since 1965.

Papua New Guinea

EILEEN WORMALD, a political sociologist, is a research fellow in the department of political science and international relations at the University of Birmingham, England. Her chapter is based on research done while teaching at the University of Papua New Guinea. Her publications on political socialization, women and politics, and women and education include *Sex Differences in Britain* (1982, coeditor) and, most recently, *Women and Education in Papua New Guinea and the South Pacific* (1988, coeditor).

Peru

VIRGINIA VARGAS, who has a background in economics and Latin American politics, has been a visiting professor at many universities. She has been involved in women's political participation in Peru since the 1960s, and she founded Flora Tristán, a center for Peruvian women. Recent publications (in Spanish) include "The Women's Movement in Peru: Streams, Spaces, and Knots" (1991), "How to Change the World Without Losing Our Way" (1992), and *Gender in Development* (1991).

VICTORIA VILLANUEVA, general director of the Manuela Ramos Movement, has been involved in trade union and political party organization for 17 years. Since 1978 she has been an activist in the feminist movement, working with women in the shantytowns of Lima and on behalf of the Women's Forum, a project that combines the efforts of the women's movement with those of women in public administration. In 1985 she ran for election to the Senate.

The Philippines

BELINDA A. AQUINO is professor of political science and Asian studies and director of the Center for Philippine Studies at the University of Hawaii at Manoa. She is the author of *Politics of Plunder—The Philippines Under Marcos* (1987) and the editor of *Presidential Leadership and Cory Aquino* (1990), *The Failed December Coup* (1990), and *Reflections on the U.S. Bases in the Philippines* (1990). She has taught courses on women and politics in Hawaii and the Philippines and was instrumental in setting up the Center for Women's Studies at the University of the Philippines.

Poland

RENATA SIEMIEŃSKA is professor at the Institute of Sociology, Warsaw University. Her recent research and publications have centered on cross-cultural analyses of the value systems of different populations, the functioning of local leaders, and women's participation in public life. She is the author of *Gender-Occupation-Politics: Women in Public Life in Poland* (1990, in Polish) and *Gender Inequality: A Comparative Study of Discrimination and Participation* (1990, written with Mino Vianello), as well as a number of articles on women's issues.

Puerto Rico

YAMILA AZIZE-VARGAS is associate professor at the University of Puerto Rico, Cayey, where she has directed the women's studies program, PRO-MUJER, since 1987. A specialist in literature, women's history, and women's health issues, she is the author of *Women in Struggle* (1985), a history of feminism in Puerto Rico, and the editor of *Women in Puerto Rico* (1987), an anthology of research essays; both are in Spanish. She received a Ford Foundation

Fellowship to pursue her graduate studies and holds a Ph.D. from the University of Pennsylvania.

South Africa

BARBARA KLUGMAN, a political activist and social anthropologist, coordinates the Women's Health Project of the Center for Health Policy at the University of Witwatersrand, Johannesburg. She was active in the anti-apartheid United Democratic Front, served on the executive board of the Federation of Transvaal Women, and in 1991 became chair of the Black Sash in the Southern Transvaal. Her research and publications concern women in connection with trade unions, reproductive rights, and population politics.

Spain

MARIA TERESA GALLEGO MENDEZ, professor of political science and director of the Women's Studies Institute at the Autonomous University of Madrid, is the author of *Women, the Falange, and Francoism* (1983, in Spanish), the coauthor of *The European Left* (1985, in Spanish) and *Violence and the Patriarchal Society* (1990, in Spanish), and the editor of *New Perspectives About Women* (1982). She has contributed (with M. A. Duran) to *The New Women's Movement in Europe and the U.S.* (1980) and (with C. Fernandez) to *The Implementation of Equal Rights for Men and Women* (1991). She has been active in the socialist feminist movement and in furthering women's studies in Spanish universities.

Sudan

MAGDA M. EL-SANOUSI is assistant researcher and coordinator of the Documentation Unit for Women's Studies at Ahfad University for Women. Her specialties are women in politics, and rural and displaced women. She is the author of "The Effect of Socialization and Education on Women's Political Participation in Sudan" (1990) and "Displaced Women in Omdurman" (1990), both in Arabic. She is head of the Relief Aid Office of the Babiker

Badri Scientific Association for Women's Studies.

NAFISA AHMED EL-AMIN, founder and head of the Documentation Unit for Women's Studies at Ahfad University for Women, Omdurman, and a founder of the Sudanese women's movement, has served as vice-minister of the Ministry of Youth and Sports and the Ministry of Social Welfare and as a member of the Political Bureau. She is the author of *The Sudanese Woman Through the Long History of Struggle, Light on the Sudanese Women's Movement,* and *Education and the Family in Islam: Between Tradition and Modernization* (all in Arabic).

Switzerland

REGULA STÄMPFLI is secretary general of the Swiss Students Unions in Bern. She specializes in research on political participation, women in politics, and quota models for women in politics. She has written numerous articles on women's representation and is the coauthor of *Take a Seat, Madam* (1990, in German), a study of women in politics in Switzerland. She is active in the Association of Feminist Research in Switzerland and in the Social Democratic Party.

Turkey

NERMIN ABADAN-UNAT, professor of political science at Bosporus University, also teaches in the Women's Research and Education Center at the University of Istanbul. She specializes in mass communication and political behavior, as well as women's studies and international migration and is the author of *Turkish Workers in Europe* (1976) and *Women in the Developing World: Evidence from Turkey* (1986). She represents Turkey on the Committee for Equality of Women and Men in the Council of Europe.

OYA TOKGÖZ is dean of the School of Journalism and Broadcasting and a professor in the department of journalism at the University of Ankara. She specializes in political communication and journalism education. She is the author of four books in Turkish—*Radio and Television Systems in Turkey and the Middle East, Political Communication and Woman* (1972), *Introduction to Journalism* (1981, 1987), and *The Impact of Television Commercials on Mother and Child Pairs* (1981)—and numerous articles in Turkish and English.

Union of Soviet Socialist Republics (former)

OLGA A. VORONINA, senior researcher at the Institute of Philosophy at the Russian Academy of Sciences, is also affiliated with the Center for Gender Studies at the academy's Institute of Socio-Economic Problems of the Population. The author of numerous journal articles on women's issues and feminism, she is a member of the feminist scholars' group LOTUS and a creator of the Foundation for Supporting Gender Studies. She was a member of the Organizing Committee for the First Independent Women's Forum, "Democracy Minus Women Is Not Democracy," held in Dubna.

United States

BARBARA J. NELSON, a political scientist, is professor of public affairs and codirector of the Center on Women and Public Policy, Humphrey Institute of Public Affairs, at the University of Minnesota. She specializes in social policy and social movements and is the author of *Wage Justice: Comparable Worth and the Paradox of Technocratic Reform* (1989, with Sara M. Evans), *Making an Issue of Child Abuse: Political Agenda Setting for Social Problems* (1984), and *American Women and Politics* (1984). She is active in the feminist antirape movement and in gender-inclusive, multicultural curriculum design.

KATHRYN A. CARVER, a lawyer and an epidemiologist, is director of the Office of Patient Advocacy of the National Marrow Donor Program. She specializes in public health policy and antidiscrimination law. She is the author of *The 1992 Handbook of Federal Agencies, Legislative Committees, Programs, and Private Foundations Interested in Adolescent Health* (1992) and "The 1985 Minnesota Indian Family Preservation Act: Claiming a Cultural

Identity" (1986). She is active in issues concerning women's rights, racial justice, access to healthcare, and AIDS and is a member of the Legal and Human Rights Committee of the Minnesota AIDS Project.

Uruguay

GRACIELA SAPRIZA works as a researcher for the Study Group on the Condition of Women (GRECMU), an autonomous center for feminist research in Uruguay. Her research has focused on social and feminist history. She is the author of *Women, State and Politics in Uruguay During the Twentieth Century* (1984, with Silvia Rodriguez Villamil) and *Memories of Revolt: Seven Life Stories* (1988) and the editor of *Women and Power* (1991), all in Spanish. She is also an activist in the feminist movement in Uruguay.

Index

Research methodology (*continued*)
structures, 31–37; definitions, 32–33, 53–55; data collection, 49–53
Revolutionary feminism, France, 250–52, 253
Rey, Georgina, 197
Rey Alvarez, Sara, 763–64
Rhee, Sung-Man, 440
Rio de Janeiro, Brazil, 134
Roakeina, Gena, 565
Robert, Marta, 630
Roca, Blas, 196, 201
Rocard, Michel, 257*n3*
Rodríguez, Eugenio, 175
Rodríguez Larreta de Gutiérrez Ruiz, Matilde, 768, 769
Rodriguez Villamil, Silvia, 767
Roe v. Wade (1973), 747–49
Roh, Tae-Woo, 438
Roja, Clarita, 598
Roman Catholic church: Brazil, 17, 129, 137, 138; Argentina, 62; Czechoslovakia, 219–20; France, 245, 258*n12*; Germany, 274, 275; Mexico, 450, 453, 455, 459; Philippines, 603; Poland, 611, 616, 619, 620, 621, 622; Spain, 661, 662, 663, 666, 667, 668; United States, 748, 754
Roman Catholicism, 12; Argentina, 62; Costa Rica, 175; Cuba, 191; Czechoslovakia, 212, 221; Hungary, 348; Netherlands, 498; United States, 747, 750, 756–57*n48*
Romania, 281*n13*
Rome, Treaty of (1957), 306, 310*n11*
Rönsch, Helga, 275
Rooney, Nahau, 570, 571
Roosevelt, Franklin D., 752
Rossanda, Rossana, 67
Roten, Iris von, 697
Roudy, Yvette, 255, 256
Ruacan, Melâhat, 716
Rubin, Gayle, 27
Ruiz, Rose Marie, 180
Ruíz Cortines, Adolfo, 451
Rumbold, Angela, 304
Russia, 723
Ryan, Susan, 82
Ryšlinková, Jana, 213

El-Saadawi, Nawal, 238, 240
Sadat, Anwar, 227, 228, 229, 231, 236

Sadat, Jehan, 236, 237
Sadauki, Pamela, 520
Al-S'aid, Amina, 234
Sakamoto Misoji, 406
Sakellaridou, Zeli, 323*n17*
Salic law, 244
Salinas de Gortari, Carlos, 458
Samana, Fungke, 569
Sancho, Nelia, 599
Sanguinetti, Julio M., 768
Santamaría, Haydée, 195
São Paulo, Brazil, 134, 136
Sapriza, Graciela, 12
Sartori, Giovanni, 26
Sati, in India, 365, 373, 375, 376–77
Saudi Arabia, 557–58, 716–17
Sawaba, Gambo, 520
Sayigh, Rosemary, 551
Schloss, Elizabeth Butler, 300
Scindia, Vijaya Raje, 377
Scotland, 301, 303–4; Parliament, 299
Secularism, 6, 7, 8; Bangladesh, 104; Turkey, 706–7, 708, 710, 711, 715, 716, 717, 718
Semenova, Galina, 732
Sen, Amartya K., 34, 428
Separate spheres, 20, 27; Bangladesh, 95; German philosophy and, 271; Japan, 404; Nigeria, 513; Turkey, 712; United States, 745. *See also* Gender roles; Labor, division of
Seregni, Liber, 768, 769
Sex education: Costa Rica, 184; Cuba, 196; Mexico, 453, 455; Poland, 621; Puerto Rico, 630
Sexism: Australia, 78; Costa Rica, 181; France, 246; Germany, 277; Ghana, 288; Mexico, 450, 455; Nigeria, 522; Puerto Rico, 635, 636; South Africa, 655, 659*n49*. *See also* Discrimination and anti-discrimination measures
Sexton, Mary, 79
Sexual harassment: France, 256; Germany, 272; India, 372, 374; Israel, 389; Mexico, 458; Nepal, 482; Peru, 584; Puerto Rico, 627, 634–35; South Africa, 651, 658*n25*; Turkey, 710
Sexuality, 149, 201, 308, 709
Shafiq, Duriya, 234
Sha'rawi, Huda, 228, 233, 234
Sharia. *See* Islamic law

Shimizu Kiyoko, 410
Shope, Gertrude, 641
Short, Claire, 308–9
Siagaru, Mina, 566
Silang, Diego, 593
Silang, Gabriela, 593, 599
Siles Zuazo, Hernán, 115, 116, 119
Silva, Benedita da, 134
Sin, Jaime Cardinal, 603
Singh, Ganesh Man, 484, 494*n14*
Sisulu, Albertina, 648
Sisulu, Walter, 641
Sivard, Ruth Leger, 49
Six-Day War, 389, 545
Slavery, 5; in Cuba, 190; African slave trade, 288, 517, 524*n8*; in United States, 738, 744
Slovakia (part of Czechoslovakia), 213, 215, 219
Slovak Republic (independent), 210
Smidovich, Sophia, 727
Smith, Lois, 206*n42*
Smith, Muriel, 151
Sobrado, Enrique, 766
Social cleavages, 9, 19
Social democracies, 37*n6*
Socialism: Hungary, 17, 348; Argentina, 62; Bolivia, 123; China, 168, 171; Cuba, 190, 192, 193, 197, 201, 203; Eastern European, 203; Czechoslovakia, 210, 215; East Germany, 269; Israel, 382; Spain, 662; Soviet Union, 722, 723, 725–26. *See also* Communism; Marxism
Socialist feminism: Australia, 77; Canada, 148–49; Great Britain, 301, 305; Netherlands, 499; Turkey, 710
Somare, Michael, 562
Somoza Debayle, Anastasio, 581
Sora, Tandang. *See* Aquino, Melchora
South Africa, 13, 639–40; state violence, 12, 641, 642, 648, 659*n46*; war in Angola, 190, 197; political parties, 639, 641, 650, 655, 656; apartheid, 640, 641–42, 643, 644–45, 650, 652; Blacks in, 640, 641–42, 644, 645, 650, 652, 657*n4*; women's political engagement, 640, 642–43, 656; legislatures, 640, 654–55; constitution, 640–41, 642, 650, 656; colonialism in, 641; National Party, 641, 642, 647, 653, 654–55; Federa-

743, 747, 749; women's suffrage, 629, 745; Comstock Act, 630; abortion rights, 635, 739, 743, 747–50, 754, 756–57n48; democracy in, 738, 739, 744; women's political engagement, 739; women's movement, 739, 741, 745; equal rights, 739, 742, 743, 744, 755n21; political action committees (PAC), 740, 741, 746; Blacks in, 740, 742, 743, 744, 745, 751, 755n10, 756–57n48; elections, 740, 745, 746; women's organizations, 741–42, 743, 746, 750; Mexican American women in, 742; antifeminist movement, 741–42, 743–44; civil rights movement, 742, 754n5; antiabortion movement, 743, 747–50, 757n50; women in public office, 745, 746–47

Universalism, 7, 742

Universidad Nacional Autónoma de México (National Autonomous University of Mexico), 452

Universities: Costa Rica, 180, 185; Germany, 283n28; South Africa, 644; Spain, 672; Switzerland, 698

University of Athens, 319

University of Costa Rica, 177

University of Minnesota, 43, 45

University of Papua New Guinea, 564, 565, 568

University of the Philippines, 597

University of Puerto Rico, 634

University of Technology (Papua New Guinea), 565

Uno Sōsuke, 408, 413n20

Uruguay, 758; military rule, 12, 759, 760, 761, 765, 766, 768–69; state terrorism, 12, 760, 766, 768–69; political parties, 758, 759, 761, 766, 767–68; independence (1817), 759; constitution, 759, 766, 769; women's political engagement, 759–60, 770, 771; democracy in, 760–61, 766, 767, 768, 770–71; women's suffrage, 761, 762, 763, 764; elections, 761, 763–64, 765, 766, 768, 769–70; Parliament, 761, 765, 768; economy, 761, 765, 771n4; welfare state, 761, 765, 771n4, 772n19; feminists in, 762; women's organizations, 762, 768; equal rights, 763, 764–65; family

law, 765; labor unions, 765, 767, 769; women in public office, 765, 768; women's employment, 766–67; women's movement, 767, 768; Immunity Law (1986), 768–70

Utilitarianism, 34

Valdés, Tapia, 771

Van Leer Foundation, 570

Vargas, Getúlio, 128, 129, 131

Vargas, Ivete, 131

Vargas Valente, Virginia, 15

Veiling. See Purdah

Velasco Alvarado, Juan, 576, 577, 579–80, 582, 585

Ver, Fabian, 600, 601

Vera, Maité, 196

Vickers, Jill McCalla, 150

Videla, Jorge Rafael, 12, 60–65, 70

Vietnam War, 76, 633

Villaflor, Azucena, 65

Villanueva, Victoria, 15

Violence against women, 11–12, 19, 23n40; Australia, 85–86, 89; Bangladesh, 105, 112n40; Brazil, 133, 136–37; Cuba, 202, 206n46; France, 256; Germany, 283–84n42; Great Britain, 301, 308; Greece, 315, 319; Hong Kong, 331, 338–41; India, 365, 369–70, 373–77; Mexico, 452, 453, 457–59; Norway, 531, 538, 539; Papua New Guinea, 567–68; Peru, 581, 583; Puerto Rico, 634, 635; South Africa, 649; Spain, 669; Turkey, 710. See also Rape

Virginity ideal: Bangladesh, 94; Nepal, 480, 481–82, 491

Vlok, Adriaan, 648

Voluntarism, 17; Bangladesh, 102; Hong Kong, 328; Norway, 539, 541

Voting rights, 14, 50, 53; Argentina, 62; Australia, 75, 81; Bangladesh, 98; Bolivia, 120; Brazil, 128, 130–31; Canada, 144, 146, 147, 148; Costa Rica, 177, 178, 188n6; Cuba, 191; Egypt, 231, 233–35, 239; France, 244, 246; Germany, 264; Great Britain, 304; Hungary, 352; India, 366; Israel, 384; Japan, 399, 408; Mexico, 449, 450, 451; Morocco, 464, 466; Netherlands, 497, 503, 504, 505; Nigeria, 516, 517; Peru,

579, 585; Philippines, 594–95, 604; Poland, 613, 618; Puerto Rico, 628–29; United States, 629, 745; Spain, 662; Sudan, 679; Switzerland, 691–92, 694–97, 703; Turkey, 707; Uruguay, 761, 762, 763, 764

Voznesenskaya, Julia, 732

Wages: Australia, 75, 86, 87–88; Bolivia, 122; Canada, 153; Czechoslovakia, 216–17, 218; Egypt, 230, 235; France, 246, 256; Germany, 272; Hungary, 355; India, 371–72; Israel, 391; Kenya, 430; South Korea, 438; Mexico, 450; Morocco, 473; Norway, 535, 537; Philippines, 596; Puerto Rico, 627–28, 631, 636–37n9; Spain, 672; Switzerland, 698; Soviet Union, 726, 729, 733; Uruguay, 766, 772n19. See also Equal pay; Incomes

Wajed, Sheikh Hasina, 96, 97, 99, 100, 110n23, 111n26

Wales, 299, 301, 303–4

Walesa, Lech, 611, 617, 621

Wan Li, 171

War, 13

Warsaw University, 618

Al-Wazir, Intissar ('Um Jihad), 554–55, 556, 557

Weber, Max, 271

Weffort, Francisco, 770

Weill-Hallé, Andrée, 253

Welfare state: Egypt, 229, 230–31; France, 245; Germany, 271, 272, 273; Norway, 530, 537, 540, 542; Uruguay, 761, 765, 771n4, 772n19

West African Currency Board, 291

Western Europe, 7, 9, 14, 18, 32

Weyrich, Paul, 747

Whitlam, Gough, 83

Wiarda, Howard J., 37n2

Widows: India, sati in, 365, 373, 375, 376–77; Israel, 393; Kenya, 428

Wingti, Paias, 562

Woleková, Helena, 214

Wollenberger, Vera, 267, 280–81n8

Womanist organizations, 19

Women: A World Survey (Sivard), 49

Women-headed households, 52, 55n11; Malawi, 6; Australia, 89; Cuba, 201